International Private Law: A Scots Perspective

Fourth Edition

International Private Law:
A Scots Perspective

Fourth Edition

Elizabeth B. Crawford
LLB (Hons), PhD, Solicitor
Professor Emeritus of International Private Law, University of Glasgow

Janeen M. Carruthers
LLB (Hons), Dip LP, PhD, Solicitor
Professor of Private Law, University of Glasgow

W. GREEN

THOMSON REUTERS

First Edition   1998
Second Edition   2006
Third Edition   2010

Published in 2015 by W. Green, 21 Alva Street, Edinburgh EH2 4PS part of Thomson Reuters
(Professional) UK Limited (Registered in England & Wales, Company No.1679046. Registered
Office and address for service: 2nd floor, 1 Mark Square, Leonard Street, London EC2A 4EG)

Typeset by Letterpart Limited, Caterham on the Hill, Surrey, CR3 5XL.

Printed and bound in Great Britain by CPI Group (UK) Ltd, Croydon,CR0 4YY.

No natural forests were destroyed to make this product; only farmed timber was used and
re-planted.

A CIP catalogue record of this book is available for the British Library.

http://www.wgreen.co.uk

ISBN: 978-0-414-03398-6

Thomson Reuters and the Thomson Reuters logo are trademarks of Thomson Reuters.

Crown copyright material is reproduced with the permission of the Controller of HMSO and
the Queen's Printer for Scotland.

In memoriam

Dr James G. Carruthers

1941–2014

Foreword

By The Right Honourable Lady Paton

International Private Law: A Scots Perspective by Professor E.B. Crawford and Professor J.M. Carruthers is, by now, a well-established authority and the first port of call in all IPL matters for Scottish legal practitioners and academics alike. In modern times, increasingly international lifestyles throw up numerous problems with an IPL aspect. That makes this fourth edition all the more welcome, whether the reader is attempting to resolve a question of jurisdiction, or family law, or cross-boundary contract, or international child abduction.

Recent developments in the law have been clearly and helpfully set out. There is an enhanced section devoted to the drive for harmonisation in the European Union. There are passages noting the courts' increased emphasis on habitual residence (rather than domicile) as a connecting factor in family, child abduction and other cases, and also references to the Supreme Court decisions on post-divorce financial matters (*Radmacher* and *Agbaje*). Chapter 7 gives all-important guidance concerning Brussels I Recast (Regulation EU No 1215/2012) which came into operation on 10 January 2015; the current approach to class actions ("collective redress") and relevant IPL instruments; and the regulations governing mediation in civil and commercial cases. Contemporary developments such as same-sex marriages and related issues (constitution, dissolution, and recognition of foreign decrees) are dealt with in Chs 11 and 12, while questions arising from electronic communication can be found in Ch.15. Updates in delict are addressed in Ch.16, including case-law on direct actions against insurers following upon the decision in *FBTO Shadeverzekeringen NV v Odenbreit* (C-463/06) [2007] ECR I-11321. Chapter 18 (Succession) discusses the possible effect which the Rome IV regulation (Regulation EU No 650/2012) might have on UK citizens, despite the UK's decision not to opt in.

Not only does this fourth edition provide a wealth of up-to-date material, but it gives a commentary on, and an analysis of, recent changes and developments and their effect on existing law. The volume is therefore particularly useful to anyone trying to assimilate and apply what is an increasingly complex area of law. The authors are to be congratulated on their major contribution to international private law jurisprudence.

Ann Paton
Parliament House, Edinburgh
23 July 2015

Preface to the Fourth Edition

Five years have elapsed since the publication of the third edition, and very many significant changes have occurred in the subject, mostly attributable to the European harmonisation agenda, an agenda which aims both to consolidate and to innovate. Both of these objectives, in the timeframe in question, have resulted in major changes by way of instruments intended to modify, refine and accelerate existing measures (the prime example being the Brussels I Recast Regulation, applicable from 10 January 2015, in place of the Brussels I Regulation), or to introduce conflict of laws provision in subject areas, such as wills and succession, hitherto untouched by European regulation. It has been remarked that the most recent 50 year period through which the subject of international private law has passed has been more productive than all 650 years which went before—a sentiment from which, at the end of our labours on this edition, we do not demur.

In writing about the law the authorial purpose must, first, be accuracy of content, and then clarity of expression. The complexity of the subject means that very close attention has been paid to the ordering of materials. Elegance of composition should be an aim, and even attempts at levity where opportunity presents. Inevitably, when dealing with EU regulations in the administrative and procedural area, earnestness is unavoidable; while we have derived great enjoyment from the whole exercise of writing this new edition, humour will not easily be detected within the EU Service Regulation.

A challenge which increasingly presents is explanation and assessment of the co-existence of the increasing number of EU instruments and international conventions, their inter-dependence and connectedness. Moreover, and especially from a UK perspective, one must be mindful of the potential impact in the UK of European regulations into the operation of which the UK has not opted. Achieving consensus and coherence between and among EU instruments is a delicate business and, as we have written elsewhere, problems of demarcation are very familiar to modern international private lawyers. We have endeavoured, throughout the book, to be on the alert for problems of this nature, and not to shirk exploration of them.

A Table of Cases which runs in excess of 50 pages to service a book of circa 700 pages is indicative of the lively state of court business in the UK and in Europe generally.

With regard to notable developments since 2010, the following may be highlighted. Chapter 6 has been subject to a re-balancing exercise in view of the increasing use of habitual residence as a connecting factor in jurisdiction and in choice of law in a variety of private law contexts. The long and loving tribute to the rules of domicile found in earlier editions of this book has been trimmed, so far as personal predilection for that topic will allow, and the treatment of habitual residence has been enlarged—generally, and subject area by subject area, particular care being given to its use in matrimonial proceedings and child law. The feverish state of judicial analysis of its meaning, and the twists and turns of the judicial mind, have been tracked closely; one cannot fail to note the degree of autonomy enjoyed by a UK judge in interpreting and applying a non-autonomous connecting factor, and in reaching his/her conclusion about the habitual residence, especially of a child.

The heart of any international private law book is its treatment of the rules of jurisdiction and judgment recognition and enforcement in civil and commercial matters. This edition has been designed to permit thorough treatment of the Brussels I Recast Regulation. There is a full account in Chs 7 and 9 of the changes brought about thereby, and analysis of the buoyant state of judicial interpretation of the Brussels I Regulation from the CJEU downwards. Ancillary procedural measures, such as the new European Account Preservation Order, are addressed in Ch.8.

In family law, much additional writing and synthesis of primary and secondary legislation was required to give due account of the introduction in Scotland and England, respectively, of same sex marriage, and the possibility of converting, with retrospective effect, civil partnership into marriage. The text sets out the complex legislative framework and seeks to put a conflict of laws gloss on the subject (even though that dimension often is not clear from the relevant legislation), addressing problems arising out of the constitution and dissolution of same sex marriage, viz. problems of capacity to marry, jurisdiction, choice of law rules pertaining to matrimonial remedies, and recognition of foreign divorces/ nullities of same sex marriages. The operation of Brussels II *bis*, in place now for over 10 years, has generated in matrimonial proceedings a great deal of case law, which is examined in Ch.12.

A good deal of extra work was required in Ch.13 as a result of the coming into effect of the EU Maintenance Regulation, the 2007 Hague Protocol on the law applicable to maintenance obligations, and the 2007 Hague Convention on the international recovery of child support and other forms of family maintenance.

Writing Ch.14 proved to be one of the most exacting tasks which the new edition demanded. The area of international child law having become what Thorpe LJ has described as a "treaty jungle", Ch.14 now is one of the longest in the book, encompassing status, parental rights and responsibilities, guardianship, abduction, parental relocation, adoption, and surrogacy. The chapter required a considerable amount of new writing on topics such as international surrogacy arrangements, as well as careful synthesis and analysis of the very high volume of cases which cross-border child law generates. Nowhere is the river of judicial creativity flowing more rapidly than in the UK Supreme Court when dealing with cases of international child abduction which require interpretation of the 1980 Hague Convention. Several distinguished judicial personages who assisted in earlier years in the illumination of the instrument have been ignominiously erased.

In the law of obligations, the Rome I and Rome II Regulations have bedded in, and Chs 15 and 16 treat the emerging jurisprudence, which, in the case of Rome II, concentrates on the classic distinction between substance and procedure, particularly in relation to the law of damages. The material on double and multiple locality delicts has been expanded, taking account, for example, of problems pertaining to defamation and related claims, violations of privacy, and rights relating to personality. Illustrative of a layering problem which affects choice of law, case law shows that there is life yet in the Private International Law (Miscellaneous Provisions) Act 1995, and in the common law.

It has been possible in this edition to take account of the Recast Insolvency Regulation, which entered into force on 26 June 2015, and which will apply, in the main, from 26 June 2017. Likewise, revision of Ch.18 necessitated examination of Regulation (EU) No.650/2012 ("Rome IV", concerning wills and succession), and speculation as to the possible effect upon the estates of British nationals, or upon the transmission of UK-situated property, of a regulation into which the UK has not opted. Rome IV exhibits a new level of hybridity in the evolving project of EU harmonisation.

Our thanks, as always, are due to the publishing team at W.Green. The depth of our account in many places, and the fullness of the footnotes, we trust will be accepted in the spirit in which they are offered. We hope that the detail which a modern treatment requires has not obscured the beguiling essence of the subject.

Work began on this book in June 2014. The writing was completed in April 2015. In personal terms, a grievous loss was sustained in September 2014. This book is dedicated to JMC's father.

2015 is a signal year for the authors, marked by the publication of this fourth edition, and by the birth of a first grandchild and the forthcoming celebrations of two (cross-border) marriages.

We have sought to state the law as at 1 July 2015.

EBC and JMC
Glasgow
31 July 2015

Preface to the Third Edition

Earlier than anticipated, we deliver the third edition of "IPL in Scotland", now as a freestanding volume rather than as part of Greens Concise Law Series, and under the title *International Private Law: A Scots Perspective*. In view of the pace of the EU programme of harmonisation of conflict of laws of Member States, a new edition is timely.

The new title is intended to convey the changed and changing nature of international private law rules, as applicable in Scotland. Many, but by no means all, of these rules are held in common with the rest of the UK and with fellow EU Member States. What is offered here, therefore, is a treatment of the intrinsically Scottish rules of international private law, together with an account and critique of those UK and EU/Hague harmonised rules which increasingly dominate the subject. The whole is viewed through the lens of Scots law, paying full respect to Scots private law and international private law sources and authorities, early and modern. Yet in the 21st century there is a notable degree of comity and mutual reliance among "UK" conflict lawyers, who work together to secure what jointly is conceived to be in the best interests of UK citizens (or domiciliaries) in a rapidly changing legal situation in which civilian practices and modes of thinking are inevitably pre-eminent.

There are few chapters unaffected by European changes, which in recent years have encompassed matters of jurisdiction, choice of law, recognition and enforcement of judgments, and related procedural topics. EU judicial co-operation in civil matters now rests upon the Treaty on the functioning of the European Union (the Lisbon Treaty). Where EU legislation already is in force, our policy has been to begin the relevant chapter with that material, on the rationale that this is the most useful manner of presentation for the reader, enabling immediate reference to the law in force. Where the EU instrument is merely proposed (as, for example, in relation to choice of law in divorce ("Rome III"), or Succession ("Rome V")), we have favoured a chronological approach.

The most active and most difficult area is that concerning the rules of civil and commercial jurisdiction. A pressing matter for Scots lawyers is to examine the extent of operation of the Brussels regime of jurisdiction and judgments, to draw a line of demarcation between "Brussels" and "non-Brussels" cases, and to keep abreast of what may be proposed as regards the relationship, in terms of jurisdiction and judgment recognition, between Member States and Third States. Also, importantly, the revised Lugano Convention ("Lugano II") has come into being, and its provisions are addressed, together with its relationship with the Brussels I Regulation. Likewise, the relationship between the rules of jurisdiction of the Brussels regime, on the one hand, and arbitration as a means of resolving international commercial disputes, on the other, has required attention. In procedure, full account is taken of the development of yet more rapid judgment enforcement procedures within the EU: Regulation 1896/2006 creating a European Order for Payment Procedure, and Regulation 861/2007 creating a European Small Claims Procedure.

In choice of law, Chapter 13 (Proprietary and Financial Consequences of Marriage and Other Adult Relationships) takes full account of the Maintenance Regulation (Regulation 4/2009); Chapters 15 (Contractual Obligations) and 16 (Non-contractual Obligations) include, respectively, analysis of the Rome I Regulation (Regulation 593/2008) and Rome II Regulation (Regulation 864/2007). In addition to applicable law rules for delict, the latter instrument contains applicable law rules for unjust enrichment, *negotiorum gestio* and *culpa in contrahendo*, which, as laid down in statutory form, are a novelty in Scots law.

Early discussion, on an EU basis, concerning the principle of *iura novit curia*, and the implications of more widespread acceptance of this principle in legal systems favouring the adversarial process (such as our own), may portend significant change as part of the project to transform national sets of conflict rules into a corpus of harmonised rules. Though the UK approach to proof of foreign law has been criticised on the ground, *inter alia*, that it curbs development of the subject, causing the conflict potential of a case to remain unfulfilled, the case law cited in this edition is more voluminous even than before. This is attributable partly to the lively state of the conflict branch of law generally, but also to the need for interpretative direction, by domestic courts and/or the CJEU, which new legislative instruments, national and European, demand. Amidst the rigour and sobriety, perhaps there is time for the *faux-naïf*:

> "I'm not going to argue with Maud" says Horace. "She's a girl. What's the real answer?"

> "Oh, the Correctional Court at Lille found for the railway company. Payelle had to reimburse them."

> "I won!" shouts Horace. "Maud got it wrong."

> "No one got it wrong," George replies, "The case could have gone either way. That's why things go to court in the first place."[1]

To this complex and rewarding branch of law has been added the complexity of seeking to ascertain the ranking *inter se*, and respective application of, different sets of rules (national, European and international; and in and across those categories), which operate within the same subject area. Unappealing though at first sight it may be, we think that the term "demarcation law", suggested as a title for the subject early in its development, has become apposite to describe a crucial part of the conflict lawyer's expertise.

Detailed, clear and accurate statement of the law is a discipline and first duty demanded of the writer. Wit and elegance of expression have to take a subordinate role, but we have enjoyed searching for *le mot juste* and the felicitous phrase, as we have enjoyed the writing task as a whole. As a reversal of the adage

---

[1] Julian Barnes, *Arthur & George* (London: Vintage reissue, 2006), p.72.

that any age is younger when one achieves it than when it is viewed in advance, the writing of each chapter has proved to be a lengthier exercise than expected; there have been many more par 5s on this golf course than usually are encountered, and lengthy ones at that, making it a challenge to get up in regulation, Regulation by Regulation.

As with the second edition, this work is entirely jointly authored, and at its completion we report our continuing enjoyment of the subject, and pleasure in the company.

We express our appreciation to the commissioning, editorial and marketing sections of W. Green, and record, in particular, our thanks to Janet Campbell, Kathy Pauline, and Alan Bett.

We are grateful to our families for their patience and their support of a demanding endeavour.

We have sought to state the law as at July 31, 2010.

EBC and JMC
Glasgow
August 2010

Preface to the Second Edition

Many changes have occurred in Scots conflict rules since publication of the first edition of this book at the end of 1998.

In the first place, the development by the European Union of an "area of freedom, security and justice" has justified and necessitated, *inter alia*, the assimilation of the conflict rules of Member States across an increasing number of areas of private law. The European programme affects all aspects of the conflict of laws, viz. jurisdiction, choice of law, and recognition and enforcement of judgments, as well as procedural matters.

A programme of work was set for the period 1999 to 2004 at an Extraordinary European Council Meeting at Tampere, Finland. Important legislative reform under the Tampere agenda includes the conversion of the 1968 Brussels Convention on jurisdiction and the enforcement of judgments in civil and commercial matters into Council Regulation (EC) No 44/2001; Council Regulation (EC) No. 1346/2000 on Insolvency Proceedings; and, significantly, moving into Family Law, Council Regulation (EC) No 2201/2003 ("Brussels II Bis") concerning jurisdiction and the recognition and enforcement of judgments in matrimonial matters and matters of parental responsibility. These are weighty changes concerning substantive conflict rules. There have been also a number of changes to procedural conflict rules, including those relating to service of documents, and taking of evidence abroad.

This programme is to be pursued without pause under the Hague Programme, adopted by the European Council in 2004, for the period 2005–2009. Negotiations continue on the conversion into a Regulation of the 1980 Rome Convention on the Law Applicable to Contractual Obligations; and upon a Proposal for a Regulation on the Law Applicable to Non-Contractual Obligations ("Rome II"). Green Papers recently have been presented by the European Commission on applicable law and jurisdiction in divorce matters; on succession and wills; and on maintenance.

Secondly, a number of important changes have been made to Scottish and English domestic law, requiring concomitant conflict rules. Where such rules are lacking, expert commentary must be provided. The prime examples in this category arise in Family Law, in particular with regard to the creation of the new status of civil partner under the Civil Partnership Act 2004; and the statutory regulation in Scots law of certain aspects of *de facto* cohabitation.

Thirdly, the Family Law (Scotland) Act 2006 has placed on a statutory basis for the first time a number of Scots conflict rules in Family Law, such as those relating to validity of marriage, and matrimonial property, thereby crystallising them, and in so doing changing conflict rules by seemingly foreclosing the operation of certain options which existed at common law. The Act has added rules on a number of particular points of conflict significance, including a new provision concerning void marriages, and a different rule for ascribing the domicile of persons under 16. It is fortunate that the publication schedule of this book has permitted us to take full account of this major new Act.

The material has been re-ordered, and the book is presented now in two parts. Part A deals with matters such as methodology; connecting factors; and the pre-eminent subject of civil and commercial jurisdiction, including full analysis of UK and ECJ case law such as *Gasser v Misat, Turner v Grovit and Owusu*. The subjects of evidence and procedure and foreign decree enforcement, included in Part A, reflect the importance of these rules, and their inter-relationship with jurisdictional rules. Part B gives a full account of the conflict rules of Scots law in all major areas of private law. Substantial re-writing has occurred, particularly in the chapters on marriage and other adult relationships; consistorial causes; property and financial consequences of adult relationships; children; contractual obligations; non-contractual obligations; and insolvency.

It has been our aim to provide a comprehensive account of Scots conflict rules in all major areas of private law. This must be done within reasonable compass, and the decision was made to excise chapters on company law and criminal law to compensate for the increase in text which the changes outlined above demand.

We wish to record our thanks to our research assistant, Michael Thomson, who ably assisted us during the summer of 2005.

As is obvious, this book is now a co-authored composition. EBC expresses her gratitude to JMC for joining her in this venture. Our friends will know that differences of opinion between us are seldom found (the most profound being Burns's/Burns' poems; by great forbearance EBC has allowed the case of *Dinwoodie's Executrix v Carruthers' Executor* to pass unchanged, in deference to Dr Carruthers's opinion). There has been no division of labour or writing tasks; the work is entirely jointly authored.

At the University of Glasgow in recent years the authors have greatly expanded the conflict of laws teaching provision. We are privileged to teach in an area which is that of our prime research interest; teaching and writing are best when they are interlinked. The authors acknowledge the benefit which accrues to them through teaching, and trust that the mutual advantage is apparent also from the student perspective.

This book is dedicated to David M. Walker, *Regius Professor Emeritus of Law in the University of Glasgow*, whose contribution to legal scholarship in Scots law and legal education is immense. For EBC, Professor Walker was an inspirational teacher; for JMC, of the next generation, a mentor in her early research; to both of us, a friend whose kind interest and encouragement we appreciate. We are honoured that Professor Walker has accepted this dedication. We have endeavoured to state the law as at 8 June 2006, although it has been possible to take account of some later developments.

EBC

JMC
University of Glasgow
June 2006

Preface to the First Edition

This book is the product of the Printed Notes provided annually for the class of International Private Law at Glasgow University. Originally, and for many years, they were the work of Alex Donaldson, my predecessor as lecturer in that class. Thereafter they were updated and enlarged by me until there came a time at which it seemed appropriate to develop them further into book form. The text is intended principally for students, but I hope that it may be of wider use and interest. I have sought to state the law as at the date of this Preface.

The account presented is of Scottish conflict rules. A Scots forum is assumed, and accordingly the substantive domestic legal background as well as the system of conflict rules is that of Scottish private law. Nevertheless, since in my view much in the conflict of laws is held in common with England, many English conflict cases are cited, for interest and by way of illustration. They may be persuasive. Differences between Scots conflict rules and English conflict rules, in common law or statute, in substance or procedure, in emphasis or in nuance, I have tried to identify at appropriate points in the text.

I am grateful to my colleagues in the Stair building for their advice and expertise in many areas of law; to my researchers—successively, Paul Sheehan, Susan Mitchell, Shaheed Fatima and Jacqueline Donald—for their help; and to the editorial team at W. Green for bringing the book to publication.

Above all, I thank Moira Smith, who has converted many versions of this text into its final form, and without whose great skill and patience the book would not have been completed.

Finally I record my gratitude to all the students over the years to whom I have had the pleasure and the privilege of speaking on the subject of International Private Law. The classes have been a joy to me, as I know they were to Alex Donaldson. Mr Donaldson's death occurred in April 1998, after the completion of the text but before production of the book. International Private Law in Scotland is dedicated to him, by a pupil to a teacher.

Elizabeth B. Crawford
University of Glasgow
30 September 1998

TABLE OF CONTENTS

CONTENTS

CONTENTS

CONTENTS

CONTENTS

CONTENTS

CONTENTS

CONTENTS

CONTENTS

CONTENTS

CONTENTS

18. The law of succession

CONTENTS

TABLE OF CASES

TABLE OF CASES

TABLE OF CASES

TABLE OF CASES

TABLE OF CASES

TABLE OF CASES

TABLE OF CASES

TABLE OF CASES

TABLE OF CASES

TABLE OF CASES

TABLE OF CASES

1

TABLE OF CASES

TABLE OF CASES

lii

TABLE OF CASES

TABLE OF CASES

liv

TABLE OF CASES

TABLE OF CASES

TABLE OF CASES

TABLE OF CASES

TABLE OF CASES

TABLE OF CASES

TABLE OF CASES

TABLE OF CASES

TABLE OF CASES

TABLE OF CASES

TABLE OF CASES

TABLE OF CASES

TABLE OF CASES

TABLE OF CASES

TABLE OF CASES

TABLE OF CASES

TABLE OF CASES

TABLE OF CASES

TABLE OF CASES

TABLE OF CASES

TABLE OF CASES

TABLE OF CASES

TABLE OF CASES

TABLE OF CASES

TABLE OF CASES

TABLE OF CASES

TABLE OF CASES

TABLE OF CASES

TABLE OF CASES

TABLE OF CASES

TABLE OF CASES

TABLE OF CASES

TABLE OF CASES

TABLE OF CASES

TABLE OF CASES

TABLE OF CASES

TABLE OF CASES

TABLE OF CASES

TABLE OF CASES

TABLE OF CASES

TABLE OF CASES

TABLE OF CASES

TABLE OF STATUTES

TABLE OF STATUTES

Acts of the Scottish Parliament

TABLE OF STATUTES

TABLE OF STATUTORY INSTRUMENTS

TABLE OF INTERNATIONAL CONVENTIONS

cxvii

TABLE OF INTERNATIONAL CONVENTIONS

TABLE OF EUROPEAN LEGISLATION

TABLE OF EUROPEAN LEGISLATION

Directives

CHAPTER 1

Nature of the subject

NATURE

International private law is that branch of the law of any system which is applied   1–01
to determine questions which involve foreign elements. More particularly, it is
the branch of the private law of any legal system which consists of the rules
which enable its courts to determine the following matters:

(a)   the rules of jurisdiction to be followed by its courts;
(b)   the system of law which is to be applied by those courts to determine the
      rights of the parties in cases involving foreign elements ("choice of law");
      and
(c)   the extent to which recognition is to be given by those courts to decrees of
      foreign courts, and the manner of enforcement of such recognised decrees,
      if enforcement be necessary; and conversely, the extent to which
      recognition of their own decrees and, if need be, enforcement thereof is to
      be accorded elsewhere.

International private law is also known as the conflict of laws and its rules are
known as conflict rules. Conflict cases are those which contain a foreign element,
though not all cases containing a foreign element are necessarily "conflict"; they
may reveal themselves on the facts to be domestic,[1] or they may be treated as
domestic cases if no offer,[2] or no timeous offer,[3] is made to prove foreign law. In
such an event, the court may proceed on the basis that the content of the foreign
law is the same as its own.[4]

   Although the process of assimilation of conflict rules among the Member
States of the European Union, and beyond, is well advanced, it must be
understood that each legal system has its own body of conflict rules, in every
substantive private law area, to deal with cross-border cases arising in its courts.

   The subject is concerned with the relationship among different systems of
private law, not with the relationship among sovereign states as political units.
Only occasionally will the subjects of public international law (which in its
nature is international and not peculiar to each legal system) and international

---

[1] *William Grant & Sons Ltd v Glen Catrine Bonded Warehouse Ltd*, 1995 S.L.T. 936.
[2] *Pryde v Proctor & Gamble Ltd*, 1971 S.L.T. (Notes) 18.
[3] *Bonnor v Balfour Kilpatrick Ltd*, 1974 S.L.T. 187; 1975 S.L.T. (Notes) 3.
[4] *De Reneville v De Reneville* [1948] P. 100; and *Rodden v Whatlings Ltd*, 1960 S.L.T. (Notes) 96.
See paras 8–28 to 8–32.

private law meet[5]; they will not usually clash with each other, pursuing, rather, parallel courses, with the result that often it will be found that their approaches differ to a problem which is common to both.[6] Sometimes, the two branches are involved jointly in a question, e.g. the extent to which English and Scots law should recognise private law "events", such as the celebration or termination of a marriage, the conclusion of a contract, and rights which normally would flow therefrom, if the event has taken place within a state the government of which is not formally recognised by the UK ("the problem of unrecognised governments"[7]).

Even if viewed originally as akin to public international law, international private law is truly a branch of the private law of a legal system. This means that different legal systems' rules of international private law will differ from one another, unless and until the harmonisation process supervenes in any given area whether to a full or limited extent. It means also that there is no affront to the sovereignty of the forum in entertaining the notion of upholding foreign acquired rights because the matter is regulated by a branch of the forum's own law.

1–02   As the twentieth century progressed, legislation in the UK showed an increasing awareness of conflict of laws issues and of the matter of territorial application of rules. Since 1970, the subject of Scots (and English) international private law has been transformed from one largely regulated by common law to one largely regulated by legislation (broadly defined to include in the 21st century international conventions and EU regulations). Some statutes have been required to enable the UK to ratify international conventions; others are the result of domestic initiatives. These legislative interventions have been concerned with all areas of the subject, personal,[8] commercial,[9] and procedural.[10] In addition some statutes contain conflict of laws provision alongside domestic law provision.[11]

---

[5] e.g. sovereign immunity from suit and from enforcement of judgments; recognition of governments; "jurisdiction" (not, perhaps, as that word is understood in a conflict of laws sense, but used to express locus standi, the legitimacy of expression of interest by a state in an incident outside its borders). For a modern examination of the relationship between public and private international law, see A. Mills, *The Confluence of Public and Private International Law: justice, pluralism and subsidiarity in the international constitutional ordering of private law* (Cambridge: Cambridge University Press, 2009).
[6] The subject of cultural property is notable for attracting international private law and public international law attention: see J.M. Carruthers, *The Transfer of Property in the Conflict of Laws* (Oxford: Oxford University Press, 2005), paras 5.23–5.32; and *Kuwait Airways Corp v Iraqi Airways Co (No.6)* [2002] UKHL 19; [2002] 3 All E.R. 209, discussed in J.M. Carruthers and E.B. Crawford (2003) 52 I.C.L.Q. 761.
[7] *Sierra Leone Telecommunications Co Ltd v Barclays Bank Plc* [1998] 2 All E.R. 821. cf. Foreign Corporations Act 1991.
[8] e.g. Recognition of Divorces and Legal Separations Act 1971, superseded by Family Law Act 1986; Domicile and Matrimonial Proceedings Act 1973; Matrimonial and Family Proceedings Act 1984; Child Abduction and Custody Act 1985; Civil Partnership Act 2004; Family Law (Scotland) Act 2006; and Adoption and Children (Scotland) Act 2007.
[9] e.g. Contracts (Applicable Law) Act 1990; Private International Law (Miscellaneous Provisions) Act 1995; Civil Jurisdiction and Judgments Acts 1982 and 1991; and Recognition of Trusts Act 1987.
[10] e.g. Prescription and Limitation (Scotland) Act 1973, as amended; and Evidence (Proceedings in Other Jurisdictions) Act 1975.
[11] e.g. Family Law (Scotland) Act 2006.

Traditionally, UK statutes do not have extra-territorial operation[12] unless this is express, or necessarily implied.[13] However, British statutes have an implicit extra-territorial dimension by virtue of the operation of choice of law rules. If Scots or English law, in the view of a UK forum, is the law governing the substance of a cross-border question (the *lex causae*), the relevant Scots or English law, common law or statutory, will apply, e.g. if the deceased died domiciled in Scotland, the distribution, testate or intestate, of his moveable estate, *wherever situated*, will be subject to the provisions of the Succession (Scotland) Act 1964.[14] Equally, a foreign statute of the *lex causae*, whatever its purported territorial scope in the view of its own legal system, will receive effect in a UK forum by reason of its status as the *lex causae*, subject to public policy.

The subject of the conflict of laws, which hitherto has been characterised by respect for territorial boundaries, must respond to the challenge of finding appropriate solutions to the growing number of legal problems of jurisdiction and choice of law prompted by technological and electronic advances, e.g. with regard to the online dissemination of defamatory[15] or otherwise offensive material; or in relation to electronic commerce and related property problems such as the transfer of securities held with an inter-mediary, where modern shareholding practice typically is "dematerialised" and "immobilised".[16]

THE NAME

The names "international private law", "private international law" and "conflict of laws" are each suitable descriptions of this branch of law, but conflict lawyers tend to disagree first on the name of their subject of study.[17] In Scotland the three terms are used interchangeably, but in certain civilian systems the term "conflict of laws" denotes that branch of the subject referred to in the UK as "choice of law". It has been said of the subject that "dispute starts from the title page". In this treatment of the subject, we shall use the term international private law, as it is believed to be the name traditionally used in Scotland, and it brings to mind more quickly and aptly the nature of the subject.

1–03

---

[12] e.g. *Att Gen for Alberta v Huggard Assets Ltd* [1953] A.C. 420, per Lord Asquith of Bishopstone at 441; *CEB Draper & Son Ltd v Edward Turner & Son Ltd* [1964] 3 All E.R. 148, per Lord Denning at 150; and *Yorke v British & Continental Steamship Co* (1945) 78 Ll. L.Rep. 181. The terms of a statute may have the effect that a foreigner is entitled to take advantage of UK legislation even if not subject to it: *Krzus v Crow's Nest Pass Coal Co Ltd* [1912] A.C. 590; and *Lawson v Serco Ltd* [2006] UKHL 3. See, in detail, para.3–11.

[13] This is especially strongly held in certain branches such as criminal law, but in recent years there have been more examples of express extra-territorial application, *especially* in criminal law, e.g. Sexual Offences (Conspiracy and Incitement) Act 1996 s.6; Criminal Justice and Immigration Act 2008 s.72; and *Serious Organised Crime Agency v Perry* [2012] UKSC 35; [2013] 1 A.C. 182. Most conflict of laws textbooks exclude from their treatment the subject of criminal law. An exception is the first edition of this work: Crawford, *International Private Law in Scotland* (Edinburgh: W. Green, 1998), Ch.20.

[14] Contrast *Kerr v Mangan*, 2015 S.C. 17.

[15] Paras 7–24 and 16–48.

[16] Para.17–35.

[17] Martin Wolff rightly predicted that the German suggestion of "demarcation law" was unlikely to become popular. He notes that Baty considered the term "polarized law" (*Private International Law*, 2nd edn (Oxford: Clarendon Press, 1950), p.10).

TERMINOLOGY

1–04 International private law has its own terminology, which traditionally has made much use of Latin phrases, though less so in recent years with the advent of the harmonisation of the subject and the setting out of conflict rules regionally by EU regulation and globally in convention form. The following is a list of expressions frequently used:

Lex fori	The *internal* (i.e. local or domestic) law of the country in which an action is raised.
Lex causae	The legal system which governs the subject matter of an action or the rights of parties, that is, the law in accordance with which the substance of a legal question is to be determined.
Lex domicilii	The law of a person's domicile.
Lex patriae	The law of a person's nationality.
Lex loci celebrationis	The law of the country where a marriage is celebrated.
Lex situs and *lex loci rei sitae*	The law of the country in which immoveable property or moveable assets are situated: the latter term used to be considered the correct one with regard to moveables, but nowadays *lex situs* tends to be used indifferently, whether the case concerns immoveable or moveable property.
Lex loci actus	The law of the country where a legal act or transaction takes place.
Lex actus	The law with which a legal act or transaction has the most real connection. This may or may not be also the *lex loci actus*.
Lex loci contractus	The law of the country in which a contract technically is said to have been made.
Lex loci solutionis	The law of the country in which performance of a contract is to take place.
Lex loci delicti	The law of the country where a delict or tort allegedly has been committed.
Lex successionis	The law in accordance with which rights of succession to the estate of a deceased are to be determined.

In recent years the following expressions have emerged:

Lex loci damni	The law of the place in which damage occurred.
Lex loci concursus	The law of the place in which insolvency proceedings are opened.
Lex loci registrationis	The law of the place where a civil partnership or equivalent was registered.

THE LAW OF A COUNTRY

The term "country" should be taken to mean law unit, or legal system, having an independent body of law.[18] The expression "the law of a country" is ambiguous because its meaning may be construed in either of the following ways:

(a) *narrow sense*: in this sense it means the purely internal, or domestic, law of a country, excluding its rules of international private law;
(b) *wide sense*: in this sense it means the internal law, including the rules of international private law of the country in question.

The term "Scots law" in its wide sense includes that body of Scots private law rules in use to decide questions which raise foreign issues, of jurisdiction, choice of law, and/or extraterritorial recognition and enforcement of judgments. While it is true to say that each body of conflict rules is peculiar to its own legal system, each is affected now more than ever before by international legal, commercial and political developments.

The expression "law of a country" will be used in this work in its narrow sense, except in the context of discussion of the methodological problems of *renvoi* and the incidental question.[19]

1–05

HARMONISATION

The subject has undergone great change. The nature of Scots and English international private law rules until as late as the end of the 20th century were, paradoxically, national in nature, despite their international purpose. A notable development in the early-mid 20th century was international co-operation in the treatment of private law problems which (literally!) cross the boundaries of legal systems, e.g. commercial codes on carriage of goods or persons, such as the conventions on the carriage of goods by sea,[20] by air,[21] by rail,[22] or by road.[23]

1–06

---

[18] Hence in the UK there are three separate law units, namely, England and Wales, Scotland, and Northern Ireland; and in the "British Islands" there are, in addition, Jersey, Guernsey, Alderney and Sark (the latter often subsumed under Guernsey), and the Isle of Man. *Dicey, Morris and Collins on the Conflict of Laws*, edited by L. Collins, 15th edn (London: Sweet & Maxwell, 2012), para.1–065. Similarly, there are Canadian provinces and Australian States, in relation to which, for some purposes, e.g. consistorial causes or company law, the substance of the law may be the same for all the component parts of a federation, and so the meaning of "country" in that context is the composite unit. The situation in the USA is doubly complex, since there may be State/Federal and US/international conflicts.

[19] Chs 4 and 5, below.

[20] e.g. Athens Convention relating to the Carriage of Passengers and their Luggage by Sea 1974 (Merchant Shipping Act 1995); Hague-Visby Rules on Carriage of Goods by Sea (Carriage of Goods by Sea Act 1971); UN Convention on the Carriage of Goods by Sea 1978 ("the Hamburg Rules"); and UN Convention on Contracts for the International Carriage of Goods Wholly or Partly By Sea 2008 (multimodal carriage of goods: "the Rotterdam Rules").

[21] e.g. Warsaw Convention for the Unification of Certain Rules relating to International Carriage by Air 1929, as amended at The Hague, 1955, supplemented by the Guadalajara Convention 1961 (Carriage by Air Act 1961), and modernised by the Montreal Convention for the Unification of Certain Rules relating to International Carriage by Air 1999. *Abnett v British Airways Plc*, 1997 S.L.T. 492 HL. See also *Quantum Corp Inc v Plane Trucking Ltd* [2002] 2 Lloyd's Rep. 25; *King v Bristow*

The outstanding feature of the modern age, and an ongoing process of fundamental importance, is the creation and development of a supranational body of international private law rules, developed intra-EU and internationally. The impetus comes principally from the EU and from the Hague Conference on Private International Law.

Europeanisation

1–07   There is an ambitious and wide-ranging programme of harmonisation of law undertaken by the EU in its Justice and Home Affairs portfolio, with the aim of creating an "Area of Freedom, Security and Justice". The central policy is the removal of barriers to the free movement of persons, goods, services and capital. The legal basis for the development of this area is founded now upon the Treaty of Lisbon. Measures in the field of judicial co-operation in civil matters having cross-border implications are authorised by art.81, "particularly when necessary for the proper functioning of the internal market".[24]

The Lisbon Treaty, which is shorthand for two treaties, viz The Treaty on the Functioning of the European Union ("TFEU")[25] and The Treaty on European Union ("TEU"), came into force on 1 December 2009, and as a consequence of which the EU's competence to propose legislation in the field of civil justice was consolidated under Title V of the TFEU, concerning the EU "Area of Freedom, Security and Justice". This is the Justice and Home Affairs ("JHA") agenda. The TFEU contains a number of new provisions pertaining to justice and home affairs. The provision on judicial co-operation in civil matters is contained in art.81 (ex-TEC art.65), viz:

> "1.   The Union shall develop judicial cooperation in civil matters having cross-border implications, based on the principle of mutual recognition of judgments and of decisions in extrajudicial cases. Such cooperation may include the adoption of measures for the approximation of the laws and regulations of the Member States.
>
> 2.   For the purposes of paragraph 1, the European Parliament and the Council, acting in accordance with the ordinary legislative procedure, shall adopt measures, particularly when necessary for the proper functioning of the internal market, aimed at ensuring:

Helicopters Ltd, 2002 S.L.T. 378; *Re Deep Vein Thrombosis and Air Travel Group Litigation* [2006] 1 All E.R. 786; *Ford v Malaysian Airline Systems Berhad* [2013] EWCA Civ 1163; *Laroche v Spirit of Adventure (UK) Ltd* [2009] 2 All E.R. 175; *Barclay v British Airways Plc* [2009] 1 All E.R. 871; *Hook v British Airways Plc (aka Stott v Thomas Cook Tour Operators Ltd)* [2014] UKSC 15; [2014] A.C. 1347; and *Dawson v Thomson Airways Ltd* [2014] EWCA Civ 845; [2015] 1 W.L.R. 883.

[22] e.g. Berne Convention concerning International Carriage by Rail 1980 (Railways (Convention on International Carriage by Rail) Regulations 2005 (SI 2005/2092)); and Railways and Transport Safety Act 2003 s.103.

[23] e.g. Geneva Convention on the Contract for the International Carriage of Goods by Road 1956 (Carriage of Goods by Road Act 1965); *Hatzl v XL Insurance Co Ltd* [2009] EWCA Civ 223; and *British American Tobacco Switzerland SA v Exel Europe Ltd* [2013] EWCA Civ 1319; [2014] 1 W.L.R. 4526.

[24] Note the change of wording from Treaty of Amsterdam art.65, which had a stricter test, namely, "insofar as necessary for the proper functioning of the internal market".

[25] Which amends and replaces the previous Treaty (of Amsterdam) establishing the European Community ("TEC").

(a)   the mutual recognition and enforcement between Member States of judgments and of decisions in extrajudicial cases;

(b)   the cross-border service of judicial and extrajudicial documents;

(c)   the compatibility of the rules applicable in the Member States concerning conflict of laws and of jurisdiction;

(d)   cooperation in the taking of evidence;

(e)   effective access to justice;

(f)   the elimination of obstacles to the proper functioning of civil proceedings, if necessary by promoting the compatibility of the rules on civil procedure applicable in the Member States;

(g)   the development of alternative methods of dispute settlement;

(h)   support for the training of the judiciary and judicial staff.

3.   Notwithstanding paragraph 2, measures concerning family law with cross-border implications shall be established by the Council, acting in accordance with a special legislative procedure. The Council shall act unanimously after consulting the European Parliament.

The Council, on a proposal from the Commission, may adopt a decision determining those aspects of family law with cross-border implications which may be the subject of acts adopted by the ordinary legislative procedure. The Council shall act unanimously after consulting the European Parliament. The proposal referred to in the second subparagraph shall be notified to the national Parliaments. If a national Parliament makes known its opposition within six months of the date of such notification, the decision shall not be adopted. In the absence of opposition, the Council may adopt the decision."

The TFEU increased the number of subject areas in respect of which voting in the European Parliament and the Council no longer is required to be unanimous, and in respect of which it is sufficient to have "qualified majority voting" ("QMV"). The entry into force of the Treaty of Lisbon had important consequences for ongoing, inter-institutional decision-making procedures[26]: since 2009, the European Parliament and the Council have acted as co-legislators in most areas of judicial cooperation in civil matters. Moreover, the Treaty made changes to the organisation and jurisdiction of the Court of Justice of the European Union ("CJEU"). The CJEU acquired general jurisdiction to give preliminary rulings in the area of freedom, security and justice.[27]

The UK opt-in

Under the Lisbon Treaty, by virtue of Protocol No.21 on the position of the UK and Ireland in respect of the area of freedom, security and justice,[28] the UK

        1–08

---

[26] Communication from the Commission to the European Parliament and the Council COM/2009/065 final.

[27] For earlier position, see E.B. Crawford and J.M. Carruthers, "Conflict of Loyalties in the Conflict of Laws: the Cause, the Means and the Cost of Harmonisation" [2005] Jur. Rev. 251, 252. See, for current procedure, "Information note on references from national courts for a preliminary ruling" [2009] O.J. C297/1; and "Recommendations to national courts and tribunals in relation to the instigation of preliminary ruling proceedings" ([2012] O.J. C338/01).

[28] Protocol No.21 [2008] O.J. C115/295. Prior to the Treaty of Lisbon the opt-in was provided by Protocol No.4 on the position of the UK and Ireland [1997] O.J. C340/99. See also Protocol No.22 on the position of Denmark (ex-Protocol No.5 on the position of Denmark [1997] O.J. C340/101), in terms of which Denmark shall not take part in the adoption of proposed measures pursuant to Title V of the TFEU.

enjoys a right not to participate in EU JHA measures. The UK secured this position in order to maintain its border controls and to protect its common law system.[29]

In terms of Protocol No.21, the default position for the UK and Ireland is one of opt-out of proposed measures pursuant to Title V of Part Three of the TFEU, but art.3 permits the UK or Ireland to notify the President of the Council, within three months after a proposal or initiative has been presented pursuant to Title V of Part Three, that it wishes to take part in the adoption and application of any such proposed measure, whereupon it shall be entitled to do so. The Protocol means that when the European Commission proposes legislation founded on a legal base or competence under Title V of the TFEU,[30] the UK does not participate in it unless it chooses to exercise its right to opt in.

The UK exercised the right not to opt in to measures including Rome III,[31] Rome IV[32] and the Regulation Establishing the Justice Programme (2014–2020),[33] and it is expected not to participate in two proposed Regulations on jurisdiction, applicable law and the recognition and enforcement of decisions regarding matrimonial property regimes and the property consequences of registered partnerships.[34] Future proposals concerning judicial cooperation in civil matters will be assessed, and a decision whether or not to opt in taken, by the UK Government on a case-by-case basis.[35]

The opt-in enjoyed by the UK and Ireland, coupled with the Danish opt-out, means that, especially in cases where the UK and/or Ireland declines to opt in, there emerges, in the private law subject area in question, a twin-track Europe. While British and Irish interests are thought to be protected by their default opt-out position, from the point of view of other Member States which do not enjoy the benefit of an automatic opt-out, failure by the UK and/or Ireland to opt in defeats the goal of a common European area of justice. Additionally, the EU rolling stock can diverge—or, as some prefer to say, proceed at different speeds—by virtue of enhanced cooperation procedure, which allows "participating Member States" to work towards a closer degree of integration and/or approximation of laws, as permitted by Title IV of the TEU.

---

[29] HM Government, "Review of the Balance of Competences between the United Kingdom and the European Union Civil Judicial Cooperation" (February 2014), para.1.17.

[30] Interpretation of the legal basis of the opt in has been controversial, in respect of which, see House of Lords, European Union Committee, 9th Report of Session 2014–15: *The UK's opt-in Protocol: implications of the Government's approach* (HL Paper 136, March 2015).The House of Lords Committee view is that a Title V legal base is required before the opt in can be triggered. The UK Government position, however, is that the opt-in Protocol applies whenever, in its view, an EU measure contains JHA content, in addition to when a Title V legal base is formally cited (Ch.1 para.7).

[31] Regulation (EU) No.1259/2010 implementing enhanced co-operation in the law applicable to divorce and legal separation (Ch.12, below).

[32] Regulation (EU) No.650/2012 of the European Parliament and of the Council on jurisdiction, applicable law, recognition and enforcement of decisions and acceptance and enforcement of authentic instruments in matters of succession and on the creation of a European Certificate of Succession ("Rome IV") (Ch.18, below).

[33] Para.1–09, below.

[34] HM Government, "Review of the Balance of Competences between the United Kingdom and the European Union Civil Judicial Cooperation" (February 2014), paras 2.51–2.56. See also Ch.13 below.

[35] HM Government, "Review of the Balance of Competences between the United Kingdom and the European Union Civil Judicial Cooperation" (February 2014), para.3.66.

This two-speed Europe (dubbed "Europe à la carte") is a new phenomenon. Until recently the UK has opted in to the major advances in the international private law harmonisation programme in the matters of civil and commercial jurisdiction and applicable law, and it is only since the programme has ventured into private law fields in respect of which, from the common law UK perspective, there is no perceived advantage in participating, that the UK has refrained from opting in. The implications and complications of this twin-track area of freedom, security and justice will unfold.

The EU Justice Agenda 2020

The EU justice agenda in the period 1999 to 2004 was pursued under the heading of the "Tampere Agenda". 2005 marked the beginning of the follow-up, "second generation" agenda, the "Hague Programme",[36] for the period to 2009. The Commission stated that the strength of the Hague Programme lay in its longer term perspective.[37] Strategic priorities for the period 2010 to 2014 were agreed sub nom the European Council's "Stockholm Programme",[38] and included revision of the Brussels I Regulation,[39] review of certain provisions of the Rome I Regulation,[40] and of the Rome II Regulation,[41] revision of the Brussels II *bis* Regulation,[42] and development of applicable law rules concerning wills and succession[43] and matrimonial property.[44]

The Stockholm Programme and the European Commission implementation plan came to term in December 2014,[45] and subsequent thereto the EU

1–09

---

[36] *The Hague Programme: Strengthening Freedom, Security and Justice in the European Union* [2005] O.J. C53/1; and the Council and Commission Action Plan Implementing the Hague Programme Strengthening Freedom, Security and Justice in the European Union [2005] O.J. C198/1. See, e.g. Communication from the Commission to the Council and the European Parliament: *Report on Implementation of the Hague Programme for 2007* COM(2008) 373 final. See, more generally, E.B. Crawford and J.M. Carruthers, "Conflict of Loyalties in the Conflict of Laws" [2005] Jur. Rev. 251.

[37] Communication from the Commission to the Council, the European Parliament, the European Economic and Social Committee and the Committee of the Regions, *Justice, Freedom and Security in Europe since 2005: An Evaluation of the Hague Programme and Action Plan* COM(2009) 263 final para.VI. See also Implementation Scoreboard SEC(2009) 756 final; Extended Report on the Evaluation of the Programme SEC(2009)766 final; and Institutional Scoreboard SEC(2009) 767 final.

[38] *"The Stockholm Programme – An open and secure Europe serving and protecting citizens"* [2010] O.J. C115/1.

[39] Regulation 44/2001 on jurisdiction and the recognition and enforcement of judgments in civil and commercial matters [2001] O.J. L12/1 ("Brussels I Regulation"). See para.7–15 et seq., below, for details of Regulation (EU) No.1215/2012 of the European Parliament and of the Council of 12 December 2012 on jurisdiction and the recognition and enforcement of judgments in civil and commercial matters (recast) ("Brussels I Recast").

[40] Regulation 593/2008 on the law applicable to contractual obligations (Rome I) [2008] O.J. L177/6. See Ch.15, below.

[41] Regulation 864/2007 on the law applicable to non-contractual obligations (Rome II) [2007] O.J. L199/40. See Ch.16, below.

[42] Regulation 2201/2003 concerning jurisdiction and the recognition and enforcement of judgments in matrimonial matters and in matters of parental responsibility [2003] O.J. L338/1. See Ch.12, below.

[43] Ch.18, below.

[44] Ch.13, below.

[45] Communication from the Commission to the European Parliament, the Council, the European Central Bank, the European Economic and Social Committee and the Committee of the Regions: *The 2014 EU Justice Scoreboard* (COM(2014) 155 final, Brussels, 17 March 2014).

institutions set the political priorities and orientations to be pursued in order to make further progress towards "a fully functioning common European area of justice oriented towards trust, mobility and growth by 2020".[46] A Justice Programme for the period 1 January 2014 to 31 December 2020 has been established,[47] setting general and (so-called) specific objectives for that six-year period.[48] The overall aim is that "by 2020, justice and citizens' rights should know no borders in the EU".[49] In terms of principles underpinning the Justice Agenda, the importance of mutual trust is reaffirmed as "the bedrock upon which EU justice policy should be built".[50]

The essence of the EU Justice Agenda 2020 is to focus on the consolidation of what has been achieved; the codification of EU law and practice when necessary and appropriate; and the complementing of the existing framework with new initiatives.[51] At the same time, full account is to be taken of the diversity of legal systems and traditions in the EU, and the principles of subsidiarity and proportionality are to be respected, all founded upon the EU Charter of Fundamental Rights.[52] With particular reference to international private law, the spectre has been raised of the codification of existing instruments in the civil and commercial field.[53] While technically it would seem to be satisfactory to have multiple instruments in cognate areas brought into a streamlined, single instrument, one senses that the EU aim will be for something more ambitious.

Very significantly, the UK, relying on Protocol No.21, is not taking part in the adoption of the Regulation by which the Justice Agenda 2020 has been set, and is not bound by it or subject to its application.[54]

Implementation of the European justice agenda

1–10   The Regulation is the legislative tool of choice in order to achieve the Europeanisation of international private law, in view of the desired speed of change and the benefits which the Regulation affords, namely, uniform date of entry into force, uniform application, and automatic right of appeal to the Court of Justice of the European Union on points of interpretation.

Although the basis of European actings in the area of harmonisation of law is regional, instruments typically adopt a principle of universality, meaning that in the forum of an EU Member State the harmonised rules must apply, even though the result of applying them is to identify as applicable the law of a non-EU

---

[46] Communication from the Commission to the European Parliament, the Council, the European Economic and Social Committee and the Committee of the Regions: *The EU Justice Agenda for 2020 – Strengthening Trust, Mobility and Growth within the Union* (COM(2014) 144, 11 March 2014), para.1 ("Commission Communication 2014").

[47] Regulation (EU) No.1382/2013 of the European Parliament and of The Council of 17 December 2013 establishing a Justice Programme for the period 2014 to 2020 ([2013] O.J. L354/73).

[48] Regulation (EU) No.1382/2013 art.3.

[49] Commission Communication 2014 para.5.

[50] Commission Communication 2014 para.3.

[51] Commission Communication 2014 para.4.

[52] Commission Communication 2014.

[53] Commission Communication 2014.

[54] Recital (34). See for details of UK reaction House of Lords European Union Committee – 13th Report of Session 2013–14: "Strategic guidelines for the EU's next Justice and Home Affairs programme: steady as she goes" (HL Paper 173, April 2014).

Member State. The link which justifies and requires the application by a forum of an EU regulation is constituted by that court's being situated in an EU Member State; "applicable law", by contrast, is not restricted to that of an EU Member State.

The instruments which are concerned with the allocation of jurisdiction and the enforcement of judgments fall under the "Brussels" family name, since in philosophy and detail they stem from the 1968 Brussels Convention on Jurisdiction and the Enforcement of Judgments in Civil and Commercial Matters.[55] The principle of mutual recognition of judgments, which is founded upon agreement as to acceptable grounds of jurisdiction within the EU, is said to be the cornerstone of judicial co-operation in civil matters. In 2001, certain amendments were made to the text of the Brussels Convention upon its conversion into a Regulation, which instrument, in turn, was superseded by Brussels I Recast, with effect from 10 January 2015.

As well as dealing with jurisdiction and judgment enforcement, the EU has enacted a number of important procedural law instruments, pertaining to civil and commercial litigation, such as Regulations on the taking of evidence abroad,[56] and the service of documents.[57] Additionally, regulations have been enacted with the aim of accelerating enforcement of Member State decrees which in their nature are uncontroversial, such as small claims[58] and uncontested claims.[59] One of the primary aims has been to complete the already advanced implementation of mutual recognition and enforcement of judgments, by abolishing all intermediate measures in the Member State where the decree is to be enforced; this is termed removal of the "*exequatur*" procedure.[60]

Measures have been introduced in family law, following the commercial model, to govern jurisdiction and the recognition of judgments emanating from Member States. The most important instrument in this area is Regulation 2201/2003 ("Brussels II *bis*").[61]

The instruments which are concerned with choice of law fall under the "Rome" patronymic. The most significant instrument in choice of law was the 1980 Rome Convention on the Law Applicable to Contractual Obligations ("Rome I"), now replaced by the Rome I Regulation.[62] This Regulation, in combination with the Rome II Regulation[63] (concerning non-contractual

---

[55] Para.7–08, below. The Lugano Convention 1988 made parallel provision for the EFTA bloc (then Austria, Finland, Iceland, Norway, Sweden and Switzerland). It was revised in 2007 in order to align it with the Brussels I Regulation: [2007] O.J. L339/3.

[56] Regulation 1206/2001 on cooperation between the courts of the Member States in the taking of evidence in civil or commercial matters [2001] O.J. L174/1 (Ch.8, below).

[57] Regulation 1393/2007 on the service in the Member States of judicial and extrajudicial documents in civil or commercial matters [2007] O.J. L324/79 (replacing Regulation 1348/2000 [2000] O.J. L160/37) (Ch.8, below).

[58] Regulation 861/2007 creating a European small claims procedure [2007] O.J. L199/1.

[59] Regulation 805/2004 creating a European Enforcement Order for uncontested claims [2004] O.J. L143/15; and Regulation 1896/2006 creating a European order for payment procedure [2006] O.J. L399/1.

[60] Ch.9, below.

[61] Repealing Regulation 1347/2000 on jurisdiction and the recognition and enforcement of judgments in matrimonial matters and in matters of parental responsibility for children of both spouses ("Brussels II") [2000] O.J. L160/19 (Chs 12 and 14, below).

[62] Ch.15, below.

[63] Ch.16, below.

obligations arising out of tort, delict, unjust enrichment, *negotiorum gestio*, and *culpa in contrahendo*), means that there is now in place a harmonised corpus of rules applicable to the great majority of conflict disputes arising in the law of obligations before EU Member State courts.

Some instruments deal with multiple aspects of the conflict of laws, namely, jurisdiction, applicable law, recognition and enforcement of decisions, and co-operative measures. A recent example is Rome IV.[64]

To facilitate the harmonisation process, there has been created the European Judicial Network (into which the UK has opted[65]), a mechanism for ensuring compliance with, and evaluation of, EU Member State legislation, with the aim of improving cooperation between judicial and legal authorities in the Member States in civil, commercial and family matters.

Continuity of interpretation among instruments

1–11 The degree of interpretative guidance differs from instrument to instrument, depending upon the availability and status of accompanying expert reports,[66] and upon the incidence of appeals to a court of overarching authority, such as the CJEU.[67] Moreover, in the evolution of the European justice agenda, account should be taken of two principles of interpretation to ensure consistency between and among instruments.[68] First, where there are consecutive instruments dealing with and refining the rules relative to a given topic, there is the principle of *vertical* continuity. Within, e.g. civil and commercial jurisdiction, where there has been historical progression from Convention to Regulation to Recast Regulation,[69] continuity of interpretation is important. There are two aspects to vertical continuity: the temporal scope of application of each succeeding instrument, including transitional provisions, must be clear; and judicial interpretation of the later/latest instrument, where an identical or similar form of words is found in succeeding instruments, should be consistent. Where a provision in a subsequent instrument is intended to be equivalent in purpose to one in a predecessor instrument (allowing for modest semantic refinement), weight should be given to

---

[64] Ch.18, below.

[65] HM Government, "Review of the Balance of Competences between the United Kingdom and the European Union Civil Judicial Cooperation" (February 2014), para.2.57.

[66] e.g. as regards interpretation of the Rome I Convention, the Giuliano and Lagarde Report may be relied upon by the courts (M. Giuliano and P. Lagarde, "Report on the Convention on the Law Applicable to Contractual Obligations" [1980] O.J. C282/23).

[67] Treaty on the Functioning of the European Union art.267 provides that the CJEU shall have jurisdiction to give preliminary rulings concerning: (a) the interpretation of the Treaties; (b) the validity and interpretation of acts of the institutions, bodies, offices or agencies of the Union. Where such a question is raised before any court or tribunal of a Member State, that court or tribunal may, if it considers that a decision on the question is necessary to enable it to give judgment, request the Court to give a ruling thereon. Where any such question is raised in a case pending before a court or tribunal of a Member State against whose decisions there is no judicial remedy under national law, that court or tribunal shall bring the matter before the Court.

[68] For detail, see E.B. Crawford and J.M. Carruthers, "Connection and Coherence between and among European Instruments in the Private International Law of Obligations" (2014) 63 International and Comparative Law Quarterly 1.

[69] Brussels I Recast recital (34). For vertical continuity between the 1968 Brussels Convention and the Brussels Regulation, see Brussels Regulation recital (19).

pre-existing decisions of the Court of Justice of the European Union and of national courts, which were interpretative of the earlier provision.

The second principle is that of *horizontal* continuity, i.e. cross-fertilisation between instruments dealing with related subjects. As the cohort of instruments extends across subjects, there may be found instances of horizontal continuity, as e.g. where a provision in an applicable law instrument ("the Rome family") clearly derives from a provision in a jurisdiction instrument ("the Brussels family'"), and may benefit from the interpretation accorded thereto.[70] Replication and reiteration of certain rules horizontally across instruments is apparent,[71] for reasons of principle, consistency and practicality. Horizontal continuity may be expressly directed in an instrument, as, for example, in recital (7) of the Rome I Regulation. Where a principle set in one instrument is imitated in another, the effect is to affirm and consolidate that principle.[72] It is desirable that there be coherence between instruments in a cognate area, such as the law of obligations (contractual and non-contractual). In addition, it may be found that there is inter-dependence between instruments, as for example, the extent to which the applicable law identified by application of the rules of the Rome I Regulation influence identification of the applicable law under the Rome II Regulation.[73]

EU accession to the ECHR

By an Opinion given in 1996,[74] the European Court of Justice concluded that, as Community law then stood, the European Community had no competence to accede to the European Convention for the Protection of Human Rights and Fundamental Freedoms ("ECHR"). Since then, however, the European Parliament, the Council of the European Union and the Commission have proclaimed the Charter of Fundamental Rights of the European Union ("the CFEU") which, by the Treaty of Lisbon when it entered into force on 1 December 2009, received the same legal standing as the Treaties. The Treaty of Lisbon amended art.6 of the EU Treaty, which now provides that fundamental rights, as guaranteed by the ECHR and as they result from the constitutional traditions common to EU Member States, constitute general principles of EU law, and that the EU should accede to the ECHR.[75] Protocol No.8 relating to art.6(2) of the Treaty on European Union on the accession of the Union to the European Convention on

1–12

---

[70] A form of parallel continuity is represented by the 1988 Lugano Convention on jurisdiction and enforcement of judgements in civil and commercial matters (horizontal continuity with the 1968 Brussels Convention), and by the 2007 Lugano II Convention (vertical continuity with Lugano I; and horizontal continuity with the Brussels Regulation).

[71] e.g. in applicable law in obligations: Rome I art.18 = Rome II art.22 (burden of proof); Rome I art.20 = Rome II art.24 (exclusion of *renvoi*); Rome I art.21 = Rome II art.26 (public policy); Rome I art.22 = Rome II art.25 (states with more than one legal system); Rome I art.23 = Rome II art.27 (other provisions of Community law); Rome I art.25 = Rome II art.28 (relationship with other international conventions); and Rome I art.27 = Rome II art.30 (review clause).

[72] e.g. in the subject of awards of damages in contractual and non-contractual disputes. cf. Rome I Regulation art.12.1.c and Rome II Regulation art.15c, both shifting power to fix the award of damages in favour of the *lex causae*.

[73] e.g. per art.4.3 of Rome II, which refers to a pre-existing relationship between the parties, *such as a contract* that is closely connected with the tort in question.

[74] Opinion of the Court of 28 March 1996 (2/94).

[75] Court of Justice of the European Union, Press Release No.180/14 (Luxembourg, 18 December 2014).

the Protection of Human Rights and Fundamental Freedoms provides that any EU accession agreement must satisfy certain conditions to preserve the specific characteristics of the EU and of EU law, and to ensure that accession does not affect EU competences or institutional powers.

The opening of negotiations for an EU accession agreement having been authorised, there was produced in April 2013 a draft accession instrument.[76] Subsequently, the European Commission sought from the CJEU its opinion on the compatibility of the draft agreement with the EU Treaties and with EU law.

In an Opinion issued in December 2014,[77] the CJEU (Full Court) concluded that, although the problem of the lack of any legal basis for the EU's accession to the ECHR had been resolved by the entry into force of the Treaty of Lisbon, the draft agreement on the accession of the EU to the ECHR is not compatible with EU law.

The position rests there; although the EU's accession to the ECHR is deemed to be very important "for the overall fundamental rights architecture around the European area of justice",[78] EU accession to the ECHR cannot proceed on the basis of the current draft agreement.

Global harmonisation

EU—Third State interface

1–13   The extent or ambit of any "intra-EU" regime, and the relationship or interface between an "EU regime" and so-called Third States (non-EU Member States) is a complex matter. One of the political priorities for the European civil justice agenda in the 2010–2014 period was "Europe in a Global World": the external dimension of freedom, security and justice. As far as judicial co-operation in civil matters is concerned, the operation of the Brussels rules in the international legal order (a subject under which is subsumed the task of setting the geographical and legal boundaries of the so-called Brussels regime, and the resolution of difficult issues regarding the relationship between the EU and Third States, including, in particular, the debate as to what should be the rights in civil litigation of European citizens against defendants resident in Third States) was a topic of controversy and concern, both to those within and those outside the EU regime.[79] It seems impossible to contain the European programme, or to effect its ambitious aims without seeping into the area beyond Europe, and without affecting non-EU citizens.[80] One of the principal concerns for future periods of development and

---

[76] Fifth Negotiation Meeting between the CDDH {Steering Committee For Human Rights} Ad Hoc Negotiation Group and The European Commission on the Accession of the European Union to the European Convention on Human Rights ... Final report to the CDDH, 10 June 2013: Appendix 1 contains: Draft revised agreement on the accession of the European Union to the Convention for the Protection of Human Rights and Fundamental Freedoms.

[77] Opinion 2/13 of The Court (Full Court) 18 December 2014.

[78] Communication from the Commission to the European Parliament, the Council, the European Economic and Social Committee and the Committee of the Regions: *The EU Justice Agenda for 2020 – Strengthening Trust, Mobility and Growth within the Union* (COM(2014) 144, 11 March 2014), para.4.

[79] See para.7–62, below.

[80] See, e.g. Regulation (EC) No 662/2009 of the European Parliament and of the Council of 13 July 2009 establishing a procedure for the negotiation and conclusion of agreements between Member

design and implementation of the European programme is to manage the relationship with non-EU Member States.

Hague Conference on Private International Law

The EU operates at a regional level among its Member States, but the Hague Conference on Private International Law functions at a global level. The Hague Conference is an inter-governmental body, founded in 1893, and dedicated to the harmonisation of the private international law rules of different legal systems, and the development and service of multilateral legal instruments.

1-14

In 1955 the Conference was put on a statutory footing, and now has 69 Member States and Regional Economic Integration Organisations ("REIO") from all continents. A REIO is defined[81] as an international organisation that is constituted solely by sovereign States and to which its Member States have transferred competence over a range of matters, including the authority to make decisions binding on its Member States in respect of those matters. Competence having been transferred, the REIO assumes the rights and obligations of a Contracting State. It is for a REIO to indicate the extent to which it has subject-matter competence, and for the REIO and its constituent States to consider whether any subsequent action has to be taken by those States in relation to relevant matters.[82]

The Hague Conference's chosen mode of proceeding is by multilateral treaty or convention, to which Member States may accede, occasionally under reservation as to particular provisions. Conventions may deal only with jurisdiction or with choice of law; or they may deal with jurisdiction and with recognition and enforcement of judgments ("double"); or possibly with all three aspects ("triple"), or even four ("quadruple").

Since 1955, 36 conventions and 2 protocols have been finalised, notable examples of which are: 1961 Convention on the Conflict of Laws relating to the Form of Testamentary Dispositions; 1970 Convention on the Taking of Evidence Abroad in Civil or Commercial Matters; 1980 Convention on the Civil Aspects of International Child Abduction; 1985 Convention on the Law Applicable to Trusts and on their Recognition; 1996 Convention on Jurisdiction, Applicable Law, Recognition, Enforcement and Cooperation in respect of Parental Responsibility Measures for the Protection of Children; 2002 Convention on the Law Applicable to Certain Rights in Respect of Securities Held with an Intermediary; 2005

States and third countries on particular matters concerning the law applicable to contractual and non-contractual obligations ([2009] O.J. L2009/200) (applicable in the UK per recital (24) thereof). Article 1 of the Regulation states that it establishes a procedure to authorise a Member State to amend an existing agreement or to negotiate and conclude a new agreement with a third country, subject to the conditions laid down in this Regulation. This procedure is without prejudice to the respective competencies of the Community and of the Member States.

[81] The 1955 Statute of the Hague Conference on Private International Law, as amended, art.3.9.

[82] Council Note 15226/08 JUSTCIV 235 entitled, "Accession by the European Community to Conventions of The Hague Conference on Private International Law" sets out a letter from the European Commission and Council to the Hague Conference on Private International Law, outlining the intended European approach to existing Hague Conventions, using the classification (a) Conventions which the European Community should join; (b) Conventions requiring further reflection; (c) Conventions which should be left aside; and (d) Conventions which should be left for the Member States to join.

Convention on Choice of Court Agreements; and 2007 Convention on the International Recovery of Child Support and other forms of Family Maintenance. A true measure of the success of a convention is the extent to which it is acceptable internationally, as expressed in the number of states acceding to the instrument. In 2015, the Hague Conference acted by way of a new legislative vehicle, namely, a statement of Principles on Choice of Law in International Commercial Contracts, intended to operate not as a Convention, nor as a Protocol, but rather as a "model for national, regional, supranational or international instruments".[83]

UK participation at the Hague Conference

1–15   The main participation by the UK in Hague Conference projects has been in the period since 1951.[84] Significantly, on 3 April 2007, the European Community was admitted to membership of the Hague Conference as a REIO.[85] With the entry into force of the Treaty of Lisbon on 1 December 2009, and by Declaration of Succession, the European Union replaced and succeeded the European Community as a member of the Conference from that date. In 2014, the European Commission indicated that "At a multilateral level, focus will be given to more efficient cooperation with the Hague Conference on Private International Law, *where the EU speaks with one voice* in areas of civil and commercial law".[86] Although the EU's membership of the Hague Conference does not supplant the membership thereof of individual EU Member States, by dint of shared competence in projects which fall within the expanding EU remit, participation by individual EU Member States in Hague Conference projects is correspondingly inhibited.

UK–EU balance of competences

1–16   In the period 2013–2014, a review of the balance of competences between the EU and the UK in the area of civil judicial cooperation (inter alia) was led by the UK Ministry of Justice,[87] as part of a wider UK Government review and audit of EU

---

[83] Preamble para.1.8 of the introduction indicates that they are a "non-binding set of principles, which the Hague Conference encourages States to incorporate into their domestic choice of law regimes in a manner appropriate for the circumstances of each State. In this way, the Principles can guide the reform of domestic law on choice of law and operate alongside existing instruments on the subject …". At the date of writing the Principles have entered into force only in Paraguay.

[84] K. Lipstein, "One Hundred Years of Hague Conferences on Private International Law" (1993) 42 I.C.L.Q. 553. For background information, and detail of conventions, see *http://www.hcch.net* [accessed 2 June 2015].

[85] A.Schulz, "The Accession of the European Community to the Hague Conference on Private International Law" (2007) 56 I.C.L.Q. 939.

[86] Emphasis added. Communication from the Commission to the European Parliament, the Council, the European Economic and Social Committee and the Committee of the Regions: *The EU Justice Agenda for 2020 – Strengthening Trust, Mobility and Growth within the Union* (COM(2014) 144, 11 March 2014), para.4.

[87] HM Government, "Review of the Balance of Competences between the United Kingdom and the European Union Civil Judicial Cooperation" (February 2014).

competence[88] (i.e. those areas where the power to legislate has been conferred by Member States upon the EU[89]) and its effect on the UK. The Review incorporated an evaluation of the current state of EU competence in civil judicial cooperation and an evaluation of the impact on the UK of measures introduced to date, and of measures proposed. With regard to civil justice cooperation, the position is not uncomplicated. Each EU Member State, as a result of opting in to the European harmonisation scheme, has lost its capacity to act autonomously in any matter concerning judicial cooperation in civil law which falls within EU competence. Extending the exclusive external competence exercised by the EU presents both a challenge and a threat to individual Member States,[90] bringing about, as it inevitably does, a measure of loss of individual state autonomy. For example, the entry by the EU into family law regulation by way of Brussels II *bis* removed from EU Member States their autonomy in the signature and ratification of Hague instruments concerning family law. In relation to cross-border maintenance, the UK Government position was to accept that, by virtue of the existence of the EU Maintenance Regulation,[91] the EU has exclusive external competence in the matters covered by the 2007 Hague Convention on the International Recovery of Child Support and Other Forms of Family Maintenance.[92] In certain matters, however, such as civil and commercial jurisdiction, and the question of acceptance of the accession of further (Third) States to any instrument, the UK Government indicated that it does not accept the assertion by the EU Commission of exclusive external competence.[93]

Engines for law reform—potential for duplication and rivalry

Clearly there is potential for over-regulation and duplication where different law reform agencies operate in the same subject area. The relationship between the Hague Conference, on the one hand, and the EU Commission, Council and Parliament and EU Member States, on the other, is of moment.[94]

    There are instances where the same subject area within international private law has been addressed at different points in time by the Hague Conference and

1–17

---

[88] FCO, "Review of the Balance of Competences between the United Kingdom and the European Union", Cm 8415 (July 2012).

[89] FCO, "Review of the Balance of Competences between the United Kingdom and the European Union", Cm 8415 (July 2012), Ch.1.para.4. For the purposes of the Review, the UK Government adopted a broader definition of competences: the Review would encompass "all the areas where the Treaties give the EU competence to act, including the provisions in the Treaties giving the EU institutions the power to legislate, to adopt non-legislative acts, or to take any other sort of action" (Ch.1, para.4).

[90] HM Government, "Review of the Balance of Competences between the United Kingdom and the European Union Civil Judicial Cooperation" (February 2014), para.3.83.

[91] Regulation 4/2009 on jurisdiction, applicable law, recognition and enforcement of decisions and cooperation in matters relating to maintenance obligations [2009] O.J. L7/1 (Ch.13, below).

[92] HM Government, "Review of the Balance of Competences between the United Kingdom and the European Union Civil Judicial Cooperation" (February 2014), para.2.42.

[93] HM Government, "Review of the Balance of Competences between the United Kingdom and the European Union Civil Judicial Cooperation" (February 2014), para.2.38.

[94] H.van Loon and A.Schulz, "The European Community and the Hague Conference on Private International Law" in B.Martenczuk and S.van Thiel (eds), *Justice, Liberty, Security: New Challenges for the External Relations of the European Union* (Brussels: Institute for European Studies of the Free University of Brussels, 2007).

by the EU.[95] The "layering phenomenon" is a complicating feature of modern conflict of laws, seen most plainly where international instruments overlap, in terms of substance and geography, giving rise to the need to rank potentially applicable sets of rules.[96]

The ranking of different instruments *inter se* in the same subject area normally is set out in a "disconnection clause" within the later instrument.[97] An overt example of a regional solution cutting across an established international treaty, so as to create a particular rule for qualifying cases is Brussels II *bis* art.11,[98] which has provided a significant overlay in instances of intra-EU child abduction, on the operation of the scheme of rules put in place by the 1980 Hague Convention on the Civil Aspects of International Child Abduction. Similarly, the operation of the 1970 Hague Convention on the Taking of Evidence Abroad in Civil or Commercial Matters, implemented in the UK by means of the Evidence (Proceedings in Other Jurisdictions) Act 1975, has been overtaken, in qualifying cases, by Regulation 1206/2001.[99] In the subject area of cross-border maintenance, there is evidence of co-operative symbiosis between Europe and the Hague.[100]

Conclusion

1–18   Insofar as efforts by the EU institutions and the Hague Conference have as their goal the harmonisation of *choice of law* rules, they aim to produce the result that the courts of all Member/Contracting States will agree as to which law shall apply in any given situation. The harmonisation of the *substantive* rules of legal systems would have the result that the issue of choice of law would matter less, because the substantive content of each law which potentially would apply would be identical.[101] Both harmonisation aims can be viewed as facilitating large-scale legal, political and economic objectives. Harmonisation of substantive rules is a longer-term and more ambitious goal. Even if, in the shorter-term, harmonisation

---

[95] Or by the EU and other international convention, such as the Geneva Convention on the Contract for the International Carriage of Goods by Road 1956: *Nipponkoa Insurance Co (Europe) Ltd v Inter-Zuid Transport BV* (C-452/12) [2014] 1 All E.R. (Comm) 288; [2014] C.E.C. 751.

[96] Thorpe L.J. in *Re G (Children) (Foreign Contact Order: Enforcement)* [2003] EWCA Civ 1607 at [32], described the area of "international child law" as a "treaty jungle".

[97] e.g. Brussels II *bis* art.60 ("Relations with certain multilateral conventions"); 2005 Hague Convention on Choice of Court Agreements art.26 ("Relationship with other international instruments"); and Brussels I Recast Ch.VII ("Relationship with other international instruments").

[98] Para.14–65 et seq., below.

[99] Para.8–24 et seq., below.

[100] Para.13–29 et seq., below.

[101] There are early examples of attempts to achieve substantive harmonisation, e.g. agreement on a uniform law on the international sale of goods available for selection by parties (under the Uniform Laws on International Sales Act 1967). More recently, there was issued in January 2009 by the Study Group on a European Civil Code and the Research Group on EC Private Law (Acquis Group) an Academic Common Frame of Reference, containing "Principles, Definitions and Model Rules of European Private Law". Similarly, see Proposal for a Regulation of the European Parliament and of the Council on (an optional) Common European Sales Law ({SEC(2011) 1165 final}) (COM(2011) 635 final 2011/0284 (COD) Brussels, 11 October 2011), which received strong backing by the Committee for Legal Affairs (JURI) in September 2013 (MEMO/13/792), and by the European Parliament in February 2014 (MEMO 14/137). For background, see T.Grädler and M.Köchel, "The parties' remedies under the proposed regulation on a common European sales law", 2013 S.L.T. (News) 69.

of international private law is "achieved" in major areas of private law, the interpretation of harmonisation instruments will vary from Member/Contracting State to Member/Contracting State. Therefore, notwithstanding the harmonisation at some future date of international private law across all major areas, and within a particular political grouping such as the EU, problems will continue to arise as to interpretation of the rules and the extent of their application, even given a central court of overarching authority.

When the modern configuration of international private law is viewed in the light of the layering phenomenon, it is clear that a key skill for the modern conflict lawyer is sensitivity to the importance of selecting, and if necessary justifying as applicable, a particular set of rules from several potentially applicable sets. Even where there are no competing international instruments, and where the UK is party to the one relevant instrument, it may be that the terms of that instrument, in leaving a gap in its scope of application, require the forum to rely on its pre-existing, national conflict rule.[102] Likewise, where the UK decides against opting in to an EU instrument on a given area of law,[103] the UK forum must rely on its pre-existing, national conflict rule. Finally, a problem may arise in the EU context concerning the application of a particular set of harmonised rules within the UK (or within any other multi-legal system Member State), i.e. in an intra-UK conflict case as between Scotland and England, do the EU harmonised rules apply? It is usual for the UK to be given the opportunity to elect not to have the harmonised rule apply in disputes arising between or among its constituent legal systems,[104] but equally, it is usual for the UK to decline to exercise this option. Evidently, the subject has passed beyond a simple layering analogy to one of millefeuille confection!

The very speed with which the text of this book has reached such a detailed account of the busy programme of harmonisation shows how fundamentally changed is the conflict of laws landscape from even a generation ago. The EU programme dominates the design, content and interpretation of the international private law rules of Member States. The harmonisation of conflict of laws rules is a handmaid to the realisation of larger European strategies, and one must be aware of political issues in narrating, analysing and forecasting the content of Scottish and UK international private law rules.

---

[102] e.g. in choice of law in contract, whether the case falls to be regulated by the Rome I Regulation, or by residual national rules, as a result of being excluded from the scope of the Regulation (art.1). Alternatively, a particular term of an instrument may not cover all situations: Rome I Regulation art.13.

[103] e.g. Rome IV; see E.B. Crawford and J.M. Carruthers, "Speculation on the Operation of Succession Regulation 650/2012: Tales of the Unexpected" (2014) 22 European Review of Private Law 847–878. See Ch.18, below.

[104] e.g. Rome I Regulation art.22 and Rome II Regulation art.25.

CHAPTER 2

History

One of the earliest examples of a system of conflict rules is to be found,   **2–01**
preserved in the Louvre Museum, carved on a black pillar: it is the Code of
Hammurabi, King of Babylon. He became king in 2400 BC. The code includes
rules of international private law in the areas of property law, family law and the
law of contract. Hammurabi distinguished between persons and things, and
applied different choice of law rules to each. Thus, Hammurabi's law governed
all contracts made in Babylon regardless of the personal law of the parties,
whereas capacity to marry was governed by the law of the religion provided that
the religion was that of the God of the sun or the God of justice. Where the
religion was neither, Hammurabi's law applied; in the earliest days, as now, the
forum preferred to keep overall control. Whatever religion, the form of marriage,
if celebrated in Babylon, was governed by the *lex loci celebrationis*. The
distinction between that which pertains to persons (deemed to be "permanent",
that is, of long term consequence, and calling for a governing law which would
transcend territorial connections as they might change from time to time), and
that which pertains to things (often thought to be "transient", that is, of
short/medium term consequence, and in respect of which a localised governing
law might be thought appropriate) is a most useful starting point in any
consideration of choice of law, and forms the basis of the distinction drawn in the
early Middle Ages by the post-Glossator, Bartolus, who distinguished between
statutes personal and statutes real. By the sixth century Hammurabi's Kingdom
drew a different distinction—that between Islam and infidel. The personal law of
the Muslim was to be the law of Islam, no matter where s/he might be domiciled.

Roman law is not a fertile source of conflict rules or thinking. Martin Wolff[1]
noted that the *Corpus Juris Civilis*, that repository of answers to "practically
every conceivable legal question", says little on the subject of the application of
foreign laws. Rome's promising circumstances, of legal ability and extensive
empire, produced little from the perspective of the conflict of laws, as Graveson
pointed out,[2] largely because Roman law was so dominant that if one party to a
dispute were a Roman citizen, the application of no other system of law would be
considered. Roman citizens alone had the privilege of being governed by the *jus
civile* of Rome; provincials were subject to their own provincial laws. Hence, the
jus civile governed the rights inter se (and against the world) of Roman citizens.
Where the dispute was between provincials from different provinces the *jus*

---

[1] Wolff, *Private International Law*, 2nd edn (1950), p.19.
[2] Ronald H. Graveson, *Private International Law*, 7th edn (London: Sweet & Maxwell, 1974), p.30.

21

gentium, the law of nations, "which bore little relation to the provincial laws of either party",[3] would regulate the outcome.

In AD 212, by the Edict of Caracalla, which increased greatly the number of persons entitled to the status of Roman citizen and liable to pay citizens' taxes, the ambit of the civil law of Rome was extended to include all people living within the Roman Empire. Hence, that system of private law became territorial—that is to say, it was the same for all people, of whatever race, living within the rule of Rome.

Next came the barbarian invasion, which overthrew the Roman Empire, and settled different tribes in territories previously Roman. Law became personal, and those few who travelled took their personal laws with them like a cloak.

The era of personal law, existing from about the 6th to 10th centuries, was succeeded by a period (11th to 12th centuries) when territorial laws prevailed. The meaningful development was the emergence of the powerful Italian city states in the 13th century. As these cities (of Bologna, Florence, Genoa, Padua, Milan, Modena, Venice and others) developed, they began to pass their own statutes or legal codes which applied over and above the common law. Problems arose in conflicts between the statutes of different cities or between statutes and the common law and the true origin of modern conflict of laws is to be found in such problems, and in the necessity to identify the applicable law. Trade has always fostered the development of conflict rules.

Likewise, scholarship advanced the development of the subject.[4] Of the Glossators and post-Glossators,[5] the greatest contribution to the development of thinking in the conflict of laws was made by Bartolus of Saxoferrato (1314–1357). He made the distinction, in his "Statute Theory", between *statutes personal* (affecting a person in his personal and domestic life wherever he might go), and *statutes real* (concerning things: such laws applied within the territory of the enacting state, so as to affect all persons transacting with things within that state, but they might be found to extend also to moveable property outside the jurisdiction belonging to subjects of that state). However difficult it may be in a particular case to make this classification, the distinction which Bartolus drew is essential to an understanding of the nature and content of orthodox conflict rules and methodology. It is important to grasp that the law which one may expect to have applied to one's situation in the fundamental things of life is not necessarily the appropriate law to govern that which is commercial and/or relatively transient.

2–02   The Statute Theory was applied by the French jurists of the 16th century, with varying approaches. D'Argentré, of the Breton (territorial) background, favoured the extension of the scope of the statute real, and the ascription of doubtful cases to that category, while Dumoulin (Molinaeus) advocated what now is termed "party autonomy", a permissive attitude towards choice of law by parties.

The developments in France were followed by a corresponding development in the Netherlands by jurists of the Dutch School, such as Burgundus (d. 1649),

---

[3] Graveson, *Private International Law*, 7th edn (1974), p.30.

[4] Wolff, *Private International Law*, 2nd edn (1950), p.21: "Private International Law was a product of the Italian Universities of the thirteenth century".

[5] Or better, "Commentators": Wolfgang Kunkel, *Roman Legal and Constitutional History* (London: Clarendon Press, 1966), pp.171, 172. Kunkel argues that the work of putting a gloss on the Roman texts was creative work and a significant contribution, not merely "laborious erudition".

Paul Voet (d. 1677), his son, John Voet (1647–1714), and Huber (1636–94). The last mentioned was a professor and judge from Friesland, whose treatise on the subject, entitled *De Conflictu Legum* (1689)[6] was only five quarto pages in length but immensely influential. By Huber's time, political considerations and notions of sovereignty had begun to impinge. Why should a sovereign admit the application within his kingdom of the laws of another sovereign? Huber provided the following guide and explanation in his maxims:

(1) the laws of every sovereign authority operate within its territorial boundaries, and are binding on all its subjects, but not beyond;
(2) those are held to be subject to a sovereign authority who are found within its boundaries, whether they be there permanently or temporarily;
(3) sovereigns will so act by way of comity that rights acquired within the limits of a sovereign authority retain their force everywhere so far as they do not cause prejudice to the power or rights of another sovereign authority or its subjects.[7]

It should be noted that in his third maxim, Huber made two suggestions to explain the extraterritorial application of law. The first is comity, which may be translated as international goodwill into which is mixed a measure of reciprocity and mutual advantage, and the second is the use of the phrase "rights acquired". The second concept later gave support to a theory, the "Vested Rights Theory", which is based upon the proposition that it is not foreign law per se, but a right acquired under a foreign legal system, which is enforced *extra territorium*.

In England, there is little trace of any attempt to apply conflict rules and principles before 1603. There could be little private law conflict between England and Scotland because the gates were closed: the Scots Act of 1431 (c.128) made it treason to live in England without permission of the King of Scotland, that of 1436 (c.145) forbade Scots from buying English goods "under pain of escheat", and that of 1587 (c.105) prohibited a Scot from marrying an Englishwoman. When the gates were opened, the differences in the domestic laws of persons of the neighbouring countries made the conflict cases particularly interesting.[8] England had not the beneficial exposure to the influence of the continental jurists. The English practice was to apply English law to all disputes coming before English courts, whether or not the case contained a foreign element.

When the Crowns were unified in 1603, a problem was posed for Huber's sovereignty theory in that the king was sovereign of two legal systems. Previously, the English courts had applied English law to all disputes whether or not foreign elements were involved, but surely some validity now must be accorded in England to the King's law in/of Scotland? In *Calvin's Case*,[9] it was held by the Exchequer Chamber in England that Scots born after the accession of James to the throne of England did not have the status of aliens in England. Many

---

[6] In full *"De Conflictu Legum Diversarum in Diversis Imperiis"*.

[7] For other translations, see Wolff, *Private International Law*, 2nd edn (1950), p 27; D.J. Llewelyn Davies, "The Influence of Huber's *De Conflictu Legum* on English Private International Law" (1937) 18 Brit. Y.B.Int'l L 49 at 56–57; and *Emory v Greenough* (1797) 3 Dallas 369.

[8] Andrew D. Gibb, *Law from Over The Border* (Edinburgh: W. Green, 1950), p.89; and more recently, Kirsty J. Hood, *Conflict of Laws within the UK* (Oxford: Oxford University Press, 2007).

[9] *Calvin's Case* (1608) 7 Co. Rep. 1; 2 St. Tr. 559.

would consider this a constitutional case rather than a conflict one. One of the earliest reported conflict cases is that of *Dungannon*[10] (upon the question of which law should govern the rate of interest under an Irish bond), indicating the beginning of a readiness to accept that some law, other than that of the English law of the forum, might apply.

In the 1760s, the great Anglo-Scottish lawyer, Lord Mansfield, made valuable contributions to early conflict of laws thinking, for example in the identification of the law which should govern substantive questions pertaining to a contract, where no choice of law has been made.[11] In these early days English courts were troubled by the taking of jurisdiction in a case of alleged civil wrongdoing where the actings complained of had been committed abroad. They devised, therefore, the fiction of "local venue", and would accept the plea that the event had taken place, "in the Parish of St Mary le Bow", thereby "laying the venue".[12] This fiction also tended to lead the English courts to the view that the *lex fori* was the natural law to apply. The consequences of this were far reaching both for England and Scotland, and even after the revision of conflict rules in tort/delict by the Private International Law (Miscellaneous Provisions) Act 1995, the influence of the *lex fori* was not extinguished.[13] The fiction of "local venue" was abandoned in English law, and was never present in Scots law which found no difficulty in assuming jurisdiction in a case relating to a foreign delict so long as a personal link would justify it.[14]

Since 1707 the systems of Scotland and England have grown together in many areas, including international private law, and in truth are closer in their conflict rules than in many other areas. The English rules in this area were slower to emerge, and developed later, in a typically pragmatic and remedy-based manner (although Morris[15] was of the view that the attention paid in deciding cases to the writings of jurists was unusual in English law). Of the Anglo-American school the greatest debt is owed to the jurist Joseph Story (1779–1845),[16] who drew the strands together. He was followed by Dicey and Westlake, a long line of learned writers,[17] and a wealth of 19th and 20th-century case law. UK conflict lawyers of

---

[10] *Dungannon v Hackett* (1702) 1 Eq. Cas. Abr. 289. See also *Cottington's Case* (1678) 2 Swans. 326; and (1607) *Wiers Case* 1 Rolle, Abridgmt. 530, 12, admitting the obligation in principle to recognise and give effect to foreign judgments: Wolff, *Private International Law*, 2nd edn (1950), p.30.

[11] *Robinson v Bland* (1760) 2 Burr. 1077.

[12] *Mostyn v Fabrigas* (1774) 1 Coup. 161; 1 S.L.C. 615, in which Lord Mansfield again brought the law forward by taking the view that a justification by the *lex loci delicti* could be pleaded as a defence to an action in England. But see R.H. Graveson, *Private International Law*, 7th edn (1974), p.135, on the matter of taking jurisdiction where the conduct complained of related to immovable property in Nova Scotia (a "local" (land) action as opposed to a "transitory" (with the potential to arise anywhere) action, in English parlance). Morse, *Torts in Private International Law* (Oxford: North-Holland Publishing Company, 1978), p.9.

[13] The common law "rule of double actionability" is retained by s.13 in relation to actions pertaining to defamation, and survives also the introduction of the Rome II Regulation. See Ch.16, below.

[14] Until 1971 it was necessary also that the defender was served within the jurisdiction. This requirement was removed by the Law Reform (Jurisdiction in Delict) (Scotland) Act 1971.

[15] J.H.C. Morris, *The Conflict of Laws*, edited by D. McClean, 4th edn (London: Sweet & Maxwell, 1993), p.6. A.V. Dicey's *Digest of the law of England with reference to the conflict of laws* (London: Stevens, 1896) is regarded as the first systematic English treatment.

[16] J. Story, *Commentaries on the Conflict of Laws* (Boston: Hilliard, Gray and Co, 1834).

[17] Through Cheshire, Graveson, Morris and Anton, the distinguished list continues up to the expertise of the present day.

the 21st century must accept, address, and master harmonised private international law rules springing mainly from an EU source.

DEVELOPMENT OF CONFLICT RULES IN SCOTLAND

In consequence of the close ties between Scotland and France before the Reformation and between Scotland and the Netherlands after the Reformation, the Scots courts dealt with conflict problems at an earlier date than the English courts.[18] The dictionaries of Morison, Kilkerran and others contain reports of Scots conflict cases[19] a century ahead of English cases.

2–03

Knowledge of conflict thinking grew through scholarship[20] and through trade, the latter perhaps, in the view of Gibb,[21] even more valuable. It is gratifyingly evident in the early case of *Stranger from Middleburg v Executors of Smith*,[22] a case concerning a bond which the deceased Smith, a Scot, had made in Flanders, but had failed to honour, and from whose estate in Scotland the Flemish creditor had been obliged to seek satisfaction. The Scots court upheld the bond as valid, though it lacked witnesses, "because the pursuer offered to prove that it was the custom of the country that such bonds, albeit wanting witnesses, yet were effectual against the subscribers thereof"[23]—a matter to be proved, not by declarations of witnesses, but by a testimonial by the judges of the country. In *A Frenchman against an Englishman*[24] it was held that the Scottish Lords of Council were competent judges between stranger and stranger, in all civil actions "even concerning transactions outside the realm", and should decide according to, "the common law, and not after the municipal law of this realme": the applicable law therefore was not to be Scots law, despite the fact that Scotland was the forum. Possibly what was intended was the application of the "Law of Nations", that is, principles of right reason generally accepted internationally.

The links achieved as a result of trade demonstrated at an early date some of the problems which international private law exists to try to solve. It was the practice in Scotland to confer upon one town in the Low Countries a monopoly of trade: this was the "Scottish Staple", established at various times at Middleburg, Campvere, Antwerp, Bruges, and from 1541, at Vere. All Scots merchants had to use the favoured town, and in return it would keep the channel safe, and provide

---

[18] A.D. Gibb, "International Private Law in Scotland in the 16th and 17th Centuries" (1927) 39 J.R. 369; A. Donaldson, "Some Conflict Rules of Scots Law" in *The Grotius Society* (London: Longmans, Green and Co); *Problems of Public and Private International Law* (1953), Vol.39, pp.145–148.

[19] See generally P.R. Beaumont and P.E. McEleavy, *Anton's Private International Law*, 3rd edn (Edinburgh: W. Green, 2011), paras 1–26 to 1–35. But also in the later Victorian years, Scotland produced significant and helpful cases: see L. MacKinnon, *Leading Cases in the International Private Law of Scotland* (Edinburgh: W. Green, 1934); and A.D. Gibb, *Law from Over The Border* (1950), pp.89–91.

[20] It is well established that many Scottish students resorted to European universities in the Low Countries such as Franeker and Leyden: D.M. Walker, *The Scottish Legal System*, 8th edn revised (Edinburgh: W. Green, 2001), p.163.

[21] A.D. Gibb, "International Private Law in Scotland in the 16th and 17th Centuries" (1927) 39 J.R. 369, 373.

[22] *Stranger from Middleburg v Executors of Smith* (1626) Mor. 12420.

[23] This accords with the modern practice: Rome I Regulation art.11(1). See Ch.13, below.

[24] *A Frenchman against an Englishman* (1550) Mor. 7323.

warehouse accommodation and wharfage.[25] Hence, there grew up a little Scottish colony which had a Governor, the Lord Conservator of the Scottish privileges, with jurisdiction to hear disputes between Scots litigants and to apply Scots law. Gibb noted how remarkable it is to find a judge exercising exclusive jurisdiction and using his own law in a foreign country.[26] There was appeal to the Scots courts. Where the parties were Scots and Dutch, a mixed court of local magistrates and arbiters appointed by the Conservator would decide the issue, but it is uncertain according to which law. We know that when a Scotsman married a Dutchwoman, she came under the jurisdiction of the Conservator and became subject to Scots law. It has been pointed out,[27] however, that there was a loophole (closed in 1696) which gave advantages for the potentially insolvent Scots merchant: if he became bankrupt, his property would escape safely to his wife.

When a community is transferred out of its usual abode, it is compelled to consider the conflict of laws. Conversely, when the gates are closed between neighbours, conditions do not encourage development of conflict thinking.

Donaldson[28] concluded that, although Scotland by the end of the 17th century could not be said to be furnished with a complete set of conflict rules, certain principles were clearly established, namely, the pre-eminence of the *lex situs* in property matters,[29] and of the *lex fori* in procedure, and the universality of bankruptcy.

HOW SCOTTISH ARE THE CONFLICT RULES OPERATIVE IN SCOTLAND?

2–04   In contrast with the early days, there has been for many years a spirit of co-operation and sympathy between English and Scots law and between their law reform agencies in the matters of the aims and content of their conflict rules. Not only can there be identified swathes of conflict rules which long have been similar in content and mutually supportive,[30] there is now also, in an increasing number of areas, uniformity attributable to the Europeanisation of the subject. Further, there is within the UK mutual recognition of consistorial decrees,[31] of parental responsibility orders and adoption orders,[32] and of confirmation and probate/letters of administration.[33] Strictly speaking, conflict decisions of one legal system of the UK are merely persuasive in the other, but the conflict decisions of the one jurisdiction are likely to be followed in the other if on a point

---

[25] A.D. Gibb, "International Private Law in Scotland in the 16th and 17th Centuries" (1927) 39 J.R. 369, 375, who comments that English merchants were never other than private adventurers.

[26] A modern instance can be cited in that in 1999, the High Court of Justiciary sat, with its usual powers, at Camp Zeist, Netherlands, in the case *HM Advocate v Al Megrahi*, 2000 S.L.T. 1393.

[27] A.D. Gibb, "International Private Law in Scotland in the 16th and 17th Centuries" (1927) 39 J.R. 369, 377.

[28] A. Donaldson, "Some Conflict Rules of Scots Law" in *Problems of Public and Private International Law* (1953), p.147.

[29] *Lamb v Heath* (1624) Mor. 4812.

[30] e.g. in family law, obligations, property and succession (while there remain many differences between the domestic laws of Scotland and England in these areas).

[31] Ch.12, below.

[32] Ch.14, below.

[33] Ch.18, below.

common to both sets of conflict rules. If the decision is of the House of Lords/Supreme Court on a matter of general principle, for all practical purposes the decisions will be of equal authority in both countries: in this way there have become "naturalised" in England, Scottish House of Lords cases and vice versa. The twin Victorian domicile pillars of *Udny v Udny*[34] and *Bell v Kennedy*[35] (both Scottish House of Lords cases) represent a very British view of the connecting factor of domicile.[36] A caveat perhaps should be inserted: where a substantial body of interpretative case law has been developed in Scotland in a particular subject matter, e.g. concerning the 1980 Hague Convention on the Civil Aspects of International Child Abduction, there is less need and less inclination to refer to English authority. The approach taken in this book is that the conflict rules of Scots and English law in many areas have more to unite them than to divide them: where there are differences, or have been differences, these will be mentioned in the text. This is not intended to detract in any way from the status of the body of Scots conflict rules as a complete and independent system, capable of providing an answer to any conflict problem.

Account must be taken of the fundamental constitutional change effected by the Scotland Act 1998 (as amended by the Scotland Act 2012), as a result of which matters of Scottish civil law fall within the legislative competence of the Scottish Parliament.[37] Section 126(4)(a) interprets the civil law of Scotland as a reference to the general principles of private law, including private international law.[38] An Act of the Scottish Parliament is not law insofar as any provision thereof is outside the legislative competence of the Parliament; reserved matters are expressly excluded from its legislative competence. The question whether a provision relates to a reserved matter is to be determined by reference to the purpose of the provision.[39] Although international private law generally is a devolved matter falling within the legislative competence of the Scottish Parliament, the private international law aspects of reserved matters likewise are reserved (s.29(4)(b); e.g. the international private law rules concerning intellectual property).

By constitutional convention, it is possible for the UK Parliament, with consent of the Scottish Parliament, by legislative consent motion (previously a "Sewel motion") to legislate for Scotland in devolved matters. In the context of the conflict of laws, particularly in family law, there may be perceivable benefits in having the UK Parliament legislate for the entire UK, thus lessening the likelihood of intra-UK conflict problems. The resultant UK legislation may contain separate provision for each legal system within the UK, but even if that is the case, it is hoped that the legislation will demonstrate internal UK coherence.[40]

---

[34] *Udny v Udny* (1869) 7 M. (H.L.) 89.

[35] *Bell v Kennedy* (1868) 6 M. (H.L.) 69.

[36] Subject now to the divergence wrought by the Scottish Parliament in s.22 of the Family Law (Scotland) Act 2006.

[37] Scotland Act 1998 s.29 (legislative competence) establishes what the Scottish Parliament may not do rather than what it may do. Section 29(2)(b) provides that reserved matters (s.30, Sch.5) are outside Scottish parliamentary competence.

[38] Family Law (Scotland) Act 2006 s.38 serves as an example of Holyrood utilisation of this competence.

[39] Scotland Act 1998 s.29(3).

[40] The Civil Partnership Act 2004, which affects reserved matters as well as devolved matters, was referred to Westminster by means of a Sewel motion. The Act, however, makes bespoke provision for

In terms of s.57 of the 1998 Act ("EU law and Convention rights"), despite the transfer to the Scottish Ministers of functions in relation to implementing obligations under EU law, any function of a Minister of the Crown in relation to any matter shall continue to be exercisable by him as regards Scotland for the purposes of s.2(2) of the European Communities Act 1972. In this context, therefore, there is "shared power" between Scottish and UK Ministers. As indicated in Ch.1, with regard to the EU Private International Law harmonisation agenda, the privilege of discretionary opt-in to proposed instruments is one extended not to individual legal systems of the UK, but rather to the UK as a whole, as the EU Member State.[41] Furthermore, Sch.5 Pt 1 para.7 to the 1998 Act reserves foreign affairs, including relations with the EU, but excepting implementation of international obligations, obligations under the Human Rights Convention and obligations under EU law.[42]

With regard to participation in and ratification of initiatives of the Hague Conference on Private International Law, it remains the case that the United Kingdom is the Hague Conference Contracting State. Nevertheless, on occasion, as a result of differences in the content of certain areas of domestic law of Scotland and England, it may happen that the United Kingdom will sign a Hague Convention on behalf of one constituent legal system only.[43]

---

the different legal systems within the UK. See Ch.11, below. cf. Matrimonial and Family Proceedings Act 1984 Pt 3 (England) and Pt 4 (Scotland) (Ch.13, below).

[41] See para.1–08.

[42] Separate secondary implementing legislation frequently is required for Scotland and England, respectively, in respect of EU Regulations.

[43] e.g. 2000 Hague Convention on International Protection of Adults, signed by the UK separately for Scotland and for England, and ratified by Scotland. For England and Wales, see Mental Capacity Act 2005.

CHAPTER 3

Operation of foreign law: theories of inclusion and rules of exclusion

Why should the domestic law of one legal system be recognised and given effect in another? It is surely a sufficient reply that there is in each developed legal system a system of rules, known as its international private law, or conflict of laws, rules, which regulates these matters: the operation of the rules of one legal system within the bounds of another stems from the law of the latter. There is therefore no affront to sovereignty. **3–01**

However, over the course of the relatively young life of the subject, various theories have been advanced to explain the extraterritorial effect of a rule:

(1)   The international theory (comity) finds the nature of the subject in the notion of international goodwill or reciprocity, a "do as you would be done by" spirit of international co-operation,[1] which is present in many modern international legislative exercises,[2] as well as in longer-established bodies of rules based on mutual assistance,[3] the more so if the legal systems involved are each members of a supranational body.[4]

(2)   The statutory or neo-statutory theory is derived from the illuminating distinction made by Bartolus[5] between statutes real (affecting only property situated within the enacting state) and statutes personal (affecting the individual in his personal life wherever he or she might go).

(3)   Savigny's theory of the natural seat of an obligation[6] holds that every relationship is by its nature connected more strongly with one legal system than any other. That legal system, therefore, being the source of rights and obligations, should determine the outcome, wherever the matter is litigated.

---

[1] L. Collins, "Comity in Modern Private International Law" in James Fawcett (ed.), *Reform and Development in Private International Law: Essays in Honour of Sir Peter North* (Oxford: Oxford University Press, 2002), Ch.4.

[2] e.g. 1980 Hague Convention on the Civil Aspects of International Child Abduction; 1993 Hague Convention on Protection of Children and Co-Operation in Respect of Intercountry Adoption; and 1996 Hague Convention on Jurisdiction, Applicable Law, Recognition, Enforcement and Cooperation in respect of Parental Responsibility Measures for the Protection of Children.

[3] e.g. in foreign judgment enforcement: Administration of Justice Act 1920 and Foreign Judgments (Reciprocal Enforcement) Act 1933; and Civil Jurisdiction and Judgments Acts 1982 and 1991.

[4] Ch.1, above.

[5] Para.2–01, above.

[6] F.C. von Savigny, translated by Sheriff W. Guthrie, *A Treatise on the Conflict of Laws* (Edinburgh: T&T Clark, 1869); cf. in similar vein, the American view expressed by Holmes and Cardozo JJ. that foreign law constitutes an *obligatio* which, "follows the person and may be enforced wherever the person may be found": *Slater v Mexican National Railway* (1904) 194 U.S. 120 at 126.

Savigny's view was "universalist" and supranational, seeking uniformity in the treatment of conflict cases. Savigny's work (adapted)[7] had a Scottish follower in James Lorimer (1818–90), writer on international law.[8]

(4) Mancini's theory of nationality. The movements for political unification of Italy and Germany in the latter part of the 19th century brought with them a natural enthusiasm for nationality as the most suitable choice of governing law in personal matters. Mancini argued that nationality was the basis of international law (propounding this at a famous lecture at the University of Turin in 1851) and that a person should be entitled, under limited exceptions, to be governed by the law of his nationality even when abroad.

(5) The territorial theory originated in the writings of the Dutch jurists and in particular those of Huber.[9] This theory, which reflects the concerns of the time at which Huber was writing (1689), and which is founded upon the dignity of sovereigns, and their power and authority within their own realms, continues to influence many areas of the subject, e.g. matters of title to property, immoveable or moveable, in respect of which the *lex situs*[10] is the pre-eminently applicable law. In effect the theory means that a state has complete power over all persons and property within its territory, that within its territory only its own law applies, and that it has no power over persons and property outside its own territory: "The Laws of a foreign State have no coercive force extra territorium".[11] It follows from this that, if foreign rights are to be recognised and enforced in Scotland, they must be regarded as being part of Scots law and/or as acquiring recognition, and justifying enforcement, under Scots conflict rules.

(6) The local law theory, which arose from the observations and writings of the American jurist Cook,[12] suggests that the forum, when asked to lend its aid to enforce a foreign right which originated in a foreign system, does not apply foreign law, but uses an analogous right of its own domestic law to achieve the same end.[13]

(7) The theory of Justice. It may be that the true basis of the subject is simply the desire and necessity to ensure that the ends of justice are served and in particular that justice is done to the individual whose personal or business life has led him to experience the conflict of laws. "Conflicts justice" would seem to include considerations such as seeking to meet reasonable party expectations, and to achieve certainty, predictability and uniformity of result, and increasingly now to permit a degree of "party autonomy" (party choice of choice of court and/or choice of law). Graveson wrote that this is the major basis of the subject.[14] It is doubtful whether the grand aim of uniformity of result regardless of forum is ever capable of being

---

[7] D.M. Walker, *The Scottish Jurists* (Edinburgh: W. Green, 1985), p.369.

[8] Walker, *The Scottish Jurists*, 1985, p.370.

[9] Para.2–02, above.

[10] As to meaning of which, see Ch.17, below.

[11] Morison's Dictionary, 4453.

[12] W.W. Cook, *The Logical and Legal Bases of the Conflict of Laws* (Cambridge, Massachusetts: Harvard University Press, 1942).

[13] Cases can be found in which the theory seems to be borne out by the circumstances and outcome, e.g. *Re Bettinson's Question* [1956] Ch. 67.

[14] Graveson, *Private International Law*, 7th edn (1974), p.7.

accomplished, but many agree that the pursuit of "private law justice" is the main aim and raison d'être of the subject.

(8)   American policy evaluation theories, discussed and debated in the USA since the 1930s (termed "The American Revolution"),[15] constituted a fundamental change in thinking, both as to theory and as to method.

There are many approaches to choice of law, and there has been much writing.[16] The traditional approach is "jurisdiction-selecting", a term used to describe the orthodox choice of law process which seeks to apply the law indicated as applicable, category by category, according to the forum's choice of law rules. It does not purport to take account of the outcome in the instant case (indeed prides itself in avoiding so doing). The term, however, is confusing because "jurisdiction" in this context must be interpreted, unusually, as a reference to application of the rules of a particular legal system and does not pertain to the allocation or exercise of civil jurisdiction by a particular forum.

Policy evaluation thinking seeks to depart from the traditional "blind" or "blinkered" selection of the law to be applied, determined in the abstract (in the view of the forum), to adjudicate on the type of problem in question. A "rule-selecting" approach has regard to the nature and desirability (in the view of the forum, presumably) of the particular outcome, i.e. it considers the effect in the concrete case of the application of such law. Every forum has to struggle against the view, conscious or subconscious, that its own law is best. Commentators and courts must be alert to incidence of "homeward trend" on the part of the forum, that is to say, a tendency of the forum to favour its "own" litigant or the application of its own law. It has been suggested that often the effect of the policy evaluation theories—or, properly, methods—is that the forum wends its way home, albeit by a circuitous route.

Examples of the policy evaluation methods include the theories of "Government Interest Analysis" (can the policies of the competing laws be ascertained? How reasonable is it for each respective state to assert an interest in the application of its law?); "Comparative Impairment" (if policies conflict, there should be applied the law of the state whose interest would be more/most gravely impaired if not applied); "Principles of Preference"[17] and "Choice Influencing Factors", which proceed on the

---

[15] Morris, *Conflict of Laws*, 6th edn (2005), Ch.21; and P.M. North, "Family Law and the American Revolution" in P.M. North, *Essays in Private International Law* (Oxford: Clarendon Press, 1993), Ch.6.

[16] Though the writing may be said to be concerned particularly with inter-state conflicts. See, in particular, B. Currie, *Selected Essays on the Conflict of Laws* (Durham, North Carolina: Duke University Press, 1963); D.F. Cavers, *The Choice of Law Process* (Ann Arbor: University of Michigan Press, 1965); and A. Shapira, *The Interest Approach to Choice of Law* (The Hague: Martinus Nijhoff, 1970). The federal structure, wherever found (but especially in the USA) is likely to produce conflict disputes. The American Law Institute brought together, in a Restatement, the most important principles. The Restatement is persuasive, not binding on states. The first Restatement (1934, with Reporter Beale) was certain in tone and favoured the Vested Rights approach (*q.v.*); the second Restatement (1971, with Reporter Reese) was more open to the new theories and methods.

[17] Cavers's suggestions are concerned principally with the law of obligations, offering guidance to the forum on grounds of general policy (the higher standard of required conduct being usually, but not always, preferred) in choosing between or among the rules of interested states.

basis that agreement on certain general aims, for example protection of justified expectations, or uniformity of result, should aid choice of law. All such policy evaluation methods involve "rule-selection", that is, "looking up to see the finishing tape", which is at odds with the orthodox or classical "jurisdiction-selection" method traditionally held to provide the benefits of neutrality and distance.

The EU's ambitious programme of harmonisation of private international law in many private law subject areas proceeds on the basis that the emerging corpus of assimilated conflict rules derives from, and demonstrates, jurisdiction-selection methodology. Quite apart from the question of acceptability in principle of a rule-selection approach, it is thought unsuitable in an international, as opposed to an inter-state, context.[18]

(9)   The theory of the vested or acquired right, based on the territorial theory, was advocated by Dicey. The premise is that, if a question should arise in Scotland as to the enforcement of a "foreign right", the Scots court must determine the origin of the foreign right and ascertain whether it is a right which has been validly acquired under its own law. If that is so, the right will be enforceable in Scotland provided that its enforcement does not fall within any of the exceptions, discussed in paras 3–02 et seq., below. Whatever the merits and standing of the theory (or of any theory of extraterritorial validity and enforceability of rights), at least the exceptions or limitations are well known and well vouched[19]: no Scots or English court will recognise or give effect to a foreign right if this would involve:

(a)   the enforcement of foreign revenue laws;

(b)   the enforcement of foreign penal laws;

(c)   the enforcement of foreign confiscatory laws; or

(d)   making a decision inconsistent with the public policy or morality of the UK, or detrimental to its political and judicial institutions.

The procedure available by Scots law must be appropriate for the enforcement of the right, and a foreign right, which is otherwise valid, will not be enforced if its enforcement would involve any question of discretion which would be exercised more appropriately by a foreign court.[20]

The vested rights theory has been the subject of trenchant criticism.[21] The germ of the theory, as well as of the comity theory, can be found in Huber's third maxim: sovereigns will so act by way of comity that rights acquired within the limits of a sovereign authority retain their force

---

[18] Morris, *Conflict of Laws*, 8th edn (2012), para.19–022 (re principles of preference): "[H]ow could a judge express a preference for the rules adopted by one country or another when those countries are not component parts of a federal system but are linked only by diplomatic relations or (perhaps) by a common cultural heritage?"

[19] Though nowadays, while the core of the exceptions holds firm, the edges, as a result of harmonisation and globalisation, are not so well defined. For a modern discussion of the topic generally, see *Iran v Barakat Galleries Ltd* [2009] Q.B. 22, per Lord Phillips at [95] et seq.

[20] cf. *Phrantzes v Argenti* [1960] 2 Q.B. 19; contrast *Shahnaz v Rizwan* [1965] 1 Q.B. 390.

[21] *Cheshire, North and Fawcett: Private International Law*, 14th edn (2008), pp.24–26; M. Wolff, *Private International Law*, 2nd edn (1950), p.2; Graveson, *Private International Law*, 7th edn (1974), p.38. Supporters are C.M. Schmitthoff, *The English Conflict of Laws* (London: Stevens & Sons Ltd, 1954), pp.32 and 35 et seq.; and J.H. Beale, *Treatise on the Conflict of Laws* (New York: Baker, Voorhis & Co, 1935).

everywhere so far as they do not cause prejudice to the power or rights of another sovereign authority or its subjects.[22]

It is predicated on the basis that it is not the foreign law per se which is being enforced *extra territorium*, but rights acquired *under* the foreign law; but it is difficult to see how the rights conferred by a legal system can be dissociated from the law which created them. Moreover, if the forum is to set itself to implement foreign acquired rights, so far as its own public policy and procedure allow, it must ascertain the law by which the right is to be tested to determine whether it has vested or has been acquired. The theory contains no choice of law rules. The forum cannot start from the right and work backwards, assuming/supposing that the right should be enforced; that law which is the origin of the right may not be (in the view of the forum) the correct choice of law to apply. Therefore, if the acquired rights theory is to be used at all, it seems suitable only for simpler cases where all seemingly relevant factors, apart from the identity of the forum, pertain to one legal system, and the remedy available in the legal system of origin is sought elsewhere. A number of cases in the conflict of laws catalogue satisfy this test,[23] but a much greater number do not. However, there is no doubt that the vested rights theory, as encapsulated in a form of words as a guide, instils the correct attitude of international co-operation and open-mindedness.[24] Novelty in itself should be no bar to the enforcement of a foreign acquired right, nor to the recognition of a foreign status unknown but unexceptionable.[25]

(10) Economic analysis of the conflict of laws.[26] A further and more modern lens through which to view the subject is that of the economic analysis theory, which examines the interrelationship of systems of private law, particularly in the law of obligations. The analysis is part of what may be called the "Law and Economics Movement". It requires the expertise of the economist and the conflict lawyer, not a commonly found combination of talents. This modern debate seeks to bring an economic efficiency perspective to bear on issues of jurisdiction and choice of law, but within the new approach there seems to be no consensus of opinion as to whether the focus should be on state interests, or individual interests. The purpose has been to ascertain whether or not such an approach can provide "more scientific, objective foundations to the discipline of private international law"[27] and promote global and individual economic welfare in the

---

[22] Para.2–02, above.

[23] e.g. *Dalrymple v Dalrymple* (1811) 2 Hag. Con. 54 at 58; *Caldwell v Van Vlissengen* (1851) 9 Hare 415 at 425; *Hooper v Gumm* (1867) L.R. 2 Ch. 282, per Turner L.J. at 289, 290; *Slater v Mexican National Railroad Co* (1904) 194 U.S. 120 at 125; *Re Bettinson's Question* [1956] Ch. 67; *Phrantzes v Argenti* [1960] 2 Q.B. 19; *Shahnaz v Rizwan* [1965] 1 Q.B. 390.

[24] *Cheshire, North and Fawcett: Private International Law*, 14th edn (2008), p.26.

[25] *Bumper Development Corp v Commissioner of Police of the Metropolis* [1991] 1 W.L.R. 1362.

[26] See, generally, M.J. Whincop and M. Keyes, *Policy and Pragmatism in the Conflict of Laws* (Aldershot: Ashgate, 2001); J. Basedow and Kono (eds) (in cooperation with Ruýhl), *An Economic Analysis of Private International Law* (Tübingen: Mohr Siebeck, 2006); and E.A. O'Hara (ed.), *Economics of Conflict of Laws* (Cheltenham: Edward Elgar Publishing, 2007). For further secondary literature, see *Cheshire, North and Fawcett: Private International Law*, 14th edn (2008), p.36.

[27] R. Michaels, in Basedow and Kono (eds), *Economic Analysis of Private International Law* (2006), p.144.

determination of conflict cases. For example, the forces of competition might be thought capable of improving the value to individual litigants of the outcome of a given dispute in that, both in jurisdiction and choice of law, states would have an incentive, through their laws, to attract parties and their business[28]—always assuming that conflict rules permit a degree of party freedom to choose the court and the law.

THE EXCLUSION OF FOREIGN LAW: EXCEPTIONS TO THE ENFORCEMENT OF FOREIGN RIGHTS

3–02 Whatever theory is adopted to explain why rights allegedly due to a party may be enforced outside the legal system which is their source, it is necessary to delineate the limits of extraterritorial enforcement.

Revenue laws

3–03 As a general rule, the revenue laws of a foreign country are not enforceable in the UK because such laws are regarded as being essentially local in their application and not appropriate for enforcement in any other country.[29] The revenue law exception applies as regards the revenue laws of all other countries, including those of the British Commonwealth,[30] but increasingly one requires to make special mention of the intra-EU situation, where exceptions to the exception can be identified.[31] Nonetheless, in *QRS 1 ApS v Frandsen*,[32] the Court of Appeal ruled that the principle of "the revenue law exception", as a fundamental of English law, could be objectively justified and was not incompatible with (then) EC law.

---

[28] O'Hara (ed.), *Economics of Conflict of Laws* (2007), p.xxii.

[29] The principal authority is *India v Taylor* [1955] A.C. 491. See also *Holman v Johnson* (1775–1802) All E.R. Rep. 98, per Lord Mansfield C.J. at 99: "no country ever takes note of the revenue laws of another"; *The Eva* [1921] P. 454; *Re Visser* [1928] Ch. 877; *Rossano v Manufacturers' Life Insurance Co* [1963] 2 Q.B. 352; *Lord Advocate v Tursi*, 1998 S.L.T. 1035; *JSC BTA Bank v Mukhtar Ablyazov* [2011] EWHC 202 (Comm); and *Revenue and Customs Commissioners v Ben Nevis (Holdings) Ltd* [2012] EWHC 1807 (Ch).

[30] *Att-Gen for Canada v William Schulze & Co*, 1901 9 S.L.T. 4, per Lord Stormonth-Darling at 5.

[31] e.g. Council Directive 2010/24/EU of 16 March 2010 concerning mutual assistance for the recovery of claims relating to taxes, duties and other measures ("MARD") is designed to effect mutual assistance between EU Member States for the recovery of claims relating to taxes, duties and other specified measures. The MARD Regulations 2011 (SI 2011/2931) make procedural, supplementary and adaptive provision for the transposition into UK law of the EU Directive, regarding both incoming claims to the UK from other EU Member States, and outgoing claims from the UK to another EU Member State. Another EU example which breaches the purity of the revenue law exception is Council Regulation 1346/2000 on Insolvency Proceedings [2000] O.J. L160/1, by art.39 of which any creditor who has his habitual residence, domicile or registered office in a Member State, other than the State of the opening of insolvency proceedings, including the tax authorities and social security authorities of Member States, shall have the right to lodge claims in the insolvency proceedings.

[32] *QRS 1 ApS v Frandsen* [1999] 3 All E.R. 289.

Classification of the nature of a claim as "revenue" or not is a matter for the forum.[33] It does not matter in what light the claim is viewed in its legal system of origin. Lord Cameron stated in *Metal Industries (Salvage) Ltd v ST Harle (Owners)*[34]:

> "It is a general rule of law that no state will act as a tax gatherer for another or permit its courts to be used for that purpose, and it is a corollary of that rule that what is a revenue or fiscal claim is to be determined by the Courts of the country where the claim is sought to be enforced and in accordance with the *lex fori*."

The forum will not knowingly be deluded by the manner in which the claim comes to court, or by its form, but rather will seek to ascertain its true nature.[35] A claim for local rates has been classified as "revenue",[36] as has a claim in a Scottish multiplepoinding for employers' contributions, unpaid, to a French government benefit scheme for seamen.[37] UK courts will not connive at an attempt to deprive a foreign government of its revenue.[38] A most instructive example is the case of *Re Norway's Application (Nos 1 and 2)*,[39] a tax investigation into the affairs of the late AJ, a Norwegian domiciliary. With the agreement of the late AJ's family, the Norwegian tax authorities sought to have evidence taken in England from two merchant bankers for use in a tax litigation in Norway. This was done by means of "letters of request" under the Evidence (Proceedings in Other Jurisdictions) Act 1975.[40] The House of Lords permitted the application on the view that this was not an attempt to collect foreign revenue, but rather a request for assistance in a tax investigation. As to the warring principles of banker/client confidentiality on the one hand, and the demands of international comity on the other, the court favoured the latter, while protecting the former by a careful monitoring of the terms of the questions to be asked. Trustees or executors who decide to pay foreign inheritance tax may be exonerated (though the foreign government could not stand in UK courts to claim the sum), if by their action they have taken the only means of giving effect to the wishes of the testator.[41]

---

[33] *Tasarruf Mevduati Sigorta Fonu v Demirel* [2006] EWHC 3354 (Ch) at [65]; affirmed without discussion of this point [2007] 1 W.L.R. 2508.

[34] *Metal Industries (Salvage) Ltd v ST Harle (Owners)*, 1962 S.L.T. 114 at 116.

[35] *Peter Buchanan Ltd v McVey* [1955] A.C. 516; [1954] I.R. 89; *Brokaw v Seatrain UK Ltd* [1971] 2 All E.R. 98, per Lord Denning at 100; citing *Holman v Johnson* [1775–1802] All E.R. Rep. 98 at 99; *QRS 1 ApS v Frandsen* [1999] 3 All E.R. 289; *JSC BTA Bank v Ablyazov* [2011] EWHC 202 (Comm); [2011] 2 All E.R. (Comm) 10; and *Revenue and Customs Commissioners v Total Network SL* [2008] 2 All E.R. 413 HL. On a related point of jurisdiction, see *Revenue and Customs Commissioners v Sunico ApS* (C-49/12) [2014] Q.B. 391; [2014] 2 W.L.R. 335.

[36] *Sydney Municipal Council v Bull* [1909] 1 K.B. 7.

[37] *Metal Industries (Salvage) Ltd v ST Harle (Owners)*, 1962 S.L.T. 114.

[38] And so, e.g. will not afford a party, who for tax reasons had divested himself in USA of shares in favour of his wife, the opportunity to attempt to prove the true position by trying to rebut the presumption of gift: *Re Emery's Investment Trusts* [1959] Ch. 410.

[39] *Re Norway's Application (Nos 1 and 2)* [1989] 1 All E.R. 745. cf. *Revenue and Customs Commissioners v Gresh* (Court of Appeal (Guernsey)) [2010] W.T.L.R. 1303.

[40] With regard to the classification of a fiscal case as being of a "civil or commercial" nature (in order to satisfy the 1975 Act s.1), the House of Lords held that classification of the proceedings was to be referred to the laws of both states (the requesting state and the state addressed).

[41] *Scottish National Orchestra Society Ltd v Thomson's Executor*, 1969 S.L.T. 325; *Re Lord Cable deceased* [1976] 3 All E.R. 417.

There are exceptions to the revenue law exception, or limitations on it. The revenue law exception applies only to the collection of money, with the result that foreign revenue laws may be recognised and receive effect indirectly. Foreign revenue laws therefore have received effect as regards currency laws,[42] sufficiency of stamp duty, or forgery of coins or banknotes. Double taxation treaties exist with the aim of ensuring that the income of corporate bodies or individuals is subjected to taxation by only one of the signatory states: they provide the detailed regulation required to assess the income according to its source.

Within the UK, as a result of the overarching jurisdiction of the Westminster Parliament and the common exchequer, British revenue laws are enforceable throughout the UK. Part 3 (ss.23–27) of the Scotland Act 2012, repealing ss.73–80 of the Scotland Act 1998, make particular provision with regard to the Scottish Parliament's power to legislate on tax, permitting it to set,[43] inter alia, a Scottish rate of income tax for "Scottish taxpayers".[44] The question which in time may require to be answered is whether the Inland Revenue in Scotland may pursue in England a claim against an erstwhile Scottish taxpayer, later resident in England, for unpaid tax due by him, arising under a provision made by the Scottish Parliament. Such a suit would be permissible, within the ratio of the revenue law exception, so long as Scotland remains part of the United Kingdom.

Penal laws

3–04 Penal laws are regarded as being strictly local and therefore are not enforceable in another state: "The courts of no country execute the penal laws of another".[45] In the sense of this rule, a penal law is a measure directed by a state against a particular individual or group of individuals. Hence it does not include a penalty in a private contract,[46] nor does it include a general enactment confiscating all property, such an enactment falling under the heading of "confiscatory laws" below.

The classic definition was given by the Privy Council in *Huntington v Attrill*[47]: the "penal law exception" refers to "a penalty imposed by the State for some criminal violation of its rules". The (excluded) claim:

---

[42] *Re Claim by Helbert Wagg & Co Ltd* [1956] Ch. 323; *Kahler v Midland Bank Ltd* [1950] A.C. 24; *Zivnostenska Banka National Corp v Frankman*[1950] A.C. 57; contrast *Indian & General Investment Trust Co v Borax Consolidated Ltd* [1920] 1 K.B. 539; and *Rossano v Manufacturers Life Insurance Co* [1963] 2 Q.B. 352.

[43] 2012 Act s.23, inserting ss.80A–80B into the 1998 Act; and s.25 ("Scottish rate of income tax") of the 2012 Act, inserting ss.80C–80H into the 1998 Act.

[44] 2012 Act s.25, inserting s.80D into the 1998 Act, and thereby importing a definition of "Scottish taxpayer" essentially on the basis of the proportion of days during which a person has resided in Scotland in the tax year in question.

[45] *The Antelope*, 10 Wheaton 123, per Marshall C.J. quoted in *Huntington v Attrill* [1893] A.C. 150. *Ogden v Folliot* (1790) 3 T.R. 726; affirming sub nom. *Folliot v Ogden* (1789) 1 Ll.Bl. 123. See more recently *Pocket Kings Ltd v Safenames Ltd* [2009] EWHC 2529. For the problems which may arise in modern electronic conditions, see *Yahoo! Inc v La Ligue Contra Le Racisme et L'Antisemitisme*, 433 F 3d.; 2006 U.S. App. Lexis 668. cf. *King v Serious Fraud Office* [2009] 1 W.L.R. 718.

[46] *SA Consortium General Textiles v Sun & Sand Agencies Ltd* [1978] Q.B. 279, per Lord Denning at 299, 300.

[47] *Huntington v Attrill* [1893] A.C. 150.

"...must be in the nature of a suit in favour of the State whose law has been infringed, and the penalties must be recoverable at the instance of the State, or a State official, or a member of the public acting in the public interest".

This means that criminal law is intraterritorial. A person should face trial (if necessary, following extradition) in the legal system where he allegedly committed the offence. There can be no conviction in Scotland on the ground of breach of a foreign criminal law, nor enforcement of a judgment given in foreign criminal proceedings.[48]

Sometimes the question of where an offence has taken place becomes of central importance for the purpose of the meaning and operation of a statute. With regard to British statutes, there is a strong, though weakening,[49] presumption against extraterritorial effect in the case of criminal statutes. Thus, on interpretation of the (English) Theft Act 1968, in circumstances where a criminal plan had been devised to bring stolen cars into Britain from Germany, it has been held that since the statutory crime of theft is a "once and for all" and not a "continuing" act, there could be no conviction in England, the criminal activity having been completed abroad.[50] It may be possible to sever the civil from the criminal aspect of a foreign award granted in a legal system which has a unified procedure, and if so there is no objection to enforcing the award of civil damages.[51]

To classify the nature of the foreign law as penal, or not, is the function of the forum.[52] In *Huntington v Attrill*, the question was whether the New York-imposed liability on promoters for making misrepresentations in company reports was penal (criminal) in nature, or remedial (protective of private interests). The Privy Council, exercising the power of classification on appeal from the Court of Ontario, found it was not penal within the relevant conflict rule (or exception). A modern instance of the same point is *United States Securities & Exchange Commission v Manterfield*,[53] in which the Court of Appeal dismissed the argument that a freezing order[54] made by an English court in support of United States proceedings amounted to the enforcement of US penal law. The approach was taken that the forum would ascertain which part of the foreign judgment it was being asked to enforce, having regard to the substance of the relief. In the circumstances the Court of Appeal concluded that what was sought was the disgorgement of the alleged proceeds of fraud for the benefit of investors, i.e. that it was remedial in nature, and so enforceable, rather than penal. Moreover, the court held that comity required the English court to lend its assistance to thwart

---

[48] Though an instance of account being taken in Scotland, for the purpose of sentencing, of an individual's criminal history in England is to be found in *Herd v HM Advocate*, 1993 G.W.D. 24-1503. cf. shrieval jurisdiction in relation to a statutory offence allegedly committed abroad: *McCarron (George Wallace) v HM Advocate*, 2001 S.L.T. 866.

[49] Para.3–11, below.

[50] *R. v Atakpu (Austin)* [1993] 4 All E.R. 215. cf. *R. (on the application of Purdy) v DPP* [2009] UKHL 45 (Suicide Act 1961).

[51] *Raulin v Fischer* [1911] 2 K.B. 93.

[52] e.g. *Larkins v National Union of Mineworkers* [1985] I.R. 671; and *Iran v Barakat Galleries Ltd* [2009] Q.B. 22 at [106].

[53] *United States Securities & Exchange Commission v Manterfield* [2009] 1 Lloyd's Rep 399.

[54] Para.8–19, below.

international fraudulent activity, notwithstanding that the fraud did not take place
in the UK, nor were British interests directly affected.

In this connection, therefore, "penal" should be understood as meaning
"criminal" rather than unfair or discriminatory.[55] A case may arise in which a
foreign law can be regarded as "penal" in both senses, as illustrated by *Banco de
Vizcaya v Don Alfonso De Borbon y Austria*.[56] The Spanish Republican
Government purported to confiscate the property in England of the former King
Alfonso, founding on a Spanish decree declaring the King guilty of high treason
and an outlaw. The English forum refused to entertain the Spanish claim, which
came to court in the form of a claim by the Spanish bank. In whatever form it
appeared, it was an attempt to enforce extraterritorially a foreign "penal" (and
confiscatory) law. Likewise, in *United States v Inkley*,[57] the attempt by the US
Government to recover an "appearance bond" (security for appearance in
forthcoming American criminal proceedings), granted by Inkley when in
America, was irrecoverable from him when resident in England, because in the
view of the English court the bond was inextricably linked with American public,
criminal procedure.

Certain foreign statutory provisions, such as prohibitions on export without
licence of historic artefacts, may be difficult to classify. In the leading case of
Attorney General of New Zealand v Ortiz,[58] Maori carvings having been removed
from New Zealand without the requisite certificate under the (New Zealand)
Historic Articles Act 1962, the plaintiff sought to restrain the sale of these articles
in London. Two principal questions arose: (1) the nature of the New Zealand
statutory provision; and (2) interpretation of the wording of the provision, and in
particular of the word "forfeit". In the Court of Appeal[59] the majority view was
that the provision was "penal" (in the sense of criminal), although Lord Denning
placed it in a broad grouping which he termed "other public law" (and hence
concurred with his brother judges in finding it not enforceable *extra
territorium*).[60] The speeches in the House of Lords were concerned only with
interpretation of the word "forfeit", and the view taken of the proper meaning was
that the carvings fell into the ownership of the Crown in right of New Zealand
only if seized within the territorial bounds of New Zealand; on interpretation,
there could be no notional forfeiture upon seizure following export from New
Zealand without a licence.[61] Hence to have acceded to the Attorney General's
claim would have amounted to giving effect extraterritorially to a foreign penal
law.

---

[55] Though early cases used it in this way: *Wolff v Oxholm* (1817) 6 M. & S. 92; and *Re Fried Krupp
AG* [1917] 2 Ch. 188.

[56] *Banco de Vizcaya v Don Alfonso De Borbon y Austria* [1935] 1 K.B. 140.

[57] *United States v Inkley* [1989] Q.B. 255.

[58] *Attorney General of New Zealand v Ortiz* [1983] 2 All E.R. 93. cf. and contrast *Iran v Barakat
Galleries Ltd* [2009] Q.B. 22.

[59] *Attorney General of New Zealand v Ortiz* [1982] 3 All E.R. 432.

[60] cf. *Att Gen v Heinemann Publishers Australia PTY Ltd* [1989] 2 F.S.R. 631; and *United States v A
Ltd* [2003] C.L.Y.B. 621; (2001-02) 4 I.T.E.L.R. 797.

[61] cf. and contrast *Spain v Christie, Manson & Woods Ltd* [1986] 1 W.L.R. 1120.

Confiscatory laws

There are three manifestations of state confiscation:

(a)   *expropriation or confiscation*: the taking by a state of property belonging to a private individual or body for public purposes without any compensation, or with inadequate compensation;

(b)   *nationalisation*: the taking of private property for public purposes in the same circumstances as in (a) above, but upon payment of compensation;

(c)   *requisitioning*: the taking of private property for public purposes with compensation for a limited period such as the duration of a war.[62]

Modern instances tend to concern the first of these.

The general principle is that the act of any recognised government[63] is accepted as being effective as regards all property situated within its territory, but as having no effect on property situated outside such territory.[64] Intraterritorial compulsory acquisitions by recognised governments are recognised, but assertion of a sovereign right, extraterritorially in the legal system of another, will not be effective without the acquiescence or imprimatur of that other.[65]

Hence, a confiscatory act directed against an individual or a class of individuals will be deemed to be completely effective as regards property belonging to such persons which is within the territory of the "confiscating" state,[66] but will not receive any effect as regards assets situated outside that territory.[67] The question, therefore, may simply be one as to the location of property, the territorial limits of the state which has purported to confiscate,[68] or as to the effective completion[69] of the purported confiscation within those limits.[70]

---

[62] As to which see anomalous wartime case of *Lorentzen v Lydden & Co Ltd* [1942] 2 K.B. 202.

[63] By parliamentary announcement in 1980, the British Government stated that it would no longer give formal recognition to new governments, although it would continue formally to recognise new states where appropriate. Thereafter, the status of a new regime must be inferred from the manner of the British Government's dealings with it, as to which the Foreign and Commonwealth Office will provide information. See R. Leslie, "The Existence of Governments and the Conflict of Laws: the Republic of Somalia Case", 1997 Jur. Rev. 110.

[64] *Spain v National Bank of Scotland*, 1939 S.C. 413.

[65] *Iran v Barakat Galleries Ltd* [2009] Q.B. 22; and *JSC BTA Bank v Mukhtar Ablyazov* [2011] EWHC 202 (Comm).

[66] *AM Luther Co v James Sagor & Co* [1921] 3 K.B. 532; *Princess Paley Olga v Weisz* [1929] 1 K.B. 718; *Frankfurther v WL Exner Ltd* [1947] Ch. 629; *Novello & Co Ltd v Hinrichsen Edition Ltd* [1951] Ch. 1026.

[67] *Bank voor Handel en Scheepvaart NV v Slatford* [1953] 1 Q.B. 248.

[68] *The Jupiter (No.3)* [1927] P. 122; [1927] P. 250.

[69] In *Iran v Barakat Galleries Ltd* [2009] Q.B. 22, Lord Phillips at [148] opined that where a foreign sovereign state has occasion to claim in England property to which it alleges it acquired ownership through confiscation or compulsory process, this can be done only where the foreign state had taken the property in question into its possession. In his Lordship's view a different situation arose in the instant proceedings in that Iran did not assert a claim based on compulsory acquisition, but rather put forward a patrimonial claim based upon legislation. Insofar as Lord Phillips took the view that, in the latter circumstances, success in an English claim did not depend on a state having reduced the property in question into its possession, one can detect a departure from the reasoning in *Ortiz*.

[70] *Williams & Humbert Ltd v W&H Trade Marks (Jersey) Ltd* [1986] A.C. 368: in complex circumstances, it was held by the House of Lords that a Spanish compulsory acquisition had been

The suggestion made in *Anglo-Iranian Oil Co v Jaffrate (The Rose Mary)*,[71] that another requirement of an effective confiscation was that the persons divested of their property must be nationals of the confiscating state, was shortlived, and was disapproved in *Re Helbert Wagg*.[72]

Should a state purport to confiscate property beyond its territorial bounds, there will be a question of interpretation as to the intended extent of the confiscatory order; but even if extraterritorial ambit is intended, it is unlikely to receive effect. In *Lecouturier v Rey*[73] a French confiscation was interpreted by the House of Lords as having been intended to be only of intraterritorial effect. However, in the words of Lord Macnaghten:

> "To me it seems perfectly plain that it must be beyond the power of any foreign
> Court or any foreign legislature to prevent the monks from availing themselves in
> England of the benefit of the reputation which the liqueurs of their manufacture
> have acquired here".

It may be asked whether any inquiry can be made by the forum of the "immoral" quality of intraterritorial confiscation,[74] so as to provide justification for the forum in refusing recognition; or, in the obverse situation, whether a "benevolent" quality of an extraterritorial confiscation should permit recognition thereof.[75] There is found in *Oppenheimer v Cattermole*[76] condemnation of Nazi removal of Jewish German citizenship.[77] There was an argument that if a confiscation be regarded as discriminatory and unfair, there might be some means of circumventing the established conflict rule as to title to property if the confiscated property should find its way to Britain.[78] It must be concluded that there is little support in case authority for this suggestion.[79]

---

completed within the territorial boundaries of Spain. But see F.A. Mann, "The Effect in England of the Compulsory Acquisition by a Foreign State of the Shares in a Foreign Company", 1987 L.Q.R. 191.

[71] *Anglo-Iranian Oil Co v Jaffrate (The Rose Mary)* [1953] 1 W.L.R. 246.

[72] *Re Helbert Wagg* [1956] Ch. 323.

[73] *Lecouturier v Rey* [1910] A.C. 262 at 265.

[74] Consider the attempt made by Nourse J. in *Williams & Humbert Ltd*, at first instance, to categorise governmental decrees according to degrees of unacceptability on moral grounds: [1985] 2 All E.R. 208 at 213–215; and see per Sir John Donaldson M.R. in *Settebello Ltd v Banco Totta and Acores* [1985] 1 W.L.R. 1050 at 1056, 1057.

[75] *Peer International Corp v Termidor Music Publishers Ltd* [2004] Ch. 212; Morris, *Conflict of Laws*, 8th edn (2012), para.13–058. Contrast the clear decision against extraterritorial effect of an (essentially uncontroversial) New Zealand statute in *Att Gen of New Zealand v Ortiz* [1983] 2 All E.R. 93.

[76] *Oppenheimer v Cattermole* [1975] 1 All E.R. 538 HL.

[77] *Oppenheimer v Cattermole* [1975] 1 All E.R. 538 HL, per Lord Hodson at 557: "The courts of this country are not in my opinion obliged to shut their eyes to the shocking nature of such legislation as the 1941 decree if and when it falls for consideration." Yet in the circumstances the removal of citizenship was held to be effective; in consequence, in this tax case, the taxpayer was not entitled to tax relief under the relevant double taxation agreement.

[78] e.g. Morris, *Conflict of Laws*, 4th edn (1993), p.388. But see *Frankfurther v WL Exner Ltd* [1947] Ch. 629, per Romer J. at 644 (strict territorial approach).

[79] However, in the case of Nazi confiscations, the pressure of international opinion seems likely to result in compensation, disbursement and/or restoration of property: e.g. Holocaust (Return of Cultural Objects) Act 2009; and Carruthers, *The Transfer of Property in the Conflict of Laws* (2005), Ch.5, on the treatment of cultural property.

The House of Lords in *Williams & Humbert Ltd* took the view that expropriation is a common occurrence and that the forum should be concerned only with the territoriality principle.[80] The position is regulated in the general case by the principle found in moveable property that he who takes a good title by the *lex situs* obtains a good title against the world.[81]

An important difficulty arises in some cases where it is not clear whether the purported confiscation took place extraterritorially or intraterritorially, the most notable example being *Kuwait Airways Corp v Iraqi Airways Co*,[82] which contained human rights arguments, and the facts of which gave rise to concerted opprobrium from the international community.

Kuwait Airways Corp v Iraqi Airways Co illustrates various points, viz: the meaning of intraterritoriality; the application of the rule of intraterritoriality; the appropriate use of public policy to recognise or not intraterritorial confiscations; the appropriate use of public policy to exclude the application of an otherwise applicable foreign law in terms of the choice of law rule in tort; application of the common law choice of law rule of double actionability in tort; application of the choice of law rule in property; and interaction of international private law and public international law. The student of the rules of jurisdiction might also note the lack of close connection between the forum and the circumstances of the alleged tort.

The case arose out of the circumstances of the 1990 Gulf War. After lengthy litigation, including a trial of jurisdictional issues, it came before the House of Lords in the form of an action laid in the English tort of conversion (wrongful interference with the property of another). Iraqi military forces having occupied Kuwait, the Iraqi authorities passed resolutions proclaiming Iraqi sovereignty over Kuwait, and seized from Kuwait airport and removed to Iraq, a number of commercial aircraft belonging to Kuwait Airways Corp ("KAC"). One month later, the Revolutionary Command Council of Iraq passed Resolution 369 dissolving KAC, and purporting to transfer all of its property, wherever situated, to the Iraqi Airways Co ("IAC"). Early in 1991, KAC began litigation against IAC and the Republic of Iraq, seeking return of the aircraft, or payment of the value, and damages.

3–06

The question of fundamental importance was whether the seizure of the aircraft was to be regarded as *intra territorium* Iraq, in light of Iraq's purported annexation of Kuwait. The purported annexation was universally condemned, and United Nations Security Council resolutions called on Member States to give no recognition, directly or indirectly, to the annexation.

Many conflict confiscation cases have arisen from turbulent events of the 20th century, such as the Russian Revolution, the Spanish Civil War, and seizure of property by the Nazi regime. An important strand in the conflict reasoning of any Scots or English forum called to adjudicate upon such cases is whether the UK recognised the authority of the government which performed the confiscation in question, or which subsequently ratified the confiscatory actings, as de jure or de

---

[80] *Williams & Humbert Ltd* [1986] A.C. 368, per Lord Templeman at 427, 428 and 431. *Contra Kuwait Airways Corp v Iraqi Airways Co (No.6)* [2002] 3 All E.R. 209.

[81] *Cammell v Sewell* (1860) 5 H. & M. 728 (Exchequer Chamber); *Princess Paley Olga v Weisz* [1929] 1 K.B. 718. Ch.17, below.

[82] *Kuwait Airways Corp v Iraqi Airways Co* [2002] 3 All E.R. 209. See E.B. Crawford and J.M. Carruthers, "*Kuwait Airways Corporation v Iraqi Airways Company*" (2003) 52 I.C.L.Q. 761.

facto in control of the territory in question.[83] A summary of the decisions of 20th
century cases must conclude that the courts in Scotland and England recognised
the actings of a governing body subsequently recognised (politically) by the UK
Government, and all the private law consequences which flowed from such initial
confiscation, without commenting upon the "morality" of the confiscatory event.

On this reasoning, had Kuwait been recognised, sooner or later, as Iraqi
territory, then precedent suggests that a Scottish or English court would have
recognised the confiscation and its private law consequences.[84] Conversely, the
annexation of Kuwait not having been accorded recognition, had the litigation
presented as a confiscation one, precedent would have required that the
confiscation be refused recognition as an extraterritorial purported seizure. But
the litigation presented in tort, and there was little discussion of these important
anterior points. On the facts, the House of Lords, by application of the common
law rule of double actionability in delict,[85] decided that KAC had not been
divested of its property, and therefore had a claim for compensation.

Act of state and sovereign immunity[86]

3–07   An act performed by the UK Government, or authorised by it, in the course of its
relations with a foreign state is not justiciable in the domestic courts of the UK,[87]
a principle which may foreclose an action to claim[88] or to defend a private law
right. Moreover, UK courts will not enquire into the legality of acts done by a
foreign government within its own territory.[89] But the act of state or
non-justiciability doctrine does not prevent examination in the UK of the extent
to which substantial justice is available and the rule of law adhered to in a foreign
sovereign state. Hence where an English court is asked to refuse to recognise a
foreign court decision on the ground of failure of substantive justice, the decision
will rest on evidence and argument and not on any principle of immunity.[90]

The act of state doctrine is founded on the principles of the sovereign equality
of states and international comity.[91] Lord Wilberforce in *Buttes Gas & Oil Co v
Hammer (No.3)*,[92] preferring to avoid arguments on terminology, thought it
desirable to consider this area of law as one illustrating the exercise of judicial
restraint or abstention. Hence, a British Act of Parliament directly or indirectly

---

[83] e.g. *Princess Paley Olga v Weisz* [1929] 1 K.B. 718.
[84] Subject to a scintilla of doubt about the proper reaction to "immoral"/evil conduct.
[85] Para.16–49, below.
[86] Para.7–04 et seq., below.
[87] British Act of State Doctrine. *Dicey, Morris & Collins*, 15th edn (2012), paras 5-043–5.053.
[88] *JSC BTA Bank v Mukhtar Ablyazov* [2011] EWHC 202 (Comm). But see *Belhaj v Straw* [2014]
EWCA Civ 1394; and *Rahmatullah v Ministry of Defence* [2014] EWHC 3846 (QB).
[89] Foreign Act of State Doctrine. *AM Luther Co v James Sagor & Co* [1921] 3 K.B. 532; *Princess
Paley Olga v Weisz* [1929] 1 K.B. 718; and *Buttes Gas & Oil Co v Hammer (No.3)* [1982] A.C. 888.
[90] *Korea National Insurance Co v Allianz Global Corporate & Specialty AG* [2008] EWCA Civ
1355; and *Yukos Capital Sarl v OJSC Rosneft Oil Co* [2012] EWCA Civ 855; [2014] Q.B. 458.
[91] *Belhaj v Straw* [2014] EWCA Civ 1394.
[92] *Buttes Gas & Oil Co v Hammer (No.3)* [1982] A.C. 888, at para 931.

may render a foreign acquired right void as regards its enforcement in the UK[93]; so too may a British act of indemnity or government declaration.[94] Lord Dyson in *Belhaj v Straw* explained that:

> "The principles of state immunity and act of state ... are clearly linked and share common rationales. They may both be engaged in a single factual situation. Nevertheless, they operate in different ways ... Act of state reaches beyond cases in which states are directly or indirectly impleaded ... and operates by reference to the subject matter of the claim rather than the identity of the parties."[95]

Historically, a Scots or English court could not proceed to hear an action against a foreign government if the foreign government had been recognised (politically) by the UK government as the de jure or de facto government, and was in peaceful possession of the property in question.[96] The subject of sovereign immunity was placed on a statutory basis following the European Convention on State Immunity (1972), resulting in the UK in the passing of the State Immunity Act 1978. The basic principle of the 1978 Act is that a foreign state[97] is immune from the jurisdiction of British courts, and effect is to be given to that immunity whether or not the state enters an appearance in proceedings.[98] Section 1(1) of the 1978 Act confers immunity upon a state from the jurisdiction of the courts of the UK subject to the principle of submission to the jurisdiction of the UK courts (s.2),[99] and with exceptions on certain grounds,[100] e.g. in respect of "commercial transactions".[101]

Where a foreign state is the pursuer, no question of immunity from suit arose at common law, or arises under the 1978 Act.[102] However, in terms of substance, a foreign state will not be able to secure from a Scottish or English court an order which gives effect extraterritorially to a foreign governmental act.[103]

---

[93] *Phillips v Eyre* (1870–71) L.R. 6 Q.B. 1; *Poll v Lord Advocate* (1899) 1 F. 823.

[94] *Dobree v Napier* (1836) 2 Bing. N.C. 781; *Buron v Denman* (1848) 2 Ex. 167; *Carr v Fracis Times & Co* [1902] A.C. 176; *Nissan v Att Gen* [1967] 3 W.L.R. 1044. Contrast *Berezovsky v Abramovich* [2011] EWCA Civ 153; [2011] 1 W.L.R. 2290.

[95] *Belhaj v Straw* [2014] EWCA Civ 1394 at [48].

[96] *Compania Naviera Vascongada v The Cristina* [1938] A.C. 485; *Spain v Owners of the Arantzazu Mendi* [1939] A.C. 256; *The Abodi Mendi* [1939] P. 178; *Zarine v Ramava* [1942] I.R. 148.

[97] With regard to the questions to whom, and in what circumstances, the immunity is extended, see para.7–06, below.

[98] *Bank of Credit and Commerce International (Overseas) Ltd (In Liquidation) v Price Waterhouse* [1997] 4 All E.R. 108; and *Mbasogo v Logo Ltd (No.1)* [2007] Q.B. 846.

[99] e.g. *NML Capital Ltd v Argentina* [2011] UKSC 31; [2011] 2 A.C. 495.

[100] Defined in ss.3–11. Further para.7–05, below.

[101] Defined in s.3(3). e.g. *Alcom Ltd v Colombia* [1984] 2 All E.R. 6, per Lord Diplock at 8; *Bank of Credit and Commerce International (Overseas) Ltd (In Liquidation) v Price Waterhouse (No.1)* [1997] 4 All E.R. 108; *Kuwait Airways Corp v Iraqi Airways Co* [1995] 1 W.L.R. 1147 HL, per Lord Goff at 1156; *AIG Capital Partners Inc v Kazakhstan* [2006] 1 All E.R. 284; and *ETI Euro Telecom International NV v Bolivia* [2009] 1 W.L.R. 665.

[102] 1978 Act s.2(3). See, e.g. *High Commissioner for Pakistan In the United Kingdom v National Westminster Bank* [2015] EWHC 55 (Ch).

[103] Para.3–05, above.

Public policy

3–08 It is a well-settled principle that UK courts will not apply a foreign rule if its terms, or the application thereof, would be contrary to British conceptions of public policy, notwithstanding that the right which is sought to be enforced is enforceable under the *lex causae*.[104] This bar to the enforcement of a foreign right may derive from policy enshrined in, or capable of being inferred from, legislation, or existing at common law.

Common law

3–09 Public policy in this sense means British conceptions of morality and justice. In practice, the courts have applied this restraint in the following circumstances:

(1) where the fundamental conceptions of British justice have been disregarded[105];
(2) where British conceptions of morality have been infringed[106];
(3) where the enforcement of a transaction would prejudice the interests of the UK or its good relations with foreign powers[107];
(4) where the recognition of a penal[108] condition of status or its incidents would offend British conceptions of human liberty and freedom of action.

It is accepted that the use of public policy in the conflict of laws should be more restricted than in domestic law, its scope narrower. The conflict of laws does not promote conflict, but is concerned rather to anticipate conflict and to resolve cross-border disputes in as fair-minded and non-partisan a manner as can be achieved by any given forum. This (even) more restrictive attitude towards public policy in the international private law context is termed "external public policy". There is a particular danger of public policy making mischief and running counter to the aims of the subject. Nevertheless, public policy must exist as a tool or a mechanism, available for use by the forum in any subject area of the conflict of laws, in order that the forum may avoid a result which, though identified as the "correct" result by its appropriate choice of law rule, is nevertheless

---

[104] See P.B. Carter, "The Role of Public Policy in English Private International Law" (1993) 42 I.C.L.Q. 1; R. Leslie, "The Relevance of Public Policy in Legal Issues Involving Other Countries and Their Laws" [1995] Jur. Rev. 477; J. Blom, "Public Policy in Private International Law and its Evolution in Time" (2003) 50 Netherlands International Law Review 393; and EU Parliament Directorate-General for Internal Policies, "Interpretation of the Public Policy Exception as referred to in EU Instruments of Private International and Procedural Law" (2011). See also para.10–05, below.

[105] *Re Hope* (1857) 8 De G.M. & G. 731; *Grell v Levy* (1864) 16 C.B. (N.S.) 73; *Roussillon v Roussillon* (1880) L.R. 14 Ch.D. 51; *Kaufman v Gerson* [1904] 1 K.B. 591; and *Crowe v Crowe* [1937] 2 All E.R. 723. Contrast *Addison v Brown* [1954] 1 W.L.R. 779.

[106] e.g. *Lemenda Trading Co Ltd v African Middle East Petroleum Co Ltd* [1988] Q.B. 448; [1988] 2 W.L.R. 735.

[107] e.g. *Foster v Driscoll* [1929] 1 K.B. 470; *Regazzione v KC Sethia* (1944) Ltd [1958] A.C. 301; *Re Emery's Investment Trusts* [1959] Ch. 410; and *Beijing Jianlong Heavy Industry Group v Golden Ocean Group Ltd* [2013] EWHC 1063 (Comm).

[108] In this sense, "penal" should be taken to mean (excessively) punitive, unfair or discriminatory. Examples arise in relation to prohibitions on marriage out of religion or out of caste: *Chetti v Chetti* [1909] P. 67; *MacDougall v Chitnavis*, 1937 S.C. 390. Para.11–29, below.

fundamentally unacceptable to it. One question which arose from *Kuwait Airways Corp v Iraqi Airways Co*[109] was whether it was justifiable for the forum to ignore a particular part of the *lex loci delicti*.[110] The dissenting speech of Lord Scott proceeded on the basis that the forum must accept and apply the whole content of the *lex loci delicti* as it stood in the eyes of Iraqi law, but the majority held that the Iraqi Resolution 369[111] constituted a fundamental breach of international law, this view strengthened by background circumstances of public international law as expressed in condemnatory UN Security Council resolutions. In this way, the Resolution could be excised and a thereby modified *lex loci delicti* applied. This case, though instructive, is more than usually special on its facts.

In this matter of policy objection, one should remember that the domestic policy of the forum upon a certain matter may change from time to time, e.g. in relation to recognition of same-sex relationships, or contingent fees,[112] or gaming contracts,[113] and further that the forum must strive so far as possible, temporal issues aside, to be consistent within and across subject areas.[114] However, in conflict cases, the ranking of policies may vary according to context and period of history.[115] The right of any forum to act in the light of its own conscience is an essential part of its conflict rules, and the availability of exercise of such discretion by the forum serves to secure participation by contracting states in international co-operative projects, since international instruments to date invariably contain a public policy discretion. Normally international instruments permit exercise of this discretion only where the rule in question is "manifestly contrary to public policy"; while this phrase has become formulaic, it is undeniable that it contains a warning against over-use. Since its exercise is a manifestation of individual state discretion, attempts to formulate a fixed, predetermined, regionally-harmonised view on a matter sub nom. public policy are inappropriate.[116]

It is possible to employ the public policy tool flexibly: the court in Scotland might accept a foreign status without being obliged to accept all its incidents, or to recognise a foreign divorce without accepting all the terms imposed by the

---

[109] *Kuwait Airways Corp v Iraqi Airways Co (No.6)* [2002] 3 All E.R. 209.
[110] J.M. Carruthers and E.B. Crawford, *"Kuwait Airways Corporation v Iraqi Airways Company"* (2003) 52 I.C.L.Q. 761, 770.
[111] Para.3–06, above.
[112] *Sibthorpe v Southwark LBC* [2011] EWCA Civ 25; [2011] 1 W.L.R. 2111.
[113] *Ferguson v Littlewoods Pools Ltd*, 1997 S.L.T. 309. But see *Robertson v Anderson,* 2003 S.L.T. 235; and now Gambling Act 2005 s.335.
[114] Consistency is not always achieved: 100 years after refusing to recognise the status of slaves (*Sommerset v Stewart* (1772) 20 St. Tr. 1), the English courts enforced a contract for the sale of slaves, because the contract was valid by its Brazilian proper law (*Santos v Illidge* (1860) 8 C.B. (N.S.) 861). See also *Corbett v Corbett* [1957] 1 All E.R. 621 in the matter of foreign prohibition of marriage between Jew and Gentile.
[115] J.M. Carruthers and E.B. Crawford, *"Kuwait Airways Corporation v Iraqi Airways Company"* (2003) 52 I.C.L.Q. 761, 768, fn.57.
[116] In the drafting of Rome II, negotiation took place on the insertion of a "Community public policy" provision; the provision was dropped from the final Regulation, but a hint of the approach can be seen in recital (32). The harmonisation exercise of the European regime may require the suppression of the normally available freedom to refuse to recognise a judgment on the ground of differing substantive law (e.g. Brussels II *bis* art.25) and therefore represents a further incursion into independent judgment by a Member State.

foreign court.[117] By the same token, pragmatism is observable: a forum may note unfair dealings between parties, e.g. in the procuring of decree of divorce, but may yet recognise the divorce as delivering, in all the circumstances, the best result.[118]

The effect of a successful plea to public policy in any given forum is normally negative, that is to say, it operates to exclude application of the rule of the otherwise applicable *lex causae*, and thereby to revert to the default position of application of the *lex fori*. But a positive use also can be envisaged, that is, where the public policy of the forum insists upon application of the domestic *lex fori*, overriding the otherwise applicable foreign law in order to supply a remedy or fill a gap.

"Other public laws"

3–10   There is a further consideration, concerning the effect of the forum's public policy upon the extent to which it might, contrary to what has been explained above, permit the operation in its territory of a "public law" of a foreign sovereign state. Until very recently, the term "other public law" of a foreign state has been used as a residual category of exception to the vested rights theory, in order to justify the forum's non-application of a law which it found difficult to characterise as penal, revenue or confiscatory, but which could be regarded as ejusdem generis, the genus being laws which purport to exercise sovereign authority beyond the territory of the enacting state. It was in this sense that Lord Denning used the term in *Ortiz* in the Court of Appeal.[119] However, in *Iran v Barakat Galleries Ltd*,[120] in which the court reviewed the exclusion of operation of foreign law in British courts, Lord Phillips examined the "other public law" exception in order to ascertain whether or not a court in the UK is bound to find that there is a rule which prevents the enforcement in the UK of all foreign sovereign rights of purportedly extraterritorial effect.[121] His Lordship favoured an interpretation which permits the enforcement of foreign sovereign rights where the state owns property in the same way as a private citizen, and so may be said to be exercising property rights akin to those of such a person and acting effectively in a "private" capacity. If the matter can be viewed in this light, the conclusion may be that it is a matter of positive policy for a UK court to uphold the right, rather than the more neutral position that there is no reason not to do so. Indeed Lord Phillips considered that it would certainly be contrary to public policy for

---

[117] e.g. *Wood v Wood* [1957] P. 254.

[118] e.g. *Newmarch v Newmarch* [1978] Fam. 79; *Golubovich v Golubovich* [2010] E.W.C.A. Civ.810; contrast *Kendall v Kendall* [1977] Fam. 208.

[119] *Att Gen of New Zealand v Ortiz* [1982] 3 W.L.R. 570, per Lord Denning M.R. at 585. Contrast Ackner and O'Connor L.JJ., in whose view the export prohibition and forfeiture provision was categorised as penal, the former doubting the existence of the residual category. For background, see *Iran v Barakat Galleries Ltd* [2009] Q.B. 22, per Lord Phillips at [112] et seq. This line of reasoning was used by the High Court of Australia in *AG(UK) v Heinemann Publishers Australia Pty Ltd (No.2)* (1988) 165 C.L.R. 30 to block enforcement in Australia of obligations owed to the UK Government, this principle rendering unenforceable actions to enforce the governmental interests of a foreign state. See also *Equatorial Guinea v Royal Bank of Scotland International* [2006] UKPC 7; *Mbasogo v Logo Ltd (No.1)* [2007] Q.B. 846; *JSC BTA Bank v Ablyazov* [2011] EWHC 202 (Comm).

[120] *Iran v Barakat Galleries Ltd* [2009] Q.B. 22.

[121] *Iran v Barakat Galleries Ltd* [2009] Q.B. 22 at [125] et seq.

such a quasi-private claim to be excluded. This important amplification of UK public policy as exercised by the courts takes place against a backdrop of growing international acceptance of the desirability of preserving cultural heritage and, arguably, may be particular to that area.

The presence and use of public policy will be discussed in context throughout this work.

THE OPERATION OF STATUTE LAW AND THE CONFLICT OF LAWS: TERRITORIAL AMBIT OF STATUTES

Both British and foreign statutes are presumed to have a strictly limited territorial effect so that in general they apply, respectively, only to persons and property on British or foreign territory.[122] In many cross-border cases it will be found that the answer to a problem depends upon the territorial scope of a statute[123] and that the real question is one of interpretation as to whether or not a particular statute is intended to apply, e.g. only to persons domiciled or resident in a particular country, or to contracts made or to be performed in, or to actings which took place in, some particular country.[124] In order to resolve a dispute involving cross-border issues, a question of interpretation may arise of a statute which Parliament did not consciously enact as a conflict of laws provision.[125] On occasion a UK statute may hint at its territorial applicability, without fully articulating the conflict of laws dimension.[126]

3–11

---

[122] *Tomalin v S Pearson and Son Ltd* [1909] 2 K.B. 61; *Yorke v British & Continental Steamship Co Ltd* (1945) 78 L1. L. Rep. 181 (Digest 144); and *Cox v Ergo Versicherung AG (formerly Victoria)* [2014] UKSC 22 (re. Fatal Accidents Act 1976). It may happen, however, that foreigners may be entitled to benefits under British statutory provisions—*Davidsson v Hill* [1901] 2 K.B. 606; *Krzus v Crow's Nest Pass Coal Co Ltd* [1912] A.C. 590; *Cox v Owners of the Esso Malaysia (The Esso Malaysia)* [1974] 3 W.L.R. 341.

[123] Statutes imposing licensing requirements are particularly likely to be intraterritorial. *Dulaney v Merry & Son* [1901] 1 Q.B. 536; *Dublin Finance Corp v Rowe* [1943] N.I. 1; *Goetschuis v Brightman*, 245 N.Y. 186, 156 N.E. 660 (1927).

[124] Consider, e.g. the scope of Age of Legal Capacity (Scotland) Act 1991; see D.I. Nichols, "Can They or Can't They? Children and the Age of Legal Capacity (Scotland) Act 1991", 1991 S.L.T. (News) 395. As to the territorial scope of UK employment law, see conjoined House of Lords decision *Lawson v Serco Ltd* [2006] UKHL 3; [2006] 1 All E.R. 823; also *Masri v Consolidated Contractors International (UK) (No.4)* [2009] UKHL 43; *Diggins v Condor Marine Crewing Services Ltd* [2009] EWCA Civ 1133; *Duncombe v Secretary of State for Children, Schools and Families* [2011] UKSC 36; [2011] 4 All E.R. 1020; *Ravat v Halliburton Manufacturing & Services Ltd* [2012] UKSC 1; [2012] 2 All E.R. 905; *Dhunna v Creditsights Ltd* [2013] I.C.R. 909; *Wittenberg v Sunset Personnal Services* Employment Appeal Tribunal (Scotland), 21 November 2013 (unreported); and *Lodge v Dignity & Choice In Dying, Compassion In Dying* [2014] Appeal No. UKEAT/0252/14/LA Employment Appeal Tribunal (2 December 2014).

[125] e.g. *Fox v Lawson* [1974] A.C. 803; *Cox v Army Council* [1963] A.C. 48; and *Duncan v Motherwell Bridge Engineering Co Ltd*, 1952 S.L.T. 433. See also *Re Paramount Airways Ltd (No.2)* [1992] 3 All E.R. 1; *R. v Atakpu* [1993] 4 All E.R. 215; *Re Seagull Manufacturing Co Ltd (In Liquidation)* [1993] 2 All E.R. 980; *Tradition Securities and Futures SA v X* [2009] I.C.R. 88; *Dolphin Drilling Personnel PTE Ltd v Alan Winks and Dolphin Drilling Ltd* [2009] EATS/0049/08/BI; and *R (on the application of Smith) v Oxfordshire Assistant Deputy Coroner* [2010] UKSC 29.

[126] e.g. Human Fertilisation and Embryology Act 2008 s.54(4) and (10).

OPERATION OF FOREIGN LAW: THEORIES OF INCLUSION AND RULES OF EXCLUSION

Traditionally, the UK Parliament passed Acts with intended extraterritorial operation only in relation to nationality, status and capacity,[127] and exchange control,[128] but it is notable that many incursions have been made into the principle of intraterritoriality of Scottish or English statutes pertaining to criminal law,[129] and more generally. Study of authorities across a range of subject areas reveals the extent of the exercise of judicial discretion in the matter of interpreting statutory or regulatory provisions so as to establish their territorial ambit, where this is not explicit. Very rarely, a change in judicial interpretation as to the territorial scope of a statute is seen, e.g. the Human Rights Act 1998 as it applies to British military personnel serving abroad.[130]

British courts apply equivalent principles to the question of the territorial operation of foreign statutes[131]: it is probable that a foreign statute dealing with a matter of nationality, status and capacity, or exchange control would receive extraterritorial effect in Scotland,[132] subject to the forum's public policy.

The corpus of Scots and English conflict rules, specifically so designated, now is largely legislative in nature. As regards UK legislation, statutes may be entirely "conflict" law,[133] or may be general in character, containing particular provisions of conflict of laws implication, which intentionally,[134] or possibly inadvertently,[135] adhere to or cut across pre-existing conflict rules or reasoning.

The final point to make at this juncture is that as a matter of technical or orthodox conflict reasoning in a Scots or English forum, any rule, common law or statutory, of the applicable law (*lex causae*) must apply, if it is substantive in nature and in its terms does not offend the policy of the forum. It is important that this point is made as a backdrop to a discussion of the territorial operation of any given law. A more complex point is that modern conflict of laws instruments frequently employ as a drafting device the concept of "mandatory rules".[136] Since the forum must give effect to these mandatory provisions of its own law or of a

---

[127] e.g. *Sussex Peerage Case* (1884) 11 Cl. & F. 85; and *Pugh v Pugh* [1951] P. 482.

[128] *Boissevain v Weil* [1950] A.C. 327.

[129] e.g. Proceeds of Crime Act 2002; and *Blue Holding (1) Pte Ltd v United States* [2014] EWCA Civ 1291. See also E.B. Crawford, *International Private Law*, 1st edn (Edinburgh: W. Green / Sweet & Maxwell, 1998), Ch.20.

[130] See *Smith v Ministry of Defence* [2013] UKSC 41, in which a 10-judge Bench held, following *Al-Skeini v United Kingdom* (55721/07) (2011) 53 E.H.R.R. 18, that the view taken in *R. (on the application of Smith) v Oxfordshire Assistant Deputy Coroner* [2010] UKSC 29; [2011] 1 A.C. 1 (that the state's armed forces abroad were not within its jurisdiction for the purposes of art.1 of the ECHR) could no longer be maintained.

[131] *Bank voor Handel en Scheepvaart NV v Slatford (No.2)* [1953] 1 Q.B. 248; and *F&K Jabbour v Custodian of Israeli Absentee Property* [1954] 1 W.L.R. 139.

[132] cf. *Starkowski v Att Gen* [1954] A.C. 155; and *Re Claim by Helbert Wagg & Co Ltd* [1956] Ch. 323.

[133] e.g. Matrimonial and Family Proceedings Act 1984; Family Law Act 1986; Contracts (Applicable Law) Act 1990; Private International Law (Miscellaneous Provisions) Act 1995.

[134] Unfair Contract Terms Act 1977 (*Trident Turboprop (Dublin) Ltd v First Flight Couriers Ltd* [2009] EWCA Civ 290; and *Air Transworld Ltd v Bombardier Inc* [2012] 1 W.L.R 349); Family Law (Scotland) Act 2006; Forced Marriage etc. (Protection and Jurisdiction) (Scotland) Act 2011; and Anti-social Behaviour, Crime and Policing Act 2014 Pt 10 Forced marriage: s.122 (Offence of forced marriage: Scotland).

[135] e.g. Timeshare, Holiday Products, Resale and Exchange Contracts Regulations 2010 (SI 2010//2960).

[136] These are specific rules, as opposed to general policy attitudes, the application of which the parties may not by their own agreement avoid. Further Ch.15, below.

third law,[137] the result is that rules, usually statutory, of legal systems other than the *lex causae*, sometimes must be applied by the forum. Hence, by reason of conflict of laws methodology, a Scots or English forum in a suitable case, potentially in any branch of law, may be required to give effect to a foreign statutory provision.

THE OPERATION OF ECHR AND THE CONFLICT OF LAWS

In conflict cases, as in all other cases arising before UK courts, the implications of the European Convention on Human Rights (ECHR) are potentially relevant by reason of the incorporation of the Convention into UK law by the Human Rights Act 1998. The effect of s.6(1) of the 1998 Act is that courts must not act in a manner which is incompatible with Convention rights, and must take into account relevant jurisprudence of the European Court of Human Rights. To date within the conflict of laws ECHR concerns have manifested themselves principally in questions of access to court, that is, in the area of jurisdiction and judgments,[138] although instances have arisen also in family law (e.g. in the matters of same sex marriage[139] and international child abduction[140]), and in relation to the protection of property.[141] Specifically, questions have arisen in relation to the operation of the Brussels regime of jurisdiction and judgment enforcement, in the light of art.6 of the ECHR which confers the right to a fair and public hearing within a reasonable time by an independent and impartial tribunal established by law.[142] The priority of process system of jurisdiction allocation within the Brussels regime (*lis pendens*)[143] secures for the court first seised the unassailable right to decide upon its own competence; until this decision is made any other interested court must stay its proceedings. The

3–12

---

[137] Paras 15–21—15–22, below.

[138] J. Fawcett, "The Impact of Article 6(1) of the ECHR on Private International Law" (2007) 56 I.C.L.Q. 1; and G. Ward, "Protection of the Right to a Fair Trial and Civil Jurisdiction: the Institutional Legitimacy in Permitting Delay" (2008) Jur. Rev. 5.

[139] *Wilkinson v Kitzinger* [2006] EWHC 2022 (Fam). See now para.11–02 et seq.

[140] e.g. *Sylvester v Austria* [2003] 2 F.L.R. 210; *Monory v Romania* (2005) 41 E.H.R.R. 37; *Maire v Portugal* [2004] 2 F.L.R. 653; (2006) 43 E.H.R.R. 13; *Raban v Romania* (25437/08) (ECHR) [2011] 1 F.L.R. 1130; [2011] Fam. Law 121; *Neulinger v Switzerland* (41615/07) [2011] 1 F.L.R. 122; [2011] 2 F.C.R. 110; *Sneersone v Italy* (1437/09) [2011] 2 F.L.R. 1322; (2013) 57 E.H.R.R. 39; [2011] Fam. Law 1188; *In re E (Children) (Abduction: Custody Appeal)* [2011] UKSC 27; [2012] 1 A.C. 144; *G v G*, 2012 S.L.T. 2; *In the Matter of S (a child)* [2012] UKSC 10; [2012] 2 A.C. 257; *X v Latvia* (27853/09) [2014] 1 F.L.R. 1135; (2014) 59 E.H.R.R. 3; [2014] Fam. Law 269; and *Povse v Austria* (3890/11) [2014] 1 F.L.R. 944; [2014] Fam. Law 31. See para.14–74, below; and P. Beaumont et al, "Child Abduction: Recent Jurisprudence of the European Court of Human Rights" (2015) 64(1) I.C.L.Q. 39.

[141] *Orams v Apostolides* [2006] EWHC 2226 (QB); and *Apostolides v Orams* (C-420/07) [2010] 1 All E.R. (Comm) 950 and 992.

[142] *Marie Brizzard et Roger International SA v William Grant & Sons Ltd (No.2)*, 2002 S.L.T. 1365; and *Baden-Wurttembergische Bank AG, Petitioner* [2009] CSIH 47. Also *Krombach v Bamberski* [2001] Q.B. 709; *Maronier v Larmer* [2003] Q.B. 620; and *Merchant International Co Ltd v Natsionalna Aktsionerna Kompaniya Naftogaz Ukrayiny* [2012] EWCA Civ 196.

[143] Ch.7, below.

ECJ/CJEU so far has not been receptive to the argument that lengthy delays in the court first seised amount to a breach of the art.6 rights of the litigants.[144]

---

[144] *Erich Gasser GmbH v MISAT Srl* (C-116/02) [2005] Q.B. 1. But see now Brussels I Recast art.31.2.

CHAPTER 4

Method

THE STAGES IN A CONFLICT CASE

(1) *Jurisdiction* over both the subject matter and the defender is always **4-01** determined by the *lex fori*, in accordance with the rules applicable in any given situation.[1]

(2) The *form of action* is determined by the *lex fori*.

(3) *Characterisation* of the issue is decided by the *lex fori*.[2]

(4) The *choice of law rule* is identified by the forum in light of characterisation of the nature of the point at issue *per* (3) above.

It may be that the question has several strands, each of which properly may be referred by the forum, in the exercise of its choice of law rules, to a different applicable law. This is termed *dépeçage*, being an "issue by issue", segregated approach to choice of law.[3]

A choice of law rule may be a national rule of the *lex fori*, either common law or statutory; or it may be a harmonised rule contained in a European or international legislative instrument. It is the function of the forum to apply the relevant choice of law rule, which is likely to involve an element of textual interpretation.

(5) The choice of law rule indicates a *connecting factor*.[4] The connecting factor is a point of contact or localising agent. It may be a personal law factor, such as domicile, habitual residence or nationality; or a territorially-based factor, e.g. *locus celebrationis*, or situation of property. It is a neutral concept which links a person, event or transaction, on the one hand, and a legal system, on the other. The connecting factor is determined by the *lex fori* with two caveats:

(a) the nature of property as moveable or immoveable is always decided by the *lex situs* and the forum must defer to characterisation of property by the *lex situs*[5];

(b) nationality (except in time of war) is always decided by the law of the country the nationality of which is in question.[6]

---

[1] See Ch.7, below, for jurisdiction in civil and commercial matters; Ch.12 for consistorial jurisdiction; and Ch.14 for jurisdiction in respect of parental responsibility matters.

[2] At least in practice. Further, see below, para 4–02.

[3] See, e.g. *Reed v Reed* (1969) 6 D.L.R. (3d.) 617 (para 11–29, below); and *Atlantic Telecom GmbH, Noter*, 2004 S.L.T. 1031, per Lord Brodie at [56].

[4] For commonly used connecting factors, see para.1–04, above.

[5] *Macdonald v Macdonald*, 1932 S.C. (H.L.) 79.

[6] *Oppenheimer v Cattermole* [1976] A.C. 249.

(6) *Procedure*.[7] The forum applies its own rules of evidence and procedure. Foreign rules of a procedural nature are not applicable in a Scots forum and so must be identified and excluded. The possibly applicable laws therefore must be classified by the forum as pertaining to procedure or substance.[8]

(7) *Substance*.[9] The existence and extent of the rights of the parties are determined in accordance with the *lex causae*, by applying the substantive law indicated by the forum's choice of law rule. Strictly, the function of the conflict lawyer is complete when he or she has answered the question of which law applies. If the *lex causae* happens to be the law of the forum, the outcome will be determined by the forum's domestic law on the point; if the *lex causae* is a foreign law, the onus lies upon the interested party to aver and prove foreign law to the satisfaction of the Scots court.

(8) *Proof of foreign law*.[10] Foreign law is a question of fact in a British court and therefore it must be proved by the party seeking to rely on it.[11] Scots and English law have adopted a presumption that the law of a foreign country is the same as the *lex fori*[12] and the onus is on a person who maintains otherwise to aver the foreign law and to prove it.[13] While Scots judges have judicial knowledge of Scots law, including its international private law rules, a judge cannot of his own initiative order proof of the content of foreign law. Hence although the court will apply the appropriate choice of law rule (even if the parties fail to plead it), in the absence of proof of foreign law, operation of the choice of law rule effectively will be frustrated. However even where the foreign law is "proved", it should not be supposed that a forum proceeds always on an accurate understanding or application of its content.

CHARACTERISATION

4–02   The problem or method (or method, with problems) of characterisation, which sometimes also is known as classification, is as old as law itself. It is the natural inclination of the lawyer to categorise a legal problem. In domestic law, the problem must be placed under a particular *nomen juris*, or more than one. The

---

[7] See in detail Ch.8, below.

[8] e.g. *Grant v Gordon, Falconer and Fairweather* 1932 48 Sh. Ct. Rep. 155; *Re Wilks* [1935] 1 Ch. 645; *Re Goenaga* [1949] P. 367.

[9] See para.8–01, below.

[10] See, for detail, Ch.8, below.

[11] See Richard Fentiman, *Foreign Law in English Courts: pleading, proof and choice of law* (Oxford: Oxford University Press, 1998), which begins: "How foreign law is pleaded and proved is the crux of the conflict of laws".

[12] Though see *Global Multimedia International Ltd v ARA Media Services* [2006] EWHC 3612 (Ch), per Sir Andrew Morritt C. at [38]: "The true proposition, I believe, is that as foreign law is in most cases a question of fact to be proved by evidence, in the absence of such evidence the court has no option but to apply English law." See also A. Briggs, *Private International Law in English Courts* (Oxford: Oxford University Press, 2014), para.3.41.

[13] *De Reneville v De Reneville* [1948] P. 100. See also *Faulkner v Hill*, 1942 J.C. 20; *Rodden v Whatlings Ltd*, 1960 S.L.T. (Notes) 96; *Scottish National Orchestra Society Ltd v Thomson's Executor*, 1969 S.L.T. 325; *Pryde v Proctor & Gamble Ltd,* 1971 S.L.T. (Notes) 18; *Bonnor v Balfour Kilpatrick Ltd*, 1975 S.L.T. (Notes) 3; *Armour v Thyssen Edelstahlwerke AG*, 1989 S.L.T. 182; 1990 S.L.T. 891 HL; and *Kraus's Administrators v Sullivan*, 1998 S.L.T. 963.

matter may cross juridical boundaries, and the problem as a whole will be likely to do so. For example, in domestic law a grievance may find its legal basis in contract or delict or both (e.g. travel accident), or in property and contract (e.g. loss of or mistaken re-sale of property entrusted for repair), or in matrimonial law and succession (e.g. testamentary provisions rendered inoperative through the occurrence of subsequent marriage by the testator). In domestic cases, advice will be offered to the potential litigant whether to sue, for example, in contract or delict (assuming both bases of action are available), according to perceived financial or tactical advantage, e.g. a head of damage may be available in delict but not in contract.

The characterisation exercise in the conflict of laws has a much deeper significance than in domestic law. In the first place, the rules of jurisdiction of the proposed forum must be satisfied, and these will vary in content according to the nature of the action, as personal or commercial,[14] and within the many subdivisions of the latter, as, for example, pertaining to contract, delict or property. At this initial stage, therefore, the subtleties of characterisation are encountered. Inevitably the court will be influenced, but it will not be bound, by the characterisation which the claimant has adopted in order to lay the action. Within the scheme of civil and commercial jurisdiction set out in the Brussels Recast Regulation,[15] there may be a ranking of rules as where a finding as to the existence of a contract precludes a court seising jurisdiction sub nom. special jurisdiction in delict, and in this way the tactical discretion of the claimant will be restricted.[16]

Any initial problem of characterisation having been surmounted, the forum will address choice of law. The forum's characterisation of the problem will dictate the choice of law rule to be applied, which, in turn, will determine availability (in principle) of remedy, and all further substantive matters concerning liability and defences.

Traditionally, though less so in the era of harmonisation and Europeanisation, the choice of law rule is likely to differ from forum to forum, a fact which brings to its proper prominence the importance of the identity of forum. Further, even if the choice of law rule of different legal systems should appear to be the same, the characterisation of issues adopted by different courts in the interpretation and application of that rule may differ. There may be wide agreement that in respect of marriage, matters of formal validity must be referred to the *lex loci celebrationis*, and matters of capacity and essentials to the personal law, but there is no reason to suppose that courts of different legal systems will assign a

---

[14] A nice example of characterisation, for the purposes of art.1.1 of the Brussels I Regulation, between a "revenue law matter" and a "civil and commercial matter" is provided by *Revenue and Customs Commissioners v Sunico ApS* (C-49/12) [2014] Q.B. 391; [2014] 2 W.L.R. 335. The CJEU concluded that the concept of "civil and commercial matters" covered an action whereby a public authority of one Member State claimed, as against natural and legal persons resident in another Member State, damages for loss caused by a tortious conspiracy to commit VAT fraud in the first Member State.

[15] Para.7–15 et seq., below.

[16] e.g. *Kalfelis v Schroder* [1988] E.C.R. 5565; [1989] E.C.C. 407; *Source Ltd v TUV Rheinland Holding AG*[1998] Q.B. 54; and *Burke v UVEX Sports GmbH, Motorrad TAF GmbH* (Record No.2003 4850P) before the Irish High Court [2005] I.L.Pr. 26. See E.B. Crawford and J.M. Carruthers, "Connection and Coherence between and among European Instruments in the Private International Law of Obligations" (2014) 63(1) I.C.L.Q. 10 and 24.

particular problem to the same legal category.[17] Moreover, the characterisation attached by the forum to a foreign rule may differ from that attached to it by its own legal system of origin.[18] Arguably the only view which matters is that of the legal system in which the case is litigated, given that decree enforcement internationally is now well regulated and leans towards the interests of the judgment creditor.[19] In matters of family law, admittedly, there are further aspects to be considered: not only is more than one court likely to be competent (leading to potential conflicts as to jurisdiction), but the outcome, if competent courts should disagree on the choice of law rule to be applied and/or upon characterisation of issues within that choice, may produce limping status.

If competent courts should agree that a matter is governed by an individual's personal law, will they agree upon the identity of that law? Nationality, domicile, and habitual residence each may be a contender. If courts should agree upon the application of habitual residence, will their respective rules for determining habitual residence, and the application thereof, be identical? It is not to be thought that one meaning is correct and another wrong, rather that the definition to be employed will depend on the identity of the forum which definition is employed. Where the connecting factor is ostensibly the same, differences in interpretation may give rise to what are known as "latent conflicts".[20] If, on the other hand, the choice of law rules, or the connecting factors *ex facie* be different, the conflict is more clearly seen and therefore is said to be "patent".

It becomes apparent that the hopes of success of litigants may vary according to forum, and that in a conflict case the problem of classification is more acute, and the importance and complexity of the task is much greater than in a purely domestic case. The importance of the characterisation exercise in traditional conflict methodology cannot be overstated.

In Scots and English courts, the characterisation exercise in practice is performed by the forum in accordance with its own law, but in a "broad internationalist spirit"[21] and taking an "enlightened" view.[22] Very few inroads upon this practice have been made,[23] but in terms of theory, there are other views

---

[17] e.g. the treatment of parental consent to marry: *Bliersbach v McEwen*, 1959 S.L.T. 81 at 85, in which the Scots forum presumed to characterise the nature of a Dutch rule. Another example is breach of promise of marriage, which might be regarded in France as civil wrongdoing, but in Scotland would have proceeded as an action founded in breach of contract, no matter that the pursuer might be "French". But such actions have been barred in UK forums by the Law Reform (Husband and Wife) (Scotland) Act 1984 s.1, and Law Reform (Miscellaneous Provisions) Act 1970 s.1.

[18] e.g. Prescription and Limitation (Scotland) Act 1973, as amended, and Foreign Limitation Periods Act 1984 respectively direct a Scots or English court, subject to public policy, to apply the limitation period prescribed by the *lex causae*, without reference to the characterisation of the foreign rule in question, as substantive or procedural, by the *lex causae* or by the *lex fori*. See also *Cox v Ergo Versicherung AG* [2014] UKSC 22; [2014] A.C. 1379, per Lord Sumption JSC at [17].

[19] Ch.9, below.

[20] cf. Kahn Freund's "hidden homonym". The English or Scots forum will insist upon deciding, according to its own rules, what is the domicile of an individual: *Re Annesley* [1926] Ch. 692 (though see Family Law Act 1986 s.46(5)).

[21] *Raiffeisen Zentralbank Österreich AG v Five Star Trading LLC* [2001] Q.B. 825 at 839, per Mance L.J.; *Macmillan Inc v Bishopsgate Investment Trust Plc (No.3)* [1996] 1 W.L.R. 387, per Auld L.J. at 403; and *Atlantic Telecom GmbH, Noter,* 2004 S.L.T. 1031, per Lord Brodie at [31] and [56].

[22] cf. *Re Bonacina* [1912] 2 Ch. 394; Private International Law (Miscellaneous Provisions) Act 1995 s.9(2).

[23] Though see Family Law Act 1986 s.46(5).

on the proper solution of the characterisation problem, most prominently the *lex causae* theory, that characterisation be performed according to the applicable law, even though this has an obvious difficulty of circularity of reasoning.[24] The literature on the subject is immense.[25]

What is characterised?

Additionally, one must ask what it is that the forum must characterise: facts, issues, and/or rules of law? Something will depend upon the nature of the action and the remedy sought. Possibly the most helpful explanation is that there are different stages in the conflict of laws process, and it seems that what the forum must characterise varies according to the stage it has reached.   **4–03**

The facts must be the starting point of any action, and they must be assessed by the claimant in order that an action can be raised. The facts lead the claimant and, in turn, the court, to the categorisation of the legal issue(s) arising.

At the stage of jurisdiction allocation, the forum must assess whether or not it accepts the jurisdictional ground founded upon by the claimant; this ground will be tied to the claimant's preferred characterisation of the problem arising. As noted above, the characterisation supplied by the claimant normally will not be challenged.

Thereafter (on the assumption that the court is properly seised), it must proceed to a consideration of choice of law. One might say that the subject of identification of a choice of law rule is a legal question arising from a factual situation and that the focus of characterisation is a legal matter, being the determination of the question to which the rule of law relates. The relationship of fact and law in this exercise is interdependent. In order to identify the correct choice of law rule, the forum must allocate the question raised by the factual situation to what it deems to be the correct legal category.[26] Recent dicta emphasise that it is not sufficient to characterise the nature of the claim, but rather that it is necessary to identify the question at issue[27]; further, that a distributive approach may be necessary so as to direct an appropriate characterisation to each one of a number of different issues[28]: "Many claims are of a complex nature and depend on the resolution of more than one issue and the authorities clearly support the conclusion that English law characterises individual issues that arise

---

[24] M. Wolff, *Private International Law*, 2nd edn (1950), pp.154–156. For an example of characterisation by the *lex causae*, see *Maldonado* [1954] P. 223. A refinement on the forum-centred approach was urged by Robertson, to the effect that the court must initially characterise according to its own law (primary characterisation), but having been led by its own choice of law rule to the foreign law which it considers relevant, it must thereafter adopt the classification by the foreign law (secondary characterisation) (A.H. Robertson, *Characterization in the Conflict of Laws* (Cambridge, Massachusetts: Harvard University Press, 1940)).

[25] A distinguished sample comprises Robertson, *Characterization in the Conflict of Laws* (1940); Falconbridge, *Selected Essays on the Conflict of Laws*, 2nd edn (Toronto: Canada Law Book Company, 1954), Chs 3–5; and Lederman, "Classification in Private International Law", 29 Can. Bar Rev. 3.

[26] *Cheshire, North and Fawcett: Private International Law*, 14th edn (2008), term this "classification of the cause of action" (p.42).

[27] *Macmillan Inc v Bishopsgate Investment Trust Plc (No.3)* [1996] 1 W.L.R. 387, per Aldous L.J. at 418. cf. *Haugesund Kommune v Depfa ACS Bank* [2012] Q.B. 549, per Aikens L.J. at [38]–[49].

[28] *Atlantic Telecom GmbH, Noter,* 2004 S.L.T. 1031, per Lord Brodie at [56].

for determination rather than seeking to characterise the claim as a whole".[29] In complex cases,[30] parties may disagree about the issue(s) presenting, and the judge may look behind the form in which the case is pleaded to ascertain the true character of the problem(s).[31]

There are a number of characterisation cases, however, which are concerned not with the characterisation of facts, nor with legal issues, but with the nature of a particular rule of law. The most significant exercise of this type concerns the classification of a rule of law as pertaining either to substance or procedure.[32]

Applications of characterisation

4–04   Wolff noted that, "each general conception has a firm and stable nucleus but an indistinct periphery, and it would be practically impossible for any legislator or court to establish a rigid and precise delimitation".[33] In more recent years, Mance L.J. has called for a "more nuanced analysis" to characterisation: " . . .the overall aim is to identify the most appropriate law to govern a particular issue. The classes or categories of issue which the law recognises . . .are man-made, not natural. They have no inherent value, beyond their purpose in assisting to select the most appropriate law".[34] The characterisation task must be undertaken with perceptiveness, and sensitivity to the goal of the choice of law process, which is to identify and apply to the problem the appropriate law in the view of the forum. But a gloss must be put on the word "appropriate": in jurisdiction selection systems such as those of the UK,[35] the forum must act within the constraints of that methodology, which means that it is precluded from choosing directly what it perceives to be, in terms of content or application, the "best" or "better" rule from home and foreign contenders, and must act through the neutral medium of the connecting factor.

The characterisation exercise is most easily understood through examples. From the law of marriage, the cases of *Apt v Apt*[36] and *Ponticelli v Ponticelli*[37] demonstrate the orthodox, jurisdiction selection approach to solving a conflict problem. Where an English domiciliary was party (the absent party) to a proxy marriage celebrated abroad, and the question of validity of the marriage came before an English court, the forum was required to categorise the problem. The forum having accommodated the problem within a legal category (formal validity

---

[29] *Maher v Groupama Grand Est* [2009] EWCA Civ 1191; [2010] 1 W.L.R. 1564, per Moore-Bick L.J. at [8].
[30] e.g. *Raiffeisen Zentralbank Osterreich AG v Five Star General Trading LLC (The Mount I)* [2001] I Lloyd's Rep. 597; *Atlantic Telecom GmbH, Noter,* 2004 S.L.T. 1031, per Lord Brodie at 1041.
[31] *Macmillan Inc v Bishopsgate Investment Trust Plc (No.3)* [1996] 1 W.L.R. 387, per Auld L.J. at 407; and *Fiona Trust & Holding Corp v Privalov* [2010] EWHC 3199 (Comm), per Andrew Smith J at [152].
[32] e.g. in tort and delict, awards of damages: *Harding v Wealands* [2006] UKHL 32; *Knight v Axa Assurances* [2009] EWHC 1900 (QB); *Maher v Groupama Grand Est* [2009] EWCA Civ 1191; [2010] 1 W.L.R. 1564; and *Cox v Ergo Versicherung AG* [2014] UKSC 22; [2014] A.C. 1379.
[33] M Wolff, *Private International Law*, 2nd edn (1950), p.150.
[34] *Raiffeisen Zentralbank Osterreich AG v Five Star General Trading LLC (The Mount I)* [2001] I Lloyd's Rep. 597 at [27], [28].
[35] Para.3–01, above.
[36] *Apt v Apt* [1948] P. 83.
[37] *Ponticelli v Ponticelli* [1958] P. 204.

of marriage), the relevant choice of law rule was applied. The connecting factor to govern the formal validity of marriage indicated by the choice of law rule under English (and Scots) conflict rules was (and is) the *lex loci celebrationis*.[38] If a proxy marriage is acceptable in form by the *lex loci celebrationis*, a marriage so celebrated will be regarded as valid in English (and Scots) law, subject only to public policy, even though by domestic English/Scots law marriages cannot be validly celebrated by proxy. An English court has held that the foreign *lex loci celebrationis* governs the formal validity of marriage where *neither* party was present, though the correctness of this approach may be doubted because though a celebration took place abroad, the better view would seem to be that the true place of celebration of such a marriage (constituted by the exchange of consent) was the English *lex loci contractus*.[39]

From the law of property, an example of the practical importance of characterisation may be cited, namely, *Re Korvine's Trust*,[40] in which a man of Russian domicile, a patient in a London hospital, transferred, in contemplation of death, money and jewellery to his mistress, and one month later died. The claims on his estate of his widow and sons, brought in an English court, depended on whether the court viewed the matter as one of succession (to be referred to the Russian last domicile of the deceased as the long-established connecting factor *per* the choice of law rule of the forum[41]), or as one of transfer of moveable property (in which case the connecting factor would be the English *lex situs* of the property at the time of the purported transfer[42]).[43] The court characterised the problem as one of property, and so applied English domestic law qua *lex situs*, by which the gift was valid. A comparable modern case is *Gorjat v Gorjat*,[44] in which the characterisation of the issue arising was, in the view of the court, one of the validity of lifetime instructions (i.e. the validity of an assignment of intangible property), notwithstanding that those instructions had succession consequences.[45] Similarly, *Joint Administrators of Rangers Football Club Plc, Noters*,[46] demonstrates difficulties of characterisation between and among the law of property, of trusts, and of contract. Within the law of contract, a subtle difficulty of characterisation arose in *Integral Petroleum SA v Scu-Finanz AG*[47] in the matter of distinguishing issues of formal validity of contract from issues of a company's capacity to act through its official registered officers.

---

[38] Para.11–20, below.

[39] *McCabe v McCabe* [1994] 1 F.C.R. 257 CA; *The Independent*, 3 September 1993. R.D. Leslie, "Foreign Consensual Marriages", 1994 S.L.T. (News) 87.

[40] *Re Korvine's Trust* [1921] 1 Ch. 343.

[41] Paras 18–14 and 18–31, below.

[42] Para.17–13, below.

[43] cf. *Connell's Trustees v Connell's Trustees*(1886) 13 R. 1175.

[44] *Gorjat v Gorjat* [2010] E.W.H.C. 1537 (Ch).

[45] *Gorjat v Gorjat* [2010] E.W.H.C. 1537 (Ch) at [8] and [15], from which can be inferred that the alternative characterisation of the issue arising, as one of succession to moveable property, was entertained and rejected. See also *Debt Collect London Ltd v SK Slavia Praha – Fotbal AS* [2010] EWHC 57 (QB), per Tugendhat J. at [27]–[31].

[46] *Joint Administrators of Rangers Football Club Plc, Noters,* 2012 S.L.T. 599.

[47] *Integral Petroleum SA v Scu-Finanz AG* [2015] EWCA Civ 144, per Floyd L.J. at [39].

On the spectrum between the law of succession and that of matrimonial property or contract lies the celebrated case of *De Nicols v Curlier (No.1)*.[48] A husband, domiciled at marriage in France, and at death in England, purported to dispose by will of his estate as if it were entirely his own property, taking no note of any community rights allegedly attaching to his wife. Clear evidence was led of French law that the community of property established by the French Civil Code transcended any change of domicile during the marriage. The court abided by the French rule that community rights were not disturbed by a change of domicile. The issue of capacity to dispose of property was classified, therefore, though not in so many words,[49] as a matter of matrimonial property or contract, rather than of succession, and the testator was held by the House of Lords not to be entitled to dispose by will of his entire estate in contravention of French rules of community of property.

From the law of succession, the case of *Re Martin*[50] concerned the classification of the English domestic rule that marriage revokes a will, unless the will is made in express contemplation of a particular marriage which subsequently takes place. Did this rule belong to the rules of marriage or of succession? The testatrix, of French domicile, made a will in England in English form. Later she married a professor of French origin, a fugitive from French justice. When the French criminal prescriptive period expired, he returned to France without her. They were not divorced, and since unity of domicile between spouses then prevailed, she, predeceasing him, died possessed of the French domicile of her husband. Had her will been revoked by her marriage? The English court held that the matter was one of marriage law, to be referred to the connecting factor of her domicile immediately after marriage (surprisingly, held to be English) and not to her French domicile at death, which was the applicable law in succession.

As observed above, one of the most important demarcations which the forum must draw is between that which is substantive and that which is procedural. In the context of succession, Uthwatt, J. held in *Re Cohn*[51] that a rule governing sequence of death in a common calamity was a matter of substantive succession law of the German *lex causae*, qua *lex successionis*. The characterisation as substantive of the equivalent presumption under English succession law did not matter because the parties having died domiciled in Germany, the rule of the German *lex causae* necessarily prevailed over the English *lex fori* in relation to substantive issues. Had both rules been categorised as procedural, the forum would have held itself entitled to follow its own rule.

Similarly in *In the Estate of Fuld (Deceased) (No.3)*,[52] the effect of "undue influence" upon a testator was a matter of substantive succession law to be

---

[48] *De Nicols v Curlier (No.1)* [1900] A.C. 21. cf. the notable case of *Anton v Bartolo* (the "Maltese Marriage case") (1891) Clunet 1171.

[49] Further, para.13–02, below. In many cases presenting a problem of characterisation, as in *De Nicols* itself, the word characterisation may not be explicitly mentioned, and the determinative rôle of the forum hardly or not expressly noticed.

[50] *Re Martin* [1900] P. 211.

[51] *Re Cohn* [1945] Ch. 5. Ch.8, below.

[52] *In the Estate of Fuld (Deceased) (No.3)* [1968] P. 675.

governed by Peter Fuld's (German) domicile at the relevant date.[53] Scarman J. assigned rules of burden of proof, in this instance at least, to the category of procedure.[54]

In the Estate of Maldonado[55] is noteworthy in that the English Court of Appeal, unusually, accepted the Spanish law characterisation of the nature of the Spanish government's claim to ownerless property in preference to the English law classification thereof. Spanish law was the *lex causae*, qua *lex successionis*: "it has been found (and the Crown has accepted the finding) that the State of Spain is, in the eye of Spanish law, the true heir",[56] and not the fiscal recipient of ownerless property. The distinction between heir and fiscal recipient normally is one to be made by the UK forum.[57]

It can be seen from these cases that the characterisation of the issue will determine the choice of law rule, and in turn the connecting factor, and thereby the substantive outcome.

Manipulative characterisation

Where a choice of law rule is inflexible, by pointing to a "hard", single-contact connecting factor (such as nationality), the forum may chafe under its restrictions and may be tempted to reclassify the problem, by taking it out of its natural category and placing it in another category, thereby delivering a different, more palatable result through operation of a different choice of law rule incorporating a different connecting factor. This is termed "manipulative characterisation". It may be argued, for example, that a rule presented as delictual in its legal system of origin, which prohibits litigation between spouses, is overlaid with a family law purpose, and that it might be argued that it was not intended to apply to a married couple only passing through the enacting state, who otherwise are strangers to its legal system.[58] If a wife should choose to sue her husband for damages arising out of his culpable lack of care, in a forum which has a choice of law rule in delict of strict application of the *lex loci delicti*, re-characterisation by the forum of the inter-spousal immunity rule of the *locus delicti* as one pertaining to family law and not to delict, may permit circumvention by the claimant of the prohibition on suit.[59]

4–05

---

[53] That is, the date of testing, presumably, rather than the date of death—though this cannot be stated with absolute certainty, as Fuld was held by the English court never at any point in his life to have lost his German domicile of origin.

[54] *Fuld (No.3)* [1968] P. 675, per Scarman J. at 696–697. However, the categorisation of burden of proof is not uncontroversial. Ch.8, below.

[55] *In the Estate of Maldonado* [1954] P. 223.

[56] *Maldonado* [1954] P. 223, per Jenkins L.J. at 250.

[57] Para.18–16 (caduciary rights), below.

[58] This is the type of factual scenario against which American conflict theorists tested their policy evaluation theories (Ch.3, above).

[59] An alternative solution in such a case, and one more commonly found, is through operation of a more flexible choice of law rule, such as provided by Private International Law (Miscellaneous Provisions) Act 1995 s.12, and Rome II art 4. Ch.16, below.

False conflicts

4–06   The conflict lawyer should be alert to the presence of "false conflicts" that is, to note that there is a conflict problem only if there is a true conflict of laws, and that there is no conflict if there would be a coincidence of outcome, no matter which of the potentially applicable laws were applied. Three examples can be provided.

First, there is a false conflict if the result of application of different connecting factors, e.g. domicile and habitual residence, by the different choice of law rules of different legal systems, would be to apply the *same* law. This is the opposite of the latent conflict outlined above; it is rather latent harmony.

Secondly, there is a false conflict if, there being two apparently contending legal systems, it is found that those two laws have a common interest that one of them be applied, on the ground that if neither law were applied the purposes of both would be frustrated. This situation can arise because of the interaction of the laws in question in the particular circumstances presenting. For example, if, by the law of country A, the loan of a car in A were to impose on the owner liability for negligent driving by the borrower, but only if the negligent driving occurred within country A, and if the borrower drove the car negligently in country B, which imposed the same liability as did A but only if the contract of loan had been made in country B,[60] then the unfortunate result would obtain that the owner would escape responsibility. If neither A law nor B law applied, the purpose of both would be frustrated, for both adhere in principle to the imposition of liability on the car owner. Hence, in the court of A or B, the enlightened forum must be prepared to waive its own requirement, in order to serve the larger purposes of the conflict of laws.

A third example of false conflict results from the interaction of certain sets of rules, choice of law and/or domestic, of different legal systems, e.g. where, by the Arcadian *locus delicti* of a road traffic accident there is inter-spousal immunity in tort, but by the Utopian *lex fori* there is a policy objection to such immunity,[61] and where by Utopian law the parties involved in that accident are husband and wife, but by Arcadian law they are not deemed to be validly married. There is no reason, by either law, why the woman, injured through the negligent driving of the man, should not sue him for damages in Utopia or in Arcadia. A similar situation arises where the principal point at issue is whether a will has been revoked by a subsequent marriage[62] in circumstances where, by the *lex causae* (the *lex successionis*, being the law which contains the revocation rule) the marriage is invalid, but by the *lex fori*, which has no such revocation rule, the marriage is valid. The forum should note the coincidence of outcome despite the different paths of reasoning, and heed should be paid to what lies in common

---

[60] This example is taken from Morris, *Conflict of Laws*, 4th edn (1993), p.422.

[61] In Scots domestic law, the prohibition upon spouse suing spouse in delict was removed by the Law Reform (Husband and Wife) Act 1962 s.2(1), except where, in the view of the court, it appears that no substantial benefit would accrue to either party from the continuation of the action (s.2(2)). See *Kozikowska v Kozikowski (No.1)*, 1996 S.L.T. 386. Although the provision was repealed by the Family Law (Scotland) Act 2006 Sch.3, the common law does not revive (J.Thomson, *Delictual Liability*, 5th edn (2014), p.259).

[62] cf. *Re Swan's Will* (1871) 2 V.L.R. (I.E.&M.) 47.

rather than to what divides. While these circumstances otherwise might have given rise to an "Incidental Question", the identity of result is justification for aborting that question.

THE INCIDENTAL QUESTION

An incidental or preliminary question may arise in a conflict problem if the choice of law rule of the forum relating to a matter refers to a foreign law, but, before the main question can be answered, it is necessary to obtain an answer to another question also containing foreign elements. The problem which arises is whether this "incidental" question is to be solved by application of the choice of law rules of that same foreign law as applies to the main question, or by application of the choice of law rules of the *lex fori* as to the incidental question. Should the forum permit its chosen law to regulate not only the main, but also the preliminary question?

4–07

This problem arises only[63] if the following conditions are present:

(a)   the main question must be referred to a foreign law under the choice of law rule of the forum;

(b)   the main question cannot be answered until an incidental question has been answered;

(c)   the choice of law rules of the *lex causae* pertaining to the main question and those of the forum produce different results as to the answer to the incidental question.

The problem seems to be an unavoidable one in certain sets of circumstances. It may be that the problem of the incidental question is present in a case, but is ignored or overlooked by the court.[64]

This deeper mystery of the conflict of laws is most readily understood if set in narrative form. The classic exposition concerns the distribution by a Scots court (qua forum) of that part of the intestate moveable estate situated in Scotland belonging to the deceased, X, who died domiciled in Attica. Since by Scots choice of law rules the distribution of moveable estate is governed by the law of the deceased's last domicile, the *lex causae* in this example is the law of Attica. But Attican law has choice of law rules of its own, which are likely to differ from those of the Scots *lex fori*.

How is the matter to be decided if, by Attican law, a portion of moveables falls to the widow of the deceased; but it is discovered that X had a complex matrimonial history, and that she who on first sight appears to be X's widow, is

---

[63]   e.g. *Re Johnson* [1903] 1 Ch. 821; *Re Stirling* [1908] 2 Ch. 344; *Re Bischoffscheim* [1948] Ch. 79; *Haque v Haque* (1962) 108 C.L.R. 230; *Schwebel v Ungar* (1963) 42 D.L.R. (2d) 622 (Ont.C.A.); affirmed (1964) 48 D.L.R. (2d) 644 (Sup. Ct. Can.); *R. v Brentwood Superintendent Registrar of Marriages Ex p. Arias* [1968] 2 Q.B. 956 (approach superseded by legislative intervention per Recognition of Divorces and Legal Separations Act 1971 s.7, itself superseded by Family Law Act 1986 s.50).

[64]   Consider, e.g. *Shaw v Gould* (1868) L.R. 3 H.L. 55; *Perrini v Perrini* [1979] 2 All E.R. 323; *Lawrence v Lawrence* [1985] 2 All E.R. 733.

X's second[65] "wife", and that the marriage to the earlier wife has been terminated by divorce or annulment, as to the validity of which the choice of law rules of Scotland and of Attica do not agree? Should the Scottish forum permit the international private law of Attica to regulate not only the intestate moveable succession with regard to the Attican domiciliary,[66] but also to answer the incidental or preliminary question of, "*who* is X's widow?" If prepared to cede to Attican law the decision upon *both* questions, the Scots court would be said to follow the *lex causae* theory in its approach to the incidental question. On the other hand, if it prefers to apply its own choice of law rule on recognition of overseas consistorial decrees, it would be said to adopt the *lex fori* theory. If it should happen that the divorce between X and his first wife had been obtained from a Scots court, a later Scots court is very unlikely to deny its own decree.[67]

There is no definitive answer to the manner in which the incidental question should be addressed. There is general agreement upon the pursuit of the aims of justice and expediency, but which manner of proceeding best serves the case and produces a positive outcome (and for whom?) is a matter of conjecture.

Parliament, in removing one related problem,[68] left unanswered the question of what is to happen when the Scots court has to consider the legal capacity to marry of an individual who is deemed to have such capacity by the law of his domicile, but who has been divorced by a decree not recognised by Scots law. No such case appears yet to have presented itself to a Scots forum, but is exactly the situation in the classic incidental question found in the case of *Schwebel v Ungar*.[69] A husband and wife, both Jews domiciled in Hungary, decided to emigrate to Israel. En route, in Italy, they were divorced by ghet (Jewish religious divorce).[70] Such a divorce was worthy of recognition by the law of Israel, but not by the law of Hungary which was the personal law of the parties at the relevant time. Each party later acquired a domicile of choice in Israel. Thereafter, the woman removed to Canada where, being still of Israeli domicile, she purported to re-marry in Toronto. Her new "husband" later sought annulment of the later "marriage" in a Canadian court.

The law of Ontario referred the woman's capacity to marry to the Israeli law of her ante-nuptial domicile, but in the matter of the incidental question—of the validity of the antecedent divorce, which was capable of having its own choice of law rule—the Ontarian court was not willing, by its *own* choice of law rules on the particular issue of religious divorces, to recognise the ghet as valid (since it was not valid by the Hungarian law of the husband's domicile at the time).

The dilemma is clear to see. The decision by the Supreme Court of Canada, affirming the Ontario Court of Appeal, was to have the Israeli law governing the main question of capacity to marry, regulate also the incidental question of

---

[65] Or third or subsequent "wife", giving rise to the possibility of multiple incidental questions.

[66] That is, domiciled in Attica in the view of Scots law; the law of Attica may not consider X to be domiciled there, and in any case may consider the law of the last nationality to be the appropriate *lex successionis*—but that is another story, told in Ch.5 and Ch.18, below.

[67] But see *R. v Brentwood Superintendent Registrar of Marriages Ex p. Arias* [1968] 2 Q.B. 956.

[68] By enacting Family Law Act 1986 s.50. Ch.12, below.

[69] *Schwebel v Ungar* (1963) 42 D.L.R. (2d) 622 (Ont. C.A.); affirmed (1964) 48 D.L.R. (2d) 644 (Sup. Ct. Can.).

[70] As to Scots and English conflict rules on recognition of religious (extrajudicial) divorces, see Ch.12, below.

validity of antecedent divorce. The case therefore provides an example of the *lex causae* approach to resolving the incidental question. But one might say that overall control was still with the forum, which chose to take that path, the choice of law rules of Ontario containing the possibility, at the option of the Ontarian forum, to defer to the choice of law rules of the foreign system which the Canadian court itself had selected to answer the main question.

Writers are divided in approach. The *lex causae* approach, as well as being internationally minded, has an attraction. It concedes that a foreign law has a conflict of laws dimension (and that that dimension is equipped with detailed choice of law rules), and is willing to remit the entirety of the problem to the entirety of that foreign law, which the forum itself has selected in the first place: perhaps that is what "application" of the *lex causae* entails.[71]

It may be that the natural approach of the Scots lawyer is to refer the entire matter to the *lex causae*. Such an approach is preferable in the interests of international harmony and universality of status, unless the price in terms of internal dissonance is too high.[72] Few, however, would advise a rigid, predetermined attitude in this area where instances, in any event, are rare. *Potior et utilior*, we might say, had we not let go of the Latin.

TIME

Time may be a relevant factor in the forum's resolution of a conflict problem.[73] The temporal dimension may be important as a result of one of a number of eventualities:

4–08

(a) *The content of the forum's choice of law rule may change* (*le conflit transitoire*), e.g. the choice of law rule in delict which is applicable in a Scots court will vary according to the date of the act or omission giving rise to the claim. If this occurred prior to 1 May 1996, the rule of double actionability must operate[74]; if it occurred after that date, but before 11 January 2009, the case will be governed by the Private International Law (Miscellaneous Provisions) Act 1995; and if the event giving rise to damage occurred after 11 January 2009, the case will be governed by the Rome II Regulation.[75]

Where change in the choice of law rule of the forum is effected by legislative means, transitional provisions normally will be found, but these too may give rise to interpretative difficulty.[76]

---

[71] Ch.5, below.

[72] Wolff, *Private International Law*, 2nd edn (1950), p.209.

[73] F. Mann, "The Time Element in the Conflict of Laws" (1954) 31 B.Y.B.I.L. 217.

[74] *Re T & N Ltd* [2005] E.W.H.C. 2990 (Ch).

[75] Rome II Regulation arts 31 and 32.

[76] e.g. unity of domicile between husband and wife was removed by the Domicile and Matrimonial Proceedings Act 1973 s.1(1) and (2), but the case of *Inland Revenue Commissioners v Duchess of Portland* [1982] Ch. 314 reveals an imperfection in the drafting of the rule governing the domicile after January 1, 1974 of women married before January 1, 1974. cf. Family Law (Scotland) Act 2006 s.22, in respect of the transitional application of which there are serious deficiencies. Para.6–05, below.

(b)   *The connecting factor may require to be defined by time.*[77] Connecting factors may be fixed, constant or static, on the one hand, or variable/ dynamic on the other. Examples of the former are the *lex situs* of immoveable property,[78] *lex loci contractus,*[79] *lex loci actus,*[80] and *lex loci celebrationis.*[81] Examples of variable/dynamic connecting factors are the *lex situs* of moveables, and the domicile/habitual residence/nationality of persons. *Locus delicti* (place of occurrence of harm) may be a fixed connecting factor, e.g. a road traffic accident, but in more complex cases of multi-locational harm the case is likely to be regarded as "spread over" space and time. Delicts, therefore, may have a continuing quality, on the facts or in their constituent elements, and may display both spatial and temporal problems.[82]

Within the category of variable/dynamic factors, a distinction perhaps can be drawn between a connecting factor such as the *situs* of moveable property which, by nature, may change from time to time, but in respect of the identification of which at any one time (*tempus inspiciendum*), only that time is relevant[83]; and a connecting factor such as domicile which also by nature may change from time to time, but in respect of the identification of which at any one time, review will have to be made of earlier (but not later) events.[84] The domicile or habitual residence of the *propositus* is a "variable" as opposed to "static" connecting factor. It is useless as a guide unless the rule of choice of law, or jurisdiction,[85] specifies the date at which domicile or habitual residence is to be determined for the particular purpose before the court. Thus, legal capacity to marry is referred to the law of the domicile *immediately before marriage*[86]; legal testamentary capacity (age, sanity) to the law of the domicile *at the date of testing*[87]; and proprietary testamentary capacity (freedom to disinherit one's family) to the law of the deceased's domicile *at death.*[88]

Various examples can be presented to demonstrate that the temporal aspect of a conflict rule may be significant.

---

[77] For the purposes of jurisdiction and/or choice of law and/or recognition of decrees.

[78] The *situs* of land obviously can never change, unless politically by means of territorial realignment, a rare occurrence.

[79] Rome I Regulation art.11: Ch.15, below.

[80] e.g. Wills Act 1963 s.1, which, however, also exemplifies the use, in the alternative, of the variable connecting factors of domicile or habitual residence or nationality, each qualified in terms of time. Ch.18, below.

[81] Except perhaps in relation to marriage by cohabitation with habit and repute; and in the rare instance of dual locality *locus celebrationis* (telephone marriages): Ch.11, below.

[82] *Soutar v Peters,* 1912 1 S.L.T. 111; *Henderson v Jaouen* [2002] 2 All E.R. 705.

[83] *Winkworth v Christie, Manson & Woods Ltd* [1980] 1 Ch. 496; Ch.17, below.

[84] cf. *Bell v Kennedy* (1868) 6 M. (H.L.) 69.

[85] cf. *Canada Trust v Stolzenburg (No.2)* [2000] 4 All E.R. 481.

[86] *Brook v Brook* (1861) 9 H.L. Cas. 193; *Mette v Mette* (1859) 1 Sw. & Tr. 416; *Re Paine* [1940] Ch. 46; *Re Bozzelli Settlement* [1902] 1 Ch. 751; *Re De Wilton* [1900] 2 Ch. 481; see Ch.11, below and now Family Law (Scotland) Act 2006 s.38(2).

[87] As noted above, this point is not completely vouched but see *Fuld (No.3)* [1968] P. 675.

[88] *Re Groos* [1915] 1 Ch. 572. A will is inchoate: one cannot say that it is the last will of the testator until his death occurs (assuming lucidity to the end). Similarly, one cannot say whether its provisions are essentially valid until that date, because its essential validity will be judged by the law of his last domicile, which can be ascertained with certainty only at the date of death, when the connecting factor crystallises.

With regard to choice of law in annulment of marriage, the court, if it chooses to apply the law of the domicile of either or both parties, should make explicit whether it seeks to apply the domicile at the date of the purported marriage or at the date of litigation. Principle suggests that the former is the correct approach,[89] but in jurisdictional terms, it has happened that the parties have benefited from a change[90] in the legal nature of their marriage, most commonly from potentially polygamous to monogamous, by the date of consistorial litigation in a UK forum.[91]

In matrimonial property questions, there is a divergence between those legal systems which adhere to the immutability approach, which is that parties' rights in moveable property are fixed, being regulated by whatever touchstone is preferred (as to which time again may be relevant)[92]; and those, principally in the USA, which consider that parties' rights in moveables may change with changes in the domicile of the spouses during the marriage.

A variation upon this theme concerns competing titles to moveable property, where identification of the *lex situs* is not necessarily conclusive if rights to that property traceable to different legal bases should conflict. For example, security rights over moveables are governed in principle by the *lex situs*; but the question arises if the governing law should be the situation of the moveables when the terms of the contract and relevant security are concluded, e.g. Germany, or the *situs*, e.g. Scotland, of the moveables when an issue of bankruptcy arises and the validity of rights in security become commercially and practically important. This, for the forum, is an issue of ranking its own choice of law rules in order of importance in a particular case. In the contest between Scots choice of law rules of property and choice of law rules of contract, the property rules have been given precedence.[93]

Rarely, a choice of law rule may contain within it a cumulative reference to more than one *tempus inspiciendum*.[94]

(c) *The substantive content of the lex causae may change*, in such a way as to have significance for the case (*le conflit mobile dans le temps*). Parties' choice of applicable law to govern their contract is a choice of that body of law as it may prevail from time to time.[95] It follows that the passage of time may bring about supervening illegality of contractual terms during the contract's currency.[96] Supervening legislation, however, is not always negative in effect, but may be enabling, e.g, so as to confer capacity

---

[89] cf. *Szechter v Szechter* [1971] P. 286.

[90] Effected through change of domicile or change of sect or other events.

[91] cf. *Cheni v Cheni* [1965] P. 85; and *Parkasho v Singh* [1968] P. 233. But see now Matrimonial Proceedings (Polygamous Marriages) Act 1972 s.2; Ch.11, below.

[92] *Re Egerton's Will Trusts* [1956] Ch. 593.

[93] Ch.17, below.

[94] e.g. the English choice of law rule concerning legitimation by subsequent marriage, which prevailed before the Legitimacy Act 1926, and which required legal capacity in the father to legitimate by this manner by his personal law both at the date of the birth of the child, and at the date of the marriage: see *Re Goodman's Trusts* (1881) L.R. 17 Ch. D. 266.

[95] Though consider in the area of trusts and truster's intentions *Wright's Trustees v Callander*, 1993 S.L.T. 556; and *Crawford*, 1994 S.L.T. (News) 225.

[96] cf. *Ralli Bros v Compania Naviera Sota y Aznar* [1920] 2 K.B. 287.

retrospectively. The most recent example of this is found in family law, which, in permitting the conversion of a civil partnership into a same sex marriage provides that such a marriage will be deemed to have commenced on the (prior) date of registration of the partnership.[97] In other cases the choice falls upon the domestic content at a defined date, e.g. in distribution of an estate, the law of the domicile at death.[98] A consequence of change of content of the applicable law may be positive, in that defects in formalities of marriage may be removed by subsequent retrospective legislation or government decree, recognised by the forum's conflict rules.[99]

(d)   *Innominate cases.* Divorce yields interesting examples of the significance of time. If the Scots forum has jurisdiction, it will apply its own domestic law to the grounds on which divorce may be obtained.[100] It does not matter whether the acts complained of had legal significance as grounds of dissolution when and/or where committed,[101] unless such a factor forms part of the domestic divorce law of the forum. Nor does it matter that they took place before a change of domicile, the divorce court having taken jurisdiction on the basis of a new domicile.[102] Grounds of annulment are quite different as they are necessarily linked as a matter of temporal and legal priority to principles relating to the essential or formal constitution of marriage.

The significance of time is easy to see when the matter is pointed out. However, though all the points made above may be important considerations, the primary dimension of choice of law is spatial.

---

[97] Marriage and Civil Partnership (Scotland) Act 2004 s.11(2); and Marriage (Same Sex Couples) Act 2013 s.9(6). Para.11–06, below.

[98] *Lynch v Provisional Government of Paraguay* (1871) L.R. 2 P. & D. 268 in which the English court, concerned to address an application for a grant of probate to the universal legatee of moveable property, situated in England, of the deceased, Lopez, who died domiciled in Paraguay, did not give effect to Paraguayan legislation which purported to confiscate all his property, wherever situate, *after* his death. It is fair to say, however, that this case equally can be explained as a refusal to give extraterritorial effect to foreign expropriatory legislation, or on policy grounds, or as a simple affirmation of our choice of ultimate domicile as *lex successionis*. But see *Nelson v Bridport* (1846) 8 Beav. 547, where the necessity to defer at all times to the *lex situs* is affirmed. Practicalities on which the theory of the supremacy of the *lex situs* is based may require recognition of even post-death changes.

[99] cf. *Starkowski v Att Gen* [1954] A.C. 155. Ch.11, below.

[100] Para.12–18, below.

[101] Contrast *Ali v Ali* [1968] P. 564 where in specialised circumstances the English court was unwilling to take into consideration any alleged matrimonial offences pre-dating the unilateral conversion by Ali, through change of domicile from Indian to English, of the nature of the marriage from potentially polygamous to monogamous, thereby enabling the English forum to take jurisdiction. Para.11–07 et seq., above.

[102] *Carswell v Carswell* (1881) 8 R. 901; *Morton v Morton*, 1897 5 S.L.T. 222. But equally (*Stavert v Stavert* (1882) 9 R. 519) commission of the matrimonial offence within the forum is not enough to found jurisdiction *ratione delicti*!

THE END OF THE BEGINNING

The aim of each system of choice of law rules is to identify the appropriate law to govern a question which has arisen for decision in the court of that system, and which contains foreign elements. The content of the choice of law rules will vary from legal system to legal system, though as the years go on, the harmonisation impetus brings about an increasing measure of agreement among consenting states as to governing law in most private law subjects, if not necessarily securing uniform interpretation and application of harmonised choice of law rules.

4–09

That which remains to be considered is the meaning of the word "law", as used in the expression "choice of law". For if every developed legal system has both domestic law rules and choice of law rules, its law "flat" and its law "in the round"—then when the Scots forum chooses, e.g. "French" law to govern an issue, should it be within the Scots court's contemplation that French choice of law rules should be proved and followed? This is the celebrated problem of *renvoi*, the pleasures of which will be tasted in Ch.5.

SUMMARY 4

1. The forum having accepted jurisdiction, the *lex fori* governs:
   (a) the form of action;
   (b) characterisation of the point at issue;
   (c) selection of the choice of law rule, including definition and identification of the connecting factor;
   (d) application of the choice of law rule; and
   (e) matters of procedure.[103]

4–10

2. With regard to characterisation, differences between/among choice of law rules of different legal systems may be obvious or may be hidden:
   (a) Different legal systems may classify the same set of facts, or the same issue arising therefrom, in different ways. This is a problem of "patent conflict".
   (b) Different legal systems may attach different meanings to the same legal term, e.g. domicile, or habitual residence. This is a problem of "latent conflict".
   (c) Some legal systems contain legal rights or remedies which are unknown in others.
   (d) The choice of law rules of two legal systems may be the same and yet the two systems may classify the same legal issue in different ways so as to produce entirely different results, e.g. whether the requirement of parental consent to marriage is one of essential or formal validity; or whether a wife's rights in property upon her husband's death should be categorised as rights of succession or rights arising out of the matrimonial relationship.

3. For foreign law to apply, it must be averred and its content proved.
4. The circumstances may present an incidental question.
5. The element of time may be relevant.

---

[103] Ch.8, below.

CHAPTER 5

Renvoi

NATURE OF THE SUBJECT

Renvoi means a dismissal, a sending away, or sending back. The word denotes a mystery which lies at the heart of the conflict of laws. The problem springs from the dual meaning of the expression "*the law of a country*". This term may be used in a narrow, "domestic law" sense or in a wide sense, "in the round", referring to a country's law including its choice of law rules. Hence, in suggesting application of the law of country X as the governing law in a given problem, one may be criticised for lack of specification: the law of X, with or without its rules of international private law?

The natural home of *renvoi* is the law of succession.[1] A classic example of the *renvoi* problem concerns the question of succession to the moveable estate in Scotland of a British subject who died domiciled in a foreign country, by the law of which succession to moveables is governed by the law of the deceased's last nationality (instead of, as by Scots choice of law rules,[2] by the law of the deceased's last domicile). If, for example, according to the Scots choice of law rule governing succession to moveable property, the estate of the deceased is to be distributed according to the French law of his domicile, ought the Scots court to include within its understanding of "the law of the domicile", the French choice of law rule concerning succession to moveable estate, so as to secure the outcome that the distribution of the moveables in Scotland will be effected according to the law of the nationality (being the desired outcome of the French *lex successionis*)?[3]

The *renvoi* problem in general may be said to arise whenever, within the permitted scope of operation of *renvoi* as explained below, a question of law is referred notionally by one law (the *lex fori*) to another law (the *lex causae*) in its entirety, i.e. including its choice of law rules; and that other law either refers it back to the original law (*renvoi* remission) or refers it on to still another law

---

[1] e.g. *Re Annesley* [1926] Ch. 692; *Re Ross* [1930] 1 Ch. 377; *Haji-Ioannou, Deceased v Frangos* [2009] EWHC 2310 (QB); and *Lambton (Earl of Durham) v Lady Lambton* [2013] EWHC 3566 (Ch). The *renvoi* process was used without success in *Fuld (No.3)* [1968] P. 675 to attempt to save two (of four) codicils from a finding of formal invalidity.

[2] In essence, by Scots choice of law rules in succession, testate or intestate, matters of substance pertaining to immoveables are governed by the *lex situs*, and those pertaining to moveables by the *lex ultimi domicilii*, the law of the last domicile of the *propositus*. For detail see Ch.18.

[3] It seems that the English forum is never prepared fully to put itself into the position of the foreign law in as much as the deceased's domicile always will be identified according to the rules of the *lex fori*. *Re Annesley* [1926] Ch. 692; and see *Re Askew* [1930] 2 Ch. 259, per Maugham J. at 273.

(*renvoi* transmission).[4] Such remissions are notional, taking place within the reasoning process of the judge of the forum. The narrow range of potentially usable connecting factors in any given problem probably accounts for the small number of instances of *renvoi* transmission.

HISTORY OF THE PROBLEM

5–02   The problem of *renvoi* entered the consciousness of the English judiciary as a means of circumventing the rigid rule then operative concerning formal validity of wills, which required that in order to be formally valid, a will had to satisfy the formal validity rules of the legal system of the last domicile of the testator.[5] The courts were reluctant to strike down a will on a point of form if, by reference to the "total" law of a country in which the deceased died domiciled, a positive outcome might be obtained by permitting onward reference to another law, thereby enlarging the number of potentially applicable laws governing formal validity and increasing the possibility of an affirmative result.

"The fountain-head of authority is *Collier v Rivaz*"[6]: "the court sitting here...must consider itself sitting in Belgium."[7] The English court, by so doing, rendered itself able to come to the view that codicils formally invalid by the Belgian law of the testator's last domicile but valid under English law, could be admitted to probate in England, for Belgian law "in the round" would have referred the matter to the English law of the nationality.

The Scots attitude to *renvoi*, in principle and in practice, is a matter of conjecture.[8] There is no grand Scottish *renvoi* case, though there is evidence that the Scots courts will accept generally the concept of transmission, that is to say, that they will be prepared to apply the law of a third country if referred thereto by the foreign law identified by the Scottish choice of law rule.[9] Many of the cases cited in this chapter are English, and are the best authority available.

---

[4] *Taczanowska v Taczanowksi* [1957] P. 301. See also, decided in the era in which the English courts adopted the single *renvoi* theory (*q.v.*): *Re Trufort* (1887) L.R. 36 Ch.D. 600; *Secretary of State for Foreign Affairs v Charlesworth Pilling & Co* [1901] A.C. 373; *Armitage v Att Gen* [1906] P. 135; *Sasson v Sasson* [1924] A.C. 1007; *Bartlett v Bartlett* [1925] A.C. 377; and *R. v Brentwood Superintendent Registrar of Marriages Ex p. Arias* [1968] 3 All E.R. 279.

[5] e.g. early cases such as: *Collier v Rivaz* (1841) 2 Curt. 855; *Laneuville v Anderson* (1860) 2 Sw. & Tr. 24; *Bremer v Freeman* (1857) 10 Moo. P.C. 306; *Frere v Frere* (1847) 5 Notes of Cases 593; *In the Goods of Lacroix* (1877) 2 P.D. 94. *Collier* was disapproved firmly but on no easily decipherable grounds in *Bremer*.

[6] *Dicey, Morris and Collins on the Conflict of Laws*, 15th edn (2012), para.4–011.

[7] *Collier v Rivaz* (1841) 2 Curt. 855, per Sir Herbert Jenner at 859.

[8] W Binchy, *Irish Conflict of Laws* (Butterworth (Ireland) Ltd, 1988), p.38, speculates that the dearth of Irish *renvoi* cases may be due to the trend for Irish emigration to take place to countries such as Canada, USA, Australia, New Zealand, South Africa and Argentina, which belong to the family of "domicile" countries. By inference, where there are personal connections with civilian countries, whose laws favour use of nationality as a connecting factor, there is greater potential for *renvoi* problems.

[9] e.g. *McKay v Walls*, 1951 S.L.T. (Notes) 6. Reference to the personal law of the institute on a question of status, as opposed to the law of the testator, shows the same "open" attitude: *Mitchell's Trustee v Rule*, 1908 16 S.L.T. 189; *Smith's Trustees v Macpherson's Trustees*, 1926 S.C. 983; cf. *Wright's Trustees v Callander*, 1992 S.L.T. 498 Ex Div; 1993 S.L.T. 556 HL. Contrast *Re Fergusson's Will* [1902] 1 Ch. 483. See too the "recognition by" mode of reasoning used to extend the range of courts considered by UK common law rules to be competent to grant divorce. cf. Family Law Act

If there is value in the *renvoi* exercise, there is no reason in principle for its exclusion from any private law subject area, although there may be persuasive reasons of time, expense, complexity and uncertainty, as well as incontrovertible reasons of prohibition of *renvoi* contained in statute, convention or regulation.

THE THEORIES

There is much writing on this acclaimed subject.[10] The following is an outline of three approaches.

5–03

(1)   Internal law theory

The legal issue arising should be resolved by the simple application of the forum-identified *lex causae* in its narrow domestic sense. This is not so much a theory of *renvoi* as a refusal to entertain it. There is little doubt that the internal law approach was taken in early cases.[11] In *Re Annesley*[12] its use was expressly commended as avoiding the "endless oscillation"[13] which other theories entail. Many new legislative instruments, q.v., expressly exclude the operation of *renvoi*, and may be said therefore to adopt an internal law approach.

5–04

(2)   Partial *renvoi*, or single *renvoi* theory

The starting point is the *lex fori* in its wide sense from which the question is referred (*envoi*) to another law, the *lex causae* (usually the law of the domicile), which in turn may refer it back (*renvoi*) to the *lex fori* (usually qua *lex patriae*). If the *lex fori* accepts the *renvoi* or reference back, at that stage the court applies its own law in its narrow sense. The essentials of this theory are that:

5–05

(a)   the starting point for the forum is the *lex fori*, whose choice of law rules enable identification of the (foreign) *lex causae*;

1986 ss.46(2)(b)(ii), 51(3)(b)(ii) (paras 12–27—12–29, below). See also, for analogous reasoning, Marriage (Scotland) Act 1977 s.3(5): certificate of legal capacity required for a foreign domiciliary intending to marry in Scotland will be acceptable if issued by a competent authority in a state other than the domicile if by the law of the latter that other state is the personal law.

[10] e.g. J.P. Bate, *Note on the Doctrine of Renvoi* (London: Stevens and Sons Ltd, 1904); Griswold, "Renvoi Revisited", 51 Harv. L.R. 1165; Falconbridge, *Conflict of Laws*, 2nd edn (1954), Chs 6–10; Munro, "The Magic Roundabout of the Conflict of Laws", 1978 J.R. 65; G. Sauveplanne, *International Encyclopaedia of Comparative Law* (Mohr Siebeck and Martinus Nijhoff, 1990), Vol.III, Ch.6; A. Briggs, "In Praise and Defence of Renvoi" (1998) 47 I.C.L.Q. 877; and K. Lipstein "The taking into consideration of foreign private international law" (1999) *Annuaire de l'Institute de Droit International*, Vol 68-1, 13–56.

[11] *Re Askew* [1930] 2 Ch. 259, per Maugham J. at 264.

[12] *Re Annesley* [1926] Ch. 692.

[13] *Re Annesley* [1926] Ch. 692, per Russell J. at 708, 709. However, this preference for the simple approach was obiter, for *Annesley* marks the beginning of the favour shown by English law to the double *renvoi* theory, q.v. The effect of applying the internal law theory and the double *renvoi* theory often may be the same.

(b) proof is required of the choice of law rules of the *lex causae,* which may be found to refer to the law of country X (the *lex fori* or the law of a third country); and

(c) at the third stage, in a remission case, assuming the law of X (being the *lex fori*) admits the doctrine and accepts the reference back, the forum will apply its own law in its narrow, domestic sense; and in a transmission case, assuming it is proved to the satisfaction of the forum that the law of X (being the law of a third country) admits the doctrine and accepts the reference on, the forum will consider itself justified in applying the law of that third country in its narrow, domestic sense.

The effect of applying this theory is that the forum defers to another legal system's choice of law rules. This apparent abasement is not a concession if the aim of the forum is, or ought to be, application of the *lex causae* in its entirety.[14] At one time the single *renvoi* theory was approved in England,[15] but it is not now applied by the English courts. There seems no particular logic in stopping the game at this point, but once having started down the road of *renvoi* reasoning, it would be hard to say when it is logical to stop.

L'Affaire Forgo[16] provides an early example of the French attitude to the problem. Forgo was a national of Bavaria who had lived in France since the age of five and who had a de facto domicile there. He was illegitimate. He died intestate. Under the Code Napoleon his whole estate fell to the French government because of his illegitimate status, but under the law of Bavaria it passed to his collaterals. The French *lex fori*, holding that the question was referred by French choice of law rules to the Bavarian law of the nationality, found that that law referred the question back to French law, as the law of the domicile or habitual residence: at that point France accepted the *renvoi* or reference back and applied its own domestic law.

(3) Foreign court theory or total *renvoi* or double *renvoi* theory

5–06 At the outset an English forum endeavours to place itself notionally in the position of the foreign court and to decide the question as that court would decide it.[17] The notional first reference is therefore from that foreign court applying its law in the wide sense, to the law thereby indicated. If the latter law notionally would refer the matter back to the law of the foreign court, the question is whether the foreign court will accept the *renvoi*. If the foreign court accepts the principle of *renvoi*, it will accept (notionally) the reference back and the English forum will consider itself entitled to apply that foreign court's law in its narrow

---

[14] But the forum's policy of honouring the *lex causae* in its entirety may clash with the forum's policy that domicile, as identified by the forum, govern matters of moveable succession. Ch.6, below.

[15] *Re Johnson* [1903] 1 Ch. 821.

[16] *L'Affaire Forgo* (1833) 10 Clunet 64.

[17] *Armitage v Att Gen* [1906] P. 135; *Bartlett v Bartlett* [1925] A.C. 377; *Re Achillopoulos* [1928] 1 Ch. 433; *Re Annesley* [1926] Ch. 692; *Re Ross* [1930] 1 Ch. 377; *Re Askew* [1930] 2 Ch. 259; *Re O'Keefe (Deceased)* [1940] Ch. 124; *Re Duke of Wellington* [1947] Ch. 506; affirmed [1948] Ch. 118; *Jaber Elias Kotia v Katr Bint Jiryes Nahas* [1941] A.C. 403; *Fuld (No.3)* [1968] P. 675. More recently, but without express reference to double *renvoi* terminology, see *Haji-Ioannou, Deceased v Frangos* [2009] EWHC 2310 (QB), per Slade J at [57]; and *Lambton (Earl of Durham) v Lady Lambton* [2013] EWHC 3566 (Ch).

sense[18]; but if it will not accept a *renvoi*, there can be no reference back. In such a case, an English court applies, in its narrow sense, the law indicated by the foreign choice of law rule which is usually the law of the nationality.[19]

Where the country of nationality comprises territorial units with different legal systems, the English courts have applied the law of the territorial unit in which the deceased had his domicile of origin, or with which he had his closest connection.[20] It has often been remarked that a *renvoi* remission may cause difficulty because there is no "British" law, nor "English" nationality. *Re O'Keefe (Deceased)*[21] provides an example of difficulties which may be encountered if the link with the *lex patriae* is tenuous and there has been a change of political status of the territory in which the *propositus* had her domicile of origin. However, the problem of ascribing the law of the nationality where the state is not unitary, and the problems of proof of foreign law, are secondary problems: one must first decide whether one is going to have any truck with the *renvoi* dimension.

The essentials of this theory are that:

(a)   The starting point is (notionally) the foreign court, whose choice of law rules are used to identify its preferred *lex causae*, viz. the law of country X.

(b)   The reference is to the law of country X in its wide sense.

(c)   It is often found that the choice of law rule of country X would refer the issue back to the law of the "original" foreign court. It is necessary then to ascertain whether or not that foreign court admits the *renvoi* doctrine in principle, and will accept in turn a *renvoi* remission from X.

(d)   If, according to the proof of the foreign *lex causae* offered, it appears to the English forum that the foreign court admits the doctrine, and will notionally accept a reference back, the English court will consider itself justified in applying that foreign law in its narrow sense. If the doctrine is not admitted, the English court has no option but to apply its own law in a narrow sense.

A major stumbling block with regard to the foreign court theory of *renvoi* is that it "works" only if the foreign court is not applying the same theory. If it should do so, the English forum would have to seek to impersonate a foreign court which is seeking to impersonate the forum: this is a problem too far even for the enthusiasts to solve. But this theoretical objection to the theory remains theoretical; there are few *renvoi* cases, and none it seems in which the English court has found the foreign court to be playing the same double *renvoi* game. Historically, the foreign court has been found to be playing single *renvoi* (France and Germany), or not to be playing at all (Italy), or not to know whether it is playing or not (Spain). Hence, the "mirror effect", or the "after you, Claud; no, after you, Montmorency"[22] scenario, or *circulus inextricabilis* has not arisen.

---

[18] *Re Annesley* [1926] Ch. 692 (France).

[19] *Re Ross* [1930] 1 Ch. 377 (Italy).

[20] *Haji-Ioannou v Frangos* [2009] EWHC 2310 (QB), *per* Slade J. at [29].

[21] *Re O'Keefe (Deceased)* [1940] Ch. 124. Para.5–20 below.

[22] A reference to the officers' eternal bowing to one another at the Battle of Fontenoy in the War of the Austrian Succession; cf. *Re Askew* [1930] 2 Ch. 259, per Maugham J. at 267.

THE SCOPE OF OPERATION OF *RENVOI*

5–07 Where *renvoi* is not expressly excluded by legislation or precedent, care must be taken to construct a reasoned view as to the possible application of *renvoi* in the given situation, if it appears advantageous to a litigant. Typically[23] in EU private international law harmonisation instruments, it is provided that the application of the law of any country specified by a regulation means the application of the rules in force in that country other than its rules of private international law. The query then arises whether the express exclusion of *renvoi* in any instrument means that incidental questions presenting within the ambit of such an instrument must be determined by the forum adopting a *lex fori* approach.[24]

By contrast, in conventions produced by the Hague Conference on Private International Law, the word "law" includes rules of private international law and reference is to a country's internal, domestic rules only if that is explicitly stated.[25] Hence, the default position is that *renvoi* reasoning may be employed in Hague Convention litigation unless it has been expressly excluded by the convention in question. In UK and Scottish legislation, the reasonable conclusion is that, if not expressly excluded, *renvoi* is available by default.

The doctrine of *renvoi* in English conflict of laws jurisprudence has been applied to questions involving intestacy, legal rights, formal and essential validity of wills, succession to immoveables, title to moveables, formal validity of marriage and other aspects of status, in particular legitimation.

Succession

5–08 In the area of succession, which provided the genesis of *renvoi* thinking, the trend recently has been expressly to exclude the operation of *renvoi*. The Wills Act 1963 s.1, provides that a will shall be treated as properly executed if its execution conformed to the *internal* law of the various possibly applicable laws regulating execution. The effect of this is expressly to eliminate *renvoi* in questions relating to formal validity of wills.[26] The Hague Trusts Convention (given effect in Scots and English law by the Recognition of Trusts Act 1987) by art.17 excludes *renvoi*. Modern English case law nonetheless reveals that arguments based upon *renvoi* are still to be found in matters pertaining to the essential validity of wills or other substantive matters arising in succession.[27]

---

[23] But not exclusively: see the elaborate *renvoi* clause in the Wills and Succession Regulation, para. 5–09, below.

[24] Ch.4, above.

[25] e.g. the Peréz-Vera Report on the 1980 Hague Abduction Convention emphasised that the applicable law includes rules of private international law, so as to expand the potential reach of the Convention.

[26] Whereas *renvoi* reasoning in the past operated to provide a wider range of possibly applicable laws, the Wills Act 1963 itself provides more than seven laws against which to judge the formal validity of a will.

[27] e.g. *Haji-Ioannou, Deceased v Frangos* [2009] EWHC 2310 (QB), per Slade J. at [57]; and *Lambton (Earl of Durham) v Lady Lambton* [2013] EWHC 3566 (Ch).

The EU Wills and Succession Regulation

Regulation (EU) No.650/2012 of the European Parliament and of the Council on **5–09** jurisdiction, applicable law, recognition and enforcement of decisions and acceptance and enforcement of authentic instruments in matters of succession and on the creation of a European Certificate of Succession (hereinafter "Rome IV") was finalised on 4 July 2012, and shall apply to the succession of persons who die on or after 17 August 2015. Recital (82) of Rome IV states that, in accordance with arts 1 and 2 of Protocol No.21, the UK and Ireland are not taking part in the adoption of Rome IV and are not bound by it or subject to its application.[28] As explained in Ch.18, however, it is likely that the UK will be drawn involuntarily into the operation of Rome IV.[29] If a UK court were to engage in *renvoi* reasoning in a case where, in its view, the *lex causae* is that of an EU Member State bound by the Regulation, that UK court would be required to apply art.34 as part of the choice of law rules of that EU Member State.

The *renvoi* provision in Rome IV is unique, viz.:

Article 34 – Renvoi
1.   The application of the law of any third State specified by this Regulation shall mean the application of the rules of law in force in that State, including its rules of private international law in so far as those rules make a *renvoi*:
    (a)   to the law of a Member State; or
    (b)   to the law of another third State which would apply its own law.
2.   No *renvoi* shall apply with respect to the laws referred to in Article 21(2),[30] Article 22,[31] Article 27,[32] point (b) of Article 28[33] and Article 30.[34]

Article 34 authorises the operation of *renvoi* outwards, that is, where the court of an EU Member State other than the UK, Ireland or Denmark identifies as the applicable law in a succession matter[35] the law of a Third State. Recital (57) provides that:

> "The conflict-of-laws rules laid down in this Regulation may lead to the application of the law of a third State. In such cases regard should be had to the private international law rules of that State. If those rules provide for *renvoi* either to the law of a Member State or to the law of a third State which would apply its own law to the succession, such *renvoi* should be accepted in order to ensure international consistency. *Renvoi* should, however, be excluded in situations where the deceased had made a *choice of law* in favour of the law of a third State."[36]

If, therefore, a Third State law "in the round" makes a remission to the law of an EU Member State (other than the UK, Ireland or Denmark), the *renvoi* process

---

[28] Para.18–41, below.
[29] Paras 18–42 et seq., below.
[30] Applicable law general rule – exception.
[31] Party choice of law.
[32] Formal validity of dispositions of property upon death made in writing.
[33] Validity as to form of a declaration concerning acceptance or waiver.
[34] Special rules imposing restrictions concerning or affecting the succession in respect of certain assets.
[35] Rome IV art.23.
[36] Emphasis added. See art.34.2.

is permitted within the parameters of and as prescribed by art.34, and recital (57) encourages that Member State to accept the reference back. Clearly it is beyond the power of the Regulation to dictate the approach which a Third State court should take to the *renvoi* process in a cross-border succession litigation.

Contract

5–10   From time to time, there have been suggestions, which have not been taken up, that *renvoi* might be applied in areas of commercial law—as for example in contract,[37] bills of exchange,[38] enforcement of arbitral awards,[39] and recognition of credit institutions.[40] In *Re United Railways of Havana and Regla Warehouses Ltd*,[41] the Court of Appeal made it clear that, "the principle of *renvoi* finds no place in the field of contract".[42] The matter was put beyond doubt by the Contracts (Applicable Law) Act 1990, bringing into UK law the Rome Convention on the law applicable to contractual obligations, art.15 of which excludes the application of *renvoi*. Article 20 of the Rome I Regulation reiterates the exclusion of *renvoi*.

Delict

5–11   Similarly, in delict, *renvoi* was not thought to be applicable at common law.[43] The point is now largely regulated by art.24 of the Rome II Regulation and, in residual cases arising in Scots and English courts, by s.9(5) of the Private International Law (Miscellaneous Provisions) Act 1995, both of which exclude the operation of *renvoi*.

In Australia, the decision of the High Court in *Neilson v Overseas Projects Corp of Victoria Ltd*[44] excited much comment in light of its acceptance of the application of *renvoi* in a case litigated in Australia, arising from a tort which

---

[37] *Vita Food Products Inc v Unus Shipping Co Ltd (In Liquidation)* [1939] A.C. 277. cf. *Amin Rasheed Shipping Corp v Kuwait Insurance Co (The Al Wahab)* [1983] 2 All E.R. 884, per Lord Diplock at 888; and *Musawi v RE International (UK) Ltd* [2007] EWHC 2981 (Ch) at [20].

[38] *Alcock v Smith* [1892] 1 Ch. 238; *Embiricos v Anglo-Austrian Bank* [1905] 1 K.B. 677; *F Koechlin et Cie v Kestenbaum Bros* [1927] 1 K.B. 889.

[39] *Dallah Real Estate & Tourism Holding Co v Pakistan* [2010] UKSC 46, per Lord Collins at [73], [123]–[125] (for the purposes of the 1958 New York Convention on the Recognition and Enforcement of Foreign Arbitral Awards and, therefore in the UK, Arbitration Act 1996 s.103(2)(b)).

[40] Strauss Q.C. in *Cinema Holdings 2 Ltd v Irish Bank Resolution Corp Ltd* [2013] EWHC 745 (Ch) at [23] was not amenable to counsel's attempt to introduce a *renvoi* element to the interpretation of regulations made pursuant to EU Directive 2001/24/EC on the recognition of credit institutions.

[41] *Re United Railways of Havana and Regla Warehouses Ltd* [1960] Ch. 52 CA; [1961] A.C. 1007 HL.

[42] *Re United Railways of Havana and Regla Warehouses Ltd* [1960] Ch. 52, per Jenkins L.J. at 96, 97, Willmer L.J. dissenting at 115. The glancing reference made by Christopher Clarke J. in *Cherney v Deripaska* [2008] EWHC 1530 (Comm) at [136] to the use of *renvoi* in determining the applicable law of a contract seems misguided.

[43] *McElroy v McAllister*, 1949 S.C. 110, per Lord Russell at 126. See also *Jacobs v Motor Insurers Bureau*[2010] EWCA Civ 1208, per Moore-Bick L.J. at [27].

[44] *Neilson v Overseas Projects Corp of Victoria Ltd* [2005] HCA 54, discussed by M. Keyes, "The Doctrine of Renvoi in International Torts: Mercantile Mutual Insurance v Neilson" (2005) 13 Torts Law Journal 1; A. Lu and L. Carroll, "Ignored No More—Renvoi and International Torts Litigated in Australia" (2005) 1 J. Priv. Int. L. 35; and R. Mortensen, "Troublesome and Obscure: The Renewal of Renvoi in Australia" (2006) 2 J. Priv. Int. L. 1.

occurred in the People's Republic of China. It may be that *renvoi* was perceived to be a useful device to circumvent the inflexibility of the Australian choice of law rule in tort. The injured party was an Australian citizen, domiciled in Western Australia, who had been living in China as a consequence of her husband's employment there. The couple had been billeted in Wuhan, China, in accommodation which took the form of a two storey apartment connected by an internal staircase with no banister. The Neilsons complained about the dangerous state of the staircase to Mr Neilson's employer, which owned the apartment, but nothing was done to remedy the situation. Mrs Neilson was injured when she was descending the stairs. She was treated in a Chinese hospital for three weeks before being advised to return to Australia. Subsequently, Mrs Neilson sued her husband's employer in contract and tort (under the head of occupiers' liability) in Western Australia. The employer's insurance company, incorporated in New South Wales, was joined as a third party. The Australian choice of law rule in tort directed strict application of the *lex loci delicti* (Chinese law) to govern questions of substance, including the matter of time bar. However, by Chinese conflict of laws rules contained in the Law of Civil Relations involving Foreigners, a remission to Australian law, being the law of the common nationality or common domicile of the claimant and defendant, might be made. The point which precipitated the discussion of *renvoi* was the question whether or not the claim in tort was time-barred. By Chinese law there was a one-year limitation period for personal injury actions, in contrast to the more generous six-year period prevailing under Australian law. Since the date of litigation was almost six years after the accident, clearly a remission to Australian law was crucial for the claimant. While the judge at first instance was sympathetic to *renvoi* reasoning, his decision was reversed by the Full Court, which held that a reference to foreign law (Chinese law) in this regard must be a reference to its domestic law only. By a clear majority, however, the High Court of Australia, on appeal from the Full Court, preferred to adopt *renvoi* reasoning in the application of the Australian choice of law rules in tort, so as to enable the foreign law indicated by the rules to be interpreted as a reference to the whole of that law. In a remarkable decision, a majority of five judges accepted the doctrine of double *renvoi*.

In legal systems which follow a more flexible choice of law rule in delict (as for example provided by Rome II), there would seem to be less need and less justification for taking this unusual line. The application of *renvoi* reasoning by an EU forum in any event is prohibited by Rome II art.24, as noted.

Unjustified enrichment

In relation to unjustified enrichment, an argument was made in *Barros Mattos Junior v MacDaniels Ltd*[45] that the applicable law should be understood as meaning the applicable law in its totality, but this argument was rejected as premature. Insofar as unjust enrichment now is governed by Rome II,[46] there is no scope for the application of *renvoi* in any relevant case arising in a European

5–12

---

[45] *Barros Mattos Junior v MacDaniels Ltd* [2005] I.L.Pr. 45, per Collins J. at [121].
[46] Rome II Ch.III: unjust enrichment, *negotiorum gestio* and *culpa in contrahendo*.

forum.[47] In this exclusion of *renvoi*, as in other important aspects of conflict of laws rules within the law of obligations as operated in Member State courts, there is now a uniform approach.

Property

5–13   *Renvoi* should be available in cases involving title to land abroad, because if there is one certainty in the conflict of laws, it is that, in matters pertaining to land, effectiveness of the conflict rule requires that the *lex situs* be entirely satisfied. Hence, application of the *lex situs* should mean application of the entirety of that law.[48]

As regards moveable property, in *Winkworth v Christie, Manson & Woods Ltd*,[49] counsel argued strongly for a departure from the *lex situs* rule in problems of ownership of moveable property. The judge of first instance, though unconvinced, expressly made it clear that, at the trial, use might be made of *renvoi* reasoning to suggest that the Italian *lex situs* itself might not consider that Italian domestic law should apply. However, such a hint of openness to the *renvoi* argument is to be contrasted with the dictum of Staughton L.J. in *Macmillan Inc v Bishopsgate Investment Trust Plc (No.3)*,[50] a case concerning ownership of intangible moveables, namely, shares.

More recently, the question of *renvoi* was raised in *Iran v Berend*[51] in the determination of title to a fragment of 5th century BC limestone relief from Persepolis. The case contains a useful consideration by Eady J. of the policy considerations affecting a judicial decision whether or not to admit the operation of *renvoi* in the resolution of a case.[52] Eady J., concerned to decide a matter of ownership of tangible property, saw no reason to depart from the resistant attitude displayed by the court in *Macmillan*: "I can find no reason to differ from Millett J. and to hold, for the first time, that public policy requires English law to introduce the notion of *renvoi* into the determination of title to movables."[53]

In 2009 further opportunity was afforded to visit the topic in the complex Admiralty case, *Dornoch Ltd v Westminster International BV*.[54] It was necessary to decide the precise meaning of "*lex situs*" in the context of determining proprietary interests in a vessel. In identifying the law of Thailand as the *lex situs*, the question remained whether the reference to Thai law should include Thai choice of law rules. After consideration, Tomlinson J. maintained a cautious line by construing Thai law in its narrow, domestic sense. However, his Lordship declined to give a definitive answer on the question whether the expression "*lex*

---

[47] Rome II art.24.
[48] Though see *Re Ross* [1930] 1 Ch. 377: the effect of application of the Italian *lex situs* "in the round" led to the application, by the English forum, of the English law of succession.
[49] *Winkworth v Christie, Manson & Woods Ltd* [1980] 1 Ch. 496. See also *Glencore International AG v Metro Trading International Inc (No.2)* [2001] 1 Lloyd's Rep. 284, per Moore-Bick J. at [41].
[50] *Macmillan Inc v Bishopsgate Investment Trust Plc (No.3)* [1996] 1 W.L.R. 387 at 405.
[51] *Iran v Berend* [2007] EWHC 132 (QB).
[52] *Iran v Berend* [2007] EWHC 132 (QB) at [22]–[33].
[53] *Iran v Berend* [2007] EWHC 132 (QB) at [26].
[54] *Dornoch Ltd v Westminster International BV (The WD Fairway)* [2009] EWHC 889 (Admlty).

situs", in the context of moveable property generally, necessarily includes or excludes the rules of international private law.[55] The essence of his judgment is captured as follows:

> "If therefore I were to decide that as a matter of English common law reference to the *lex situs* as being the law governing the incidence of proprietary rights in movable property includes reference to the choice of law or private international law rules of the *situs*, I would I think be rowing against a strong tide. Moreover, in the commercial context in which the question arises here I should be loath to assimilate the law to that hitherto applicable only in fields such as the formal and intrinsic validity of wills, intestate succession and legitimation by subsequent marriage when in the fields of contract, tort, restitution and trusts a deliberate decision has apparently been taken to eschew the doctrine of *renvoi*."[56]

Further useful consideration of the operation of *renvoi* in the context of property rights is provided by *Blue Sky One Ltd v Mahan Air*,[57] a complex litigation concerning the property implications of the sanctions imposed by the US government preventing the sale or lease of US aircraft manufactured in the US to Iranian individuals or companies. Beatson J. in *Blue Sky*, in pondering counsel's submissions in favour of the application of the *renvoi* doctrine on a case by case analysis, depending upon identification of the policy underlying the private international law rule in question,[58] concluded that, despite the attractiveness of the suggestion, the consequence would be the construction of a very uncertain legal regime: "[I]ndeed it could lead to a Tennysonian wilderness of single instances".[59] For this and other more practical reasons, Beatson J. inclined to follow the line traced by Millett J. in *Macmillan Inc*, Eady J. in *Berend*, and Tomlinson J. in *Dornoch Ltd*, and decided that the reference to the *lex situs* in the case of a transfer of title to tangible movables such as aircraft means the domestic law of the place of the *situs* of the aircraft on the relevant date, and not the entirety of that law.

Family law

The Family Law (Scotland) Act 2006 appears generally, and in s.38 in particular, to be *renvoi*-blind.[60] This must leave open the possibility of *renvoi*-based argument in all matters pertaining to the formal and essential validity of marriage. In the background Law Commission reports, it was observed[61] that *renvoi*

5–14

---

[55] *Dornoch Ltd v Westminster International BV (The WD Fairway)* [2009] EWHC 889 (Admlty) at [28].
[56] *Dornoch Ltd v Westminster International BV (The WD Fairway)* [2009] EWHC 889 (Admlty) at [87].
[57] *Blue Sky One Ltd v Mahan Air* [2010] EWHC 631 (Comm).
[58] *Blue Sky One Ltd v Mahan Air* [2010] EWHC 631 (Comm) at [157]–[185].
[59] *Blue Sky One Ltd v Mahan Air* [2010] EWHC 631 (Comm) at [172].
[60] The reference in s.38(3) to Scots internal law ("If a marriage entered into in Scotland is void under a rule of Scots internal law, then, notwithstanding subsection (2), that rule shall prevail over any law under which the marriage would be valid.") serves a different purpose of preserving as a mandatory rule the operation of Scots domestic marriage law in the matters of capacity and consent.
[61] Law Commission and Scottish Law Commission, *Private International Law: Choice of Law Rules in Marriage* (HMSO, 1985), Law Com. Working Paper No.89; Scot. Law Com. Memo. No.64, paras 2.12, 2.13, 2.39–2.42.

reasoning may be useful when referring to the *lex loci celebrationis* in the context of ascertaining whether or not a marriage is formally valid,[62] in order to promote greater uniformity of status. *Renvoi* reasoning may be of assistance to avoid "limping marriages".

> "On the whole, we think that these arguments should prevail [against those of inconvenience, delay and cost in litigation, and theoretical problems]. Our provisional recommendation is that the reference made by our choice of law rules to the law of the country of celebration should in the case of marriages celebrated abroad be construed as a reference to the whole law of that country (including its choice of law rules) and not merely to its domestic rules."[63]

Similarly, in the matter of capacity to marry, the Law Commissions were open to *renvoi* argument.[64]

Notably the Civil Partnership Act 2004 s.124(10) provides that, in testing the validity of civil partnerships registered outside Scotland, where reference is made to the "relevant law", that means "the law of the country or territory where the overseas relationship was registered (including its rules of private international law)".

In view of the default position in interpretation of Hague Conference instruments, *renvoi* reasoning is available for the purposes of the 1980 Hague Convention on the Civil Aspects of International Child Abduction, operative in the UK by virtue of the Child Abduction and Custody Act 1985. Whether the result of admitting *renvoi* reasoning is positive or not will depend upon the litigant's perspective. In *Re JB (Child Abduction) (Rights of Custody: Spain)*,[65] the English forum permitted application of Spanish law "in the round", resulting in a remission to English law in terms of which the bereft father, unmarried, was found to have no parental rights such as to justify a petition for return of the child under the 1980 Convention on the grounds of wrongful removal.[66]

A more recent English Court of Appeal case, *Re K (Children) (Rights of Custody: Spain)*,[67] reveals, in this specific context, that a remission can be conditional: a reference made by the English forum from the Spanish law of the child's habitual residence "in the round" to English law qua law of the nationality resulted in the English court's accepting that the content of English law on parental rights would be offensive to Spanish law in terms of public policy, and would not therefore be applied.

---

[62] *Taczanowska v Taczanowski* [1957] P. 301; and *Hooper v Hooper* [1959] 1 W.L.R. 1021.

[63] Law Commission and Scottish Law Commission, *Choice of Law Rules in Marriage*, 1985, Law Com. Working Paper No.89; Scot. Law Com. Memo. No.64, para.2.39.

[64] Law Commission and Scottish Law Commission, *Choice of Law Rules in Marriage*, 1985, Law Com. Working Paper No.89; Scot. Law Com. Memo. No.64, para.3.39.

[65] *Re JB (Child Abduction) (Rights of Custody: Spain)* [2004] 1 F.L.R. 796. See K. Beevers and J. Perez Milla, "Convention 'Rights of Custody'—Who Decides? An Anglo-Spanish Perspective" (2007) 3 J. Priv. Int. L. 201.

[66] Contrast, on the facts, *Re E (A Child) (Abduction: Rights of Custody)* [2005] EWHC 848 (Fam), per Sir Mark Potter P at [36].

[67] *Re K (Children) (Rights of Custody: Spain)* [2009] EWCA Civ 986.

Perspective

The status of *renvoi* as an intellectual plaything in the subject is renowned, and its **5–15** potential for use as a tool to positive effect (e.g. to soften the perceivedly harsh effects of a strict choice of law rule), or as a corrective (i.e. to seek to neutralise the effects of forum-shopping)[68] should be recognised. But *renvoi* reasoning is convoluted and the process is the antithesis of the certainty and speed that business requires, and therein must lie the explanation for its exclusion generally from the commercial sphere. It is otherwise in family law where the consensus is that recourse to the *renvoi* doctrine may be justified on an *in favorem* rationale. It has been a notable claim of *renvoi* supporters that the operation of the doctrine is capable of producing uniformity of result regardless of forum. However, consideration of the particular problem of intestate moveable succession reveals that uniformity does not always result; it depends upon the approach to *renvoi* taken in each interested legal system (i.e. the various countries in which is situated estate belonging to the deceased).[69] Perhaps the best approach to this abstruse subject is the pragmatic one of entertaining the notion of *renvoi*, at the prompting of an interested party, in a subject area where its use is not prohibited.

RENVOI CASES

The following is a summary of important English cases in which the foreign court **5–16** theory of *renvoi* has been applied.

Re Annesley [1926] Ch. 692

Mrs Annesley, an Englishwoman, lived in France from 1866 until her death there **5–17** in 1924. By the date of her death, she had not taken the steps prescribed by the French Civil Code to acquire French domicile; the requisite form, not completed, was found among her papers. She made a will in France in English form in which she declared that she intended to remain a British subject, and that she had not any intention of abandoning her English domicile. By this will she left the residue of her estate to one daughter absolutely, but she had another child who was excluded from the will. By English law she could dispose of all her estate as she wished, but by French law she could dispose by will of only one-third of her moveable estate. The question at issue was whether her will had effectively conveyed the whole of the residue to the favoured daughter.

The question giving rise to the *renvoi* issue was the devolution of her moveable property, and the essential validity of her testamentary provisions pertaining thereto, which, by the choice of law rule of English law, was to be (and is still) determined by the law of the ultimate domicile of the testatrix. Russell J. arrived at his decision that Mrs Annesley's freedom of testation was governed by French law, by the following reasoning:

---

[68] A.Briggs, "In Praise and Defence of Renvoi" (1998) 47 I.C.L.Q. 877.
[69] C.Munro, "The Magic Roundabout of the Conflict of Laws", 1978 J.R. 65, 78–80.

(a)   The connecting factor was domicile, which must be interpreted and identified by the English law of the forum.

(b)   By English law, Mrs Annesley died domiciled in France.

(c)   Applying the law of France as the law of the domicile, the English court must endeavour notionally to place itself in the same position as a French court and decide the matter as a French court would decide it. Starting from French law as the law of the domicile in its wide sense, that law referred the matter of the essential validity of the will to "British law" as the law of the nationality. The only meaning which could be given to "British law" in the circumstances was English law, which, in turn, would refer the matter back to the law of France. According to expert evidence preferred by Russell J., French law accepted a reference back. The English court, sitting as it were in the position of the French court, applied French law in its narrow sense, with the result that it was held that Mrs Annesley's will could dispose of only one-third of her moveable estate.

It would have been possible to have arrived at the same result by ignoring *renvoi* reasoning and by simply applying French law directly in its narrow sense as the law of the domicile. Russell J. commended this route, but nonetheless, single-handedly, it seems, introduced into English conflict rules by this decision the double *renvoi* approach.

Re Ross [1930] 1 Ch. 377

5–18   Mrs Ross was a British subject of English domicile of origin, who died domiciled in Italy leaving English and Italian wills. By those wills, she bequeathed the residue of her moveable estate in England to a niece and her moveable and immoveable estate in Italy to a grand-nephew. In so doing, she excluded her son from the succession. The son raised an action in England for payment of the indefeasible rights of succession due to him under Italian law. Luxmoore J. decided as follows:

(a)   As regards moveables, the connecting factor was domicile. In the view of the English forum, by English law, the deceased died domiciled in Italy.

(b)   Starting with Italian law in its wide sense, that law referred the question to "British law" as the law of the nationality which, as in *Annesley*, could mean only English law, because the testatrix had her domicile of origin in England and had no other connection with Britain. English law would refer the question back to the law of Italy. The expert evidence, however, showed that the law of Italy could *not* accept the *renvoi*, so the matter could not proceed beyond the reference from Italian law, as the starting point, to "British law". As the Italian court could not accept a *renvoi* remission, it would insist upon applying "British law". The English court, therefore, applied English law in its narrow, domestic sense. In effect, the court applied the law of the domicile of origin in preference to the law of the last domicile. Was this the result of excessive care and politeness, or did the English court truly give effect to its conception of Italian law as the *lex successionis*?

(c) As regards immoveable property in Italy, the same decision was arrived at by the same reasoning, the starting point again being the law of Italy, this time qua *lex situs*.[70]

The difference in result between *Annesley* and *Ross* lies in the fact that French law accepted the principle of *renvoi* and notionally accepted the remission from English law, whereas Italian law did not do so.

Re Askew [1930] 2 Ch. 259

Under an English marriage contract the husband, who was domiciled in England, had a power of appointment of a trust fund among the children of his marriage and of any subsequent marriage which he might make. Later in life he went to Germany where he acquired a domicile and became the father of an illegitimate daughter. He divorced his wife and married the child's mother. Subsequently, he purported to appoint the income upon trust after his death to be paid to his second wife, and after her death, to the children of the second marriage. A question having been raised about the propriety of the exercise of the power in relation to the daughter above-mentioned (a matter which depended on her status being established as a child legitimated by subsequent marriage), the court followed the reasoning set out below:

5–19

(a) The question at issue was one of status, and so the connecting factor was domicile. The father was taken by the English court to have a German domicile at the date of birth of the daughter in question.
(b) Starting with German law in its wide sense, that law referred the matter to the law of the father's nationality, "British law", which, once again, could mean only English law.
(c) English law referred the matter back to the law of Germany, which accepted the principle of *renvoi* and notionally accepted the remission in question, with the result that the English court applied German law in its narrow sense. As the child had been legitimated by that law, it could succeed despite its adulterine status in the eyes of English law. This was a positive outcome for the child, the more so because by English domestic law at the time the child was not capable of being legitimated.

Re O'Keefe (Deceased) [1940] Ch. 124

This case often is cited to demonstrate that the operation of *renvoi* may have artificial results.

5–20

Miss O'Keefe died intestate in Italy in 1937. Her father was born in County Clare, Ireland. He lived first in India for many years and then in other countries. Miss O'Keefe, born in Calcutta, lived in India, France, England, Spain, Tangier and the Channel Islands, but for the last 47 years of her life in Italy, where she acquired a domicile in the view of the English forum. Her domicile of origin was

---

[70] This produced the result—odd to British eyes, if not to continental lawyers familiar with a unitary rather than a scissionist system: para.18–05, below—that rights of succession to land in Italy were governed by the law of England.

in Ireland, in the part which became Eire (now the Republic of Ireland), but she had not been in Ireland since a holiday visit when she was 18 years of age. At the time of her death she was a British—not Irish—subject. This case concerned the intestate succession to her estate, in respect of which the law of Ireland was applied, by the same reasoning as in *Ross*, as follows:

(a) In the view of English law, as the law of the forum (where the assets were situated), domicile was the connecting factor and Miss O'Keefe died domiciled in Italy.

(b) Italian law in its wide sense referred the matter to "British law" as the law of the nationality. "British law" would refer the matter back to the law of Italy, but Italian law would not accept the *renvoi* remission. The question, therefore, had to be decided according to "British law", whatever that might mean.

(c) Following *Ross*, the judge held that the law of the domicile of origin, the law of Ireland, was the only law which could be applied (though Miss O'Keefe was not a citizen of Ireland).

The case attracts comment because Irish law had little connection with the facts of the deceased's life, and in technical terms the English court could hardly be said to be applying the law of her nationality as was the rule of Italian law. Nevertheless, the unusual outcome reflects the unusual personal and political circumstances of the case. The task of applying the law of the nationality in relation to a multi-legal system state will not normally be productive of such difficulty.

Re Duke of Wellington [1947] Ch. 506; affirmed [1948] Ch. 118

5–21 The sixth Duke of Wellington, domiciled in England, left assets in England and Spain, and made two wills dealing respectively with those assets. By the Spanish will he left his land in Spain to the person who was to succeed jointly to the English dukedom and the Spanish dukedom. He died unmarried and it transpired that, while his uncle succeeded to the English title, it was his sister who succeeded to the Spanish title, with the result that the destination in the Spanish will failed because there was no one beneficiary to succeed to both titles.

The question arose in England as to the determination of the law in accordance with which the Spanish estate, moveable and immoveable, should devolve. By Spanish law succession to estate, moveable and immoveable, was governed by the law of the nationality. Wynn-Parry J. held that in these circumstances the Spanish property, moveable and immoveable (ineffectually disposed of by the Spanish will), fell to be distributed in accordance with the English will which the sixth Duke had made in order to dispose of the remainder of his property, specifically excepting the property competently disposed of under the Spanish will.

The court at first instance dealt with the case of moveable property on the simple view that it would descend in accordance with the English law of the ultimate domicile of the deceased. Therefore, by inference, it can be deduced that the English court felt under no obligation to dwell upon the consequences of the Spanish preference for a unity of succession rule and for application of the *lex patriae*.

The significance of the case resides in the treatment of the succession to immoveables which provoked a notable *renvoi* discussion. In relation to immoveable property, Wynn-Parry J., starting with Spanish law as the *lex situs*, held that that law referred the matter to "British law" as the law of the nationality, which could mean only English law. English law would refer the matter back to the *lex situs*, but each side in the litigation produced conflicting expert evidence as to whether or not Spanish law would accept the *renvoi*. One of the experts died before the hearing, but no objection was taken to his affidavit being read and relied on on behalf of the current Duke. The judge had to decide the point for himself and held, on balance, that Spanish law did not accept the reference back, and so he applied English law to the substantive issues. In the Court of Appeal the only matters raised pertain to the construction and effect of the two wills in English law; by application of English law the seventh Duke was entitled under the English will to succeed to the Spanish property, moveable and immoveable, comprised in (but ineffectually disposed of by) the Spanish will. English law regulated the devolution of Spanish immoveable property, and in the view of the English court, the Spanish courts would be bound to register the title of the seventh Duke as the absolute owner of the Spanish immoveable property.[71]

The judgment of Wynn-Parry J. contains a very well-known conflict of laws lament:

> "[I]t would be difficult to imagine a harder task than that which faces me, namely, of expounding for the first time either in this country or in Spain the relevant law of Spain as it would be expounded by the Supreme Court of Spain, which up to the present time has made no pronouncement on the subject, and having to base that exposition on evidence which satisfies me that on this subject there exists a profound cleavage of legal opinion in Spain, and two conflicting decisions of courts of inferior jurisdiction".[72]

SUMMARY 5

Renvoi: remission and transmission: 5–22

1. The classic example of the *renvoi* problem presents in a question of succession to moveable estate in England or Scotland belonging to a British subject who has died intestate and domiciled in a foreign country, the law of which refers questions of succession to the law of the nationality.
2. Theories:
    (a) internal law theory;
    (b) single *renvoi* theory;
    (c) foreign court theory—which requires knowledge of:
        (i)   the choice of law rule of the foreign '*lex causae*'; and
        (ii) whether or not that foreign law accepts a *renvoi* remission.

---

[71] *Re Duke of Wellington* [1947] Ch. 506, per Wynn-Parry J. at 524.
[72] *Re Duke of Wellington* [1947] Ch. 506 at 515.

3. English courts have applied the foreign court theory, though not necessarily by name. The starting point notionally is the foreign court: if the foreign law accepts the principle of *renvoi* and the *renvoi* remission in the instant case, that foreign law in the narrow sense is applied by the English court. If the foreign law does not accept that principle, then in the reported cases the forum is 'rebuffed' and reverts to the application of its own domestic law.

4. The Scottish view of *renvoi* is untested in case law.

5. Historically the doctrine has been applied in succession cases, and also to questions of status. Where benefit can be conferred on a party, modern English litigators apparently do not feel inhibited from seeking to employ *renvoi* arguments, where such arguments are not expressly prohibited by legislation. As a matter of drafting practice, European instruments typically exclude *renvoi* by stipulating that the application of the law of any country specified by the instrument means the rules of law in force in that country other than its rules of private international law. In instruments made under the auspices of the Hague Conference on Private International Law, the default position is that *renvoi* arguments may be deployed unless specifically excluded by the terms of the instrument.

CHAPTER 6

Domicile and other personal law connecting factors

THE NATURE OF DOMICILE

Every person in the course of his life becomes concerned in matters with legal implications, some of which are transient or temporary, and others of a more permanent nature. It is necessary to find a sufficiently weighty connecting factor for the regulation of the latter. The country to which a person "belongs" suggests itself as suitable. In civilian European countries such matters have tended, in the past at least, to be governed by the law of the nationality, but in English speaking countries, which usually contain various states, provinces or units, each with its own legal system, there is no such thing as the "law of nationality". As a result, generally in English speaking countries, questions of status and personal law are governed by the law of a person's domicile, which is the place where he is deemed in law to have his home. It has been estimated that allegiance to the connecting factors of nationality and domicile, respectively, is equally divided, but the scope of operation of both factors is diminishing in view of the fact that all European states now must employ principally the connecting factor of habitual residence, as a result of the high incidence of its use in modern harmonisation instruments.

6–01

In *Udny v Udny*,[1] which, with *Bell v Kennedy*,[2] forms the pillars on which the Scots and English rules of domicile rest, there is found the classical exposition:

> "The law of England, and of almost all civilised countries, ascribes to each individual at his birth two distinct legal states or conditions; one by virtue of which he becomes the subject of some particular country, binding him by the tie of natural allegiance, which may be called his political status; another by virtue of which he has ascribed to him the character of a citizen of some particular country, and as such is possessed of certain municipal rights, and subject to certain obligations, which latter character is the civil status or condition of the individual, and may be quite different from his political status, for the political status may depend upon different laws in different countries, whereas the civil status is governed universally by one specific principle. Domicile or the place of settled residence of an individual is the criterion established by law for the purpose of determining the legal condition of the person, for it is on this basis that the personal rights of the parties—that is, the law which determines his majority or minority, marriage, succession, testacy or intestacy—must depend."

---

[1] *Udny v Udny* (1869) 7 M. (H.L.) 89, per Lord Westbury at 99.
[2] *Bell v Kennedy* (1868) 6 M. (H.L.) 69.

A modern formulation is found in *Gaines-Cooper v Revenue and Customs Commissioners*[3]:

> "Given that many people move about the world from one country to another, it is essential to have a means of establishing under which system of law and within the jurisdiction of which country's courts questions relating to their civil status (such as marriage, divorce and legitimacy) and some aspects of their property (such as the devolution of moveable property on their intestacy) fall to be determined. It is to accomplish that purpose that the concept of domicile has been developed. It is a neutral rule of law for determining that system of personal law with which an individual has the appropriate connection, so that it will govern his personal status and questions relating to him and his affairs. Its essential feature is that it attempts to connect a person so far as it is possible with the country in which he has his permanent home or in which he lives indefinitely."

DOMICILE, NATIONALITY AND RESIDENCE COMPARED

6–02   *Domicile* is the tie or connection between an individual and a territorial unit governed by a common body of law. Because domicile implies a connection between a person and a legal system, it follows that there is no such thing as British, Canadian, Australian or American domicile. A person may have a domicile only in a territory subject to a single system of law such as Scotland, England (and Wales), the Provinces of Quebec or Ontario, etc. in Canada, the States of New South Wales, Victoria, etc. in Australia,[4] New York, Ohio, etc. in USA or one of the Channel Islands.

Domicile is a personal rather than administrative matter and is changed without state authorisation or formal documentation. Cases of doubt can be resolved only by adjudication of the court, for there is no paper "evidence" of a person's domicile. It is, in general, the country which is in fact his home, but in some cases it is the country which, whether it is in fact his home or not, is determined to be such by rule of law.

Nationality is the tie of allegiance which binds an individual to a state and involves reciprocal duties of obedience and protection. State authorisation is required before nationality may be changed.[5]

Residence is a mere physical fact independent of will or intention, but it may involve legal consequences such as liability to pay income tax or rendering oneself subject to the jurisdiction of a particular court.

---

[3] *Gaines-Cooper v Revenue and Customs Commissioners* [2007] EWHC 2617 (Ch); [2008] S.T.C. 1665, per Lewison J. at [1].

[4] By way of exception, for certain purposes (e.g. divorce), legislation within a non-unitary state may refer to, say, "Australian domicile", *Cheshire, North and Fawcett: Private International Law*, 14th edn (2008), p.156.

[5] i.e. for a person desiring change of nationality, the outcome (acquisition of the new; continuance of the old?) will depend on the laws of the states involved, including their attitudes to dual nationality. Further, the decision on who is a national of a state is a matter for the law of the state the nationality of which is in question: *Oppenheimer v Cattermole* [1975] 1 All E.R. 538.

Habitual residence is a modern contender for the role of personal law.[6] It might be thought that the use of the adjective "habitual" denotes substantial factual connection, not only more than sojourn,[7] but also more than mere "residence" or "ordinary residence". This, however, may be too simplistic a thought, for there is absence of agreement on the definition of habitual residence, and its meaning is likely to vary according to context. This will be examined in detail later in the chapter.

CLASSES OF DOMICILE

Introduction

Every person sui juris (the *"propositus"*) has a domicile. Prior to the Family Law (Scotland) Act 2006 (hereinafter "the 2006 Act"), it was well established that a *domicile of origin* was ascribed by law to every person at birth and was involuntary. Even if superseded by the acquisition of a new domicile, the domicile of origin was never entirely extinguished and, if the new domicile subsequently was lost, the domicile of origin would revive. *Domicile of choice* is the domicile which a person sui juris may acquire by a change of residence and intention. It is a matter of note that the rules of domicile in Scots and English law respectively diverge.

6–03

DOMICILE OF ORIGIN / "UNDER-16 DOMICILE"

Scots law prior to the Family Law (Scotland) Act 2006[8]

A domicile of origin was the domicile ascribed by law to every person at birth[9] in accordance with the following rules:

6–04

(1) *Legitimate child*—The domicile was that of the child's father as at the date of the child's birth.[10] Place of birth had no necessary relevance. On the argument that a child was legitimate by English and Scots domestic law if his parents were married at the time of his conception or the time of his

---

[6] e.g. Child Abduction and Custody Act 1985; Family Law Act 1986 s.41; Children (Scotland) Act 1995 s.14; Brussels II *bis*Regulation; 1996 Hague Convention on the Protection of Children; and Rome IV Regulation.

[7] M. Wolff, *Private International Law*, 2nd edn (1950), p.110 defines residence as, "habitual physical presence in a place …more than sojourn (physical presence) and less than domicile. It is a purely factual conception and requires no legal capacity". In *Winans v Att Gen (No.1)* [1904] A.C. 287, Lord Macnaghten at 298 described Winans as "a sojourner and stranger" when he came to England, and "a sojourner and a stranger in it" when he died, i.e. not domiciled in England at death, though resident there.

[8] And current rules of English Law.

[9] *Woodbury v Sutherland's Trustees*, 1939 S.L.T. 93; and *Re Craignish* [1892] 3 Ch. 180. The only example of ascription of domicile of origin at a date later than birth is that of adoption.

[10] *Udny v Udny* (1869) 7 M. (H.L.) 89.

birth, it was arguable[11] that a child conceived during marriage, but born after the divorce of his parents, would take his father's domicile as a domicile of origin. However, if thereafter the child had his home with his mother, he would take his mother's domicile of dependency.[12]

(2) *Illegitimate or posthumous child*—The domicile was that of the child's mother as at the date of the child's birth.[13] Changes brought about in Scottish domestic rules concerning illegitimacy and legal equality of children by the Law Reform (Parent and Child) (Scotland) Act 1986 were not accompanied by any alteration in the rules governing the ascribing of domicile of origin or dependence (q.v.).[14]

(3) *Child legitimated per subsequens matrimonium*—The domicile of origin was that of the mother as at the date of the child's birth, but the child would take the domicile of the father as from the date of the marriage as a derivative or dependent domicile.

(4) *Child of putative marriage*—The domicile was that of the innocent party to the "marriage".[15]

(5) *Adopted child*—An adopted child would acquire from the date of the adoption the domicile of the adoptive father and on the latter's death the domicile of the child would follow that of the adoptive mother. Generally, since an adopted child was treated as the legitimate child of the adoptive parent(s), his domicile would be determined in accordance with the legitimate child rule.

It was found on occasion that a court was required to trace a family history in order to provide a reasoned judgment as to the domicile of origin of the *propositus*.[16]

Family Law (Scotland) Act 2006

6–05   One of the aims of the 2006 Act was to complete the process of removal from the law of Scotland of the status of illegitimacy. Abolition of that status was effected by s.21.[17] In consequence, there should, "no longer be a link between a child's domicile and that of his parent's marital status in relation to both the domicile of origin and dependant [sic] domicile."[18]

The express purpose of s.22 ("Domicile of persons under 16") is to effect the ascription of domicile of persons under 16, according to the following rules:

---

[11] However, *Dicey, Morris and Collins on the Conflict of Laws*, 15th edn (2012), para.6–028, say that this is an open question, and that such a child may be thought to take as his domicile of origin the domicile of his mother.

[12] See in English law (and in Scots law until the advent of the 2006 Act) DMPA 1973 s.4.

[13] *Udny v Udny* (1869) 7 M. (H.L.) 89.

[14] Law Reform (Parent and Child) (Scotland) Act 1986 s.9(1)(a); and DMPA 1973 s.4.

[15] *Smijth v Smijth*, 1918 1 S.L.T. 156. But see A.E. Anton, *Private International Law: A treatise from the standpoint of Scots law*, 1st edn (Edinburgh: SULI/W. Green, 1967), pp.343, 344.

[16] *Grant v Grant*, 1931 S.C. 238; *Re Flynn (No.1)* [1968] 1 W.L.R. 103; and *Sekhri v Ray* [2014] EWCA Civ 119; [2014] 2 F.L.R. 1168.

[17] In cases where the person's status is governed by Scots law. See further para.14–01, below.

[18] Explanatory notes to Family Law (Scotland) Bill, para.30.

A child shall be domiciled in the same country as his parents[19] where:

(a)   his parents are domiciled in the same country as each other; and

(b)   he has a home with a parent or a home (or homes) with both of them.

Where these conditions are not satisfied (s.22(3)), the child shall be domiciled in the country with which he has for the time being the closest connection. The following observations may be made:

Reliance is placed on the test "having a home with", which may suggest an emotional tie, rather than, or in addition to, a purely factual tie based on ordinary residence. One would assume that where a child is sent away from his parents' home to another country for education, or for reasons of safety, his "home" (notional) must yet be held to be with his parents. Speculation would suggest that, on the basis of s.22, such a child would be held to "have his home with" his parents, although he may not generally reside with them on a day-to-day basis, and so his domicile will follow that of his parents, who may or may not be domiciled in the place to which they have been posted. This example underlines the importance of interpretation of the key test of "having a home with".[20]

The Act makes no reference to the terms "domicile of origin" and "domicile of choice". It is regrettable that full consideration was not given to the implications of this ad hoc statutory incursion into the framework of the domicile rules. Silence about the name of the under-16 domicile, and its place in the general scheme, is damaging to the coherence of the domicile rules. As will be explained below, in Scots law prior to the 2006 Act, and still in English law, the domicile of origin so termed acted/acts as an "anchor" domicile, providing certainty at times of uncertainty. Domicile of origin has been in Scotland, and remains in England, the default position. Seeking to legislate under the heading "Domicile of persons under 16", without appreciating its repercussions on the ascertainment of domicile at subsequent points in an individual's life, was ill-advised. The Law Commissions' 1987 proposals, whatever view one takes of their desirability, contained a suggested corpus of rules on domicile, including the abolition of domicile of origin,[21] whereas that which is contained in the 2006 Act purports to be restricted to the alteration of particular rules. Rules of domicile exist to supply an appropriate legal system to govern important matters of status and capacity which may arise at any point in the life of the *propositus*.

The tacit assumption is that s.22 applies, not only for the purposes of ascription of domicile at birth, but at any time during the first 16 years of the *propositus*'s life. Express repeal of the statutory amendment to dependent domicile effected by the Domicile and Matrimonial Proceedings Act 1973 ("DMPA 1973") s.4, means that s.22 governs situations which previously in a Scots court were governed by s.4. This provides a shifting test according to changing factual circumstances.

---

[19] The 2006 Act does not provide a special rule for adopted children; nor does the Act make it clear whether or not the word "parent" includes adoptive parent.

[20] cf. *Williams, Petitioner*, 1977 S.L.T. (Notes) 2.

[21] *Private International Law: The Law of Domicile*, 1987, Law Com. No.168; Scot. Law Com. No.107, para.4.24.

Drafting transitional provisions is notoriously difficult, perhaps especially in domicile.[22] The Act does not make plain the time at which the s.22 rule is to take effect. One would have hoped that it would take effect from its date of commencement (4 May 2006) forward,[23] to regulate the domiciles of those who, at the date of coming into force of the Act, were under 16 and those at that date not yet born. Regrettably, however, by inference of the Family Law (Scotland) Act 2006 (Commencement, Transitional Provisions and Savings) Order 2006, litigation to determine the ultimate domicile of an octogenarian *propositus* who dies after commencement of the Act, may require to be carried out according to the new rules contained in the Act.[24] The point is as yet untested. The difficulty of establishing, at the time of death of a nonagenarian, for the purpose, say, of distribution of his estate, his "under-16" domicile does not seem to have been appreciated[25]; identification of the childhood "home" of such a person in many cases may be impossible to prove. Even less predictable may be the decision of a court seeking to identify the country with which the child had "for the time being the closest connection".

DOMICILE OF DEPENDENCE

Scots law prior to the Family Law (Scotland) Act 2006

6–06   A person who is not sui juris does not have legal capacity to acquire a new domicile.[26] However a child's domicile might be changed through the actings of a parent. Since such a change in domicile results from the actings of another person and is involuntary on the part of the *incapax*, it was known at common law as a derivative or dependent domicile. Such a domicile was acquired, therefore, independently of the residence and intention of the *propositus*.

6–07   The DMPA 1973 s.4 (which until the coming into force of the 2006 Act applied to Scotland, England and Northern Ireland, but now applies only to the latter two jurisdictions), provides as follows:

---

[22] 1987 Law Commission proposals, *Private International Law: The Law of Domicile*, Law Com. No.168; Scot. Law Com. No.107, para.8.7 and cll.1(2), 2(3). It was suggested that with regard to the drafting of transitional provisions, changes in the rules of domicile should apply to determine the domicile of a person as at any time *after* the legislation comes into force; and that the "new" rules should apply also to times *before* the legislation comes into force, but only for the purpose of determining where, at a time *after* the legislation comes into force, a person is domiciled. Were this approach to have been applied to the transitional problems associated with s.22, the new rules for ascription of first domicile would apply in the matter of determining the domicile at death of an individual born in 1920 and dying, say, in 2007.

[23] Though this is by no means borne out by the Family Law (Scotland) Act 2006 (Commencement, Transitional Provisions and Savings) Order 2006 (SSI 2006/212), which in art.4 merely enacts that the provisions of s.22, inter alia, shall not apply in relation to any proceedings which commenced before 4 May 2006.

[24] P. McEleavy, "Regression and Reform in the Law of Domicile" (2007) 56(2) I.C.L.Q. 453.

[25] cf. *Cyganik v Agulian* [2006] EWCA Civ 129, per Mummery L.J., at para.46, quoting Kierkegaard: "[l]ife must be lived forwards, but can only be understood backwards".

[26] See also paras 6–27 and 6–28 below re married women and *incapaces*.

(1)   when his father and mother are alive, but living apart, a child's domicile shall be that of his mother if:
   (a)   he then has his home with her and has no home with his father[27]; or
   (b)   he has at any time had his mother's domicile under rule (a) above and has not since had a home with his father;
(2)   if a child's mother is dead, his domicile shall be the domicile which she had at her death, if he then had her domicile under rule (a) above and has not since had a home with his father.

This statutory change, limited to domicile of dependence, applied only to legitimate and adopted children.

Prior to the 2006 Act, and still in English law, it was/is thought that the domicile of a person under the age of 16, both of whose parents are dead, probably cannot be changed until the individual attains 16 years.

Family Law (Scotland) Act 2006

The 2006 Act repeals s.4 of the 1973 Act, on the rationale that the domicile rule for persons under 16 inserted by s.22 shall cover all questions pertaining to the domicile of such persons, without making the distinction between domicile of origin and domicile of dependence. Subsequent to the 2006 Act, s.22 provides for the domicile of a child from birth until the child attains 16 years. Therefore a court required to ascertain the domicile of a child during the years of dependence must determine the *tempus inspiciendum*, and apply s.22 accordingly.   6–08

As regards the domicile of a person under the age of 16, both of whose parents are dead, though the 2006 Act is silent on the point, the situation must fall within s.22(3), permitting a court to find the child domiciled in the country with which he has for the time being the closest connection.

DOMICILE OF CHOICE

Section 22 of the 2006 Act does not purport to apply to any person over the age of 16, and by inference, the rules contained therein cease to be applicable to a person once he attains that age.   6–09

A person over the age of 16 has legal capacity, in the view of Scots law,[28] to change his pre-existing domicile, i.e. his under-16 domicile, to a different domicile, a domicile of choice, and to effect any number of subsequent changes in that domicile. It is assumed that where the individual has made no such change after he has attained 16 years, he will be held to have retained his under-16 domicile.[29]

---

[27] *Williams, Petitioner*, 1977 S.L.T. (Notes) 2.
[28] Authority for this rests now not on the Age of Legal Capacity (Scotland) Act 1991 s.7 (repealed by 2006 Act Sch.3), but rather on the 2006 Act s.22(4). For English law, see DMPA 1973 s.3(a): capacity is conferred at age 16, or upon marriage before that age by a party who necessarily must not be of English domicile, since by English law persons do not have legal capacity to marry before 16.
[29] cf. *Harrison v Harrison* [1953] 1 W.L.R. 865; and *Henderson v Henderson* [1967] P. 77.

Every person who is sui juris may acquire a domicile of choice in any country which has a system of law of its own. This is achieved only by combination of residence (*factum*) and intention (*animus*) to reside in the new country for as long as can be seen ahead:

— *acquisition* of a domicile of choice requires a change of *both* residence *and* intention[30];
— *retention* of a domicile of choice is maintained by retention of *either* residence *or* intention;
— *loss* of a domicile of choice requires a change of *both* residence *and* intention.

Revival of domicile of origin

6–10   At common law, acquisition of a domicile of choice merely supersedes the domicile of origin, but does not obliterate it because, if the former is lost, the latter will revive. Hence, if, in the view of the court, the *propositus* has established a domicile of choice *animo et facto* in legal system A, a change of heart or mind the next day will change nothing: the change must be acted upon sufficiently, that is, by departure in a final manner beyond the territorial limits of legal system A.[31] The position is quite different from departure in a final manner from the domicile of origin, which effects no change unless and until domicile of choice is established clearly elsewhere.[32] Only in the latter context is there a "continuance" rule, i.e. continuance of domicile of origin until displaced. In contrast, where a domicile of choice is lost *animo et facto*, the domicile of origin revives to fill any gap. This is the rule of revival of domicile of origin, which has been favoured in the UK. It is *not* the case that one domicile of choice subsists until a new one is acquired.[33] Although the revival rule has been criticised, it has not been removed.

Revival of "under-16 domicile"

6–11   Since the domicile of origin rules cannot co-exist with s.22, the question arises whether or not the principle of revival of domicile of origin can be said to have survived for use by a Scots court. If a person having a Scottish "under-16" domicile acquires a "post-16" domicile in New South Wales, and then departs

---

[30] "[W]here intention is absolutely clear, a minimum of residence in the ordinary case at any rate is enough": *Willar v Willar*, 1954 S.C. 144, per Lord Justice-Clerk Thomson at 147; and *King v Foxwell* (1876) L.R. 3 Ch. D. 518. Consider the extreme circumstances of *White v Tennant*, 31 W.Va. 790, 8 S.E. 596 (1888) in which "residence" of a few hours' duration, as evidenced by deposit of belongings in the new house in the new US state, was sufficient for the *propositus* to have acquired domicile in that state, although that night, having returned to the state of his previous residence to lodge with relatives, he died there. See also the special circumstances of *Plummer v Inland Revenue Commissioners* [1988] 1 All E.R. 97.
[31] cf. *Re Raffenel* (1863) 3 Sw. & Tr. 49.
[32] *Bell v Kennedy* (1868) 6 M. (H.L.) 69.
[33] Contrast US rule in *Re Jones' Estate* (1921) 182 N.W. 227 Supreme Court of Iowa. The difference between the two systems (USA and UK) stems from the different attitudes of a country whose sons went out to travel the world and were expected to return, and those of an immigrant country from which people were not expected to depart.

that place in a final manner, and meets his death shortly thereafter on a visit to Tasmania, the question would be whether he died domiciled in Scotland (with his "under-16" domicile in place) or in New South Wales (on the basis of a continuance rule). The 2006 Act is silent as to the solution.

Revival of the "under-16" domicile, though analogous to the solution adopted by UK courts with regard to revival of domicile of origin, is not without complication insofar as domicile of origin is a fixed connecting factor whereas the "under-16" domicile might vary during the years from infancy to 16; which "under-16" domicile would revive—that which was ascribed at birth, or the one latest held? The alternative to a revival rule would be to hold that the last acquired over-16 domicile (New South Wales in the instant case) should be held to continue—even where this would lead to the application of a legal system from which the *propositus* had chosen to depart. The doubt which attends this conjecture demonstrates the inadequacies of incomplete drafting.

Proof of acquisition of domicile of choice

A person averring a change of domicile either of himself or of a third party must show that there has been a change of *both residence* and *intention*.[34] All relevant factors regarding these two matters must be considered.[35]

6–12

Standard of proof

The standard of proof of change of domicile is the normal civil standard of the balance of probabilities. Prior to the 2006 Act (and in England still) a variation in difficulty of proof could be seen in relation to different types of domicile. The domicile of dependence held by the young adult emerging into legal maturity was the easiest domicile to lose.[36] At the other extreme, at common law, the most striking feature of the domicile of origin was its "limpet-like quality", and the difficulty of discharging the burden of showing that a domicile of choice had replaced it[37]; the standard of proof in such cases tended to go beyond "a mere balance of probabilities".[38] Stronger evidence was required to establish a change from a domicile of origin to a domicile of choice than from one domicile of

6–13

---

[34] *Bell v Kennedy* (1868) 6 M. (H.L.) 69; *Vincent v Earl of Buchan* (1889) 16 R. 637; *Lord Advocate v Brown's Trustees*, 1907 S.C. 333; *Casey v Casey*, 1968 S.L.T. 56; *Spence v Spence*, 1995 S.L.T. 335; *Moynihan v Moynihan* [1997] 1 F.L.R. 59; *Reddington v Riach's Executor*, 2002 S.L.T. 537; *Cyganik v Agulian* [2006] EWCA Civ 129; *Munro v Munro* [2007] EWHC 3315 (Fam); *Morgan v Cilento* [2004] EWHC 188 (Ch); *Gaines-Cooper v Revenue and Customs Commissioners* [2007] EWHC 2617 (Ch); and *Re N (Jurisdiction)* [2009] I.L.Pr. 8.

[35] The case of *Brooks v Brooks's Trustees* (1902) 4 F. 1014 is a useful example which has been set in poetic form by William M. Gloag, *Carmina Legis* (Glasgow: Maclehose, Jackson and Co, 1920): "A domicile at birth we all acquire, True, we may change it if we so desire".

[36] *Harrison v Harrison* [1953] 1 W.L.R. 865; and *Henderson v Henderson* [1967] P. 77, per Sir Jocelyn Simon, at 82, 83: "[t]he abandonment of a domicile of choice acquired dependently in favour of a domicile of origin reacquired by personal volition must, in the nature of things, generally be of all changes of domicile, the one least onerous of proof."

[37] *Cyganik v Agulian* [2006] EWCA Civ 129. See at shrieval level *Williamson v Williamson*, 2009 G.W.D. 14–220.

[38] *Munro v Munro* [2007] EWHC 3315 (Fam), per Bennett J. at [32]. But see also *Re N (Jurisdiction)* [2009] I.L.Pr. 8, per Hedley J. at [8].

choice to a new domicile of choice. In all cases it was possibly easier to establish a change from one law unit to another within the same political state than to a legal system in which one would be an alien.[39]

The extent to which s.22 of the 2006 Act has de-stabilised the common law position is a matter of debate. Whether or not the same approach will apply to the replacement of an individual's "under-16" domicile as applied to the loss of a child's domicile of dependence is not known. Equally, whether or not a "limpet-like" quality will be deemed to attach to "under-16" domicile is not known; something may depend on whether a child has had a single, i.e. constant, "under-16" domicile, or more than one such domicile.

Value of authorities

6–14 Domicile decisions necessarily entail a review of the life of an individual, sometimes at a particular point in the course of it,[40] and frequently at the end of that life. Since all lives are unique, it is said that the corpus of domicile cases does not form a body of precedent in the normal way and that each decision is a guide only.[41] Yet, common themes recur and similar mind-sets are found, and so a wide knowledge of domicile decisions is the foundation of a convincing domicile opinion.

Residence

6–15 Actual physical residence of some kind is necessary; taking lodgings is less positive a step than renting, and renting less strong than purchase.[42] But residence by itself, no matter for how long, is ineffective without intention.[43] Graveson remarked[44] that the word does not command its Victorian meaning of a 10-roomed villa. Nourse, J. in *Inland Revenue Commissioners v Duchess of Portland*[45] said that: "Residence in a country for the purposes of the law of domicile is physical presence in that country as an inhabitant of it."

---

[39] cf. *Reddington v Riach's Executor*, 2002 S.L.T. 537.

[40] e.g. *Bell v Kennedy* (1868) 6 M. (H.L.) 69.

[41] *Lord Advocate v Brown's Trustees*, 1907 S.C. 333 per Lord McLaren at 338: "In view of the weight which is so often attributed to authorities in such questions it may not be superfluous that I should begin by stating what is almost a truism, that every question of domicile is essentially a question of fact. Judicial expositions, I need hardly say, may be of great value as guides to the relative weights to be attributed to different elements of a life history in the question of domicile; but in the determination of the whole question of the domicile, each case, as I think, must be considered by itself and in the light of the facts proved."

[42] *Re Capdevielle* (1864) 2 H. & C. 985.

[43] *Jopp v Wood* (1865) 34 L.J. Ch. 212; *Brooks v Brooks's Trustees* (1902) 4 F. 1014; *Re Almeda* (1902) 18 T.L.R. 414; *Winans v Att Gen (No.1)* [1904] A.C. 287; *Ross v Ross*, 1930 S.C. (H.L.) 1; *Liverpool Royal Infirmary v Ramsay*, 1930 S.C. (H.L.) 83; *Grant v Grant*, 1931 S.C. 238; and *Willar v Willar*, 1954 S.C. 144.

[44] R.H. Graveson, *Private International Law*, 7th edn (1974), p.201.

[45] *Inland Revenue Commissioners v Duchess of Portland* [1982] 1 Ch. 314 at 318, 319.

Lawfulness of residence

In the case of *Puttick*,[46] the view was expressed firmly by Sir George Baker, President of the Family Division, that acquisition of domicile of choice in a country cannot be founded upon residence which is unlawful by the law of that country. This statement now is qualified by the unanimous decision of the House of Lords in *Mark v Mark*,[47] a divorce jurisdiction case, in which the parties were Nigerian nationals. The wife issued a divorce petition in an English forum, relying initially for jurisdiction solely upon her habitual residence in England over the previous 12 months, but her petition later was amended so as to include the claim that she had acquired a domicile of choice in England. Having first admitted that the English court had jurisdiction, the husband later changed his mind on the point, and applied for a stay of the English proceedings, on the basis that he had commenced proceedings already in Nigeria. The husband argued that the habitual residence of the wife in England for 12 months prior to the petition could not clothe the court with jurisdiction because her presence in England was unlawful. She was classed as an "overstayer", i.e. a person whose leave to remain in the UK had expired. The judge at first instance held that while the wife could not be regarded as habitually resident in England, by reason of the unlawfulness of her presence, she could rely upon presence in England as a basis for the acquisition of a domicile of choice. The Court of Appeal dismissed the husband's appeal, finding that the wife not only had acquired an English domicile of choice by the time of litigation, but also had been habitually resident in England for the previous 12 months. In the House of Lords, on the residence point, Baroness Hale held that for the purpose of the 1973 Act s.5(2) (but not necessarily for other statutory provisions), the residence of the petitioner need not be lawful residence.

On the question of domicile, her Ladyship found that there was little English case authority until *Puttick*, though she drew on authorities from other Commonwealth jurisdictions. Treating the matter, therefore, as one of principle, and having regard to the object of the rules of domicile (which, in her Ladyship's view, is to discover the system of law with which the *propositus* is most closely connected for a range of purposes), Baroness Hale concluded that there was no reason in principle why a person whose presence in England is unlawful cannot acquire a domicile of choice there. She took a purposive approach; recognising the appropriateness of England as a divorce forum in the instant case did not offend any general principle that a person cannot be allowed to benefit from his own criminal conduct. Lady Hale took the view that in the circumstances presented, the state had no particular interest, one way or another.[48] As a matter of fact, the wife's position was precarious, and comparable to the situations of the petitioner in each of *Boldrini*[49] and *Cruh*.[50] In view of the unanimous decision in *Mark*, previously held views based upon *Puttick* must be regarded with caution.

6–16

---

[46] *Puttick v Att Gen* [1979] 3 All E.R. 463.

[47] *Mark v Mark* [2005] 3 All E.R. 912.

[48] *Mark v Mark* [2005] 3 All E.R. 912 at [44]. Contrast peerage claim *Re Barony of Moynihan* [2000] 1 F.L.R. 113.

[49] *Boldrini v Boldrini* [1932] P. 9 (re illegal alien).

[50] *Cruh v Cruh* [1945] 2 All E.R. 545 (re party subject to deportation order).

Intention

6–17　There must be an intention to settle in a new country having a separate body of law. Although a person must regard his new home as being in that country for the foreseeable future, such an intention need not be irrevocable because an everlasting intention cannot reasonably be required of anybody. However, there will not be a change of domicile to country B if the person always had at the back of his mind the intention to leave country B at some indefinite future date, for example, on retiral or death of a spouse, and to go back to his original country.[51] The decision in *Re Capdevielle*[52] in 1864 marked the change to a stricter test; from that date the Scots and English courts required "conscious adoption" of the new legal system as home, whereas before then residence of indefinite duration sufficed. Hence, lingering doubts and wishes are important, and may preclude acquisition of a domicile of choice.[53]

Motive is not a bar to change of domicile so long as the *propositus*, for whatever reason, had the requisite intention to settle in the new country.[54] The individual must be capable mentally of forming that intention, though no specialised knowledge of the significance of forming such intention is necessary.

The court will not draw the inference of sufficient intention for acquisition of a domicile of choice if it appears that an individual lives "between" legal systems, and if "his complex hesitant mind" has not decided between them[55]: in such a case, domicile of origin remains. In technical terms, the burden of proof of change will not have been discharged to the satisfaction of the court. It must not be thought that the test for acquisition of a domicile of choice is impossibly high nor that it cannot be satisfied in a relatively short time.[56] In the Scots decision of *Spence v Spence*,[57] a nicely balanced case, the court took the view that a period of 10 years' residence in Spain and connections through business and family (though without social connection) was not sufficient to justify a finding of acquisition of a Spanish domicile of choice. However, in *Reddington v Riach's Executor*[58] the domicile of the deceased (who died in Bournemouth, England, at the age of 95) was held to have been changed by him to that of an English domicile of choice. His domicile of origin had been Scottish, but from 1976 he

---

[51] *Inland Revenue Commissioners v Bullock* [1976] 3 All E.R. 353; cf. *Re De Hosson* [1937] I.R. 467. Contrast the outcome in *Inland Revenue Commissioners v Duchess of Portland* [1982] 1 Ch. 314.

[52] *Re Capdevielle* (1864) 2 H. & C. 985.

[53] *Whicker v Hume* (1858) 7 H.L. Cas. 124; *Winans v Att Gen (No.1)* [1904] A.C. 287; *Liverpool Royal Infirmary v Ramsay*, 1930 S.C. (H.L.) 83; *Gulbenkian v Gulbenkian* [1937] 4 All E.R. 618; *Re Clore (Deceased) (No.2)* [1984] S.T.C. 609; *Inland Revenue Commissioners v Bullock* [1976] 3 All E.R. 353; *Lord v Colvin* (1859) 4 Drew 366 at 376; *Re Sillar* [1956] I.R. 344; *Re Furse (Deceased)* [1980] 3 All E.R. 838; and *Sekhri v Ray* [2014] EWCA Civ 119; [2014] 2 F.L.R. 1168.

[54] Intention is not compromised by the reason for entertaining the intention; *Carswell v Carswell* (1881) 8 R. 901; *Stavert v Stavert* (1882) 9 R. 519; *Morton v Morton* (1897) 5 S.L.T. 222; *Sellars v Sellars*, 1942 S.C. 206; *McLelland v McLelland*, 1943 S.L.T. 66; *Marchant v Marchant*, 1948 S.L.T. 143; and *Re A (Parental Order: Domicile) v SA* [2013] EWHC 426 (Fam).

[55] *Fuld (No.3)* [1968] P. 675, per Scarman J. at 689.

[56] *McNeill v McNeill*, 1919 2 S.L.T. 127; *Elmquist v Elmquist*, 1961 S.L.T. (Notes) 71; *Rankin v Rankin*, 1960 S.L.T. 308; *Gould v Gould (No.2)*, 1968 S.L.T. 98; *McEwan v McEwan*, 1969 S.L.T. 342; contrast *Brown v Brown*, 1967 S.L.T. (Notes) 44.

[57] *Spence v Spence*, 1995 S.L.T. 335. Also *Marsh v Marsh*, 2002 S.L.T. (Sh.Ct.) 87; and *A v L* [2009] EWHC 1448 (Fam).

[58] *Reddington v Riach's Executor*, 2002 S.L.T. 537.

had been resident in Bournemouth, continuing to reside there after the death of his wife in 1987, visiting Scotland only once or twice after 1976 and never having expressed a desire to return. Arguably, a distinguishing factor between *Spence* and *Reddington* is that the alleged change of domicile in *Reddington* was between legal systems of one territorial unit of the UK to another. The similarity of circumstance and difference of outcome between the cases of *Liverpool Royal Infirmary v Ramsay*[59] and *Reddington v Riach's Executor* is striking, and may be explicable not only in terms of the differing states of mind of the *propositus* in each case, but also by reason of the elapse of time between the two decisions, perhaps exemplifying a softening in the attitude of the courts.

Factors which have to be considered in assessing intention

(1) NATIONALITY

There is no necessary link between domicile and nationality.[60] Nonetheless in *Munro v Munro*,[61] the fact that the *propositus* had never contemplated applying for Spanish citizenship was persuasive in a finding that he had not acquired a domicile of choice in Spain.

6–18

(2) RESIDENCE

Residence may throw light on intention[62] and expressed intention may throw light on residence; for example, intention may grow as residence lengthens. The two factors are interconnected,[63] but should be considered separately, at least in the first instance.

6–19

(3) EXERCISE OF POLITICAL RIGHTS, ENTRY INTO SOCIAL LIFE, CUSTOM

Wholehearted entry into the political and social life of a country is a significant factor in acquisition of domicile there.[64] One may contrast the adoption by a Frenchman of the customs of an English village, in the old case of *Drevon*, with Winans' enforced and aloof residence in Brighton. The *propositus* in *Lord*

6–20

---

[59] *Liverpool Royal Infirmary v Ramsay* [1930] A.C. 588.

[60] *Hamilton v Dallas* (1875) 1 Ch.D. 257; *Doucet v Geoghegan* (1879) L.R. 9 Ch. D. 441; *Bell v Bell* [1992] 2 I.R. 152; *Ross*, 1930 S.C. (H.L.) 1; *Haldane v Eckford (No.2)* (1869) L.R. 8 Eq. 631; *Brunel v Brunel* (1871) L.R. 12 Eq. 298; *Drevon* (1834) 34 L.J. Ch. 129; *Bradfield v Swanton* [1931] I.R. 446; *Wahl v Att Gen* (1932) 147 L.T. 382; *Casey*, 1968 S.L.T. 56; and *Fuld (No.3)* [1968] P. 675.

[61] *Munro v Munro* [2007] EWHC 3315 (Fam).

[62] *Aitchison v Dixon* (1870) L.R. 10 Eq. 589; *Haldane v Eckford (No.2)* (1869) L.R. 8 Eq. 631; *Platt v Att Gen of New South Wales* (1877–1888) L.R. App. Cas. 336; *Re Garden (Deceased)* (1895) 11 T.L.R. 167; *Hope, Todd and Kirk v Bruce* (1899) 6 S.L.T. 310; *Att Gen v Yule and Mercantile Bank of India* (1931) 145 L.T. 9; *Wahl v Att Gen* (1932) 147 L.T. 382; *Willar*, 1954 S.C. 144.

[63] cf. *Haldane v Eckford (No.2)* (1869) L.R. 8 Eq. 631, as expressed in the rubric derived from Lord Westbury's judgment in *Udny*: "Residence originally temporary, and intended for a limited period, may afterwards become general and unlimited, and in such a case, so soon as the change of purpose, or animus manendi, can be inferred, the fact of domicil is established."

[64] *Drevon* (1834) 34 L.J. Ch. 129; compare generally *Doucet* (1879) L.R. 9 Ch. D. 441. Also *Liverpool Royal Infirmary v Ramsay* 1930 S.C. (H.L.) 83.

Advocate v Brown's Trustees was "at home" in the social life of Ceylon; contra, Lord Cullen noted in *Spence*,[65] that the pursuer's uncontradicted evidence was that her husband's social circles in Spain were made up of British people. Nevertheless, a person who has entered into the local community may remain, in law, a stranger in a strange land, and may not be held to be domiciled there.[66]

(4) DECLARATION OF INTENTION

6–21   A declaration as to domicile or as to intention to settle in a particular country may be relevant, but too much reliance should not be placed on such a declaration without first considering any possible reason behind it. In many cases declarations have been disregarded. Moreover, it is not the prerogative of the individual, but rather of the court, to pronounce conclusively upon domicile.[67] The dictum of Lord Buckmaster in *Ross* is often quoted:

> "Declarations as to intention are rightly regarded in determining the question of a change of domicile, but they must be examined by considering the person to whom, the purposes for which, and the circumstances in which they are made, and they must further be fortified and carried into effect by conduct and action consistent with the declared intention."[68]

In many cases, declarations assert the acquisition of a new domicile, but in others,[69] declarations profess retention of an old domicile. Declarations may be made inter vivos, or *mortis causa*, usually as the last clause in a will,[70] but in no case can they be regarded as more than a dubious guide for the court. Declarations may be tactical, or tactful, to please the listener. They may be contradictory (to please different listeners), and the court may consider some to be persuasive and others not. If made many years previously, by a speaker now dead, there is the problem of incomplete recollection or bias in the listener/witness.[71] Their value as dispassionate assessments of domicile is diminished by perceived self-interest,[72] or by ignorance of the law,[73] the author or

---

[65] *Spence*, 1995 S.L.T. 335 at 338; *Cyganik v Agulian* [2006] EWCA Civ 129; and *Morris v Davies* [2011] EWHC 1773 (Ch).

[66] *Sellars*, 1942 S.C. 206.

[67] Though see *Re M* [1937] N.I. 151 where the highly unusual step in unusual circumstances was taken of permitting the petitioner to choose whether his domicile was that of the Irish Free State or of Northern Ireland. He chose the latter, thereby clothing the court with jurisdiction to hear his petition of divorce.

[68] *Ross*, 1930 S.C. (H.L.) 1 at 6. See also *De Bonneval* (1838) 1 Curt. 856; *Whicker v Hume* (1858) 7 H.L. Cas. 124; *Crookenden v Fuller* (1859) 1 Sw. & Tr. 441; *Woodbury v Sutherland's Trustees*, 1939 S.L.T. 93; *Latta, Petitioner*, 1954 S.L.T. (Notes) 74; *Scappaticci v Att Gen* [1955] P.47; *Re Sillar* [1956] I.R. 344; *Tennekoon v Duraisamy* [1958] A.C. 354; *Rev Comms v Matthews* (1958) 92 I.T.L.R. 44; and *Lambton (Earl of Durham) v Lady Lambton* [2013] EWHC 3566 (Ch).

[69] *Re Steer* (1858) 3 H. & N. 594; *Re Liddell-Grainger's Will Trusts* [1936] 3 All E.R. 173; *Re Sillar* [1956] I.R. 344.

[70] *Reddington v Riach's Executor*, 2002 S.L.T. 537.

[71] *Cyganik v Agulian* [2006] EWCA Civ 129.

[72] Though few have been regarded as dismissively as the statements of the *propositus* in *Puttick v Att Gen* [1979] 3 All E.R. 463, per Sir George Baker at 18.

[73] *Wilson v Jones (Preliminary Issue)* unreported, HC99/00157 High Court of Justice, Chancery Division (8 June 2000).

speaker using the term domicile where he may not be aware of the technical meaning and legal implications thereof. Nevertheless, on occasion,[74] declarations may tip the balance.

(5) DEPOSITING CASH OR VALUABLES

Depositing moveables in a particular place or leaving them there in a time of emergency may indicate a mental attitude displaying "permanent" attachment to that place.[75]

6–22

(6) INFIRMITY AND OLD AGE

An individual may be compelled to remain in a place for reasons of poor health or advancing years. Each case must be considered on its own merits. With regard to illness and infirmity, the test in *Hoskins v Matthews*[76] is whether the person was exercising a preference and not acting upon a necessity; in the former case, a domicile of choice might be acquired. Moreover, the intention to stay for an indefinite time in a beneficial climate may transmute into the *animus* requisite for a change of domicile and, if so, that change will occur when *animus manendi* (intention to remain for as long as can be seen ahead) is established.

6–23

Diminishing physical strength may preclude departure from a country. Place of death may be found to have a significance in domicile litigation which place of birth rarely has. If the view be taken that the *propositus* lived (and died) in the legal system of his domicile of origin, wishful thinking by him for life in another country can avail nothing.

If, being of Scots domicile of origin, the *propositus* lived abroad without an intention to acquire a domicile of choice there, the occurrence of death abroad will not alter retention at death of the domicile of origin. However, if being of, say, French domicile of choice, the *propositus* living in France wished fervently to return to Scotland (the place of his domicile of origin) and was unable physically to do so, his French domicile will remain at death.[77]

If the *propositus* should set up conditions for his departure from the country which arguably is his domicile of choice, in order to return "home", and seems loath to see these fulfilled, not only may such a condition (ever less likely to be satisfied) not preclude a finding of domicile of choice in that system, but also

---

[74] *Woodbury v Sutherland's Trustees*, 1939 S.L.T. 93.

[75] *Curling v Thornton* (1823) 2 Add. 6; *Att Gen v Dunn* (1840) 6 M. & W. 511; *Willar*, 1954 S.C. 144; *Rev Comms v Matthews* (1958) 92 I.T.L.R. 44; and *Haldane v Eckford (No.2)* (1869) L.R. 8 Eq. 631.

[76] *Hoskins v Matthews* (1855) 25 L.T. (O.S.) 78; *Johnstone v Beattie* (1843) 10 Cl. & F. 42 at 139; *Moorhouse v Lord* (1863) 10 H.L. Cas. 272; *Lauderdale Peerage Case* (1885) 10 App. Cas. 692 at 740; *Re Garden (Deceased)* (1895) 11 T.L.R. 167; *Winans* [1904] A.C. 287; *Re James* (1908) 98 L.T. 438; and *Re Haji-Ioannou (Deceased), sub nom. Haji-Ioannou v Frangos* [2009] EWHC 2310 (QB).

[77] *Re Raffenel* (1863) 3 Sw. & Tr. 49. See, generally, *Ramsay v Liverpool Royal Infirmary*, 1930 S.C. (H.L.) 83; and *Winans* [1904] A.C. 287. Contrast *Re Furse* [1980] 3 All E.R. 838 where Fox J. at 843 concluded that the deceased's intention to return to the US from Sussex only when he was physically unable to continue an active life on the farm had become increasingly unlikely to be fulfilled. His intention was to live out his days in England subject to a contingency so vaguely expressed that it could not preclude a finding of domicile at death in England (at 848).

such a finding, once made, will mean that the *propositus* would be required physically to leave the system of his adoption before domicile of origin could revive.[78]

Domicile of choice, loss of which is later rued, cannot be reinstated except on the usual rules.[79]

(7) LAIRS AND DIRECTIONS FOR BURIAL OR CREMATION

6–24 Such directions may be relevant insofar as they show that the person contemplated burial or a scattering of ashes in a particular district, but the whole surrounding circumstances must be considered including the time interval between the direction and the date of death.[80]

Loss of domicile of choice

6–25 A domicile of origin (and presumably, though not expressly so stated in the 2006 Act, an "under-16" domicile) is retained until a domicile of choice has been acquired. In accordance with the best established rule of all, departure from the domicile of origin, whether under duress or not, effects no change unless or until a new domicile is acquired.

A domicile of choice is retained unless and until it is abandoned by a change of *both* residence and intention, whereupon either:

(1)   the domicile of origin revives;[81] or
(2)   (rarely) a new domicile of choice is acquired immediately.

Loss of both elements, physical and mental, is required.[82] A domicile of choice is lost by leaving a country *animo non revertendi*,[83] i.e. with the (definite) intention of not returning (or possibly *sine animo revertendi*, i.e. without the intention of returning—a less definite frame of mind). How clear a negative is required? Megarry J. obiter in *Re Flynn*[84] took the view that a "withering away" of intention would suffice to demonstrate loss of intention. The difficulty arises where the *tempus inspiciendum* is found to be at a point before death. In other cases, the whole life will be laid before the court and the *propositus's* intention

---

[78] *Re Furse* [1980] 3 All E.R. 838.
[79] *Fleming v Horniman* (1928) 44 T.L.R. 315.
[80] *Hodgson v De Beauchesne* (1858) 12 Moore. P.C. 285; *Drevon* (1834) 34 L.J. Ch. 129; *Haldane v Eckford (No.2)* (1869) L.R. 8 Eq. 631; *Brunel* (1871) L.R. 12 Eq. 298; *Douglas v Douglas* (1871) L.R. 12 Eq. 617; *Kerr v Richardson's Trustees*, 1898 6 S.L.T. 245; *Re Garden (Deceased)* (1895) 11 T.L.R. 167; *Re Baron Emanuel de Almeda* (1902) 18 T.L.R. 414; *Liverpool Royal Infirmary v Ramsay*, 1930 S.C. (H.L.) 83; *Bradfield v Swanton* [1931] I.R. 446; *Munster and Leinster Bank Ltd v O'Connor* [1937] L.R. 462; *Latta, Petitioner*, 1954 S.L.T. (Notes) 74; *Spence*, 1995 S.L.T. 335; *Reddington v Riach's Executor*, 2002 S.L.T. 537.
[81] In relation to "under-16" domicile, see para.6–11, above.
[82] *Re Raffenel* (1863) 3 Sw. & Tr. 49 (loss of intention, but no sufficient loss of residence); *Re Marrett* (1887) 36 Ch. D. 400; *Re Lloyd Evans* [1947] Ch. 695 (loss of residence, but continuing intention); *Morgan v Cilento* [2004] EWHC 188 (Ch); and *Divall v Divall* [2014] EWHC 95 (Fam); [2014] 2 F.L.R. 1104.
[83] *Labacianskas v Labacianskas*, 1949 S.C. 280.
[84] *Re Flynn (No.1)* [1968] 1 W.L.R. 103 at 113. See also *Tee v Tee* [1974] 1 W.L.R. 213.

then will be clear. However, nice questions can arise. At what point can domicile of choice be said to be lost in a situation in which the enthusiasm of the *propositus* for the adopted country is waning, and he has established a residence in more than one legal system? Such a case was *Morgan v Cilento*,[85] where the deceased, of English domicile of origin, had acquired a domicile of choice in Queensland, Australia, but whose links with England persisted. He was found by Lewison J. to be domiciled at death in Queensland:

> "I must attempt to assess [the *propositus's*] state of mind up to the day he died. To use the language of Megarry J., it may be that his intention to return to Queensland was withering. But I do not consider that it died before Anthony did. I conclude that Anthony died domiciled in Queensland."[86]

Hence, if a significant event such as death occurs when the *propositus* has an ambivalent attitude towards the adopted legal system and before the *animus* for the domicile of choice can be said to have disappeared, that domicile of choice will remain in place at the point of death.

Death in itinere

In the unlikely event of death occurring on the very journey to the legal system which the *propositus* intends to adopt as his new domicile of choice, there may or may not be a change of domicile. If a person, in course of leaving a domicile of choice *animo non revertendi*, dies before leaving the territorial bounds of the country of departure, the domicile of choice remains. If death occurs outside the territorial waters of that country, the domicile of origin will revive.[87] If, however, death occurs inside the territorial waters of the destination country, then it can be argued that domicile of choice in the new country has been established.

6–26

Particular cases

(1) Mental incapaces

There is little authority, but the rule appears to be that a mentally *incapax* person retains the domicile which he had at the date when he became mentally incapacitated. His domicile can be changed only through the actings of a parent, not through the actings of a non-related guardian,[88] and even then probably only if the *incapax* became incapacitated before adulthood.[89]

6–27

The Adults with Incapacity (Scotland) Act 2000 makes no provision with regard to the domicile of incapable persons. The 2006 Act governs the domicile of all persons under 16, but makes no further or specific provision for the domicile of *incapaces* in their lives thereafter.

---

[85] *Morgan v Cilento* [2004] EWHC 188 (Ch).
[86] *Morgan v Cilento* [2004] EWHC 188 (Ch) at [76].
[87] *In the Goods of Luigi Bianchi* (1862) 3 Sw. & Tr. 16; contrast *Re Raffenel* (1863) 3 Sw. & Tr. 49.
[88] Appointed, e.g. under the Adults with Incapacity (Scotland) Act 2000.
[89] *Sharpe v Crispin* (1869) L.R. 1 P.&D. 611; *Crumpton's Judicial Factor v Finch-Noyes*, 1918 S.C. 378.

(2) Married women

6–28 At common law, there was a unity of domicile between husband and wife, the wife taking her husband's domicile as a matter of law at the point of marriage. The law was changed by the DMPA 1973. In order to appreciate the effect of that Act, it is helpful to state the law up to December 31, 1973 which still affects questions relating to the domicile of women married before January 1, 1974:

(a) If the marriage was valid, a wife's domicile followed that of her husband as a matter of law.[90] If the marriage was void, her domicile did not become that of her alleged husband, but she might acquire a new domicile of choice, in the same way as a single woman, in the legal system in which she was living with him. If the marriage was voidable, the wife's domicile changed with that of the husband, and she would retain that domicile even after pronouncement of a nullity decree, unless and until she changed it, *animo et facto*.[91]

(b) Separation. The domicile of a wife changed with that of her husband after a separation whether the separation was voluntary or judicial.[92]

(c) Widows and divorcées. In this case a woman, being sui juris, might acquire a new domicile, in the usual way, by a change of residence and intention, upon the termination of the marriage. However, there would be no change if she continued to live in "his" legal system.[93]

(d) As domicile is determined by the *lex fori*, it was irrelevant that a wife might have been able to acquire a domicile separate from her husband according to the law of the country where she resided.[94]

By s.1 of the 1973 Act the position now is as follows:

"(1) Subject to subsection (2) below, the domicile of a married woman as at any time after the coming into force of this section shall, instead of being the same as her husband's by virtue only of marriage, be ascertained by reference to the same factors as in the case of any other individual capable of having an independent domicile.

(2) Where immediately before this section came into force a woman was married and then had her husband's domicile by dependence, she is to be treated as retaining that domicile (as a domicile of choice, if it is not also her domicile

---

[90] *Re Cooke's Trustees* (1887) 56 L.T. 737; *Low v Low* (1891) 19 R. 115; *Le Mesurier v Le Mesurier* [1895] A.C. 517; *Re Mackenzie* [1911] 1 Ch. 578; *Mackinnon's Trustees v Lord Advocate*, 1920 S.C. (H.L.) 171; *Att Gen for Alberta v Cook* [1926] A.C. 444; *Dunne v Saban*[1955] P. 178; *Re Scullard* [1957] Ch. 107; *Faye v Inland Revenue Commissioners* (1961) 40 T.C. 103.

[91] *De Reneville* [1948] P. 100.

[92] *Att Gen for Alberta v Cook* [1926] A.C. 444; *Mackinnon's Trustees v Lord Advocate*, 1920 S.C. (H.L.) 171.

[93] *Re Raffenel* (1863) 3 Sw. & Tr. 49; *Re Wallach (Deceased)* [1950] 1 All E.R. 199. But see *Re Scullard* [1957] Ch. 107, in which the separated spouses had been living in different jurisdictions; upon the death of the husband, albeit unknown to the wife, she became sui juris and her newly validated intention when added to her residence in Guernsey created acquisition of Guernsey domicile of choice which she held at her death six weeks later. Until two weeks before her death she retained all her mental faculties. Sufficient mental capacity being present, her status as a widow rendered her intention effective.

[94] *Att Gen for Alberta v Cook* [1926] A.C. 444.

of origin) unless and until it is changed by acquisition or revival of another domicile, either on or after the coming into force of this section.
(3)   This section extends to England and Wales, Scotland and Northern Ireland."

This change, expected to be the last word on the matter, proved not to be so. **6–29** Where a woman was married before 1 January 1974, her domicile would change, on the interpretation of s.1(2) given in *Inland Revenue Commissioners v Duchess of Portland*,[95] only in accordance with the usual rules for loss of domicile of choice. There is to be no more lenient rule.[96] Hence, in the case of the Duchess, while it was always clear that her intention was to return ultimately to Canada, her practice of taking long holidays in Quebec did not mean, after 1 January 1974 upon a proper construction of the Act, that she had ceased to reside in England. Her English deemed domicile of dependence remained.

(3)   *Persons seeking asylum*[97]

Where the *propositus* has fled his domicile of origin/"under-16" domicile, it will **6–30** survive his departure, and will remain until clearly superseded, on the principle of *Bell v Kennedy*.[98] Where the *propositus* is forced to leave his domicile of choice, the enforced nature of his leaving will mean that he retains that domicile by *animus* alone; political or other conditions in his domicile of choice will explain his departure therefrom and may explain his disinclination to return.[99] Strictly, in all such cases where lack of free will is a factor, there is no need to justify failure to return, for the onus of proof lies on the party averring change from pre-existing established domicile. However, it may be necessary to try to refute the argument that the intention of the *propositus* for his domicile of choice has "withered away".[100] Continuing spiritual attachment to the domicile of choice may be easier to show, against a background of hostile political conditions.

A refugee has had the difficult option of remaining in adverse circumstances, or of flight; the state of mind of the *propositus* might be one of desire positively to adopt the legal system of refuge, or one simply of seeking a safe haven, careless of the legal system in which such refuge might be found. In the latter case, domicile of choice will not be acquired.[101]

Liability to be deported does not preclude the acquisition of a domicile in the country where the *propositus*'s residence is subject to termination,[102] nor even does the grant of a deportation order until it is carried out.[103] Such residence

---

[95] *Inland Revenue Commissioners v Duchess of Portland* [1982] Ch. 314.

[96] *Inland Revenue Commissioners v Duchess of Portland* [1982] Ch. 314, per Nourse J. at 318.

[97] *De Bonneval* (1838) 1 Curt. 856; *Re Martin* [1900] P. 211; *Boldrini* [1932] P. 9; *May v May* [1943] 2 All E.R. 146; *Cruh* [1945] 2 All E.R. 545; *Zanelli* [1948] 64 T.L.R. 556; *Re Lloyd Evans* [1947] Ch. 695; *Rev Comms v Matthews* (1958) 92 I.L.T.R. 44; *Puttick v Att Gen* [1979] 3 All E.R. 463.

[98] *Bell v Kennedy* (1868) 6 M. (H.L.) 69.

[99] *Re Lloyd Evans* [1947] Ch. 695; and *Rev Comms v Matthews* (1958) 92 I.L.T.R. 44.

[100] *Re Flynn (No.1)* [1968] 1 W.L.R. 103; *Tee* [1974] 1 W.L.R. 213; *Morgan v Cilento* [2004] EWHC 188 (Ch).

[101] *In re Martin* [1900] P. 211.

[102] *May* [1943] 2 All E.R. 146.

[103] *Cruh* [1945] 2 All E.R. 545, per Lord Denning at 546. Contrast *Re Lloyd Evans* [1947] Ch. 695. Consider also *Puttick* [1979] 3 All E.R. 463; and *Mark v Mark* [2005] 3 All E.R. 912 (para.6–16, above).

would be "precarious", and the *propositus* could entertain validly the intention of remaining so long as the authorities permit.

(4) Prisoners[104]

6–31 If a party's freedom to choose his residence for the time being is constrained by reason of the fact that he has been imprisoned, residence in the place of incarceration is involuntary and this is likely to preclude acquisition of a domicile of choice insofar as the nature of the residence will tend to indicate absence of intention to settle in that country.

(5) Debtors[105]

6–32 Flight from creditors may be a sufficient reason to doubt that free will prompts the actings of the *propositus*, yet in *Udny* there is no suggestion that Colonel Udny retained his English domicile of choice (if indeed he had acquired such a domicile) because of the enforced nature of his departure from England.[106] Udny's departure from England was final, and voluntary in a sense; but equally no attempt was made to persuade the court that in these circumstances he had acquired a domicile of choice in his place of refuge, France.

(6) Diplomatic and service personnel

6–33 A member of the diplomatic corps[107] or armed forces may acquire a domicile in a country to which he has been posted if there is the necessary change of intention as well as residence[108]:

"... there may co-exist with a residence, which has begun and is continued under military orders, facts and circumstances which establish a residence voluntary in

---

[104] *Burton v Fisher* (1828) Milward's Rep. 183; *Dunstan v Dunstan* (1858) 28 L.J.C.P. 97. The judgment in *Re the late Emperor Napoleon Bonaparte* (1853) 2 Rob. Ecc. 606, concerning the custody of Napoleon's will and codicils, concluded, not surprisingly, that he formed no voluntary intention to settle in the British territory of St Helena, and that he died domiciled in France. Napoleon was born in Corsica; after his defeat at Leipzig, he abdicated and was given the right to rule Elba. Having escaped from Elba he advanced on Paris and ruled for the "100 days" ending at the Battle of Waterloo. Then he was conveyed to St Helena as a prisoner of war and died there six years later, perhaps as a result of poison ("Scheele's Green", arsenic dye) leaking out of the wallpaper (or perhaps not).
[105] *Udny v Udny* (1869) 7 M. (H.L.) 89.
[106] cf. *Re Lloyd Evans* [1947] Ch. 695; *Rev Comms v Matthews* (1958) 92 I.T.L.R. 44.
[107] *Heath v Samson* (1851) 14 Beav. 441; *Att Gen v Kent* (1862) 1 H. & C. 12; *Sharpe v Crispin* (1869) L.R. 1 P. & D. 611; *Niboyet v Niboyet* (1878) L.R. 4 P.D. 1; *Udny* (1869) 7 M. (H.L.) 89 (the father of Col Udny was British Consul at Leghorn (Livorno) in Italy at the time of his son's birth, but Col Udny had Scottish domicile of origin).
[108] *Yelverton v Yelverton* (1859) 1 Sw. & Tr. 574; *Campbell v Campbell* (1861) 23 D. 256; *Brown v Smith* (1852) 15 Beav. 444; *Re Mitchell Ex p. Cunningham* (1884) L.R. 13 Q.B.D. 418; *Re Patience* (1885) L.R. 29 Ch. D. 976; *Re Macreight* (1885) L.R. 30 Ch. D. 165; *Sellars*, 1942 S.C. 206; *Donaldson v Donaldson* [1949] P. 363; *Willar*, 1954 S.C. 144; *Cruickshanks v Cruickshanks* [1957] 1 W.L.R. 564; and *Stone v Stone* [1958] 1 W.L.R. 1287.

character and chosen by the soldier, although it is a residence in the place in which he is stationed by the order of his military superiors."[109]

In principle, the same reasoning is applicable to posted workers.[110]

(7) Taxation

For UK Inland Revenue purposes, an artificial conception of domicile was introduced by the Finance Act 1975 s.45 (now repealed). This now is contained in the Inheritance Tax Act 1984 s.267,[111] which provides that a person who is not domiciled in the UK[112] at any given time shall be treated for inheritance tax purposes as if he were domiciled in the UK (and not elsewhere) at the relevant time if either:

6–34

(a)   he was domiciled in the UK within the three years immediately preceding the relevant time; or
(b)   he was resident in the UK in not less than 17 of the 20 years of assessment ending with the year of assessment in which the relevant time falls.

INSTANCES OF THE USE OF DOMICILE

Domicile is the connecting factor of choice in the areas of status and succession. It has long been used to judge legal capacity to marry,[113] consent to marry,[114] and associated applicable law issues in nullity proceedings. Likewise, for many years, domicile has been a connecting factor for the purposes of jurisdiction in consistorial proceedings.[115] It serves also in the matter of foreign divorce recognition,[116] operating in particular to protect "UK" domiciliaries purportedly divorced by extrajudicial means[117]; and in the related matter of applications for financial provision in Scotland following overseas divorce.[118]

6–35

---

[109] *Sellars*, 1942 S.C. 206, per Lord President Normand at 211.

[110] cf. Old cases concerning servants and officials such as government officials: *Inland Revenue Commissioners v Gordon's Executors* (1850) 12 D. 657; *Att Gen v Pottinger* (1861) 6 H. & N. 733; *Att Gen v Rowe* (1862) 1 H. & C. 31; *Fairbairn v Neville* (1897) 25 R. 192; *Cooney v Cooney*, 1950 S.L.T. (Notes) 1; and *Clarke v Newmarsh* (1836) 14 S. 488.

[111] See also Income Tax Act 2007 Pt 14 Chs 2 (Residence) and 2A (Domicile), and guidance on residence and domicile contained in HM Revenue and Customs, *Residence, Domicile and the Remittance Basis* (The Stationery Office, 2013), HMRC 6.

[112] In this connection, exceptionally, domicile is that of the "United Kingdom".

[113] e.g. *Mette* (1859) 1 Sw. & Tr. 416; *Brook* (1861) 9 H.L. Cas. 193; *Webster v Webster's Trustee* (1886) 14 R. 90; *Re De Wilton* [1900] 2 Ch. 481; *Re Bozzelli's Settlement* [1902] 1 Ch. 751; *Despatie v Tremblay* [1921] 1 A.C. 702; *Re Paine* [1940] Ch. 46; *Pugh v Pugh* [1951] P. 482; *Rojas, Petitioner*, 1967 S.L.T. (Sh. Ct.) 24; and now, s.38(2) of the Family Law (Scotland) Act 2006. Ch.11, below.

[114] *Szechter v Szechter* [1971] P. 286; *Sohrab v Kahn*, 2002 S.L.T. 1255; and *Singh v Singh*, 2005 S.L.T. 749; and s.38(2) of the Family Law (Scotland) Act 2006.

[115] DMPA 1973 ss.7–8; and Brussels II *bis* art.3.1(b). e.g. *Sekhri v Ray* [2014] EWCA Civ 119; [2014] 2 F.L.R. 1168; and *Divall v Divall* [2014] EWHC 95 (Fam); [2014] 2 F.L.R. 1104. Ch.12, below.

[116] Family Law Act 1986 s.46. Ch.12, below.

[117] Family Law Act 1986 s.46(2)(b).

[118] Matrimonial and Family Proceedings Act 1984 s.28. Ch.13, below.

In relation to children, domicile has a role to play in determining status as legitimate or not (insofar as that is still relevant), and in inter-country adoption. As regards recognition of foreign adoptions at common law, there is support for application of a principle of recognition on the basis of domicile,[119] that is, the domicile of the adoptive parents. Hedley J. in *In Re R (A Child) (Recognition of Indian Adoption)*[120] was required to interpret this area of law in light of abolition of spousal unity of domicile. Also within child law, domicile plays a significant part in cases concerning cross-border surrogacy. Such cases as presently come before UK courts tend to present as applications under s.54 of the Human Fertilisation & Embryology Act 2008 for a "parental order", namely, one which provides "for a child to be treated in law as the child of the applicants". It is a prerequisite of granting such an order that at the time of the application and the making of the order either or both of the applicants must be domiciled in the UK or in the Channel Islands or the Isle of Man.[121] In innominate and unusual circumstances in which there is no certain precedent, a UK court is likely to have resort to application of the law of the domicile of the affected party.[122]

A significant number of domicile cases arise within the area of wills and succession. According to Scots (and English) law, the connecting factor to regulate the succession, testate[123] or intestate,[124] to the moveable property of the deceased, is the *lex ultimi domicilii*, that is, the law of the domicile of the deceased at death.

In the same way that domicile acts as a gateway to a statutory remedy in the Human Fertilisation & Embryology Act 2008, so too domicile in England and Wales is used as a pre-condition for claims made in an English court under the Inheritance (Provision for Family and Dependants) Act 1975. By English domestic law, provision is made under that Act,[125] for claims to be made by a qualifying person who is dissatisfied by the terms of a will, and/or by the effect of the operation of the rules of intestacy, for a discretionary order for payment or property transfer out of the estate. This possibility exists only where the deceased

---

[119] *Re Wilson (Deceased)* [1954] Ch. 733; *Re Wilby* [1956] P. 174; *Re Marshall* [1957] Ch. 507; *Re Valentine's Settlement* [1965] Ch. 831; *Re N (Recognition of Foreign Adoption Order)* [2010] 1 F.L.R. 1102; [2010] Fam. Law 12; and *T v OCC* [2010] EWHC 964 (Fam); [2011] 1 F.L.R. 1487; [2011] Fam. Law 337.

[120] *In Re R (A Child) (Recognition of Indian Adoption)* [2012] EWHC 2956 (Fam); [2013] 1 F.L.R. 148 at [14].

[121] Human Fertilisation & Embryology Act 2008 s.54(4)(b). e.g. *Z v C (Parental Order: Domicile)* [2011] EWHC 3181 (Fam); [2012] 2 F.L.R. 797; *Re A (Parental Order: Domicile) v SA* [2013] EWHC 426 (Fam); *Re Q (A Child) (Parental Order: Domicile)* [2014] EWHC 1307 (Fam); [2014] Fam. Law 1256; and *Re G (Parental Orders)* [2014] EWHC 1561 (Fam); [2014] Fam. Law 1114.

[122] e.g. *Re S (Hospital Patient: Foreign Curator)* [1995] 4 All E.R. 30.

[123] *Groos v Groos* [1915] 1 Ch. 572 (and earlier *In the Estate of Groos* [1904] P. 269).

[124] *Lashley v Hog* (1804) 4 Pat. 581; *Maxwell v McClure* (1857) 20 D. 307; affirmed 3 Macq. 852. In England: *Lynch v Provisional Government of Paraguay* (1871) L.R. 2 P. & D. 268; and *Re Haji-Ioannou (Deceased)*, sub nom. *Haji-Ioannou v Frangos* [2009] EWHC 2310 (QB).

[125] As amended by the Inheritance and Trustees' Powers Act 2014.

died domiciled in England and Wales[126]: the so-called "domicile gateway".[127] A number of such claims presenting domicile issues arises annually before the English courts.[128]

THE RULES OF DOMICILE—A PRÉCIS

The development of the rules of domicile in Scots and English law has been characterised by steady common law progression, punctuated by legislative intervention on particular matters. The rules are largely a construct of the common law, and statutory reform of the classic domicile rules, though significant in content, is late in date and specific in nature. Knowledge of the subject of domicile requires not only a grasp of its technical rules, but also familiarity with cases, in which the topic is rich.

6–36

The rules, summarised, are set out below[129]:

(a)   Domicile is a unitary concept, meaning that its rules remain the same, in whichever area of private law it is called into play—marriage, succession, child law or other area of personal law.

(b)   No person can be without a domicile, though they may lack a home in fact[130] and/or may have no knowledge of the concept of a legal home. Equally, where an individual has two or more homes, the fact that his chief and favourite residence is situated in country A may not dissuade a court from finding him to be domiciled, by application of the forum's rules, in country B.

(c)   No person can have more than one domicile (in the classic sense) at any one time.

(d)   Prior to the coming into force of the 2006 Act, *domicile of origin* was ascribed according to fixed rules, which rested on the distinction between legitimacy and illegitimacy. The Law Reform (Parent and Child) (Scotland) Act 1986, by s.9(1)(a)[131] retained the rule of law whereby a child born outside marriage took as a domicile of origin the domicile possessed by his mother at the date of his birth, affirming therefore the common law rule (applying still in England), that domicile of origin is ascribed according to status as legitimate or illegitimate.

(e)   Section 22 of the 2006 Act effected a change in the domicile rules of Scots law concerning the domicile of persons under 16 years of age ("*under-16*

---

[126] Inheritance (Provision for Family and Dependants) Act 1975 s.1(1).

[127] E.B. Crawford and J.M. Carruthers, "The Law of Unintended Consequences: The Inheritance and Trustees' Powers Bill", 2014 Edin.L.R. 18(1) 133.

[128] e.g. *Wilson v Jones (Preliminary Issue)* unreported, HC99/00157 High Court of Justice, Chancery Division (8 June 2000); *Gully v Dix* [2004] 1 W.L.R. 1399; *Robinson v Bird* [2003] EWHC 30 (Ch); *Morgan v Cilento* [2004] EWHC 188 (Ch); *Agulian v Cyganik* [2006] EWCA Civ 129; *Holliday v Musa* [2010] EWCA Civ 335; *Peters v Pinder* [2011] WTLR 1399; and *Sylvester v Sylvester* [2014] WTLR 127.

[129] cf. *Sekhri v Ray* [2014] EWCA Civ 119, McFarlane L.J. at [10]; citing Arden L.J. in *Barlow Clowes International Limited v Henwood* [2008] EWCA Civ 77 at [8].

[130] Thus, where the *propositus* was found to have led a nomadic existence, living in lodgings or with friends, she was held not to have lost her Scots domicile of origin: *Arnott v Groom* (1846) 9 D. 142.

[131] Repealed by Family Law (Scotland) Act 2006 Sch.3.

domicile"). The general rule is that if a child's parents are domiciled in the same country as each other, and the child has a home with either or both parent(s), the child shall be domiciled in the same country as his parents. Where these conditions are not satisfied, the child shall be domiciled in the country with which he has for the time being, in the view of the Scots forum, the closest connection. The tacit assumption is that s.22 applies, not only for the purposes of ascription of domicile at birth, but at any time during the first 16 years of the *propositus's* life. The Act does not make plain the effect of the change wrought by s.22 in temporal terms, beyond the basic rule that s.22 applies in cases arising in a Scots court after May 4, 2006.

(f)   In Scots law prior to the 2006 Act, and in English law still, an individual's domicile, during nonage, would/will be dependent upon the domicile of his father or mother, depending on the child's status, and on the application if appropriate of s.4 of the DMPA 1973, in terms of which the domicile of an under-age party will change if a change should occur in the domicile of the relevant parent. By virtue of s.22 of the 2006 Act, an individual's domicile at any given point under the age of 16 will be determined by application of that section. The 2006 Act, in Sch.3, repeals, only for Scotland, s.4 of the DMPA 1973.

(g)   Legal capacity in Scots law to have an independent domicile depends upon having attained the age of 16 and upon being of sufficient mental capacity to form the requisite intention.

(h)   Every person sui juris may acquire a *domicile of choice* by combination of change of residence to a different legal system and the intention to reside in that system for as long as can be seen ahead. At common law, unless and until a domicile of choice was acquired, the domicile of origin remained: a continuance principle. Under the 2006 Act, the under-16 domicile will continue in equivalent circumstances. Any circumstances, even the seemingly trivial, which seem to bear upon residence and/or intention may be considered by the court in assessing acquisition of domicile of choice, and it is the duty of counsel to bring all potentially relevant matters to the attention of the court.

(i)   Domicile of choice is lost by a combination of loss of residence in, *and* loss of intention for, a legal system. Retention of *either* residence or intention will result in retention of domicile of choice. When a domicile of choice is lost, the domicile of origin revives to fill the gap and remains in place unless/until a new domicile of choice is acquired.[132] It is not known whether or not a principle of revival of "under-16" domicile will operate, by way of analogy.

(j)   There is a presumption in favour of an existing domicile. The onus of proof of change of domicile lies on the party arguing that change has taken place.

(k)   All conflict of laws rules which use the connecting factor of domicile must be qualified as to time, and a *tempus inspiciendum* specified, e.g. capacity to marry—*ante-nuptial* domicile of each party, cumulatively applied;

---

[132] *Udny v Udny* (1869) 7 M. (H.L.) 89.

succession to moveables—deceased's domicile *at death*. In the ascertainment of intention, the court is precluded from taking into account factors pertaining to residence or deemed intention which post-date that time.[133]

(l)   Until 1 January 1974 the domicile of a married woman depended upon the domicile of her husband, but s.1 of the DMPA 1973 abolished the "unity of domicile" rule in the case of persons married after that date.

(m)   In questions which have arisen in the courts of Scotland and England, domicile is always ascertained in accordance with the rules of the *lex fori*.[134] This will include determination of legal capacity to acquire a new domicile.

REFORM

The Scots and English rules of domicile, often criticised, provide a delicate tool to aid the securing of an appropriate result in certain important areas of status, family law and succession. In 1985, proposals were made to reform the rules,[135] and after consultation, the Law Commissions produced in 1987 recommendations contained in *Private International Law: The Law of Domicile*. The Commissions concluded that domicile should be retained as a connecting factor in the international private law of England and Wales, Scotland and Northern Ireland. However, they suggested the making of substantial changes in the detail of the then law. These changes were not implemented.[136]

6–37

The problem of taxation of "non-domiciliaries", i.e. long-term British residents who, under the current rules of domicile argue that they have not acquired English/Scots domicile of choice, has been addressed not by changing the rules of burden or standard of proof of acquisition of domicile of choice, but by exacting from such persons an annual lump sum payment to the UK Treasury in exchange for permitting them the tax advantages of their status in respect of earnings outside the UK.

As has been seen above, the domicile change effected in Scots law by the Family Law (Scotland) Act 2006, prompted by the desire to treat all children equally, in domicile as in other matters, has weakened, by inadvertence or design, the previously strong structure of the domicile rules. The expanding European conflict of laws family law programme, which favours the connecting factor of

---

[133] *Lynch v Provisional Government of Paraguay* (1871) L.R. 2 P.&D. 268; *Bell v Kennedy* (1868) 6 M. (H.L.) 69; *Morgan v Cilento* [2004] EWHC 188 (Ch); and *Cyganik v Agulian* [2006] EWCA Civ 129, per Mummery L.J. at [46].

[134] *Re Annesley* [1926] Ch. 692. See, however, exceptionally Family Law Act 1986 s.46(5).

[135] Law Commission and Scottish Law Commission, *Private International Law: The Law of Domicile* (HMSO, 1985), Law Com. Working Paper No.88; Scot. Law Com. Memo. No.63. There had been earlier attempts to reform the rules. The report of the Wynn-Parry Committee (HMSO, 1954), Cmd. 9068 had recommended abolition of domicile of origin, a continuance rule, independent domicile for judicially separated wives, and the dependence of a child's domicile upon that of the party having custody. Domicile Bills had been introduced in 1958 and 1959, but each was withdrawn. Further recommendations on domicile, not acted on, were contained in the Private International Law Committee, *Seventh Report of the Lord Chancellor's Private International Law Committee, 1963* (HMSO, 1963), Cmnd.1955.

[136] *Private International Law: The Law of Domicile*, 1987, Law Com. No.168; Scot. Law Com. No.107, para.8.7.

habitual residence (q.v.), may mean that the failure to adopt the Law Commissions' recommendations to "modernise" the rules of domicile is less significant than would have been thought, because the area in which domicile in its traditional sense is used as a connecting factor is subject to erosion.

SPECIAL STATUTORY DEFINITION OF DOMICILE FOR CIVIL AND COMMERCIAL JURISDICTION

6–38   A different meaning and usage of the term "domicile" is found as a major connecting factor in the framework of rules of civil and commercial jurisdiction and judgment enforcement known as the Brussels regime.[137] Article 2 of the Brussels I Regulation/art.4 of the Brussels I Recast Regulation establish as the pre-eminent ground of jurisdiction the "domicile" of the defender.[138] "Domicile" in this context bears no relation to domicile in its classic meaning. The purpose of ascribing domicile in this connection is to clothe a court with jurisdiction in a civil or commercial matter, as opposed to a matter of status, and therefore it is appropriate that the criterion should be presumptively established after the expiry of only a short period of time. The definition or indicia of domicile in its classic sense, including capacity to acquire domicile, is the prerogative of the forum to decide. But an EU Member State forum's role with regard to the meaning of domicile within the Brussels regime is different, viz.: art.59.1 of the Brussels I Regulation/art.62.1 of the Brussels I Recast Regulation provides that in order to determine whether a party is domiciled in a Member State whose courts are seised of the matter, the court shall apply its internal law. The definition of the "domicile" of natural persons is left to the discretion of individual Member States. For the UK, the statutory definition, found in CJJO 2001 Sch.1 para.9,[139] is to the effect that an individual is domiciled in the UK or part thereof if and only if he is resident there, and the nature and circumstances of his residence indicate that he has a substantial connection with the UK. "Substantial connection" is presumed to be fulfilled, unless the contrary is proved, if the individual has been resident in the UK or part thereof for the last three months.[140] There is no bar to substantial connection being found on the basis of less than three months residence.

Article 59.2 of the Brussels I Regulation/art.62.2 of the Brussels I Recast Regulation provide, by contrast, that if a party is (alleged) not to be domiciled in the Member State of the forum, then in order to determine whether the party is domiciled in another Member State, the forum shall apply the law of that other Member State.[141]

---

[137] Ch.7, below.

[138] Civil Jurisdiction and Judgments Act 1982 ss.41–46; and now Civil Jurisdiction and Judgments Order 2001 (SI 2001/3929) Sch.1 reg.9. Ch.7, below.

[139] Amending CJJA 1982 s.41.

[140] CJJO 2001 Sch.1 para.9(6).

[141] e.g. *Haji-Ioannou v Frangos* [1999] 2 All E.R. (Comm) 865. This is worthy of remark from the perspective also that in the usage of classic domicile, the forum applies its own law to all determinations of domicile: *Re Annesley* [1926] Ch. 692.

NATIONALITY

Although in English speaking countries the law of domicile applies generally in **6–39** questions of personal law, nationality is a connecting factor employed by the conflict rules of many other countries. Historically, domicile was pre-eminent, but nationality was substituted as the preferred personal law in France by the Code Napoleon 1804, and this approach was adopted in Belgium and Luxembourg, with similar provisions following in Austria and Holland.

Each country has its own rules as to nationality and when any question arises as to whether a person is a subject of a particular state, the matter is determined by the law of that state and (unlike domicile) not by the law of the forum.[142] This is subject only to the exception that changes of nationality are not regarded as being effective during times of war,[143] although they become effective on the termination of war.

The rules regarding British nationality were based on two principles: birth **6–40** within the territory of Great Britain; and descent. The modern period of the law on this subject might be said to begin with the British Nationality Act 1948 which introduced the status of citizen of the United Kingdom and Colonies. The position is governed now by the British Nationality Act 1981,[144] which abolished that citizenship and substituted three categories of citizenship, namely, British citizenship (Pt I of the 1981 Act); British Overseas Territories citizenship (Pt II of the 1981 Act); and British Overseas citizenship.[145]

It is has been said that domicile yields an appropriate, but sometimes **6–41** unpredictable result, whereas nationality normally is easily ascertained, but may not be appropriate as a connecting factor for the purposes of status and capacity. Each factor has certain demerits. As far as a person's domicile is concerned, it may be found to be in a place which has little or no connection with his home in the colloquial sense. Likewise, a person's nationality may have no connection with the country where he lives. The rule of revival of domicile of origin may produce anomalies. Long residence in a country in itself is of no avail, leading to unpredictability, and intention is difficult to prove. Consequently, in a complex case, uncertainty exists until judicial decision on domicile. Judicial consideration of the life in question will be sensitive and careful, but lengthy and expensive. Moreover, the effect of s.22 of the 2006 Act is destabilising. With nationality, however, the problem of statelessness[146] and possibility of dual nationality mean that the apposite connecting factor may not be obvious, or might even be absent. Most problematically, nationality cannot be applied to questions of personal law in countries such as the UK, which contain different units each having a different system of law.

---

[142] *Stoeck v Public Trustee* [1921] 2 Ch. 67.

[143] *Oppenheimer v Cattermole* [1975] 1 All E.R. 538.

[144] For a full review of earlier authorities, see *Att Gen v HRH Prince Ernest Augustus of Hanover* [1957] A.C. 436; affirming [1956] Ch. 188; reversing [1955] Ch. 440.

[145] See also British Nationality (Hong Kong) Act 1997; British Overseas Territories Act 2002; Nationality, Immigration and Asylum Act 2002; Immigration, Asylum and Nationality Act 2006; and Borders, Citizenship and Immigration Act 2009 Pt 2.

[146] *Kramer v Att Gen* [1923] A.C. 528; *Re Chamberlain's Settlement* [1921] 2 Ch. 533.

RESIDENCE

6–42   Residence increasingly is found to be a useful connecting factor in legislation. From the mid-20th century onwards,[147] its importance has tended to assert itself in the area of consistorial jurisdiction, and consequently in the rules of recognition of foreign decrees, where the granting court had assumed jurisdiction on a corresponding basis.[148] In some instances Parliament specified the length of time necessary to satisfy the residence rule in question; in such cases the main problem likely to arise is the necessary qualifying period and the extent to which interruptions can be tolerated.[149] Such time specifications ensure the existence of what is thought to be a sufficient link between the petitioner and the court to which he seeks access, or the decree which he wishes to have enforced.

HABITUAL RESIDENCE

Introduction

6–43   Increasingly in modern conflict rules, the connecting factor of *habitual residence* is employed, particularly in family law: divorce and nullity jurisdiction and recognition; custody and abduction; guardianship and protection of children; and adoption. It has a role also in the commercial sphere. The factor has achieved a favoured status in international harmonisation instruments, and is now a favourite of convention and regulation.

From the 1970s onwards British judges have attempted to define the concept, e.g. "a regular physical presence which must endure for some time".[150] "In our opinion a habitual residence is one which is being enjoyed voluntarily for the time being and with the settled intention that it should continue for some time".[151] "An appreciable period of time and a settled intention will be necessary to enable him or her to become [habitually resident]."[152]

The words habitual residence should bear their ordinary and natural meaning; the term is not a term of art, but rather a matter of fact. There is a wealth of academic discussion upon the meaning and nature of "habitual residence",[153]

---

[147] e.g. Matrimonial Causes Act 1937 s.13; Law Reform (Miscellaneous Provisions) Act 1949 ss.1, 2.

[148] *Travers v Holley* [1953] P. 246.

[149] *Land v Land*, 1962 S.L.T. 316 (cf. *Hopkins v Hopkins* [1951] P. 116); contrast *Cabel v Cabel*, 1974 S.L.T. 295 (cf. *Stransky v Stransky* [1954] P. 428).

[150] *Cruse v Chittum* [1974] 2 All E.R. 940.

[151] Lord President Hope in *Dickson v Dickson*, 1990 S.C.L.R. 692 at 703, agreeing with Lord Scarman in *R. v Barnet LBC Ex p. Shah* [1983] 2 A.C. 309 at 342, 343, that the concept is the same for all practical purposes as ordinary residence. Doubt, however, was cast upon the rationale of *Shah* vis-à-vis a child's habitual residence in *A v A (Children: Habitual Residence) (Reunite International Child Abduction Centre and others intervening)* [2013] UKSC 60, per Baroness Hale of Richmond at [54].

[152] *Re J (A Minor) (Abduction: Custody Rights)* [1990] 2 A.C. 562 (in the House of Lords sub nom. *C v S* [1990] 2 All E.R. 961 HL, per Lord Brandon at 965).

[153] See E.B. Crawford, "'Habitual Residence of the Child' as the Connecting Factor in Child Abduction Cases: A Consideration of Recent Cases", 1992 J.R. 177; E.B. Crawford "A Day is Not Enough: Further Views on the Meaning of Habitual Residence", 2000 J.R. 89; E.B. Crawford, "Case Analysis: *Gingi v Secretary of State for Work and Pensions*" (2003) 10 J.S.S.L. 52; E.B. Crawford,

debates upon whether its meaning differs from that of "residence" or "ordinary residence",[154] and upon its indicia generally in matters such as the necessity for "voluntariness" (at the outset? or throughout?); for "settled intention"; for "lawfulness" of residence[155]; the conditions required for its acquisition and loss; the hunt for guidelines as to how long residence takes to qualify as habitual as opposed to ordinary; whether a person can be without an habitual residence, or whether he can have more than one habitual residence simultaneously.[156] In other words, it seems necessary to furnish this connecting factor with a number of fixed rules, of the type of which domicile has been possessed for more than a century; and this despite the fact it is the vaunted characteristic of habitual residence that it is a factual, common sense notion, readily understandable by the person in the street.

In addition to these general points, it must be asked whether, unlike domicile, the meaning of habitual residence varies according to context. Habitual residence decisions, like domicile cases, are particular to their facts, and so their status as precedents must be treated with caution. It is a fragmented concept, certainly as between subject areas in which it is used (e.g. as between child law and contract law), albeit of late there has been an attempt in the higher courts to settle upon its meaning within a given area of private law (e.g. conflict rules affecting children). Although there are instances of autonomous definitions within legislation, the concept has been left largely to judicial interpretation.

At the start of its use in the modern era, its meaning inevitably varied from one national forum to another, but as the connecting factor has become embedded in European law, a common European interpretation is beginning to emerge, at least within discrete subject areas. It cannot be said, however, that an EU meaning for one purpose, e.g. jurisdiction in parental responsibility matters, can be transposed to another, e.g. choice of law in delict per Rome II.

Matters of parental responsibility

Habitual residence of a child plays an important role in relation to jurisdiction in matters of parental responsibility.[157] The concept of habitual residence is not defined in either Brussels II *bis* or in the 1996 Hague Children Convention, but will be determined by the judge in each case on the basis of factual elements, and in light of the objectives and purpose of the instrument. The ECJ in *Proceedings Brought by A*[158] gave an autonomous definition of habitual residence for the purpose of Brussels II *bis* art.8, viz.:

6–44

"Payment postponed: exploring the extent of *Nessa's* authority", 2003 JSSL 10(1), 52; E. Clive, "The Concept of Habitual Residence", 1997 J.R. 137; E. Clive, "The New Hague Convention on Children", 1998 J.R. 169; and P. Rogerson, "Habitual Residence: The New Domicile?" (2000) 49 I.C.L.Q. 86.

[154] The English Court of Appeal in *In Re P-J (Children)*[2009] EWCA Civ 588 held that, for purposes of child abduction, "habitual residence" and "ordinary residence" are interchangeable concepts and there is no difference in the core meaning to be given to the two phrases.

[155] The view that lawfulness of presence was not a prerequisite of a finding of habitual residence received support from the House of Lords decision in *Mark v Mark* [2005] 3 All E.R. 912, at least with regard to its meaning for the purposes of s.5 of the DMPA 1973.

[156] *C v FC* [2004] 1 F.L.R. 362.

[157] Brussels II *bis* art.8; and 1996 Hague Convention art.5. See also ss.9 and 41 of the Family Law Act 1986.

[158] *Proceedings Brought by A* (C-523/07) [2009] I.L.Pr. 39.

"[I]n addition to the physical presence of the child in a Member State other factors must be chosen which are capable of showing that that presence is not in any way temporary or intermittent .... *the concept of 'habitual residence' under Article 8(1) of Regulation No 2201/2003 must be interpreted as meaning that it corresponds to the place which reflects some degree of integration by the child in a social and family environment.* To that end, in particular the duration, regularity, conditions and reasons for the stay on the territory of a Member State and the family's move to that State, the child's nationality, the place and conditions of attendance at school, linguistic knowledge and the family and social relationships of the child in that State must be taken into consideration. It is for the national court to establish the habitual residence of the child, taking account of all the circumstances specific to each individual case."[159]

In *Mercredi v Chaffe*[160] the CJEU held that:

"53. The social and family environment of the child, which is fundamental in determining the place where the child is habitually resident, comprises various factors which vary according to the age of the child. The factors to be taken into account in the case of a child of school age are thus not the same as those to be considered in the case of a child who has left school and are again not the same as those relevant to an infant.

54. As a general rule, the environment of a young child is essentially a family environment determined by the reference person(s) with whom the child lives, by whom the child is in fact looked after and taken care of.

55. That is even more true where the child concerned is an infant. An infant necessarily shares the social and family environment of the circle of people on whom he or she is dependent."

These principles, expressed in relation to infants and young children, have been endorsed by the UK Supreme Court in *Re LC (Children) (International Abduction: Child's Objections to Return)*[161] and *A v A (Children: Habitual Residence) (Reunite International Child Abduction Centre and others intervening)*.[162]

International child abduction

6–45   The impetus for the upsurge in the use of habitual residence as a connecting factor can be traced to the 1980 Hague Convention on the Civil Aspects of International Child Abduction, where the "habitual residence of the child" is the key factor, prompting in many forums consideration of the characteristics of

---

[159] *Proceedings Brought by A* (C-523/07) [2009] I.L.Pr. 39, summary, [2], [3]; also [33], [35], [38], [44] (Emphasis added).
[160] *Mercredi v Chaffe* (C-497/10 PPU) [2011] I.L.Pr. 23 at [53]–[55] (and subsequently, in the English Court of Appeal, [2011] EWCA Civ 272; [2011] 2 F.L.R. 515). See also *C v M* (Case C-376/14PPU) [2015] 2 W.L.R. 59. See also *Re LC (Children) (International Abduction: Child's Objections to Return)* [2014] UKSC 1; [2014] A.C. 1038, per Lord Wilson at [35].
[161] *Re LC (Children) (International Abduction: Child's Objections to Return)* [2014] UKSC 1; [2014] A.C. 1038, per Lord Wilson at [35]–[36].
[162] *A v A (Children: Habitual Residence) (Reunite International Child Abduction Centre and others intervening)* [2013] UKSC 60, per Baroness Hale at [54]. See also *Re F (A Child) (Care Proceedings: Habitual Residence)* [2014] EWCA Civ 789.

habitual residence, how it may be lost, and how it may be gained.[163] Since it is not usual for a child to be financially independent, his residence is almost always dependent (factually; and therefore legally?) upon the wishes and actings of the parent upon whom he depends.

The factor is in a state of constant refinement in the light of circumstances presenting. In *Re P-J (Children)*[164] the English Court of Appeal held it to be "established" that the expression "habitually resident" is not to be treated as a term of art with some special meaning, but is to be understood according to the ordinary and natural meaning of the two words which it contains; and further, that whether or not a person is habitually resident in a specified country is a question of fact to be decided by reference to all the circumstances of the particular case.

Despite the assertion that the factor is a common sense one, it should never be thought that the judicial resolution of an habitual residence point will be predictable.[165]

It is in the nature of abduction cases that the family circumstances are abnormal. Such a case was *A v A (Children) (Habitual Residence)*,[166] in which there was posed to the UK Supreme Court the question whether or not it was right to attribute to a child an habitual residence in England and Wales, when that child had not ever been present in the UK, but where his mother and elder siblings ("the family unit") was habitually resident there. A resolution to the instant case was found in the *parens patriae* jurisdiction of the English court qua nationality, obviating the need formally to decide the habitual residence question. Baroness Hale seized the opportunity which the case presented to draw together a summary of the principles concerning habitual residence of a child[167]:

> "[54] Drawing the threads together, therefore:
> (i)   All are agreed that habitual residence is a question of fact and not a legal concept such as domicile. There is no legal rule akin to that whereby a child automatically takes the domicile of his parents.
> (ii)   It was the purpose of the [Family Law Act] 1986 … to adopt a concept which was the same as that adopted in the Hague and European [Child Abduction] Conventions. The [Brussels II *bis*] Regulation must also be interpreted consistently with those Conventions.
> (iii)   The test adopted by the European court is 'the place which reflects some degree of integration by the child in a social and family environment' in the country concerned. This depends on numerous factors, including the reasons for the family's stay in the country in question.
> (iv)   It is now unlikely that that test would produce any different results from that hitherto adopted in the English courts under the 1986 Act and the Hague Child Abduction Convention.

---

[163] *Re J (A Minor) (Abduction: Custody Rights)* [1990] 2 A.C. 562 at 578, 579; *Re N (Child Abduction: Habitual Residence)* [1993] 2 F.L.R. 124; *Re R (Wardship: Child Abduction) (No.2)* [1993] 1 F.L.R. 249; *Al-H v F* [2001] EWCA Civ 186; [2001] 1 F.L.R. 951; *Re R (Abduction: Habitual Residence)* [2003] EWHC 1968; [2004] 1 F.L.R. 216; *Re D (Abduction: Habitual Residence)* [2005] EWHC 518; [2005] 2 F.L.R. 403; *Re A (Abduction: Consent: Habitual Residence: Consent)* [2005] EWHC 2998; [2006] 2 F.L.R. 1; *E v E* [2007] EWHC 276; [2007] Fam. Law 480; and *W v F* [2007] EWHC 779 (Fam); (2007) 104(18) L.S.G. 28.

[164] *Re P-J (Children) (Abduction: Habitual Residence: Consent)* [2009] EWCA Civ 588.

[165] *Re S (A Child) (Habitual Residence)* [2009] EWCA Civ 1021.

[166] *A v A (Children) (Habitual Residence)* [2013] UKSC 60; [2014] A.C. 1.

[167] *A v A and another (Children: Habitual Residence) (Reunite International Child Abduction Centre and others intervening)* [2013] UKSC 60, per Baroness Hale of Richmond at [54]–[58].

(v)   In my view, the test adopted by the European court is preferable to that earlier adopted by the English courts, being focussed on the situation of the child, with the purposes and intentions of the parents being merely one of the relevant factors. The test derived from *R v Barnet London Borough Council, Ex p Nilish Shah* [1983] 2 AC 309 should be abandoned when deciding the habitual residence of a child.

(vi)   The social and family environment of an infant or young child is shared with those (whether parents or others) on whom he is dependent. Hence it is necessary to assess the integration of that person or persons in the social and family environment of the country concerned.

(vii)   The essentially factual and individual nature of the inquiry should not be glossed with legal concepts which would produce a different result from that which the factual inquiry would produce.

(viii)   As the Advocate General pointed out in opinion, para 45 and the court confirmed in judgment, para 43 of *Proceedings brought by A* (Case C-523/07) [2010] Fam 42, it is possible that a child may have no country of habitual residence at a particular point in time.[55] So which approach accords most closely with the factual situation of the child – an approach which holds that presence is a necessary precursor to residence and thus to habitual residence or an approach which focusses on the relationship between the child and his primary carer? In my view, it is the former. It is one thing to say that a child's integration in the place where he is at present depends on the degree of integration of his primary carer. It is another thing to say that he can be integrated in a place to which his primary carer has never taken him. It is one thing to say that a person can remain habitually resident in a country from which he is temporarily absent. It is another thing to say that a person can acquire a habitual residence without ever setting foot in a country. It is one thing to say that a child is integrated in the family environment of his primary carer and siblings. It is another thing to say that he is also integrated into the social environment of a country where he has never been. [56] However, I cannot be confident that this is *acte clair* for the purpose of European Union law … .. … [58] Hence I would not feel able to dispose of this case on the basis that Haroon was not habitually resident in England and Wales on [the relevant date] without making a reference to the Court of Justice. But we can only refer a question to the court if it is necessary for us to determine the case before us. For the reasons which will appear below, it is not at present so necessary."

Therefore the apparent possibility held out in *A v A (Children) (Habitual Residence)*,[168] that a young child might be held in law habitually resident in a place where he has never been present, should be regarded as no more than a possibility.

Notably, UK courts, including the Supreme Court in *A v A (Children) (Habitual Residence)*,[169] have adopted in cases falling to be decided under the 1980 Hague Convention, the meaning of habitual residence as formulated by the ECJ in relation to art.8(1) of Brussels II *bis* in *Proceedings Brought by A*.[170] This synthesis is desirable. Less desirable is the notion introduced by the Supreme Court in *Re LC (Children) (International Abduction: Child's Objections to*

---

[168] *A v A (Children) (Habitual Residence)* [2013] UKSC 60; [2014] A.C. 1.
[169] *A v A (Children) (Habitual Residence)* [2013] UKSC 60; [2014] A.C. 1.
[170] *Proceedings Brought by A* (C-523/07) [2009] I.L.Pr. 39.

Return),[171] particularly in relation to adolescent children,[172] that "... [the child's] state of mind is relevant to whether or not they have acquired a habitual residence in the place where they are living."[173] It is the use by the ECJ of the word "integration" which has led the UK Supreme Court to the view that the state of mind of (adolescent) children during their residence in a place may affect whether that residence is to be regarded as habitual. This gloss, introducing a mental element, seems to be at odds with the assertion that habitual residence is to be understood according to the ordinary and natural meaning of the two words which it contains.

Unilateralism

Where wrongful removal or retention[174] is said to have occurred, the question whether the removing parent may establish for the child an habitual residence in the "new" country is a crucial one. Examples can be found of legislative provisions designed to secure (for a limited period, by means of a "deeming" provision)[175] in favour of the court of the abandoned legal system, continuing jurisdiction to adjudicate upon the case.

    It was established early[176] in the corpus of case law interpretative of the 1980 Hague Convention that it should not be possible for a parent to effect a change in the habitual residence of a child through unilateral wrongful actings, that is to say, although as a matter of fact, the child might be residing in the legal system to which he has been removed, in law his habitual residence remains the legal system from which he has been taken. This was reiterated in *B v D*,[177] in the form that no unilateral action by a parent can change a child's habitual residence except by agreement or acquiescence over time by the bereft parent, or by judicial determination. Further support was provided by Lord Glennie in *A v N*.[178] The rule that the court addressed must take account of the fact that the child may have "settled" in its new environment, and also of factors such as alleged acquiescence by the bereft parent, means that provisions of the 1980 Hague Convention may operate to produce a situation in which the elapse of time produces a new status quo, resulting effectively in a (potentially) unwelcome incursion into the principle that a child's habitual residence may not be affected by wrongful actings. There will come a point in a life history at which it would be perverse to regard a person as habitually resident at any place other than that of his established physical presence, whatever view be taken of the need for free will at

6-46

---

[171] *Re LC (Children) (International Abduction: Child's Objections to Return)* [2014] UKSC 1; [2014] A.C. 1038 at [30]–[37] and [57]–[58].

[172] But also, per Baroness Hale, in relation to a younger child: *Re LC (Children) (International Abduction: Child's Objections to Return)* [2014] UKSC 1; [2014] A.C. 1038 at [57]–[58].

[173] *Re LC (Children) (International Abduction: Child's Objections to Return)* [2014] UKSC 1; [2014] A.C. 1038 at [58].

[174] Ch.14, below.

[175] That the child will be deemed still to be habitually resident in the erstwhile habitual residence. See, e.g. Family Law Act 1986 s.41(1)(b) and Brussels II *bis* art.10. Ch.14, below.

[176] *Re J (A Minor) (Abduction: Custody Rights)* [1990] 2 A.C. 562; in the House of Lords sub nom. *C v S* [1990] 2 All E.R. 961.

[177] *B v D* [2008] EWHC 1246 (Fam). cf. *Re ML and AL (Children) (Contact Order: Brussels II Regulation) (No.1)* [2006] EWHC 2385 (Fam).

[178] *A v N*, 2007 G.W.D. 01-02.

the outset (inception) of residence. This would mean that habitual residence initially brought about by residence through coercion of any kind must take longer to establish, but must be capable of being established. But there is an observable drift towards unilateralism, i.e. that a change in a child's habitual residence is capable of being effected by the unilateral actings of one parent.

The way was paved by Baroness Hale in *DL v EL (Hague Abduction Convention: Effect of Reversal of Return Order on Appeal)*[179]: "Both Lord Hughes JSC and I also questioned whether it was necessary to maintain the rule, hitherto firmly established in English law, that (where both parents have equal status in relation to the child) one parent could not unilaterally change the habitual residence of a child . . . such a bright line rule certainly furthers the policy of discouraging child abductions, but if not carefully qualified it is capable of leading to absurd results . . .".[180]

In 2015, the UK Supreme Court, in *In re R (Children) (Reunite International Child Abduction Centre and others intervening)*,[181] upheld the decision of the Extra Division of the Inner House in *R, Petitioner*,[182] to the effect that the Lord Ordinary had erred in identifying a shared parental intention to move permanently to Scotland as an essential element in any alteration in the children's habitual residence from France to Scotland; and in failing to consider whether or not on all the evidence the residence had the necessary quality of stability. The Supreme Court considered that the Extra Division[183] had considered the evidence on a proper understanding of the nature of habitual residence. Accordingly, the conclusion that the children were habitually resident in Scotland at the material time was one which the Extra Division had been entitled to reach, and in the light of that conclusion, it could not be said that the children had been wrongfully retained in Scotland.

Echoing its own recent pronouncements, the Supreme Court stated that habitual residence is a question of fact which requires an evaluation of all the relevant circumstances; and that there is no requirement for a finding of habitual residence that a child should have been resident in the country in question for a particular period of time or that there should be an intention on the part of one or both parents to reside there permanently or indefinitely. In the Supreme Court's determination, that which is important is the stability of the residence and not whether it is of a permanent character. The focus ought to be on the situation of the child, the parents' purposes and intentions being merely one of the (subsidiarily) relevant factors. On the important question of unilateralism, the

---

[179] *DL v EL (Hague Abduction Convention: Effect of Reversal of Return Order on Appeal)* [2013] UKSC 75; [2014] A.C. 1017 at [21].

[180] *DL v EL (Hague Abduction Convention: Effect of Reversal of Return Order on Appeal)* [2013] UKSC 75; [2014] A.C. 1017 at [22].

[181] *In re R (Children) (Reunite International Child Abduction Centre and others intervening)* [2015] UKSC 35, [2015] 2 W.L.R. 1583.

[182] *In re R (Children) (Reunite International Child Abduction Centre and others intervening)* [2014] CSIH 95, 2014 SLT 1080.

[183] Which had been expressly influenced by Baroness Hale's affirmation in *DL v EL (Hague Abduction Convention: Effect of Reversal of Return Order on Appeal)* [2013] UKSC 75; [2014] A.C. 1017, at [21] that there is no rule that a child's habitual residence must reflect a shared parental intent. See, e.g. per Lord Malcolm, at [17]: "[I]f parents have agreed to only a time limited residence in another country with one parent, that does not prevent a change in their children's habitual residence once they are living and settled in their new home."

Supreme Court held that since the essentially factual and individual nature of the inquiry is not to be glossed with legal concepts which would produce a different result from that which the factual inquiry would produce, there is no rule that one parent could not unilaterally change the habitual residence of a child. The articulation of this principle is highly significant in international child abduction cases.

Matrimonial proceedings

Habitual residence is the pivotal connecting factor in the context of jurisdiction in matrimonial proceedings,[184] and has an important function also in recognition of overseas consistorial decrees.[185]

6–47

In relation to jurisdiction and recognition of matrimonial decrees among EU Member States, almost total reliance has been placed upon the concept of habitual residence. For example,[186] it is enacted that jurisdiction shall lie with the court of the Member State in which, inter alia, there is joint spousal habitual residence, or recent habitual residence by both spouses with continuing residence by one spouse, or habitual residence of either.

Habitual residence is not defined in Brussels II *bis*. In 2014, in the English Court of Appeal in *Tan v Choy*,[187] Aikens L.J. said that, "Brussels II does not define 'habitually resident', although in European law the concept of 'habitual residence' is well recognised and means the place where a person has established on a fixed basis the permanent or habitual centre of his interests, with all the relevant factors being taken into account." This derives from the definition in the Borras Report.[188] The term has an autonomous meaning for the purposes of Brussels II *bis*,[189] and its meaning in that context, which is to be distilled from ECJ jurisprudence, is not necessarily the same as the meaning in UK law, nor the meaning for the purposes, e.g. of international child abduction as developed in the UK through Hague Convention jurisprudence.

An English gloss on the Borras definition was given in *LK v K*,[190] in which the English court was satisfied that there existed between the parties and the English forum a "genuine connection" such as to render them habitually resident in England.

Article 3 of Brussels II *bis* contains bases of jurisdiction where, in particular situations, the drafters added a time requirement, e.g. where the applicant is habitually resident if he resided there for at least a year before the application was made.[191] Such provisions exemplify the use to which, in a modern context, the

---

[184] In detail, para.12–06 et seq., below.

[185] Paras 12–28 and 12–37, below.

[186] Brussels II *bis* art.3.

[187] *Tan v Choy* [2014] EWCA Civ 251; [2014] Fam. Law 807, per Aikens L.J. at [29]; and *Marinos v Marinos* [2007] EWHC 2047 (Fam).

[188] A. Borras, "Explanatory Report on the Convention on Jurisdiction and the Recognition and Enforcement of Judgments in Matrimonial Matters" [1998] O.J. C221/27, para.32. The suggested definition in the Borras Report was cited with approval in *Marinos v Marinos* [2007] EWHC 2047 (Fam), per Munby J. at [33].

[189] *Marinos v Marinos* [2007] EWHC 2047 (Fam), per Munby J. at [17], [18]; and *Z v Z (Divorce: Jurisdiction)* [2009] EWHC 2626 (Fam).

[190] *L-K v K (No.2)* [2006] EWHC 3280 (Fam), per Singer J. at [35].

[191] Brussels II *bis* art.3 indent 5.

factor of habitual residence can be put, and its versatility. It is not the concept itself which varies as to meaning in a list such as that contained in art.3, but rather that the draftsmen, seeking justice in each situation, make different demands in different circumstances.

Questions have arisen as to the degree of continuity required to establish habitual residence. In *Ikimi v Ikimi*,[192] an instructive case concerning divorce jurisdiction under s.5(2) of the Domicile and Matrimonial Proceedings Act 1973, Thorpe L.J., having in mind the purpose of the finding on habitual residence, favoured a liberal rather than a restrictive approach: if the residence test is too hard, a spouse who divides his time equally between countries might not be able to invoke an habitual residence in any, whereas setting the bar too low would allow him to invoke the jurisdiction of more than one. Aikens L.J. in *Tan v Choy*[193] made clear that, "It is ... established, in European law, that one cannot habitually reside in two places at once".[194] Even so, under European law, there is no guarantee that different forums will identify the same legal system as the habitual residence at the *tempus inspiciendum*.[195] The European law position is in contrast with English and Scots law, in terms of which, as a matter of fact and as a matter of law, one may be habitually resident contemporaneously in two different countries.[196]

Study of the connecting factor of habitual residence suggests that it is not yet safe to use a cross-fertilisation technique, that is, to transplant authorities and principles from one area of law for use in another. Nonetheless, it is natural that in family law litigation, divorce issues and child custody issues may be intertwined, and it may not be unreasonable, therefore, to make reference in this context to authorities from the international child abduction area. In *Re R (Abduction: Habitual Residence)*,[197] a custody case where one parent was seconded from one country to another for purposes of work, for a temporary period, for a particular project and for a short time, Munby J. held that it was no bar to acquisition of a new habitual residence in Germany that the individual had by no means decided to abandon the English habitual residence obtaining immediately before. This comes close to suggesting that dual habitual residence may exist for the purposes of child abduction,[198] something of an awkward conclusion for the operation of the 1980 Hague Convention, and an unsatisfactory conclusion for the conceptual coherence of habitual residence as a connecting factor. It would be a most undesirable outcome if an adult could be deemed to have only one habitual residence for the purpose of art.3 of Brussels II *bis*, but to be capable of having two habitual residences for the purpose of art.11 thereof. Harmonisation of meaning is a work in progress.

---

[192] *Ikimi v Ikimi* [2002] Fam.72.

[193] *Tan v Choy* [2014] EWCA Civ 251; [2014] Fam. Law 807. See earlier *Marinos v Marinos* [2007] EWHC 2047 (Fam).

[194] *Tan v Choy* [2014] EWCA Civ 251; [2014] Fam. Law 807 at [29].

[195] Though see Munby J. in *Marinos* at [17], [18]; and Singer J. in *L-K v K (No.2)* [2006] EWHC 3280 (Fam) at [35].

[196] *Marinos v Marinos* [2007] EWHC 2047 (Fam), per Munby J. at [38].

[197] *Re R (Abduction: Habitual Residence)* [2003] EWHC 1968 (Fam).

[198] cf. Munby J. in *Marinos v Marinos* [2007] EWHC 2047 (Fam).

Social security

Within the broad area of social security law a difference may be discernible between national forum and ECJ/CJEU favoured "definitions" of the term.[199]   **6–48**

A significant case is *Nessa v Chief Adjudication Officer*,[200] in which the point at issue was whether or not Mrs Nessa, recently arrived in the UK from Bangladesh, was entitled to claim an income support payment from the British authorities. She was considered to be entitled only if habitually resident in the UK. The House of Lords held that, for the purpose of the Income Support (General) Regulations 1987,[201] residence *for a period* is required to constitute habitual residence.

Within the same subject area, the later case of *Gingi v Secretary of State for Work and Pensions*[202] demonstrates that the European Community interpretation of habitual residence in the area of social law may vary from the interpretation favoured domestically in the UK. If the issue were to be regarded as affected by Regulation 1408/71[203] (concerning social security payments to persons moving within the Community), Miss Gingi's case would be affected by the ECJ decision of *Swaddling v Adjudication Officer*.[204] In *Swaddling*, it was held in the interpretation of art.10a.1 of Regulation 1408/71 that length of residence in a Member State cannot be regarded as an intrinsic or constituent element of the concept of residence. The Court of Appeal in *Gingi*, having decided that Miss Gingi's situation was *not* governed by Regulation 1408/71, was free to follow the English domestic interpretation of habitual residence set down by the House of Lords in *Nessa*.

These cases illustrate the divergence of opinion in the matter of interpretation which may arise between the ECJ/CJEU and UK national courts in the area of social law. Conceivably also, the term may require to be interpreted differently as between different types of social security allowance.[205]

Wills and succession

Under Scots (and English) choice of law rules, habitual residence of the deceased plays no part in the substantive aspect of the devolution of his estate. In terms of the Wills Act 1963 s.1, the habitual residence of the testator at the time of the execution of his will, or at his death, provide two of the criteria against which the formal validity of his will may be adjudged.   **6–49**

---

[199] E.B. Crawford, "A Day is not Enough: Further Views on the Meaning of Habitual Residence", 2000 J.R. 89; and E.B. Crawford, "Payment postponed: exploring the extent of Nessa's authority", 2003 J.S.S.L. 10(1), 52–61.

[200] *Nessa v Chief Adjudication Officer* [1999] 1 W.L.R. 1937; [1999] 4 All E.R. 677; and *Abdirahman v Secretary of State for Work and Pensions* [2007] 4 All E.R. 882.

[201] Income Support (General) Regulations 1987 (SI 1987/1967).

[202] *Gingi v Secretary of State for Work and Pensions* [2001] EWCA Civ 1685.

[203] Regulation (EEC) No.1408/71 of the Council of 14 June 1971 on the application of social security schemes to employed persons and their families moving within the Community ([1971] O.J. L149/2).

[204] *Swaddling v Adjudication Officer* (C90/97) [1999] E.C.R. I-1075.

[205] e.g. *Patmalniece v Secretary of State for Work and Pensions (AIRE Centre intervening)* [2011] UKSC 11.

The UK Government's decision[206] not to opt in to the Rome IV Regulation[207] was influenced in large measure by disquiet about that instrument's adoption of habitual residence of the deceased as the primary connecting factor for the purposes of jurisdiction and applicable law. Unlike the Rome I and Rome II Regulations, Rome IV does not provide for its own purposes an autonomous definition of the term. Recitals (24) and (25) indicate, however, that, in the context of Rome IV, habitual residence can be established after short residence and in the face of the existence of a legal system of manifestly closer connection to the deceased.

The law of obligations

6–50   Habitual residence has some application in the commercial sphere.[208] In contract, art.4 ("Applicable law in the absence of choice") of the Rome I Regulation, adopts habitual residence as the preferred connecting factor in relation to contract-specific choice of law rules (art.4.1). By art.4.2, where a contract is not covered by art.4.1, or where the elements of the contract would be covered by more than one of the contract-specific rules, the contract shall be governed by the law of the country where the party required to effect the characteristic performance of the contract has his habitual residence.[209] Habitual residence is a favoured criterion in certain types of contract on policy grounds, usually with protective purposes.[210]

An innovation contained in art.19.1 of the Rome I Regulation is the definition, for the purposes of the Regulation, of the habitual residence of companies and other bodies, corporate or unincorporated, as the place of central administration.[211] Further, art.19.1 defines the habitual residence of a natural person acting in the course of his business activity as his principal place of business. With regard to *tempus inspiciendum*, the relevant point in time shall be the time of conclusion of the contract.[212] The habitual residence of a natural person acting otherwise than in the course of business activity will be construed by the forum in accordance with existing ECJ/CJEU jurisprudence and its own national law.

Where a contract is concluded in the course of the operations of a branch, agency or any other establishment, or if, under the contract, performance is the

---

[206] Hansard, HL Vol.502, Pt No.17, col.141 (16 December 2009); and House of Lords European Union Committee, *6th Report of Session 2009–10, The EU's Regulation on Succession: Report with Evidence* (The Stationery Office, 2010), HL Paper No.75 (Session 2009/10), paras 54–65. Para.18–41, below.

[207] Regulation (EU) No.650/2012 of the European Parliament and of the Council on jurisdiction, applicable law, recognition and enforcement of decisions and acceptance and enforcement of authentic instruments in matters of succession and on the creation of a European Certificate of Succession.

[208] e.g. Rome I Regulation arts 4.2, 5, 6, 10, 13, 19; Rome I Convention arts 4.2, 8, 11; and Rome II Regulation arts 4.2, 5.1, 10.2, 11.2, 12.2, 23.

[209] cf. Rome I Convention art.4.2, in terms of which the principal presumption to establish the applicable law in the absence of choice was the habitual residence of the party whose performance was characteristic of the contract. Litigation on interpretation of art.4.2 tended to concern identification of the performance which was characteristic of the contract, rather than of the habitual residence of the party to effect such performance. Ch.15, below.

[210] e.g. Rome I Regulation arts 4.1, 5, 6, 7, 8, 10.2; and Rome I Convention arts 5.2, 8.2.

[211] Recital (39).

[212] Rome I Regulation art.19.3.

responsibility of such a branch, agency or establishment, the place where the branch, agency or any other establishment is located shall be treated as the place of habitual residence.[213]

Likewise, in art.23 of the Rome II Regulation concerning non-contractual obligations, a definition is provided of the habitual residence of companies and other bodies corporate or unincorporated (the same as that in art.19 of Rome I, mutatis mutandis). Separately, in Rome II, one can note the use of "commonality" (the fact that claimant and defendant have a common habitual residence at the time of occurrence of damage) as a principal exception (art.4.2) to application of the general rule in art.4.1.[214]

THE RULES OF HABITUAL RESIDENCE—A PRÉCIS

Study of the use of habitual residence across the spectrum of international private law shows it to be a weasel factor which does not always live up to its reputation as a common sense, factual criterion. It has proved to be a fruitful source of discussion and litigation. Examination of the connecting factor reveals the degree to which opinion varies on the topic, and serves to identify the various contexts in which increasingly the concept is used. Though use of the concept normally is authorised by statute, convention or regulation, its meaning typically is undefined. A summary of that which, with reasonable confidence, can be said to be agreed, is as follows:

6–51

(a)   A person may cease to be habitually resident in country A in a single day if there is settled intention not to return to A.

(b)   Such a person, having left country A with the settled intention not to return, probably cannot become habitually resident in country B in a single day.[215]

(c)   While acquisition of a new habitual residence in most cases will extinguish an earlier habitual residence, concurrent habitual residences seem possible in some contexts, but not in others.[216]

(d)   A person can be without an habitual residence. There is no rule of continuance of habitual residence. The loss of an existing habitual residence may leave a vacuum.

(e)   "Voluntariness" is a question of degree. While free will may be necessary at the outset to establish residence, and while a complete lack of consent may preclude "settled intention", it is arguable that, over time, factual residence overrides other subjective factors.

(f)   Matrimonial proceedings: the term has an autonomous meaning for the purposes of Brussels II *bis*.[217] In European law the concept of 'habitual residence' means the place where a person has established on a fixed basis

---

[213] Rome I Regulation art.19.2.
[214] Ch.16, below.
[215] *C v S* [1990] 2 All E.R. 961 HL, per Lord Brandon at 965.
[216] *Tan v Choy* [2014] EWCA Civ 251; [2014] Fam. Law 807. See earlier *Marinos v Marinos* [2007] EWHC 2047 (Fam).
[217] *Marinos v Marinos* [2007] EWHC 2047 (Fam), per Munby J. at [17], [18]; and *Z v Z (Divorce: Jurisdiction)* [2009] EWHC 2626 (Fam).

the permanent or habitual centre of his interests, with all the relevant factors being taken into account. This derives from the definition in the Borras Report.[218]

(h) Children: the authoritative (context-specific) interpretation handed down by the ECJ in *Proceedings Brought by A*[219] is to the effect that a child's habitual residence corresponds to the place which reflects some degree of integration by the child in a social and family environment. In *Mercredi v Chaffe*[220] the CJEU said: "The social and family environment of the child … comprises various factors which vary according to the age of the child. The factors to be taken into account in the case of a child of school age are thus not the same as those to be considered in the case of a child who has left school and are again not the same as those relevant to an infant."[221]

In the absence of uniform definition, the malleability of the concept of habitual residence in the hands of judges raises the possibility of result-selection. Over time, subject area by subject area, decisions of the CJEU can be expected to have a harmonising influence, and there is likely to result, in certain swathes of law, a coalescence of meaning. Currently, however, and for some time to come, the meaning of the concept is likely to be fragmented, and the result in any given litigation unpredictable—even as unpredictable as a domicile decision is alleged to be, and with fewer signposts to guide.

SUMMARY 6

6–52

1. Domicile is a relationship between a person and a territory with a common body of law. Every person must have a domicile, but cannot have more than one domicile for the same purpose at any one time. There are no formalities for acquisition of domicile.

2. Prior to the Family Law (Scotland) Act 2006, and still in England, a domicile of origin was/is acquired at birth from a person's father's domicile at that date if the child is legitimate. Otherwise, and if posthumous, domicile of origin was/is acquired at birth from his mother's domicile.

3. Domicile at birth, and up to the age of 16 years, is ascribed in Scots law in accordance with s.22 of the 2006 Act. A child shall be domiciled in the same country as his parents where:
   (a) his parents are domiciled in the same country as each other; and
   (b) he has a home with a parent or a home (or homes) with both of them.
      Where these conditions are not satisfied, the child shall be domiciled in the country with which he has for the time being the closest connection.

4. Onus of proof of a change of domicile rests on the person averring a change.

5. Prior to the Family Law (Scotland) Act 2006, a derivative or dependent domicile was/is acquired from the actings of another person and was

---

[218] Borras Report, para.32.
[219] *Proceedings Brought by A* (C-523/07) [2009] I.L.Pr. 39.
[220] *Mercredi v Chaffe* (C-497/10 PPU) [2011] I.L.Pr. 23.
[221] *Mercredi v Chaffe* (C-497/10 PPU) [2011] I.L.Pr. 23 at [53].

independent of the *propositus*'s intention. Domicile up to 16 years is ascribed now in Scots law in accordance with s.22 of the 2006 Act.

6. By inference of s.22(4) of the 2006 Act, an individual becomes *sui juris* with regard to domicile at the age of 16.

7. Domicile of choice is acquired by a combination of residence and intention.

8. Domicile of choice is retained unless and until it is abandoned by a change of *both* residence and intention, whereupon either:

   (a)   the domicile of origin revives; or

   (b)   (rarely) a new domicile of choice is acquired immediately.

9. A different meaning and usage of the term "domicile" is found as a major connecting factor in the framework of rules of civil and commercial jurisdiction and judgment enforcement known as the Brussels regime. Article 2 of the Brussels I Regulation/art.4 of the Brussels I Recast Regulation establishes as the pre-eminent ground of jurisdiction the "domicile" of the defender. "Domicile" in this context bears no relation to domicile in its classic meaning. For the UK, the statutory definition, found in CJJO 2001 Sch.1 para.9, is to the effect that an individual is domiciled in the UK or part thereof if and only if he is resident there, and the nature and circumstances of his residence indicate that he has a substantial connection with the UK. "Substantial connection" is presumed to be fulfilled, unless the contrary is proved, if the individual has been resident in the UK or part thereof for the last three months.

10. Increasingly in modern conflict rules, the connecting factor of *habitual residence* is employed, particularly in family law: divorce and nullity jurisdiction and recognition; custody and abduction; guardianship and protection of children; and adoption. It has a role also in the commercial sphere. The factor frequently is utilised in international harmonisation instruments, but there is an absence of uniform definition.

11. While an autonomous definition is provided in the Rome I and Rome II Regulations, the concept is not defined in any instrument in its area of greatest use, namely, family law.

12. In matters of parental responsibility, the ECJ has defined habitual residence thus:

> "[habitual residence] corresponds to the place which reflects some degree of integration by the child in a social and family environment".

13. In matters of international child abduction, the factor is in a state of constant refinement in the light of circumstances presenting. The UK Supreme Court has held that the essentially factual and individual nature of the inquiry should not be glossed with legal concepts which would produce a different result from that which the factual inquiry would produce. Further, there is no rule that one parent may not unilaterally change the habitual residence of his/her child.

14. In the context of jurisdiction in matrimonial proceedings, habitual residence is the pivotal connecting factor. It has an important function also in recognition of overseas consistorial decrees. In this context, it means the

place where a person has established on a fixed basis the permanent or habitual centre of his interests, with all the relevant factors being taken into account.

15. In general, the UK view appears to be that a person may cease to be habitually resident in country A in a single day if there is settled intention not to return there, but such a person probably cannot become habitually resident in country B in a single day. Concurrent habitual residences seem possible in some contexts, but not in others. A person can be without an habitual residence. The loss of an existing habitual residence may leave a vacuum.

CHAPTER 7

Jurisdiction in civil and commercial matters

INTRODUCTION

This chapter deals with that area of the conflict of laws which is of greatest moment to litigants and their advisers. The subject of conflict of laws is built upon the three pillars of jurisdiction, choice of law, and recognition of foreign decrees. Although all three areas are likely to contribute to the securing of a remedy in a conflict dispute, attention at the outset is directed to securing the most advantageous forum, and enforcement[1] of the remedy there granted.

7–01

Rules of jurisdiction clothe the forum with significant powers to classify the nature of the problem, segregate the substantive from the procedural, provide pre-trial safeguards, identify the applicable law, and exercise its policy discretion, most of which will be utilised in justifying the exercise of its ultimate power, to provide or withhold the remedy which the pursuer seeks.

OVERVIEW

Jurisdiction means the entitlement of a court to hear an action and make a decision. With regard to civil and commercial jurisdiction, the power is conferred by common law or statute of the legal system of which the putative forum forms part, and most importantly now by international instrument, principally by Regulation (EU) No.1215/2012 of the European Parliament and of the Council of 12 December 2012 on jurisdiction and the recognition and enforcement of judgments in civil and commercial matters (recast)[2] (henceforth "Brussels I Recast"). Brussels I Recast operates where the defender is "domiciled" in an EU Member State (art.4) or, regardless of the domicile of the defender, if the court of a Member State has special jurisdiction (art.7—by nature of the subject-matter of the dispute), or exclusive jurisdiction (art.24), or jurisdiction by choice of the parties (art.25), or by their submission (art.26).

7–02

In a conflict of laws context, the subject of jurisdiction connotes the allocation of jurisdiction between courts, internationally, or between the constituent legal systems of a multi-legal system state. Problems of ascertainment and allocation of jurisdiction arise also in domestic law, as, for example, in Scotland,

---

[1] In respect of which, see Ch.9, below.
[2] Brussels I Recast [2012] O.J. L351/1.

geographically among sheriffdoms,[3] or hierarchically, in civil and criminal matters, between the lower and higher courts.

In general terms, the grounds upon which UK courts exercise jurisdiction depend on three basic principles:

(a) *actor sequitur forum rei*[4];
(b) effectiveness of any decree which may be pronounced; and/or
(c) submission by the defender to the jurisdiction.

Forum actoris rules of jurisdiction, based upon a personal link between the pursuer and the court, have no place in "national"[5] Scots rules of jurisdiction. In general there must be a connection between the defender, or the subject-matter of the dispute, and the court before which it is heard. If the connection is fragile, a rule of jurisdiction based upon it may be regarded internationally as objectionable.[6] Outside the ambit of Brussels I Recast, the effect of such jurisdictional rules may be mitigated by rules of *forum non conveniens*, so as to confer on the court seised the discretion to cede jurisdiction to a court which it is persuaded is more appropriate to hear the case. It is not always necessary that the defender be resident in the jurisdiction in question for the case to proceed there, for there are certain rules, based on the subject-matter of the litigation, which permit identification of a different court(s) as (equally) suitable, a fact which may afford the pursuer an alternative forum in which to sue.

RESTRICTIONS ON SUIT

7–03   Certain restrictions may operate on parties to preclude actions being brought by or against them in the UK. For example, by virtue of the Visiting Forces Act 1952, visiting forces may not be tried in UK courts. Further, enemy aliens may not be pursuers in a Scots forum,[7] unless resident in Scotland,[8] but it is open to such persons to defend actions. These cases apart, the court in Scotland or England will not be restrictive in attitude, but will seek to act in accordance with

---

[3] In respect of which, see G. Maher and B.J. Rodger, *Civil Jurisdiction in the Scottish Courts* (ThomsonReuters, 2010).

[4] Literally, that the pursuer must have recourse to the court where the subject matter of the dispute is situated; and broadly, that the pursuer must seek out the defender in the place of the latter's place of residence or business.

[5] i.e. those rules of jurisdiction of Scots law existing before, and continuing to co-exist with, the system of jurisdictional rules put in place by the 1968 Brussels Convention, q.v., largely replaced by the Brussels I Recast. The Brussels system contains examples of *forum actoris* rules where these are considered justified to protect disadvantaged parties (ss.3, 4, 5).

[6] See, e.g. the residual national English rules of jurisdiction which permit "service out of the jurisdiction" in "non-Brussels cases", upon a defendant resident abroad, if the subject matter of the litigation and the facts of the case, in the discretion of the English court, warrant this. This is an example of "long arm" jurisdiction. See for detail para.7–79.

[7] *Weber's Trustees v Riemer*, 1947 S.L.T. 295; *Netz v Ede* [1946] Ch. 224; and *R. v Bottrill Ex p. Kuechenmeister* [1947] K.B. 41.

[8] *Schulze Gow & Co v Bank of Scotland*, 1914 2 S.L.T. 455; *Weiss v Weiss*, 1940 S.L.T. 447; and *Sovfracht (V/O) v Van Udens Scheepvaart en Agentuur Maatschappij (NV Gebr)* [1943] A.C. 203.

the principles of comity, so far as public policy permits.[9] However, there is one important restriction on suit which repays closer study, namely, immunity under the State Immunity Act 1978.

Immunity from suit—State Immunity Act 1978[10]

The subject of state immunity was placed on a statutory basis following the 1972 European Convention on State Immunity, resulting in the passing of the State Immunity Act 1978. The basic principle of the 1978 Act is that a foreign state is immune from the jurisdiction of UK courts, and effect is to be given to that immunity whether or not the state enters an appearance in proceedings.[11] Since state immunity is a rule of international law, and Brussels I Recast is subject to the international law of state immunity, reliance upon state immunity is not precluded within the Brussels regime (q.v.).[12] The crucial distinction latterly at common law was between a state's actions in the exercise of its sovereign authority (*acta jure imperii*—in relation to which immunity was conferred), and its actions in the course of its commercial activities (*acta jure gestionis*—which did not attract immunity); the 1978 Act takes the same approach, though the distinction is less clear-cut.

7–04

Statutory exceptions to state immunity

Section 1(1) of the 1978 Act confers immunity upon a state from the jurisdiction of the courts of the UK subject to certain exceptions, such as upon submission by the state to the jurisdiction.[13] A further important exception concerns commercial transactions[14] and contracts to be performed in the UK (s.3); such matters are justiciable in the UK.[15] Equally, a state is not immune in respect of litigation concerning a contract of employment between the state and an individual where

7–05

---

[9] e.g. *Bumper Development Corp Ltd v Commissioner of Police of the Metropolis* [1991] 4 All E.R. 638, where the English Court of Appeal permitted a Hindu temple to sue in England to recover its property, the temple having legal personality under the law where it was situated. It was entitled to sue in the person of the officer properly appointed under its own law.

[10] See also para.3–07, above.

[11] *Bank of Credit and Commerce International (Overseas) Ltd (In Liquidation) v Price Waterhouse* [1997] 4 All E.R. 108; *Mbasogo v Logo Ltd (No.1)* [2007] Q.B. 846; and *Korea National Insurance Co v Allianz Global Corporate & Specialty AG* [2008] EWCA Civ 1355.

[12] *Grovit v De Nederlandsche Bank* [2006] 1 All E.R. (Comm) 397.

[13] 1978 Act ss.1–2; and e.g. *NML Capital Ltd v Argentina* [2011] UKSC 31; [2011] 2 A.C. 495.

[14] 1978 Act s.3(3); e.g. *Alcom Ltd v Colombia* [1984] 2 All E.R. 6, per Lord Diplock at 8; *Kuwait Airways Corp v Iraqi Airways Co* [1995] 1 W.L.R. 1147 HL, per Lord Goff at 1156; *Bank of Credit and Commerce International (Overseas) Ltd (In Liquidation) v Price Waterhouse (No.1)* [1997] 4 All E.R. 108; *Svenska Petroleum Exploration AB v Lithuania (No.2)* [2006] EWCA Civ 1529; [2007] Q.B. 886; *AIG Capital Partners Inc v Kazakhstan* [2006] 1 All E.R. 284; *ETI Euro Telecom International NV v Bolivia* [2009] 1 W.L.R. 665; and *NML Capital Ltd v Argentina* [2011] UKSC 31; [2011] 2 A.C. 495 (in which the UK Supreme Court held that proceedings "relating to…a commercial transaction" within the meaning of s.3 of the 1978 Act did not extend to proceedings for the *enforcement* of a foreign judgment which itself related to a commercial transaction).

[15] By s.13(2)(b) of the 1978 Act the property of a state shall not be subject to any process for the enforcement of a judgment or arbitration award or, in an action in rem, for its arrest, detention or sale, except in respect of property which is in use or intended for use for commercial purposes: *SerVaas Inc v Rafidain Bank* [2012] UKSC 40.

the contract was made in the UK or the work is to be wholly or partly performed there (s.4).[16] Nor is a state immune as regards proceedings in respect of death or personal injury, or damage to or loss of tangible property, caused by act or omission in the UK (s.5). Likewise, there is no immunity as respects proceedings relating to any interest of the state in immoveable property in the UK (s.6). Further where a state has agreed to submit a dispute to arbitration, the state is not immune as regards proceedings in the courts of the UK relating to the arbitration (s.9).[17]

To whom is immunity extended?

7–06   This question is addressed by s.14 of the 1978 Act, which provides that references to "a state" include references to (a) the sovereign or other head of that state in his public capacity[18]; (b) the government of that state[19]; and (c) any department of that government[20]; but not to any entity which is distinct from the executive organs of the government of the state and capable of suing or being sued.[21] However, by s.14(2), a separate entity is immune from the jurisdiction of the courts of the UK (provided it does not submit[22]), if and only if (a) the proceedings relate to anything done by it in the exercise of sovereign authority; and (b) the circumstances are such that a state would have been so immune.

By s.20 of the 1978 Act, the Diplomatic Privileges Act 1964 is extended to (a) a sovereign or other head of state; (b) members of his family forming part of his household[23]; and (c) his private servants, as it applies to the head of a diplomatic mission, to members of his family forming part of his household and to his private servants.[24] Immunity exists so long as the relevant party acts in his

---

[16] cf. *Benkharbouche v Embassy of Sudan* [2015] EWCA Civ 33.

[17] The following also are justiciable: s.7—proceedings relating to patents and trade marks; s.8—proceedings relating to a state's membership of a body corporate incorporated under the law of the UK; s.10—admiralty proceedings; and s.11—state liability for value added tax, customs duty or excise duty.

[18] *R. (on the application of Sultan of Pahang) v Secretary of State for the Home Department* [2011] EWCA Civ 616.

[19] See *Jones v Ministry of the Interior Al-Mamlaka Al-Arabiya AS Saudiya* [2006] UKHL 26.

[20] See *Owners of Cargo Lately on Board the Playa Larga v Owners of the I Congreso del Partido* [1981] 2 All E.R. 1064; *Alcom Ltd v Colombia* [1984] 2 All E.R. 6; and *Jones v Saudi Arabia* [2006] UKHL 26; [2007] 1 A.C. 270; [2006] 2 W.L.R. 1424. See also *Belhaj v Straw* [2014] EWCA Civ 1394.

[21] In *Wilhelm Finance Inc v Ente Administrador del Astillero Rio Santiago* [2009] EWHC 1074 (Comm), the question whether a shipyard was a sufficiently state-owned entity to come within the definition of "a State" for the purposes of the 1978 Act was answered in the negative. See also *La Generale des Carrieres et des Mines v FG Hemisphere Associates LLC* [2012] UKPC 27; [2013] 1 All E.R. 409.

[22] 1978 Act s.14(3).

[23] *Apex Global Management Ltd v Fi Call Ltd* [2014] 1 W.L.R. 492 re (non-)extension of diplomatic privileges to the nephew and half-brother of the Saudi Arabian King, both of whom were adults living apart from the King with households of their own.

[24] e.g. *Al-Malki v Reyes* [2015] EWCA Civ 32 (an employment contract pertaining to the provision of services incidental to family, domestic or diplomatic life is not to be interpreted as "commercial", meaning therefore in the instant case that the immunity was intact). Contrast *Benkharbouche v Embassy of Sudan* [2015] EWCA Civ 33. A foreign state's unilateral action in purporting to confer some similar status upon an individual did not bind the court in England to accept that such a person

"official" capacity.[25] Upon his functions coming to an end, privileges and immunities normally will cease when he leaves the receiving country, or on expiry of a reasonable period in which to do so.[26]

Immunity may be waived expressly or impliedly.[27] Institution of proceedings by a state is an implied waiver.[28] Waiver of diplomatic immunity must be express, and by the state, not the individual.[29]

LEGISLATIVE OVERVIEW OF RULES OF JURISDICTION APPLICABLE IN SCOTLAND

There are four legislative regimes regulating the rules applicable in Scotland concerning civil and commercial jurisdiction, namely: **7–07**

(a)   the Brussels regime, which comprises Brussels I Recast (building on the predecessor instruments, the 1968 Brussels Convention[30] and the Brussels I Regulation[31]) and the EC-Denmark Agreement,[32] with auxiliary primary legislation in the UK in the form of the Civil Jurisdiction and Judgments Act 1982, as amended by secondary legislation;

(b)   the Lugano II Convention,[33] with auxiliary primary legislation in the UK in the form of the Civil Jurisdiction and Judgments Acts 1982 and 1991;

(c)   Civil Jurisdiction and Judgments Act 1982 Sch.4: the Modified Convention, allocating jurisdiction within the UK[34]; and

(d)   Civil Jurisdiction and Judgments Act 1982 Sch.8: the residual national, Scottish rules.[35]

Each of these regimes will be examined in turn, as well as the inter-relationships between and among them.

---

had diplomatic status and immunity from suit: *R. v Governor of Pentonville Prison Ex p. Teja* [1971] 2 Q.B. 274; and *R. v Secretary of State for Home Department Ex p. Bagga* [1991] 1 Q.B. 485.

[25] *Wokuri v Kassam* [2012] EWHC 105 (Ch); [2013] Ch. 80.

[26] *Shaw v Shaw* [1979] 3 All E.R. 1; and *Harb v Aziz* [2014] EWHC 1807 (Ch).

[27] See generally M.N. Shaw, *International Law*, 6th edn (Cambridge: Cambridge University Press, 2008).

[28] *London Steam Ship Owners Mutual Insurance Association Ltd v Spain* [2015] EWCA Civ 333.

[29] *Al-Fayed v Al-Tajir* [1987] 2 All E.R. 396.

[30] 1968 Brussels Convention on jurisdiction and the enforcement of judgments in civil and commercial matters [1972] O.J. L299/32.

[31] Council Regulation (EC) No.44/2001 on jurisdiction and the recognition and enforcement of judgments in civil and commercial matters [2001] O.J. L12/1.

[32] Agreement between the European Community and Denmark on jurisdiction and the recognition and enforcement of judgments in civil and commercial matters [2005] O.J. L299/62.

[33] Para.7–72, below.

[34] Para.7–76, below.

[35] Para.7–78, below.

The Brussels regime

1968 Brussels Convention on jurisdiction and the enforcement of judgments in civil and commercial matters

7–08   The 1968 Convention was intended to regulate the jurisdiction of courts of Contracting States, and the enforcement in one Contracting State of judgments given in another. It is known for this reason as a "double" Convention, the two sets of rules having an interdependent relationship.[36] There has been much less litigation concerning interpretation of the enforcement provisions than of the jurisdiction provisions.

   The committee of experts engaged in drafting the 1968 Convention identified certain grounds of jurisdiction used in Contracting States which were unlikely to meet international standards of acceptability. These "exorbitant" grounds (e.g. the nationality of the pursuer—a *forum actoris* rule; service during temporary presence of the defendant in the UK; presence within the UK of property belonging to the defendant in actions not concerning such property) could not be used against "persons domiciled in a Contracting State",[37] a category which includes a defendant "domiciled" elsewhere in the UK, and a defender "domiciled" in Scotland. In addition to proscribing exorbitant rules, the Brussels Convention prescribed the only grounds of jurisdiction, as from time to time interpreted and amended, which could be used against such persons.

From 1968 Convention through the Brussels I Regulation to Brussels I Recast

7–09   The completion and implementation of the 1968 Brussels Convention and subsequent accession conventions[38] were signal achievements. Although certain of the rules of the Brussels Convention, particularly those concerning jurisdiction, generated much interpretative litigation,[39] when the Convention was succeeded by the Brussels I Regulation,[40] with effect from 1 March 2002, there was no fundamental change in its structure or provisions, but rather a process of refinement of its terms in the light of experience.

---

[36] P. Jenard, Report on the Convention on Jurisdiction and the Enforcement of Judgments in Civil and Commercial Matters [1979] O.J. C59/1 (henceforth "the Jenard Report").

[37] 1968 Convention art.3.

[38] UK, Danish and Irish Accession Convention 1978 [1978] O.J. L304/1 (Schlosser Report [1979] O.J. C59/71); Greek Accession Convention 1982 [1982] O.J. L388/1; Spanish and Portuguese Accession Convention 1989 [1989] O.J. L285/1; and Austrian, Finnish and Swedish Accession Convention 1996 [1997] O.J. C15/1.

[39] See 1971 Protocol on Interpretation of the Brussels Convention.

[40] The function of the 1968 Convention is all but spent. For residual application, see J.J. Fawcett and J.M. Carruthers, *Cheshire, North & Fawcett's Private International Law*, 14th edn (2008), p.342.

The EC–Denmark Agreement

Denmark did not participate in the adoption of the Brussels I Regulation,[41] and **7–10**
therefore was not bound by it. Thus, the allocation of jurisdiction and
enforcement of judgments vis-à-vis Denmark continued to be governed by the
1968 Convention until the conclusion of an Agreement between the European
Community and Denmark on Jurisdiction and the Recognition and Enforcement
of Judgments in Civil and Commercial Matters,[42] which extended, as between the
EC and Denmark, the provisions of the Brussels I Regulation, with certain
amendments of a fairly minor nature.

In terms of art.3.2 of the EC–Denmark Agreement, whenever amendments
were adopted to the Brussels I Regulation, Denmark was required to notify the
Commission of its decision whether or not to implement the content of such
amendments. By letter of 20 December 2012 Denmark notified the Commission
of its decision to implement the contents of Brussels I Recast, and so the recast
regulation applies to relations between the EU and Denmark.[43]

Brussels I Recast

European Union Member State rules of jurisdiction and judgment enforcement **7–11**
are contained primarily in Brussels I Recast, recital (6) of which states that in
order to attain the objective of free circulation of judgments in civil and
commercial matters, it is necessary and appropriate that the rules governing
jurisdiction and the recognition and enforcement of judgments be governed by a
legal instrument of the Union which is binding and directly applicable.

Legal opinion in Britain had been braced for fundamental change to certain of
the rules of jurisdiction allocation contained in the Brussels I Regulation, and
there had been doubt as to the wisdom of the UK's participation in the recasting
exercise.[44] The principal concern arose from the European Commission's desire
to arm an EU-domiciled claimant in his pursuit of a claim against a non-EU
domiciled defendant within the geographical boundaries of the EU, and the
consequential proposal to override residual national rules in Member States and
replace them with a set of harmonised rules. On the other hand, there was concern
about the prudence of standing aside from a process of refinement of the rules,

---

[41] Danish citizens having rejected the Maastricht Treaty in 1992, Denmark does not participate in the
adoption of measures under the head of judicial co-operation in civil and commercial matters. See
now Treaty of Lisbon, Protocol No.22 on the position of Denmark [2010] O.J. C/83/299 (Ch.1,
above).
[42] Agreement between the European Community and Denmark on Jurisdiction and the Recognition
and Enforcement of Judgments in Civil and Commercial Matters [2005] O.J. L299/62. See further
Council of the European Union Press Release 8402/06 (re Luxembourg meeting, April 2006), noting
agreement concerning the extension to Denmark of the Brussels I Regulation (Decision 6922/06); and
The Civil Jurisdiction and Judgments Regulations 2007 (SI 2007/ 1655).
[43] Agreement between the European Community and the Kingdom of Denmark on jurisdiction and
the recognition and enforcement of judgments in civil and commercial matters [2013] O.J. L79/4.
[44] House of Lords EU Committee (21st Report of Session 2008/09, HL Paper 148); Ministry of
Justice/Scottish Government/Department of Justice (Northern Ireland) Consultation Paper: Revision
of the Brussels I Regulation—How should the UK approach the negotiations? CP18/10 (22 December
2010); and "Response to Consultation/Call for Evidence" CP(R) 18/10, 12 December 2011: Pt 2,
Summary of Responses.

which process, when crystallised, would result in rules applicable almost universally in other Member State forums.

In April 2011, the UK Government confirmed its intention to opt into the proposed recast instrument, in whatever form ultimately it should take, the stance being that, while the Brussels I Regulation fulfilled an essential function and generally worked well, the effect of the recast proposal would be to attempt to resolve recognised problems and to effect improvements.[45] Fears as to the content of the instrument were unfounded, for, as things transpired, Brussels I Recast is a muted version of earlier proposals, and generally is thought to be an improvement on an already highly successful scheme of rules.

Temporal issues

7–12   Brussels I Recast entered into force on 9 January 2013, the twentieth day following its publication on 20 December 2012. In accordance with art.81, the regulation applies from 10 January 2015. Since Brussels I Recast repeals the Brussels I Regulation,[46] clarity as to the practical meaning of the "date of application" of the instrument is fundamental. In terms of art.66.1 the recast regulation shall apply only to legal proceedings instituted on or after 10 January 2015, and to authentic instruments formally drawn up or registered, and to court settlements approved or concluded, on or after that date.

By art.66.2, notwithstanding art.80, the Brussels I Regulation shall continue to apply to judgments given in legal proceedings instituted before 10 January 2015, and to authentic instruments formally drawn up or registered, and court settlements approved or concluded, before that date. Article 66.2 encompasses two scenarios: first, the scenario where proceedings are instituted and judgment is handed down before 10 January 2015 (a scenario which, without doubt, falls to be regulated by the Brussels I Regulation); and, secondly, the scenario where proceedings are instituted before 10 January 2015, but where the judgment is handed down after that date. Construing art.66 in its entirety, the second scenario falls also to be regulated by the Brussels I Regulation. The critical date for the purpose of determining which instrument applies is the date of institution of proceedings, and not the date of handing down the judgment.[47] It does not matter in the second scenario, in terms of the application of the rules of jurisdiction of the Brussels I Regulation, whether proceedings were instituted before the date of entry into force of Brussels I Recast (9 January 2013) or during the "overture" (9 January 2013–10 January 2015), for in each case jurisdiction must be founded upon the rules contained in the Brussels I Regulation.

Article 80 of Brussels I Recast provides that references to the Brussels I Regulation henceforth shall be construed as references to the recast regulation.

---

[45] HL 5 Apr 2011: col.WS139; HC 5 Apr 2011: cols 60WS and 61WS. See also Brussels I Recast recital (40).

[46] Brussels I Recast art.80.

[47] This is a change of approach from that taken in the transitional provisions included in the Brussels I Regulation (art.66.2).

Continuity of interpretation

As explained in Ch.1,[48] in the evolution of the European justice agenda, account   **7–13**
must be taken of two principles of interpretation to ensure consistency between
and among instruments. Important in this subject area is the principle of vertical
continuity,[49] applicable where there has been historical progression from
Convention to Regulation to Recast Regulation. Vertical continuity has two
aspects: the temporal scope of application of each succeeding instrument,
including transitional provisions, must be clear; and judicial interpretation of the
later/latest instrument, where an identical or similar form of words is found in
succeeding instruments, should be consistent with the earlier/earliest. Where a
provision in a subsequent instrument is intended to be equivalent in purpose to
one in a predecessor instrument (allowing for modest semantic refinement),
weight should be given to pre-existing decisions of the European Court of
Justice/ Court of Justice of the European Union ("ECJ"/"CJEU") and of national
courts, interpretative of the earlier provision.

Vertical continuity is readily seen in the evolution of jurisdictional provisions
from the 1968 Brussels Convention through the Brussels I Regulation to Brussels
I Recast. General approbation of the principle of vertical continuity was
contained in the Brussels I Regulation vis-à-vis the 1968 Brussels Convention,[50]
and, by recital (34) of Brussels I Recast, continuity should be ensured between
the 1968 Brussels Convention, the Brussels I Regulation and the recast
regulation.

Brussels I Recast follows the Brussels I Regulation in structure. The content of
a number of provisions is repeated verbatim, although many of the core
jurisdiction provisions have been renumbered.[51] There are many examples of
vertical continuity of expression extending back to the 1968 Brussels
Convention; where there has been vertical continuity over three generations of an
instrument, the interpretative approach is likely to be entrenched. It is noteworthy
that the wording and import of many provisions have not changed markedly over
50 years.

It was a feature of the 1968 Convention that certain key terms were allotted a
"Community" or autonomous definition for use in all Contracting States.
Definition and interpretation of certain other provisions were left to the discretion
of individual states, in accordance with their own conflict rules. The incidence of
ascription of autonomous, that is, Community, meanings to particular terms
increased in the Brussels I Regulation,[52] but in Brussels I Recast has levelled out.

Civil Jurisdiction and Judgments Act 1982

The Civil Jurisdiction and Judgments Act 1982 ("CJJA 1982") gave the force of   **7–14**
law within the UK to the 1968 Brussels Convention. The Act has been greatly
amended in the years since 1982, as more countries were admitted to membership

---

[48] Para.1–11, above.
[49] For detail see E.B. Crawford and J.M. Carruthers, "Connection and Coherence between and among
European Instruments in the Private International Law of Obligations" (2014) 63 I.C.L.Q. 1.
[50] Brussels I Regulation recital (19). cf. Rome I Regulation recital (17).
[51] Brussels I Recast Annex III (Correlation Table).
[52] e.g. Brussels I Regulation arts 5.1(b), 30 and 60.

of the EC/EU and as more countries became Contracting States to the Brussels Convention, and as the Convention was revised and superseded by successor instruments. Necessary changes to the CJJA 1982, pursuant to the Brussels I Regulation, were implemented in the UK by means of the Civil Jurisdiction and Judgments Order 2001 ("CJJO 2001").[53] Further amendments to the CJJA 1982 were effected by the Civil Jurisdiction and Judgments Regulations 2009[54]; and, in light of Brussels I Recast, by the Civil Jurisdiction and Judgments (Amendment) Regulations 2014[55] and the Civil Jurisdiction and Judgments (Amendment) (Scotland) Regulations 2015.[56]

In any dispute thought to fall within the Brussels regime, it is necessary to find the date of commencement of proceedings to ascertain which instrument or version thereof applies. Brussels I Recast, like the Brussels I Regulation, by virtue of its nature as a regulation, applies to any new EU Member State automatically upon its entry to the EU.

The scheme of CJJA 1982 is:

Part I: Implementation of the Conventions, i.e. 1968 Brussels Convention and subsequent Accession Conventions, and the Lugano Convention.

Part II: Jurisdiction, and recognition and enforcement of judgments, within the United Kingdom (i.e. subordinate to the 1968 Convention; Sch.4, "Modified" Convention).

Part III: Jurisdiction in Scotland (subordinate to Pts I and II; Sch.8).

Part IV: Miscellaneous Provisions.

Part V: Supplementary and General Provisions.

BRUSSELS I RECAST

Scope

Article 1

7–15   Brussels I Recast applies in civil and commercial matters, whatever the nature of the court or tribunal. It shall not extend, in particular, to revenue, customs or administrative matters or to the liability of the State for acts and omissions in the exercise of State authority (*acta iure imperii*).

Specifically excluded from its scope are:

(a)   the status or legal capacity of natural persons,[57] rights in property arising out of a matrimonial relationship or out of a relationship deemed by the law applicable to such relationship to have comparable effects to marriage;

---

[53] CJJO 2001 (SI 2001/3929).

[54] SI 2009/3131 (in light of implementation of Lugano II).

[55] Civil Jurisdiction and Judgments Regulations 2009 (SI 2014/2947).

[56] Civil Jurisdiction and Judgments (Amendment) (Scotland) Regulations 2015 (SSI 2015/1).

[57] *Proceedings Brought by Schneider* (C-386/12) [2014] Fam. 80; [2014] 2 W.L.R. 1048.

(b)   bankruptcy, proceedings relating to the winding-up of insolvent companies or other legal persons,[58] judicial arrangements, compositions and analogous proceedings;

(c)   social security;

(d)   arbitration[59];

(e)   maintenance obligations arising from a family relationship, parentage, marriage or affinity;

(f)   wills and succession, including maintenance obligations arising by reason of death.

An important term at the outset is "civil and commercial matters". One aid to interpreting this phrase is the negative one of noting the specific exclusions from the scope of the Regulation. In *Land Berlin v Sapir*,[60] the ECJ held that the concept of "civil and commercial matters" is defined essentially by the elements which characterise the nature of the legal relationships between the parties to the dispute or the subject matter thereof. Apart from such expressly excluded cases, ECJ concern has been to distinguish, and exclude, public law from private law cases, and to ensure that this is done according to a distinction made by European law, rather than by individual legal systems. The test has been said to be functional, rather than institutional, and classification of potentially "public law" cases depends upon whether a public authority is or is not acting in exercise of its public law powers.[61]

In *Revenue and Customs Commissioners v Sunico ApS*[62] the CJEU ruled that although proceedings brought by a public authority in the exercise of its public powers did not come within the scope of the Brussels I Regulation, the concept of "civil and commercial matters" within the meaning of art.1(1) covered an action whereby a public authority of one Member State claimed, as against natural and legal persons resident in another Member State, damages for loss in tort, caused by a tortious conspiracy to commit VAT fraud in the first Member State. The nature of the claim was judged to be the defendants' alleged involvement in a conspiracy to defraud, and not based in UK tax law.

---

[58] The question of exclusion depends on whether or not the action derives directly from and is closely connected with insolvency proceedings, e.g. *SCT Industri AB i likvidation v Alpenblume AB* (C-111/08) [2009] O.J. C205/8; *F-Tex SIA v Lietuvos-Anglijos UAB Jadecloud-Vilma* (C-213/10) [2012] I.L.Pr. 24; and *Nickel & Goeldner Spedition GmbH v "Kintra" UAB* (C-157/13) [2015] Q.B. 96.

[59] See para.7–69, below.

[60] *Land Berlin v Sapir* (C-645/11) [2013] C.E.C. 947; [2013] I.L.Pr. 29.

[61] Reference should be made to *Lufttransportunternehmen GmbH & Co KG v Organisation Européenne pour la Securité de la Navigation Aérienne (Euro-Control)* (29–76) [1976] E.C.R. 1541, distinguished in *R. v Harrow Crown Court Ex p. Unic Centre Sarl* [2000] 1 W.L.R. 2112.

[62] *Revenue and Customs Commissioners v Sunico ApS* (C-49/12) [2014] Q.B. 391; [2014] 2 W.L.R. 335.

General rule

Article 4[63]

7–16   "1.   Subject to this Regulation, persons domiciled in a Member State shall, whatever their nationality, be sued in the courts of that Member State.

2.   Persons who are not nationals of the Member State in which they are domiciled shall be governed by the rules of jurisdiction applicable to nationals of that Member State."

Article 4 is the pre-eminent jurisdictional provision, to which all others are derogations. Moreover, should other optional grounds of jurisdiction fail for any reason, art.4 remains the default basis.[64] Recital (15) of the preamble to the Regulation states that rules of jurisdiction in the Regulation should be highly predictable. Jurisdiction must always be available on the ground of defendant's domicile, but in a few well defined situations (q.v.), additional or alternative grounds exist.

The 1968 Brussels Convention left the definition of the "domicile" of natural persons to the discretion of individual Conracting States. Now, for the UK, the definition of domicile of individuals is found in CJJO 2001 Sch.1 para.9 ("Domicile of indivduals—section 41"),[65] in the manner of a cascade provision: a definition is created first for the domicile of an individual in the UK[66]; next, for the domicile of an individual in a particular part of the UK[67]; and then in a particular place within the UK.[68]

The requirements for domicile in the UK, etc. are satisfied if and only if the individual is resident in the UK (or a part of the UK; or the part of the UK in which that place is situated), and the nature and circumstances of his residence indicate that he has a substantial connection with the UK, part thereof, or place therein. The requirement of a substantial connection is presumed to be fulfilled, unless the contrary is proved, if the individual has been resident in the UK, part thereof, or place therein, for the last[69] three months or more.[70] Analysis of these terms suggests, however, that there is no reason in law why an individual might not be found "domiciled" in the UK, etc. before the elapse of a three month period. The purpose of ascribing domicile in this connection is to clothe the court with jurisdiction in a civil or commercial matter, as opposed to a matter of status, and therefore it is reasonable that the criterion should be presumptively established after the expiry of a short period of time.

A relatively small number of cases exemplifies the approach of the Scots and English courts to the interpretation of domicile for this purpose. This is surprising given the central importance of the jurisdictional ground. Decisions have been required on matters such as the *tempus inspiciendum*, the effect of interruption of

---

[63] ex Brussels I Regulation art.2.
[64] cf. *Kleinwort Benson Ltd v Glasgow City Council (No.2)* [1997] 4 All E.R. 641.
[65] Amending CJJA 1982 s.41. See Ch.6, above.
[66] CJJO 2001 Sch.1 para.9(2).
[67] CJJO 2001 Sch.1 para.9(3).
[68] CJJO 2001 Sch.1 para.9(4).
[69] An undefined term, but meaning the period ending on the date on which the court is seised, which must be taken to be the date of initiation of proceedings.
[70] CJJO 2001 Sch.1 para.9(6).

the running of the period, the significance of enforced residence, and the fact of dual residence, such issues representing the type of interpretative problem which arises whenever a jurisdictional requirement is tied to a specific length of time.

The House of Lords in *Canada Trust Ltd v Stolzenberg (No.2)*,[71] in addressing itself[72] to the interpretation of the word "sued" as it appeared in art.2 of the Brussels Convention,[73] recognised that the formulation of the general rule potentially subjects the claimant to the task of "shooting at a moving target". The House held that it was in accordance with reasonable canons of interpretation to construe "sued" as a reference to the date of initiation of proceedings, which, translated into English procedure rules, is the date of issue of the writ. Therefore, the domicile of the main defendant was to be ascertained at the date of issue of the writ, and not at the later date on which the proceedings were served on him.

Where residence is coerced, as e.g. where an individual was bailed to remain in the UK until trial, domicile in the place of effective imprisonment will not normally be found.[74]

In *Daniel v Foster*,[75] Sheriff Palmer assumed jurisdiction, in a Sch.4 ("Modified Convention") case where jurisdiction was at issue as a result of the defender's pattern of life. The defender spent regular, but intermittent, periods of time within the sheriffdom attending to his business interests, and the remainder of his time at his principal residence in Sussex, without it being able to be shown that he was resident continuously within the sheriffdom. The sheriff in effect held that the requisite period of three months' residence need not be continuous. Hence, dual "domicile" or even multiple "domicile" is a possibility in this context.[76] An abundance of residences may produce the effect that the owner thereof is not "domiciled" for the purpose of art.4 in any of them; and if so, he may be beyond the reach of the Brussels regime, which is something of an achievement.[77]

Article 62.1 of Brussels I Recast provides that in order to determine whether a party is domiciled in the Member State whose courts are seised of a matter, the court shall apply its internal law. By contrast, art.62.2 provides that if a party is (alleged) not to be domiciled in the Member State of the forum, then in order to determine whether the party is domiciled in another Member State, the forum shall apply the law of that other Member State.[78]

---

[71] *Canada Trust Ltd v Stolzenberg (No.2)* [2000] 4 All E.R. 481.

[72] In advance of the autonomous definition of "date at which a court shall be deemed to be seised", provided by art.30, Brussels I Regulation, and contained now in Brussels I Recast art.32 (q.v.).

[73] Contained now in art.4 of Brussels I Recast.

[74] *Petrotrade Inc v Smith* [1999] 1 W.L.R. 457.

[75] *Daniel v Foster,* 1989 S.L.T. (Sh. Ct.) 90 (Sch.4 case). See also *Relfo Ltd (In Liquidation) v Varsani* [2010] EWCA Civ 560; and *Work Legal E-Ltd v Allen Court of Session* [2015] CSOH 12; 2015 G.W.D. 6-115.

[76] *Gruppo Torras SA v Al-Sabah (No.1)* [1995] 1 Lloyd's Rep. 374 at 444–446; and *Haji-Ioannou v Frangos* [1999] 2 All E.R. (Comm) 865, where the question arose, inter alia, of the application of the Brussels Convention art.2 in circumstances where the defendant was resident in Monaco, a non-Contracting State, but arguably might have been considered by Greek law (as to which expert evidence was offered) also to have a special business domicile in Greece.

[77] e.g. *Cherney v Deripaska* [2007] I.L.Pr. 49.

[78] e.g. *Haji-Ioannou v Frangos* [1999] 2 All E.R. (Comm) 865. This is worthy of remark from the perspective that in the usage of classic domicile, the forum applies its own law to all determinations of domicile: *Re Annesley* [1926] Ch. 692.

The definition of the "domicile" of juristic persons has received an autonomous Community definition, in art.63, viz. that a company or other legal person is domiciled where it has its (a) statutory seat[79]; (b) its central administration[80]; or (c) principal place of business.[81] Recital (15) of the Regulation provides that the domicile of a legal person must be defined autonomously so as to make the common rules more transparent and to avoid conflicts of jurisdiction.

Significance of defendant's domicile

Article 5

7–17

"1.   Persons domiciled in a Member State may be sued in the courts of another Member State only by virtue of the rules set out in Sections 2 to 7 of this chapter.

2.   In particular, the rules of national jurisdiction…shall not be applicable as against the persons referred to in paragraph 1."

Article 5.2[82] is intended to exclude the application of exorbitant national grounds of jurisdiction of Member States against EU domiciliaries. Unacceptable "UK" grounds are those which enable jurisdiction to be founded on:

(a)   service of the document instituting the proceedings on the defendant during his temporary presence in the UK; or

(b)   the existence within the UK of property belonging to the defendant; or

(c)   the seizure by the claimant of property situated in the UK.

Article 6

7–18   Article 6 preserves the residual national rules of jurisdiction of Member States, viz.:

"1.   If the defendant is not domiciled in a Member State, the jurisdiction of the courts of each Member State shall, subject to Article 18(1), Article 21(2) and Articles 24 and 25, be determined by the law of that Member State.[83]

---

[79] Brussels I Recast art.63.2 states that for the purposes of the UK, Ireland and Cyprus, "statutory seat" means the registered office or where there is no such office anywhere, the place of incorporation or, where there is no such place anywhere, the place under the law of which the formation of the entity took place.

[80] *Young v Anglo American South Africa Ltd* [2014] EWCA Civ 1130: the "central administration" of a company is the place where, through its relevant organs according to its own constitutional provisions, it took the essential decisions of its entrepreneurial management.

[81] *King v Crown Energy Trading AG* [2003] EWHC 163; and *889457 Alberta Inc v Katanga Mining Ltd* [2009] I.L.Pr. 14. See also CJJO 2001 Sch.1 para.10 (seat of company or other legal person or association for purposes of art.24.2).

[82] See also art.76.

[83] i.e. by the residual national rules of the Member State. One consequence of this provision is that it enables a UK court to defer to another Member State court, sub nom. *forum non conveniens*, so long as the defendant is not domiciled in a Member State, even though in principle the plea of *forum non conveniens* has no place within the Brussels regime: *The Xin Yang and The An Kang Jiang* [1996] 2 Lloyd's Rep. 217. See para.7–81, below.

2.   As against such a defendant, any person domiciled in a Member State may, whatever his nationality, avail himself in that Member State of the rules of jurisdiction there in force, and in particular those of which the Member States are to notify the Commission pursuant to point (a) of Article 76(1), in the same way as nationals of that State."

The subject of residual, national jurisdiction is a controversial and complex one, considered in detail later in this chapter.[84] There has been much speculation as to the proper delineation of the European legal space. The process of measuring the extent of the Brussels regime in the aftermath of Brussels I Recast must be achieved by scrutiny, provision by provision, of those articles of the regulation which impinge upon a Member State's relations with Third States (i.e. non-EU Member States) and with Third State defendants (i.e. non-EU domiciled defendants).

The bold European proposal to harmonise the residual national rules of Member States was not realised. The limits imposed by Brussels I Recast on the use of residual national rules against Third State defendants are that the operation of such rules shall not contravene arts 18.1 (consumers), 21(2) (employer defendants), 24 (exclusive jurisdiction), and 25 (prorogation).[85]

Special jurisdictions

Article 7 of Brussels I Recast permits a claimant to pursue his claim in a forum other than that of the defendant's domicile, according to the nature of the litigation. Special jurisdiction is deemed to be justified by the existence, in certain well-defined circumstances, of a close link between a dispute and the court which might be called upon to hear and determine the case.[86]   **7–19**

These derogations from art.4 provide a useful alternative at the disposal of the claimant. There might be procedural or substantive law advantages to the claimant of suing in a particular forum.

The options available under art.7 are available only where the defendant is a person domiciled in a Member State. The most important special jurisdictions concern contract and delict, respectively.

Article 7.1—matters relating to a contract[87]

"A person domiciled in a Member State may be sued in another Member State: **7–20**
(1)(a) in matters relating to a contract, in the courts for the place of performance of the obligation in question;
(b)   for the purpose of this provision and unless otherwise agreed, the place of performance of the obligation in question shall be:
—   in the case of the sale of goods, the place in a Member State where, under the contract, the goods were delivered or should have been delivered,

---

[84] Para.7–75 et seq., below.
[85] Para.7–62, below.
[86] e.g. *Krejci Lager & Umschlagbetriebs GmbH v Olbrich Transport und Logistik GmbH* (C-469/12) [2014] C.E.C. 654; [2014] I.L.Pr. 8.
[87] cf. Brussels I Regulation art.5.1.

> — in the case of the provision of services, the place in a Member State where, under the contract, the services were provided or should have been provided;
>
> (c) if point (b) does not apply then point (a) applies..."

Since 1968, there has been a significant amount of litigation regarding interpretation of the neighbouring phrases, "matters relating to a contract"[88] and "obligation in question",[89] to the point where it could be said that Member State courts have to abide by a Community approach. These concepts must be interpreted independently, regard being had to the general scheme and objectives of the Regulation, in order to ensure that they are applied uniformly in all the Member States.[90]

Application of the rule in art.7.1 presupposes the establishment of a legal obligation freely assumed by one person towards another and on which the claimant's action is based.[91] The disputed existence of a contract is a "matter relating to a contract" so long as the claimant can satisfy the court that there is a "good arguable case" that a matter relating to a contract is in issue between the parties.[92] Similarly, repudiation of a contract is a "matter relating to a contract". This has an obvious tactical implication in a *lis pendens* system (q.v.), which tolerates the use of negative actings to initiate litigation in an available jurisdiction by a party who wishes to deny the existence of a contract.[93] Where the parties to a contract have agreed to refer "disputes arising therefrom, or in connection therewith", to arbitration, any subsequent claim made by one of the parties in relation to the contract, which the other does not admit, is a relevant dispute which the claimant is both entitled and bound to refer to arbitration. The belief or contention by the claimant that the defendant has no arguable defence does not take the matter out of the category of "dispute between the parties".[94]

In contrast, with regard to interpretation of the phrase "place of performance", each forum putatively seised under the 1968 Convention was directed to use its own choice of law rules.[95] This necessitated the forum adopting a two-step

---

[88] e.g. *Martin Peters Bauunternehmung GmbH v Zuid Nederlandse Aannemers Vereniging* [1983] E.C.R. 987; *Arcado SPRL v Haviland SA* (9/87) [1988] E.C.R. 1539; *Powell Duffryn Plc v Petereit* [1992] E.C.R. I-1745; *Jakob Handte & Co GmbH v Traitements Mecano-Chimiques des Surfaces SA (TCMS)* [1992] E.C.R. I-3967; *Boss Group Ltd v Boss France SA* [1996] 4 All E.R. 970; *Source v TUV Rheinland Holding* [1998] Q.B. 54; *Belgian International Insurance Group SA v McNicoll*, 1999 G.W.D. 22–1065; and *Assitalia SpA v Frahuil SA* (C265/02) [2004] All E.R. (EC) 373 ECJ (ostensible authority to enter into contract); and *Kolassa v Barclays Bank Plc* (C-375/13) [2015] I.L.Pr. 14.

[89] e.g. *A De Bloos SPRL v Bouyer SA* (C-14/76) [1976] E.C.R. 1497; *Union Transport Group Plc v Continental Lines SA* [1992] 1 All E.R. 161 (where there are several obligations, the "obligation in question" is the principal one); *Agnew v Lansforsakringbolagens AB* [1996] 4 All E.R. 978 (no express distinction between obligations arising during negotiation of a contract, and those arising under or after the contract); *AIG Group (UK) Ltd v Ethniki* [2000] 2 All E.R. 566; *RPS Prodotti Sidrurgici Srl v Owners of the Sea Maas (The Sea Maas)* [2000] 1 All E.R. 536; and *Bitwise Ltd v CPS Broadcast Products BV*, 2003 S.L.T. 455.

[90] *Ceska Sporitelna, AS v Feichter* (Case C-419/11) [2013] I.L.Pr. 22.

[91] *OFAB, Ostergotlands Fastigheter AB v Koot* (C-147/12) [2015] Q.B. 20.

[92] *Boss Group Ltd v Boss France SA* [1996] 4 All E.R. 970.

[93] See para.7–59, below.

[94] *The Halki* [1997] 3 All E.R. 833; and *Benincasa v Dentalkit Srl* (C-269/95) [1998] All E.R. (EC) 135.

[95] e.g. *Industrie Tessili Italiana Como v Dunlop AG* (12/76) [1976] E.C.R. 1473; *Ivenel v Schwab* (133/81) [1982] E.C.R. 1891; *Shenavai v Kreischer* (266/85) [1987] E.C.R. 239; *Fisher v Unione*

method of reasoning: (i) the applicable law of the contract was ascertained by means of application of the forum's choice of law rules; and (ii) the applicable law thereby identified was used to identify the place of performance. If the place of performance so determined was the legal system of the forum, the forum concluded that it had jurisdiction in terms of art.5.1 of the Convention.[96]

One of the refinements introduced by the Brussels I Regulation,[97] to remove the complexities which arose under the Convention version of the text, was the ascription of an autonomous Community meaning to the phrase "place of performance". This constituted an improvement, and it is not surprising that the change effected by the Brussels I Regulation has been repeated in Brussels I Recast. However, if the case does not fall within art.7.1(b), art.7.1(c) directs that art.7.1(a) applies, which means that the default position and reasoning remains the same as the original Brussels Convention approach.

In the case of sale of goods, where the place of delivery of goods is identified in the contract, the place of performance shall be that place.[98] Where delivery is to be made on the basis of an FOB contract, the place of delivery is the port of shipment.[99] Only exceptionally will the court look behind the technical terms of the contract in order to discover the true state of contractual affairs.[100] If there is more than one place of delivery within one Member State, and the national court cannot determine the principal place of delivery, the ECJ has ruled that the claimant may bring proceedings in whichever of those places he wishes.[101]

With regard to "provision of services",[102] it is well established that the concept of service implies, at least, that the party who provided the service carried out a particular activity in return for remuneration.[103] Where services are provided in several EU Member States, the place of performance is the place of the main provision of services.[104] The decision of the ECJ in *Rehder v Air Baltic Corp*[105] is

---

Italiana de Riassicurazione Spa [1998] 8 C.L. 71 (denial of obligation to perform); *GIE Groupe Concorde v Master of the Vessel Suhadiwarno Panjan* (C-440/97) [2000] All E.R. (EC) 865; *Montagu Evans (A Firm) v Young*, 2000 S.L.T. 1083; *Ennstone Building Products Ltd v Stanger (No.1)* [2002] C.L.Y.B. 624; *Besix SA v Wasserreinigungsbau Alfred Kretzschmar GmbH & Co KG (WABAG)* (C256/00) [2003] 1 W.L.R. 1113 ECJ; *Prifti v Musini Sociedad Anonima de Suguros y Reaseguros* [2003] EWHC 2796; and *Engler v Janus Versand GmbH* (27/02) [2005] 7 C.L. 76 ECJ.

[96] *William Grant & Sons International Ltd v Marie Brizard Espana SA*, 1998 S.C. 536; and *Ferguson Shipbuilders Ltd v Voith Hydro GmbH & Co KG*, 2000 S.L.T. 229.

[97] Note that in Sch.4 (the Modified Convention) para.3(a), wording equivalent to the Brussels Convention art.5.1 remains: *JS Swan (Printing) Ltd v Kall Kwik UK Ltd*, 2009 G.W.D. 27–431; and *Commercial Marine Piling Ltd v Pierse Contracting Ltd* [2009] 2 Lloyd's Rep. 659.

[98] *DPT (Duroplast Technik Verwaltungs) GmbH v Chemiplastica SpA* [2009] I.L.Pr. 15 Court of Cassation (Italy).

[99] *Re Place of Performance of an FOB Contract* [2010] I.L.Pr. 17 Federal Supreme Court (Germany).

[100] *Scottish & Newcastle International Ltd v Othon Ghalanos Ltd* [2008] UKHL 11; and *Electrosteel Europe SA v Edil Centro SpA* (C-87/10) [2011] I.L.Pr. 28.

[101] *Color Drack GmbH v Lexx International Vertriebs GmbH* (C-386/05) [2008] All E.R. (EC) 1044.

[102] A phrase which has been held by the CJEU to extend to distribution agreements (*Corman-Collins SA v La Maison du Whisky SA* (C-9/12) [2014] Q.B. 431; [2014] 2 W.L.R. 494), and to storage contracts (*Krejci Lager & Umschlagbetriebs GmbH v Olbrich Transport und Logistik GmbH* (C-469/12) [2014] C.E.C. 654; [2014] I.L.Pr. 8).

[103] *Falco Privatstiftung und Rabitsch v Weller-Lindhorst* (C-533/07) [2009] E.C.R. I-3327; and *Krejci Lager & Umschlagbetriebs GmbH v Olbrich Transport und Logistik GmbH* (C-469/12) [2014] C.E.C. 654; [2014] I.L.Pr. 8.

[104] *Wood Floor Solutions Andreas Domberger GmbH v Silva Trade SA* (C-19/09) [2010] I.L.Pr. 21.

[105] *Rehder v Air Baltic Corp* (C-204/08) [2009] I.L.Pr. 44.

to the effect that when an air passenger who intended to travel from one Member State to another suffered the cancellation of his flight, he could bring proceedings for compensation either in the court of the jurisdiction of the Member State place of departure, or that of the place of arrival. The rationale offered is that, where services are provided in different Member States, the jurisdiction must be found which has the closest linking factor with the contract, and in that scenario each place was deemed to be equally closely linked.

Inevitably, circumstances can arise in which obligations for the provision of services *and* for the sale of goods present. In *Societe ND Conseil SA v Societe le Meridien Hotels et Resorts World Headquarters*,[106] the service element of the contract trumped the sale of goods element; whereas in *Car Trim GmbH v KeySafety Systems Srl*,[107] the dominant characteristic of the "mixed" contract was the supply of goods, even though the purchaser had given detailed specifications with regard to his requirements as to the components to be produced.

Nullity of contract

7–21   There is no bespoke special jurisdiction rule for cases of unjust enrichment.[108] As will be seen in the examination of choice of law rules in contract, the interface between contract and unjust enrichment presents difficulties, both in domestic and conflict terms.[109]

The House of Lords held in *Kleinwort Benson Ltd v City of Glasgow City Council (No.2)*[110] that a claim arising in restitution from a *void* contract did not fall under special jurisdiction in contract. On the other hand, as has been seen, matters relating to a contract can include matters relating to a disputed contract.[111] *Kleinwort* is not an ECJ decision,[112] and it may be that, in the event of a reference for a preliminary ruling, the CJEU might take a different view.

---

[106] *Societe ND Conseil SA v Societe le Meridien Hotels et Resorts World Headquarters* [2007] I.L.Pr. 39: the French *Cour de Cassation* accepted the reasoning of the Versailles *Cour d'Appel* that the contractual obligation consisted of the provision of intellectual services and the delivery of goods in the form of advertising material, and that the latter was merely an accessory obligation to the provision of services; the whole constituted a single obligation, led by the services component which, having been provided in London, conferred jurisdiction on the English court.

[107] *Car Trim GmbH v KeySafety Systems Srl* [2009] I.L.Pr. 33.

[108] See, however, *Stevens v Hamed* [2013] EWCA Civ 911. Contrast the choice of law position in Rome II, Ch.III of which deals with non-contractual obligations arising out of unjust enrichment, *negotiorum gestio*, and *culpa in contrahendo*: para.16–56 et seq., below.

[109] See Ch.15, below.

[110] *Kleinwort Benson Ltd v City of Glasgow City Council (No.2)* [1999] 1 A.C. 153 (a case under CJJA 1982 Sch.4). Lord Goff, delivering the leading speech, further stated that such a claim could not fall under special jurisdiction in tort (q.v.), since, in general, unjust enrichment does not presuppose a harmful event or a threatened wrong. Ante-dating this decision is a shrieval decision, *Strathaird Farms Ltd v GA Chattaway Co*, 1993 S.L.T. (Sh. Ct.) 36 that a claim under the *condictio indebiti* does not qualify as a "matter relating to a contract".

[111] *Boss Group Ltd v Boss Group France SA* [1996] 4 All E.R. 970; *The Halki* [1997] 3 All E.R. 833; *Belgian International Insurance Group SA v McNicoll*, 1999 G.W.D. 22–1065; and *Stevens and Hamed* [2013] EWCA Civ 911.

[112] The question whether restitution was to be regarded as falling under quasi-delict was referred by the Court of Appeal to the ECJ in *Barclays Bank Plc v City of Glasgow DC*; sub nom. *Kleinwort Benson Ltd v Glasgow City Council (No.1)* [1994] 2 W.L.R. 466, but the ECJ held that it had no jurisdiction to give a ruling on the interpretation of the Modified Convention (Sch.4): *Kleinwort Benson Ltd v Glasgow City Council* (C346/93) [1995] All E.R. (EC) 514.

Arguably (especially from a European perspective), the consequences of nullity of a contract *should* be characterised as contractual for the purposes of jurisdiction, chiming with the Rome I Regulation for choice of law. It is hoped that the matter will be considered by the CJEU in such a way as to place a restitutionary claim of this sort under art.7.1 of Brussels I Recast. It seems not unreasonable that in all Member State courts the remedy for such claims be regulated by the content of what must be the putative applicable law of the void contract, and that the court properly seised to implement this remedy be, as it were, the "putative court" under art.7.1. To say that claims resulting from *void* contracts fall outside the ambit of art.7.1, but those which arise out of *voidable or unenforceable* contracts fall within its ambit, is not a helpful dividing line, and is one which is likely to be productive of uncertainty.

Culpa in contrahendo

As to the jurisdiction aspect of pre-contractual obligations (a matter left open in *Kleinwort*), the House of Lords in *Agnew*[113] was prepared to hold that special jurisdiction in contract applied. The justification for utilising this ground is likely to be strongly fact-dependent. While a misrepresentation on the way to the conclusion of a contract might justify engaging art.7.1, allegations of breach of a "duty" not to use undue influence or duress, or other negative obligation, would seem to be a less persuasive case for special jurisdiction in contract[114] (but surely would not altogether foreclose an argument for the engagement of art.7.2, q.v., assuming that the forum putatively seised was that of the occurrence of actual or anticipated harm). For example, where it was alleged that a party unjustifiably broke off negotiations, the ECJ held in *Fonderie Officine Meccaniche Tacconi SpA*[115] that no obligation having been assumed by one party to another, there was no obligation assumed by the defendant which could justify application of the special jurisdiction in contract rule. Any alleged breach of the duty of good faith imposed by the Italian Civil Code upon which the claimant sought to rely would require to be placed in jurisdictional terms under the special rule of jurisdiction in tort. In *Fonderie*, no contract resulted, and so *Agnew* might be distinguished on that ground. These are very nice distinctions.

7–22

Article 7.2—matters relating to tort, delict or quasi-delict[116]

A person domiciled in a Member State[117] may be sued in another Member State:

7–23

> "2.   in matters relating to tort, delict or quasi-delict, in the courts for the place where the harmful event occurred or may occur".[118]

---

[113] *Agnew v Lansforsakringsbolagens AB* [2001] 1 A.C. 223 (re Lugano).
[114] *Cheshire, North and Fawcett: Private International Law*, 14th edn (2008), pp.231, 232.
[115] *Fonderie Officine Meccaniche Tacconi SpA v Heinrich Wagner Sinto Machinenfabrik GmbH* (C-334/00) [2002] E.C.R. I-7357.
[116] cf. Brussels I Regulation art.5.3.
[117] *G v de Visser* (C-292/10) [2013] Q.B. 168; [2012] 3 W.L.R. 1523.
[118] cf. Under CJJA 1982 Sch.4 (q.v.), *Bonnier Media Ltd v Kestral Trading Corp*, 2002 S.C.L.R. 977. See also Reference from German Federal Court of Justice to the ECJ: *eDate Advertising GmbH v X* (Case C-509/09) [2010] O.J. C134/14.

"Tort, delict or quasi-delict" has an independent Community meaning.The concept of "matters relating to tort, delict or quasi-delict" within the meaning of art.7.2 covers all actions which seek to establish the liability of a defendant and do not concern "matters relating to a contract" within the meaning of art.7.1.[119] Whether an event is harmful is to be decided by the domestic law of the legal system chosen to govern the issue by the choice of law rules of the court seised.[120]

It is said that the "place where the harmful event occurred" must have a high degree of predictability for all parties.[121] However, interpretative difficulties have arisen in jurisdiction (and in choice of law)[122] in identifying the locus of double or multi-locality delicts, that is, where elements of the delict occur in different legal systems, most commonly where the place of acting differs from the place of effect; and also where an act or omission giving rise to injury in one jurisdiction, is followed in another legal system by deterioration of the victim's condition,[123] and/or further consequential damage.

The point was famously discussed in *Bier BV v Mines de Potasse d'Alsace SA*[124] (in circumstances where the pollution of the Rhine in France harmed the plants of a market gardener in Holland), to the effect that the rule of special jurisdiction in delict confers jurisdiction on the courts *both* for the place of acting (the place of the event giving rise to the damage), *and* the place where the effect(s) is/are felt (the place where the damage occurs), affording an option, within the option of special jurisdictions, to the aggrieved party to sue in either.

In the context of product liability, the CJEU held in *Kainz v Pantherwerke AG*,[125] that, where a manufacturer faces a claim of liability for a defective product, the "place of the event giving rise to the damage" (i.e. the place of acting) is the place where the product in question was manufactured. In an earlier case examining the meaning of the place where the damage occurred, *Zuid Chemie BV v Philippo's Mineralenfabriek NV/SA*,[126] the ECJ, in response to a reference from the Dutch Hoge Raad asking whether the initial damage would be the damage which arose by virtue of delivery of a defective product, or the

---

[119] *Kalfelis v Bankhaus Schroder Munchmeyer Hengst & Co (t/a HEMA Beteiligungsgesellschaft GmbH)* [1988] E.C.R. 5565; *Swithenbank Food Ltd v Bowers* [2002] 2 All E.R. (Comm) 974; *Verein fur Konsumenteninformation v Henkel* (C-167/00) [2003] All E.R. (EC) 311; *Danmarks Rederiforening v Landsorganisationen i Sverige* (C18/02) [2004] All E.R. (EC) 845; *Brogsitter v Fabrication de Montres Normandes EURL* (C-548/12) [2014] Q.B. 753; and *Kolassa v Barclays Bank Plc* (C-375/13) [2015] I.L.Pr.14. cf. para.7–27, below re relationship between arts 7.1 and 7.2.

[120] *Kitechnology BV v Unicor GmbH Plastmaschininen* [1994] I.L.Pr. 568; and *Dumez France and Tracoba v Hessische Landesbank* (C220/88) [1990] E.C.R. I–49.

[121] *OFAB, Ostergotlands Fastigheter AB v Koot* (C-147/12) [2015] Q.B. 20.

[122] Para.16–10, below.

[123] e.g. *Henderson v Jaouen* [2002] 2 All E.R. 705; and *Dolphin Maritime & Aviation Services Ltd v Sveriges Angfartygs Assurans Forening* [2009] I.L.Pr. 52.

[124] *Bier BV v Mines de Potasse d'Alsace SA* [1976] E.C.R. 1735. See also *Mecklermedia Corp v DC Congress GmbH* [1998] 1 All E.R. 148; *Reunion Europeene SA v Spliethoff's Bevrachtingskantoor BV* (C51/97) [1998] CLYB 769; *Raiffeisen Zentral Bank Osterreich AG v Tranos* [2001] I.L.Pr. 9; *Ennstone Building Products Ltd v Stanger (No.1)* [2002] C.L.Y.B. 624; *Kronhofer v Maier* (C168/02) [2004] All E.R. (EC) 939; *Mackie (t/a 197 Aerial Photography) v Askew*, 2009 S.L.T. (Sh. Ct.) 146; and *Future Investments SA v Federation Internationale de Football Association* [2010] EWHC 1019 Ch and *Cartel Damage Claims (CDC) Hydrogen Peroxide SA v Azko Nobel NV* (Case C-352/13).

[125] *Kainz v Pantherwerke AG* (C-45/13) [2015] Q.B. 34; [2014] 3 W.L.R. 1292.

[126] *Zuid Chemie BV v Philippo's Mineralenfabriek NV/SA* (C-189/08) [2009] O.J. C220/11.

damage which arose when normal use was made of the product, the Court held that the words "the place where the harmful event occurred" designated the place where the initial damage occurred as a result of the normal use of the product for the purpose for which it was intended. Accordingly, the place where the product was used for the purpose for which it was intended, and thereby caused damage, was the place of initial damage.

As regards the "place where damage occurred", so long as some primary harm occurred within a Member State, that will suffice to confer jurisdiction upon the courts thereof,[127] but consequential, tangential or secondary economic loss suffered in a Member State will not be enough to confer art.7.2 jurisdiction.[128] In *Deutsche Bahn AG v Morgan Advanced Materials Plc (formerly Morgan Crucible Co Plc)*,[129] the English Court of Appeal made clear that, although special jurisdiction in tort points to the place where direct damage occurred, it can be relied upon by *any* putative claimant. Tomlinson L.J. stated that there was no justification for imposing upon art.5.3 of the Brussels I Regulation:

> "a gloss to the effect that, in order to be a relevant connecting factor between defendant and putative jurisdiction, a harmful event must be one of which the putative claimant is an immediate victim. That would seem to involve a search for a connecting factor between the claimant and the putative jurisdiction, rather than a connecting factor between the defendant and the putative jurisdiction, which is what the regulation is concerned with."[130]

This case concerned an action by 30 claimants for damages under the Competition Act 1998 against six defendants, following a 2003 decision by the European Commission that the defendants had been engaged in a cartel.

The mere fact that a claimant has suffered adverse financial consequences does not justify the attribution of jurisdiction to the courts of his domicile, where both the events causing loss and the loss itself occurred in the territory of another Member State. The position is different (i.e. jurisdiction will be attributed by art.7.2) if the claimant's domicile coincides with the place where the events giving rise to the loss took place or the loss occurred.[131]

---

[127] *Minster Investments Ltd v Hyundai Precision & Industry Co Ltd* [1988] 2 Lloyd's Rep. 621; and *Equitas Ltd v Wave City Shipping Co Ltd* [2005] 2 All E.R. (Comm) 301.

[128] *Dumez France SA v Hessische Landesbank* (220/88) [1990] E.C.R. I-49; and *Marinari v Lloyd's Bank Plc* [1996] All E.R. (EC) 84. cf. Case C-12/15: Request for a preliminary ruling from the Hoge Raad der Nederlanden (Netherlands) lodged on 14 January 2015 – *Universal Music International Holding BV v Michael Tétreault Schilling*[2015] O.J. C89, in which the following question has been referred, "Must Article 5(3) be interpreted as meaning that the 'place where the harmful event occurred' can be construed as being the place in a Member State where the damage occurred, if that damage consists exclusively of financial damage which is the direct result of unlawful conduct which occurred in another Member State?".

[129] *Deutsche Bahn AG v Morgan Advanced Materials Plc (formerly Morgan Crucible Co Plc)* [2013] EWCA Civ 1484. See also *AMT Futures Ltd v Marzillier, Dr Meier & Dr Guntner Rechtsanwaltsgesellschaft mbH* [2015] EWCA Civ 143.

[130] *Deutsche Bahn AG v Morgan Advanced Materials Plc (formerly Morgan Crucible Co Plc)* [2013] EWCA Civ 1484 at [20].

[131] *Kronhofer v Maier* (C-168/02) [2004] E.C.R. I-6009; [2004] I.L.Pr. 27; *Coty Germany GmbH v First Note Perfumes NV* (C-360/12) [2014] Bus. L.R. 1294; [2014] E.T.M.R. 49; [2015] I.L.Pr. 14; and *Kolassa v Barclays Bank Plc* (C-375/13) [2015] I.L.Pr. 14.

Defamation claims

7–24 *Shevill v Presse Alliance SA*[132] is authority for the proposition that a claimant may sue a publisher, under art.2 of the Brussels Convention (cf. Brussels I Recast art.4), for defamation, in the publisher's place of business, for all damage, wherever it is alleged to have been suffered. Alternatively, the defendant may be sued (using *Bier* reasoning) in the jurisdiction where any (even small) circulation of the allegedly defamatory matter occurred, but only to the extent of the damage allegedly suffered by the claimant in that jurisdiction. This means that the publication of only a few copies of allegedly defamatory material in Scotland is in principle sufficient to clothe the Scots court with jurisdiction to determine the defamation claim and award relief for damage sustained within the jurisdiction.

This "separate" or "pluralist" or "mosaic" approach, rather than "global" or "universal" approach, has been favoured also in non-EU cases.[133] But in an attempt to address the problem of "libel tourism", a term used to describe a claimant seeking to sue in a forum with which the case, and/or the parties, has/have only a tenuous connection, s.9 of the Defamation Act 2013 has been introduced for England and Wales.[134] Section 9 applies only to actions for defamation against parties who are not domiciled in the UK, in another EU Member State, or in a Lugano II Contracting State. By s.9(2), a court in England and Wales is not entitled to exercise jurisdiction in respect of such an action unless the court is satisfied that "of all the places in which the statement complained of has been published, England and Wales is clearly the most appropriate place in which to bring an action in respect of the statement".[135] This apparently simple, common sense approach, albeit conferring much discretion on the forum, can address libel tourism cases falling outside the scope of the Brussels/Lugano regime. Many signal cases spring from that non-EU source.[136]

Warby J. in *Sloutsker v Romanova*[137] commented that "As the law stands, the same principles apply to internet publication as apply to hard copy publication, except that the court's discretion in an internet context 'will tend to be more open-textured than otherwise'." Against this background it is interesting to observe the failure of the aggrieved parties in *Clark v TripAdvisor LLC*[138] to

---

[132] *Shevill v Presse Alliance SA* [1996] 3 All E.R. 929.

[133] e.g. *Barclay v Sweeney* [1999] I.L.Pr. 288 Court of Appeal (Paris); *Berezovsky v Michaels (No.1)* [2000] 1 W.L.R. 1004; *Godfrey v Demon Internet Ltd* [2001] Q.B. 201; *Bonnier Media Ltd v Smith*, 2003 S.C. 36; *King v Lewis* [2004] I.L.Pr. 31; *Applause Stores Ltd v Raphael* [2008] EWHC 1781 QB; and *Lockton Companies International v Persons Unknown* [2009] EWHC 3423 QB.

[134] By s.17(3) of the 2013 Act, s.9 extends only to England and Wales and not to Scotland.

[135] According to the Explanatory Memorandum to the Act, the range of factors which the court may wish to take into account include the amount of damage to the claimant's reputation in England compared to elsewhere, the extent to which the publication was targeted at a readership in England compared to elsewhere, and whether or not there is reason to think that the claimant would not receive a fair hearing elsewhere (para.66).

[136] e.g. *Sloutsker v Romanova* [2015] EWHC 545 (QB), concerning a Russian claimant who brought libel proceedings in England against a defendant resident in Russia. The English court regarded itself as a proper forum for the claim because the claimant had a reputation which was significant and widespread enough to make it likely that the publication in England of seriously defamatory allegations would lead to serious harm.

[137] *Sloutsker v Romanova* [2015] EWHC 545 (QB) at [43]; with reference to *King v Lewis* [2004] EWCA Civ 1329 at [31].

[138] *Clark v TripAdvisor LLC*, 2015 S.L.T. 59.

secure their desired remedy. The owners of a Scottish guest house petitioned the Scots court for an order ordaining the operators of a website to disclose information as to the identity of persons who posted on the site unfavourable and *ex facie* defamatory reviews of the guest house. At first instance, the respondents' plea of no jurisdiction was sustained, in circumstances where the defendant was an American company, incorporated under the law of the State of Massachusetts, and having no place of business in the UK. Moreover, the respondents averred that the registration process in respect of the TripAdvisor website required users expressly to accept certain terms of use which promulgated the exclusive jurisdiction of the courts of the State of Massachusetts. At first instance and on appeal, the petition proceedings were held to fall within the scope of the jurisdiction clause.

Infringements of personality rights

Related to, but different from, defamation, is the subject of infringement of personality rights. Victims of such wrongs are particularly vulnerable when the defamatory communication or infringement is by online means.   **7–25**

In *eDate Advertising GmbH v X* (C-509/09)[139] the CJEU was required to interpret the *Shevill* principle in the context of online media. The Court held that a person who considered that his personality rights had been infringed by means of content placed online on an internet website may bring an action (i) in respect of all the damage caused, before the courts of either the Member State in which the publisher of the content is established or the Member State in which the centre of the claimant's interests are based; or (ii) in respect only of the damage caused within the territory of the forum, before the court of each Member State in the territory of which content placed online was or had been accessible. In so doing, the Court gave a ruling which "reconciled the interests of the media with the need to safeguard the legal position of the holder of personality rights".[140] The place where a person has the centre of his interests "corresponds in general to his habitual residence. However, a person may also have the centre of his interests in a member state in which he does not habitually reside, in so far as other factors, such as the pursuit of a professional activity, may establish the existence of a particularly close link with that state."[141] In the Court's judgment, conferring jurisdiction on the court of the place where the alleged victim has the centre of his interests accords with the aim of predictability of the rules governing jurisdiction, from the perspective of the claimant and also, it is said, from that of the defendant since the publisher of harmful content, at the time at which that content is placed online, is in a position to know the centres of interests of the persons who are the subject of that content.[142]

---

[139] *Martinez v MGN Ltd* (C-161/10)) (aka *E-Date Advertising GmbH v X* (C-509/09)) [2012] Q.B. 654.

[140] *Martinez v MGN Ltd* (C-161/10)) (aka *E-Date Advertising GmbH v X* (C-509/09)) [2012] Q.B. 654, per Advocate General Cruz Villalón at [49]. Cf. *Vidal-Hall v Google Inc* [2015] EWCA Civ 311.

[141] *Martinez v MGN Ltd* (C-161/10)) (aka *E-Date Advertising GmbH v X* (C-509/09)) [2012] Q.B. 654, judgment of the Court, [49]. See also Opinion of Advocate General Cruz Villalón at [58]–[59].

[142] *Martinez v MGN Ltd* (C-161/10)) (aka *E-Date Advertising GmbH v X* (C-509/09)) [2012] Q.B. 654, judgment of the Court, [50].

Alleged infringement of intellectual property rights

7–26   The CJEU in *Wintersteiger AG v Products 4U Sondermaschinenbau GmbH*[143] drew a distinction between the approach to jurisdiction with regard to infringement of personality rights and the approach in respect of infringements of intellectual property rights. Generally protection of the latter is provided on a territorial basis. Hence, for reasons of foreseeability, jurisdiction should lie with the courts of the Member State in which the trade mark at issue was registered, since such courts are best able to assess whether a situation infringes the protected national mark. However, "an action relating to alleged infringement of a trade mark registered in a Member State through the use, by an advertiser, of a keyword identical to that trade mark on a search engine website operating under a country-specific top-level domain of another Member State" might also be brought before the courts of the Member State of the place of establishment of the advertiser.[144]

In *Pinckney v KDG Mediatech AG*,[145] a case concerning alleged copyright infringement,[146] an action was brought by the author of a work against a company established in another Member State, which company in the latter State, reproduced the work, for subsequent sale by companies established in a third Member State. The sale was to be conducted through an internet site accessible also within the jurisdiction of the court seised. The CJEU held that, in the event of alleged infringement of copyrights protected by the Member State of the court seised, that court had jurisdiction to determine only such damage as was caused within its own territory. The Court, referring to *Wintersteiger*, approved the distinction in jurisdictional terms between infringements of personality rights and infringement of intellectual and industrial property rights.[147]

Relationship between article 7.1 and article 7.2

7–27   The special jurisdiction rules have generated a great deal of interpretative case law, and in particular the rule of special jurisdiction in tort, delict and quasi-delict. Partly this is attributable to the fact that delicts are many and varied, and the categories of negligence never closed, but also to difficulties in applying the *Bier* principle to wrongdoing allegedly committed online.

The ECJ's significant decision in *Kalfelis v Bankhaus Schroder Munchmeyer Hengst & Co*,[148] that the phrase "matters relating to tort, delict or quasi-delict" in art.5.3 of the Brussels Convention (cf. Brussels I Recast art.7.2), must be regarded as an, "independent concept covering all actions which seek to establish the liability of a defendant and which are not related to a 'contract' within the

---

[143] *Wintersteiger AG v Products 4U Sondermaschinenbau GmbH* (C-523/10) [2012] I.L.Pr. 23.

[144] *Wintersteiger AG v Products 4U Sondermaschinenbau GmbH* (C-523/10) [2012] I.L.Pr. 23 at [39].

[145] *Pinckney v KDG Mediatech AG* (C-170/12) [2014] I.L.Pr. 7.

[146] See also *Hi Hotel HCF SARL v Spoering* (C-387/12) [2014] 1 W.L.R. 1912; [2015] C.E.C. 74; and *Melzer v MF Global UK Ltd* (Case C-228/11) [2013] QB 1112.

[147] See also *Hejduk v EnergieAgentur.NRW GmbH* Case C-441/13 [2015] O.J. C107/7.

[148] *Kalfelis v Bankhaus Schroder Munchmeyer Hengst & Co* (189/87) [1988] E.C.R. 5565; [1989] E.C.C. 407 (a case under the Brussels Convention). See also *Source Ltd v TUV Rheinland Holding AG* [1998] Q.B. 54.

meaning of Article 5(1)"[149] (cf. Brussels I Recast art.7.1), has had the consequence that particular care must be taken in giving advice to a litigant who potentially has a claim arising both under contract and under delict, from the same circumstances, according to whether the litigation in view can be said to be purely domestic or having a conflict of laws dimension.

In the domestic case, an aggrieved party is quite likely to be entitled to sue in the alternative, or at least to have a free choice as to the category of law under which he wishes to proceed to his best advantage. In contrast, in a cross-border case within the Brussels regime, the supremacy of the contract special jurisdiction rule over the tort/delict special jurisdiction rule, appears to preclude suit under the head of tort/delict if there exists a contractual link between the parties.

The decision of the Irish High Court in *Burke v Uvex Sports GmbH*[150] arose from simple facts: Burke claimed for personal injuries to his face caused when his motorcycle helmet visor broke when he skidded and struck the roadside in Tipperary, Ireland. His claim was framed solely in tort against two defendants, both domiciled in Germany: first, the manufacturer, and secondly, the party from whom Burke had bought the helmet and visor. With regard to the second defendant, there was necessarily a contractual relationship with Burke. The court could not overlook the existence of that contractual element,[151] with the result that it could not properly take jurisdiction over the second defendant on the basis of art.5.3 (occurrence of the tort in Ireland). It did not matter that in these circumstances, by the national law of Ireland, the contractual element of the claim did not foreclose the claim in tort; nor could account be taken of the possible detriment to the claimant (Burke) if, as a result of time limit rules, he was unable to sue the second defendant in Germany under art.2.

If the general rule of jurisdiction is used (Brussels I Recast art.4; ex-Brussels I Regulation art.2), one advantage for the claimant is that he may frame his action in contract *or* delict in the alternative, to hedge his risk or better his chances. Moreover, the general rule is available where the circumstances cannot be said to fall into any of the special categories, in particular neither within contract nor tort/delict. But if special jurisdiction be used, then the claimant's case would appear to be limited to an argument in contract or delict, respectively.

Other special jurisdictions

"A person domiciled in a Member State may be sued in another Member State: **7–28**

  (3)   as regards a civil claim for damages or restitution which is based on an act giving rise to criminal proceedings, in the court seised of those proceedings, to the extent that that court has jurisdiction under its own law to entertain civil proceedings;

---

[149] *Brogsitter v Fabrication de Montres Normandes EURL* (C-548/12) [2014] I.L.Pr. 20; and *Kolassa v Barclays Bank Plc* (C-375/13) [2015] I.L.Pr. 14. See also at shrieval level *MacRitchie Bros Ltd v Commercial Power Ltd*, 2011 G.W.D. 2-82.

[150] *Burke v Uvex Sports GmbH* [2005] I.L.Pr. 26 High Court (Ireland) (re Brussels I Regulation). See contra, *Re Mail Order Promise of Win in a Draw* [2003] I.L.Pr. 46 Federal Supreme Court (Germany).

[151] It was agreed between the parties, and accepted by Herbert J., that the contract between Burke and the second defendant was *not* a consumer contract within the provisions of arts 15–17 of the Brussels I Regulation (*Burke v UVEX Sports GmbH* [2005] I.L.Pr. 26 at [31]).

(4)   as regards a civil claim for the recovery, based on ownership, of a cultural object as defined in point 1 of Article 1 of Directive 93/7/EEC initiated by the person claiming the right to recover such an object, in the courts for the place where the cultural object is situated at the time when the court is seised;[152]

(5)   as regards a dispute arising out of the operations of a branch, agency or other establishment, in the courts for the place where the branch, agency or other establishment is situated;[153]

(6)   as regards a dispute brought against a settlor, trustee or beneficiary of a trust created by the operation of a statute, or by a written instrument, or created orally and evidenced in writing, in the courts of the Member State in which the trust is domiciled;[154]

(7)   as regards a dispute concerning the payment of remuneration claimed in respect of the salvage of a cargo or freight, in the court under the authority of which the cargo or freight in question:

(a)   has been arrested to secure such payment; or

(b)   could have been so arrested, but bail or other security has been given;
          provided that this provision shall apply only if it is claimed that the defendant has an interest in the cargo or freight or had such an interest at the time of salvage."

Related actions

Article 8[155]

7–29   A person domiciled in a Member State may also be sued:

"1.   where he is one of a number of defendants in the courts for the place where any one of them is domiciled provided the claims are so closely connected that it is expedient to hear and determine them together to avoid the risk of irreconcilable judgments resulting from separate proceedings;[156]

2.   as a third party in an action on a warranty or guarantee or in any other third-party proceedings,[157] in the court seised of the original proceedings, unless these were instituted solely with the object of removing him from the jurisdiction of the court which would be competent in his case;

3.   on a counter-claim arising from the same contract or facts on which the original claim was based, in the court in which the original claim is pending;

4.   in matters relating to a contract, if the action may be combined with an action against the same defendant in matters relating to rights in rem in immovable property, in the court of the Member State in which the property is situated."

---

[152] This provision in Brussels I Recast is novel.
[153] cf. *Latchin (T/A Dinkha Latchin Associates) v General Mediterranean Holdings SA* [2003] C.L.Y.B. 601; and *Anton Durbeck GmbH v Den Norske Bank ASA* [2003] Q.B. 1160. Although this provision expands the claimant's options, the branch, etc. must be situated in a Member State.
[154] e.g. *Gomez v Gomez-Monche Vives* [2008] EWHC 259 (Ch).
[155] cf. Brussels I Regulation art.6.
[156] *Gascoine v Pyrah* [1994] I.L.Pr. 82; *Canada Trust v Stolzenberg (No.2)* [2000] 4 All E.R. 481; *Watson v First Choice Holidays & Flights Ltd* [2001] 2 Lloyd's Rep. 339; *Daly v Irish Group Travel Ltd (t/a Crystal Holidays)* [2003] I.L.Pr. 38; *Andrew Weir Shipping Ltd v Wartsila UK Ltd* [2004] 2 Lloyd's Rep. 377; *Et Plus SA v Welter* [2005] EWHC 2115; *Masri v Consolidated Contractors International (UK) Ltd* [2006] 1 W.L.R. 830; *Latmar Holdings Corp v Media Focus Ltd (aka Linuzs v Latmar Holdings Corp)* [2013] EWCA Civ 4; [2013] I.L.Pr. 19; and *Cartel Damage Claims (CDC) Hydrogen Peroxide SA v Azko Nobel NV* (Case C-352/13).
[157] e.g. *Kinnear v Falconfilms MV* [1994] 3 All E.R. 42.

Since art.8 is a rule of special jurisdiction which derogates from the principle in art.4, it is to be strictly interpreted.[158]

The relevant time for determining whether the court has jurisdiction under art.8 is the time at which the jurisdiction is invoked, i.e. the date of issue of proceedings.[159] Under art.8, a claimant who sues a person in the courts for the place where he is domiciled ("the anchor claim") may sue another person in that court, subject to the requirement that the anchor claim and the other claim are so closely connected that it is expedient to hear and determine them together to avoid the risk of irreconcilable judgments resulting from separate proceedings.[160]

In order to sue a co-defendant before the courts of a Member State on the basis of art.8, it is necessary that the co-defendant should be domiciled in another Member State. Article 8 is not intended to apply to defendants who are not domiciled in another Member State, in the case where they are sued in proceedings brought against several defendants, some of whom are domiciled in the EU.[161]

Of the related actions rules, that which has given rise to most litigation is para.1. An instructive early example is *Gascoine v Pyrah*,[162] in which the Court of Appeal considered it reasonable to permit the claimants, who had brought an action in England against the first defendant (domiciled in England), claiming financial loss resulting from negligent professional advice in the matter of the purchase of a showjumping horse, to conjoin with the first defendant, a second defendant, a veterinary expert domiciled in Germany, whose advice by telephone allegedly endorsed the wisdom of the purchase. Article 6.1 of the Brussels Convention (cf. Brussels I Recast art.8.1) applied so as to avoid the risk of irreconcilable judgments resulting from separate proceedings. The content of the telephone conversation between the first and second defendants was a vital issue of fact upon which courts might easily have differed were separate proceedings to ensue.

The ECJ held in *Land Berlin v Sapir*,[163] that in determining whether or not claims are "closely connected", there is no requirement that the actions brought against different defendants should have identical legal bases[164]; such an identity is only one relevant factor among others.

The risk of irreconcilability of judgments is the principal consideration when applications under para.1 are in issue.[165] Satisfaction of the condition in art.8, that it is expedient to hear and determine the claims together in order to avoid the risk of irreconcilable judgments resulting from separate proceedings, is for the national court in question to verify.[166] The question whether there is such a risk of irreconcilability must be tested objectively.[167]

---

[158] *Painer v Standard Verlags GmbH* (C-145/10) [2011] E.C.D.R. 13; and *Land Berlin v Sapir* (Case C-645/11) [2013] I.L.Pr. 29.
[159] *Latmar Holdings Corp v Media Focus Ltd* [2013] EWCA Civ 4; [2013] I.L.Pr. 19.
[160] A.G. Trstenjak in *Painer v Standard Verlags GmbH* (C-145/10) [2011] E.C.D.R. 13.
[161] *Land Berlin v Sapir* (C-645/11) [2013] C.E.C. 947; [2013] I.L.Pr. 29.
[162] *Gascoine v Pyrah* [1994] I.L.Pr. 82.
[163] *Land Berlin v Sapir* (C-645/11) [2013] C.E.C. 947; [2013] I.L.Pr. 29.
[164] *Freeport Plc v Arnoldsson* (C-98/06) [2008] Q.B. 634.
[165] cf. Brussels I Recast art.30 (*lis pendens* in related actions), below.
[166] *Gard Marine and Energy Ltd v Tunnicliffe* [2010] EWCA Civ 1052; [2011] 2 All E.R. (Comm) 208 (re Lugano).
[167] *FKI Engineering Ltd v De Wind Holdings Ltd* [2007] I.L.Pr. 17.

If there is clear evidence of collusion or abuse by the claimant, a court can refuse an application which otherwise meets the requirements of art.8.1.[168]

Disadvantaged parties

7–30   A feature of the Brussels Convention and the Brussels I Regulation was the inclusion of rules providing grounds of jurisdiction protective of potentially disadvantaged parties. While the 1968 Convention afforded special protection to consumers and to insured parties, and the Lugano Convention contained a provision favouring employees, the Brussels I Regulation gathered these provisions together, creating a protective framework for insured parties (including, under the Regulation, the beneficiaries under insurance policies, if different from the policyholder), consumers, and employees, respectively.[169] Under Brussels I Recast, the protective policy has been continued, indeed strengthened.[170]

These sets of rules share common characteristics, for example, in restricting parties' ability to contract out of them to their detriment[171]; and in the principle that the "weak" party may be sued only in his domicile, whereas he may sue the "strong" party in his own domicile, as an alternative to suing in the state where the "strong" defendant is domiciled.

A central principle of the Brussels regime is that at the enforcement stage the jurisdiction of the court of the Member State of origin may not be reviewed,[172] and to this principle the "weaker parties" protections are the only exceptions. A significant protection afforded to "weak" parties was contained in Ch.3 (recognition and enforcement) art.35.1 of the Brussels I Regulation, to the effect that a Member State judgment should not be recognised if the jurisdictional provisions contained in ss.3 (insured parties), 4 (consumers) or 6 (exclusive jurisdictions[173]) (q.v.) had not been honoured. A change brought about by Brussels I Recast is that, per art.45.1(e)(i), this protection (i.e. permission to contest the jurisdiction of the EU Member State court of origin) is extended to cases falling under s.5 (jurisdiction over individual contracts of employment). The exclusion of employees from this protection in the text of the Brussels I Regulation was something of a mystery and may have been explicable on the ground that it was thought any re-visiting of the jurisdictional competence would favour the employer not the employee, who is the perceived weaker party whom these rules are designed to protect.

In relation to submission to the jurisdiction, art.26 of Brussels I Recast (ex-Brussels I Regulation art.24) incorporates a protective device of a soft law nature (art.26.2), to the effect that where the defendant in the proposed litigation

---

[168] *Sibir Energy Ltd v Chalva Pavlovich Tchigirinski* [2012] EWHC 1844 (QB) [2012] I.L.Pr. 52 at [31] (re Lugano II art.6).
[169] cf. special choice of law rules for such contracts in Rome I Regulation arts 6, 7, 8. See further E.B. Crawford and J.M. Carruthers, "Connection and Coherence between and among European Instruments in the Private International Law of Obligations" (2014) 63 I.C.L.Q. 1.
[170] Brussels I Recast arts18.1 and 45.1(e).
[171] *Sherdley v Nordea Life and Pensions SA* [2012] EWCA Civ 88, per Rix L.J. at [59]: the protections cannot be "bartered away by any agreement prior to the outbreak of a dispute".
[172] Brussels I Regulation art.35.3.
[173] *Weber v Weber* (C-438/12) [2015] Ch. 140.

is an insured party, a consumer, or an employee, the Member State court, before assuming jurisdiction on the basis of submission, should ensure that the defendant is informed of his right to contest the jurisdiction, and of the consequences of entering or not entering an appearance.

Articles 10–16 (jurisdiction in matters relating to insurance)[174]

Article 11

"1.   An insurer domiciled in a Member State may be sued: **7–31**
    (a)   in the courts of the Member State in which he is domiciled;
    (b)   in another Member State, in the case of actions brought by the policy-holder, the insured or a beneficiary, in the courts for the place where the claimant is domiciled;
    (c)   if he is a co-insurer, in the courts of a Member State in which proceedings are brought against the leading insurer.
2.   An insurer who is not domiciled in a Member State, but has a branch, agency or other establishment in one of the Member States shall, in disputes arising out of the operations of the branch, agency or establishment, be deemed to be domiciled in that Member State."[175]

The victim of an accident was assisted by creative interpretation of art.9 of the Brussels I Regulation (cf. Brussels I Recast art.11). In its decision in *FBTO Shadeverzekeringen NV v Odenbreit*[176] the ECJ effectively added to the categories of specially protected parties under art.9.1(b), by extending its *forum actoris* benefits to the injured party in an accident, thereby allowing him to sue, in his own legal system, the wrongdoer's insurance company, so long as that is permitted by the national law of the court in question. Looking more closely at this condition, it was held in *Mapfre Mutualidad compania de Seguros y Reaseguros SA v Keefe*[177] that, on the issue of whether a direct action against the insurer is permitted, the law to be referred to is the law of the forum, meaning not the internal law thereof, but the *lex fori*, including its rules of private international law. Therefore the private international law of the forum will identify the applicable law of the insurance contract, per Rome I Regulation art.7, and ascertain whether or not, by that law, such suit is permitted.

Articles 12 and 13 lay down special provisions in respect of liability insurance, and insurance of immoveable property.

Article 14 completes, with arts 15 and 16, the protective structure which Brussels I Recast provides for insurance cases. In terms of art.14.1, an insurer

---

[174] Cf. Brussels I Regulation art.12–18.

[175] The concept of "deemed domicile" in this provision operates potentially to draw into the regime a defendant domiciled in a Third State. Article 11 has left virtually unchanged the wording of its predecessor provisions. Notably, unlike the position under arts 18.1 and 21.2 (q.v.), there has been no equivalent extension of jurisdiction with regard to non-EU domiciled insurers beyond the pre-existing "branch, agency" concession contained in art.11.2 (ex-Brussels I Regulation art.9.2).

[176] *FBTO Shadeverzekeringen NV v Odenbreit* (C-463/06) [2007] E.C.R. I-11321; [2008] I.L.Pr. 12. See also *Re Jurisdiction in a Direct Action against an Insurer* (VI ZR 200/05) [2008] I.L.Pr. 52; *Thwaites v Aviva Assurances* [2010] I.L.Pr. 47.

[177] *Mapfre Mutualidad compania de Seguros y Reaseguros SA v Keefe* [2015] EWCA Civ 598, per Gloster LJ at [35], taking the same line as HH Judge Birtles in *Jones v Assurances Generales de France (AGF) SA* [2010] I.L.Pr. 4.

may bring proceedings only in the courts of the Member State in which the defendant is domiciled, irrespective of whether he is the policyholder, the insured or a beneficiary. Article 14.2 states that the provisions of s.3 shall not affect the right to bring a counter-claim in the court in which, in accordance with the section, the original claim is pending.

There follow in art.15 rules concerning the extent to which the "beneficiaries" of the provisions of Section 3 may depart from them,[178] namely, only by an agreement which:

> "1.   ...is entered into after the dispute has arisen; or
> 2.   ...allows the policyholder, the insured or a beneficiary to bring proceedings in courts other than those indicated in this Section; or
> 3.   ...is concluded between a policyholder and an insurer, both of whom are at the time of conclusion of the contract domiciled or habitually resident in the same Member State, and...has the effect of conferring jurisdiction on the courts of that Member State even if the harmful event were to occur abroad, provided that such an agreement is not contrary to the law of that Member State; or
> 4.   ...is concluded with a policyholder who is not domiciled in a Member State, except in so far as the insurance is compulsory or relates to immoveable property in a Member State; or
> 5.   ...relates to a contract of insurance in so far as it covers one or more of the risks set out in Article 16."

Article 16 excludes certain categories of risk, such as loss to seagoing ships, and "large" risks,[179] because certain specific risks are governed by sector-specific instruments.

Articles 17–19 (jurisdiction over consumer contracts)[180]

Article 17

7–32

> "1.   In matters relating to a contract concluded by a person, the consumer, for a purpose which can be regarded as being outside his trade or profession, jurisdiction shall be determined by this Section, without prejudice to Article 6 and point 5 of Article 7, if:
> (a)   it is a contract for the sale of goods on instalment credit terms;
> (b)   it is a contract for a loan repayable by instalments, or for any other form of credit, made to finance the sale of goods; or
> (c)   in all other cases, the contract has been concluded with a person who pursues commercial or professional activities in the Member State of the consumer's domicile or, by any means, directs such activities to that Member State or to several States including that Member State, and the contract falls within the scope of such activities.
> 2.   Where a consumer enters into a contract with a party who is not domiciled in the Member State but has a branch, agency or other establishment in one of

---

[178] *Societe Financiere et Industrielle du Peloux v Axa Belgium* [2006] Q.B. 251 ECJ.
[179] As defined in Directive 73/239/EEC on the coordination of laws, regulations and administrative provisions relating to the taking-up and pursuit of the business of direct insurance other than life insurance [1973] O.J. L228/3, as amended.
[180] cf. Brussels I Regulation arts 15–17.

the Member States, that party shall, in disputes arising out of the operations of the branch, agency or establishment, be deemed to be domiciled in that Member State.[181]

3.   This Section shall not apply to a contract of transport other than a contract which, for an inclusive price, provides for a combination of travel and accommodation."

Article 17 applies if three conditions are met, namely that (i) a party to a contract is a consumer who was acting in a context which could be regarded as being outside his trade or profession[182]; (ii) the contract between such a consumer and a professional[183] had actually been concluded; and (iii) such a contract falls within one of the categories referred to in art.17(1)(a) to (c). If any of the three conditions is not met, jurisdiction cannot be founded under the rules relating to consumer contracts.[184]

Doubt arose as to whether or not the advantageous consumer jurisdiction provisions are triggered in a situation in which an individual has received from a mail order company a letter, the terms of which suggest that she has won a prize, which can be claimed simply by returning a signed and numbered voucher. This question was referred to the ECJ for a preliminary ruling in *Ilsinger*.[185]

The facts of *Ilsinger* were on all fours with the prior case of *Engler v Janus Versand GmbH*,[186] decided by the ECJ upon the meaning and scope of application of art.13.1.3 of the Brussels Convention, a provision which was substantially re-enacted in the Brussels I Regulation art.15.1(c), and which is reiterated in art.17.1(c) of Brussels I Recast. Although the threshold wording in the Regulation was somewhat simpler than that in the Convention, both instruments demanded, as does Brussels I Recast, that a contract shall have been *concluded* by the consumer with a commercial or professional party. The ECJ in *Engler* delivered, in answer to a question identical to that posed in *Ilsinger*, the decision that since the vendor's initiative was not followed by the conclusion of a contract between the (admitted) consumer and the vendor, the litigation brought

---

[181] cf. n.175 (re art.11.2): use of the concept of "deemed domicile" has the micro effect of assisting the consumer, and the macro effect of extending the reach of the provisions of the regime.

[182] See *Benincasa v Dentalkit Srl* (C-269/95) [1998] All E.R. (EC) 135; *Engler v Janus Versand GmbH* (C27/02) [2005] 7 C.L. 76 ECJ. Contrast *Chris Hart (Business Sales) Ltd v Niven*, 1992 S.L.T. (Sh. Ct.) 53; *BJ Mann (Advertising) Ltd v Ace Welding & Fabrications Ltd*, 1994 S.C.L.R. 763; *Standard Bank London Ltd v Apostolakis* (No.1) [2000] I.L.Pr. 766; *Davies v Rayner* [2002] 1 All E.R. (Comm) 620; *Semple Fraser WS v Quayle*, 2002 S.L.T. (Sh. Ct.) 33; *Prostar Management Ltd v Twaddle*, 2003 S.L.T. (Sh. Ct.) 11; and *Verein fur Konsumenteninformation v Henkel* (C-167/00) [2003] All E.R. (EC) 311 ECJ.

[183] cf. *Vapenik v Thurner* (Case C-508/12) [2014] 1 W.L.R. 2486 re Regulation (EC) No.805/2004 of the European Parliament and of the Council of 21 April 2004 creating a European Enforcement Order for uncontested claims art.6.1.d: the consumer provision is inapplicable where the contract is between two parties, neither of whom is engaged in commercial or professional activities.

[184] *Ceska sporitelna as v Feichter* (C-419/11) [2013] C.E.C. 923; [2013] I.L.Pr. 22 (in which the contract in question failed to satisfy the first criterion, rendering art.15 of the Brussels I Regulation inapplicable); and *Kolassa v Barclays Bank Plc* (C-375/13) [2015] I.L.Pr. 14.

[185] *Ilsinger v Dreschers* (C-180/06) [2009] O.J. C153/3. See E.B. Crawford, "*Ilsinger v Dreschers*" (2009) 4 E.J.C.L. 861.

[186] *Engler v Janus Versand GmbH* (C-27/02) [2005] E.C.R. I-481. See however *Re Mail Order Promise of Win in a Draw* [2003] I.L.Pr. 46 Federal Supreme Court (Germany).

by the disappointed party could *not* be regarded as being (consumer) contractual for the purposes of art.13.1.3 of the Brussels Convention.[187]

In *Ilsinger*, it was necessary to decide whether art.15.1(c) of the Brussels I Regulation must be interpreted in the same way, or whether that provision might be interpreted differently by reason of its partially different wording.[188] In the particular instance, when the old and the new consumer jurisdiction provisions were compared, it could be seen that there was no substantive difference between them. The important point, as noted above, is that a contract shall have been concluded between the parties. In *Ilsinger*, it was observed[189] that, since the Brussels I Regulation largely replaces the Brussels Convention, the Court's interpretation of the Convention extended also to the Regulation, where its provisions and those of the Brussels Convention might be treated as equivalent. It is testament to the edifice that has been built that a case interpretative of the 1968 Convention will be influential in deciding like cases under Brussels I Recast.

There has been interpretative case law on the question of "directing activities" for the purposes of art.15.1.c of the Brussels I Regulation,[190] which will extend to interpretation of art.17.1.c of Brussels I Recast. Agreement on these words was hard to obtain, the consumer and the supplier lobbies being opposed in the matter of the crafting of jurisdiction rules which would be apt to cover internet trading. The same form of words has been adopted for choice of law in contractual obligations in the Rome I Regulation art.6.1(b).

In *Pammer v Reederei Karl Schluter GmbH & Co KG*[191] in order to determine whether a trader whose activity was presented on its website or that of an intermediary was "directing" its activity to the Member State of a consumer's domicile, within the meaning of art.15.1.c, the ECJ held that it should be ascertained whether, before the conclusion of any contract with the consumer, it was apparent from those websites and the trader's overall activity that the trader was envisaging doing business with consumers domiciled in one or more Member States, including the Member State of that consumer's domicile, in the sense that it was minded to conclude a contract with them. It is for national courts to ascertain whether such evidence exists. However, the mere accessibility of the trader's or the intermediary's website in the Member State in which the consumer was domiciled was held to be insufficient evidence, as was the mention of an email address or other contact details, or the use of a language or a currency which were the language or currency generally used in the Member State in which the trader was established.[192]

---

[187] It was accepted that the circumstances were sufficient to satisfy art.5.1 of the Brussels I Regulation (cf. Brussels I Recast art.7.1) (*Engler*, at [60]).

[188] *Ilsinger v Dreschers* (C-180/06) [2009] O.J. C153/3, opinion of the Advocate General at [36], [37].

[189] *Ilsinger v Dreschers* (C-180/06) [2009] O.J. C153/3 at [41].

[190] See *Pammer v Reederei Karl Schlüter GmbH & Co KG* (C-585/08) [2009] O.J. C44/40; and *Hotel Alpenhof GesmbH v Heller* (C-144/09) [2009] O.J. C153/26.

[191] *Pammer v Reederei Karl Schluter GmbH & Co KG* (C-585/08) [2011] 2 All E.R. (Comm) 888. See also *Oak Leaf Conservatories Ltd v Weir* [2013] EWHC 3197 (TCC) (on CJJA 1982 Sch.4 para.8).

[192] *Pammer v Reederei Karl Schluter GmbH & Co KG* (C-585/08) [2011] 2 All E.R. (Comm) 888 at [81], [83]–[84], [93]–[94].

Two further important points were decided, respectively, in *Muhlleitner v Yusufi*[193] and *Emrek v Sabranovic*,[194] namely, whether art.15.1.c is satisfied in circumstances where, the professional party having directed its activities to the Member State of the consumer's domicile, the contract in question is concluded in person rather than at a distance; and secondly, whether there requires to be a causal link between the directing of the activities and the conclusion of the contract.

In *Muhlleitner* the consumer, domiciled in Austria, searched on the internet for a car of a German make. After connecting to the German search platform www.mobile.de, she contacted the defendants, who operated a motor vehicle retail business in Germany. She used the telephone number, which included an international dialling code, stated on the business's website. Ms Mühlleitner went to Germany and, by a contract of sale signed on 21 September 2009 in Hamburg, bought another vehicle from the defendants. On her return to Austria, she discovered that the vehicle was defective, and consequently asked the defendants to repair it. When the defendants refused to repair it, she brought proceedings in Austria for rescission of the contract of sale, which she claimed to have concluded as a consumer with an undertaking directing its commercial or professional activities to Austria, i.e. within art.15.1.c. The defendants contested Ms Mühlleitner's status of "consumer" and argued that the dispute should be brought before the German courts. They also submitted that they did not direct their activities to Austria and that Ms Mühlleitner had concluded the contract at the seat of their undertaking in Germany. The ECJ held, on a reference from the Austrian court, that art.15.1.c did not require the contract between the consumer and the trader to be concluded at a distance. To have reached the opposite conclusion would have run counter to the objective of protecting consumers as the weaker parties to the contract.

In *Emrek*, the CJEU held that it is sufficient for the application of art.15.1.c that the trader has directed his activities to the Member State of the consumer's domicile, even if such activities were not the basis for conclusion of the contract in question. To insist on the existence of a causal link between the directing of the activities and the conclusion of the contract would be contrary to the objective pursued by art.15.1.c. Although the causal link was not an unwritten condition to which the application of art.15.1.c is subject, such a link could constitute evidence which could be taken into consideration by the national court when determining whether the activity was in fact directed to the Member State in which the consumer was domiciled.

Article 18

"1.   A consumer may bring proceedings against the other party to a contract either in the courts of the Member State in which that party is domiciled or, regardless of the domicile of the other party, in the courts for the place where the consumer is domiciled.   **7–33**

2.   Proceedings may be brought against a consumer by the other party to the contract only in the courts of the Member State in which the consumer is domiciled.

---

[193] *Muhlleitner v Yusufi* (C-190/11) [2013] C.E.C. 595; [2012] I.L.Pr. 46.
[194] *Emrek v Sabranovic* (C-218/12) [2014] I.L.Pr. 39.

3. This Article shall not affect the right to bring a counter-claim in the court in which, in accordance with this Section, the original claim is pending."

Article 18 concerns litigation brought by a consumer against the other party to a consumer contract. Since 1968 consumers, insured persons and, to a lesser extent, employees have had the benefit of *forum actoris* rules. In *Hypotecni Banka AS v Lindner*,[195] the ECJ was prepared, in a case of doubt as to the consumer's domicile, and in the absence of any firm evidence that he was domiciled outside the EU, to treat his last known domicile within the EU as affording a ground of jurisdiction for the purposes of art.16.2 of the Brussels I Regulation. In *Maletic v lastminute.com GmbH*[196] the CJEU held that the concept of "other party to the contract" in art.16 of the Brussels I Regulation extended to a contracting partner of the professional party with whom the consumer concluded that contract (in the instant case, the holiday operator, which supplied the relevant holiday package to the travel agent, through whom the consumer booked the holiday) and which had its registered office in the Member State in which the consumer was domiciled, with the result that the claimant consumers were able to sue both defendants before their local court.

Under the Brussels I Regulation, the beneficial provisions applied only on the basis that *both* parties to the contract were EU-domiciled (ex-art.16.1) or that the "non-consumer" party had a branch or agency in the EU (ex-art.15.2). In a significant expansion of the protection afforded these weaker parties, Brussels I Recast, by inclusion of the words "regardless of the domicile of the other party", provides that the consumer shall enjoy the benefit of suing in the Member State of his own domicile not only an EU-domiciled defendant (or *deemed*-EU-domiciled defendant: art 17.2), but also a *non*-EU domiciled defendant (art.18.1). This extends the privilege of the *forum actoris* rule.

Article 19

7–34 "The provisions of this Section may be departed from only by an agreement:
1. which is entered into after the dispute has arisen;
2. which allows the consumer to bring proceedings in courts other than those indicated in this Section; or
3. which is entered into by the consumer and the other party to the contract, both of whom are at the time of conclusion of the contract domiciled or habitually resident in the same Member State, and which confers jurisdiction on the courts of that Member State, provided that such an agreement is not contrary to the law of that Member State."

Articles 20–22 (jurisdiction over individual contracts of employment)[197]

7–35 Section 5 governs individual contracts of employment,[198] including the situation (art.20.2) where an employee enters into an individual contract of employment

---

[195] *Hypotecni Banka AS v Lindner* (C-327/10) [2011] E.C.R. I-11543; [2012] C.E.C. 975.
[196] *Maletic v lastminute.com GmbH* (C-478/12) [2014] Q.B. 424.
[197] cf. Brussels I Regulation arts 18–20. cf. Under 1968 Convention, *Weber v Universal Ogden Services Ltd* (C-37/00) [2002] Q.B. 1189 (ECJ).
[198] In relation to the meaning of which, see *Alfa Laval Tumba AB v Separator Spares International Ltd* [2012] EWCA Civ 1569.

with an employer who is not domiciled in a Member State, but has a branch, agency or other establishment in one of the Member States. In such cases, the employer shall be deemed,[199] in disputes arising out of the operations of the branch, agency, or establishment, to be domiciled in that Member State.[200] Thus:

Article 21

"1.   An employer domiciled in a Member State may be sued: **7–36**
    (a)   in the courts of the Member State in which he is domiciled; or
    (b)   in another Member State:
        (i)   in the courts for the place where or from where the employee habitually carries out his work or in the courts for the last place where he did so; or
        (ii)   if the employee does not or did not habitually carry out his work in any one country, in the courts for the place where the business which engaged the employee is or was situated.
2.   An employer not domiciled in a Member State may be sued in a court of a Member State in accordance with point (b) of paragraph 1."

In the same way that art.18.1 extends the privilege of the *forum actoris* rule for a consumer seeking to sue a non-EU domiciled defendant, so too art.21.2 permits an employee to sue a *non*-EU domiciled employer in a court of the Member State in which the employee habitually carries out his work, or last did so, or of the situation of the business which engaged the employee. Residual national rules of jurisdiction no longer may be applied in relation to non-EU domiciled defendants in these two disadvantaged party scenarios.

Article 22

"1.   An employer may bring proceedings only in the courts of the Member State   **7–37**
in which the employee is domiciled.
2.   The provisions of this Section shall not affect the right to bring a counter-claim in the court in which, in accordance with this Section, the original claim is pending."

Article 23

"The provisions of this Section may be departed from only by an agreement: **7–38**
1.   which is entered into after the dispute has arisen; or
2.   which allows the employee to bring proceedings in courts other than those indicated in this Section."

Exclusive jurisdiction

Article 24 allocates jurisdiction in circumstances where it is thought that certain   **7–39**
courts are uniquely well placed to deal with the subject-matter of the litigation. The focus is on territorial connection. The significance of exclusive jurisdiction is

---

[199] cf. notes 175 (re art.11.2) and 181 (re. art.17.2) re use of the concept of "deemed domicile".
[200] *Mahamdia v Algeria* (C-154/11) [2014] All E.R. (EC) 96: the Algerian embassy in Germany qualified as an "establishment" within the meaning of Brussels I Regulation art.18.2.

that it trumps other bases of jurisdiction, including art.4. However, to keep the article in check, it has been strictly construed, for its effect is to oust the jurisdiction of other potentially interested courts.

Article 24[201]

7–40   "The following courts of a Member State shall have exclusive jurisdiction, regardless of the domicile of the parties:

1.   in proceedings which have as their object rights *in rem* in immovable property or tenancies of immovable property, the courts of the Member State in which the property is situated.[202]

However, in proceedings which have as their object tenancies of immovable property concluded for temporary private use for a maximum period of six consecutive months, the courts of the Member State in which the defendant is domiciled shall also have jurisdiction, provided that the tenant is a natural person and that the landlord and the tenant are domiciled in the same Member State;

2.   in proceedings which have as their object the validity of the constitution, the nullity or the dissolution of companies or other legal persons or associations of natural or legal persons, or the validity of the decisions of their organs, the courts of the Member State in which the company, legal person or association has its seat. In order to determine that seat, the court shall apply its rules of private international law;[203]

3.   in proceedings which have as their object the validity of entries in public registers, the courts of the Member State in which the register is kept;

4.   in proceedings concerned with the registration or validity of patents, trade marks, designs, or other similar rights required to be deposited or registered, irrespective of whether the issue is raised by way of an action or as a defence, the courts of the Member State in which the deposit or registration has been applied for, has taken place or is under the terms of an instrument of the Union or an international convention deemed to have taken place.
    …;

5.   in proceedings concerned with the enforcement of judgments, the courts of the Member State in which the judgment has been or is to be enforced."

Article 24 applies only where the subject-matter of the action is connected with a Member State.[204] Exclusive jurisdiction is mandatory in nature; jurisdiction conferred by this provision cannot be excluded by the voluntary submission by a defender to the courts of another Member State, nor by agreement of the parties to purported opposite effect.

The exclusive jurisdiction provision pertaining to immovable property is that which has generated the most litigation. Exclusive jurisdiction under art.24.1

---

[201] cf. Brussels I Regulation art.22.

[202] *Rosler v Rottwinkel* [1986] Q.B. 33; *Scherrens v Maenhout* (158/87) [1988] E.C.R. 3791; *Hacker v Euro-Relais GmbH* [1992] E.C.R. I-1111; and *Jarrett v Barclays Bank Plc* [1997] 2 All E.R. 484.

[203] For this purpose, the seat is to be determined by national conflict rules. For the UK, see CJJA 1982 s.43 (and s.43A re Lugano II), and CJJO 2001 Sch.1 para.10; cf. Brussels I Recast art.63. See *Bambino Holdings Ltd v Speed Investments Ltd* [2004] EWCA Civ 1512; and contrast *Berliner Verkehrsbetriebe (BVG) v JP Morgan Chase Bank NA, Frankfurt Branch* (C-144/10) [2011] 1 W.L.R. 2087.

[204] Though see para.7–63, below (*effet réflèxe*).

pertains only in proceedings which have as their object[205] rights in rem,[206] rendering significant the distinction between rights in rem and rights in personam[207] (e.g. pertaining to legal capacity of natural persons).

With regard to tenancies,[208] it can be seen from the current and earlier versions of the short-term tenancy provision contained in art.24.1 that liberties have been taken with use of the word "exclusive". It is clear on the face of the provision that "exclusive" in this context does not mean "unique". This is the explanation for art.31.1 (*lis pendens*), which allocates jurisdiction among courts with "exclusive" jurisdiction on a priority in date basis.

Article 27 of Brussels I Recast is significant in imposing a duty on a court to act *ex proprio motu*, viz.: "Where a court of a Member State is seised of a claim which is principally concerned with a matter over which the courts of another Member State have exclusive jurisdiction by virtue of Article 24, it shall declare of its own motion that it has no jurisdiction."

Article 45 regulates the very limited extent to which, at the stage of judgment enforcement, the jurisdiction of the Member State court of origin (i.e. the court issuing the judgment) may be reviewed by the Member State court addressed (i.e. the enforcing court). Bolstering the strength of art.24, art.45.1(e)(ii) provides that a judgment shall not be recognised if it conflicts, inter alia, with s.6 of Ch.II, i.e. with the exclusive jurisdiction rule set out in art.24.

Choice of court clauses: prorogation of jurisdiction

Prorogation of jurisdiction is authorised by art.25 of Brussels I Recast.If parties, one or more of whom is domiciled in a Member State, have agreed that the court of a Member State is to have jurisdiction in any dispute arising between them, art.25 provides that that court shall have jurisdiction, which jurisdiction shall be exclusive unless the parties have agreed otherwise. The article provides certain requirements, set out below, as to form, which must be complied with before the agreement will qualify as a valid prorogation.

7–41

---

[205] *Sanders v Van der Putte* (73/77) [1977] E.C.R. 2383; *Barratt International Resorts Ltd v Martin*, 1994 S.L.T. 434; and *Land Oberosterreich v CEZ AS* (C-343/04) [2006] I.L.Pr. 25 ECJ.

[206] See, e.g. *Reichert v Dresdner Bank* (C115/88) [1990] E.C.R. I-27; *Barratt International Resorts Ltd v Martin*, 1994 S.L.T. 434; *Webb v Webb* [1994] Q.B. 696; *Lieber v Gobel* (C292/93) [1994] I.L. Pr. 590; *Re Hayward (Deceased)* [1997] 1 All E.R. 32; *Cambridge Bionutritional Ltd v VDC Plc*, 2000 G.W.D. 6–230; *Gaillard v Chekili* (C518/99) [2001] I.L.Pr. 33 ECJ; *Dansommer A/S v Gotz* (C8/98) [2001] 1W.L.R. 1069 ECJ; *Ashurst v Pollard* [2001] 2 W.L.R. 722; *Prazic v Prazic* [2007] I.L.Pr. 31; *R v R (Bankruptcy Jurisdiction concerning Real Property Abroad: Setting Aside Consent Order: Estoppel)* [2007] EWHC 2589 (Fam); *Wellington Pub Co Plc v Hancock* [2009] 48 E.G. 108; *Depfa Bank Plc v Provincia di Pisa* [2010] EWHC 1148 (Comm); and *JP Morgan Chase Bank NA v Berliner Verkehrsbetriebe (BVG) Anstalt des Offentlichen Rechts* [2010] EWCA Civ 390.

[207] *Webb v Webb* [1994] 3 All E.R. 911; *Re Hayward (Deceased)* [1997] 1 All E.R. 32; *Ashurst v Pollard* [2001] 2 W.L.R. 722; *R v R (Bankruptcy Jurisdiction concerning Real Property Abroad: Setting Aside Consent Order: Estoppel)* [2007] EWHC 2589 (Fam); *Byers v Yacht Bull Corp* [2010] EWHC 133 (Ch); *Proceedings Brought by Schneider* (C-386/12) [2014] Fam. 80; [2014] 2 W.L.R. 1048; *Stevens v Hamed* [2013] EWCA Civ 911; and *Weber v Weber* (C-438/12) [2015] Ch. 140. See, on the "in personam" loophole, Carruthers, *The Transfer of Property in the Conflict of Laws* (2005), paras 2.39–2.50.

[208] *Sanders v Van der Putte* (73/77) [1977] E.C.R. 2383; *Klein v Rhodos Management Ltd* (C73–04) [2006] I.L.Pr. 2; and (on CJJA 1982 Sch.8) *Sauchiehall Street Properties One Ltd v EMI Group Ltd*, 2015 G.W.D. 1-3.

Article 25[209]

7–42

"1.   If the parties, regardless of their domicile, have agreed[210] that a court or the courts of a Member State are to have jurisdiction to settle any disputes which have arisen or which may arise in connection with a particular legal relationship, that court or those courts shall have jurisdiction unless the agreement is null and void as to its substantive validity under the law of that Member State. Such jurisdiction shall be exclusive unless the parties have agreed otherwise. The agreement conferring jurisdiction shall be either:

(a)   in writing or evidenced in writing;[211]

(b)   in a form which accords with practices which the parties have established between themselves; or

(c)   in international trade or commerce, in a form which accords with a usage of which the parties are or ought to have been aware and which in such trade or commerce is widely known to, and regularly observed by, parties to contracts of the type involved in the particular trade or commerce concerned.[212]

2.   Any communication by electronic means which provides a durable record of the agreement shall be equivalent to 'writing'.

3.   The court or courts of a Member State on which a trust instrument has conferred jurisdiction shall have exclusive jurisdiction in any proceedings brought against a settlor, trustee or beneficiary, if relations between those persons or their rights or obligations under the trust are involved.

4.   Agreements or provisions of a trust instrument conferring jurisdiction shall have no legal force if they are contrary to Articles 15, 19 or 23, or if the courts whose jurisdiction they purport to exclude have exclusive jurisdiction by virtue of Article 24.

5.   An agreement conferring jurisdiction which forms part of a contract shall be treated as an agreement independent of the other terms of the contract.

The validity of the agreement conferring jurisdiction cannot be contested solely on the ground that the contract is not valid."

---

[209]   cf. ex-Brussels I Regulation art.23, in respect of which, see *Siboti K/S v BP France SA* [2003] 2 Lloyd's Rep. 364; and contrast *OT Africa Line Ltd v Hijazy (The Kribi) (No.1)* [2001] 1 Lloyd's Rep. 76; *Comsite Projects Ltd v Andritz AG* [2003] EWHC 958; and *Standard Steamship Owners Protection & Indemnity Association (Bermuda) Ltd v GIA Vision Bail* [2005] 1 All E.R. (Comm) 618.

[210]   *Deutsche Bank AG v Asia Pacific Broadband Wireless Communications Inc* [2009] I.L.Pr. 36 addresses the question of the extent to which the appearance of consensus on the face of the deed is conclusive. See also *UBS AG v HSH Nordbank AG* [2009] EWCA Civ 585; *Deutsche Bank AG v Sebastian Holdings Inc* [2009] EWHC 3069 (Comm); and (re Lugano II) *Aeroflot - Russian Airlines v Berezovsky* [2013] EWCA Civ 784. See further L. Merrett, "Article 23 of the Brussels I Regulation: A Comprehensive Code for Jurisdiction Agreements?" (2009) 58 I.C.L.Q. 545, who concludes, at 564, that the requirements laid down in art.23 are both necessary and sufficient conditions for the material validity of jurisdiction agreements under the Brussels I Regulation, i.e. in favour of holding parties to the objective appearance of agreement.

[211]   *Franke GmbH v Fallimento Rubinetterie Rapetti SpA* [2009] I.L.Pr. 13: the Italian Court of Cassation held that the requirement of written form was satisfied, in a case where a jurisdiction clause featured among the standard general conditions of one of the contracting parties, only if the documentation was signed by both of the parties, and contained an express reference to those general conditions; and further that the requirement was not satisfied where a clause was inserted in a form signed by only one of the contracting parties. cf. in England, *Polskie Ratownictwo Okretowe v Rallo Vito & C SNC* [2009] EWHC 2249 (Comm); and *Calyon v Wytwornia Sprzetu Komunikacynego PZL Swidnik SA* [2009] EWHC 1914 (Comm). See also, on "chick-wrapping", *Jaouad El Majdoub v Cars On The Web* (Case C-322/14) (21 May, 2015).

[212]   cf. *Coreck Maritime GmbH v Handelsveen BV* (C-387/98) [2001] C.L.Y.B. 795; and *Erich Gasser Gmbh v Misat Srl* [2005] Q.B. 1.

Just as the exclusive jurisdiction conferred on Member State courts by art.24 operates regardless of the domicile, EU or non-EU, of parties, so too per art.25.1, the prorogation rule shall apply to parties "regardless of their domicile". In light of this clarification, a provision equivalent to that contained in art.23.3 of the Brussels I Regulation (applicable where an agreement in favour of a Member State court is concluded by parties "none of whom is domiciled in a Member State") would have been otiose.

The recast instrument has harmonised the choice of law rule applicable to the substantive validity of a choice of court agreement. If parties have agreed that a court of a Member State is to have jurisdiction, that court shall have (presumed exclusive) jurisdiction "unless the agreement is null and void as to its substantive validity under the law of that Member State". The law of that chosen forum—even if that does not coincide with the contractual *lex causae*—shall govern questions of substantive validity.

In *Refcomp SpA v Axa Corporate Solutions Assurance SA*,[213] the CJEU, noting that the wording of art.23.1 of the Brussels I Regulation did not indicate whether a jurisdiction clause could be transmitted beyond the circle of the parties to a contract to a third party, held that it is consensus between the parties which justifies the primacy of jurisdiction granted, in the name of the principle of the freedom of choice, to the choice of a court other than that which might have had jurisdiction under the regulation. Consequently, art.25(1) of Brussels I Recast, being limited to cases in which the parties have "agreed" on a court, will not bind a successor to a party to the initial contract unless that successor himself has agreed to the choice of court clause.

Article 25.5, an innovation in the recast instrument in providing that a jurisdiction agreement forming part of a contract shall be treated as an agreement independent of the other terms of the contract, takes the same approach as is found in the Hague Choice of Court Convention (q.v.).[214] This usefully separates the issues of the validity of a choice of court clause from the validity of the contract within which the clause is found. Hence, the fact that doubt may attend the validity of the main contract will not prevent the chosen court from adjudicating upon that or any other contractual issue.

Exclusivity of choice

Under the Brussels Convention, there was no presumption of exclusivity of jurisdiction, and a number of case authorities demonstrate the drafting difficulty for the parties of securing that end.[215] This defect was remedied in art.23 of the

7–43

---

[213] *Refcomp SpA v Axa Corporate Solutions Assurance SA* (C-543/10) [2013] 1 All E.R. (Comm) 1201.

[214] cf. at common law in the UK *Mackender v Feldia AG* [1967] 2 Q.B. 590; *Zapata Offshore Co v Bremen and Unterweser Reederei Gmbh (The Chaparral)* [1968] 2 Lloyd's Rep. 158; [1972] 2 Lloyd's Rep. 315 (US Sup. Ct.); *Belgian International Insurance Group SA v McNicoll*, 1999 G.W.D. 22–1065; *Astilleros v Zamakona SA v MacKinnons*, 2002 S.L.T. 1206; and *Cavell USA Inc v Seaton Insurance Co* [2009] EWCA Civ 1363. See E.B. Crawford, "The Uses of Putativity and Negativity in the Conflict of Laws" (2005) 54 I.C.L.Q. 829.

[215] *Dresser UK Ltd v Falcongate Freight Management Ltd (The Duke of Yare)* [1992] 2 All E.R. 450; *MT Group v James Howden & Co Ltd*, 1993 S.L.T. 409; *Barratt International Resorts Ltd v Martin*, 1994 S.L.T. 434; *Morrison v Panic Link Ltd*, 1994 S.L.T. 232; *Continental Bank NA v Aeakos Compania Naviera SA* [1994] 2 All E.R. 540; *Mainshiffarts Genossenschaft eG (MSG) v Les*

Brussels I Regulation, which introduced the rebuttable presumption of exclusivity of chosen forum. The presumption has been carried into art.25 of Brussels I Recast.

The promise of exclusivity must bow before the provisions of arts 24 and 26. Likewise, art.25 is subject to the limitations on disadvantaged parties' capacity to depart by agreement from what is provided for their benefit in the Regulation.[216] The celebrated problem discovered under the Brussels I Regulation that party choice of court was trumped by the *lis pendens* system has been addressed in art.31.2 of Brussels I Recast, discussed below.

One distinction between the prorogation rules contained in Brussels I Recast and those in Sch.4 (the Modified Convention, q.v.)[217] is that in the latter there is no presumption of exclusivity of jurisdiction.[218]

Harlequin clauses and unilateral clauses

7–44   The ECJ has long accepted "harlequin" jurisdiction clauses, as, e.g. in *Meeth v Glacetal*,[219] viz.:

> "If Meeth sues Glacetal the French courts alone shall have jurisdiction. If Glacetal sues Meeth the German courts alone have jurisdiction".

The Court held that, "Although, with regard to an agreement conferring jurisdiction, article 17 of the Brussels Convention, as it is worded, refers to the choice by the parties to a contract of a single court or the courts of a single state, that wording cannot be interpreted as prohibiting an agreement under which the two parties to a contract, who are domiciled in different states, can be sued only in the courts of their respective states." Article 25 makes no reference to harlequin choice of court clauses, and it is to be taken that they are still permitted.

More contentious, however, are unilateral dispute resolution clauses, to which also art.25 makes no reference. The validity of assymetric, or one-sided, choice of court clauses is more debateable.[220] They vary in shape and nature, but have in common a one-sided character whereby only one party to the contract enjoys the choice in which forum to bring the dispute. Such a dispute resolution clause grants to one party, A, the ability to choose among several jurisdictions when suing the other, B; and grants to B the ability, if suing A, to sue only in a single

---

Gravieres Rhenanes Sarl (C-106/95) [1997] All E.R. (EC) 385; *Hough v P&O Containers Ltd* [1998] 2 All E.R. 978; *AIG Europe (UK) Ltd v Ethniki* [2000] 2 All E.R. 566. *McGowan v Summit at Lloyds*, 2002 S.L.T. 1258; and *Astrazeneca UK Ltd v Albemarle International Corp* [2010] EWHC 1028 (Comm).

[216] See para.7–61, above.

[217] Modified Convention Sch.4 r.12.

[218] *Breitenbucher v Wittke* [2008] CSOH 145. cf. *Morrison v Panic Link Ltd*, 1994 S.L.T. 232; and *Scotmotors (Plant Hire) Ltd v Dundee Petrosea Ltd*, 1982 S.L.T. 181.

[219] *Meeth v Glacetal* Case 23/78 (1978).

[220] *Ms X v Banque Privée Edmond de Rothschild, Cour de Cassation (Chambre Civile 1)* (25.3.2015, N° de pourvoi: 13-27264) (confirming *Cour de Cassation*, 26 September 2012, No.11-26.022) and *Credit Suisse v Danne, Cour de Cassation* (Chambre Civile 1) (25.3.2015), both to the effect that the unilateral jurisdiction clauses are not enforceable in France; to be contrasted with *Mauritius Commercial Bank Ltd v Hestia Holdings Ltd* [2013] EWHC 1328 (Comm), where the English court rejected the challenge to the validity of a unilateral jurisdiction clause).

jurisdiction. The clauses are commonly used in international banking and finance agreements, and a typical clause will give the bank/financer considerable flexibility, while simultaneously restricting the options of the borrower/debtor. The purpose typically is to protect the financing party from being sued by a recalcitrant borrower before the courts of the borrower's domicile, and also to give the financer the flexibility of suing the borrower in the jurisdiction where the speediest and most effective relief is to be had. The validity of such clauses is of critical importance to banks and lenders. The position, at least in English law,[221] is that unilateral jurisdiction clauses are valid, UK lawyers taking the view that rendering a unilateral dispute resolution clause unenforceable would be an unacceptable interference with the principle of party autonomy.

Choice of a non-EU Member State court

Article 25, though indifferent to the domicile, EU or non-EU, of the prorogating parties, is limited in its scope to choice of Member State courts. To that extent, the provision is strictly geographically based; the Brussels regime has no *locus standi* to seek to regulate choice-of-court agreements nominating a non-EU forum, except possibly by virtue of reflexive reasoning.[222] If a Third State court is specified in the prorogation agreement, it falls outside the scope of art.25. The instrument does not *require*, therefore, any Member State court to decline jurisdiction in a case where the parties have prorogated the courts of a Third State. The new international *lis pendens* rule (q.v.) may assist, but only in the discretion of the Member State court.

7–45

Prorogation clauses are found also outside the Brussels regime. These will usually,[223] but not always,[224] be enforced, if necessary, by English or Scots court order[225] enjoining one party to desist from conducting legal proceedings in defiance of the clause. But under the Brussels regime, in light of *Turner v Grovit* (q.v.),[226] the use by an English or Scottish forum of an anti-suit injunction to seek to prevent a party from reneging on an agreement by suing in a different Member State, in defiance of the prorogation clause, is incompetent.

---

[221] *Mauritius Commercial Bank Ltd v Hestia Holdings Ltd* [2013] EWHC 1328 (Comm).

[222] Para.7–63, below.

[223] *Continental Bank NA v Aeakos Compania Naviera SA* [1994] 2 All E.R. 540; *Reichhold Norway ASA v Goldman Sachs International* [2000] 1 W.L.R. 173; *Messier Dowty Ltd v Sabena SA* [2000] 1 W.L.R. 2040; *The Kribi* (No.1) [2001] 1 Lloyd's Rep. 76; *Import Export Metro Ltd v Compania Sud Americana de Vapores SA* [2003] 1 All E.R. (Comm) 703; *Sabah Shipyard (Pakistan) Ltd v Pakistan* [2003] 2 Lloyd's Rep. 571; and *Beazley v Horizon Offshore Contractors Inc* [2005] I.L.Pr. 11.

[224] *Standard Bank London Ltd v Apostolakis (No.2)* [2001] Lloyd's Rep. Bank. 240; *Donohue v Armco Inc* [2002] 1 All E.R. 749; *Deutsche Bank AG v Highland Crusader Offshore Partners LP* [2009] EWCA Civ 725; and *Morgan Stanley & Co International Plc v China Haisheng Juice Holdings Co Ltd* [2009] EWHC 2409 (Comm).

[225] Order restraining foreign proceedings/anti-suit injunction: see para.7–83, below.

[226] *Turner v Grovit* [2005] 1 A.C. 101.

2005 HAGUE CONVENTION ON CHOICE OF COURT AGREEMENTS[227]

7–46   This Convention[228] represents that which could be salvaged of international co-operation and agreement generated in advance of the collapse of negotiations instigated by the Hague Conference on Private International Law to achieve a "worldwide" convention on jurisdiction and the enforcement of judgments. It was admitted in 2003 that the ambitious "worldwide" project should be laid aside. Thereafter the more restricted aim was to build upon a basis of what could be agreed at the broadest level of generality. What emerged is a Convention, the provisions of which seek to ensure the effectiveness of exclusive choice of court agreements between parties to commercial transactions, and which govern the recognition and enforcement thereof.

Although the rationale of the Hague rules is in striking contrast with the position which was expressed in the judgments of the ECJ in *Gasser v Misat*[229] and *Turner v Grovit*,[230] the EU took a leading part in negotiations prior to the creation of the 2005 Convention. In the strict system of *lis pendens* under the Brussels I Regulation, the initiative lay with the court first seised to adjudge its own jurisdiction, both generally and in light of argument that the parties had made an exclusive choice of court in favour of another jurisdiction. By contrast, the Hague Convention, after setting out[231] a lengthy list of excluded matters to which its provisions shall not apply, defines[232] "exclusive choice of court agreement" (with a presumption of exclusivity) and provides, usefully, that an exclusive choice of court agreement that forms part of a contract shall be treated as an agreement independent of the other terms of the contract. The validity of the choice of court agreement cannot be contested solely on the ground that the "principal" contract is not valid.[233] The rules of the Brussels regime did not

---

[227] See T. Hartley and M. Dogauchi, "Explanatory Report on the Convention of 30 June 2005 on Choice of Court Agreements" (The Hague, Permanent Bureau of the Hague Conference, 2007) (hereafter "Hartley and Dogauchi Report"); and M. Pertegas, "The Brussels I Regulation and the Hague Convention on Choice of Court Agreements" (2010) 11(1) ERA-Forum 19.

[228] The Convention has been acceded to by Mexico, and signed by the USA and Singapore, and by the EC (replaced and succeeded by the EU) on behalf of Member States. It shall enter into force on the first day of the month following the expiration of three months after the deposit of the second instrument of ratification, acceptance, approval or accession (art.31). By declaration of the EU under art.30, the Member States of the EU will not sign, ratify, accept or approve the Convention, but shall be bound by it by virtue of its conclusion by the EC, the Convention falling within the competence of the EU. On 4/5 December 2014, the Council of the EU adopted a decision on the approval, on behalf of the EU, of the 2005 Convention, thereby completing the internal EU approval process (Press Release 16526/14: Council Decision of 4 December 2014 on the approval, on behalf of the European Union, of the Hague Convention of 30 June 2005 on Choice of Court Agreements (2014/887/EU) [2014] O.J. L353/5). On 11 June, 2015 the EU deposited its instrument of approval, meaning that the Hague choice of Court Convetion will enter into force for Mexico and the EU on 1 October, 2015.

[229] *Erich Gasser Gmbh v Misat Srl* [2005] Q.B. 1. See para.7–58, below.

[230] *Turner v Grovit* [2005] 1 A.C. 101. See para.7–84, below.

[231] Hague Convention art.2.

[232] Hague Convention art.3.

[233] Hague Convention art.3(d).

necessarily differ on this point.[234] Brussels I Recast, by effectively removing the *Gasser* problem by means of art.31.2, and by providing in art.25.5 for the severance of a prorogation agreement from the contract of which it forms part, aligned itself with the Hague Convention. Accordingly, the adoption of Brussels I Recast paved the way for the approval of the 2005 Convention, on behalf of the Union, by ensuring coherence between the rules of the EU on choice of court in civil and commercial matters and the rules of the Convention.[235]

The essence of the 2005 Convention (arts 5 and 6) is that it places the court selected by the parties in a position of authority, even though that authority sometimes is shared with the court "first seised but not chosen".

Article 5 (Jurisdiction of the chosen court)

"1.   The court or courts of a Contracting State designated in an exclusive choice of court agreement shall have jurisdiction to decide a dispute to which the agreement applies, unless the agreement is null and void under the law of that State.

2.   A court that has jurisdiction under paragraph 1 shall not decline to exercise jurisdiction on the ground that the dispute should be decided in a court of another State."

7–47

These provisions therefore set down the power and the duty of the court selected.

Article 6 (Obligations of a court not chosen)

"A court in a Contracting State other than that of the chosen court shall suspend or dismiss proceedings to which an exclusive choice of court agreement applies unless:

(a)   the agreement is null and void under the law of the State of the chosen court;

(b)   a party lacked the capacity to conclude the agreement under the law of the State of the court seised;[236]

(c)   giving effect to the agreement would lead to a manifest injustice or would be manifestly contrary to the public policy of the State of the court seised;[237]

(d)   for exceptional reasons beyond the control of the parties, the agreement cannot reasonably be performed; or

(e)   the chosen court has decided not to hear the case."

7–48

Articles 19 ("Declarations limiting jurisdiction") and 20 ("Declarations limiting recognition and enforcement") open the possibility of state reservations. Article 19 is remarkable in permitting a state to declare that its courts may refuse to determine disputes to which an exclusive choice of court agreement applies if, except for the location of the chosen court, there is no connection between that

---

[234] *Benincasa v Dentalkit Srl* (C-269/95) [1997] E.C.R. I-3767. See also *Knorr-Bremse Systems for Commercial Vehicles Ltd v Haldex Brake Products GmbH* [2008] I.L.Pr. 26; and *Skype Technologies SA v Joltid Ltd* [2009] EWHC 2783 (Ch).

[235] Council Decision of 4 December 2014 on the approval, on behalf of the EU, of the Hague Convention of 30 June 2005 on Choice of Court Agreements, recital (5).

[236] The question of capacity (mental and legal, presumably) is to be governed by the law of the court seised, but not chosen. Contrast, at the stage of judgment recognition, the rule under art.9(b) that one reason for the requested state's refusal to recognise or enforce a resulting judgment is that a party lacked capacity to conclude the choice of court agreement under the law of the requested state.

[237] Note the power which the public policy discretion gives to the court seised.

state and the parties or the dispute. If a state were to enter such a reservation, it would effectively be adding a mandatory rule of its own to the principal jurisdiction provision contained in art.5.1, and would be curtailing party autonomy in choice of court to an unprecedented degree. Choice of neutral court and neutral law have always been regarded in UK conflict rules as explicable and not unreasonable.

Recognition and enforcement under the 2005 Convention

7–49   With regard to recognition and enforcement of judgments, art.8 of the 2005 Convention provides that a judgment given by a court of a Contracting State designated in an exclusive choice of court agreement shall be recognised in other Contracting States, and may be refused effect only on the grounds specified in the Convention. In general, there shall be no review of the merits of the judgment, except insofar as necessary for the application of the provisions of the Convention. The court addressed shall be bound by the findings of fact on which the court of origin based its jurisdiction, unless that judgment was given by default. A number of the grounds of refusal of recognition rest upon natural justice, but the relationship of power between the chosen court and the court seised, as expressed in arts 6(a) and (b) and 9(a) and (b), repays study.[238] It is important, additionally, to note the possibility of state reservation offered by art.20, namely, that the courts of a state may refuse to recognise or enforce a judgment given by a court in another Contracting State if the parties were resident in the requested state, and the relationship of the parties and all other elements relevant to the dispute, other than the location of the chosen court, were connected only with the requested state.[239]

Relationship between the Brussels regime and the 2005 Hague Convention

7–50   Article 26 of the 2005 Convention ("Relationship with other international instruments") should be considered. This disconnection clause, which is lengthy and opaque, begins in very general terms, by stating in art.26.1 that the Convention shall be interpreted so far as possible to be compatible with other treaties in force for Contracting States, whether concluded before or after this Convention. Thereafter, art.26.2 provides that the Convention shall not affect the application by a Contracting State of a treaty, whether concluded before or after the Convention, in cases where none of the parties is resident in a Contracting State that is not a party to the treaty. The effect is that where all parties to the litigation are residents of EU Member States, application of Brussels I Recast will

---

[238] i.e. validity of agreement is determined by the law of the chosen court, at the stages both of jurisdiction allocation and judgment recognition; but the question of capacity is referred, at the stage of jurisdiction allocation, to the law of the court seised, and at the stage of judgment recognition, to the law of the court requested.

[239] This is an interesting insight into the anticipated objection by some states to parties' unfettered choice of court. It militates against forum shopping, and in spirit has something in common with the anti-avoidance provision in the Rome I Regulation art.3.3, which inhibits complete freedom of choice of law in contract.

not be affected.[240] Similarly, Brussels I Recast prevails where one party is an EU resident and the other resident in a Third State which is not party to the Hague Convention. But, where one party is an EU resident and the other resident in a Third State which is a party to the Hague Convention (i.e. Mexico, USA or Singapore), the Hague Convention shall prevail.[241]

With regard to the provisions in each instrument concerning recognition and enforcement of judgments, the Convention is in keeping with the rules contained in Brussels I Recast, but certain peculiarities have been appended in view of the particular purpose of the Convention. Article 26.4 provides, in effect, that for the purposes of obtaining recognition or enforcement of a judgment given by a court of a Contracting State which is also an EU State, Brussels I Recast shall apply; however, it further provides that the judgment shall not be recognised or enforced to a lesser extent than it would be under the Convention.[242] Further, when approving the Convention, it is intended that the EU shall make the declaration allowed under art.21 of the 2005 Convention, excluding from the scope of the Convention insurance contracts in general, subject to certain well-defined exceptions.[243] The objective of the declaration is to preserve the protective jurisdiction rules available to the policyholder, the insured party or a beneficiary in matters relating to insurance under Brussels I Recast. The exclusion should not cover reinsurance contracts nor contracts relating to large risks.

Submission to the jurisdiction

Brussels I Recast honours the well-established principle of founding jurisdiction upon the basis of submission.

7–51

Article 26[244]

"1.   Apart from jurisdiction derived from other provisions of this Regulation, a court of a Member State before which a defendant enters an appearance shall have jurisdiction. This rule shall not apply where appearance was entered to contest the jurisdiction, or where another court has exclusive jurisdiction by virtue of Article 24."

7–52

---

[240] cf. art.26.6(b) (concerning Regional Economic Integration Organisations).

[241] Hartley and Dogauchi Report, para.271 ("First 'give-way' rule"); and Pertegas, "The Brussels I Regulation and the Hague Convention on Choice of Court Agreements" (2010) 11(1) ERA-Forum 19, 22, 23.

[242] Hartley and Dogauchi Report, paras 286, 287, explain the "Third 'give-way' rule" thus: "This rule is of significance only when both States concerned are Parties to both the Convention and the other treaty: the Convention would not apply unless both States were Parties to it and the other treaty would not apply unless both were Parties to it. The purpose of the rule is to promote the recognition and enforcement of judgments. If the other treaty does this more efficiently, or to a greater extent, it would be better to allow its application. It is only where the judgment would be recognised or enforced to a lesser extent under the other treaty that the Convention should apply. Unless the law of the requested provides otherwise, the judgment creditor can choose whether to enforce the judgment under the Convention or under the other treaty." Also Pertegas, "The Brussels I Regulation and the Hague Convention on Choice of Court Agreements" (2010) 11(1) ERA-Forum 19, 23.

[243] Council Decision of 4 December 2014 on the approval, on behalf of the European Union, of the Hague Convention of 30 June 2005 on Choice of Court Agreements, recital (7).

[244] cf. Brussels I Regulation art.24.

It is an important principle of the Regulation that a defendant must be allowed to appear, without prejudice, to argue for its proper application in his case, which includes allowing him to challenge or contest jurisdiction if he thinks the court has been wrongly seised. If the defendant argues in the alternative (i.e. he avers, first, that there is no jurisdiction over him, and further that, even if there is jurisdiction, there is a defence on the merits), it seems that the defendant is not deemed to have submitted to the jurisdiction.[245] But a defendant cannot append challenges to the jurisdiction to what is essentially a defence on the merits, merely in order to evade the operation of art.26.1. For the defendant to evade the suggestion of submission, it must be clear to the claimant and to the court from the outset of the defence that the defendant intends to challenge the court's jurisdiction under art.26.[246] The ECJ, in *Elefanten Schuh GmbH*,[247] held, on a reference from the Belgian Court of Cassation, that the simultaneous raising by the defendant of a complaint as to the jurisdiction (i.e. not later than the submission of its first substantive defence) prevented the defendant's appearance in the Belgian court from being regarded as submission thereto.

The principle of submission under art.26 does not apply where another Member State court has exclusive jurisdiction by virtue of art.24. In contrast, art.25 is subservient to art.26; the defendant's submission to the courts of a Member State under art.26 overrides an art.25 agreement. This is logical: a subsequent selection of jurisdiction by means of submission trumps an earlier agreed jurisdiction.

As explained above in relation to weaker parties, art.26.2 introduces a protective device of a soft law nature,[248] to the effect that where the defendant in the proposed litigation is an insured party, a consumer, or an employee, the Member State court, before assuming jurisdiction on the basis of submission, shall ensure that the defendant is informed of his right to contest the jurisdiction, and of the consequences of entering or not entering an appearance.

CONFLICTS OF JURISDICTION UNDER BRUSSELS I RECAST: *LIS PENDENS*

7–53   The rules in s.9 comprise the system which the Brussels regime has adopted since 1968 to deal with problems of concurrent, conflicting jurisdiction. As will be seen, it is a system of strict priority of process, notably different from that discretionary system which operated in the UK at common law, and now operates when permitted. i.e. "outside the Brussels regime".[249]

---

[245] *Marc Rich & Co AG v Societa Italiana Impianti pA (The Atlantic Emperor) (No.2)* [1992] 1 Lloyd's Rep. 624 at 633.

[246] *Harada Ltd (t/a Chequepoint UK) v Turner (No.2)* [2003] EWCA Civ 1695 at [29]; and *Maple Leaf Macro Volatility Master Fund v Rouvroy* [2009] 1 W.L.R. 475; [2009] EWCA Civ 1334.

[247] *Elefanten Schuh GmbH v Jacqmain* [1981] E.C.R. 1671. See also *Deutsche Bahn AG v Morgan Advanced Materials Plc (formerly Morgan Crucible Co Plc)* [2013] EWCA Civ 1484; *Future New Developments Ltd v B&S Patente Und Marken GmbH* [2014] EWHC 1874; and *Deutsche Bank AG London Branch v Petromena ASA* [2015] EWCA Civ 226.

[248] See, under art.24 of Brussels I Regulation, *Ceska Podnikatelska Pojistovna as, Vienna Insurance Group v Bilas* (C-111/09) [2010] Lloyd's Rep. I.R. 734, especially at paras 30–32.

[249] Para.7–81, below.

CONFLICTS OF JURISDICTION UNDER BRUSSELS I RECAST: LIS PENDENS

Article 29[250]

> "1.   Without prejudice to Article 31(2), where proceedings involving the same   **7–54**
> cause of action and between the same parties are brought in the courts of
> different Member States,[251] any court other than the court first seised[252] shall
> of its own motion stay its proceedings until such time as the jurisdiction of
> the court first seised is established.
>
> 2.   In cases referred to in paragraph 1, upon request by a court seised of the
> dispute, any other court seised shall without delay inform the former court of
> the date when it was seised in accordance with Article 32.
>
> 3.   Where the jurisdiction of the court first seised is established, any court other
> than the court first seised shall decline jurisdiction in favour of that court."

There are many essential, and essentially simple, characteristics of the rule of priority of process. However, the *lis pendens* system of jurisdiction allocation has generated a significant body of often complex case law interpretative of important phrases such as "same cause of action"[253] and "same parties".[254]

Lord Bingham, in *Haji-Ioannou v Frangos*,[255] ruled that actions have the same cause if they have the same facts and rule of law as their basis, or if they have the same end in view. Article 29 applies if the actions are mirror images of one another and thus are legally irreconcilable, or the "heart" of the claims are the same.[256] If the actions are not incompatible, art.29 does not apply.[257]

As regards the parties to the action, it was held in *The Tatry*[258] that on a proper construction of art.21 of the Brussels Convention (cf. art.29 of Brussels I Recast), where two actions involve the same cause of action and some, but not all, of the

---

[250] cf. Brussels I Regulation art.27.

[251] The question is whether the courts in the different Member States have jurisdiction on a Brussels ground, not (necessarily, therefore) whether either or both party(ies) is/are domiciled in a Member State: *Overseas Union Insurance Ltd v New Hampshire Insurance Co* [1992] 2 All E.R. 138.

[252] As to which, see art.32. See operation of *lis pendens* system per Court of Appeal in *Royal & Sun Alliance Insurance Plc v MK Digital FZE (Cyprus) Ltd* [2006] EWCA Civ 629.

[253] e.g. *Gubisch Maschinenfabrik KG v Palumbo* [1987] E.C.R. 4861 (in which the ECJ held that an action for the rescission or discharge of a contract involved the same cause of action as an action to enforce the same contract); *Mecklermedia Corp v DC Congress GmbH* [1998] 1 All E.R. 148; *Owners of Cargo Lately Laden on Board the Tatry v Owners of the Maciej Rataj* [1999] Q.B. 515; *Haji-Ioannou v Frangos* [1999] 2 All E.R. (Comm) 865; *Gantner Electronic GmbH v Basch Exploitatie Maatschappij BV* (C-111/01) [2003] I.L.Pr. 37 ECJ; *Bank of Tokyo-Mitsubishi Ltd v Baskan Gida Sanayi Ve Pazarlama AS* [2004] 2 Lloyd's Rep. 395; and *Royal & Sun Alliance Insurance Plc v MK Digital FZE (Cyprus) Ltd* [2005] EWHC 1408.

[254] e.g. *Drouot Assurances SA v Consolidated Metallurgical Industries (CMI Industrial Sites)* [1998] All E.R. (EC) 483 (there may be such a degree of identity between the interests of insurer and insured that they must be considered to be the same party). Contrast *Mecklermedia Corp v DC Congress GmbH* [1998] 1 All E.R. 148; *Glencore International AG v Metro Trading International Inc (No.1)* [1999] 2 All E.R. (Comm) 899; *Glencore International AG v Shell International Trading & Shipping Co Ltd* [1999] 2 All E.R. (Comm) 922; *The Tatry* [1999] Q.B. 515; *Tavoulareas v Alexander G Tsavliris & Sons Maritime Co (No.2)* [2005] EWHC 2643 (Comm); *Re Claim by a German Lottery Company* [2005] I.L.Pr. 35; *JP Morgan Europe Ltd v Primacom AG* [2005] 2 All E.R. (Comm) 764; and *Kolden Holdings Ltd v Rodette Commerce Ltd* [2008] 3 All E.R. 612.

[255] *Haji-Ioannou v Frangos* [1999] 2 Lloyd's Rep. 337 at 351.

[256] *Football Dataco Ltd v Sportradar GmbH* [2011] EWCA Civ 330.

[257] *Starlight Shipping Co v Allianz Marine & Aviation Versicherungs AG (The Alexandros T)* [2013] UKSC 70; [2014] 1 All E.R. 590, per Lord Clarke of Stone-Cum-Ebony JSC (with whom Lord Sumption and Lord Hughes JJSC agreed) at [30].

[258] *The Tatry* [1999] Q.B. 515.

parties to the second action are the same as the parties to the action commenced earlier in another Contracting State, the second court seised is required to decline jurisdiction only to the extent to which the parties to the proceedings before it are also parties to the action previously commenced; it does not prevent the proceedings from continuing between any other parties.

The facts of *Starlight Shipping Co v Allianz Marine & Aviation Versicherungs AG (The Alexandros T)*[259] take the interpretative task beyond that reached in *The Tatry*, on a point which, had it been required for decision in the instant case, necessarily, in the view of the Supreme Court, would have been referred to the CJEU, viz.: whether or not the court first seised remains first seised of the proceedings even where those proceedings are subsequently amended by the addition of new claims. While there is a principle at common law of "once seised, always seised", the question arises whether this should hold true where the claim originally litigated suffers substantial change.[260] The point remains unanswered.

Only in 2014, in *Cartier parfums - lunettes SAS v Ziegler France SA*,[261] did the CJEU hand down its decision on the meaning of "such time as the jurisdiction of the court first seised is established". The Court held that it was clear both from the overall scheme and the purpose of the Brussels I Regulation that, in order for the jurisdiction of the court first seised to be established within the meaning of art.27(2), it was sufficient that the court first seised had not declined jurisdiction of its own motion and that none of the parties had contested that jurisdiction before or up to the time at which a position was adopted which was regarded by national procedural law as being the first defence. At that point, any court second seised must decline jurisdiction, unless the case falls within the exclusive jurisdiction of that court.[262]

Article 30[263]

7–55

"1.   Where related actions are pending in the courts of different Member States, any court other than the court first seised may stay its proceedings.

2.   Where the action in the court first seised is pending at first instance, any other court may also, on the application of one of the parties, decline jurisdiction if the court first seised has jurisdiction over the actions in question and its law permits the consolidation thereof.[264]

3.   For the purposes of this Article, actions are deemed to be related where they are so closely connected that it is expedient to hear and determine them together to avoid the risk of irreconcilable judgments resulting from separate proceedings.[265]"

---

[259] *Starlight Shipping Co v Allianz Marine & Aviation Versicherungs AG (The Alexandros T)* [2013] UKSC 70; [2014] 1 All E.R. 590.

[260] cf. *FKI Engineering Ltd v Stribog Ltd* [2011] EWCA Civ 622.

[261] *Cartier parfums – lunettes SAS v Ziegler France SA* (C-1/13) [2014] I.L.Pr. 25.

[262] As in, e.g. *Overseas Union Insurance Ltd v New Hampshire Insurance Co* [1992] 2 All E.R. 138; and *Weber v Weber* (C-438/12) [2015] Ch. 140.

[263] cf. Brussels I Regulation art.28.

[264] e.g. *Jacobs & Turner Ltd v Celsius Sarl*, 2007 S.L.T. 722.

[265] *Nomura International Plc v Banca Monte Dei Paschi Di Siena SpA* [2013] EWHC 3187 (Comm); [2014] 1 W.L.R. 1584.

This manner of drafting provides a type of autonomous definition, but one in which a great deal is left to the discretion of the individual state forum.[266] The discretion conferred is two-fold; first, the value judgment to decide whether or not the two sets of proceedings are "related"[267]; and separately, if they are related, the discretion conferred on the forum to stay its own (i.e. the later) proceedings.[268]

In *FKI Engineering Ltd v Stribog Ltd*,[269] the English Court of Appeal held that where a court is asked, pursuant to art.28 of the Brussels I Regulation, to stay an action, it must determine (a) whether it and the court of another Member State are both seised of an action, rather than a particular issue in an action; (b) where both are seised, it must ascertain in accordance with art.32 whether it or the court of the other Member State was the first to be seised, in order to determine which court has jurisdiction to impose a stay; (c) if the court were not the first seised, it must compare the two proceedings to see whether there are related issues; and (d) in carrying out the comparative exercise, it must look at all the circumstances, and not merely those as at the date of institution of the proceedings in the forum, in order to determine how closely related the actions are and whether or not there exists a risk of irreconcilable judgments in separate proceedings.[270]

Article 30 effectively covers circumstances which fall outside art.29. It is not necessary under art.30 that the parties in the related actions, or even the subject matter, be identical.[271]

Articled 30 is a direction to courts other than that first seised, offering a discretion to such a court. If a court is first seised, it has no discretion to stay under art.30.

Article 32[272]

Article 32 provides an autonomous definition of the date at which a court shall be deemed to be seised. It is essential in a priority of process system that there be clarity on this matter.[273] The rule is bifurcated to reflect two differing modes of practice among Member States:

7–56

---

[266] *Jacobs & Turner Ltd v Celsius Sarl*, 2007 S.L.T. 722; and *Cooper Tire & Rubber Co Europe Ltd v Shell Chemicals UK Ltd* [2009] EWHC 1529 (Comm).

[267] *Haji-Ioannou v Frangos* [1999] 2 All E.R. (Comm) 865; *Mecklermedia Corp v DC Congress GmbH* [1998] 1 All E.R. 148; *Blue Nile Shipping Co Ltd v Iguana Shipping & Finance Inc (The Happy Fellow)* [1998] 1 Lloyd's Rep. 13; *Evialis SA v SIAT* [2003] 2 Lloyd's Rep. 377; *Research in Motion UK Ltd v Visto Corp* [2008] EWCA Civ 153; *FKI Engineering Ltd v Stribog Ltd* [2010] EWHC 1160 (Comm); *Rahman v GMAC Commercial Finance Ltd* [2012] EWCA Civ 1467; and *Nomura International Plc v Banca Monte Dei Paschi Di Siena SpA* [2013] EWHC 3187 (Comm).

[268] *Starlight Shipping Co v Allianz Marine & Aviation Versicherungs AG (The Alexandros T)* [2013] UKSC 70; [2014] 1 All E.R. 590; and *Trademark Licensing Co Ltd v Leofelis SA* [2010] I.L.Pr. 16, per Sir William Blackburne at [38].

[269] *FKI Engineering Ltd v Stribog Ltd* [2011] EWCA Civ 622.

[270] Mummery L.J. and Rix L.J. differed as to the order of addressing these questions, but not as to substance.

[271] *Sarrio SA v Kuwait Investment Authority* [1999] 1 A.C. 32.

[272] cf. Brussels I Regulation art.30.

[273] Identification of the point at which the court is seised proved contentious under the 1968 Brussels Convention: *Neste Chemicals SA v DK Line SA (The Sargasso)* [1994] 3 All E.R. 180; *The Duke of*

"1. For the purposes of this Section, a court shall be deemed to be seised[274]:
   (a) at the time when the document instituting the proceedings or an equivalent document is lodged with the court, provided that the claimant has not subsequently failed to take the steps he was required to take to have service effected on the defendant; or
   (b) if the document has to be served before being lodged with the court, at the time when it is received by the authority responsible for service, provided that the claimant has not subsequently failed to take the steps he was required to take to have the document lodged with the court.

The authority responsible for service referred to in point (b) shall be the first authority receiving the documents to be served.

2. The court, or the authority responsible for service, referred to in paragraph 1, shall note, respectively, the date of the lodging of the document instituting the proceedings or the equivalent document, or the date of receipt of the documents to be served."

Articles 33 and 34

7–57   These two new provisions in Brussels I Recast are worthy of note. They address directly one aspect of the "turf war" between "Brussels cases" and "non-Brussels cases".[275] The model for these provisions is arts 29 and 30 of the Recast Regulation, insofar as art.33 operates where conflicting proceedings involve the same cause of action and are conducted between the same parties, and art.34 where conflicting proceedings concern related actions.

The novelty is that arts 33 and 34 provide an exception to the otherwise strict operation of the priority of process system and, significantly, apply only where the conflicting proceedings take place, respectively, in a (first seised) Third State court and in a (second seised) Member State court whose jurisdiction is founded on particular provisions of Brussels I Recast.

This concession to discretionary reasoning does not go so far as to cover, for example, the situation in *Owusu v Jackson (t/a Villa Holidays Bal Inn Villas)*,[276] in which the defendants hoped to persuade the English forum to defer to a court in Jamaica, where litigation had not been commenced. In terms of art.33, where a Member State court's jurisdiction is based on general jurisdiction per art.4, or under the special jurisdiction provisions in arts 7, 8 or 9, and proceedings involving the same cause of action and between the same parties are pending before the court of a Third State at the time when the Member State court is seised of an action, the Member State court may stay its proceedings if (a) it is expected that the Third State court will give a judgment capable of recognition and, where applicable, of enforcement in that Member State; and (b) the Member State court is satisfied that a stay is necessary for the proper administration of justice.

On the other hand, per art.33.2, the Member State court may continue its proceedings if (a) the proceedings in the Third State court are stayed or

---

Yare [1992] 1 Q.B. 502, overtaken by *Canada Trust v Stolzenberg (No.2)* [2000] 4 All E.R. 481; and *Zelger v Salinitri* [1984] E.C.R. 2397. As to the Lugano Convention, see *Phillips v Symes (A Bankrupt)* [2006] I.L.Pr. 9; and Lugano II art.30.

[274] e.g. *Debt Collect London Ltd v SK Slavia Praha-Fotbal AS* [2010] EWCA Civ 1250.

[275] cf. *Goshawk Dedicated Ltd v Life Receivables Ireland Ltd* [2009] I.E.S.C.7.

[276] *Owusu v Jackson (t/a Villa Holidays Bal Inn Villas)* [2005] Q.B. 801; [2005] 2 W.L.R. 942; [2005] 2 All E.R. (Comm) 577.

discontinued; or (b) it appears to the Member State court that the Third State court proceedings are unlikely to be concluded within a reasonable time; or (c) such continuation of proceedings in the Member State court is required for the proper administration of justice. Further, by art.33.3, the Member State court shall dismiss its proceedings if the Third State court proceedings are concluded and have resulted in a judgment capable of recognition and, where applicable, of enforcement in that Member State. Article 33 may be triggered on application by one of the parties or by the Member State court on its own initiative, where this is possible under that court's national law (art.33.4).

Article 34 provides that where Member State court jurisdiction is based on general jurisdiction per art.4, or under the special jurisdiction provisions in arts 7, 8 or 9, and proceedings involving a *related* cause of action are pending before the court of a Third State at the time when the Member State court is seised of the action, the Member State court may stay its proceedings if (a) it is expedient to hear and determine the related actions together to avoid the risk of irreconcilable judgments resulting from separate proceedings; (b) it is expected that the Third State court will give a judgment capable of recognition and, where applicable, of enforcement in that Member State; and (c) the Member State court is satisfied that a stay is necessary for the proper administration of justice.

On the other hand, per art.34.2, the Member State court may continue its proceedings if (a) it appears to the Member State court that there is no longer a risk of irreconcilable judgments; (b) the proceedings in the Third State court are stayed or discontinued; (c) it appears to the Member State court that the Third State court proceedings are unlikely to be concluded within a reasonable time; or (d) such continuation of proceedings in the Member State court is required for the proper administration of justice.

Articles 34.3 and 34.4 mirror arts 33.3 and 33.4, explained above. Articles 33.2(c) and 34.2(d) both refer to the "proper administration of justice", a concept in respect of which elaboration is given in recital (24). The recital urges a Member State court to assess all the circumstances of the case before it—an unusual notion in a civilian inspired instrument—including connections between the facts of the case and the parties and the Third State; the stage to which the Third State proceedings have progressed by the time proceedings are initiated in the Member State court; and whether or not the Third State court can be expected to give a judgment within a reasonable time. Lord Goff of Chieveley would have no difficulty in accommodating these considerations within the guidance laid down in his seminal speech on the operation of the plea of *forum non conveniens* in *Spiliada*,[277] examined below.[278]

---

[277] *Spiliada Maritime Corp v Cansulex ("The Spiliada")* [1987] A.C. 460; [1986] 3 W.L.R. 972; [1986] 3 All E.R. 843.
[278] Para.7–80, below.

RANKING OF THE JURISDICTIONAL RULES IN BRUSSELS I RECAST

Choice of court agreements and priority of process—the background

Erich Gasser GmbH v Misat Srl[279]

7–58   Misat, an Italian company, based in Rome, and Gasser, an Austrian company, had done business together for a number of years in the supply by Gasser, and purchase by Misat, of children's clothing. In April 2000, Misat brought proceedings against Gasser in a court in Rome (arguing apparently that, in the circumstances, its jurisdiction was available under art.2 of the 1968 Brussels Convention), seeking, essentially, "negative declarations" (q.v.) to the effect that the contract between the parties had terminated by operation of law, or as a result of disagreement between the two companies; and further, a finding that Misat had not failed to perform the contract; and seeking also an order for damages plus expenses against Gasser in relation to its failure to fulfil its obligations of good faith.

In December 2000, Gasser brought an action against Misat in the Regional Court in Austria for payment of outstanding invoices, asserting that the jurisdiction of the Austrian court was established, not only on the basis of the 1968 Brussels Convention art.5.1 (special jurisdiction in contract), but also on the basis that the parties had agreed a choice of court for Austria, as evidenced by a prorogation clause appearing on the back of all invoices sent by Gasser to Misat without any objection having been raised in that matter by Misat.[280] Misat denied this, contending that there had been no choice of court agreement, and further, that the litigation in Italy, being earlier in time, must take precedence.

The Austrian court decided of its own motion to stay its proceedings until the jurisdiction of the Italian court had been established. The Austrian court's view was that it had jurisdiction under art.5.1 as the court for the place of performance of the contract, but it did not rule upon the question whether there had been an agreement to confer jurisdiction on the Austrian court. On appeal against that decision by Gasser, the Oberlandesgericht Innsbruck referred these questions of interpretation to the ECJ for a preliminary ruling. In essence, this was a request for a ranking of art.17 of the Brussels Convention (prorogation of jurisdiction)[281] and art.21 (court first seised).[282]

It was decided that a national court could refer to the ECJ a request for interpretation even where the basis for the reference, factual and legal, relied upon submissions the merits of which had not yet been examined, i.e. in this case, that the choice of court clause printed on the back of the invoices, neither

---

[279] *Erich Gasser GmbH v Misat Srl* [2005] Q.B. 1; [2004] 3 W.L.R. 1070; [2005] All E.R. (EC) 517. See application of *Gasser* in *JP Morgan Europe Ltd v Primacom AG* [2005] 2 All E.R. (Comm) 764.
[280] cf. *MSG v Les Gravières Rhenanes Sarl* (C-106/95) [1997] All E.R. (EC) 385.
[281] cf. Brussels I Regulation art.23.
[282] cf. Brussels I Regulation art.27.

acknowledged nor denied by Misat, was sufficient to satisfy art.17 as a choice of court which was in accordance with the parties' practice and trade usage prevailing between Austria and Italy.[283]

The decision of the ECJ was that the system set in place by the *lis pendens* rule was pre-eminent. The effect of *Gasser* was to subordinate art.23 (choice of court) to art.27 (*lis pendens*). Where a court had been first seised, any court second seised, even one the jurisdiction of which the parties allegedly had prorogued, was required to stay its proceedings until the court first seised ruled upon its own jurisdiction. If the court first seised decided that it had jurisdiction, the court second seised was required to decline jurisdiction in favour of that court. This was the case even where the proceedings before the court first seised were protracted.

Negative declarations

The initiative taken by Misat took the form of actings of a negative nature.[284] A system of priority of process which brooks no exception lends itself to such behaviour,[285] placing in an advantageous position a party who is able to initiate the process in a forum of his choice, so far as the facts admit use of (another) Member State forum within the rules of the regime. The question arises as to the extent to which it is reasonable for a litigant to seize the initiative by seising a forum in which to seek a declaration of a negative nature, e.g. that he has not breached the contract: a declaration of non-liability. The device seems to be indulged, or tolerated, so long as, in the view of the instant forum, there has not been a gross abuse of process. But what is an abuse of process?[286]

7–59

The English courts in their operation of the English residual rules (q.v.),[287] are not inexperienced in dealing with this matter. Increasingly, while advocating caution, the effect of recent pronouncements has been to suggest that negative actings in litigation should not necessarily be viewed negatively.[288] Sometimes justice requires acceptance of the seeking of a negative declaration in order to avoid further, perhaps indefinite, delay and prevarication.[289] It is difficult to avoid the conclusion that the matter must be treated on a case-by-case basis.

---

[283] See *Erich Gasser Gmbh v Misat Srl* [2005] Q.B. 1 at [42].

[284] Attracting comment from AG Léger: *Erich Gasser Gmbh v Misat Srl* [2005] Q.B. 1 at [68], [69]. The ECJ in its judgment ([53] and also at [68]) declined to engage with the negativity problem.

[285] A.S. Bell, *Forum Shopping and Venue in Transnational Litigation* (Oxford: Oxford University Press, 2002), Ch.4 ("Reverse Forum Shopping").

[286] *Messier Dowty Ltd v Sabena SA* [2000] 1 W.L.R. 2040; and *Toropdar v D* [2009] EWHC 567 (QB).

[287] Use of negative tactics to initiate litigation is not limited to the Brussels scheme: see *Bristow Helicopters Ltd v Sikorsky Aircraft Corp* [2004] 2 Lloyd's Rep. 150; *Swiss Reinsurance Co Ltd v United India Insurance Co* (Jurisdiction) [2004] I.L.Pr. 4; and *Ark Therapeutics Plc v True North Capital Ltd* [2006] 1 All E.R. (Comm) 138.

[288] e.g. *Bank of Tokyo-Mitsubishi Ltd v Baskan Gida Sanayi Ve Pazarlama AS* [2004] 2 Lloyd's Rep. 395.

[289] *Swiss Reinsurance Co Ltd v United India Insurance Co (Jurisdiction)* [2004] I.L.Pr. 4.

Choice of court agreements and priority of process—the solution to *Gasser*

7–60   Under the Brussels I Regulation, the strength of the priority of process system, as interpreted by the ECJ in *Gasser*, was such that an anterior choice of court clause in favour of one Member State court could not prevail against the claim to jurisdiction of another Member State court which had been seised first by either party, albeit in apparent breach of the alleged choice of court agreement.

Under art.27 of the Brussels I Regulation, the court first seised was not required, as a matter of principle, to defer to a court earlier chosen by the parties. The principle of mutual trust and confidence demanded that trust be reposed in the court of the Member State first seised to adjudicate upon its jurisdiction, competently and in good faith, and to defer to the court exclusively chosen, if persuaded that the prorogation clause is valid and applicable. Any argument on the subject-matter applicability of the choice of court clause or as to its essential, formal or material validity was required to be laid before the court first seised. In the Brussels scheme of rules, the foundations of which are mutual trust and comity among Member States, it was to be taken for granted that the first seised court, if convinced that a valid and applicable exclusive choice of court clause existed, would defer to the court therein identified. There was, however, no requirement that the court first seised should arrive at its decision with reasonable speed. A notorious problem lay in the length of time which the first forum might take to ponder jurisdiction—the so-called "Italian torpedo"—and in the resultant uncertainty and expense which was likely to be suffered by the thwarted contracting party.

Considerable dismay was felt in the UK as a result of the decision in *Gasser*.[290] It was too easy under the ranking of rules in the Brussels I Regulation for an individual to renege on a prorogation agreement to which he was party and, if he deemed it advantageous so to do, to initiate litigation in another forum available under the rules.

Reversal of the ranking of the relevant provisions of the Brussels I Regulation suggested itself as the simplest remedy to this state of affairs. This is the solution which has been adopted in Brussels I Recast, and, as noted above, being in keeping with that found in the 2005 Hague Convention on Choice of Court Agreements, enables the EU to approve and become bound by that Convention.

Accordingly, the *lis pendens* rule in art.29.1 of Brussels I Recast (ex-Brussels I Regulation art. 27.1) is qualified by reference to a new provision, art.31.2, which provides that:

> "2.   Without prejudice to Article 26,[291] where a court of a Member State on which an agreement as referred to in Article 25 confers exclusive jurisdiction is seised, any court of another Member State shall stay the proceedings until such time as the court seised on the basis of the agreement declares that it has no jurisdiction under the agreement."

---

[290] e.g. T. Hartley, "The European Union and the Systematic Dismantling of the Common Law of Conflict of Laws" (2005) 54 I.C.L.Q. 813.
[291] Submission to the jurisdiction.

The objective, set out in recital (22) is plain, namely, to enhance the effectiveness of exclusive choice of court agreements, and to avoid abusive litigation tactics. The recast rule is likely to reduce the incidence of litigation tactics such as the institution of proceedings for negative declaratory relief; it should torpedo the torpedo. In terms, art.31.2. is restricted to cases where the choice of court clause confers exclusive jurisdiction, but by virtue of the presumption of exclusivity contained in art.25.1, this will be the case in most instances.

By art.31.3, where the court designated in the choice of court agreement has established jurisdiction in accordance therewith, any court of another Member State shall decline jurisdiction in favour of the chosen court. This refinement upon the *lis pendens* rule should ensure that the court designated in an exclusive choice of court agreement has priority to decide on the validity thereof and on its applicability in the circumstances. The new rule is likely to reduce the incidence of (arguably) abusive litigation tactics such as the institution of proceedings for negative declaratory relief.

This exception to the rigour of the *lis pendens* system shall not apply in cases where the choice of court agreement in question purportedly has been entered into by a consumer, an employee or a party qualifying for protection under Ch.II S.3 (insured persons), and is an agreement which is not valid by dint of those protective provisions (art.31.4). If it should happen that an action comes within the exclusive jurisdiction of several courts (such being the cavalier use of the adjective "exclusive" in the Brussels regime), any court other than the court first seised shall decline jurisdiction in favour of that court (art.31.1).

Ranking of other rules

As regards other provisions of Brussels I Recast, art.25 (prorogation of jurisdiction) yields to art.26 (submission to the jurisdiction), on the rationale that submission by a party, other than merely to contest the jurisdiction, amounts to acquiescence in the jurisdiction of that court. When submission post-dates the making of a choice of court agreement, the appearance by both parties, or by one party at the behest of the other, in a different court than that agreed is taken to constitute later agreement (the latest indication) of a party's intentions as to choice of court, superseding earlier agreement.[292]

7–61

Neither an agreement under art.25, nor submission under art.26, can override the jurisdiction conferred "exclusively" on certain courts by art.24.

With regard to the relationship between art.8[293] and the protective jurisdictions, the ECJ has held that when the special jurisdictional rules concerning employees are engaged, and an action is brought by an employee against companies established in different Member States, which the employee considered to be his joint employers, the provisions of Ch.II S.5 of Brussels I Recast (jurisdiction over individual contracts of employment), because of their specific and exhaustive nature, could not be supplemented by art.6 of the Brussels I Regulation or other rules of jurisdiction contained therein, unless this

---

[292] *Elefanten Schuh GmbH v Jacqmain* (C-150/80) [1981] E.C.R. 1671.
[293] Jurisdiction over multiple defendants through the domicile of the "anchor" defendant.

had been specifically authorised.[294] Since there is no such authorisation in S.5, use of art.8.1 of Brussels I Recast in conjunction with that Section, is not justified. This is an interesting example of the fact that certain provisions of the Regulation are interdependent, and other bodies of rules within the Regulation are hermetically sealed.

It would seem reasonable to assume that this ECJ decision would apply equally to Ss.3 (insurance) and 4 (consumers). The ECJ decision was reached on a literal construction of the instrument, but the court additionally took the view that the sound administration of justice would imply that art.6.1 of the Brussels I Regulation ought to be open to both employees and employers (a policy conclusion which would be at odds with the general policy pertaining to the protection of weaker parties). Hence, the rule of special jurisdiction provided for in art.8.1 of Brussels I Recast may not be applied to a dispute under Ch.II Ss.3 and 4.

Finally, on the theme of the interrelationship of articles within one instrument, one might query the relationship between Ch.II S.7 (arts 25 and 26) with Ss.3, 4 and 5. Although there is no overt indication in Brussels I Recast that S.7 is outranked by the Sections containing protective provisions for disadvantaged persons,[295] nor any authoritative ECJ interpretation thereon, it must surely be the case that agreements made under art.25 have no legal force if they are contrary to the protective rules enshrined in arts 15 (insured persons), 19 (consumers) and 23 (employees). In contrast, it was generally thought that the principle of submission without protest as found in art.24 of the Brussels I Regulation applied with full force to disadvantaged parties.[296] The rationale of art.24 was that, since it represented a later choice by a party, it superseded any choice of court made earlier; and if art.24 affects disadvantaged parties in like manner, this must have been taken to mean that no account should be taken, upon the later eventuality of submission, of such parties' lack of full freedom to choose in the first instance. No special treatment was afforded on the second occasion. It was presumed that to provide otherwise would be seen as benefiting the disadvantaged twice—a benefit too far, there being no intention, seemingly, to buttress such parties' pre-existing protection. The situation was explicable also on the argument that, after the dispute had arisen, weaker parties, it appeared, were to be treated as not being in need of special protection, and therefore it was consistent to regard them as fully *capax* and to have completely regained their freedom[297] in the matter of choice of jurisdiction,[298] whether that choice was made expressly or tacitly through actings.

However, Brussels I Recast has softened the position without altering the substance of the law, in providing by art.26.2 that the court before which a weaker party has entered appearance shall ensure, before assuming jurisdiction on the basis of submission, that the defendant has been informed of his right to

---

[294] *Glaxosmithkline v Rouard* (C-462/06) [2008] E.C.R. I-3965 (reference from *Cour de Cassation*).

[295] Contrast the specific exception from the application of art.26.1 of art.24.

[296] e.g. *Cheshire, North and Fawcett: Private International Law*, 14th edn (2008), pp.268, 272, 275. As to case law, see *Re Jurisdiction in a Consumer Contract* (2U 1788/99) [2002] I.L.Pr. 14 Regional Court of Appeal (Koblenz) at [11].

[297] Jenard Report, p.34.

[298] But not as to choice of law—for Rome I Regulation art.6 still will apply, conferring special protection.

contest the court's jurisdiction and of the consequences of entering or not entering an appearance. This soft law provision is at best precatory.

THE OPERATION OF BRUSSELS I RECAST IN THE INTERNATIONAL LEGAL ORDER

Delineation of the European legal space, or measuring the extent of the Brussels regime,[299] is far from easy. To measure the full extent of the Brussels regime, it is necessary to include in the computation temporal and subject-matter scope, territorial boundaries,[300] the personal law connecting factor of domicile, "deemed domicile" created through branches or agencies, and those binding ECJ/CJEU decisions interpretative of the provisions of the Brussels instruments, which have a bearing on patent and latent extent.

7–62

One particular problem which has come to the forefront is the extent to which it is proper for the interests of an EU-domiciled claimant to have the effect of pushing outwards the reach of the Brussels regime. The background is that the favoured child of the Brussels regime was, for many years, the EU Member State-domiciled defendant. The 1968 Convention and the Brussels I Regulation, in turn, applied, even where the claimant was domiciled in a non-Contracting/ Member State, so long as the defendant was domiciled within a Contracting/ Member State at the date of institution of proceedings (or a special or exclusive ground of jurisdiction was/is available). Concern grew, however, for Member State-domiciled claimants, particularly in their dealings with non-EU domiciled defendants ("Third State defendants"), whom perforce they were required to sue according to the national rules of a defendant's domicile.

The exercise of measuring the extent of the Brussels regime following entry into force of Brussels I Recast must be done by scrutiny of its terms, so as to identify those articles of the Regulation which impinge upon a Member State's relations with Third State legal systems. As noted above, art.6.1 states that if the defendant is not domiciled in a Member State, the jurisdiction of the courts of each Member State shall be determined, subject to arts 18.1, 21.2, 24 and 25, by the law of that Member State. This provision, in effect, preserves, therefore, for most cases the residual national rules of jurisdiction of Member States.[301]

Article 18 concerns litigation brought by a consumer against the other party to the consumer contract. Since 1968 consumers, insured persons and, to a lesser extent, employees, all deemed to be disadvantaged, have had the benefit of *forum actoris* rules. Whilst under the Brussels I Regulation, these beneficial provisions applied only on the basis that *both* parties to the contract are EU-domiciled (art.16.1) or that the "non-consumer" party has a branch or agency in the EU (art.15.2), the extension effected by Brussels I Recast is that the consumer has the benefit of suing in the Member State of his own domicile not only an EU-domiciled defendant, but also a *non*-EU domiciled defendant (art.18.1).

---

[299] E.T. Winter, "Measuring the extent of the Brussels regime" [2010] J.R. 163. See also para.9–38, below re extent of operation of Brussels regime of recognition and enforcement.

[300] *Orams v Apostolides* [2010] I.L.Pr. 20: para.9–38, below.

[301] Para.7–75, below.

Equally, by art.21.2, a non-EU domiciled employer may be sued by his employee in a court of the Member State in which the employee habitually carries out his work, or last did so, or of the situation of the business which engaged the employee. There is no equivalent extension of jurisdiction with regard to non-EU domiciled insurers beyond the pre-existing "branch, agency" concession contained in art.11.2 (ex-art.9.2).

The exclusive jurisdiction conferred on Member State courts by art.24 (ex-art.22) operates regardless of the domicile (EU or non-EU) of parties. Article 24 exclusive jurisdiction applies regardless of the domicile of the parties. The unfortunate interpretation in *Choudhary v Bhatter*,[302] of the equivalent provision (Brussels I Regulation art.22), to the effect that the Brussels rule did not extend to cases where the defendant was not domiciled in an EU Member State, has been discredited. The interpretation was ill-founded and based on misunderstanding of the Regulation.[303]

So too in art.25 (ex-art.23), the prorogation rules shall apply to parties regardless of their domicile. Article 25, though indifferent to the domicile (EU or non-EU) of the prorogating parties, is limited in its scope to choice of Member State courts. To that extent, the provision is strictly geographically based; the regime has no locus standi to seek to regulate choice of court agreements nominating a non-EU forum, except possibly by virtue of reflexive reasoning.

Effet réflèxe

7–63   "Reflexive application is a term of art in the field of conflicts of law."[304] The possible reflexive effect of the Brussels Convention and its descendants has been under discussion since 1972.[305] The theory is that where, for example, proceedings before an EU Member State court concern a question of title to land in a Third State, or where an EU Member State court is seised second in a matter which already is the subject of litigation before the courts of a Third State—both of the above being situations for which the Brussels regime has rules—it is most improbable that the EU Member State court is obliged to exercise its jurisdiction in the face of a stay sought by the defendant on the ground that the Third State is the *forum conveniens*.

It is perplexing to decide whether a Member State court which cedes jurisdiction in such a case to a Third State court (thereby "reflecting" the rationale and practice of the Brussels regime, like the beam of a torch, into the dark regions which, geographically, are beyond the purlieu of the EU) pays full obeisance to the regime; or, on the other hand, if a Member State court which proves amenable to reflexive reasoning, causing it to yield to the Third State court, is being duped by sophistry, and is unjustifiably deprived of its prima facie jurisdiction. Certainly, the concept has been seised upon with enthusiasm by those in the

---

[302] *Choudhary v Bhatter* [2010] I.L.Pr. 8.

[303] Brussels I Regulation art.22 operated to override art.4, and therefore, transcended the residual national rules of jurisdiction.

[304] *Law Debenture Trust Corp Plc* [2015] EWHC 43 (Ch), per Proudman J. at [65].

[305] G.A.L. Droz, *La competence judiciaire et effet de jugements dans le Marché Commun* (Etude de la Convention de Bruxelles du 27 septembre 1968), *Bibliothèque de droit international privé*, Dalloz, Vol.XIII, 1972, pp.429–453.

common law camp, as a means of turning to their own advantage the rules of the
civilian game; using the ideology of the Brussels regime in order to evade the
regime.

The silence of the 1968 Convention and the Brussels I Regulation on this
matter was taken by some to serve as justification for employing the argument; to
turn traditional ECJ reasoning against itself, by drawing an inference from the
observation that, "nothing in the Regulation forbids reflexive reasoning". But a
stronger case can be made, on the argument that the relevant articles of the
Regulation can be read in such a way as to provide positive justification for a
Member State court staying its proceedings in such cases. Brussels I Regulation
art.2, although the foundation article of the instrument, was required to defer to
arts 22, 23, 27 and 28. Why then should it not be argued that a court seised under
art.2 was under a duty to defer to a Third State court where the circumstances
equated to those covered by arts 22, 23, 27 and 28?

Such authority as can be discerned to be in favour of application of reflexive
effect of the Brussels I Regulation is fragmentary and fragile, and perhaps is best
monitored by category. It may be that the strongest case for application of *effet
réflèxe* is in relation to Third State proceedings where jurisdiction is taken on
grounds comparable to those covered by art.22 (exclusive jurisdiction).[306]
Secondly, a fairly strong case may be made out in favour of upholding an
exclusive choice of court clause for a Third State,[307] although this in itself is odd,
since *Gasser* showed that there could be no such guarantee *within* the regime.
However, greater doubt attends the strength of the reflexive argument in the plain
operation of the *lis pendens* rules.[308]

The English court in *Catalyst Investment Group Ltd v Lewinsohn*[309] was not
well disposed to reflexive effect argument. The court having been properly seised
under art.2 of the Brussels I Regulation, Barling J. was not persuaded that, by
reason of the existence of litigation pending in the USA, the appropriate reflexive
application of art.27.2 was that the English forum was entitled to apply its
national rules on *forum conveniens* in order to decide whether to stay proceedings
in favour of those in the Third State. The English forum was not prepared to take
so bold a step in the matter of interpretation of art.27,[310] and distinguished the
situation from that in which an EU court might defer to a Third State court by
reflexive effect of art.23. It is difficult not to agree with Barling J. that the
argument proffered was strained.

The reflexive effect debate has been conducted largely within the UK, without
reference having been made (assuming that would be competent—and that's the
rub) to the CJEU. Brussels I Recast does not make any explicit reference to
reflexive reasoning, and the final version of the text has drawn back from the

---

[306] See, e.g. *Ferrexpo AG v Gilson Investments Ltd*[2012] EWHC 721 (Comm), in which Smith J.
supported a flexible approach to the reflexive application of art.22. See further E.B. Crawford and
J.M. Carruthers, "*Ferrexpo AG v Gilson Investments Ltd and ors*: A Flexible Interpretation of the
Reflexive Doctrine" (2013) 78 The Edinburgh Law Review 78.
[307] *Konkola Copper Mines Plc v Coromin Ltd* [2006] EWHC 1093, per Colman J.
[308] cf. *Goshawk Dedicated Ltd v Life Receivables Ireland Ltd* [2009] I.E.S.C. 7. But see *Law
Debenture Trust Corp Plc* [2015] EWHC 43 (Ch), per Proudman J. at [90].
[309] *Catalyst Investment Group Ltd v Lewinsohn* [2009] EWHC 1964 (Ch).
[310] See, however, Smith J., obiter, in *Ferrexpo AG v Gilson Investments Ltd* [2012] EWHC 721
(Comm), to the effect that, in a suitable case, art.27 could be reflexively applied.

challenge of addressing hybrid situations, that is, the relationship of the regime with Third State legal systems. Certain of the very few English cases which exemplify use of reflexive reasoning display arguably a desire to exercise discretion to cede jurisdiction to a more appropriate court, that is, to retain something of a *forum non conveniens* discretion. To a very limited extent, Brussels I Recast in arts 33 and 34 has begun to satisfy this desire. In the absence of a comprehensive set of rules to deal with hybrid situations, reflexive reasoning cannot be regarded as redundant. *Ferrexpo* and *Plaza BV v Law Debenture Trust Corp Plc*,[311] both single judge English decisions, evidence receptiveness to arguments based on reflexive effect.

ONGOING REFINEMENT OF THE BRUSSELS REGIME

7–64 As witnessed by the very existence of Brussels I Recast, the rules of the Brussels regime are subject to constant revisal/refinement in the light of experience. Interpretative questions continue to arise about the meaning of terms of the Brussels I Regulation and, over time, will emerge regarding Brussels I Recast. The CJEU responds to such references as it receives, eschewing hypothetical questions, and restricting its rulings to the issues in point and to the questions asked; inevitably the body of jurisprudence accrues only incrementally.

Article 79 of Brussels I Recast provides that by 11 January 2022 the Commission shall present a report (accompanied, where appropriate by a proposal to amend the instrument) to the European Parliament, Council and European Economic and Social Committee, on the application of the Regulation. The report shall include an evaluation of the possible need for a further extension of the rules on jurisdiction to defendants not domiciled in a Member State, taking into account possible developments at international level.

COLLECTIVE REDRESS

7–65 On 11 June 2013, the European Commission issued a non-binding Recommendation on common principles for injunctive and compensatory collective redress mechanisms in the Member States concerning violations of rights granted under Union Law.[312] The Recommendation should be read in conjunction with Directive 2014/104/EU of the European Parliament and of the Council of 26

---

[311] *Ferrexpo* and *Plaza BV v Law Debenture Trust Corp Plc* [2015] EWHC 43 (Ch). cf. *Winnetka Trading Corp v Julius Baer International Ltd*[2008] EWHC 3146 (Ch).

[312] Recommendation on common principles for injunctive and compensatory collective redress mechanisms in the Member States concerning violations of rights granted under Union Law 2013/396/EU [2013] O.J. L201/60. See also European Commission, Communication from the Commission to the European Parliament, the Council, the European Economic and Social Committee and the Committee of the Regions, "Towards a European Horizontal Framework for Collective Redress" (COM(2013) 401 final) (Strasbourg, 11 June 2013).

November 2014 on certain rules governing actions for damages under national law for infringements of the competition law provisions of the Member States and of the European Union.[313]

The Recommendation constitutes a rather weak result of protracted and controversial debate on the reform of the European system of enforcement of consumer rights and the rights of tort victims in mass harm situations. "Recommendations" have a lowly standing as compared with a European Directive or Regulation, and neither they nor Directive 2014/104/EU will oblige Member States fundamentally to reform their existing systems.[314] From a UK Government perspective, however, the "light touch" approach is desirable.[315]

Commission Recommendation

Recommendation II.3(a) defines "collective redress" as meaning:

7–66

> "(i) a legal mechanism that ensures a possibility to claim cessation of illegal behaviour collectively by two or more natural or legal persons or by an entity entitled to bring a representative action (injunctive collective redress); (ii) a legal mechanism that ensures a possibility to claim compensation collectively by two or more natural or legal persons claiming to have been harmed in a mass harm situation or by an entity entitled to bring a representative action (compensatory collective redress)."

In essence collective redress permits multiple claims relating to the same cause to be consolidated into one court action, for reasons of procedural economy and/or efficiency of enforcement. The objective is to facilitate access to justice, especially where the value of any individual claim is considered too small to justify the expense of legal action, and also to strengthen the claim by enhancing the overall negotiating power of the claimant[316]; and to contribute to the efficient administration of justice, by avoiding numerous proceedings concerning claims resulting from the same infringement.

The Commission's recommendation falls short of a proposal to harmonise Member States' rules as to collective redress, but advocates that all Member States should have collective redress mechanisms at national level for both

---

[313] Directive 2014/104/EU [2014] O.J. L349/2. Directive 2014/104/EU is intended to assist victims of infringements of EU anti-trust rules, such as cartels or abuses of dominant market positions, to obtain compensation. Recital (13) states that the right to compensation is recognised for any natural or legal person, irrespective of the existence of a direct contractual relationship with the infringing undertaking, and regardless of whether or not there has been a prior finding of an infringement by a competition authority. Importantly, the Directive does not require Member States to introduce collective redress mechanisms for the enforcement of arts 101 and 102 TFEU, and leaves to Member States the decision whether or not to introduce collective redress actions in the context of private enforcement of competition law.

[314] European Law Institute, "Statement on Collective Redress and Competition Damages Claims" (approved by ELI Council on 12 December 2014), p.12.

[315] UK Response to EU Consultation on Collective Redress (http://ec.europa.eu/competition/consultations/2011_collective_redress/uk_en.pdf [accessed 22 June 2015]).

[316] European Commission, "Towards a European Horizontal Framework for Collective Redress" (COM(2013) 401 final) (Strasbourg, 11 June 2013), para.1.2.

injunctive and compensatory relief.[317] It sets out in aspirational terms a number of common European principles that Member States ought to respect.

Recommendation III.4 envisages that Member States should designate representative entities to bring representative actions on the basis of clearly defined conditions of eligibility. In terms of Recommendation III.17, Member States should ensure that where a dispute concerns persons from several Member States, a single collective action in a single forum should not be prevented by national rules on admissibility or standing of the foreign groups of claimants or the representative entities originating from other national legal systems. The Commission recommends a system which, as a general rule, is based on an "opt-in" principle, in terms of which the claimant party should be formed on the basis of express consent of the natural or legal persons claiming to have been harmed.[318] Collective alternative dispute resolution is promoted insofar as Member States should ensure that collective alternative dispute resolution is available to the parties before and throughout the litigation.[319]

Member States should have a system of collective redress that enables private individuals and entities to seek injunctive relief requiring cessation or prohibition of a violation of rights granted under Union law, and the efficient enforcement of injunctive orders.[320] Moreover, Member States ought to have a system which permits the award of compensatory relief for harm caused by such infringements.[321] The bold, substantive recommendation is made (V.3) to the effect of a prohibition on punitive damages.[322]

Although the Recommendations are in the main precatory, follow-up action is required on the part of Member States by virtue of Recommendations VI and VII, namely: the setting up of a national registry of collective redress actions (VI.35–37); implementation of the principles set out in the Recommendation no later than 26 July 2015 (VII.38); and the collection and communication of statistical information concerning collective redress procedures (VII.39–40). No later than 26 July 2017, the Commission should assess the implementation of the Recommendation.

Relationship between the Recommendations and existing international private law instruments

Jurisdiction

7–67   Viewing these recommendations against the backdrop of current international private law rules of jurisdiction in civil and commercial matters, it is conceded that, from the outset, the Brussels regime of rules was predicated principally upon proceedings by individual natural or legal persons against individual natural or legal persons subject to the important exception, contained now in art.8 of

---

[317] Recommendation I.2.
[318] Recommendation V.21. It is also recommended that having opted in, a member of the claimant party should be free to leave at any time, without prejudice to his right to pursue his claim in any other form: recommendation V.22.
[319] Recommendation V.26.
[320] Recommendations IV.19 and 20.
[321] Recommendation V.
[322] See comment below at para.7–68.

Brussels I Recast. Article 8 permits a claimant to conjoin in the court of one Member State an action against a number of defendants on the basis of the forum being the domicile of any one of them, and provided that the claims are so closely connected that it is expedient to hear and determine them together. The emphasis in Brussels I Recast is upon multiple defendants, not multiple claimants, even though, in recent years, concern has been expressed about the proper treatment of EU-domiciled claimants.

In principle, it is apt for the Commission to devise recommendations to accommodate collective redress actions, and to seek to ensure that Member State legal systems have in place appropriate mechanisms for dealing with them. It is noteworthy that Brussels I Recast does not include any harmonised rule of jurisdiction to facilitate collective litigation. Rather, the Commission has stated that the rules in the existing Brussels regime "should be fully exploited".[323]

But a consumer who opts in to a collective redress action, thereby becoming a member of the claimant party, seemingly will lose the (presumed) benefit of the *forum actoris* rules contained in arts 17–19 of Brussels I Recast. By reason of art.35(1) of the Brussels I Regulation, it is arguable that a consumer would have been unable to waive the protection which Ch.II S.4 of that instrument conferred upon him. The terms of art.45.1(e)(i) of Brussels I Recast, however, render it probable that a consumer is able to cede the advantage which that instrument offers him, for the provision operates only where the consumer is the defendant and not the claimant.

Choice of law

In existing choice of law rules for non-contractual obligations, there is no overt reference to mass claims or actions for collective redress. Application of the harmonised rules in Rome II might lead to the application of several different laws to the substance of claims arising out of one grievance.[324] To date, the European Commission has not been persuaded that it would be appropriate to introduce into Rome II a tort-specific rule for collective claims, requiring the forum to apply a single *lex causae*.

7–68

Recommendation V.31, however, intrudes on choice of law principles by proposing the prohibition of punitive damages. It provides that:

> "The compensation awarded to natural or legal persons harmed in a mass harm situation should not exceed the compensation that would have been awarded, if the claim had been pursued by means of individual actions. In particular, punitive damages, leading to overcompensation in favour of the claimant party of the damage suffered, should be prohibited."

---

[323] European Commission, Communication from the Commission to the European Parliament, the Council, the European Economic and Social Committee and the Committee of the Regions, "Towards a European Horizontal Framework for Collective Redress" (COM(2013) 401 final) (Strasbourg, 11 June 2013), para.3.7.

[324] "Towards a European Horizontal Framework for Collective Redress" COM(2013) 401 final (Strasbourg, 11 June 2013), para.3.7.

The relationship between this recommendation and Rome II art.15.1(c),[325] is unclear. As noted in Ch.16,[326] during the negotiations of Rome II, there was an attempt by the European Parliament to include a rule directing Member State courts on the manner of treatment of awards of non-compensatory, exemplary or punitive damages of an excessive nature. The clause as originally drafted by the Commission did not survive, but a residue remains in recital (32), which provides that, "...the application of a provision of the law designated by this Regulation which would have the effect of causing...punitive damages of an excessive nature to be awarded may, depending on the circumstances of the case and the legal order of the Member State of the court seised, be regarded as being contrary to the public policy (ordre public) of the forum." The Commission clearly is exercised about the subject of punitive damages, and seems determined to circumscribe their availability. The manner of its seeking to achieve that end through the recommendations is questionable.

THE LITIGATION/ARBITRATION INTERFACE[327]

7–69   The European Commission proposal[328] to recast the Brussels I Regulation identified as one of the main shortcomings in that instrument the uncertain boundary between the civil jurisdiction rules of the regulation and the operation of arbitration, the latter subject being excluded from the regulation, *ex facie*. Notable and well documented tensions arose on the interface between the Brussels I Regulation and arbitration. The exclusion from the scope of the regulation of arbitration by art.1.2(d) proved deceptive and disappointing for those who, for whatever reason (including a desire to avoid the operation of the regulation's *lis pendens* system) would go to arbitration in preference to going to court. This was demonstrated most keenly by the decision of the ECJ in *West Tankers Inc v Allianz SpA*.[329]

West Tankers

7–70   The charterparty between West Tankers, the owner of a vessel (*The Front Comor*), and the charterer, Erg Petroli SpA, contained a clause providing that any disputes were to be resolved by arbitration in London. *The Front Comor* collided with a jetty in Syracuse, Sicily, which was owned by Erg. Erg claimed upon its insurers, RAS Riunione Adriatica di Securta, up to the limit of its insurance cover, and began arbitration proceedings in London against West Tankers for the

---

[325] Para.16–38.
[326] Para.16–39.
[327] See T.C. Hartley, "The Brussels I Regulation and Arbitration" (2014) 63 I.C.L.Q. 843.
[328] European Commission proposal COM (2010) 748 final.
[329] *West Tankers Inc v Allianz SpA* [2009] 1 A.C. 1138; [2009] 3 W.L.R. 696; [2009] All E.R. (EC) 491 (and see earlier *West Tankers Inc v RAS Riunione Adriatica di Securta SpA*[2007] UKHL 4; [2007] 1 All E.R. (Comm) 794). For earlier authorities, see *Marc Rich & Co AG v Societa Italiana Impianti SpA* (C190-89) [1992] 1 Lloyd's Rep. 342; *Navigation Maritime Bulgare v Rustal Trading Ltd (The Ivan Zagubanski)* [2002] 1 Lloyd's Rep. 106; *Electronic Arts CB v CTO SpA* [2003] EWHC 1020; and *Through Transport Mutual Insurance Association (Eurasia) Ltd v New India Assurance Co Ltd (The Hari Bhum)* [2004] 1 Lloyd's Rep. 206; [2005] 1 Lloyd's Rep. 67.

excess. West Tankers counterclaimed that it was not liable for any of the damage caused by the collision. Adriatica, having been subrogated to Erg's claim, brought a delictual action in Italy against West Tankers, seeking to recover the amount which had been paid to Erg in terms of the insurance policies. In response, West Tankers disputed the jurisdiction of the Italian court on the ground of the existence of the arbitration agreement, and in a parallel action raised in London sought declaration that the dispute was to be settled by arbitration pursuant to the agreement, and an order requiring Adriatica to desist from pursuing the Italian action. The English High Court granted the orders sought, and on appeal by the insurers, the House of Lords, noting that art.1.2(d) of the Brussels I Regulation excluded arbitration from its scope, referred for a preliminary ruling from the ECJ the question whether an anti-suit injunction to give effect to an arbitration agreement was incompatible with the Brussels I Regulation.

The Advocate General's opinion[330] was that although art.1.2(d) specifically excluded arbitration, the decisive question was not whether the English proceedings concerning the anti-suit injunction in support of arbitration fell within the scope of the Regulation, but rather whether the Italian proceedings against which the anti-suit injunction was directed, did so.[331] In the circumstances, the subject-matter of the litigation in Italy was a claim in tort, and possibly in contract, jurisdiction being founded therefore on art.5 of the Brussels I Regulation. The existence and applicability of the arbitration clause merely constituted a preliminary issue which that court had to address when examining whether it had jurisdiction. In the opinon of the Advocate General, the use of the anti-suit injunction would amount to an interference with proceedings falling within the scope of the Regulation, and following *Turner v Grovit*[332] was proscribed.

The decision of the ECJ, handed down in February 2009,[333] adhered to the opinion of Advocate General Kokott, that it is incompatible with the Brussels I Regulation for the court of a Member State to make an order to restrain a person from commencing or continuing proceedings before the courts of another Member State on the ground that such proceedings would be contrary to an arbitration agreement.

The reasoning employed en route to the ECJ's decision is true to type, encapsulated in the following statement:

> "Nor is it a prerequisite of infringement of the principle of mutual trust, on which the judgment in *Turner v Grovit* was substantially based, that both the application for an anti-suit injunction and the proceedings which would be barred by that injunction should fall within the scope of the Regulation. Rather, the principle of mutual trust can also be infringed by a decision of a court of a Member State which does not fall within the scope of the Regulation obstructing the court of another Member State from exercising its competence under the Regulation."[334]

---

[330] *Allianz SpA (formerly Riunione Adriatica di Sicurta SpA) v West Tankers Inc* (C-185/07) [2008] 2 Lloyd's Rep. 661.

[331] See also *Youell v La Reunion Aerienne* [2009] EWCA Civ 175.

[332] *Turner v Grovit* (C-159/02) [2005] 1 A.C. 101.

[333] *West Tankers Inc v Allianz SpA* [2009] 1 A.C. 1138.

[334] *West Tankers Inc v Allianz SpA* [2009] 1 A.C. 1138 at [34].

The ECJ held that it was incompatible with the regulation for one Member State court to make an order restraining a person from commencing or continuing proceedings before the courts of another Member State on the ground that such proceedings would be contrary to the terms of an arbitration agreement. The court's rationale was that, "...the principle of mutual trust can...be infringed by a decision of a court of a Member State which does not fall within the scope of the regulation obstructing the court of another Member State from exercising its competence under the regulation".[335] Thus if a Member State court were seised in a delictual issue pertaining to a matter which the contending parties previously had agreed would be settled by arbitration, the existence and applicability of the arbitration clause would become a preliminary issue of which it was the function of that Member State forum to dispose; and attempted enforcement of the arbitration clause by means of, for example, an anti-suit injunction obtained in London (if an English court had personal jurisdiction over those who have dishonoured the agreement to arbitrate) was a remedy which belonged to (recent) history.

The *West Tankers* decision gave rise to consternation in the UK, for reasons which included the fear that, commercially, London could lose valuable arbitration business to centres of arbitration such as New York and Singapore, which operate beyond EU strictures.[336] Such concern was summarily dismissed by the ECJ.[337] The European Commission, however, acknowledged that by challenging an arbitration agreement before a Member State court, a party was capable of undermining that very agreement.

The rationale behind the exclusion of arbitration from the scope of the regulation (namely, that the recognition and enforcement of such agreements is governed by the 1958 New York Convention on the Recognition and Enforcement of Foreign Arbitral Awards, to which all Member States are parties) is as good now as it was in 1968 at the time of conclusion of the Brussels Convention, and the UK Government was rightly concerned not to compromise the operation of the New York Convention. More importantly perhaps, the UK Government, acutely conscious of the importance of arbitration to international commerce, was anxious to enhance the effectiveness of arbitration agreements within the EU to prevent parallel litigation and arbitration proceedings, and to avoid sabotaging London's place as an arbitration seat.

It was not long before the ramifications of the *West Tankers* decision were seen in the UK. In the English Court of Appeal in *National Navigation Co v Endesa Generacion SA (The Wadi Sudr)*,[338] the implications of *West Tankers* were felt in the matter of recognition of the judgment of a Spanish court, i.e. whether a Spanish judgment on the particular point of whether or not an arbitration clause had been incorporated into a contract gave rise to an issue estoppel in arbitration proceedings in the Commercial Court in London. The Spanish judgment had

---

[335] *West Tankers Inc v Allianz SpA* [2009] 1 A.C. 1138.

[336] *West Tankers Inc v RAS Riunione Adriatica di Securta SpA (The Front Comor)* [2007] UKHL 4 at [21], [22]; and per Lord Mance at [29], [30]. See also expert evidence from the Ministry of Justice to the House of Lords European Union Committee, *Green Paper on the Brussels I Regulation: Report with Evidence*, 2009, HL Paper No.148 (Session 2008/09), paras 98 et seq.

[337] *West Tankers Inc v Allianz SpA* [2009] 1 A.C. 1138 at [66]: "...aims of a purely economic nature cannot justify infringements of Community law".

[338] *National Navigation Co v Endesa Generacion SA (The Wadi Sudr)* [2009] EWCA Civ 1397.

ruled that the arbitration clause had not been incorporated in the contract. Reversing the decision of the judge of first instance, the Court of Appeal held that the English court was bound by the Spanish decision on the incorporation or not of the clause. The Court of Appeal took the view that the decision on incorporation of an arbitration clause into a contract, in most instances, would be very closely tied to the merits of a contractual dispute; the situation therefore was comparable with the *West Tankers* decision, in which the Italian court was seised under the art.5 special jurisdiction. This decision of the Court of Appeal stems directly from the ECJ decision in *West Tankers* (a *jurisdiction* case), that a preliminary ruling as to the applicability of an arbitration clause in proceedings in which the main subject-matter was within the Regulation was itself to be categorised as within the Regulation. *The Wadi Sudr* concerns the extent to which the ratio of *West Tankers* can affect decisions in national courts at the *enforcement* stage. In sum, the Court of Appeal held that a judgment of a Member State court on the preliminary issue of whether an arbitration clause is validly incorporated is a judgment under the Brussels I Regulation, despite the arbitration exception in art.1.2(d), if that judgment formed part of proceedings, the main scope of which fell within the Regulation.

Recasting the arbitration exclusion

Consideration was given at the Green Paper[339] stage (and support for the idea was forthcoming in the House of Lords EU Committee[340]) to the partial deletion of the arbitration exclusion from the recast regulation's scope, and to the conferral of exclusive jurisdiction on the courts of the Member State of the seat of the proposed arbitration to determine issues relating to the existence (including validity), scope and applicability of the agreement. In response to the Green Paper, the UK Government indicated that, although initially attracted to a modified exclusion rule, it had become aware of opposition among certain Member States, principally on the basis that this would necessitate ceding external competence on arbitration matters to the EU. In light of this, the UK Government expressed a preference for expansion of the art.1.2(d) arbitration exclusion, so as to remove completely the arbitral process from the scope of the regulation, leaving the matter to be regulated entirely by the New York Convention regime and Member States' national arbitration laws.

7–71

As matters turned out, the bald, if deceptive, exclusion of "arbitration" from the scope of the Brussels I Regulation is repeated in art.1.2(d) of Brussels I Recast. In the recast instrument, resort must be had to the recitals, specifically recital (12), in order to understand the approach settled on to attempt to solve the notorious difficulties emanating from the litigation/arbitration interface.

Recital (12) advises that nothing in Brussels I Recast shall prevent a Member State court, when seised of an action in a matter in respect of which the parties have entered into an arbitration agreement, from referring the parties to arbitration, from staying or dismissing the proceedings, or from examining whether the arbitration agreement is null and void, inoperative, or incapable of

---

[339] Green Paper on the Review of Regulation 44/2001 COM(2009)175 final.
[340] Green Paper on the Brussels I Regulation: Report with Evidence, 2009, HL Paper No.148 (Session 2008/09, paras 86–98).

being performed, in accordance with its own national law. Such a ruling on the question of the validity of the arbitration agreement will not be subject to the rules of recognition and enforcement laid down in Brussels I Recast, regardless of whether the court decided that point as a principal issue or as an incidental question. But where a Member State court has determined that an arbitration agreement is null and void, this should not preclude that court's judgment on the substance of the matter from being recognised or, as the case may be, enforced in accordance with the Regulation. Yet again, the recital states that this should be without prejudice to the competence of Member State courts to decide on the recognition and enforcement of arbitral awards in accordance with the New York Convention 1958, which takes precedence over Brussels I Recast.

The position reached is less bold, and correspondingly less protective of arbitration agreements, than would have been achieved by the early proposal partially to delete the arbitration exclusion from the instrument's scope, and to confer exclusive jurisdiction on the courts of the Member State of the seat of the proposed arbitration to determine issues relating to the existence (including validity), scope and applicability of the agreement. It is debateable whether the new provisions, contained in the shade of the recitals rather than the bright light of the rules themselves, will effect anything more than an illusion of improvement.

Recital (12) provides that the Recast Regulation shall not apply to any action or ancillary proceedings relating to what might be termed curial matters, e.g. powers of arbitrators, and conduct of arbitration procedure.

LUGANO II CONVENTION

7–72   A parallel scheme of rules of jurisdiction and judgment enforcement was brought into force for the European Free Trade Association (EFTA) area[341] by the 1988 Lugano ("Parallel") Convention on Jurisdiction and Enforcement of Judgments in Civil and Commercial Matters, which was extended to operate in the UK by means of the Civil Jurisdiction and Judgments Act 1991. To a large extent, the Lugano Convention repeated the text of the 1968 Brussels Convention, but the provisions, though similar, were not identical. Nor did the Lugano Convention benefit from the advantages of speed and certainty which in the Brussels regime followed from the transformation of the Brussels Convention into a Regulation.

It was necessary therefore to effect equivalent changes to the Lugano regime to align it with the Brussels I Regulation. "Lugano II" refers to the Convention on jurisdiction and the recognition and enforcement of judgments in civil and commercial matters, between the European Community and the Republic of Iceland, the Kingdom of Norway, the Swiss Confederation and the Kingdom of Denmark, signed on behalf of the European Community on 30 October 2007.[342] It replaces the 1988 Lugano Convention in terms which, in general, are parallel to

---

[341] Now comprising, for the purposes of Lugano II, Iceland, Norway and Switzerland. The principality of Liechtenstein, an EFTA Contracting State, did not ratify the Lugano I or II Conventions.

[342] See Decision 2007/712/EC on the signing, on behalf of the Community, of the Convention on jurisdiction and the recognition and enforcement of judgments in civil and commercial matters [2007] O.J. L339/1; and Decision 2009/430/EC concerning the conclusion of the Convention on jurisdiction

those contained in the Brussels I Regulation. Lugano II entered into force for the EU, including Denmark, and Norway on 1 January 2010; for Switzerland, on 1 January 2011; and for Iceland, on 1 May 2011.[343]

Lugano II is accompanied by an Explanatory Report.[344] The Pocar Report stresses the importance of simplification of procedures for judgment enforcement, as a necessary contribution to the development of the single judicial area, an area which, "lends itself so well to extension to the EFTA countries".[345] Everything possible must be done to facilitate the free movement of judgments, and further reduce the obstacles which still exist.

With regard to interpretation of Lugano II, reference should be made to Protocol 2 on the Uniform Interpretation of the Convention and on the Standing Committee. The Standing Committee, comprising representatives of the Contracting Parties, is convened as required. Within its remit fall questions concerning revision of the instrument; and the relationship between the Convention and other international instruments.

As a result of Lugano II having become part of Community rules (the Convention having been signed and ratified by the Community, and succeeded to by the European Union), the CJEU has jurisdiction to give interpretative rulings on its provisions upon application to the Court by the courts of EU Member States.[346] States bound by Lugano II which are not EU Member States (i.e. the EFTA States of Iceland, Norway and Switzerland), though not entitled to make application to the CJEU for interpretative rulings on Lugano II, are entitled, in terms of art.2 of the Protocol to submit statements of case or written observations to that Court where the court of an EU Member State has made such an application. Article 1 of Protocol 2 requires any court applying and interpreting Lugano II to pay due account to relevant jurisprudence upon Lugano I, Lugano II, and the Brussels I Regulation and amendments thereof, handed down by the ECJ/CJEU and courts bound by these instruments, respectively.

Jurisdiction provisions of Lugano II[347]

Title II of Lugano II deals with jurisdiction. The provisions were almost completely aligned with those in the Brussels I Regulation. One difference between the instruments concerned maintenance. In light of Council Regulation 4/2009 on jurisdiction, applicable law, recognition and enforcement of decisions and cooperation in matters relating to maintenance obligations ("the Maintenance

7–73

---

and the recognition and enforcement of judgments in civil and commercial matters [2009] O.J. L147/1. See Civil Jurisdiction and Judgment Act 1982, as amended by the Civil Jurisdiction and Judgments Regulations 2009 (SI 2009/3131).

[343] Lugano II art.69.5.

[344] F. Pocar, Explanatory Report [2009] O.J. C319/1 ("Pocar Report").

[345] Pocar Report, para.128.

[346] While the position is clear, and the reason for CJEU jurisdiction convincing insofar as the Lugano II and Brussels I Regulation texts have been aligned, rendering divergent interpretations undesirable, the immediate authority rests only on the preamble to Protocol 2, and is not visible anywhere in the text of the articles. See also Pocar Report, para.196.

[347] Title III of Lugano II is concerned with recognition and enforcement of judgments. There is little change in this section of the instrument as compared with the 1988 Lugano Convention. Para.9–40, below.

Regulation"[348]), which has applied in EU Member States, including the UK,[349] from 18 June 2011, art.1.2(e) of Brussels I Recast has excluded from that instrument's scope "maintenance obligations arising from a family relationship". At its meeting on 3 May 2011, the Lugano Standing Committee stated that it would not require, for the time being, a protocol in relation to the law on maintenance, since its ordinary revision mechanisms could be used as necessary in order to resolve possible inconsistencies.

Relationship between Lugano II and Brussels I Recast

7–74   This subject is addressed in Lugano II Title VII art.64. In this difficult area of delimitation of ambit of Brussels I Recast[350] and Lugano II,[351] the courts of EFTA States are obliged always to apply Lugano II. Courts in Member States bound by Brussels I Recast may find themselves having to apply both instruments.

Article 64.1 of Lugano II in effect provides that the scope of Brussels I Recast, and of the EC–Denmark Agreement, remains unaltered, not limited by Lugano II. Hence, with regard to persons domiciled in States bound by Brussels I Recast, or the EC-Denmark Agreement, the jurisdiction of EU Member State courts continues to be exercised in accordance with the rules contained in those instruments; these rules also continue to apply with regard to persons domiciled in Third States, which are not party to Lugano II.[352]

In matters of jurisdiction, by art.64.2, Lugano II is applicable, "...in all cases, by the courts of any State bound by the Convention, including the courts of States bound by the Brussels I Regulation, if the defendant is domiciled in the territory of a State where the Convention applies and the Regulation does not."[353] Essentially, therefore, if the defendant in proceedings in Scotland is domiciled, e.g. in Iceland, the Scots court shall apply Lugano II. Likewise, Lugano II shall apply where, by Lugano arts 22 (exclusive jurisdiction) or 23 (prorogation), jurisdiction is conferred on a Lugano State, e.g. a Scots court seised on the ground of domicile under art.4 of Brussels I Recast, in proceedings concerning rights in rem in immoveable property in Iceland, must cede jurisdiction to the Icelandic courts on the basis of the respect due to the exclusive jurisdiction principle, but this would be done in terms of art.22 of Lugano II, not art.24 of Brussels I Recast.

In terms of art.64.2(b), Lugano II shall apply in a situation where proceedings are instituted in a Lugano State, say, Norway, and proceedings in respect of the same or a related cause of action are instituted in Scotland; if, in terms of the *lis*

---

[348] Maintenance Regulation [2009] O.J. L7/1.
[349] The UK did not take part in the adoption of the Maintenance Regulation, and therefore initially was not bound by it, or subject to its application (recital (47)). However, in accordance with art.4 of Protocol No.4 on the position of the UK and Ireland ([1997] OJ C340/99) the UK later notified its intention to accept the Regulation (Note from General Secretariat of the Council to the Council JUSTCIV 262). Para.13–18, below.
[350] Having regard to the wording of Lugano II art.64.1, and Brussels I Recast art.80.
[351] Pocar Report, para.18.
[352] Pocar Report, para.19.
[353] Pocar Report, para.20.

pendens system, the Scots court must or may defer to the Norwegian court, this shall be done under Lugano II arts 27 and 28, and not under the corresponding provisions of the Brussels I Recast.

At its meeting on 25 September 2013, the Lugano Standing Committee considered possible modification of Lugano II, to align it with Brussels I Recast. The Standing Committee made no recommendation on the possible amendment of Lugano II, and no proposed revisals have been forthcoming.[354]

PRESERVATION OF RESIDUAL NATIONAL RULES

As against non-EU domiciliaries (or in cases against EU domiciliaries which fall outside the subject-matter scope of Brussels, per art.1), residual national rules can be utilised.   **7–75**

The Nuyts Study[355] was commissioned by the European Commission to produce a comparative analysis of the national rules of jurisdiction of Member States (operative in civil and commercial areas, and in matrimonial and parental responsibility proceedings)[356]; and to make recommendations for possible harmonisation of the rules. The study considered whether the absence of common rules determining jurisdiction against defendants domiciled in Third States could jeopardise the application of mandatory Community legislation, or the objectives of the Community.

Of the five options identified as possible solutions to the alleged problem, the one favoured in the Nuyts Study was extension of the jurisdictional rules contained in the Brussels I Regulation to claims against defendants domiciled in Third States. This would have been blatant aggrandisement by the Brussels regime. The main advantage of such an option was said to be ease of implementation, and convenience for judges and lawyers. Nuyts recommended that such a change should be accompanied by the creation of additional grounds of jurisdiction and the crafting of new rules concerning declining jurisdiction in favour of the courts of Third States. Hence Nuyts, while not suggesting "sanctifying" exorbitant national rules by introducing them into Community law, advanced three additional grounds of jurisdiction,[357] viz.: a jurisdiction based on the carrying out of activities in the forum by the Third State domiciled defendant, provided that the dispute relates to such activities; on the location of assets belonging to such a defendant within the territory of an EU Member State, provided the claim relates to such assets; and the so-called *forum necessitatis*, permitting proceedings to be brought against such a defendant when there is no other jurisdiction available in the EU or outside the EU.

---

[354] https://www.bj.admin.ch/bj/en/home/wirtschaft/privatrecht/lugue-2007.html (Swiss Federal Office of Justice) [accessed 22 June 2015].

[355] A.Nuyts et al, "Study on Residual Jurisdiction (Review of the Member States' rules concerning the "Residual Jurisdiction" of their courts in civil and commercial matters, pursuant to the Brussels I and II Regulations): General Report" (JLS/C4/2005/07-30-CE) (*Universite Libre de Bruxelles*, 2007) (henceforth "Nuyts Study").

[356] The study concluded that recommendations for proposed harmonisation of residual jurisdiction would require to distinguish between the Brussels I and Brussels II *bis* regimes: Executive Summary, p.7.

[357] Executive Summary, p.9.

In the proposal for a recast regulation, the Commission expressed the view that diversity of national laws rendered access to justice in the EU unsatisfactory as regards disputes involving non-EU domiciled defendants. It came as no surprise, therefore, that the Commission proposed to act on something long threatened, namely, extension of the jurisdiction rules of the regulation to disputes involving Third State defendants. In what was a brash manoeuvre, even by its own standards, the Commission aimed to harmonise the national ("residual" or "subsidiary") rules of Member States. The UK Government's resistance to this proposed extension of Brussels grounds of jurisdiction to Third State defendants was predictable.[358] As events transpired, concern was misplaced because the ambitious proposal to harmonise the residual national rules of Member States was not realised. As noted above, the changes brought about by Brussels I Recast affecting Third State defendants are those contained in arts 18.1, 21.2, 24 and 25.

Civil Jurisdiction and Judgments Act 1982 Schedule 4: the Modified Convention, allocating jurisdiction within the UK[359]

7–76   Part II of CJJA 1982 is headed "Jurisdiction, and recognition and enforcement of judgments, within United Kingdom". By s.16, the provisions set out in Sch.4, which contain a modified version of the Brussels I Recast,[360] have effect for determining, for each part of the UK, whether the courts of that part, or any particular court in that part, have/has jurisdiction, where (a) the subject-matter of the proceedings is within the scope of Brussels I Recast, per art.1 thereof; and (b) the defendant or defender is domiciled in the United Kingdom or the proceedings are of a kind mentioned in art.24 of Brussels I Recast (i.e. exclusive jurisdiction regardless of domicile).

Schedule 4, therefore, has two main functions: first, where, under Brussels I Recast, jurisdiction is allotted to the "UK" generally, but not to a particular territorial unit thereof,[361] Sch.4 supplies the lack. Secondly, it is utilised in cases which arise within the UK, but are related to more than one territorial unit within the UK.

The provisions of Sch.4 follow those of Brussels I Recast, and in approach and detail are frequently the same, or similar. However, there are certain differences between the detail of Brussels I Recast and Sch.4. For example, while protective rules for consumers and employees are contained in Sch.4, provisions for insured parties and beneficiaries equivalent to those found in Brussels I Recast are not present in Sch.4. The autonomous Community definition of "place of performance" of a contract, provided first in art.5.1 of the Brussels I Regulation

---

[358] e.g. *Green Paper on the Brussels I Regulation: Report with Evidence*, 2009, HL Paper No.148 (Session 2008/09), paras 86–98.

[359] As amended by CJJO 2001 Sch.2.

[360] CJJA 1982 s.1, as amended by Civil Jurisdiction and Judgments (Amendment) Regulations 2014 (SI 2014/2947) Sch.1 para.2.

[361] e.g. for the provision of jurisdiction on the basis of the defendant's domicile under art.4 of Brussels I Recast, the international allocation of jurisdiction per the Regulation is satisfied by a finding that the defendant is domiciled in the UK. Thereafter, identification of the domicile of the defendant as, e.g. between Scotland, and England and Wales, is determined by Sch.4: *Daniel v Foster*, 1989 S.C.L.R. 378.

and reiterated in art.7.1 of Brussels I Recast, was not extended by the CJJO 2001 to Sch.4 r.3(a).[362] Similarly, the presumption of exclusivity of choice of court clauses, found in the prorogation provision of art.25 of Brussels I Recast, is not found in Sch.4 r.12 (prorogation).

National rules of jurisdiction of Member States proscribed by the 1968 Brussels Convention and its descendants may not be used against persons domiciled in a Member State, or in a territorial unit within a Member State. This means that a Scots rule such as arrestment to found jurisdiction can be utilised only if the property sought to be arrested is situated in Scotland, and the owner/defender is not domiciled in Scotland, elsewhere in the UK or in any other Member State. There remains one ground of jurisdiction which does not feature in Brussels I Recast, but yet is not a proscribed ground, and therefore deserves mention as an example of a distinction between Brussels I Recast and Sch. 4, namely, the special jurisdiction conferred on the parts of the UK in which the relevant property is situated, where the proceedings concern a debt secured on immoveable property, or which are brought to assert, declare, or determine proprietary or possessory rights, or rights of security, in or over moveable property, or to obtain authority to dispose of moveable property.[363]

Direct recourse cannot be had to the CJEU for interpretation of the provisions of Sch.4.[364]

Residual national rules for Scotland

Historical background: Scots common law rules of jurisdiction

At common law the grounds upon which the Scots courts assumed jurisdiction were, with only a few exceptions, grounds which generally were recognised in other countries. The likely result was that a Scots decree would be recognised and enforced internationally. The grounds were as follows:

7–77

(a)   domicile of succession[365] (for use in consistorial actions and actions involving status);

(b)   domicile of citation (i.e. residence);

(c)   in relation to itinerants, presence of defender in Scotland, if personally cited;

(d)   place of performance of contract[366] (*ratione contractus*)[367];

---

[362] cf. the position re. Sch.8 (para.7–78, below): *Fishers Services Ltd v All Thai'd Up Ltd (t/a Richmond House Hotel)*, 2013 S.L.T. (Sh Ct) 121.

[363] CJJA 1982 Sch.4 r.3(h).

[364] TFEU art.267 (ex-EC Treaty art.234); and now, re jurisdiction of the CJEU. See *Kleinwort Benson Ltd v Glasgow City Council (No.2)* [1997] 4 All E.R. 641.

[365] i.e. domicile in the classic sense. See Ch.6, above.

[366] *Dallas & Co (Transport Ltd) v McArdle*, 1949 S.L.T. 375, per Lord President Cooper at 378.

[367] Jurisdiction *ratione contractus* (regarded as meaning that either the place of execution or the place of performance of the contract was within the jurisdiction) was subject to the essential condition that there had to be personal service within Scotland or within the sheriffdom: Sheriff Courts (Scotland) Act 1907 s.6(f) (repealed to the extent that it determines jurisdiction in respect of any matter to which the Civil Jurisdiction and Judgments Act 1982 Sch.8 applies).

(e)   place of occurrence of delict (*ratione delicti*)[368];
(f)   moveables situated in Scotland[369] (*ratione rei sitae*);
(g)   prorogation (party choice of forum)[370];
(h)   reconvention[371];
(i)   interdict to prevent the commission of a wrong in Scotland, on that ground alone, or a wrong abroad, if possessed of jurisdiction over the defender on another ground[372]; and
(j)   in relation to trusts, the place of the domicile of a trust.

At common law, the courts of the *situs* alone had jurisdiction in questions relating to title to immoveable property because they alone had power to grant effective decrees. Certain grounds of jurisdiction did not receive approval internationally, namely, possession of heritage in Scotland in an action unrelated to the heritage[373]; and arrestment of moveable property of the defender in Scotland in order to found jurisdiction.[374]

Civil Jurisdiction and Judgments Act 1982 Schedule 8

7–78   The residual rules of jurisdiction in use in Scotland, per s.20 of the Civil Jurisdiction and Judgments Act 1982, as amended, are set out in Sch.8 to that Act. Schedule 8 takes effect, subject to Brussels I Recast,[375] Lugano II (allocating jurisdiction among EU/EFTA Member States), and Sch.4 (the "Modified Convention", allocating jurisdiction within the UK). By reason of the Europeanisation and internationalisation of the rules of civil and commercial jurisidiction, the ambit of operation of these native Scots rules is much attenuated.

The introduction of this set of rules for Scotland was advocated by the Maxwell Committee,[376] which recommended that the grounds of jurisdiction in use in Scotland be rationalised and set out in a single code.[377] The scheme of jurisdiction for Scotland introduced by the CJJA 1982, as now amended[378]

---

[368] The need for personal citation was removed by the Law Reform (Jurisdiction in Delict) (Scotland) Act 1971; also *Russell v FW Woolworth & Co Ltd*, 1982 S.L.T. 428. But see *Wendel v Moran*, 1993 S.L.T. 44.

[369] *Muir v Matassa*, 1935 S.L.T. (Sh. Ct.) 55.

[370] Agreement supplied a lack of jurisdiction over the *person*, not the type of action or subject-matter.

[371] Jurisdiction which a foreign litigant, by raising an action in Scotland, was held to call down upon himself, in order to permit the defender to raise a counter-action, if the latter is necessary to do justice between the parties.

[372] D.M. Walker, *Principles of Scottish Private Law*, 4th edn (Oxford: Clarendon, 1988), p.157. cf. CJJA 1982 Sch.8 r.2(10).

[373] *Baron Hume's Lectures, 1786–1822*, edited by G. Campbell H. Paton (Edinburgh: Stair Society, 1939–1958), Vol.V, p.249. cf. In English law *Emanuel v Symon* [1908] 1 K.B. 302.

[374] Baron Hume's Lectures, Vol.V, p.250. *Agnew v Norwest Construction Co Ltd*, 1935 S.C. 771.

[375] Including incursions made by that instrument, per arts 18.1, 21.2, 24 and 25 re Third State defendants.

[376] Scottish Committee on Jurisdiction and Enforcement, *Report of the Scottish Committee on Jurisdiction and Enforcement* (HMSO, 1980) ("Maxwell Report").

[377] Maxwell Report, paras 2.16(h), 2.23, 2.24.

[378] By Civil Jurisdiction and Judgments Order 2001 (SI 2001/3929); Civil Jurisdiction and Judgments Regulations 2009 (SI 2009/3131); and Civil Jurisdiction and Judgments (Maintenance) Regulations 2011 (SI2011/1484).

supersedes all pre-existing rules of jurisdiction in matters covered by the Act, subject to retention of the *nobile officium* of the Court of Session. Although Sch.8 contains the "Scottish rules",[379] the key to operation of these rules is not the Scottish location of the putative litigation, but rather the legal characteristic of the defender, or the subject matter of the litigation.

Schedule 8 also contains those native or idiosyncratic rules of Scots law which are capable of being utilised against persons not domiciled in an EU or EFTA Member State. A defence which can be offered for retention of these native grounds is that their effect may be mitigated by the plea of *forum non conveniens*, where it remains available and competent. There is another, unexceptional ground in cases concerning moveable property, jurisdiction being based on the situation thereof,[380] which may be used not only against persons domiciled in a non-Member State, but also against persons domiciled in any part of the UK.

Some rules in Sch.8 are identical in substance to their counterpart in Brussels I Recast[381]; some rules in Sch.8 remain in the original Brussels Convention form, unamended to reflect the modifications effected subsequently by the Brussels I Regulation and Brussels I Recast[382]; and some rules in Sch.8 are similar to those in Brussels I Recast, but not identical.[383]

In determining any question as to the meaning or effect of any provision contained in Sch.8, the Scottish courts must have regard to relevant principles and decisions handed down by the CJEU, and to the expert reports (Jenard and Schlosser, etc.).[384]

Residual national rules for England

Unlike the Scottish "residual" rules, the English "residual" rules are not contained in a Schedule to the Civil Jurisdiction and Judgments Act 1982. Rather, the pre-existing rules[385] remain operative wherever the Brussels regime does not apply. In such cases, jurisdiction is assumed on a wide, liberal and discretionary basis, namely presence of the defendant within the jurisdiction[386]; submission of the defendant to the jurisdiction of the court; and "service out" of the English jurisdiction in cases in which the Civil Procedure Rules permit such service at the discretion of the court.[387]

7–79

---

[379] The provisions of Sch.8 are termed "rules", not "articles".

[380] cf. corresponding provision in Sch.4 r.3(h).

[381] e.g. Sch.8 r.2(c) (special jurisdiction in matters relating to a delict) and r.2(f) (branch or agency).

[382] e.g. Sch.8 r.2(b) (special jurisdiction in matters relating to a contract).

[383] Notably, sch.8 r.6 (prorogation) does not include a presumption of exclusivity.

[384] Civil Jurisdiction and Judgments Act 1982 s.20(5).

[385] For Civil Procedure Rules, see https://www.justice.gov.uk/courts/procedure-rules/civil/rules [accessed 22 June 2015]. For commentary, see R.Fentiman, *International Commercial Litigation*, 2nd edn (OUP, 2015), paras 8.26 et seq.

[386] See, famously, *Maharanee Seethadevi Gaekwar of Baroda v Wildenstein* [1972] 2 Q.B. 283 ("temporary presence" in England only long enough for the service of a writ). Temporary presence within the jurisdiction was never a feature of Scots common law rules (jurisdiction over itinerants, that is, persons of no fixed abode, being different in purpose and nature).

[387] CPR r.6.36 and CPR PD 6B (Service out of the Jurisdiction). See, e.g. *Seaconsar (Far East) Ltd v Bank Markazi Jomhouri Islami Iran* [1993] 1 Lloyd's Rep. 236. See also *Konamaneni v Rolls Royce Industrial Power (India) Ltd* [2002] 1 W.L.R. 1269; *Morin v Bonhams & Brooks Ltd* [2003] 2 All E.R. (Comm) 36; *Apple Corps Ltd v Apple Computer Inc* [2004] EWHC 768; *Ophthalmic Innovations International(UK) Ltd v Ophthalmic Innovations International Inc* [2005] I.L.Pr. 10; *Marconi*

In English law, the Civil Jurisdiction and Judgments Act 1982 s.30, abolished the rule in *British South Africa Co v Companhia de Mocambique*[388] which had excluded (though there were always certain exceptions) the jurisdiction of the English court to entertain an action concerning damages for trespass to foreign land, even though no question of title was involved. Under s.30, the court in England and Wales or Northern Ireland has jurisdiction to hear proceedings for trespass to immoveable property situated outside that part of the UK (and hence in another part of the UK, as well as outside the UK), unless the proceedings principally are concerned with title to, or right to possession of, the property (and subject also to the terms of s.30(2)).

RESIDUAL NATIONAL RULES OF JURISDICTION: CONFLICTS OF JURISDICTION OUTSIDE THE BRUSSELS REGIME

The plea of *forum non conveniens*

7–80   Use of residual national rules opens the way to the plea of *forum non conveniens* (q.v.),[389] with the result that when a Scots or English court is seised under such rules of jurisdiction, it might find itself deferring sub nom. *forum non conveniens* to a court in another EU Member State.[390]

Choice of forum is a fiercely fought issue because the same forum is unlikely to be in the best interests of all the parties. The starting point for Scots law is taken to be the famous dictum by Lord Kinnear in *Sim v Robinow*,[391] where his Lordship said:

> "...the plea can never be sustained unless the Court is satisfied that there is some other tribunal, having competent jurisdiction, in which the case may be tried more suitably for the interests of all the parties and for the ends of justice."

Communications International Ltd v PT Pan Indonesia Bank TBK [2005] 2 All E.R. (Comm) 325; *Ark Therapeutics Plc v True North Capital Ltd* [2006] 1 All E.R. (Comm) 138; *Masri v Consolidated Contractors International Co SAL* [2009] 4 All E.R. 847; *Wink v Croatia Osiguranje DD* [2013] EWHC 1118 (QB); *Vidal-Hall v Google Inc.* [2015] EWCA Civ 311; and *Brownlie v Four Seasons Holdings Inc.* [2015] EWCA Civ 665.

[388] *British South Africa Co v Companhia de Mocambique* [1893] A.C. 602. Upheld by the House of Lords in *Hesperides Hotels Ltd v Muftizade* [1978] 3 W.L.R. 378. See, for Scotland, *Hewit's Trustees v Lawson* (1891) 18 R. 793; and *Cathcart v Cathcart* (1902) 12 S.L.T. 182.

[389] Brussels I Recast art.6.

[390] *Sarrio SA v Kuwait Investment Authority* [1999] 1 A.C. 32; and *Haji-Iannou v Frangos* [1999] 2 Lloyd's Rep. 337. See Morris, *Conflict of Laws*, 7th edn, 2009, para.5–046.

[391] *Sim v Robinow* (1892) 19 R. 665, 668. Later notable Scottish cases are *Longworth v Hope* (1865) 3 M. 1049 (where the court noted the infelicity of the formerly used term *forum non competens*; still, *conveniens* should not be translated as convenient, but rather as appropriate, fit for, or suitable; *Société du Gaz de Paris v Armateurs Francais*, 1926 S.C. (H.L.) 13; *Jubert v Church Commissioners of England*, 1952 S.L.T. 99; *Argyllshire Weavers Ltd v A Macaulay (Tweeds) Ltd (No.1)*, 1962 S.C. 388; *Crédit Chemique v James Scott Engineering Group Ltd*, 1979 S.C. 406; *De Mulder v Jadranska Linijska (Jadrolinija)*, 1989 S.L.T. 269; *Shell (UK) Exploration and Production Ltd v Innes*, 1995 S.L.T. 807; *FMC Corp v Russell*, 1999 S.L.T. 99; *Compagnie Commerciale Andre SA v Artibell Shipping Co Ltd (No.1)*, 1999 S.L.T. 1051; and *Banks v CGU Insurance Plc*, 2005 S.C.L.R. 556.

This form of words was quoted with approval by Lord Goff[392] in *Spiliada
Maritime Corp v Cansulex Ltd*,[393] which decision of the House of Lords
represents the acceptance by English law that its position in this area is
indistinguishable from the Scots plea.[394] Useful consideration of the subject in
Scotland is found in *De Mulder v Jadranska Linijska (Jadrolinija)*,[395] where the
considerations appeared to be relatively straightforward or neutral, for example,
convenience of witnesses, and language difficulties. Conflicting interests may
present acutely or controversially and the question for the forum is how, if at all,
judicial discretion should weigh these interests.

The onus of proof is shared in the following manner: the case having been
properly laid in Scotland, the onus is on the defender[396] making the plea, to show
that there is a competent and more appropriate forum elsewhere. If this is
established to the satisfaction of the original forum, in terms of expense and
convenience of witnesses, etc.[397] the onus shifts to the pursuer to show
"objectively by cogent evidence"[398] that to require him to litigate abroad would
remove from him a personal or juridical advantage of such importance that it
would be unjust to him to deprive him of it.[399] A general principle may be
derived, namely, "if a clearly more appropriate forum overseas has been
identified, generally speaking the plaintiff will have to take that forum as he finds
it, even if it is in certain respects less advantageous to him than the English
forum".[400] Only if the plaintiff can establish that substantial justice cannot be
done in the appropriate forum will the court refuse to grant a stay.[401] However,
availability in England of legal aid, or the benefit of a conditional fee agreement

---

[392] Tracing the line of English judicial thinking to *Spiliada* from the strict or avid *St Pierre v South
American Stores (Gath & Chaves) Ltd* [1936] 1 K.B. 382, through *Owners of the Atlantic Star v
owners of the Bona Spes (The Atlantic Star)* [1973] 2 All E.R. 175; *MacShannon v Rockware Glass
Ltd* [1978] A.C. 795 (the "natural forum"); *Castanho v Brown & Root (UK) Ltd* [1981] A.C. 557;
Trendtex Trading Corp v Credit Suisse [1982] A.C. 679; *Smith Kline & French Laboratories v Bloch*
[1983] 2 All E.R. 72; *The Atlantic Song* [1983] 2 Lloyd's Rep. 394; *Owners of the Las Mercedes v
Owners of the Abidin Daver* [1984] 2 W.L.R. 196 HL.

[393] *Spiliada Maritime Corp v Cansulex Ltd (The Spiliada)* [1986] 3 All E.R. 843 at 853.

[394] Important post-*Spiliada* cases include: *Connelly v RTZ Corp Plc (No.2)* [1998] A.C. 854 HL;
Radhakrishna Hospitality Service Private Ltd v EIH Ltd [1999] 2 Lloyd's Rep. 249; *Askin v Absa
Bank Ltd* [1999] I.L.Pr. 471; *Lubbe v Cape Plc* (No.2) [2000] 1 W.L.R. 1545; *XN Corp Ltd v Point of
Sale Ltd* [2001] I.L.Pr. 35; *Ceskoslovenska Obchodni Banka AS v Nomura International Plc* [2003]
I.L.Pr. 20; *Dornoch Ltd v Mauritius Union Assurance Co Ltd* [2006] EWCA Civ 389; *Ark
Therapeutics Plc v True North Capital Ltd* [2006] 1 All E.R. (Comm) 138; *Pacific International
Sports Clubs Ltd v Soccer Marketing International Ltd* [2009] EWHC 1839 (Ch); and *Rattan v Bank
of Singapore Ltd* [2015] EWHC 1549 (Ch.).

[395] *De Mulder v Jadranska Linijska (Jadrolinija)*,1989 S.L.T. 269.

[396] A pursuer having selected a forum will not normally be permitted, upon a change of mind, to
plead *forum non conveniens* with a view to having his chosen Scots court defer to another court:
Marodi Service de D Mialich v Mikkal Myklebusthaug Rederi A/S, 2002 G.W.D. 13–398.

[397] If this is not established (e.g. *Banks v CGU Insurance Plc*, 2005 S.C.L.R. 556), the argument will
not continue.

[398] *De Mulder v Jadranska Linijska (Jadrolinija)*, 1989 S.L.T. 269, per Lord Kincraig at 274.

[399] The principles which govern identification of the appropriate forum in non-Brussels consistorial
cases are similar: see Ch.12, below.

[400] *Connelly v RTZ Corp Plc (No.2)* [1998] A.C. 854, per Lord Goff at 872.

[401] *Connelly v RTZ Corp Plc (No.2)* [1998] A.C. 854, per Lord Goff at 853.

was held in two House of Lords cases to be good reason not to defer to the jurisdiction of the objectively natural forum.[402]

Levels of damages, nature of the system of discovery of evidence, and content of the rules of evidence will not normally be suitable factors to be taken into account. Expiry of a limitation period in the alternative forum is an ambivalent factor, the weight attributed depending on circumstances, especially the court's assessment of the conduct of the party potentially disadvantaged by it, for example degree of culpability or motive or excuse in failing to act expeditiously.[403] The court may take into account the amount of legal and technical work done in one jurisdiction, or in one jurisdiction in relation to a similar case (the "Cambridgeshire factor").[404] The existence of a jurisdiction clause in favour of the forum will render it unlikely that the forum would accede to a plea of *forum non conveniens*.[405]

Hence, assessment by the forum of what constitutes personal or juridical advantage is the crucial and most difficult issue, but there arises also the question *when* particular factors ought to be considered, i.e. at the first, or second, stage of the plea.[406] It is thought that at the first stage availability of alternative forum means availability in principle; at the second stage, it will be open to the claimant to seek to establish that, in reality, the alternative forum is not open to him, by reason for example of: time bar; absence of public funding; or that for political or other reasons the claimant will not be afforded a fair hearing, or any hearing at all, or will be in danger of his life in the alternative forum.[407]

In*AK Investment CJSC v Kyrgyz Mobil Tel Ltd*,[408] a case arising out of a coup d'état in Kyrgyzstan, the Privy Council held that the standard of proof to be satisfied by a party who asserts that he will not obtain justice in a foreign jurisdiction is that there is a "real risk" that justice will not be obtained in the foreign court. On the facts, the Court held that although Kyrgyzstan was undoubtedly the natural forum for determination of those issues, there was substantial evidence of specific irregularities, breach of principles of natural justice, and irrational conclusions by the Kyrgyz court, sufficient to justify a conclusion that there was considerably more than a real risk that the claimant Manx companies would not obtain justice in Kyrgyzstan. Allegations of political,

---

[402] *Lubbe v Cape Plc* [2000] 1 W.L.R 1545; and *Connelly v RTZ Corp Plc (No.2)* [1997] 4 All E.R. 335 (Lord Hoffman dissenting).

[403] *The Spiliada* [1986] 3 All E.R. 843 at 860; and *Banks v CGU Insurance Plc*, 2005 S.C.L.R. 556.

[404] At the time of the *Spiliada* decision, litigation was ongoing in England concerning a similar action for damage to a cargo of sulphur, involving the same defendant shippers, but a different ship, *The Cambridgeshire* (hence, this factor has become known as the "Cambridgeshire factor"), and many of the same lawyers and expert witnesses.

[405] *Horn Linie GmbH & Co v Panamericana Formas e Impresos SA (The Hornbay)* [2006] EWHC 373 (Comm). Cf. *Standard Chartered Bank (Hong Kong) Ltd v Independent Power Tanzania Ltd* [2015] EWHC 1640 (Comm), in which the English Commercial Court held that a non-exclusive jurisdiction clause combined with a *forum non conveniens* waiver clause does not preclude the forum from granting a stay of English proceedings. But a stay should be granted only if there are exceptional grounds, unforeseeable at the time of the agreement.

[406] See L. Merrett, "Uncertainties in the First Limb of the Spiliada Test" (2005) 54 I.C.L.Q. 211.

[407] *Askin v Absa Bank Ltd* [1999] I.L.Pr. 471; and *Mohammed v Bank of Kuwait and the Middle East KSC* [1996] 1 W.L.R. 1483.

[408] *AK Investment CJSC v Kyrgyz Mobil Tel Ltd* [2012] 1 W.L.R. 1804.

governmental or judicial impropriety in foreign jurisdictions should not be made,
and will be rejected outright, unless there is clear and cogent evidence to support
them.[409]

In *OJSC Oil Co Yugraneft v Abramovich*,[410] Christopher Clarke J. commented
that "The litigation in which Yugraneft…engaged does not bear tell tale indicia of
impropriety such as repeated determinations of different cases by the same judge
without good reason, departure from normal curial practice, irrational conclusions or the like."

The Court of Appeal in *Deripaska v Cherney*,[411] noting the increased risks to
Mr Cherney in Russia, namely, assassination, prosecution on trumped-up charges
and state interference in the judicial process, upheld the judgment of Christopher
Clarke J. that England was the jurisdiction in which the action could most
suitably be tried in the interests of all the parties and for the ends of justice. The
position would seem to be that the party seeking to continue litigation in the UK
will be required to show that the foreign system in question is susceptible, in
principle, to corruption, and that in the instant case, there is a demonstrable risk
to that party of a denial of justice in the foreign court.

The court may grant or refuse the sist; and if the former, it may dismiss or
sist[412] the Scottish proceedings. In *VTB Capital Plc v Nutritek International
Corp*,[413] the UK Supreme Court held, in the context of debate on permission to
serve out of the jurisdiction in a matter of tort, that where a judge at first instance
has made an evaluative judgment as to whether England was the appropriate
forum, an appellate court should refrain from interfering with the decision unless
satisfied that a significant error had been made. The case also warns that there
should not be a "stage trial" before the "main trial" in cases of this type; judges
hearing applications for a stay should ensure that the evidence and argument are
kept within proportionate bounds and do not get out of hand.

When may the plea be used?

Section 49 of the CJJA 1982, enacts that: 7–81

> "Nothing in this Act shall prevent any court in the United Kingdom from staying,
> sisting, striking out or dismissing any proceedings before it, on the ground of *forum
> non conveniens* or otherwise, where to do so is not inconsistent with the 1968
> Convention, or as the case may be, the Lugano Convention."

Generally, a stay will be inconsistent with the Brussels/Lugano regime, but the
question which has arisen in England is whether the plea can be used in an
English/Scottish (CJJA 1982 Sch.4) context. There are two conflicting decisions
of the same judge on the question, the later decision favouring the continuing

---

[409] *Dornoch Ltd v Mauritius Union Assurance Co Ltd* [2005] EWHC 1887 (Comm), per Aikens J. at
[97].
[410] *OJSC Oil Co Yugraneft v Abramovich* [2008] EWHC 2613 (Comm) at [496].
[411] *Deripaska v Cherney* [2009] EWCA Civ 849.
[412] *De Mulder v Jadranska Linijska (Jadrolinija)*, 1989 S.L.T. 269: litigation in Scotland was sisted,
in case the alternative forum in the former Yugoslavia should cede to the Scots court.
[413] *VTB Capital Plc v Nutritek International Corp* [2013] UKSC 5; [2013] 2 A.C. 337. See also
Faraday Reinsurance Co Ltd v Howden North America Inc [2012] EWCA Civ 980.

competence of the plea within the UK being preferred,[414] and so far uncontradicted. Lady Smith gave no indication that the plea would not be competent within the UK, in her judgment in *Banks v CGU Insurance Plc*.[415]

Subject to the UK situation in Sch.4, it can be said that the plea of *forum non conveniens* is not available within the Brussels/Lugano regime, since that regime resolves conflicts of jurisdiction on a strict priority of process basis.[416] By contrast, when a Scots or English court is seised under residual national rules of jurisdiction, it might find itself deferring sub nom. *forum non conveniens* to another court in another EU Member State.[417] It is particularly important to be clear therefore as to the ground upon which a Scots court has taken jurisdiction.

A doubt which arose about availability of the *forum non conveniens* discretion where it was attempted to use the plea in the court of a Member State, where the alternative forum was in a non-EU/non-EFTA state,[418] was resolved by the ECJ in the negative in *Owusu v Jackson (t/a Villa Holidays Bal Inn Villas)*.[419]

Owusu v Jackson (t/a Villa Holidays Bal Inn Villas)

7–82

The claimant, a "UK domiciliary", who rented from the first defendant, also domiciled in "the UK", a holiday villa in Jamaica with access to a private beach, suffered severe injuries following a diving accident. Mr Owusu walked into the sea and, diving under the water when it was at waist level, struck his head against a submerged sandbank, sustaining grave injuries rendering him tetraplegic. A similar accident, with the same outcome, allegedly occurred two years earlier to another English holidaymaker.

In 2000, Mr Owusu brought an action in England against Mr Jackson, the owner of the holiday villa, in contract; and against several Jamaican companies, including the owner and licensed users of the beach, in tort. The ground of argument in contract was that there was an implied term that the beach would be reasonably safe, or free from hidden dangers; and in tort, that it was the duty of the owner/occupier of the beach to warn swimmers of the unseen hazard constituted by the submerged sandbank.

Proceedings were commenced in Sheffield District Registry of the High Court, served on Jackson in the UK, and leave granted to serve the proceedings out of

---

[414] *Foxen v Scotsman Publications, The Times*, February 17, 1994; and *Cumming v Scottish Daily Record, The Times*, June 8, 1995, both per Drake J., the latter in favour of use of the plea as not inconsistent with CJJA 1982 s.49.

[415] *Banks v CGU Insurance Plc*, 2005 S.C.L.R. 556. See also *Ennstone Building Products Ltd v Stanger (No.1)* [2002] C.L.Y.B. 624; and *Lennon v Scottish Daily Record & Sunday Mail Ltd* [2004] EWHC 359 (QB).

[416] Brussels I Recast arts 29–32; *Arkwright Mutual Insurance Co v Bryanston Insurance Co Ltd* [1990] 2 All E.R. 335; *S&W Berisford Plc v New Hampshire Insurance Co Ltd* [1990] 2 All E.R. 321; and *Aiglon Ltd v Gau Shan Co Ltd* [1993] 1 Lloyd's Rep. 164.

[417] *Sarrio SA v Kuwait Investment Authority* [1999] 1 A.C. 32; and *Haji-Ioannou v Frangos* [1999] 2 Lloyd's Rep. 337.

[418] *BP International Ltd v Energy Infrastructure Group Ltd* [2003] EWHC 2924; *Navigators Insurance Co v Atlantic Methanol Production Co LLC* [2004] Lloyd's Rep. I.R. 418; *Bristow Helicopters Ltd v Sikorsky Aircraft Corp* [2004] 2 Lloyd's Rep. 150; *Royal & Sun Alliance Insurance Plc v Retail Brand Alliance Inc* [2005] Lloyd's Rep. I.R. 110; and *OT Africa Line Ltd v Magic Sportswear Corp* [2005] EWCA Civ 710.

[419] *Owusu v Jackson (t/a Villa Holidays Bal Inn Villas)* [2005] Q.B. 801. Decided under the 1968 Brussels Convention, even though a 2005 decision.

the jurisdiction on the other defendants in Jamaica. In response, a number of the six defendants, including Jackson, applied to the English court for a declaration that it should not exercise its jurisdiction in relation to them, on the argument that the case had closer links with Jamaica, and that Jamaica constituted a competent forum in which the case might be tried more suitably for the interests of all the parties and the ends of justice.[420]

The question for the court was whether or not it was competent for an English court to accede to the plea of *forum non conveniens* in these circumstances.[421] How "European" must a case be before the plea is incompetent? In an entirely European case[422] (which, however, it seems, does not include an intra-UK case) the plea is inappropriate.

The matter had been in doubt in the UK since the case of *Re Harrods (Buenos Aires) Ltd (No.2)*,[423] in which the English Court of Appeal, seised as the seat of a company registered in England, but conducting its business in Argentina, held itself entitled, within the terms of s.49 of the CJJA 1982, to stay its proceedings in favour of Argentina as the more appropriate forum for trial of the issues. In *Owusu*, the judge at first instance, having no power to refer the question to the ECJ, ruled that the application to a dispute of the jurisdictional rules in the 1968 Brussels Convention depended, in principle, on whether the defendant had its seat or was domiciled in a Contracting State, and that the Convention applied to a dispute between a defendant domiciled in a Contracting State and a claimant domiciled in a non-Contracting State[424]; and on the facts that it was not open to him to stay the action because Jackson was domiciled in a Contracting State. Similarly, he held that he could not stay the action in relation to the other defendants, notwithstanding the fact that they were Jamaican domiciled, because of the risk of conflicting decisions in related actions.[425] On that basis of reasoning, he held (using non-Brussels terminology) that a court in the UK was a more appropriate forum than one in Jamaica.

Jackson and the other defendants appealed to the Court of Appeal, which stayed its proceedings in order to refer the following question to the ECJ for a preliminary ruling:

> "(1)   Is it inconsistent with the Brussels Convention, where a claimant contends that jurisdiction is founded on article 2,[426] for a court of a contracting state to exercise a discretionary power, available under its national law, to decline to

---

[420] *Owusu v Jackson (t/a Villa Holidays Bal Inn Villas)* [2005] Q.B. 801 at [15].

[421] cf. *Lubbe v Cape Plc* [2000] 1 W.L.R. 1545, per Lord Bingham at 1563.

[422] Which, for present purposes, could be taken to be one where each available contending court is a court in an EU Member State and is seised on a Brussels ground.

[423] *Re Harrods (Buenos Aires) Ltd (No.2)* [1992] Ch. 72 (in which appeal to the ECJ was abandoned). The decision was followed in *Owners of the Bowditch v Owners of the Po (The Po)* [1991] 2 Lloyd's Rep. 206 (where the HL referred the question to the ECJ, but again the case settled); and *Hamed el Chiaty & Co (t/a Travco Nile Cruise Lines) v Thomas Cook group Ltd (The Nile Rhapsody)* [1994] 1 Lloyd's Rep. 382. See also *Ace Insurance SA-NV v Zurich Insurance Co* [2001] 1 All E.R. (Comm) 802; and *Travelers Casualty & Surety Co of Europe Ltd v Sun Life Assurance Co of Canada (UK) Ltd* [2004] I.L.Pr. 50. The ECJ position as expressed in *Owusu* was foreshadowed in relation to the Lugano Convention in *Mahme Trust Reg v Lloyds TSB Bank Plc* [2004] 2 Lloyd's Rep. 637.

[424] *Owusu v Jackson (t/a Villa Holidays Bal Inn Villas)* [2005] Q.B. 801 at [16].

[425] The potentially conflicting Jamaican and English judgments producing a difficult hybrid situation in terms of enforcement.

[426] The rule of general jurisdiction, now contained in Brussels I Recast art.4.

hear proceedings brought against a person domiciled in that state in favour of the courts of a non-contracting state, (a) if the jurisdiction of no other contracting state under the 1968 Convention is in issue, (b) if the proceedings have no connecting factors to any other contracting state? (2) If the answer to question 1(a) or (b) is yes, is it inconsistent in all circumstances or only in some and if so which?"

In relation to the first question, the ECJ held that on the interpretation and applicability of art.2, nothing in the wording thereof suggested that application of the general rule of jurisdiction there laid down on the basis of the defendant's domicile in a Contracting State was subject to the condition that there should be a legal relationship involving only the courts of Contracting States. Article 2 was mandatory in nature (meaning that the English court could not stay its proceedings against a defendant domiciled in a Contracting/Member State when it took the view that another forum in a non-Contracting/Member State was more appropriate),[427] and there could be no derogation from the principle it laid down, except in the cases expressly provided for by the Convention.[428] No exception on the basis of *forum non conveniens* was provided by the authors of the Convention. Respect for the principle of legal certainty would not be fully guaranteed if the court having jurisdiction under the Convention was allowed to apply the *forum non conveniens* doctrine. Application of the doctrine would undermine predictability, and affect the uniform application of the rules within the Community since the doctrine of *forum non conveniens* is recognised only in a limited number of Member States. The ECJ held that to permit any incursion of judicial discretion into the system would undermine the legal protection of persons established in the Community (although it is notable that the UK-domiciled defendant wished to have the case proceed in Jamaica in this instance).

In summary, it was held in *Owusu* that the Brussels Convention (and consequently the Brussels I Regulation and Brussels I Recast) precludes a court of a Contracting State from declining the jurisdiction conferred on it by art.2 (art.4 of Brussels I Recast), on the ground that the court of a non-Contracting/ Member State would be a more appropriate forum for the trial of the action, even if the jurisdiction of no other Contracting/Member State is in issue, or the proceedings have no connections with any other Contracting/Member State.

Owusu raised complex questions about the applicability of the Brussels regime given different permutations of circumstance and identity of parties. The decision resolved, in a negative way, points of dubiety. Strictly, the decision was concerned with the ambit of authority of art.2 of the Convention, the key provision of in personam jurisdiction under Brussels. But to suggest faintly[429]

---

[427] *Owusu v Jackson (t/a Villa Holidays Bal Inn Villas)* [2005] Q.B. 801 at [20].
[428] e.g. *Blue Tropic Ltd v Chkhartishvili* [2014] EWHC 2243 (Ch); and *Plaza BV v Law Debenture Trust Corp Plc* [2015] EWHC 43 (Ch).
[429] But less faintly when there is evidence of an exclusive jurisdiction clause: *Konkola Copper Mines Plc v Coromin Ltd* [2006] EWCA Civ 5, per Rix L.J. at [71]–[73]. See re reflexive effect, para.7–63, above; also *Viking Line ABP v International Transport Workers Federation* [2006] I.L.Pr. 4.

that the plea of *forum non conveniens* yet might be utilised in a future case in
which jurisdiction is founded on a ground of special jurisdiction under art.7,
seems to invite disappointment.[430]

The decision in *Owusu* is a notable, if not necessarily welcome, contribution to
our understanding of the reach of the Brussels regime and the relationship
between the Brussels regime and the legal systems of Third States. At a simple
level, if the claimant sues a defendant on the basis of art.4 of Brussels I Recast,[431]
it is his legitimate expectation that all the rules and principles of the Brussels
regime should apply.

The anti-suit injunction: restraint of foreign proceedings

By way of contrast with *forum non conveniens*, the plea for restraint of foreign   **7–83**
proceedings or, as it has come to be known, the grant of an anti-suit injunction,
relates to the power of a Scots[432] or English[433] court to prevent a person who is
subject to its jurisdiction from raising, or proceeding with, an action in a foreign
court between the same parties and relating to the same subject-matter as that
before the Scots court. Although the Scots/English courts have no power to
restrain a foreign court from proceeding to hear any action, they have power to
restrain a person subject to their jurisdiction from proceeding with an action in a
foreign court. The lively use of this remedy in England is not matched in
Scotland.

If an order is granted restraining foreign proceedings, the foreign court still
may hear the action (for it is part of its sovereignty so to do), but if the party
against whom the order of restraint is granted proceeds with the action abroad, he
will be acting in contempt of the British court and will receive no assistance in
attempting to enforce the resultant decree.

Generally, a court will not exercise this power if to do so would deprive a
party of an advantage in the foreign court which the Scots forum considers
legitimate. There is greater likelihood of the power being exercised in a case in
which the pursuer in the UK is also the pursuer abroad.[434] Further, if no choice of
forum is open to the claimant in that in only the foreign court is a remedy
available, the claimant remaining also amenable to the home court, the English
court has shown that it will hesitate before making an order to restrain the party:

---

[430] Where Aberdeen Sheriff Court was seised on art.5 grounds, the sheriff refused to accede to a plea
of *forum non conveniens*, considering himself to be bound by *Owusu* reasoning: *Oceanfix
International Ltd v AGIP Kazakhstan North Caspian Operating Co NV*, 2009 G.W.D. 17–266. See
also *Skype Technologies SA v Joltid Ltd* [2009] EWHC 2783 (Ch); *Equitas Ltd v Allstate Insurance
Co* [2009] Lloyd's Rep. I.R. 227; and *Jefferies International Ltd v Landesbanki Islands HF* [2009]
EWHC 894 (Comm).

[431] Or art.63: *889457 Alberta Inc v Katanga Mining Ltd* [2009] I.L.Pr. 14.

[432] *Young v Barclay* (1846) 8 D. 774; *Dawson's Trustees v Macleans* (1860) 22 D. 685; *Pan American
World Airways Inc v Andrews*, 1992 S.L.T. 268, per Lord Kirkwood at 271; *Shell UK Exploration &
Production Ltd v Innes*, 1995 S.L.T. 807; and *FMC Corp v Russell*, 1999 S.L.T. 99.

[433] Senior Courts Act 1981 s.37.

[434] In *Cohen v Rothfield* [1919] 1 K.B. 410 (where the test "vexatious or oppressive" is used)
Scrutton L.J. at 414 said: "It is not prima facie vexatious for the same plaintiff to commence two
actions relating to the same subject-matter, one in England and one abroad. The applicant must prove
a substantial case of vexation resulting from the identity of proceedings, remedies, and benefits, or
from the existence of some motive other than a bona fide desire to determine disputes." cf. *Insurance
Co of the State of Pennsylvania v Equitas Insurance Ltd* [2013] EWHC 3713 (Comm).

it would have to be shown that the defendant's being sued in the foreign forum would infringe a legal or equitable right of the defendant not to be sued.[435] An injunction will not be granted by a UK court if it has insufficient interest in, or connection with, the matter in question, such as would justify the interference, having been seised only on a quirk of jurisdiction.[436] Comity requires restraint.[437]

The modern interest arises principally in commercial matters.[438] In *SNIA v Lee Kui Jak*,[439] on appeal from Brunei, the Privy Council ordered a party to desist from her suit in Texas because Brunei was the natural forum and the defendants would be unfairly disadvantaged if prevented from presenting their defence in Brunei. The leading opinion was given by Lord Goff who said that the principles governing an order by the English court to restrain foreign proceedings were not the same as those which govern the decision whether or not to accede to a plea under *forum non conveniens*. The restraint, it was said, would be ordered only if the parallel double procedure were regarded as vexatious and oppressive,[440] a rigorous test, once applied,[441] but abandoned in English law in relation to *forum non conveniens*.

In an important judgment in *Deutsche Bank AG v Highland Crusader Offshore Partners LP*[442] Toulson L.J. reviewed the authorities and revisited the criteria upon which English judicial discretion ought to be exercised in the grant or withholding of anti-suit injunctions, producing eight "key principles" in relation to anti-suit injunctions. His Lordship's second and third guidelines are as follows:

> "(2) It is too narrow to say that such an injunction may be granted only on grounds of vexation or oppression, but, where a matter is justiciable in an English and a foreign court, the party seeking an anti-suit injunction must *generally*[443] show that

---

[435] *British Airways Board v Laker Airways Ltd* [1984] 3 All E.R. 39; *Midland Bank Plc v Laker Airways Ltd* [1986] 1 All E.R. 526; *South Carolina Insurance Co v Assurantie Maatschappij De Zeven Provincien NV* [1986] 3 All E.R. 487; *Societe Nationale Industrielle Aerospatiale (SNIA) v Lee Kui Jak* [1987] 3 All E.R. 510; *Channel Tunnel Group Ltd v Balfour Beatty Construction Ltd* [1993] A.C. 334; *Donohue v Armco Inc* [2002] 1 All E.R. 749; *Royal Bank of Canada v Cooperatieve Centrale Raiffeisen-Boerenleenbank BA* [2004] 1 Lloyd's Rep. 471; and *Morgan Stanley & Co International Plc v China Haisheng Juice Holdings Co Ltd* [2009] EWHC 2409 (Comm).

[436] *Airbus Industrie GIE v Patel* [1999] I.L.Pr. 238.

[437] *Star Reefers Pool Inc v JFC Group Co Ltd* [2012] EWCA Civ 14; and *Jewel Owner Ltd v Sagaan Developments Trading Ltd* [2012] EWHC 2850 (Comm).

[438] *Smith Kline & French Laboratories Ltd v Bloch* [1983] 2 All E.R. 72; *SNIA v Lee Kui Jak* [1987] 3 All E.R. 510; *El Du Pont de Nemours & Co v Agnew (No.2)* [1988] 2 Lloyd's Rep. 240 CA; *Sohio Supply Co v Gatoil (USA) Inc* [1989] 1 Lloyd's Rep. 588; *Société Commerciale de Reassurance v Eras International Ltd (No.2)* [1995] 2 All E.R. 278; *Airbus Industrie GIE v Patel* [1999] I.L.Pr. 238; and *Horn Linie GmbH & Co v Panamericana Formas e Impresos SA (The Hornbay)* [2006] EWHC 373 (Comm).

[439] *SNIA v Lee Kui Jak* [1987] 3 All E.R. 510.

[440] The English Court of Appeal in *Deutsche Bank AG v Highland Crusader Offshore Partners LP* [2009] EWCA Civ 725 held that there is no general presumption that where there is a non-exclusive jurisdiction clause, parallel proceedings in a different jurisdiction are to be regarded as vexatious or oppressive. Where non-exclusive jurisdiction has been agreed, parties must be taken to have accepted the possibility of parallel proceedings, and the grant of anti-suit injunction is a matter within the court's discretion.

[441] *St Pierre v South American Stores (Gath & Chaves) Ltd* [1936] 1 K.B. 382.

[442] *Deutsche Bank AG v Highland Crusader Offshore Partners LP* [2009] EWCA Civ 725 at [49] et seq.

[443] Emphasis added.

proceeding before the foreign court is or would be vexatious or oppressive. (3) The courts have refrained from attempting a comprehensive definition of vexation or oppression…".

Significantly, Toulson L.J. was of the view that: "(6) The prosecution of parallel proceedings in different jurisdictions is undesirable but not necessarily vexatious or oppressive."

In *Stichting Shell Pensioenfonds v Krys*[444] the Privy Council held that, on an application for an injunction to restrain foreign proceedings which were calculated to give a creditor prior access to any part of an insolvent estate, it was not necessary to show that the creditor had acted vexatiously or oppressively by invoking the jurisdiction of the foreign court; as with any injunction, the court had a discretion to refuse relief if in the particular circumstances it would not serve the ends of justice. *Per curiam*, it was stated that the true principle which applies to all injunctions, and not just anti-suit injunctions in the course of insolvency proceedings, is that English courts will not as a matter of discretion grant injunctions affecting matters outside their territorial jurisdiction if they are likely to be disregarded or would be *"brutum fulmen"*.

English courts "cheerfully" used the tool of the anti-suit injunction in order to hold parties to their choice of court bargain[445]: if a contracting party should renege on the choice of court agreement, such an injunction seemed to the UK courts to be the appropriate remedy, on the principle of *pacta sunt servanda*. However, the ECJ decisions in *Gasser* and *Turner v Grovit* reinforced the strict operation of the *lis pendens* system, and the unavailability within the Brussels regime of the anti-suit injunction.

Turner v Grovit[446]

Opportunity arose in *Turner v Grovit* for the ECJ to consider whether or not the   **7–84** use by one EU forum of an anti-suit injunction to seek to restrain a party from litigating in the court of another Member State was acceptable.

Turner, an English solicitor, was an employee of Harada Ltd, a company incorporated in Ireland and having its place of central management in England, and under the control of a group of companies of which Grovit was the director. The companies carried on the business of operating *bureaux de changes* in Spain. In 1997, Turner was sent to work in Madrid at the office of Changepoint SA, a Spanish company in the same group of companies as Harada. Turner remained employed by Harada Ltd, though Changepoint paid Harada for his services. Shortly after commencing work in Madrid, Turner resigned because he alleged his work involved collusion in illegal conduct (tax fraud). Having returned to England, Turner brought constructive unfair dismissal proceedings against Harada Ltd before an English employment tribunal (which considered that it had jurisdiction under arts 2, 5.1 and 5.5 of the 1968 Brussels Convention). In response, Grovit (in the name of Changepoint) sued Turner in Spain for substantial damages for "unjustified departure" and for professional misconduct.

---

[444] *Stichting Shell Pensioenfonds v Krys* [2014] UKPC 41; [2015] 2 W.L.R. 289.
[445] *Continental Bank NA v Aekos Compania Naviera SA* [1994] 1 W.L.R. 588.
[446] *Turner v Grovit* (C-159/02) [2005] 1 A.C. 101. See also *Research in Motion UK Ltd v Visto Corp* [2008] EWCA Civ 153.

On the basis that the litigation brought in Spain was vexatious and oppressive, the Court of Appeal, at the request of Turner, granted an anti-suit injunction against Grovit. Grovit appealed to the House of Lords, which, in turn, referred the matter to the ECJ for a preliminary ruling on the following question:

> "Is it inconsistent with the Convention on Jurisdiction and the Enforcement of Judgments in Civil and Commercial Matters signed at Brussels on 27 September 1968 (subsequently acceded to by the United Kingdom) to grant restraining orders against defendants who are threatening to commence or continue legal proceedings in another Convention country when those defendants are acting in bad faith with the intent and purpose of frustrating or obstructing proceedings properly before the English courts?"

The decision of the ECJ was that a prohibition issued by one Member State court upon the commencement or continuation of legal proceedings in another is tantamount to interference with the jurisdiction of the foreign court and, having regard to the 1968 Brussels Convention, incompatible with the principle of mutual trust between legal systems of Contracting States, and the general prohibition of review of the jurisdiction of the court of one Contracting State by the court of another.

Therefore the Brussels Convention, and by implication, its descendants, precludes the grant by a court in a Contracting/Member State of an injunction prohibiting a party to proceedings pending before it, from commencing or continuing proceedings before a court of another Contracting/Member State, even where that party is acting in bad faith.

This decision, like *Gasser*, provoked comment and criticism in the UK,[447] although its content was not unexpected, and the two decisions are coherent and consistent inter se.

Somewhat surprisingly, in view of the stern disapproval shown by the ECJ to the remedy of anti-suit injunction and its prohibition "within the Brussels regime", the English Court of Appeal in *Samengo-Turner v J&H Marsh & McLennan (Services) Ltd*[448] acceded to the request for the grant of an anti-suit injunction to require parties to desist from proceedings undertaken in New York, in order that the employee protection provisions contained in S.5 of the Brussels I Regulation (jurisdiction over individual contracts of employment) might be engaged. This action was alleged to be justified because it was thought the only way to give effect to the Brussels-endowed employee rights (over employees who were domiciled in England) was to seek to restrain the New York proceedings.

In *The Angelic Grace*,[449] the English Court of Appeal held that there was no difference in principle between restraining a party from commencing/continuing foreign proceedings in breach of an exclusive jurisdiction clause and doing likewise in respect of foreign proceedings raised in contravention of an arbitration clause: the restraint should be effected as promptly as possible and

---

[447] e.g. Hartley, "The European Union and the Systematic Dismantling of the Common Law of Conflict of Laws" (2005) 54 I.C.L.Q. 813.

[448] *Samengo-Turner v J&H Marsh & McLennan (Services) Ltd* [2007] EWCA Civ 723.

[449] *Aggeliki Charis Compania Maritima SA v Pagnan SpA (The Angelic Grace)* [1994] 1 Lloyd's Rep. 168.

without diffidence.[450] The unfolding of events has revealed, however, that just as there may be no difference in principle between these two instances, neither is there any difference in practice in the grant of such a remedy by the UK courts in support of an arbitration clause or in support of a choice of court clause; each is *verboten* "within the Brussels regime".[451]

The use of anti-suit injunctions to order parties to desist from pursuing proceedings in the courts of a non-Member State, that is to say geographically "outside the Brussels regime", in such a way as to flout an exclusive jurisdiction clause,[452] or an agreement to arbitrate, remains available,[453] and the English courts are not afraid to grant such injunctive relief.[454] The burden of proof is on the party in breach of an arbitration clause to show that there are strong reasons for not granting an anti-suit injunction.[455]

THE LITIGATION/MEDIATION INTERFACE[456]

Concept of mediation

Mediation is a process in which parties seek to resolve their dispute with the assistance of a mediator acting as an impartial third party. In general mediation is voluntary and aims to offer the disputing parties the opportunity to reach a consensual solution. It is one of several, non-adversarial methods of alternative dispute resolution utilised in the UK in a wide range of subject areas, including family law, consumer disputes, small claims, employment disputes, professional disputes, and construction. There is no primary legislative basis in the UK establishing or regulating mediation. In practice, mediation is a flexible process,

7–85

---

[450] *Through Transport Mutual Insurance Association (Eurasia) Ltd v New India Assurance Co Ltd (The Hari Bhum) (No.1)* [2004] 1 Lloyd's Rep. 206; [2005] 1 Lloyd's Rep. 67.

[451] *Transfield Shipping Inc v Chiping Xinfa Huayu Alumina Co Ltd* [2009] EWHC 3629 (QB); and *Midgulf International Ltd v Groupe Chimiche Tunisien* [2009] 2 Lloyd's Rep. 411. At the time of writing, two judgments are awaited from the CJEU concerning the status of arbitration and anti-suit injunctions: see Opinion of AG Wathelet delivered on 4 December 2014 re. *"Gazprom" OAO* (Case C-536/13) (Lithuanian request for a preliminary ruling; and *Cartel Damage Claims Hydrogen Peroxide SA (CDC) v Evonik Degussa GmbH* (Case C-352/13) [2013] O.J. C298/2 (German request for a preliminary ruling). The hope is that the Court will clarify the relationship between EU law and international arbitration.

[452] *Bank St Petersburg v Arkhangelsky* [2014] EWCA Civ 593; and *Caresse Navigation Ltd v Zurich Assurances MAROC* [2014] EWCA Civ 1366. See also *Royal Bank of Scotland Plc v Highland Financial Partners LP* [2013] EWCA Civ 328.

[453] *Shashoua v Sharma* [2009] EWHC 957 (Comm) (India), per Cooke J. at [717], [718].

[454] *AES Ust-Kamenogorsk Hydropower Plant LLP v Ust-Kamenogorsk Hydropower Plant JSC* [2013] UKSC 35; [2013] 1 W.L.R. 1889; *Joint Stock Asset Management Co Ingosstrakh-Investments v BNP Paribas SA* [2012] EWCA Civ 644; and *Sulamerica Cia Nacional de Seguros SA v Enesa Engenharia SA* [2012] EWCA Civ 638.

[455] *Ecom Agroindustrial Corp Ltd v Mosharaf Composite Textile Mill Ltd* [2013] EWHC 1276 (Comm), per Hamblen J at [19].

[456] For full treatment, see C. Esplugues, J. Iglesias and G. Palao (eds), *Civil and Commercial Mediation in Europe, Vol.1 – National Mediation Rules and Procedures* (Intersentia, 2013); in particular E.B. Crawford and J.M. Carruthers "UK National Report" at p.515; and C. Esplugues, J. Iglesias and G.Palao (eds), *Civil and Commercial Mediation in Europe, Vol.II – Cross-Border Mediation* (Intersentia, 2014); in particular E.B. Crawford and J.M. Carruthers "UK National Report" at p.461.

which can operate on an "out-of-court" basis, as a litigation-avoidance device, or as part of a court-annexed scheme. Party autonomy cannot override legal principles. Hence unless expressly permitted by domestic law, parties cannot violate, by means of contracting out, domestic law. Within an international private law context, parties cannot privately agree, e.g. to disapply the Rome I Regulation.[457] A court will not interpone its authority to a mediation settlement, the terms of which contravene the forum's public policy generally, or as expressed in its substantive private law, but the essence of mediation being consent, not all mediation resolutions will require to be judicially endorsed, and so questions of enforceability may not arise.

Cross-Border Mediation (EU Directive) Regulations 2011

7–86 The Cross-Border Mediation (EU Directive) Regulations 2011[458] came into force on 20 May 2011, and apply in respect of mediations relating to cross-border disputes, as defined, commencing on or after that date. They implement Directive 2008/52/EC of the European Parliament and of the Council of 21 May 2008 on certain aspects of mediation in civil and commercial matters.[459] Part 1 of the Mediation Regulations extends to the whole of the UK; Part 2 to England and Wales; and Pts 3 and 4 to the same extent as the provisions that they amend.[460] The Mediation Regulations were supplemented for Scotland by the Cross-Border Mediation (Scotland) Regulations 2011,[461] which came into force on 6 April 2011.

"Cross-border disputes"

7–87 There was concern in the UK to limit the territorial scope of application of Directive 2008/52/EC to disputes having cross-border implications. The definition of cross-border disputes, contained in art.2 of the Directive, has been adopted by the UK for the purposes of the Mediation Regulations,[462] i.e. only if a mediation satisfies the art.2 definition will a court in the UK apply to it the Mediation Regulations, and Scottish Regulations, as appropriate. Article 2(1) defines a cross-border dispute, for its purposes, as one in which at least one of the parties is domiciled[463] or habitually resident in a Member State other than that of any other party on the date on which:

(a)   the parties agree to use mediation after the dispute has arisen;
(b)   mediation is ordered by a court;
(c)   an obligation to use mediation arises under national law; or

---

[457] Regulation (EC) No. 593/2008 of the European Parliament and of the Council of 17 June 2008 on the law applicable to contractual obligations ("the Rome I Regulation").

[458] Cross-Border Mediation (EU Directive) Regulations 2011 (SI 2011/1133).

[459] Directive 2008/52/EC [2008] O.J. L136/3.

[460] See generally Explanatory Memorandum to the Cross-Border Mediation (EU Directive) Regulations 2011 (SI 2011/1133) ("Explanatory Memorandum").

[461] Cross-Border Mediation (Scotland) Regulations 2011 (SSI 2011/234).

[462] Cross-Border Mediation (EU Directive) Regulations 2011 (SI 2011/1133) reg.8(b); and Cross-Border Mediation (Scotland) Regulations 2011 (SSI 2011/234) reg.2.

[463] To be determined in accordance with arts 62 and 63 of Brussels I Recast.

(d)   for the purposes of art.5 (judicial invitation to the parties to have recourse to mediation), an invitation to go to mediation is made to the parties.

Further, art.2.2 provides that, for the purposes of arts 7 (confidentiality) and 8 (effect of mediation on limitation and prescription periods) of the Directive, a cross-border dispute also shall be one in which judicial proceedings or arbitration following mediation between the parties are/is initiated in a Member State other than that in which the parties were domiciled or habitually resident on the date on which the parties agreed to use mediation, or on which mediation is ordered by a court, or on which an obligation to use mediation arises under national law.

Implementation of Cross-Border Mediation (Scotland) Regulations 2011[464]

Of the specific provisions in the Directive, specific implementation of arts 7 and 8 was required in Scotland. Regulation 3 of the Mediation (Scotland) Regulations 2011 implements art.7 (confidentiality of mediation), by providing that a mediator or person involved in the administration of mediation in relation to a relevant cross-border dispute is not to be compelled in any civil proceedings or arbitration to give evidence, or produce anything, regarding any information arising out of or in connection with that mediation, except where all the parties to the mediation otherwise agree; or in the circumstances set out in art.7.1(a) or (b) of the Directive, namely, overriding public policy considerations; or where disclosure is necessary to implement the terms of the agreement. Regulations 4–9 of the Regulations implement art.8 of the Directive (effect of mediation on limitation and prescription periods), by amending prescription and limitation periods in primary legislation, most importantly in the Prescription and Limitation (Scotland) Act 1973, to ensure that if a prescription or limitation period would have expired while cross-border mediation is ongoing, or within 8 weeks after the mediation has ended,[465] that period will be extended until 8 weeks *after* the end of the mediation[466] and the parties' rights to go to court are not prejudiced.

7–88

Choice of law analysis

While it is relevant in a chapter on civil and commercial jurisdiction to consider the litigation/mediation interface, it is not appropriate to offer a comprehensive international private law analysis of mediation per se. It suffices to note that such an analysis must disentangle the various contracts which are identifiable in the course of the mediation process, viz.:

7–89

—   the agreement between the disputing parties to go to mediation, whether voluntary or court-directed;

---

[464] Cross-Border Mediation (Scotland) Regulations 2011 (SSI 2011/234).
[465] For these purposes, a mediation is taken to have ended on the first of several eventualities stated in reg.5 of the 2011 Regulations.
[466] Mediation (Scotland) Regulations 2011 reg.5.

— the agreement between the disputing parties (together, party A), the mediation services provider (party B), and the individual mediator (party C); essentially, by this agreement, A engages the services of B and, in turn, C, although where the mediator is a sole practitioner/small organisation, the contract is likely to be directly between A and C;

— if the mediation services are provided through the offices of a mediation services provider, there will be a contract between that mediation services provider and the individual mediator; and

— the mediation settlement; this may be bilateral between the disputing parties, or multilateral among parties A, B and C.

In Scots and English law, respectively, there is no corpus of conflict of laws rules dedicated to the agreement to employ the services of a mediator, nor to the regulation and enforcement of the agreement which constitutes the mediation settlement, and a court in the UK, therefore, would employ relevant conflict of laws rules from the law of contractual obligations.[467]

SUMMARY 7

7–90 1.   Allocation of jurisdiction.
There are four legislative regimes regulating the rules applicable in Scotland concerning civil and commercial jurisdiction, namely:

(a)   The Brussels regime, which comprises Brussels I Recast (building on the predecessor instruments, the 1968 Brussels Convention and the Brussels I Regulation) and the EC–Denmark Agreement, with auxiliary primary legislation in the UK in the form of the Civil Jurisdiction and Judgments Act 1982, as amended by secondary legislation;

(b)   The Lugano II Convention, with auxiliary primary legislation in the UK in the form of the Civil Jurisdiction and Judgments Acts 1982 and 1991;

(c)   Civil Jurisdiction and Judgments Act 1982 Sch.4: the Modified Convention, allocating jurisdiction within the UK; and

(d)   Civil Jurisdiction and Judgments Act 1982 Sch.8: the residual national, Scottish rules.

2.   Allocation of jurisdiction among EU Member States is governed by Brussels I Recast:

(a)   The main ground of jurisdiction is "domicile" of the defendant (art.4), which, for this purpose, for the UK, is defined in CJJO 2001 Sch.1 para.9 (amending CJJA 1982 s.41). In terms of personal jurisdiction, art.4 is the pre-eminent ground to which all others are derogations.

(b)   There are alternative "special" grounds of jurisdiction, most importantly in matters relating to contract and delict (art.7).

---

[467] For a full exposition of the principles, see E.B. Crawford and J.M. Carruthers "UK National Report" in C. Esplugues, J. Iglesias and G. Palao (eds), *Civil and Commercial Mediation in Europe, Vol.II – Cross-Border Mediation* (Intersentia, 2014), at pp.465 et seq.

(c)   There are protective jurisdictional rules for disadvantaged parties (arts.10–23) (insured parties, consumers and employees).

(d)   Article 24 contains rules conferring exclusive jurisdiction on a court of a Member State in specified cases, most importantly on the court of the *situs* in proceedings which have as their object rights *in rem* in immoveable property.

(e)   Article 25 permits prorogation of jurisdiction by parties.

(f)   Article 26 endows with jurisdiction the court of a Member State before which a party has entered appearance, provided appearance was not solely for the purpose of contesting the jurisdiction.

(g)   The *lis pendens* system of priority of process (arts 29–34) regulates problems of conflicting jurisdiction.

(h)   The hierarchy of provisions is as follows:
—   art.24 takes precedence over arts 25 and 26;
—   art.26 takes precedence over art.25.;
—   arts 10–23 take precedence over art.25, but are subordinate to art.26;
—   by art.31.2, the rule of *lis pendens* is subject to an exception, namely, where an agreement under art.25 confers exclusive jurisdiction on an EU Member State court, any court of another Member State shall stay its proceedings until such time as the court seised on the basis of the agreement declares that it has no jurisdiction.

3.   The Hague Conference in 2005 concluded the Convention on Choice of Court Agreements. The Convention was signed by the EU in 2009, and in December 2014, the Council of the EU adopted a decision on the approval, on behalf of the EU, of the 2005 Convention, thereby completing the internal EU approval process.

4.   Resolution of conflicts of jurisdiction occurring "outside the Brussels regime" are treated by Scots and English courts as a matter arising within judicial discretion, expressed in the acceding to, or refusing of, a plea by the defender of *forum non conveniens*.

5.   "Outside the Brussels regime", the Scots/English courts have power to order a party who is subject to Scots/English jurisdiction to desist from commencing or continuing proceedings abroad. This power is expressed by means of grant of an anti-suit injunction.

6.   The Cross-Border Mediation (EU Directive) Regulations 2011 came into force on 20 May 2011, and apply in respect of mediations relating to cross-border disputes commencing on or after that date. They implement Directive 2008/52/EC of the European Parliament and of the Council of 21 May 2008 on certain aspects of mediation in civil and commercial matters, and are supplemented in Scotland by the Cross-Border Mediation (Scotland) Regulations 2011.

CHAPTER 8

Evidence and procedure

INTRODUCTION

There is a crucial distinction in the conflict of laws between *substance* or *right* and *procedure* or *remedy*.[1] **8-01**

Substance is governed by the *lex causae*, the law which governs the right, such as the applicable law of the contract, or the applicable law in delict.

Procedure is governed by the *lex fori*. Foreign rules of procedure are ignored by Scots and English forums. The reason for this rule was explained in *De la Vega v Vianna*[2] by Lord Tenterden, who said that if a person comes to raise an action in England he must take the procedural law as he finds it; he cannot enjoy a procedural advantage over a native-born or resident litigant, nor should he be deprived of such advantages as normally are available. Further, it is feared that if a Scots or English forum should attempt to apply foreign procedural law, it may tear it out of context, misunderstand and misapply it. It would not be suitable to have litigations proceeding in Scotland according to a variety of legal systems' rules of evidence and procedure. Moreover, how "foreign" would a case have to be before application of foreign procedure seemed appropriate to apply? Hence, although a party sometimes may be able to choose the forum to his perceived best advantage, he is not entitled to choose the procedure which that forum will use to resolve the dispute.[3]

There is a danger that a forum may be too quick to categorise a foreign rule as procedural. This is one means of justifying disapplication of a rule of the *lex causae*, clearing the way for application of the *lex fori*. The wording of a foreign rule may be deceptive, and the forum must look to the true nature of the rule. The worst cases of rough justice may be eliminated by a careful delimitation of what is procedural.[4] Sometimes the UK Parliament has intervened to insist upon a characterisation as, for example, in the case of foreign limitation of action rules, where the English and Scots courts are directed to apply the prescription/limitation rule of the *lex causae* without attempting to classify its nature either by Scots law or by the foreign law.[5]

---

[1] See, famously, *Re Cohn* [1945] Ch. 5; and more recently, e.g. *Cox v Ergo Versicherung AG (formerly Victoria)* [2014] UKSC 22, per Lord Sumption at [12]. Also *Actavis Uk Ltd v Eli Lilly & Co.* [2015] EWCA Civ 555, per Floyd LJ obiter at [136]–[149].

[2] *De la Vega v Vianna* (1830) 1 B. & Ad. 284.

[3] Even though he may try to do so: *Hamlyn and Co v Talisker Distillery* (1894) 21 R. (H.L.) 21, per Lord Herschell L.C. at 24.

[4] Anton, *Private International Law*, 1st edn (1967), p.542.

[5] Para.8–07, below.

Frequently European Regulations, in particular the Rome I and Rome II Regulations,[6] contain provisions which impinge upon the substance/procedure distinction.[7] In each of these instruments, in terms of their subject-matter scope, it is provided that the Regulation shall not apply to evidence and procedure,[8] but as ever, there will be questions of definition and demarcation.[9]

MEANING OF "PROCEDURE"

8–02   There are few definitions of procedure. One which may serve is per Lush L.J. in *Poyser v Minors*,[10] as follows: "'Practice'...like 'procedure'...denotes the mode of proceeding by which a legal right is enforced, as distinguished from the law which gives or defines the right."[11] Lord Murray in *Naftalin v London Midland & Scottish Railway Co*[12] described procedure thus:

> "No doubt procedure is a term of somewhat indefinite connotation but in his [Dicey's] opinion the true view is that any rule of law which affects, not the enforcement of a right, but the nature of the right itself, does not come under the head of procedure; or, in other words, is not governed by the *lex fori*."

All are agreed upon the fundamental distinction between substance and procedure, but modern writers are sceptical of the possibility of making a definitive categorisation between matters of substance and matters of procedure.[13] Moore Bick L.J. in *Maher v Groupama Grand Est*[14] held that:

> "For the purposes of resolving problems in the conflicts of laws English law recognises a distinction between substantive rules of law, which are governed by the *lex causae*, and procedural rules, which are governed by the *lex fori*. Many claims are of a complex nature and depend on the resolution of more than one issue and the authorities clearly support the conclusion that English law characterises individual issues that arise for determination rather than seeking to characterise the claim as a whole."[15]

The term "procedure" is used in a wide sense to cover forms of action and remedies, including the laws of evidence, and diligence; of this one can be confident. However, subjects such as actionability, and title to sue, have a mixed quality, and with regard to other topics, for example, onus of proof and presumptions, opinions vary as to the proper categorisation.

---

[6] Paras 15–43 and 16–44, below.

[7] e.g. Rome I Regulation arts 12, 17, 18; and Rome II Regulation arts 15, 22.

[8] Rome I Regulation art.1.3; and Rome II Regulation art.1.3.

[9] e.g. *Wall v Mutuelle de Poitiers Assurances*[2014] EWCA Civ 138; [2014] 1 W.L.R. 4263.

[10] *Poyser v Minors* (1881) L.R. 7 Q.B.D. 329 at 333.

[11] See also per Lord Brougham in *Don v Lippmann* (1837) 5 Cl. & F. (HL) 13 at 13, 14.

[12] *Naftalin v London Midland & Scottish Railway Co*, 1933 S.L.T. 193 at 200.

[13] W.W. Cook, "Substance and Procedure in the Conflict of Laws" (1932–1933) 42 Yale L.J. 333; and J.M. Carruthers, "Substance and Procedure in the Conflict of Laws: A Continuing Debate in relation to Damages" (2004) 53 I.C.L.Q. 691, 694.

[14] *Maher v Groupama Grand Est* [2009] EWCA Civ 1191 at [8].

[15] Moore Bick L.J. cited *Macmillan Inc v Bishopsgate Investment Trust Plc (No.3)* [1996] 1 W.L.R. 387, per Auld L.J. at 407. See also per Floyd, LJ in *Actavis Uk Ltd v Eli Lilly & Co.* [2015] EWCA Civ 555 at [132].

MISCELLANEOUS MATTERS PERTAINING TO LITIGATION

In treating the subject of "evidence and procedure", a variety of topics will be considered, taking the subjects in the order in which they are encountered in the course of litigation.

8–03

Actionability

The question whether or not an action may be raised is determined by the *lex fori*. This can be seen, for example, from the Scottish and English prohibition upon suits for damages for breach of promise of marriage, no matter the identity and content of the law governing the promise.[16] This is a matter of policy of the forum, not procedure.

8–04

But the preliminary, procedural side of an issue soon may segue into the substantive: actionability in the broader sense of whether or not a cause of action arises between claimant and defender, becomes a substantive matter for decision by the *lex causae*, as identified by the choice of law rules of the forum, and proved to the forum. Thus, a rule of the foreign *lex causae* which prohibits inter-spousal litigation in principle will bar such a suit, even if the claim is actionable per the *lex fori*.

Form of action

This is purely a matter of procedure to be decided by the *lex fori*.[17]

8–05

Title to sue/parties

Title to sue and liability to be sued each contain elements both of the substantive and the procedural; the law governing the right indicates the party who has the right or title to sue and the party who should be called as defender.[18] It is necessary, of course, to comply with the procedural requirements of the *lex fori*; by the procedural law of the forum, certain bodies or persons may be immune from suit, or prohibited from suing.[19]

8–06

The forum's requirements on occasion may reflect anxieties about the difficulties likely to be encountered in the place of enforcement. Thus in *Brianchon v Occidental Petroleum (Caledonia) Ltd*,[20] it was thought prudent for the Court of Session to appoint a curator *ad litem* to represent the children of a victim of the Piper Alpha North Sea oil platform disaster in litigation in Scotland,

---

[16] Law Reform (Husband and Wife) (Scotland) Act 1984 s.1; and Law Reform (Miscellaneous Provisions) Act 1970 s.1 (England).

[17] *Hansen v Dixon* (1906) 23 T.L.R. 56; and *Phrantzes v Argenti* [1960] 2 Q.B. 19.

[18] cf. *FMC Corp v Russell*, 1999 S.L.T. 99; in respect of which see E.B. Crawford, "The Adjective and the Noun: Title and Right to Sue in International Private Law", 2000 Jur. Rev. 347. See also *Maher v Groupama Grand Est* [2009] EWCA Civ 1191, per curiam: a claimant who brings a direct action against a foreign insurer pursuant to Brussels I Recast art.13.2, is entitled to join the insured as an additional defendant to the same action, pursuant to art.1(3), where it is necessary to do so to avoid the risk of irreconcilable judgments (paras 21, 42, 43).

[19] See paras 7–03—7–06, above.

[20] *Brianchon v Occidental Petroleum (Caledonia) Ltd*, 1990 S.L.T. 322.

where the principal litigant was their mother, in order that no question of conflict of interest should be raised later in the American courts. On the other hand, restrictions imposed by the foreign law upon a party's capacity to sue may be disregarded in Scotland as being local (of application only in the foreign jurisdiction), or penal.[21]

Unusual situations may arise, as for example, in *Toprak Enerji Sanayi AS v Sale Tilney Technology Plc*,[22] in which the claimant foreign company ceased to exist during the course of the proceedings. In *Bumper Development Corp v Commissioner of Police of the Metropolis*,[23] the Court of Appeal recognised, in accordance with the principle of comity of nations, the title to sue of a Hindu temple which had legal personality under its *lex situs*. Novelty was no objection since the matter remained within the discretion and power of the forum.

Rules of prescription and limitation of actions

Prescription

8–07 From a conflict of laws standpoint, the important distinction is between those rules concerning the effect of lapse of time which extinguish the right (rules of prescription), and those which merely bar the remedy (rules of limitation).

An early illustration is provided by *Huber v Steiner*,[24] in which the English court interpreted the rule of the French *Code de Commerce* (that actions on promissory notes "prescribe themselves" after five years, reckoning from the day of protest if there had been no judgment or acknowledgment of the debt in that period), as no more than a limitation of the remedy and not an extinction of the contract, and therefore concluded that the enforceability of the French contract in England was governed by the limitation rule of the *lex fori*, the matter being characterised as one of remedy.

The common law rule has been altered by statutory intervention, in Scotland and in England and Wales,[25]respectively. In Scots domestic law, the rules on prescription were rationalised by the Prescription and Limitation (Scotland) Act 1973, as amended by the Prescription and Limitation (Scotland) Act 1984 s.4.[26] The choice of law rule contained in s.23A requires the Scots forum to apply, subject to public policy, any relevant rules upon extinction of obligations of the *lex causae*, in preference to domestic rules of the *lex fori*.

Section 23A of the 1984 Act in turn was amended to take account of the European harmonisation instruments in the law of obligations. Section 23A(4) provides that that section shall not apply in any case where the law of a country

---

[21] *Bernaben and Co v Hutchison* (1902) 18 Sh. Ct. Rep. 72.

[22] *Toprak Enerji Sanayi AS v Sale Tilney Technology Plc* [1994] 3 All E.R. 483. See also *Kamouh v Associated Electrical Industries International Ltd* [1980] Q.B. 199.

[23] *Bumper Development Corp v Commissioner of Police of the Metropolis* [1991] 4 All E.R. 638.

[24] *Huber v Steiner* (1835) 2 Bing. N.C. 202, Tindal C.J.; also [1835–42] All E.R. 159. See also *Westminster Bank v McDonald*, 1955 S.L.T. (Notes) 73; and *Rodriguez v Parker* [1967] 1 Q.B. 116.

[25] In England and Wales, the position rests on the Foreign Limitation Periods Act 1984. See, e.g. *OJSC Oil Co Yugraneft v Abramovich* [2008] EWHC 2613 (Comm); *Harley v Smith* [2010] EWCA Civ 78; and *Bank St Petersburg v Arkhangelsky* [2014] EWCA Civ 593. As to s.2(3) (exceptions to application of foreign law), see *Iraqi Civilian Litigation v Ministry of Defence* [2015] EWHC 116 (under appeal).

[26] Inserting into the 1973 Act s.23A.

other than Scotland falls to be applied by virtue of any choice of law rule contained in the Rome I (contractual obligations)[27] or Rome II (non-contractual obligations)[28] Regulations.[29] No change, however, is substantively effected because the relevant rules in the Rome I and Rome II Regulations[30] are to the effect that the rules of prescription and limitation of actions are subsumed under the scope of the law applicable per the Regulation, and governed therefore by the *lex causae*, subject, as at common law, to the public policy of the forum.[31]

Classification, therefore, in a conflict of laws case in the law of obligations is effected by the Rome I and Rome II Regulations, so as to place the matter into the substantive category. The 1973 Act for Scotland, unlike its English counterpart, the Foreign Limitation Periods Act 1984, is limited to "obligations" and does not include "property rights".[32] Clearly, the Rome I and Rome II Regulations concern contractual and non-contractual obligations. Equally clearly, the contractual and the proprietary may be commixed in any question. With regard to property questions, from a Scottish domestic perspective, the classification, so far as it continues to be relevant, appears to be as follows:

Positive prescription

This involves acquisition of title to, or interest in, property (usually land) and is a matter of substance governed by the *lex situs*.[33]

8–08

Negative prescription[34]

The long negative prescription extinguishes an obligation. Hence, it is a matter of substance and is governed by the proper law of the right. The 1973 Act replaced

8–09

---

[27] See also Law Applicable to Contractual Obligations (Scotland) Regulations 2009 (SSI 2009/410). For England, Foreign Limitation Periods Act 1984 s.8, modified by Law Applicable to Contractual Obligations (England and Wales and Northern Ireland) Regulations 2009 (SI 2009/3064).

[28] See also Law Applicable to Non-contractual Obligations (Scotland) Regulations 2008 (SSI 2008/404). For England, Foreign Limitation Periods Act 1984 s.8, added by Law Applicable to Non-Contractual Obligations (England and Wales and Northern Ireland) Regulations 2008 (SI 2008/2986).

[29] There has been discussion of European harmonisation of foreign limitation periods in EU Commission Consultation Paper on the Compensation of Victims of Cross-border Road Traffic Accidents in the European Union (MARKT/H2/RM markt.h.2 (2009) 61541). Views were sought on nine proposed options to address the fact that limitation periods vary among Member States. The UK Government favoured the status quo: UK Government Response to a Consultative Document issued by the European Commission dated 26 March 2009 (June 2009). See also European Commission Public Consultation on Limitation Periods for Compensation Claims of Victims of Cross-Border Road Traffic Accidents in the European Union (2012) (*http://ec.europa.eu/justice/newsroom/civil/opinion/121031_en.htm* [accessed 17 June 2015]).

[30] Rome I Regulation art.12.1(d); Rome II Regulation art.15(h).

[31] Rome I Regulation art.21; Rome II Regulation art.26.

[32] See J.M. Carruthers, *Transfer of Property in the Conflict of Laws* (2005), para.8.55; and D.M. Walker, *The Law of Prescription and Limitation of Actions in Scotland*, 6th edn (Edinburgh: W. Green, 2002).

[33] Carruthers, *Transfer of Property in the Conflict of Laws* (2005), paras 8.52–8.66.

[34] *Alexander v Badenoch* (1843) 6 D. 322; *Low v Low* (1893) 1 S.L.T. 43; *Re Low* [1894] 1 Ch. 147; *Higgins v Ewing's Trustees*, 1925 S.C. 440; and *Stirling's Trustees v Legal & General Assurance Society Ltd*, 1957 S.L.T. 73.

a variety of earlier short prescriptions with a short negative prescription which, being substantive in nature, applies where the *lex causae* is Scots.

Limitation

8–10   At common law, the nature of the limitation had to be ascertained by the forum by referring to the (foreign) statute or rule in question to find out whether it affected the substance (and therefore the existence of the right) no matter where a party might seek to vindicate it, or whether it was merely a rule of procedure, effective only within the territory covered by the statute in question.[35] However, as noted, since the coming into effect of the Prescription and Limitation (Scotland) Act 1984, the matter has been governed by statute, as amended, and assigned to the category of the substantive, insofar at least as concerns obligations.

Citation and service of writs

Service of documents within the EU

8–11   Service of documents within the EU is governed by Regulation 1393/2007 on the service in the Member States of judicial and extrajudicial[36] documents in civil or commercial matters (service of documents), and repealing Regulation 1348/2000.[37] The aim of Regulation 1348/2000 was to improve efficiency and speed in the transmission of such documents, in order to aid the proper functioning of the internal market. Following a study upon implementation of that instrument,[38] the European Commission adopted a Report on the application thereof,[39] concluding that while Regulation 1348/2000 generally had improved the transmission and service of documents between Member States, the application of certain provisions was not fully satisfactory.[40] Following consultation, a revised proposal was issued, and the resulting instrument is Regulation 1393/2007, applicable

---

[35] *Huber v Steiner* (1835) 2 Bing. N.C. 202; *British Linen Co v Drummond* (1830) 10 B.C. 903; *Don v Lippmann* (1837) 2 Sh. & Macl. 682; *Harris v Quine* (1869) L.R. 4 Q.B. 653; *Goodman v LNWR* (1877) 15 S.L.R. 449; *McElroy v McAllister*, 1949 S.C. 110.

[36] In respect of the meaning of "extrajudicial document", see *Roda Golf & Beach Resort SL* (Case C-14/08) [2008] O.J. C92, in which the ECJ clarified that the concept of 'extrajudicial document' within the meaning of art.16 of Regulation 1348/2000 (which is the same as art.6 of the 2007 Regulation) is a Union concept which should be interpreted autonomously. The service of a notarial act, in the absence of legal proceedings, was held to fall within the scope of the Regulation.

[37] In accordance with art.3.2 of EC-Denmark Agreement, Denmark, by letter of 20 November 2007, notified the Commission of its decision to implement Regulation 1393/2007. In accordance with art.3.6 of the Agreement, the Danish notification creates mutual obligations between Denmark and the EC. Regulation 1393/2007 is considered to be annexed to the EC-Denmark Agreement [2008] O.J. L331/21. See, subsequently, Council Decision of 30 November 2009 (2009/943/EC) amending Decision 2006/326/EC to provide for a procedure for the implementation of art.5(2) of the Agreement between the European Community and the Kingdom of Denmark on the service of judicial and extrajudicial documents in civil or commercial matters.

[38] Study on Application of Council Regulation (EC) No.1348/2000 (FINAL REPORT – 1348 – B5 – 03052204, May 2004).

[39] Report on the application of Regulation 1348/2000 on the service in the Member States of judicial and extrajudicial documents in civil or commercial matters (COM(2004) 603 final).

[40] Regulation 1393/2007 recital (5).

from 13 November 2008. The Regulation takes precedence over the 1965 Hague Convention on the Service Abroad of Judicial and Extra-Judicial Documents in Civil and Commercial Matters, to which the UK is a party.[41]

In terms of Regulation 1393/2007, the transmission of documents is effected directly between "local bodies" (termed the transmitting and receiving agencies), rather than through the medium of "central bodies", as provided in the 1965 Convention. While in Scotland the central body is the Constitution, Law and Courts Directorate of the EU and International Law Branch of the Scottish Government, the transmitting agencies (i.e. local bodies) are the messengers-at-arms.[42] The central body shall supply information and assist the transmitting agencies.

The document to be transmitted must have appended to it a form completed in the language of the Member State addressed, or in another language indicated by that Member State to be acceptable.[43] The use of all appropriate means of transmission is permitted,[44] provided that the content of the document received is true and faithful to that of the document forwarded, and that all information in it is legible. The receiving agency will serve, or have served, the document in accordance with the law of the Member State addressed, or by a particular form requested by the transmitting agency, unless such a method is incompatible with the law of that Member State.[45] The receiving agency shall take all necessary steps to effect the service of the document as soon as possible, and in any event within one month of receipt.[46] The receiving agency must inform the addressee that s/he may refuse to accept the document if it is in a language other than the official language of the Member State addressed, or a language of the transmitting state which the addressee understands.[47] When service has been effected, a certificate of completion will be sent to the transmitting agency.[48] If it does not prove possible to effect service within one month of receipt, the receiving agency shall inform the transmitting agency by means of a standard form certificate.[49]

The date of service shall be the date on which it is served in accordance with the law of the Member State addressed.[50] However, where a document must be served within a particular period the date to be taken into account with respect to the applicant shall be that fixed by the law of that Member State.[51]

---

[41] Recital (23) and art.20.

[42] Information communicated by Member States under art.23 of Regulation (EC) No.1393/2007 of the European Parliament and of the Council of 13 November 2007 on the service in the Member States of judicial and extrajudicial documents in civil or commercial matters (service of documents), and repealing Council Regulation (EC) No.1348/2000 (*http:ec.europa.eu/justice_home/ judicialatlascivil/html/pdf/vers_consolide_en_1393.pdf* [accessed 21 April 2015]).

[43] Regulation 1393/2007 art.4.3.

[44] Regulation 1393/2007 art.4.2.

[45] Regulation 1393/2007 art.7.1.

[46] Regulation 1393/2007 art.7.2.

[47] Regulation 1393/2007 arts 5 and 8; e.g. *Ingenieurburo Michael Weiss und Partner GbR v Industrie- und Handelskammer Berlin* (C-14/07) [2008] E.C.R. I-3367; [2009] I.L.Pr. 24; *Re Contractual Claims for Damages* [2015] I.L.Pr. 6; and *Agco (Societe) v Airmeex (Societe)* Cour de Cassation (France) [2013] I.L.Pr. 14.

[48] Regulation 1393/2007 art.10.

[49] Regulation 1393/2007 art.7.2(a).

[50] Regulation 1393/2007 srt.9.1; e.g. *C v A*(*Cour de Cassation*, Luxembourg) [2015] I.L.Pr. 4.

[51] Regulation 1393/2007 art.9.2.

Other means of service remain competent: by consular or diplomatic channels,[52] post,[53] or direct service through the judicial officers, officials or other competent persons of the Member State addressed.[54]

Where a writ of summons has been transmitted under the provisions of the Regulation, and the defendant has not appeared, judgment shall not be given until it is established that the document was served by a method prescribed by the internal law of the Member State addressed for the service of documents in domestic actions upon persons within its territory; or the document was actually delivered to the defendant, or to his residence, by another method provided for by the Regulation; and that in either case, service or delivery was effected in sufficient time to enable the defendant to defend.[55] However, each Member State shall be free to make it known to the Commission that the judge, notwithstanding art.19.1, may give judgment, even if no certificate of service or delivery has been received, if three conditions have been fulfilled, namely: (a) the document was transmitted by one of the methods provided for in the Regulation; (b) a period of not less than six months, considered adequate by the judge in the particular case, has elapsed since the date of the transmission; and (c) no certificate of any kind has been received, even though every reasonable effort has been made to obtain it through the competent authorities of the Member State addressed.[56]

Extrajudicial documents may be transmitted for service in another Member State in accordance with the Regulation.[57]

Proposed reform

8–12 In December 2013, pursuant to art.24 of Regulation 1393/2007, there was issued a Report from the Commission to the European Parliament, the Council and the European Economic and Social Committee on the application of that regulation.[58] The Report is to the effect that the Regulation has been applied satisfactorily by Member State authorities, but "the increasing judicial integration of Member States has brought to light the limits of the current text of the Regulation. In the light of the role of the Regulation in the entire framework of judicial cooperation

---

[52] Regulation 1393/2007 arts 12 and 13.

[53] Regulation 1393/2007 art.14. The Regulation does not establish any hierarchy between the method of transmission and service under arts 4–11 and that in art.14. It is therefore possible to serve a judicial document by one or other or both of those methods: *Plumex v Young Sports NV* (C473/04) [2006] E.C.R. I-1417 ECJ. See also *Caisse Regionale de Credit Agricole Mutuel du Languedoc v X(Cour de Cassation,* France) [2015] I.L.Pr. 17.

[54] Regulation 1393/2007 art.15.

[55] Regulation 1393/2007 art.19.1.

[56] Regulation 1393/2007 art.19.2. See also art.19.4 concerning expiry of time for appeal after non-appearance by the defendant. Consider also the inter-relationship between the detail of Regulation 1393/2007, and the Brussels I Recast art.45.1(b) (defence to enforcement on grounds of natural justice).

[57] Regulation 1393/2007 art.16.

[58] COM(2013) 858 final (Brussels, 4 December 2013). For background analysis, see MainStrat, "Study on the application on the application of Regulation (EC) No 1393/2007 on the service of judicial and extrajudicial documents in civil and commercial matters: final report" (1393_v150) (July 2012).

in civil justice matters, particularly in the light of the abolition of *exequatur* a deeper integration within the Union, for instance by way of minimum standards on service, may be considered."[59]

Significantly, the Report notes that the rules of Member States differ substantially on fundamental points such as which documents are served on the parties in proceedings; in which circumstances documents are served; by whom documents are served; on whom documents are served; and the legal consequences attached to service, e.g. commencement of limitation periods.[60] These differences, coupled with the abolition of *exequatur* in Brussels I Recast, indicate that there may be a need for better protection of foreign defendants, to be achieved, in the view of the European Commission, by further harmonisation concerning national civil procedural rules, in general, and concerning rules on service of documents, in particular.[61]

Service of documents outside the EU

As regards service of documents in non-EU states, citation "furth of Scotland" is governed by the Rules of Court,[62] assuming that the method of service does not contravene the local law or contradict the 1965 Hague Convention, where applicable.

8–13

Security for expenses

A foreign pursuer may be called upon to "sist a mandatory" as security for expenses. The function of a mandatory, appointed by the foreign party on the instruction of the court, is to perform any order of the court made during the litigation, and to be personally liable for the expenses of the action. The matter is within the discretion of the court.[63] Alternatively, provision of caution (security) may be ordered. A balance must be kept between taking reasonable precautions to ensure that any decree pronounced against a foreign party can be satisfied, and avoiding the imposition of unreasonably onerous conditions not applicable to native litigants. Where there is no reason to doubt the financial standing of the foreign parties, caution will not be required.[64] The imposition of a requirement to

8–14

---

[59] COM(2013) 858 final (Brussels, 4 December 2013) para.5.
[60] COM(2013) 858 final (Brussels, 4 December 2013) para.3.1.4.
[61] COM(2013) 858 final (Brussels, 4 December 2013).
[62] Act of Sederunt (Rules of the Court of Session 1994) 1994 (SI 1994/1443) r.16.2 (service furth of UK) and r.16.2A (service under the EC Service Regulation). For rules concerning service, intimation and diligence generally, see RCS Ch.16. For sheriff court actions, see Act of Sederunt (Sheriff Court Ordinary Cause Rules) 1993 (SI 1993/1956) r.5.5 (service on persons furth of Scotland), as amended.
[63] *Renfrew and Brown v Magistrates of Glasgow* (1861) 23 D. 1003; *Gunn and Co v Couper* (1871) 10 M. 116; *NV Ondix International v Landay Ltd*, 1963 S.L.T. (Notes) 68; *Masinimport v Scottish Medical Light Industries Ltd*, 1972 S.L.T. (Notes) 76; *Re Little Olympian Each Ways Ltd (No.2)* [1994] 4 All E.R. 561, per Lindsay J. at 576; and *Rossmeier v Mounthooly Transport*, 2000 S.L.T. 208.
[64] *Kaiser Bautechnik GmbH v GA Group Ltd*, 1993 S.L.T. 826; and *Medicopharma (UK) BV v Cairns*, 1993 S.L.T. 386.

sist a mandatory, or to order security or caution,[65] may be unjustified in terms of the Brussels jurisdiction and judgments regime.[66]

PROVISIONAL AND PROTECTIVE MEASURES

8–15   The purpose of such rules and remedies in any legal system is, first, to preserve evidence for the litigation and, secondly, to preserve the defender's assets for satisfaction of the claim and expenses.

Preservation of evidence

8–16   Evidence may be obtained under authority of a commission and diligence authorised by the Scots court at common law. Further, the Administration of Justice (Scotland) Act 1972 s.1,[67] permits the Scots court in its discretion to order commission and diligence[68] for the inspection, photographing, etc. and custody of documents or other property, including land, which appear to the court to be property in respect of which a question may arise in civil proceedings. This is the process of "recovery" in Scots law ("discovery" in English law).

The First Division of the Court of Session in *Iomega Corp v Myrica (UK) Ltd (No.2)*,[69] overruling *Dailey Petroleum Services Corp v Pioneer Oil Tools Ltd*,[70] permitted material so recovered to be used in foreign proceedings.[71] While the party recovering evidence was impliedly restricted in his use of the evidence to the proceedings in respect of which it had been recovered, the court had power to permit such evidence to be used in other proceedings in Scotland or elsewhere, provided it was satisfied that such use was in the interests of justice.[72]

By s.19 of the Law Reform (Miscellaneous Provisions) (Scotland) Act 1985, the court is empowered to order a party to disclose such information as he possesses as to the identity of possible witnesses or defenders.

---

[65] But see opinion of Lord Hamilton in *La Pantofola D'Oro SpA v Blane Leisure Ltd (No.2)* 2000 S.L.T. 1264 at 1269.

[66] *Rossmeier v Mounthooly Transport*, 2000 S.L.T. 208; *Nguyen v Searchnet Associates Ltd*, 2000 S.L.T. (Sh. Ct.) 83; *De Beer v Kanaar & Co (No.1)* [2003] 1 W.L.R. 38; and *Bell Electric Ltd v Aweco Appliance Systems GmbH & Co KG* [2003] 1 All E.R. 344.

[67] See, in cases of urgency, s.1(3), the "dawn raid": *British Phonographic Industry Ltd v Cohen*, 1983 S.L.T. 137 (application for such remedy granted ex parte where there is danger that the possessor is likely to remove or destroy the property); and *Ted Jacob Engineering Group Incorporated v Robert Matthew, Johnson-Marshall and Partners*, 2014 S.C. 579.

[68] *Union Carbide Corp v BP Chemicals Ltd*, 1995 S.L.T. 972. As to human rights challenge, see *Narden Services Ltd v Inverness Retail and Business Park Ltd*, 2006 S.L.T. 338.

[69] *Iomega Corp v Myrica (UK) Ltd (No.2)*,1999 S.L.T. 796.

[70] *Dailey Petroleum Services Corp v Pioneer Oil Tools Ltd*, 1994 S.L.T. 757.

[71] See extension of powers of Court of Session by Civil Jurisdiction and Judgments Act 1982 (Provisional and Protective Measures) (Scotland) Order 1997 (SI 1997/2780), as amended.

[72] *Iomega Corp v Myrica (UK) Ltd (No.2)*, 1999 S.L.T. 796, per Lord President Rodger at 804, admitting the lack of precedent.

Preservation of assets

By virtue of art.35 of Brussels I Recast,[73] application may be made to the court of **8–17** a Member State for such provisional, including protective, measures as may be available under that law, even if the court of another Member State has jurisdiction as to the substance of the matter.

In relation to art.31 of the Brussels I Regulation (the precursor to art.35 of Brussels I Recast), the ECJ in *Van Uden Maritime BV (t/a Van Uden Africa Line) v Kommanditgesellschaft in Firma Deco-Line*,[74] emphasised that authorisation of provisional measures under art.31 required to be founded upon a "real connection" between the subject-matter of the action in respect of which the measures are sought and the territorial jurisdiction of the requested forum. This principle presumably applies to art.35 of Brussels I Recast by reason of vertical continuity of interpretation, but also must be understood in the light of recital (33), which provides that where provisional, including protective, measures are ordered by a court having jurisdiction as to the substance of the matter, their free circulation should be ensured. However, provisional, including protective, measures which were ordered by such a court without the defendant being summoned to appear should not be recognised and enforced under the Regulation unless the judgment containing the measure is served on the defendant prior to enforcement. This should not preclude the recognition and enforcement of such measures under national law. But where the provisional, including protective, measures are ordered by a court of a Member State *not* having jurisdiction as to the substance of the matter, the effect of such measures should be confined to the territory of that Member State.

Article 31 of the Brussels I Regulation was taken to refer to such measures as might be available prior to judgment on the merits. Hence, not only does the Brussels system provide an effective procedure for enforcing judgments, it provides also a system of safeguarding the claimant's interests before and during litigation or arbitration.

By art.42.2 of Brussels I Recast, for the purposes of enforcement in a Member State of a judgment given in another Member State ordering a provisional, including a protective, measure, the applicant shall provide the competent enforcement authority with (a) a copy of the judgment which satisfies the conditions necessary to establish its authenticity; (b) any certificate issued pursuant to art.53, containing a description of the measure and certifying that (i) the court has jurisdiction as to the substance of the matter; (ii) the judgment is enforceable in the Member State of origin; and (c) where the measure was ordered without the defendant being summoned to appear, proof of service of the judgment.

---

[73] cf. art.31 of Brussels I Regulation, and art.31 of Lugano II. See, for England and Wales, CJJA 1982 s.25 (Interim relief in England and Wales and Northern Ireland in the absence of substantive proceedings); and, e.g. *Thomas Cook Tour Operations Ltd v Louis Hotels SA* [2013] EWHC 2469 (QB).

[74] *Van Uden Maritime BV (t/a Van Uden Africa Line) v Kommanditgesellschaft in Firma Deco-Line* (C-391/95) [1998] E.C.R. I-7091; [1999] Q.B. 1225. See also *Mietz v Intership Yachting Sneek BV* (C-99/96) [1999] I.L.Pr. 541; and *Cruz City 1 Mauritius Holdings v Unitech Ltd* [2014] EWHC 3704 (Comm).

As far as the UK is concerned, provisional and protective measures which may be offered by Scots and English law are as outlined below.[75]

Remedies afforded by Scots law

8–18 Scots law offers the remedies of attachment (in respect of corporeal moveable property which is in the possession of the debtor, rather than a third party),[76] land attachment and residual attachment[77]; inhibition[78] (which prevents a defender from disposing of, or burdening, his heritable property to the prejudice of the inhibitor); diligence on the dependence[79]; interdict (interim or permanent) granted, like the English injunction,[80] against reasonable apprehension of wrong; money attachment[81]; diligence against earnings[82]; arrestment in execution[83]; and arrestment (which attaches only assets held by a third party arrestee, such as a bank or financial institution).

By arrestment, a litigant may restrain the payment to his opponent of money or property, in the hands of a third party, due to the opponent.[84] Arrestment of the defender's property in the hands of a third party, to await the outcome of litigation, is a provisional security measure, frequently manifested in the attaching of a credit balance held by the defender at a bank, to the amount sought in the decree. There is a triangular relationship among arrester, arrestee and debtor. The arrestee (e.g. bank) must not permit operation on the account by the defender, and will be liable to the arrester should this occur.[85] While the debtor at the outset may be unaware that the creditor intends to effect, or has effected, arrestment on the dependence,[86] it is open to the debtor to apply to the court for recall of any arrestment made, on the ground that it is nimious and oppressive.[87] Arrestment on the dependence depends upon litigation having commenced.[88]

---

[75] cf. *Reichert v Dresdner Bank* [1992] E.C.R. I-2149 (measures "intended to preserve a factual or legal situation so as to safeguard rights").

[76] Debt Arrangement and Attachment (Scotland) Act 2002 Pt 2. On interim attachment, see Pt 1A.

[77] Bankruptcy and Diligence etc. (Scotland) Act 2007 ("2007 Act") Pt 4.

[78] 2007 Act Pt 5.

[79] 2007 Act Pt 6. See, previously, *Marie Brizard et Roger International SA v William Grant & Sons Ltd (No.1)*, 2001 G.W.D. 33–1302; and *China National Star Petroleum Co v Tor Drilling (UK) Ltd*, 2002 G.W.D. 12–348.

[80] See *G v Caledonian Newspapers Ltd*, 1995 S.L.T. 559, in which the Scots court was prepared to match an injunctive remedy granted by an English court in parallel proceedings.

[81] 2007 Act Pt 8.

[82] 2007 Act Pt 9.

[83] 2007 Act Pt 10.

[84] e.g. *Hydraload Research & Developments Ltd v Bone Connell & Baxters Ltd*, 1996 S.L.T. 219; *Dramgate Ltd v Tyne Dock Engineering Ltd*, 1999 S.L.T. 1392; and *China National Star Petroleum Co v Tor Drilling (UK) Ltd*, 2002 S.L.T. 1339; cf. in English law the making of a third party debt order (ex-garnishee order): Cheshire, North and Fawcett: *Private International Law*, 14th edn (2008), pp.1238–1240.

[85] cf. duty of care owed by a bank in terms of an English freezing order: *Customs and Excise Commissioners v Barclays Bank Plc* [2004] EWCA Civ 1555.

[86] i.e. a court order granting (until a final court decision) a temporary security over goods, or funds, e.g. in a bank account, held on behalf of the defender by a third party.

[87] *Fab Tek Engineering Ltd v Carillion Construction Ltd*, 2002 S.L.T. (Sh. Ct.) 113.

[88] *Oceaneering International AG, Petitioners*, 2011 S.L.T. 667; *Fish & Fish Ltd v Sea Shepherd UK*, 2012 S.L.T. 156; and *Prosper Properties Ltd and Inkersall Investments Ltd v Scottish Ministers (No.3)*, 2014 S.C. 25.

Dramgate Ltd v Tyne Dock Engineering Ltd[89] demonstrates that, in a conflict of laws case, the provisional safeguard of arrestment on the dependence cannot be sought or granted unless and until the jurisdiction of the Scots court over the defender is properly founded. The safeguard sought was premature and contained an inherent vice. Absence of malice made no difference. Diligence is strict law; formalities must be observed.[90]

Remedies afforded by English law

English remedies of freezing orders (formerly "Mareva injunctions")[91] and search warrants (formerly "Anton Piller orders"),[92] exist respectively to prevent dissipation or removal of a defendant's assets,[93] i.e. to preserve them in order to satisfy the anticipated judgment and expenses; and to permit inspection of premises to discover documents relevant to the forthcoming litigation.

8–19

There must be shown to the court to be a risk of dissipation before a defendant will be ordered not to remove his assets from the jurisdiction.[94] An upper limit is set on the value of the assets frozen. The claimant normally must give an undertaking to compensate any third party who suffers damage as a result of the injunction, but where a third party holding the defendant's property, and having notice of the injunction,[95] knowingly aids and abets the defendant to breach the injunction, he is guilty of contempt of court. The claimant may be required to guarantee that he will not seek to litigate abroad with regard to the defendant's assets without the court's permission, i.e. the English court may seek to control the proliferation of foreign proceedings by the terms in which it grants its order.[96]

The freezing injunction as a remedy has proceeded apace, in an attempt to keep abreast of defendant ingenuity and electronic advances.[97] It has developed significantly from its starting point as an injunction preventing the defendant from disposing of his assets wherever situated, granted in the discretion of the English forum in a case where, in its view, the remedy was merited, and where

---

[89] *Dramgate Ltd v Tyne Dock Engineering Ltd*, 1999 S.L.T. 1392.

[90] *Anglo-Dutch Petroleum International Inc v Ramco Energy Plc*, 2006 S.L.T. 334.

[91] *Mareva Compania Naviera SA v International Bulk Carriers SA (The Mareva)* [1975] 2 Lloyd's Rep. 509. Also *Z Ltd v A-Z* [1982] 1 All E.R. 556; *Babanaft International Co SA v Bassatne* [1989] 2 W.L.R. 232; *Rosseel NV v Oriental Commercial & Shipping Co (UK) Ltd* [1990] 1 W.L.R. 1387; *S&T Bautrading v Nordling* [1997] 3 All E.R. 718; *Maimann v Maimann* [2001] I.L.Pr. 27; *Bank of China v NBM LLC* [2002] 1 All E.R. 717; and *Lakatamia Shipping Co Ltd v Su* [2014] EWCA Civ 636.

[92] *Anton Piller KG v Manufacturing Processes Ltd* [1976] Ch. 55; *Haiti v Duvalier (No.2)* [1989] 1 All E.R. 456; *Derby & Co Ltd v Weldon (No.1)* [1989] 1 All E.R. 469; *Balkanbank v Taher (No.2)* [1995] 2 All E.R. 904; *Camdex International Ltd v Bank of Zambia (No.2)* [1997] 1 All E.R. 728; and *A/S D/S Svenborg v Wansa* [1997] 1 C.L. 122.

[93] *JSC BTA Bank v Ablyazov* [2013] EWCA Civ 928 (under appeal).

[94] *Congentra AG v Sixteen Thirteen Marine SA (The Nicholas M)* [2008] 2 Lloyd's Rep. 602.

[95] See the safeguard known as the "Babanaft proviso" to identify and guide third parties: *Babanaft International SA v Bassatne* [1988] 2 Lloyd's Rep. 435. Also *Derby & Co Ltd v Weldon (Nos 3 and 4)* [1990] Ch. 65, per Lord Donaldson at 84; and *Bank of China v NBM LLC* [2002] 1 W.L.R. 844.

[96] *Dadourian Group International Inc v Simms* [2006] 1 W.L.R. 2499.

[97] See *Derby & Co Ltd v Weldon (Nos 3 and 4)* [1989] 2 W.L.R. 412, per Lord Donaldson at 420: "We live in a time of rapidly growing commercial and financial sophistication and it behoves the courts to adapt their practices to meet the current wiles of those defendants who are prepared to devote as much energy to making themselves immune to the courts' orders as to resisting the making of such orders on the merits of their case." See also *El-Ajou v Dollar Land Holdings Plc (No.1)* [1994] 2 All E.R. 685; and *Eliades v Lewis (No.9)* [2005] EWHC 2966.

the principal litigation was to take place in England. It was extended to include cases where, if the litigation was to take place abroad, the matter was justiciable in England. The point has been reached where the English court has power to make such an order in support of foreign arbitral[98] or judicial[99] proceedings, where the defendant is personally subject, on some ground, to the jurisdiction of the English court, even though the issue is not justiciable in England.[100] The jurisdiction *in personam* is the justification for this extraordinarily powerful remedy; an element of controversy may arise where the connection of the defendant with the English jurisdiction is tenuous.[101] The English court may grant an injunction restraining a party from leaving the country pending proceedings.[102]

Metaphors of war often are employed in this branch of the subject. While the use of negative declarations within the Brussels regime has been compared to the use of a torpedo, the English remedy of granting a worldwide freezing injunction has been termed the nuclear weapon in the litigation armoury. The injunction is a powerful remedy, and the English court will not always grant it.[103] The remedy will not be granted unless litigation is in active contemplation. A wrongly obtained freezing order may be discharged on appeal.[104]

European account preservation order

8–20   Regulation (EU) No.655/2014 of the European Parliament and of the Council of 15 May 2014 establishing a European Account Preservation Order procedure to facilitate cross-border debt recovery in civil and commercial matters[105] entered into force on 18 July 2014 and will apply from 18 January 2017.[106] It aims to help creditors by preserving funds, and assisting in the recovery of bad debts.

Recital (50) narrates that the UK has not taken part in the adoption of the Regulation and is not bound by it or subject to its application. As with Rome IV,[107] in respect of which the UK exercised its right under Protocol No.21 to the

---

[98] Arbitration Act 1996 s.2; *ETI Euro Telecom International NV v Bolivia* [2008] EWCA Civ 880; and *Mobile Telesystems Finance SA v Nomihold Securities Inc* [2011] EWCA Civ 1040.

[99] Brussels I Recast art.35, in combination with CJJA 1982 s.25 (interim relief in England and Wales and Northern Ireland in the absence of substantive proceedings): *United States Securities & Exchange Commission v Manterfield* [2009] EWCA Civ 27. See also s.24 (interim relief and protective measures in cases of doubtful jurisdiction).

[100] *Credit Suisse Fides Trust SA v Cuoghi* [1997] 3 All E.R. 724; departing from the decision in *Owners of the Cargo Lately Laid on Board the Siskina v Distos Compania Naviera SA* [1979] A.C. 210 which had been followed in *Mercedes-Benz AG v Leiduck* [1995] 3 All E.R. 929. See also *Channel Tunnel Group Ltd v Balfour Beatty Construction Ltd* [1993] A.C. 334; and *Haiti v Duvalier (No.2)* [1989] 1 All E.R. 456.

[101] *Haiti v Duvalier (No.2)* [1989] 1 All E.R. 456; *Motorola Credit Corp v Uzan (No.6)* [2004] 1 W.L.R. 113.

[102] *Morris v Murjani* [1996] 2 All E.R. 384; and *B v B (Injunction: Restraint on leaving Jurisdiction)* [1997] 3 All E.R. 258 (consistorial).

[103] *Mobil Cerro Negro Ltd v Petroleos de Venezuela SA* [2008] EWHC 532.

[104] *Fourie v Le Roux* [2007] 1 W.L.R. 320; and *IOT Engineering Projects Ltd v Dangote Fertilizer Ltd* [2014] EWCA Civ 1348.

[105] Regulation (EU) No.655/2014 of the European Parliament and of the Council of 15 May 2014 establishing a European Account Preservation Order procedure to facilitate cross-border debt recovery in civil and commercial matters [2014] O.J. L189/59.

[106] Regulation (EU) No.655/2014 art.54.

[107] Para.18–42.

TEU and to the TFEU, to refrain from opting in,[108] it would be wrong to assume that Regulation 655/2014 has no implications for UK-based individuals. The ways in which UK creditors and debtors may be affected will be examined below.[109] Denmark, by dint of its entitlement under Protocol No.22 to the TEU and to the TFEU,[110] is not taking part in the adoption of the Regulation and is not bound by it or subject to its application. Ireland, unlike the UK, has notified its wish to take part in the adoption and application of the Regulation.[111]

The purpose and provisions of Regulation 655/2014

The underlying purpose of the Regulation is to enable a creditor to obtain a protective European (as opposed to national) measure in the form of a European Account Preservation Order ("EAPO"), preventing the transfer or withdrawal of funds held by his debtor in a bank account[112] maintained in a Member State, if there is a risk that, without such a measure, the subsequent enforcement of his claim against the debtor will be impeded or made substantially more difficult. While the EAPO is described as being available to a creditor as an alternative to preservation measures under national law,[113] recital (6) explains that the procedure established by Regulation 655/2014 is intended to serve, in fact, as an additional and optional means for the creditor, who remains free to make use of any other procedure for obtaining an equivalent measure under national law. The preservation of funds will have the effect of freezing the account, and preventing its operation not only by the debtor, but also by persons authorised by him to make payments through that account, by way of standing order, direct debit or the use of a credit card.[114]

8–21

The Regulation does not apply to the preservation of accounts maintained in the Member State of the court seized of the application for the preservation order if the creditor's domicile is also in that Member State.[115] It is apparent therefore that the instrument shall apply only to cross-border cases,[116] which are defined as cases in which the bank account to be preserved is maintained in a Member State other than the Member State of the court seised of the application for the EAPO pursuant to art.6; or the Member State in which the creditor is domiciled.

The EAPO is intended to operate flexibly in terms of its availability: a creditor may seek a preservation order, per art.5, before initiating proceedings in a Member State against the debtor on the substance of the matter; at any stage during such proceedings until the issuing of the judgment; or after obtaining a Member State judgment, which requires the debtor to pay the creditor's claim.[117]

---

[108] Para.1–08.

[109] Para.18–42 et seq.

[110] Para.1–08.

[111] Regulation 655/2014 recital (49).

[112] Defined in art.4.1 as any account containing funds which is held with a bank in the name of the debtor or in the name of a third party on behalf of the debtor. It is arguable that this could extend to funds held by a solicitor on behalf of a client in the firm's client account.

[113] Regulation 655/2014 art.1(2).

[114] Regulation 655/2014 recital (7) and art.1.

[115] Regulation 655/2014 recital (10).

[116] Regulation 655/2014 art.3.

[117] Regulation 655/2014 recitals (11) and (12).

In terms of art.6, jurisdiction to issue a preservation order shall lie with the courts of the Member State which have jurisdiction to rule on the substance of the matter in accordance with the relevant rules of jurisdiction applicable. However, where the debtor is a consumer, jurisdiction is restricted to the courts of the Member State of the consumer-debtor's domicile. In circumstances where the creditor has already obtained a judgment, jurisdiction to issue an EAPO for the claim specified therein shall lie with the courts of the Member State in which the judgment was issued.

In order to procure an EAPO, the creditor must satisfy the court that there is an urgent need for the order in light of the real risk that, without it, the subsequent enforcement of his claim against the debtor will be "impeded or made substantially more difficult",[118] e.g. because of a real risk that, by the time the creditor is able to have the existing/future judgment enforced, the debtor may have dissipated, concealed or destroyed his assets or have disposed of them under value.[119] In cases where the order is sought in advance of judgment, the creditor must satisfy the court also that he is likely to succeed on the substance of his claim against the debtor.[120]

An EAPO is to be obtained ex parte; the debtor shall not be notified of the application for a preservation order or be heard prior to the issuing of the Order.[121] The court seised of the application, having examined whether the decisions and requirements have been fulfilled, shall decide on the application without delay.[122]

In view of the potentially punitive effects of the EAPO, and in light of its being granted ex parte, and to guard against abuse, it is important that there are certain safeguards to protect the debtor's rights.[123] Article 12.1 provides for security to be provided by a creditor who has not yet obtained judgment, to ensure compensation is available for any damage suffered by the debtor as a result of the EAPO. Where the creditor has already obtained a judgment, the court may require that the creditor provide security if it considers this necessary and appropriate in the circumstances of the case.[124] Secondly, to protect the debtor, art.13 provides that the creditor shall be liable for any damage caused to the debtor by the EAPO due to fault on the creditor's part.[125] The burden of proof shall lie with the debtor, except in prescribed cases.[126]

Article 14 empowers a creditor who has obtained in a Member State an enforceable judgment,[127] and who has experienced practical difficulties in obtaining information about the whereabouts in a specific Member State of the debtor's account(s), to ask the court with which the application is lodged to

---

[118] Regulation 655/2014 art.7.1.
[119] Regulation 655/2014 recital (14).
[120] Regulation 655/2014 art.7.2.
[121] Regulation 655/2014 art.11 and recital (15).
[122] Regulation 655/2014 art.17.
[123] Regulation 655/2014 recital (17).
[124] Regulation 655/2014 art.12.2 and recital (18).
[125] Regulation 655/2014 recital (19).
[126] Regulation 655/2014 art.13.2.
[127] See also recital (20).

request that the information authority[128] of the Member State of enforcement obtain the information necessary to allow the bank or banks and the debtor's account or accounts to be identified.

By reason of its status as a holistic European rather than national remedy, a creditor may not submit to several courts, simultaneously, parallel applications for a preservation order against the same debtor aimed at securing the same claim.[129] An EAPO shall remain operative until revocation, termination, or until a judgment enforcement measure has taken effect with respect to the funds preserved thereby.[130]

An EAPO issued in one Member State shall be recognised in the other Member States without any special procedure being required, and shall be enforceable in the other Member States without the need for a declaration of enforceability.[131] The nub of the remedy is found in art.24.1, in terms of which a bank to which a EAPO is addressed shall implement it without delay following receipt of the order.[132] An obligation is imposed on the bank in question to declare whether and, if so, to what extent the order has led to the preservation of any funds of the debtor,[133] and a parallel obligation is imposed on the creditor to ensure the release of any funds preserved that exceed the amount specified in the order.[134] Article 28 mandates that the EAPO shall be served on the debtor in accordance with that article.

Article 33 provides remedies for the debtor against the preservation order, namely its revocation or modification on cause shown. The right of third parties to contest an EAPO shall be governed by the law of the Member State of origin, namely, the Member State in which the preservation order was issued; and the right to contest the enforcement of an order shall be governed by the law of the Member State of enforcement, namely, the Member State in which the bank account to be preserved is maintained.[135]

The order shall have the same rank, if any, as an equivalent national order in the Member State of enforcement.[136] It is significant that, per art.2.2, the Regulation does not apply to claims against a debtor in relation to whom bankruptcy proceedings, proceedings for the winding-up of insolvent companies or other legal persons, judicial arrangements, compositions, or analogous proceedings have been opened. By recital (8) this should mean that no preservation order can be issued against a debtor once insolvency proceedings as defined in Council Regulation (EC) No.1346/2000[137] have been opened in relation to him. Insofar as a debtor subject to an EAPO easily and predictably may slip into bankruptcy, the relationship between the Insolvency Regulation and

---

[128] Defined in art.4.13.
[129] Regulation 655/2014 art.16.1.
[130] Regulation 655/2014 art.20.
[131] Regulation 655/2014 art.22.
[132] Regulation 655/2014 art.24.1.
[133] Regulation 655/2014 art.25 and recital (29).
[134] Regulation 655/2014 art.27.
[135] Regulation 655/2014 art.39.
[136] Regulation 655/2014 art.32.
[137] Para.17–43, below. In view of the repeal of the Insolvency Regulation, references to that instrument shall be construed as references to Regulation (EU) 2015/848 of the European Parliament and of the Council of 20 May, 2015 in Insolvency Proceedings (recast) (art.91); see Correlation Table in Annex D.

Regulation 655/2014 requires to be clearly delineated. Regulation 655/2014 is stated to be without prejudice to the Insolvency Regulation (inter alia),[138] and presumably in the event of a clash, the provisions of the Insolvency Regulation will prevail.

UK opt out

8–22   In common with Rome IV, Regulation 655/2014 refers only to "Member State", without differentiating in terminology between participating Member State and non-participating Member State. The question arises whether creditors and debtors, respectively, domiciled in the non-participating Member State of the UK are affected, and if so, to what extent. The meaning of the UK's non-participation in this scheme has to be worked out according to arts 3–6.

Article 4(7) defines "debtor" as "a natural person or a legal person … having legal capacity to sue or be sued under the law of a Member State, against whom or which the creditor seeks to obtain, or has already obtained, a Preservation Order relating to a claim." Article 4(6) defines "creditor" as a "natural person domiciled in a Member State or a legal person domiciled in a Member State … having legal capacity to sue or be sued under the law of a Member State, who or which applies for, or has already obtained, a Preservation Order relating to a claim". Insofar as an application for an EAPO is concerned, the important connecting factor is the creditor's domicile in a Member State. Domicile for this purpose means domicile as determined in accordance with arts 62 and 63 of Brussels I Recast.[139] Whether or not art.4(6) is to be construed as domicile in a participating Member State is not clear from the articles of the Regulation, but the recitals make clear that that is the intended interpretation. Recital (48) states, first, that the procedure for obtaining an EAPO is available only to creditors who are domiciled in a Member State bound by the Regulation and, secondly, that orders issued under the Regulation should relate only to the preservation of bank accounts which are maintained in such a Member State. The effect of this is to exclude Scots and English domiciled creditors from utilising the remedy. Likewise, bank accounts maintained in the UK are exempt from the reach of a preservation order. The effect of the UK decision not to opt in has had the effect, therefore, of depriving UK creditors of this European remedy. Any creditor, however, if circumstances permit, is able to seek from a Scots or English court such pre-trial freezing injunctions or other protective remedy as the legal system of the forum affords.[140]

But looked at the other way, since art.4(7) does not define "debtor" by reference to his domicile, if a Scots domiciled debtor has a bank account located in a participating Member State and is pursued by a creditor domiciled in a participating Member State, the debtor's foreign account (but not any UK account) is vulnerable to an EAPO granted by a court of a participating Member State having jurisdiction under art.6. Accordingly, in spite of the UK decision not to opt in, British debtors may be vulnerable to the grant of an EAPO.

---

[138] Regulation 655/2014 art.48(c).
[139] Regulation 655/2014 art.4(15). Para.7–16, above.
[140] Para.8–17 et seq., above.

The Regulation was concerned to strike an appropriate balance between the interest of the creditor in obtaining an order and the interest of the debtor in preventing abuse of the order. From the outset, the UK was concerned that the measures were too claimant-friendly, and insufficiently debtor-protective.[141] The Regulation in its final form contains more safeguards and protections than were originally devised, but even so, the published text leaves unanswered questions, e.g. ranking among EAPOs granted to different creditors in respect of the same funds (do these "stack" on the same funds, ranked according to date, or will there be distribution among creditors on a pro rata basis?).

There is no indication to date that the UK will seek to opt-in to the instrument post-adoption.

Evidence

All questions as to the requirements, extent and sufficiency of evidence are determined by the *lex fori* alone, irrespective of the governing law of the substantive dispute.   **8–23**

Article 18.2 of the Rome I Regulation, and art.22.2 of the Rome II Regulation, which are in the same terms, mutatis mutandis, provide that a contract or an act[142] intended to have legal effect may be proved by any mode of proof recognised by the law of the forum, or by any of the laws identified by either instrument to govern issues of formal validity[143] under which that contract or act is formally valid, provided such mode of proof can be administered by the forum.

As noted above, the province of the *lex causae*/governing law extends to all matters which involve substance rather than procedure. A distinction must be drawn between "the facts to be proved" (determined by the *lex causae*) and "the proof of the facts" (governed by the *lex fori*).[144]

The "whole point" of an evidential rule was said in *Fuld (No.3)*[145] to be one "concerned with the approach required of the court to the evidence submitted for its consideration".

In *Immanuel v Denholm and Co*[146] the question for the Scots court was whether the information contained in a bill of lading pertaining to a contract with a Danish proper law was conclusive on this matter, a point on which the *lex causae* and the *lex fori* differed. Since that point was classified by the Scots forum as one of evidence, the Scots rule prevailed. There are many other cases which illustrate the rule.[147]

---

[141] HM Government, "Review of the Balance of Competences between the United Kingdom and the European Union Civil Judicial Cooperation" (February 2014), para.2.54.

[142] Falling, respectively, within the scope of the Rome I or Rome II Regulation.

[143] Rome I Regulation art.11; Rome II Regulation art.21.

[144] *The Gaetano and Maria* (1882) L.R. 7 P.D. 137: "Now the manner of proving the facts is matter of evidence, and, to my mind, is matter of procedure, but the facts to be proved are not matters of procedure; they are the matters with which the procedure has to deal", per Brett L.J. at 144.

[145] *Fuld (No.3)* [1968] P. 675, per Scarman J. at 697.

[146] *Immanuel v Denholm and Co* (1887) 15 R. 152.

[147] e.g. *Leroux v Brown* (1852) 12 C.B. 801; *Bain v Whitehaven and Furness Junction Railway Co* (1850) 3 H.L. 1; *Bristow v Sequeville* (1850) 5 Ex. 275; *Mahadervan v Mahadervan* [1964] P. 233; *Fuld (No.3)* [1968] P. 675; and *Caltex Singapore Pte Ltd v BP Shipping Ltd* [1996] 1 Lloyd's Rep. 286.

The following are particular aspects of the rule, the question in each case being whether the point truly involves substance or procedure:

(a) the *lex fori* determines whether or not a document is admissible in evidence, irrespective of whether or not it may be so under any other law[148];

(b) the *lex fori* determines whether extrinsic evidence will be allowed with a view to varying the terms of a contract, irrespective of the governing law, but its admissibility to interpret the terms of a contract is determined by the proper/applicable law of the contract[149];

(c) at common law, proof of a death abroad was a matter of fact to be decided by the *lex fori*,[150] but in terms of the Presumption of Death (Scotland) Act 1977 s.10, where a foreign judgment of presumed death emanates from a court in a foreign country in which the person was domiciled or habitually resident on the date when he was last known to be alive, this raises a (rebuttable) presumption of death.

Professional conduct investigation/disciplinary procedure in respect of the medical profession has been held by the Privy Council[151] to be governed by English law (even though in the case in question the disciplinary committee sat in Glasgow), with the aim of having a single set of rules of evidence no matter where the committee might sit.[152] Similarly, British Army discipline by court-martial, wherever held, is governed by specialised UK rules.[153]

Taking of evidence abroad

Taking of evidence within the EU

8–24 The matter is regulated by Regulation 1206/2001 on cooperation between the courts of the Member States in the taking of evidence in civil or commercial matters. Regulation 1206/2001 entered into force on 1 July 2001,[154] creating a

---

[148] cf. *Henaff v Henaff* [1966] 1 W.L.R. 598.

[149] cf. at common law *Thomson* (1917) 33 Sh. Ct. Rep. 84. See Rome I Regulation art.12.1(a).

[150] *Simpson's Trustees v Fox*, 1951 S.L.T. 412. See also *In the Goods of Spenceley* [1892] P.255; *Re Schulhof* [1948] P. 66; *In the Estate of Arthur Dowds* [1948] P. 256; and *Kamouh v AEI International* [1980] 1 Q.B. 199.

[151] *McAllister v General Medical Council* [1993] 2 W.L.R. 308 PC.

[152] cf. *Prescription Pricing Authority v Ferguson*, 2005 S.L.T. 63, concerning the jurisdiction of an industrial tribunal.

[153] Army Act 1955, as amended: see *R. v Martin (Alan)* [1998] 1 All E.R. 193.

[154] See Report on the Application of Regulation 1206/2001 on cooperation between the courts of Member States in the taking of evidence in civil or commercial matters COM(2007) 769 final. The Report concluded that Regulation 1206/2001 has achieved, to a satisfactory extent, its two main objectives, viz. simplification of co-operation between Member States, and acceleration of the performance of taking evidence; and that accordingly, no modifications of the Regulation are required (para.3). See, however, Resolution 2008/2180(INI) on cooperation between the courts of the Member States in the taking of evidence in civil or commercial matters [2010] O.J. C87E/21. See also European Commission *Practice Guide for the Application of the Regulation on the Taking of Evidence* (2011). In 2012 there was produced the Mainstrat Study on "The Application of Articles 3(1)(C) and 3, and Articles 17 and 18 of the Council Regulation (EC) No 1206/2001" (June 2012, Final_Report_1206_A). No further Commission Report has been forthcoming.

system for the rapid transmission and execution of requests for the taking of evidence between Member State courts (except Denmark) and laying down precise criteria as to the form and content of such requests. The Regulation applies in civil and commercial cases where a court of a Member State requests the competent court of another Member State to obtain evidence, or asks to take evidence directly in another Member State.[155] Unusually, since the purpose of the Regulation is to improve and accelerate procedures for taking evidence in other Member States, and not to deprive those states of pre-existing judicial powers, or to provide an exclusive means for a court in one Member State to obtain information or evidence located in another Member State, use of the procedures provided by the Regulation is not mandatory.[156] The CJEU has confirmed that Regulation 1206/2001 applies only if the court of a Member State decides to take evidence according to one of the two methods provided for by the Regulation, in which case it is required to follow the procedures relating to those methods.[157]

A list of courts competent for the purposes of the Regulation must be drawn up by each Member State. A request shall not be made to obtain evidence which is not intended for use in judicial proceedings, commenced or contemplated.[158]

(a) Taking of evidence by request[159]

Where evidence is to be taken by request, the request must be made using a specific form[160] and must contain certain specific details such as details of the parties, and the nature of the case. The request and all documents accompanying it shall be exempted from authentication or any equivalent formality.[161] The request must be presented in one of the official languages of the Member State requested, or in another language indicated by that state to be acceptable.[162] It is an aim of the new legislation that the taking of evidence should be done without delay. If it is not possible for the request to be executed by the requested court within 90 days of receipt of the request, the requested court should inform the requesting court, stating reasons. Representatives of the requesting court and of the parties may be physically present at the taking of evidence, but if this is not possible, aids such as video conferencing may be used to permit their participation.

8–25

Communications pursuant to the Regulation shall be transmitted by the swiftest possible means, and may be carried out by any appropriate means provided that the document received accurately reflects the content of the document forwarded, and that all information in it is legible.[163]

Where the request does not fall within the jurisdiction of the court to which it was transmitted, the latter shall forward the request to the competent court of its

---

[155] *Dendron GmbH v University of California* [2004] I.L.Pr. 35.
[156] *Secretary of State for Health v Servier Laboratories Ltd* [2013] EWCA Civ 1234; and *ProRail BV v Xpedys NV* (C-332/11) [2013] C.E.C. 879.
[157] *Lippens v Kortekaas* (C-170/11) [2012] I.L.Pr. 42.
[158] Regulation 1206/2001 art.1.2.
[159] Regulation 1206/2001 Ch.II ss.1–3.
[160] Regulation 1206/2001 art.4.
[161] Regulation 1206/2001 art.4.2.
[162] Regulation 1206/2001 art.5.
[163] Regulation 1206/2001 art.6.

Member State, and shall inform the requesting court.[164] If the request cannot be executed because it does not contain all information required by art.4, the requested court shall inform the requesting court thereof without delay, and at the latest within 30 days of receipt, using a particular form, and shall request it to send the missing information.[165] Similarly, if a request cannot be executed because a deposit or advance is necessary, the requested court shall inform the requesting court without delay, and at the latest within 30 days of receipt, using a particular form and informing the requesting court how the deposit or advance should be made.[166] With regard to the time limit (of execution of the request without delay and at the latest within 90 days of receipt) contained in art.10, such time limit shall begin to run when the requested court receives the request duly completed.[167] The requested court shall execute the request in accordance with the law of its Member State, although if the requesting court calls for execution in accordance with a special procedure provided for by the law of its Member State, the requested court shall comply unless this procedure is incompatible with its law, or would raise major practical difficulties.[168]

The requesting court may ask the requested court to use communications technology at the taking of evidence, in particular by using video conferencing and tele-conferencing.[169]

If, by the law of the requesting court, the parties and their representatives have the right to be present at the taking of evidence, this shall be facilitated by the requested court.[170] If it is compatible with the law of the requesting court, representatives of the requesting court (including judicial personnel or experts) have the right to be present at the taking of evidence. If participation of such representatives is requested by the requesting court, the conditions under which such participation may take place shall be determined by the requested court.[171] Where necessary in executing a request, the requested court shall apply the appropriate coercive measures to the extent provided for by its law.[172]

With regard to refusal to give evidence, the Regulation provides in art.14 that the request for the hearing of a person shall not be executed where s/he claims the right to refuse to give evidence, or to be prohibited from giving evidence, under the law of the requested court, or under the law of the requesting court (subject to confirmation by the requesting court).

The execution of a request may be refused by the requested court only in exceptional circumstances, namely[173]:

(a)   the request does not fall within the scope of the Regulation; or

(b)   under the law of the requested court the execution of the request does not fall within the function of the judiciary; or

---

[164] Regulation 1206/2001 art.7.2.
[165] Regulation 1206/2001 art.8.1.
[166] Regulation 1206/2001 art.18.
[167] Regulation 1206/2001 art.9.
[168] Regulation 1206/2001 arts 10.2 and 10.3.
[169] Regulation 1206/2001 art.10.4
[170] Regulation 1206/2001 art.11.
[171] Regulation 1206/2001 art.12.4.
[172] Regulation 1206/2001 art.13.
[173] Regulation 1206/2001 art.14.2.

(c)   the requesting court does not comply within 30 days with the request by the requested court to complete the request pursuant to art.8; or

(d)   a deposit or advance asked for in accordance with art.18.3 has not been made within 60 days.[174]

Importantly, art.14.3 provides that execution may not be refused by the requested court solely on the ground that under the law of its Member State a court of that state has exclusive jurisdiction over the subject-matter of the action, or that the law of that Member State would not admit the right of action on it.[175] If execution of the request is refused on any of the grounds in art.14.2, the requested court shall notify the requesting court thereof within 60 days of receipt.[176]

In terms of art.16, the requested court shall send without delay to the requesting court the documents establishing the execution of the request, and where appropriate return documents received.

(b)   Direct taking of evidence[177]

Where a court requests to take evidence directly in another Member State, it shall submit a request to the central body, or competent authority.[178] Direct taking of evidence may take place only if it can be performed on a voluntary basis without the need for coercive measures; the requesting court shall inform participating persons that their performance shall take place on a voluntary basis.[179]

8–26

The taking of such evidence shall be performed by a member of the judicial personnel, or designated expert, of the requesting court, in accordance with that court's law. The central body of the requested Member State shall advise within 30 days of receipt if the request is accepted, and, if necessary, under what conditions the performance is to be carried out. In particular, the central body may assign a court of its Member State to take part to ensure the proper application of this provision, and compliance with conditions.[180]

The central body may refuse direct taking of evidence only if[181]:

(a)   the request does not fall within the scope of the Regulation; or

(b)   the request does not contain all the necessary information pursuant to art.4; or

(c)   the direct taking of evidence requested is contrary to fundamental principles of law in its Member State.

Without prejudice to the conditions mentioned above, the requesting court shall execute the request in accordance with the law of its Member State.

---

[174] Regulation 1206/2001 art.18 concerns costs: the execution of the request shall not give rise to a claim for any reimbursement of taxes or costs. cf. *Werynski v Mediatel 4B Spolka z oo* (C-283/09) [2012] Q.B. 66.

[175] Note the subservient position of the requested court in this regard.

[176] Regulation 1206/2001 art.15.

[177] Regulation 1206/2001 Ch.II s.4.

[178] Regulation 1206/2001 art.3.

[179] Regulation 1206/2001 art.17.2.

[180] Regulation 1206/2001 art.17.

[181] Regulation 1206/2001 art.17.5.

In terms of art.21, Regulation 1206/2001 prevails over bilateral or multilateral agreements, and in particular, over the 1970 Hague Convention on the Taking of Evidence Abroad in Civil or Commercial Matters (to which the UK is a party), in relations between the Member States party thereto.

Taking of evidence outside the EU

8–27 As regards taking of evidence from non-EU Member States, evidence in the form of testimony, or documents[182] or both[183] may be obtained under the authority of, and by complying with the provisions in, the Evidence (Proceedings in Other Jurisdictions) Act 1975, implementing in the UK the 1970 Hague Convention on the Taking of Evidence Abroad in Civil or Commercial Matters.

Under the 1975 Act, the Court of Session, at the instance of a foreign court/tribunal, by "letter of request" may order witnesses in Scotland to give evidence to be remitted abroad to aid foreign litigation.[184] The leading case is *Re Norway's Application (Nos 1 and 2)*,[185] in which the House of Lords held, inter alia, that for the process to be initiated under the 1975 Act, the proceedings for which evidence was sought to be gathered must be regarded as concerning a "civil or commercial matter" in the view of both the requesting and the requested court, since there was no internationally acceptable classification.[186] The Extra Division in *Lord Advocate, Petitioner*,[187] refused to accede to four incoming letters of request from a Texas court, on the ground that the material sought related to pre-trial discovery which might lead to a line of inquiry ultimately resulting in deposition testimony, and did not relate directly to evidence for use at a trial.

---

[182] *Stewart v Callaghan*, 1996 S.L.T. (Sh. Ct.) 12; *Panayiotou v Sony Music Entertainment (UK) Ltd* [1994] 1 All E.R. 755; *Refco Capital Markets Ltd v Credit Suisse First Boston Ltd* [2001] EWCA Civ 1733; and *APA Excelsior v Premiere Technologies Inc* [2002] EWHC 2205 (QB).

[183] *Rio Tinto Zinc Corp v Westinghouse Electric Corp (Nos 1 and 2)* [1978] 1 All E.R. 434; *Boeing Co v PPG Industries* [1988] 3 All E.R. 839; and *Charman v Charman* [2006] 1 W.L.R. 1053.

[184] *Lord Advocate, Petitioner*, 1994 S.L.T. 852; but see *Lord Advocate, Petitioner*, 1998 S.L.T. 835; *Minnesota v Philip Morris Inc* [1998] I.L.Pr. 170 (request refused because terms of letter of request from Minnesota District Court too wide ranging); and *Smith v Phillip Morris Companies Inc* [2006] EWHC 916 (QB).

[185] *Re Norway's Application (Nos 1 and 2)* [1989] 1 All E.R. 745.

[186] Contrast *Lufttransportunternehmen GmbH & Co KG v Organisation Europeene pour la Securite de la Navigation Aerienne (Eurocontrol)* [1976] E.C.R. 1541 at 1552. See also *Pharaon v Bank of Credit and Commerce International SA (In Liquidation)* [1998] 4 All E.R. 455 as regards limits of disclosure; and *Cambridge Gas Transport Corp v Official Committee of Unsecured Creditors of Navigator Holdings Plc* [2007] 1 A.C. 508.

[187] *Lord Advocate, Petitioner*, 1998 S.L.T. 835. Contrast *Lord Advocate, Petitioner*, 1994 S.L.T. 852. See in England, refusal to accede to letter of request from US District Court of Columbia, on the ground that the width of the questions made the letter oppressive. A balance had to be struck between international co-operation and oppression of witnesses: *First American Corp v Al-Nahyan* [1999] 1 W.L.R. 1154.

Outside the scope of the EU Regulation, there is precedent for use of video conferencing[188] and the sitting of a Scots court abroad. The former is an acknowledgment of the benefit in suitable cases of advances in technology; the latter is an exceptional event.[189]

Proof of foreign law[190]

Where foreign law arguably is applicable in a British court, its content requires to be pleaded and proved to the court as a matter of fact by the party who seeks to rely upon it. The content of foreign law may be proved, or accepted to have been proved,[191] by the methods of admission on record,[192] or submission of expert evidence,[193] usually delivered orally to the court,[194] or remit to a foreign court or foreign lawyer for an opinion.[195] Copies of Acts of Parliament of a "British possession" may be received in evidence without further procedure, in terms of the Evidence (Colonial Statutes) Act 1907. A case may be stated to a foreign court of the Commonwealth under the British Law Ascertainment Act 1859. Finally, a request for information may be made under the 1968 European Convention on Information on Foreign Law ("London Convention"). Though the UK has ratified the London Convention, it has never been implemented in

8–28

---

[188] As to which in English law, see *R. v Horseferry Road Magistrates' Court Ex p. Bennet (No. 3)*, *The Times*, 14 January 1994; *R. v Forsyth, The Times*, 8 April 1997 CA.

[189] e.g. in 1992, when the Court of Session, in recognition of the age and frailty of witnesses, removed to Vilnius, Lithuania in order to hear a trial of alleged war crimes. More recently the Scots High Court removed to Camp Zeist in the Netherlands for the purposes of the Lockerbie trial, the territory being deemed part of Scotland for the purposes of the trial. cf. *Peer International Corp v Termidor Music Publishers Ltd (No.3)* [2005] EWHC 1048.

[190] See C. Esplugues Mota, J. Iglesias, and G. Palao Moreno (eds), *Application of Foreign Law* (Sellier, 2011); and, in particular, E.B. Crawford and J.M. Carruthers, "UK National Report", at p.391; R. Fentiman, *Foreign Law in English Courts* (1998); S. Geeroms, *Foreign Law in Civil Litigation: A Comparative and Functional Analysis* (Oxford: Oxford University Press, 2004); and B.J. Rodger and J. van Doorn, "Proof of Foreign Law: The Impact of the London Convention" (1997) 46 I.C.L.Q. 151.

[191] See, for England and Wales only, the Civil Evidence Act 1972 s.4(2), which provides that where any question as to the law of any country outside the UK, or of any part of the UK other than England and Wales, with respect to any matter, has been determined in any English proceedings which have been reported or recorded in citable form, that determination shall be admissible in evidence for the purpose of proving the law of that country, unless the contrary is proved.

[192] *Black v Black's Trustees*, 1950 S.L.T. (Notes) 32.

[193] e.g. *Re E (A Child) (Abduction: Rights of Custody)* [2005] EWHC 848 (Fam); and *Re K (Children) (Rights of Custody: Spain)* [2009] EWCA Civ 986.

[194] Civil Evidence Act 1972 s.4(1) declares that a person who is suitably qualified on account of his knowledge or experience is competent to give expert evidence as to the law of any country outside the UK, or of any part of the UK other than England and Wales, irrespective of whether he has acted or is entitled to act as a legal practitioner there. In Scots law, there is no statutory equivalent to the 1972 Act. The question of who is competent to act as an expert witness rests on the common law, and is context-dependent. The qualification of the expert witness to testify to the point in issue is a matter for the judge's discretion in each individual case. For further details, see *Cheshire, North and Fawcett: Private International Law*, 14th edn (2008), pp.115, 116.

[195] *Welsh v Milne* (1844) 7 D.213. A more modern and specific instance is provided by art.15 of the 1980 Hague Convention on the Civil Aspects of International Child Abduction, which permits the judicial or administrative authorities of a Contracting State, prior to the making of an order for the return of the child, to request that the applicant obtain from the authorities of the state of the child's habitual residence a decision that his removal or retention was wrongful within the meaning of art.3: *Re D (A Child) (Abduction: Rights of Custody)* [2007] 1 A.C. 619 HL.

primary legislation, nor have there been any ensuing UK rules concerning court practice thereunder. Resort to the Convention is unlikely for it does not eliminate the need for expert evidence to be submitted, and even if an opinion is received, its content will not take into account the circumstances of the individual case. Moreover, the Convention's procedures may serve to increase the cost, complexity and duration of proceedings in the UK.

By way of exception, a foreign law may be so notorious that a judge is entitled to take "judicial notice" of it[196]; for example, the fact that roulette is not unlawful in Monte Carlo.[197] Likewise, although an unusual occurrence, the court may take judicial notice of foreign law if legislation so provides.[198] In particular, a Scots court may be required by legislation to take judicial notice of a provision of English law. The UK Supreme Court, whatever its composition in a particular case, has knowledge of each one of the laws of the constituent jurisdictions in the UK,[199] and must develop them.[200] Hence, the Supreme Court, when dealing with the law of any part of the UK, has judicial notice of that law; that which was required to be proved as a matter of fact during the course of the litigation becomes a matter of law in the Supreme Court. In addition, all UK judges must take judicial notice of certain matters of European law. Section 3 of the European Communities Act 1972, as amended, provides as follows:

> "3.— Decisions on, and proof of, Treaties and EU instruments etc.
> (1)   For the purposes of all legal proceedings any question as to the meaning or effect of any of the Treaties, or as to the validity, meaning or effect of any EU instrument, shall be treated as a question of law (and, if not referred to the European Court, be for determination as such in accordance with the principles laid down by and any relevant decision of the European Court).
> (2)   Judicial notice shall be taken of the Treaties, of the Official Journal of the European Union and of any decision of, or expression of opinion by, the European Court on any such question as aforesaid; and the Official Journal shall be admissible as evidence of any instrument or other act thereby communicated of the EU or of any EU institution.
> (3)   Evidence of any instrument issued by a EU institution , including any judgment or order of the European Court, or of any document in the custody of a EU institution , or any entry in or extract from such a document, may be given in any legal proceedings by production of a copy certified as a true copy by an official of that institution; and any document purporting to be such a copy shall be received in evidence without proof of the official position or handwriting of the person signing the certificate."

In the event of failure of proof of foreign law by any of the permitted methods, there is a presumption in the UK that the law of a foreign country is the same as the *lex fori*[201]; or, alternatively, it may be said, that on failure of proof of foreign

---

[196]   i.e. acceptance of evidence without proof. Although, in the adversarial system, a court cannot find as a fact that which has not been proved, judicial notice allows a court to declare that a fact exists even though it has not been established by evidence.

[197]   *Saxby v Fulton* [1909] 2 K.B. 208 at 211.

[198]   e.g. Maintenance Orders Act 1950 s.22(2).

[199]   *Elliot v Joicey*, 1935 S.C. (H.L.) 57, per Lord MacMillan at 68.

[200]   *Bank of East Asia Ltd v Scottish Enterprise*, 1997 S.L.T. 1213.

[201]   Though see *Global Multimedia International Ltd v ARA Media Services* [2006] EWHC 3612 (Ch), per Sir Andrew Morritt C. at [38]: "The true proposition, I believe, is that as foreign law is in most cases a question of fact to be proved by evidence, in the absence of such evidence the court has no

law, the *lex fori* applies by default.[202] The onus is on a person who maintains otherwise to aver the foreign law and to prove it.[203] If the foreign law is not pleaded and proved to the court's satisfaction, then the court will not have judicial knowledge of that law and will treat the case as a purely domestic one. Not only may the content of a foreign *lex causae* be assumed to be the same as the *lex fori*, through default of proof to the contrary, but also, rarely, an outcome may be based upon an assumption or hypothesis about the content of foreign law, for example, where the point may be said to be incidental to the main issue.[204] A UK court does not take notice of foreign laws; the judge is treated as neither knowing, nor being able to know of his own volition, the content of the foreign law to be applied, and cannot investigate and apply foreign law ex officio.

While Scots judges have judicial knowledge of Scots law, and English judges of English law, including their conflict of laws rules, a court cannot of its own initiative order a proof of the content of foreign law. Hence although the court will apply the appropriate choice of law rule (even if the parties fail to plead it), in the absence of proof of foreign law, operation of the choice of law rule of the forum effectively will be frustrated. Accordingly, this approach in Scots and English law has fundamental implications for the conduct of litigation in UK courts; by inadvertence, negligence or tacit consent between the adversaries, the conflict of laws dimension of a case may be lost. It has to be said that the subject, as a body of law, does not seem to have been impoverished.

Yet proof of foreign law must be regarded as a matter of fact of a peculiar kind in English and Scots courts.[205] In the UK, an appellate court always is slow to interfere with a trial court's finding of fact; but where an appeal principally or subsidiarily involves a point of foreign law, the superior court is less reluctant to revisit that issue of fact.[206] Thus, when the content of the foreign law becomes the

---

option but to apply English law." See also A. Briggs, *Private International Law in English Courts* (Oxford: Oxford University Press, 2014), para.3.41.

[202] "In default of proof. . .an English judge still has to adjudicate; and his default position is that he will apply English law, *faute de mieux*": A. Briggs, *Conflict of Laws*, 2nd edn (2008), p.6. But see later A. Briggs, *Private International Law in English Courts* (OUP) (2014), para.341.

[203] *Mostyn v Fabrigas* (1774)1 Coup. 161, per Lord Mansfield at 174; *Lloyd v Guibert* (1865) L.R. 1 Q.B. 115; *Stuart v Potter, Choate & Prentice*, 1911 1 S.L.T. 377; *Ertel Bieber & Co v Rio Tinto Co Ltd* [1918] A.C. 260. *Naftalin v London Midland & Scottish Railway Co*, 1933 S.C. 259; *Faulkner (Michael Stanislaus) v Hill*, 1942 J.C. 20; *De Reneville v De Reneville* [1948] P. 100; *Pryde v Proctor & Gamble Ltd*, 1971 S.L.T. (Notes) 18; *Bonnor v Balfour Kilpatrick Ltd*, 1975 S.L.T. (Notes) 3; *Rodden v Whatlings Ltd*, 1960 S.L.T. (Notes) 96; *Scottish National Orchestra Society Ltd v Thomson's Executor*, 1969 S.L.T. 325; *Armour v Thyssen Edelstahlwerke AG*, 1989 S.L.T. 182 IH; 1990 S.L.T. 891 HL; *Bumper Development Corp v Commissioner of Police of the Metropolis* [1991] 1 W.L.R. 1362 CA; *Kraus's Administrators v Sullivan*, 1998 S.L.T. 963; and *Wilmington Trust Co v Rolls Royce Plc*, 2011 G.W.D. 1-15.

[204] See, e.g. *Duhur-Johnson v Duhur-Johnson* [2005] 2 F.L.R. 1042 (despite absence of evidence that the divorce obtained by the husband was effective by the law of Nigeria, the English court assumed, for the purposes of the application for a stay of English proceedings, that the requirements of the Family Law Act 1986 s.46(1) had been met, and that the divorce was effective by Nigerian law).

[205] *Parkasho v Singh* [1968] P. 233, per Cairns J. at 246.

[206] *Parkasho v Singh* [1968] P. 233 at 250; *Dalmia Dairy Industries v National Bank of Pakistan* [1978] 2 Lloyd's Rep. 223 at 286 CA; *Att Gen of New Zealand v Ortiz* [1984] A.C. 1; *The Saudi Prince (No.2)* [1988] 1 Lloyd's Rep. 1 at 3 CA; *Bumper Development Corp v Commissioner of Police of the Metropolis* [1991] 1 W.L.R. 1362 at 1368 CA; *Grupo Torras SA v Al-Sabah (No.1)* [1996] 1 Lloyd's Rep. 7 at 18 CA; and *Re K (Children) (Rights of Custody: Spain)* [2009] EWCA Civ 986, per Thorpe LJ at [18].

subject of an appeal to a higher court, it is treated not merely as a question of fact, but is reviewed in much the same way as if it were an issue of law.[207] However, the appeal court cannot ascertain the foreign law ex officio by initiating an investigation de novo; all it can do is to review the expert evidence submitted to the lower court, and make its own assessment of whether the foreign law was proved adequately, and which version, if any, of the foreign law it prefers.

The civilian-based practice in European countries varies, but generally stands in contrast to the UK approach. Even where the foreign law is sought to be "proved", by any method, whether initiated by the parties, or one of them, *ex officio* by the judge, or by the judge assisted by the litigants, it should not be supposed that a forum proceeds always on an accurate understanding of its content.

Role of the parties in the matter of proof of foreign law

8–29   The UK position is that the party who wishes to rely on the point of foreign law should bear the onus of pleading and proving its content. Currently in the UK, pleading foreign law is voluntary. The principle of party autonomy is influential, but in this context it stems from UK (domestic) adversarial procedure, and not from its sanction in an EU instrument, of jurisdiction[208] or choice of law.[209] Some would say it operates as a covert choice of law (even a *fraudem legis*), through passivity, ignorance, or complicity of litigants, colluded in, in effect, by the judge, perforce of the system, and to be viewed, therefore, as an excessive use of party autonomy. In mitigation, it may be that parties' conduct is motivated by a desire to reduce expense, and in that and other ways, their expectations may be met by application of domestic law.

Where a party seeks to rely on foreign law, a "best endeavours" approach may be said to apply. If the parties can agree on the content of foreign law,[210] that is a resolution which a UK judge will accept. The burden of proof of asserting foreign law lies on the party(ies) seeking to rely on it.[211] Within the limits of honesty,[212] a party may take advantage of errors or weaknesses or lacunae in the pleadings of the other party in the particular of proof of foreign law, as in any other matter.

There is no obligation of co-operation between parties, for their interests are opposed, or between judge and parties.

---

[207] *Macmillan Inc v Bishopsgate Investment Trust Plc (No.4)* [1999] C.L.C. 417. See R. Fentiman, *Foreign Law in English Courts* (1998), pp.201, 202.

[208] e.g. Brussels I Regulation art.25 (Brussels I Recast, art.27).

[209] e.g. Rome I Regulation art.3; Rome II Regulation art.14.

[210] e.g. *Beatty v Beatty* [1924] 1 K.B. 807; *Iran v Barakat Galleries Ltd* [2007] EWHC 705; and *Iran v Berend* [2007] EWHC 132 (QB).

[211] *Brown v Gracey* (1821) Dow & Ry N.P. 41; *Schapiro v Schapiro* [1904] T.S. 673; *Ertel Bieber & Co v Rio Tinto Co Ltd* [1918] A.C. 260 at 295 HL; *Guaranty Trust Co of New York v Hannay & Co* [1918] 2 K.B. 623 at 655 CA; and *Ascherberg, Hopwood & Crew v Casa Musicale Sonzogno* [1971] 1 W.L.R. 173.

[212] *Arrow Nominees Inc v Blackledge* [2000] 2 B.C.L.C 167.

Role of the judge in the matter of proof of foreign law

A UK judge's role is that of umpire, not investigator. The foreign law must be   **8–30**
pleaded and proved to the court's satisfaction before the court can apply it.[213] The
judge is not entitled to, "search for himself into the sources of knowledge from
which the witnesses have drawn, and produce for himself the fact which is
required to be proved as a part of the case before him."[214] There is no tradition,
therefore, of the UK judge applying foreign law ex officio. The principle of *iura
novit curia* is not applicable in the UK in the case of foreign law. The role of the
judge with regard to the proof of foreign law is, in general, largely passive, but, in
a litigation having conflict of laws potential, s/he is not *entirely* neutral, for it is
the task of the judge to identify the applicable law according to the pleadings and,
having done so, to adjudicate upon whether or not the relevant points of the *lex
causae* have been sufficiently proved.[215]

Consequences of failure to prove foreign law

A distinction must be drawn between "gaps" or deficiencies in the parties' proof   **8–31**
of the law; and gaps or lacunae in the rules of the applicable law itself for the
purpose of determining the instant question. As explained, under the UK system,
the effect of absence of proof of foreign law, or of proof being incomplete, is that
the *lex fori* supplies the lack.[216]

If the litigant provides a seemingly convincing and complete account of the
content of the relevant foreign law, the judge will proceed to apply that law as
detailed.[217] If, however, either or both litigant(s) fail(s) to provide for the court, in
the court's view, a suitably persuasive account, with the result that the judge is
uncertain as to content, the forum will assume that the content of the foreign law

---

[213] For guidance on the judicial role in this context, see Purchas L.J. in *Bumper Development Corp v
Commissioner of Police of the Metropolis* [1991] 1 W.L.R. 1362. See also *Gotha City v Sotheby's
(No.2)* unreported 9 September 1998, per Moses J.; and *Harley v Smith* [2010] EWCA Civ 78 (it being
ultra vires the English judge to interpret Sharia law without hearing evidence).

[214] *Di Sora v Phillipps* (1863) H.L.C. 624, per Lord Chelmsford at 640.

[215] See, e.g. *In Re Duke of Wellington* [1947] Ch. 506; *Fuld (No.3)* [1968] P. 675, per Scarman J. at
700–703; *Re K (Children) (Rights of Custody: Spain)* [2009] EWCA Civ 986; and *Lupofresh Limited
v Sapporo Breweries Ltd* [2013] EWCA Civ 948, per Tomlinson L.J. at [9].

[216] *Faulkner v Hill*, 1942 J.C. 20; *Stafford Allen & Sons Ltd v Pacific Steam Navigation Co* [1956] 1
Lloyd's Rep. 104; [1956] 1 Lloyd's Rep. 166; *Winkworth v Hubbard* [1960] 1 Lloyd's Rep. 150;
Schneider v Eisovitch [1960] 2 Q.B. 430; *Suisse Atlantique Societe d'Armement SA v NV
Rotterdamsche Kolen Centrale* [1967] 1 A.C. 361; *Czarnikow Ltd v Koufos (The Heron II)* [1969] 1
A.C. 350; *Pryde v Proctor & Gamble Ltd*, 1971 S.L.T. (Notes) 18; *R Pagnan & Fratelli v Corbisa
Industrial Agropacuaria Ltd* [1970] 1 All E.R. 165; *Bonnor v Balfour Kilpatrick Ltd*, 1975 S.L.T.
(Notes) 3; *Aluminium Industrie Vaassen BV v Romalpa Aluminium Ltd* [1976] 1 W.L.R. 676; *Emerald
Stainless Steel Ltd v South Side Distribution Ltd*, 1983 S.L.T. 162; *Deutz Engines Ltd v Terex Ltd*,
1984 S.L.T. 273; *Armour v Thyssen Edelstahlwerke AG* [1991] 2 A.C. 339 HL; and *Parker v TUI UK
Ltd* [2009] EWCA Civ 1261.

[217] *Asaad v Kurter* [2013] EWHC 3852 (Fam), per Moylan J. at [93]. Sed pace *Neilson v Overseas
Projects Corporation of Victoria Ltd* [2005] HCA 54 (Australia).

is the same as its own domestic law.[218] This also will happen if the litigant(s) fail(s) entirely to raise and prove the relevant point.[219]

In respect of the second situation, where the forum finds the foreign *lex causae* to be defective or deficient, the forum should not supplement the foreign *lex causae* with its own domestic law solution/remedies. Parties ought to be on their guard at the pre-litigation stage as to the outcome of application of the applicable law; if it has no domestic right or remedy which suits their needs and purpose, then a party should endeavour to formulate his pleadings/submissions, so as to persuade the court that a different law is applicable (i.e. at the choice of law stage, *not* the proof of law stage). If the foreign *lex causae* as a matter of policy is found *not* to contain a particular cause of action or remedy, which happens, however, to exist in the law of the forum, it would not be right for the forum to interpone the cause of action/remedy of the *lex fori*, for that would amount, in effect, to non-application or contradiction of the *lex causae*, an outcome which is not justified except under the head of public policy. This situation must be distinguished sharply from the situation where proof fails and the *lex fori* applies by default.

There is a third situation, where foreign law is proved adequately, and is not found to be lacking in provision, but those provisions in some particular are offensive to the forum. In these circumstances, the effect will be that the *lex fori* will apply, either in a negative way by overruling application of the *lex causae* or, very rarely, in a positive way by supplying a remedy that the *lex causae* lacks.[220] The applicable law having been identified per the forum's choice of law rule, the forum, therefore, is entitled to exercise a public policy discretion to disapply that foreign law, as proved. *Ex hypothesi*, this can be done only after proof of what turns out to be, in the view of the forum, the unacceptable content of foreign law. There is no scope at the point of proof of foreign law (i.e. when establishing, as a matter of fact, what is the content of the foreign law) for the forum to "censor" the foreign law, since the task of proof is purely a "fact"-finding exercise.

The Madrid Principles

8–32   It is recognised that the different approaches taken by EU Member States to the matter of proof of foreign law, and in particular the "out-of-line" UK attitude, may frustrate the desired goal of harmonisation of applicable law rules, which, typically, are framed in a mandatory form of words.[221] Article 30 of the Rome II

---

[218] *Lloyd v Guibert* (1865) L.R. 1 Q.B. 115; *Ertel Bieber & Co v Rio Tinto Co Ltd* [1918] A.C. 260; *Faulkner v Hill*, 1942 J.C. 20; *Rodden v Whatlings Ltd*, 1960 S.L.T. (Notes) 96; *Pryde v Proctor & Gamble Ltd*, 1971 S.L.T. (Notes) 18; *Bonnor v Balfour Kilpatrick Ltd*, 1975 S.L.T. (Notes) 3; and *Bumper Development Corp v Commissioner of Police of the Metropolis* [1991] 4 All E.R. 638, per Purchas L.J. at 643–646.

[219] *De Reneville v De Reneville* [1948] P. 100.

[220] Instances of this third situation are difficult to find, but one might cite the example of a foreign rule of spousal immunity from suit in tort, adequate proof of which has been led, but the content of which the forum chooses to reject, thereby conferring upon an injured spouse (through default application of the forum's own law) the right to sue the offending spouse.

[221] e.g. Rome II Regulation art.4.1, "...the law applicable to a non-contractual obligation arising out of a tort/delict shall be the law of the country..."; Rome I Regulation art.4.1: "To the extent that the law applicable to the contract has not been chosen...the law governing...shall be determined as follows...".

Regulation laid down that, not later than August 20, 2011, the European Commission should submit to the European Parliament, the Council and the European Economic and Social Committee, a report on the application of that instrument, to include a study on the effects of the way in which foreign law is treated in the different Member States, and on the extent to which courts in the Member States apply foreign law in practice pursuant to the Rome II Regulation.

A Report, with "Principles for a future EU Regulation on the Application of Foreign Law" (the "Madrid Principles") was published in 2011.[222] The Principles begin by recommending that a regulation should be produced on the ascertainment of content and manner of application of foreign law; and proceed by recommending inter alia that:

- the regulation should have a general scope of application so as to include the application of Third countries' laws;
- application of foreign law should be made *ex officio* by the forum, which must use its best endeavours to ascertain the content of foreign law;
- the ascertainment of foreign law will not exclude its non-application on grounds of public policy; and
- if, in the view of the forum, there has been no adequate ascertainment of the content of foreign law in a reasonable time, or it is found upon ascertainment to be inadequate to address the issue in question, the *lex fori* shall be applied.

Although there is a strong case for addressing the perceived anomaly of Member State courts applying their own national rules in respect of the proof of foreign law, UK courts would not welcome such an intrusion into the longstanding practice of adversarial procedure.

Onus of proof

There is doubt whether this matter truly pertains to substance or procedure. **8–33** Writers in their earlier editions[223] favoured classification of the topic as substantive. Latterly views are equivocal.[224]

Scarman J. in *In the Estate of Fuld (Deceased) (No.3)*[225] assigned the topic of burden of proof to the category of procedure: the English Probate Court, "must in all matters of burden of proof follow scrupulously its own *lex fori*",[226] though this procedural characterisation is not one about which all authorities agree.[227]

Article 18.1 of the Rome I Regulation, and art.22.1 of the Rome II Regulation, which are in the same terms, mutatis mutandis, support the substantive

---

[222] C. Esplugues Mota, J. Iglesias, and G. Palao Moreno (eds), *Application of Foreign Law* (Sellier, 2011).

[223] e.g. M.Wolff, *Private International Law*, 2nd edn (1950), pp.234, 235; and *Cheshire's Private International Law*, 8th edn (1970), p.699; and 9th edn (1974), p.693.

[224] The 10th edn of *Cheshire and North on Private International Law* (1979), at p.707, does not express a firm view, nor does the latest, *Cheshire, North and Fawcett: Private International Law*, 14th edn (2008), at p.89.

[225] *In the Estate of Fuld (Deceased) (No.3)* [1968] P. 675.

[226] *Fuld (No.3)* [1968] P. 675 at 697. See also *Mackenzie v Hall* (1854) 17 D. 164, which prefers to assign the topic to procedure. cf. R.H. Graveson, *Private International Law*, 7th edn (1974), p.602.

[227] *Re Cohn* [1945] Ch. 5 supports the view that burden of proof is substantive.

characterisation: the instruments provide that the law governing a contractual/non-contractual obligation, as identified by either instrument, shall apply to the extent that, in matters of contractual/non-contractual obligations falling within the scope of each Regulation, it contains rules which raise presumptions of law or determine the burden of proof.

Presumptions

8–34 Graveson[228] regarded all presumptions of law and of fact as procedural, governed by the *lex fori*, but, as has been seen above, this position has been overtaken, at least in relation to the particular (contractual and non-contractual, respectively) matter with which they deal, by art.18(1) of Rome I Regulation and art.22(1) of Rome II Regulation.

Aside from the European instruments, it is thought that irrebuttable presumptions contained within the *lex causae* are matters of substance. As regards rebuttable presumptions it is suggested that they also should receive effect as matters involving substance unless they are clearly (foreign) rules of procedure.

Damages[229]

8–35 In principle, according to the traditional approach of Scots and English conflict of laws rules, there are two elements in the assessment of damages,[230] namely:

(a) liability,[231] a matter of substance, to be determined by the *lex causae*; and
(b) quantification of damages, a matter of procedure, to be determined by the *lex fori*.

At common law and under the Private International Law (Miscellaneous Provisions) Act 1995,[232] the availability of a particular head of damages was governed, therefore, by the *lex causae* (in contract, delict, or restitution, etc.); and the monetary calculation of damages was a matter purely for the *lex fori*.[233]

---

[228] R. Graveson, *Private International Law*, 7th edn (1974), p.602.

[229] See generally J.M. Carruthers, "Substance and Procedure in the Conflict of Laws: A Continuing Debate in relation to Damages" (2004) 53 I.C.L.Q. 691, 694; and "Damages in the Conflict of Laws: The Substance and Procedure Spectrum: *Harding v Wealands*" (2005) J. Priv. Int. L. 1.

[230] *Chaplin v Boys* [1971] A.C. 356; and *Harding v Wealands* [2007] 2 A.C. 1.

[231] *J D'Almeida Araujo LDA v Sir Frederick Becker & Co Ltd* [1953] 2 Q.B. 329.

[232] For the pre-Rome II position on damages in delict, see para.16–37, below. In *Maher v Groupama Grand Est* [2009] EWCA Civ 1191, on the characterisation by an English court (before the advent of Rome II) of the question whether or not interest is payable pre-judgment on the damages awarded to the claimant, the Court of Appeal held the matter to be one pertaining to remedy, and referable to the English *lex fori*. See also *Kuwait Airways Corpn v Iraqi Airways Co (Nos 4 and 5)* [2002] 2 A.C. 883; *Knight v Axa Assurances* [2009] EWHC 1900 (QB); *Wylie v Omniasig SA*, 2013 S.L.T. 46; and *Cox v Ergo Versicherung AG (formerly Victoria)* [2014] UKSC 22.

[233] *Fyffe v Ferguson* (1841) 2 Rob. 267; *Kendrick v Burnett (Owners of the SS Marsden)* (1897) 25 R. 82; *pace Chaplin v Boys* [1971] A.C. 356, the ratio of which is, notoriously, a matter of individual opinion; and *Mapfre Mutilidad Compania De Seguros Y Reaseguros SA v Keefe* [2015] EWCA Civ 598.

This statement of the traditional choice of law rule is subject to the changes introduced by the Rome I and Rome II Regulations, in respect of contractual and non-contractual obligations. Rome I Regulation art.12.1(c), within the limits of the powers conferred on the forum by its procedural law, allocates to the scope of the *lex causae* the consequences of a total or partial breach of obligations, including the assessment of damages, insofar as it is governed by rules of law.[234] This provision expands the province of the governing law, and curtails the power of the *lex fori*.

A similar, though further reaching change, took place in the treatment of awards of damages in non-contractual obligations, by virtue of art.15(c) of the Rome II Regulation. Article 15(c) allocates to the scope of the law applicable, "the existence, the nature and the assessment of damage or the remedy claimed". This provision wrought a significant change for UK courts.[235] The forum is thus enjoined to apply the *lex causae* to all aspects of the award of damages, subject only to public policy, and in the case of contractual[236] (though not expressly in non-contractual) cases, to the procedural constraints of the forum.[237]

In spite of the wording of art.15(c), there may yet be matters in the area of the award of damages which remain the province of the *lex fori*, on the rationale that the point is procedural, "evidence and procedure" being excluded from the scope of Rome II per art 1.3. For example, in *Wall v Mutuelle de Poitiers Assurances*,[238] the English Court of Appeal held that, in the assessment of damages for negligence in a claim brought in England by a claimant who had been injured in a road traffic accident in France, the issue of whether there should be a single joint expert or several experts fell to be determined by reference to English law, the law of the forum, on the basis that it was an issue of "evidence and procedure" within art.1(3) of Rome II. Elsewhere, sectoral provision may operate to dislodge the application of the *lex causae* per Rome II, as occurred in *Jacobs v Motor Insurers Bureau*[239] and *Bloy v Motor Insurers' Bureau*.[240]

The European provisions are extremely significant. The wide subject-matter scope of the remit of the Rome I and Rome II Regulations must be

---

[234] According to the Giuliano & Lagarde Report on the Convention on the Law Applicable to Contractual Obligations [1980] O.J. C282/1 at 33, the phrase of significance is "by rules of law": questions of fact in assessment of damages always will be for the forum, but international conventions or the terms of the contract itself may have provided "rules" for application in the instant matter, and these would be substantive. See para.15–39, below.

[235] Though the change was foreshadowed in the judgment of Arden L.J. in the Court of Appeal in *Harding v Wealands* [2005] All E.R. 415 (decision reversed by HL [2007] 2 A.C. 1). See para.16–37, below.

[236] Rome I Regulation art.12.1.c.

[237] See, for detail, para.16–38, below; and *Jacobs v Motor Insurers Bureau* [2010] EWCA Civ 1208; [2011] 1 W.L.R. 2609; *Bloy v Motor Insurers' Bureau* [2013] EWCA Civ 1543; *Actavis UK Ltd v Eli Lilly & Co* [2015] EWCA Civ 555; and *Wall v Mutuelle de Poitiers Assurances* [2014] EWCA Civ 138; [2014] 1 W.L.R. 4263.

[238] *Wall v Mutuelle de Poitiers Assurances* [2014] EWCA Civ 138; [2014] 1 W.L.R. 4263. The manner in which expert evidence was to be offered was classified by the court as procedural. The defendant's contrary submission, that art.15 should receive a broad construction so as to include within the scope of the (French) applicable law practices regularly used by the French court in assessing damages under French law, did not find favour with the English Court of Appeal.

[239] *Jacobs v Motor Insurers Bureau* [2010] EWCA Civ 1208; [2011] 1 W.L.R. 2609. Discussion at para.16–38, below.

[240] *Bloy v Motor Insurers' Bureau* [2013] EWCA Civ 1543. See also *Moreno v Motor Insurer's Bureau* [2015] EWHC 1002 (QB).

acknowledged; the majority of contentious damages claims in EU Member State courts will arise within the law of obligations, and most of those claims, though not all, will fall within the scope of either one of the Regulations. Where the claim does not fall within the technical scope of the Regulations, it will be interesting to see whether UK courts adhere to their traditional reasoning.

Currency in which judgment is given

8–36 This area concerns the answers which the conflict of laws provides to the problem of currency value fluctuation. It is important to distinguish between the substance of an obligation, on the one hand, and, on the other, the currency which, by agreement of the parties, is to be used to make payment in respect thereof.[241] *Money of account* (which measures the substance of an obligation)[242] is a substantive matter governed by the *lex causae*, but *money of payment* (in which the debt is discharged) is procedural.[243] In modern practice the money of account and money of payment usually are the same, agreed between the parties at the outset. A party to a contract may cover the risk of changes in the exchange rate between his own currency and the currency of payment by arranging a forward exchange contract with a third party, usually a bank, to hedge the exchange risk. In earlier decades, this aim was achieved by use of "gold clauses", linking the obligation to the value of gold, but in more recent years a substantial body of law and practice has developed in the structuring of derivatives as the basic concept of covering forward exchange risk. Parties may make a forward purchase of currency to safeguard their exposure, or if the period of time is considerable, seek, through a bank, a swap contract, if an equal and opposite risk can be found.

For centuries it had been assumed without argument in Scotland[244] and England[245] that a British court could grant a decree for payment of money only as a sum of money expressed in sterling. In 1974,[246] however, the Court of Appeal decided unanimously that within the "Common Market" a judgment might be given in a foreign currency (namely, the currency of the governing law of the contract in question), and that to do otherwise would be contrary to the spirit and intent of the Treaty of Rome. Lord Denning also thought that there was no reason why a court should not now grant such a judgment in the currency of the governing law, whether or not the parties were from countries within the "Common Market".

This initiative was followed in many later cases, with refinements and advances, first and notably in *Miliangos v George Frank (Textiles) Ltd*.[247] Later

---

[241] *Adelaide Electric Supply Co Ltd v Prudential Assurance Co Ltd* [1934] A.C. 122; *Mayor of Auckland v Alliance Assurance Co Ltd* [1937] A.C. 587; *Mount Albert BC v Australasian Temperance & General Mutual Life Assurance Society* [1938] A.C. 224; *Bonython v Australia* [1951] A.C. 201; and *National Mutual Life Assurance of Australasia v Att Gen of New Zealand* [1956] A.C. 369.

[242] *Woodhouse v Nigerian Produce Marketing Co Ltd* [1971] 2 Q.B. 23, per Lord Denning at 54; affirmed [1972] A.C. 741.

[243] See further para.15–40, below.

[244] *Hyslops v Gordon* (1824) 2 Sh. App. 451.

[245] *Re United Railways of Havana and Regla Warehouses Ltd* [1961] A.C. 1007.

[246] *Schorsch Meier GmbH v Hennin* [1975] Q.B. 416; [1974] 3 W.L.R. 823.

[247] *Miliangos v George Frank (Textiles) Ltd* [1975] Q.B. 487.

the same year, in *The Halcyon the Great (No.1)*,[248] the court ordered that a ship be sold and the proceeds paid in dollars into the English court. There was a number of decisions in the 1970s,[249] leading to the conjoined contract/tort House of Lords decision, *The Folias*,[250] which held in tort (the tort aspect having been reserved by the House of Lords in *Miliangos*) that the plaintiff should have his judgment in the currency which best expressed his loss; and in contract, that the fact that payments under a contract were in a particular currency did not necessarily mean that damages for breach need be awarded in that same currency.

In Scotland, these issues arose at the same point in the 1970s, first, tentatively, in *L/F Foroya Fiskasola v Charles Mauritzen Ltd*,[251] and soon after in *Commerzbank AG v Large*,[252] in which the point was made that there was no reason why a foreign creditor suing for an undisputed money debt in the country of his debtor's residence should be disadvantaged by fluctuations in currency. He should be entitled to have his decree expressed in the currency of the debt. If conversion be necessary, it should take place at the latest date practicable, which would be the date of extracting the decree.[253] In *Fullemann v McInnes's Executors*,[254] which concerned an award of damages to a Swiss pursuer injured in a road accident in Scotland as a result of the admitted fault of the other driver, the pursuer suffered physical and patrimonial loss. *Solatium* was valued at £42,500, but the award for patrimonial loss was expressed in Swiss francs, or the sterling equivalent at the date of payment or of extracting decree, whichever was the earlier.[255]

It can be seen that there was a "moving staircase" of judicial development, and in recognition of this the Law Commission concluded that it was inappropriate to propose substantial legislation, though minor amendments were suggested (but not implemented).[256] This then is one of the few areas of modern UK conflict rules in which the legislature has refrained from itself effecting change where change was deemed necessary.

---

[248] *The Halcyon the Great (No.1)* [1975] 1 W.L.R. 515.

[249] e.g. *Jugoslavenska Oceanska Plovidba v Castle Investment Co Inc (The Kozara)* [1974] Q.B. 292 (arbitration); *Barclays Bank International Ltd v Levin Bros (Bradford) Ltd* [1977] Q.B. 270; and *Jean Kraut AG v Albany Fabrics Ltd* [1977] Q.B. 182.

[250] *Services Europe Atlantique Sud (SEAS) v Stockholms Rederi AB Svea (The Folias)* [1979] Q.B. 491; [1978] 2 All E.R. 764.

[251] *L/F Foroya Fiskasola v Charles Mauritzen Ltd,* 1977 S.L.T. (Sh. Ct.) 76; 1978 S.L.T. (Sh. Ct.) 27.

[252] *Commerzbank AG v Large,* 1977 S.L.T. 219.

[253] See *Carnegie v Giessen* [2005] 1 W.L.R. 2510, in which the Court of Appeal stated that conversion should be made as close as practicable to the date of payment, "having regard to realities of enforcement procedures".

[254] *Fullemann v McInnes's Executors,* 1993 S.L.T. 259.

[255] *Fullemann v McInnes's Executors,* 1993 S.L.T. 259, per Lord Cullen at 267; contrasting *North Scottish Helicopters Ltd v United Technologies Corp Inc (No.2),* 1988 S.L.T. 778. See J. Blaikie, "Personal Injuries Claims: Damages in Foreign Currency", 1993 S.L.T. (News) 184.

[256] Law Commission, *Private International Law, Foreign Money Liabilities* (HMSO, 1983), Law Com. No.124. The question of interest on foreign currency judgment debts and arbitral awards was identified as an area where procedural change was needed: see now, for England and Wales only, Private International Law (Miscellaneous Provisions) Act 1995 Pt I.

Diligence

8–37   In Scots conflict of laws, this is governed at present entirely by the law of the place where a decree is to be enforced.[257]

Set-off/compromise

8–38   This subject, concerning methods of extinguishing, wholly or partly, an indebtedness, tended to be placed in early authorities under the heading of procedure or remedy, to be governed by the *lex fori*.[258] However, a persuasive argument can be made for treating the topic as pertaining to substance, whether it be referred to the applicable law in contract,[259] property, restitution, or insolvency.[260] Rome I Regulation contains, in art.17, a rule on set-off as it affects the subject-matter scope of that instrument.[261] In the absence of agreement of the parties, set-off shall be governed by the law applicable to the claim against which the right to set-off is asserted. If the right to set-off is the subject of an agreement between or among the parties, the applicable law of that agreement arrived at through application of art.3 (or potentially arts 5–8), must govern since, in terms of art.12.1(d), "the various ways of extinguishing obligations" fall under the scope of the law applicable, as a substantive matter.

It is clear that rights in this area may be seen often to arise out of principles of property, or the fact of possession, for example lien.[262] It could be that earlier decisions and later thoughts might meet on the rationalisation that an unpaid party's right to retain custody of an object of property pending payment for work done or a debt due, falls within the category of remedy or procedure, and frequently will be governed by the *lex fori* qua *lex situs*. Similarly, the right of a party to set off what he owes against what he is owed (as for example arising out of several contracts forming a course of dealing between two parties), arguably should be governed by the common applicable law, if there is one; and if there is not, it might be that the remedies available to the parties should be determined by the *lex fori* qua *situs* of the debt.[263]

Any confusion which has arisen under this heading probably stems from the variety of circumstances which can be subsumed under it. Some of these issues are plainly procedural, for example, whether a counterclaim may be brought by

---

[257] *Stewart v Royal Bank of Scotland Plc*, 1994 S.L.T. (Sh Ct) 27; *Union Carbide Corp v BP Chemicals Ltd*, 1995 S.L.T. 972. See also *Camdex International Ltd v Bank of Zambia Ltd* [1997] 1 C.L. 123; and *Bankers Trust International v Todd Shipyards Corp (The Halycon Isle)* [1981] A.C. 221 PC. In Scots domestic law, see Debt Arrangement and Attachment (Scotland) Act 2002, and Bankruptcy and Diligence etc. (Scotland) Act 2007, para.8–18, above.

[258] *Mitchell v Burnett and Mowat* (1746) Mor. 4468; *Robertson's Trustees v Bairds* (1852) 14 D. 1010; *Macfarlane v Norris* (1862) 2 B.J. 783; and *Meyer v Dresser* (1864) 16 C.B. (N.S.) 646.

[259] At least if the circumstances involve only two parties in a matter which could be said to arise out of a contract or putative contract between them.

[260] *Joint Administrators of Heritable Bank Plc v Winding up Board of Landsbanki Islands hf* [2013] UKSC 13.

[261] Para.15–41, below.

[262] See minority position of Lords Scarman and Salmon, in *The Halycon Isle* [1981] A.C. 221 PC.

[263] These suggested solutions beg several questions, chief among them being "which debt?" (if the debts had different governing laws) and "which forum?" In practice, however, the forum probably would be that of the domicile (i.e. residence) of the debtor first sued.

the defender in an action against the pursuer without raising separate proceedings; and whether and under what circumstances an action may be settled by compromise.

SUMMARY 8

1. Substance is governed by the *lex causae*; procedure by the *lex fori*. Classification between the two is for the forum in each instance. Certain matters are clearly procedural: form of action, evidence, and diligence. There is doubt about the classification of other issues, such as onus of proof. The treatment of damages, originally partly substantive and partly procedural in character, has been changed by EU instrument to render the existence, the nature and the assessment of damages as regards contractual action—contractual obligations a subject for the *lex causae*.
    8–39

2. Foreign prescriptive or limitation periods: the forum must defer to the rules of the *lex causae*, at least in matters relating to obligations, in terms of the Prescription and Limitation (Scotland) Act 1973, as amended.

3. Service of judicial and extrajudicial documents within the EU is governed by Regulation 1393/2007. Service furth of Scotland outside the EU is governed by Rules of Court of the Court of Session/Sheriff Court Rules.

4. Provisional and protective measures

    Evidence may be obtained under authority of a commission and diligence authorised by the Scots court at common law, or in terms of the Administration of Justice (Scotland) Act 1972 s.1.

    Regarding the preservation of assets, by art.35 of Brussels I Recast application may be made to the court of a Member State for such provisional, including protective, measures as may be available under that law, even if the court of another Member State has jurisdiction as to the substance of the matter.

    The UK did not opt in to Regulation (EU) No.655/2014 of the European Parliament and of the Council of 15 May 2014 establishing a European Account Preservation Order procedure to facilitate cross-border debt recovery in civil and commercial matters. Scots domiciled creditors are not able to utilise the remedy afforded by the regulation, but a Scots domiciled debtor having a bank account located in a participating Member State may be vulnerable to the grant of an EAPO by a court of a participating Member State having jurisdiction under the regulation.

5. Among EU Member States evidence from another Member State may be obtained under authority of Regulation 1206/2001.

    Evidence from non-EU Member States, or to be remitted abroad, may be obtained/provided by the "letter of request" procedure laid down by the Evidence (Proceedings in Other Jurisdictions) Act 1975.

6. The content of foreign law, if relied upon and not admitted, must be proved. In the absence of proof, it is presumed to be the same as the *lex fori*.

7. Decrees expressed in foreign currency may be awarded by a Scots or English court.

CHAPTER 9

Enforcement of foreign decrees

INTRODUCTION

The rules for enforcement in the UK of judgments from abroad depend upon the identity of the court of origin, i.e. the territory whence the judgment originated, and the necessity for enforcement varies according to type of decree. There are different classes of judicial decree, with different consequences for enforcement. Not all judicial decrees are suitable for, or require, enforcement *extra territorium*. Recognition of the foreign decree is a precursor to enforcement, but sometimes recognition alone suffices. Occasionally reliance is placed on a foreign judgment in a negative way, as a defence to an action in Scotland or England, under the heading of res judicata.

9–01

Classes of decree

Decrees may be divided into the following classes:

9–02

(a) Declarators of fact

The courts in Scotland or England are not bound by findings of fact in a foreign decree. A foreign declarator which purports merely to establish a fact is not necessarily conclusive, but may be accepted in non-contentious matters.[1]

9–03

(b) Interdicts

A decree of this class generally is enforceable only within the territorial limits of the court which granted it,[2] at least at common law, and in cases falling outside the ambit of the Brussels/Lugano regime.[3] Under that regime, orders for specific implement and interdict, as well as those which are purely money judgments, have the advantage of the enforcement scheme provided thereby among Member/Contracting States.[4]

9–04

---

[1] *Simpson's Trustees v Fox*, 1951 S.L.T. 412.
[2] *Waygood and Co v Bennie* (1885) 12 R. 615; *British Nylon Spinners v ICI* [1953] Ch. 19; and *Waste Systems International Inc v Eurocare Environmental Services Ltd*, 1998 G.W.D. 6-260.
[3] See Ch.7, above.
[4] *Barratt International Resorts Ltd v Martin*, 1994 S.L.T. 434, per Lord Sutherland at 437: "An interdict [granted in Scotland] therefore can be rendered effective even though the events being interdicted may occur in Spain." Also *G v Caledonian Newspapers Ltd*, 1995 S.L.T. 559 (intra-UK enforcement).

(c) Judgments in rem

9–05 Decrees of this class establish rights in property which are effective against the world at large, not simply between the two parties to a dispute.

The test of validity of such a decree turns upon the strength of the claim to jurisdiction of the issuing court ("court of origin"), which, in turn, depends upon the presence of the res within the jurisdiction,[5] with the result that if the res was within the jurisdiction at the time of pronouncement of the judgment, it is thought that the only ground upon which the judgment may be challenged is that of fraud.[6] It follows that the title of a third party who has acquired the res in compliance with that *lex situs* cannot be challenged.[7]

(d) Judgments affecting status

9–06 Judgments of this class although treated separately (i.e. possessing special statutory rules in conflict of laws, contained in the Family Law Act 1986 Pt II (non-EU decrees) and Brussels II *bis*[8] (EU decrees)) are regarded as being equivalent in many respects to decrees in rem in that they establish rights which should be recognised internationally without the aid or intervention of a foreign court, and have a status in unrelated litigation. The decision of the House of Lords in *Administrator of Austrian Property v Von Lorang*[9] is instructive as it demonstrates that an annulment of marriage granted by a court in Wiesbaden, Germany, recognised by the Scots forum, had a direct effect upon a property dispute taking place by way of multiplepoinding (diligence on assets) in Edinburgh. Viscount Dunedin in that case said: "A metaphysical idea, which is what the status of marriage is, is not strictly a *res*, but, to borrow a phrase, it savours of a *res*, and has all along been treated as such."[10]

If there is doubt as to the validity in Scotland of a foreign, non-EU consistorial judgment, a party may seek declarator of status from the Court of Session.[11] In principle, however, it follows from the decision in *Von Lorang*, above, that no such procedure should be necessary.

In relation to EU judgments affecting marital status, in terms of art.21 of Brussels II *bis*, a judgment given in a Member State shall be recognised in the other Member States without any special procedure being required. Under the

---

[5] Contrast *Castrique v Imrie* (1870) L.R. 4 H.L. 414 and *McKie v McKie* [1933] I.R. 464.

[6] *Ellerman Lines Ltd v Read* [1928] 2 K.B. 144.

[7] *Cammell v Sewell* (1858) 3 Hurl. & N. 617; *Doglioni v Crispin* (1866) L.R. 1 H.L. 301; *Castrique v Imrie* (1870) L.R. 4 H.L. 414; *Ballantyne v Mackinnon* [1896] 2 Q.B. 455; *Minna Craig Steamship Co v Chartered Mercantile Bank of India London and China* [1897] 1 Q.B. 55; *Enochin v Wyllie* (1882) 10 H.L. Cas. 1; *Orr-Ewing's Trustees v Orr-Ewing* (1885) 13 R. (H.L.) 1; and *Re Trepca Mines Ltd* [1960] 1 W.L.R. 1273. See Ch.17, below.

[8] Chs 12 and 14, below.

[9] *Administrator of Austrian Property v Von Lorang,* 1927 S.C. (H.L.) 80.

[10] *Administrator of Austrian Property v Von Lorang,* 1927 S.C. (H.L.) 80 at 92.

[11] Family Law (Scotland) Act 2006 s.37 amends the Domicile and Matrimonial Proceedings Act 1973 s.7 (jurisdiction of Court of Session in certain consistorial causes), to the effect of conferring jurisdiction on the Court of Session in actions for declarator of recognition of a "relevant foreign decree" (meaning a decree of divorce, nullity or separation granted by a non-EU state). Shrieval jurisdiction to grant such a declarator is conferred by s.37(3). In English law a declaration may be sought under the Family Law Act 1986 s.55.

head of enforceable judgments, art.28 of Brussels II *bis* provides that a judgment on the exercise of parental responsibility given in a Member State and enforceable there shall be enforceable in another Member State when, on the application of any interested party, it has been declared enforceable there.[12] Hence, a "declaration of enforceability" is required in such parental responsibility judgments; but the Regulation makes no mention of the use of such declarations in relation to any other type of judgment covered by the Regulation.[13]

(e)   Judgments in personam

Judgments of this class,[14] such as claims for debts or for damages for breach of contract, establish personal rights between the litigants: a foreign decree in personam, if not complied with by the defender, may be enforced in Scotland only by the holder of the personal right invoking the assistance of the courts.

9–07

LEGAL BASIS OF ENFORCEMENT

The original bases of enforcement of any foreign decree in Scotland were comity and reciprocity, but it is now accepted that comity alone is inadequate as a reason for enforcement, though reciprocity remains relevant.[15] There later arose the doctrine that a foreign judgment imposed an obligation[16] enforceable in another jurisdiction, the burden lying on the defender to show why it should not be enforced.

9–08

Originally in English conflict of laws, as contrasted with its domestic law, a foreign decree was not regarded as consuming the cause of action. Hence, a claimant holding a foreign decree which he wished to enforce in England might sue either upon the decree itself, or ignore the decree and sue on the cause of action (the best course being to sue on both grounds as alternatives).[17] However, this non-merger rule was abolished by the Civil Jurisdiction and Judgments Act

---

[12] i.e. a form of *exequatur* (registration) procedure. Such a judgment shall be enforced in England and Wales, in Scotland or in Northern Ireland only when, on the application of any interested party, it has been registered for enforcement in that part of the UK.

[13] See Chs 12 and 14, below.

[14] See *Pattni v Ali* [2007] 2 A.C. 85 PC (Isle of Man). cf. *Rubin v Eurofinance SA and New Cap Reinsurance Corp Ltd (in Liquidation) v Grant* [2013] 1 A.C. 236.

[15] The statutory structure of foreign judgment recognition and enforcement inter-country (in terms of 1920 and 1933 Acts; and also under the Civil Jurisdiction and Judgments Act 1982) rests on reciprocity. See, e.g. Foreign Judgments (Reciprocal Enforcement) Act 1933 ss.1, 9.

[16] *Schibsby v Westenholz* (1870) L.R. 6 Q.B. 155.

[17] See *East India Trading Co Inc v Carmel Exporters and Importers Ltd* [1952] 2 Q.B. 439; and *Carl Zeiss Stiftung v Rayner & Keeler Ltd* [1967] A.C. 853.

1982 s.34.[18] The section does not apply to Scotland, possibly because it was not required since the rule which it effected was already the rule in Scotland.[19]

Essentially, an unimpeachable foreign judgment creates rights and imposes obligations which should be enforceable across frontiers,[20] especially where a net of reciprocity has been woven, as by the 1920 and 1933 Acts (q.v.) and by the Brussels regime. The aim and rationale within the EU is the free movement of judgments, thereby facilitating the operation of the internal market.

Various principles of natural justice operate in the subject of judgment enforcement. For example, there should be finality in judgments so that a person is not required to "hawk his defence round Europe". It follows from this that the "enforcing" court, known as the "court addressed", will not act as a further court of appeal from the foreign court, the "court of origin". As a general rule, under any of the systems of judgment enforcement operative in the UK, review of substance will not be undertaken, nor will allegations of error on the part of the foreign court be investigated. The one important exception to this general rule against the re-opening of proceedings is in relation to alleged fraud, and even there the opportunity to re-open on this ground is significantly more restricted under the Brussels rules. Review of jurisdictional competence is permitted under the common law rules and older statutory schemes, but under the Brussels regime only to a very limited extent:[21] the absence of a right to query the jurisdiction of the court of origin is a *leitmotif* of the Brussels regime.

In Scotland, a civil and commercial judgment may be enforced in one of the following ways:

(1)   By action for decree conform.

(2)   By judgment registration ("judgment extension") under the Administration of Justice Act 1920 or the Foreign Judgments (Reciprocal Enforcement) Act 1933.

(3)   By use of the system of judgment enforcement provided by Brussels I Recast for judgments from EU Member States, and by the Lugano II Convention, for judgments from EFTA States, all per the Civil Jurisdiction and Judgments Acts 1982 and 1991.[22] There are significant differences between the rules of the Brussels/Lugano regime and the rules which apply at common law and under the 1920 and 1933 Acts.

---

[18] Section 34: "No proceedings may be brought by a person in England and Wales, or Northern Ireland on a cause of action in respect of which a judgment has been given in his favour in proceedings between the same parties, or their privies, in a court in another part of the United Kingdom or in a court of an overseas country, unless that judgment is not enforceable or entitled to recognition in England and Wales, or, as the case may be, in Northern Ireland." See *Fraser v HLMAD Ltd* [2007] 1 All E.R. 383; and *Blyth-Whitelock v de Meyer* [2009] EWHC 2839 (Ch). *Sed contra Black v Yates* [1992] Q.B. 526.

[19] Maxwell Report para.6.186.

[20] *Williams v Jones* (1845) 13 M. & W. 633; *Schibsby v Westenholz* (1870) L.R. 6 Q.B. 155; *Grant v Easton* (1883) L.R. 13 Q.B.D. 302.

[21] Namely, to ensure that the rules with regard to disadvantaged parties and exclusive jurisdiction have been complied with: Brussels I Recast art.45.1.e (paras 9–28 and 9–32, below).

[22] See also Civil Jurisdiction and Judgments Order 2001 (SI 2001/3929); Civil Jurisdiction and Judgments Regulations 2007 (SI 2007/1655); and Civil Jurisdiction and Judgments Regulations 2009 (SI 2009/3131), discussed in Ch.7, above.

(4)   By means of Schs 6 and 7 to the Civil Jurisdiction and Judgments Acts 1982 and 1991, in order to enforce English and Northern Irish judgments in Scotland and vice versa.
(5)   By use of any of the European enforcement procedures, viz.:
    (a)   European Enforcement Order for Uncontested Claims Procedure;
    (b)   European Order for Payment Procedure;
    (c)   European Small Claims Procedure.

Enforcement of judgments at common law

Enforcement via the common law route is required when a judgment emanates from a foreign country which is not bound by the Brussels/Lugano regime, nor linked by reciprocal arrangements with the UK in terms of the Administration of Justice Act 1920[23] or the Foreign Judgments (Reciprocal Enforcement) Act 1933.[24] Generally speaking, common law enforcement is required in respect of judgments from the USA,[25] Africa (except for Commonwealth countries), the Middle East and the Far East (including now Hong Kong).[26]   **9–09**

A foreign decree is enforced in Scotland by raising "an action for decree conform" to the decree of the foreign court. Certified translation of the foreign decree may be required. Decree conform may be granted only against a person who was party to the foreign proceedings. Such an action may be raised only in the Court of Session because it is regarded as falling under the *nobile officium*.[27]

The conditions set out below must be complied with in order that a foreign decree in personam may be enforceable in Scotland under the common law procedure:

(a)   the foreign court of origin must have had jurisdiction in the international sense;
(b)   the decree must have been granted in a judicial process. It is not clear whether the judgment must emanate from a "superior" court[28];
(c)   the decree must be final and res judicata;
(d)   the decree must be for payment of a definite sum of money (a foreign decree for an indefinite sum or a decree *ad factum praestandum* is not enforceable at common law in Scotland);

---

[23] If decree conform is sought in circumstances where judgment extension under the 1920 Act is available, expenses will not be awarded: Administration of Justice Act 1920 s.9(5).
[24] Under the Foreign Judgments (Reciprocal Enforcement) Act 1933 s.6, it is incompetent to proceed at common law if registration per that Act is possible.
[25] e.g. *First Fidelity Bank NA v Hudson*, 1995 G.W.D. 28-1499; *Wendel v Moran*, 1993 S.L.T. 44; *Elf Caledonia Ltd v London Bridge Engineering Ltd*, 1997 G.W.D. 33-1686; and *Clarke v Fennoscandia Ltd (No.3)*, 2008 S. L.T. 33.
[26] [1997] 12 C.L. 90.
[27] *O'Connor v Erskine* (1905) 13 S.L.T. 530; and *Geiger v D&J Macdonald Ltd*, 1932 S.L.T. 70.
[28] It is arguable that, to found enforcement proceedings in Scotland/England, the decree must be "incapable of revision by the Court which pronounced it": *Ascot Commodities NV v Northern Pacific Shipping (The Irini A) (No.2)* [1999] 1 Lloyd's Rep. 189 (issue estoppel). Taking a purposive approach, it seems unlikely that objection would be raised as to the rank of the court of origin in its own hierarchy so long as the judgment in question meets the common law requirements as to the "finality" of the judgment.

(e)   the subject-matter of the decree must not fall within any of the areas which form exclusions or exceptions to the extraterritorial effect of foreign law (revenue or penal laws, etc.).[29]

Grounds of challenge to actions for decree conform

(a)   No jurisdiction

9–10   This always will be the first challenge to be considered. In considering the sufficiency of the ground of jurisdiction assumed by a foreign court, there would be no point in referring only to the law of the foreign court because clearly that court regarded itself as having had jurisdiction; nor would there be any point in considering only the grounds assumed by the court addressed because that would restrict enforceability to cases where the two laws coincided. In practice, courts in the UK test the ground of jurisdiction in the court of origin according to whether or not it complies with a broad international standard of justice. By this standard certain grounds of jurisdiction (domicile, residence,[30] presence,[31] place of performance of contract or occurrence of delict,[32] prorogation or submission, reconvention) generally are recognised,[33] whereas other bases of jurisdiction considered exorbitant (nationality,[34] arrestment to found jurisdiction, ownership of heritage in an action unrelated to the heritage)[35] are not recognised.[36]

The case of appearance under protest to contest the jurisdiction of the putative forum is one which requires special consideration.[37] The final decision on whether the judgment debtor submitted to the jurisdiction of the court of origin is for the court addressed.[38] A controversy arose in England upon the question whether appearance simply to deny that the court had jurisdiction amounted to submission. The matter was settled by the Civil Jurisdiction and Judgments Act 1982 s.33[39] (which does not apply to Scotland), to the effect that a person shall not be regarded as having submitted to the jurisdiction of the court by reason only

---

[29] See Ch.3, above.

[30] *Schibsby v Westenholz* (1870) L.R. 6 Q.B. 155.

[31] *Adams v Cape Industries Plc* [1991] 1 All E.R. 929; and *Lucasfilm Ltd v Ainsworth* [2011] UKSC 39.

[32] Though see *Wendel v Moran*, 1993 S.L.T. 44.

[33] *Emanuel v Symon* [1908] 1 K.B. 302.

[34] *Rainford v Newell Roberts* [1962] I.R. 95; *Singh v Rajah of Faridkote* [1894] A.C. 670; though see *Ashbury v Ellis* [1893] A.C. 339.

[35] Possession of heritable property in Scotland is a general ground of jurisdiction in the Court of Session (Civil Jurisdiction and Judgments Act 1982 Sch.8 r.2(h)(ii)). Accordingly, a Scots court might be expected to recognise foreign decrees based on an equivalent ground of jurisdiction.

[36] See in English law *Emanuel v Symon* [1908] 1 K.B. 302, per Buckley L.J. at 309; see also *Re Trepca Mines Ltd* [1960] 1 W.L.R. 1273; and *Buchanan v Rucker* (1808) 9 East. 192.

[37] Common law cases in England before Civil Jurisdiction and Judgments Act 1982 s.33, demonstrating the controversy: *Copin v Adamson* (1874) L.R. 9 Ex. 345; *Guiard v De Clermont & Donner* [1914] 3 K.B. 145; *Harris v Taylor* [1915] 2 K.B. 580; *Re Dulles Settlement (No.2)* [1951] Ch. 842; *Blohn v Desser* [1962] Q.B. 116; *NV Daarnhouwer & Co NV, Handelmaatschappij v Boulos* [1968] 2 Lloyd's Rep. 259; and *Henry v Geoprosco International Ltd* [1976] Q.B. 726.

[38] *Akai Pty Ltd v People's Insurance Co Ltd* [1998] 1 Lloyd's Rep. 90.

[39] See *Tracomin SA v Sudan Oil Seeds Ltd (No.1)* [1983] 3 All E.R. 137; *Starlight International Inc v Bruce* [2002] EWHC 374 (Ch); and *AES UST-Kamenogorsk Hydropower Plant LLP v UST-Kamenogorsk Hydropower Plant JSC* [2010] EWHC 722 (Comm).

of the fact that he appeared (conditionally or otherwise) in the proceedings (a) to contest the jurisdiction of the court; and/or (b) to ask the court to dismiss or stay the proceedings on the ground that the dispute in question should be submitted to arbitration or to the determination of the courts of another country, or to protect, or obtain the release of, property seized or threatened with seizure in the proceedings.[40]

(b) Other grounds of challenge

As a foreign decree which, on the face of it, complies with "international" standards of jurisdiction, is regarded as conferring rights on the holder thereof, those rights generally will be recognised in Scotland, unless the other party satisfies the court that it would not be proper for it to recognise them. A Scots or English court will not act as a further court of appeal in relation to a foreign decree. The foreign court must be regarded as having been able to try the case and as having pronounced a valid judgment.   9–11

The result is that, broadly speaking, the grounds upon which a foreign decree may be challenged are restricted to those cases in which the court should be deemed not to have had jurisdiction in the international sense, as explained, or where it would be contrary to public policy to recognise the decree. A foreign judgment will be subject to challenge in Scotland or England only on some ground which goes to the very root and essence:

> "If a judgment is pronounced by a foreign Court over persons within its jurisdiction and in a matter with which it is competent to deal, English courts never investigate the propriety of the proceedings of the foreign Court unless they offend against English views of substantial justice."[41]

The following are the only available defences in addition to that of "no jurisdiction":   9–12

(1) Judgment not final and conclusive.[42] Particular attention should be paid to the meaning at common law of this challenge. A foreign judgment will not be enforced in Scotland or England if the merits have not been exhausted,[43] but the fact that the judgment is appealable,[44] or even that an appeal is pending, will not necessarily render it unenforceable in Scotland or England at common law. However, a Scots court would be likely to sist the

---

[40] cf. Brussels I Recast art.26.

[41] *Pemberton v Hughes* [1899] 1 Ch. 781, per Lindley M.R. at 790.

[42] *Paul v Roy* (1852) 15 Beav. 433; *Shedden v Patrick* (1854) 1 Macq. 535; *Sheey v Professional Life Assurance Co* (1857) 2 C.B. (N.S.) 211; *Scott v Pilkington* (1862) 2 B. & S. 11; *Harris v Quine* (1869) L.R. 4 Q.B. 653; *Blohn v Desser* [1962] 2 Q.B. 116; *Colt Industries Inc v Sarlie (No.2)* [1966] 1 W.L.R. 1287; *Berliner Industriebank AG v Jost* [1971] 2 Q.B. 463; *Black-Clawson International Ltd v Papierwerke Waldhof-Aschaffenburg AG* [1975] A.C. 591.

[43] *Nouvion v Freeman* (1889) L.R. 15 App. Cas. 1.

[44] *Colt Industries Inc v Sarlie (No.2)* [1966] 1 W.L.R. 1287.

action for decree conform if foreign appeal were imminent.[45] The court addressed must rely upon the court of origin in order to determine whether, by that foreign law, the judgment is final and binding.[46]

(2) Decree for an indefinite amount[47] or *ad factum praestandum*[48]; or for enforcement of a foreign revenue or penal or other public law excluded by Scots conflict rules from extraterritorial operation.[49]

(3) Judgment no longer extant (e.g. time-barred in the foreign system, or satisfied, or otherwise no longer enforceable).[50]

(4) Fraud: fraus omnia corrumpit.

Fraud may relate to the substantive issue, or it may reside in the fraudulent quality of the behaviour of the parties (collateral fraud).[51] Within the latter, another distinction[52] may be made, namely that between *dolus praesens* (by fraudulent use of the judgment as, for example, by falsely promising not to enforce it) and *dolus praeteritus* (consisting, for example, in fraud in the getting of the judgment, as by bribing the judge or producing perjured evidence).[53]

The alleged presence of fraud (by the court; on the court; or by one party against another)[54] may vitiate a judgment. In domestic law, a judgment may be impugned only if new evidence suggestive of fraud has been discovered since the hearing. In the conflict of laws, at least in cases falling outside the Brussels/Lugano regime, there seems to be no such requirement. Indeed, a defence relating to fraud may have been kept back in the original (foreign) proceedings, to be used in the subsequent enforcement proceedings,[55] and may then be admitted to proof.

The right, or duty, of the enforcing/requested court to consider and pronounce upon the effect of some allegedly fraudulent element, brought to the notice of, and perhaps dismissed by, the court of origin, was upheld by the Court of Appeal in *Jet Holdings Inc v Patel*,[56] itself approved by the

---

[45] As to the statutory position with regard to this matter, see Administration of Justice Act 1920 s.9(2)(e) (e.g. *NML Capital Ltd v Argentina* [2010] EWCA Civ 41); and the Foreign Judgment (Reciprocal Enforcement) Act 1933 s.1(2)(a) (*Aerotel Ltd v Wavecrest Group Enterprises Ltd* [2005] EWHC 2539 (Pat)).

[46] *Joint Stock Co 'Aeroflot-Russian Airlines' v Berezovsky* [2014] EWCA Civ 20.

[47] *Sadler v Robins* (1808) 1 Camp. 253.

[48] *Beatty v Beatty* [1924] 1 K.B. 807.

[49] See para.3–02 et seq., above.

[50] It is not an abuse of process for a judgment creditor to seek a second judgment on its original judgment with a view to avoiding difficulties in enforcing the original judgment abroad as a result of the expiry of limitation periods: *Kuwait Oil Tanker Co SAK v Al Bader* [2008] EWHC 2432 (Comm).

[51] e.g. *Ochsenbein v Papelier* (1873) L.R. 8 Ch. App. 695.

[52] Made in *Jacobson v Frachon* (1924) 44 T.L.R. 103: see M. Wolff, *Private International Law*, 2nd edn (1950), p.268.

[53] M. Wolff, *Private International Law*, 2nd edn (1950), p.268; *Macalpine v Macalpine* [1958] P. 35; *Middleton v Middleton* [1967] P.62; and more recently, *Clarke v Fennoscandia Ltd (No.2)*, 2001 S.L.T. 1311; and *Clarke v Fennoscandia Ltd (No.3)*, 2005 S.L.T. 511.

[54] *Wilson v Robertson* (1884) 11 R. 893; *Price v Dewhurst* (1837) Sim. 279; *Abouloff v Oppenheimer and Co* (1882) L.R. 10 Q.B.D. 295; *Vadala v Lawes* (1890) L.R. 25 Q.B. 310; *Habib Bank Ltd v Ahmed* [2002] 1 Lloyd's Rep. 444; and *Noble v Owens* [2010] EWCA Civ 224.

[55] *Syal v Hayward* [1948] 2 K.B. 443.

[56] *Jet Holdings Inc v Patel* [1990] 1 Q.B. 335.

House of Lords in *Owens Bank Ltd v Bracco*.[57] But the same latitude to the defendant in permitting him to raise a defence previously held back in the foreign proceedings was not evident where the not dissimilar issue of undue influence was alleged,[58] nor in the Brussels/Lugano context does the challenge under the head of *ordre public* allow such a wide challenge.[59] An addition to the corpus of cases is the English Court of Appeal decision in *Gelley v Shephard*[60] to the effect that a foreign judgment should not be refused effect, even though it was tainted by fraud, if it is shown that the court of origin would have made the same disposal even if it had been aware of the attempt to mislead it.

Clearly, there are warring principles of roughly equal weight: the desirability of finality of judgments is set against the undesirability of permitting a party to profit from his own wrongdoing. A modern understanding of comity, together with a desire for consistency, internally and in conflict of laws rules, may lead to a revision of the position when a suitable opportunity arises in the Supreme Court to place greater faith in the decision of the foreign court in such a matter.[61]

(5)   Decree contrary to natural justice.[62]

The Scottish and English courts have recognised that it is unreasonable to expect Scottish/English procedural rules[63] to be replicated abroad. Though breach of natural justice always must be one of the prime justifications for refusal to enforce a foreign decree, the requested forum must be satisfied, before refusing to enforce, that substantial justice was not done in the granting of the decree. A complaint that the defendant in the foreign court was not allowed to give evidence on his own behalf may be answered sufficiently by an explanation that neither party, in the circumstances, was entitled by the law of the forum to give evidence.[64] The ends of comity are not served if one legal system is too quick to criticise the standards of another.[65]

Procedural irregularities may result in unfairness, as for example where no translation services are provided, as in *Det Norske v McLaren*.[66]

If, in the foreign system, there is a ladder of appeal which was not used by the party then or later declaring himself aggrieved, that fact will tell

---

[57] *Owens Bank Ltd v Bracco* [1992] 2 All E.R. 193 HL (enforcement sought by means of 1920 Act); [1994] 1 All E.R. 336 ECJ; though contrast *House of Spring Gardens Ltd v Waite (No.2)* [1991] 1 Q.B. 241 (res judicata/estoppel).

[58] *Israel Discount Bank of New York v Hadjipateras* [1984] 1 W.L.R. 137. Undue influence would be likely to be subsumed under public policy.

[59] *Interdesco SA v Nullifire Ltd* [1992] 1 Lloyd's Rep. 180.

[60] *Gelley v Shephard* [2013] EWCA Civ 1172.

[61] cf. *Owens Bank Ltd v Etoile Commerciale SA* [1995] 1 W.L.R. 44 PC, e.g. per Lord Templeman at 48–51.

[62] *Jeannot v Fuerst* (1909) 25 T.L.R. 424; *Robinson v Fenner* [1913] 3 K.B. 835; *Re Macartney (No.2)* [1921] 1 Ch. 522; *Macalpine* [1958] P. 35; *Pemberton v Hughes* [1899] 1 Ch. 781; *Re Arbitration between the Owners of the Steamship Catalina and the Owners of the Motor Vessel Norma* (1938) 61 Ll. L. Rep. 360 (prejudice of arbitrator openly expressed).

[63] e.g. on matters such as days of notice: *Jeannot v Fuerst* (1909) 25 T.L.R. 424.

[64] *Scarpetta v Lowenfeldt* (1911) 27 T.L.R. 509.

[65] *Igra v Igra* [1951] P. 404.

[66] *Det Norske v McLaren* (1885) 22 S.L.R. 861.

against him.[67] On the other hand, force and fear imposed on a litigant to persuade him/her to seek the remedy[68] may result in non-enforcement. Where a Texas court awarded a global sum of damages, to be divided among a number of plaintiffs at the discretion of the plaintiffs' lawyers, the Texan judge making no decision upon the defendants' liability to each plaintiff, this constituted one of the grounds upon which the Court of Appeal refused to enforce the judgment.[69]

(6)   Decree contrary to public policy.[70]

At common law, there is always the possibility of a public policy challenge to meet any circumstances which arise. Frequently, public policy defences merge with those founded on fraud, or unfair treatment of a litigant as a result of foreign rules of procedure. It is very rare in commercial circumstances for a Scots or English court as the court addressed to refuse recognition on the ground of objection to some rule of substance on which the foreign decree is founded. However, an example of an objection to the substance of a foreign decree (in family law) can be found in the case of *Re Macartney (No.2)*,[71] in which the English court refused to enforce a Maltese award of "perpetual" aliment for a posthumously born child, out of the estate of her putative father. It has been questioned whether it is right for a British forum to direct its attention to the policy acceptability of the underlying ground of decree, rather than of the judgment. In any event, the public policy challenge to a commercial judgment rarely is found.

(7)   Infringements of human rights.

These venerable principles which guide courts in Scotland and England in the matter of refusing enforcement of a judgment which, in the view of the court addressed, is tainted by an element of what might generally be termed, "injustice to the judgment debtor" must be set against[72] the background of UK accession to the European Convention on Human Rights, which entails that UK courts must not permit enforcement in the UK of a foreign judgment which is not compliant with art.6 (right to a fair and public hearing within a reasonable time by an independent and impartial tribunal established by law). Article 6 applies both to the original proceedings in another ECHR State and to the enforcement proceedings in the UK.[73] It must be asked whether the body of guidelines accumulated in UK practice in this area meets the test which the human rights jurisprudence imposes. Might it be that the protection provided by traditional conflict of laws jurisprudence falls short of what is now required? Comparable with the principles of mutual trust which are

---

[67] *Cooney v Dunne*, 1925 S.L.T. 22; and *Jacobson v Frachon* (1924) 44 T.L.R. 103. Moreover, the decision of the foreign court on a procedural matter may bar the raising of that issue in the enforcement proceedings: *Desert Sun Loan Corp v Hill* [1996] 2 All E.R. 847.

[68] *Re Meyer* [1971] 2 W.L.R. 401; *Hornett v Hornett* [1971] P. 255.

[69] *Adams v Cape Industries Plc* [1991] 1 All E.R. 929.

[70] As to which, see generally Ch.3, above.

[71] *Re Macartney (No.2)* [1921] 1 Ch. 522. Also *Buchler v Al-Midani* [2006] B.P.I.R. 620; *United States Securities & Exchange Commission v Manterfield* [2009] 2 All E.R. 1009.

[72] J.J. Fawcett, "The Impact of Article 6(1) of the ECHR on Private International Law" (2007) 56 I.C.L.Q. 1; G. Ward, "Protection of the Right to a Fair Trial and Civil Jurisdiction" (2008) J.R. 15.

[73] *Citibank NA v Rafidian Bank* [2003] I.L.Pr. 49.

applicable among EU Member States, it appears that there has emerged a presumption that proceedings which have taken place in states which are party to the ECHR are compliant with art.6.[74]

Arguably, the UK court addressed is entitled to overlook technical breaches of art.6 if substantive justice in its view was done in the court of origin. The authority for this proposition is a decision of the House of Lords in *United States v Montgomery (No.2)*.[75] Montgomery's ex-husband, Barnette, was convicted on a charge of having defrauded the US Government of approximately $15 million. Shortly before conviction, Barnette transferred shares in a company, through which he had laundered the fraudulent proceeds, to his then wife. The US Government sought a tracing and confiscation order in relation to the funds, on the argument that the Government's title to the shares ante-dated Barnette's transfer of them to Montgomery, and that consequently the shares were forfeited and had to be surrendered to the Government. Barnette, being a fugitive from US justice, was not permitted under US "fugitive disentitlement" law to appear in the relevant proceedings in the United States. When the US Government sought to enforce the resultant confiscation order against Montgomery, by that date resident in the UK, Barnette argued before the English court that if the ECHR had applied in the United States, the confiscation proceedings would have breached art.6(1), and that, therefore, if the English court registered the US order, it would contravene s.6 of the Human Rights Act 1998. Lord Carswell, having referred to earlier House of Lords authority,[76] to the effect that only a case of extreme unfairness to the applicant would suffice to permit a case of indirect effect to be made out, took the view that no different proposition had yet emerged from the Strasbourg jurisprudence. The US "fugitive disentitlement" doctrine, while not in conformity strictly with art.6, was defensible, and did not fall within the "flagrant denial of justice" precept. It was not an arbitrary deprivation of a party's right to a hearing.

In light of this decision, the approach taken in international private law jurisprudence would not appear to be notably defective.

(8)   Decree taken contrary to agreement.

Under the Civil Jurisdiction and Judgments Act 1982 s.32,[77] a judgment given by a court in an overseas country[78] shall not be recognised or enforced in the UK if the bringing of those proceedings was contrary to an agreement,[79] by which the dispute in question was to be settled otherwise

---

[74] cf. *Merchant International Co Ltd v Natsionalna Aktsionerna Kompaniya Naftogaz Ukrayiny* [2012] EWCA Civ 196.

[75] *United States v Montgomery (No.2)* [2004] 1 W.L.R. 2241. See criticism by J.J. Fawcett, "The Impact of Article 6(1) of the ECHR on Private International Law" (2007) 56 I.C.L.Q. 1, 33.

[76] *R. (on the application of Ullah) v Special Adjudicator* [2004] UKHL 26; and *R. (on the application of Razgar) v Secretary of State for the Home Department* [2004] UKHL 27, per Lord Carswell at [26].

[77] e.g. *Cavell United States Inc v Seaton Insurance Co* [2008] EWHC 876 (Comm); and *Youell v La Reunion Aerienne* [2009] EWCA Civ 175.

[78] i.e. outside UK (s.32(4)), but not a judgment falling within the Brussels regime: *Partenreederei M/S Heidberg v Grosvenor Grain & Feed Co Ltd (The Heidberg) (No.2)* [1994] 2 Lloyd's Rep. 287.

[79] So long as the agreement was not illegal, void, unenforceable or incapable of being performed for reasons not attributable to the fault of the party bringing the proceedings in which the judgment was given (s.32(2)).

than by proceedings in the courts of that country; and those proceedings were not brought in that court by or with the agreement of the party against whom the judgment was given; and that party did not counterclaim in the proceedings or otherwise submit to the jurisdiction of that court.[80]

(c) Unavailable defences

9–13 (1) Defence omitted.[81]
Except in relation to the defence of fraud,[82] the defender must make available all his defences in the court of origin.[83] If he fails to do so, he will not be allowed to plead them afterwards in the court addressed.
(2) Error in fact by the court of origin.
(3) Error in law by the court of origin as to its own law.[84] Whether the error is as to the substantive law of that court, or as to its rules of jurisdiction, it does not serve as a defence against enforcement unless the "judgment" is a nullity by its own law.
(4) Error as to Scots or English law.[85]
(5) Defective procedure. It behoves the court addressed to pay regard to the de minimis principle. Natural justice must be secured, but the question is always whether substantial justice has been done in the instant case.[86]

Res judicata

9–14 A foreign decree may be founded upon as a defence to an action in Scotland[87] or England[88] if the decree was in favour of the defender in the Scottish or English action. If in such a case the pursuer maintains that the decree should not be recognised, it may still be scrutinised, but the grounds on which it may be challenged are fewer in number; for example, the pursuer in a foreign action who is suing again in Scotland can hardly plead that the court which he himself selected had no jurisdiction. The case of *Showlag v Mansour*[89] is Privy Council authority for the view that, where there are two conflicting foreign (necessarily now, non-EU) judgments on the same matter, apparently of equal standing, the first in date should be preferred.

---

[80] *Tracomin SA v Sudan Oil Seeds Ltd (No.1)* [1983] 3 All E.R. 137.
[81] *Ellis v McHenry* (1871) L.R. 6 C.P. 228. cf. *Henderson v Henderson* (1843) 3 Hare. 100.
[82] See para.9–10, above.
[83] *Clydesdale Bank Ltd v Schroder & Co* [1913] 2 K.B. 1.
[84] *Henderson* (1843) 3 Hare. 100; *Scott v Pilkington* (1862) 2 B. & S. 11; *Dent v Smith* (1869) L.R. 4 Q.B. 414, per Cockburn C.J. at 446; *De Cosse Brissac v Rathbone* (1861) 6 H. & N. 301; *Merker v Merker* [1963] P. 283.
[85] *Castrique v Imrie* (1870) L.R. 4 H.L. 414; *Godard v Gray* (1870) L.R. 6 Q.B. 139; cf. *Dallal v Bank Mellat* [1986] 1 All E.R. 239 (arbitration).
[86] *Pemberton v Hughes* [1899] 1 Ch. 781, e.g. per Lindley M.R. at 789–791.
[87] *Boe v Anderson* (1857) 20 D. 11; *Phosphate Sewage Co v Molleson* (1878) 5 R. 1125; and *Comber v Maclean* (1881) 9 R. 215.
[88] *Ricardo v Garcias* (1845) 12 Cl. & F. 368; 65 R.R. 585; *Vanquelin v Bouard* (1863) 15 C.B. (N.S.) 341; *Castrique v Imrie* (1870) L.R. 4 H.L. 414; *Godard v Gray* (1870) L.R. 6 Q.B. 139; *Taylor v Hollard* [1902] 1 K.B. 676; *Jacobson v Frachon* (1924) 44 T.L.R. 103; *Kohnke v Karger* [1951] 2 K.B. 670; *Carl Zeiss Stiftung v Rayner & Keeler Ltd* [1967] 1 A.C. 853; and *Air Foyle Ltd v Center Capital Ltd* [2004] I.L.Pr. 15.
[89] *Showlag v Mansour* [1994] 2 All E.R. 129 PC.

Direct enforcement of foreign judgments

In terms of the Judgments Extension Act 1868, and the Inferior Courts Judgments **9–15**
Extension Act 1882, a system was established of registration in Edinburgh in a
Register of English and Irish Decrees of the Supreme (and, by the 1882 Act, the
inferior) Courts of England and Ireland. After registration these decrees had the
same effect as decrees of the Court of Session, and might be enforced in the same
way. Both Acts were repealed by the Civil Jurisdiction and Judgments Act 1982.

There remain applicable to judgments emanating from countries outside the
geographical ambit[90] of the Brussels/Lugano regime two Acts concerning the
registration of foreign judgments. These are the Administration of Justice Act
1920 and the Foreign Judgments (Reciprocal Enforcement) Act 1933. The 1933
Act is more detailed than the 1920 Act, and is much more important in terms of
geographical reach. Both Acts depend on reciprocity. Applicability of their
provisions depends on their extension by Order in Council in suitable cases[91] to
the country whence the judgment came.

The Administration of Justice Act 1920

Part II provides for the enforcement of judgments[92] of superior courts[93] within **9–16**
Commonwealth countries,[94] by means of registration, which is a matter of
discretion and not of right. The provisions undernoted (paraphrased and
abbreviated) are those of principal importance.

A judgment of a superior court of the Dominions may be enforced on
application to the High Court in England or Northern Ireland or the Court of
Session in Scotland at any time within 12 months after its date or within such
longer period as the court addressed may allow. On any such application the court
may order the judgment to be registered and enforced in the UK if it thinks it just
and convenient to do so.[95]

No judgment may be registered if[96]:

(a)   the original court acted without jurisdiction[97]; or

---

[90] Where a judgment from an EU Member State falls outside the scope of Brussels I Recast, and
likewise where a judgment from an EFTA country falls outside the scope of Lugano II, the 1933 Act
continues to apply.
[91] i.e. that in such country satisfactory reciprocal provision for enforcement of UK judgments has
been made: Administration of Justice Act 1920 s.14.
[92] *Platt v Platt*, 1958 S.L.T. 94; and *Standard Chartered Bank v Zungera Power Ltd* [2014] EWHC
4714 (QB).
[93] *Ivory, Petitioner,* 2006 S.L.T. 758.
[94] New Zealand, Falkland Islands, Jamaica, Trinidad, Ghana, Nigeria, Kenya, Tanzania, Uganda,
Zimbabwe, Zambia, Malawi, Botswana, Sri Lanka, Malaysia, Singapore. No countries will be added
to the list. Gibraltar is now governed by the Civil Jurisdiction and Judgments Act 1982 (Civil
Jurisdiction and Judgments Act 1982 (Gibraltar) Order 1997 (SI 1997/2602)). Enforcement of Hong
Kong judgments, previously falling under the Administration of Justice Act 1920, now proceeds at
common law.
[95] 1920 Act s.9(1).
[96] 1920 Act s.9(2).
[97] *Chief Harry Akande v Balfour Beatty Construction Limited* [1998] I.L.Pr. 110.

(b)   the defender, being neither a person carrying on business nor ordinarily resident in the jurisdiction of the court of origin, did not voluntarily appear or submit or agree to submit to the jurisdiction of that court[98]; or

(c)   the defender was not duly served with the process of the original court and did not appear, notwithstanding that he was ordinarily resident or was carrying on business within the jurisdiction of that court or agreed to submit to the jurisdiction of that court; or

(d)   the judgment was obtained by fraud; or

(e)   the defender satisfies the registering court either that an appeal is pending, or that he is entitled and intends to appeal against the judgment;[99] or

(f)   the judgment was in respect of a cause of action which for reasons of public policy or some other similar reason could not have been entertained by the registering court.

When registered the decree shall have as from the date of registration the same force and effect, and proceedings may be taken thereon, as if it had been a judgment originally obtained in the registering court.[100] If an action for decree conform is raised on a decree which could have been registered the pursuer shall not be entitled to expenses unless an application for registration was refused or the court orders otherwise.[101] When a judgment has been obtained in a superior court in the UK and the judgment creditor wishes to secure the enforcement of the judgment in a part of the Commonwealth outside the UK to which the Act extends, the court shall issue to the judgment creditor a certified copy of the judgment to enable him to enforce it.[102]

The Foreign Judgments (Reciprocal Enforcement) Act 1933

9–17   The 1933 Act applies to certain non-Commonwealth countries as well as to Commonwealth countries,[103] the hope being that ultimately it would supersede the 1920 Act. The Australian states have transferred from the 1920 to the 1933 system. European countries, in respect of which enforcement of decrees originally was governed by the 1933 Act, transferred to the Brussels system upon accession to the EU.[104] The system of reciprocity echoes that operative under s.14 of the 1920 Act.[105]

The 1933 Act governs the enforcement in the UK of judgments under certain sector-specific conventions to which the UK is party, but it does not cover the

---

[98] *Sfeir & Co v National Insurance Co of New Zealand Ltd* [1964] 1 Lloyd's Rep. 330; and *Beach Petroleum NL v Johnson* [1996] C.L.Y. 1104.

[99] Contrast common law position, and the rule under 1933 Act s.1(3).

[100] 1920 Act s.9(3).

[101] 1920 Act s.9(4).

[102] 1920 Act s.10; *Consolidated Contractors International Company SAL v Masri Privy Council* [2011] UKPC 29; and *Bank of British West Africa Ltd, Petitioners*, 1931 S.L.T. 83.

[103] The list comprises Australia, Bangladesh, Canada (except Quebec), India, Isle of Man, Israel, Jersey, Guernsey, Pakistan, Surinam and Tonga. Norway was on the original list, but Lugano II applies now to Norwegian judgments. See special circumstances of the Bahamas in *B v T (No.1)*, 2002 C.L.Y.B. 637.

[104] Austria, Belgium, France, Germany, Italy, Netherlands. However, where the matter falls outside the scope of Brussels I Recast, the 1933 Act continues to apply.

[105] 1920 Act s.9.

enforcement of a judgment of a relevant foreign country if the latter was simply for the enforcement of a judgment given in a third country.[106]

The Act may not be used for the recognition or enforcement of a foreign decree which does not relate to a commercial matter.[107] The 1933 scheme of registration is mandatory: foreign decrees which can be registered under the Act are not enforceable by other means, i.e. action for decree conform is incompetent.[108]

Unlike the 1920 Act, registration is a matter of right not discretion, subject only to the provisos (s.2(1)) that registration shall not take place if at the date of the application: (a) a judgment has been wholly satisfied[109]; or (b) it could not be enforced by execution in the country of the court of origin.

The Act applies to foreign countries, specified by Order in Council,[110] which give reciprocal treatment with regard to decrees of UK courts. The Act applies only to a judgment of a recognised court which post-dates the coming into force of the relevant Order in Council and is (a) either final and conclusive[111] as between the judgment debtor and the judgment creditor, or requires the former to make an interim payment to the latter; and (b) there is payable thereunder a sum of money, not being a sum payable in respect of taxes or other charges of a like nature, or in respect of a fine or other penalty.[112]

By s.2(1), application for registration may be made by the judgment creditor to the Court of Session within six years of the date of the decree or last judgment in the appeal proceedings; and upon registration the decree has the same force and effect as a decree of the courts of this country.[113]

Section 4(1)(a) contains grounds upon which the registration shall be set aside[114] by the registering court, viz.:

(i)   the Act does not apply to the judgment in question, or the judgment was registered in contravention of the above provisions of the Act; or

(ii)   the courts of the country of the original court had no jurisdiction in the circumstances of the case[115]; or

---

[106] 1933 Act s.1(2A), added by Civil Jurisdiction and Judgments Act 1982 Sch.10, pertaining to judgments at one remove, e.g. judgments of the foreign court on appeal from a court which is not a recognised court, or a judgment regarded as a judgment of the foreign court but made in another country.

[107] *Maples v Maples* [1987] 3 All E.R. 188 (concerning a Jewish divorce).

[108] 1933 Act s.6. See also *Rubin v Eurofinance SA and New Cap Reinsurance Corp Ltd (in Liquidation) v Grant* [2013] 1 A.C. 236.

[109] If, at the date of application for registration, the judgment has been partially satisfied, judgment shall be registered only in respect of the balance remaining payable at that date: s.2(4).

[110] 1933 Act s.1(1).

[111] 1933 Act s.1(3): a judgment shall be deemed to be final and conclusive notwithstanding that an appeal may be pending against it, or that it may still be subject to appeal, in the courts of the country of the original court.

[112] 1933 Act s.1(2).

[113] 1933 Act s.2(2): *Re A Judgment Debtor* [1939] 1 All E.R. 1; *Ferdinand Wagner v Laubscher Bros & Co* [1970] 2 Q.B. 313.

[114] *Société Cooperative Sidmetal v Titan International Ltd* [1965] 3 All E.R. 494; *Northern Electricity Supply Corp (Private) Ltd v Jamieson*, 1971 S.L.T. 22 (expenses).

[115] 1933 Act s.4(2)(a), (b), (c): recognised grounds of jurisdiction in the court of origin are in essence *in personam*—submission by voluntary appearance by the judgment debtor; or the debtor's residence or place of business in that place.

(iii) the defender (even if duly served in accordance with the law of the country of the original court) did not receive notice of the proceedings in sufficient time to enable him to defend the proceedings, and did not appear; or

(iv) the judgment was obtained by fraud; or

(v) the enforcement of the judgment would be contrary to public policy in the country of the registering court[116]; or

(vi) the rights under the judgment are not vested in the person by whom the application for registration was made.

Section 4(1)(b) states that the registration may be set aside if the registering court is satisfied that the matter in dispute in the proceedings in the original court had previously to the date of the judgment in the original court been the subject of a final and conclusive judgment by another court having jurisdiction in the matter (res judicata).

Section 5(1) provides that on an application to set aside registration, if the applicant satisfies the registering court either that an appeal is pending, or that he is entitled and intends to appeal against the judgment, the court may set aside the registration or adjourn the application until after the expiration of such period as appears to the court to be reasonably sufficient to enable the applicant to take the necessary steps to have the appeal disposed of by the competent tribunal.[117]

The setting aside of a registered judgment shall not prejudice a further application to register the judgment when the appeal has been disposed of or if and when the judgment becomes enforceable by execution in that country.[118]

Section 8(1) provides for finality of judgment: a judgment to which Part I applies or would have applied if a sum of money had been payable thereunder, whether it can be registered or not, or whether, if it can be registered, it is registered or not, shall be recognised in any court in the UK as conclusive between the parties thereto in all proceedings founded on the same cause of action and may be relied on by way of defence or counterclaim.[119]

The Protection of Trading Interests Act 1980

9–18 The 1920 and 1933 Acts provide rules which, in substance, resemble those of the common law. Common law authorities, therefore, may be useful. Each of the systems so far considered envisages the enforcement in the UK of fixed money judgments from a court of a foreign legal system which has jurisdiction according to an international test; and a registration system caters for those countries which have entered into reciprocal arrangements with the UK.

The enforcement system described, at common law and under the Acts of 1920 and 1933, is subject to the Protection of Trading Interests Act 1980 s.5, in terms of which no judgment to which s.5 applies shall be registered under the Acts of 1920 or of 1933, nor shall common law enforcement proceedings be entertained by any UK court.[120] The judgments affected are:

---

[116] *SA Consortium General Textiles v Sun & Sand Agencies* [1978] 2 All E.R. 339.

[117] *Walton, Petitioner* [2012] CSIH 53.

[118] 1933 Act s.5(2).

[119] *Black Clawson International Ltd v Papierwerke Waldhof-Aschaffenburg AG* [1975] 1 All E.R. 810. But see now for England the Foreign Limitation Periods Act 1984 s.3.

[120] *British Airways Board v Laker Airways Ltd* [1985] A.C. 58.

Section 5(2) (paraphrased and abbreviated):

(a) a judgment for multiple damages, i.e. a judgment for an amount arrived at by doubling, trebling or otherwise multiplying a sum assessed as compensation for the loss or damage sustained by the person in whose favour the judgment is given[121];

(b) a judgment based on a provision or rule of law specified or described in an order under s.5(4)[122];

(c) a judgment on a claim for contribution in respect of damages awarded by a judgment falling within (a) or (b) above.

Section 6 applies where such a judgment for multiple damages has been made against a UK citizen, or company incorporated in the UK or person carrying on business in the UK, and where such a defendant has paid (or has yielded through process of execution (s.6(6)) an amount on account of the damages. In such circumstances, unless the party (the "qualifying defendant") was ordinarily resident in the overseas country at the time of the institution of the judgment proceedings, or is a body corporate with its principal business there, or carried on business in the overseas country and the judgment proceedings concerned activities exclusively carried on in that country, the qualifying defendant shall be entitled to recover from the judgment creditor so much of the amount as exceeds the part attributable to compensation.[123] Further, by s.6(5), a court in the UK may entertain proceedings on such a claim even though the person against whom the proceedings are brought is not within the jurisdiction of the court.

This legislation, unusual in nature, and unusually specific, is designed to protect British individuals and companies from American anti-trust legislation which makes possible an award of multiple damages for losses caused by anti-competitive actings.[124] Section 5 (and consequently s.6) does not apply within the Brussels/Lugano ambit, nor, generally, does it appear to strike at other foreign awards of exemplary damages which do not fall within the definition provided by s.5(3).[125]

---

[121] 1933 Act s.5(3). Although on a literal interpretation of s.5, such a judgment would be wholly unenforceable, *Lewis v Eliades (No.2)* [2004] 1 W.L.R. 692 is authority for the segregation and enforcement of the compensatory (i.e. non-punitive) element of an award in a case where the judgment pertains to several causes of action in respect of some, but not all, of which punitive multiplication has been applied. See also *Service Temps Inc v MacLeod,* 2014 S.L.T. 375; and contrast *Pace Europe Ltd v Dunham* [2012] EWHC 852 (Ch).

[122] i.e. a judgment appearing to the Secretary of State to be concerned with the prohibition or regulation of agreements, arrangements or practices designed to restrain, distort or restrict competition in the carrying on of business of any description or to be otherwise concerned with the promotion of such competition.

[123] As defined: s.6(2).

[124] For explanation of background and details, see *Cheshire, North and Fawcett: Private International Law,* 14th edn (2008), pp.561–563.

[125] *SA Consortium General Textiles v Sun & Sand Agencies* [1978] 2 All E.R. 339.

Judgments rendered in EU Member States or EFTA States

Civil Jurisdiction and Judgments Acts 1982 and 1991[126]

9–19   It falls to consider the system of "free flow of judgments" regulated by Brussels I Recast,[127] associated European regulations, and the Lugano II Convention. Since the foundation instrument, the 1968 Brussels Convention,[128] was a double convention, concerned to reach agreement on jurisdiction and then to proceed to a relatively simple enforcement method, certain differences from the common law and statutory registration systems described above are immediately apparent, one being the small scope for challenging the jurisdiction of the court of the Member State of origin. Further, the Brussels mechanism is not limited to the enforcement of money judgments, but may extend to decrees *ad factum praestandum*. Moreover it does not matter that the judgment is not final, nor is the level of the hierarchy whence the decree comes significant.

Brussels I Recast

Introduction

9–20   The 1968 Brussels Convention laid down its own procedure for recognition and enforcement, a procedure which was streamlined, but was not, in essentials, changed by the Brussels I Regulation.[129] Rather more change was introduced by Brussels I Recast, which, as explained in Ch.7, applies to legal proceedings instituted on or after 10 January 2015, and to authentic instruments[130] formally drawn up or registered, and to court settlements[131] approved or concluded, on or after that date.[132]

Where the Brussels regime is operative, no other procedure is competent[133]; the Brussels system is obligatory. The rules apply only to judgments from EU Member States,[134] and only to such judgments as fall within the scope of the Regulation, that is, judgments in civil and commercial matters not specifically excluded by art.1. The rules of recognition and enforcement vis-à-vis all Member States except Denmark are contained in Ch.III arts 36–57 of Brussels I Recast.

---

[126] As amended by the Civil Jurisdiction and Judgments Order 2001 (SI 2001/3929), and Civil Jurisdiction and Judgments Regulations 2009 (SI 2009/3131).

[127] Regulation (EU) No.1215/2012 of the European Parliament and of the Council of 12 December 2012 on jurisdiction and the recognition and enforcement of judgments in civil and commercial matters (recast) [2012] O.J. L351/1 (henceforth "Brussels I Recast").

[128] 1968 Brussels Convention on jurisdiction and the enforcement of judgments in civil and commercial matters [1972] O.J. L299/32.

[129] Council Regulation (EC) No.44/2001 on jurisdiction and the recognition and enforcement of judgments in civil and commercial matters [2001] O.J. L12/1.

[130] Defined in art.2(c).

[131] Defined in art.2(b).

[132] For transitional provisions, see para.7–12, above.

[133] *De Wolf v Harry Cox BV* [1976] E.C.R. 1759.

[134] There can be no "laundering" of non-EU judgments: *Owens Bank Ltd v Bracco (No.2)* [1994] 1 All E.R. 336. The Brussels regime enforcement procedures do not apply to judgments from a court of a non-Member State (cf. exclusion of laundering in 1933 Act s.1(2A)).

The EC–Denmark Agreement

Denmark did not participate in the adoption of the Brussels I Regulation,[135] and therefore was not bound by it. Thus, the allocation of jurisdiction and enforcement of judgments vis-à-vis Denmark continued to be governed by the 1968 Convention until the conclusion of an Agreement between the European Community and Denmark on Jurisdiction and the Recognition and Enforcement of Judgments in Civil and Commercial Matters,[136] which extended, as between the EC and Denmark, the provisions of the Brussels I Regulation, with certain amendments of a fairly minor nature. In terms of art.3.2 of the EC–Denmark Agreement, whenever amendments were adopted to the Brussels I Regulation, Denmark was required to notify the Commission of its decision whether or not to implement the content of such amendments. By letter of 20 December 2012, Denmark notified the Commission of its decision to implement the contents of Brussels I Recast, and so the recast regulation applies to relations between the EU and Denmark.[137]

9–21

Qualifying judgments

The recognition and enforcement rules of Brussels I Recast apply to "judgments", defined as any judgment given by a court or tribunal of a Member State, whatever the judgment may be called, including a decree, order, decision or writ of execution, as well as a decision on the determination of costs or expenses by an officer of the court.[138]

9–22

The enforcement mechanism applies to all qualifying judgments, whether or not the defendant was "domiciled" in a Member State, or in Denmark. This feature of the 1968 Brussels Convention made it necessary to provide therein for the possibility of bilateral agreements between Contracting States and non-Contracting States whose nationals lived in Contracting States, in order to ensure that in the former states the enforcement procedures might not be used against such nationals in the territory of Contracting States.[139] If a judgment emanates from a European court, seised on a non-Brussels ground, the judgment creditor

---

[135] See Protocol No.22 on the position of Denmark [2010] O.J. C83/299 (Ch.1, above).

[136] Agreement between the European Community and Denmark on Jurisdiction and the Recognition and Enforcement of Judgments in Civil and Commercial Matters [2005] O.J. L299/62. See further Council of the European Union Press Release 8402/06 (re Luxembourg meeting, April 2006), noting agreement concerning the extension to Denmark of the Brussels I Regulation (Decision 6922/06); and The Civil Jurisdiction and Judgments Regulations 2007 (SI 2007/1655).

[137] Agreement between the European Community and the Kingdom of Denmark on jurisdiction and the recognition and enforcement of judgments in civil and commercial matters [2013] O.J. L79/4.

[138] Brussels I Recast art.2(a). For the purposes of Ch.III (recognition and enforcement), "judgment" includes provisional, including protective, measures ordered by a court or tribunal which by virtue of Brussels I Recast has jurisdiction as to the substance of the matter. It does not include a provisional, including protective, measure which is ordered by such a court or tribunal without the defendant being summoned to appear, unless the judgment containing the measure is served on the defendant prior to enforcement. For provisions in Brussels I Recast concerning authentic instruments and court settlements, see Ch.IV (arts 58–60). See *Gothaer Allgemeine Versicherung AG v Samskip GmbH* (C-456/11) [2013] Q.B. 548.

[139] Brussels Convention art.59.

may enforce any resulting EU judgment in any EU Member State in which the defendant has assets, using the Brussels enforcement scheme.[140]

Henceforth in this chapter, reference shall be to the terms of Brussels I Recast, but, necessarily, illustrative cases are drawn from earlier instruments.

Article 80 of Brussels I Recast provides that references to the Brussels I Regulation henceforth shall be construed as references to the recast regulation, and vertical continuity of reasoning applies.[141]

Background to changes

9–23   On 14 December 2010, the European Commission published its proposal to recast the Brussels I Regulation.[142] Most of the perceived shortcomings in the existing Regulation pertained to jurisdiction, but one important matter related to judgment enforcement, namely, the removal of obstacles of time and cost associated with the *exequatur* procedure (q.v.) in respect of the recognition and enforcement in one Member State of a judgment given in another Member State. The proposal sought to address this deficiency by pursuing the aim of an *exequatur*-free zone. The beginning of the removal of the *exequatur* procedure had already taken place in relation to related European regulations in the areas of uncontested and small claims.[143] The principle of abolition of *exequatur* is an example of the onward march of the harmonisation agenda.

Scope

9–24   The scope of Brussels I Recast encompasses civil and commercial matters.[144] It shall not extend, in particular, to revenue, customs or administrative matters or to the liability of the State for acts and omissions in the exercise of State authority (*acta iure imperii*).[145] The Regulation does not apply to judgments pertaining to the following matters[146]:

(a)   the status or legal capacity of natural persons, rights in property arising out of a matrimonial relationship or out of a relationship deemed by the law applicable to such relationship to have comparable effects to marriage;

---

[140] Under the 1968 Convention and Brussels I Regulation, non-Contracting/Member States, especially USA, expressed concern about this matter. For this reason, art.59 of the Convention was inserted to enable non-Contracting States to make bilateral arrangements with Contracting States to protect their nationals; relevant treaties were concluded between the UK and Canada (Reciprocal Enforcement of Foreign Judgments (Canada) Order 1987 (SI 1987/468), as amended), and between the UK and Australia (Reciprocal Enforcement of Foreign Judgments (Australia) Order 1994 (SI 1994/1901), as amended). Bilateral agreements made under art.59 of the 1968 Convention were honoured in art.72 of the Brussels I Regulation, and will be honoured, in turn, by art.72 of Brussels I Recast.

[141] Para.7–13 (re continuity of interpretation); and recital (34), Brussels I Recast.

[142] (COM (2010) 748 final).

[143] Paras 9–49 et seq. and 9–62, below.

[144] e.g. *Realchemie Nederland BV v Bayer CropScience AG* (C-406/09) [2011] E.C.R. I-9773.

[145] Brussels I Recast art.1.1.

[146] Brussels I Recast art.1.2.

(b)   bankruptcy, proceedings relating to the winding-up of insolvent companies or other legal persons, judicial arrangements, compositions and analogous proceedings;

(c)   social security;

(d)   arbitration[147];

(e)   maintenance obligations arising from a family relationship, parentage, marriage or affinity;

(f)   wills and succession, including maintenance obligations arising by reason of death.

Chapter III contains the rules for recognition and enforcement: Section 1 (Recognition: arts 36–38); Section 2 (Enforcement: arts 39–44); Section 3 (Refusal of recognition and enforcement: arts 45–51); and Section 4 (Common Provisions: arts 52–57). Recognition of a judgment is a precursor to enforcement thereof.

Recognition rules in Brussels I Recast

It is a pillar of the Brussels regime that mutual trust in the administration of justice in the EU justifies the principle that judgments given in one Member State shall be recognised in all Member States without the need for any special procedure.[148] As a result, a judgment given by the courts of a Member State should be treated as if it had been given in the Member State addressed. Under Brussels I Recast, for the purposes of the free circulation of judgments, a judgment given in a Member State should be recognised and enforced in another Member State even if it is given against a person not domiciled in a Member State.[149]

9–25

Article 36[150]

"1.   A judgment given in a Member State shall be recognised in the other Member States without any special procedure being required.[151]

2.   Any interested party may, in accordance with the procedure provided for in Subsection 2 of Section 3, apply for a decision that there are no grounds for refusal of recognition as referred to in Article 45.

3.   If the outcome of proceedings in a court of a Member State depends on the determination of an incidental question of refusal of recognition, that court shall have jurisdiction over that question."

9–26

Refusal of recognition (and enforcement)—Article 45[152]

The substance and tenor of art.45 differs little from its predecessor articles.

9–27

---

[147] Paras 7–69 et seq. and 9–47 et seq.

[148] Brussels I Recast recital (26).

[149] Brussels I Recast recital (27).

[150] cf. Brussels I Regulation art.33.

[151] Where a judgment is given against a state by a court in another state, this, to be enforceable, must be in conformity with the State Immunity Act 1978. See *NML Capital Ltd v Argentina* [2009] 1 Lloyd's Rep. 378.

[152] cf. Brussels I Regulation arts 34 and 35.

Article 45

9–28
"A judgment shall not be recognised:
1. On the application of any interested party, the recognition of a judgment shall be refused:
   (a) if such recognition is manifestly contrary to public policy (ordre public) in the Member State addressed;[153]
   (b) where the judgment was given in default of appearance, if the defendant was not served with the document which instituted the proceedings or with an equivalent document in sufficient time and in such a way as to enable him to arrange for his defence, unless the defendant failed to commence proceedings to challenge the judgment when it was possible for him to do so;
   (c) if the judgment is irreconcilable with a judgment given between the same parties in the Member State addressed;
   (d) if the judgment is irreconcilable with an earlier judgment given in another Member State or in a third State involving the same cause of action and between the same parties, provided that the earlier judgment fulfils the conditions necessary for its recognition in the Member State addressed; or
   (e) if the judgment conflicts with:
       (i) Sections 3, 4 or 5 of Chapter II where the policyholder, the insured, a beneficiary of the insurance contract, the injured party, the consumer or the employee was the defendant; or
       (ii) Section 6 of Chapter II.
2. In its examination of the grounds of jurisdiction referred to in point (e) of paragraph 1, the court to which the application was submitted shall be bound by the findings of fact on which the court of origin based its jurisdiction.
3. Without prejudice to point (e) of paragraph 1, the jurisdiction of the court of origin may not be reviewed. The test of public policy referred to in point (a) of paragraph 1 may not be applied to the rules relating to jurisdiction.
4. The application for refusal of recognition shall be made in accordance with the procedures provided for in Subsection 2 and, where appropriate, Section 4."

Public policy

9–29
The first of the four grounds of refusal of recognition of a judgment is the widest of the challenges in art.45. Although under this heading of public policy/*ordre public* there will be subsumed allegations of fraud, the challenge is a muted version of the stronger one which is available at common law.[154]

---

[153] *Viking Line ABP v International Transport Workers' Federation* [2006] I.L.Pr. 4 at [78]–[81]; and, earlier, under Brussels Convention, *Societe d'Informatique Service Realisation Organisation (SISRO) v Ampersand Software BV* [1994] I.L.Pr. 55; and *Materiel Auxiliaire d'Informatique v Printed Forms Equipment Ltd* [2006] I.L.Pr. 44.

[154] *Interdesco SA v Nullifire Ltd* [1992] 1 Lloyd's Rep. 180. Equally, the ECJ in *Regie Nationale des Usines Renault SA v Maxicar SpA* [2000] E.C.R. I-2973 displayed disinclination to revisit alleged error in the application of Community law by the Member State court of origin; the public policy challenge under the Brussels regime is to be interpreted strictly, and for it to be invoked, there would have to exist a manifest breach of a rule of law viewed as essential, or manifest breach of a right acknowledged as fundamental in the legal order of the Member State addressed. See also Opinion of AG Szpunar delivered on 3 March 2015 in *Diageo Brands BV v Simiramida-04 EOOD* (Case C-681/13). cf. at common law, para.9–12, above.

As to the human rights dimension, is the public policy challenge as evidenced in the development of jurisprudence thereon under the Brussels regime[155] co-extensive with the challenge which may be made to the conduct of a court process in terms of the ECHR art.6,[156] or does it fall short of what the ECHR requires?

In *Maronier v Larmer*,[157] in 1984, a Dutch national began proceedings in the Netherlands against the defendant for damages for allegedly negligent dental treatment. The defendant filed a defence, but in 1986 the proceedings were stayed on the application of the claimant. In 1991, the defendant moved to reside in the UK. In 1998, the claimant sought to reactivate the case, by which time the defendant's solicitors had lost contact with him. The claimant made no attempt to contact the defendant, and in due course he obtained decree in absence from a Dutch court. After expiry of the time period for appeal in the Netherlands, the claimant applied ex parte to enforce the Dutch judgment in the UK under the Brussels Convention. An appeal by the claimant, against a first instance decision to refuse to register the Dutch decree, failed. The Court of Appeal, holding that the defendant manifestly had been denied a fair trial within the terms of ECHR art.6 opined that the Brussels aim of simple and rapid enforcement would be frustrated if the court addressed were required to carry out a detailed review of whether the procedure in the court of origin was art.6-compliant. Rather, the court addressed should apply a strong, but rebuttable presumption that the court procedures of states which are party to the ECHR are compliant with art.6. Further, the Brussels Convention itself, in art.2, expressly recognises the right of a defendant to have a fair opportunity to defend.

The Court of Appeal decision in *Maronier*[158] has been criticised for paying insufficient attention to the jurisprudence of the European Court of Human Rights,[159] in contrast with the earlier Scottish case of *SA Marie Brizzard et Roger International v William Grant & Sons Ltd (No.2)*.[160] In *Marie Brizzard*, upon registration having been granted by a Scots court of a judgment of the *Cour D'Appel de Bordeaux*, the judgment debtors appealed under art.36 of the Brussels Convention, on the argument that the judgment should not be recognised and enforced in Scotland, being contrary to public policy in terms of art.27, with particular reference to art.6.1 of the ECHR. The judgment debtors alleged that their rights under art.6 had been infringed. Their complaint pertained to the constitution of the court of first instance, the *Tribunal de Commerce de Bordeaux*, which they alleged lacked objective impartiality. Their appeal on that ground was refused. In the judgment of Lord Mackay of Drumadoon, which took proper account of Strasbourg jurisprudence, it was right to look objectively at the whole

---

[155] e.g. *Krombach v Bamberski* [2001] Q.B. 709; *Pordea v Times Newspapers Ltd* [2001] C.L.Y.B. 818; *Marie Brizard et Roger International SA v William Grant & Sons Ltd (No.2)*, 2002 S.L.T. 1365; and *Gambazzi v DaimlerChrysler Canada Inc* (C-394/07) [2009] 1 Lloyd's Rep. 647.

[156] The right to a fair and public hearing within a reasonable time by an independent and impartial tribunal established by law. See at common law, para–9.12.

[157] *Maronier v Larmer* [2003] Q.B. 620. See also *Merchant International Co Ltd v Natsionalna Aktsionerna Kompaniya Naftogaz Ukrayiny* [2012] EWCA Civ 196.

[158] *Maronier v Larmer* [2003] Q.B. 620.

[159] J. Fawcett, "The Impact of Article 6(1) of the ECHR on Private International Law" (2007) 56 I.C.L.Q. 1 at 27.

[160] *SA Marie Brizzard et Roger International v William Grant & Sons Ltd (No.2)*, 2002 S.L.T. 1365. See generally Fentiman, *International Commercial Litigation* (2010), paras 18–28, 18–29.

history of the French proceedings. It was a question of fact whether any infringement of ECHR rights at an early stage could be, and in fact had been, cured on appeal; there was no doubt that the proceedings in the *Cour D'Appel* were fully compliant with art.6. On that basis, the judgment debtors had been afforded their full rights conferred by art.6. Lord Mackay, therefore, rejected the argument by the respondents, William Grant, that the judgment sought to be enforced was tainted by the original judgment of the *Tribunal*, which was its genesis. For such cases arising in Scots courts, it may be predicted that a court will follow Lord Mackay's example, not only in the attention he paid to human rights case law, but also, importantly, in his Lordship's approach of considering the entirety of the foreign proceedings in coming to his conclusion that there had been no breach of art.6 such as to preclude recognition and enforcement of the French decree in Scotland.

Due service

9–30   In the Brussels Convention, the word "duly" preceded "served".[161] In *Pendy Plastic Products BV v Pluspunkt*,[162] a Convention case, the ECJ decision was that "due service" was to be tested against the law of the court of origin, and the concept of service in "sufficient time" by the law of the court addressed. The adverb "duly" has been omitted from art.34.2 of the Brussels I Regulation, and from art.45.1.b of Brussels I Recast. Although one of the aims of the later instruments is to streamline the system of judgment enforcement, there is no question of there being any undermining of the right to a fair trial and the opportunity to prepare a defence.[163] Hence, the omission of the adverb "duly" probably is not significant in drafting terms; rather, with the advent of the Service Regulation,[164] the question has arisen whether service which does not meet the rules set out therein can found a ground of challenge under art.45.1.b, i.e. whether, in effect, "duly" has been silently reinstated with more technical meaning. In *Tavoulareas v Tsavliris (The Atlas Pride)*[165] it was argued that the defendant had to be served in accordance with the concept of service under the Service Regulation in order to forestall any challenge under art.34.2 of Brussels I Regulation.

In *Reeve v Plummer*,[166] in the English High Court, Simler J. rejected submissions that the focus must be on whether the manner of service is in

---

[161] See Brussels Convention art.27.2. See *Scania Finance France SA v Rockinger Spezialfabrik fur Anhangerkupplungen GmbH* (C-522/03) [2006] I.L.Pr. 1; *Arctic Fish Sales Co Ltd v Adam (No.2)*, 1995 G.W.D. 25-1351; *Selco Ltd v Mercier*, 1996 S.L.T. 1247; and *Verdoliva v JM van der Hoeven BV* (C-3/05) [2006] I.L.Pr. 31.

[162] *Pendy Plastic Products BV v Pluspunkt Handelsgesellschaft mbH* (C-228/81) [1982] E.C.R. 2723. See also *Debaecker v Bouwman* [1985] E.C.R. 1779; *TSN Kunststoffrecycling GmbH v Jurgens* [2002] 1 W.L.R. 2459.

[163] *ASML Netherlands BV v Semiconductor Industry Services GmbH (Semis)* (C-283/05) [2007] I.L.Pr. 4 ECJ; *ASML Netherlands BV v Semiconductor Industry Services GmbH* [2009] I.L.Pr. 29 Supreme Court (Austria).

[164] Regulation 1348/2000; and now Regulation 1393/2007.

[165] *Tavoulareas v Tsavliris (The Atlas Pride)* [2006] EWCA Civ 1772. See also *Scania Finance France SA v Rockinger Spezialfabrik fur Anhangerkupplungen GmbH & Co* (C-522/03) [2006] I.L.Pr. 1.

[166] *Reeve v Plummer* [2014] EWHC 4695 (QB).

accordance with the law of the court of origin, and if that is the case, that will be sufficient, provided that, as a matter of fact, such service was in time to enable the defendant to arrange for his defence. His Lordship preferred the argument that it is no longer sufficient to show due service, rather it is now necessary to show service "in such a way" as to enable the defendant to arrange for his defence—a question of substance, not form.[167] "[E]ven if service has been validly effected in a manner which constitutes "due" service in the member state concerned, the court, considering whether the judgment should be recognised, must consider all the relevant circumstances to determine whether actual or sufficient service has been effected in advance of the hearing and in a manner that enables the defendant to arrange for his defence."[168]

Irreconcilability

Article 45.1.c enjoins refusal of recognition of a foreign Member State judgment   9–31
if it is irreconcilable with a judgment (earlier or later) given between the same parties in the Member State addressed.

    Article 45.1.d enjoins refusal of recognition of a Member State judgment if it is irreconcilable with a judgment, earlier given, in another Member State or in a Third State, involving the same cause of action and between the same parties, provided that the earlier judgment must be recognised by the Member State addressed. The foreign judgment first handed down takes precedence in accordance with the maxim *prior tempore, potior jure*.[169]It would be inconsistent with the principle of mutual trust, on which the rules on recognition and enforcement of judgments are based, to interpret the provision as covering conflicts between two judgments given in one Member State, since such an interpretation would allow a court in a Member State in which recognition was sought to substitute its own assessment of a judgment's lawfulness for that of the court in the Member State of origin.[170]

Breach of jurisdiction rules

Article 45.1.e provides that the recognition of a judgment shall be refused if the   9–32
judgment conflicts with ss.3, 4 or 5 of Ch.II, that is to say, jurisdiction in matters relating to insurance (3); jurisdiction over consumer contracts (4); and jurisdiction over individual contracts of employment; (5) where such disadvantaged party was the defendant in the court of origin.

    The provision embraces employees. Under the Brussels I Regulation, the sanction to contest jurisdiction contained in art.35.1 did not extend to cases concerning jurisdiction over individual contracts of employment. The probable reason for this was that it was thought that any re-visiting of jurisdictional competence would favour an employer rather than an employee, who is the

---

[167] *Reeve v Plummer* [2014] EWHC 4695 (QB) at [27] and [28].

[168] *Reeve v Plummer* [2014] EWHC 4695 (QB) at [29].

[169] cf. Brussels I Regulation art.34(4). *Salzgitter Mannesmann Handel GmbH v SC Laminorul SA* (C-157/12) [2014] 1 W.L.R. 904; and *Hoffmann v Krieg* (Case 145/86) [1988] E.C.R. 645 (in the context of divorce).

[170] *Trade Agency Ltd v Seramico Investments Ltd*(Case C-619/10) [2012] O.J. C331/3; and *Salzgitter Mannesmann Handel GmbH v SC Laminorul SA* (C-157/12 [2014] 1 W.L.R. 904.

perceived weaker party, whom these rules are designed to protect. The provenance of the clarification in Brussels I Recast that the protection applies (only) where the disadvantaged party was the defendant, therefore, is easy to trace.

Likewise, the recognition of a judgment shall be refused if the judgment conflicts with S.6 of Ch.III, the rule of exclusive jurisdiction set out in art.24. This reiterates the position under the Brussels I Regulation.

Article 45.1.e, together with art.45.2 and 45.3, represents the limits of the power of the court addressed to review the jurisdiction of the court of origin.

Article 52[171]

9–33

"Under no circumstances may a judgment given in a Member State be reviewed as to its substance in the Member State addressed."[172]

Article 38[173]

9–34

"The court or authority before which a judgment given in another Member State is invoked may suspend the proceedings, in whole or in part, if:
(a)   the judgment is challenged in the Member State of origin; or
(b)   an application has been submitted for a decision that there are no grounds for refusal of recognition as referred to in Article 45 or for a decision that the recognition is to be refused on the basis of one of those grounds."

Enforcement rules in Brussels I Recast

Abolition of *exequatur*

9–35   Chapter III S.2 (arts 39–44) addresses the subject of enforcement of judgments. The enforcement rules in Brussels I Recast are markedly different from those in the Brussels I Regulation as a result of the abolition of *exequatur*.

Article 38 of the Brussels I Regulation provided that, in the UK, a judgment given in a Member State and enforceable in that State should be enforced in England and Wales, in Scotland, or in Northern Ireland when, on the application of any interested party, it had been registered for enforcement in that part of the UK. This was the form which the *exequatur* procedure ("declaration of enforceability") took in the UK.[174] In terms of art.53 of the Brussels I Regulation, a party seeking recognition or applying for a declaration of enforceability was required to produce a copy of the judgment, which satisfied the conditions necessary to establish its authenticity, together with a certificate.[175] No

---

[171] cf. Brussels I Regulation art.36.
[172] *Prism Investments BV v van der Meer* (C-139/10) [2012] I.L.Pr. 13.
[173] cf. Brussels I Regulation art.37.
[174] For the UK, reference was to the process of registration rather than to the declaration of enforceability: Jenard-Möller Report on the Lugano Convention [1990] O.J. C189/79 (para.68). This difference was attributable to the lack of an *exequatur* procedure per se in the UK, and was largely one of terminology.
[175] The decision of Slade J. in *Haji-Ioannou v Frangos* [2009] EWHC 2310 (QB) shed light on the qualification as "an interested party" to register a judgment for enforcement. It was held that the

legalisation or other similar formality was required in respect of the copy judgment, certificate, or translation thereof, or in respect of a document appointing a representative *ad litem*.[176]

From the outset of the recasting exercise one of the central aims of the European Commission was to abolish the *exequatur* procedure, and to consign it to history. On the argument that challenges to the grant of declarations of enforceability were very small in number and only rarely successful (there being a very low incidence of recorded refusal by Member States of declarations of enforceability/registration), the European Commission, in the Green Paper,[177] put forward the view that it was difficult to justify in an internal market without frontiers the expense, by way of time and cost, occasioned to individuals and to businesses by the *exequatur* procedure.[178]

The central provision in the new instrument is art.39,[179] which gives effect to the Commission's long desired aim, and states that:

Article 39

"A judgment given in a Member State which is enforceable in that Member State shall be enforceable in the other Member States without any declaration of enforceability being required."

Notably, the abolition in Regulation 1215 has been effected "across the board"; an earlier proposal that judgments in defamation and collective redress actions should be excepted from the abolition was abandoned.

Procedure for enforcement is governed by the law of the Member State addressed

Article 41[180]   9–36

"1. Subject to the provisions of this Section, the procedure for the enforcement of judgments given in another Member State shall be governed by the law of the Member State addressed. A judgment given in a Member State which is enforceable in the Member State addressed shall be enforced there under the same conditions as a judgment given in the Member State addressed.

2. Notwithstanding paragraph 1, the grounds for refusal or of suspension of enforcement under the law of the Member State addressed shall apply in so far as they are not incompatible with the grounds referred to in Article 45.

---

applicants acquired the requisite interest in the judgment for the purposes of art.38 of the Brussels I Regulation only when they formally accepted their inheritance rights under Greek law.

[176] Brussels I Regulation art.56.

[177] Green Paper on the review of Council Regulation (EC) No.44/2001 on jurisdiction and the recognition and enforcement of judgments in civil and commercial matters (COM (2009)175 final).

[178] Green Paper on the review of Council Regulation (EC) No.44/2001 on jurisdiction and the recognition and enforcement of judgments in civil and commercial matters (COM (2009)175 final), p.2; and Brussels I Recast recital (26).

[179] See also, for detail, Rules of Court of Session, Ch.62: Part VA–Recognition and Enforcement of Judgments under Regulation (EU) No.1215/2012 of the European Parliament and of the Council of 12 December 2012 on Jurisdiction and the Recognition and Enforcement of Judgments in Civil Matters (Recast).

[180] cf. Brussels I Regulation art.40.

3.   The party seeking the enforcement of a judgment given in another Member State shall not be required to have a postal address in the Member State addressed. Nor shall that party be required to have an authorised representative in the Member State addressed unless such a representative is mandatory irrespective of the nationality or the domicile of the parties."

Under art.42, the applicant shall provide the competent enforcement authority with (a) a copy of the judgment which satisfies the conditions necessary to establish its authenticity; (b) the certificate from the court of origin issued pursuant to art.53, containing a description of the measure and certifying that: (i) the court has jurisdiction as to the substance of the matter; (ii) the judgment is enforceable in the Member State of origin; and (c) where the measure was ordered without the defendant being summoned to appear, proof of service of the judgment. Such certificate shall be served on the judgment debtor prior to the first enforcement measure (art.43.1). Abolition of *exequatur* means that an enforceable judgment shall carry with it the power to proceed to any protective measures existing under the law of the Member State addressed.[181]

Refusal of enforcement

9–37   Article 46

"On the application of the person against whom enforcement is sought, the enforcement of a judgment shall be refused where one of the grounds referred to in Article 45 is found to exist."[182]

In terms of art.47, the application for refusal of enforcement shall be submitted to the appropriate court of the Member State addressed, which shall decide on the matter without delay (art.48). The decision on the application for refusal of enforcement may be appealed against by either party to the appropriate court of the Member State addressed (art.49), and further appeal from that decision is authorised in terms of art.50. Proceedings in the court addressed under arts 49 or 50 may be stayed if an appeal has been lodged against the judgment in the Member State of origin, or if the time for such an appeal has not yet expired (art.51).

By art.54, in a new provision (the "equivalence provision"), if a judgment contains a measure or an order not known in the law of the state addressed, that measure or order shall, to the extent possible, be adapted to a measure or order known in the law of that Member State (the state addressed), which has equivalent effects attached to it, and which pursues similar aims. Such adaptation shall not result in effects going beyond those provided for in the state of origin.

The *exequatur* performed an imprimatur function, that is, by giving a stamp of approval by the state addressed of the foreign decree. Much has been written on the desirability and the dangers of removing the *exequatur* process, but examination of the new provisions shows that although one procedural step has

---

[181] See para.8–15 et seq. re protective measures.
[182] Narrated at para.9–28, above.

been removed from the enforcement process, no noticeably prejudicial diminution in the rights of the judgment debtor to object to enforcement appears to have occurred.[183]

Extent of operation of Brussels regime of recognition and enforcement

Delimiting the extent of the Brussels regime of jurisdiction and judgments has been addressed in Ch.7, above, from the standpoint of the extent of operation of the rules of jurisdiction, and their possible reflexive effect.[184] The case of *Orams v Apostolides*,[185] which was the subject of a reference for a preliminary ruling from the ECJ,[186] addressed this difficult point from the perspective of judgment enforcement.

9-38

Apostolides, a Cypriot national, sought, from an English court, recognition and enforcement of two judgments obtained by him against Mr and Mrs Orams, British nationals, from a court in Nicosia, in the southern, Greek-controlled, Republic of Cyprus, which became part of the EU in 2004. In principle, the recognition and enforcement of its judgments by other Member States should be governed by the Brussels I Regulation, as above described. However, the orders in question concerned land situated in that part of Cyprus controlled by the Turkish Cypriot administration and not, therefore, within the area over which the Government of the Republic of Cyprus exercised effective control, and not, accordingly, within the EU. The Turkish Republic of Northern Cyprus is not recognised by the international community, with the exception of Turkey. By a protocol annexed to the act of accession by Cyprus to the EU, the application of Community law in northern Cyprus has been suspended.[187] The Orams had purchased part of the land in question from a third party, who was the registered owner under Turkish Cypriot law, and had built a villa on the plot. By the terms of the Nicosian judgment, the Orams were required to demolish the villa, and to deliver free possession of the property to Apostolides, on the basis that his family had been compelled to abandon the land in question at the time of partition of the island in 1974. Apostolides was pronounced the rightful owner of the land in the judgment of the Cypriot court. The first judgment obtained by him was given in default of appearance by the Orams, but was confirmed by a later judgment on appeal brought by them.

The English Court of Appeal, the court addressed, referred to the ECJ the question whether the fact that the judgment concerned land situated in an area over which the Government of Cyprus does not exercise effective control had an effect on the recognition and enforcement of the judgment and, in particular, whether the court of origin could be said to have had jurisdiction, and, further, what might be the effect of the public policy of the Member State addressed upon the enforceability of the judgment. There were also issues concerning procedural

---

[183] For further consideration, see X.E. Kramer: "Cross-Border Enforcement and the Brussels I-bis Regulation: Towards a New Balance between Mutual Trust and National Control over Fundamental Rights" (2013) 60 N.I.L.R. 343–373.

[184] See para.7–63, above.

[185] *Orams v Apostolides* [2010] EWCA Civ 9.

[186] *Orams v Apostolides* (C-420/07) [2010] 1 All E.R. (Comm) 950 and 992.

[187] Article 1.1 of Protocol No.10 on Cyprus to the Act concerning Conditions of Accession to the EU of a Number of States (2004).

correctness; although the document instituting proceedings in the Nicosian court was not served on the defendants in sufficient time to enable them to arrange for their defence, the defendants, as noted above, were able to bring an appeal against the initial judgment.

The term "hybrid case" is particularly apt in these circumstances because there presented in *Apostolides* a judgment from an EU Member State court which in its nature was largely an in rem judgment, having certain in personam provisions, and which, in its in rem character, purported to affect a res which technically was situated outside its territory. The case was hybrid in the fact that it concerned both in rem and in personam rights, but more importantly because the court of origin and the court addressed both were in EU Member States, but the land which the decree purported to affect was outside the territorial bounds of the EU.

By use of a manner of reasoning which has become familiar, the ECJ ruled that art.35.1 of the Brussels I Regulation (cf. art.45.1.e of the Brussels I Recast) did not authorise the court of a Member State to refuse recognition or enforcement of a judgment given by a court of another Member State concerning land situated "therein" but over which its government did not exercise effective control. It is often the case that the ECJ/CJEU in its reasoning relies upon, and draws inferences from, the silence of the instrument in question; indeed it draws succour from that silence in order to achieve an aim which is in accordance with the overarching nature and purpose of the Brussels regime.[188] The result in *Orams* seems counterintuitive, at least according to traditional thinking,[189] which holds that the court of the *lex situs* is clothed with jurisdiction in the matter of pronouncing decrees in rem concerning immoveable or moveable property by virtue of the property being situated within the territorial limits of that court. In *Orams*, however, the matter of overriding importance, it seems, was that the court seised was that of an EU Member State.

The ECJ ruled further that, as a practical matter, the fact that the judgment concerning land could not be enforced where the land was situated did not constitute a ground for refusal of recognition or enforcement under art.34.1 of the Brussels I Regulation (cf. art.45.1.a of Brussels I Recast), nor could it be said to fail the test set in art.38.1 of the Regulation, the wording of which began "a judgment given in a Member State *and enforceable in that State* . . .".[190] With regard to the natural justice aspect of the case, a default judgment could not be refused effect under art.34.2 (cf. art.45.1.b of Brussels I Recast), in circumstances where the defendants had been able to commence proceedings to challenge the default judgment.

---

[188] cf. The negative attitude evinced by the ECJ in relation to a reference concerning the competence of the plea of *forum non conveniens* in a case where the alternative forum was in a Third State and there were no connections with the EU apart from the first court seised being an EU Member State: *Owusu v Jackson (t/a Villa Holidays Bal Inn Villas)* [2005] Q.B. 801.

[189] *Castrique v Imrie* (1870) L.R. 4 H.L. 414; affirmed in Brussels regime thinking, e.g. Brussels I Recast art.24.1.

[190] Emphasis added.

document appointing a representative *ad litem*.[201] The judgment shall be declared enforceable immediately upon completion of these formalities (art.41). The declaration of enforceability[202] shall be served on the party against whom enforcement is sought (art.42.2). Thereafter any defence to enforcement must be adduced within the terms of arts 34 and 35 of Lugano II.

Relationship between Lugano II and the Brussels I Regulation

This subject is addressed in Lugano II Title VII art.64. In the difficult area of delimitation of ambit of Brussels I Recast[203] and Lugano II,[204] the courts of EFTA States are obliged always to apply Lugano II. Courts in Member States bound by Brussels I Recast may find themselves having to apply both instruments. **9–42**

Article 64.1 of Lugano II in effect provides that the scope of Brussels I Recast, and of the EC–Denmark Agreement, remains unaltered, not limited by Lugano II. As between States bound by Brussels I Recast, judgments delivered in one State must be recognised and enforced in accordance with the terms of the Recast.

In the matter of recognition and enforcement, Lugano II applies where both states are party to the Lugano Convention alone, or when only one is a party to Lugano II and the other is bound by Brussels I Recast. While Lugano II shall not prejudice the application by EU Member States of Brussels I Recast, and amendments thereof (including the EC–Denmark Agreement), Lugano II shall be applied in matters of recognition and enforcement, where either the state of origin or the state addressed is not applying Brussels I Recast.[205] However, in addition to the grounds of refusal of recognition set out in arts 34 and 35 of Lugano II, recognition or enforcement may be refused if the ground of jurisdiction on which the judgment has been based differs from that set out in Lugano II and the judgment debtor is domiciled in a Lugano State, unless the judgment may otherwise be recognised or enforced under any rule of law in the state addressed.[206]

Article 68 remains, permitting bilateral arrangements to be made between a Lugano State and a Third State, whereby it is agreed not to recognise and enforce judgments given in other Lugano States against defendants domiciled or habitually resident in the Third State, where the judgment in question could be founded only on a ground of jurisdiction specified in art.3.2 (i.e. so-called exorbitant jurisdictions).[207]

---

[201] Lugano II art.56.

[202] The decision on the application for a declaration of enforceability may be appealed against by either party (art.43).

[203] Having regard to the wording of Lugano II art.64.1, and Brussels I Recast art.80.

[204] Pocar Report para.18.

[205] Lugano II art.64.2(c).

[206] Lugano II art.64.3; as to which see Pocar Report para.21.

[207] However, a Lugano State may not assume an obligation towards a Third State not to recognise a judgment given in another Lugano State by a court basing its jurisdiction on the presence within that state of property belonging to the defendant or the seizure by the plaintiff of property situated there: (1) if the action is brought to assert or declare proprietary or possessory rights in that property, seeks to obtain authority to dispose of it, or arises from another issue relating to such property; or (2) if the property constitutes the security for a debt which is the subject matter of the action (art.68.2). Contrast, Brussels I Recast art.72.

Reciprocal enforcement within the UK

9–43 The Civil Jurisdiction and Judgments Act 1982 s.18 and Schs 6 and 7, replace rules contained in the Judgments Extension Act 1868 and the Inferior Courts Judgments Extension Act 1882 in respect of intra-UK enforcement of civil and commercial judgments. They apply to money (Sch.6) and non-money (Sch.7) judgments, and include, therefore, orders of interdict and specific implement. Arbitration awards also are included.[208]

"Judgment" is defined positively in s.18(2), beginning (s.18(2)(a)), "any judgment or order (by whatever name called) given or made by a court of law in the United Kingdom", with derogations therefrom in s.18(3)–(7), excluding judgments inter alia regarding insolvency, confiscation of the proceeds of certain criminal offences, maintenance, status or capacity, management of affairs of *incapaces*, and foreign judgments which have achieved status as UK judgments by virtue of legislation under statute, for example, the 1920 or 1933 Acts.

Schedule 6 (money provisions)[209]

9–44 Any interested party who wishes to secure the enforcement in another part of the UK of any money provisions contained in a judgment may apply for a certificate under Sch.6, in the manner prescribed by para.2(2).[210]

A certificate shall not be issued under Sch.6 in respect of a judgment unless under the law of the part of the UK in which the judgment was given either the time for bringing an appeal against the judgment has expired, no such appeal having been brought within that time, or, such an appeal having been brought within that time, that appeal has been finally disposed of, and provided further that the enforcement of the judgment is not for the time being stayed or suspended, and the time available for its enforcement has not expired.[211]

The proper officer shall issue to the applicant a certificate stating the sum payable and such other particulars as may be prescribed, and stating that the above conditions have been satisfied.[212]

Where a certificate has been issued under Sch.6 in any part of the UK, any interested party, within six months from the date of its issue, may apply in the prescribed manner to the proper officer of the superior court[213] in any other part of the UK (i.e. Court of Session or, in relation to England and Wales, or Northern Ireland, the High Court) for the certificate to be registered in that court.[214] A certificate registered under Sch.6 shall, for the purposes of its enforcement, be of the same force and effect, the registering court shall have in respect of its enforcement the same powers, and proceedings for or with respect to its

---

[208] Civil Jurisdiction and Judgments Act 1982 s.18(2)(e).
[209] See, in detail, Rules of Court of Session Ch.62 Pt V–Recognition and Enforcement of Judgments under the Civil Jurisdiction and Judgments Act 1982 or under the Lugano Convention of 30 October 200 rr.62.37, 62.41. See also *Parkes v MacGregor*, 2008 S.C.L.R. 345.
[210] Civil Jurisdiction and Judgments Act 1982 Sch.6 para.2.1.
[211] Civil Jurisdiction and Judgments Act 1982 Sch.6 para.3.
[212] Civil Jurisdiction and Judgments Act 1982 Sch.6 para.4.
[213] Even if the court of origin of the judgment was an inferior court.
[214] Civil Jurisdiction and Judgments Act 1982 Sch.6 para.5.

enforcement may be taken, as if the certificate had been a judgment originally given in the registering courts and had (where relevant) been entered.[215]

Where a certificate in respect of a judgment has been registered under Sch.6, the registering court (if satisfied that any person against whom it is sought to enforce the certificate is entitled and intends to apply, under the law of the part of the UK in which the judgment was given, for any remedy which would result in the setting aside or quashing of the judgment) may stay/sist proceedings for the enforcement of the certificate, on such terms as it thinks fit, for such period as appears to the court to be reasonably sufficient to enable the application to be disposed of.[216]

Where a certificate has been registered under Sch.6, the registering court:

> "(a) shall set aside the registration if, on an application made by any interested party, it is satisfied that the registration was contrary to the provisions of this Schedule[217];
>
> (b) may set aside the registration if, on an application so made, it is satisfied that the matter in dispute in the proceedings in which the judgment in question was given had previously been the subject of a judgment by another court or tribunal having jurisdiction in the matter."[218]

Schedule 7 (non-money provisions)[219]

Any interested party who wishes to secure the enforcement in another part of the UK of any non-money provisions contained in a judgment may apply for a certified copy of the judgment (to the proper officer of the original court, who shall issue the certified copy, subject, however, to the same provisos as set out above regarding appeals, etc.).[220]   **9–45**

Where a certified copy of a judgment has been issued in any part of the UK, any interested party may apply in the prescribed manner to the superior court in any other part of the UK (i.e. Court of Session or, in relation to England and Wales, or Northern Ireland, the High Court) for the judgment to be registered in that court.[221] However, a judgment shall not be so registered by the superior court in any part of the UK if compliance with the non-money provisions contained in the judgment would involve a breach of the law of that part of the UK.[222]

The non-money provisions contained in a judgment registered under Sch.7 shall, for the purposes of their enforcement, be of the same force and effect, the registering court shall have in relation to their enforcement the same powers, and

---

[215] Civil Jurisdiction and Judgments Act 1982 Sch.6 para.6.1.

[216] Civil Jurisdiction and Judgments Act 1982 Sch.6 para.9.

[217] For unsuccessful petition for reduction of a certificate, *Parkes v Cintec International Ltd*, 2010 GWD 12-208.

[218] Civil Jurisdiction and Judgments Act 1982 Sch.6 para.10.

[219] See, in detail, Rules of Court of Session Ch.62 Pt V–Recognition and Enforcement of Judgments under the Civil Jurisdiction and Judgments Act 1982 or under the Lugano Convention of 30 October 2007 rr.62.38, 62.42.

[220] Civil Jurisdiction and Judgments Act 1982 Sch.7 para.2.1.

[221] Civil Jurisdiction and Judgments Act 1982 Sch.7 para.5.1.

[222] Civil Jurisdiction and Judgments Act 1982 Sch.7 para.5.5.

proceedings for or with respect to their enforcement may be taken, as if the judgment containing them had been originally given in the registering court and had (where relevant) been entered.[223]

Where a certificate in respect of a judgment has been registered, the registering court, if it is satisfied that any person against whom it is sought to enforce the certificate is entitled and intends to apply under the law of the part of the UK in which the judgment was given for any remedy which would result in the setting aside or quashing of the judgment, may stay/sist proceedings for the enforcement of the certificate, on such terms as it thinks fit, for such period as appears to the court to be reasonably sufficient to enable the application to be disposed of.[224]

Where a certificate has been registered under Sch.7, the registering court:

> "(a)   shall set aside the registration if, on an application made by any interested party, it is satisfied that the registration was contrary to the provisions of this Schedule;
>
> (b)   may set aside the registration if, on an application so made, it is satisfied that the matter in dispute in the proceedings in which the judgment in question was given had previously been the subject of a judgment by another court or tribunal having jurisdiction in the matter."[225]

Summary

9–46   Judgments to which s.18 applies may not be enforced except by registration under Sch.6 or Sch.7.[226] Moreover, reasons for refusal to register are strictly limited under both schedules. Judgments to which s.18 apply, in the matter of intra-UK recognition only, are governed by the Civil Jurisdiction and Judgments Act 1982 s.19: subject to the definition of judgment, and exclusions thereto contained in s.18, recognition of judgments in another part of the UK shall not be refused solely on the ground that the court of origin was not a court of competent jurisdiction according to the rules of private international law in force in that other part of the UK.

Arbitration

9–47   The Arbitration (Scotland) Act 2010 came into effect on 7 June 2010,[227] placing on a legislative basis the Scots rules of arbitration which previously were piecemeal. The Act contains certain provisions of conflict of laws significance. Section 2 expressly includes, under the term "arbitration", not only domestic (Scottish) arbitration, but also arbitration between persons residing, or carrying on business, anywhere in the UK; and international arbitration (undefined). Under s.3 an arbitration is "seated" in Scotland if:

---

[223] Civil Jurisdiction and Judgments Act 1982 Sch.7 para.6.1.
[224] Civil Jurisdiction and Judgments Act 1982 Sch.7 para.8.
[225] Civil Jurisdiction and Judgments Act 1982 Sch.7 para.9.
[226] Civil Jurisdiction and Judgments Act 1982 s.18(8).
[227] Arbitration (Scotland) Act 2010 (Commencement No.1 and Transitional Provisions) Order 2010 (SSI 2010/195).

"(a)   Scotland is designated as the juridical seat of the arbitration—
         (i)   by the parties,
         (ii)   by any third party to whom the parties give power to so designate, or
         (iii)   where the parties fail to designate or so authorise a third party, by the
                 tribunal, or
(b)   in the absence of any such designation, the court determines that Scotland is
         to be the juridical seat of the arbitration."

By s.3(2), the fact that an arbitration is seated in Scotland does not affect the substantive law to be used to decide the dispute.[228] Enforcement of arbitral awards is governed by s.12 of the Arbitration (Scotland) Act 2010.

The conflict of laws aspects of resolution of commercial disputes by arbitration is important, complex and many-faceted. Brussels I Recast excludes arbitration from its scope,[229] as does Lugano II.[230] In terms of residual national rules of jurisdiction, under the Civil Jurisdiction and Judgments Act 1982 s.20 Sch.8 r.2(m), the Court of Session has jurisdiction in proceedings concerning an arbitration if it was conducted in Scotland, or if the arbitration procedure was governed by Scots law.

With regard to choice of law, as a result of the exclusion from the scope of the Rome I Regulation of "arbitration agreements and agreements on the choice of court",[231] the validity of an arbitration clause in a contract, in the view of a Scots court, is determined by its own (common law ascertained) proper law, separate from the applicable law which governs the contract of which it forms a part. Nevertheless, the existence in a contract of an arbitration clause may be an indication of the applicable law under the Rome I Regulation arts 3.1[232] or 4.4.

If, after the parties have proceeded to arbitration as agreed, an attempt is made to have the arbitral award enforced as a judgment under the Brussels regime, the attempt should fail. However, if, in the face of an arbitration clause, a court in a Member State gives a judgment on the substance—perhaps on the basis that the clause is essentially invalid or not incorporated in the agreement, or if persuaded that the matter in dispute does not fall within the arbitration clause—is this to be enforceable in accordance with the Brussels/Lugano enforcement procedure and with its attendant benefits? Perhaps the party against whom the judgment was made unwisely submitted to the jurisdiction, but even if so, and especially if not, what is the position? The matter has attracted debate,[233] and circularity of argument can occur.[234] Since arbitration is excluded from the scope of Brussels I Recast and Lugano II, it is perhaps surprising that within the UK, an arbitration award from one jurisdiction is enforceable in another in terms of the Civil

---

[228] Para.15–14, below.
[229] Brussels I Recast art.1.2(d).
[230] Lugano II art.1.2(d).
[231] Rome I Regulatio art.1.2(e).
[232] See, under the Rome I Convention, *Egon Oldendorff v Libera Corp (No.2)* [1996] 1 Lloyd's Rep. 380, where English law was identified as both the applicable law and the curial (i.e. procedural) law. The curial law of the arbitration and the applicable/proper law to be applied by the arbiter to the substance of the dispute may differ, as happened in *James Miller & Partners Ltd v Whitworth Street Estates (Manchester) Ltd* [1970] 1 All E.R. 796. The curial law will govern matters such as whether there can be an appeal to the court from the decision of the arbiter.
[233] *Marc Rich & Co AG v Societa Italiana Impianti SpA* [1991] E.C.R. I-3855 ECJ.
[234] *Alfred C Toepfer International GmbH v Société Cargill France* [1998] 1 Lloyd's Rep. 379.

Jurisdiction and Judgments Act 1982 s.18 Schs 6 and 7.[235] In relation to enforcement of foreign judgments outwith the Brussels regime, a judgment obtained in breach of an arbitration agreement is not enforceable in the UK.[236]

Until the decision in *West Tankers*, it was the hope of common lawyers that one benefit of arbitration was that it remained competent for the courts of EU Member States to seek to enforce arbitration agreements by means of anti-suit injunction,[237] a remedy which, in view of *Turner v Grovit*,[238] has ceased to be a competent policing remedy within the Brussels regime. It has become apparent that this was too simple a view,[239] and that arbitration agreements though ex facie excluded from the scope of the Brussels/Lugano regime, nonetheless are not immune from the regime.

Enforcement of foreign arbitration awards

9–48
Although a foreign arbitral award may be enforced at common law, or under the judgment extension legislation,[240] a scheme for recognition and enforcement of arbitration awards is contained in the New York Convention on the Recognition and Enforcement of Foreign Arbitral Awards 1958 (replacing the Geneva Protocol 1923 and Geneva Convention 1927, except in relation to awards issued in countries which are parties thereto and not party to the New York Convention, which cases remain governed by the Arbitration Act 1950 Pt III). The New York Convention was brought into UK law by the Arbitration Act 1975. The Arbitration (Scotland) Act 2010 repeals *in toto* the Arbitration Act 1975,[241] and so reference must be made, in relation to New York Convention awards, to the 2010 Act ss.18–21 and 26.

---

[235] Civil Jurisdiction and Judgments Act 1982 s.18(2)(e): "judgment" includes an arbitration award which has become enforceable in the part of the UK in which it was given in the same manner as a judgment given by a court of law in that part.

[236] Civil Jurisdiction and Judgments Act 1982 s.32. See *Tracomin SA v Sudan Oil Seeds Co (No.1)* [1983] 1 W.L.R. 1026. But note that s.32 does not extend to authorise the non-recognition of a judgment which is required to be recognised in terms of the Brussels regime. See also *Cavell United States Inc v Seaton Insurance Co* [2008] EWHC 876 (Comm); *DHL GBS (UK) Ltd v Fallimento Finmatica SpA* [2009] EWHC 291 (Comm); *National Navigation Co v Endesa Generacion SA (The Wadi Sudr)* [2010] 1 Lloyd's Rep. 193; and *AES UST-Kamenogorsk Hydropower Plant LLP v UST-Kamenogorsk Hydropower Plant LLP JSC* [2013] UKSC 35.

[237] *Through Transport Mutual Insurance Association (Eurasia) Ltd v New India Assurance Co Ltd (The Hari Bhum) (No.2)* [2005] 2 Lloyd's Rep. 378. Another advantage of exclusion from the Brussels regime was that the related actions rule contained in art.28 of the Brussels I Regulation (cf. Brussels I Recast art.30) clearly would not apply where the subject matter though related or identical is being addressed by different means, judicial and arbitral, respectively.

[238] *Turner v Grovit* [2005] 1 A.C. 101.

[239] See para.7–84, above.

[240] An arbitration award made in a country the judgments of which are enforceable under the Administration of Justice Act 1920 or the Foreign Judgments (Reciprocal Enforcement) Act 1933, but which is not a party to the New York Convention, is enforceable in Scotland in the same way as a judicial decree. See also Arbitration (Scotland) Act 2010 s.22.

[241] See Arbitration (Scotland) Act 2010 s.29 Sch.2. The Law Reform (Miscellaneous Provisions) (Scotland) Act 1990 s.66 Sch. 7, which gave effect in Scots law to the UNCITRAL Model Law on International Commercial Arbitration, likewise has been repealed. See, in detail, Rules of Court of Session Ch.62—recognition, registration, and enforcement of foreign judgments, etc.—Pt IX—Enforcement of Arbitral Awards under the New York Convention on the Recognition and Enforcement of Foreign Arbitral Awards. Recognition and enforcement of foreign arbitration awards under the New York Convention is governed in English law by the Arbitration Act 1996 ss.100–104.

By the 2010 Act s.19(1) an award made in pursuance of a written arbitration agreement in the territory of a state which is party to the New York Convention ("a Convention award") is to be recognised as binding on the persons between whom it was made, and accordingly may be relied on by those persons in any legal proceedings in Scotland. By s.19(2), the court may order that a Convention award be enforced as if it had been granted by that court. Recognition or enforcement may be refused only in accordance with s.20, on the grounds that the defendant proves:

"(a)   that a party was under some incapacity under the law applicable to the party,
(b)   that the arbitration agreement was invalid under the law which the parties agree should govern it (or, failing any indication of that law, under the law of the country where the award was made),[242]
(c)   that the person—
      (i)   was not given proper notice of the arbitral process or of the appointment of the tribunal, or
      (ii)   was otherwise unable to present the person's case,
(d)   that the tribunal was constituted, or the arbitration was conducted, otherwise than in accordance with—
      (i)   the agreement of the parties, or
      (ii)   failing such agreement, the law of the country where the arbitration took place."

By s.20(3) recognition or enforcement of a Convention award also may be refused if the defendant proves that the award:

"(a)   deals with a dispute not contemplated by or not falling within the submission to arbitration,
(b)   contains decisions on matters beyond the scope of that submission,
(c)   is not yet binding on the person, or
(d)   has been set aside or suspended by a competent authority."

Further, by s.20(4), recognition or enforcement of a Convention award may be refused if:

"(a)   the award relates to a matter which is not capable of being settled by arbitration, or
(b)   to do so would be contrary to public policy."[243]

By s.21, a party seeking recognition or enforcement of a Convention award must produce (a) the duly authenticated original award (or a duly certified copy of it); and (b) the original arbitration agreement (or a duly certified copy of it); together with a translation if the agreement is in a language other than English.

---

[242] cf. in England *Dallah Real Estate & Tourism Holding Co Pakistan* [2010] 1 All E.R. 592.

[243] e.g. as where the arbitration agreement was valid, but the contract to which it pertained was illegal by its governing law or the law of place of performance. See *Soleimany v Soleimany* [1999] Q.B. 785, decided with reference to Arbitration Act 1950 s.26.

European Enforcement Order for uncontested claims

9–49   Regulation 805/2004 creating a European Enforcement Order for uncontested claims[244] has applied generally from 21 October 2005.[245] Its purpose is to ensure, by laying down minimum procedural standards, that judgments, court settlements and authentic instruments on uncontested claims, can circulate freely throughout the Member States of the EU, without the need for intermediate proceedings in the Member State addressed prior to recognition and enforcement.[246] The Regulation applies to all Member States, including the UK and Ireland,[247] but excluding Denmark.[248]

Background

9–50   Whilst the Brussels I Regulation represented notable progress in the development of procedures for the recognition and enforcement of judgments in civil and commercial matters, as has been noted, it left in place the requirement for *exequatur* (declaration of enforceability) procedure.[249] To simplify and expedite procedures for the recognition and enforcement of judgments among Member States, it was agreed that there should be introduced a form of automatic recognition without any intermediate proceedings, or grounds for refusal of enforcement, for certain specific types of claim.[250] The abolition of *exequatur* for uncontested claims was identified as one of the Community's priorities. As explained above, this represented the beginning of the removal of the *exequatur* procedure, a process significantly advanced by the coming into effect of Brussels I Recast.[251]

Regulation 805/2004 has two distinct components, first, the creation of the European Enforcement Order; and secondly, the laying down of minimum procedural standards.

Scope of instrument

9–51   Regulation 805/2004 applies to judgments, court settlements and authentic instruments on uncontested claims,[252] in civil and commercial matters, whatever the nature of the court or tribunal. It does not extend, however, to revenue,

---

[244] Regulation 805/2004 [2004] O.J. L143/15.

[245] Regulation 805/2004 art.33. Article 26 provides that the Regulation applies only to judgments given, settlements approved and documents formally drawn up or registered as authentic instruments after the entry into force of the Regulation.

[246] Regulation 805/2004 art.1.

[247] Regulation 805/2004 recital (24).

[248] Regulation 805/2004 recital (25).

[249] "[The Regulation] does not remove all the obstacles to the unhindered movement of judgments within the EU and leaves intermediate measures that are still too restrictive" (Proposal for a Council Regulation creating a European Enforcement Order for Uncontested Claims, Explanatory Memorandum, COM (2002) 159 final, p.2 (henceforth "Explanatory Memorandum")).

[250] Explanatory Memorandum p.2.

[251] Para.9–35, above.

[252] Regulation 805/2004 recital (7); and arts 3, 24 and 25. See, in respect of the latter, *GE Capital Bank AG v Fell-Neumeyr* QBD (Commercial Court) unreported 22 February 2013; *Vogel v Lotschutz* [2012] EWHC 3411; and *Lothschutz v Vogel* [2014] EWHC 473 (QB).

customs or administrative matters or the liability of the state for acts and omissions in the exercise of state authority.[253]

Uncontested claims

An uncontested claim is one[254]:   **9–52**

(a)   to which the debtor has expressly agreed by admission or by means of a settlement which has been approved by a court or concluded before a court in the course of proceedings; or

(b)   to which the debtor has never objected, in compliance with the relevant procedural requirements under the law of the Member State of origin, in the course of the court proceedings; or

(c)   in which the debtor has not appeared or been represented at a court hearing regarding that claim after having initially objected to the claim in the course of the court proceedings, provided that such conduct amounts to a tacit admission of the claim or of the facts alleged by the creditor under the law of the Member State of origin; or

(d)   to which the debtor has expressly agreed in an authentic instrument.

The concept of "uncontested claims" is intended to cover:

> "... all situations in which a creditor, given the verified absence of any dispute by the debtor as to the nature or extent of a pecuniary claim,[255] has obtained either a court decision against that debtor or an enforceable document that requires the debtor's express consent, be it a court settlement or an authentic instrument."[256]

In other words, a claim will be treated as uncontested if the debtor has failed to object to it in the course of court proceedings (i.e. if decree were passed in absence, or by default), or if he has expressly agreed (in court proceedings, or by means of a settlement or in an authentic instrument), that the claim exists and is justified.

European Enforcement Order

Article 6 lays down the requirements for certification as a European Enforcement   **9–53**
Order ("EEO") by the Member State of origin,[257] of a judgment delivered in that state on an uncontested claim.[258] Such a judgment, upon application at any time to the court of origin, shall be certified as an EEO if:

---

[253] Regulation 805/2004 art.2.

[254] Regulation 805/2004 art.3.

[255] Amplified in recital (6), to the effect that the absence of objections from the debtor may take the form of decree by default (default of appearance at a court hearing), or decree in absence (failure to comply with an invitation by the court to give written notice of an intention to defend the case).

[256] Regulation 805/2004 recital (5).

[257] Defined in art.4(4): the Member State of origin is the Member State in which the judgment has been given, the court settlement has been approved or concluded, or the authentic instrument has been drawn up or registered, and is to be certified as a European Enforcement Order.

[258] Regulation 805/2004 art.8 provides that if only parts of the judgment meet the requirements laid down in art.6, a partial EEO certificate shall be issued for those parts.

(a)   the judgment is enforceable in the Member State of origin; and

(b)   the judgment does not conflict with the rules on jurisdiction as laid down in ss.3[259] and 6[260] of Ch.II of the Brussels I Regulation[261]; and

(c)   the court proceedings in the Member State of origin meet the requirements of Ch.III of Regulation 805/2004 (minimum standards for uncontested claims procedures); and

(d)   if the claim relates to a consumer contract[262] and the debtor is the consumer, the judgment was given in the Member State of the debtor's domicile within the meaning of art.59 of the Brussels I Regulation.[263]

By art.9, the EEO shall be issued in the standard form provided in Annex I of Regulation 805/2004, and in the language of the judgment.

Abolition of exequatur

9–54   By virtue of art.5, a judgment which has been certified as an EEO in the Member State of origin shall be recognised and enforced in the other Member State (the Member State of enforcement),[264] without the need for a declaration of enforceability, and without any possibility of opposing its recognition. Thus, it can be said that the certification of a judgment as an EEO "renders obsolete" the *exequatur* procedure which, under the Brussels I Regulation (but not Brussels I Recast) was a precondition of enforcement of a judgment in another Member State.

Satisfaction of minimum procedural standards

9–55   As a corollary to the abolition of *exequatur* for uncontested claims, and to ensure that the debtor is duly informed about the court action against him,[265] Regulation 805/2004 lays down in Ch.III minimum standards with regard to the service of documents, covering admissible methods of service, the time of service enabling the preparation of a defence and the proper information concerning the debtor.

Article 12 states that a judgment on an uncontested claim can be certified as an EEO only if the court proceedings in the Member State of origin satisfied the procedural requirements set out in the Regulation. It is said that due to differences among Member States regarding their rules of civil procedure, and especially those governing the service of documents,[266] it is necessary to lay down a specific

---

[259] Insured persons; to be read now as referring to S.3 of Brussels I Recast, per art.80 of that instrument.

[260] Exclusive jurisdiction; to be read now as referring to S.6 of Brussels I Recast, per art.80 of that instrument.

[261] Brussels I Regulation S.5 (employees) is omitted also in the protective provisions contained in Brussels I Regulation art.35.1. Notably, however, Brussels I Recast art.45.1.e, which replaces art.35 of the predecessor, brings into the scope of protection the category employed persons. This constitutes a small anomaly between Regulation 805/2004 and Brussels I Recast.

[262] On application of art.6.1.d, see *Vapenik v Thurner* (C-508/12) [2014] 1 W.L.R. 2486.

[263] To be read now as referring to art.62 of Brussels I Recast, per art.80 of that instrument.

[264] Regulation 805/2004 art.4(5).

[265] Regulation 805/2004 recital (12).

[266] Though see Regulation 1348/2000; and see para.8–11, above.

and detailed definition of those minimum standards.[267] Accordingly, arts 13 and 14 provide for methods of service which are characterised,[268] respectively, by full certainty,[269] or by a very high degree of likelihood that the document served reached its addressee.[270]

The courts competent for scrutinising full compliance with the minimum procedural standards should, if satisfied, issue a standardised EEO certificate that makes that scrutiny and its result transparent.[271] The point to note is that it is the court of the Member State of origin, rather than that of the Member State of enforcement, which is responsible for scrutiny of the judgment, and for deciding whether the judgment satisfies the conditions precedent to its being certified as an EEO.[272]

Recital (19) states that the Regulation does not imply an obligation upon Member States to ensure that their national legislation meets the minimum procedural standards set out therein, but rather it provides an incentive to that end, by making available a more efficient and rapid enforceability of judgments in other Member States only if those minimum standards are met.[273] For Scotland, provision to satisfy minimum procedural standards has been made,[274] whereby rules consequential upon the introduction of Regulation 805/2004 create a procedure for certifying certain judgments as EEOs,[275] and for enforcing EEOs in Scotland,[276] Act of Sederunt (Sheriff Court European Enforcement Order Rules) 2005,[277] pertains to applications under the Regulation where the sheriff court is the court of origin and introduces rules of equivalent procedure for applications for EEO certificates for enforcement of judgments in other Member States.

---

[267] Regulation 805/2004 recital (13).

[268] Regulation 805/2004 recital (14).

[269] Regulation 805/2004 art.13: service with proof of receipt by the debtor.

[270] Regulation 805/2004 art.14: service without proof of receipt by the debtor.

[271] Regulation 805/2004 recital (17).

[272] Contrast the position under the *exequatur* procedure, where responsibility rested with the court of the Member State addressed, not the Member State of origin, to determine whether the conditions for a declaration of enforceability were met. This characteristic of the EEO procedure is worthy of comment in that it is novel for the court addressed in effect to lose its power of scrutiny, but such a loss is inherent in the purpose of the Regulation and the mode adopted to fulfil it.

[273] "It is up to the Member States to decide whether or not to adjust their national legislation to the minimum standards of Chapter III in order to ensure the eligibility of the largest possible number of decisions on uncontested claims for certification as a European Enforcement Order" (Explanatory Memorandum p.4).

[274] Rules of Court of Session Ch.62—recognition, registration, and enforcement of foreign judgments, etc.—Pt XII. See also Act of Sederunt (Sheriff Court European Enforcement Order Rules) 2005 (SSI 2005/523), pertaining to applications under the Regulation where the sheriff court is the court of origin and introducing rules of equivalent procedure for applications for EEO certificates for enforcement of judgments in other Member States.

[275] See procedure for certification under art.6(1) (judgment on uncontested claim) or art.8 (partial EEO) of decree in absence or decree by default (r.62.82); for certification under art.24 of court settlement (r.62.83); and for certification under art.25(1) of authentic instrument (r.62.84).

[276] Registration for enforcement of a judgment, court settlement or authentic instrument certified as an EEO: r.62.88.

[277] Act of Sederunt (Sheriff Court European Enforcement Order Rules) 2005 (SSI 2005/523).

Enforcement

9–56   A judgment that has been certified as an EEO by a court of the Member State of origin should be treated, for enforcement purposes, as if it had been delivered in the Member State in which enforcement is sought.[278] Arrangements for the enforcement of judgments should continue to be governed by national law. Hence, recital (8) specifically provides that:

> "In the United Kingdom, for example, the registration of a certified foreign judgment will therefore follow the same rules as the registration of a judgment from another part of the UK".

In terms of art.20, the creditor shall be required to provide the competent enforcement authorities of the Member State of enforcement with (a) a copy of the judgment; (b) a copy of the EEO certificate; and (c) where necessary, a transcription of the EEO certificate.

The grounds for refusal of enforcement, per art.21, are very restricted,[279] being limited to the existence of irreconcilable judgments.[280] On application by the debtor, enforcement shall be refused by the competent court in the Member State addressed if the judgment certified as an EEO is irreconcilable with an earlier judgment given in another (Member State or non-Member State) country, provided that: (a) the earlier judgment involved the same cause of action and was between the same parties; and (b) the earlier judgment was given in the Member State of enforcement or is recognised in that state; and (c) the irreconcilability was not and could not have been raised as an objection in the court proceedings in the Member State of origin.

Under no circumstances may a judgment or its certification as an EEO be reviewed as to its substance in the Member State of enforcement.[281]

Relationship with other Community instruments

9–57   Regulation 805/2004 provides Member States and, in turn, creditors, with an additional, optional means of seeking recognition and enforcement of a judgment, court settlement or authentic instrument on an uncontested claim.[282] In suitable cases, creditors can choose whether to proceed by means of Brussels I Recast, or to utilise the more expeditious procedure laid down in Regulation 805/2004. The removal by Brussels I Recast of the *exequatur* procedure means that the advantages of the EEO procedure set out in recital (9) of Regulation 805/2004 are less apparent.

---

[278] Regulation 805/2004 recital (8).
[279] *Lothschutz v Vogel* [2014] EWHC 473.
[280] Regulation 805/2004 art.23 provides, in exceptional cases, for the stay of enforcement proceedings, or for the limitation thereof to protective measures.
[281] Regulation 805/2004 art.21(2).
[282] Regulation 805/2004 art.27; cf. recital (20).

In terms of art.28, Regulation 805/2004 shall not affect the application of Regulation 1348/2000, and now Regulation 1393/2007, concerning service of documents.[283]

European order for payment procedure

Regulation 1896/2006 creating a European order for payment procedure has applied from 12 December 2008. The UK and Ireland opted into this instrument,[284] but Denmark is not participating.[285]

9–58

The purpose of this Regulation is to:

> "... simplify, speed up and reduce the costs of litigation in cross-border cases concerning uncontested pecuniary claims by creating a European order for payment procedure, and to permit the free circulation of European orders for payment throughout the Member States by laying down minimum standards, compliance with which renders unnecessary any intermediate proceedings in the Member State of enforcement prior to recognition and enforcement."[286]

It is said that the expeditious recovery of uncontested outstanding debts is of paramount importance to economic operators within the EU and for the proper functioning of the internal market.[287]

Scope

The Regulation applies in cross-border cases,[288] in civil and commercial matters, whatever the nature of the court or tribunal. It does not apply, however, to revenue, customs or administrative matters, or to what may be termed "standard" excluded matters.[289]

9–59

Procedure

Article 4 states the general aim and purpose of Regulation 1896/2006, viz.: collection of pecuniary claims for a specific amount that have fallen due at the time when the application for a European order for payment ("EOP") is submitted. In other words, the efficient recovery of outstanding debts over which

9–60

---

[283] See Ch.8, above. Recital (21) provides that when a document has to be sent from one Member State to another for service there, Regulation 805/2004 should apply together with the Service Regulation.

[284] Regulation 1896/2006 recital (31). See Act of Sederunt (Sheriff Court European Order for Payment Procedure Rules) 2008 (SSI 2008/436).

[285] Regulation 1896/2006 recital (32).

[286] Regulation 1896/2006 recital (9).

[287] Proposal for a Regulation creating a European order for payment procedure COM (2004) 173 final/3, para.2.1.1.

[288] Defined in art.3 as one in which at least one of the parties is domiciled or habitually resident in a Member State other than the Member State of the court or tribunal seised, at the date when the application for a European order for payment is submitted.

[289] Regulation 1896/2006 art.2.2. Mention should be made, however, of art.2(d)(i) and (ii), viz. the Regulation shall not apply to claims arising from non-contractual obligations, unless: (i) they have been the subject of an agreement between the parties or there has been an admission of debt; or (ii) they relate to liquidated debts arising from joint ownership of property.

no legal controversy exists.[290] Therefore, the context in which this operates is where the claimant has a debt or pecuniary claim, but one which, unlike the claims in Regulation 805/2004 and Regulation 871/2007 (q.v.), has not yet been adjudicated upon by a court, and so is not the subject of a court decision, or court settlement, or authentic instrument. This, therefore, is an effort which can only be applauded, to assist the unpaid creditor against the prevaricating debtor.

Regulation 1896/2006 provides thus a further additional, optional means for the claimant by which to seek to recover his debt. It neither replaces, nor harmonises the existing mechanisms for the recovery of uncontested claims under national law.[291]

With regard to the opaque relationship between Regulation 1896/2006 and Regulation 805/2004, the Commission indicated that:

> "The Commission has decided to pursue both objectives—the mutual recognition of decisions on uncontested claims on the one hand and the creation of a specific procedure for the attainment of decisions on the other—in two different legislative instruments. This two-tiered strategy does not entail the risk of an overlap or of contradictions between both projects since they are clearly demarcated by their strict limitation to the stages before (creation of an order for payment procedure) and after (recognition and enforcement) the delivery of the enforceable decision, respectively. Quite on the contrary, this approach offers a number of significant advantages over a legislative initiative combining both aspects. For example, it allows a broader scope of application for the abolition of *exequatur*, extending it to all judgments handed down in the verifiable absence of any dispute over the nature and extent of a debt and not only to decisions delivered in one specific procedure."[292]

Whereas the EEO is a certificate relating to a judgment, authentic act or court settlement which is issued in a national procedure, the EOP can be issued only in a single procedure common to EU Member States.[293] For the purpose of applying Regulation 1896/2006, jurisdiction shall be determined according to the rules contained in Brussels I Recast. The court shall examine the issues of jurisdiction and evidence in order to come to a view of the prima facie merits of the claim, and to exclude clearly unfounded claims,[294] but recital (16) states that this examination need not be carried out by a judge and may take the form of an automated procedure.[295] The claimant shall declare in his application for a European order for payment, that the information provided is true to the best of his knowledge and belief and shall acknowledge that any deliberate false statement could lead to appropriate penalties under the law of the Member State of origin.[296] The procedure shall be based, to the largest extent possible, on the use of standard forms in any communication between the court and the parties.[297]

---

[290] *Cheshire, North and Fawcett: Private International Law*, 14th edn (2008), p.644.

[291] See Regulation 1896/2006 recital (10).

[292] Proposal for a Regulation creating a European order for payment procedure COM (2004) 173 final/3; Explanatory Memorandum para.1.1.

[293] European Commission Practice Guide for the Application of the Regulation on the European Order for Payment (2011), p.5.

[294] Regulation 1896/2006 recital (16).

[295] Regulation 1896/2006 art.8.

[296] Regulation 1896/2006 art.7.3.

[297] Regulation 1896/2006 recital (11).

The application must include such information as suffices clearly to identify and support the claim in order to allow the defendant to make a well informed choice either to oppose the claim or to leave it uncontested. The court seised of the application shall examine, as soon as possible, whether the requirements set out in arts 2 (scope), 3 (cross-border requirement), 4 (procedure), 6 (jurisdiction), and 7 (formal requirements) are satisfied.

Assuming that all requirements are fulfilled, the court shall issue expeditiously a European order for payment. The defendant shall be informed that the order was issued solely on the basis of the information which was provided by the claimant and was not verified by the court; and that the order will become enforceable unless a statement of opposition has been lodged with the court in accordance with art.16.[298] In the EOP, the defendant shall be advised of his options, (a) to pay to the claimant the amount indicated in the order; or (b) to oppose the order by lodging with the court of origin a statement of opposition, to be sent within 30 days of service of the order on him.[299]

If the defendant lodges a statement of opposition, the proceedings shall continue before the competent courts of the Member State of origin (i.e. the Member State in which the EOP was issued).[300] If no statement of opposition is lodged, the court of origin without delay shall declare the EOP enforceable,[301] and shall send the order to the claimant. The order from the Member State of origin shall be recognised and enforced in the other Member States without the need for a declaration of enforceability, and without any possibility of opposing its recognition.[302] Enforcement procedures shall be governed by the law of the Member State of enforcement.[303] The grounds for refusal of enforcement, listed in art.22, are minimal and lie only in the area of res judicata. There can be no review of substance.[304]

Proposed reform

Reform of the European Order for payment procedure has been proposed in conjunction with reform of the European Small Claims Procedure, and is discussed below, at para.9–67.

9–61

---

[298] Regulation 1896/2006 art.12.4. See *Goldbet Sportwetten GmbH v Sperindeo* (C-144/12) [2014] I.L.Pr. 1.
[299] Regulation 1896/2006 art.12.3. See on the matter of alleged failure in proper service of EOP: *eco cosmetics GmbH & Co KG v Dupuy* and *Raiffeisenbank St Georgen reg Gen mbH v Bonchyk* (Joined Cases C-119/13, C-120/13) [2015] 1 W.L.R. 678. See, however, proposal to amend art.17 of Regulation 1896/2006 (COM(2013) 794 final; 2013/0403 (COD), (Brussels, 19.11.2013)).
[300] Regulation 1896/2006 arts 5, 12.4.
[301] Regulation 1896/2006 art.18.1.
[302] Regulation 1896/2006 art.19.
[303] Regulation 1896/2006 art.21.
[304] Regulation 1896/2006 art.22.3.

European Small Claims Procedure

9–62   There was introduced in 2007, with effect from 1 January 2009,[305] Regulation 861/2007.[306] The UK and Ireland opted into this instrument,[307] but Denmark is not participating.[308]

Objective

9–63   The objective of Regulation 861/2007 is to simplify and speed up litigation concerning small claims in cross-border cases, by establishing a European procedure for small claims ("EPSC"), and to reduce the costs associated with pursuing such a claim.[309] The Regulation is also intended to eliminate, by means of the EPSC, the intermediate measures which currently are necessary[310] to enable recognition and enforcement in one Member State of judgments given in another Member State. The Regulation does not prejudice the application of Brussels I Recast.

Scope

9–64   The Regulation applies in cross-border cases,[311] in civil and commercial matters, whatever the nature of the court or tribunal, where the value of the claim (excluding interest, expenses and disbursements), does not exceed EUR 2000 at the time when the claim form is received by the court. The small claims limit under Scots law, at the time of writing, is £3,000.[312] The Regulation does not apply, however, to revenue, customs or administrative matters, or to "standard" excluded matters.[313]

Nature of the EPSC

9–65   A relatively tight timescale is set out in art.5, in accordance with which the claim must be served on the defendant, his response submitted, and judgment delivered

---

[305] Article 29. Reg.861/2007. See European Commission Practice guide for the application of the European Small Claims Procedure under Regulation (EC) No.861/2007 of the European Parliament and of the Council of 11 July 2007 establishing a European Small Claims Procedure (2013).

[306] Regulation 861/2007 establishing a European Small Claims Procedure [2007] O.J. L199/1. See also Act of Sederunt (Sheriff Court European Small Claims Procedure Rules) 2008 (SSI 2008/435).

[307] Regulation 861/2007 recital (37).

[308] Regulation 861/2007 recital (38).

[309] Regulation 861/2007 art.1. Recital (7) narrates that the, "costs, delay and complexities connected with litigation do not necessarily decrease proportionally with the value of the claim. The obstacles to obtaining a fast and inexpensive judgment are exacerbated in cross-border cases. It is therefore necessary to create a European Procedure for Small Claims. The objective of such a European procedure should be to facilitate access to justice."

[310] Except as otherwise provided for by Regulation 805/2004 (European Enforcement Order for uncontested claims) and Regulation 1896/2006 (EU order for payment procedure).

[311] Defined in art.3 as one in which at least one of the parties is domiciled or habitually resident in a Member State other than the Member State of the court or tribunal seised, at the date on which the claim form is received by the court.

[312] Small Claims (Scotland) Amendment Order 2007 (SSI 2007/496).

[313] Regulation 861/2007 art.2.

by the court or tribunal.[314] The claimant commences the claim procedure[315] by completing a claim form in the style provided in the Regulation, and by lodging it with relevant supporting documents at the competent court or tribunal.[316] Upon receipt of the claim form, the court or tribunal completes the answer form,[317] and the two forms will be served, within 14 days of receipt of the claim form, on the defendant. The defendant has 30 days in which to make a response, which, within 14 days of receipt thereof by the court, must be dispatched to the claimant. The claimant has 30 days in which to respond to any counterclaim by the defendant. All documents must be submitted in the language or one of the languages of the court of tribunal.[318]

Article 5 makes plain the EPSC is a written procedure, unless, for some reason, an oral hearing is deemed by the court or tribunal to be necessary.[319] In terms of art.7, the court or tribunal shall give a judgment within 30 days of receipt of the documentation, unless it demands further details, wishes to take evidence, or summons the parties to an oral hearing, which must be held within 30 days of the summons. Article 8 permits, if the parties should agree, the holding of a hearing through audio, video or email conference.[320] Article 9.3 directs that the court or tribunal shall use the simplest and least burdensome method of taking evidence, and representation by a lawyer is not mandatory. Where an oral hearing is held, the court or tribunal shall give the judgment within 30 days of the hearing.

Under art.19, the EPSC shall be governed by the procedural law of the forum.

Enforceability of judgments

Article 15 provides that a judgment rendered shall be immediately enforceable, notwithstanding any possible appeal.[321] A judgment shall be recognised and enforced without the need for a declaration of enforceability (*exequatur* procedure).[322] Moreover, there is no possibility whatsoever (even, it seems, on a public policy basis) of opposing recognition of the judgment.

9–66

Enforcement procedures shall be governed by the law of the Member State of enforcement.[323] Any judgment given in the EPSC shall be enforced under the same conditions as a judgment given in the Member State of enforcement. As

---

[314] Regulation 861/2007 art.5.3. A degree of flexibility is proposed in art.14, by which, in "exceptional circumstances", the court or tribunal may extend the time limits otherwise laid down, if that is necessary in order to safeguard the rights of the parties.

[315] Regulation 861/2007 art.4.

[316] Regulation 861/2007 art.3.1.

[317] Regulation 861/2007 Annex III.

[318] Regulation 861/2007 art.6.

[319] Regulation 861/2007 art.5.1.

[320] cf. Article 9 by which the court or tribunal may determine the means of proof (including taking evidence via telephone, written witness statements and audio/video/email conference) and the extent to which evidence is taken, according to its discretion. It may be expected that this could give rise to certain practical problems.

[321] cf. Regulation 861/2007 recital (30).

[322] Regulation 861/2007 art.20.1.

[323] Regulation 861/2007 art.21.1.

with Regulation 1896/2006, the grounds for refusal of enforcement, listed in art.22, are minimal and lie only in the area of res judicata. There can be no review of substance.

Proposed reform

9–67 Mention should be made of Proposal for a Regulation of the European Parliament and of the Council amending Regulation (EC) No.861/2007 of the European Parliament and the Council of 11 July 2007 establishing a European Small Claims Procedure; and Regulation (EC) No.1896/2006 of the European Parliament and of the Council of 12 December 2006 creating a European order for payment procedure.[324] The Commission has observed that the ESCP is "little known and remains under-used several years after the entry into application of the Regulation".[325]

The main elements of the proposed revision include extension of the scope of the EPSC to cross-border claims up to EUR 10,000; extension of the definition of cross-border cases (so as to include disputes, excluded from the scope of the instrument in its original form, involving parties domiciled in the same Member State which have an important cross-border element and which could therefore benefit from the European simplified procedure); improving the use of electronic communication, including for service of certain documents; imposing an obligation on courts to use video-conferencing, tele-conferencing and other means of distance communication for the conduct of oral hearings and taking of evidence; and providing a maximum limitation on court fees charged for the procedure.[326] An increase in the upper limit of small claims is the change most likely to promote greater use of the remedy.

SUMMARY 9

9–68 1. At common law, decrees in rem establish rights in property against all comers and stand unaided on their own strength: challenge of a foreign decree in rem is limited to the challenges of "no jurisdiction in the foreign court", or fraud.

2. Judgments affecting status are treated as equivalent to decrees in rem, but recognition is governed by special statutory provision, namely, the Family Law Act 1986 Pt II and Brussels II *bis*.

3. Decrees in personam establish personal rights. Foreign decrees of this type, if not complied with where pronounced, require the assistance of the Scottish courts in order to be enforced in Scotland (by granting of decree conform to the foreign decree or by process of registration as described below) to be in compliance with Brussels/Lugano procedure.

---

[324] COM(2013) 794 final; 2013/0403 (COD), (Brussels, 19 November 2013). This is pursuant to Report from the Commission to the European Parliament, the Council and the European Economic and Social Committee on the application of Regulation (EC) No.861/2007 of the European Parliament and of the Council establishing a European Small Claims Procedure (COM(2013) 795 final), Brussels, 19 November 2013.

[325] COM(2013) 794 final; 2013/0403 (COD), (Brussels, 19 November 2013), para.1.2.

[326] COM(2013) 794 final; 2013/0403 (COD), (Brussels, 19 November 2013), para.3.1.

4.	Action for decree conform is necessary if the judgment emanates from a state with which the UK has no reciprocal arrangement of judgment enforcement under the Administration of Justice Act 1920 or the Foreign Judgments (Reciprocal Enforcement) Act 1933, and which is not an EU Member State or an EFTA State.

5.	A number of defences may be raised to an action for decree conform, on jurisdictional or natural justice/public policy grounds.

6.	"Direct" enforcement may be effected of Commonwealth (1920 Act) or other foreign (1933 Act) judgments, by means of registration ("judgment extension"). Under the 1920 Act, registration is a matter of discretion and will not be permitted if the defender can establish any one of a number of defences of a jurisdictional or natural justice/public policy nature. Registration under the 1933 Act is of right, but may be set aside later on application by the defender if any one of a number of challenges of a jurisdictional or natural justice/public policy nature can be made. Challenges at common law and under each of these statutes are similar to each other, but care must be taken as there are differences in detail, for example, the effect of pending or possible appeal.

7.	The Protection of Trading Interests Act 1980 constitutes a specialised caveat to the above.

8.	Judgments rendered by a court of an EU Member State are enforced in another Member State in accordance only with the procedures laid down by Brussels I Recast (and subsequent Regulations per 10, below), subject to the proviso that the matter falls within the scope of the instrument. Enforcement is not limited to money judgments, nor to judgments of superior courts.

9.	There is a parallel regime, contained in Lugano II, for enforcement of judgments rendered by the courts of an EFTA State.

10.	Among EU Member States, specialised procedures are available under the following Regulations:

	(a)	Regulation 805/2004 (European Enforcement Order for uncontested claims);

	(b)	Regulation 1896/2006 (European order for payment procedure); and

	(c)	Regulation 861/2007 (European small claims procedure).

11.	Reciprocal enforcement of money and non-money judgments within the UK is governed by the Civil Jurisdiction and Judgments Act 1982 s.18 and Schs 6 and 7, as amended.

12.	Enforcement of arbitral awards is governed principally by the New York Convention on the Recognition and Enforcement of Foreign Arbitral Awards 1958. See, for Scotland, the Arbitration (Scotland) Act 2010, and for England, the Arbitration Act 1996.

CHAPTER 10

Status and capacity

STATUS

At any particular time every person has at least one status in law. Status may be   **10–01**
defined as a person's legal condition in society: "The status of an individual, used
as a legal term, means the legal position of the individual in or with regard to the
rest of a community."[1] Status may result either from a natural condition such as
age or insanity, or from a legal condition such as marriage. It is a condition which
has attached to it the capacity (or incapacity) of an individual to acquire and
exercise legal rights and to perform legal acts and duties. The effect of allocation,
by application of the forum's choice of law rules, of a particular status to an
individual automatically results in the acquisition by that individual of
corresponding rights and duties, powers and disabilities, and capacities and
incapacities.

THE THEORY OF UNIVERSALITY OF STATUS

The ideal is that status should be universal so that a condition of status which   **10–02**
Scots conflict rules regard as having been validly conferred in one country
(particularly if it is the country of a person's domicile) should be recognised in all
other countries.[2] This theory or ideal is the basis of a legal theory known as the
theory of universality of status.[3] The theory is an excellent starting point: modern
times still produce unprecedented cases[4] and cases of international complexity
which cross the boundaries of other branches of legal knowledge,[5] where
recourse to first principles is the best help. However, Viscount Simonds in
National Bank of Greece and Athens SA v Metliss[6] attributes recognition of a
foreign status to comity rather than to the universal quality of the status. Further,
the theory of universality of status is now not sufficiently strong, subtle or
detailed a guide to provide solutions to modern problems of family law. Rather,

---

[1] *Niboyet v Niboyet* (1878) L.R. 4 P.D. 1, per Brett L.J. at 11.
[2] *Mackie v Darling* (1871) L.R. 12 Eq. 319 (but see *Johnstone v Beattie* (1843) 10 Cl. & F. 42); and
Green v Montagu (aka Re Duchy of Manchester English Settled Estates) [2011] EWHC 1856 (Ch).
[3] *Re Luck's Settlement Trusts* [1940] Ch. 864, per Scott L.J. at 885–919, especially 889–891.
[4] e.g. *Bumper Development Corp v Commissioner of Police of the Metropolis* [1991] 4 All E.R. 638;
Re S (Hospital Patient: Foreign Curator) [1995] 4 All E.R. 30; and *W v H (Child Abduction:
Surrogacy)* [2002] 1 F.L.R. 1008.
[5] e.g. *Arab Monetary Fund v Hashim (No.3)* [1991] 1 All E.R. 871 HL; and *Westland Helicopters Ltd
v Arab Organisation for Industrialisation* [1995] 2 All E.R. 387.
[6] *National Bank of Greece and Athens SA v Metliss* [1958] A.C. 509 at 525.

resort must be had to technical conflict of laws rules, such as those of jurisdiction and recognition enshrined in the Family Law Act 1986[7] and Brussels II *bis*[8]—which, however, may be said to be inspired by the theory of universality.

General points as to status

10–03   The general rule is that a natural[9] person's status is determined by his personal law. Traditionally in the view of Scots law, the pre-eminent personal law connecting factor has been, and in places continues to be, the law of a person's domicile. Likewise, historically, in jurisdictional terms, the court of the domicile[10] has been regarded as the appropriate court to determine the existence and effects of any status, or alteration therein, and prior to the Europeanisation of the subject a Scots court exercising jurisdiction on the basis of domicile was unlikely to yield to another court its pre-eminence in this area. The status or legal capacity of natural persons falls outside the scope of the 1968 Brussels Convention and its descendants.[11] When the Brussels Convention was concluded, the rules of the Member States on jurisdiction in matrimonial matters, "were considered so disparate as to preclude their effective unification in the 1968 Convention without major change to its nature".[12] However, account now must be taken of the encroachment, notably into the rules of jurisdiction in matrimonial matters and matters of parental responsibility, by the personal law factor of habitual residence.[13]

    Since 1 March 2001, matrimonial status[14] has been regulated by Regulation 1347/2000 ("Brussels II"), itself superseded by Regulation 2201/2003 ("Brussels II *bis*"), as of 1 March 2005.[15] In terms of Brussels II *bis*, an EU Member State forum is clothed with jurisdiction in matrimonial matters, and in matters of parental responsibility, principally upon the basis of habitual residence and only residually on the basis of nationality or domicile.[16] Similarly, under the 1980 Hague Convention on the Civil Aspects of International Child Abduction, and the 1996 Hague Convention on Jurisdiction, Applicable Law, Recognition, Enforcement and Co-operation in respect of Parental Responsibility and Measures for the Protection of Children, the habitual residence of the child is the pivotal

---

[7] Para.12–28, below.

[8] Paras 12–05, 12–37 and 14–09 et seq., below.

[9] With regard to non-natural persons, see generally para.8–06, above.

[10] Hence the Court of Session has jurisdiction to entertain a petition to determine status if the petitioner avers sufficient evidence of a Scots domicile.

[11] 1968 Brussels Convention Title 1 art.1; Brussels I Regulation art.1.2.a; and Brussels I Recast Regulation art.1.2.a.

[12] House of Lords European Communities Committee, *Fifth Report of the European Communities Committee*, "Brussels II: The Draft Convention on Jurisdiction, Recognition and Enforcement of Judgments in Matrimonial Matters" (The Stationery Office, 1997), Pt 1 para.1.

[13] Regulation 2201/2003. See Chs 6 and 12.

[14] Insofar as concerns the allocation of jurisdiction, and recognition of judgments, in cases concerning divorce, legal separation, and marriage annulment, but not concerning capacity to marry which remains governed by Scots conflict rules. See Ch.11, below.

[15] See in detail Ch.12, below.

[16] See in detail Ch.14, below.

connecting factor.[17] This accumulation of legislation, therefore, has had the effect of reducing the hitherto central significance of a person's domicile in this regard.[18]

With regard to debtor status, Regulation 1346/2000 on insolvency proceedings applies to such proceedings, whether the debtor is a natural person or a legal person.[19] It applies so as to identify the law applicable to insolvency proceedings, and their effects. In providing rules on jurisdiction and choice of law, it presupposes the existence of a qualifying debtor,[20] but makes no provision for the determination of debtor status itself, a matter apparently left for decision by the law(s) governing the alleged debt(s).[21]

CAPACITY

Choice of law issues will be determined according to the context in which they arise. They are likely to concern the matter of legal capacity. Status is the basis of capacity or incapacity so that a person's capacity to have legal rights and to perform legal acts depends upon his status. Status is a legal condition while capacity is a power, and incapacity a disability, which result from status.[22] Although one law determines any particular status, different laws may determine different questions of capacity within the same status. Thus, under Scots choice of law rules, although the law of first recourse in a matter of status is that of an individual's domicile (which applies, e.g. to determine capacity to marry), different laws are likely to determine his capacity to enter into a contract, to purchase land, and to test.

Moreover, a person may stand in a number of legal conditions of status at one and the same time; thus he may be in nonage, married, and bankrupt. The question whether he is in nonage for the purposes, respectively, of marriage and bankruptcy is likely to be referred to a different law for each purpose. This is so, even though strictly speaking, it is meaningless to say that a status of nonage

10–04

---

[17] Brought into effect in the UK by the Child Abduction and Custody Act 1985. See generally Ch.14, below.

[18] See generally Ch.6, below.

[19] Regulation 1346/2000 recital (9). See also Regulation (EU) 2015/848 (Insolvency Regulation Recast) recital (9).

[20] Regulation 1346/2000 recitals (12)–(14), art.3.2; Regulation 2015/848 recital (23)–(25), art.3.2.

[21] See, in respect of the Cross-Border Insolvency Regulations 2006 (SI 2006/1030), *Rubin v Eurofinance SA* [2010] 1 All E.R. (Comm) 81 (and later on appeal: [2013] 1 A.C. 236), in which the single judge held that, having regard to the definition of "foreign proceedings" under those regulations, it would be perverse to give the word "debtor" any other meaning than that given to it by the foreign court in those foreign proceedings, i.e. the USA court in which the main proceedings took place. Therefore, the argument that, under English law, the foreign bankruptcy proceedings related to a debtor who had no legal personality, either as an individual or as a body corporate, was discounted (a trust was a debtor for the purposes of the 2006 Regulations and the Model Law, even though by English law it had no legal personality as an individual or a body corporate).

[22] *Integral Petroleum SA v SCU-Finanz AG* [2014] EWHC 702 (Comm), per Popplewell J. at [53]; confirmed [2015] EWCA Civ 144. See *Haugesund Kommune v Depfa ACS Bank* [2012] Q.B. 54 (esp. Aikens L.J. at [38]), where lack of power of a Norwegian local authority resulted in lack of capacity to enter into a contract. Also, on the question of the legal capacity of an international organisation, see *Westland Helicopters Ltd v Arab Organisation for Industrialisation* [1995] 2 All E.R. 387; and the International Organisations Act 2005.

exists except in relation to particular capacities, with regard to each of which a choice of law rule will provide a governing connecting factor. Thus according to Scots choice of law rules, the capacity of a person to test with regard to moveables is governed by the law of his domicile at the time of testing,[23] whereas his capacity to test with regard to immoveables is referred to the *lex situs*.[24] Therefore choice of law rules direct to different legal systems, by means of different connecting factors, the question of capacity in respect of each "transaction" as it may arise. Some rules are more complex[25] and/or uncertain than others.

As in the case of penal or discriminatory conditions of status, penal incapacities are not recognised by a Scots forum.[26] An incapacity imposed by the personal law may be found to have created an incapacity of strictly limited territorial extent and may not affect that person when outside the jurisdiction of his personal law.[27] The broad rule, however, is that a person's capacity to perform acts and have legal rights depends upon the law of his domicile in relation to personal matters and matters concerning moveable property,[28] while, in general, matters relating to immoveable property depend upon the *lex situs*.[29]

PUBLIC POLICY

10–05   Status and its incidents normally are governed by an individual's personal law, but the forum retains discretion under the heading of public policy. By way of exception, common law or legislative, to the principle of recognition, the forum may refuse, on grounds of public policy, to accept a particular status conferred by another law, or any of its incidents.[30]

The exercise of discretion by the (English) forum is seen in the innominate and unusual case of *Re S*,[31] concerning a physical *incapax* whose domicile and nationality were Norwegian and whose residence was in England. The presence of the *incapax* in England was held to clothe the English court with jurisdiction.[32] Further, even though an appointment of a guardian by the date of litigation had been made under the Norwegian personal law, the English court retained discretion to act in the best interests of the *incapax*. However, comity suggested

---

[23]   See Ch.18, below.

[24]   See, e.g. *Black v Black's Trustees*, 1950 S.L.T. (Notes) 32; *Bank of Africa Ltd v Cohen* [1909] 2 Ch. 129.

[25]   e.g. Rome I Regulation art.13 (ex-art.11 of Rome I Convention). Ch.15, below.

[26]   *MacDougall v Chitnavis*, 1937 S.C. 390. cf. *Chetti v Chetti* [1909] P. 67.

[27]   *Bernaben and Co v Hutchison* (1902) 18 Sh. Ct. Rep. 72; and *Kaye (Peter) v HM Advocate*, 1957 J.C. 55.

[28]   *Doglioni v Crispin* (1866) L.R. 1 H.L. 301; *Orlando v Earl of Fingall* [1940] I.R. 281; *Sawrey-Cookson v Sawrey-Cookson's Trustees* (1905) 8 F. 157; and *Ogilvy v Ogilvy's Trustees*, 1927 S.L.T. 83.

[29]   *Black v Black's Trustees*, 1950 S.L.T. (Notes) 32; *Bank of Africa Ltd v Cohen* [1902] 2 Ch. 129; and *Ogilvy v Ogilvy's Trustees*, 1927 S.L.T. 83.

[30]   Paras 3–08, above.

[31]   *Re S (Hospital Patient: Foreign Curator)* [1995] 4 All E.R. 30.

[32]   See now Mental Capacity Act 2005, and discussion thereof in J.J. Fawcett and J.M. Carruthers, *Cheshire, North & Fawcett's Private International Law*, 14th edn (2008), Ch.26. cf. In Scotland, Adults with Incapacity (Scotland) Act 2000 s.85 and Sch.3, in respect of which see P.B. Beaumont and P.E. McEleavy, *Anton's Private International Law*, 3rd edn (2011), Ch.18.

that the *incapax* should be returned to Norway, the burden of proof lying on those who asserted the contrary. Surprisingly, no reference appears to have been made to the case of *Re Langley's Settlement Trusts*[33] where, after some doubt, the English court concluded that the status of "incompetent" (and its concomitant incapacities), conferred by the Californian court of the domicile upon a person mentally capable but physically incapable, did not offend the forum's public policy, but rather was to be recognised by the forum as being protective of the individual, and not punitive.

Sometimes British courts have been inconsistent in their views. A century after it had been agreed that the status of slavery could not be recognised in the UK, the English court in *Santos v Illidge*[34] enforced a contract for the sale of slaves (despite the provision of the Slave Trade Act 1824 s.2, making it unlawful for "any person" to purchase, sell or contract for the purchase or sale of slaves, a provision in its nature of intra-territorial effect only), because the contract was governed by the law of Brazil, by which it was valid. Both then[35] and now,[36] a provision valid by the proper/applicable law of the contract, but offensive to the public policy of the forum may be refused enforcement. Moreover, use today is made by European draftsmen of the concept of "overriding mandatory provision", to secure the operation in any given EU Member State court of rules (of the forum or of a law of close connection) which, by reason of their nature and purpose, are superimposed upon the otherwise applicable law. Use of this tool is an example of permitted discretion by the forum, both in interpretation of what constitutes an "overriding mandatory provision" and in application of the safeguarding provision.[37]

Inconsistency, on occasion, also is seen in family law jurisprudence. While prohibitions on re-marriage after divorce[38] and those concerning marriage out of caste[39] are rejected by Scots and English courts as imposing incapacities unacceptable on public policy grounds, it is possible to cite a case of overseas nullity recognition[40] in which a ground of nullity used by the court in Jerusalem was that the Jewish faith of the woman precluded marriage with a Christian, the resulting annulment being recognised by the English court. On the other hand, Nazi-compelled divorces of marriages between Jew and Gentile were not recognised by British courts.[41] Examples of historical interest can be noted, in all of which recognition was denied on the ground that the status was penal in the sense of discriminatory, or contrary to UK public policy: slavery[42]; civil death (i.e. removal of all civil rights); monastic celibacy; conviction for treason abroad;

---

[33] *Re Langley's Settlement Trusts* [1961] 1 All E.R. 78.

[34] *Santos v Illidge* (1860) 8 C.B. (N.S.) 861.

[35] *Grell v Levy* (1864) 16 C.B. (N.S.) 73.

[36] Rome I Regulation art.21.

[37] This is seen notably in contract: Rome I Regulation art.9. Para.15–22, below.

[38] *Warter v Warter* (1890) L.R. 15 P.D. 152; *Martin v Buret*, 1938 S.L.T. 479. But see *Buckle v Buckle* [1956] P. 181; *Scott v Att Gen* (1886) L.R. 11 P.D. 128. As to re-marriage after divorce, see Ch.12, below.

[39] *MacDougall v Chitnavis*, 1937 S.C. 390.

[40] *Corbett v Corbett* [1957] 1 W.L.R. 486.

[41] *Re Meyer* [1971] P. 298; but see *Igra v Igra* [1951] P. 404.

[42] cf. *Somerset v Stewart* (1772) 20 St. Tr. 1; *Knight v Wedderburn* (1778) Mor. 14545; *Santos v Illidge* (1860) 8 C.B. (N.S.) 861.

and the prodigal status.[43] Account has to be taken now of grounds of non-recognition contained in relevant European instruments, such as arts 22 and 23 of Brussels II *bis*, which impose a closely worked system of rules which impact upon a person's status.[44]

Both at common law, and under legislation, one should be aware of the dangerous potential of the public policy discretion, insofar as it may frustrate the aims of this branch of law and, in the particular matter of marital status, may produce limping status.[45] However, it is generally appreciated by courts that delicacy and scrupulousness must be exercised in relation to public policy in international private law issues ("external public policy").[46]

STATUS AND ITS INCIDENTS

10–06   Status must be distinguished from its incidents, that is, from the effects, rights and duties, powers or disabilities which attach to it or result from it. Although a condition of status may be recognised in general, consequences following from it may or may not be recognised in certain circumstances, with the result that a condition of status may be recognised for some purposes but not for others. The question is always whether it will be recognised for the particular purpose before the court. Thus, a foreign divorce may be recognised as having terminated a marriage,[47] but the financial consequences thereof, exceptionally, may not be recognised.[48] Further, as noted above,[49] a condition attached to a divorce, which otherwise is worthy of recognition, may be considered by the forum to be penal and regarded as *pro non scripto*.

SUMMARY 10

10–07   1.   Status in general is determined by the law of the domicile. A condition of status conferred by that law, in principle, should be recognised everywhere, subject to express legislative provision (especially in consistorial and child-related areas, which have had the effect of raising the profile of habitual residence as a determinant of status) and to public policy.

---

[43] *Worms v De Valdor* (1880) 49 L.J. Ch. 261; *Re Selot's Trusts* [1902] 1 Ch. 488; *Re Langley's Settlement Trusts* [1962] 1 Ch. 541.

[44] Paras 12–38—12–39, below; and 14–25.

[45] i.e. where a person's status as married is recognised in one legal system, but not in another.

[46] Ch.3, above; and P.B. Carter, "The Rôle of Public Policy in English Private International Law" (1993) 42 I.C.L.Q. 1; N. Enonchong, "Public Policy in the Conflict of Laws: A Chinese Wall Around Little England?" (1996) 45 I.C.L.Q. 633; R.D. Leslie, "The Relevance of Public Policy in Legal Issues Involving Other Countries and Their Laws", 1995 J.R. 477; and J. Blom, "Public Policy in Private International Law and Its Evolution in Time" (2003) 50 Netherlands International Law Review 373.

[47] Scots conflict rules assume that this is a defining feature of a divorce decree. cf. Family Law Act 1986 s.50 and *Lawrence v Lawrence* [1985] 2 All E.R. 733.

[48] *Wood v Wood* [1957] P. 254 (pre-existing English award of maintenance kept in being by English court after pronouncement of Nevada divorce recognised in England). See now Brussels II *bis* recitals (8) and (11).

[49] Note 38, above.

2. As a general guide, capacity is governed by the law of the domicile or habitual residence as regards matters of personal law and as regards dealings with moveable property, and by the *lex situs* as regards immoveable property. However, legal capacity to perform a particular act is determined by the law applicable to the act or transaction in question.

3. Status must be distinguished from its incidents. Not all incidents of a recognised status may be recognised by the forum for the purpose in hand.

CHAPTER 11

The law of marriage and other adult relationships

NATURE OF THE RELATIONSHIP

Marriage

In order that a decision can be made upon the validity of a marriage in the view of **11–01** Scots conflict law, it is necessary first that the relationship presented amount in its nature to the Scots conception of marriage. If that test is satisfied, the adequacy of the "marriage" in terms of its essential and formal validity must be examined.

Lord Penzance, in *Hyde v Hyde and Woodmansee*, famously stated that: "I conceive that marriage, as understood in Christendom, may for this purpose be defined as the voluntary union for life of one man and one woman, to the exclusion of all others."[1] Though long accepted as the benchmark for marriage as understood in the UK, a profound change was made to Scots law through the enactment of the Marriage and Civil Partnership (Scotland) Act 2014, and likewise to English law by the Marriage (Same Sex Couples) Act 2013. These changes in the laws of marriage in Scotland and England, respectively, have significant conflict of laws repercussions.

The gender aspect of the definition aside, it follows from Lord Penzance's famous criteria, widely accepted in the common law world, that the nature of the union must be such that it is recognised as conferring the status of married persons on the parties thereto in a relationship intended to be permanent.[2] Except in the special case of the recognition, under Scots and UK rules, of polygamous marriages,[3] the relationship of married persons must be exclusive. The law will not recognise a sub-normal marriage,[4] that is, a union under which one party has the status of "spouse", but the other does not have equivalent status. Nor will it recognise a "non-marriage" which, though it may have had apparently the trappings of marriage, was not intended to be a marriage, being in the nature of a charade.[5] Whether both parties must be alive at the date of the celebration of the

---

[1] *Hyde v Hyde and Woodmansee* (1866) L.R. 1 P. & D. 130 at 133.
[2] Ease of dissolution does not invalidate original intention: *Nachimson v Nachimson* [1930] P. 217.
[3] And even there, the forum must decide whether the situation presented amounts to polygamy or concubinage; the forum's view will prevail over that of the *lex loci celebrationis*: *Lee v Lau* [1967] P. 14. See para.11–14, below.
[4] Wolff, *Private International Law*, 2nd edn (1950), p.316.
[5] e.g. *Hudson v Leigh* [2009] EWHC 1306 (Fam): in such a case, decree of nullity was neither necessary nor appropriate. Also *Gandhi v Patel* [2002] 1 F.L.R. 603.

marriage is a matter which would be referred to the domiciliary laws of the parties,[6] and would be subjected to the public policy of any given forum.

Marriage must be entered into voluntarily, "with an agreeing mind". Marriage induced by coercion[7] (to be distinguished from arranged marriage), or without matrimonial intent,[8] or under error,[9] is void.[10]

The advent of same sex marriage

11–02   Prior to the entry into force of the Marriage and Civil Partnership (Scotland) Act 2014,[11] no same sex marriage could be celebrated in Scotland, nor, as a result of the dual domicile theory,[12] did a Scottish domiciliary have capacity to enter into "same sex marriage" elsewhere, no matter that the *lex loci celebrationis* or the personal law of the other party permitted such a "marriage".[13] The same was true mutatis mutandis of an English locus and English domiciliary before the introduction of the Marriage (Same Sex Couples) Act 2013.[14]

The aims of the 2014 Act[15] are, inter alia, to make provision for the marriage of persons of the same sex; to make provision as to the persons who may solemnise marriage and as to procedure and venue; and to make provision for the conversion of civil partnerships to marriage.[16]

---

[6] cf. French Civil Code art.171: a marriage may be authorised in French law though one of the parties is dead, if certain conditions are satisfied, in order to safeguard the succession rights of children. The Hague Marriage Convention 1976 (not signed or ratified by the UK, nor by many other countries) excludes from its scope posthumous marriage and proxy marriage.

[7] *Szechter v Szechter* [1971] P. 286; *Mahmud v Mahmud*, 1977 S.L.T. (Notes) 17; *Mahmood v Mahmood*, 1993 S.L.T. 589; *Mahmud v Mahmud*, 1994 S.L.T. 599; and *Sohrab v Kahn*, 2002 S.L.T. 1255. Para.12–52, below for detail.

[8] *Akram v Akram*, 1979 S.L.T. (Notes) 87; and *Hakeem v Hussain*, 2003 S.L.T. 515; on appeal, sub nom. *SH v KH*, 2005 S.L.T. 1025.

[9] *Lendrum v Chakravarti*, 1929 S.L.T. 96; *Mehta v Mehta* [1945] 2 All E.R. 690; and *Noble v Noble*, 1947 S.L.T. (Notes) 62.

[10] See more fully at para.11–30, and at paras 12–52—12–55, below.

[11] In respect of which see The Marriage and Civil Partnership (Scotland) Act 2014 (Commencement No.1) Order 2014 (SSI 2014/121); The Marriage and Civil Partnership (Scotland) Act 2014 (Commencement No.2 and Saving Provisions) Order 2014 (SSI 2014/212); The Marriage and Civil Partnership (Scotland) Act 2014 (Commencement No.2 and Saving Provisions) Amendment Order 2014 (SSI 2014/218); The Marriage and Civil Partnership (Scotland) Act 2014 (Commencement No.3, Saving, Transitional Provision and Revocation) Order 2014 (SSI 2014/287); and The Marriage (Same Sex Couples) Act 2013 (Consequential and Contrary Provisions and Scotland) Order 2014 (SI 2014/560).

[12] Explained below at paras 11–28—11–29, below.

[13] Whether same sex "marriages" contracted outside the UK between parties neither of whom was domiciled in a part of the UK, but the domicile of each of whom conferred capacity to enter into such a "marriage", would be recognised by Scots courts as equivalent to heterosexual marriages was a matter of conjecture. The question now has been overtaken by the 2014 Act.

[14] Para.11–05, below.

[15] K. McKNorrie, "Now the Dust has Settled: the Marriage and Civil Partnership (Scotland) Act 2014" (2014) 2 Juridical Review 135.

[16] Registered same sex civil partnerships have been permitted by Scots and English law since 2004 by virtue of the Civil Partnership Act 2004. Paras 11–33—11–38, below.

Same sex marriage celebrated in Scotland

Same sex marriage has been permitted to take place in Scotland since December 2014.[17] This change has been effected by s.2 of the 2014 Act, in its repeal of s.5(4)(e) of the Marriage (Scotland) Act 1977 (in which was found the objection to marriage in Scotland on the ground that the parties were of the same sex). This is all that is patent. The domestic law of Scotland concerning marriage having changed, the inference must be that any person of Scots domicile at the point of marriage has capacity by his personal law[18] to enter a same sex marriage in Scotland.

11–03

As regards a party not domiciled in Scotland, but who purports to marry in Scotland, the 2014 Act must be read in conjunction with the Family Law (Scotland) Act 2006 ("the 2006 Act") s.38. Reference should be made in the first place to s.38(2), which refers the question of capacity to marry to the law of the ante-nuptial domicile. Section 38(2) itself is subject to s.38(4).[19] Section 38(4) enacts that the capacity of an individual to enter into a marriage shall not be determined by his/her ante-nuptial domicile in ofar as it would be contrary to public policy in Scotland for such capacity to be so determined. If, therefore, by the law of a party's non-Scottish domicile, there is a prohibition on same sex marriage, the question will arise as to whether such a marriage involving such a person should be permitted to take place in Scotland. The Marriage (Scotland) Act 1977 s.3(5) has been amended by s.3(2)(c) of the 2014 Act, to the effect that the requirement, imposed upon a non-UK domiciliary intending to enter a marriage to be solemnised in Scotland, to submit a certificate of capacity, falls away if no such certificate has been issued by reason only of the fact that the parties to the intended marriage are of the same sex.

The implication of the above must be that an incapacity to enter a same sex marriage, imposed by a party's (or both parties') non-Scottish *lex domicilii*, may be disregarded if the purported marriage takes place in Scotland.[20]

Same sex marriage celebrated outside the UK

Prior to the entry into force of the 2014 Act, same sex marriage could not take place in Scotland. It was possible nonetheless for a Scots domiciliary to purport to enter into such a marriage in a foreign jurisdiction which permitted such form of marriage. Principle directed that, in accordance with the dual domicile theory outlined below, any same sex marriage, purportedly entered into anywhere in the world, where at least one of the parties was of Scots domicile, would not be regarded as valid in a Scots court, by reason of lack of legal capacity. But where same sex "marriage" was valid by the *lex loci celebrationis*, and where, by his/her personal law, each contracting party had legal capacity to enter into such a

11–04

---

[17] The Marriage and Civil Partnership (Scotland) Act 2014 (Commencement No.3, Saving, Transitional Provision and Revocation) Order 2014 (SSI 2014/287).

[18] Capacity to marry being a matter for the law of the ante-nuptial domicile. Para.11–28, below.

[19] Para.11–29, below.

[20] This is supported by the statement in the Explanatory Memorandum to the 2014 Act, at para.11, that, even if a same sex marriage would be void according to the law of the domicile of one (or both) of the parties, that is *not* a barrier to the parties entering into a same sex marriage in Scotland.

union, recognition was likely to be afforded in Scotland to the status, or at least to certain of the incidents thereof, albeit only sub nom. civil partnership.[21]

As stated, it is a necessary inference of the 2014 Act that any person of Scots domicile at the point of marriage has capacity by his/her personal law to enter a same sex marriage. The further inference is that such a person has legal capacity by his/her personal law to enter into a same sex marriage in *any* jurisdiction. Whether such a marriage celebrated abroad will be regarded as valid by Scots law will depend on a number of matters of form, capacity and essentials (q.v.).

If a Scots court should have occasion to adjudicate upon the validity of a marriage celebrated overseas, it will use the choice of law rules contained in s.38 of the Family Law (Scotland) Act 2006. Where one or both of the parties lacks capacity to enter into a same sex marriage by reason of a prohibition in his/her personal law, it may be necessary for the Scots court to consider its public policy and the operation of s.38(4) of the 2006 Act.[22] To date, s.38(4) has been understood to provide a protective discretion to a Scots judge to refuse to recognise capacity to marry conferred by the law of the domicile which offends Scots policy, i.e. to prevent recognition of marriage where the domicile permits it, as for example in the case of marriage where one or both parties is underage or within the prohibited degrees of relationship by Scots domestic law. In light of the 2014 Act, s.38(4) could be invoked by a Scots court equally in a case where the law of a party's domicile does *not* permit him/her to enter into a same sex marriage, to the effect of overriding that personal law and positively conferring capacity to enter such a marriage. In terms of precedent, the examples which Scots or English conflict of laws provide are few. Cases can be cited in which a Scots court has refused to recognise an incapacity to marry on the ground that it is penal,[23] but the classification as penal of an incapacity to marry in a same sex relationship would be a new development and a strong exercise of the public policy tool by the forum. But the fact that the policy of Scots law on same sex marriage has changed would not authorise per se a Scots court to disregard an incapacity imposed by the law of the domicile of either party.

Complex temporal questions might arise. If, for example, it should happen that a Scots court, after 31 December 2014, is asked to adjudicate on a same sex marriage celebrated abroad before that date, that marriage being valid as to form and essentials in all respects other than legal capacity of a Scots domiciled party to enter a same sex relationship, is it likely that a Scots court could be persuaded to apply to the issue of legal capacity the relevant law at the time the matter comes in issue, rather than at the date of the purported marriage? Could lack of

---

[21] In terms of s.215 of the Civil Partnership Act 2004, the effect of recognition in the UK of a specified overseas relationship qualifying under Sch.20 was to treat such a union as equivalent to a UK civil partnership. See, e.g. the English High Court decision in *Wilkinson v Kitzinger* [2006] EWHC 2022 (Fam); and also *P.B. and J.S. v Austria* (Application No.18984/02), 22 July 2010. See now, s.26 of the 2014 Act, above, para.11–32. See also Registration of overseas relationships treated as civil partnerships: Ch.2.

[22] 2006 Act s.38(4) authorises a Scots court to override under the banner of public policy an individual's capacity to enter into a marriage by the law of his/her ante-nuptial domicile. Para.11–29, below.

[23] Para.11–29, below. The case of *Sottomayor v De Barros (No 2)* [1874 – 80] All E.R. Rep. 97, in which an unknown foreign incapacity was regarded by the English forum as quasi-penal by that fact alone and thereby able to be disregarded, became discredited. See E.B. Crawford, *International Private Law in Scotland* (1998), para.9.18.

capacity at the point of contracting "marriage" be cured retrospectively in the same manner that a defect of form was cured in *Starkowski v Attorney General*?[24] The *Starkowski* principle has not to date in England or Scotland been extended to matters of essential validity, and although it would seem an unwarranted extension, it would not be out of line with the backdating mechanism which operates when a civil partnership is translated into marriage.[25]

Same sex marriage—English law

The same significant change in the matter of same sex marriage was made in English law by the Marriage (Same Sex Couples) Act 2013. The aims of the Act, inter alia, are to make provision for the marriage of same sex couples in England and Wales; to make provision about gender change by married persons and civil partners; to make provision about consular functions in respect of marriage and the marriage of armed forces personnel overseas; and for the review of civil partnership and of survivor benefits under occupational pension schemes.

11–05

By s.1(1), it is enacted that, with effect from 13 March 2014,[26] "Marriage of same sex couples is lawful". By s.20(1), the 2013 Act extends principally to England and Wales, but s.20(2) extends a number of provisions to Scotland.[27] The terseness of s.1(1) gives rise to many conflict of laws questions. First, it can be assumed that s.1(1) is territorially limited to marriages celebrated in England and Wales. Next, by s.10(1) a marriage under (a) the law of any part of the UK other than England and Wales; or (b) the law of any country or territory outside the UK, is not prevented from being recognised under English law only because it is the marriage of a same sex couple.[28] In terms of s.11, in English law marriage is to have the same effect in relation to same sex couples as it has in relation to opposite sex couples.

From this bare legislative framework, it must be concluded that persons domiciled in England and Wales have legal capacity to enter into a same sex marriage in England or elsewhere. The English applicable law rules on capacity to marry rest on the common law, there being no equivalent to s.38 of the Family Law (Scotland) Act 2006, and so an English court in judging the validity of a

---

[24] *Starkowski v Attorney General* [1954] A.C. 155. See para.11–23, below.

[25] Para.11–38, below.

[26] The Marriage (Same Sex Couples) Act 2013 (Commencement No.2 and Transitional Provisions) Order 2014 (SSI 2013/93) art.3. See also The Marriage (Same Sex Couples) Act 2013 (Commencement No.1) Order 2014 (SSI 2013/2789); The Marriage (Same Sex Couples) Act 2013 (Commencement No. 3) Order 2014 (SI 2014/1662); and The Marriage (Same Sex Couples) Act 2013 (Consequential and Contrary Provisions and Scotland) and Marriage and Civil Partnership (Scotland) Act 2014 (Consequential Provisions) Order 2014 (SI 2014/3168).

[27] Namely, in Pt 1 s.10(3) and Sch.2 (Extraterritorial matters); Pt 2 (ss.12–16, except for ss.14 and 15); and Pt 3 (final provisions).

[28] By s.10(2), the time at which same sex marriage is provided for in the alternative jurisdiction is irrelevant. English law having permitted same sex marriage in advance of Scots law, Sch.2 Pt 1 makes interim provision whereby a marriage of a same sex couple under English law is to be treated in Scots law as a civil partnership.

same sex marriage celebrated in England or abroad between parties one or both of whom is under a legal incapacity by the law of his/her domicile, must be guided by common law precedent.[29]

Conversion of civil partnerships into same sex marriage

11–06   Section 11 of the Marriage and Civil Partnership (Scotland) Act 2014 is concerned with the situation where the parties to a qualifying[30] civil partnership (a) marry in accordance with the procedure set out in s.8 of the 2014 Act; or (b) change their civil partnership into a marriage in accordance with s.10(1) thereof. Section 11(2) incorporates an unusual backdating mechanism, whereby a qualifying civil partnership, once converted into same sex marriage by s.8 or by s.10(1), is to be deemed a marriage which commenced on the date of registration of the partnership. The effect of this is to enlarge the legal capacity to marry of persons who take advantage of these provisions, this enlargement being conferred retrospectively, i.e. capacity to enter a same sex marriage is imputed even though such marriage was not a recognised status in Scots law pre-2014.

Under English law, by s.9(1) of the Marriage (Same Sex Couples) Act 2013, the parties to an "England and Wales civil partnership"[31] may convert their civil partnership into a marriage.[32] As under Scots law, the resulting marriage is to be treated as having subsisted from the date of formation of the civil partnership.[33]

The special case of polygamous relationships

11–07   Polygamous marriages now are recognised for practically all purposes, but such recognition is of relatively recent origin.[34] The older view was that such "marriages" should not be recognised at all.[35] The foundation for this view is found in the judgment of Lord Penzance in *Hyde*.[36] Courts and commentators placed emphasis upon the first excerpt from his judgment cited below, to the expense of the second, viz.[37]:

> "Now, it is obvious that the matrimonial law of this country is adapted to the Christian marriage, and it is wholly inapplicable to polygamy"; but: "[t]his Court does not profess to decide upon the rights of succession or legitimacy which it

---

[29] Which may include the connecting factor of intended matrimonial home, q.v., and *Sottomayor* reasoning (*Sottomayor v De Barros (No 2)* [1874 – 80] All E.R. Rep. 97).

[30] Defined in s.8(6) and (7) of the 2014 Act. But see also s.9 of the 2014 Act.

[31] Defined in s.9(7) of the 2013 Act. But see also s.9(3) of the 2013 Act.

[32] See The Marriage of Same Sex Couples (Conversion of Civil Partnership) Regulations 2014 (SI 2014/3181); The Marriage (Same Sex Couples) Act 2013 and Marriage and Civil Partnership (Scotland) Act 2014 (Consequential Provisions) Order 2014 (SI 2014/3061); and The Marriage (Same Sex Couples) Act 2013 (Consequential and Contrary Provisions and Scotland) and Marriage and Civil Partnership (Scotland) Act 2014 (Consequential Provisions) Order 2014 (SI 2014/3168).

[33] 2013 Act s.9(6).

[34] Much of what follows describes the development of this subject in the English conflict of laws, but there is no reason to suppose that our smaller jurisdiction was not in agreement, if less often required to comment. See denial of matrimonial remedy in *Muhammed v Suna*, 1956 S.C. 366.

[35] *Hyde* (1866) L.R. 1 P. & D. 130; *Armitage v Armitage* (1866) L.R. 3 Eq. 343; *Re Bethell* (1888) 38 Ch. D. 220; *Brinkley v Att Gen* (1890) L.R. 15 P.D. 76.

[36] *Hyde* (1866) L.R. 1 P. & D. 130.

[37] *Hyde* (1866) L.R. 1 P. & D. 130 at 135.

might be proper to accord to the issue of the polygamous unions, nor upon the rights or obligations in relation to third persons which people living under the sanction of such unions may have created for themselves. All that is intended to be here decided is that as between each other they are not entitled to the remedies, the adjudication, or the relief of the matrimonial law of England."[38]

After 1945, it was realised that there was a growing case for the recognition, for some purposes, of polygamous marriage if valid by the law under which it was celebrated, and it began to be appreciated that the question was not whether such a marriage should be recognised in general or in the abstract, but whether it should be recognised *for the particular purpose before the court*; that is, that the issue of recognition concerns the incidents of the status, not the status itself. This change was seen first in *The Sinha Peerage Claim*,[39] in which, in a peerage claim with no precedent, the son of a Hindu marriage was held entitled to succeed to the title. The marriage at its inception was potentially polygamous, but was never actually polygamous and had changed its nature through a change of religious sect by the parties before the birth of the son and, obviously, therefore, before the litigation.[40] From that date, polygamous marriages began to be recognised gradually over an increasingly wide field. The cases fall into the following groups:

(a) Consistorial actions

The consistorial remedies provided by Scots and English law were regarded as being essentially adapted to the concept of monogamous marriage and accordingly were not available initially to parties to a polygamous marriage.[41] But if the marriage had changed its character to monogamous by the date of litigation in Scotland or England, the courts would not be precluded from taking jurisdiction.[42]

11–08

Nevertheless, such a marriage was regarded as conferring upon the parties thereto the status of married persons, to the effect that such persons, being married, could not enter into subsequent monogamous unions. Hence annulments were granted of purported monogamous unions entered into by persons who previously had entered into polygamous marriages.[43] To this extent, therefore, the polygamous marriage was recognised.

The position was altered materially by the Matrimonial Proceedings (Polygamous Marriages) Act 1972,[44] s.2 of which provides that the fact that a

---

[38] *Hyde* (1866) L.R. 1 P. & D. 130 at 138.
[39] *The Sinha Peerage Claim*, 1939, reported [1946] 1 All E.R. 348.
[40] Hence, mutability of nature of a marriage received recognition as a concept, and mutation on the facts was accepted. The importance of *tempus inspiciendum* is clearly seen. See paras 11–15—11–16, below relating to mutability.
[41] *Mehta* [1945] 2 All E.R. 690; *Risk v Risk* [1951] P. 50; *Sowa v Sowa* [1961] P. 70; *Ohochuku v Ohochuku* [1960] 1 W.L.R. 183; *Muhammad v Suna*, 1956 S.C. 366; Webb, "Potentially Polygamous Marriages and Capacity to Marry" (1963) 12 I.C.L.Q. 672; Cohen, "A Note on Potentially Polygamous Marriages" (1963) 12 I.C.L.Q. 1407. See also A.E. Anton, "The 'Christian Marriage' Heresy", 1956 S.L.T. (News) 201.
[42] *Cheni v Cheni* [1965] P.85; and *Parkasho v Singh* [1968] P. 233.
[43] *Srini Vasan v Srini Vasan* [1946] P. 67; *Baindail v Baindail* [1946] P. 122.
[44] The equivalent English provisions are contained now in the Matrimonial Causes Act 1973 s.47.

marriage was entered into under a law which permits polygamy shall not preclude a Scots court from entertaining proceedings for:

(a)   divorce;
(b)   nullity of marriage;
(c)   dissolution of marriage on the ground of presumed death;
(d)   judicial separation;
(e)   separation and aliment, adherence and aliment or interim aliment;
(f)   declarator of marriage (that a marriage is valid or invalid);
(g)   any other action involving a decision on the validity of a marriage.

Section 2 also states that it shall apply whether or not either party has taken an additional spouse, but that provision may be made by rules of court for requiring notice of the proceedings to be given to any such other spouse, and conferring on such a person the right to be heard.

(b)   Legitimacy and succession

11–09   The children of polygamous marriages are regarded as having the status of legitimate persons for the purpose of status generally, and of succession in particular, if they have such a status by the law of their domicile (that is, in view of the circularity problem, by the law(s) of the domicile(s) of each parent).[45]

(c)   General

11–10   Polygamous marriages now are recognised as creating the status of marriage in a large number of different areas of law, from criminal law to taxation.[46] Specialties arise with regard to the following matters:

Succession to titles of honour, or of an heir in intestacy to immoveables

11–11   In such cases it must be ascertained whether the law of the title, or the *lex situs*, requires the heir to be legitimate. If so, he must be legitimate in the view of that law. This does not necessarily preclude claims by children of a polygamous marriage.[47]

---

[45] *Khoo Hooi Leong v Khoo Hean Kwee* [1926] A.C. 529; [1930] A.C. 346; *The Sinha Peerage Claim*, 1939, reported [1946] 1 All E.R. 348; *Bamgbose v Daniel* [1955] A.C. 107; *Coleman v Shang* [1961] A.C. 481; *Dawodu v Danmole* [1962] 1 W.L.R. 1053. See Ch.14, below; and Ch.6, above, for current Scots rules of domicile.

[46] *Mawji v The Queen* [1957] A.C. 126; *Din v National Assistance Board* [1967] 2 Q.B. 213; *Alhaji Mohamed v Knott* [1969] 1 Q.B. 1; [1968] 2 All E.R. 563; *Chaudhry v Chaudhry* [1975] 3 All E.R. 687; affirmed [1976] 1 All E.R. 805; *Shahnaz v Rizwan* [1964] 2 All E.R. 993; *Nabi v Heaton* [1983] 1 W.L.R. 626 CA; *Rampal v Rampal* [2001] 3 W.L.R. 795 (ancillary relief on divorce); and *Ben Hashem v Ali Shayif* [2009] 1 F.L.R. 115 (ancillary relief on divorce).

[47] cf. *Bamgbose v Daniel* [1955] A.C. 107.

Bigamy

The offence of bigamy is committed if a person who already has the status of a **11–12** "married person" purports to enter into a subsequent marriage. In English law bigamy is a statutory offence under the Offences Against the Person Act 1861 s.57. Extraterritorial effect is explicit in s.57, so as to affect the actings of a British subject in England or elsewhere, meaning that a charge of bigamy in English law may be preferred even if the second marriage takes place abroad.

In Scots law, until the coming into effect of the Marriage and Civil Partnership (Scotland) Act 2014, bigamy was a crime at common law, and therefore a charge of bigamy could be preferred only if the second "marriage" took place in Scotland since Scots common law could not apply elsewhere. Section 28(3) of the 2014 Act abolishes the common law offence of bigamy. Instead, from 1 September 2014,[48] s.24 of the Marriage (Scotland) Act 1977 was amended by the insertion of s.24(A1)–(A2), to the effect that a person, A, commits an offence if he purports to enter a marriage with another person, B, knowing that either or both: A is already married to, or in a civil partnership with, a person other than B; or B is already married to, or in a civil partnership with, a person other than A. Section 28, and the Explanatory Memorandum thereon, are conflict of laws-blind. The general principle that British statutes have strictly limited territorial effect[49] suffers many exceptions. It is unknown whether charges could be brought in Scotland on the basis of an allegedly bigamous marriage celebrated abroad.

In the case of a person who is already a party to a polygamous marriage, there is a question as to what is meant by a "married person" in this (criminal) context, that is whether a party to a polygamous marriage is to be regarded as "married" in this sense, so as to forbid (or not) a subsequent "marriage". In English civil law, at a point in the development of the conflict rules at which recognition was not generally afforded to potentially or actually polygamous marriages, the existence of a prior marriage of such a type was recognised to the extent of barring the celebration of a valid marriage in England (necessarily monogamous in nature) by one of the parties. The first marriage would be recognised, therefore, as regards civil law, to the effect of making the second marriage void,[50] but criminal charges for bigamy in respect of the second "marriage" did not follow. In *R. v Sagoo*,[51] overruling *R. v Sarwan Singh*,[52] it was held that the offence of bigamy had been committed when the first (potentially polygamous) marriage had become monogamous by statute or by change of domicile before the second

---

[48] See savings set out in The Marriage and Civil Partnership (Scotland) Act 2014 (Commencement No.2 and Saving Provisions) Order 2014 (SSI 2014/212) (as amended by The Marriage and Civil Partnership (Scotland) Act 2014 (Commencement No.2 and Saving Provisions) Amendment Order 2014 (SSI 2014/218)).

[49] Para.3–11, above.

[50] cf. *Baindail* [1946] P. 122 (civil action).

[51] *R. v Sagoo (Mohinder Singh)* [1975] 2 All E.R. 926.

[52] *R. v Sarwan Singh* [1962] 3 All E.R. 612.

marriage, but there has been no decision in a case where the first marriage has remained potentially polygamous. The disinclination of the authorities to prosecute is noteworthy.[53]

Social security

11–13 Against a background in benefits regulations whereby a potentially polygamous marriage will be treated as monogamous for every day that the marriage remains actually monogamous,[54] it should be noted that there are more recent exceptions which operate in favour of parties to actually polygamous marriages,[55] provided that the marriages in themselves are valid by Scots and English conflict of laws, i.e. contracted abroad between parties having legal capacity by their personal law to enter into such a marriage. UK law, apparently, will recognise marriages actually polygamous in nature as qualifying marriages for the purpose of certain benefits, though social security benefits will not be paid to spouses of such marriages who are permanently resident outside the UK. Generally in this area of allowances and taxation, the landscape is complex, and any advice must be benefit-specific, but the discernible trend overall is not to discriminate against parties to polygamous marriages.

The result is therefore that a polygamous marriage now will be recognised for most purposes.[56]

Finally, attention must be paid in any conflict of laws treatment of polygamy to the interrelated matters of (a) characterisation; and (b) capacity.

---

[53] R.D. Leslie, "Polygamous Marriages and Bigamy", 1972 J.R. 113. Also Law Commission and Scottish Law Commission, *Polygamous Marriages (Capacity to Contract a Polygamous Marriage and the Concept of the Potentially Polygamous Marriage)* (HMSO, 1982), Law Com. No.83; Scot. Law Com. Memo. No.56, para.4.46; and further Private International Law (Miscellaneous Provisions) Act 1995 s.7 (explained below at para.11–17).

[54] e.g. Child Benefit Act 1975 s.9(2)(a); Social Security Act 1975 s.162(b); Inland Revenue Decision Makers Guides: DMG 11105; CG 22072-*Transfer of Assets between Husband and Wife: Polygamy* (to the effect that transfers between a husband and any wife with whom he is living will be at no gain/no loss); DMG 41003-*Polygamy*; and CBTM 11020-*General and supplementary provisions: Polygamous marriages*. The British fisc refused to pay widows' benefit to two widows in Decision No.R(G) 1/93; and refused to pay invalidity benefit to one wife of a marriage proved to the satisfaction of the commissioners to be polygamous in nature in Decision No.R(S) 2/92. See also *Bibi v Chief Adjudication Officer, The Times* 10 July 1997 CA, in which one wife of an actually polygamous marriage contracted in Bangladesh was held not to be entitled to widowed mother's allowance under the Social Security Act 1975 s.25 (now Social Security Contributions and Benefits Act 1992 s.37); it would have been different if the marriage had been merely potentially polygamous. See further Social Security and Family Allowances (Polygamous Marriage) Regulations 1975 (SI 1975/561).

[55] e.g. Income Support (General Regulations) 1987 (SI 1987/1967) regs 2(3), 18, 23(3). See for detail House of Commons Standard Note on Polygamy (SN/HA/5051, 8 May 2014).

[56] Consider post-1972 cases in England of *Chaudhry v Chaudhry* [1975] 3 All E.R. 687 (extending to the polygamously married the remedy in English law provided by Married Women's Property Act 1882 s.17); *Re Sehota (Deceased)* [1978] 3 All E.R. 385 (permitting one of two widows of the same man to claim under the Inheritance (Provision for Family and Dependants) Act 1975 in the estate of the husband, domiciled at death in England, he having favoured the other wife in his will); and *Official Solicitor to the Senior Courts v Yemoh* [2010] EWHC 3727 (Ch); [2011] 1 W.L.R. 1450. Why then should not such a wife (wives), validly married to a man who died domiciled in Scotland, claim legal rights?

Characterisation of the nature of a marriage

Which law characterises?

According to the balance of authorities, the character of a union as monogamous **11–14** or polygamous is determined initially by the *lex loci celebrationis*,[57] though later, for the purpose before the court, the decision upon classification is for the forum.[58] A marriage bears a mark, but not an indelible mark.

The nature of a marriage celebrated in Scotland is monogamous despite scope for a wide variation in locus and form of ceremony,[59] and regardless of the personal law(s) of the parties (or their expectations).

Until the decision by the Court of Appeal in *Hussain v Hussain*,[60] the assumption always was made that the initial character of any marriage was determined by the *lex loci celebrationis* (though there was some support for the application of the matrimonial domicile),[61] but in *Hussain* the marriage was categorised as monogamous because the capacity of each party at the marriage (English male domiciliary; Pakistani female domiciliary) precluded the possibility of any other type of marriage. In other words, the test of the nature of the marriage was legal capacity of parties, and the capacity of neither party[62] extended to permit entry into a potentially polygamous union, notwithstanding that it was entered into in Pakistan. However, this decision may be regarded as a creative judicial solution to a problem solved shortly thereafter by Parliament by means of ss.5–7 of the Private International Law (Miscellaneous Provisions) Act 1995 (q.v.).

Mutability: change of character of marriage

The nature of any marriage may *change*, from actually or potentially polygamous **11–15** to monogamous[63]; less commonly the other way.[64] A change in character may result from a change in the parties' personal circumstances, religion, religious sect, or joint change of domicile,[65] or a change by statutory provision. Such a change will not affect the marriage's validity, though in the past it would affect the jurisdiction of the UK courts, and, consequently, available remedies. In

---

[57] *R. v Hammersmith Superintendent Registrar of Marriages Ex p. Mir-Anwaruddin* [1917] 1 K.B. 634; *R. v Naguib (Mark Mahommed)* [1917] 1 K.B. 359; *Lendrum v Chakravarti*, 1929 S.L.T. 96; *MacDougall v Chitnavis*, 1937 S.C. 390; *Qureshi v Qureshi* [1971] 1 All E.R. 325 (obiter); cf. wording of Matrimonial Proceedings (Polygamous Marriages) Act 1972 s.2.

[58] *Lee v Lau* [1967] P. 14, per Cairns J. at 20.

[59] Marriage (Scotland) Act 1977, as amended by the Marriage (Scotland) Act 2002 and the Marriage and Civil Partnership (Scotland) Act 2014.

[60] *Hussain v Hussain* [1982] 3 All E.R. 369.

[61] *Warrender v Warrender* (1835) 2 Cl. & F. 488, per Lord Brougham at 535; *Harvey v Farnie* (1882) L.R. 8 App. Cas. 43, per Lord Selborne; *De Reneville v De Reneville* [1948] P. 100, per Lord Greene M.R.; *Kenward v Kenward* [1951] P. 124, per Denning L.J. at 144, 146.

[62] The personal law of the woman did not permit polyandry.

[63] e.g. *Cheni* [1965] P. 85; *Parkasho v Singh* [1968] P. 233; *Quoraishi v Quoraishi* (1983) 13 Fam. Law 86.

[64] *Drammeh v Drammeh* (1970) 78 Cey. L.W. 55; *Att Gen of Ceylon v Reid* [1965] A.C. 720. cf. *Onobrauche v Onobrauche* (1978) 8 Fam. Law 107.

[65] *Ali v Ali* [1968] P. 564.

Drammeh v Drammeh,[66] a Gambian case upheld by the Privy Council, it was decided that the change from monogamous to polygamous, effected unilaterally by the husband through reversion to his original domicile and religion, did not affect the monogamous nature of the original wife's marriage.

Date of determination of character of marriage

11–16   It was held in *Cheni v Cheni*[67] that, if a question arises as to the character of a marriage, it is determined at the date, and for the purpose, of the litigation: if the marriage was monogamous at that date, it was no objection for jurisdictional purposes that the marriage was potentially polygamous when it was entered into.

These matters, although of interest, are of less importance in view of the 1972 Act which removes the necessity for the marriage to come before the court in monogamous form.

Capacity to enter into a potentially or actually polygamous marriage

Potential polygamy

11–17   The effect of s.7 of the Private International Law (Miscellaneous Provisions) Act 1995[68] is that a person of Scots domicile may enter into a *potentially* polygamous marriage, which marriage shall be treated as a monogamous marriage for every day that it remains so.[69] This removes doubt about the validity of marriages entered into abroad by persons of British residence and uncertain domicile, where, by the *lex loci celebrationis*, the nature of all marriages at the point of celebration is potentially polygamous, i.e. giving the husband the legal entitlement to take concurrently more than one wife.

Actual polygamy

11–18   No Scottish or English domiciliary has legal capacity by his or her personal law to enter an actually polygamous marriage, wherever purportedly contracted.[70] Hence, if the dual domicile theory (q.v.) is used, no such purported marriage by someone whose personal law is Scots can be regarded as valid by Scots law. Authority exists for applying the intended matrimonial home theory (q.v.),[71] but the decision is an isolated one, and is not highly regarded. Moreover, in a Scots

---

[66] *Drammeh v Drammeh* (1970) 78 Cey. L.W. 55.

[67] *Cheni v Cheni* [1965] P. 85.

[68] As to England and Wales, see ss.5, 6 (retrospective effect, subject to conditions therein contained).

[69] Unlike the equivalent English provisions, the Scots rule is not retrospective: see B.J. Rodger, annotations to statute. The precursor to this provision is the Law Commissions' joint report entitled *Private International Law—Polygamous Marriages: Report on Capacity to Contract a Polygamous Marriage and Related Issues* (HMSO, 1985), Law Com. No.146; Scot. Law Com. No.96. See also *Hussain* [1982] 3 All E.R. 369.

[70] Scots law: *MacDougall v Chitnavis*, 1937 S.C. 390; Law Commission and Scottish Law Commission, *Private International Law—Polygamous Marriages*, 1985, Law Com. No.146; Scot. Law Com. No.96, paras 4.2–4.9. Marriage (Scotland) Act 1977 ss.2(3)(b), s.5(4)(b). English law: see Matrimonial Causes Act 1973 s.11(d); and *Hussain* [1982] 3 All E.R. 369.

[71] *Radwan (No.2)* [1972] 3 All E.R. 1026. Contrast *Lendrum v Chakravarti*, 1929 S.L.T. 96, per Lord Mackay at 99.

court, the possibility of utilising the latter theory appears to be precluded by the Family Law (Scotland) 2006 s.38(2)(a) of which directs that the question of capacity to enter into a marriage shall be determined by the law of the place where, immediately before the marriage, that person was domiciled.[72]

MARRIAGE: THE DISTINCTION BETWEEN ESSENTIALS AND FORM

Until about 1860, marriage was regarded as a matter of contract, the rights of the contracting parties being governed by the law of the place where the contract was entered into, that is, the *lex loci celebrationis*. The result of this was that the *lex loci celebrationis* was applied to determine all questions as to the validity of a marriage. As the rules developed, however, it was recognised that marriage involves more than contract insofar as it creates a new status, and that the law of the domicile has an interest in being applied. When, after 1860,[73] questions concerning the validity of a marriage arose, UK courts began to distinguish between essentials and form, in order to avoid making decisions inconsistent with the "Gretna Green cases",[74] applying different choice of law rules to each aspect.[75]

11–19

Although essentials and form are quite distinct in theory, in some cases it may be difficult in practice to distinguish between them; examples are the need for parental consent,[76] and marriage by proxy. The classification of a particular matter or element as pertaining to essentials or form is determined by the *lex fori*.

Formal validity

Form includes not only required length of residence (and how to count the days), notice periods and ceremony, but also irregular forms of marriage, such as marriage by cohabitation with habit and repute,[77] proxy marriage,[78] and marriage lacking the presence of either party.[79]

11–20

---

[72] Para.11–28, below.

[73] *Brook v Brook* (1861) 9 H.L. Cas. 193; and *Mette v Mette* (1859) 1 Sw. & Tr. 416.

[74] Marriages at Gretna had become popular since the *lex loci celebrationis* was applied to all aspects of the validity of a marriage, with the result that any incapacity of either party per the law of their (English) domicile did not render the marriage invalid in the view of Scots (and, it seems, English) law. See further Anton and Francescakis, "Modern Scots Runaway Marriages", 1958 J.R. 253; and Anton, *Private International Law*, 1st edn (1967), pp.273, 274.

[75] A different policy is evinced in American practice. Dyer has explained the American preference for permitting the place of celebration to judge both form and substance as the natural preference of an immigrant society whose members were far from their original home and did not intend to return. (A Dyer, "The Hague Convention on celebration and recognition of the validity of marriages in perspective", *Grensoverschrijdend Privaatrecht*, p.102).

[76] *Bliersbach v McEwen*, 1959 S.L.T. 81; see also and contrast the English cases of *Simonin v Mallac* (1860) 2 Sw. & Tr. 67; and *Ogden v Ogden* [1908] P. 46. Para.11–32, below.

[77] The 2006 Act s.3 abolished this form of irregular marriage in Scots domestic law. Older conflict cases on this matter include *Cullen v Gossage* (1850) 12 D. 633; *Rooker v Rooker* (1863) 3 Sw. & Tr. 526; *Re Green, Noyes v Pitkin* (1909) 25 T.L.R. 222. Modern instances include *Kamperman v MacIver*, 1994 S.L.T. 763; *Dewar v Dewar*, 1995 S.L.T. 467; *Walker v Roberts*, 1998 S.L.T. 1133;

The Family Law (Scotland) Act 2006 s.38(1) confirms the common law position[80] that, subject to s.13(1) of, and Sch.6 to, the Marriage (Same Sex Couples) Act 2013,[81] the question of formal validity of a marriage shall be determined by the law of the place where it was celebrated. In order for a marriage to be valid as to form there must be, therefore, compliance with the requirements of the *lex loci celebrationis*. On the other hand, it matters not if it is found that there has not been compliance with the formal requirements of the law(s) of the domicile of either or both party(ies). As stated by Lord Dunedin in *Berthiaume v Dame Dastous*[82]:

> "If a marriage is good by the laws of the country where it is effected, it is good all the world over, no matter whether the proceeding or ceremony which constituted marriage according to the law of the place would or would not constitute marriage in the country of the domicil of one or other of the spouses".

There may be advantage in remembering that since the 2006 Act does not expressly exclude the operation of *renvoi*, a Scots court might be persuaded to apply the *lex loci celebrationis* in its entirety, i.e. including its choice of law rules.[83]

Determining the locus celebrationis

11–21 On occasion identification of the *locus celebrationis* may be difficult. In *A v K*,[84] a marriage purportedly took place between A, a 20 year old woman of UK nationality and Pakistani ethnicity, then resident in Edinburgh, and K, a 27 year old man having a postal address in Karachi, Pakistan, but resident apparently in Dubai. A "met" K on the internet, but the parties never met in person, before, during or following the purported union. The proceedings before Lord Stewart concerned the formal (in)validity of the marriage. It was accepted that A was in Scotland during the telephone call, and that A believed K to be in Pakistan. According to the copy of the marriage "certificate" and "true translation" subsequently received by A and produced to the court, the "place of

---

Ackerman v Logan's Executors (No.1), 2002 S.L.T. 37; and *Sheikh v Sheikh*, 2005 G.W.D. 11–183. The transitional provisions are contained in s.3(2) and (3), and attention should be paid to the protective provisions in s.3(4).

[78] Marriage by proxy has been classified by English courts as a matter of form, with the result that such marriages have been accepted if this form of marriage is permitted by the foreign *lex loci celebrationis: Apt v Apt* [1948] P. 83; *Ponticelli v Ponticelli* [1958] P. 204; and *Pazpena di Vire v Pazpena di Vire* [2001] 1 F.L.R. 460.

[79] *McCabe v McCabe* [1994] 1 F.L.R. 410.

[80] *Bliersbach v McEwan*, 1959 S.C. 43; *Simonin v Mallac* (1860) 2 Sw. & Tr. 67; *Administrator of Austrian Property v Von Lorang*, 1927 S.C. (H.L.) 80; *Pepper v Pepper* (1921) L.J. 413; *Kenward* [1951] P. 124; *Pilinski v Pilinska* [1955] 1 W.L.R. 329; *Burke v Burke*, 1983 S.L.T. 331.

[81] Inserted by the Consular Marriages and Marriages under Foreign Law Order 2014/1110 Pt 4, art.18. By s.13 of the Marriage (Same Sex Couples) Act 2013, the Foreign Marriage Act 1892 is repealed, and in its place Sch.6 to the 2013 Act has effect. Para 11–24 below.

[82] *Berthiaume v Dame Dastous* [1930] A.C. 79 at 83. More recently, see *Asaad v Kurter* [2013] EWHC 3852 (Fam).

[83] Para.5–14, above; R.D. Leslie, *Stair Memorial Encyclopaedia*, para.221. See also *Taczanowska v Taczanowski* [1957] P. 301; and *Hooper v Hooper* [1959] 2 All E.R. 575.

[84] *A v K*, 2011 S.L.T. 873.

solemnisation"[85] was Pakistan; the bridegroom and witnesses were present in Pakistan; the dowry was payable in Pakistani currency (though there was no evidence as to whether or not it was paid); and it appears that the marriage was registered or "intended to be registered"[86] in Pakistan. Seemingly the celebrant was physically present in Pakistan; during the proceedings A spoke by telephone to an individual who claimed to be a priest.[87] At the Scottish end, A subsequently received what she described as the marriage certificate, with a translation. The certificate showed the marriage to have been registered in Pakistan. Having signed the certificate in Scotland, A, as directed, took it on 3 February 2005 to the Pakistani Consulate in Glasgow. The Consulate stamped the certificate on the reverse, and A "returned" the documentation (presumably) to K. In 2011, A commenced proceedings in the Court of Session, seeking to have her marriage to K annulled. Lord Stewart, refusing the declarator, rejected counsel's arguments in favour of a dual locality approach, taking the view that the marriage took place wholly in Pakistan.[88]

The judge's opinion in *A v K* decides, for its own circumstances, the meaning of *locus celebrationis* where parties, physically present in different jurisdictions, consent to marry. The facts afforded an opportunity to clarify and refine Scots law on the issue, but the opportunity was squandered. If elements of marriage procedure take place in more than one jurisdiction, it could be argued either that the *locus celebrationis* is single locality; or that it is dual locality. If it is to be judged as single, the question arises whether the procedure should be localised in the legal system where the procedure was instigated, or where concluded, or perhaps in the legal system wherein the preponderance of connections lie.

If, however, the *locus* in these cases is to be judged as dual locality, there is a question whether the two *leges loci celebrationis* should be applied cumulatively (i.e. requiring both *leges causae* to be satisfied), or in the alternative (i.e. requiring only one *lex causae* to be satisfied). Where a legal procedure comprises two or more (equal or unequal) elements, and where those component parts take place in different jurisdictions, the maxim *locus regit actum* should be re-written *loci regunt actum*[89]; a dual rule of cumulative application, in the same way as occurs with regard to the essential validity of marriage. Such a rule would bar marriages by telephone where one party is physically in Scotland at the time of the marriage (such an informal means not satisfying Scots law), an outcome which seems desirable in terms of the individuals themselves, and protective of the larger interests of the UK legal systems. This approach, advanced by the authors, was commended in England in *SB v The Secretary of State for Work and Pensions (BB)*.[90]

---

[85] *A v K*, 2011 S.L.T. 873 at [51].

[86] *A v K*, 2011 S.L.T. 873 at [51].

[87] *A v K*, 2011 S.L.T. 873 at [10].

[88] *A v K*, 2011 S.L.T. 873 at [58].

[89] E.B. Crawford and J.M. Carruthers, "Dual locality events: marriage by telephone", 2011 S.L.T. (News) 227–234.

[90] *SB v The Secretary of State for Work and Pensions (BB)* [2014] UKUT 0495 (AAC) at [40]. See also the decision of the Court of Appeal in *KC v City of Westminster Social and Community Services Department* [2008] EWCA Civ 198, where a marriage ceremony was conducted by telephone call between one party (a British national of Bangladeshi descent, and an English domiciliary) and the second party, a woman of presumed Bangladeshi domicile. For the purposes of the case, the marriage was accepted to have taken place in Bangladesh, by the law of which it was formally valid.

Religious or customary ceremonies

11–22   In giving effect to the *lex loci celebrationis* at common law, the settled position was that the *lex loci* required to be complied with if it demanded observance of the rules of the parties' religious denomination(s), but not if it required compliance with the rules of some other denomination. One can expect the rule to continue that compliance or non-compliance with the religious beliefs of the parties does not affect the validity of a marriage unless the *lex loci celebrationis* insists upon observance of such forms.[91] A customary marriage proved[92] to have been carried out according to the forms of the *lex loci celebrationis* is likely to suffice.[93]

Tempus inspiciendum

11–23   Section 38(1) of the 2006 Act, in directing application of the *lex loci celebrationis*, does not specify the *tempus inspiciendum*, that is, does not expressly address the question of the time at which the content of the *lex loci* is to be ascertained and applied. The common law position, it is presumed, continues to prevail. The House of Lords, in *Starkowski v Att Gen*,[94] held that if the formal validity of a marriage is called in issue, this falls to be determined in accordance with the content of the *lex loci celebrationis* at that date, not at the date of the marriage ceremony. The reason for this is that, although as a general rule the validity of a marriage must be determined as at the date of the ceremony (at which the formalities either have been complied with or not), in exceptional circumstances its validity may be affected for the better by subsequent legislation of the *lex loci*. Yet *Starkowski*, though long established and of high authority, is regarded as a case tied very closely to its facts, viz. a marriage celebrated only by religious ceremony in Austria in 1945, at which date such a form of ceremony was insufficient by the Austrian *lex loci celebrationis* to constitute a valid marriage. Soon afterwards, however, an Austrian law was passed, providing that such marriages might be validated (retrospectively), if they were registered. The marriage in question was not registered until 1949. By that date, following the parties' separation, each of them, originally of Polish domicile, was held by the English court to have acquired a domicile of choice in England, whatever the status of the marriage. In 1950 the woman married another man in England. The Austrian legislation was held by the House of Lords to have validated the 1945 marriage. However, had the "second" marriage in England ante-dated the rectification of the "first" marriage in Austria, and had it been celebrated validly as to form and with no incapacity as to persons by their then domicile, it is hard to see how a British court could have denied the validity of that "second" marriage.

---

[91] *Re Alison's Trusts* (1874) 31 L.T. 638; *Usher v Usher* [1912] 2 I.R. 445; *Papadopoulos v Papadopoulos* [1930] P. 55; *Hooper v Hooper* [1959] 1 W.L.R. 1021; *Gray v Formosa* [1963] P. 259; and *R v M* [2011] EWHC 2132 (Fam).

[92] On the question of difficulties of proof, see *MO v RO (Declaration of Marital Status)* [2013] EWHC 392 (Fam).

[93] cf. *Alfonso-Brown v Milwood* [2006] EWHC 642 (Fam); and *K v A* [2015] Fam Law 137. See also *McCabe* [1994] 1 F.L.R. 410; and commentary per R.D. Leslie, "Foreign Consensual Marriages", 1994 S.L.T. (News) 87; and *N v D* [2015] EWFC 28.

[94] *Starkowski v Att Gen* [1954] A.C. 155. Contrast *Pilinski v Pilinska* [1955] 1 W.L.R. 329.

Any suggestion that the later removal, by the law(s) of the domicile(s), of incapacities existing by that/those laws at the date of "marriage" can be effected *ratione Starkowsi*, would appear unjustified, given that the decision concerns rectification of defects of form.[95]

Exceptions to the rule on formal validity

Marriage overseas

By s.13 of the Marriage (Same Sex Couples Act) 2013,[96] the Foreign Marriage Act 1892 is repealed, and in its place Sch.6 to the 2013 Act has effect. Schedule 6, headed "Marriage overseas", provides rules in Pt 1 for "consular marriage under UK law"; in Pt 2 for "marriage under foreign law: certificates of no impediment"; and in Pt 3 for "marriage of forces personnel under UK law". In light of this, s.38(1) of the Family Law (Scotland) Act 2006 required to be amended.[97] The effect is that the detail of the sole statutory exception to the *lex loci celebrationis* rule, for consular marriages and marriages of service personnel, now is found in Sch.6 to the 2013 Act. This complex legislative framework has extended to same-sex couples the privilege of the rules on marriage of service personnel and marriages at foreign embassies. Consular marriages and marriages of service personnel will be valid as to form if they comply with formalities laid down in Sch.6, irrespective of whether or not there is compliance with the *lex loci celebrationis*.[98]

11–24

Common law exceptions

Section 38(1) makes no reference to other exceptions which exist at English common law, and which may have existed in Scots common law, under the headings "belligerent occupation" and "local form impossible". These operated as benevolent exceptions in qualifying cases for the purpose of upholding the formal validity of a marriage otherwise defective. The former exception was to the effect that a marriage celebrated in accordance with the "requirements of common law"[99] in a country under the occupation of military forces and where

11–25

---

[95] However, a different approach may be taken with regard to the removal of an incapacity to enter into a same sex marriage. Para.11–06, above.

[96] Which extends to Scotland, by virtue of s.20(2) thereof.

[97] By virtue of art.18 of The Consular Marriages and Marriages under Foreign Law Order 2014 (SI 2014/1110). See also The Marriage (Same Sex Couples) Act 2013 (Consequential and Contrary Provisions and Scotland) Order 2014 (SI 2014/560) art.1(3) and Sch.1 para 31.

[98] For equivalent provision for civil partnerships, see Civil Partnership Act 2004 ss.210, 211.

[99] The basic minimum, one presumes, is mutual voluntary exchange of consent, in the presence of at least one witness. cf. the Scots irregular form of marriage by declaration *de praesenti* (removed with effect from 1 July 1940), in respect of which no witness was required, nor proof of time nor place at which consent was given, provided that the court was satisfied that the parties' true intention was to be married to each other.

one of the parties is a member of these forces, was formally valid.[100] The benefit of the exception was not extended to those who attempted to comply with the local law, and who failed so to do.[101]

Secondly, a number of cases stand as authority, for English law,[102] that a marriage celebrated as nearly as possible in accordance with the "requirements of common law" in a country in which the use of the local form is impossible or in which there is no such form, is formally valid.

The likelihood in Scots law is that no further exception to that specified in s.38(1) will be admitted.

Presumption in favorem matrimonii

11–26 The common law presumption is that if a marriage has been celebrated, registered and a formal certificate produced, it will be formally valid, and the onus of proving otherwise rests upon any person who so avers.[103] There is no reason to think that the Family Law (Scotland) Act 2006 has removed this presumption.

Essential validity

11–27 The term "essentials" covers matters such as whether parties have legal capacity to marry, whether they consented to marry, and the incidents of marriage, i.e. the rights and duties arising during marriage.[104] The majority of problems concern capacity to marry and consent to marry.

Capacity to marry

11–28 Since 4 May 2006, much of Scots conflict law pertaining to the constitution of marriage, both formal and essential, has rested upon the statutory basis of the Family Law (Scotland) Act 2006.

---

[100] *Taczanowska v Taczanowski* [1957] P. 301; *Kochanski v Kochanska* [1958] P. 147; *Merker v Merker* [1963] P. 283; *Preston v Preston* [1963] P. 141.

[101] *Lazarewicz v Lazarewicz* [1962] P. 171.

[102] *Lord Cloncurry's Case* (1811), cited in 6 St. Tr. (N.S.) 87 (evidence of exchange of consent by Protestants in Rome held sufficient since local law made no provision for Protestant marriage); *Catterall v Sweetman* (1845) 1 Rob. Ecc. 304; *Beamish v Beamish* (1861) 9 H.L. Cas. 274 at 348, 352; *Lightbody v West* (1903) 19 T.L.R. 319; *Phillips v Phillips* (1921) 38 T.L.R. 150; *Wolfenden v Wolfenden* [1946] P. 61 ("a British Subject takes to a colony only so much of English law as is applicable to his situation"); *Penhas v Tan Soo Eng* [1953] A.C. 304 (in the absence of a form appropriate to both, the parties devised a composite ceremony which they used in Singapore: the English forum accepted that a valid marriage had resulted, monogamous in nature).

[103] *Hill v Hill* [1959] 1 W.L.R. 127; *Mahadervan v Mahadervan* [1964] P 233; *Pazpena di Vire* [2001] 1 F.L.R. 460; *Al-Saedy v Musawi* [2010] EWHC 3293 (Fam); *G v M* [2011] EWHC 2651 (Fam); *El Gamal v El-Maktoum* [2011] EWHC 3763 (Fam); *A v A (Attorney General intervening)* [2012] EWHC 2219 (Fam); [2013] 2 W.L.R. 606; and *Galloway v Goldstein* [2012] EWHC 60 (Fam). cf. Marriage (Scotland) Act 1977 s.23A: *omnia praesumuntur rite et solemniter acta esse.*

[104] As to matrimonial property matters see Ch.13, below.

With regard to legal capacity to marry, e.g. in matters of consanguinity, sanity and nonage,[105] the common law view that the Scottish forum defers to the law(s) of the parties' domicile(s), cumulatively applied, and subject to a public policy discretion, was given legislative approval by the Marriage (Scotland) Act 1977, and more recently, and expressly, by s.38(2) of the 2006 Act.[106] By the predominant theory at common law, the "dual domicile" theory, each party was required to have legal capacity to marry in general, and to marry the other party, in particular, by the law of his/her domicile immediately before the marriage (the ante-nuptial domicile). It has been said that "this theoretical construct tumbles over its own heels in hilarious circularity",[107] for the reality is the cumulative application of the parties' personal laws, with the result that the stricter rule (if two rules are involved) will prevail. Taking the example of the proposed marriage of an uncle and his niece; what does it benefit the uncle if his law permits him to marry his niece, but her law does not reciprocate?

Section 38(2)(a), in stating that the question whether a person who enters into a marriage had capacity to enter into it shall be determined by the law of the place where, immediately before the marriage, that person was domiciled, affirms in statutory form the common law approach. In so doing, it appears to have excluded the possibility in Scotland of advancing an alternative argument on choice of law which might produce an *in favorem matrimonii* result where application of the dual domicile theory would yield a negative, i.e. a finding of lack of capacity on the part of either or both parties. The minority approach at common law, attributed first to Cheshire,[108] and manifested by a small number of English cases, is termed the "matrimonial domicile theory". On this approach, the relevant law is argued to be the law of the place where the parties intended to live their married life, that is, the law of the intended matrimonial domicile. The intended matrimonial domicile was presumed to be the husband's domicile, but that presumption might be rebutted if it could be inferred that the parties, at the point of marriage, intended to settle in a different country, and proved that they did so within a reasonable time.[109]

According to the matrimonial domicile theory all questions of essentials arising before, as well as after, the marriage ceremony were governed by the law of the matrimonial domicile. Authority in favour of the matrimonial theory is scarce,[110] and sometimes specialised,[111] and criticism of it not hard to find.[112] There was the problem, seen too in the context of commercial contractual

---

[105] *Mette* (1859) 1 Sw. & Tr. 416; *Brook* (1861) 9 H.L. Cas. 193; *Webster v Webster's Trustee* (1886) 14 R. 90; *Re De Wilton* [1900] 2 Ch. 481; *Re Bozzelli's Settlement* [1902] 1 Ch. 751; *Despatie v Tremblay* [1921] 1 A.C. 702; *Re Paine* [1940] Ch. 46; *Pugh v Pugh* [1951] P. 482; *Rojas, Petitioner*, 1967 S.L.T. (Sh. Ct.) 24.

[106] The conflict rules of England and Wales in this area remain largely common law.

[107] C.A. Dyer, First Secretary of the Hague Conference on Private International Law, "The Hague Convention on celebration and recognition of the validity of marriages in perspective", *Grensoverschrijdend Privaatrecht*, p.102.

[108] Geoffrey C. Cheshire, *Private International Law*, 5th edn (London: Clarendon Press, 1957), pp.305–320.

[109] Cheshire, *Private International Law*, 5th edn (1957), p.307.

[110] *De Reneville* [1948] P. 100, per Greene M.R., especially at 114; *Kenward* [1951] P. 124, per Denning L.J. at 144, 146; *Re Swan's Will* (1871) 2 V.L.R. (I.E.&M.) 47 (Victoria, Australia); *Radwan (No.2)* [1972] 3 All E.R. 1026 (polygamous marriage); *Bliersbach v McEwen*, 1959 S.C. 43, per Lord Sorn at 55; Clive M. Schmitthoff, *The English Conflict of Laws*, 3rd edn (London: Stevens & Sons Ltd, 1954), pp.312–314 (supportive of Cheshire's theory).

capacity,[113] of seeming to permit parties to confer legal capacity on themselves by virtue merely of their own choice. Further, there was the danger[114] of creating uncertainty: how soon after the ceremony must matrimonial domicile be established, and what was the status of the parties should they have died en route? That said, dicta to support Cheshire's view can be produced, and certain decisions can be cited in which it is difficult to say whether the law was applied qua matrimonial domicile or qua ante-nuptial domicile(s), because the two coincided.[115] A study of the case of *Lawrence v Lawrence*,[116] especially in the first instance judgment of Anthony Lincoln J.,[117] reveals approval of the intended matrimonial home theory, or at least of a criterion of "real and substantial connection" and a *favor matrimonii* approach, to the extent of expression of the view that there is equal support for each theory, but it may be that the exigencies of the case, and the state of the conflict rule principally under consideration[118] in that case contributed to the stance taken.

11–29   In sum, the balance of authority at common law favoured the traditional dual domicile theory. Though the Law Commissions reviewed[119] the matter in the 1980s, and concluded[120] that the dual domicile test is preferable to the intended matrimonial domicile test and should be adopted as the test for all issues of legal capacity, as yet there is no statutory provision in England equivalent to s.38(2)(a) of the Family Law (Scotland) Act 2006, which latter provision appears to have the effect of excluding the operation of the matrimonial domicile theory.

The rule in s.38(2)(a) is subject to a saving, in s.38(3), to the effect that, if a marriage entered into in Scotland is void in terms of Scots domestic law, the Scots rule shall prevail over any contrary rule of the law(s) of the party/ies' domicile(s). This reflects the position under the Marriage (Scotland) Act 1977

---

[111] *Radwan (No.2)* [1972] 3 All E.R. 1026 supports Cheshire's theory, but is drawn from the specialty of polygamous marriage, and is itself not well regarded.

[112] See current evaluation in *Cheshire, North and Fawcett: Private International Law*, 14th edn (2008), pp.897, 898. Also Graveson, *Private International Law*, 7th edn (1974), pp.265–269; Wolff, *Private International Law*, 2nd edn, (1950), pp.335, 356; and Bresler, "Note on *Pugh v Pugh*" (1951) 4 I.C.L.Q. 478, where it is noted that the celebrated South African case in matrimonial property of *Frankel v CIR* (1950) 1 S.A.L.R. 220 is firmly against the use of the intended matrimonial home theory at least in the matrimonial property connection.

[113] G.C. Cheshire, "David Murray lecture on International Contracts", University of Glasgow, 4 March 1948, pp.45, 46.

[114] Similarly, in the matrimonial property context: *Re Egerton's Will Trusts* [1956] Ch. 593; see para.13–10, below.

[115] See pre-eminently *Brook* (1861) 9 H.L. Cas. 193, in which, though it was one of the early leading authorities cited in support of the dual domicile theory, Lord Campbell, in order to determine the validity of a purported marriage in Denmark between a man and his deceased wife's sister, at a time when such marriages were void by English law, applied the law of England qua ante-nuptial domicile of the parties but also as the law "in which the matrimonial residence is contemplated".

[116] *Lawrence v Lawrence* [1985] 2 All E.R. 733, per Sir David Cairns at 746.

[117] *Lawrence v Lawrence* [1985] 1 All E.R. 506 at 510–512.

[118] Recognition of Divorces and Legal Separations Act 1971 s.7, now repealed and replaced by Family Law Act 1986 s.50.

[119] Law Commission and Scottish Law Commission, *Private International Law: Choice of Law Rules in Marriage*, 1985, Law Com. Working Paper No.89; Scot. Law Com. Memo. No.64, paras 3.3, 3.4.

[120] Law Commission and Scottish Law Commission, *Private International Law: Choice of Law Rules in Marriage* (HMSO, 1987), Law Com. No.165; Scot Law Com. No.105; *Private International Law: Choice of Law Rules in Marriage*, 1985, Law Com. Working Paper No.89; Scot. Law Com. Memo. No.64, para.3.36.

s.2(1). The effect is to insist upon legal capacity by the Scots *lex loci celebrationis*, as well as by the law(s) of the domicile(s). Despite consideration by the Scottish Law Commission on the question whether there should be any requirement of capacity by a *foreign lex loci celebrationis*,[121] the 2006 Act is silent on the question. Accordingly, whether a Scots court, reviewing the validity of a marriage celebrated abroad, would require capacity by the foreign *lex loci* was, and remains, a matter of conjecture. It may be argued that the role of the *lex loci* should be confined[122] to matters of form and ceremony (including the evidencing of consent, and registration of the event), and that marriages in Scotland are a special case justifying on policy grounds the cumulative application of the Scots *lex loci* with the law(s) of the parties' domicile(s).

A difficulty may arise in a foreign *lex loci celebrationis* if, by the domestic rules of that legal system, divorce is prohibited; or if that law is opposed to the re-marriage within its jurisdiction of divorced persons. Increasingly, however, such problems are more theoretical than real. The solution in these situations is that if the antecedent divorce is worthy of recognition by the conflict rules of the *lex loci celebrationis*, its domestic policy objections must yield to direction by its conflict rules.[123] A related problem of the validity of a purported re-marriage, in respect of which one or both of the parties was previously divorced from (an)other person(s) by virtue of divorce(s) not recognised by the personal law(s), will be solved now in the UK by use of the Family Law Act 1986 s.50 (q.v.). Where the antecedent divorce is not worthy of recognition by the conflict rules of the *lex loci celebrationis*, but is valid by the law of the domicile, an incidental question will arise for decision by the forum qua *lex loci*.[124]

From the coming into effect of the 2006 Act, the public policy exception in Scots law rests upon s.38(4) of that Act, to the effect that the capacity of a person to enter into marriage shall not be determined by the law of his/her domicile in so far as it would be contrary to public policy in Scotland for such capacity to be so determined. Thus, the Scots forum retains its discretion not to require capacity by, or not to give effect to, a provision of the party/ies' personal law, if it is offensive to conscience[125] or common sense. Section 38(4) without doubt applies in relation to marriages celebrated in Scotland. With regard to marriages celebrated overseas, it must be presumed that the public policy challenge remains available,

---

[121] Law Commission and Scottish Law Commission, *Private International Law: Choice of Law Rules in Marriage*, 1987, Law Com. No.165; Scot Law Com. No.105, para.2.6. Also Scottish Law Commission, *Family Law: Pre-Consolidation Reforms* (HMSO, 1990) Scot. Law Com. D.P. No.85, paras 9.5, 9.6, 9.21. Also Scottish Law Commission, *Report on Family Law*, 1992, Scot. Law Com. No.135, paras 14.5, 14.6, 14.22.

[122] See the instructive Canadian case of *Reed v Reed* (1969) 6 D.L.R. (3d.) 617, which directed the issue of consanguinity to the domicile of British Columbia, and the issue of parental consent to the *lex loci celebrationis* in the State of Washington. By this reasoning, the purported marriage of first cousins, the female party according to her personal law being under the age of marriage without parental consent, avoided all difficulties and was held to be valid in a nullity petition brought by the female party in the British Columbian court of their (common) domicile. The case illustrates the process of teasing out the issues from the skein of a legal problem and treating them in the conflict of laws to different choice of law rules: dépeçage (para.4–01, above).

[123] *Breen v Breen* [1964] P. 144.

[124] *Schwebel v Ungar* (1964) 48 D.L.R. (2d.) 644, Sup.Ct. (Can); para.4–07, above.

[125] See discussion in *Cheni* [1965] P. 85, per Sir Jocelyn Simon P. at 99.

and that the reference in s.38(4) to "the marriage" (pursuant to s.38(3), "a marriage entered into in Scotland") is not intended to restrict the challenge to marriages entered into in Scotland.

The 2006 Act makes no reference to other exceptions which were argued to exist at common law. The most important of these[126] was termed "penal incapacity", whereby a marriage celebrated in Scotland or England was not invalid on account of any incapacity, which, although existing under the law of the domicile of either/ both party/ies, was penal in the sense of being discriminatory. Penal incapacities included restrictions or incapacities attributable to colour or race, rules of caste, or religion,[127] religious rules of celibacy, or prohibitions on re-marriage. A restriction on the re-marriage of one party (usually the "guilty" party) at any time, or within the lifetime of the other (usually the "innocent" party), would be regarded in Scots law as penal,[128] and therefore would not be recognised in Scotland; but a restriction upon each party's re-marriage within a certain time limit, or until certain formalities have been complied with, would be regarded as affecting the capacity of either party to remarry, and such a condition would be respected, being an integral part of the divorce proceedings (probably imposed for the avoidance of doubt about paternity) and not uneven in application or otherwise objectionable.[129] It is very likely that incapacities of this nature would fall to be treated in Scots law within the terms of s.38(4).

Parties' consent to marry

11–30 While evidencing consent is a matter for regulation by the *lex loci celebrationis*, the nature and extent of free will necessary to create a valid marriage are matters of substance for decision by the parties' personal law(s).

The first aspect of consent is that of free will. Parties might enter a marriage in mental states varying from joyful acceptance to rueful resignation, whether under

---

[126] The others were the Royal Marriage exception and the "unknown incapacity" exception. The former of these, to the effect of invalidating a marriage if either of the parties, being a descendant (as defined) of George II, married in contravention of the Royal Marriages Act 1772, requires the consent of the sovereign to the marriage of such persons, no matter where the purported marriage may take place. See *The Sussex Peerage Case* (1844) 11 Cl. & F. 85. But see Farran, "The Royal Marriages Act 1772" (1951) 14 M.L.R. 53, cited in Wilson, "Validation of Void Marriages in Scots Law" (1964) J.R. 199. See more recently Pugh and Samuels, "The Royal Marriages Act 1772: Its Defects and the Case for Repeal" (1994) 15 Statute Law Review 46; Cretney, "The Royal Marriages Act 1772: A Footnote" (1995) 16 Statute Law Review 195. The "unknown incapacity" exception, which probably was not part of Scots law, and which the Law Commission proposed be removed from English law (*Private International Law: Choice of Law Rules in Marriage*, 1985, Law Com. Working Paper No.89; Scot. Law Com. Memo. No.64, and *Private International Law: Choice of Law Rules in Marriage*, 1987, Law Com. No.165; Scot Law Com. No.105, para.3.48), rests upon *Sottomayor v De Barros (No.2)* (1879) L.R. 5 P.D. 94, the ratio of which is that a marriage celebrated in England, according to local form, between parties of whom one has an English domicile and the other a foreign domicile, is not invalid on account of an incapacity affecting the foreign party under the law of his/her domicile, which does not exist under English law.

[127] *Chetti v Chetti* [1909] P. 67; *MacDougall v Chitnavis*, 1937 S.C. 390.

[128] *Beattie v Beattie* (1866) 5 M. 181 (prohibition upon any subsequent marriage by adulteress); *Scott v Att Gen* (1886) L.R. 11 P.D. 128 (prohibition upon the re-marriage of the guilty party while the innocent party remained unmarried).

[129] *Warter v Warter* (1890) L.R. 15 P.D. 152; *Martin v Buret*, 1938 S.L.T. 479; but see *Buckle v Buckle* [1956] P. 181; and *Wall v De Thoren* (1874) 1 R. 1036.

the influence of ideals of family obedience and family honour, or under duress. A "sham" marriage may be entered into for non-matrimonial purposes. Scots domestic law, while requiring "a willing mind" will not generally be prepared to give effect, by means of subsequent grant of an annulment, to unilateral mental reservation at the point of marriage. On the other hand, where it is clear that one party never had any intention to marry, as for example where s/he took part in a ceremony which s/he did not understand, there will be no marriage in the Scots or English view.[130] There are many fine distinctions, which are multiplied when the case is a conflict one giving rise to a number of choice of law options within the power of the forum to select.[131] The reported cases at common law display a variety of approaches, from application by the forum of its own law without argument,[132] through application of the *lex fori* after useful argument,[133] and application of the *lex fori* as interpreted in the light of a cultural background foreign to the *lex fori*,[134] to application by the forum of the law(s) of the parties' domicile(s).[135]

The second aspect of consent is mental capacity to consent. In cases where it is alleged that an individual is not capable of understanding the nature of marriage or giving his/her consent to be married, difficult factual questions may arise, which may operate to obfuscate the choice of law process.[136]

The Family Law (Scotland) Act 2006 s.38(2)(b) provides a rule on party consent, which directs that the question whether a person who enters into a marriage consented to enter into it shall be determined (subject to s.38(3) and (4) and to s.50 of the Family Law Act 1986)[137] by that person's ante-nuptial domicile. The rule is supplemented by s.2 of the 2006 Act, which inserts, as s.20A of the Marriage (Scotland) Act 1977, a provision on void marriages. This provision shall apply only in relation to marriages solemnised in Scotland; the territorial limitation of s.20A must be noted. Section 20A(2) and (3) make clear, with regard to marriages solemnised in Scotland, that where a party was capable of consenting and purported to give consent, but did not only by reason of duress

---

[130] *Alfonso-Brown v Milwood* [2006] EWHC 642 (Fam).

[131] There is even the possibility of conflict within the forum between and among the *lex fori* (also qua *lex loci celebrationis*), the law(s) of the parties' domicile(s), and their religious laws: *Di Rollo*, 1959 S.C. 75. cf. Decision of Tribunal Supremo (Spain) in *Re Recognition of a Canon Law Judgment* [2008] I.L.Pr. 31.

[132] *Buckland v Buckland* [1968] P. 296; *Kassim v Kassim* [1962] P. 224; or, oddly, of its own law qua *lex loci celebrationis* (or *lex loci contractus*—Davies J.), *Parojcic v Parojcic* [1958] 1 W.L.R. 1280.

[133] *H v H* [1954] P. 258.

[134] *Mahmud v Mahmud*, 1994 S.L.T. 599; *Mahmood v Mahmood*, 1993 S.L.T. 589. See also *Mahmud v Mahmud*, 1977 S.L.T. (Notes) 17.

[135] *Szechter v Szechter* [1971] P. 286 (all parties of Polish domicile at date of marriage of expediency/mercy in Poland).

[136] e.g. *KC v City of Westminster Social and Community Services Department* [2008] EWCA Civ 198, where it was found that the individual whose mental capacity was under scrutiny was severely intellectually impaired, to such an extent that by the English *lex fori* he lacked mental capacity to consent to marry. In the view of English law, since the male party lacked the mental capacity to consent, the marriage was void. While this result might have been reached by application of the *lex domicilii* of the impaired party, the decision rests expressly on the exercise of the public policy of the English forum. See also *M v B* [2005] EWHC 1681 (Fam); *Re SA (Vulnerable Adult with Capacity: Marriage)* [2005] EWHC 2942 (Fam); *X City Council v MB* [2006] EWHC 168 (Fam); and *XCC v AA* [2013] 2 All E.R. 988. Such questions may be found to arise in relation to purported marriage for reasons connected with immigration: *A v M* [2013] EWHC 4020 (COP).

[137] Para.12–36, below.

or error, or where a party was incapable of understanding the nature of marriage and of consenting, the marriage shall be void. Section 20A(4) states that if a party purported to give consent other than by reason only of duress or error, the marriage shall not be void by reason only of that party's having tacitly withheld consent to the marriage at the time of its solemnisation. These provisions constitute mandatory rules of the Scots *lex loci celebrationis*.[138] Further legal protection against being forced into marriage is afforded to "protected persons" by the Forced Marriage etc. (Protection and Jurisdiction) (Scotland) Act 2011.[139] This Act, and the subject of applicable law pertaining to matrimonial consent generally will be treated in detail in Ch.12, below.

Other matters of essential validity

11–31   The Family Law (Scotland) Act 2006 makes no provision on matters of essential validity beyond capacity and consent to marry. Hence it may be presumed that the common law continues to apply to the rights and duties of the spouses during the subsistence of the married relationship,[140] to the effect that those rights shall be governed by the law of the matrimonial domicile at the time in question, namely, the place where the parties have their home in the legal sense, most probably where the parties have their primary matrimonial residence. Questions of the extent of property rights in wealth inherited by one spouse during the marriage, or as to ownership of items acquired by the parties during the marriage are within the province of conflict rules of matrimonial property.[141]

Third parties' consent to marry

11–32   Cases in which the validity of a marriage is dependent upon the consent of a third party, and of a parent in particular, require special consideration. In some legal systems parental consent to marriage is required up to the age of 21, in others to 25. In some, absence of consent makes a marriage void wherever it is celebrated, whilst in others, it may make a marriage voidable within a certain period, again wherever it is celebrated. In some, it may be overcome by following certain procedure; in others, lack of consent may have different effects according to whether the individual is under or above 21.

The Scots choice of law rule now is contained[142] in the Family Law (Scotland) Act 2006 s.38(5) which provides that:

> "If the law of the place in which a person is domiciled requires a person under a certain age to obtain parental consent before entering into a marriage, that requirement shall not be taken to affect the capacity of a person to enter into a

---

[138] For further discussion of their mandatory nature and effect, paras 12–52—12–54, below.

[139] Para.12–55, below.

[140] e.g. selection of home and allocation of the costs of running it, and duty to adhere. Occupancy rights in the matrimonial home fall within the interest of the *lex situs*.

[141] Ch.13, below.

[142] For background: Scottish Law Commission, *Report on Family Law*, 1992, Scot. Law Com. No.135, paras 14.8–14.10, recommendation 70(a), which was to the effect that a foreign parental consent rule should be regarded as resulting in a legal incapacity if, but only if, it precluded marriage by the person affected, anywhere in the world.

marriage in Scotland unless failure to obtain such consent would render invalid[143] any marriage that the person purported to enter into in any form anywhere in the world."

At common law in Scotland, it appeared that the Scots courts derived assistance from the Canon law classification of impediments to marriage, viz.:

(a)　irritant impediment (*impedimentum dirimens*), being one which is so fundamental that it bars a marriage altogether and makes any union void (arguably substantive, to be referred to the personal law); and

(b)　prohibitive impediment (*impedimentum impeditivum*), being one which is not so important, merely prohibiting marriage until the impediment is removed (arguably procedural, to be referred to the *lex loci celebrationis*).

In *Bliersbach v McEwan*[144] the consent of parents required by the Dutch Civil Code was regarded as falling under class (b), with the result that the proposed marriage in Scotland of a Dutch couple without such consent was permitted to proceed. The opinions in the case suggest a potentially different result if the requirement of consent were to fall within class (a). The decision as far as it goes is to the same effect as the English cases.

Of the two notable cases in English law, the foreign parental consent required by French law in the circumstances of *Simonin v Mallac*,[145] in which lack of parental consent operated merely to postpone the marriage, was of quite a different nature from that required in *Ogden v Ogden*,[146] but in both cases it was held that the requirement was to be regarded as a foreign rule affecting form, having no effect upon the valid celebration of a marriage in England. In effect, the English courts decided that, no matter what might be the domicile of the parties, whether or not parental consent is a necessary condition for the validity of a marriage celebrated in England was a matter to be classified by English law (the *lex fori*), and was held to be a matter of form, governed by the *lex loci celebrationis*.

Under the 2006 Act, in qualifying cases in Scotland, s.38(5) will require proof of content of the party's domiciliary law on this matter, and its intended ambit.

CIVIL PARTNERSHIP

Since December 2005 the laws of Scotland and England have provided the *de iure* institution of civil partnership, by virtue of the Civil Partnership Act 2004 ("the 2004 Act"), which contains not only domestic, but also conflict of laws rules. This legislative provision was modelled upon existing provision concerning marriage. A civil partnership is defined in s.1 of the 2004 Act as a legal relationship between two people of the same sex which is formed when they register as civil partners of each other, in accordance with the relevant provisions

11–33

---

[143]　i.e. invalid by the law of the party's domicile.
[144]　*Bliersbach v McEwan*, 1959 S.L.T. 81.
[145]　*Simonin v Mallac* (1860) 2 Sw. & Tr. 67.
[146]　*Ogden v Ogden* [1908] P. 46.

of the 2004 Act, and which ends only on death, dissolution, annulment, or (since the introduction in the UK of same sex marriage) transmutation of the civil partnership to marriage.

Civil Partnership Act 2004

11–34   The Act[147] is in 8 parts and has 30 Schedules. Part 1 establishes the requirements for the creation of a formally and essentially valid civil partnership. Separate provision is laid down for the different jurisdictions of the UK: Pt 2 (England and Wales), Pt 3 (Scotland), and Pt 4 (Northern Ireland). Determination of when each Part shall apply appears to depend upon the place of registration (*locus registrationis*) of the civil partnership in question.[148]

Within each Part are special rules concerning formation and eligibility, registration, occupancy rights and tenancies, dissolution and financial arrangements. Part 5, containing the conflict of laws provisions, is concerned with civil partnerships formed or dissolved abroad, and is of particular relevance here.

Civil partnerships registered in Scotland: Part 3

Eligibility—section 86[149]

11–35   Legal capacity to enter a civil partnership is placed under the heading of "eligibility". Under s.86(1), two parties are not eligible to register in Scotland[150] as civil partners of each other if:

(a)   they are not of the same sex;
(b)   they are related in a forbidden degree[151];
(c)   either has not attained the age of 16 years;
(d)   either is married or already in civil partnership; or
(e)   either is incapable of understanding the nature of civil partnership, or validly consenting to its formation.[152]

It appears from s.86 that eligibility to register a civil partnership in Scotland depends only upon compliance with these provisions. This means that the statutory rules in Pt 3 demonstrate a basic territorial approach, applicable to all registrations in Scotland, to matters of form (s.85) and matters of capacity (s.86) alike, and to all persons registering a partnership, regardless of their domicile(s).

---

[147] As amended by the Marriage and Civil Partnership (Scotland) Act 2014 Pt 2.
[148] 2004 Act s.1(1)(a).
[149] As amended by Family Law (Scotland) Act 2006 s.33.
[150] As regards formation of partnership, and eligibility to register a partnership in England, see ss.2, 3; and in Northern Ireland, ss.137, 138.
[151] The forbidden degrees are set out in s.86 of and Sch.10 to the Act in a similar manner to that found in the Marriage (Scotland) Act 1977, as amended (mutatis mutandis).
[152] Section 123 provides that absence of consent is a ground rendering the civil partnership void.

Civil partnerships formed abroad: Part 5

Registration at British consulates, or by armed forces personnel: Chapter 1

Section 210 makes provision for the registration by persons as civil partners in prescribed countries outside the UK, and in the presence of a prescribed officer of HM Diplomatic Service, if certain conditions are satisfied, viz.: at least one of the proposed civil partners is a UK national, the parties would have been eligible to register as civil partners in the UK, the authorities of the country in question do not object, and insufficient facilities exist for them to enter into an overseas relationship under the law of that country. Section 211 makes equivalent provision, mutatis mutandis, for the registration of a civil partnership in a country outside the UK where at least one of the proposed civil partners is a member of HM Forces serving in that country.

11–36

Registration of overseas relationships treated as civil partnerships: Chapter 2

Sections 212–218 of the 2004 Act, and Sch.20 to the Act, provide for the recognition in the UK as civil partnerships of qualifying overseas relationships. An overseas relationship is either a relationship specified in Sch.20 (s.213[153]), or is one which satisfies the general conditions set out in s.214. By s.215, two people are to be treated as having formed a civil partnership as a result of having registered an overseas relationship,[154] if under the relevant law they had capacity to enter into the relationship, and met all requirements necessary per the *lex loci registrationis* to ensure the formal validity of the relationship. The "relevant law" means, in terms of s.212(2), the law of the country of registration of the relationship, including its rules of private international law. Thus, if by the *lex loci registrationis*, parties are required to have capacity also by their personal law, this will constitute an extra requirement.

11–37

It should be noted that two people shall not be treated in "UK law" as having formed a civil partnership upon the registration of an overseas relationship if, at the date of registration, they were not of the same sex under "UK law".[155]

Importantly, s.217 makes certain mandatory provision in cases where at least one of the parties to the overseas relationship was domiciled in a part of the UK at the date of registration. By s.217(3) and (4), a person domiciled in Scotland shall not be treated as having formed a civil partnership as a result of having entered into an overseas relationship, if at the date of registration (i) s/he was related to the other party in a forbidden degree; (ii) s/he had not attained the age of 16 years; or (iii) s/he was incapable of understanding the nature of civil

---

[153] In respect of which, see Civil Partnership Act 2004 (Overseas Relationships) Order 2012 (SI 2012/2976).

[154] As defined in ss.212, 213, Sch.20. See Civil Partnerships Act 2004 (Overseas Relationships) Order 2012 (SI 2012/2976), which adds to the number of relationships set out in Sch.20 to be treated as civil partnerships.

[155] 2004 Act s.216.

partnership, or validly consenting to its formation. In this way, Pt 5[156] imposes upon persons domiciled in Scotland all the requirements as to eligibility which would apply to them were they to seek to register a civil partnership in Scotland. This means that a Scottish domiciliary cannot evade, for example, Scottish rules of consanguinity or nonage by going abroad to register the partnership; this safeguard has an ancient lineage.[157]

Although the safeguard provided by s.217 appears sufficient, s.218 further provides that two people are not to be treated as having formed a civil partnership as a result of having entered into an overseas relationship if it would be manifestly contrary to (Scots/English) public policy to recognise the capacity, of one or both of them, under the *lex loci registrationis*, to enter into the relationship.

Prior to the introduction of the Marriage and Civil Partnership (Scotland) Act 2014, ss.212–218 of the 2004 Act and Sch.20 authorised the recognition in the UK as civil partnerships of overseas same sex marriages and same sex civil unions. Section 26 of the 2014 Act, however, amends this approach so that as from 16 December 2014, the recognition arrangements relate only to same sex civil unions (i.e. other than marriage); overseas same sex marriage will be recognised in Scotland only if it satisfies s.38 of the Family Law (Scotland) Act 2006.

Conversion of civil partnership into marriage

11–38 One purpose of the 2014 Act is to make provision for the conversion of qualifying civil partnerships into marriage. Section 11(2) of the Marriage and Civil Partnership (Scotland) Act 2014 is concerned with the situation where the parties to a qualifying[158] civil partnership (a) marry in accordance with the procedure set out in s.8 of the 2014 Act; or (b) change their civil partnership into a marriage in accordance with s.10(1) thereof. Section 8(3)(a) amends the Marriage (Scotland) Act 1977 s.5(4)(b), to the effect that parties being in a qualifying civil partnership with each other is not a legal impediment to their marrying each other. Section 8(3)(b) inserts new subs.(6) into s.5 (objections to marriage) of the 1977 Act, to the effect of defining a "qualifying civil partnership" as one which was registered in Scotland, and has not been dissolved, annulled or ended by death.[159]

Section 9 of the 2014 Act, further extending the category of civil partnerships which can be converted into marriage in Scotland, authorises the Scottish Ministers to order that the meaning of qualifying civil partnership shall include civil partnerships registered outside Scotland. Accordingly, civil partners in a partnership registered outside Scotland may be permitted, in Scotland, to change their partnership to a marriage, if Scottish Ministers so order. Section 10(1) of the 2014 Act facilitates the conversion of a qualifying civil partnership into a same sex marriage.

---

[156] Per ss.214(a), 216(1), 217(4).

[157] Ch.2, below, re statutes personal in the writings of Bartolus. cf. *Sussex Peerage Case* (1844) 11 Cl. & F. 85; and *Brook* (1861) 9 H.L. Cas. 193.

[158] Defined in s.8(6) and (7) of the 2014 Act. But see also s.9 of the 2014 Act.

[159] See also s.5(7) of the 1977 Act re partnerships registered outside the UK at a British consulate or by British armed forces personnel.

By s.11(2), where such parties marry in accordance with the 1977 Act, or change their civil partnership into a marriage in accordance with s.10(1) of the 2014 Act, the qualifying civil partnership ends on the date on which the marriage was solemnised or the change took effect, and the change of status is backdated so that the parties are to be treated as having been married to each other since the date of registration of the qualifying civil partnership. The effect of this is retrospectively to enlarge the legal capacity to contract a same sex marriage of persons who take advantage of these provisions.

In England, s.15 of the Marriage (Same Sex Couples) Act 2013 makes provision for the review of the operation and future of the Civil Partnership Act 2004 in England and Wales. By s.9(1) of the Marriage (Same Sex Couples) Act 2013, the parties to an "England and Wales civil partnership"[160] may convert their civil partnership into a marriage.[161] As under Scots law, the resulting marriage is to be treated as having subsisted from the date of formation of the civil partnership.[162]

DE FACTO COHABITATION

Until the Family Law (Scotland) Act 2006, there was no single body of rules in Scots domestic law governing the definition, constitution, and proprietary and other consequences, of de facto cohabitation, although particular claims by one partner of a cohabiting couple occasionally might be recognised.[163] Provision was haphazard.

11–39

The 2006 Act introduced in ss.25–30 a set of rules which, after defining "cohabitant" (s.25) provides certain rights for such persons in household goods (s.26); in money and property (s.27); upon termination of the relationship otherwise than by death (s.28); and upon termination of the relationship upon death intestate of one cohabitant (s.29[164]).

The statutory meaning of "cohabitant", as enacted, was as follows: either member of a couple consisting of (a) a man and a woman who are (or were) living together as if they were husband and wife; or (b) two persons of the same sex who are (or were) living together as if they were civil partners. By s.4(2) and (3) of the Marriage and Civil Partnership (Scotland) Act 2014, however, s.25(1)(a) of the 2006 Act must be read now as extending equally to two people of the same sex who are (or were) living together as if they were married to each other.

---

[160] Defined in s.9(7) of the 2013 Act. But see also s.9(3) of the 2013 Act.
[161] See The Marriage of Same Sex Couples (Conversion of Civil Partnership) Regulations 2014 (SI 2014/3181), and also The Marriage (Same Sex Couples) Act 2013 and Marriage and Civil Partnership (Scotland) Act 2014 (Consequential Provisions) Order 2014 (SI 2014/3061); The Marriage (Same Sex Couples) Act 2013 (Consequential and Contrary Provisions and Scotland); and the Marriage and Civil Partnership (Scotland) Act 2014 (Consequential Provisions) Order 2014 (SI 2014/3168).
[162] 2013 Act s.9(6).
[163] e.g. Home Owner and Debtor Protection (Scotland) Act 2010; the claim of a partner under the Damages (Scotland) Act 2011; and the Housing (Scotland) Act 1988 s.31(4).
[164] *Kerr v Mangan* [2014] CSIH 69; 2014 G.W.D. 25-509 (IH (Ex Div)); *Savage v Purches*, 2009 S.L.T. (Sh. Ct.) 36; and *Chebotareva v Khandro (King's Executrix)*, 2008 Fam. L.R. 66. See also The Cross-Border Mediation (Scotland) Regulations 2011 (SSI 2011/234) reg.9.

The Act takes the approach of providing in s.25(1) an abstract definition of those who are eligible to be regarded as "cohabitant", and of providing in s.25(2) factors which may be taken as sufficient to establish cohabitation so as to "trigger" ss.26–30. Section 25(2) states that the court shall have regard to (a) the length of the period during which A and B have been living together (or lived together); (b) the nature of their relationship during that period; and (c) the nature and extent of any financial arrangements subsisting, or which subsisted, during that period. It is therefore not possible to advise with certainty as to whether the law would regard a particular couple as being cohabitants for the purposes of the Act. On the other hand, it may be difficult for a couple to evade the status of cohabitant under the 2006 Act, even if that should be their choice, an outcome which is an affront to party autonomy.

A problem with regard to the definition of cohabitation generally is that of identifying the date of commencement, and possibly the date of termination; whilst both dates are questions of fact, the former is likely to be more difficult of proof. A particular problem of time may arise, e.g. in circumstances where a same sex cohabitation commenced many years prior to the coming into effect of s.4 of the 2014 Act. In contrast with the provision concerning transformation of civil partnership into marriage,[165] nothing is said in s.4 about the dating back or not of a same sex cohabitation. In other words, it is unclear whether or not, in deciding whether to make an award, e.g. under s.28 of the 2006 Act, a sheriff may take into account the fact that a period of cohabitation "as if they were married to each other" accumulated over a time when same sex marriage in Scots law was not competent, and when such financial consequences as the 2006 Act bestows were not bestowed upon same sex cohabitants. If the qualifying criterion is "as if they were married", it may be difficult to persuade a court to take account of pre-existing cohabitation since the parties were unable to be married to each other by Scots law until the coming into effect of the 2014 Act. Section 25(2), which requires the court, when determining for the purposes of any of ss.26–29 if one person is a cohabitant of another, to have regard to the length of the period during which they have been living together (or lived together), and not the period during which they have been living together (or lived together) "as husband and wife" would seem to permit account to be taken of the pre-existing cohabitation.

Conflict problems arising from the incidence of de facto cohabitation

11–40 These notable changes in domestic family law have the potential to generate conflict of laws problems, but in general ss.25–30 are "conflict of laws blind", except that for application to be made for succession rights under s.29 the deceased cohabitant must have been domiciled in Scotland at death. It is implicit that application may be made for the rights provided for in the Act whenever Scots law is the *lex causae*. However, since generally the Act contains no jurisdiction or choice of law rules with regard to de facto cohabitation, it remains uncertain, e.g. which law governs an individual's legal capacity to attain the status of cohabitant, or indeed when Scots law is to be considered to be the *lex*

---

[165] 2014 Act s.11(2)(b).

causae. The essential antecedent question, not addressed in the Act, is in what circumstances the Scottish courts have jurisdiction to rule on these matters in the first place.[166]

Furthermore, as conflict rules now stand, what arguments might a party approaching the Scots court deploy to persuade the court that a law other than Scots law should apply, assuming such other law is furnished with rules containing property rights for cohabitants? Arguably, the starting point might be that Scots law is the governing law where the parties have, or last had, their principal place of cohabitation in Scotland, i.e. a simple territorial basis akin to the "matrimonial domicile". There is a strong argument for application, by the court of the country in which the parties cohabit, of the law of that country to the consequences of cessation of de facto cohabitation. Presumably that law also would determine when, and in what circumstances, such cohabitation is deemed to have ceased.[167] The conflict dimension of cohabitants' property rights is dealt with further at Ch.13, below.

SUMMARY 11

1. Nature of the relationship   **11–41**
    This must be tested by the indicia of marriage according to the *lex fori*.
    Same sex marriage: Scots and English domestic law have introduced same sex marriage by means of the Marriage and Civil Partnership (Scotland) Act 2014 and the Marriage (Same Sex Couples) Act 2013, respectively.
    Polygamous marriages: polygamous marriages are recognised for most purposes. In particular, consistorial actions between the parties to such a marriage have been competent since the Matrimonial Proceedings (Polygamous Marriages) Act 1972. Although no Scottish or English domiciliary has legal capacity to enter into an actually polygamous marriage, the Private International Law (Miscellaneous Provisions) Act 1995 s.7 provides that such a person has legal capacity to enter into a marriage which is potentially polygamous.
2. Formal validity of marriage
    Matters of form are governed by the *lex loci celebrationis* in terms of s.38(1) of the Family Law (Scotland) Act 2006.
3. Essential validity of marriage
    In terms of the Family Law (Scotland) Act 2006 s.38(2)(a), each party must have capacity to marry by the law of his/her domicile immediately before the marriage. Likewise, in terms of s.38(2)(b), the question whether a party has consented to enter into a marriage is to be determined by his/her ante-nuptial domicile, subject however to the provisions on void marriages

---

[166] J.M. Carruthers in K. Boele-Woelki (ed.), *Perspectives for the Unification and Harmonisation of Family Law in Europe* (Antwerp/Oxford/New York: Intersentia, 2003), p.322.

[167] 2006 Act s.28 gives lengthy consideration to the types of order which may be made on cessation of cohabitation and the criteria for awarding them, but no guidance to ascertain that cessation has occurred.

inserted by s.2 of the Act. The rule in each case is subject to s.38(3) (application of Scots law where the *locus celebrationis* is Scots), and s.38(4) (public policy of the forum).

4. Third parties' consent to marriage

In terms of s.38(5) of the Family Law (Scotland) Act 2006, a requirement of the law of a party's domicile that parental consent must be obtained to his/her marriage if s/he is under a certain age shall not be taken to affect his/her capacity to enter into a marriage in Scotland unless failure to obtain such consent would render invalid by the personal law of the party any marriage that s/he purported to enter into in any form anywhere in the world.

5. Civil Partnership Act 2004

Part 3 contains rules on the formation of civil partnerships in Scotland. Part 5 contains conflict of laws provision in respect of civil partnerships formed abroad.

6. De facto cohabitation

The Family Law (Scotland) Act 2006 sets out rules of Scots law in respect of the rights and duties of cohabitants. No jurisdiction provisions for de facto cohabitation disputes are contained in the Act, and only one such choice of law rule is visible.

CHAPTER 12

Matrimonial causes

12–01

In addressing each of the topics of divorce, judicial separation, and annulment of marriage, the following aspects will be considered in turn:

(1)   jurisdiction of the Scots courts;
(2)   choice of law rules in use in Scots courts; and
(3)   recognition of foreign decrees by the Scots courts.

The topics of matrimonial remedies for same sex marriage and of dissolution of civil partnership will be treated thereafter.

DIVORCE

The jurisdiction of Scots courts

Common law grounds of jurisdiction and statutory extension

12–02

There is a natural tendency towards interdependence between the rules of jurisdiction in consistorial causes utilised by a forum and its approach to the recognition of foreign decrees in that area.[1] At one time the Scots courts assumed jurisdiction in divorce on a wide basis, including residence, but Scots decrees were not recognised in England unless the husband was domiciled in Scotland at the date of the action.[2] The Scots courts did not adopt such a strict view as to (non-) recognition at that time. Between 1852 and 1895,[3] they developed a doctrine of matrimonial domicile, that is, that the parties should be regarded as being domiciled in the country where they resided, for the purpose of consistorial actions only, and that the courts of that country should be regarded as having jurisdiction in such actions. In *Le Mesurier*,[4] however, the Privy Council, on an appeal from Ceylon, held that there was no such thing for jurisdictional purposes as matrimonial domicile and that only the courts of the husband's domicile had jurisdiction in actions of divorce. This decision was accepted as applying both to Scotland and England, and in Scotland the doctrine of matrimonial domicile as a

---

[1] *Travers v Holley* [1953] P. 246; and *Indyka v Indyka* [1969] 1 A.C. 33, per Lord Pearce at 78.
[2] *Lolley's Case* (1812) Russ. & Ry. 237; and *Shaw v Gould* (1868) L.R. 3 H.L. 55.
[3] *Shields v Shields* (1852) 15 D. 142; *Jack v Jack* (1862) 24 D. 467; *Pitt v Pitt* (1864) 2 M. (H.L.) 28; *Dombrowitzki v Dombrowitzki* (1895) 22 R. 906.
[4] *Le Mesurier v Le Mesurier* [1895] A.C. 517.

ground of jurisdiction subsequently was abandoned.[5] The practical difficulties of having to make resort to the court of the domicile, the problem of the deserted wife in England,[6] and the occurrence of wartime marriages to "foreigners", combined to demonstrate the undue strictness of the rule in *Le Mesurier*. As a result, a number of statutory extensions were made to permit access by the wife to the Scots or English courts on the basis of her residence in the jurisdiction.[7]

Modern grounds of jurisdiction

Rules of jurisdiction up to 1 March 2001

12–03   The earlier statutory provisions were replaced by the Domicile and Matrimonial Proceedings Act 1973 ("the 1973 Act"). The 1973 Act specified a ground of jurisdiction additional to that of domicile. Section 7 provided that the Court of Session should have jurisdiction in actions of divorce, separation and declarators of freedom and putting to silence if and only if: (a) either party was domiciled in Scotland at the date when the action began; or (b) either party was habitually resident in Scotland throughout the period of one year ending with the date when the action was begun.[8]

Divorce jurisdiction was extended to the sheriff court by the Divorce Jurisdiction, Court Fees and Legal Aid (Scotland) Act 1983.[9]

Regulation 1347/2000: Brussels II

12–04   From 1 March 2001, there was put in place a discrete system of allocation of jurisdiction in matrimonial matters and consistorial decree recognition among the then Member States of the EU, in the form of Regulation[10] 1347/2000 on jurisdiction and recognition and enforcement of judgments in matrimonial matters and in matters of parental responsibility for children of both spouses (colloquially known as "Brussels II").[11] The matrimonial system depends, as does the Regulation's commercial law precursors, the 1968 Brussels Convention ("Brussels I") and Regulation 44/2001 ("Brussels I Regulation") (the latter of which provides the structure for the family law instrument), upon Member States

---

[5] J.A. Maclaren, *Court of Session Practice* (Edinburgh: W. Green & Son Ltd, 1916), pp.57, 58.

[6] In desertion cases, the English courts regarded the husband's domicile at the date of the raising of the action as being determinant of jurisdiction: *H v H* [1928] P. 206; and *Herd v Herd* [1936] P. 205. In such cases in Scotland, however, the courts assumed jurisdiction if the husband was domiciled in Scotland at the date of desertion.

[7] Indian and Colonial Divorce Jurisdiction Acts 1926 and 1940; and Colonial and Other Territories (Divorce Jurisdiction) Act 1950; Matrimonial Causes Act 1937 (A.P. Herbert's Act) (introducing residence as a ground of jurisdiction in England for a deserted wife); and Matrimonial Causes (War Marriages) Act 1944 s.1 (England), s.2 (Scotland). The last and most useful was the Law Reform (Miscellaneous Provisions) Act 1949 s.1 (England), s.2 (Scotland).

[8] Equivalent provisions were introduced in ss.5 and 13 as regards the courts of England and Northern Ireland, respectively.

[9] Also 1973 Act s.8(1), (2). As to the interpretation of habitual residence such as to confer jurisdiction on the sheriff, see *Williamson v Williamson*, 2010 S.L.T. (Sh. Ct.) 41.

[10] The original plan had been to produce a Brussels II Convention, but this plan was superseded by the proposal for a Regulation.

[11] Brussels II [2000] O.J. L160/19.

agreeing, first, a set of rules of jurisdiction. Thereafter, if the decree in question emanates from a court of competent jurisdiction in terms of the instrument, recognition thereof is almost certain to follow in the other Member States.

However, the life of Brussels II was short. It was succeeded rapidly by Regulation 2201/2003 concerning jurisdiction and the recognition and enforcement of judgments in matrimonial matters and matters of parental responsibility ("Brussels II *bis*"),[12] which came into force fully on 1 March 2005, repealing Brussels II. Brussels II *bis* came about as a result of the view that the scope of Brussels II, as it affected children, was too narrow. The more ambitious aim of Brussels II *bis* was to create a single European instrument securing the free movement, both of matrimonial judgments and parental responsibility judgments.[13] The "Brussels rules" apply, with direct effect, among all Member States of the EU,[14] with the exception of Denmark.[15]

Rules of jurisdiction after 1 March 2005: Brussels II *bis*

The starting point is the 1973 Act, as amended first by the European Communities (Matrimonial Jurisdiction and Judgments) (Scotland) Regulations 2001[16] (taking account of Brussels II[17]), and later by the European Communities (Matrimonial and Parental Responsibility Jurisdiction and Judgments) (Scotland) Regulations 2005[18] (taking account of Brussels II *bis*[19]).[20]   **12–05**

---

[12] Brussels II *bis* [2003] O.J. L338/1. See also Regulation 2116/2004 concerning jurisdiction and the recognition and enforcement of judgments in matrimonial matters and the matters of parental responsibility, repealing Regulation 1347/2000, as regards treaties with the Holy See [2004] O.J. L367/1). For specialist treatment, see M. Ni Shuilleabhain, *Cross-Border Divorce Law: Brussels II bis* (2010) Oxford University Press.

[13] The draft Brussels II Convention was accompanied by an Explanatory Report by Dr Alegria Borras, *Explanatory Report on the Convention on Jurisdiction and the Recognition and Enforcement of Judgments in Matrimonial Matters* [1998] O.J. C221/27 ("Borras Report"). No separate explanatory memorandum was issued to accompany Brussels II or Brussels II *bis*, but the Borras Report can be used to shed light on certain of the provisions in the Regulation, which echo those contained in the draft Convention.

[14] 1973 Act s.12(5)(b).

[15] Protocol No.22 on the position of Denmark (consolidated versions of the TEU and the TFEU: [2008] O.J. C115/299), in terms of which Denmark shall not take part in the adoption of proposed measures pursuant to Title V of Pt 3 of the Treaty on the Functioning of the European Union; and formerly Protocol No.5 ([1997] O.J. C340/101), in terms of which Denmark shall not take part in the adoption of proposed measures pursuant to Title IIIa of the Treaty establishing the European Community.

[16] European Communities (Matrimonial Jurisdiction and Judgments) (Scotland) Regulations 2001 (SSI 2001/36).

[17] See also Act of Sederunt (Ordinary Cause Rules) Amendment (European Matrimonial and Parental Responsibility Jurisdiction and Judgments) 2001 (SSI 2001/144).

[18] European Communities (Matrimonial and Parental Responsibility Jurisdiction and Judgments) (Scotland) Regulations 2005 (SSI 2005/42).

[19] See generally Commission Services in consultation with the European Judicial Network in Civil and Commercial Matters, *Practice Guide for the Application of the Brussels IIa Regulation* (2014). Further, for Scotland see Act of Sederunt (Rules of the Court of Session Amendment) (Jurisdiction, Recognition and Enforcement of Judgments) 2005 (SSI 2005/135).

[20] For the rules of jurisdiction applicable to divorce of same sex marriage, see paras 12–57—12–58, below.

The currently applicable Scottish rules of jurisdiction[21] are contained in s.7 (Court of Session) and s.8 (sheriff court) of the 1973 Act.

Section 7(2A) is to the effect that the Court of Session has jurisdiction to entertain, inter alia, an action for divorce or separation,[22] if and only if:

(1)   the Scottish courts have jurisdiction under Brussels II *bis*; or
(2)   the action is an excluded action and either of the parties to the marriage is domiciled in Scotland on the date when the action is begun.

Likewise, s.8 confers jurisdiction on the sheriff court to entertain, inter alia, an action for divorce or separation,[23] if and only if:

(1)   the Scottish courts have jurisdiction under Brussels II *bis*; or
(2)   the action is an excluded action and either of the parties to the marriage is domiciled in Scotland on the date when the action is begun; and
(3)   either party to the marriage—(i) was resident in the sheriffdom for a period of 40 days ending with that date; or (ii) had been resident in the sheriffdom for a period of not less than 40 days ending not more than 40 days before the said date, and has no known residence in Scotland at that date.

The first point of reference, therefore, is Brussels II *bis*.

BRUSSELS II *BIS* ARTICLE 3

12–06   Turning first to jurisdiction under the Regulation, the bases of jurisdiction are contained in art.3, to the following effect: in matters relating to divorce, legal separation or marriage annulment, jurisdiction shall lie with the courts of the Member State:

> "(a)   in whose territory:
> — the spouses are habitually resident, or
> — the spouses were last habitually resident, insofar as one of them still resides there, or
> — the respondent is habitually resident, or
> — in the event of a joint application, either of the spouses is habitually resident, or
> — the applicant is habitually resident if he or she resided[24] there for at least a year immediately before the application was made,[25] or
> — the applicant is habitually resident if he or she resided there for at least six months immediately before the application was made, and is either a national of the Member State in question or, in the case of the UK and Ireland, has his or her 'domicile' there;[26]

---

[21] For England, see s.5(2).
[22] There continue to be special rules of jurisdiction for actions of declarator of marriage: 1973 Act s.7(3).
[23] Special rules of shrieval jurisdiction for actions of declarator of marriage are contained in 1973 Act s.8(2ZA).
[24] e.g. *Tan v Choy* [2014] EWCA Civ 251; [2014] Fam. Law 807.
[25] e.g. *V v V (Divorce)* [2011] EWHC 1190 (Fam); [2012] I.L.Pr. 3.
[26] In terms of art.3.2, for the purposes of the Regulation, "domicile" shall have the same meaning as it has under the legal systems of the UK and Ireland.

(b) of the nationality of both spouses or, in the case of the UK and Ireland, of the 'domicile' of both spouses.[27]"

ARTICLE 3.1(A)

Why the focus on habitual residence, and why so many bases of jurisdiction? The Borras Report explains that:

12–07

"The grounds adopted are based on the principle of *genuine connection* between the person and a Member State. The decision to include particular grounds reflects their existence in various national legal systems and their acceptance by the other Member States or the effort to find points of agreement acceptable to all."[28]

The notion of genuine connection is one which has been accorded some credence in England. In *Ikimi v Ikimi*,[29] Thorpe L.J. in the Court of Appeal, reviewing the history of jurisdiction in divorce, explained that in the late 1960s the Law Commissions wished to extend consistorial jurisdiction beyond domicile on a base of jurisdiction that met the interests of the state and of those who, "genuinely belong here, refusing access to transients and forum shoppers."[30] The Law Commissions favoured a "belonging test" which could tolerate periods of absence but which required more than occasional or casual residence. "Habitual" residence was chosen instead of "ordinary" residence in order to provide a uniform test in family law and to conform with international conventions, but there was not thought to be any difference between the two in this area of the law.[31] So the idea of genuine connection between a litigant and the court is apparently the rationale, both in UK law and in EU thinking.

Ikimi is an instructive case concerning the meaning of habitual residence for the purpose of divorce jurisdiction under s.5(2) of the Domicile and Matrimonial Proceedings Act 1973. In terms of the quality of residence required, the Court of Appeal took the view that the bodily presence required to form a basis for habitual residence, for the purposes of jurisdiction in divorce in the pre-Brussels era, had to be more than merely token in duration, probably amounting to residence for, "an appreciable part of the relevant year".[32] The point in issue was the degree of continuity required to establish habitual residence for the purposes of divorce jurisdiction. The court had to consider whether a Nigerian wife, who filed a petition for dissolution of marriage in England on the basis of habitual residence there, had two such residences. The family had two matrimonial homes, of equal status, in Nigeria and in England, and the wife had spent 161 days of the year in England. The submission, that it was not possible to be habitually resident

---

[27] e.g. *Divall v Divall* [2014] EWHC 95 (Fam).
[28] Borras Report para.30.
[29] *Ikimi v Ikimi* [2002] Fam. 72.
[30] *Ikimi v Ikimi* [2002] Fam. 72 at [21]. And refusing access also to fraudsters: in *Rapisarda v Colladon (also known as Re 180 Irregular Divorces)* [2014] EWFC 35, Sir James Munby set aside decrees obtained by false claims of habitual residence in England, commenting at [34] that, "... given the dimensions of the mail box it is clear that not even a single individual, however small, could possibly reside in it."!
[31] *Ikimi* [2002] Fam. 72, per Thorpe L.J. at [31]; and *Armstrong v Armstrong* [2003] EWHC 777 (Fam), per Butler-Sloss L.J.
[32] *Ikimi* [2002] Fam. 72, per Thorpe L.J. at [35].

in two places simultaneously, was rejected by the Court of Appeal. On the facts, the court found there was just sufficient residence in England by the wife, looking at all the comings and goings. Interestingly, having in mind the purpose of the finding on habitual residence, Thorpe L.J. favoured a liberal rather than a restrictive approach to the determination of habitual residence, whilst noting that one consequence of this approach might be forum shopping. If the residence test is too hard, a spouse who divides his time equally might not be able to invoke a habitual residence in either. On the other hand, setting it too low would allow the spouse to invoke the jurisdiction of both.

Habitual residence is not defined in Brussels II *bis*, and is not easy to define. Recently in the Court of Appeal[33] Aikens L.J. said that, "Brussels II does not define 'habitually resident', although in European law the concept of 'habitual residence' is well recognised and means the place where a person has established on a fixed basis the permanent or habitual centre of his interests, with all the relevant factors being taken into account." This derives from the definition in the Borras Report.[34]

The term has an autonomous meaning for the purposes of Brussels II *bis*,[35] and its meaning, which is to be derived from ECJ jurisprudence, is not necessarily the same as the UK domestic meaning, nor the meaning for the purposes, e.g. of international child abduction as developed in the UK through Hague Convention jurisprudence.

The interpretation of habitual residence adopted by the French Cour de Cassation in *Moore v Moore*[36] is in keeping with the spirit of the Borras definition, viz.: "The place where the party involved has fixed, with the wish to vest it with a stable character, the permanent or habitual centre of his or her interests." In *Moore*, the husband brought divorce proceedings in a French court, and a question arose as to whether or not that court had jurisdiction under Brussels II art.2,[37] on the basis of the wife's habitual residence in France. The couple were English nationals who had moved to their second home in France for a pre-determined 18-month period. The principal purpose of the move was to have their child schooled in France. The husband argued that habitual residence for the purpose of Brussels II included "temporary installation for a definite period", and required only an objective attachment to the place. The French judge at first instance declined jurisdiction. In the Cour de Cassation, habitual residence was defined and applied in such a way that the conclusion was reached that evidence did not show that W had transferred the "centre of her interests" to France. This French decision is demonstrably stricter than many of the English authorities, and it may be that the French court detected an inappropriate evasion of the natural forum.

An English gloss on the Borras definition was given in the case of *LK v K*.[38] The case involved a peripatetic husband and wife, both French nationals, who

---

[33] *Tan v Choy* [2014] EWCA Civ 251; [2014] Fam. Law 807, per Aikens L.J. at [29].

[34] Borras Report para.32. The suggested definition was cited with approval in *Marinos v Marinos* [2007] EWHC 2047 (Fam), per Munby J. at [33].

[35] *Marinos v Marinos* [2007] EWHC 2047 (Fam), per Munby J. at [17], [18]; and *Z v Z (Divorce: Jurisdiction)* [2009] EWHC 2626 (Fam).

[36] *Moore v Moore* [2006] I.L.Pr. 29.

[37] Equivalent to Brussels II *bis* art.3.

[38] *L-K v K (No.2)* [2006] EWHC 3280 (Fam), per Singer J. at [35].

married in Singapore. They arrived in England in late 2004 to live in rented property, the move occasioned by the husband's employment. His work commenced in February the following year. In March the wife began divorce proceedings in England. The husband submitted that neither party was habitually resident in England. Singer J. held that the issue of habitual residence is fact dependent, to be judged against the pattern of the couple's lives. Given the husband's work patterns, neither spouse had entered England as a transient, but with the settled intention of being resident in England for the duration of the husband's employment. The court was satisfied that there existed between the parties and the English forum the "genuine connection" referred to above, and both spouses were deemed to be habitually resident in England. This is a decision resting on "centre of interests", not on length of time.

An important English case is *Marinos v Marinos*,[39] in which it fell to be decided whether or not, for the purposes of Brussels II *bis*, a person can be habitually resident in two different countries at the same time. The husband was of Greek, and the wife of British, nationality. The husband went to Greece in October 2002 to work, and his wife and children followed in December that year, on something of a trial basis, the wife claiming the removal was a temporary relocation. In fact she and the children did not return to England until January 2007, and the day after arrival she petitioned for divorce in England, relying on Brussels II *bis* art.3 indent 6. It was not disputed that she satisfied the domicile requirement of indent 6; the case turned entirely on whether she could prove that she was habitually resident in England and had resided there for the preceding six months. Munby J. held, in what was a very evenly balanced case, that the wife's centre of gravity was located in England, not Greece, and he found that she was both resident[40] and habitually resident in England at all material times. Significantly, Munby J. considered that while it was clear that, for the purposes of English domestic law, one could be habitually resident contemporaneously in two different countries,[41] "the same is not necessarily true of the law laid down by the ECJ nor, specifically, for the purposes of the Regulation".[42]

The single judge decision in *Marinos* is at odds with another single judge decision handed down four years earlier in *Armstrong v Armstrong*[43] by the then President of the English Family Division of the High Court, Dame Elizabeth Butler-Sloss. In that (Brussels II) case, the President accepted that, as a matter of fact, a person can have two habitual residences simultaneously and she concluded that the correct approach to the degree of continuity required to establish habitual residence in a country, "cannot just be a counting of the days spent in the country. There has to be an element of quality of residence".[44] Her Ladyship, however, did count the days, and on the facts, noted that the husband had spent 171 days in

---

[39] *M v M* [2007] EWHC 2047 (Fam).
[40] See later, *Tan v Choy* [2014] EWCA Civ 251; [2014] Fam. Law 807, per Aikens L.J. at [29], "There is no definition of 'residence' or 'resides' in either Article 2 or 3 of Brussels II Revised."
[41] *Marinos v Marinos* [2007] EWHC 2047 (Fam) at [38].
[42] *Marinos v Marinos* [2007] EWHC 2047 (Fam) at [38].
[43] *Armstrong v Armstrong* [2003] EWHC 777 (Fam); [2003] 2 F.L.R. 375.
[44] *Armstrong v Armstrong* [2003] EWHC 777 (Fam); [2003] 2 F.L.R. 375 at [30]. The pattern of the respondent's visits to England, together with the number of days spent in the country—one-fifth of the year—did not demonstrate in the court's view sufficient residence to meet the statutory requirement of habitual residence in the 1973 Act and Brussels II.

South Africa as against 71 in England. Could it be said that the husband was habitually resident in South Africa *and* in England? The court found in the negative; the husband was clearly habitually resident in South Africa, but was only resident in England, and accordingly, the English court had no jurisdiction. The husband's voluntary presence in England on a regular basis did not amount to a settled intention to make England his habitual residence, or one of his habitual residences. England was merely a stopping off place for work or holidays. The character, in fact, of the residence was not sufficient to found, in law, habitual residence.

Munby J. in *Marinos* suggested that the point of interpretation of art.2 of Brussels II in *Armstrong* was inadequately argued and addressed, and that the decision of Dame Elizabeth Butler-Sloss P. rested on a "frail foundation".[45] Munby J. concluded in *Marinos*,[46] that:

". . . the language of Article 3(1)(a) of the Regulation [Brussels II *bis*][47] is clear, as is the ECJ case-law. For the purposes of the Regulation, one cannot be habitually resident in more than one country at the same time."

Of the conflicting interpretations, *Marinos* is perhaps the more persuasive.[48] In 2014 Aikens L.J. in the Court of Appeal in *Tan v Choy*[49] affirmed that, "It is ... established, in European law, that one cannot habitually reside in two places at once."[50] Even so, there is no guarantee that different forums will identify the same legal system as the habitual residence at the *tempus inspiciendum*.[51]

12–08   Study of the connecting factor of habitual residence suggests that it is not safe to use a cross-fertilisation technique, that is, to transplant authorities and principles from one area of law for use in another. Nonetheless, it is natural that in family law litigation, child custody issues and divorce issues may be intertwined, and it may not be unreasonable, therefore, to make reference in this context to authorities from the international child abduction area.

On that basis then, there may be examined *Re R (Abduction: Habitual Residence)*,[52] a custody case which prompted discussion of the implications of the not uncommon situation where one parent is seconded from one country to another for purposes of work, for a temporary period, for a particular project and for a short time. The father, a financier, was seconded from London to Germany for what the father claimed was an indefinite period intended to extend into the foreseeable future and for a minimum period of six months, but which the mother argued was a temporary posting, of short-term duration, at maximum six months. Munby J. concluded that for a person to be regarded in law as habitually resident in any country, he must have lived there for a period; but that period is not a fixed period and may be short—a month can be an appreciable period of time. On the facts, the judge concluded that the father's "temporary" posting to Germany was

[45] *Marinos v Marinos* [2007] EWHC 2047 (Fam) at [42].
[46] *Marinos v Marinos* [2007] EWHC 2047 (Fam) at [43].
[47] Article 3 of which is in identical terms to art.2 of Brussels II.
[48] *Marinos v Marinos* [2007] EWHC 2047 (Fam) at [40].
[49] *Tan v Choy* [2014] EWCA Civ 251; [2014] Fam. Law 807.
[50] *Tan v Choy* [2014] EWCA Civ 251; [2014] Fam. Law 807 at [29].
[51] Though see Munby J. in *Marinos* at [17], [18]; and Singer J. in *L-K v K (No.2)* [2006] EWHC 3280 (Fam) at [35].
[52] *Re R (Abduction: Habitual Residence)* [2003] EWHC 1968 (Fam).

sufficient to confer on him, his wife and their child, an habitual residence in Germany. The family's residence there was for a settled purpose, albeit a purpose of short duration. Munby J. paid some attention[53] to the state of mind necessary to permit acquisition of a new habitual residence, in particular, the suggestion that one cannot acquire a habitual residence in a foreign country unless one has a settled intention not to return to the country from which one is departing. His view was that it is wrong to suggest that a person does not lose his habitual residence in a particular country unless he has a settled intention not to return there; that would be to confuse habitual residence with domicile. Rather, in his opinion, it was no bar to acquisition of a new habitual residence in Germany that the individual had by no means decided to abandon the English habitual residence obtaining immediately before. This comes close to suggesting that dual habitual residence may exist,[54] an awkward conclusion in child abduction cases. Lifestyles such as this are likely to raise the possibility of dual or concurrent habitual residence, assuming that the family retains a home in the state of origin. If this fairly liberal approach were to be transposed to legal issues affecting the adult community, then it could have quite significant implications for the mobile international population.

While the suggestion of rapidly and easily alternating (i.e. consecutive not concurrent) habitual residences has its attractions for the adult community,[55] one would have to assess its suitability against the family situation as a whole in circumstances such as *Re R*, and ask whether the rapid acquisition of a new habitual residence in, say, Germany extends also to the child. It will not serve if it were to lead to the situation in which divorce jurisdiction under Brussels II *bis* might be easily established, based on a new habitual residence; but that a mother who wished, on termination of the marriage, to return with the children of the family to the English jurisdiction whence they had come, would be in danger of being found to have wrongfully removed the children from their deemed habitual residence in Germany, the "new" country. The shifting meaning of habitual residence in the international child abduction context is visible in recent judgments of the UK Supreme Court.[56]

ARTICLE 3.1(B)

Article 3.1(b) confers jurisdiction on the courts of the Member State of the nationality of both spouses or, in the case of the UK and Ireland, of the "domicile" of both spouses. Some states had wanted the condition to attach to one spouse only, but this was rejected on the ground that it would amount to a pure "*forum actoris*" approach.[57] The phrases in art.3.1(b) must be read disjunctively so as to produce one provision for the UK and Ireland, and another for all other Member States; it does not provide an additional gateway for the UK and Ireland.[58]

12–09

---

[53] *Re R (Abduction: Habitual Residence)* [2003] EWHC 1968 (Fam) at [40].
[54] cf. Munby J. in *Marinos v Marinos* [2007] EWHC 2047 (Fam); para.12–07, above.
[55] e.g. *Z v Z (Divorce: Jurisdiction)* [2009] EWHC 2626 (Fam).
[56] Paras 14–55—14–57, below.
[57] Borras Report para.33.
[58] *Re N (Jurisdiction)*; sub nom. *NDO v JFO* [2009] I.L.Pr. 8.

A difficulty of interpretation has arisen in relation to parties of dual nationality. In *Re Hadadi*,[59] the French Cour de Cassation referred for a preliminary ruling the question whether art.3.1(b) is to be interpreted as meaning that where spouses hold both the nationality of the court seised, and the nationality of another Member State, the nationality of the court seised must prevail. The ECJ held that where spouses have the same dual nationality, the court seised cannot overlook the fact that the individuals concerned hold the nationality of another Member State, with the result that persons with the same dual nationality are treated as if they had only the nationality of the Member State of the court seised. On the contrary, the courts of those Member States of which the spouses hold nationality have jurisdiction under that provision and between the two the spouses may seise the court of the Member State of their choice.[60]

PARTY AUTONOMY IN JURISDICTION

12–10   Brussels II *bis* does not provide the possibility for spouses to designate the court competent to determine their action, i.e. there is very limited scope for party autonomy. Specifically, arts 16 (seising of the court) and 19 (lis pendens) of the Brussels II *bis* system are prescriptive, and are not susceptible to being overridden by private agreement between the parties. However, as Vos L.J. in the Court of Appeal in *Jefferson v O'Connor*[61] explained:

> "If the parties wish to agree that jurisdiction over their divorce shall be in a particular Member State having jurisdiction under article 3 of the Council Regulation, it is still open to them to achieve that result. They can simply start only one set of proceedings in that Member State or, if there are already two sets, withdraw or discontinue the proceedings they do not wish to pursue. Thus, whilst it is true that the Council Regulation prevents the parties contracting out of the jurisdiction of the court in the first Member State seised, it does not prevent them giving effect to an agreement if they still wish to do so."[62]

For a number of years, consideration has been given to the question whether or not party autonomy in this respect ought to be permitted.[63] The most recent communication from the European Commission[64] and the accompanying Questionnaire on the operation of the instrument invited responses to the question whether or not it should be possible for spouses to choose the court, and if it should be possible, whether or not that choice should be limited to courts of an EU country with which one or both spouses have a substantial connection. The

---

[59] *Re Hadadi*; sub nom. *Re Hadady* (C-168/08) [2008] O.J. C158/11.

[60] *Re Hadadi* (C-168/08) [2009] O.J. C220/11.

[61] *Jefferson v O'Connor* [2014] EWCA Civ 38.

[62] *Jefferson v O'Connor* [2014] EWCA Civ 38 at [38].

[63] e.g. European Commission Green Paper on Applicable Law and Jurisdiction in Divorce Matters ("Rome III") (Brussels, 14 March 2005; COM(2005) 82 final; {SEC(2005) 331}), s.3.6; and Proposal for a Council Regulation amending Regulation (EC) No.2201/2003 as regards jurisdiction and introducing rules concerning applicable law in matrimonial matters (presented by the Commission) (Brussels, 17 July 2006; COM(2006) 399 final; 2006/0135 (CNS)), art.3a. The 2006 proposal lapsed, in view of developments re Rome III (para.12–19 below).

[64] Report on the application of the Brussels II bis Regulation (COM (2014) 225 final) (15 April 2014).

Commission's response to the consultation is awaited.[65] The trend in recent instruments in civil and commercial and family law matters is in favour of party autonomy,[66] and the introduction of restricted party autonomy in Brussels II *bis*, to allow spouses to agree on the competent court, could be useful.[67]

"EXCLUDED ACTION"

By Article 6 of Brussels II *bis*, a spouse who: (a) is habitually resident in the territory of a Member State; or (b) is a national of a Member State, or, in the case of the United Kingdom and Ireland, has his or her "domicile" therein, may be sued in another EU Member State only in accordance with arts 3, 4 (counterclaim) and 5 (conversion of legal separation into divorce). By art.7.1 ("residual jurisdiction"), where no court of a Member State has jurisdiction pursuant to arts 3, 4 and 5, jurisdiction shall be determined, in each Member State, by the laws of that State. This provides, in effect, for the continuing application of residual national rules of jurisdiction.[68]

12–11

The Scottish courts will have jurisdiction under the 1973 Act s.7(2A) if the action is an "excluded action" and either party is domiciled in Scotland on the date when the action is begun.[69] An understanding of this qualification requires, therefore, an examination of the meaning of "excluded action", which is defined in s.12(5)(d) of the 1973 Act,[70] as:

> "... an action in respect of which no court of a Contracting State has jurisdiction under the Council Regulation and the defender is not a person who is (i) a national of a Contracting State (other than the United Kingdom or Ireland); or (ii) domiciled in Ireland."

In order to access the residual rules of jurisdiction of Scots law, the judge has to assure himself that there is no ground on which he (nor any other judge of an EU Member State) may take jurisdiction under Brussels II *bis*. The residual ground of jurisdiction under the 1973 Act is the domicile of either party in Scotland on the date when the action is begun, taking no account of that party's residence or habitual residence. Domicile is a connecting factor which can operate to confer jurisdiction under art.3 of Brussels II *bis*. For art.3.1(b) to confer jurisdiction,

---

[65] Article 65 of Brussels II *bis* requires, no later than 1 January 2012, the Commission to present a report on the application of the instrument. On 15 April 2014, the European Commission published its Report on the application of the Brussels II *bis* Regulation (COM (2014) 225 final), and issued its "Consultation on the functioning of the Brussels IIa Regulation (EC 2201/2003)". A summary of the responses to the Consultation may be viewed at http://ec.europa.eu/eusurvey/publication/BXLIIA [accessed 20 June 2015]. To date, no proposal to amend Brussels II *bis* has been published.

[66] See J.M. Carruthers, "Party Autonomy in the Legal Regulation of Adult Relationships: What Place for Party Choice in Private International Law?" (2012) 61 I.C.L.Q. 881.

[67] cf. operation of Rome III, and authorisation of party choice of law: paras 12–23—12–24, below.

[68] See *A v L*; sub nom. *F v F* [2009] EWHC 1448 (Fam); and *Sundelind Lopez v Lopez Lizazo* (C-68/07) [2008] I.L.Pr. 4, in which the ECJ made clear that jurisdiction cannot be regulated by national law under art.7.1 unless no court of a Member State has jurisdiction pursuant to arts 3–5.

[69] See also, for England, s.5(2); and *Sekhri v Ray* [2014] EWCA Civ 119; [2014] 2 F.L.R. 1168.

[70] Introduced by reg.2(5)(d) of European Communities (Matrimonial Jurisdiction and Judgments) (Scotland) Regulations 2001 (SSI 2001/36), and substituted by European Communities (Matrimonial and Parental Responsibility Jurisdiction and Judgments) (Scotland) Regulations 2005 (SSI 2005/42) reg.8.

both parties must be domiciled in Scotland. Article 3.1(a) indent 6 confers jurisdiction on the basis that the applicant (alone) is domiciled in Scotland, coupled with his/her being resident for at least six months immediately before the application. Only if the applicant is domiciled in Scotland, but resident immediately before the application elsewhere, should the Scots judge utilise the residual ground of jurisdiction per the 1973 Act.[71] The pre-existing (that is, pre-1 March 2001) Scottish jurisdictional ground of one year's habitual residence of either party in Scotland has ceased to be available.

Jurisdiction to reduce a decree of divorce granted by a court in Scotland is conferred on the Court of Session whether or not at that later date the court has jurisdiction independently to pronounce on the parties' status.[72]

Conflicting jurisdictions

12–12 The common law position was that if a Scots or English court had jurisdiction in consistorial proceedings brought by one party and the other party was proceeding with another action in a foreign court, that fact would not prevent the first party from proceeding with the first action unless a very strong case was submitted.[73]

The 1973 Act set out for England[74] and Scotland,[75] respectively, a dual system of mandatory and discretionary sists for the treatment of instances of conflicting jurisdictions in consistorial causes. In terms of Sch.3 para.7, there is a duty on the pursuer or on any other person who has entered appearance in a consistorial action, in either the Court of Session or the sheriff court, in which proof has not begun, to give notice of any proceedings relating to, or capable of affecting the validity of, the marriage in another jurisdiction, whether within or outside Great Britain.

It has been seen in Ch.7, above, that there has been much debate in the commercial arena concerning the continuing competence, and extent of competence, in the era of European harmonised private international law rules, of the plea of *forum non conveniens* among the legal systems of the UK; and how far the plea can be utilised by UK forums in favour of a non-EU forum. The same problem arises in the context of matrimonial causes.

Mandatory sists

12–13 The 1973 Act rule is that a Scottish court must sist an action of divorce where, before proof has begun in the Court of Session, or sheriff court, a party shows that, first, an action of divorce or nullity relating to the same marriage is proceeding in a related jurisdiction (that is within England and Wales, Northern

---

[71] *Olafisoye v Olafisoye (Jurisdiction)* sub nom. *O v O* [2010] EWHC 3539 (Fam); [2011] 2 F.L.R. 553.

[72] Law Reform (Miscellaneous Provisions) (Scotland) Act 1980 s.20. See previously *Acutt v Acutt*, 1935 S.C. 525. cf. approach in Family Law Act 1986 s.47(2) and Wills Act 1963 s.2(1)(c); and *Leon v Leon* [1967] P. 275: "once seised, always seised".

[73] *Sealey v Callan* [1953] P. 135.

[74] 1973 Act s.5(5A), (6) and (6A) and Sch.1 (amended in light of the Marriage (Same Sex Couples) Act 2013 (Consequential and Contrary Provisions and Scotland) and Marriage and Civil Partnership (Scotland) Act 2014 (Consequential Provisions) Order 2014/3168 Sch.1 para.7).

[75] 1973 Act s.11 and Sch.3.

Ireland, Jersey, Guernsey (including Alderney and Sark) or Isle of Man)[76]; and, secondly, that the parties resided together after the marriage and last resided together in that other jurisdiction, and either party was habitually resident in that other jurisdiction throughout the year ending with the date on which they last resided together before that other action was begun.[77]

The mandatory stay system which applies under the 1973 Act Sch.3 para.8 does not differ in essence from that which applies per Brussels II *bis* art.19.

Discretionary sists

It is in respect of discretionary sists that the differences between the Brussels system and the residual, national system are striking. Where, before proof has begun in any consistorial action in the Court of Session or sheriff court, it appears that there are other proceedings relating to the marriage in another jurisdiction and that the balance of fairness, including convenience, between the parties is such that it is appropriate for those other proceedings to be disposed of before further steps are taken in the Scottish action, the court may if it thinks fit sist the action.[78]

12–14

There may be cultural considerations as a result of which a UK forum may think that the balance of fairness and convenience lies in permitting an action to proceed in Scotland/England, for example, if the litigant has little hope of a satisfactory remedy in the competing jurisdiction.[79] However, many cases do not exhibit a cultural clash, and in such cases the controversial issue is the extent to which personal or juridical advantage to one party ought to be taken into account in making the decision to sist/stay, or not.

The need for a judicial disposal with regard to heritable property within the Scots jurisdiction is likely to dissuade the forum from sisting.[80]

The Matrimonial and Family Proceedings Act 1984[81] changed the situation to a significant extent, in that from 1984 a party may apply to a Scots or English court for financial provision despite the existence of an antecedent foreign divorce worthy of recognition in Scotland or England. Use of the 1984 Act is subject to strict jurisdictional rules. Nevertheless, the provision was intended to result in a smaller number of divorce cases being defended, ex facie on

---

[76] 1973 Act Sch.3 para.3.

[77] 1973 Act Sch.3 para.8.

[78] 1973 Act Sch.3 para.9. See Schuz, "The Further Implications of Spiliada in Light of Recent Case Law: Stays in Matrimonial Proceedings" (1989) 38 I.C.L.Q. 946. See operation of the plea in the following (English) cases: *Shemshadfard v Shemshadfard* [1981] 1 All E.R. 726; *De Dampierre v De Dampierre* [1987] 2 All E.R. 1; *Thyssen-Bornemisza v Thyssen-Bornemisza* [1986] Fam. 1; *Breuning v Breuning* [2002] 1 F.L.R. 888; *A v S (Financial Relief after Overseas US Divorce)* [2002] EWHC 1157 (Fam); *B v B (Divorce: Stay of Foreign Proceedings)* [2002] EWHC 1711 (Fam); [2003] 1 F.L.R. 1; *O v O (Appeal against Stay: Divorce Petition)* [2003] 1 F.L.R. 192; *T v M-T* [2005] EWHC 79 (Fam); *Ella v Ella* [2007] EWCA Civ 99; *M v M* [2010] EWHC 982 (Fam); *AB v CB (Divorce and Maintenance: Discretion to Stay)* (also known as *Mittal v Mittal*) [2014] Fam 102; and *Chai v Peng* [2015] Fam Law 37.

[79] e.g. *Shemshadfard v Shemshadfard* [1981] 1 All E.R. 726; and *A v L* [2009] EWHC 1448 (Fam).

[80] *Mitchell v Mitchell*, 1993 S.L.T. 123. cf. *Butler v Butler (No.2)* [1997] 2 All E.R. 822 CA.

[81] See para.13–42, below.

jurisdiction, when the true motive is financial.[82] Some cases which pre-date the 1984 Act, and which bear upon judicial advantage, are no longer a safe guide.[83]

The rules concerning sists are a manifestation in consistorial actions of a system of allocation of jurisdiction which depends on the use of judicial discretion. It stands in contrast to the continental European preference for a system of ranking concurrent proceedings on the basis of priority of process (*lis pendens*).

Lis pendens system under Brussels regime

12–15   When the Brussels regime was extended, in operation and influence, from commercial law to family law,[84] it followed that the Brussels-preferred system of allocating jurisdiction among competing legal systems[85] should operate to solve the equivalent problem in consistorial litigation in qualifying cases. The Brussels system must apply in cases where the interested legal systems are EU Member States,[86] but difficulties have arisen in delimiting the ambit of operation of each of the EU and non-EU systems of rules (q.v.).

The rules on *lis pendens* are contained in Brussels II *bis* art.19: where proceedings relating to divorce, legal separation or marriage annulment between the same parties are brought before the courts of different Member States, the court second seised shall of its own motion[87] stay its proceedings until such time as the jurisdiction of the court first seised is established.[88] Article 16 provides a bifurcated autonomous definition of the date at which a court shall be deemed to be seised, in terms which are equivalent to art.30 of the Brussels I Regulation/art.32 of the Brussels I Recast Regulation.[89] By art.17, where a court of a Member State is seised of a case over which it has no jurisdiction per Brussels II *bis*, and over which a court of another Member State has jurisdiction

---

[82]   Consider *Quazi v Quazi* [1980] A.C. 744; and contrast *Tahir v Tahir*, 1993 S.L.T. 194 (and *Tahir v Tahir (No.2)*, 1995 S.L.T. 451).

[83]   e.g. *K v K* [1986] Fam. Law 329; and *Gadd v Gadd* [1985] 1 All E.R. 58. See *forum non conveniens* argument in context of litigation under the Matrimonial and Family Proceedings Act 1984 in *Agbaje v Agbaje* [2010] 2 All E.R. 877.

[84]   See para.1–09, above.

[85]   See para.7–53, above.

[86]   1973 Act s.11(2).

[87]   Upon proof, by the party interested, of the existence of prior proceedings in another Member State court: *Trussler v Trussler* [2003] EWCA Civ 1830.

[88]   This is a re-working of the rule contained in Brussels II art.11. The rule of priority applies whether or not the conflicting proceedings concern the same matrimonial remedy, e.g. divorce proceedings in France and an annulment petition in England.

[89]   A good example of interpretation of the priority of process rule, against the background of the technicalities of French process, is *Chorley v Chorley (Divorce: Jurisdiction)*; sub nom. *C v C (Brussels II: French Conciliation and Divorce Proceedings)* [2005] EWCA Civ 68; [2005] 1 W.L.R. 1469) in which the question posed in both conflicting jurisdictions (England and France), was whether the first phase of French divorce proceedings, termed the "*requête*", was to be taken to be an initiation of "proceedings" or a separate process. The Court of Appeal upheld the husband's argument that the commencement of the French "*requête* process" rendered the French court first seised in law. See also *Re N (Jurisdiction)*; sub nom. *NDO v JFO* [2009] I.L.Pr. 8.

by Brussels II *bis*, it shall declare of its own motion that it has no jurisdiction: it is for the forum putatively seised to decide whether it has been properly seised (and seised first[90]).

The system of priority of process in this context, mirroring that in commercial causes, is intended to "ensure that jurisdiction is swiftly established, that cases are swiftly heard and that irreconcilable judgments are avoided".[91] But the untidiness of life, compounded by different procedures in different European legal systems (perhaps even more in matrimonial than in commercial matters), has the capacity to frustrate the system.[92]

Such were the circumstances of *S v S (Brussels II Revised: Articles 19(1) and (3): Reference to ECJ)*,[93] a case arising as a result of the passivity of the husband in failing proactively to procure a decree of divorce in France following his seising of the court for judicial separation, and thereby stymieing the wife in her pursuit of a decree of divorce in England. Mostyn J. has referred to the Court of Justice questions as to the interpretation, for the purposes of art.19(1) and (3), of "established" and, in particular, whether the word "established" imports that the applicant in the first proceedings must take steps to progress those proceedings with due diligence and expedition to a resolution of the dispute (whether by the Court or by agreement), or that the applicant in the first proceedings, having once secured jurisdiction under arts 3 and 19(1), is free thereafter to take no substantive steps at all towards resolution of the first proceedings and thereby to secure a stop of the second proceedings and a stalemate in the dispute as a whole. Mostyn J. remarked that the state of affairs with which he was presented "cannot have been in the contemplation of the architects of Brussels II (in its original form) or Brussels II Revised. ...The history of this case demonstrates that none of [the] goals [of the Brussels regime] will be achieved, and that lengthy litigation in two jurisdictions potentially awaits these unfortunate parties."[94]

His Lordship criticised, reasonably, the absence in Brussels II *bis* of any discretionary transfer mechanism, akin to that which operates in the instrument, per art.15, for proceedings concerning parental responsibility matters:

> "There is no comparable provision within Brussels II Revised which allows a court to transfer a divorce to the courts of another member state on the basis that the courts of that latter member state would be best placed to hear the case. Nor to my knowledge are there any proposals to alter Brussels II Revised to incorporate such a power ... So one can see that in relation to divorce cases the anomalous situation arises that there are no powers, in contrast to civil claims and children claims, to achieve a transfer to a court which is better placed to hear the case or otherwise is a more convenient forum. It is in the face of this iron inflexibility that the parties in divorce cases engage in such extensive, expensive and futile manoeuvres as have been demonstrated in this case."[95]

---

[90] *Bentinck v Bentinck* [2007] EWCA Civ 175; [2007] I.L.Pr. 32.

[91] *S v S (Brussels II Revised: Articles 19(1) and (3): Reference to ECJ)* [2014] EWHC 3613 (Fam); [2015] Fam. Law 130, per Mostyn J at [10].

[92] e.g. *Jefferson v O'Connor* [2014] EWCA Civ 38.

[93] *S v S (Brussels II Revised: Articles 19(1) and (3): Reference to ECJ)* [2014] EWHC 3613 (Fam); [2015] Fam. Law 130.

[94] *S v S (Brussels II Revised: Articles 19(1) and (3): Reference to ECJ)* [2014] EWHC 3613 (Fam); [2015] Fam. Law 130 at [10].

[95] *S v S (Brussels II Revised: Articles 19(1) and (3): Reference to ECJ)* [2014] EWHC 3613 (Fam); [2015] Fam. Law 130 at [17]. cf. *CC v NC (Maintenance Pending Suit)* [2014] EWHC 703 (Fam);

A more technical question, but one which broadly comes within the area addressed by *S v S*, is the question of the temporal extent of seisin per arts16 and 19. The cases of *C v S (Divorce: Jurisdiction)*;[96] and *de Barge v China*,[97] show that in Italian procedure an Italian court retains seisin after the ending of separation proceedings but before divorce proceedings are instigated (by Italian law separation being a necessary precursor to divorce); on the other hand, where an Italian court had declared a petition for separation void, leaving the possibility of application to revive those proceedings, the Italian court, in the view of English law, was no longer to be regarded as seised of the matter.

Demarcation between the 1973 Act Schedule 3 paragraph 9 and Brussels II *bis* article 19

12–16   There is no difficulty in appreciating the differences between the Brussels system and that provided by the 1973 Act, and their respective strengths and weaknesses. Rather, the challenging task is to form a defensible view of which set of rules applies in hybrid or borderline cases, for example, where one spouse initiates a divorce action in the court of a Member State, founding on a ground under art.3 of Brussels II *bis*; and in response the other spouse argues that the court of a non-EU country is a more appropriate forum, and seeks a sist of the Scottish proceedings. Whilst the UK courts are experienced in using their discretion to adjudicate between contending courts on the grounds of suitability and justice, the question arises whether a Scots court would be entitled to accede to a plea for a sist in these circumstances, since it could be argued that by doing so it would be defeating the legitimate expectations of the pursuer and would be adopting a "non-Brussels" plea in litigation which the pursuer legitimately has founded as a Brussels case. This difficulty is familiar, indeed notorious, in the commercial sphere,[98] where it was decided by the ECJ in *Owusu v Jackson*[99] that it would be incompatible with the Brussels regime for the court addressed to exercise its discretion in the manner requested. The ambit of the *lis pendens* rule has been shown to be wider than at first thought.[100]

[2014] Fam. Law 96, per Mostyn J. at [13]. See, earlier, European Commission Green Paper on Applicable Law and Jurisdiction in Divorce Matters ("Rome III") (Brussels, 14 March 2005; COM(2005) 82 final; {SEC(2005) 331}), s.3.7. It is likely that in the ongoing review of Brussels II *bis* attention will be paid to the virtues and vices of the *lis pendens* system, and consideration given to the possibility of allowing, in exceptional circumstances, transfer of jurisdiction in a divorce action to a court of another Member State. On art.15, see para.14–21, below.

[96] *C v S (Divorce: Jurisdiction)* [2010] EWHC 2676 (Fam). cf. *H v W (divorce; jurisdiction)* [2010] All E.R. (D) 70 (Sep).

[97] *de Barge v China* [2014] EWHC 3975 (Fam).

[98] *Re Harrods (Buenos Aires) Ltd (No.2)* [1992] Ch 72.

[99] *Owusu v Jackson (t/a Villa Holidays Bal Inn Villas)* [2005] 1 Lloyd's Rep. 452. See para.7–82, above.

[100] The problem was perhaps capable of arising in *Breuning v Breuning* [2002] 1 F.L.R. 888, but does not appear to have been noticed by the court; though jurisdiction was laid in England one month after the coming into force of Brussels II, no diffidence was felt about the possible incompetence of acceding to a request for a discretionary stay in favour of the courts of South Africa. It has also to be said that discussion of jurisdiction focussed in that case upon domicile in the classic sense, and upon habitual residence with reference to the 1973 Act s.5, rather than upon Brussels II art.2. See also *Cook v Plummer* [2008] EWCA Civ 484.

The problem arose for determination in the matrimonial sphere in *JKN v JCN*.[101] By the date of their separation, the spouses in question were living in New York, neither having any intention to return to England. The wife's choice of English forum arose because, in the circumstances, the residence requirements for New York jurisdiction were not met. One month later, the husband issued divorce proceedings in New York, prompting his application for a stay of the English divorce proceedings brought by his wife. This presented squarely the question whether the English court competently could accede to his plea in light of *Owusu*. The judge, Theis Q.C., stated that:

"If the *Owusu* doctrine applies to [Brussels II *bis*] then the discretion to order a stay on principles of *forum non conveniens* in accordance with para 9 of Schedule 1 to the Domicile and Matrimonial Proceedings Act 1973 ('DMPA 1973') is now no longer available if the jurisdiction is founded on Article 3 [Brussels II *bis*]."[102]

In face of the wife's argument[103] that it was inconceivable that the *Owusu* doctrine could apply to the Brussels I Regulation, but not apply to Brussels II *bis*, Judge Theis nonetheless held that it was neither necessary nor desirable to extend the principle of *Owusu* to the situation of parallel matrimonial proceedings arising under Brussels II *bis*. In granting the stay, on the basis that New York was clearly the more appropriate forum, the judge proceeded on two grounds, namely, that if the principle of *Owusu* were extended such as to preclude the English court from granting a stay, there was a risk of irreconcilable judgments, because both sets of proceedings would continue; and, secondly, in the alternative, that there was no need to extend the principle of *Owusu* to Brussels II *bis* because there was no direct connection between the two Regulations, and there were differences between them, e.g. that the transfer jurisdiction with regard to children available under art.15 made it plain that the plea of *forum non conveniens* was not anathema to Brussels II *bis*.[104] The natural and preferable construction of "proceedings governed by the Council Regulation" referred to competing proceedings between Member States; consequently, the English court's discretion to stay under Sch.1 para.9 remained in place where the competing proceedings were in a non-Member State. The judge garnered support from the wording of art.19 of Brussels II *bis*, which in terms provides a mechanism to resolve conflicting consistorial proceedings arising before courts of different Member States.

The tenor of the Theis judgment is that which one might imagine would have been utilised had counsel wished to distinguish a commercial case and thereby exclude it from the operation of *Owusu*, on the basis that the Brussels I Regulation ground on which the case was laid was not art.2, but, for example, art.5.1 or 5.3; the futility of such an argument is evidenced by the absence of any attempt to advance it.

---

[101] *JKN v JCN* [2010] EWHC 843 (Fam).

[102] *JKN v JCN* [2010] EWHC 843 (Fam) at [126].

[103] Relying on *Cheshire, North and Fawcett: Private International Law*, 14th edn (2008), pp.962, 963; H.H.J. Karsten Q.C., "The State of International Family Law Issues: A View from London" [2009] I.F.L. 35; and Baroness Hale of Richmond in *Re I (A Child) (Contact Application: Jurisdiction)* [2010] 1 A.C. 319 at [40].

[104] The transfer jurisdiction, as explained, is particular to children, and Brussels II *bis*'s admission of the use of discretion in that context is consciously and carefully contained.

Although the reasoning of Theis Q.C. seems doubtful insofar as the risk of irreconcilable judgments is no different from that which pertains in the commercial sphere, her approach has been supported in the English Court of Appeal. In *AB v CB (Divorce and Maintenance: Discretion to Stay)* (also known as *Mittal v Mittal*),[105] the Court of Appeal approved the dicta of Judge Theis, in the matter of non-applicability of *Owusu*-reasoning in the consistorial context, and held that the English court had jurisdiction to stay a wife's divorce proceedings on the ground of *forum non conveniens*, in favour of proceedings already commenced by the husband in India. In a robust judgment, Lewison L.J. stated that:

> "[*Owusu*] was concerned with a different Convention regulating jurisdiction in a very different field of activity. ... Second, the legislative language under consideration in Owusu was very different from the language of [Brussels II *bis*] ... whereas the language of article 2 of [the Brussels I Regulation] is mandatory, transitive, and prescriptive, the language of article 3(1) of BIIR is intransitive and facilitative ... Third, ... *Owusu* ... could ... only be applied to BIIR by way of analogy. The analogy would have to found itself on the policy underlying both the Judgments Regulation and BIIR. But fourth, the policy objectives of the Brussels Convention (and latterly the Judgments Regulation) were different from those of BIIR. Fifth, BIIR itself recognises diversity in different legal systems, which was one of the objections in the *Owusu* case. Sixth, the policy underlying the Judgments Regulation has itself changed. The new Judgments Regulation (Parliament and Council Regulation (EU) No 1215/2012 of 12 December 2012 on jurisdiction and the recognition and enforcement of judgments in civil and commercial matters), due to operate from 10 January 2015, now recognises a discretionary power to stay proceedings."[106]

In *A v L*,[107] a hybrid case of some complexity which pre-dates *JKN v JCN*, the husband asked the court in England to withdraw his wife's English divorce petition on the ground of lack of jurisdiction, or alternatively to stay those divorce proceedings under the discretionary stay provisions of the 1973 Act, on the ground that the husband previously had commenced divorce proceedings in Cairo, and the balance of fairness and convenience between the parties made it appropriate for such a stay to be granted. In response, the wife asserted that the English forum had jurisdiction under Brussels II *bis* art.3, on the ground that she was habitually resident in England, having resided there for at least a year (indent 5), or on the ground that she had been habitually resident in England for six months and was of English domicile (indent 6); or, if the court was not satisfied as to the contentions in favour of application of art.3, that, in effect, the case was an excluded action[108] because no court of a Member State had jurisdiction, and the wife at the date of the petition was domiciled in England. Sir Mark Potter, having decided that it was plausible that the wife had acquired a domicile in England,[109] went on to conclude that since, on the facts, she was not habitually resident there, jurisdiction could not be established in England on the basis of art.3, and therefore the case fell to be determined by the national rules of

---

[105] *Mittal v Mittal* [2014] Fam 102.
[106] *Mittal v Mittal* [2014] Fam 102 at [37].
[107] *A v L* [2009] EWHC 1448 (Fam).
[108] Brussels II *bis* art.7.
[109] *A v L* [2009] EWHC 1448 (Fam) at [49].

England, which conferred jurisdiction on the court by s.5(2)(b) of the 1973 Act. That being so, on the question of conflicting jurisdiction, the law to be applied was Sch.1 para.9 to the 1973 Act, i.e. discretionary stays. Thereafter, the question became a balancing exercise as to the merits of the husband's application to stay the proceedings. Sir Mark Potter refused a stay of the English proceedings, on the argument that it would not be fair or convenient for the wife to have to litigate in Egypt, where there would be, at the outset, doubt about jurisdiction; a slow court process; and, per Egyptian choice of law rules, a Libyan applicable law under which the wife's putative financial provision as compared with her position in England would be meagre.

It is interesting to speculate on the interpretative approach likely to be taken in a suitable case by the CJEU. It is probable that that court would follow *Owusu*-reasoning and that the plea of *forum non conveniens* would be deemed incompetent when a Member State court is seised on a Brussels II *bis* ground, with the result that the priority of process rule in art.19 would apply. In *A v L*, the husband's proceedings in Egypt were commenced before the wife petitioned for divorce in England, and so would have taken priority. Even were *Owusu*-type reasoning to be extended to the matrimonial sphere, it is questionable whether art.19 should be invoked in such a scenario in favour of a Third State. It may be that this could be done only reflexively.[110] This question is of some subtlety, because it is unclear whether by giving effect to the *effet réflexe* of the Regulation, the Member State forum would be honouring the regime (by applying the *lis pendens* principle) or dishonouring it (by ceding jurisdiction to the court of a Third State when a Member State clearly is seised).

Finally, with regard to recognition of judgments, if, by virtue of the factual circumstances, no Member State court has jurisdiction under art.3, and for this reason, or for reasons of practical convenience, the parties (say, a "European" married couple who are not of common nationality or domicile, and who have been habitually resident in a non-EU state, say Iowa, USA) resort to the court of Iowa which, by its own rules, may take jurisdiction in the case, recognition in an EU state of the resultant Iowa decree will be governed, not by Brussels II *bis*, but by the pre-existing (residual) divorce recognition rules of that EU state.

Hemain injunctions

In *Hemain v Hemain*,[111] a wife petitioned for divorce in England. Her husband, having earlier petitioned for divorce in France, applied for a stay of the English proceedings. In response the wife sought from the English court an injunction to restrain her husband from pursuing legal proceedings in France until such time as his application for a stay of the English proceedings had been determined. The husband was unsuccessful in his appeal against the grant of such an injuction. The Court of Appeal held that the English court had jurisdiction to restrain a party from commencing or pursuing legal proceedings in a foreign country where such

12–17

---

[110] i.e. that which would have been done "inside" the regime, ought to be done "outside" the regime. See para.7–63, above.
[111] *Hemain v Hemain* [1988] 2 F.L.R. 388. See earlier *Thornton v Thornton* (1886) L.R. 11 P.D. 176; *Armstrong v Armstrong* [1892] P. 98; *Vardopulo* (1909) 25 T.L.R. 518; *Orr Lewis v Orr Lewis* [1949] P. 347; *Sealey v Callan* [1953] P. 135.

proceedings would be vexatious or oppressive. Such jurisdiction must be exercised with caution, and the court must be mindful of potential injustice to both parties. In the immediate case, the effect of the husband's continuation of the French proceedings was oppressive because, on the facts, it precluded the wife from pursuing her English proceedings. This decision was handed down at the same point in the decade of the 1980s as the cardinal decisions of the House of Lords and Privy Council, respectively, in *Spiliada Maritime Corp v Cansulex Ltd*[112] and *Societe Nationale Industrielle Aerospatiale (SNIA) v Lee Kui Jak*,[113] and embraces the same rationale. Here again one sees English judges chafing against the civilian regime and as in *AB v CB (Divorce and Maintenance: Discretion to Stay)* (also known as *Mittal v Mittal*),[114] seeking to restrict its operation to the minimum in consistorial cases.

Further guidance emerges from *R v R (Divorce: Hemain Injunction)*,[115] a decision of Munby J. granting the application in part, on the principle that where there are parallel proceedings in different jurisdictions, fairness requires that neither party should be allowed to litigate the substantive issues until both courts, having disposed of any preliminary issues as to jurisdiction, are ready to embark upon a consideration of substance. The *Hemain* injunction, in Munby J.'s opinion, aimed to ensure that neither party could get a "head start" on the other by manipulating both sets of proceedings to his own forensic advantage. The question in *R v R* was whether Danish proceedings unfairly delayed English proceedings.[116] It was not necessary for the wife in England to demonstrate at that stage that England was the natural forum.

The *Hemain* injunction has been developed in the English courts. There is no reported Scots case on attempted restraint of foreign consistorial proceedings, but there is no reason in principle why the remedy should not be sought in a Scots court. Certainly in the commercial sphere, there is familiarity with the remedy, usually termed restraint of foreign proceedings or simple interdict, but generally now referred to, at least in England, as anti-suit injunction.

Although available, in principle, in the Scots as well as English courts, the usual doubt arises as to the continuing competence of its use in the Brussels era, where a UK court is asked to restrain proceedings which have commenced in the courts of an EU Member State. This matter has been famously litigated in the commercial sphere in *Turner v Grovit*,[117] where the ECJ held that the prohibition by a Member State court of the commencement or continuation of legal proceedings in another Member State country is tantamount to interference with the jurisdiction of that foreign court, and hence, so far as concerned the Brussels regime, is incompatible with the principles of mutual trust and comity which underpin it. Accordingly, the regime precludes the grant by a court in a Member State of an injunction prohibiting a party to proceedings pending before it from

---

[112] *Spiliada Maritime Corp v Cansulex Ltd (The Spiliada)* [1987] A.C. 460.

[113] *Societe Nationale Industrielle Aerospatiale (SNIA) v Lee Kui Jak* [1987] A.C. 871.

[114] *Mittal v Mittal* [2014] Fam 102.

[115] *R v R (Divorce: Hemain Injunction)* [2003] EWHC 2113 (Fam).

[116] See *T v T (Hemain Injunction)*[2012] EWHC 3462 (Fam); [2014] 1 F.L.R. 96; *B v B (Divorce: Stay of Foreign Proceedings)* [2003] 1 F.L.R. 1; and *Golubovich v Golubovich* [2010] EWCA Civ 810.

[117] *Turner v Grovit* (C-159/02) [2005] 1 A.C. 101. See also *Cheshire, North and Fawcett: Private International Law*, 14th edn (2008), pp.962–965.

commencing or continuing proceedings before a court of another Member State, even where that party was acting in bad faith with a view to frustrating the proceedings in the first state.[118] It is impossible to conceive that the CJEU would adopt a different stance in the matrimonial context.

Choice of law in Scots courts

At common law, when only the courts of the husband's domicile had jurisdiction in divorce proceedings, no problem of choice of law arose because the *lex domicilii* and the *lex fori* were the same, and the potentially applicable laws necessarily coincided. Under statutory jurisdiction, and in view of the breaking of the unity of domicile rule, however, those laws may be different. It may be contrary to principle to apply the *lex fori* both to substance and procedure, but in practice, the courts in Scotland and England, once seised of jurisdiction, always apply their own domestic law to grounds of divorce.[119]

12–18

The reasons for this longstanding rule are threefold. First, there is the belief that substantive divorce rules reflect the policy of the forum at any given time[120]: "the question of the conditions under which the nuptial tie may be loosened or destroyed touches fundamental English conceptions of morality, religion and public policy."[121] Yntema viewed application of the *lex fori* as a form of legal self-defence.[122] Secondly, at common law, the coincidence of *lex fori* and *lex domicilii* meant that application of the *lex fori* to matters of status could be justified *qua* application of the *lex domicilii*. When the bases of matrimonial jurisdiction increased in number, however, the choice of law rule was left untouched, and until recently, unchallenged.[123] The third reason commonly cited in support of the *lex fori* rule in divorce is practical convenience and the financial savings that follow as a result of there being no need to offer proof of foreign law. As has been firmly expressed, however, "There is danger in these arguments. It is always easier (and cheaper) to apply the *lex fori*; but that argument is not permitted to prevail elsewhere in private international law."[124] In any event, it was the belief that departure from the *lex fori* choice of law rule would be a grave mistake that led the UK, ultimately, to decide against opting into Rome III.

---

[118] See, in detail, para.7–84, above.

[119] *Zanelli v Zanelli* (1948) 64 T.L.R. 556; and *Warrender v Warrender* (1835) 2 Cl. & F. 488. Thus a Scots court with jurisdiction in an action of divorce will apply the Divorce (Scotland) Act 1976, as amended by the Marriage and Civil Partnership (Scotland) Act 2014. cf. Approach in Cyprus, Denmark, Finland, Ireland and Sweden (House of Lords EU Committee, *Rome III – Choice of Law in Divorce: Report with Evidence*, HL Paper 272 (2006), para 8).

[120] The situation is different in relation to choice of law in nullity cases, where the ground of nullity must refer back to some earlier stage of the matrimonial history, and that stage is likely to have a conflict rule of its own (e.g. an alleged defect of form, which must be referred to the *lex loci celebrationis*, or a defect of legal capacity, which must be referred to the ante-nuptial domicile of each). See nullity, para.12–48 et seq.

[121] M Wolff, *Private International Law* (2nd edn) (1950), pp.373–374. cf. P.M. North (1980) 1 *Hague Recueil* 9 at 87–88.

[122] H.E. Yntema, "'Autonomy' in Choice of Law" (1952) 1(4) American Journal of Comparative Law 342 at 358.

[123] See, however, academic discussion in P.M. North (1980) 1 *Hague Recueil* 9 at 87–88.

[124] P.M. North (1980) 1 *Hague Recueil* 9 at 164.

Rome III[125]

12–19   Council Regulation (EU) No.1259/2010 of 20 December 2010 implementing enhanced cooperation in the area of the law applicable to divorce and legal separation ("Rome III") came into effect on 21 June 2012 in "participating Member States", of which the UK is not one.[126] There is an option for non-participating states subsequently to accept the instrument, but no enthusiasm in the UK for such a course of action. Rome III is the only fruit of difficult debate and negotiation stemming from the European Commission's 2005 Green Paper on applicable law and jurisdiction in divorce matters.[127] By 2008, a divergence of view across Member States as to substantive divorce law, from the liberal to the conservative, had become apparent, making it impossible for certain states to accept the Commission's Proposal for a Council Regulation amending Regulation (EC) No.2201/2003 as regards jurisdiction and introducing rules concerning applicable law in matrimonial matters.[128] This proved problematic insofar as the Proposal related to judicial co-operation in civil matters having "aspects relating to family law", a legal basis requiring unanimity of decision-making. It was clear, however, that a significant number of Member States strongly favoured the settlement of harmonised rules on applicable law. By June 2008, it was concluded that there was no unanimity among Member States to proceed, and that insurmountable difficulties existed with regard to introducing a Regulation. Shortly thereafter nine Member States addressed a request to the Commission, indicating that they wished to establish enhanced co-operation among themselves in the restricted area of applicable law.[129] In March 2010, the Commission responded to that request by producing a Proposal for a Council Regulation implementing enhanced cooperation in the area of the law applicable to divorce and legal separation,[130] and an accompanying Proposal for a Council Decision authorising such enhanced co-operation.[131] The authority for the Proposal for a Council Decision rested upon art.329(1) of the Treaty on the Functioning of the European Union, and the Proposal for a Council Regulation on art.81(1) of the TFEU. The Proposal for a Council Decision admitted[132] that, from the institutional standpoint, enhanced co-operation was a better outcome than would

---

[125] See A.Fiorini, "Rome III – Choice of Law in Divorce: Is the Europeanization of Family Law Going Too Far?" (2008) International Journal of Law, Policy and the Family 178; and A.Fiorini, "Harmonizing the Law Applicable to Divorce and Legal Separation – Enhanced Co-operation as the Way Forward?" (2010) 59 I.C.L.Q. 1143.

[126] The UK exercised its right not to opt-in to the proposed measure: Hansard 18 Apr 2007: Col WS7. For background, see House of Lords EU Committee (2005-06) "Rome III – Choice of Law in Divorce, Report with Evidence" (2006).

[127] Green Paper on Applicable Law and Jurisdiction in Divorce Matters (March 2005, COM (2005) 82 final).

[128] COM (2006) 399 final. See also Commission Staff Working Document, Annex to the Proposal (19 July 2006) (JUSTCIV 174, 11818/06).

[129] Article 20(2) of the TEU establishes that the enhanced co-operation device can be adopted by the Council only as a last resort, "when it has established that the objectives of such cooperation cannot be attained within a reasonable period by the Union as a whole, and that at least nine Member States participate in it": Proposal for a Council Decision authorising enhanced cooperation in the area of the law applicable to divorce and legal separation COM(2010) 104 final/2, para.10.

[130] COM(2010) 105 final (hereinafter "Proposal for a Council Regulation").

[131] COM(2010)104final/2 (hereinafter "Proposal for a Council Decision").

[132] Proposal for a Council Decision art.30.

be the negotiating by the interested Member States of a freestanding international agreement, because even if the acts adopted in the enhanced co-operation procedure can bind only participating Member States, they fall under EU control, and specifically under the jurisdiction of the CJEU.

The result is that the current framework of European rules for matrimonial proceedings extends to harmonised rules of jurisdiction and judgment recognition and enforcement (Brussels II *bis*), which bind all Member States (except Denmark); and harmonised rules of applicable law for divorce and separation (Rome III), which bind only the limited number of participating Member States[133]—two-speed Europe in action, or inaction, as the case may be; a twin-track area of freedom, security and justice.[134] The British and Irish interests are always protected by their default opt-out position.[135] From the point of view of non-participating Member States which do not enjoy the benefit of an automatic opt-out position, the enhanced co-operation procedure is advantageous in allowing them to preserve their autonomy. Hence, although the Commission frankly admitted its own interests in this manner of proceeding, there are, it seems, advantages from the perspective of participating and non-participating Member States alike.

In terms of substantive provision the alleged advantages of Rome III include the strengthening of legal certainty and predictability, allied, it is said, with flexibility (normally the antithesis of certainty); flexibility is said to be introduced by permitting a degree of party autonomy, a characteristic feature of recent EU harmonisation instruments in applicable law. The specific apologia for the Rome III Proposal was that by reducing the possibility of one party's being prejudiced by the "random" application to the grounds of divorce of the choice of law rule of any given forum (whatever it may be), there would be applied to the dissolution of the marriage a law with which both spouses have some connection.

Scope of instrument

Rome III shall apply, in situations involving a conflict of laws, to divorce and legal separation (art.1.1), and so applies only in an "international situation", viz. where the spouses are of different nationalities or live in different Member States, or in a Member State of which at least one of them is not a national. Hence it is not open to a couple divorcing in a participating state to utilise the provisions of Rome III if their divorce is a "domestic" one[136] (subject to art.16). The instrument is confined to the substantive grounds of divorce, and by art.1.2 shall not apply to the following matters, inter alia, even if they arise merely as a preliminary

12–20

---

[133] Austria, Bulgaria, France, Spain, Italy, Luxembourg, Hungary, Romania, Slovenia, Germany, Belgium, Latvia, Malta and Portugal. Greece, which had been one of the petitioners, withdrew its request to participate in the instrument on (Rome III recital (6)). The legal systems of those 14 Member States (with the possible exception of Malta) in their national conflict rules on divorce already accepted the potential application of foreign law.

[134] cf. and contrast the position of compliant and non-compliant Member States with regard to Regulation (EU) No.650/2012 of the European Parliament and of the Council on jurisdiction, applicable law, recognition and enforcement of decisions and acceptance and enforcement of authentic instruments in matters of succession and on the creation of a European Certificate of Succession ("Rome IV"): para.18–42, below.

[135] Protocol 21 on the Position of the UK and Ireland [2008] O.J. C115/295.

[136] Proposal for a Council Regulation, Explanatory Memorandum para.6.

question within the context of divorce or legal separation proceedings: the existence, validity or recognition of a marriage; the annulment of a marriage; the property consequences of the marriage; or maintenance obligations. The Regulation's scope is restricted to applicable law, and does not affect the application of Brussels II *bis* (art.2).

Principle of universal application

12–21 The main problem for the UK in considering whether or not to participate in Rome III was that it adopts a principle of universal application (art.4), whereby the divorce law of a participating Member State, or of a non-participating Member State, or of a Third State may require to be applied through operation of the rules which enjoin the honouring of party choice.[137] The foreign divorce law may be more stringent than the forum's own law (e.g. requiring evidence of fault), or more liberal (e.g. permitting divorce upon unilateral request), and offence to public policy, feasibly, could be triggered in both scenarios. The UK had particular concern regarding this principle, especially regarding the possibility of party choice (q.v.) of a Third State law.[138]

Exclusion of renvoi

12–22 By art.11 any reference in Rome III to the law of a State means the rules of law in force in that State other than its rules of private international law.

Law applicable to divorce and legal separation – choice of applicable law by parties

12–23 Recital (15) of Rome III expressly promotes the principle of party autonomy in divorce and legal separation by giving parties a limited possibility to choose the law applicable to their divorce or legal separation. Accordingly, in the cascade of choice of law rules, priority is given to party autonomy.

The primary rule, contained in art.5 (choice of applicable law by the parties), provides that the spouses may agree to designate the law applicable to divorce and legal separation from a limited list of potentially applicable laws, viz.: the law of the state where they are habitually resident at the time the agreement is concluded[139]; or the law of the state where they were last habitually resident, insofar as one of them still resides there at the time the agreement is concluded; or the law of the state of nationality of either spouse at the time the agreement is concluded; or the law of the forum. Parties, therefore, are empowered to choose as the governing law only the law of a country with which they have a "special

---

[137] Rome III recital (12) and art.4.

[138] For example, if W, of English domicile and Iranian background, married to H, of Iranian domicile, were prevailed upon by H to agree to the application of Iranian divorce law to regulate their divorce, to be heard in an English court, it is quite possible that the substantive applicable law would offend the public policy of the forum. However, the initiative would lie with W to persuade the forum of the public policy objection, placing a new burden on the respondent party, and a necessary but possibly distasteful onus on the forum to adjudge the rule of foreign law in terms of substantive policy.

[139] See issues in respect of time, below.

connection"[140] at the time their choice is exercised, or the law of the forum. *Ex facie* harmonisation of applicable law rules in the manner permitted brings certainty, but interpretation and application of an amorphous connecting factor such as habitual residence is inherently uncertain.

An agreement as to choice of law may be concluded and modified at any time up to the seising of the court, except that such a choice may also be made during the course of the proceedings if the *lex fori* so provides. By art.6, the existence and validity of an agreement as to choice of law shall be determined by the putative applicable law per Rome III. The rules concerning formal validity are contained in art.7.

Restrictions on choice of law

Choice is permitted only of "State" law.[141] Acceptance of the principle of party autonomy, even amongst participating Member States, has not extended so far as to permit parties to evade the operation of civil (secular) law, by opting into, e.g. the religious (i.e. non-State) law of his/her choosing. In no context does UK law permit bespoke application of a party's religious law (unless that law happens to coincide with, i.e. constitutes, the law of his/her domicile), and reference to an individual's personal law is always a reference only to the civil law (which, however, in many instances, will demonstrate sensitivity to religious issues).

The UK fear engendered by the prospect of having to apply a Third State law was not mitigated by the inclusion of other restrictions on choice. First, the law chosen by the spouses under Rome III must be consonant with the fundamental rights recognised by the Treaties and the Charter of Fundamental Rights of the European Union.[142] Secondly, since it is stated that the informed choice of both spouses is a basic principle of the Regulation, "Each spouse should know exactly what are the legal and social implications of the choice of applicable law."[143] Potentially artificial though this may be (for how would spousal knowledge be tested, or affirmed?), the Regulation states that, "[t]he possibility of choosing the applicable law by common agreement should be without prejudice to the rights[144] of, and equal opportunities for, the two spouses. Hence judges in the participating Member States should be aware of the importance of an informed choice on the part of the two spouses concerning the legal implications of the choice-of-law agreement concluded."[145]

12–24

Law applicable to divorce and legal separation—applicable law in the absence of choice by parties

In the absence of party choice of law, art.8 subjects the divorce or legal separation to the law of the state where the spouses are habitually resident at the time the court is seised; failing which, the law of the state where the spouses were last

12–25

---

[140] Rome III recital (16).
[141] Likewise, the applicable law in the absence of choice must be that of a State: art.8.
[142] Rome III recital (16).
[143] Rome III recital (18).
[144] By what law?
[145] Rome III recital (18).

habitually resident, provided that the period of residence did not end more than one year before the court was seised, insofar as one of the spouses continues to reside in that state at the time the court is seised; failing which, the law of the common nationality at the time the court is seised; failing which, the *lex fori*.

Application of the law of the forum

12–26   If it should be found that the applicable law under arts 5 or 8 makes no provision for divorce, or does not treat the spouses equally, art.10 provides that the law of the forum shall apply. While art.10 is useful in allaying the misgivings of "liberal" states, art.12 (public policy) provides a more general exit route for any forum having a fundamental objection of any kind, i.e. from any perspective, to the ground of divorce which it is directed to apply by means of these choice of law rules. Furthermore, art.13 provides that nothing in the Regulation obliges the courts of a participating Member State whose law does not provide for divorce, or does not deem the marriage in question to be valid, to pronounce a divorce by virtue of application of the Regulation.

Recognition of foreign divorces

Recognition of foreign decrees of divorce at common law

12–27   The basic principle underlying the recognition of foreign divorces at common law was universality of status, based upon the connecting factor of domicile.

At common law, a foreign decree of divorce which had been granted by a court of competent jurisdiction and was not subject to challenge on any of certain grounds (no notice, fraud, duress, ground of divorce against public policy) would be regarded as having the same effect in Scotland as a decree granted by the Court of Session. A foreign decree of divorce granted by the court of the husband's domicile was recognised at common law as emanating from the court regarded as pre-eminently appropriate and, being equivalent to a decree in rem,[146] received extraterritorial recognition. The number of courts regarded as competent increased gradually, from the court of the husband's domicile,[147] a court recognised by that of the husband's domicile,[148] through *Travers v Holley*,[149] to the decree of a court the jurisdictional basis of which was similar to that of the English or Scots court (even though the foreign court had not proceeded on that ground).[150] English and Scots courts also recognised decrees of divorce granted

---

[146] cf. *Salvesen (otherwise Von Lorang) v Administrator of Austrian Property* [1927] A.C. 641, per Viscount Dunedin at 662, 663 in the matter of decrees of nullity.

[147] *Le Mesurier* [1895] A.C. 517; *Shaw v Gould* (1868) L.R. 3 H.L. 55.

[148] *Armitage v Att Gen* [1906] P. 135; but not further—*Mountbatten v Mountbatten (No.1)* [1959] P. 43.

[149] *Travers v Holley* [1953] P. 246, in terms of which recognition of a New South Wales decree was granted where the foreign court took jurisdiction on grounds similar to those available in the circumstances, mutatis mutandis, in England.

[150] In divorce recognition the forum addressed is not concerned with the grounds upon which the foreign court assumed jurisdiction (*Robinson-Scott v Robinson-Scott* [1958] P. 71), but rather with whether the foreign court is competent in terms of UK recognition rules. The inroad made upon this principle by *Travers v Holley* [1953] P. 246, is now historical.

in the Dominions or Colonies where the courts assumed jurisdiction under the Indian and Colonial Divorce Jurisdiction Acts. The common law development culminated in the famous case of *Indyka*[151] in which the House of Lords, by a variety of lines of reasoning including wife's nationality, wife's residence, and real and substantial connection of the marriage with the court which granted the decree, recognised a Czechoslovakian decree of divorce, even though by the date of that decree and at the date of the English litigation the husband was domiciled in England. It could be said that this decision reinstated the so-called ground of matrimonial domicile which had been in abeyance since *Le Mesurier* in 1895. The fame and influence of *Indyka* was short-lived because deliberations on the subject of divorce recognition conducted at the Eleventh Session of the Hague Conference resulted in a degree of international agreement, implemented in the United Kingdom by the Recognition of Divorces and Legal Separations Act 1971. The 1971 Act was said to retain the liberality of *Indyka*, but to produce greater certainty than had obtained at common law after *Indyka*.

The 1971 Act was repealed *in toto* by the Family Law Act 1986.

Recognition of overseas (non-EU) divorces, etc. under the Family Law Act 1986[152]

Although recognition in Scotland of a divorce granted by a court of an EU Member State (apart from Denmark) depends now upon the scheme of jurisdiction and recognition contained in Brussels II *bis*, the Family Law Act 1986 continues to regulate recognition of Danish decrees, and non-EU decrees. In the absence of any legislative initiative by the Scottish and/or Westminster Parliaments to expand on the guidance given in art.66 of Brussels II *bis*, in relation to Member States having two or more legal systems, it is presumed that the Family Law Act 1986 s.44(2) (effectively providing a system of mutual recognition) still regulates the matter of recognition in one part of the UK of a consistorial decree granted in another part.   **12–28**

In terms of s.44(1) of the 1986 Act, no divorce or annulment obtained in any part of the British Islands shall be regarded as effective in any part of the United Kingdom unless granted by a court of civil jurisdiction. Under s.44(2), subject to s.51 of the Act, the validity of any divorce, annulment or judicial separation granted by a court of civil jurisdiction in any part of the British Islands shall be recognised throughout the United Kingdom.[153] No extrajudicial divorces pronounced in the UK can be recognised.

Overseas divorces (annulments and legal separations)

Sections 44–51 apply only to overseas divorces, etc. obtained outside the EU, and in Denmark.[154] The Family Law Act 1986, in its treatment of the recognition of   **12–29**

---

[151] *Indyka* [1969] 1 A.C. 33. Scots cases following this trend shortly thereafter are *Galbraith v Galbraith*, 1971 S.C. 65; and *Bain v Bain*, 1971 S.C. 146.
[152] For the rules of recognition of non-EU divorces of same sex marriages, see para.12–60, below.
[153] Note intra-UK mutual recognition (also found in 1971 Act), subject to s.51(1) and (2) (prior irreconcilable decision or "no marriage to terminate"). Contrast *Shaw v Gould* (1868) L.R. 3 H.L. 55.
[154] 1986 Act s.45(2).

non-EU consistorial decrees, differentiates between divorces, annulments or legal separations obtained by means of proceedings (s.46(1)) and divorces, annulments or legal separations[155] obtained otherwise than by means of proceedings (s.46(2)).

In terms of s.46:

"(1) The validity of an overseas divorce, annulment or legal separation obtained by means of proceedings shall be recognised if—

    (a) the divorce, annulment or legal separation is effective under the law of the country in which it was obtained[156]; and

    (b) at the relevant date either party to the marriage—

        (i) was habitually resident in the country in which the divorce, annulment or legal separation was obtained; or

        (ii) was domiciled in that country; or

        (iii) was a national of that country.

(2) The validity of an overseas divorce, annulment or legal separation obtained otherwise than by means of proceedings shall be recognised if—

    (a) the divorce, annulment or legal separation is effective under the law of the country in which it was obtained;

    (b) at the relevant date—

        (i) each party to the marriage was domiciled in that country; or

        (ii) either party to the marriage was domiciled in that country and the other party was domiciled in a country under whose law the divorce, annulment or legal separation is recognised as valid; and

    (c) neither party to the marriage was habitually resident in the United Kingdom throughout the period of one year immediately preceding that date.

(3) In this section 'the relevant date' means—

    (a) in the case of an overseas divorce, annulment or legal separation obtained by means of proceedings, the date of the commencement of the proceedings;

    (b) in the case of an overseas divorce, annulment or legal separation obtained otherwise than by means of proceedings, the date on which it was obtained."

A stricter test for recognition applies in the case of divorces, etc. obtained otherwise than by means of proceedings because there is concern that before such divorces may be recognised in the UK, there must be a strong connection between both parties and a legal culture which provides such relatively informal methods of divorce. Hence, s.46(2) provides that the divorce must be effective under the law of the country in which it was obtained and at the relevant date (i.e. the date on which it was obtained)[157] each party must have been domiciled[158] in that country or either party domiciled in that country and the other party domiciled in a country the law of which would recognise the divorce as valid, and

---

[155] See para.12–56 relating to nullities.

[156] *Kellman v Kellman* [2000] 1 F.L.R. 785; *Emin v Yeldag* [2002] 1 F.L.R. 956; *H v H (Validity of Japanese Divorce)* [2006] EWHC 2989 (Fam); [2007] 1 F.L.R. 1318; and *H v H (Talaq Divorce)* [2007] EWHC 2945 (Fam).

[157] See 1986 Act s.46(3)(b).

[158] See 1986 Act s.46(5).

neither party[159] must have been habitually resident in the UK throughout the period of one year immediately preceding the date on which the divorce was obtained.

With regard to the meaning in this context of the connecting factor of domicile, s.46(5) provides that a party to a marriage shall be treated as domiciled in a country if he was domiciled in that country either according to the law of that country in family matters or according to the law of the part of the United Kingdom in which the question of recognition arises. It is unusual for the forum to yield to any other law in the interpretation of connecting factors generally, and of this factor in particular.[160]

Conversion of judicial separation

Section 47 regulates cross-proceedings and divorces following legal separations. With regard to the conversion of legal separations into divorces, s.47(2) provides that where a legal separation, the validity of which is entitled to recognition by virtue of the provisions of s.46 of the Act, is converted, in the country in which it was obtained, into a divorce which is effective under the law of that country, the validity of the divorce shall be recognised in Scotland whether or not it would itself be entitled to recognition by virtue of that provision.[161] **12–30**

Proof of facts relevant to recognition

For the purpose of ss.46 and 47 of the 1986 Act, s.48 provides that any finding of fact on the basis of which jurisdiction was assumed in the proceedings shall, if both parties to the marriage took part in the proceedings, be conclusive evidence of the fact found; and in any other case, shall be sufficient proof unless the contrary is shown.[162] **12–31**

Refusal to recognise

Section 51 narrates the bases on which recognition may be refused: **12–32**

> "(1)   Subject to section 52 of this Act, recognition of the validity of—
>
> (a)   a divorce, annulment or judicial separation granted by a court of civil jurisdiction in any part of the British Islands, or
>
> (b)   an overseas divorce, annulment or legal separation,
>
> may be refused in any part of the United Kingdom if the divorce, annulment or separation was granted or obtained at a time when it was irreconcilable with a decision determining the question of the subsistence or validity of the marriage of the parties previously given (whether before or after the commencement of this Part) by a court of civil jurisdiction in that part of the

---

[159] The prior rule had withheld recognition only if both parties had been habitually resident in the UK for one year before pronouncement of divorce (1973 Act s.16) and so the current formulation of this rule is stricter.

[160] cf. *Re Annesley* [1926] Ch. 692.

[161] See analogous provision in Brussels II *bis* art.5.

[162] By s.48(2) a "finding of fact" includes a finding that either party to the marriage (a) was habitually resident in the country in which the divorce, annulment or legal separation was obtained; (b) under the law of that country was domiciled there; or (c) was a national of that country.

United Kingdom or by a court elsewhere recognised or entitled to be recognised in that part of the United Kingdom.[163]

(2) Subject to section 52 of this Act, recognition of the validity of—

    (a) a divorce or judicial separation granted by a court of civil jurisdiction in any part of the British Islands, or

    (b) an overseas divorce or legal separation,

may be refused in any part of the United Kingdom if the divorce or separation was granted or obtained at a time when, according to the law of that part of the United Kingdom (including its rules of private international law and the provisions of this Part), there was no subsisting marriage between the parties.

(3) Subject to section 52 of this Act, recognition by virtue of section 45 of this Act of the validity of an overseas divorce, annulment or legal separation may be refused if—

    (a) in the case of divorce, annulment or legal separation obtained by means of proceedings, it was obtained—

        (i) without such steps having been taken for giving notice of the proceedings to a party to the marriage as, having regard to the nature of the proceedings and all the circumstances, should reasonably have been taken[164]; or

        (ii) without a party to the marriage having been given (for any reason other than lack of notice) such opportunity to take part in the proceedings as, having regard to those matters, he should reasonably have been given; or

    (b) in the case of a divorce, annulment or legal separation obtained otherwise than by means of proceedings—

        (i) there is no official document certifying that the divorce, annulment or legal separation is effective under the law of the country in which it was obtained; or

        (ii) where either party to the marriage was domiciled in another country at the relevant date, there is no official document certifying that the divorce, annulment or legal separation is recognised as valid under the law of that other country; or

    (c) in either case, recognition of the divorce, annulment or legal separation would be manifestly contrary to public policy."[165]

The ground of a foreign divorce is potentially or in theory a ground for non-recognition, but in practice UK courts have accepted foreign divorces on grounds unknown to them.[166]

---

[163] *Shagroon v Sharbatly (also known as W v H)* [2012] EWCA Civ 1507; [2013] Fam. 267; and *K v A* [2015] Fam Law 137.

[164] *Duhur-Johnson v Duhur-Johnson* [2005] 2 F.L.R. 1042; and *X v Y* [2015] EWHC 1462 (Fam). Cf. generally *Akhtar v Rafiq* [2006] 1 F.L.R. 27.

[165] See, e.g. *Ahmed v Ahmed*, 2006 S.L.T. 135; *Abbassi v Abbassi* [2006] EWCA Civ 355 (talaq documentation alleged by the wife to have been forged; decision of judge of first instance to remit the case to be determined by a court in Islamabad upheld by the Court of Appeal); *Golubovich v Golubovich* [2010] EWCA Civ 810; *NP v KRP (Recognition of Foreign Divorce)* [2013] Fam. Law 1385; and *Ivleva (formerly Yates) v Yates* [2014] EWHC 554 (Fam). Older cases, decided in relation to the 1971 Act s.8 still may be helpful: *Hack v Hack* (1976) 6 Fam. Law 177; *Newmarch v Newmarch* [1978] 1 All E.R. 1; *Joyce v Joyce and O'Hare* [1979] 2 All E.R. 156; and *Kendall v Kendall* [1977] Fam. 208.

[166] *Perin v Perin*, 1950 S.L.T. 51; *Pemberton v Hughes* [1899] 1 Ch. 781. It is otherwise if coercion is used: *Re Meyer* [1971] P. 298. But possibly means and ground may merge in the case of a person divorced against his will (and against his spouse's will) for reasons such as alleged heresy or apostasy (Muslim hisbah divorces). cf. *Viswalingham v Viswalingham* (1980) 1 E.L.R. 15 CA.

Declarators

Although a decree in rem stands on its own strength and requires no further **12–33** approbation in any legal system where recognition or application is desired, nevertheless in order to test the validity of a foreign decree of divorce in a case of doubt, the proper procedure is not to raise an action of declarator with a crave specifically directed to the validity of the foreign decree, but rather a declarator as to the status of the petitioner, e.g. that the petitioner is free to marry.[167] The Registration of Births, Deaths and Marriages (Scotland) Acts apply only to births, deaths and marriages having a Scottish locus, but even if a marriage took place in Scotland, a foreign decree of divorce cannot be registered or made effective indirectly in such a manner.[168]

Though strictly, a foreign consistorial decree is equivalent to a decree in rem, for the avoidance of doubt, the Family Law (Scotland) Act 2006 has endowed the Scots courts with power to grant such declarators. In terms of s.37 of that Act, amending the Domicile and Matrimonial Proceedings Act 1973, jurisdiction to grant declarator of recognition of decrees of divorce, nullity or separation granted outwith a Member State of the EU, is given to the Court of Session and sheriff court.[169]

Recognition of overseas (non-EU) extrajudicial divorces

Not all foreign divorces are judicial: it may be found rather that a divorce has **12–34** been obtained by legislative process,[170] or by religious or other[171] process, the most common of which are the Muslim talaq (or talak) and the Jewish ghet[172] (or gett). Initial non-recognition by the English courts of extrajudicial divorces[173] gave way quickly to a less strict attitude, which would recognise such divorces provided that they were competent by the law of the husband's domicile,[174] no matter that the marriage[175] and/or the divorce[176] had taken place in England.[177]

---

[167] *Arnott v Lord Advocate*, 1932 S.L.T. 46; *McKay v Walls*, 1951 S.L.T. (Notes) 6; *Sim v Sim*, 1968 S.L.T. (Notes) 15.

[168] *Smart v Registrar General*, 1954 S.C. 81.

[169] cf. for England, Family Law Act 1986 s.55. See, e.g. *Abbasi v Abbasi* [2006] EWCA Civ 355; *NP v KRP (Recognition of Foreign Divorce)* [2013] Fam Law 1385; *K v A* [2015] Fam Law 137; and *N v D* [2015] EWFC 28.

[170] *Manning v Manning* [1958] P. 112.

[171] *Lee v Lau* [1964] 2 All E.R. 248 gives an example of the Chinese chop (document signed by parties agreeing to dissolve their marriage was authenticated by the "chop" or seal); *Quazi* [1979] 3 All E.R. 897 contains reference to a Thai 'khula'; and *H v H (Validity of Japanese Divorce)* [2006] EWHC 2989 (Fam); [2007] 1 F.L.R. 1318 refers to the Japanese "kyogi rikon" administrative procedure.

[172] See D. Levine, "Divorce Law, the Jewish Client and the Get", 2009 S.L.T. (News) 61; and *AI v MT* [2013] EWHC 100 (Fam).

[173] *R. v Hammersmith Superintendent Registrar of Marriages Ex p. Mir-Anwaruddin* [1917] 1 K.B. 634.

[174] See, e.g. *Maher v Maher* [1951] 2 All E.R. 37; and *Russ v Russ* [1963] P. 87. The decision in *Makouipour v Makouipour*, 1967 S.L.T. 101 suggests that the Scots rule was the same as the English one.

[175] *Har-Shefi v Har-Shefi (No.2)* [1953] P. 220.

[176] *Sasson v Sasson* [1924] 1 A.C. 1007.

The test of recognition against the law of the husband's domicile was retained by ss.2–6 of the 1971 Act. As has been noted, the 1971 Act was repealed *in toto* by the Family Law Act 1986.[178] Nevertheless, not only have some interpretative decisions[179] survived to guide later cases, but also the interpretation of the word "proceedings" handed down in two important cases decided under the 1971 Act (*Quazi*[180] and, by way of contrast, *Chaudhary*[181]) remain as the key interpretative guidance to distinguish between cases falling respectively now under the Family Law Act 1986 s.46(1) and under s.46(2). In *Chaudhary*, concerning a "bare" talaq, Oliver L.J. attempted to make such a distinction and produced a form of words which often is quoted:

> "In the context . . . of a solemn change of status, it does seem to me that the word ['proceedings'] must import a degree of formality and at least the involvement of some agency, whether lay or religious, of or recognised by the state, having a function that is more than simply probative, although *Quazi v Quazi* clearly shows that it need have no power of veto."[182]

In *Quazi*, the House of Lords held that compliance with the Pakistan Muslim Family Laws Ordinance 1961 involving notification to the wife and to a public authority and the compulsory elapse of a 90-day reconciliation period (but with no compulsion to attempt to achieve reconciliation), amounted to "proceedings", although essentially the divorce was a unilateral act by the husband and was a remedy which no Pakistani public authority could deny him.

The subject of recognition of overseas extrajudicial divorces emanating from outside the EU resolves itself into a consideration of whether the religious divorce can be said to be a "proceedings" divorce or an "otherwise than by means of proceedings" divorce; whether, if the latter, s.46(2) (jurisdiction) and s.51(3)(b) (authentication) can be satisfied; whether s.51(3)(c) (public policy) can be said to have any application; and finally whether the Matrimonial and Family Proceedings Act 1984 has any part to play in the situation.[183] Section 51(3)(b), which applies only to non-proceedings divorces, states that recognition may be

---

[177] In *Qureshi v Qureshi* [1972] Fam. 173 both the marriage and the religious divorce, which was recognised by the English court, took place in England. By this point in the development of the subject area, it was felt that legislative intervention was necessary.

[178] *Maples v Maples* [1987] 3 All E.R. 188 made clear that no extrajudicial divorce can be tested for recognition in the UK except by reference to the terms of the 1986 Act.

[179] *Hack v Hack* (1976) 6 Fam. Law 177; *Newmarch v Newmarch* [1978] 1 All E.R. 1; *Joyce v Joyce and O'Hare* [1979] 2 All E.R. 156; *Kendall v Kendall* [1977] Fam. 208.

[180] *Quazi v Quazi* [1979] 3 All E.R. 897. cf. *Ahmed v Ahmed*, 2006 S.L.T. 135; *Abbassi v Abbassi* [2006] EWCA Civ 355; and *H v H (Talaq Divorce)* [2007] EWHC 2945 (Fam).

[181] *Chaudhary* [1984] 3 All E.R. 1017.

[182] *Chaudhary* [1984] 3 All E.R. 1017, per Oliver L.J. at 1031 (distinguishing, at 1030, "proceedings" from "procedure" or "ritual", and the latter two terms from each other). See also *El-Fadl v El-Fadl* [2000] 1 F.L.R. 175, wherein there was sufficient to constitute proceedings for the purposes of s.46(1), on a *Chaudhary* test, with the consequence that a talaq performed in accordance with Lebanese law, and registered with a Sharia court in Lebanon, was afforded recognition by an English court, despite the fact that the wife had remained in ignorance for 16 years of the occurrence of the divorce; pragmatism was the pre-eminent policy. cf. *Newmarch v Newmarch* [1978] 1 All E.R. 1; *Igra v Igra* [1951] P. 404; *H v H (Validity of Japanese Divorce)* [2006] EWHC 2989 (Fam); [2007] 1 F.L.R. 1318; *H v S (Recognition of Overseas Divorce)* [2012] Fam. Law 271; and *NP v KRP (Recognition of Foreign Divorce)* [2013] Fam. Law 1385.

[183] *Tahir v Tahir*, 1993 S.L.T. 194. See para.13–42 et seq., below.

refused if there is no official document certifying that the divorce is effective under the law of the country in which it was obtained or, where either party was domiciled in another country at the relevant date, there is no official document certifying that the divorce is recognised as valid under the law of that other country. Opinion in the religious communities whence such divorces spring are thought not to be convinced of the rightness of the "proceedings" distinction, nor of the feasibility of obtaining official certificates to satisfy s.51(3)(b). Section 51(3)(a), which concerns itself with challenges on grounds of lack of notice or lack of opportunity to take part in the case of "proceedings" divorces, was thought not suited to non-judicial divorces.

The impulse behind the *Quazi* litigation was financial[184] in that, if the Pakistan talaq was recognised, the British court, as the law then stood, could not add financial provisions to it. Now, in terms of the Matrimonial and Family Proceedings Act 1984, such provision may be made after any divorce or annulment in a case where the Scots or English court satisfies the strict terms of that Act. Consequently the validity of religious divorces is less often the subject of debate.

One notable development in English conflict rules was the enactment of the Divorce (Religious Marriages) Act 2002. By s.1 an insertion was made (s.10A) in the Matrimonial Causes Act 1973, to the following effect: if a decree of divorce has been granted but not made absolute, and the parties to the marriage: (a) were married in accordance with: (i) the usages of the Jews; or (ii) any other prescribed religious usages; and (b) must co-operate if the marriage is to be dissolved; then on the application of either party, the court may order that a decree of divorce is not to be made absolute until a declaration made by both parties that they have taken such steps as are required to dissolve the marriage in accordance with those usages is produced to the court. Such an order may be made by the court only if it is satisfied that in all the circumstances of the case it is just and reasonable to do so. The order may be revoked at any time.

The background to this legislation is the importance attached to religious divorce in certain religious laws, particularly those of Judaism, where if the religious divorce is not obtained, the wife, in the view of her religion, would have the status of a "chained woman" (agunah), a status which forbids her re-marriage under Jewish law, and holds any issue of a subsequent union as illegitimate unto the tenth generation.[185]

The Family Law (Scotland) Act 2006 s.15[186] makes equivalent provision for Scotland. It amends the Divorce (Scotland) Act 1976 s.3, to permit postponement of the grant of a decree of divorce where religious impediment to re-marry exists. If, in any Scots divorce action in which irretrievable breakdown of a marriage has been established, one party ("the applicant") is prevented from entering into a religious marriage by virtue of a requirement of the religion of that marriage [sic], and the other party to the divorce can act so as to remove, or enable or contribute to the removal of, the impediment which prevents that marriage, that Scots divorce court may, upon application by the applicant, and if satisfied that it is just

---

[184] cf. *Ahmed v Ahmed*, 2006 S.L.T. 135.
[185] Levine, "Divorce Law, the Jewish Client and the Get", 2009 S.L.T. (News) 61.
[186] See also the Divorce (Religious Bodies) (Scotland) Regulations 2006 (SSI 2006/253).

and reasonable to do so, postpone the grant of decree until it is satisfied that the other party has so acted to remove the impediment, etc.

Transnational divorces

12–35   In terms of s.44(1) of the 1986 Act, no divorce or annulment obtained in any part of the British Islands shall be regarded as effective in any part of the UK unless granted by a court of civil jurisdiction.[187] Should the divorce, being part of a religious and/or legal procedure, be seen to have taken place in two countries, in order to qualify for recognition in the UK, it is essential that no part of the "proceedings" have taken place in the UK.[188] Although the wording of s.46 of the 1986 Act might suggest that what matters is whether the divorce is valid where it is completed,[189] case law shows that dual location divorces do not commend themselves as complying with the Act.[190] Arguably the question of recognition of transnational divorces no part of which take place in the UK remains open.

Re-marriage: Family Law Act 1986 section 50

12–36   When recognition of a foreign consistorial decree depended upon the decree having emanated from the court of the parties' (necessarily common) domicile, and capacity to marry also (as now) was governed by the law of the domicile, there would usually be a coincidence of the two laws (unless a new domicile had been acquired in the interval between the granting of a divorce and the date of re-marriage), and no conflict would arise with regard to a person's legal capacity to (re-)marry.

However, since the recognition rule in Scots and English conflict of laws widened under the Family Law Act 1986 to accept consistorial decrees from the domicile (in either sense[191]), habitual residence, or nationality, of either party to the marriage, while the capacity to marry rule has remained the same (requiring of the party intending to marry capacity to marry by his/her ante-nuptial domicile),[192] a problem may arise for the forum in prioritising its own rules in this area. Tension inevitably will occur on occasion.

---

[187] *Sulaiman v Juffali* [2002] 1 F.L.R. 479: irrespective of parties' domicile(s), an informal divorce obtained in the UK otherwise than by way of proceedings in a court of civil jurisdiction is not to be recognised. The policy applies indiscriminately to all informal divorces, regardless of the parties' religious or other beliefs. See also *Asaad v Kurter* [2013] EWHC 3852 (Fam); [2014] 2 F.L.R. 833; and *Solovyev v Solovyeva* [2014] EWFC 1546; [2014] Fam. Law 1240.

[188] *R. v Secretary of State for the Home Department Ex p. Fatima* [1984] 2 All E.R. 458 (transnational talaq).

[189] Pilkington, "Transitional Divorces under the Family Law Act 1986" (1988) 37 I.C.L.Q. 131. See, however, *Berkovits v Grinberg* [1995] 2 All E.R. 681, per Wall J. at 692–694.

[190] *Sulaiman v Juffali* [2002] 1 F.L.R. 479; and *Berkovits* [1995] 2 All E.R. 681 (in both of which part of the divorce took place in England).

[191] That is to say, a party to a marriage shall be treated as domiciled in a country if he was domiciled in that country either according to the law of that country in family matters or according to the law of the part of the United Kingdom in which the question of recognition arises (Family Law Act 1986 s.46(5)).

[192] Family Law (Scotland) Act 2006 s.38(2)(a).

At common law,[193] a persuasive case was made to the effect that a person whose personal law considered him to be already married, should be regarded as legally incapable of re-marriage in the UK no matter that the Scots or English court might view as valid a purported divorce pre-dating the desired re-marriage. In other words, the forum would defer to the personal law in the matter of recognition of antecedent decrees. In *Perrini*,[194] however, with little argument, Sir George Baker, President of the Family Division, upon finding the antecedent New Jersey nullity worthy of recognition by English conflict rules, concluded that a party thereto might re-marry in England.

In a provision now repealed, namely, Recognition of Divorces and Legal Separations Act 1971 s.7, it was enacted that the recognition rule of the forum should take precedence over the capacity to marry rule, where the antecedent decree was that of divorce and where the re-marriage took place in the UK.[195]

The matter now is governed by the Family Law Act 1986 s.50, which provides that:

"Where, in any part of the United Kingdom—
(a)   a divorce or annulment has been granted by a court of civil jurisdiction, or
(b)   the validity of a divorce or annulment is recognised by virtue of this Part,
the fact that the divorce or annulment would not be recognised elsewhere shall not preclude either party to the marriage from re-marrying in that part of the United Kingdom or cause the re-marriage of either party (wherever the re-marriage takes place) to be treated as invalid in that part."

The opposite situation (where the divorce is recognised by a party's personal law but not by the forum) is not catered for under statute, but help may be had by reference to discussions of the incidental question,[196] and in particular to *Schwebel v Ungar*,[197] in which the Canadian forum, using a *lex causae* approach, deferred to the Israeli law of the ante-nuptial domicile of the woman, where Ontarian law and Israeli law differed as to the validity of an Israeli ghet, and by this reasoning the Ontarian court held valid a re-marriage of the woman in Ontario.

Recognition of EU divorces under Brussels II bis[198]

In terms of art.21 of Brussels II *bis*, a judgment given in an EU Member State   **12–37** shall be recognised in the other Member States without any special procedure being required; in particular, no special procedure shall be required for updating the "civil-status records" of a Member State, on the final award of a consistorial judgment from another Member State. However, any interested party may apply for a decision that the judgment be or be not recognised.[199]

---

[193] *Padolecchia v Padolecchia* [1968] P. 314. See *R. v Brentwood Superintendent Registrar of Marriages Ex p. Arias* [1968] 2 Q.B. 956.
[194] *Perrini v Perrini* [1979] Fam. 84.
[195] United Kingdom restriction caused difficulties in *Lawrence v Lawrence* [1985] Fam. 106.
[196] See para.4–07, above.
[197] *Schwebel v Ungar* (1964) 48 D.L.R. (2d.) 644.
[198] For the rules of recognition of EU divorces of same sex marriages, see para.12–62, below.
[199] This must be read subject to an understanding that the rules governing recognition under Brussels II *bis* admit few opportunities for challenge.

12–38   The grounds of non-recognition, therefore, are very limited, and are contained in art.22. They are concerned solely with public policy, natural justice, due process, and res judicata. The grounds of challenge available are as follows:

Article 22

12–39   A judgment relating to a divorce, legal separation or marriage annulment shall not be recognised:

(a)   if such recognition is manifestly contrary to the public policy of the Member State in which recognition is sought;

(b)   where it was given in default of appearance, if the respondent was not served with the document which instituted the proceedings or with an equivalent document in sufficient time and in such a way as to enable the respondent to arrange for his or her defence unless it is determined that the respondent has accepted the judgment unequivocally;

(c)   if it is irreconcilable with a judgment given in proceedings between the same parties in the Member State in which recognition is sought; or

(d)   if it is irreconcilable with an earlier judgment given in another Member State or in a non-Member State between the same parties, provided that the earlier judgment fulfils the conditions necessary for its recognition in the Member State in which recognition is sought.

12–40   A defining feature of any Brussels instrument, commercial or consistorial, is the general prohibition of review of jurisdiction of the court of origin by the legal system in which recognition is sought. Article 24 of Brussels II *bis* states that the jurisdiction of the court of the Member State of origin may not be reviewed and, further, that the test of public policy may not be applied to the jurisdiction rules set out in the Regulation.[200] There is no opportunity to challenge the decision of the court of the Member State of origin in its application of art.3 to the facts of the case.[201] Article 24 is consonant with the overarching principle contained in recital (21), that the recognition and enforcement of judgments given in a Member State should be based on the principle of mutual trust, and that the grounds for non-recognition be kept to a minimum. Moreover, recognition of a judgment may not be refused because the law of the Member State in which recognition is sought would not allow divorce, legal separation or marriage annulment on the same facts. Further, a judgment may never be reviewed as to its substance.[202]

---

[200] However, see exceptionally *Rapisarda v Colladon* (also known as *Re 180 Irregular Divorces*) [2014] EWFC 35, in which, on the intervention of the Queen's Proctor, Sir James Munby, President of the Family Division, set aside decrees nisi and absolute which had been obtained by fraud on the English court in the matter of its jurisdiction. The court had been deceived into accepting jurisdiction by false claims of habitual residence in England by European nationals, and the decrees were therefore void. See, earlier, *Moynihan v Moynihan (Nos 1 and 2)* [1997] 1 F.L.R. 59; [1997] Fam. Law 88.

[201] Therefore examination of the facts of the case against the relevant jurisdictional rules is no longer permissible in this branch of the subject. Contrast opportunity, strictly limited, for challenge on this ground in civil and commercial matters under the Brussels I Regulation art.35(1), and Brussels I Recast art.45(1)(e).

[202] See art.26. Contrast *Gray v Formosa* [1963] P. 259.

Extrajudicial divorces[203]

It is necessary to determine the extent of application, if any, of Brussels II and Brussels II *bis*, to recognition of extrajudicial divorces. This must be done by reference to the terms of the Regulations, and to their respective preambles.

    Recital (9) of Brussels II stated that the scope of the Regulation should cover, "civil proceedings and non-judicial proceedings in matrimonial matters in certain States, and exclude purely religious procedures." Article 1.2 of Brussels II states that, "[o]ther proceedings officially recognised in a Member State shall be regarded as equivalent to judicial proceedings."

    The preamble to Brussels II *bis* omits specific reference to religious procedures, and in recital (7) advises that the scope of this Regulation covers "civil matters, whatever the nature of the court or tribunal". There has been no attempt to date to apply the Regulation to recognition of a religious divorce.[204] Article 1.1 of Brussels II *bis* (Scope) states that the Regulation shall apply, "whatever the nature of the court or tribunal, in civil matters relating to divorce, legal separation or marriage annulment." The system of recognition depends upon jurisdiction having been assumed in terms of art.3 of the Regulation, which states that jurisdiction shall lie with the courts of a Member State, broadly speaking, on the grounds of habitual residence of one or both parties. In sum, the terms of Brussels II *bis* are somewhat ambivalent, and might be apt to include divorces involving the participation by a religious court or tribunal, such as the Jewish letter of divorcement (ghet) issued by the rabbinical court. A case could be presented that art.1.1 can be interpreted so as to include religious divorces. For a ghet, for example, to fall under Brussels II *bis*, the rabbinical court would have to satisfy art.1.1 (Scope), which ex facie it would seem to do.

12–41

Re-marriage[205]

There is no provision equivalent to s.50 of the Family Law Act 1986 in Brussels II *bis*, presumably because in a situation where it is intended that recognition of EU divorces among Member States will be almost automatic, such provision would be unnecessary. However, it is not impossible that a "s.50 situation" could arise in a European context; the answer in the instant case would depend upon the conflict rules of the forum in which the problem arose.

12–42

---

[203] See para.12–34, above re recognition of non-EU extrajudicial divorces.

[204] But see *Sulaiman v Juffali* [2002] 1 F.L.R. 479 in which the question whether the English court had jurisdiction in the wife's petition for divorce (contested by the husband on the ground that the marriage already had been validly dissolved by bare talaq pronounced in England and registered in Saudi Arabia in the Sharia court three days later), was determined by the Family Division of the High Court according to art.2 of Brussels II. The recognition issue was settled by application of the Family Law Act 1986 s.44(1). It was sufficient to preclude recognition that talaq had been pronounced in England (cf. *Berkovits* [1995] 2 All E.R. 681).

[205] See para.12–36, above re s.50.

JUDICIAL SEPARATION

12–43   Judicial or legal separation is a remedy almost extinct domestically, and a foreign judicial/legal separation in relation to the validity of which there lingers a conflict of laws doubt is a poor remedy indeed. That said, all rules which govern in divorce, jurisdiction, choice of law (including Rome III Regulation), and recognition of foreign decrees, apply also, mutatis mutandis, to judicial separation. Note should be made of s.47(2) of the 1986 Act, concerning conversion of legal separation into divorce.[206]

ANNULMENT OF MARRIAGE

The jurisdiction of Scots courts

Introduction

12–44   The treatment of annulment of marriage in the conflict of laws has been attended by greater complexity, doubt and difficulty than has the treatment of divorce. One reason is the void/voidable marriage distinction which is not found in all systems or, if present, may differ in content. Some systems may have other classifications peculiar to themselves.[207] Some systems may grant an annulment where others would grant divorce, e.g. in the area of physical incapacity. It is no longer necessary for a UK court to classify the genus of foreign consistorial decree in order to know which rules of recognition, common law or statutory, to apply, because the rules of recognition of divorces and nullities are the same, both intra- and extra-EU, resting upon Brussels II *bis* and the Family Law Act 1986 Pt II, respectively.

While, as has been noted, the grounds of divorce available in a system at any time will reflect its policy at that time, the grounds of annulment will be linked to an anterior matter such as alleged lack of capacity, physical or legal, or alleged absence of consent. Each of these factors will attract the application of a choice of law rule of the forum which is called upon to judge the validity of the marriage. Therefore, while reasons of cost and convenience, to say nothing of policy, may justify application by the forum of its own law in judging a divorce petition, the subject of choice of law in nullity rightly demands a different approach.

Further, while an annulment of a void marriage merely declares the position which always has existed, legal systems will vary in the effect which they accord (prospective only, or dating back to date of purported marriage) to a nullity decree pertaining to a voidable marriage. This is a matter properly for the forum which grants the decree: the recognising court should accept the effect as an integral part of the decree.[208]

---

[206]   cf. Brussels II *bis* art.5.
[207]   e.g. *Merker v Merker* [1963] P. 283; *M v M (Divorce: Jurisdiction: Validity of Marriage)* [2001] 2 F.L.R. 6; and *Ghandi v Patel* [2002] 1 F.L.R. 603.
[208]   *Social Security Decision No. R (G) 1/85.*

Jurisdiction at common law

A decree of nullity of a voidable marriage clearly effected a change in the status **12–45** of the parties, but a decree of nullity of a void marriage did not have any such effect because the parties never were married. For this reason, in the past, both Scots and English courts assumed jurisdiction on a wider basis in actions of nullity involving void marriages[209] than in voidable marriages.[210] The distinction between void and voidable, which might not have been present in the law of the granting country, created difficulties as to jurisdiction edn that a preliminary decision had to be made upon the nature of the marriage as void or voidable (by which law?) before it could be said whether or not the Scots forum had jurisdiction.[211] This is a variation on the problem of circularity which not infrequently arises in conflict problems.

Development of grounds of jurisdiction

Rules of jurisdiction up to 1 March 2001

The position was simplified by the 1973 Act which provided in ss.5 (England), 7 **12–46** (Scotland), and 13 (Northern Ireland) that the only competent grounds of jurisdiction for a declarator of marriage, or a declarator of nullity of marriage, were as follows:

(1)   domicile of either party in Scotland on the date when the action was begun; or
(2)   habitual residence of one year of either party prior to the date when the action was begun; or
(3)   if one party has died, that he or she either—
        (a)   was domiciled in Scotland at death, or
        (b)   had been habitually resident in Scotland throughout the period of one year ending with the date of death.

This eliminated any distinction between void and voidable marriages as regards jurisdiction.

---

[209] e.g. in Scots law, the assumption of jurisdiction by the forum qua *locus celebrationis* was permitted if the marriage was thought to be void (*Prawdziclazarska v Prawdziclazarski*, 1954 S.C. 98). In England that ground initially was used with regard to both void and voidable marriages, but was rejected in respect of voidable marriages by the House of Lords in *Ross Smith v Ross Smith* [1963] A.C. 280, though it continued to be used with regard to void marriages, as can be seen from *Padolecchia v Padolecchia* [1968] P. 314.

[210] Scots authorities at common law include: *Miller v Deakin*, 1912 1 S.L.T. 253; *Lendrum v Chakravarti*, 1929 S.L.T. 96; *MacDougall v Chitnavis*, 1937 S.C. 390; *Prawdziclazarska*, 1954 S.C. 98; *Aldridge v Aldridge*, 1954 S.C. 58; *Woodward v Woodward*; sub nom. *AB v CD*, 1957 S.C. 415; 1958 S.L.T. 213; *Orlandi v Castelli*, 1961 S.L.T. 119; *Balshaw v Kelly*, 1967 S.C. 63; and F.P. Walton, *A Handbook of Husband and Wife According to the Law of Scotland*, 3rd edn (Edinburgh: W. Green & Son, 1951), p.410.

[211] *Prawdziclazarska*, 1954 S.C. 98.

Rules of jurisdiction after 1 March 2001

12–47   As with jurisdiction in divorce, the starting point is the 1973 Act, as amended first by the European Communities (Matrimonial Jurisdiction and Judgments) (Scotland) Regulations 2001[212] (taking account of Brussels II[213]), and later by the European Communities (Matrimonial and Parental Responsibility Jurisdiction and Judgments) (Scotland) Regulations 2005[214] (taking account of Brussels II *bis*[215]).[216]

The rules of jurisdiction of the Court of Session[217] in actions of *declarator of marriage* are contained in s.7(3) of the 1973 Act, and, being unaffected by Brussels II *bis*, remain the same as the pre-1 March 2001 position.[218]

Jurisdiction in actions for *declarator of nullity of marriage*, however, are affected by Brussels II *bis*. Section 7(3A) is to the effect that the Court of Session has jurisdiction to entertain such an action, if and only if:

(1)   the Scottish courts have jurisdiction under Brussels II *bis*;[219] or

(2)   the action is an excluded action[220] and either of the parties to the marriage is domiciled in Scotland on the date when the action is begun.

There continue to be special rules where one party was dead at the date of the action, and that party was domiciled at death in Scotland, or had been habitually resident there for one year before death.[221]

By s.8(1)(c) and 8(2A)[222] the sheriff court has jurisdiction to entertain an action for *declarator of nullity of marriage*, if and only if:

(1)   either party to the marriage— (i) was resident in the sheriffdom for a period of forty days ending with the date when the action was begun; or (ii) had been resident in the sheriffdom for a period of not less than forty days

---

[212] European Communities (Matrimonial Jurisdiction and Judgments) (Scotland) Regulations 2001 (SSI 2001/36).

[213] See also Act of Sederunt (Ordinary Cause Rules) Amendment (European Matrimonial and Parental Responsibility Jurisdiction and Judgments) 2001 (SSI 2001/144).

[214] European Communities (Matrimonial and Parental Responsibility Jurisdiction and Judgments) (Scotland) Regulations 2005 (SSI 2005/42).

[215] See also Act of Sederunt (Rules of the Court of Session Amendment) (Jurisdiction, Recognition and Enforcement of Judgments) 2005 (SSI 2005/135).

[216] See para.12–05, above. For the rules of jurisdiction applicable to same sex annulments, see para.12–57 et seq., below.

[217] For shrieval jurisdiction, see ss.8(1)(c) and 8(2ZA).

[218] Para.12–03, above. Similarly, the rules of jurisdiction of the Scots court in a petition for declarator of death continue to be governed by the Presumption of Death (Scotland) Act 1977 s.1.

[219] See paras 12–06 to 12–09, above. See *Singh v Singh*, 2005 S.L.T. 749, in which Temporary Judge Macdonald Q.C. held that the fact that the marriage in question was celebrated in India did not affect the issue of jurisdiction as Brussels II was not restricted to cases where both parties could found jurisdiction under art.2(1), and applied in a case such as the present where the respondent was not habitually resident or domiciled in, or a national of, a Member State.

[220] 1973 Act s.7(3B). Para.12–11, above.

[221] 1973 Act s.7(3A)(b)(b).

[222] Shrieval jurisdiction in declarators of nullity of marriage was extended by s.15(2) of the Forced Marriage etc (Protection and Jurisdiction) (Scotland) Act 2011.

ending not more than forty days before said date, and has no known residence in Scotland at that date; and either

(2)   the Scottish courts have jurisdiction under Brussels II *bis*;or

(3)   the action is an excluded action and either of the parties to the marriage is domiciled in Scotland on the date when the action is begun.[223]

Choice of law in Scots courts

Which law is the court to apply in determining the validity of a marriage in an action of declarator of nullity of marriage? At the current date, the rules of choice of law to be used by a Scots court rest partly still on the common law, and partly on statute, namely, the Family Law (Scotland) Act 2006, according to the nature of the defect alleged.   **12–48**

Common law principle indicated that the court should look at the defect alleged and decide whether it related to essentials or form. If it related to form, reference was made to the *lex loci celebrationis*, and if it related to essentials, reference was made to the law of the domicile. But which domicile was to apply where the parties did not have a common domicile? The law of the domicile of each party applied as regards capacity to marry and matters up to the date of the ceremony, but as regards essentials and matters after the ceremony (e.g. impotence), the only law which could have been applied during the days of unity of domicile was that of the domicile of the alleged husband. Such a statement elicited immediately the response that there would be no unity of domicile if the marriage was void and today the domiciles of women, married or not, are ascertained independently of the domicile of any other person. It should be borne in mind when reading the older cases that an added difficulty was that the unity of domicile rule between husband and wife required that the domicile of the wife followed that of the husband *ex lege* if the marriage was valid or voidable,[224] but not if the marriage was void, although in that case it might be found, in any event, on the facts that the woman had changed her domicile upon going to live with the man. Where the parties had different domiciles, reference was made to the law of the domicile of the party alleged to lack capacity, but if, by that law, the marriage was valid, reference then was made to the law of the domicile of the other party. In principle, then as now, there was no reason why, subject to public policy, a Scots court should not grant the remedy of annulment on a ground unknown to it, if it is a ground of the *lex causae* (be that the common domicile, the domicile of the complainer, or possibly the domicile of the defender).

---

[223] For shrieval jurisdiction in declarators of nullity of marriage where one of the parties has died, see s.8(2B) and (2D).

[224] And if so would not change upon pronouncement of declarator of nullity, but only upon independent acquisition thereafter of a different domicile—*De Reneville* [1948] 1 All E.R. 56. Such difficulties are to be seen in Maltese marriage cases, *Chapelle* [1950] P. 134; *Lepre* [1965] P. 52; and *Gray v Formosa* [1963] P. 259.

Formal invalidity

12–49 As explained in Ch.11,[225] a Scots court, in accordance with s.38(1) of the Family Law (Scotland) Act 2006, will determine the question whether a marriage is formally valid by applying the law of the place where the marriage was celebrated.

Legal incapacity

12–50 As explained in Ch.11,[226] a Scots court, in accordance with s.38(2) of the Family Law (Scotland) Act 2006, will determine the question whether a person who entered into a marriage (heterosexual or same sex[227]) had legal capacity so to do by the law of the place where, immediately before the marriage, that person was domiciled. The rule is applied cumulatively.[228]

Physical incapacity

12–51 The point is well made in *Ross Smith v Ross Smith*,[229] per Lord Reid, that the ground of wilful refusal may found an action of divorce for desertion in some systems, and in others may give rise to no remedy, and that it is wrong for the forum, applying its own law, to grant a remedy where none is available by a law of closer connection.[230]

Generally among legal systems, impotence is likely to found an action for nullity. In Scots law it will render a marriage voidable. The two grounds of impotence and wilful refusal to consummate are different in nature and while it might be thought appropriate to have different applicable laws, it is simpler to apply one choice of law rule for all alleged defects of physical incapacity. It may be argued that a remedy should be given if such is available under the personal law of either party.

Mental element: error, lack of consent, unilateral mental reservation

12–52 At common law particular difficulty was encountered where the defect alleged was absence of consent, or physical incapacity. It was found that sometimes the forum applied its own law without question,[231] often because the matter of application of foreign law was not raised. The decision in *Szechter v Szechter*[232]

---

[225] See, in detail, para.11–20 et seq.

[226] See, in detail, paras 11–04 and 11–28.

[227] The introduction into Scots and English domestic law, respectively, of same sex marriage impacts upon the legal capacity of Scots and English domiciliaries, respectively, to enter such a marriage.

[228] cf. *Asaad v Kurter* [2013] EWHC 3852 (Fam); [2014] 2 F.L.R. 833.

[229] *Ross Smith v Ross Smith* [1963] A.C. 280 at 306.

[230] Also *Ponticelli v Ponticelli* [1958] P. 204, a case of physical incapacity, to which the court applied the domicile of the aggrieved party.

[231] *Buckland v Buckland* [1968] P. 296; *Kassim v Kassim* [1962] P. 224.

[232] *Szechter v Szechter* [1971] P. 286, a marriage of compassionate convenience, to which the court applied the law of the Polish domicile of all parties at the time of the marriage. This decision presented no true conflict, English law and Polish law concurring in the view that the marriage was void.

favoured the application of the personal law, whereas in *H v H*[233] the English forum, finding the possibly applicable laws, those of England and of Hungary, to be similar, stemming from the common parentage of the canon law, explicitly chose to apply its own law as the law with which it was familiar.

In domestic Scots law of marriage, there must be "an agreeing mind". Scots law does not favour giving legal effect to unilateral mental reservation, yet Lord Dunpark in *Akram*[234] was required by the facts of the case to grant an annulment to Muslim parties who had "married" in a civil ceremony in Glasgow, upon evidence given that neither had considered the formalities to amount to marriage from the viewpoint of their religion.

Parties may marry out of a sense of family duty if that is the pattern of their cultural background. In each of the cases of *Mahmud*[235] and *Mahmood*,[236] the Court of Session granted an annulment of a Muslim arranged marriage, at the instance of pursuers who argued that s/he had entered into marriage without the Scottish requisite of free will, and out of a sense of family loyalty or under threat of being cut off from the family.[237] It does not appear that in either case was the issue of domicile raised; nor did the Scots court make any reference to foreign law. Seemingly the Scots domestic law of the forum was used, but the court in each case was mindful of the cultural background: in both, the parties were of Pakistani culture living in Scotland, and it was appreciated that each petitioner's will would be more easily overborne as a result of the family piety which formed part of their background. Hence, the forum appears to have interpreted its own law in the light of circumstances acknowledged to be different. It did not purport to apply the law of the domicile, but in any event no query as to the possibility of domicile being other than Scots was raised. Paradoxically, the care accorded to the background may have resulted in a decision at odds with that which would have been reached in a legal system of Muslim culture. The approach is hybrid therefore in these two cases and there is no discussion of choice of law.

Similarly in *Sohrab v Kahn*,[238] Lord McEwan granted decree of nullity of a purported marriage on the ground of the woman's lack of consent, induced by duress, and for reasons of defects of formal validity. There was much evidence on the detail of the Muslim wedding ceremony, and marriage customs. Although his Lordship's decision on lack of consent was reached after careful consideration of factual evidence of Muslim practice and parties' actings and statements in relation thereto, there is no indication that Lord McEwan applied any law other than Scots to determine the quality of consent which he deemed requisite for a valid marriage.

---

[233] *H v H* [1954] P. 258.

[234] *Akram v Akram*, 1979 S.L.T. (Notes) 87. cf. *Orlandi v Castelli*, 1961 S.C. 119.

[235] *Mahmud v Mahmud*, 1994 S.L.T. 599.

[236] *Mahmood v Mahmood*, 1993 S.L.T. 589.

[237] A more extreme variation is exemplified by parental wishes to take a daughter out of a UK jurisdiction in order to arrange a marriage in Pakistan: *M v B* [2005] EWHC 1681 (consent to remove refused where the adult daughter had learning difficulties such that she was incapable of understanding the meaning of consent to marry); or where the party who, it is surmised, may be coerced into marriage, is under the age of 16 years, in which event the case may present as an abduction or wardship case: *Re KR (A Child) (Abduction: Forcible Removal by Parents)* [1999] 4 All E.R. 954. cf. *P (Forced Marriage)* [2010] EWHC 3467 (Fam); [2011] 1 F.L.R. 2060.

[238] *Sohrab v Kahn*, 2002 S.L.T. 1255.

Notable for its raising of the conflict implications is the decision of R.F. Macdonald Q.C. in *Singh v Singh*,[239] to the effect that the law governing the issue of consent to marry is the law of the domicile of the party alleging lack of consent. This decision provided discussion of choice of law upon the issue of duress relating to marriage. The judge declined to follow an obiter dictum of Lord Guthrie in *Di Rollo v Di Rollo*,[240] which had favoured the application of the *lex loci celebrationis* to the question of consent. In *Singh*, the pursuer, a UK citizen, had been brought up in Edinburgh and expressed the intention to live in Scotland for the foreseeable future; there was no challenge to the inference of Scots domicile. She had accompanied her mother to India to visit relations, only to be coerced into marriage at the mother's insistence during the holiday in India. The judge applied Scots law, being the law of the pursuer's domicile, in the matter of the requirement and content of consent to marry.[241] Hence this decision brought Scots law further along a path which, it is submitted, is the correct one *quoad* choice of law; but it does not afford an example of application by the Scots forum, after proof, of a foreign marriage law qua *lex causae*. In the instant case, the court was satisfied that the threat from the pursuer's mother was sufficient to cause the will of the pursuer to be overborne and to vitiate her consent to marry.

The robust English law view of consent to marriage, namely that parties of sound mind should be held to their bargain, is seen in the notable House of Lords decision of *Vervaeke v Smith*.[242]

Sham marriage

12–53 A significant decision (reversed, however, on appeal) is that of *Hakeem v Hussain*,[243] in which Lord Clarke held, at first instance, that a civil marriage was not void merely because the parties to it did not regard it as having any religious significance. A distinction was drawn between consent to marriage for the purposes of the civil law; and the parties' private views on the relationship of a Scottish civil marriage ceremony and a religious marriage prescribed by their own faith. This distinction, while useful (e.g. when contrasted with the outcome in *Akram v Akram*[244]) in effectively preventing the exploitation of Scots civil marriage, is a fine one, some would say almost too fine to make. Reliance was placed on a statement by Professor Clive that:

> "Everything turns on the distinction between an intention to assume the legal relationship of husband and wife and an intention not to get married at all. If the parties intended to get married . . .then they will be married even if their marriage was for a limited purpose and they had no intention of living together or assuming

---

[239] *Singh v Singh*, 2005 S.L.T. 749.
[240] *Di Rollo v Di Rollo*, 1959 S.L.T. 278.
[241] Making reference to *Mahmood*, 1993 S.L.T. 589; and *Mahmud*, 1994 S.L.T. 599.
[242] *Vervaeke v Smith* [1983] 1 A.C. 145.
[243] *Hakeem v Hussain*, 2003 S.L.T. 515; and on appeal, sub nom. *SH v KH*, 2005 S.L.T. 1025.
[244] *Akram v Akram*, 1979 S.L.T. (Notes) 87.

the normal social roles of husband and wife. If they intended not to get married at all, but merely to go through an empty ceremony they will not be married."[245]

While Clive admits that parties may not draw this distinction clearly in their minds, he writes that it is the crucial distinction. But it is difficult to grasp; the difference between marrying without the intention of assuming the normal roles, on the one hand, and, on the other, merely going through a ceremony with no intention to get married at all, is one which may not convince. Perhaps the inference which could be taken from Lord Clarke's decision (which, however, was overturned) was that marriages entered into in Scotland for an identifiable— albeit not "matrimonial"—purpose[246] (e.g. so that a defender's visa could be granted if immigration authorities consider him to be married), should not be annulled upon request of either party. This still may be the case, but it must now be noted that in a long and careful judgment on appeal,[247] Lord Penrose, while agreeing with Lord Clarke that parties' motives on entering into marriage are not a determinative factor, nevertheless held that:

> "... there may be cases in which the religious convictions of the parties may affect the consent exchanged in a regular marriage ceremony to the extent of wholly undermining it."[248]

Lord Penrose was in no doubt that the parties wished it to be understood that the registry office ceremony was a formal marriage; but the critical question in an annulment is whether at the moment of seeming acceptance of, or acquiescence in, the civil ceremony, the parties intended to become husband and wife. Since, in the view of the appellate court, an agreement that the parties would not become husband and wife in any real sense until some further condition was satisfied in the indefinite future was not a marriage, the appeal was allowed, and decree of nullity granted.

This has been an active area of consideration in Scots family law. In all cases of this type in which annulment has been granted, the forum has been conscious of the public policy aspect, in particular, of the abuse or exploitation of the Scots institution of marriage, as entered into by means of a civil ceremony, with accompanying formalities. Insofar as this decision on appeal reverted to a criterion of assessing the existence of matrimonial consent on a subjective basis, it was in line with earlier Scots law marriage precedents.[249] While it was an established rule of domestic Scots law that unilateral mental reservation to marriage with a particular person cannot found an action of nullity, the court in cases such as those under discussion is required to deal with instances of bilateral

---

[245] E.M. Clive, *The Law of Husband and Wife in Scotland*, 4th edn (Edinburgh: W. Green, 1997), para.07.047. A further variation is that the argument is advanced that one or both parties believed that the ceremony was merely an engagement ceremony: *Alfonso-Brown v Millwood* [2006] EWHC 642 (Fam).

[246] As in *Hakeem v Hussain*, 2003 S.L.T. 515.

[247] The main opinion was delivered by Lord Penrose, Lords Marnoch and Macfadyen concurring (*SH v KH*, 2005 S.L.T. 1025).

[248] *SH v KH*, 2005 S.L.T. 1025 at [36]. Lord Penrose made reference to *Brady v Murray*, 1933 S.L.T. 534.

[249] Such as *Akram*, 1979 S.L.T. (Notes) 87, per Lord Dunpark at 88; and *Brady v Murray*, 1933 S.L.T. 534.

mental reservation on the ground that, at best, the Scottish civil ceremony is merely a precursor to a marriage ceremony fully recognised as such by the parties in terms of their religious views.[250] On the other hand, it is impossible not to sympathise with the distinction which Lord Clarke made at first instance: if the parties register themselves as married persons, having utilised Scottish marriage procedures, they have purported to consent to enter the institution for which the formalities were designed, viz. marriage in Scots law. Such marriage has public law and private law consequences. It is unreasonable that parties should hope to enjoy the public law consequences of the married status in Scotland, but should choose not to accept the private law consequences. In these cases, the parties appear to wish to have the benefit of the incidents of marriage without acquiring the status of married parties.

A statutory response

12–54   The Family Law (Scotland) Act 2006 seeks to address the problems encountered in this area in the following manner[251]:

Section 38(2) directs the question whether a person has consented to enter into a marriage to the law of the domicile of that person immediately before the marriage. This provision will make clear the basic rule in the general case, but the inclusion in s.2 of the Act of a particular rule concerning void marriages (inserted as s.20A of the Marriage (Scotland) Act 1977) represents an attempt to address the problems which have troubled the Scots courts in this area. Section 2 provides a rule which insists upon its own operation, i.e. is of an overriding nature, where the marriage, the validity of which is in question, was solemnised in Scotland. It introduces a mandatory provision of the *lex loci celebrationis*, where the *lex loci* is Scottish.[252]

Such a marriage shall be void if, at the time of the marriage ceremony, a party to the marriage who was capable of consenting to the marriage purported to give consent, but did so by reason only of duress or error (i.e. coerced marriage: s.20A(2)). Error is defined for the purposes of the legislation as (a) error as to the nature of the ceremony; or (b) a mistaken belief held by a person that the other party at the ceremony with whom the first party purported to enter into a marriage was the person whom the first party had agreed to marry (s.20A(5)).

---

[250]   i.e. a form of betrothal or condition precedent to "full" religious marriage.

[251]   For measures in immigration law seeking to tackle the problem of sham marriages, see the Asylum and Immigration (Treatment of Claimants etc.) Act 2004 ss.19–24 (as amended, following the House of Lords decision in *R. (on the application of Baiai) v Secretary of State for the Home Department* [2009] 1 A.C. 287, by The Asylum and Immigration (Treatment of Claimants, etc) Act 2004 (Remedial) Order 2011 (SI 2011/1158) to remove the incompatibility of s.19(1) with a Convention right); and Immigration (Procedure for Marriage) Regulations 2011 (SI 2011/2678), as amended. The legislation establishes procedures where a marriage is to be solemnised in the UK and a party to the marriage is subject to immigration control. See also *R. (on the application of Aguilar Quila) v Secretary of State for the Home Department* [2011] UKSC 45. Further: Immigration Act 2014 s.55, amending Immigration and Asylum Act 1999, to make provision (re. duty to report suspicious marriages) for "sham marriage", as defined therein.

[252]   This, at least, would be the view taken by a Scots forum. One may speculate how this mandatory, but territorially limited, rule of Scots law would be regarded by a court, say, in England, if a party to the alleged marriage (say, of Pakistan domicile) were to seek an annulment there. If such a party at the point of marrying in Scotland had unilaterally reserved consent, the English forum will take account of s.20A of the 1977 Act only if it classifies that rule as a mandatory rule of form of the *lex loci*.

Further, the marriage shall be void if at the time of the marriage ceremony, a party to the marriage was incapable of (a) understanding the nature of marriage; and (b) consenting to the marriage (s.20A(3)). However, thirdly, if a party to a marriage purported to give consent to the marriage other than by reason only of duress or error, the marriage shall not be void by reason only of that party's having tacitly withheld consent to the marriage at the time when it was solemnised (s.20A(4)).

Forced Marriage etc. (Protection and Jurisdiction) (Scotland) Act 2011[253]

The Forced Marriage etc. (Protection And Jurisdiction) (Scotland) Act 2011 **12–55** enables the Court of Session or sheriff court to make forced marriage protection orders to protect persons from being forced into marriage without their free and full consent; and for protecting persons who have been forced to enter into marriage without such consent. Section 1(6) of the Act defines "force" as including (a) coercion, by physical, verbal or psychological means, threatening conduct, or harassment; and (b) knowingly taking advantage of a person's incapacity to consent to marriage or to understand the nature of the marriage.

Section 2 states that a forced marriage protection order (which may be sought by the "protected person", or any relevant third party,[254] or may be granted *ex proprio motu* by the court[255]) may contain such prohibitions, restrictions or requirements, and other terms, as the court considers appropriate for the purposes of the order. Notably, the terms of the order may relate to conduct outside, as well as/instead of conduct within Scotland.

Importantly, s.9 provides that any person who, knowingly and without reasonable excuse, breaches a forced marriage protection order commits a criminal offence and is subject to criminal penalties. The Act does not affect the law of marriage,[256] and so any matrimonial remedy to be sought by the protected person must be pursued separately.[257]

Recognition of foreign decrees of annulment[258]

Until 1986, recognition of foreign decrees of annulment developed at common **12–56** law, following a pattern similar to that found in relation to recognition of foreign divorces prior to 1971.[259] The only challenges were on the grounds of no

---

[253] See also Forced Marriage etc. (Protection and Jurisdiction) (Scotland) Act 2011 (Commencement) Order 2011 (SSI 2011/352). cf. in England and Wales, Forced Marriage (Civil Protection) Act 2007. Further: Anti-social Behaviour, Crime and Policing Act 2014, Pt 10, Forced marriage: s.121 (Offence of forced marriage: England and Wales) and s.122 (Offence of forced marriage: Scotland).

[254] Forced Marriage etc. (Protection and Jurisdiction) (Scotland) Act 2011 s.3(1). On interpretation and application of the 2011 Act, see *City of Edinburgh Council v S*, 2015 S.L.T. (Sh.Ct) 69 (application for a forced marriage protectopm order dismissed).

[255] Forced Marriage etc. (Protection and Jurisdiction) (Scotland) Act 2011 s.4.

[256] Forced Marriage etc. (Protection and Jurisdiction) (Scotland) Act 2011 s.12(2)(g).

[257] e.g., under the Forced Marriage (Civil Protection) Act 2007 in England, *Re P (Forced Marriage)* [2010] EWHC 3467 (Fam); [2011] 1 F.L.R. 2060.

[258] For the rules of recognition of annulments of same sex marriages, paras 12–60 and 12–62, below.

[259] e.g. cf. *Law v Gustin* [1976] 1 All E.R. 113 with *Indyka* [1969] 1 A.C. 33: law of close connection. See also *Perrini v Perrini* [1979] 2 All E.R. 323.

jurisdiction, fraud, or that the ground on which the foreign annulment was granted was *contra bonos mores*.[260] Error by the foreign court as to its own law or any other law was not a ground of challenge.[261]

The Law Commissions concluded[262] that there was no convincing argument for retaining common law regulation of recognition of nullity decrees. As a result, the Family Law Act 1986 ss.44–54, was applied to the recognition of foreign annulments as well as foreign divorces.[263]

Since the coming into force of Brussels II and Brussels II *bis*, the 1986 Act applies only to the recognition of annulments obtained outside the EU, and in Denmark. The Brussels regime applies to recognition of annulments granted in EU Member State courts in the same manner as it applies to recognition of EU divorces.[264]

SAME SEX MARRIAGE: MATRIMONIAL REMEDIES

Jurisdiction

12–57 Section 8A(1)[265] of the Domicile and Matrimonial Proceedings Act 1973 states that ss.7 and 8 do not apply in relation to marriages between persons of the same sex. Rather, s.8A(2) of the 1973 Act makes special provision for jurisdiction of the Scottish courts regarding same sex marriages. By s.8A(2), Sch.1B[266] to the 1973 Act (jurisdiction in relation to same sex marriages (Scotland)) applies.[267] Schedule 1B has effect with respect to the jurisdiction of the Court of Session and of the sheriff court to entertain, in relation to same sex marriages, proceedings for divorce, separation, declarator of marriage, declarator of nullity of marriage, and

---

[260] *Gray v Formosa* [1963] P. 259; *Lepre* [1965] P. 52; *Chapelle* [1950] P. 134. These cases provide rare instances of a successful challenge on policy grounds of the substance of the foreign ground of nullity.
[261] *Merker v Merker* [1963] P. 283.
[262] Law Commission and Scottish Law Commission, *Private International Law: Recognition of Foreign Nullity Decrees and Related Matters* (HMSO, 1984), Law Com. No.137; Scot. Law Com. No.88, Cmnd.9341.
[263] The rules explained at para.12–28 et seq., above apply to the recognition of non-EU annulments. Instances of foreign extrajudicial annulments are rare, though see, e.g. *Di Rollo v Di Rollo*, 1959 S.C. 75.
[264] 1986 Act s.45(2). The rules explained at para.12–37, above apply to the recognition of EU annulments. Whether a religious annulment is capable now of being governed by Brussels II *bis* is debateable. See Spanish decision in *Re Recognition of a Canon Law Judgment* [2008] I.L.Pr. 31. In the case of the Roman Catholic Rota, see also Council Regulation (EC) No.2116/2004 of 2 December 2004 amending Regulation (EC) No.2201/2003 concerning jurisdiction and the recognition and enforcement of judgments in matrimonial matters and the matters of parental responsibility, repealing Regulation (EC) No.1347/2000, as regards treaties with the Holy See.
[265] Added by Marriage and Civil Partnership (Scotland) Act 2014 Sch.1 para.1(2).
[266] Inserted by Marriage and Civil Partnership (Scotland) Act 2014 Sch.1 para.1(4).
[267] With regard to jurisdiction in England and Wales, see s.11(4) and Sch.4 (paras 5 and 8) to the Marriage (Same Sex Couples) Act 2013, which amends the DMPA 1973 as it applies to England and Wales. Schedule 4(8) inserts into the 1973 Act Sch.A1 (Jurisdiction [in England and Wales] in relation to marriage of same sex couples). See also Marriage (Same Sex Couples) (Jurisdiction and Recognition of Judgments) Regulations 2014 (SI 2014/543).

declarator of recognition, or non-recognition, of a relevant foreign decree, which by virtue of para.1(3) means a non-EU decree of divorce, separation or nullity.[268]

By dint of the 1973 Act Sch.1B para.2, The Marriage (Same Sex Couples) (Jurisdiction and Recognition of Judgments) (Scotland) Regulations 2014[269] ("the 2014 Regulations") have been introduced. Regulation 2 of the 2014 Regulations provides that the Scottish courts have jurisdiction in two circumstances: *first*, in proceedings for the declarator of recognition, or non-recognition, of a relevant foreign (i.e. non-EU) decree; and *secondly*, in proceedings for the divorce of, or declarator of nullity of a marriage of, or the judicial separation of a married same sex couple.

Jurisdiction re divorce or separation of same sex marriage

The rules of jurisdiction[270] are to the effect that the Court of Session[271] has jurisdiction to entertain an action for divorce or separation of parties to a same sex marriage, if and only if: **12–58**

(1)   the Scottish courts have jurisdiction under the 1973 Act Sch.1B para.2; or
(2)   no court has, or is recognised as having, jurisdiction under those regulations[272] and either party to the marriage is domiciled in Scotland on the date on which the proceedings are begun.[273]

Therefore, the first gateway is the 1973 Act Sch.1B para.2, which provides that the Scottish court has jurisdiction if one of the criteria in paras (a)–(f) is satisfied, namely:

(a)   both spouses are habitually resident in Scotland;
(b)   both spouses were last habitually resident in Scotland and one of the spouses continues to reside there;
(c)   the defender is habitually resident in Scotland;
(d)   the pursuer is habitually resident in Scotland and has resided there for at least one year immediately preceding the date on which the action is begun;
(e)   the pursuer is domiciled and habitually resident in Scotland and has resided there for at least six months immediately preceding the date on which the action is begun; or
(f)   both spouses are domiciled in Scotland.

These provisions clearly are based on the grounds of jurisdiction set out in art.3 of Brussels II *bis*.

---

[268] Marriage and Civil Partnership (Scotland) Act 2014 Sch.1 para.1(1).
[269] The Marriage (Same Sex Couples) (Jurisdiction and Recognition of Judgments) (Scotland) Regulations 2014 (SSI 2014/362).
[270] 1973 Act Sch.1B para.3(1).
[271] As to shrieval jurisdiction, see 1973 Act Sch.1B paras 2 and 3(2) and (3).
[272] i.e. is equivalent to an "excluded action".
[273] 1973 Act Sch.1B para.3(1)(b). cf. 1973 Act s.7(2A), para.12–05, above.

Jurisdiction re nullity of same sex marriage

12–59 Similarly, the Court of Session[274] has jurisdiction to entertain an action for declarator of nullity of a same sex marriage, if and only if:

(1) the Scottish courts have jurisdiction under the 1973 Act Sch.1B para.2; or

(2) no court has, or is recognised as having, jurisdiction under those regulations[275] and either party to the marriage (a) is domiciled in Scotland on the date on which the proceedings are begun[276]; or (b) died before that date and either was at death domiciled in Scotland or had been habitually resident in Scotland throughout the period of one year ending with the date of death.

As with jurisdiction in divorce and separation, therefore, the first gateway is the 1973 Act Sch.1B para.2, which provides that the Scottish court has jurisdiction if one of the criteria in paras (a)–(f) thereof is satisfied.[277]

Jurisdiction in proceedings for the declarator of recognition, or non-recognition, of a non-EU decree

12–60 By the 1973 Act Sch.1B para.6(1), the Court of Session[278] has jurisdiction to entertain proceedings for declarator of recognition, or non-recognition, of a relevant foreign (i.e. non-EU) decree relating to a same sex marriage if (and only if):

(1) the Scottish courts have jurisdiction under the 1973 Act Sch.1B para.2; or

(2) no court has, or is recognised as having, jurisdiction under those regulations[279] and either party to the marriage is domiciled in Scotland on the date on which the proceedings are begun, or died before that date and either was at death domiciled in Scotland or had been habitually resident in Scotland throughout the period of one year ending with the date of death.

Choice of law

12–61 Currently in divorce and separation actions in Scotland, the choice of law made by the forum is always the *lex fori*.[280] There is no reason to depart from this practice vis-à-vis the dissolution by Scots decree of same sex marriages. Equally the choice of law approach to annulment of marriage should extend, mutatis mutandis, to same sex marriage.[281]

---

[274] 1973 Act Sch.1B paras 5(1). As to shrieval jurisdiction, see 1973 Act Sch.1B paras 2 and 5(2) and (3).

[275] i.e. is equivalent to an "excluded action".

[276] 1973 Act Sch.1B para.5(1)(b). cf. 1973 Act s.7(3A).

[277] Detailed at para.12–58, above.

[278] As to shrieval jurisdiction, see 1973 Act Sch.1B para.6(2).

[279] i.e. is equivalent to an "excluded action".

[280] Para.12–18, above.

[281] Paras 11–03—11–05 re capacity to enter same sex marriage.

Recognition, or non-recognition, of a foreign divorce, annulment or separation of a same sex marriage

Part 2 of the Marriage (Same Sex Couples) (Jurisdiction and Recognition of Judgments) (Scotland) Regulations 2014 provides additional rules (corresponding to those contained in Brussels II *bis*) concerning recognition and refusal of recognition of EU Member State judgments. Part 2 of the 2014 Regulations is restricted to recognition of judgments of a court of an EU Member State.[282]

12–62

With regard to the recognition, or non-recognition, of a non-EU divorce, annulment or separation of a same sex marriage, reference must be made to the Family Law Act 1986 ss.45 – 54.[283]

Regulations 3 and 4 of the 2014 Regulations provide that if a court of an EU Member State (other than the UK) gives judgment in respect of the divorce of, annulment of the marriage of, or the judicial separation of a married same sex couple, that judgment is to be recognised in Scotland unless one of the grounds specified in reg.5 applies, permitting refusal of recognition of such a judgment.

In terms of reg.5(1), recognition of the validity of a judgment may be refused if the judgment was obtained at a time when it was irreconcilable with a decision determining the question of the subsistence or validity of the marriage (a) previously given by a court of civil jurisdiction in Scotland; or (b) previously given by a court elsewhere and recognised or entitled to be recognised in Scotland. Under reg.5(2), recognition of the validity of a judgment may be refused if the judgment was obtained at a time when the law of Scotland did not recognise marriages of same sex couples (i.e. did not, in domestic law, provide for such marriages). Regulation 5(2) does not prevent the recognition of a judgment if, at the time the judgment was obtained, the marriage would have been treated as a subsisting civil partnership according to the law of Scotland.[284] By reg.5(4)(a), recognition of the validity of a judgment obtained by means of proceedings, may be refused if it was obtained (i) without such steps having been taken for giving notice of the proceedings to a spouse as, having regard to the nature of the proceedings and all the circumstances, should reasonably have been taken; or (ii) without a spouse having been given (for any reason other than lack of notice) such opportunity to take part in the proceedings as, having regard to those matters, that spouse should reasonably have been given. By reg.5(4)(b),

---

[282] 2014 Regulations (SSI 2014/362) regs 1(3) and 3. It is of note that recognition of an EU divorce of a same sex marriage is not to be effected using Brussels II *bis* even though it is arguable that, since neither "divorce" nor "marriage" is defined in Brussels II *bis*, same sex divorces could have been treated as falling within the scope of that instrument.

[283] By Family Law Act 1986 s.11(3) and Sch.3. Part 1 of the Marriage (Same Sex Couples) Act 2013, in interpretation of "existing England and Wales legislation" (a) a reference to marriage is to be read as including a reference to marriage of a same sex couple; (b) a reference to a married couple is to be read as including a reference to a married same sex couple; and (c) a reference to a person who is married is to be read as including a reference to a person who is married to a person of the same sex. It must be assumed, therefore, that at least insofar as Pt II of the 1986 Act concerns the recognition (or otherwise) by an English court of a non-EU consistorial decree, the court will apply the same rules as it would apply to heterosexual marriage. The Marriage and Civil Partnership (Scotland) Act 2014 does not contain a provision corresponding to Sch.3 Pt 1 (mutatis mutandis), but it is to be thought that a Scots court, charged with recognising a non-EU consistorial decree of a same sex marriage, would apply the Family Law Act 1986 on a teleological basis.

[284] 2014 Regulations reg.5(3).

recognition of the validity of a judgment obtained otherwise than by means of proceedings, may be refused if there is no official document certifying the judgment is effective under the law of the country in which it was obtained. By reg.5(4)(c), recognition of a judgment, obtained by means of proceedings or otherwise, may be refused where recognition would be manifestly contrary to public policy.[285]

In terms of reg.6, the recognising court may not review the jurisdiction of the court which issued the judgment. Nor may a judgment be reviewed as to its substance. Further, by reg.7, the recognition of a judgment may not be refused on the grounds that Scots law would not allow divorce, declarator of nullity or judicial separation on the same facts.[286]

DISSOLUTION OF CIVIL PARTNERSHIP

Jurisdiction of Scots courts under the Civil Partnership Act 2004

12–63   Part 3 of the Act applies to civil partnerships registered in Scotland, and Pt 5 applies to civil partnerships formed and dissolved abroad (dissolution and separation: ss.117–122; and nullity: ss.123, 124).

Part 3—dissolution in Scotland of a civil partnership: jurisdiction

12–64   In terms of s.117, an action for the dissolution of a civil partnership may be brought in the Court of Session or in the sheriff court. Though s.117 in its terms does not restrict the jurisdiction which it confers to actions concerning civil partnerships registered in Scotland, Pt 5 of the Act (ss.225–227) lays down particular rules of jurisdiction of the Scottish courts in respect of civil partnerships formed abroad, and so by inference it would seem that Pt 3 jurisdiction must be restricted to those civil partnerships registered in Scotland, or possibly in the UK.[287] The jurisdictional link, therefore, for the first time in the treatment of the subject of jurisdiction in personal status, is based on the location of the occurrence of an event, rather than upon a personal connection between one or both parties and the forum.[288]

Under s.117, the Scottish court may grant decree of dissolution if, but only if, it is established that the civil partnership has broken down irretrievably or an interim gender recognition certificate under the Gender Recognition Act 2004 has been issued, after the date of registration of the civil partnership, to either of the civil partners. Irretrievable breakdown is taken to be established by proof of certain factors such as unreasonable behaviour, desertion, or non-cohabitation, all on the model of the domestic divorce law of Scotland as contained in the Divorce

---

[285] The drafting provenance of regs 3–5 is the Family Law Act 1986 s.46, as adapted for the recognition of dissolutions of civil partnerships obtained abroad (as contained in the Civil Partnership (Jurisdiction and Recognition of Judgments) (Scotland) Regulations 2005 (SSI 2005/629)).

[286] The drafting provenance of regs 6–7 is Brussels II *bis* arts 24–26.

[287] "Abroad" is not defined. Section 225(1)(c) confers residual jurisdiction on the Scottish courts.

[288] As has been seen, *locus registrationis* in Scotland will regulate capacity and form, but domicile safeguards are inserted where the *locus registrationis* is overseas. Paras 11–35—11–37, above.

(Scotland) Act 1976, as amended. A register of decrees of dissolution will be maintained at the General Register Office.

Part 5—civil partnerships formed or dissolved abroad

This Part makes provision for "overseas relationships", which are defined as specified relationships,[289] or as relationships which meet the general conditions,[290] *and* which are registered in a country outside the UK by two people who under the relevant law (q.v.) are of the same sex at the time when they do so, and neither of whom is already a civil partner or lawfully married. The Act describes in these provisions a set of factual/legal circumstances which is a sufficient approximation to the institution of civil partnership in UK law as to justify the attachment to those circumstances of (a) recognition in the UK; and (b) availability of domestic remedy. Thus: 12–65

Chapter 2—overseas relationships treated as civil partnerships

(i) General rule—section 215

In order to have an overseas relationship treated as a civil partnership, the parties must have had legal capacity under the *locus registrationis*,[291] and have met all the formal requirements of the locus. 12–66

(ii) Persons domiciled in a part of the UK—section 217

By s.217 persons domiciled in Scotland will not be treated as having formed a civil partnership if, at the time of registration, they were not eligible in terms of s.86[292] to register such a relationship in Scotland.[293] This section reinstates for parties domiciled in a part of the UK the traditional rule that the law of the domicile regulates legal capacity to enter into domestic relationships. In this way, the registration of an overseas relationship receives a different treatment from the registration of a civil partnership within the UK, in respect of the latter of which essential validity (including capacity) and formal validity are both governed by the *lex loci registrationis*. 12–67

By inference, it must be that a Scots court in seeking to establish whether parties (neither of whom was, at the point of registration, domiciled in a part of the UK) have validly created a civil partnership abroad, must apply the *lex loci registrationis*, including its rules of private international law.

(iii)Public policy—section 218

---

[289] Defined in s.213, and by reference to Sch.20, as augmented by the Civil Partnership Act 2004 (Overseas Relationships) Order 2005 (SI 2005/3135).

[290] The general conditions per s.214 (as amended by the Marriage and Civil Partnership (Scotland) Act 2014 s.26(2)) are that, under the relevant law: (a) the relationship may not be entered into if either of the parties is already a party to a relationship of that kind or lawfully married; (b) the relationship is of indeterminate duration; and (ba) the relationship is not one of marriage; (c) the effect of entering into it is that the parties are: (i) treated as a couple either generally or for specified purposes, but are not treated as married.

[291] Being the law of the place of registration, including its rules of private international law (ss.212, 215), although by s.216(1) the parties are not to be treated as having formed a civil partnership in such circumstances if at the time of registration they were not at that date of the same sex under UK law.

[292] Para.11–35, above.

[293] The same principle applies to English domiciliaries (s.217(2)) and Northern Irish domiciliaries (s.217(5)).

12–68   All of the above is subject to the usual public policy discretion of the forum, which will justify non-recognition of a capacity existing under the *lex loci registrationis*.

Part 5 Chapter 3—dissolution of civil partnerships formed abroad: jurisdiction of the Scottish courts

12–69   Section 225 provides that the Court of Session and, in qualifying cases, the sheriff court, has jurisdiction to entertain an action for the dissolution of a civil partnership formed abroad, or for separation of such partners,[294] if (and only if):

(a)   the court has jurisdiction under regulations made under s.219 of the Act (that is, to correspond to Brussels II *bis* art.3)[295]; or

(b)   if no court has jurisdiction under (a) above, and either civil partner is domiciled in Scotland on the date when the proceedings are begun; or

(c)   the following conditions are met—

    (i)   the two people concerned registered their partnership in Scotland[296];

    (ii)   no court has jurisdiction under (a) above; and

    (iii) it appears to the court to be in the interests of justice to assume jurisdiction in the case.[297]

Conflicting jurisdictions

12–70   Given that the bases of jurisdiction adopted for dissolution of civil partnerships are modelled on the rules found in Brussels II *bis*, it would have been reasonable to expect that the rule on conflicting jurisdictions would have followed the *lis pendens* system. In fact, provision is made in s.226, and accompanying secondary legislation,[298] for the resolution of cases of conflicting jurisdiction in a manner which corresponds to the system of mandatory and discretionary sists contained in Sch.3 to the 1973 Act. This is an odd amalgam of Brussels and non-Brussels rules.

---

[294] For declarators of nullity, jurisdiction is restricted to the Court of Session; see s.225(3). Contrast shrieval jurisdiction in respect of nullity of same sex marriage: n.274, above.

[295] Detailed rules, laid under s.219 of the 2004 Act, are set out in the Civil Partnership (Jurisdiction and Recognition of Judgments) (Scotland) Regulations 2005 (SSI 2005/629) reg.4. These rules, which align the rules on jurisdiction in respect of dissolution and annulment of civil partnerships, and separation of partners, with the corresponding rules for dissolution of marriage contained in Brussels II *bis*, came into force on December 5, 2005. Equivalent rules applying in England and Wales, and Northern Ireland, are contained in the Civil Partnership (Jurisdiction and Recognition of Judgments) Regulations (SI 2005/3334).

[296] There is a precedent for this in that at common law in Scotland *locus celebrationis* was regarded as a good ground of jurisdiction in annulment of marriage if it was averred that the marriage was void: *Prawdziclazarska*, 1954 S.C. 98.

[297] i.e. the residual rules of national jurisdiction. cf. Brussels II *bis* art.7.

[298] Act of Sederunt (Ordinary Cause Rules) Amendment (Civil Partnership Act 2004) 2005 (SSI 2005/638) Pt XIII (sisting of civil partnership actions) (rr.33A.79–33A.84). For equivalent rules for England and Wales, see the Family Procedure (Civil Partnership: Staying of Proceedings) Rules 2010 (SI 2010/2986) (r.3: obligatory stays; r.4: discretionary stays).

Choice of law rules for dissolution, separation and nullity of civil partnership

There is no direct reference in the 2004 Act to choice of law.

12–71

Currently in divorce and separation actions in Scotland, the choice of law made by the forum is always the *lex fori*. It is assumed that this approach will apply also in relation to dissolution and separation of civil partnerships.[299]

With regard to annulment,[300] in the case of civil partnerships registered in Scotland, the civil partnership is void if, and only if, the parties were not eligible to register (see s.86), or, being eligible, either of them did not validly consent to its formation.[301]

The minor differences between the body of provisions governing civil partnerships registered in England and Wales, and Northern Ireland, from those which are to obtain with regard to civil partnerships registered in Scotland, have resulted in a latent choice of law direction in s.124, viz.: where two people have registered as civil partners of each other in England and Wales, or Northern Ireland, and wish to have that relationship declared null in Scotland, it is enacted that their civil partnership is to be regarded as void (or voidable) if it would be void (or voidable) in England and Wales, or Northern Ireland, respectively.[302] This must mean that a Scottish dissolution forum must apply to a civil partnership registered in England and Wales, or Northern Ireland, those provisions in the Act which have been particularly crafted for those jurisdictions.

By the same token where (by implication of the Act) two people seek a dissolution of their partnership in a Scots court (per ss.225–227), said partnership being "an apparent or alleged overseas relationship", s.124(7) directs that the civil partnership is void if the relationship is not an overseas relationship or, being an overseas relationship, the parties are not to be regarded under Ch.2 of Pt 5 (overseas relationships treated as civil partnerships) as having formed a civil partnership. Further, s.124(8), in regard to overseas relationships, provides that the civil partnership is voidable if it is voidable under the relevant law,[303] or, either of the parties being domiciled in England and Wales or Northern Ireland, if the circumstances fall within ss.50 or 174 (grounds on which a civil partnership is voidable, in England and Wales, and Northern Ireland, respectively).

---

[299] The rules of the Scots *lex fori* pertaining to grounds of dissolution and separation are contained in ss.117–122 of the 2004 Act.

[300] The rules of the Scots *lex fori* pertaining to grounds of nullity are contained in ss.123 and 124 of the 2004 Act.

[301] 2004 Act s.123.

[302] For grounds of voidability, see ss.50 and 51. cf. ss.174, 175 for Northern Ireland.

[303] 2004 Act s.124(10) defines relevant law as the law of the country or territory where the overseas relationship was registered, including its rules of private international law. This therefore amounts to reference to the use of that law, including its conflict rules.

Recognition of foreign decrees of dissolution, separation and nullity of civil partnership

Decrees obtained in the UK

12–72 By s.233,[304] no dissolution or annulment of a civil partnership obtained in one part of the UK is effective in any part of the UK unless obtained from a court of civil jurisdiction. Likewise[305] if such a judicial dissolution, etc. is obtained from a court in one part of the UK, it shall be recognised throughout the UK subject to the principles of res judicata and avoidance of irreconcilable judgments.

Decrees obtained overseas

12–73 Section 234(2) permits rules of recognition of EU decrees to be introduced, mirroring those which obtain in relation to matrimonial decrees under Brussels II *bis*.[306] With regard to the recognition in Scotland of judgments from EU Member States,[307] the Civil Partnership (Jurisdiction and Recognition of Judgments) (Scotland) Regulations 2005 regs 6 and 7, lay down rules for obtaining a declarator of recognition, and the grounds for refusal of the same. Notably, these provisions apply to all judgments even if the date of the judgment is earlier than the date on which s.219 and the 2005 Regulations came into force.

The rules of recognition of non-EU decrees[308] follow closely the provisions for recognition (and refusal thereof) of overseas consistorial decrees which are contained in the Family Law Act 1986 ss.46 and 51. The mirroring continues in ss.237 and 238,[309] but one notable novelty is contained in s.237(2)(b)(ii), which addresses the interesting issue of the proper resolution of the following situation: what is to happen where (i) a party has purported to enter into a civil partnership in a jurisdiction in which he is not domiciled; and (ii) one or both parties to the purported partnership is/are domiciled in a country which does not recognise such relationships between two persons of the same sex; (iii) this relationship, presumably legally constituted according to the *lex loci registrationis*,[310] has broken down; (iv) the parties have obtained a dissolution order from a court in the *locus registrationis*, and now seek to have that order recognised in the UK? Section 237(2) permits the Lord Chancellor or the Scottish Ministers to make provision for such cases,[311] but it is uncertain whether provision is necessary, and it is difficult to predict the nature of the modifications to be made. If the difficulty

---

[304] cf. Family Law Act 1986 s.44(1).

[305] cf. Family Law Act 1986 s.44(2).

[306] Civil Partnership (Jurisdiction and Recognition of Judgments) (Scotland) Regulations 2005 (SSI 2005/629); and, for England and Wales, and Northern Ireland, the Civil Partnership (Jurisdiction and Recognition of Judgments) Regulations (SI 2005/3334).

[307] Defined in the Civil Partnership (Jurisdiction and Recognition of Judgments) (Scotland) Regulations 2005 (SSI 2005/629) reg.5; and the Civil Partnership (Jurisdiction and Recognition of Judgments) Regulations (SI 2005/3334) reg.6. Notably Denmark is included as a Member State for this purpose.

[308] 2004 Act s.235 (grounds for recognition); s.236 (refusal of recognition).

[309] cf. Family Law Act 1986 ss.46(5) and 50, respectively.

[310] Bearing in mind s.124(10).

[311] e.g. Civil Partnership (Supplementary Provisions relating to the Recognition of Overseas Dissolutions, Annulments or Separations) (Scotland) Regulations 2005 (SSI 2005/567); and Civil

in the case described is one of capacity to enter into a new partnership, s.238 already provides a solution. If it is rather a matter of the wisdom of according recognition to such a dissolution, s.236(3)(c) permits withholding recognition on the grounds of public policy. However, if the effect of withholding recognition of a dissolution would be to recognise the continuing existence (according to Scots conflict rules) of a legal relationship which is forbidden by the domicile of one of the parties, such an outcome seems counter-productive.

Since there is to be a dual system, with provision for one set of rules for recognition of EU decrees, and another set for non-EU decrees, it will be important to delimit the scope of operation of each set of rules. Moreover, it will require to be clarified, as regards, e.g. the recognition of EU decrees, when s.234 of Pt 5 of the 2004 Act applies, and when Pt 2 of the Marriage (Same Sex Couples) (Jurisdiction and Recognition of Judgments) (Scotland) Regulations 2014[312] which provide additional rules (corresponding to those contained in Brussels II *bis*) concerning recognition and refusal of recognition of EU Member State judgments, applies. By which law is the relationship to be characterised as "marriage" or "partnership"? Upon that categorisation rests the decision as to which set of jurisdiction and recognition rules apply. A further dilemma of delimitation might arise in relation to conflicting proceedings concerning the same relationship, in order to decide which set of conflicting jurisdiction rules should apply.

This body of primary and secondary legislation, complex and voluminous as it is, nonetheless fails to deal clearly and comprehensively with the conflict of laws dimension. Much time has been spent on drafting legislation in this area, but to date there are no reported cases.

Cessation of de facto cohabitation

De facto relationships, by definition, do not require formalities at the point of commencement, or conclusion, but a court may be asked to make proprietary and/or financial provision to a "cohabitant", during or at the cessation of the de facto relationship, and therefore must ascertain by the relevant applicable law, whether the claimant qualifies as a cohabitant. For this purpose, the length of the period, and nature, of the alleged cohabitation will be relevant.[313] The Family Law (Scotland) Act 2006 s.28, empowers the court to make certain financial provision orders, "where cohabitants cease to cohabit otherwise than by reason of the death of one (or both) of them". The test of cessation therefore is a factual one.[314] Similarly, application to the court by the survivor for provision on intestacy will be possible upon proof of the death intestate of a predeceasing cohabitant, domiciled in Scotland.

12–74

Partnership (Supplementary Provisions relating to the Recognition of Overseas Dissolutions, Annulments or Legal Separations) (England and Wales and Northern Ireland) Regulations 2005 (SI 2005/3104).

[312] Marriage (Same Sex Couples) (Jurisdiction and Recognition of Judgments) (Scotland) Regulations 2014 (SSI 2014/362).

[313] For Scots law, see Family Law (Scotland) Act 2006 ss.25–30. Ch.11, above.

[314] The problem is that the applicability of these provisions in a conflict of laws sense is not clear. Para.11–40, above.

SUMMARY 12

12–75   1.   Divorce and judicial separation

Allocation of jurisdiction—Domicile and Matrimonial Proceedings Act 1973 ss.7 and 8, as amended to ensure compliance with Brussels II *bis*.

Conflicting jurisdiction—Outside the Brussels regime: a discretionary sist system applies (Domicile and Matrimonial Proceedings Act 1973 Sch.3). Under Brussels II *bis*: a *lis pendens* system operates (art.19).

Choice of law—Scots law as the *lex fori* determines grounds as well as procedure. Council Regulation (EU) No.1259/2010 implementing enhanced cooperation with regard to the law applicable to divorce and legal separation ("Rome III") came into effect on 21 June 2012 in participating Member States, of which the UK is not one.

Recognition of foreign divorces, including extrajudicial divorces—Outside the Brussels regime, and within the United Kingdom: the matter is governed by ss.44–51 of the Family Law Act 1986. Under Brussels II *bis*: arts 21–27 apply.

2.   Annulment of marriage

Allocation of jurisdiction—Domicile and Matrimonial Proceedings Act 1973 ss.7 and 8, as amended to ensure compliance with Brussels II *bis*.

Conflicting jurisdiction—Outside the Brussels regime: a discretionary sist system applies (Domicile and Matrimonial Proceedings Act 1973 Sch.3). Under Brussels II *bis*: a *lis pendens* system operates (art.19).

Choice of law—grounds of annulment in a Scots forum correspond to the Scots choice of law rules on constitution of marriage in the matters of formal invalidity, legal incapacity, physical incapacity and defective consent. Particular note should be taken of the Family Law (Scotland) Act 2006 ss.2 and 38.

Recognition of foreign annulments—Outside the Brussels regime, and within the United Kingdom: the matter is governed by ss.44–51 of the Family Law Act 1986. Under Brussels II *bis*: arts 21–27 apply.

3.   Same sex marriage: matrimonial remedies

Allocation of jurisdiction—per Domicile and Matrimonial Proceedings Act 1973 s.8A, as amended to ensure compliance with Marriage and Civil Partnership (Scotland) Act 2014; and The Marriage (Same Sex Couples) (Jurisdiction and Recognition of Judgments) (Scotland) Regulations 2014 (SSI 2014/362).

Choice of law—as per divorce and annulment rules pertaining to heterosexual marriage.

Recognition of foreign dissolutions—Part 2 of the Marriage (Same Sex Couples) (Jurisdiction and Recognition of Judgments) (Scotland) Regulations 2014 for recognition and refusal of recognition of EU Member State judgments; and, with regard to the recognition, or non-recognition, of a non-EU divorce, annulment or separation of a same sex marriage, Family Law Act 1986 ss.45–54.

4.   Dissolution of civil partnership

SUMMARY 12

Allocation of jurisdiction—Civil Partnership Act 2004 ss.117–122 (dissolution and separation), 123 (annulment), and 225–227 (jurisdiction of Scottish courts).

Conflicting jurisdictions—A discretionary sist system applies per Civil Partnership Act 2004 s.226.

Choice of law—limited guidance is contained in the Civil Partnership Act 2004 s.124.

Recognition of foreign decrees of dissolution, annulment and separation—Intra-UK decrees, and non-EU decrees: Civil Partnership Act 2004 ss.233 and 234(1), respectively; EU decrees: Civil Partnership Act 2004 s.234(2) applies.

CHAPTER 13

Proprietary and financial consequences of marriage and other adult relationships

PROPRIETARY CONSEQUENCES

Property rights of married persons

The effect of marriage upon the property rights of parties differs from one legal **13–01** system to another. Certain systems imply that, in the absence of an express marriage contract between the parties, marriage creates a "community of goods" between the spouses.

Under domestic Scots law, marriage per se has no effect upon the property rights of spouses. The Family Law (Scotland) Act 1985 s.24 states that marriage shall not of itself affect the respective rights of parties to the marriage in relation to their property.[1]

The different approaches taken by legal systems to the effect of marriage upon the property rights of spouses have the potential to produce conflict of laws problems. Attempts to resolve such problems, and to reconcile the differences in approach, were made by the Hague Conference on Private International Law in 1978, resulting in a Convention on the Law Applicable to Matrimonial Property Regimes, which, however, the United Kingdom did not sign.[2] The subject of matrimonial property is the focus of renewed international harmonisation efforts, on a European basis.[3]

When dealing with a question of matrimonial property rights having cross-border implications, one of the first issues to ascertain is whether a "matrimonial property regime" was established upon marriage, either by operation of law, or by contract. There are three possibilities:

(1) a (default) statutory system imposing some version of a community of goods regime;
(2) private marriage contract; or
(3) absence of statutory or private contractual provision.

---

[1] There is therefore in Scots law a system of separation of property, except for (i) piecemeal legislative provision, such as the Family Law (Scotland) Act 1985 s.25 (presumption of equal share in household goods); (ii) "equalisation" provisions which obtain at termination of marriage by divorce per Family Law (Scotland) Act 1985 ss.8–17; and (iii) the modifying effect of a surviving spouse's claim for legal rights in the moveable estate of the predeceaser on his/her death intestate, a very long-established feature of Scots law.

[2] The Convention is of very limited effect, entering into force in only three countries.

[3] Para.13–17, below.

Scots applicable law rules of matrimonial property have been placed on a legislative footing in terms of the Family Law (Scotland) Act 2006 s.39. By virtue of s.39(6)(b), the Scots choice of law rules provided thereby concerning matrimonial property are subject to the spouses' contrary agreement. It is therefore apparent that these rules do not trump private marriage contract provisions. Since, as will be explained below, the traditional approach of Scots and English conflict rules has been to assimilate the effect of statutory codes to that of private marriage contracts, and since any other construction would be productive of great difficulty, it is assumed that the provisions contained in s.39 are subject also to rights which have vested under a statutory scheme (though it has to be conceded that the Act nowhere makes such a specific assertion).[4]

Marriage contracts: statutory community of goods

13–02   In certain countries there is a statutory code which, in the absence of a private marriage contract, establishes a community of goods between husband and wife. Such a code is likely to have the same legal effect as a private marriage contract. In order to avoid the operation of statutory community of goods, parties by contract may exclude the community of goods if permitted so to do by the statutory regime.[5]

The leading case of *De Nicols v Curlier*[6] shows that failure by spouses to enter into a private marriage contract may mean that, by default, they become subject to the property regime laid down by the law in terms of which they may be presumed to have entered the marriage relationship.[7] The rights which spouses acquire under the statutory regime are thought to vest at the point of contracting: no matter where the parties subsequently may reside, their property rights are not affected by subsequent change(s) of domicile.[8] This doctrine is known as immutability of property rights. The most famous Scottish (House of Lords) case on the topic, *Lashley v Hog*,[9] appears prima facie to be inconsistent with the theory of immutability. In *Lashley*, Hog of Newliston, domiciled in Scotland, removed to England and became domiciled there. While in England he married an Englishwoman and the parties had a number of children, including Thomas Hog, and a daughter who became Mrs Lashley (the litigants). Upon his wife's death in 1760, Hog returned to Scotland where he died domiciled. Mrs Lashley then claimed not only *legitim* (due to a child of the marriage), but also a share in

---

[4] See further para.13–11, below.

[5] *Shand-Harvey v Bennet-Clark*, 1910 1 S.L.T. 133 Sh. Ct.

[6] *De Nicols v Curlier (No.1)* [1900] A.C. 21 (moveables); *De Nicols v Curlier (No.2)* [1900] 2 Ch. 410 (immoveables).

[7] There may be argument about the basis on which this law, when identified, is to apply. Any given regime of community rules will provide for the extent of its own application, e.g. *De Nicols (No.1)* [1900] A.C. 21, per Lord Macnaghten at 33: "Community of goods in France is constituted by a marriage in France according to French law, not by married people coming to France and settling there. And the community must commence from the day of the marriage. It cannot commence from any other time." "Late entry" usually therefore will be precluded.

[8] At the dates when the grand illustrative cases of *Lashley v Hog* (1804) 4 Pat. 581; *De Nicols (No.1)* [1900] A.C. 21; and *Shand-Harvey v Bennet-Clark*, 1910 1 S.L.T. 133 were handed down, the conjugal unit had one conjoined domicile. This no longer being the case, the property rules are accordingly more difficult to state.

[9] *Lashley v Hog* (1804) 4 Pat. 581.

the *communio bonorum* of her parents' marriage to which at that date (and until (Dunlop's) Marriage Act 1855)[10] the representatives of a predeceasing wife could lay claim, standing in their mother's place.[11] This so-called *communio bonorum* was vestigial evidence of community of property in Scots law[12]; the law of England had no equivalent. The House of Lords, in upholding Mrs Lashley's claim, might be thought to have admitted the possibility that matrimonial property rights may change upon change of domicile, since the law of England, the domicile at marriage, would have admitted no such property claim.[13] If, on the other hand, the case is regarded as a succession case, which is plausible, it was proper for Scots law, as the law of the deceased's domicile at death, to regulate Mrs Lashley's claim.[14]

If it is to be argued by one or both parties that the foreign community of property regime has extraterritorial effect, such as to purport to extend to foreign immoveable property, this, if not admitted,[15] must be proved, the onus lying on the married pair, or the survivor as the case is more likely to be.[16] The *lex situs* in its discretion may accept that the devolution of land within its territory is to be regulated by some legal system other than its own, i.e. the *lex situs* may acquiesce in a foreign community of property regime.[17]

Although it seems clear that the survivor may claim under the terms of a matrimonial regime, private or statutory, no matter that the predeceaser died domiciled in another legal system (that is to say, it can confidently be expected that the matter will be regarded as one of matrimonial property rather than succession), if, rather, the question is whether the survivor has the option to choose between the rights conferred by a matrimonial property regime, on the one hand, and rights conferred by means of succession to the deceased's estate, on the other, the point seems to be regarded as one of succession, to be determined, in principle and in detail, by the law of the deceased's last domicile.[18]

---

[10] Intestate Moveable Succession (Scotland) Act 1855 s.6.

[11] Of the surviving three children, Mrs Lashley alone claimed under this head, her brother Alexander having received advances from their father during his lifetime. In the circumstances, it was not in the succession interests of her brother Thomas to argue in favour of the application of Scots law on this point.

[12] It was a claim by Mrs Bell's daughter for her deceased mother's share in the "goods in communion" which occasioned the House of Lords decision on continuance of domicile of origin: *Bell v Kennedy* (1868) 6 M. (H.L.) 69.

[13] There was never a matrimonial property regime in England, a fact which enabled the House of Lords 100 years later in *De Nicols* to distinguish *Lashley*.

[14] See Ch.18, below. cf. Walton, *A Handbook of Husband and Wife according to the Law of Scotland*, 3rd edn (Edinburgh: W. Green, 1951), pp.352–354.

[15] *De Nicols (No.2)* [1900] 2 Ch. 410.

[16] *Callwood v Callwood* [1960] A.C. 659: widow unable to prove that Danish community of property regime extended to Great Thatch Island in the British Virgin Islands.

[17] *De Nicols (No.2)* [1900] 2 Ch. 410; *Chiwell v Carlyon* (1897) 14 S.C. (S.A.) 61 (South Africa) (land in Cornwall, being community property by the law of South Africa, devolved according to that law) (details to be found at *Cheshire, North and Fawcett: Private International Law*, 14th edn (2008), p.1303).

[18] *Re Mengel's Will Trusts* [1962] Ch. 791; contrast *Re Allen's Estate* [1945] 2 All E.R. 264.

13–03 In the absence of a default system of community of goods, or even within such a system if the system itself permits, parties may enter into a private marriage contract, selecting for example a system of community of property of their choosing and on their own terms, or of separation of property.

Proper/governing law

13–04 "Obligations arising out of matrimonial property regimes, [and] property regimes of relationships deemed by the law applicable to such relationships to have comparable effects to marriage" are excluded from the Rome I Regulation.[19] Hence, marriage contracts are governed by Scots and English common law choice of law rules, though a marriage contract involving trusts will be regulated by the Recognition of Trusts Act 1987.[20] Consequently, the proper law of a private marriage contract, following the common law rules for commercial contracts, is either the law by which the parties expressly, or by implication, agree that it is to be governed, or failing any such express or implied agreement, the law with which the contract has the most real and substantial connection.[21]

Capacity to enter into a marriage contract

13–05 As regards immoveables, capacity to enter into a marriage contract is governed by the *lex situs*.[22] As regards moveables there is no recent case law, but arguing by analogy from the topic of commercial contracts, application of the putative proper law (that is, the law which would govern the contract if it were valid) commends itself.

In earlier days, an argument was adduced that a distinction could be drawn between void and voidable marriage contracts. In the former case, capacity to grant a marriage contract was referable to the law of the domicile of the granter at the date of the purported grant,[23] and in the latter, the question was whether, by the law of the domicile of the granter at the date of the purported revocation, s/he had capacity to revoke.[24] It may still be thought best to express the matter in the form that revocability is an issue for the putative proper law of the contract, whereas capacity to revoke is an issue for the *lex domicilii* at the time of the purported revocation of the party/parties wishing to revoke. Later English

---

[19] Rome I Regulation art.1.2(c). cf. "Rights in property arising out of a matrimonial relationship", Rome I Convention art.1.2.6.

[20] Para.18–67, below.

[21] e.g. *Chamberlain v Napier* (1880) L.R. 15 Ch. D. 614; *Re Fitzgerald* [1904] 1 Ch. 573; *Re Mackenzie* [1911] 1 Ch. 578; *Re Hewitt's Settlement* [1915] 1 Ch. 228; *Brown v Brown*, 1913 2 S.L.T. 314; *Eadie's Trustees v Henderson*, 1919 1 S.L.T. 253; *Goold Stuart's Trustees v McPhail*, 1947 S.L.T. 221; *Earl Iveagh v Inland Revenue Commissioners* [1954] Ch. 364; *Duke of Marlborough v Att Gen* [1945] Ch. 78 ("presumption" in favour of matrimonial, i.e. husband's, domicile applied); *Re Bankes* [1902] 2 Ch. 333 ("presumption" rebutted); *R v R* [1995] 1 F.C.R. 745.

[22] *Black v Black's Trustees*, 1950 S.L.T. (Notes) 32.

[23] *Re Cooke's Trusts* (1887) 3 T.L.R. 558; *Cooper v Cooper* (1888) 15 R. (H.L.) 21; *Black v Black's Trustees*, 1950 S.L.T. (Notes) 32.

[24] *Viditz v O'Hagan* [1900] 2 Ch. 87; *Sawrey-Cookson v Sawrey-Cookson's Trustees* (1905) 8 F. 157.

consensus[25] construes all cases as supporting a reference to the putative proper law, but the case of *Cooper v Cooper*[26] (in which the House of Lords held that a wife of Scots domicile was entitled, by Irish law, to repudiate an ante-nuptial contract made by her when a minor domiciled in Ireland) strictly remains authoritative in Scotland, although the decision is open to different interpretation.[27]

The case of *Sawrey-Cookson v Sawrey-Cookson's Trustees*[28] is instructive in a number of aspects: a Scotswoman granted in Scotland a unilateral ante-nuptial marriage settlement in Scots form in anticipation of her marriage to an Englishman. A few years later, she wished to revoke it. As the proper law of the deed was Scots, Scots law determined its revocability, but her capacity to revoke was to be referred to her English domicile at the date of proposed revocation. She also had executed in England, after her marriage, a ratification of the settlement: that deed had an English proper law, and its effect and its revocability, as well as her legal capacity to revoke, were to be determined by the law of England.

Formal validity

It is sufficient that the deed complies in form either with the proper law or with the law of the place where the marriage contract was executed.[29]   **13–06**

Essential validity

Essential validity is governed by the *lex situs* as regards immoveables.[30] As   **13–07** regards moveable property, the proper law applies,[31] being the law with reference to which the contract was made, and which the parties intended to govern their rights and liabilities, or failing such ascertainable or deemed intention, by the law

---

[25] *Dicey, Morris and Collins on the Conflict of Laws*, 15th edn (2012), para.28–042; *Cheshire, North and Fawcett: Private International Law*, 14th edn (2008), pp.1304–1306. See also Morris, "Capacity to Make a Marriage Settlement Contract in English Private International Law" (1938) 54 L.Q.R. 78.

[26] *Cooper v Cooper* (1888) 15 R. (H.L.) 21.

[27] e.g. Morris, *Conflict of Laws*, 7th edn (2009), para.16–011; *Dicey, Morris and Collins on the Conflict of Laws*, 15th edn (2012), para.28–039.

[28] *Sawrey-Cookson v Sawrey-Cookson's Trustees* (1905) 8 F. 157.

[29] *Guepratte v Young* (1851) 4 De G. & Sm. 217; *Van Grutten v Digby* (1862) 31 Beav. 561; *Re Bankes* [1902] 2 Ch. 333.

[30] *Tezcan v Tezcan* (1992) 87 D.L.R. 503 BC CA.

[31] Scottish cases: *Countess of Findlater and Seafield v Seafield Grant*, 8 February 1814, F.C.; *Williamson v Taylor* (1845) 8 D. 156; *Scott v Sinclair* (1865) 3 M. 918; *Earl of Stair v Head* (1844) 6 D. 904; *Corbet v Waddell* (1879) 7 R. 200; *Brown's Trustees* (1890) 17 R. 1174; *Brown v Brown*, 1913 2 S.L.T. 314; *Lister's Judicial Factor v Syme*, 1914 S.C. 204; *Battye's Trustee v Battye's Administrator*, 1917 S.C. 385; *Montgomery v Zarifi*, 1918 S.C. (H.L.) 128; *Eadie's Trustees v Henderson*, 1919 1 S.L.T. 253; *Goold Stuart's Trustees v McPhail*, 1947 S.L.T. 221; *Stevenson v Currie* (1905) 13 S.L.T. 457; *Black v Black's Trustees*, 1950 S.L.T. (Notes) 32; *Lashley v Hog* (1804) 4 Pat. 581. English cases: *Van Grutten v Digby* (1862) 31 Beav. 561; *Chamberlain v Napier* (1800) L.R. 15 Ch. D. 614; *Re Hernando* (1884) 27 Ch. D. 284; *Re Fitzgerald* [1904] 1 Ch. 573; *Re Mackenzie* [1911] 1 Ch. 578; *Re Hewitt's Settlement* [1915] 1 Ch. 228; *Duke of Marlborough v Att Gen* [1945] Ch. 78. Irish case: *Re Lord Cloncurry's Estate* [1932] I.R. 687.

of most real and substantial connection, objectively construed.[32] Thus the proper law applies to all questions of substance such as:

(1)   the validity of the provisions of the deed;
(2)   the property rights of the parties; and
(3)   whether the deed is revocable *sua natura*.

The meaning of the terms of the contract, including possibly identification of the property to be affected by the contract, is determined by the law governing interpretation of the contract (which might be expressed by the parties, or could be inferred from the language of the deed; failing which the putative proper law will apply).[33]

Effect of a change of domicile on a private marriage contract

13–08   A change of domicile, while it may affect the capacity of the parties to revoke an existing agreement, does not affect the contractual rights of the parties.[34] This means that the rights of third parties, for example the husband's creditors, whose claims may be good by their own laws, i.e. by the law(s) governing the debt(s), may be prejudiced by the pre-existing rights of the debtor's spouse under another law governing the debtor's marriage contract or matrimonial regime, in terms of which the spouse's rights have vested.[35]

The powers of the parties v. the powers of the divorce forum

13–09   Any UK forum, if properly seised of jurisdiction in divorce, will apply its own law to grounds of divorce and to the rules of property distribution upon divorce. In domestic Scots law, a degree of party autonomy by way of private ordering has long been permitted.[36] A Scots court generally will endeavour to give effect to parties' wishes as expressed in their contract, provided that the contract is valid, essentially and formally, and that the parties had capacity to enter into it. A straightforward approach is taken, namely, that a private agreement[37] should be:

> "construed and enforced on precisely the same principles as any commercial agreement … [T]he parties to a marriage can oust the jurisdiction of the courts to make financial provision on divorce if they want to. Assuming that their agreement was not reducible on the contractual grounds of force and fear, facility or

---

[32] See paras 15–04 and 14–20, below. Consider *Re Bankes* [1902] 2 Ch. 333; and see also *Chamberlain v Napier* (1880) L.R. 15 Ch. D. 614 (Scots and English law, respectively, governed different parts of the deed).

[33] *Corbet v Waddell* (1879) 7 R. 200; *Hope Vere v Hope Vere* (1907) 13 S.L.T. 774; affirmed (1907) 15 S.L.T. 361 HL; and *Drummond v Bell-Irving*, 1930 S.C. 704.

[34] *Shand-Harvey*, 1910 1 S.L.T. 133 Sh. Ct.

[35] *Shand-Harvey*, 1910 1 S.L.T. 133 Sh. Ct.

[36] Subject to limited judicial control: Family Law (Scotland) Act 1985 s.14(2)(h) (power to grant an incidental order, including an order setting aside or varying any term in an antenuptial or postnuptial marriage settlement—but such an order may be made only if justified by the principles set out in s.9 of the Act); and ss.16, 17 (judicial power to vary contractual terms agreed by parties to come into effect in the event of divorce or nullity).

[37] Pre- or post-nuptial: *Kibble v Kibble,* 2010 S.L.T. (Sh Ct) 5.

circumvention, the only question is whether it was fair and reasonable when it was entered into. This is a fairly broad test, as it allows all the circumstances when the contract was entered into to be examined."[38]

But a legal system may have policy objections to agreements which envisage, or seek to regulate ante-nuptially, the property effects of termination of the marriage about to be entered into. Doubts in English law rested on two different strands of policy, viz., that ante-nuptial provision might be inimical to the stability of a marriage and, secondly, that in principle the wishes of the parties should not be capable of ousting the jurisdiction of the court to make such financial/proprietary provision as it thinks fit upon dissolution of the marriage.

Traditionally English courts have been more antagonistic than Scots courts of arrangements made by private contract. The legitimacy and effect of the exercise of party autonomy in relation to matrimonial property was subject to UK Supreme Court scrutiny in the seminal English case of *Radmacher v Granatino*,[39] concerning the principles to be applied when a court, in considering post-marital breakdown financial arrangements, must decide what weight should be given to a pre-nuptial agreement. The Supreme Court showed favour to a pre-nuptial agreement which was valid and enforceable by the foreign national laws of each party. The parties (of French and German nationality, respectively), at the wife's request had made a pre-nuptial agreement, valid by French and German law, waiving any claims for maintenance after divorce. The court, noting that the subject area was ripe for reform by Parliament, took the view that under the then current state of the law, an English court, in ordering a financial settlement upon divorce, could give weight to the existence of the marital property regime which the parties freely had chosen, as part of the wide discretion given to the court by the Matrimonial Causes Act 1973 s.25. On the subject of autonomy, the President of the Court, Lord Phillips, stated that:

"The reason why the court should give weight to a nuptial agreement is that there should be respect for individual autonomy. The court should accord respect to the decision of a married couple as to the manner in which their financial affairs should be regulated. It would be paternalistic and patronising to override their agreement simply on the basis that the court knows best. This is particularly true where the parties' agreement addresses existing circumstances and not merely the contingencies of an uncertain future."[40]

Contemporary *mores* place a high value on personal autonomy. As Thorpe L.J. remarked earlier in the Court of Appeal, "Due respect for adult autonomy suggests that, subject of course to proper safeguards, a carefully fashioned contract should be available as an alternative to the stress, anxieties and expense of a submission to the width of the judicial discretion."[41] The judgment of the Supreme Court ushered in a new era for party autonomy in cases heard in

---

[38] Speech by Lord Hope to the Family Law Association Conference, "Family Law in the UK Supreme Court" (18 November 2011).
[39] *Radmacher v Granatino (also known as G v R (Pre-Nuptial Contract))* [2010] UKSC 42; [2011] 1 A.C. 534.
[40] *Radmacher v Granatino (also known as G v R (Pre-Nuptial Contract))* [2010] UKSC 42; [2011] 1 A.C. 534 at [78].
[41] *Radmacher v Granatino* [2009] EWCA Civ 649 at [27].

England, recognising as it does the weight and "new respect"[42] to be given to the
exercise of party freedom of choice in the context of marriage contracts.

The position now in the UK, therefore, is that the English approach has drawn
closer to the Scots approach, although still there are instances in which the
English forum will ignore[43] the terms of a marriage contract, or modify it,[44] e.g.
by ordering additional capital transfer to the perceivedly disadvantaged party. The
fundamental policy objections held by English courts have fallen away. The
matter in England rests with Parliament. In 2009, the Law Commission
commenced a project to examine the status and enforceability of marital property
agreements, and in 2011 it opened a consultation to review the law of marital
property agreements and discuss options for reform. The scope of the project was
extended in 2012 to cover two further issues of financial provision arising on
divorce or the dissolution of a civil partnership. In 2014, following consultation,
the Law Commission published its final report, "Matrimonial Property, Needs
and Agreements",[45] incorporating a draft Nuptial Agreements Bill. It recommended inter alia the introduction of "qualifying nuptial agreements" as
enforceable contracts which would enable couples to make binding arrangements
for the financial consequences of divorce or dissolution. The matter awaits
parliamentary debate.[46]

No marriage contract

13–10   At common law, where parties did not make a private marriage contract, and did
not impliedly consent to be governed by a statutory code, the rights of the
husband and wife in immoveables were governed by the *lex situs*.[47] With regard
to moveables, the test was more complex. It was essential to distinguish two
different issues: first, what was the touchstone against which parties' rights were
to be tested?[48]; secondly, could parties' rights change through the course of their
marriage, following, for example, changes of domicile?[49]

---

[42] *V v V (Ancillary Relief: Pre-Nuptial Agreement)*[2011] EWHC 3230 (Fam); [2012] 1 F.L.R. 1315,
per Charles J. at [36].

[43] e.g. *Kremen v Agrest* [2012] EWHC 45 (Fam); [2012] 2 F.L.R. 414 (in which the court held that a
party would not usually be taken to have freely entered into a marital agreement with full appreciation
of its implications where there had been no independent legal advice and no full disclosure). cf. *Y v Y
(Financial Remedy: Marriage Contract)* [2014] EWHC 2920 (Fam); and *AH v PH (Scandinavian
Marriage Settlement)* [2013] EWHC 3873 (Fam); [2014] 2 F.L.R. 251.

[44] e.g. *Z v Z (Financial Remedy: Marriage Contract)* [2011] EWHC 2878 (Fam); [2012] 1 F.L.R.
1100; *V v V (Ancillary Relief: Pre-Nuptial Agreement)* [2011] EWHC 3230 (Fam); [2012] 1 F.L.R.
1315; and *B v S (Financial Remedy: Marital Property Regime)* [2012] EWHC 265 (Fam); [2012] 2
F.L.R. 502. See also *Gray v Work* [2015] EWHC 384 (Fam.).

[45] Law Com. No.343, 26 February 2014.

[46] The Government postponed a final response on nuptial agreements from February 2015 to the next
Parliament: House of Commons Library Paper: C. Fairbairn, "Pre-nuptial agreements" (SN/HA/3752,
25 November 2014).

[47] *Welch v Tennent* (1891) 18 R. (H.L.) 72.

[48] i.e. what was the first regulator of rights in moveables, at the point of marriage? Did rights
"crystallise" at that point, or could the regulator, fixed or flexible, be set at some point after marriage
(the *Egerton* issue: *Re Egerton's Will Trusts* [1956] Ch. 593)?

[49] i.e. was it possible that their rights in moveables acquired at different times during the marriage
were governed by different laws?

Initially, there was a presumption to the effect that the rights of parties are/were to be determined by the law of the husband's domicile at the time of the marriage, but it seems clear that this presumption, or any more modern formulation of it, might be rebutted if there was express agreement that another law would govern, or if there was implied agreement to that effect, in that there was proof that the parties intended to set up home shortly in another legal system having a distinct matrimonial property regime (or having none), and they did in fact carry out their intention reasonably promptly. The guide was *Re Egerton's Will Trust*,[50] where not only did the parties after the marriage fail to effect their proposed removal to France, from the husband's domicile in England, until two years had elapsed, but it was held also that mere agreement to change to French domicile did not carry any inference that the parties had agreed to adopt French matrimonial property law. Nevertheless, Roxburgh J. left open the possibility of the use of intended matrimonial home as the base test in a suitable case.[51] In the normal case, though, the most likely applicable law would have been the matrimonial domicile (that is, in this context, the domicile of the married pair immediately after the marriage).

The question whether the rights of parties in property acquired during the marriage must be referred always and only to that law first "chosen" was something other than the *Egerton* issue. Civilian systems typically prefer the "immutability" rule, by which the law governing matrimonial property rights at the outset, whatever that law may be, continues to regulate rights in acquisitions, wherever and whenever acquired, and no matter that the parties have changed domicile once or several times since marriage. The question was argued with full and learned citation of authority in the South African case of *Frankel v The Master*,[52] in which the decision (that the German law of the husband's domicile at the date of marriage would regulate the parties' rights in property inter se at all times thereafter even though within four months of marriage they had settled in Johannesburg, South Africa) was described as, "a tribute which logic pays to certainty". Immutability is a principle which has merits and demerits: it has the merit of certainty, but the governing law thus identified may be that of the one legal system in the world to which the parties, erstwhile refugees, would not return. The South African case of *Sperling v Sperling*[53] reveals that the South African conflict rules are disposed to apply the rules of that (initial and continuing) *lex causae* as they may prevail from time to time, i.e. if retrospective changes are made in the *lex causae*, the forum, subject to public policy, would accept them. In the United States, mutability prevails, so that rights of parties in acquisitions during the course of marriage are referred to the domicile of the parties at the time of each acquisition.[54]

---

[50] *Re Egerton's Will Trust* [1956] Ch. 593.

[51] Though the legal system to which the parties remove, at whatever speed and with whatever degree of decisiveness, may not admit "late entry". cf. fn.7, above.

[52] *Frankel v The Master* (1950) 1 S.A.L.R. 220 (South Africa).

[53] *Sperling v Sperling,* 1975 (2) S.A. 707.

[54] See E. Kahn, "Conflict of Laws" 1975 Annual Survey of South African Law 521; and Davie, "Matrimonial Property in English and American Conflict of Laws" (1993) 42 I.C.L.Q. 855.

It is probable that a middle path was taken in England and Scotland.[55] The only House of Lords guide was the old case of *Lashley v Hog*,[56] which, on one reading, might be said to support the argument that property rights of spouses may change upon a change of domicile. It is just as likely, however, that *Lashley*, as noted,[57] is properly understood as a succession case.

The Scots position immediately before the 2006 Act, therefore, probably was that although (future) rights might change with a change of domicile, the domicile change must be effected by both parties, and vested rights in earlier acquired property would not be prejudiced.

Family Law (Scotland) Act 2006 section 39

13–11   The following rules are laid down in s.39 (subject, by s.39(6)(b), to the spouses' contrary agreement):

By s.39(1), the rights of spouses to each other's immoveable property arising by virtue of the marriage shall be determined by the *lex/leges situs*.[58] Moreover, by s.39(4), any question relating to the use of the contents of a matrimonial home, or to the use or occupation of a moveable matrimonial home, shall be determined by the law of the country in which the home is situated (for the time being, it is presumed!).

By s.39(2), the rights of spouses to each other's moveable property arising by virtue of the marriage shall be determined by the law of the common domicile. The relevant time at which domicile is to be ascertained is not specified: it may be a reference to the domicile of the spouses at the date of acquisition of the property in question, or possibly to the immediate post-nuptial domicile. Section 39(5) provides that a change of domicile by one or both spouses shall not affect a right in moveable property which, immediately before the change, has vested in either spouse.[59] By s.39(3), where the parties are domiciled in different countries (when?), the spouses shall be taken to have the same rights in each other's moveable property arising by virtue of the marriage as they had immediately before the marriage (by which law?). This obscure provision is subject also to the provision on vested rights contained in s.39(5). It may mean that the parties are to

---

[55] See *Cheshire, North and Fawcett: Private International Law*, 14th edn (2008), pp.1299, 1300; and consider *Slutsker v Haron Investments Ltd* [2013] EWCA Civ 430.

[56] *Lashley v Hog* (1804) 4 Pat. 581; though see also *Clarke v Newmarsh* (1836) 14 S. 488; *Duchess of Buckingham v Winterbottom* (1851) 13 D. 1129; *Roe v Roe*, 1916 32 Sh.Ct Rep. 30; *Frankel v The Master* (1950) 1 S.A.L.R. 220 (South Africa); *Chiwell v Carlyon* (1897) 14 S.C. (S.A.) 61; *Re Bettinson's Question* [1956] Ch. 67; *Re Egerton's Will Trusts* [1956] Ch. 593; cf. *Dicey, Morris and Collins on the Conflict of Laws*, 15th edn (2012), r.167.

[57] See para.13–02.

[58] Ex facie this appears simply to be a reiteration of the common law position. The advisability of encasing it in legislation is not beyond doubt since the phrase, "arising by virtue of the marriage" not only begs the question, but raises the spectre of an incidental question on the point whether the marriage itself is valid. Admittedly, the same could be said of the rule at common law, but the absence of case law suggests that few problems have arisen. Further, would s.39(1) be capable, by referring to the *lex situs*, to have the parties subjected to a statutory scheme of community if the reference led, for example, to a system of law which imposed such a regime?

[59] This was thought to be the common law rule of Scots and English law where there is no statutory or private regulation of matrimonial property.

be taken to have adopted for the future the matrimonial property rules existing in their respective ante-nuptial domiciles; but what if these systems are mutually inconsistent?

Section 39 shall not apply in relation to the law on aliment, financial provision on divorce, transfer of property on divorce or succession.

The need to legislate on these matters, introducing, after many years of quiescence, provisions of variable clarity and completeness, is not obvious.

Property rights arising from other adult relationships

Types of cohabitation—"de facto" and "de jure"

In the following discussion, de facto cohabitation is intended to mean relationships not formalised by legal ceremony or registration process, but nevertheless attracting, to a greater or lesser extent as the case may be, financial and proprietary consequences which arise by operation of law where the relationship in question satisfies the definition of cohabitation laid down by the legal system purporting to regulate that relationship. Of such a type is the cohabitation relationship to which are attached property, etc. consequences by the Family Law (Scotland) Act 2006 ss.25–30.   **13–12**

De jure cohabitation, on the other hand, denotes a relationship which is formally registered in accordance with the legal system which creates and regulates it. Of such a type is registered partner status.

De facto cohabitants, cohabiting in Scotland

In terms of Scots domestic law, ss.25–30 of the Family Law (Scotland) Act 2006 endow "cohabitants"[60] with certain rights (e.g. in household goods, per s.26 and, per s.27, in money derived from a household allowance or property acquired out of such money). Section 28[61] states that where cohabitation ends otherwise than by death, a Scottish court may award a capital sum to the applicant, and grant an order in respect of any economic burden of caring for a child of the cohabitants. Application is permitted to the court, per s.29,[62] by the survivor for provision on the death intestate of his/her cohabitant.   **13–13**

---

[60] "Cohabitant" means either member of a couple consisting of (a) a man and a woman who are (or were) living together as if they were husband and wife; or (b) two persons of the same sex who are (or were) living together as if they were civil partners: s.25(1). There has been no adjustment as yet to the definition to take account of the Marriage and Civil Partnership (Scotland) Act 2014. Further, per s.25(2), in determining whether a person is a cohabitant of another person, the court shall have regard to (a) the length of the period during which the parties have been living together (or lived together); (b) the nature of their relationship during that period; and (c) the nature and extent of any financial arrangements subsisting, or which subsisted during that period. It is unclear whether a Scottish forum will be prepared to take into account any period of cohabitation spent abroad (cf. and contrast *Walker v Roberts*, 1998 S.L.T 1133; and *Toner-Boyd v Secretary of State for Work and Pensions* [2010] CSIH 7; 2010 G.W.D. 9-167).

[61] e.g. *C v S*, 2008 S.L.T. 871; *Jamieson v Rodhouse*, 2009 G.W.D. 3–54; *Lawley v Sutton*, 2010 G.W.D. 14–257; and *Gow v Grant* [2012] UKSC 29.

[62] e.g. *Chebotareva v Khandro*, 2008 Fam. L.R. 66; *Windram, Applicant*, 2009 G.W.D. 36–617; *Savage v Purches*, 2009 S.L.T. (Sh. Ct.) 36; and *Kerr v Mangan*, 2014 S.L.T. 866.

It is implicit that application may be made for the rights provided for in the Act whenever Scots law is the *lex causae*. But the Act does not specify, from a conflict of laws perspective, when, or in what circumstances, the rights created therein should apply. By inference, and arguing by analogy from the use of the matrimonial domicile in marriage cases, Scots law would be the *lex causae* in relation to rights arising during the cohabitation where the cohabitation is occurring in Scotland. This immediately raises temporal issues which, given the mobility of persons, are not academic. At least it is clear that in respect of the rights of the survivor on the death intestate of the predeceaser, Scots law, if it is the *lex ultimi domicilii*, must be the *lex causae*.[63]

If a case were to arise with an actual or potential conflict of laws dimension, e.g. as regards the property consequences of cohabitation in Scotland of one or more foreign domiciliaries, guidance in solving such problems will require to be drawn from general conflict principles governing capacity to enter into legal relationships, recognition of status and its incidents, and public policy.

The 2006 Act contains no jurisdiction or choice of law rules with regard to de facto cohabitation. Thus, it remains uncertain in Scots law which law, for example, governs an individual's legal capacity to attain the status of cohabitant (for the purposes of s.25); and in what factual circumstances a Scottish court would be entitled to apply the provisions in the Act covering the personal, financial and proprietary consequences of cohabitation. The essential antecedent question, not addressed in the Act, is in what circumstances the Scottish courts have jurisdiction to rule on the financial/proprietary rights of cohabitants (including the question as to the extent of competence of the Scottish courts to regulate the distribution of cohabitants' foreign assets upon termination of their relationship).[64]

At this point one might summarise the position by stating that the 2006 Act introduced into Scots domestic law significant rules relating to cohabitation, without enacting when those rules shall apply; the provisions are incomplete. This is not to say that Scots conflict of laws unaided cannot provide guidance and remedy, but it is regrettable to leave these important matters to speculation. Silence about jurisdiction is the most difficult deficiency to fill.[65]

De facto cohabitants, cohabiting outside Scotland

13–14   With regard to the proprietary consequences of a foreign de facto cohabitation, and in particular, the effect, if any, upon moveable and immoveable property situated in Scotland, it is likely that, in the first instance, the Scottish court would apply the "proper law of the cohabitation" (law of closest connection) to determine whether the statutory regime imposed by that law purported to have extraterritorial effect upon property belonging to the cohabitants and situated abroad. If a foreign statutory regime (say, of community of property between

[63] 2006 Act s.29(1)(b)(i). In *Chebotareva* [2008] Fam. L.R. 66 the sheriff held that the domicile requirement of s.29 was not satisfied, the applicant having failed to persuade the court that the deceased, at the date of his death, had changed his domicile to a Scots domicile. In the view of the court the deceased's English domicile of origin remained.

[64] J.M. Carruthers, *The Transfer of Property in the Conflict of Laws* (2005), paras 2.51–2.62; and *McKie v McKie* [1933] I.R. 464.

[65] Presumably jurisdiction could be established upon the presence of property within Scotland.

cohabitants), or a private contractual arrangement between the cohabitants, purported to affect all property belonging to the couple, the Scottish *lex situs* nevertheless would retain absolute control over any immoveable property situated within Scotland, and moveable property situated there from time to time, and would have an undeniable right to recognise, or not, the purported extraterritorial proprietary effects of the statutory regime, and the purported effect of the parties' contractual arrangements. It is probable that the Scottish *lex situs* would recognise the purported proprietary effects of a de facto cohabitation, inter partes, but possibly not in the event of a competing claim to property in Scotland by a third party such as a creditor.[66]

The question whether a Scottish court would be entitled to apply the provisions of the Family Law (Scotland) Act 2006 to cohabitants would seem to rest upon the Scottish court having jurisdiction (the basis of which is not clear), and upon the individuals satisfying the s.25 meaning of cohabitants.

Foreign "de jure" cohabitants

Scots domestic law currently does not make provision for registered heterosexual partnerships. With regard to foreign de jure cohabitants, it is probable that the attitude of the Scots court would be similar to that outlined above in relation to de facto cohabitants cohabiting outside Scotland. In both instances, the likelihood of recognition is greater now that Scots law contains provision regulating certain proprietary and financial consequences of cohabitation, and same sex civil partnership.

13–15

Civil partnership

In the case of civil partnerships registered in England, the property and financial consequences are detailed in the Civil Partnership Act 2004 Pt 2 Ch.3 (ss.65–72).

13–16

Part 3 of the 2004 Act (civil partnership: Scotland) does not contain a direct equivalent to Pt 2 Ch.3. Instead, Pt 3 Ch.3 makes provision with regard to occupancy rights and tenancies.[67] As regards the financial consequences of a civil partnership (registered in Scotland?), or of the death intestate of a civil partner (by inference, domiciled at death in Scotland), s.261(2) of and Sch.28 to the 2004 Act extend to civil partners, mutatis mutandis, the rules contained in the Succession (Scotland) Act 1964 concerning intestate and testate succession; rights in moveable property and money conferred by the Family Law (Scotland) Act 1985, and also the financial relief provisions of that Act upon dissolution of a relationship; and certain other miscellaneous legislative provisions concerning,

---

[66] At least where the third party, say, the creditor, is relying on Scots law. If, however, the proper law of the debt between the creditor and the debtor (i.e. the cohabitant) were, say, Dutch law, it would not be contrary to the reasonable expectations of the creditor to apply Dutch law rather than Scots law, and therefore, to prefer the claim to moveable property in Scotland of, say, the Dutch cohabitant (cf. *North Western Bank v John Poynter, Son and MacDonalds* (1894) 22 R. (H.L.) 1; *Scottish Provident Institution v Robinson* (1892) 29 S.L.R. 733).

[67] The conflict dimension is not clear: occupancy rights and tenancies in respect of properties situated in Scotland? Or in respect of Scottish domiciliaries?

inter alia, bankruptcy, damages, and housing. Rights under the 2004 Act will arise whenever Scots law is the governing law, though there may well be doubt as to when this will be the case.

Proposed EU harmonisation measures

13–17   The Stockholm Programme, detailing European strategic priorities for the period 2010–2014,[68] identified matrimonial property law as an area for development. In 2006 the European Commission published a Green Paper on conflict of laws in matrimonial property regimes.[69] According to the Commission, broad consensus emerged during the consultations, in favour of according parties a degree of freedom in choosing the applicable law for their matrimonial property regime, so long as the option is closely regulated to prevent choice of a law having little relation "to the couple's real situation or past history".[70] After considerable delay, two proposals were published in 2011, namely, a Proposal for a Council Regulation on jurisdiction, applicable law and the recognition and enforcement of decisions in matters of matrimonial property regimes ('the Matrimonial Property Proposal'),[71] and a parallel Proposal for a Council Regulation on jurisdiction, applicable law and the recognition and enforcement of decisions regarding the property consequences of registered partnerships ('the Registered Partnerships Proposal').[72]

The common goal of the Proposals was to establish a clear European legal framework for determining jurisdiction and the law applicable to matrimonial property/registered partnership regimes and facilitating the movement of decisions and instruments among Member States. Following the visible trend in recent European proposals, party autonomy is a dominant feature of the two proposals, both as to jurisdiction and in choice of law. By art.4 of the Matrimonial Property Proposal, parties can exercise (restricted) freedom of choice of court insofar as they can empower the courts of a Member State "divorce forum" to rule on matters concerning the parties' matrimonial property. In relation to choice of law, art.16 enables spouses/future spouses to choose as the law[73] applicable to their matrimonial property regime, any one of the law of the common habitual residence of the parties, or the law of the nationality or habitual residence of

---

[68] Communication on Delivering an Area of Freedom, Security & Justice for Europe's Citizens: Action Plan Implementing the Stockholm Programme COM(2010) 175 final. See also Draft Presidency Note Multiannual Programme for an Area of Freedom, Security and Justice Serving the Citizen: the Stockholm Programme 14449/09 JAI 679.

[69] COM (2006) 400 final. See also Annex (SEC (2006) 952), partially comprising the fruits of an EU-commissioned study entitled, 'Matrimonial Property Regimes and the Property of Unmarried Couples in Private International Law' (JAI/A3/2001/03).

[70] Explanatory Memorandum para 5.3.

[71] COM (2011) 126 final; 2011/0059 (CNS); and Commission Staff Working Document Impact Assessment (16.3.2011, SEC(2011) 327 final); and, subsequently, European Parliament Committee on Legal Affairs, *Report on the proposal for a Council regulation on jurisdiction, applicable law and the recognition and enforcement of decisions in matters of matrimonial property regimes* (COM(2011)0126 – C7-0093/2011 – 2011/0059(CNS), Rapporteur: A. Thein (A7-0253/2013, 20 August 2013).

[72] COM (2011) 127 final; 2011/0060 (CNS).

[73] Article 21 guarantees the principle of universality.

either party at the time the choice is made.[74] Freedom of choice of law is not extended to registered partners. The reason for denying even limited freedom of choice to registered partners is not explained, and the logic of so doing is not apparent: "While not all Member States recognise the concept of such partnerships it is not clear why, in appropriate circumstances, partners could not choose the law of a Member State where the law did provide for the concept of registered partnerships."[75]

In 2011, stakeholders in the UK were invited to express views on how the UK should approach these European proposals, and specifically on whether or not it would be in the UK's national interests to opt in to the negotiations on the Commission's proposed Regulations.[76] It is not difficult to criticise the detail of the proposals (and it is the detail that matters), or to disregard them as being tailored to the civilian mindset and legal traditions, and on their face ill-suited to UK culture, social and legal. Not surprisingly, the UK Government announced in June 2011 its decision not to opt-in to the Matrimonial Property/Registered Property Proposals, and indicated that, on account of the significant differences in EU legal systems, it is unlikely that the UK will participate in the proposals post-adoption.

FINANCIAL CONSEQUENCES

Maintenance obligations

The Maintenance Regulation

Council Regulation 4/2009 on jurisdiction, applicable law, recognition and enforcement of decisions and cooperation in matters relating to maintenance obligations ("the Maintenance Regulation"[77]) has applied in EU Member States, including the UK,[78] from 18 June 2011. In light of the coming into force of the Regulation, art.1.2(e) of Brussels I Recast excludes from that instrument's scope **13–18**

---

[74] Also recitals (19) and (20). By art.5.2, parties can confer jurisdiction on the Member State whose law has been chosen under art.16. A form of (limited) indirect choice rests in this relationship between party choice of court, and choice of law.

[75] Joint consultation by the Ministry of Justice, Scottish Government, and the Northern Ireland Department of Finance & Personnel, "Matrimonial Property Regimes and the property consequences of registered partnerships – How should the UK approach the Commission's proposals in these areas?" (Consultation Paper CP 8/2011, 2011), para 39.

[76] Joint consultation by the Ministry of Justice, Scottish Government, and the Northern Ireland Department of Finance & Personnel, "Matrimonial Property Regimes and the property consequences of registered partnerships – How should the UK approach the Commission's proposals in these areas?" (Consultation Paper CP 8/2011, 2011), para 39.

[77] Maintenance Regulation [2009] O.J. L7/1. See also Commission Implementing Regulation (EU) 2015/228 of 17 February 2015 replacing Annexes I to VII to Council Regulation (EC) No.4/2009 on jurisdiction, applicable law, recognition and enforcement of decisions and cooperation in matters relating to maintenance obligations. For background, see Green Paper on Maintenance Obligations COM(2004) 254 final; and Proposal for a Regulation on jurisdiction, applicable law, recognition and enforcement of decisions and cooperation in matters relating to maintenance obligations COM(2005) 649 final.

[78] The UK did not take part in the adoption of the Maintenance Regulation, and therefore at that point was not bound by it, or subject to its application (recital (47)). However, in accordance with art.4 of

"maintenance obligations arising from a family relationship".[79] One of the underlying themes of the Maintenance Regulation is that a maintenance creditor, i.e. any individual to whom maintenance is owed or is alleged to be owed,[80] should be able to obtain easily in a Member State a maintenance decision[81] which will be automatically enforceable in another Member State without further formalities.[82]

13–19 Application of the Maintenance Regulation in the UK is facilitated by The Civil Jurisdiction and Judgments (Maintenance) Regulations 2011 (hereinafter "CJJOMR 2011").[83]

Scope of instrument

13–20 The concept of maintenance obligation is to be interpreted autonomously for the purposes of the Maintenance Regulation, but is intended to cover all maintenance obligations which arise from a family relationship, parentage, marriage or affinity, in order to guarantee equal treatment of all maintenance creditors.[84]

Under the 1968 Brussels Convention (as also under the Brussels I Regulation), difficulties emerged regarding interpretation of the phrase a "matter relating to maintenance". According to *Van den Boogaard v Laumen*,[85] if a court judgment were designed to enable one spouse to provide for himself or herself or if the needs and resources of each of the spouses were taken into consideration in the determination of the amount, the decision was concerned with maintenance. On the other hand, where the provision awarded was solely concerned with dividing property between spouses, the decision was concerned with rights in property arising out of the matrimonial relationship and was not therefore enforceable under the Brussels regime.[86]

Protocol No.4 on the position of the UK and Ireland ([1997] O.J. C340/99) the UK later notified its intention to accept the Regulation (Note from General Secretariat of the Council to the Council JUSTCIV 262).

[79] Prior to the coming into force of the Maintenance Regulation, a maintenance order could be enforced under the Brussels regime in the same way as an ordinary commercial debt. The main enforcement route within the EU was the general commercial enforcement procedure provided in the Brussels I Regulation, but there was an alternative European Enforcement Order for Uncontested Claims (Regulation 805/2004), which includes claims for maintenance payments. The Brussels II *bis* Regulation does not apply to the "property consequences of the marriage or any other ancillary measures" (recital (8)), or to "maintenance obligations" (recital (11)).

[80] Maintenance Regulation art.2.1.10.

[81] By art.2.1.1, "decision" shall mean a decision given by a court, which term itself is defined in art.2.2 to include administrative authorities of Member States.

[82] Maintenance Regulation recital (9).

[83] CJJOMR 2011 (SI 2011/1484). See also Civil Jurisdiction and Judgments (Maintenance) (Rules of Court) Regulations 2011 (SI 2011/1215); and for England, Practice Direction 34C (Fam Div: Applications for Recognition and Enforcement to or from European Union Member States) [2012] 1 F.L.R. 1075.

[84] Maintenance Regulation recital (11); and art.1.

[85] *Van den Boogaard v Laumen* (C-220/95) [1997] All E.R. (EC) 517. Also *De Cavel v De Cavel (No.1)* (143/78) [1979] E.C.R. 1055; *De Cavel v De Cavel* (No.2) (120/79) [1980] E.C.R. 731; *Farrell v Long* (C295/95) [1997] All E.R. (E.C.) 449; and *Moore v Moore* [2007] I.L.Pr. 36.

[86] Brussels I Regulation/Brussels I Recast art.1.2(a). cf. Regulation 2201/2003 art.1.3(e) recital (8).

Jurisdiction

Before the entry into force of the Maintenance Regulation, the allocation of **13–21** jurisdiction intra-EU was determined by the Brussels I Regulation. In terms of that Regulation, a person normally was sued in the country in which s/he was domiciled (art.2), but per the rule of special jurisdiction in art.5.2:

> "A person domiciled in a Member State may, in another Member State, be sued . . . in matters relating to maintenance, in the courts for the place where the maintenance creditor is domiciled or habitually resident or, if the matter is ancillary to proceedings concerning the status of a person, in the court which, according to its own law, has jurisdiction to entertain those proceedings, unless that jurisdiction is based solely on the nationality of one of the parties."

Thus, maintenance creditors could opt to sue either in the court for the Member State where the debtor was domiciled, or in the Member State where the creditor was domiciled or habitually resident.[87] The option was thought to confer an advantage on the maintenance creditor, who was perceived as the weaker party, and was comparable to the *forum actoris* rules provided in Ss.3 (insured parties), 4 (consumers) and 5 (employees) of the Brussels I Regulation.

Now, rules of jurisdiction are set out in Ch.II of the Maintenance Regulation, the most important of which are arts 3 (general provisions), 4 (choice of court), 5 (appearance of defendant), 6 (subsidiary jurisdiction where no court of a Member State has jurisdiction pursuant to arts 3–5), 7 (*forum necessitatis*), and 8 (limit on proceedings, i.e. jurisdiction to modify a previous award).

GENERAL RULE

The general rule of jurisdiction is to be found in art.3, in terms of which: **13–22**

> "In matters relating to maintenance obligations in Member States, jurisdiction shall lie with:
> (a) the court for the place where the defendant is habitually resident, or
> (b) the court for the place where the creditor[88] is habitually resident, or
> (c) the court which, according to its own law, has jurisdiction to entertain proceedings concerning the status of a person if the matter relating to maintenance is ancillary to those proceedings, unless that jurisdiction is based solely on the nationality of one of the parties, or
> (d) the court which, according to its own law, has jurisdiction to entertain proceedings concerning parental responsibility if the matter relating to maintenance is ancillary to those proceedings, unless that jurisdiction is based solely on the nationality of one of the parties."

No reference in art.3 is made to the domicile of the defendant or the maintenance creditor; the looser criterion of habitual residence is thought, presumably, to be more suitable for the purpose.

---

[87] e.g. *Sawicki v Sawicka* [2008] I.L.Pr. 3; *T v L* [2009] I.L.Pr. 5 (Irish Supreme Court).
[88] Or potential creditor: *M v W* [2014] EWHC 925 (Fam), per Coleridge J. at [39].

13–23   Article 4 permits prorogation of court by agreement of the parties, the choice falling upon the court(s) of the habitual residence or nationality (i.e. to be interpreted in a UK court as referring to domicile[89]) of either party. In the case of spouses or former spouses, the parties may choose the court having jurisdiction in matrimonial matters, or the court of the Member State of the spouses' last common habitual residence for a period of at least one year. There is a presumption of exclusivity, i.e. that jurisdiction conferred by agreement shall be exclusive unless the parties have agreed otherwise. The choice of court provision in art.4 shall not apply to a dispute relating to a maintenance obligation towards a child under the age of 18.

Article 4.1 contains a useful *tempus inspiciendum* provision, laying down that the relevant time for ascertaining the personal law connecting factor is the time the choice of court agreement is concluded or the time the court is seised.

SUBMISSION

13–24   Submission by the defendant without protest as to jurisdiction will confer jurisdiction upon a Member State court.[90]

SUBSIDIARY JURISDICTION AND JURISDICTION OF NECESSITY

13–25   "Article 6
Subsidiary jurisdiction
Where no court of a Member State has jurisdiction pursuant to Articles 3, 4 and 5 and no court of a State party to the Lugano Convention which is not a Member State has jurisdiction pursuant to the provisions of that Convention, the courts of the Member State of the common nationality of the parties shall have jurisdiction."

This significant provision can be seen as a notable step in the creation of EU rules to treat hybrid cases, and in effect to safeguard the position of the claimant. Recital (15) explains that the fact that the defendant is habitually resident in a Third State should no longer rule out the application of Community rules so as to permit application of national rules. Rather, the Maintenance Regulation itself imposes a rule in this situation, namely, that the courts of the Member State of the common nationality (in a UK court, common domicile) of the parties shall have jurisdiction. Admittedly, the newly created rule insists upon a strong connection of both parties with a Member State.

Should there be no such common nationality (or domicile in the case of the UK), and where no court of a Member State has jurisdiction under arts 3, 4 or 5, art.7 provides that the courts of a Member State, on an exceptional basis, may hear the case if proceedings cannot reasonably be brought or conducted or would be impossible in a Third State with which the dispute is closely connected. Under art.7, headed *"forum necessitatis"*, the dispute must have a close connection with

---

[89] Maintenance Regulation recital (18); cf. in choice of law, art.9 of the 2007 Hague Protocol on the Law Applicable to Maintenance Obligations (q.v.).

[90] Maintenance Regulation art.5. cf. Brussels I Regulation art.24; Brussels I Recast art.26.

the Member State of the court seised. Recital (16) explains that the provision of jurisdiction *necessitatis* has been conferred in order to remedy a denial of justice.

Articles 6 and 7, read together, comprise a further aggrandisement of the EU's own jurisdiction to deal with Third States and hybrid cases.

LIMIT ON PROCEEDINGS

It is characteristic of awards of maintenance that, in their nature, they are subject to change. So, too, in a conflict situation, the habitual residence of the parties, in particular of the maintenance debtor, may change. Article 8 addresses this feature as follows:

13–26

> "1.   Where a decision is given in a Member State or a 2007 Hague Convention Contracting State where the creditor is habitually resident, proceedings to modify the decision or to have a new decision given cannot be brought by the debtor in any other Member State as long as the creditor remains habitually resident in the State in which the decision was given.
>   2.   Paragraph 1 shall not apply:
> (a)   where the parties have agreed in accordance with Article 4 to the jurisdiction of the courts of that other Member State;
> (b)   where the creditor submits to the jurisdiction of the courts of that other Member State pursuant to Article 5;
> (c)   where the competent authority in the 2007 Hague Convention Contracting State of origin cannot, or refuses to, exercise jurisdiction to modify the decision or give a new decision; or
> (d)   where the decision given in the 2007 Hague Convention Contracting State of origin cannot be recognised or declared enforceable in the Member State where proceedings to modify the decision or to have a new decision given are contemplated."

Article 8.1 safeguards the maintenance creditor against uncertainty or possible prejudice resulting from a change in the habitual residence of the debtor. Article 8.1 is subject to parties' agreement in accordance with art.4, submission without protest,[91] and cases where the original court refuses to modify the decision or give a new decision or where the original decision cannot be recognised or declared enforceable in the Member State where the fresh proceedings are contemplated.

ARTICLES 9–14

The remaining provisions of Ch.II of the Maintenance Regulation incorporate the familiar indicia of the system of *lis pendens* put in place in the 1968 Brussels Convention, and replicated in the Brussels I Regulation,[92] namely, autonomous definitions of the time at which a court shall be deemed to be seised (art.9)[93]; examination by the court seised of its own jurisdiction (art.10)[94]; examination as

13–27

---

[91] Maintenance Regulation art.8.2 in its terms refers to submission by the creditor pursuant to art.5. Article 5, however, refers to submission by the defendant, being the maintenance debtor.
[92] There has been no modification of Ch.II in light of art.31.2 of the Brussels I Recast.
[93] cf. Brussels I Regulation art.30; Brussels I Recast art.32.
[94] e.g. *EA v AP* [2014] I.L.Pr. 17. cf. Brussels II *bis* art.17; and also Brussels I Regulation arts 25 and 26/Brussels I Recast arts 27 and 28.

to admissibility (art.11)[95]; and *lis pendens* (same cause of action: art.12[96]; and
related actions: art.13)[97]; and art.14 (provisional, including protective measures).[98] However, as was readily appreciated at common law, decrees of aliment
are inherently variable. The classic operation of the *lis pendens* system is not
always suited to maintenance issues.[99]

Applicable law

13–28   The provisions on applicable law are contained in Ch.III of the Maintenance
Regulation, and are restricted to the determination of the law applicable to
maintenance obligations, and should not determine the law applicable to the
establishment of the family relationships on which the maintenance obligations
are based.[100]

THE 2007 HAGUE PROTOCOL ON THE LAW APPLICABLE TO MAINTENANCE OBLIGATIONS

13–29   Article 15 of the Maintenance Regulation provides that, in Member States bound
by the 2007 Hague Protocol on the Law Applicable to Maintenance Obligations,[101] the law applicable to maintenance obligations shall be determined in
accordance with that Protocol. The Protocol was signed by the EC on 8 April
2010, and came into force in Member States, excluding the UK and Denmark, on
1 August 2013.[102] By declaration under art.24 of the Protocol, the EC undertook
to apply the rules of the Protocol from 18 June 2011,[103] the date of application of
the Maintenance Regulation.

In the subject of maintenance, therefore, instead of producing competing
instruments, the harmonisation exercises initiated in Europe and at the Hague,
respectively, were streamlined, so that the resulting Regulation and Protocol are
not contradictory, but complementary. The manner in which the Hague and the
European projects on the same subject-matter have been dovetailed denotes
significant progress in the harmonisation of harmonisation efforts themselves.
However, some violence has been done to classic conflicts methodology, and

---

[95] Brussels II *bis* art.18.
[96] cf. Brussels I Regulation art.27/ Brussels I Recast art.29.
[97] cf. Brussels I Regulation art.28/ Brussels I Recast art.30.
[98] cf. Brussels I Regulation art.31/ Brussels I Recast art.35.
[99] *AA v BB* [2015] Fam. Law 265.
[100] Maintenance Regulation recital (21).
[101] A. Bonomi, *Explanatory Report on the Hague Protocol of 23 November 2007 on the Law
Applicable to Maintenance Obligations* (HccH, 2009) ("*Explanatory Report*").
[102] The EC declared, in accordance with art.24 of the Protocol, that it exercised competence over all
the matters governed by the Protocol, and that its Member States shall be bound by the Protocol by
virtue of its conclusion by the EC. For the purpose of the declaration, the term "European
Community" does not include Denmark or the United Kingdom.
[103] Protocol art.76. The EC declared that it would apply the rules of the Protocol also to maintenance
claimed in one of its Member States relating to a period prior to the entry into force or the provisional
application of the Protocol in the Community in situations where, under the Maintenance Regulation,
proceedings were instituted, court settlements approved or concluded and authentic instruments
established as from 18 June 2011.

even to modern drafting, as a result of the desire to safeguard the interests of the maintenance creditor and to provide for him/her the best of all possible rules and outcome.

APPLICABLE LAW IN A SCOTS COURT

The primary purpose of the Protocol was to introduce uniform international rules **13–30** for the determination of the law applicable to maintenance obligations. The UK decision not to participate in the 2007 Protocol reflects the UK Government's view that in maintenance cases the expense of proving the content of foreign law would be disproportionate to the value of the great majority of maintenance claims. More self-interestedly perhaps, the UK was conscious that nothing should be done which would undermine the current position of the English courts as a forum of choice in contested matrimonial proceedings. The UK agreed to participate in the Maintenance Regulation only on the basis that applicable law rules were removed from the EU instrument; and further that EC accession to the 2007 Protocol would be done on the basis that the UK was not obliged to participate therein. Accordingly, where a Scots court has jurisdiction in respect of a maintenance claim, it will apply Scots domestic law to the substance of the question.[104] This choice of law rule has been placed on a statutory basis by the Family Law (Scotland) Act 2006 s.40, and is subject to the Maintenance Orders (Reciprocal Enforcement) Act 1972 (q.v.).

APPLICABLE LAW—MEMBER STATES BOUND BY THE 2007 HAGUE PROTOCOL

The 2007 Protocol essentially replaces the 1973 Hague Convention on the Law **13–31** Applicable to Maintenance Obligations (to which the UK was not a Contracting State). The choice of law rules contained in the Protocol provide for universal application,[105] and exclusion of *renvoi*.[106] The general rule (art.3) is that maintenance obligations shall be governed by the law of the state of the habitual residence of the maintenance creditor, a rule deemed appropriate because, " . . .it allows a determination of the existence and amount of the maintenance obligation with regard to the legal and factual conditions of the social environment in the country where the creditor lives and engages in most of his or her activities."[107]

Temporal issues being of particular importance in this area, art.3.2 provides that where that habitual residence changes, the law of the state of the new habitual residence shall apply as from the moment when the change occurs.[108] Article 3 in its entirety is subject to an important caveat in respect of spouses and ex-spouses, contained in art.5, to the effect that art.3 shall not apply if one of the

---

[104] i.e. those rules contained in Family Law (Scotland) Act 1985 ss.1–7.

[105] 2007 Protocol art.2.

[106] 2007 Protocol art.12.

[107] *Explanatory Report* 2009 para.37.

[108] While the inclusion of a temporal provision is welcome, it is notorious that the connecting factor of habitual residence is difficult to define, and there is a particular difficulty in the temporal dimension of ascertaining at what "particular moment" a change occurs. The *Explanatory Report* 2009 para.42 notes that change of residence of a temporary nature is not sufficient to dislodge the pre-existing habitual residence of the creditor.

parties objects and the law of another state, in particular the state of their last common habitual residence, has a closer connection with the marriage. In such a case the law of that other state shall apply. Article 5 is intended to protect the maintenance debtor from the effects of a unilateral and self-serving change of residence by the maintenance creditor, which might lead to an outcome which is contrary to the debtor's expectations.[109]

Article 3 proves to be subject also to art.4.3, although there is no express mention of this in art.3 itself. Article 4 confers upon certain maintenance creditors, in particular children against their parents (and vice versa), favourable rules insofar as if a creditor is unable, by virtue of the law applicable under art.3, to obtain maintenance from the debtor, the law of the forum[110] shall apply.[111] Article 4.3 is novel in that it provides that if the creditor has seised the competent authority of the state of the debtor's habitual residence,[112] the law of that state shall apply. However, if the creditor is unable thereunder to obtain maintenance, the forum shall revert to the general rule in art.3.1 of the Protocol and apply the habitual residence of the creditor. Similarly, if the creditor is unable to obtain maintenance from the debtor under any of the laws of the habitual residence of the creditor, or the debtor, or of the *lex fori* (whatever the forum may be), the law of the state of the common nationality, if there is one, shall apply.[113] This produces a complex construct which appears to be result-driven and does violence to the traditional approach to applicable law; it is not orthodox to re-visit choice of law if the outcome of applying a particular law does not result in benefit to the party favoured by the policy of the instrument.[114] A simpler approach, achieving much the same outcome ("*favor creditoris*"), would have been to direct the forum to apply the law most beneficial to the maintenance creditor.

CHOICE OF LAW BY PARTIES

13–32 Articles 7 and 8, permitting "designation" of applicable law by parties, are in line with the trend in EU modern instruments of jurisdiction and choice of law to allow party autonomy.

Article 7, the narrower provision, permits the maintenance creditor and debtor to choose the applicable law for the purpose only of a particular proceeding in a given state. The parties may choose only the law of the forum. It is anticipated that this provision would be useful in cases of legal separation and divorce, permitting the spouses to choose the *lex fori* in the matter of maintenance as well as substance.

Article 8, which is of broader compass, permits the parties,[115] notwithstanding the provisions of arts 3–6 to choose, at any time, as applicable law one of the following:

---

[109] *Explanatory Report* 2009 para.77. Contrast the counterbalancing provision in art.8.1 of the Maintenance Regulation.
[110] Maintenance Regulation arts 3–8 contain the rules for identification of forum.
[111] 2007 Protocol art.4.2.
[112] Maintenance Regulation art.3(a).
[113] 2007 Protocol art.4.4.
[114] Orthodox choice of laws methodology is result-blind: para.3–01, above.
[115] Subject to compliance with arts 8.2 (formal validity) and 8.3 (non-age).

"a)   the law of any State of which either party is a national (or, in the case of the UK, a domiciliary) at the time of the designation;

b)   the law of the State of the habitual residence of either party at the time of designation;

c)   the law designated by the parties as applicable, or the law in fact applied, to their property regime;

d)   the law designated by the parties as applicable, or the law in fact applied, to their divorce or legal separation."

Article 8.4 states that, notwithstanding such a choice, the question whether the creditor can renounce his/her right to maintenance shall be determined by the law of the habitual residence of the creditor at the time of the choice.

Article 8.5 appears to undo much of the value of that which precedes it by stipulating that, "...unless at the time of the designation the parties were fully informed and aware of the consequences of their designation, the law designated by the parties shall not apply where the application of that law would lead to manifestly unfair or unreasonable consequences for any of the parties". This begs many questions and raises incidental questions. The purpose of art.8.5 seems to be to permit parties to undo a choice of law if the consequences of application of that law would lead, in the view of the forum,[116] to manifest unfairness "for any of the parties". Hence, that which can be undone is the *choice* of law. The province of art.8.5 marches closely to, and might trespass on, the territory of art.13 (public policy), which states that the application of the *law chosen* may be refused only to the extent that its effects would be manifestly contrary to the public policy of the forum. Their effects coincide in the matter of the consequences of application of the *lex causae*, by whatever process that governing law was identified. The forum could strike out a provision of the *lex causae* even where both parties were shown to have been fully informed and aware of the consequences of choice.

As a matter of (a different) policy, there is very little point in giving party autonomy if that autonomy is so hedged about with protections[117] for one or other or both contracting parties that the choice can easily be rendered nugatory. By what law(s) will the forum assess whether the parties (either or both?) were "fully informed" and aware of the consequences of their choice?

SCOPE OF APPLICABLE LAW

The non-exhaustive scope of application of the applicable law per art.11 of the Protocol is: **13–33**

"a)   whether, to what extent and from whom the creditor may claim maintenance;

b)   the extent to which the creditor may claim retroactive maintenance;

c)   the basis for calculation of the amount of maintenance, and indexation;

---

[116] Bearing in mind the number of forums which are potentially available in this context: Maintenance Regulation arts 3–8.

[117] Protections are routinely inserted into instruments which allow for party choice of court or party choice of law, but to date the protections have been of a different timbre, being typically related to exclusion of choice, time of choice, formal validity of choice, and impositions upon choice, rather than displeasure at the consequences of one's choice.

d) who is entitled to institute maintenance proceedings, except for issues relating to procedural capacity and representation in the proceedings;

e) prescription or limitation periods;

f) the extent of the obligation of a maintenance debtor, where a public body seeks reimbursement of benefits provided for a creditor in place of maintenance."

It is interesting that art.11(d) assigns title to sue, except for procedural issues, to the *lex causae*.

Given that, "matters arising from the obligation to maintain" frequently may depend upon whether the parties were or are married, reference should be made to recital (21) of the Maintenance Regulation, which makes clear that the rules in the Regulation, and therefore, via art.15, the rules in the Protocol, determine only the law applicable to the maintenance obligation, and do not determine the law applicable to the establishment of the family relationships on which the maintenance obligations are based.[118] In respect of the latter, the national rules of Member States, including their rules of private international law, will continue to apply.

With regard to art.11(c) of the Protocol (the basis for calculation of the amount of maintenance), it becomes apparent from the terms of art.14 of the Protocol that the applicable law is not necessarily conclusive on the amount of maintenance. Article 14 directs the forum, even if the applicable law provides otherwise, to take into account in the matter of determining the amount of maintenance the needs of the creditor and the resources of the debtor, as well as any compensation which the creditor was awarded in place of periodical maintenance payments.[119] The Explanatory Report[120] comments that art.14 is "a substantive rule", binding on Contracting States. One consequence is that if the applicable law is that of the forum, the forum may be required to deny its own law.

MULTI-LEGAL SYSTEM CONTRACTING STATES

13–34 Article 15 of the Protocol permits multi-legal system Contracting States to opt out of applying the rules of the Protocol to conflicts solely between such different systems. The Maintenance Regulation itself does not contain the customary clause dealing with states with more than one legal system. By reg.8 of the CJJOMR 2011, Sch.6 (containing rules for the allocation of jurisdiction within the UK in relation to maintenance) has effect.

---

[118] Maintenance Regulation art.22, in providing that, "[t]he recognition and enforcement of a decision on maintenance under this Regulation shall not in any way imply the recognition of the family relationship, parentage, marriage or affinity underlying the maintenance obligation which gave rise to the decision", is consistent with the attempt to confine the applicable law of maintenance to matters strictly limited thereto. But, on the other hand, see art.23.3, which states that if the outcome of proceedings in a court of a Member State depends on the determination of an incidental question of recognition, the court shall have jurisdiction over that question. Consider *T v L* [2009] I.L.Pr. 5 (Irish Supreme Court).

[119] cf. Rome II Regulation recital (33), discussed at para.16–20, below.

[120] *Explanatory Report* 2009 para.179.

Recognition, enforceability and enforcement of decisions

Chapter IV of the Maintenance Regulation lays down two different sets of rules, according to whether or not the decision[121] to be recognised and given effect was handed down in a Member State bound by the 2007 Hague Protocol. By reg.3 of CJJOMR 2011, Sch.1 to the Regulations, containing provisions relating to the enforcement of maintenance decisions pursuant to the Maintenance Regulation, has effect.

13–35

DECISIONS GIVEN IN A MEMBER STATE BOUND BY THE 2007 HAGUE PROTOCOL[122]

Chapter IV section 1 of the Maintenance Regulation provides a set of rules governing recognition and enforcement where the decision in question was given in a Member State bound by the 2007 Hague Protocol (i.e. all Member States except Denmark and the UK). Such a decision shall be recognised in another Member State without any special procedure being required and without any possibility of opposing its recognition.[123] Such a decision shall be enforceable in another Member State without the need for a declaration of enforceability[124]; for this category of case *exequatur* is abolished. By art.18, protective measures existing under the law of the state of enforcement will attach to such a decision.

13–36

The right of the defendant to apply in the court of origin for a review of the decision of that court is set out in art.19. The right to apply for such a review arises[125] where the defendant (a) was not served with the document instituting the proceedings or an equivalent document in sufficient time and in such a way as to enable him to arrange for his defence; or (b) was prevented from contesting the maintenance claim by reason of force majeure or due to extraordinary circumstances without any fault on his part; unless he failed to challenge the decision when it was possible for him to do so. If the court of origin accepts the application for review, the maintenance decision shall be null and void. If, however, the decision is to the opposite effect and the court rejects the application for review, its decision on the matter of maintenance shall remain in force, and will be enforced in another Member State upon production of relevant documents specified in art.20. Article 21 lays down such grounds of refusal or suspension of enforcement under the law of the Member State addressed as are compatible with a system of virtually automatic recognition. These grounds are, first, extinction by the effect of prescription or limitation of action of the right to enforce the maintenance decision,[126] under the law either of the Member State of origin or the Member State of enforcement, whichever limitation period is the longer;

---

[121] By art.48 of the Maintenance Regulation, court settlements and authentic instruments enforceable in the Member State of origin shall be recognised in another Member State and be enforceable there in the same way as decisions, in accordance with Ch.IV. See also CJJOMR 2011 reg.5 and Sch.3.

[122] See also CJJOMR 2011 Sch.1 Pt 2.

[123] Maintenance Regulation art.17.1.

[124] Maintenance Regulation art.17.2. Para.9–35, above.

[125] Subject to time limit: art.19.2.

[126] Maintenance Regulation art.21.2 concerns the extinction by prescription of the *decision* of the court of origin. By contrast art.11(e) of the Hague Protocol assigns prescription and limitation of the maintenance obligation to the scope of its applicable law.

secondly, irreconcilability of the decision of the court of origin with a decision given in the Member State of enforcement or with a decision given in another Member State or in a Third State which requires to be recognised by the Member State of enforcement[127]; and thirdly, where the debtor shows that the substantive decision of the court of origin is subject to review or suspension in the court of origin.[128]

DECISIONS GIVEN IN A MEMBER STATE NOT BOUND BY THE 2007 HAGUE PROTOCOL[129]

13–37   Chapter IV S.2 of the Maintenance Regulation establishes that in cases concerning decisions on maintenance obligations given in a Member State which is not bound by the 2007 Hague Protocol (i.e. Denmark and the UK[130]), the procedures for recognition and declaration of enforceability are modelled on the procedures and the grounds for refusing recognition set out in the Brussels I Regulation. Recital (26) adds that, to accelerate proceedings and enable the creditor to recover his claim quickly, the court seised should be required to give its decision within a set time, unless there are exceptional circumstances.

By art.23, a decision given in a Member State not bound by the 2007 Hague Protocol shall be recognised in another Member State without any special procedure being required. The grounds of refusal of recognition of the maintenance decision, contained in art.24, are the same as those in art.34 of the Brussels I Regulation (based on public policy, natural justice and res judicata), with the additional proviso that a decision which modifies an earlier decision on maintenance on the basis of changed circumstances shall not be considered an irreconcilable decision within the meaning of art.24. The significant distinction between S.1 and S.2 cases lies in the fact that in respect of the latter a decision given in a Member State not bound by the 2007 Protocol shall be enforceable in another Member State (only) when, on the application of any interested party it has been declared enforceable.[131] Assuming compliance with the formalities required by art.28, the maintenance decision shall be declared enforceable without any review; and this shall be done expeditiously.[132] The maintenance debtor may not make any submissions at this stage. The declaration of enforceability shall be served on the defendant (art.31). The procedures essentially are the same as those set out in Ch.III of the Brussels I Regulation/ Brussels I Recast.[133] The decision on the application for a declaration of enforceability may be appealed by either party.[134] The court with which an appeal is lodged shall refuse or revoke a declaration of enforceability only on one of the grounds specified in art.24.[135]

---

[127] Maintenance Regulation art.21.2.
[128] Maintenance Regulation art.21.3.
[129] CJJOMR 2011 Sch.1 Pt 3.
[130] CJJOMR 2011 Sch.1 para.5(b).
[131] 2007 Protocol art.26.
[132] 2007 Protocol art.30: within 30 days of the completion of art.28 formalities, barring exceptional circumstances.
[133] Paras 9–36—9–37, above.
[134] 2007 Protocol art.32.
[135] 2007 Protocol art.34.

Implementation and administration of the provisions of the Regulation is assisted by a network of central authorities, amongst which cooperation is expected (Ch.VII). Conscious of the practical, as well as legal, difficulties which this subject area entails, the Maintenance Regulation seeks to remove international barriers to the successful recovery of maintenance, making provisions in Ch.V (entitled "Access to Justice") concerned with laying the obligation on Member States to provide legal aid of a level which corresponds at least to that available in an equivalent domestic case.

Interaction among instruments

Where EU Member States which are bound by the Maintenance Regulation are Contracting States also to the 1956 New York (UN) Convention on the Recovery Abroad of Maintenance and/or the 2007 Hague Convention on the International Recovery of Child Support and Other Forms of Family Maintenance (q.v.), questions of priority of instrument will arise. Such questions are answered by art.69 of the Maintenance Regulation, to the effect that the Maintenance Regulation shall not affect the application of bilateral or multilateral conventions and agreements to which one or more Member States are party at the time of adoption of this Regulation (art.69.1), but in relations between Member States (i.e. in intra-EU disputes), the Regulation takes precedence over the conventions and agreements to which Member States are party.

13–38

Enforcement of maintenance orders intra-UK

Part II of the Maintenance Orders Act 1950[136] governs the registration and enforcement of aliment or maintenance orders intra-UK.

13–39

Reciprocal treatment of applications for maintenance under Maintenance Orders (Reciprocal Enforcement) Act 1972[137]

As between Great Britain and the Commonwealth there have been reciprocal statutory provisions since 1920,[138] but these were never entirely satisfactory,[139] and the 1920 Act did not apply to Scotland. The Maintenance Orders (Reciprocal Enforcement) Act 1972, providing for accession by the UK to the 1956 United Nations (New York) Convention on the Recovery Abroad of Maintenance, was intended to facilitate the recovery of maintenance by or from persons in the UK, from or by persons in other (mainly Commonwealth) countries by setting in place a scheme for the reciprocal treatment of applications for maintenance (rather than the enforcement thereof).

Part I of the 1972 Act provides a system of registration and enforcement in the United Kingdom of maintenance orders made in reciprocating countries. The 1972 Act contains both "incoming" and "outgoing" registration provisions.

13–40

---

[136] As amended by reg.9 of the CJJOMR 2011 Sch.7 para.1(3).

[137] As amended by the Maintenance Orders (Reciprocal Enforcement) Act 1992, and by reg.9 of the CJJOMR 2011 Sch.7 para.5.

[138] Maintenance Orders (Facilities for Enforcement) Act 1920.

[139] *Peagram v Peagram* [1926] 2 K.B. 165; *Harris v Harris* [1949] 2 All E.R. 318.

Incoming orders are governed by ss.6–11 (s.6: registration in Scotland, per sheriff court, of maintenance order from reciprocating country; s.8: enforcement thereof; s.9: variation and revocation thereof).[140] Under these statutory rules, no provision is made to permit refusal to enforce such an order on the ground of public policy. This matter was raised in *Sethi v Sethi*,[141] in which the husband sought reduction of the 1986 registration in Scotland of a maintenance order obtained against him by his wife in India. Lord Weir refused to accede to his request, holding that the terms of s.6 were mandatory, and observing that the pursuer ought to have challenged the original order (rather than its enforcement) as contrary to public policy.

Part II of the 1972 Act provides for reciprocal enforcement of claims for the recovery of maintenance in "Convention countries", being countries party to the 1956 New York (UN) Convention on the Recovery Abroad of Maintenance. Part II provides a procedure for the transmission, not of maintenance orders (as in Pt I), but of maintenance claims.

Part III of the 1972 Act deals with countries which are neither reciprocating countries, nor "Convention countries". Special bilateral arrangements may be made with countries, and if this is done, an Order in Council may be made under Pt III, applying modified provisions of the 1972 Act to the country in question.[142] Where the maintenance order emanates from a foreign legal system which does not fall to be regulated by the 1972 Act, the holder may seek "decree conform" from the Court of Session.[143]

2007 Hague Convention on the International Recovery of Child Support and Other Forms of Family Maintenance

13–41   The 2007 Hague Convention on the International Recovery of Child Support and Other Forms of Family Maintenance, and the 2007 Protocol on the Law Applicable to Maintenance Obligations, are the culmination of work to review earlier Hague Conventions concerning maintenance and the 1956 New York Convention on the Recovery Abroad of Maintenance. The 2007 Convention was signed by the EU on 6 April 2011, and came into force in EU Member States, including the UK, on 1 August 2014. Its object is "to ensure the effective international recovery of child support and other forms of family maintenance"[144] by establishing a comprehensive system of co-operation among Contracting States; making available applications for the establishment of maintenance decisions; providing for the recognition and enforcement of maintenance decisions; and requiring effective measures for the prompt enforcement of such decisions. The Convention applies on a mandatory basis to child support cases,

---

[140] *Killen v Killen*, 1981 S.L.T. (Sh. Ct.) 77.

[141] *Sethi v Sethi*, 1995 S.L.T. 104.

[142] e.g. Reciprocal Enforcement of Maintenance Orders (United States of America) (Scotland) Order 2007 (SSI 2007/354). Of particular significance are the arrangements made under this Part in relation to countries signatory to the 1973 Hague Convention on the Recognition and Enforcement of Decisions relating to Maintenance Obligations: see, e.g. Reciprocal Enforcement of Maintenance Orders (Hague Convention Countries) Order 1993 (SI 1993/593), and Reciprocal Enforcement of Maintenance Orders (Hague Convention Countries) (Variation) Order 2002 (SI 2002/2838).

[143] Para.9–09, above.

[144] 2007 Convention art.1.

and by declaration the EU resolved to extend the application of Chs II and III to spousal support. The instrument's raison d'être is to assist the judgment creditor both in the encouragement of amicable solutions and in the facilitation of enforcement, together with the collection of maintenance payments. The aim is to streamline procedures at the stage of recognition and enforcement, reducing delays and costs.

The International Recovery of Maintenance (Hague Convention 2007) (Scotland) Regulations 2012[145] facilitate the application of the 2007 Convention in Scotland.[146] Regulation 3 designates the Scottish Ministers as the Scottish Central Authority for the purposes of art.4 of the Convention. Regulation 4 provides for the recognition and enforcement in Scotland of maintenance decisions[147] made by courts in Contracting States. By reg.4(2) jurisdiction in relation to an application for registration of a maintenance decision lies with the courts[148] of Scotland if (a) the judgment debtor is resident in Scotland; or (b) has assets which are susceptible to enforcement situated there. Regulation 4(7) has the effect that a maintenance decision registered in Scotland shall be of the same force and effect as if the decision had originally been made by the registering court.

Financial provision upon termination of marriage and other adult relationships

Termination of marriage by foreign divorce

Provided that a foreign divorce is recognised in Scotland as valid, any lack in the terms of the foreign decree in the matter of property distribution/financial provision now may be supplied,[149] so long as the Scots court has jurisdiction.[150] It was not always so. There used to be a difficulty in that, if a foreign divorce was entitled to recognition in Scotland, the Scots courts could not award financial provision to one of the parties, since *ex hypothesi* the parties were no longer married to each other, and s/he had no title to ask, nor the Scottish/English court any jurisdiction to grant, an order which it thought desirable to append to the foreign decree. The problem was compounded by the proper reluctance of any foreign court otherwise competent to terminate the marriage (in the view of Scots/English law), to make an award in relation to immoveable property outside its territory. Hence, no provision would be made with regard to immoveable

13–42

---

[145] International Recovery of Maintenance (Hague Convention 2007) (Scotland) Regulations 2012 (SSI 2012/301).

[146] See also Act of Sederunt (Rules of the Court of Session and Sheriff Court Rules Amendment) (Miscellaneous) 2014 (SSI 2014/201); and The International Recovery of Maintenance (Hague Convention 2007 etc) Regulations 2012 (SI 2012/2814), which primarily make provision to facilitate the application of the Convention in England and Wales, but extend also to Scotland in relation to enforcement of international maintenance decisions by way of driving disqualification, and regarding the sharing of information by certain Government departments to facilitate establishment and enforcement of maintenance decisions to which the 2007 Hague Convention applies.

[147] 2012 Regulations reg.8 makes equivalent provision for the recognition and enforcement in Scotland of maintenance arrangements, as defined in art.3(e) of the 2007 Convention.

[148] The sheriff court: reg.4(1).

[149] Matrimonial and Family Proceedings Act 1984 s.29.

[150] Matrimonial and Family Proceedings Act 1984 s.28.

property in Scotland or England. As a result, as happened in *Torok v Torok*,[151] an unseemly race to the courthouse door might ensue. Law Commission discussion followed[152] and resulted in the enactment of provisions clothing the Scots and English courts with jurisdiction to make property provision in suitable cases. All were agreed that the rules must be strict, but separate legislative provision within the Matrimonial and Family Proceedings Act 1984 was made for Scotland and England, respectively, with the result that the same end was achieved by different rules. The English provisions are contained in Pt III of the 1984 Act, and the Scottish provisions in Pt IV.

Financial provision in Scotland

13–43 The Scottish Law Commission did not believe that actions for financial provision after foreign divorce would be frequent in Scotland, a forecast which, some decades on, can be confirmed as accurate. A rare example in Scots law of the use of these provisions is *Tahir v Tahir*.[153] The Scottish provisions are available after foreign divorce, or annulment,[154] and are contained in ss.28 and 29, stipulating a number of strict jurisdictional criteria,[155] and additional conditions[156] which must be satisfied before an award may be made.

The jurisdictional criteria are as follows:

"(a) the applicant was domiciled or habitually resident in Scotland on the date when the application was made; and

(b) the other party to the marriage—

(i) was domiciled or habitually resident in Scotland on the date when the application was made; or

(ii) was domiciled or habitually resident in Scotland when the parties last lived together as husband and wife; or

(iii) on the date when the application was made, was an owner or tenant of, or had a beneficial interest in, property in Scotland which had at some time been a matrimonial home of the parties; and

(c) where the court is the sheriff court, either—

(i) one of the parties was, on the date when the application was made, habitually resident in the sheriffdom; or

(ii) paragraph (b)(iii) above is satisfied in respect of property wholly or partially within the sheriffdom."

The additional conditions are:

"(a) the divorce falls to be recognised in Scotland;

(b) the other party to the marriage initiated the proceedings for divorce;

(c) the application was made within five years after the date when the divorce took effect;

[151] *Torok v Torok* [1973] 1 W.L.R. 1066.
[152] Law Commission, *Family Law: Financial Relief after Foreign Divorce* (HMSO, 1980), Law Com. Working Paper No.77.
[153] *Tahir v Tahir*, 1993 S.L.T. 194; and *Tahir v Tahir (No.2)*, 1995 S.L.T. 451.
[154] Matrimonial and Family Proceedings Act s.29A, inserted by Family Law (Scotland) Act 1985.
[155] Matrimonial and Family Proceedings Act s.28(2).
[156] Matrimonial and Family Proceedings Act s.28(3).

(d)   a court in Scotland would have had jurisdiction to entertain an action for divorce between the parties if such an action had been brought in Scotland immediately before the foreign divorce took effect;

(e)   the marriage had a substantial connection with Scotland; and

(f)   both parties are living at the time of the application."

The remedy may be sought in the Court of Session or sheriff court.[157] In disposing of an application under s.28, the court shall exercise its powers so as to place the parties, insofar as it is reasonable and practicable to do so, in the financial position in which they would have been if the application had been disposed of, in an action for divorce, etc. in Scotland, on the date on which the foreign divorce took effect. In determining what is reasonable and practicable, the court shall have regard in particular to (a) the parties' resources, present and foreseeable at the date of disposal of the application; and (b) any order made by a foreign court in or in connection with the divorce proceedings for the making of financial provision in whatever form, or the transfer of property, by one of the parties to the other. Where jurisdiction has been exercised solely on the basis of s.28(2)(b)(iii), the Scottish court's powers are restricted to making an order relating to the former matrimonial home and its contents, or a capital sum not exceeding the value of the defender's interest therein.

Financial relief in England

For England, the Law Commission preferred a solution which permitted the court, guided by a list of factors, to eliminate at the outset cases where an award would be inappropriate. Hence, in England, a party first must seek, per s.13, leave of the court to apply for financial relief, which leave shall not be granted unless the court thinks there is substantial ground for the making of an application for such an order; further, the leave may be conditional. Unless it is clear that a respondent can deliver "a knockout blow" at this stage, the application should proceed.[158] Once leave to apply has been granted, a second filter operates whereby, per s.16, no order for financial relief shall be made unless in all the circumstances of the case the court is satisfied that it is appropriate for such an order to be made.

    Under the English rules, parties may apply for financial provision after foreign divorce, annulment or legal separation. A number of cases on the operation of the English provisions can be cited,[159] often to the effect that it is inappropriate to supply the remedy,[160] or that the English court should not interfere where a foreign appropriate forum has made satisfactory provision and the applicant is seeking merely a "second bite at the cherry".[161] As a matter of public policy, the

13–44

---

[157] Matrimonial and Family Proceedings Act s.30.

[158] *Agbaje v Agbaje* [2010] 2 All E.R. 877. For a case in which the "knockout blow" was delivered, see *M v W* [2014] EWHC 925 (Fam).

[159] e.g. *Macaulay v Macaulay* [1991] 1 All E.R. 865; *Chebaro v Chebaro* [1987] Fam. 127; *Garcia v Garcia* [1991] 3 All E.R. 451; *M v M* [1995] 7 C.L. 64; *Jordan v Jordan* [2000] 1 W.L.R. 2010; *Emin v Yeldag* [2002] Fam. Law 419; *A v S (Financial Relief after Overseas US Divorce)* [2002] EWHC 1157 (Fam); *T v M-T* [2005] EWHC 79 (Fam); *Moore v Moore* [2007] I.L.Pr. 36; *Agbaje v Agbaje* [2010] 2 All E.R. 877; and *Traversa v Freddi* [2011] EWCA Civ 81.

[160] *Hewitson v Hewitson* [1995] 1 All E.R. 472 (and later [1999] Fam. Law 450).

[161] *Holmes v Holmes* [1989] 3 All E.R. 786; and *M v W* [2014] EWHC 925 (Fam).

Court of Appeal has held that there should be judicial collaboration where parties
have divorced in one jurisdiction and all consequential matters have been decided
in that jurisdiction, but where there are pension funds rooted and funded in
another jurisdiction, so that an applicant in the former jurisdiction will not be
deprived of pension rights.[162]

Part III of the Act was considered for the first time by the UK Supreme Court
in *Agbaje v Agbaje*,[163] a landmark English case concerning a couple of dual
Nigerian and British citizenship. They married in England in 1967, and were
divorced in Nigeria in 2005. They had strong connections with England, the five
children of the marriage having been born and educated there, and the wife
having lived continuously in England since the breakdown of the marriage in
1999. The parties had assets both in Nigeria and England; two houses in London
accounted for a large proportion of their wealth. The effect of the Supreme Court
order, restoring the award of the High Court, was to supplement the award made
to the wife by the Nigerian court by conferring upon her a proportion of the value
of the sale price of the UK properties. Lord Collins made clear that while the
factors which an English court must take into account in making or withholding
an award have much in common with those which would be relevant in a *forum
non conveniens* enquiry, they are not directed to the question of which of two
jurisdictions is appropriate, but rather whether the making of an order by an
English court would be appropriate when, *ex hypothesi*, there have already been
proceedings in a foreign country in which financial provision may have been
made.[164]

The decision in *Agbaje* means that the English courts will be more receptive to
applications for an order for financial relief after a foreign divorce, leading to
greater use of the remedy which the Act affords.[165]

*Relationship between maintenance awards and financial provision upon
termination of marriage*

13–45   The 1984 Act was introduced as a national measure, in the pre-harmonisation era,
and the advent of the Brussels and Lugano regimes rendered the jurisdiction
provisions in the 1984 Act subject to the harmonisation instruments.[166] In
Agbaje,[167] Lord Collins issued a warning regarding the relationship between the
Brussels regime governing maintenance decisions and the 1984 Act. He
explained that if an award of maintenance[168] had been made in another EU
Member State, the question might arise as to whether the application for financial
provision in England under Pt III (or, Scotland under Pt IV) would be precluded

---

[162] *Schofield v Schofield* [2011] EWCA Civ 174; [2011] 1 F.L.R. 2129.

[163] *Agbaje v Agbaje* [2010] 2 All E.R. 877.

[164] *Agbaje v Agbaje* [2010] 2 All E.R. 877 at [50].

[165] e.g. *Traversa v Freddi* [2011] EWCA Civ 81.

[166] Lord Collins in *Agbaje v Agbaje* [2010] 2 All E.R. 877 at [55] made clear that "maintenance" was
within the scope of the Brussels I Regulation (art.5.2), and that "rights in property arising out of a
matrimonial relationship" were expressly excluded from the scope thereof. These were autonomous
concepts: *De Cavel (No.1)* (143/78) [1979] E.C.R. 1055; *De Cavel (No.2)* (120/79) [1980] E.C.R.
731.

[167] *Agbaje v Agbaje* [2010] 2 All E.R. 877 at [55]. Also *M v W* [2014] EWHC 925 (Fam).

[168] *Van den Boogaard v Laumen* (C-220/95) [1997] Q.B. 759.

on the basis that the issue of maintenance had been determined in the other jurisdiction, that determination being entitled to recognition as an EU judgment. This important point was raised obiter, and no answer given, though it seemed that a UK court might properly be inhibited from acting on the basis of the 1984 Act to supplement the award of an EU Member State court, at least where account had been taken in the overseas proceedings of assets in the UK, and insofar as the application under the 1984 Act concerned maintenance.

The introduction of the Maintenance Regulation, with accompanying secondary legislation in the UK, necessitated clarification of the ranking of legislative instruments for the UK. By s.28(1) of the 1984 Act, a court's ability to entertain an application for financial provision is subject to section 28(3A).[169] Section 28(3A) establishes that if an application or part of an application relates to a matter where jurisdiction falls to be determined by reference to the jurisdictional requirements of the Maintenance Regulation and Sch.6 to the Civil Jurisdiction and Judgments (Maintenance) Regulations 2011, those requirements are to be satisfied in respect of the application (or part thereof), instead of the jurisdictional requirements set out in s.28(2).[170] Moreover, in such circumstances, with regard to the conditions to be satisfied per s.28(3), the condition set out in s.28(3)(e) (that the marriage had a substantial connection with Scotland) does not apply.

Termination of civil partnership by foreign dissolution

In relation to financial provision available upon the foreign dissolution of a civil partnership, the Civil Partnership Act 2004 provides, in s.125 and Sch.11, that where a civil partnership has been dissolved or annulled abroad, and the dissolution or annulment is entitled to be recognised as valid in Scotland, the Scots court may entertain an application by one of the former civil partners, or former ostensible civil partner, for an order for financial provision. The jurisdictional requirements and conditions clearly are modelled upon those contained in the Matrimonial and Family Proceedings Act 1984 ss.28 and 29. In such a case, the Scots court may make property orders in terms of the provisions of the Civil Partnership Act 2004.[171] As with divorce, after taking jurisdiction in terms of s.125 of the Civil Partnership Act 2004[172] (financial provision after overseas proceedings), the court will apply its own domestic law. As regards civil partnerships dissolved or annulled in Scotland, there is provision in the 2004 Act in Sch.28 Pt 2 (and s.261), in terms of which the benefits conferred upon married persons by the Family Law (Scotland) Act 1985 are extended, mutatis mutandis, to civil partners. Financial provision on termination of de facto cohabitation otherwise than by death is discussed at paras 13–13 to 13–14, above.

13–46

---

[169] Civil Jurisdiction and Judgments (Maintenance) Regulations 2011 (SI 2011/1484) Sch.7 para.10(4)(a).
[170] Civil Jurisdiction and Judgments (Maintenance) Regulations 2011 (SI 2011/1484) Sch.7 para.10(4)(b).
[171] Para.13–16, above (civil partnership).
[172] Civil Partnership Act 2004 Sch.11 Pt 3 (disposal of applications).

SUMMARY 13

13–47 1. Proprietary consequences of marriage.

The Family Law (Scotland) Act 2006 s.39 places Scots applicable law rules of matrimonial property on a legislative footing.

By s.39(6)(b), the Scots choice of law rules provided in the 2006 Act concerning matrimonial property are subject to the spouses' contrary agreement.

When dealing with a question of matrimonial property rights having cross-border implications, one of the first issues to ascertain is whether a "matrimonial property regime" was established upon marriage, either by operation of law, or by contract. There are three possibilities:

(1) A (default) statutory system imposing some version of a community of goods regime:

a foreign community of goods may have the same effect as a private marriage contract, by creating indefeasible contractual rights in moveable and immoveable property, in the latter case subject to the acquiescence of the *lex situs*.

(2) Private marriage contract:

The Rome I Regulation has no application.

The proper law is the law intended by the parties either expressly or by implication and, failing that, the law with which the deed has its closest connection. This law will govern the essential validity of the contract, subject to compliance with (or acquiescence of) the *lex situs* in the case of immoveables.

A private marriage contract is formally valid if it complies with the proper law of the contract, or with the law of the place of execution.

A Scots forum properly seised of a divorce action will apply the provisions of its own domestic law to the distribution of property between the spouses upon termination of marriage, but it is likely that a Scots forum will endeavour to respect the terms of the marriage contract.

(3) Absence of statutory or private contractual provision:

The Family Law (Scotland) Act 2006 s.39 has laid down a statutory rule providing applicable law rules in relation to the rights of spouses to each other's immoveable and moveable property arising by virtue of the marriage.

Questions in relation to immoveable property shall be determined by the *lex situs*(s.39(1)).

Questions in relation to the contents of a matrimonial home shall be determined by the *lex situs* of the home (s.39(4)).

Rights of a spouse in the moveable property of the other which arise by virtue of the marriage shall be determined by the law of the common domicile (without specification as to *tempus inspiciendum*) (s.39(2)); and failing such common domicile, the spouses shall be taken to have the same rights to such property as they had immediately before the marriage (s.39(3)).

A change of domicile by one or both spouses shall not affect a right in moveable property which immediately before the change has vested in either spouse (s.39(5)).

Section 39 shall not apply to the law on aliment, financial provision on divorce, or transfer of property on divorce or succession (s.39(6)(a)); nor shall it apply to the extent that spouses agree otherwise (s.39(6)(b)).

2. Proprietary consequences of other adult relationships.

Provision is made in the Family Law (Scotland) Act 2006, to confer upon cohabitants certain rights in property and upon death intestate of a predeceasing cohabitant, exigible where Scots law is the *lex causae*.

3. Financial consequences of adult relationships: maintenance obligations.

Maintenance Regulation

Council Regulation 4/2009 on jurisdiction, applicable law, recognition and enforcement of decisions and cooperation in matters relating to maintenance obligations ("the Maintenance Regulation") has applied in EU Member States, including the UK, from 18 June 2011.

Rules of jurisdiction are set out in Ch.II, the most important of which are arts 3 (general provisions), 4 (choice of court), 5 (appearance of defendant), 6 (subsidiary jurisdiction where no court of a Member State has jurisdiction pursuant to arts 3–5), 7 (*forum necessitatis*), and 8 (limit on proceedings, i.e. jurisdiction to modify a previous award).

Article 15 of the Maintenance Regulation provides that, in Member States bound by the 2007 Hague Protocol on the Law Applicable to Maintenance Obligations, the law applicable to maintenance obligations shall be determined in accordance with that Protocol. Since the UK Government decided not to participate in the Protocol, where a Scots court has jurisdiction in respect of a maintenance claim, it will apply Scots domestic law to the substance of the question: Family Law (Scotland) Act 2006 s.40.

With regard to recognition and enforcement of Member State maintenance decisions, Ch.IV of the Maintenance Regulation lays down two different sets of rules, according to whether or not the decision to be recognised and given effect was handed down in a Member State bound by the 2007 Hague Protocol.

Part II of the Maintenance Orders Act 1950 governs the registration and enforcement of aliment or maintenance orders intra-UK.

Reciprocal treatment of applications for maintenance under *Maintenance Orders (Reciprocal Enforcement) Act 1972*: the 1972 Act, as amended, applies Pt I to reciprocating (mainly Commonwealth) countries; Pt II to 1956 New York Convention countries; and Pt III to countries with which the UK has made bilateral arrangements.

2007 Hague Convention on the International Recovery of Child Support and Other Forms of Family Maintenance

The 2007 Convention was signed by the EU on 6 April 2011, and came into force in EU Member States, including the UK, on 1 August 2014. Its object is "to ensure the effective international recovery of child support and other forms of family maintenance" by establishing a comprehensive system of co-operation between Contracting States; making available applications for the establishment of maintenance decisions; providing for the recognition and enforcement of maintenance decisions; and requiring effective measures for the prompt enforcement of such decisions.

The Convention applies on a mandatory basis to child support cases, and by declaration the EU resolved to extend the application of Chs II and III to spousal support.

The International Recovery of Maintenance (Hague Convention 2007) (Scotland) Regulations 2012 facilitate the application of the 2007 Convention in Scotland.

4.   Financial consequences of adult relationships: provision upon termination of relationships.

Part IV of the Matrimonial and Family Proceedings Act 1984 permits a Scots court to make an award of financial provision following recognition of a foreign divorce or nullity.

Section 125 of the Civil Partnership Act 2004 endows the court with equivalent power in relation to civil partnerships dissolved overseas.

CHAPTER 14

Conflict rules affecting children: status, parental rights and responsibilities, guardianship, abduction, adoption, and surrogacy

STATUS

Legitimacy

Questions of legitimacy are most likely to arise now in relation to matters of **14–01** testate succession, where the testator's intention must first be ascertained before identification of those who are entitled to succeed.[1]

The status of legitimacy may continue to be relevant in Scots conflict cases, even though in domestic law the Law Reform (Parent and Child) (Scotland) Act 1986 began a process of removing distinctions between children on the basis of their having been born within or outside marriage. This process was completed by the Family Law (Scotland) Act 2006 ("the 2006 Act"), which, by s.21, abolished the status of illegitimacy. Section 21(2)(a) enacts a substitution in the 1986 Act (s.1: legal equality of children), to the following effect:

> "No person whose status is governed by Scots law shall be illegitimate; and accordingly the fact that a person's parents are not or have not been married to each other shall be left out of account in—
> (a) determining the person's legal status; or
> (b) establishing the legal relationship between the person and any other person."

This begs the question of when a person's status is governed by Scots law. There is a mutually dependent relationship between domicile and status, domicile being ascribed at birth according to status, but (until the advent of the 2006 Act in Scotland, and still in England) the status of the individual being required to be identified before domicile can be ascribed. Identification of domicile of origin depended upon legitimacy, but, as domicile of origin determined status, legitimacy depended upon domicile. There was, therefore, a problem of circularity of reasoning.[2]

---

[1] Para.18–32, below.
[2] See solutions suggested by Wolff, *Private International Law*, 2nd edn (1950), p.109; and Anton, *Private International Law*, 1st edn (1967), pp.345, 346.

Since, in terms of s.22 of the 2006 Act, the domicile of a child at birth is ascribed according to the rules contained therein, and not according to status as having been born inside marriage or not, one must conclude that if, in terms of s.22, a child's domicile is Scots, his status cannot be one of illegitimacy. But if, by s.22, his domicile is found to be other than Scots, his status must be determined by that other personal law, which may contain a distinction between legitimate and illegitimate.[3]

The Scots choice of law rule, traditionally stated, was[4] as follows:

— A child born anywhere of a marriage valid by Scots choice of law rules was legitimate.

— A child not born of a marriage valid by Scots choice of law rules[5] was legitimate if legitimate by the law of the domicile of each parent at the date of his birth. This rule was subject to the qualification that in the case of intestate succession to immoveables or succession to a title of honour, the child must be legitimate also by the *lex situs* or the law of the title, if such law so required[6] (that is to say, the requirements of the *lex situs* or the law of the title, whatever they may be, must be satisfied).[7]

— In the case of the child of a putative marriage,[8] his status would depend upon the law of the domicile of the innocent "spouse"; that is, he would be legitimate if that law recognised such marriages, and/or conceded that the issue thereof were legitimate.[9]

The position now falls to be regulated by s.41 ("Effect of parents' marriage in determining status to depend on law of domicile") of the 2006 Act. Section 41 provides that:

"Any question arising as to the effect on a person's status of—
(a)   the person's parents being, or having been, married to each other; or
(b)   the person's parents not being, or not having been, married to each other,

---

[3] Whether the status of illegitimacy by a foreign legal system would be found to be against Scots public policy would depend upon the matter being capable of being raised in a Scots forum, and upon the context in which the matter arose. The existence of 2006 Act s.41 suggests that a foreign status of illegitimacy, per se, would not offend Scots public policy.

[4] See still for England, *Dicey, Morris and Collins on the Conflict of Laws*, 15th edn (2012), r.113. Separation of the issue of status from the issue of validity of marriage was a late development in English law, not seen until *Re Bischoffsheim* [1948] Ch. 79. See also *Green v Montagu (aka Re Duchy of Manchester English Settled Estates)* [2011] EWHC 1856 (Ch). Children of polygamous marriages were considered legitimate in English law in advance of changes in the law permitting full recognition of the marriages whence they sprang: *Khoo Hooi Leong v Khoo Hean Kwee* [1926] A.C. 529; *Bamgbose v Daniel* [1955] A.C. 107; and *Hashmi v Hashmi* [1971] 3 All E.R. 1253: para.11–09, above.

[5] cf. in England, *Azad v Entry Clearance Officer (Dhaka)* [2001] Imm. A.R. 318.

[6] As to succession to, or devolution of, titles, see saving made by Family Law (Scotland) Act 2006 (Commencement, Transitional Provisions and Savings) Order 2006 (SSI 2006/212) art.11; and cf. in England *Re Barony of Moynihan* [2000] 1 F.L.R. 113.

[7] *Birtwhistle v Vardill* (1840) 7 Cl. & F. 895; *Re Don's Estate* (1857) 4 Drewry 194; and *Shedden v Patrick* (1854) 1 Macq. 535. *Sed contra Re Grey's Trusts* [1892] 3 Ch. 88 (re testate succession to land).

[8] According to Scots law, one contracted in the bona fide, but erroneous, belief on the part of one or both parties that they are free to marry; the error must be one of fact and not of law.

[9] *Smijth v Smijth*, 1918 1 S.L.T. 156.

shall be determined by the law of the country in which the person is domiciled at the time at which the question arises."

It would appear that this provision, though not heralded as a conflict of laws provision, must represent the current Scots choice of law rule. The status of an individual will be referred to his domicile, as discovered by reference to s.22 of the 2006 Act and/or common law rules of domicile. Where the *lex situs* and/or the law of the title require(s) that an heir be legitimate by such laws, the Scots court would give effect to those requirements.[10]

Declarators of status

The Law Reform (Parent and Child) (Scotland) Act 1986 makes provision for declarators of status. By the 2006 Act Sch.2, the declarators which may be sought, in terms of s.7 of the 1986 Act, in the Court of Session or sheriff court, are those of "parentage or non-parentage", the concept of illegitimacy, and associated terminology, having been removed from domestic Scots law. **14–02**

Legitimation

Legitimation is the means by which the status of legitimacy is acquired by an illegitimate person subsequent to birth. The concept is no longer relevant in Scots domestic law, but may be relevant where there is a foreign *lex causae*. There are two principal methods of legitimation. The Scots choice of law rules are as follows: **14–03**

Legitimation by subsequent marriage (per subsequens matrimonium)

The choice of law rule of Scots common law required capacity in the father so to legitimate the child by the law of the father's domicile at the date of the marriage (and not at any earlier date).[11] What mattered was whether or not the law of the father's domicile at marriage contained a doctrine of legitimation.[12] **14–04**

Legitimation was not part of English common law. English domestic law was opposed to legitimation, cleaving to the doctrine of indelibility of bastardy and being particularly hostile where the matter concerned succession to English land. It followed that the English choice of law rule was strict. A child would be regarded as legitimated by the marriage of its parents only if the father had capacity so to legitimate by the law of his domicile *both* at the date of the child's birth *and* at the date of the subsequent marriage.[13] This rule was altered by the

---

[10] Given the terms of s.21(2) of the 2006 Act.

[11] *Udny v Udny* (1869) M. (H.L.) 89; *Munro v Munro* (1837) 16 S. 18; confirmed on appeal (1840) 1 Rob. 492 HL; *McDouall v Adair* (1852) 14 D. 525; *Aikman v Aikman* (1859) 21 D. 757; affirmed (1861) 23 D. (H.L.) 3; *Blair v Kay's Trustees*, 1940 S.L.T. 464; and *Kelly v Marks*, 1974 S.L.T. 118.

[12] This was confirmed by the somewhat circuitously worded s.5(2) of the Legitimation (Scotland) Act 1968. This Act was repealed, subject to savings per the Family Law (Scotland) Act 2006 (Commencement, Transitional Provisions and Savings) Order 2006 (SSI 2006/212) art.11.

[13] *Re Goodman's Trusts* (1881) L.R. 17 Ch. D. 266; and *Re Askew* [1930] 2 Ch. 259 (since English law at the date in question would not have considered the child to be legitimate, the benefit of legitimate status was conveyed to the child through operation of the doctrine of *renvoi*).

Legitimacy Act 1926, which, by s.1, introduced legitimation into English domestic law. In terms of s.8, the father need have such capacity by the law of his domicile only at the date of the marriage. The English rules now are contained in the Legitimacy Act 1976 ss.2, 2A and 3.

Legitimation by recognition (per rescriptum principis)

14–05   The English common law choice of law rule still applies so that a child will be regarded as having been legitimated by recognition only if his father had power so to legitimate him both at the date of the child's birth and at the date of the act of recognition.[14] The Scots choice of law rule, less strict, is the same as that which obtains in cases of legitimation by subsequent marriage, requiring capacity to legitimate only at the date of the act of recognition.

PARENTAL RIGHTS AND RESPONSIBILITIES

14–06   The Borras Report[15] stated that family law, including the law in relation to children, should form part of the project of European legal integration. For many years there has existed a number of international conventions dealing with child matters,[16] including: the 1961 Hague Convention concerning the Powers of Authorities and the Law Applicable in respect of the Protection of Minors (to which the UK is not a party); the 1980 Hague Convention on the Civil Aspects of International Child Abduction[17]; the 1980 Council of Europe Convention on the Recognition and Enforcement of Decisions concerning Custody of Children[18]; and the 1996 Hague Convention on Jurisdiction, Applicable Law, Recognition, Enforcement and Co-operation in respect of Parental Responsibility and Measures for the Protection of Children.[19] Arguably, no European intervention in relation to parental rights and responsibilities would have been necessary had all EU Member States been willing to ratify the 1996 Hague Convention, but in 1995 the Council of Ministers of the EU concluded that it was necessary to make European provision for parental responsibility matters, in the form of measures supplementary to those laid down in the 1996 Convention.[20] The only perceived benefit of introducing special European rules in addition to the Hague rules was that it would fill the gap where any Member State decided not to ratify the 1996 Hague Convention, and also that it would confer jurisdiction on the European Court of Justice ("ECJ"/"CJEU") to interpret the provisions and thereby bring some uniformity of interpretation. The Borras Report concluded in 1998 that the

---

[14] *Re Luck's Settlement Trusts* [1940] Ch. 864.

[15] A. Borras, *Explanatory Report on the Convention on Jurisdiction and the Recognition and Enforcement of Judgments in Matrimonial Matters* [1998] O.J. C221/27 ("Borras Report") (in respect of which, see para.12–04, above).

[16] Thorpe L.J. in *Re G (Children) (Foreign Contact Order: Enforcement)* [2003] EWCA Civ 1607 at [32], described the area as a "treaty jungle". See further P. McEleavy, "Luxembourg, Brussels and now The Hague: Congestion in the Promotion of Free Movement in Parental Responsibility" (2010) 59 I.C.L.Q. 505.

[17] Para.14–50, below.

[18] Para.14–49, below.

[19] Para.14–29, below.

[20] Borras Report para.9.

negotiating and drafting work had been laborious, but fruitful[21]: the result was Council Regulation (EC) No.1347/2000 on jurisdiction and the recognition in matrimonial matters and in matters of parental responsibility for children of both spouses.[22]

Background

Regulation 1347/2000: Brussels II

Brussels II set out rules for jurisdiction and recognition and enforcement of judgments in matrimonial matters and matters of parental responsibility for the children of both spouses rendered on the occasion of the matrimonial proceedings. The instrument, evidently, did not cater for all children, or for all parental responsibility issues. Whilst it covered both biological and adopted children of a couple, it did not provide for the more general concept of "children of the family." It was soon apparent that a further instrument was required, with a wider remit concerning children.

14–07

French Access Initiative[23]

In summer 2000, France presented an initiative for a Council Regulation on the mutual enforcement of judgments on rights of access to children. The initiative was to facilitate, through the abolition of (*exequatur*) procedural hurdles, the exercise of cross-border rights of access in the case of divorced or separated couples. However, the Justice and Home Affairs Council of the EU considered that work on the French initiative could proceed only in parallel with extension of the scope of Regulation 1347/2000. Therefore the Commission presented in spring 2001 a working document on the mutual recognition of decisions on parental responsibility. Ultimately, Regulation 1347/2000 was repealed by Council Regulation (EC) No.2201/2003 concerning jurisdiction and the recognition and enforcement of judgments in matrimonial matters and matters of parental responsibility (repealing Regulation (EC) No.1347/2000[24]), referred to in this book as "Brussels II *bis*", but also known as "Brussels IIa".

14–08

---

[21] Borras Report para.10.

[22] Regulation 1347/2000 (henceforth "Brussels II").

[23] Initiative of the French Republic with a view to adopting a Council Regulation on the mutual enforcement of judgments on rights of access to children [2000] O.J. C234/7.

[24] Regulation 2201/2003. See Commission Services in consultation with the European Judicial Network in Civil and Commercial Matters, *Practice Guide for the Application of the Brussels IIa Regulation* (2014) (henceforth "Practice Guide").

Brussels II *bis*

14–09 Since March 1, 2005, jurisdiction, recognition and enforcement of judgments on parental rights and responsibilities have been governed in UK courts[25] by Brussels II *bis*.[26] The prime importance of Brussels II *bis quoad* proceedings relating to children lies in its severing of the link with matrimonial proceedings. Brussels II *bis* covers judgments on parental responsibility over a child, irrespective of his parents' marital status, thereby ensuring equality of treatment for all children in the matters to which the Regulation pertains. The objective of Community action[27] in Brussels II *bis* is to protect the child's best interests, and to give expression to the child's fundamental right to maintain on a regular basis a personal relationship and direct contact with both parents, as laid down in art.24 of the Charter of Fundamental Rights of the EU.[28]

Scope

14–10 Brussels II *bis* lays down rules on jurisdiction (Ch.II), recognition and enforcement (Ch.III), and co-operation between central authorities (Ch.IV) in the field of parental responsibility, and contains specific rules on child abduction and access rights. The Regulation applies to all civil matters concerning the "attribution, exercise, delegation, restriction or termination of parental responsibility."[29]

"Parental responsibility"

14–11 For the purposes of Brussels II *bis*, "parental responsibility" means:

> "... all rights and duties relating to the person or property of a child which are given to a natural or legal person by judgment, by operation of law or by an agreement having legal effect. The term shall include rights of custody and rights of access."[30]

The list of matters in art.1.2 concerning the attribution, exercise, delegation, restriction or termination of "parental responsibility" is illustrative, not exhaustive. The expression covers not only rights of custody[31] and access,[32] but also matters such as guardianship and the placement of a child in a foster family,

---

[25] The Court of Appeal in *AD v CD* [2008] I.L.Pr. 11 held that a Romanian contact order made in October 2006 was unenforceable under Brussels II *bis* because it pre-dated Romania's accession to the EU on January 1, 2007.

[26] The instrument is currently subject to a revision exercise: art.65 of Brussels II *bis* requires, no later than 1 January 2012, the Commission to present a report on its application. On 15 April 2014, the European Commission published its Report on the application of the Brussels II *bis* Regulation (COM (2014) 225 final), and issued its "Consultation on the functioning of the Brussels IIa Regulation (EC 2201/2003)". A summary of the responses to the Consultation may be viewed at http://ec.europa.eu/eusurvey/publication/BXLIIA [accessed 20 June 2015]. To date, no proposal to amend Brussels II *bis* has been published.

[27] Imposing "international obligations": *Re S (A Child)* [2009] EWCA Civ 1471.

[28] Brussels II *bis* Proposal Explanatory Memo, p.2.

[29] Brussels II *bis* art.1.1(b).

[30] Brussels II *bis* art.2.7.

[31] Brussels II *bis* art.2.9: "Rights of custody" shall include rights and duties relating to the care of the person of a child, and in particular the right to determine the child's place of residence.

or in institutional care (covering cases where a specific matter of parental responsibilities is a "public law" measure).[33] The holder of parental responsibilities may be a natural person, or a legal person. The term "parental responsibilities" is used in the 1996 Hague Convention (q.v.), and the Borras Report says that it has a "degree of unifying potential".[34]

"Civil matters"

The interpretation of "civil matters" arose for decision by the ECJ in *Proceedings*   **14–12**
Brought by A,[35] a case in which a mother, her three children and their stepfather moved from Sweden to Finland in 2005, where they lived on campsites and with relatives. The children did not attend school. Later in 2005, the children were taken into care in Finland on the grounds of the stepfather's violence, and by reason of their having been abandoned. On application by the mother for the care order to be lifted, the question of the jurisdiction of the Finnish court arose, and was referred to the ECJ for a preliminary ruling. The ECJ held that "civil matters" had to be interpreted autonomously, and to the effect of including measures which, from the point of view of the national law of the Member State, might fall under public law.[36] A decision to take a child into care, such as that in issue in the main proceedings, was inherently an act of the public authorities the aim of which was to satisfy the need to protect and assist young persons and was therefore a "civil matter" for the purposes of the Regulation.

Similarly, in *Re C (Recognition and Enforcement of Decision to Take Child Into Care)*,[37] on a reference for a preliminary ruling from the Finnish *Korkein Hallinto-Oikeus*, the ECJ held that a single decision ordering a child to be taken into care and placed in a foster family was covered by the term "civil matters", even though that decision was adopted in the context of public law rules relating to child protection.

In contrast with Brussels II, Brussels II *bis* applies to all decisions on parental responsibility issued by a court of a Member State. However, the following matters are not included in the scope of the Regulation: criminal aspects of child protection; criminal offences committed by children; adoption; emancipation; the child's names; measures taken as a result of criminal offences committed by children; and maintenance obligations.[38] The Regulation does not apply to general public law issues concerning education, health, immigration or asylum. Nor does it apply, within private law, to paternity issues, since establishing parenthood is quite different from the matter of attributing parental responsibility.[39]

---

[32] Brussels II *bis* art.2.10: "Rights of access" shall include the right to take a child to a place other than his habitual residence for a limited period of time.

[33] Brussels II *bis* art.1.2.

[34] Borras Report para.24.

[35] *Proceedings Brought by A* (C-523/07) [2009] I.L.Pr. 39.

[36] *Proceedings Brought by A* (C-523/07) [2009] I.L.Pr. 39 at summary, [1], [29].

[37] *Re C (Recognition and Enforcement of Decision to Take Child Into Care)* (C-435/06) [2008] I.L.Pr. 1.

[38] Brussels II *bis* recitals (10), (11), art.1.3. Although maintenance obligations and parental responsibilities often are dealt with in the same court action, maintenance obligations now are covered by Regulation 4/2009, discussed at para.13–18, above.

[39] Brussels II *bis* recital (10).

Mostly parental responsibilities relate to a child's person, but they may relate also to a child's property.[40] It may be necessary to take certain protective measures concerning a child's property, for example, to appoint a person or group to assist and represent the child in relation to that property. The Regulation applies to any such protective measure that may be necessary for the administration or sale of the property, e.g. if the child's parents are in dispute about the property. Measures relating to the child's property which are not protective in nature are not covered by the Regulation[41]; whether or not a measure is protective will be decided by the forum on a case-by-case basis.

Rules of jurisdiction in Brussels II bis

14–13 Chapter II s.2 lays down rules of jurisdiction concerning parental responsibility in respect of all children. The rules listed in arts 8–15 establish a system of grounds of jurisdiction to determine the courts of which Member States are competent. The question which court is competent within a particular Member State (e.g. sheriff court or Court of Session) is answered by domestic procedural rules.[42] The grounds of jurisdiction in matters of parental responsibility are said to be shaped in light of the best interests of the child, "in particular the criterion of proximity".[43]

Article 8—general jurisdiction[44]

14–14 "The courts of a Member State shall have jurisdiction in matters of parental responsibility over a child who is habitually resident in that Member State at the time the court is seised."[45]

"The fundamental principle of the jurisdiction rules of the Regulation in matters of parental responsibility is that the most appropriate forum is the relevant court of the Member State of the habitual residence of the child".[46] The concept of habitual residence is not defined, but will be determined by the judge in each case on the basis of factual elements, and in light of the objectives and purpose of the instrument. The ECJ in *Proceedings Brought by A*[47] gave an autonomous definition of habitual residence for the purpose of art.8, viz.:

"Since Article 8(1) of Regulation No 2201/2003 . . .does not make any express reference to the law of the Member States for the purpose of determining the meaning and scope of the concept of 'habitual residence', the determination of that concept must be made in the light of the context of the provisions and the objective of the regulation, in particular that which is apparent from Recital 12 in the

---

[40] Paras 14–46—14–47, below.
[41] Such measures will be governed by the Brussels I Regulation (failing which as to scope, by s.14 of the 1995 Act, para.14–47, above).
[42] Practice Guide para.3.2.1. See para.14–36, below.
[43] Brussels II *bis* recital (12).
[44] Practice Guide para.3.2.3.
[45] Brussels II *bis* art.8.1. e.g. *Re B (A Child) (Care Proceedings: Jurisdiction)* [2013] EWCA Civ 1434; [2014] Fam. 139; and *N v K (Jurisdiction: International Liaison)* [2013] EWHC 2774 (Fam).
[46] Practice Guide para.3.2.3.
[47] *Proceedings Brought by A* (C-523/07) [2009] I.L.Pr. 39.

preamble, according to which the grounds of jurisdiction which it establishes are shaped in the light of the best interests of the child, in particular on the criterion of proximity. Thus, in addition to the physical presence of the child in a Member State other factors must be chosen which are capable of showing that that presence is not in any way temporary or intermittent .... Therefore, *the concept of 'habitual residence' under Article 8(1) of Regulation No 2201/2003 must be interpreted as meaning that it corresponds to the place which reflects some degree of integration by the child in a social and family environment.* To that end, in particular the duration, regularity, conditions and reasons for the stay on the territory of a Member State and the family's move to that State, the child's nationality, the place and conditions of attendance at school, linguistic knowledge and the family and social relationships of the child in that State must be taken into consideration. It is for the national court to establish the habitual residence of the child, taking account of all the circumstances specific to each individual case."[48]

If the forum decides that it does not have jurisdiction under art.8, it must declare this of its own motion; it is not required to transfer the case to another court.[49]

Once a competent court is seised, in principle it retains jurisdiction even if the child acquires habitual residence in another Member State during the course of the proceedings, an example of the operation of the principle of *perpetuatio fori.* This important principle is effected by art.9.

Article 9—continuing jurisdiction of child's former habitual residence[50]

The Practice Guide made clear that when a child moves from one Member State **14–15** to another, it is often necessary to review access or contact arrangements. The policy of art.9 is that "the holders of parental responsibility are encouraged to agree the necessary adjustments of previously-ordered access rights and arrangements before the move takes place and, if this proves impossible, to apply to the court of the country of the child's former habitual residence to resolve the dispute."[51] Any person who can no longer exercise access rights (because of the lawful removal of the child to a new habitual residence) can apply for an appropriate adjustment of access rights by the court which granted them (i.e. the former habitual residence of the child) for a period of three months following the move. During this three-month period, the courts of the new Member State do not have jurisdiction in matters of access rights. Article 9 deals only with access rights, and does not apply to other matters of parental responsibility.

For art.9 to apply, the following conditions must be satisfied[52]:

(1) the courts of the Member State of origin must have issued a judgment on access rights (otherwise the Member State of the child's new habitual residence would have jurisdiction under art.8);

---

[48] *Proceedings Brought by A* (C-523/07) [2009] I.L.Pr. 39 at summary, [2], [3]; also [33], [35], [38], [44] (Emphasis added). See also *Mercredi v Chaffe* (C-497/10 PPU) [2011] I.L.Pr. 23 (and subsequently, in the English Court of Appeal, [2011] EWCA Civ 272; [2011] 2 F.L.R. 515); and *C v M* (Case C-376/14PPU) [2015] 2 W.L.R. 59. In England, see, e.g. *Re F (A Child) (Care Proceedings: Habitual Residence)* [2014] EWCA Civ 789.
[49] Brussels II *bis* art.17. Contrast art.15.
[50] Practice Guide para.3.2.4.1.
[51] Practice Guide para.3.2.4.1.
[52] Practice Guide para.3.2.4.2.

(2)   the removal of the child to the new habitual residence must be lawful (otherwise, see art.10);

(3)   it is operative only during the three-month period immediately following the child's physical removal;

(4)   the child must have acquired habitual residence in the new Member State during the three-month period (otherwise the Member State of origin would have art.8 jurisdiction);

(5)   the holder of the access rights must still be habitually resident in the Member State from which the child was removed (the Member State of origin); and

(6)   the holder of the access rights must not have accepted the change of jurisdiction.

Articles 10 and 11—jurisdiction in cases of child abduction; return of the child

14–16   These provide special rules, examined below.[53]

Article 12—prorogation of jurisdiction

14–17   Article 12 grants very limited scope to seise a court of a Member State in which the child is not habitually resident.[54] The basis of prorogation is that the matter of parental responsibility is connected with a related, pending matrimonial proceeding (art.12.1 and 12.2[55]), or that the child has a substantial connection with that Member State (art.12.3).[56] The reference in art.12.1(b) to the "superior interests of the child" differs from the term "best interests of the child" in art.12.3(b),[57] but since the non-English versions of the Regulation employ identical wording in both paragraphs, no significance attaches to the difference in wording in the English text. The CJEU has ruled that where parents agreed to bring proceedings in a particular Member State, the jurisdiction of the courts in that Member State ends once a final judgment in those proceedings has been delivered.[58]

---

[53] Paras 14–65—14–73.

[54] e.g. *L v M* (Case C-656/13); [2015] W.L.R. 801.

[55] e.g. *Re S-R (Contact: Jurisdiction)* [2008] 2 F.L.R. 1741; *Bush v Bush* [2008] EWCA Civ 865; *AP v TD (Relocation: Retention of Jurisdiction)* [2010] EWHC 2040 (Fam); and *Re LR (A Child) (Jurisdiction: Habitual Residence: Acceptance of Jurisdiction)* [2014] EWCA Civ 1624; [2015] Fam. Law 273. See, under Brussels II, *X v Y* [2009] I.L.Pr. 22 *Cour de Cassation* (France).

[56] Practice Guide para.3.2.6.1. cf. *C v FC (Brussels II: Freestanding Application for Parental Responsibility)* [2004] 1 F.L.R. 317; and *Re ED (A Child) (Jurisdiction: Undertaking to Return Child) (aka A v D)* [2014] EWHC 2731 (Fam).

[57] e.g. *W v W (A Minor) (Mirror Order)* [2011] EWCA Civ 703; [2014] 1 F.L.R. 1530; and *VC v GC (Jurisdiction: Brussels II Revised art.12)* [2012] EWHC 1246 (Fam); [2013] 1 F.L.R. 244.

[58] *E v B* (C-436/13) [2014] 3 W.L.R. 1750; [2015] 1 F.L.R. 64.

PARTIES RESIDENT IN THIRD STATES

The doubts and controversies which have been seen in relation to the extent of **14–18** jurisdiction and the reach of the Brussels regime in commercial matters are now visible in the family law arena.

In the case of *Re I (A Child) (Contact Application: Jurisdiction),*[59] the Supreme Court held that nothing in the wording of Brussels II *bis* art.12 limited the jurisdiction therein conferred to children resident in the EU. While this interpretative approach has a familiar, ambitious European ring to it,[60] support can be gleaned from the wording of art.12.4, which suggests that the article extends to children habitually resident in the territory of a Third State. In the instant case, the requirements of art.12.3 were satisfied: the child could be said to have a substantial connection with the English court since the child was a British national and both parents had been habitually resident in the UK. On the facts, both parents had accepted the jurisdiction of the English court. On a welfare criterion (art.12.4), the jurisdiction of the English court was in the best interests of the child. It was accepted that the habitual residence of the child was in Pakistan.[61] His parents were divorced in 2003, and in 2004 the father received leave of the court to take the child to Pakistan, but agreed to facilitate visits by the child to the UK to see his mother. In 2008 the mother applied in England to enforce and vary the contact order, so as to ensure that the child was in the UK to facilitate contact. The mother had invoked the jurisdiction of the English court, and the father had accepted it.

In Baroness Hale's opinion, as a matter of fact, there must be many cases in which matrimonial jurisdiction is present under art.3 of Brussels II *bis* (jurisdiction in divorce, etc.) on the basis of the connection of one spouse to the forum, while the other spouse and children are resident outside the EU.

Article 12.1 permits the divorce court to exercise jurisdiction in any matter related to parental responsibility, provided that at least one of the spouses has parental responsibility and the jurisdiction of the divorce court has been accepted unequivocally by the spouses at the time the court is seised,[62] and that jurisdiction

---

[59] *Re I (A Child) (Contact Application: Jurisdiction)* [2009] UKSC 10. See also *Re Z (A Child) (aka X v Y)* [2014] EWHC 2147 (Fam).

[60] cf. *Owusu v Jackson (t/a Villa Holidays Bal Inn Villas)* [2005] Q.B. 801 at [24].

[61] The concern expressed in the Court of Appeal about any possible contradiction of the terms of the 2003 UK-Pakistan Judicial Protocol on Children Matters (q.v.) was allayed in the Supreme Court by Baroness Hale, *Re I (A Child) (Contact Application: Jurisdiction)* [2009] UKSC 10 at [42]–[44], on the basis that the Protocol was not directly applicable to the case, there having been no abduction or wrongful retention of the child: moreover, in her Ladyship's view, the terms of an agreement between the judiciaries of one Member State and a non-Member State could not affect the proper interpretation of an EU Regulation. See also Council Regulation No.664/2009 establishing a procedure for the negotiation and conclusion of agreements between Member States and third countries concerning jurisdiction, recognition and enforcement of judgments and decisions in matrimonial matters, matters of parental responsibility and matters relating to maintenance obligations, and the law applicable to matters relating to maintenance obligations (and Corrigendum thereto at [2011] O.J. L241/35).

[62] The wording of art.12.3 raises a nice question of interpretation the answer to which did not affect the instant case on the facts. The Justices of the Supreme Court agreed that there might have to be a reference to the CJEU on the question whether the proper interpretation was that there required to be acceptance by all the parties of the jurisdiction "at the time the court is seised", or whether acceptance (at any time) of the jurisdiction had to be had of those who were parties to the proceedings at the time the court was seised.

is in the superior interests of the child. In Lady Hale's view, there was nothing to differentiate art.12.3 from art.12.1; there was nothing to suggest that its provisions be restricted to children residing in a Member State.

Article 13—jurisdiction based on child's presence

14–19   If it should be impossible to determine the child's habitual residence, and if art.12 does not apply, art.13 allows a Member State court to decide matters of parental responsibilities in relation to a child who is present in that Member State.[63] This would be capable of applying to refugee and asylum children.[64]

Article 14—residual jurisdiction

14–20   If no court has jurisdiction pursuant to arts 8–13, a Member State court may found jurisdiction on the basis of its own national rules.[65]

Article 15—transfer to a court better placed to hear the case

14–21   Exceptionally,[66] a court which is seised of a case (the court of origin) may transfer it, in whole or in part, to a court of another Member State if that Member State is "better placed" to hear the case.[67] Once a case has been transferred to the second Member State,[68] it cannot be further transferred to a third Member State (recital (13)). This admission of the principle of judicial discretion, though tentative, at the heart of a Brussels regime instrument, is worthy of remark. The circumstances in which the discretion may be exercised, and how it shall be done,[69] are set out in art.15.2–15.6.[70]

---

[63] Practice Guide para.3.2.7.

[64] cf. ss.10 and 12 of the Family Law Act 1986; and at common law in Scotland *Oludimu v Oludimu*, 1967 S.L.T. 105.

[65] i.e. Family Law Act 1986 ss.9–18, at paras 14–36—14–42, below. cf. the operation of the 1973 Act in cases where consistorial jurisdiction cannot be exercised under art.3 of Brussels II *bis. Sed contra* Regulation 4/2009 art.6 (subsidiary jurisdiction).

[66] Transfer was refused, e.g. in *Re P (A Child)*[2013] EWCA Civ 1216 (although the mother was a Bulgarian national and the child had Bulgarian and British nationality, the jurisdiction of England and Wales was better placed than the Bulgarian court to hear an application for care and placement orders since the fact-finding process had already taken place there, the family's habitual residence was in England, and the sources of evidence and the circumstances to be evaluated were in England). cf. *Re D (A Child) (Transfer of Proceedings) (aka Re M (Brussels II Revised: Art.15))* [2014] EWCA Civ 152.

[67] For examples of incoming transfers, see *Re M (A Child) (Foreign Care Proceedings: Transfer) (aka Re LM (A Child) (Transfer of Irish Proceedings))* [2013] EWHC 646 (Fam); [2013] Fam. 308; and *Re Application in respect of A and B* [2014] Fam. L.R. 137; 2014 G.W.D. 38-698.

[68] e.g. *Re T (A Child) (Care Proceedings: Request to Assume Jurisdiction)* [2013] EWCA Civ 895; [2014] Fam. 130 (transfer to Slovakian court); *Re ED (A Child) (aka A v D)* [2014] EWHC 3851 (Fam) (transfer to Polish court); and *Barking and Dagenham LBC v C* [2014] EWHC 2472 (Fam).

[69] See *In Re J (A Child) (Brussels II Revised: Article 15: Practice and Procedure) (aka Islington LBC v R)* [2014] EWFC 41, in which the view was expressed that judicial cooperation is essential.

[70] Practice Guide para.3.3. See Act of Sederunt (Jurisdiction, Recognition and Enforcement of Judgments in Matrimonial Matters and Matters of Parental Responsibility Rules) 2006 (SSI 2006/397); and, in England, *Practice Direction (Family Proceedings: Allocation and Transfer)* [2008] 1 W.L.R. 2651. See also *B v B (Brussels II Revised: Article 15)* [2008] EWHC 2965 (Fam); *Re H*

Conflicting jurisdictions

Generally, the treatment of allocation of jurisdiction in a case of concurrent proceedings is determined by the *lis pendens* principle.[71] Hence, where proceedings relating to parental responsibility concerning the same child and involving the same cause of action are brought before courts of different Member States, the court second seised shall of its own motion stay its proceedings until such time as the jurisdiction of the court first seised is established.[72]

14–22

Article 16 provides an autonomous definition of the time at which a court shall be deemed to be seised, in terms which are equivalent, mutatis mutandis, to art.30 of the Brussels I Regulation/art.32 of the Brussels I Recast Regulation.[73]

Provisional, including protective, measures

In urgent cases, the courts of a Member State may take such provisional, including protective, measures in respect of persons or assets in that state as may be available under the law of that state, even if, under Brussels II *bis*, the court of another Member State has jurisdiction as to the substance of the matter.[74]

14–23

In *Proceedings Brought by A*,[75] the ECJ indicated that a protective measure, such as the taking into care of children, may be decided by a national court under art.20 if the following three conditions are satisfied: the measure must be urgent; it must be taken in respect of persons in the Member State concerned; and it must be provisional. The taking of that measure, adopted in the best interests of the child, and its binding nature are determined in accordance with national law. After the protective measure has been taken, the national court is not required to transfer the case to the court of another Member State having jurisdiction. However, since provisional or protective measures are temporary, circumstances related to the physical, psychological and intellectual development of the child may require early intervention by the court having jurisdiction in order for definitive measures to be adopted.

Protective measures shall cease to apply when the court of the Member State having jurisdiction as to substance has taken the measures it considers appropriate.[76]

(Abduction) [2009] EWHC 1735 (Fam; and *DR v MB (otherwise Re AB (A Child) (Abduction: Art.15: Procedure and Evidence))* [2014] EWHC 276 (Fam)).

[71] Brussels II *bis* art.19. Para.12–15, above.

[72] Para.12–16 re implications of *Owusu v Jackson (t/a Villa Holidays Bal Inn Villas)* [2005] Q.B. 801. See also *Purrucker v Valles Perez* (Case C-296/10) [2011] I.L.Pr. 14.

[73] e.g. *Re G (A Child) (Jurisdiction: Brussels II Revised)* [2014] EWCA Civ 680; [2015] 1 F.L.R. 276.

[74] Brussels II *bis* art.20; cf. art.31 of the Brussels I Regulation/ art.35 of the Brussels I Recast Regulation.

[75] *Proceedings Brought by A* (C-523/07) [2009] I.L.Pr. 39; at [47], [56], [59], [64], [65].

[76] *Re S (Care Proceedings: Jurisdiction)* [2008] EWHC 3013 (Fam); and *Deticek v Sgueglia* Case (C-403/09 PPU) [2010] All E.R. (EC) 313.

Choice of law

14–24   Brussels II *bis* does not lay down choice of law rules. However, by reason of secondary legislation,[77] if a Scots court exercises jurisdiction over a parental responsibility matter under Brussels II *bis*, it will apply the applicable law provisions (q.v.) contained in the 1996 Hague Convention.

Recognition and enforcement of judgments

14–25   As in the case of matrmonial decrees, mutual recognition is a main objective of Brussels II *bis*. In terms of art.21, a judgment given in a Member State shall be recognised in the other Member States without any special procedure being required. However, any interested party may apply for a decision that the judgment be or be not recognised.[78] The grounds of non-recognition of judgments relating to parental responsibility are relatively few, and are contained in art.23. A judgment relating to parental responsibility shall not be recognised:

(a)   if such recognition is manifestly contrary to the public policy of the Member State in which recognition is sought taking into account the best interests of the child;

(b)   if it was given, except in case of urgency, without the child having been given an opportunity to be heard, in violation of fundamental principles of procedure of the Member State in which recognition is sought;

(c)   where it was given in default of appearance if the person in default was not served with the document which instituted the proceedings or with an equivalent document in sufficient time and in such a way as to enable that person to arrange for his or her defence unless it is determined that such person has accepted the judgment unequivocally;

(d)   on the request of any person claiming that the judgment infringes his or her parental responsibility, if it was given without such person having been given an opportunity to be heard;

(e)   if it is irreconcilable with a later judgment relating to parental responsibility given in the Member State in which recognition is sought;

(f)   if it is irreconcilable with a later judgment relating to parental responsibility given in another Member State or in the non-Member State of the habitual residence of the child provided that the later judgment fulfils the conditions necessary for its recognition in the Member State in which recognition is sought; or

(g)   if the procedure laid down in art.56 (re placement of a child in another Member State) has not been complied with.

The "public policy" clause in art.23(a) is unusual in the qualification, "taking into account the best interests of the child". By which law are the best interests of the

---

[77] The Parental Responsibility and Measures for the Protection of Children (International Obligations) (Scotland) Regulations 2010 (SSI 2010/213) reg.6.

[78] This must be read subject to an understanding that the rules governing recognition under Brussels II *bis* admit few opportunities for successful challenge. See *Rinau v Rinau* (C-195/08 PPU) [2008] I.L.Pr. 51.

child to be determined? Presumably this must lie within the discretion of the forum.[79] A heavy onus rests on a parent who seeks to re-open welfare issues, and the English Court of Appeal has held that a foreign judgment will not be subverted save in the most exceptional of circumstances: "a high degree of disparity is required between the effects of the order if enforced and the child's welfare interests".[80]

The jurisdiction of the court of the Member State of origin may not be reviewed, nor may the test of public policy be applied to the rules relating to jurisdiction (art.24).

Enforceability

Article 28: Enforceable judgments

A judgment on the exercise of parental responsibility in respect of a child given in a Member State which is enforceable in that Member State and has been served, shall be enforced in another Member State when, on the application of any interested party, it has been declared enforceable there. However, in the UK, such a judgment shall be enforced in England and Wales, in Scotland or in Northern Ireland only when, on the application of any interested party, it has been registered for enforcement in that part of the UK.

Where application for a declaration of enforceability has been made, the court shall give its decision without delay. Submissions by the child, or by the person against whom enforcement is sought, will not be admitted at this stage. The judgment may not be reviewed as to its substance,[81] and the application may be refused only on the ground of one of the reasons specified in arts 22–24. Article 33 sets out the rules for appealing against the decision.[82]

14–26

Rights of access

The 1980 Hague Convention (q.v.) does not guarantee the enforcement of access rights in the same way as it seeks to uphold custody rights, but art.21 of that instrument binds central authorities to promote the peaceful enjoyment of access rights and the fulfilment of any conditions to which the exercise of those rights shall be subject. They shall take steps, "to remove, as far as possible, all obstacles to the exercise of such rights".[83] The French Initiative on Rights of Access[84] having expedited agreement on parental responsibilities generally, it is not surprising to find specific provision in Brussels II *bis*, concerned with the enforceability of rights of access[85] and practical arrangements in relation thereto.[86]

14–27

---

[79] e.g. *Re L (A Child) (Recognition of Foreign Order)* [2012] EWCA Civ 1157; and *Re D (Recognition and Enforcement of Romanian Order) (aka MD v AA)* [2014] EWHC 2756 (Fam).
[80] *Re A (Removal Outside Jurisdiction: Habitual Residence) (aka ES v AJ)* [2011] EWCA Civ 265.
[81] Brussels II *bis* art.31.
[82] *Re S (A Child) (Enforcement of Foreign Judgment)* [2009] EWCA Civ 993.
[83] Hague Convention art.21.
[84] Para.14–08, above.
[85] Brussels II *bis* art.41.
[86] Brussels II *bis* art.48.

International co-operation

14–28   Implementation of Brussels II *bis* is facilitated by the provisions of Ch.IV (co-operation between central authorities in matters of parental responsibility).

1996 Hague Convention

14–29   An important development in this area of the conflict of laws is the 1996 Hague Convention on Jurisdiction, Applicable Law, Recognition, Enforcement and Co-operation in respect of Parental Responsibility and Measures for the Protection of Children.[87] The 1996 Convention was signed on 1 April 1 2003 by the then 14 EU Member States. No further steps were taken for several years regarding ratification of the Convention,[88] but in June 2008, the EU Council adopted a decision authorising certain EU Member States to ratify or accede to the Convention.[89] In consequence, in the UK, there was introduced the European Communities (Definition of Treaties) (1996 Hague Convention on Protection of Children etc.) Order 2010,[90] which had the effect of rendering the Convention an EU Treaty, and enabling secondary legislation to be put in place in Scotland and England to implement all aspects of the Convention. For ratification to proceed, all EU Member States were required to be ready to proceed en bloc.[91] Ultimately, the Convention was ratified by the UK on 27 July 2012 and entered into force on 1 November 2012. Its implementation in Scotland is facilitated by The Parental Responsibility and Measures for the Protection of Children (International Obligations) (Scotland) Regulations 2010.[92]

    The Convention, which was intended to replace the 1961 Hague Convention concerning the powers of authorities and the law applicable in respect of the protection of infants (an instrument to which the UK was not a Contracting State), and to reinforce the operation of the 1980 Hague Convention on the Civil Aspects of International Child Abduction (q.v.), is quadruple in nature and establishes uniform rules on jurisdiction, applicable law, the recognition and enforcement of judgments, and co-operation in respect of parental responsibility and measures for the protection of children.

---

[87] For commentary, see Hague Conference on Private International Law, *Practical Handbook on the Operation of the 1996 Child Protection Convention* (2014) ("Hague Practical Handbook").

[88] Essentially due to political conflict over the position of Gibraltar.

[89] Justice and Home Affairs Council, *EU Council Factsheet: Decisions in Civil Law Matters*, 6 June 2008.

[90] European Communities (Definition of Treaties) (1996 Hague Convention on Protection of Children etc.) Order 2010 (SI 2010/232).

[91] House of Lords Grand Committee, per Lord Bach (15 December 2009: cols GC124–GC128).

[92] The Parental Responsibility and Measures for the Protection of Children (International Obligations) (Scotland) Regulations 2010 (SSI 2010/213). Although the effect of s.2(1) of the European Communities Act 1972 is that the Convention applies directly in Member States, without further legislation, the 2010 Regulations amend existing provision and assist the working of the Convention in Scotland. See also Act of Sederunt (Rules of the Court of Session Amendment No. 3) (Miscellaneous) 2011 (SSI 2011/190) r.4; and Act of Sederunt (Jurisdiction in Respect of Parental Responsibility and Measures for the Protection of Children Rules) 2011 (SSI 2011/192). For England and Wales, see Parental Responsibility and Measures for the Protection of Children (International Obligations) (England and Wales and Northern Ireland) Regulations 2010 (SI 2010/1898).

Scope

One of the merits of the 1996 Convention is its comprehensive scope in terms of   **14–30**
subject matter, applying equally to the protection of a child's person and property.
By art.2, it applies to all children, from birth to 18 years, and deals with both
public law and private law matters, where these are not expressly excluded from
the Convention as having been covered already by other Hague Conventions.
Significantly, unlike the 1980 Hague Abduction Convention, a child does not
need to be habitually resident in a Contracting State to fall within the scope of the
1996 Convention.[93]

Article 3 details, in non-comprehensive fashion, those matters which fall
within the Convention's scope, including, importantly, (a) the attribution,
exercise, termination or restriction of parental responsibility, as well as its
delegation; (b) rights of custody, including rights relating to the care of the person
of the child and, in particular, the right to determine the child's place of residence,
as well as rights of access including the right to take a child for a limited period
of time to a place other than the child's habitual residence; (c) guardianship; and
(g) the administration, conservation or disposal of the child's property. Article 4,
in contrast, lists matters which are expressly excluded from the scope of the
instrument, including, (a) the establishment or contesting of a parent-child
relationship; and (e) maintenance obligations.

Jurisdiction

The provisions on jurisdiction and recognition and enforcement of judgments   **14–31**
concerning parental responsibility are similar in design and content to those in
Brussels II *bis*. The main ground of jurisdiction under the 1996 Convention is the
Contracting State of the habitual residence of the child (art.5[94]), and there are
various subsidiary bases of jurisdiction (arts 7–14).

The judicial or administrative authorities of the Contracting State of the
habitual residence of the child have jurisdiction to take measures directed to the
protection of the child's person or property. Notably, by art.5(2), subject to art.7
(concerning the continuing jurisdiction of the courts of the child's habitual
residence in cases of wrongful removal/retention), in the event of a change of the
child's habitual residence from one Contracting State to another, the authorities of
the State of the new habitual residence have jurisdiction. Unlike the position
secured by art.9 of Brussels II *bis*, the principle of *perpetuatio fori* generally does
not apply.[95]

Article 6(1) lays down a special rule of jurisdiction, based on presence in a
Contracting State, for refugee children and children who, due to disturbances
occurring in their country, are internationally displaced, as well as for children
(art.6(2)) whose habitual residence cannot be established. Similarly, art.11

---

[93] Hague Practical Handbook para.3.11.

[94] cf. Brussels II *bis* art.8.

[95] See, however, art.7, which, like art.10 of Brussels II *bis*, establishes a rule of jurisdiction for cases
of wrongful removal or retention of the child. In such cases, the authorities of the Contracting State in
which the child was habitually resident immediately before the removal or retention keep their
jurisdiction until the child has acquired a habitual residence in another State.

provides, in all cases of urgency, for jurisdiction based upon presence in a Contracting State of the child or property belonging to the child.

Articles 8 and 9 operate by way of a (limited) transfer jurisdiction[96] where, by way of exception, the authority of a Contracting State having jurisdiction under arts 5 or 6, considers that the authority of another Contracting State would be better placed in the particular case to assess the best interests of the child. By art.8(4), the authority addressed[97] may assume jurisdiction, in place of the authority having jurisdiction under arts 5 or 6, if it considers that this is in the child's best interests.

Article 10 permits prorogation of jurisdiction[98] in favour of the authorities of a Contracting State exercising jurisdiction to decide upon an application for divorce or legal separation of the parents of a child habitually resident in another Contracting State, or for annulment of their marriage.

Article 12, like art.20 of Brussels II *bis*, permits, subject to art.7, the authorities of a Contracting State in whose territory the child or property belonging to the child is present to exercise jurisdiction to take provisional measures to protect the person or property of the child, so long as the effect of those measures is territorially limited to the State in question, and insofar as they are not incompatible with measures already taken by authorities having jurisdiction under arts 5–10.

Article 13(1) establishes a rule of *lis pendens* whereby the authorities of a Contracting State which have jurisdiction under arts 5–10 must abstain from exercising jurisdiction if, at the time of the commencement of the proceedings, corresponding measures have been requested from the authorities of another Contracting State having jurisdiction thereunder and are still under consideration.

Applicable law

14–32 Unlike Brussels II *bis*, the 1996 Hague Convention lays down rules concerning applicable law (arts 15–22). On the face of art.15, the applicable law rules therein shall apply only where the forum is exercising jurisdiction under the Convention, and not, e.g. when it is exercising jurisdiction under Brussels II *bis*. By secondary legislation in the UK, however, it has been made clear that the reference to Ch.II in art.15(1) of the Convention is to be read as including a reference to Ch.II of Brussels II *bis* (arts 8–20).[99] Accordingly, the applicable law provisions of the 1996 Convention will apply also where a UK forum is exercising jurisdiction in parental responsibility matters under Brussels II *bis*.

The general rule under art.15(1) is that the forum, in exercising jurisdiction under Ch.II (arts 5–14) of the Convention, shall apply its own law. By way of

---

[96] cf. Brussels II *bis* art.15.

[97] Hague Convention art.8(2): the Contracting States whose authorities may be addressed are (a) a State of which the child is a national; (b) a State in which property of the child is located; (c) a State whose authorities are seised of an application for divorce or legal separation of the child's parents, or for annulment of their marriage; or (d) a State with which the child has a substantial connection.

[98] cf. Brussels II *bis* art.12.

[99] The Parental Responsibility and Measures for the Protection of Children (International Obligations) (Scotland) Regulations 2010 (SSI 2010/213) reg.6; and, for England and Wales, The Parental Responsibility and Measures for the Protection of Children (International Obligations) (England and Wales and Northern Ireland) Regulations 2010 (SI 2010/1898) reg.7.

exception to art.15(1), art.15(2) provides that, insofar as the protection of the person or the property of the child requires, the court may apply or take into consideration the law of another State with which the situation has a substantial connection, even if the law designated is the law of a non-Contracting State.[100]

Notably, art.16 (which operates generally in a Contracting State and is not, seemingly, restricted to cases where the forum is exercising jurisdiction per the Convention), provides that the attribution or extinction of parental responsibility by operation of law, without the intervention of a judicial or administrative authority, is governed by the law of the State of the habitual residence of the child (art.16(1)). Likewise, the attribution or extinction of parental responsibility by an agreement or a unilateral act, without intervention of a judicial or administrative authority, is governed by the law of the State of the child's habitual residence at the time when the agreement or unilateral act takes effect (art.16(2)).

Parental responsibility which exists under the law of the State of the child's habitual residence subsists after a change of that habitual residence to another State (art.16(3)). If the child's habitual residence changes, the attribution of parental responsibility by operation of law to a person who does not already have such responsibility is governed by the law of the State of the new habitual residence (art.16(4)).

Article 21(1) makes clear that the forum shall apply its own internal law, i.e. *renvoi* is not available. However, by art.21(2), if the law applicable according to art.16 is that of a non-Contracting State, and if the choice of law rules of that State designate the law of another non-Contracting State which would apply its own law, the law of the latter State applies. If that other non-Contracting State would not apply its own law, the applicable law shall be that designated by art 16.

The application of the law designated by the Convention can be refused only if application would be manifestly contrary to public policy (presumably of the forum), taking into account the best interests of the child.[101]

Recognition and enforcement

Article 23 provides a rule of recognition whereby measures taken by the authorities of a Contracting State shall be recognised by operation of law in all other Contracting States. Recognition may be refused on six grounds similar to those set out in art.23 of Brussels II *bis*. By art.28 measures taken in one Contracting State and declared enforceable,[102] or registered for the purpose of enforcement, in another Contracting State shall be enforced in the latter State as if they had been taken by the authorities of that State. Enforcement takes place in accordance with the law of the requested State to the extent provided by such law, taking into consideration the best interests of the child.

14–33

Cooperation

Chapter V of the Convention emphasises cooperation, both between central authorities processing applications and between competent authorities, such as

14–34

---

[100] Hague Convention art.20.
[101] Hague Convention art.22.
[102] Hague Convention art.26.

courts, in Contracting States taking measures for the protection of children. This should provide better continuity of protection for children across international borders. For example, the Convention increases the effectiveness of any temporary measures ordered by a judge under the 1980 Convention returning a child to the country from which the child was wrongfully taken or in which s/he was retained, by making those orders enforceable until the authorities in the country to which the child is returned are able to put in place necessary measures of protection.

Disconnection

14–35   It is hoped that the 1996 Convention will make a valuable contribution to the protection of children in parental responsibility and child protection cases that transcend the boundaries of Europe, and that it will complement Community rules. The relationship between the Convention and Brussels II *bis*, however, is not uncomplicated, for both instruments lay down rules concerning jurisdiction and the recognition and enforcement of judgments in parental responsibility matters, and co-operation in relation thereto.

Article 52(1) of the Convention provides that it does not affect any international instrument to which Contracting States are Parties and which contains provisions on matters governed by the Convention, unless a contrary declaration is made by the States Parties to such instrument.

Article 61 of Brussels II *bis* ranks the Regulation above the relevant provisions of the 1996 Convention where the child in question is habitually resident in an EU Member State. The Regulation shall apply: (a) where the child concerned has his habitual residence on the territory of a Member State; (b) as concerns the recognition and enforcement of a judgment given in a court of a Member State on the territory of another Member State, even if the child concerned has his habitual residence on the territory of a third State which is a contracting Party to the said Convention. If, however, the child in question is not habitually resident in an EU Member State, but is habitually resident in a (non-EU) state which is a Contracting State to the 1996 Hague Convention, the Convention will apply.

Where neither Brussels II *bis*, nor the 1996 Hague Convention, applies, the residual rules of Scots law are available.[103]

Intra-UK cases

Family Law Act 1986

14–36   The Family Law Act 1986, when brought into force, made provision for the allocation of jurisdiction within the UK in all matters relating to children, including rules for deferring to a court more appropriate, and for mutual recognition and enforcement, after registration, of Scots parental responsibility orders in England and vice versa. In light of the coming into force of Brussels II *bis*, and amending secondary legislation,[104] and of the 1996 Hague Convention,

---

[103] Family Law Act 1986 s.17A.

[104] The European Communities (Matrimonial and Parental Responsibility Jurisdiction and Judgments) (Scotland) Regulations 2005 (SSI 2005/42).

and relevant secondary legislation,[105] Pt I ("Child Custody") of the Family Law Act 1986 now must be taken to apply only where jurisdiction cannot be founded under Brussels II *bis*[106] or the 1996 Convention. By s.17A of the 1986 Act, the provisions of Ch.III ("Jurisdiction of Courts in Scotland") thereof are subject to Ss.2 (parental responsibilities) and 3 (common provisions) of Ch.II (jurisdiction) of Brussels II *bis*, and to the 1996 Hague Convention. The provisions in Ch.III of the 1986 Act, therefore, are relegated to the status of residual national rules.

Brussels II *bis* is to be taken to effect allocation of jurisdiction between the territorial units of a Member State, as well as between Member States.[107] Although the position is not entirely clear, to assume the operation of the jurisdiction rules in Brussels II *bis* in intra-UK cases is the less complex interpretative option.[108] The European Communities (Matrimonial and Parental Responsibility Jurisdiction and Judgments) (Scotland) Regulations 2005 make no mention, however, of ss.27–29 of the 1986 Act, covering registration and enforcement of parental responsibility orders intra-UK, and so it is to be assumed that these provisions continue to operate intra-UK, in qualifying cases (*q.v.*), irrespective of the recognition and enforcement provisions in Brussels II *bis* (Ch.III).[109]

Residual national rules

For the reduced number of cases to which the 1986 Act now applies, the most important provisions of the Act are as follows:

14–37

Chapter III—Jurisdiction of court in Scotland

Section 9: Habitual residence of the child[110]

An application for a parental responsibilities order otherwise than in matrimonial proceedings[111] may be entertained by (a) the Court of Session if, on the date of the application, the child[112] concerned is habitually resident in Scotland; or (b) the sheriff, if, on that date, the child concerned is habitually resident in the sheriffdom.

14–38

---

[105] The Parental Responsibility and Measures for the Protection of Children (International Obligations) (Scotland) Regulations 2010 (SSI 2010/213).

[106] Hague Convention art.14 (residual jurisdiction).

[107] Art.66; see also N. Lowe [2002] Fam. Law 39; K. Beevers and D. McClean, "Intra-UK Jurisdiction in Parental Responsibility Cases" [2005] I.F.L.129; *Cheshire, North and Fawcett: Private International Law*, 14th edn (2008), p.1085; and A. Inglis, 2009 J.R. 285, 287, 288; and *S v D*, 2007 S.L.T. (Sh. Ct.) 37. *Contra* Maher, 2007 S.L.T. (News) 117; and *B v B*, 2009 S.L.T. (Sh. Ct.) 24.

[108] cf. *Re W-B (A Child)* [2012] EWCA Civ 592; [2013] 1 F.L.R. 394.

[109] See, however, changes to Family Law Act 1986 made per The Parental Responsibility and Measures for the Protection of Children (International Obligations) (Scotland) Regulations 2010 (SSI 2010/213) Sch.1 paras 2–5.

[110] cf. jurisdiction per Brussels II *bis* art.8, which will prevail over s.9.

[111] *Dorward v Dorward*, 1994 S.C.L.R. 928. Section 13 provides for jurisdiction ancillary to matrimonial proceedings.

[112] A person who has not attained the age of 16: s.18(1).

Section 10: Presence of the child[113]

14–39   An application for a parental responsibilities order may be entertained by (a) the Court of Session if, on that date, the child is: (i) present in Scotland; and (ii) not habitually resident in any part of the UK; or (b) the sheriff if, on that date, the child is: (i) present in Scotland; (ii) not habitually resident in any part of the UK; and (iii) either the pursuer or the defender in the application is habitually resident in the sheriffdom.

Section 11: Relevant matrimonial proceedings

14–40   The jurisdiction of a court to entertain an application under ss.9, 10, or 15(2) is excluded if, on the date of the application, matrimonial proceedings in respect of the marriage of the parents of the child are continuing in a court in any part of the UK (unless that other court has made an order under the 1986 Act enabling the custody proceedings to be taken in Scotland). Arguably, of the residual bases of jurisdiction afforded by the 1986 Act, the s.11 ground is the only one which, since not directly coinciding with a Brussels II *bis* or Hague Convention ground,[114] exceptionally may confer jurisdiction on the Scottish courts.

Section 12: Emergency jurisdiction[115]

14–41   Notwithstanding that any other court, within or outside Scotland, has jurisdiction to entertain an application for a parental responsibilities order, the Court of Session or the sheriff shall have jurisdiction if: (a) the child concerned is present in Scotland or in the sheriffdom on the date of the application; and (b) the Court of Session or sheriff considers that, for the protection of the child, it is necessary to make such an order immediately.[116]

Section 14: Power to refuse application or sist proceedings

14–42   Where application is made to a Scots court for a Pt I order, and it appears to the court that (a) proceedings with respect to the same matter are continuing outside Scotland or in another court in Scotland; or (b) it would be more appropriate for those matters to be determined in those other proceedings; or (c) it should exercise its powers under Article 15 of Brussels II *bis* to transfer the proceedings to a court better placed to hear the case; or (d) it should exercise its powers under art.8 of the Hague Convention to request the authorities in another Contracting State to assume jurisdiction, the court may sist the proceedings on that application[117] or, as the case may be, exercise its powers under art.15 or art.8, as appropriate.

---

[113]   cf. Brussels II *bis* art.13, which will prevail over s.10.

[114]   cf. Brussels II *bis* art.12, which, however, is restrictively drafted.

[115]   cf. Brussels II *bis* art.13, which will prevail over s.10.

[116]   *Carroll v Carroll* [2005] Fam. L.R. 99.

[117]   *Messenger v Messenger*, 1992 S.L.T. (Sh. Ct.) 29; *Al-Najjar, Petitioner*, 1993 G.W.D. 27-1661; *Hill v Hill*, 1991 S.L.T. 189; and *B v B*, 1998 S.L.T. 1245.

Section 17: Orders for delivery of child

This empowers the Court of Session or sheriff court to make an order for delivery **14–43** of a child from one parent to the other when the order is not sought to implement a parental responsibility order, if, but only if, the Court of Session or sheriff would have had jurisdiction to make a parental responsibilities order.

Chapter V—Recognition and enforcement

Section 25(1): a parental responsibilities order made by a court in any part of the **14–44** UK in force in respect of a child who has not attained 16 years, shall be recognised (except for its enforcement provisions) in any other part of the UK as if made by the appropriate court in that part. Section 25(3): a court in a part of the UK in which a parental responsibility order is recognised shall not enforce the order unless it has been registered in that part of the UK as if made by the appropriate court in that part.

Section 26: an order relating to parental responsibilities or parental rights in relation to a child which is made outside the UK shall be recognised in Scotland if the order was made in the country where the child was habitually resident.[118]

Section 27(1) and (2): any person on whom rights are conferred by a parental responsibility order may apply to the court which made it for the order to be registered in another part of the UK.[119]

Section 29(1): where a parental responsibility order has been registered under s.27, the registering court shall have the same powers to enforce the order as if it had itself made the order and had jurisdiction to make it; and proceedings for enforcement may be taken accordingly.

Section 32: "the appropriate court" in relation to England and Wales or Northern Ireland means the High Court, and in relation to Scotland, means the Court of Session.

Chapter VI—Miscellaneous and supplemental

Various miscellaneous powers are granted to safeguard the child and ensure the **14–45** effective operation of the Act:

Section 33: power to order disclosure of a child's whereabouts (from any person whom the court has reason to believe may have relevant information).[120]

Section 34: power to order recovery of a child, including authority to enter and search any premises where the person acting in pursuance of the order has reason

---

[118] Note statutory change to common law rule of recognition of decree of domicile of father. The residual statutory rule now is subject to arts 21–27, 41.1 and 42.1 of Brussels II *bis* and arts 23–28 of the 1996 Hague Convention.

[119] It became clear in *Woodcock v Woodcock*, 1990 S.L.T. 848 that, in the view of the Scots court, s.29 does not deprive the court of its discretion and duty to ensure that natural justice was observed. See D. Edwards, "A Domestic Muddle: Custody Orders in the United Kingdom" (1992) 41 I.C.L.Q. 444. See also *Rellis v Hart*, 1993 S.L.T. 738; *Messenger*, 1992 S.L.T. (Sh. Ct.) 29; and *Re B (Minors) (Residence Order)* [1992] 3 All E.R. 867.

[120] *Re G (Children) (Residence: Same Sex Partner)* [2006] UKHL 43.

to believe the child may be found, and to use such force as may be necessary to give effect to the purpose of the order.[121]

Section 35: powers to restrict removal of a child from the jurisdiction of the court.[122]

Section 37: where there is in force an order prohibiting or otherwise restricting the removal of a child from the UK or from any specified part of it, the court by which the order was made may require any person to surrender any UK passport which has been issued to, or contains particulars of, the child.

Section 41 (habitual residence after removal without consent, etc.) provides as follows:

(1)   Where a child who:
    (a)   has not attained the age of 16; and
    (b)   is habitually resident in a part of the UK, becomes habitually resident outside that part of the UK in consequence of circumstances of the kind specified in s.41(2) below, he shall be treated for the purposes of Pt II of the Act as continuing to be habitually resident in the UK for the period of one year beginning on the date on which those circumstances arise.
(2)   The circumstances referred to in (1) above exist where the child is removed from or retained outside, or himself leaves or remains outside, the part of the UK in which he was habitually resident before his change of residence:
    (a)   without the agreement of the person or all the persons having, under the law of that part of the UK, the right to determine where he is to reside; or
    (b)   in contravention of an order made by a court in any part of the UK.
(3)   A child shall cease to be treated by virtue of s.41(1) as habitually resident in a part of the UK if, during the period there mentioned:
    (a)   he attains the age of 16; or
    (b)   he becomes habitually resident outside that part of the UK with the agreement of the person(s) mentioned in s.41(2)(a) above and not in contravention of an order made by a court in any part of the UK.

This provision is an early example of "continuing jurisdiction", inserted to offset the advantage of the passage of time which otherwise generally operates in favour of a parent who removes a child.[123] It has been held in the English Court of Appeal in *Re S (A Child) (Abduction: Residence Order)*[124] that s.41 regulates only jurisdictional or enforcement conflicts between the constituent jurisdictions

---

[121] 1986 Act s.34 was enacted without prejudice to any existing power of the court. The Scots court has common law powers: *Edgar v Fisher's Trustees* (1893) 21 R. 59; *Guthrie v Guthrie*, 1954 S.L.T. (Sh. Ct.) 58; *Fowler v Fowler (No.2)*, 1981 S.L.T. (Notes) 78; and *Abusaif v Abusaif*, 1984 S.L.T. 90.

[122] Para.14–80, above, re international parental relocation.

[123] cf. Brussels II *bis* art.10, and art.7 of the 1996 Hague Convention. See A. Inglis, "A Muckle Midden Cleared: Brussels II *bis* and section 41 Family Law Act 1986", 2009 J.R. 285, written with reference to *RAB v MIB*, 2009 S.C. 58.

[124] *Re S (A Child) (Abduction: Residence Order)* [2002] EWCA Civ 1941; [2003] 1 F.L.R. 1008, per Thorpe L.J. at [31].

of the UK,[125] and that it has no application to "international" conflicts as between the UK and any jurisdiction that is not a constituent jurisdiction of the UK.

GUARDIANSHIP AND ADMINISTRATION OF A CHILD'S PROPERTY

Guardianship

At common law in Scotland, there were three classes of guardians, viz.: (1) tutors; (2) curators; and (3) curators *bonis* and/or *ad litem*. The Age of Legal Capacity (Scotland) Act 1991 removed the common law classification of children into pupils and minors, and replaced tutors and curators with "guardians" (defined as parent-substitutes). Curators *ad litem* and curators *bonis* still may be appointed by the court.[126] Many important changes in substance and terminology were made by the Children (Scotland) Act 1995: appointment and removal of guardians came to be regulated by s.7 (appointment), s.8 (revocation and other termination of appointment), and s.11(2)(h) (judicial appointment or removal of guardians). Under the 1995 Act, an application can be made to the Court of Session or sheriff court for an order in relation to parental responsibilities and rights, by any person who claims an interest (s.11(3)(a)(i)). Such an interest may be genetic or emotional or professional and might include, therefore, a step-parent, grandparent, medical/social services professional, or even the child himself or herself.[127]

    Under Brussels II *bis*, the definition of parental responsibility, and of the holder thereof, is apt to cover a person who in Scots law would be regarded as a guardian.[128] Likewise, under art.3(c) of the 1996 Hague Convention, the measures referred to in art.1 as protecting the person or property of a child, may deal with guardianship, curatorship and analogous institutions. Accordingly, the pre-existing jurisdictional rules of Scots law contained in the Family Law Act 1986 ss.9–12, and in the 1995 Act ss.9, 11, 13 and 14, now take the function, in relation to guardianship, as for other aspects of parental responsibility, of residual national rules.[129] Section 14 of the 1995 Act has not been expressly amended so as to render it subject to the 1996 Hague Convention, but that must be the necessary interpretation.

Jurisdiction to administer a child's property[130]

At common law, jurisdiction in the Scots courts to appoint a guardian by whatever name, was founded on the child's domicile or residence in Scotland, or on the ownership by the child of property in Scotland.[131] Section 16 of the Family

14–46

14–47

---

[125] e.g. *T v K* 2014 GWD 26-522.
[126] Age of Legal Capacity (Scotland) Act 1991 s.1(3)(f).
[127] e.g. *S v S* 2011 Fam. L.R. 86; 2010 G.W.D. 34-704.
[128] Brussels II *bis* art.1.2(b), (e).
[129] Brussels II *bis* art.14; and 1995 Act s.14(5).
[130] Brussels II *bis* recital (9) art.1.2(e).
[131] *Hay v Hay* (1861) 23 D. 1291; and *Reid v Reid* (1887) 24 S.L.R. 281.

Law Act 1986 conferred jurisdiction on the Scots court to entertain an application for guardianship, if the child in question was habitually resident in Scotland. With regard to orders concerning the administration of a child's property, the Children (Scotland) Act 1995 ss.9, 10, and 14 now apply, the last of which has conflict of laws implications. Section 14 provides that:

> "(1)   The Court of Session shall have jurisdiction to entertain an application for an order relating to the administration of a child's property if the child is habitually resident in, or the property is situated in, Scotland.
>
> (2)   A sheriff shall have jurisdiction to entertain such an application if the child is habitually resident in, or the property is situated in, the sheriffdom.
>
> (3)   Subject to subsection (4) below, any question arising under this Part of this Act—
>
> (a)   concerning—
>
> (i)   parental responsibilities or parental rights; or
>
> (ii)   the responsibilities or rights of a guardian,
>
> in relation to a child shall, in so far as it is not also a question such as is mentioned in paragraph (b) below, be determined by the law of the place of the child's habitual residence at the time when the question arises[132];
>
> (b)   concerning the immediate protection of a child shall be determined by the law of the place where the child is when the question arises; and
>
> (c)   as to whether a person is a validly appointed or constituted guardian of a child[133] shall be determined by the law of the place of the child's habitual residence on the date when the appointment was made (the date of death of the testator being taken to be the date of appointment where an appointment was made by will), or the event constituting the guardianship occurred."

For residual cases, s.14(3) directs the forum to apply the law of the child's habitual residence, subject to a discretionary power, in terms of the 1995 Act, to regard the welfare of the child as the paramount consideration. This residual national rule does not coincide with the applicable law rule set out in art.15(1) of the 1996 Hague Convention, whereby the forum is directed to apply its own (domestic) law.[134]

INTERNATIONAL CHILD ABDUCTION

14–48   International child abduction disputes now fall into three categories: cases falling under the 1980 Hague Convention on the Civil Aspects of International Child Abduction; cases regulated by Brussels II *bis*; and cases governed by common law rules. The rules to be applied will depend largely on the identity of the country(ies) to/in and from which the child has been wrongfully removed or retained. In the context of the international instruments, not only must the

---

[132] *S v D*, 2007 S.L.T. (Sh. Ct.) 37.
[133] This amounts to a rule of recognition.
[134] Para.14–32, above. That said, by Art.5 of the 1996 Hague Convention as by Art.8 of Brussels II *bis*, jurisdiction rests in the state of the habitual residence.

circumstances fall within those covered by the particular instrument, but the date of the circumstances must post-date the coming into effect of the instrument in the relevant country(ies).[135]

Child Abduction and Custody Act 1985

The 1980 Hague Convention on the Civil Aspects of International Child Abduction, and the 1980 Council of Europe ("Luxembourg") Convention on Recognition and Enforcement of Decisions concerning Custody of Children and on the Restoration of Custody of Children brought about great change in the civil law governing cross-border child abduction cases. The Hague Convention, which applies to persons under 16,[136] seeks to uphold custody rights (whether or not there has been a "custody order"), where there has been wrongful removal of a child habitually resident in a Contracting State from the legal system of his habitual residence, or wrongful retention of him outside the legal system, whereas the Council of Europe Convention is concerned with registration and enforcement of custody decisions.

    The United Kingdom (like a number of countries) became party to both Conventions, by virtue of the Child Abduction and Custody Act 1985. Part 1 Sch.1 to the Act implements the Hague Convention, and Pt 2 Sch.2 implements the Council of Europe Convention. If a case were capable of falling under both instruments, a litigant might choose which to invoke.[137] Of the two, the Hague Convention was always the more prominent. Importantly, both Conventions now are subject to the overriding authority of Brussels II *bis* in a qualifying EU case.[138] While the 1980 Hague Convention continues to have a very important role, and is discussed in detail in this chapter, the same cannot be said of the Luxembourg Convention. Brussels II *bis*, in its application to parental responsibility matters, principally is concerned with recognition and enforcement of parental responsibility orders emanating from EU Member States. Since usage of the European Convention now is so rare, its detail is not recounted in this chapter, and reference should be made to the second edition of this book.

Substance of the 1980 Hague Abduction Convention

By s.4 of the Child Abduction and Custody Act 1985, the courts having jurisdiction to entertain applications under the 1980 Hague Convention shall be, in Scotland, the Court of Session, and in England and Wales, or in Northern Ireland, the High Court.

    The following provisions of the Convention are of prime importance:

14–49

14–50

---

[135] *Kilgour v Kilgour*, 1987 S.L.T. 568.
[136] By art.4, the Convention shall apply to any child who was habitually resident in a Contracting State immediately before any breach of custody or access rights. The Convention shall cease to apply when the child attains the age of 16 years.
[137] *Re S (A Minor) (Custody: Habitual Residence)* [1997] 4 All E.R. 251.
[138] Brussels II *bis* art.60. See *Proceedings Brought by Rinau* (C-195/08 PPU) [2008] I.L.Pr. 51; and *Re G (Children) (Foreign Contact Order: Enforcement)* [2004] 1 W.L.R.521.

Article 3

14–51 The removal or the retention of a child is to be considered wrongful where:

(a) it is in breach of rights of custody[139] attributed to a person, an institution[140] or any other body, either jointly or alone, under the law of the state in which the child was habitually resident immediately before the removal or retention; and

(b) at the time of removal or retention those rights were actually exercised,[141] either jointly or alone, or would have been so exercised but for the removal or retention.

Wrongful removal[142] and retention[143]

14–52 The removal or retention of a child is wrongful where it is in breach of custody rights attributed to any person(s) under the law of the state in which the child was habitually resident. In *Perrin v Perrin*,[144] it was held that the determination of wrongfulness means something less than a full legal determination of the custodial rights of the parents and whether they have been breached.[145]

Wrongful retention is quite distinct from wrongful removal; the concepts are mutually exclusive, and a child can be wrongfully retained only if he has first been lawfully removed.[146] In *Findlay v Findlay (No. 2)*,[147] the court made clear that removal and retention, respectively, are events which occur on a specific date, and refer to the removal or retention of a child from the state in which he is habitually resident. Importantly, retention is not to be regarded as a continuing state of affairs begun on a particular day and continuing from day to day thereafter. It is necessary to establish the date of retention in order to fix the *terminus a quo* for the running of the one-year period under art.12.[148]

Rights of custody

14–53 The rights of custody mentioned in sub-para.(a) above may arise by operation of the law of the habitual residence of the child, as proved to the court,[149] or by

---

[139] Hague Convention art.5.1.

[140] e.g. *Z, Petitioner*, 2010 S.L.T. 285. In the view of the Scots court, the claim by a Dutch public authority that it had rights of custody in terms of art.3 was not sufficiently made out.

[141] *Urness v Minto*, 1994 S.L.T. 988.

[142] *Taylor v Ford*, 1993 S.L.T. 654; *McCarthy v McCarthy*, 1994 S.L.T. 743; *Perrin v Perrin*, 1995 S.L.T. 81; *Seroka v Bellah*, 1995 S.L.T 204; and *Hunter v Murrow* [2005] EWCA Civ 976.

[143] *Findlay v Findlay (No.1)*, 1994 S.L.T. 709; *Findlay v Findlay (No.2)*, 1995 S.L.T. 492; *Moran v Moran*, 1997 S.L.T. 541; *Watson v Jamieson*, 1998 S.L.T. 180; *M, Petitioner*, 2000 G.W.D. 32-1242; and *Re H (Minors) (Abduction: Custody Rights)* [1991] 3 All E.R. 230.

[144] *Perrin v Perrin*, 1995 S.L.T. 81.

[145] Lord Murray was entitled to conclude that the removal was wrongful; a letter from the French Ministry of Justice stated it was wrongful as in breach of art.372 of the French Civil Code, which awarded both parents joint custody.

[146] *McCarthy*, 1994 S.L.T. 743; *Findlay (No.1)*, 1994 S.L.T. 709.

[147] *Findlay v Findlay (No. 2)*, 1995 S.L.T. 492.

[148] *Re H (Minors) (Abduction: Custody Rights)* [1991] 3 All E.R. 230.

[149] *Re D (A Child) (Abduction: Rights of Custody)* [2007] 1 A.C. 619.

reason of a judicial or administrative decision, or by reason of an agreement having legal effect under the law of that state.[150]

The UK Supreme Court, in *Re K (A Child) (Abduction: Rights of Custody)*,[151] held that, for the purposes of the Convention, rights of custody bear an autonomous meaning independent of that given in the domestic law of any individual state, and are to be interpreted as applying consistently in all such states. Further, the Convention is not essentially concerned with the merits of custody rights, and will characterise a removal or retention as wrongful only where it interferes with the existence of a custody right giving legal content to a situation which had been changed by the removal or the retention. Moreover, the Court held that art.3, in contemplating that rights of custody might arise "in particular" by operation of law, by judicial or administrative decision, or by an agreement having legal effect under the law of the relevant state party, indicates that such rights might arise in other ways.[152] Specifically in the context of the case, "rights of custody" were judged capable of including the "inchoate" rights of persons (in the instant case, grandparents[153]), who carried out custodial duties where the person with legal rights of custody had abandoned the child or delegated primary care to others.

The House of Lords in *Re D (A Child) (Abduction: Custody Rights)*,[154] in holding that no obligation to return the child arose because the father did not enjoy rights of custody sufficient to satisfy art.3, further held that, in considering the content of the law of the legal system of the child's habitual residence, the foreign court of that system was much better placed than the English court to understand the true meaning and effect of its own law in Convention terms; only if its characterisation of the parent's rights were clearly out of line with the international understanding of the Convention's terms should the court in the requested state decline to follow it.[155] This was so even though the Hague Convention terms are autonomous, and intended to be applied consistently by all Contracting States. In particular, the fact that the non-custodial parent, in the view of the Romanian court, did not have a right of veto over measures taken by the custodial parent in relation to the child's person, the removal of the child from

---

[150] *Findlay (No.1)*, 1994 S.L.T. 709; *Findlay (No.2)*, 1995 S.L.T. 492; *Perrin*, 1995 S.L.T. 81; *Seroka v Bellah*, 1995 S.L.T. 204; *Bordera v Bordera*, 1995 S.L.T. 1176; *McKiver v McKiver*, 1995 S.L.T. 790; *Urness v Minto*, 1994 S.L.T. 988; *Zenel v Haddow*, 1993 S.L.T. 975; *Taylor v Ford*, 1993 S.L.T. 654; *McCarthy v McCarthy*, 1994 S.L.T. 743; *Dickson v Dickson*, 1990 S.C.L.R. 693; *Cameron (No.1)*, 1996 S.L.T. 306; *Moran*, 1997 S.L.T. 541; *Pirrie v Sawacki*, 1997 S.L.T. 1160; *Re S (A Minor) (Custody: Habitual Residence)* [1997] 4 All E.R. 251 HL; *Fourman v Fourman*, 1998 G.W.D. 32-1638; *Re H (A Minor) (Abduction: Rights of Custody)* [2000] 2 All E.R. 1 HL; *Re G (Abduction: Rights of Custody)* [2002] 2 F.L.R. 703; *Re P (A Child) (Abduction: Acquiescence)* [2004] 2 F.L.R. 1057; *F v B-F* [2008] EWHC 272 (Fam); *A v B (Abduction: Rights of Custody: Declaration of Wrongful Removal)* [2008] EWHC 2524 (Fam); *A v H* [2009] 4 All E.R. 641; *Re K (Children) (Rights of Custody: Spain)* [2009] EWCA Civ 986; and *Z, Petitioner*, 2010 S.L.T. 285.
[151] *Re K (A Child) (Abduction: Rights of Custody)* [2014] UKSC 29; [2014] A.C. 1401.
[152] cf. *A v B (Abduction: Rights of Custody: Declaration of Wrongful Removal)* [2008] EWHC 2524 (Fam) (the mere making of an ex parte order constituted the conferral of rights of custody despite the fact that it had not been served on the mother); and *A v H* [2009] 4 All E.R. 641.
[153] cf. *Re O (A minor) (Child Abduction: Custody Rights)*, The Times, 24 June 1997, per Cazalet J.; and *Re D (A Minor) (Contact: Interim Order)* [1995] 1 F.L.R. 495 CA.
[154] *Re D (A Child) (Abduction: Custody Rights)* [2007] 1 A.C. 619.
[155] *Re D (A Child) (Abduction: Custody Rights)* [2007] 1 A.C. 619, per Lord Hope of Craighead at 638.

Romania to England could not be viewed as wrongful by Romanian law (an interpretation of Romanian law which the House of Lords was prepared to accept).

Renvoi

14–54   A question arises as to the meaning of "law" in the context of art.3. It is a rule of Hague Convention drafting that a reference to "law" includes rules of private international law. Only if it is explicitly stated shall a reference to "law" mean a legal system's internal or domestic law rules. The Peréz-Vera Report on the 1980 Hague Abduction Convention emphasised that the applicable law includes rules of private international law, so as to expand the potential reach of the Convention. This opens the door to *renvoi* reasoning in child abduction cases, as was seen in *Re JB (Child Abduction: Rights of Custody: Spain)*[156] in which the English court, in referring to "Spanish law" as the law of the habitual residence of the child in the matter of the existence or not of custody rights, accepted a referral back to English law qua law of the nationality, with the effect that the unmarried bereft father, had no parental rights such as to justify a petition for return of the child under the 1980 Hague Convention on the grounds of wrongful removal. So too in *Re K (Children) (Rights of Custody: Spain)*,[157] the English judge at first instance, following the same approach, found himself required to take a view on the content of Spanish law as between the conflicting expert evidence produced by the contending parents. The investigation of Spanish law in this case went a stage further than that seen in *Re JB*. While it was accepted that Spanish law would refer the matter to the law of England qua nationality, it was contended successfully by the father that the result of application of English law, in depriving an unmarried father of parental responsibility and in attributing custody to the mother without taking into account the children's welfare interests, would be contrary to the public policy of Spain. This statement of Spanish law was accepted, and the English Court of Appeal made no criticism of the judge's treatment of proof of foreign law. On the facts, removal of the child by the mother was, by circuitous reasoning, in breach of the father's rights of custody under art.5.

Habitual residence of the child

14–55   This connecting factor has been discussed in detail in Ch.6. In recent years, one of the most prominent manifestations of the use of the factor has been in international child abduction cases under the Hague Convention.[158] The factor is

---

[156] *Re JB (Child Abduction: Rights of Custody: Spain)* [2004] 1 F.L.R. 796; discussed by K. Beevers and J. Perez Milla, "'Convention Rights of Custody'—Who Decides? An Anglo-Spanish Perspective" (2007) 3 J. Priv. Int. L.201.

[157] *Re K (Children) (Rights of Custody: Spain)* [2009] EWCA Civ 986.

[158] e.g. *Robertson v Robertson*, 1988 S.L.T. 468; *Dickson v Dickson*, 1990 S.C.L.R. 692; *Cameron (No.1)*, 1996 S.L.T. 306; *Cameron v Cameron (No.2)*, 1997 S.L.T. 206; *Watson v Jamieson*, 1998 S.L.T. 180; *D v D*, 2001 S.L.T. 1104; *Al-H v F* [2001] EWCA Civ 186; *W v H (Child Abduction: Surrogacy)* [2002] 1 F.L.R. 1008; *W, Petitioner*, 2003 G.W.D. 28-772; *M, Petitioner*, 2005 S.L.T. 2; *Re F (Abduction: Unborn Child)* [2006] EWHC 2199 (Fam); *Re ML and AL (Children) (Contact Order: Brussels II Regulation) (No.1)* [2006] EWHC 2385 (Fam); *A v N*, 2007 G.W.D. 01-02; *B v D*

in a state of constant refinement in the light of circumstances presenting. In *Re P-J (Children)*[159] certain principles were put forward by the Court of Appeal as "established", viz.:

(a) the expression "habitually resident" is not to be treated as a term of art with some special meaning, but is to be understood according to the ordinary and natural meaning of the two words which it contains;

(b) "habitual residence" and "ordinary residence" are interchangeable concepts and there is no difference in the core meaning to be given to the two phrases;

(c) there is a distinction to be made between being settled in a new place or country, and being resident there for a settled purpose which might be fulfilled by meeting a purpose of short duration or one conditional upon future events; and

(d) whether or not a person is or is not habitually resident in a specified country is a question of fact to be decided by reference to all the circumstances of the particular case.

While it may be recognised that these principles, under exception perhaps of (c), have become generally accepted, or truisms, the exigencies of cases demand that they be mapped on to complex domestic living "patterns", those patterns possibly inadequately vouched by evidence. Moreover, habitual residence decisions, like domicile cases, are particular to their facts, even assuming that these facts can be established. Thus the decision by the Court of Appeal in *Re S*,[160] that habitual residence in England had been established after residence in the jurisdiction by the child's family for only seven or eight weeks, combined with some evidence of intention at the outset to remain, was said to be justified on its facts (though finely balanced), but must be confined to the particular circumstances of the case, and not elevated to a statement of general principle. Despite the assertion that the factor is a common sense one, it should never be thought that the judicial resolution of an habitual residence point will be predictable.

A striking example of life's circumstances presenting a challenge to one's understanding of habitual residence as a legal concept is provided by *A v A (Children) (Habitual Residence)*,[161] in which a mother of English habitual residence and Pakistani background was forced to "reconcile" with her husband in Pakistan, as a result of which she bore him a fifth child there. The question for the UK Supreme Court was the attribution to this child of an habitual residence, and in particular whether it was legitimate to attribute to him an habitual residence in England and Wales, even though he had never set foot there (albeit the mother, at the date of the hearing, had returned to England, and it could be said that the family unit was habitually resident there[162]). The Court was inclined

---

[2008] EWHC 1246 (Fam); *Re P-J (Children) (Abduction: Habitual Residence: Consent)* [2009] EWCA Civ 588; *Re S (A Child) (Habitual Residence)* [2009] EWCA Civ 1021; and *Proceedings Brought by A* (C-523/07) [2009] I.L.Pr. 39.

[159] *Re P-J (Children) (Abduction: Habitual Residence: Consent)* [2009] EWCA Civ 588.

[160] *Re S (A Child) (Habitual Residence)* [2009] EWCA Civ 1021. See also *Re P-J (Children) (Abduction: Habitual Residence: Consent)* [2009] EWCA Civ 588.

[161] *A v A (Children) (Habitual Residence)* [2013] UKSC 60; [2014] A.C. 1.

[162] *A v A (Children) (Habitual Residence)* [2013] UKSC 60; [2014] A.C. 1, per Lord Hughes at [90].

to ascribe English habitual residence to a child who had no personal physical connection with the English legal system, but the need so to find was obviated by reason of the inherent jurisdiction which the Supreme Court was able to exercise as *parens patriae* in the case of a British national, justifying an order for return of the child to England.

The test or preferred definition employed by UK courts in cases falling to be decided under the 1980 Hague Convention is that formulated by the ECJ in *Proceedings Brought by A*,[163] in relation to art.8(1) of Brussels II *bis*, and meaning *"the place which reflects some degree of integration by the child in a social and family environment"*.[164]

An adroit judicial gloss upon this has been put by Lord Wilson and Baroness Hale in *Re LC (Children) (International Abduction: Child's Objections to Return)*,[165] by introducing the notion, particularly in relation to an adolescent child,[166] that "... their state of mind is relevant to whether or not they have acquired a habitual residence in the place where they are living."[167] "[T]he inquiry into [the child's] integration in the new environment [must] encompass more than the surface features of her life there."[168] This embroidering of the vaunted "factual" connecting factor of habitual residence seems harsh in its effects in the instant case (in which the mother and four children had lived in a settled fashion in Spain, the instant proceedings being precipitated by the father's wrongful retention of the children in England after an agreed holiday there), and is significant in its repercussions for subsequent cases.

14–56   It was established, seemingly at least, early[169] in the *corpus* of case law interpretative of the Convention that it should not be possible for a parent to effect a change in the habitual residence of a child through unilateral wrongful actings, that is to say, although as a matter of fact, the child might be residing in the legal system to which he has been removed, in law his habitual residence remains the legal system from which he has been taken. This principle was reiterated in *B v D*,[170] in the form that no unilateral action by a parent can change a child's habitual residence except by agreement or acquiescence over time by the bereft parent, or by judicial determination. Further support was provided by Lord Glennie in *A v N*.[171] As detailed in Ch.6, however, there is an observable drift towards unilateralism, i.e. change in a child's habitual residence capable of being

---

[163] *Proceedings Brought by A* (C-523/07) [2009] I.L.Pr. 39.

[164] Emphasis added. *Proceedings Brought by A* (C-523/07) [2009] I.L.Pr. 39 at summary, [2], [3]; also [33], [35], [38], [44]. e.g. *Re LC (Children) (International Abduction: Child's Objections to Return)* [2014] UKSC 1; [2014] A.C. 1038; and *Re R (A Child) (Habitual Residence)* [2014] EWCA Civ 1032. Para.14–14, above.

[165] *Re LC (Children) (International Abduction: Child's Objections to Return)* [2014] UKSC 1; [2014] A.C. 1038 at [30]–[37] and [57]–[58].

[166] But also, per Baroness Hale, in relation to a younger child: *Re LC (Children) (International Abduction: Child's Objections to Return)* [2014] UKSC 1; [2014] A.C. 1038 at [57]–[58].

[167] *Re LC (Children) (International Abduction: Child's Objections to Return)* [2014] UKSC 1; [2014] A.C. 1038 at [58].

[168] *Re LC (Children) (International Abduction: Child's Objections to Return)* [2014] UKSC 1; [2014] A.C. 1038, per Lord Sumption at [37].

[169] *Re J (A Minor) (Abduction: Custody Rights)* [1990] 2 A.C. 562; in the House of Lords sub nom. *C v S* [1990] 2 All E.R. 961; and *Re P (GE) (An Infant)* [1965] Ch. 568.

[170] *B v D* [2008] EWHC 1246 (Fam). cf. *Re ML and AL (Children) (Contact Order: Brussels II Regulation) (No.1)* [2006] EWHC 2385 (Fam).

[171] *A v N*, 2007 G.W.D. 01-02.

effected by the unilateral actings of one parent. The way was paved by Baroness Hale in *DL v EL (Hague Abduction Convention: Effect of Reversal of Return Order on Appeal)*[172]:

> "Both Lord Hughes JSC and I also questioned whether it was necessary to maintain the rule, hitherto firmly established in English law, that (where both parents have equal status in relation to the child) one parent could not unilaterally change the habitual residence of a child....As the US Court of Appeals for the Ninth Circuit pointed out in *Mozes v Mozes* (2001) 239 F 3d 1067, 1081, such a bright line rule certainly furthers the policy of discouraging child abductions, but if not carefully qualified it is capable of leading to absurd results . . .".[173]

In 2014, the Extra Division in *R, Petitioner*[174] found that the Lord Ordinary had erred in identifying a shared parental intention to move permanently to Scotland as an essential element in any alteration in the children's habitual residence from France to Scotland. The case addresses the controversial situation in which one parent contends a removal from one country to another is temporary, and the other argues it is settled. The Scottish Bench was expressly influenced by recent UK Supreme Court jurisprudence, and particularly by Baroness Hale's affirmation that there is no rule that a child's habitual residence must reflect a shared parental intent.[175] Not surprisingly the decision of the Extra Division was upheld by the UK Supreme Court in *In re R (Children) (Reunite International Child Abduction Centre and others intervening)*.[176]

The application of these rules to unborn children arose in *Re F (Abduction: Unborn Child)*,[177] in which the parents of the child in question had lived together in Wales before the mother, while pregnant with the child, left Wales in order to live in Israel, it being alleged by the father that there was an agreement between them that the mother would return in due course to live in Wales. The child was born in Israel. Although the child had never lived in Wales, it was argued, in abduction proceedings brought by the father, that England and Wales was the child's habitual residence, because she had been wrongly retained in Israel from the date when the mother (in the father's view) reneged on the agreement to return to the UK. These facts present a further challenge to the meaning in law of habitual residence. Hedley J. held that habitual residence requires some degree of physical presence; there was no wrongful retention within art.3, for it was not possible in law to abduct a foetus.[178]

---

[172] *DL v EL (Hague Abduction Convention: Effect of Reversal of Return Order on Appeal)* [2013] UKSC 75; [2014] A.C. 1017 at [21]. Para.6–46, above.

[173] *DL v EL (Hague Abduction Convention: Effect of Reversal of Return Order on Appeal)* [2013] UKSC 75; [2014] A.C. 1017 at [22].

[174] *R, Petitioner* [2014] CSIH 95, 2014 SLT 1080.

[175] *R, Petitioner* [2014] CSIH 95, 2014 SLT 1080, per Lord Malcolm, at [12]. *Contra Dickson v Dickson*, 1990 S.C.L.R. 692.

[176] [2015] UKSC 35, [2015] 2 W.L.R. 1583. See, in the Inner House *sub nom. R, Petitioner* [2014] CSIH 95, 2014 SLT 1080, per Lord Malcolm, at [17]. "[I]f parents have agreed to only a time limited residence in another country with one parent, that does not prevent a change in their children's habitual residence once they are living and settled in their new home."

[177] *Re F (Abduction: Unborn Child)* [2006] EWHC 2199 (Fam).

[178] *W v H (Child Abduction: Surrogacy)* [2002] 1 F.L.R. 1008.

Article 12

14–57   Where a child has been wrongfully removed or retained in terms of art.3 and, at the date of the commencement of the proceedings before the judicial or administrative authority of the Contracting State where the child is, a period of less than one year has elapsed from the date of the wrongful removal or retention, the authority concerned shall order the return[179] of the child forthwith.[180]

The judicial or administrative authority, even where the proceedings have been commenced after the expiration of the period of one year referred to in the preceding paragraph, shall also order the return of the child, unless it is demonstrated that the child is now settled in its new environment.

Where the judicial or administrative authority in the requested state has reason to believe that the child has been taken to another state, it may stay the proceedings or dismiss the application for the return of the child.

Settlement of the child

14–58   With regard to settlement, each case must be considered on its own facts.[181] The court must look for physical, emotional and psychological stability and security of a non-transient nature likely to continue into the future. This will include consideration of home, school, friends, activities, and opportunities, and need not be wholly associated with the children's relationship with the abducting parent.[182] The Family Division in *Re E (Abduction: Intolerable Situation)*[183] held that a child had settled physically and emotionally in the UK, clear evidence being given of his integration into family and school life, despite the fact that he and his mother were overstayers in the UK, of insecure immigration status.

Article 12 was the subject of detailed examination by the House of Lords in *Re M (Children) (Abduction: Rights of Custody)*.[184] The circumstances afforded an opportunity for the House to scrutinise the operation of art.12, in particular, the question whether, and if so under what authority (Convention or otherwise), and in accordance with what principles, there is a discretion to return the children to their habitual residence, if it be established that they are settled in the new jurisdiction. The majority (Lord Rodger of Earlsferry dissenting) held that once a child has become settled for the purposes of art.12 the court retains a discretion to return him within the Convention procedures.[185] Thereafter, the Convention discretion is "at large" and the court is entitled to take into account the various

---

[179] That is to say, return to the jurisdiction of the child's habitual residence, not to the custody of the other parent; *Findlay (No.1)*, 1994 S.L.T. 709; and *Findlay (No.2)*,1995 S.L.T. 492.

[180] *Re S (Minors) (Child Abduction; Wrongful Retention)* [1994] 1 All E.R. 237, per Wall J. at 249.

[181] *Re F v M (Abduction: Acquiescence: Settlement)* [2008] EWHC 1525 (Fam); *C v C*, 2008 S.C. 571; *Perrin*, 1995 S.L.T. 81; *Soucie v Soucie*, 1995 S.L.T. 414; *O'Connor v O'Connor*, 1995 G.W.D. 3-113; and *Cannon v Cannon* [2004] EWCA Civ 1330 (concealment of child); and *Re C (A Child) (Abduction: Settlement)* [2006] EWHC 1229 (Fam).

[182] *Re H (Children)* unreported 27 February 2010.

[183] *Re E (Abduction: Intolerable Situation)* [2008] EWHC 2112 (Fam). cf. *B, Petitioner,* 2014 G.W.D. 2-43.

[184] *Re M (Children) (Abduction: Rights of Custody)* [2008] 1 A.C. 1288.

[185] *Re M (Children) (Abduction: Rights of Custody)* [2008] 1 A.C. 1288, per Baroness Hale of Richmond at [29]–[31].

aspects of Convention policy alongside the circumstances which gave the court a discretion in the first place, and the wider considerations of the child's rights and welfare.[186] Lady Hale indicated,[187] that:

". . . a view has crept in that 'exceptional' is not merely a description, to be applied to the small number of exceptions in which the court has power to refuse to order a return, but also an additional test to be applied, after a ground of opposition has been made out, to the exercise of the court's discretion".

Her Ladyship concluded that:

"I have no doubt at all that it is wrong to import any test of exceptionality into the exercise of discretion under the Hague Convention. The circumstances in which return may be refused are themselves exceptions to the general rule. That in itself is sufficient exceptionality. It is neither necessary nor desirable to import an additional gloss into the Convention."[188]

Therefore, the House of Lords, taking into account the firm views of the children (aged 13 and 10 years, respectively, at the date of appeal) that they had settled in England and wished to stay there, reversed the decision of the court below, which appeared to have been taken on the basis that a judge in the court addressed required to find something exceptional in a case before he could refuse to order return under the Convention.

Defences available under arts 12 and 13 typically coalesce, and frequently the cases display a "scattergun" approach. In law, as in life, one defence may strengthen inadequacies in another defence, or indeed there may be a symbiotic relationship between or among them, as for example in *W v W*,[189] where the objections to return to Ireland expressed by a very young child were bolstered by the fact of the family having settled into life in London for nine months. Equally, during that period, the court had to assess whether the bereft father had acquiesced in the child's wrongful removal. The English Court of Appeal concluded that though he had not acquiesced, nonetheless he had allowed time to pass in knowledge of the family's London address.

Article 13

Notwithstanding the provisions of the preceding article, the judicial or administrative authority of the requested state is not bound to order the return of the child if the person, institution or other body which opposed its return establishes that:

14–59

---

[186] *Re M (Children) (Abduction: Rights of Custody)* [2008] 1 A.C. 1288 at [43].
[187] *Re M (Children) (Abduction: Rights of Custody)* [2008] 1 A.C. 1288 at [37].
[188] *Re M (Children) (Abduction: Rights of Custody)* [2008] 1 A.C. 1288, per Baroness Hale of Richmond at [40].
[189] *W v W* [2010] EWHC 332 (Fam); and on appeal sub nom. *Re W (Children)* [2010] EWCA Civ 520.

(a)   the person, institution or other body having the care of the person of the child was not actually exercising the custody rights at the time of removal or retention, or had consented to or subsequently acquiesced in the removal or retention; or

(b)   there is a grave risk that his or her return would expose the child to physical or psychological harm or otherwise place the child in an intolerable situation.

The judicial or administrative authority may also refuse to order the return of the child if it finds that the child objects to being returned and has attained an age and degree of maturity at which it is appropriate to take account of its views.

In considering the circumstances referred to in this Article, the judicial and administrative authorities shall take into account the information relating to the social background of the child provided by the Central Authority or other competent authority of the child's habitual residence.

Article 12 is to be read subject to art.13; hence art.13 can be invoked irrespective of the length of time which has elapsed since the alleged wrongful removal or retention.

Consent and acquiescence

14–60   These concepts, referring to the state of mind of the bereft parent, are related. Consent[190] can be given only in advance of the wrongful removal or retention, whereas acquiescence inevitably must follow the wrongful event.

In the cases concerning the alleged consent of the non-abducting parent[191] prior to the wrongful event, much will depend on evidence and credibility of witnesses. The cases are fact-specific.[192] That which appears to be consent may be vitiated if it was based upon a delusion as to the good faith of the other parent, as where the bereft parent erroneously believed that a contact agreement would be honoured.[193]

Notable difficulties have arisen in relation to conditional consent, that is, where consent to removal is given in the event that a particular set of circumstances should transpire, such as a failed reconciliation. Consent of this type was accepted as effective consent by the majority in *Zenel v Haddow*,[194] the court holding that agreement to removal does not require to be connected in time to the actual removal, i.e. can be open-ended. A similar set of circumstances arose in *Re P-J (Children)*,[195] where the English Court of Appeal accepted that consent

---

[190] *Zenel v Haddow*, 1993 S.C. 612; *Robertson v Robertson*, 1998 S.L.T. 468; *Re C (Minors) (Abduction: Consent)* [1996] 1 F.L.R. 414; *C v C*, 2003 S.L.T. 793; *H v H*, 2006 G.W.D. 18-361.

[191] Consent can be given only by the party whose rights of custody are at risk of being breached: *C v H (Abduction: Consent)* [2009] EWHC 2660 (Fam).

[192] *Re L (Abduction: Future Consent)* [2007] EWHC 2181 (Fam).

[193] *M v T (Abduction)* [2008] EWHC 1383 (Fam).

[194] *Zenel v Haddow*, 1993 S.C. 612 (Lord Morton of Shuna dissenting).

[195] *Re P-J (Children) (Abduction: Habitual Residence: Consent)* [2009] EWCA Civ 588.

to the removal of a child, while it must be clear and unequivocal,[196] may be given in respect of some future, but unspecified time, or on the happening of some future event.

To be used as an art.13 defence, such advance consent requires still to be operative and in force at the time of the actual removal. Fulfilment of the condition must be reasonably capable of ascertainment, and not dependent on the subjective determination of one party. Since the situation is not completely analogous with the law of contract, but rather must be viewed against the background of the disintegration of family life, consent can be withdrawn at any time before the actual removal of the child. Once consent has been acted upon, however, change of mind by the consenter comes too late.[197] The burden of proving consent rests on the party who asserts its existence.

The House of Lords decision in *Re H*[198] established for UK jurisprudence that acquiescence[199] depends on the actual state of mind and subjective intention of the bereft parent, although this approach will be subordinated to any impression that parent had given by clear and unequivocal actings. Acquiescence cannot be inferred from oral or written[200] remarks made by someone who has newly suffered the wrongful removal or retention of a child.

The court addressed must consider carefully the fact of delay on the part of the bereft parent in instituting proceedings under the Hague Convention, and the reasons for this delay.[201] A parent cannot be said to have acquiesced in unlawful removal/retention unless s/he was aware of the facts and of the law.[202] In a number of cases, for a number of reasons, inaction or delay on the part of the bereft parent in issuing proceedings has been held not to amount to acquiescence.[203] Acquiescence obtained by fraud, or based on misunderstanding as to fact or intention, or non-disclosure by the abducting parent, will not suffice as an art.13 defence. What is required is clear subjective acceptance of the situation, evidenced by words and actions.[204] The court will take into account the fact that the bereft parent may have difficulty ascertaining the true intention of the abducting parent, which itself may not be constant, and in obtaining legal advice.

---

[196] *VK v JV (Abduction: Consent)* [2012] EWHC 4033 (Fam); [2013] 2 F.L.R. 237.

[197] *K v K (Abduction: Consent)* [2009] EWHC 2721 (Fam). *Sed contra K v K (Abduction: Hague Convention: Adjournment)* [2009] EWHC 3378 (Fam).

[198] *Re H (Minors) (Abduction: Acquiescence)* [1997] 2 All E.R. 225.

[199] *Soucie*, 1995 S.L.T. 414; *Re M (Abduction: Acquiescence)* [1996] 1 F.L.R. 315; *Re B (Abduction) (Article 13 Defence)* [1997] 2 F.L.R. 573; *Robertson*, 1998 S.L.T. 468; *J v K*, 2002 S.C. 450; *T v T*, 2003 S.L.T. 1316; *M v M*, 2003 S.L.T. 330; and *Re P (A Child) (Abduction: Acquiescence)* [2004] 2 F.L.R. 1057.

[200] Contrast *Re A (Minors) (Abduction: Custody Rights)* [1992] 1 All E.R. 929.

[201] *Re W (Children)* [2010] EWCA Civ 520.

[202] *J, Petitioner*, 2002 S.C. 450; *Re F (Abduction: Rights of Custody)* [2008] EWHC 272 (Fam).

[203] *Re G (Children) (Abduction: Withdrawal of Proceedings, Acquiescence, Habitual Residence)* [2007] E.W.H.C. 2807 (Fam); *Re F (Abduction: Rights of Custody)* [2008] E.W.H.C. 272 (Fam); *Re Z (Abduction)* [2008] E.W.H.C. 3473 (Fam); and *B v D* [2008] E.W.H.C. 1246 (Fam).

[204] *T v T* [2008] EWHC 1169 (Fam); *B-G v B-G* [2008] EWHC 688 (Fam).

Grave risk

14–61 Case law indicates that the courts in Scotland and England are slow to find grave risk proved.[205] In *Re E (Children) (Abduction: Custody Appeal)*,[206] however, the UK Supreme Court held that, "The exceptions to the obligation to return are by their very nature restricted in their scope. They do not need any extra interpretation or gloss."[207] The onus lies on the party averring risk, that is, the abducting parent. The focus is on grave risk to the child were he ordered to return to his habitual residence, not risk to the abducting parent.[208] The judgment about the level of risk which is required to be made by art.13(b) is one which falls to the judge at first instance.[209] The *tempus inspiciendum* is the time at which the case comes to the Scots court: in a Hague Convention case it is not open to the court to ponder the effect of improvements which might be made in conditions in the legal system of habitual residence.[210] The terms of art.13 mean that the child may have to be returned even though conditions are not ideal.[211] The test, therefore, is high, but it can be reached.[212] The symbiosis among the art.12 and art.13 defences, observed above, is seen also in *S v S*,[213] where the court found that the child was settled in his new life, and return to his habitual residence would be devastating to such an extent as to constitute an intolerable situation.

Child's objection

14–62 The judicial or administrative authority may refuse to order the return of the child if it finds that the child objects to being returned and has attained an age and degree of maturity at which it is appropriate to take account of his/her views.[214]

---

[205] *Slamen v Slamen*, 1991 G.W.D. 34-2041; *Whitley v Whitley*, 1992 G.W.D. 15-843; 1992 G.W.D. 22-1248; *Murphy v Murphy*, 1994 G.W.D. 32-1893; *Matznick v Matznick*, 1998 S.L.T. 636; *Starr v Starr*, 1999 S.L.T. 335; *I, Petitioner*, 1999 G.W.D. 21-972; *Q, Petitioner*, 2001 S.L.T. 243; *D v D*, 2001 S.L.T. 1104; *I, Petitioner*, 2004 S.L.T. 972; *M, Petitioner*, 2007 S.L.T. 433; and *B, Petitioner* 2014 G.W.D. 2-43. The first English decision upholding the grave risk argument was as late as 1995: *Re F (A Minor) (Child Abduction: Rights of Custody Abroad)* [1995] 3 All E.R. 641, per Butler Sloss L.J. at 648. See also now *Re F (A Child) (Abduction: Art.13(b): Psychiatric Assessment)* [2014] EWCA Civ 275.

[206] *Re E (Children) (Abduction: Custody Appeal)* [2011] UKSC 27; [2012] 1 A.C. 144, per Baroness Hale and Lord Wilson at [52].

[207] cf. *In re M (Children) (Abduction: Rights of Custody)* [2007] UKHL 55; [2008] 1 A.C. 1288.

[208] *M, Petitioner*, 2007 S.L.T. 433.

[209] *Re S (A Child) (Abduction: Rights of Custody)* [2012] UKSC 10; [2012] 2 A.C. 257, per Lord Wilson at [35].

[210] *Macmillan v Macmillan*, 1989 S.L.T. 350. But contrast Brussels II *bis* art.11.4, q.v.

[211] *Viola v Viola*, 1988 S.L.T. 7: the principle of paramountcy of the child's best interests does not apply. But see *Re C (A Child) (Child Abduction: Settlement)* [2006] EWHC 1229 (Fam).

[212] e.g. *Q, Petitioner*, 2001 S.L.T. 243 (sexual abuse); *K v K* [2007] EWCA Civ 533 (domestic violence); *Re E (Abduction: Intolerable Situation)* [2008] EWHC 2112 (Fam); and *Re H (Abduction)* [2009] EWHC 1735 (Fam) (the court addressed was persuaded that siblings should not be returned to their father in Spain, there being a real risk in the view of the court that the elder child, who previously had attempted suicide, would commit suicide if ordered to return, and that the younger child would suffer damage to his psychological and emotional development).

[213] *S v S (Abduction: Wrongful Retention)* [2009] EWHC 1494 (Fam).

[214] *Urness v Minto*, 1994 S.L.T. 988; *O'Connor*, 1995 G.W.D. 3-113; *Marshall v Marshall*, 1996 S.L.T. 429; *Cameron (No.2)*, 1997 S.L.T. 206; *Matznick*, 1998 S.L.T. 636; *Singh v Singh*, 1998 S.L.T. 1084; *W v W*, 2003 S.L.T. 1253; and *Re H* [2005] EWCA Civ 319. Also *Re S (A Minor) (Child*

The House of Lords in *Re M (Children) (Abduction: Rights of Custody)*[215] made clear that "taking account of a child's views" does not mean that those views are determinative. The older the child, the greater the weight a child's objections to return may carry.[216] Article 13 refers to the child's objections, rather than to the expression of a preference; preference, it seems, may be expressed only after an objection is raised.[217]

An important re-evaluation of this defence was made by the English Court of Appeal in *Re M (Children) (Child's Objections: Joinder of Children as Parties to Appeal)*.[218] Black L.J. explained the normal judicial approach to the child's objections exception, viz. first, the "gateway stage" and, secondly, the discretion stage. The gateway stage comprises two parts: (a) the child objects to being returned; and (b) the child has attained an age and degree of maturity at which it is appropriate to take account of his or her views. If the gateway elements are not established, the court is bound to return the child in accordance with art.12. If the gateway elements are established, the court may return him or her, but is not obliged so to do. Her Ladyship usefully pointed out, however, that this traditional approach requires to be applied in the light of important developments, namely, implementation of Brussels II *bis*, and in particular art.11(2) thereof (q.v.); the decisions of the House of Lords in *In re D (A Child)(Abduction: Rights of Custody)*,[219] and in *In re M (Children)(Abduction: Rights of Custody)*[220]; and the growing relevance and influence of the child's state of mind, as highlighted by the Supreme Court in *Re LC (Children) (International Abduction: Child's Objections to Return)*[221] in relation to a finding as to a child's habitual residence. In sum, there appeared to Her Ladyship to be an inconsistency of approach at the gateway stage:

> "On the one hand, a highly technical, structured, approach is described which requires the court to go in considerable detail into the circumstances in which the children object (I will call this 'the *Re T* approach'[222]). On the other hand, there is

---

Abduction: Delay) [1998] 1 F.C.R. 17; *W v W*, 2003 S.L.T. 1253; *Re J (Children) (Abduction: Child's objections to return)* [2004] EWCA Civ 428; *Re M (Children) (Abduction: Rights of Custody)* [2008] 1 A.C. 1288; *C v C*, 2008 S.C. 571; *Re E (Abduction:Intolerable Situation)* [2008] EWHC 2112 (Fam); *M v F* [2008] EWHC 2049 (Fam); *Re Z (Children) (Abduction)* [2008] EWHC 3473 (Fam); *Re G (Abduction)* [2008] EWHC 2558 (Fam); *Re R (A Child) (Abduction: Child's Objections)* [2009] EWHC 3074 (Fam); *M v B* [2009] EWHC 3477 (Fam); and *W v W* [2010] EWHC 332 (Fam).

[215] *Re M (Children) (Abduction: Rights of Custody)* [2008] 1 A.C. 1288.

[216] *W v W* [2010] EWHC 332 (Fam); and on appeal sub nom. *Re W (Children)* [2010] EWCA Civ 520, per Wilson L.J. at [22].

[217] J.M. Carruthers, "Party Autonomy and Children: A View from the UK" *Nederlands Internationaal Privaatrect*, Special Issue 2012: Party Autonomy and International Family Law, pp.562–568 (ISSN 0167-7594).

[218] *Re M (Children) (Child's Objections: Joinder of Children as Parties to Appeal)* [2015] EWCA Civ 26.

[219] *In re D (A Child)(Abduction: Rights of Custody)* [2007] 1 A.C. 619.

[220] *In re M (Children)(Abduction: Rights of Custody)* [2007] UKHL 55.

[221] *Re LC (Children) (International Abduction: Child's Objections to Return)* [2014] UKSC 1, [2014] A.C. 1038.

[222] *Re T (Children) (Abduction: Child's Objections to Return)* [2000] 2 F.L.R. 192 at 204 (followed, e.g. by Sir Mark Potter in *Re R (A Child) (Abduction: Child's Objections)* [2009] EWHC 3074 (Fam) at [66]); and *Re K* [2010] EWCA Civ 1546. Essentially the *Re T* approach necessitated a 4-pronged enquiry, viz.: (i) the child's own perspective of what is in his own short, medium or long term interests; (ii) the extent to which the reasons for objection are rooted in reality or might reasonably

support for a much simpler exercise at the gateway stage, with the detail of the case being considered if and when it comes to determining whether return should be ordered ('the more basic approach')."[223]

Importantly, the Court of Appeal, in the person of Black L.J., has given clear direction:

> "We know now that the child's views are not determinative of the application or even presumptively so; they are but one of the factors to be considered at the discretion stage. We also know that the discretion is at large; there is no requirement of exceptionality, and the court is entitled to take into account the various aspects of Convention policy, the circumstances which gave the court discretion in the first place, and wider considerations of the child's rights and welfare . . . .I am persuaded that the *Re T* approach is unhelpful . . .[it] might, in some cases, rob the discretionary stage of its proper role[224] ... In the light of all of this, the position should now be, in my view, that the gateway stage is confined to a straightforward and fairly robust examination of whether the simple terms of the Convention are satisfied in that the child objects to being returned and has attained an age and degree of maturity at which it is appropriate to take account of his or her views. Sub-tests and technicality of all sorts should be avoided. In particular, the *Re T* approach to the gateway stage should be abandoned."[225]

Black J. in *W v W*[226] stated that there was no absolute threshold below which a child could not be sufficiently mature for the purposes of the child's objections defence. The judge found it appropriate to take into account the views of children aged eight and six. On (unsuccessful) appeal by the father, the Court of Appeal, having examined the issue, concluded that it could not be said that the age of the younger child per se foreclosed the possibility that she had objections to returning.[227] Nonetheless, Wilson L.J. expressed concern that lowering the age at which a child's objections might be taken into account might gradually have the effect of eroding the principal objective of the Convention, which is swift restoration of a child to the state of his habitual residence. In the matter of age, the Family Division in *Re Z (Children) (Abduction)*,[228] examining the views of siblings, held that the younger child, aged five years, was too young to have his view taken into consideration, whereas the views of the seven year old could be

---

appear to be so grounded; (iii) the extent to which those views have been shaped or coloured by undue parental pressure, direct or indirect; and (iv) the extent to which the objections would be modified on return and/or the child's removal from the pernicious influence of the abducting parent.

[223] *Re M (Children) (Child's Objections: Joinder of Children as Parties to Appeal)* [2015] EWCA Civ 26, per Black L.J. at [50].

[224] *Re M (Children) (Child's Objections: Joinder of Children as Parties to Appeal)* [2015] EWCA Civ 26 at [63].

[225] *Re M (Children) (Child's Objections: Joinder of Children as Parties to Appeal)* [2015] EWCA Civ 26 at [69]; and *Re U-B (A Child)* [2015] EWCA Civ 60.

[226] *W v W* [2010] EWHC 332 (Fam); and on appeal sub nom. *Re W (Children)* [2010] EWCA Civ 520.

[227] cf. *Re W (Children)* [2010] EWCA Civ 520, in which account was taken of the views of a 6 year old child.

[228] *Re Z (Children) (Abduction)* [2008] EWHC 3473 (Fam). Contrast siblings of 12 and 9 years in *M v B* [2009] EWHC 3477 (Fam).

given some weight. A strong example of the court taking full account of the clearly held views of a 13 year old is provided by *Re R (A Child) (Abduction: Child's Objections)*.[229]

At whatever age, but especially with regard to younger children, the court must take into account the influence which the abducting parent may have exercised upon the child in the stance the child is taking, and in the expression of his views,[230] albeit being alert to the fact that it would be unnatural for a parent not to air with the child the options available in the circumstances, and the benefits and drawbacks of each.

The court must be sure it understands the child's view, and that the child understands its options: his true wish may be to stay with one parent, wherever that parent may choose to be.[231] Yet again, the reality of the situation is that it will be a rare child who would choose a place over a parent.[232] A child might be more inclined to express his view in a negative way, by saying that he does not wish to return to a given place, which is the home of the less favoured parent.[233] The difficulty can readily be seen that the "child's objection to return to a country" defence is likely to segue into a more personal preference, the denial of which, in the child's view, might be to place him in an intolerable situation.[234]

In *Re A (Abduction: Child's Objections to Return)*[235] the Court of Appeal held that during that part of the meeting in which the judge is listening to what the child has to say, the judge's role should be largely that of a passive recipient of whatever communication the young person wishes to transmit, and he should not, therefore, probe or seek to test what the child says.[236] The court on appeal will be reluctant to disturb the weight attributed by the trial judge to the various factors considered in the exercise of his discretion, and to his view of the evidence, and will depart from the judge's decision only if it was plainly wrong in the view of the appellate court, and the reasoning aberrant: "for it is of the essence of the [trial judge's] discretion that the exercise of attributing weight is committed to her or him".[237] Where an older child might be able to contribute relevant evidence, which is not easily given by either parent, or is incapable of being represented by either parent, the Supreme Court has indicated that the child should be made a party to the proceedings.[238]

---

[229] *Re R (A Child) (Abduction: Child's Objections* [2009] EWHC 3074 (Fam); with reference to Ward L.J. in *Re T (Children) (Abduction: Child's Objections to Return)* [2000] 2 F.L.R. 192 at 204.

[230] *C v C*, 2008 S.C. 571; *Re R (A Child) (Abduction: Child's Objections)* [2009] EWHC 3074 (Fam).

[231] *Re G (Abduction)* [2008] EWHC 2558 (Fam).

[232] Though see *W v W* [2010] EWHC 332 (Fam), and on appeal sub nom. *Re W (Children)* [2010] EWCA Civ 520, per Wilson L.J. at [20].

[233] *M v B* [2009] EWHC 3477 (Fam).

[234] *S v S (Abduction: Wrongful Retention)* [2009] EWHC 1494 (Fam).

[235] *Re A (Abduction: Child's Objections to Return)* [2014] EWCA Civ 554; [2014] 1 W.L.R. 4326.

[236] Black L.J. in *Re U-B (A Child)* [2015] EWCA Civ 60 stated at [52] that, "The appeal court cannot be used as a vehicle for conducting in effect an entire rehearing in such circumstances."

[237] *Re W (Children)* [2010] EWCA Civ 520, per Wilson L.J. at [25]; and *Re F (A Child) (Abduction: Refusal to Order Summary Return)* [2009] EWCA Civ 416. Also, in a non-Convention case, *Re J(A Child) (Custody Rights: Jurisdiction)* [2006] 1 A.C. 80.

[238] *Re LC (Children) (International Abduction: Child's Objections to Return)* [2014] UKSC 1; [2014] A.C. 1038.

Sibling solidarity

14–63 Scots courts in international, as in domestic cases, normally favour a solution which does not divide siblings.[239] This preferred stance may be strengthened by the expression, by one or more siblings, of objections to the prospect of return to their country of habitual residence. The objections of an older sibling may affect the outcome of proceedings for a younger child who is deemed insufficiently old and mature to express an objection.[240] In *B, Petitioner*,[241] for example, the objections to return to France expressed by a 14 year old brother were taken into account, whereas it was considered that the 10 year old brother was not mature enough to state an objection to a return to France for the purpose of art.13. As it was specifically conceded on the younger child's behalf that an intolerable situation would be created for him were he to be returned to France alone, the court considered itself competent to exercise discretion in relation to both brothers, and in the circumstances neither child was returned to France.

Conversely, but rarely, the strongly held objection of one child, usually the eldest, may have the effect of persuading the court to separate siblings.[242] Moreover, in the specialties of any given set of circumstances, the best outcome in the view of the court on the basis of the personalities of the children may be to split parental responsibilities for different children between the father and mother.[243]

Role and function of central authorities

14–64 Article 7 provides for the involvement of Central Authorities. Their function, in summary, is to facilitate the smooth working of the Convention by helping a parent locate a child, and obtain legal advice. The Central Authority for Scotland is the EU and International Law Branch of the Scottish Government, and for England and Wales is the Child Abduction Unit of the Office of Official Solicitor and Public Trustee.

Central Authorities exist in every Contracting State, but the speed with which applications for assistance are dealt with varies from country to country. Central Authorities shall bear their own costs, and shall not require payment from applicants towards the costs and expenses of proceedings.[244] However, a Contracting State may limit its assumption of costs to those covered by its system of legal aid and advice.[245]

---

[239] *Urness v Minto*, 1994 S.C. 249; and *Ontario Court v M and M (Abduction: Children's Objections)* [1997] 1 F.L.R. 475.

[240] e.g. *Re LC (Children) (International Abduction: Child's Objections to Return)* [2014] UKSC 1; [2014] A.C. 1038.

[241] *B, Petitioner* [2013] CSOH 187; 2014 Fam. L.R. 41; 2014 G.W.D. 2-43.

[242] *Singh v Singh,* 1998 S.C. 68.

[243] *H v H,* 2010 S.L.T. 395, in which the eldest child's welfare was secured by remaining in Scotland with her mother, whereas the welfare of the younger child was judged to be best secured by making a residence order in favour of his father in Australia.

[244] Though they may require payment of expenses incurred or to be incurred in implementing the return of the child: art.26.

[245] *Matznick*, 1998 S.L.T. 636.

Intra-EU abductions: inter-relationship between 1980 Hague Convention and Brussels II *bis*[246]

The 1980 Hague Convention has been ratified by all EU Member States and applies in relations between Member States. However, the 1980 Convention now is supplemented by certain provisions of Brussels II *bis*, which operate in cases of child abduction between Member States, and which take precedence over the Hague Convention in those cases. In relations between EU Member States, in matters covered by Brussels II *bis*, the rules of the Regulation prevail over the rules of the 1980 Hague and Council of Europe Conventions. This means that where child abduction matters arise under international instruments, the rules of the 1980 Hague Convention are subject to the overriding direction of Brussels II *bis* in a qualifying[247] case.

14–65

Brussels II *bis* aims to deter wrongful removal or retention of children between Member States, and if abduction should occur, to ensure the prompt return of a child to his Member State of origin.[248] The existence of the Regulation provides another example of the "layering" of potentially relevant conflict rules, which is characteristic of many areas of international private law at this period of its development. The instant example is a case of "overlay", for it leaves in place the existing, well established Hague structure, and operates on top of that foundation.

Recital (17) of Brussels II *bis* states that in cases of wrongful removal or retention of a child, the child must be returned without delay; to this end, it is expressly stated that the 1980 Hague Convention continues to apply, as complemented by the provisions of Brussels II *bis*, and by art.11 in particular.[249]

The courts of the Member State to/in which the child has been wrongfully removed/retained[250] should be able to oppose the child's return in specific, duly justified cases, in the normal way under the 1980 Hague Convention.

In sum, where a child is "abducted" from one Member State (Member State of origin) (henceforth "MSO") to another Member State (the requested Member State) (henceforth "RMS"), the Regulation ensures that the courts of the MSO retain jurisdiction to decide on the question of custody, notwithstanding the abduction. Once a request for the return of the child is lodged with a court in the RMS, the RMS will apply the 1980 Hague Convention as complemented by the Regulation in order to make a decision. Where the RMS decides not to return a child by reason of art.12 or art.13 of the 1980 Hague Convention, it must inform the court of the MSO (recital (18)). However, the decision not to return the child is little more than a provisional protective decision because it may be superseded

---

[246] P. McEleavy, "The Brussels II Regulation: How the European Community has moved into Family Law" [2002] I.C.L.Q. 883; P. McEleavy, "The New Child Abduction Regime in the European Union: Symbiotic Relationship or Forced Partnership?" (2005) 1 J.P.I.L. 5; and A. Schulz, "The enforcement of child return orders in Europe: where do we go from here?" [2012] International Family Law March 2012 (special issue).

[247] i.e. abduction of a child from one EU Member State to another EU Member State, both of which are parties to the 1980 Hague Convention.

[248] Practice Guide para.4.1.2.

[249] *Vigreux v Michel* [2006] EWCA Civ 630, the first case governed by the Regulation to reach the Court of Appeal. For Scotland, see rules in Act of Sederunt (Rules of the Court of Session Amendment) (Jurisdiction, Recognition and Enforcement of Judgments) 2005 (SSI 2005/135).

[250] Defined in art.2.11.

by a subsequent decision of the court of the MSO. If that subsequent decision by the MSO requires that the child be returned to his habitual residence, return must take place without special procedure for decree recognition or enforcement of that decision in the court of the state to/in which the child was wrongfully removed/retained.

Article 10—jurisdiction in cases of child abduction

14–66   The 1980 Hague Convention does not contain direct or indirect rules of jurisdiction. Article 10 of Brussels II *bis* lays down rules for intra-EU child abduction cases, to determine which EU Member State has jurisdiction to decide "custody issues".[251] As a deterrent to intra-EU child abduction, art.10 safeguards the principle of *perpetuatio fori*[252] and regulates its operation in this context by ensuring that the courts of the MSO (the state in which the child was habitually resident before the abduction) remain competent after the abduction, to decide on matters of custody.[253]

While the opening words of the article uphold the claim of the court of the jurisdiction whence or in which the child has been wrongfully removed/retained, the remaining parts of the article afford justifications for departing from that position. Article 10 recognises the conceptual difficulties which the factor of habitual residence contains, namely, that as time goes on, it may be perverse to refuse to recognise a situation which in factual terms is incontestable. The RMS (the state to which the child has been abducted) may exercise jurisdiction over the child only in narrowly defined circumstances, namely, if:

(a)   the child has acquired habitual residence in the RMS,[254] *and* all those with custody rights have acquiesced in the abduction; *or*

(b)   the child has acquired habitual residence in the RMS and has resided there for at least one year after those persons with custody rights learned, or should have learned,[255] of the child's whereabouts[256]; *and* the child has settled in the new environment; *and* one of the following conditions is met:

    (i)   the bereft parent has not lodged a request for return of the child within a year of being able to locate the child[257];

    (ii)   the bereft parent has lodged a request for return of the child, but has withdrawn that request;

    (iii)   art.11.7 (*q.v.*) has been satisfied;

    (iv)   the MSO has issued a judgment[258] which allows the child to remain in the RMS.

---

[251] *B v D* [2008] EWHC 1246 (Fam).

[252] cf. *Leon v Leon* [1967] P. 275: once seised, always seised.

[253] e.g. *H v B (Wardship: Jurisdiction)* [2014] EWCA Civ 1101; [2015] 1 W.L.R. 863; and *Re B (A Child) (Hague Convention Proceedings)* [2014] EWCA Civ 375; [2015] 1 F.L.R. 389.

[254] By inference this presupposes that wrongful removal by a parent can effect change in habitual residence of the child; but as art.10 proceeds, it can be seen that this assumption is qualified.

[255] Practice Guide para.4.2.1.2.

[256] *M v F* [2008] EWHC 2049 (Fam).

[257] Note the imposition upon a parent of a duty of enquiry by this term of the Regulation.

[258] i.e. a final judgment. The ECJ held in *Povse v Alpago* (C-211/10 PPU) ECJ (Third Chamber) [2011] Fam. 199; [2011] 3 W.L.R. 164 that a provisional measure does not constitute a "judgment" within the meaning of art.10(b)(iv). cf. *G v G,* 2012 S.L.T. 2.

Under art.10(a), if no habitual residence has been acquired in the RMS, the child would require to be returned to the court of his habitual residence in the MSO, meaning that the outcome is in line with the Hague regime.

Article 10(b), which enumerates rules of specificity, is intended to keep a jurisdictional balance. It is extremely difficult to tear jurisdiction away from the courts of the child's original habitual residence, a feature which is a great help to the bereft parent. Jurisdictional competence will shift to the RMS only if the bereft parent acquiesces, or is indifferent, or does not discharge the duty of enquiry.[259]

From the "abductor's" point of view, one assumes that if acquiescence is not proved for jurisdiction purposes under art.10, the matter still could be argued for larger purposes under art.13 of the 1980 Hague Convention, since Brussels II *bis*, although demoting the Hague Convention,[260] does not extinguish it.

Article 11—return of the child

In any case brought in an EU Member State under the 1980 Hague Convention, in respect of the wrongful removal or retention of a child to or in another Member State, the provisions of art.11.2–11.8 of Brussels II *bis* apply.

14–67

Article 11.2—child's opportunity to be heard

Brussels II *bis* reinforces[261] the child's right to be heard. Recital (19) lays down the principle that giving audience to the child plays an important role in the application of the Regulation. When a court is applying arts 12 and 13 of the 1980 Hague Convention, it may refuse to order the child's return if it finds that the child objects to being returned, and has attained an age and maturity at which it is appropriate to take account of his/her views. Article 11.2 of the Regulation goes further than art.13 of the Hague Convention, by "ensuring"[262] that the child is given the opportunity to be heard, "unless this appears inappropriate having regard to his or her age or degree of maturity". A shift in emphasis in favour of the rights of the child can be discerned.[263]

14–68

Article 11.3—six-week deadline

Article 11.3 is tautological: the court "shall act expeditiously . . .using the most expeditious procedures available in national law." The RMS must issue a decision

14–69

---

[259] Under the Hague regime also, unexplained inactivity by the bereft parent may give rise to judicial comment, and sometimes may contribute to a defence of acquiescence. Sed *contra J v K*, 2002 S.C. 450.

[260] Brussels II *bis* art.60.

[261] Practice Guide para.4.3.4, and Ch.6.

[262] In *Re F (A Child) (Abduction: Child's Wishes)* [2007] EWCA Civ 468 the English judge erred in failing to comply with art.11.2 by neglecting to give the child (seven years old) the opportunity to be heard. See also *Re M (A Child) (Abduction: Child's Objections: Appeal)* [2014] EWCA Civ 1519; [2015] Fam. Law 121.

[263] e.g. *Re S (A Child) (Abduction: Hearing the Child)* [2014] EWCA Civ 1557; [2015] 1 F.C.R. 223.

(and, implicitly, enforce that decision) no later than six weeks after the lodging of the application for return of the child.[264]

Article 11.4—future arrangements

14–70   This is an interesting provision, showing how strictly art.13(b) of the Hague Convention is to be construed in intra-EU cases. Brussels II *bis* reinforces the principle that the RMS shall order the immediate return of the child by restricting the art.13(b) exceptions to a minimum.[265] The Regulation requires the return of the child to the MSO even in cases where a return would expose the child to physical or psychological harm, so long as the authorities of the MSO have made "adequate arrangements" to secure the child's protection following his return. The RMS cannot refuse to return a child on art.13(b) grounds if it is shown that, "adequate arrangements have been made to secure the protection of the child after his or her return".The child should always be returned to the MSO if he can be adequately protected there.[266]

How will it be established that adequate arrangements have been made? Is this an evidentiary issue? Adequate arrangements under art.11.4 mean more than procedures existing in theory in the MSO to safeguard the child; it must be established that the authorities in the MSO have taken definite measures to protect the child in question. Central Authorities will play a vital role in assessing whether or not adequate protective measures are in place.

Article 11.5—bereft parent's opportunity to be heard

14–71   As well as the child having an opportunity to be heard, so too a court cannot refuse to return a child unless the bereft parent (the party requesting return of the child) has been given the opportunity to be heard. Arguably the application for return of the child is itself an opportunity for the parent to be heard, but art.11.5 seems to envisage something more.

Article 11.6 and 11.7—RMS's refusal to return the child

14–72   In most cases, the RMS is likely to order return of the child to the MSO (i.e. it will not find an art.13 ground to be established). But, in exceptional cases, where the RMS decides that the child shall not be returned to the MSO, special procedures must be followed, as laid down in art.11.6 and 11.7.[267]

---

[264] Practice Guide para.4.3.5.

[265] Practice Guide para.4.3.3.

[266] *S v S (Abduction: Wrongful Retention)* [2009] EWHC 1494 (Fam); and *A, Petitioner* [2011] CSOH 215; 2012 S.L.T. 370.

[267] e.g. *HA v MB (Brussels II Revised: Article 11(7) Application)* [2007] EWHC 2016 (Fam); *Re H (Abduction: Jurisdiction)* [2009] EWHC 2280 (Fam); *Re F (A Child) (Abduction: Refusal to Order Summary Return)* [2009] EWCA Civ 416; *Re N (Jurisdiction)* [2009] I.L.Pr. 8; and *Re RC (Child Abduction) (Brussels II Revised: Article 11(7))* [2009] 1 F.L.R. 574 (application under art.11.7 refused as the foreign court had made no non-return order under art.13, but rather had decided that the father's retention of the child was not wrongful in terms of art.3; the gateway to art.11.7 of Brussels II *bis* is a non-return order per art.12 or art.13 of the Convention).

Within one month of the (provisional protective[268]) decision not to return the child, the RMS must transmit a copy of its decision to the court of the MSO (either directly or via the Central Authorities). The MSO must notify the parties, and invite them to make submissions within three months, as to whether or not they wish the MSO to examine the question of custody. If no submissions are made, the MSO shall close the case. However, if one or both parties make(s) submissions, the MSO must examine the case, in which event all parties (including, if appropriate, the child) must be given an opportunity to be heard.[269] The judge in the MSO is expected to take account of the reasons of the judge in the RMS for not returning the child. This process may result in a peremptory order for return to the MSO, as explained.

Article 11.8—subsequent decision of MSO

Article 11.8 is the crucial provision of art.11. Following the judgment[270] issued by the RMS, if the court of the MSO, upon application by the bereft parent, makes a decision which entails the child's return to that state, this decision must be directly recognised and enforced in the RMS, without need for further procedure. It is not possible for the RMS to oppose the recognition and enforcement of such a judgment, which is to be directly recognised and enforceable in the other Member States. Article 11.8 allows, in effect, for the non-return order of the RMS to be subverted.

    14–73

This significant provision is buttressed by art.42, which provides that an enforceable judgment by the MSO ordering the return of a child under art.11.8 shall be recognised and enforceable in another Member State (i.e. in particular the RMS) without the need for a declaration of enforceability and without the possibility of opposing recognition, so long as the judgment has been certified in the MSO.[271] Such certification by the MSO judge can be issued only if:

(a) the child was given an opportunity to be heard, unless a hearing was considered inappropriate having regard to his or her age or degree of maturity[272];

(b) the parties were given an opportunity to be heard; and

(c) the court has taken into account in issuing its judgment the reasons for and evidence underlying the order issued pursuant to art.13 of the 1980 Hague Convention.[273]

---

[268] *Proceedings Brought by Rinau* (C-195/08 PPU) [2008] I.L.Pr. 51.

[269] Brussels II *bis* art.42.

[270] The CJEU held in *Povse v Austria*(3890/11) [2014] 1 F.L.R. 944; [2014] Fam. Law 31 that art.11(8) had to be interpreted as meaning that a judgment of the court with jurisdiction ordering return of the child fell within the scope of that provision, even if it was not preceded by a final judgment of that court relating to rights of custody of the child. cf. *Proceedings Brought by Rinau* (C-195/08 PPU) [2008] I.L.Pr. 51.

[271] Brussels II *bis*art.42(1).

[272] In view of the MSO; it is not beyond possibility that a judge in the MSO will take a different view as to a child's age and maturity than will a judge in the RMS.

[273] Brussels II *bis* art.42(2).

In the event that the court or any other authority takes measures to ensure the protection of the child after its return to the state of habitual residence, the certificate shall contain details of such measures.

Human rights implications[274]

14–74 There have been many references in this chapter to the welfare and paramount interests of children, and to the need to hear the views of the child. It would be an incomplete treatment were no reference to be made to the rights bestowed on children by international instruments. There are various sources of children's rights, namely, the European Convention on Human Rights 1950, implemented in UK law by the Human Rights Act 1998; the United Nations Convention on the Rights of the Child (signed by the UK in 1990, and in force as of 15 January 1992, with the effect that all UK government policies and practices must comply with the "UNCRC"); and the Charter of Fundamental Rights of the EU ("CFEU"),[275] which enshrines in EU law certain political, social, and economic rights for EU citizens/residents, and requires EU institutions and Member States to act and legislate consistently with the Charter. Specifically, art.24(1) of the CFEU provides that "Children shall have the right to such protection and care as is necessary for their well-being. They may express their views freely. Such views shall be taken into consideration on matters which concern them in accordance with their age and maturity."[276] The collective effect of these instruments is that children are entitled, inter alia, to maintain regular contact with both parents,[277] to have their views heard,[278] and to enjoy family life.[279]

With regard to the 1980 Hague Convention, s.1(2) of the Child Abduction and Custody Act 1985 provides that the provisions of that Convention set out in Sch.1 to the Act shall have the force of law in the United Kingdom. Article 20 of the Convention, which provides that, "The return of the child under the provisions of Article 12 may be refused if this would not be permitted by the fundamental principles of the requested State relating to the protection of human rights and fundamental freedoms" is not incorporated in Sch.1 to the Act, since the 1985 Act was enacted before the ECHR had force of law in the UK.[280] However, although art.20 is not incorporated by the 1985 Act, nonetheless it is available by operation of the Human Rights Act 1998.[281]

---

[274] See also L. Walker and P. Beaumont, "Shifting the Balance Achieved by the Abduction Convention: The Contrasting Approaches of the European Court of Human Rights and the European Court of Justice" (2011) 7 J.P.I.L. 231–249; and P. Beaumont et al, "Child Abduction: Recent Jurisprudence of the European Court of Human Rights" (2015) 64(1) I.C.L.Q. 39.

[275] Charter of Fundamental Rights of the EU [2007] O.J. C303/01.

[276] Recital (33) of Brussels II *bis* states that the Regulation recognises the fundamental rights and observes the principles of the CFEU and, in particular, that it seeks to ensure respect for the fundamental rights of the child as set out in art.24. cf. art.3(3) TEU (Consolidated Version [2008] O.J. C115/13), which sets protection of the rights of the child as a core EU objective.

[277] UNCRC arts 9, 10, 11; ECHR art.8; CFEU arts 7 and 24.

[278] UNCRC art.9(2), 12, 13; ECHR art.6; CFEU arts 11, 24 and 47.

[279] UNCRC art.8; ECHR art.8; CFEU arts 3 and 7.

[280] *In re D (A Child) (Abduction: Rights of Custody)* [2006] UKHL 51; [2007] 1 A.C. 619, per Lord Hope of Craighead at [65].

[281] *SP v EB* [2014] EWHC 3964 (Fam), per Mostyn J. at [2], citing Lord Hope, ibid.; and *X v Latvia* [2014] 1 F.L.R. 1135 at [106] and [107].

In abduction cases, the inter-relationship between, on the one hand, the 1980 Hague Convention and (where applicable) Brussels II *bis*, and, on the other, the international "rights" treaties, has generated a new tranche of abduction jurisprudence, which has revealed a dichotomy between the approach to children's rights adopted by the ECtHR and the essence of the 1980 Abduction Convention.

The tension was brought to prominence in *Neulinger v Switzerland*,[282] in which the ECtHR held that in matters of international child abduction, the obligations under art.8, ECHR were to be interpreted in the light of, inter alia, the 1980 Hague Convention. The Court held that art.8 required that a child's return could not be ordered mechanically whenever the Hague Convention was applicable, and that what was in the child's best interest had to be assessed in each case. Domestic courts were required to carry out an "in-depth examination of all relevant factors", and to make a balanced assessment of the respective interests of each person, particularly taking into account the best interests of the child.[283] The adoption by the ECtHR of the test of an "in-depth examination", being one entirely at odds with the philosophy of the Hague scheme, caused consternation in the UK.[284] In turning the "swift, summary decision making which is envisaged by the Hague Convention into the full-blown examination of the child's future in the requested state which it was the very object of the Hague Convention to avoid",[285] the ECtHR jurisprudence was inimical—albeit superior—to the Hague rationale.

Soon after the *Neulinger* decision, the ECtHR in *Sneersone v Italy*[286] endorsed the point that the Hague decision-making process involved an in-depth examination of the family situation. Having emphasised that it had power to review the procedure followed by domestic courts to uphold the child's best interests as the primary consideration (thereby constituting, in effect, a court of further appeal), the Court declared that a child's return could not be ordered automatically or mechanically.[287] In so doing, it might be said that its judgment afforded some relief to domestic courts in that decisions made nowadays under the Hague Convention are rarely, if ever, made mechanically.[288]

The decision in *X v Latvia*[289] brought a welcome modification of the *Neulinger* principle insofar as the ECtHR Grand Chamber held that the judicial authorities of the requested state are subject to a duty to undertake an "effective examination" of allegations made by a party on the basis of one of the exceptions expressly provided for in the 1980 Hague Convention. Due to the failure of the Latvian court to carry out an effective examination of the applicant's allegations, or to consider whether it was possible for the mother in the instant case to follow her daughter to Australia and to maintain contact with her, there had been a

---

[282] *Neulinger v Switzerland* (41615/07) [2011] 1 F.L.R. 122; [2011] 2 F.C.R. 110.

[283] *Neulinger v Switzerland* (41615/07) [2011] 1 F.L.R. 122; [2011] 2 F.C.R. 110 H10(g); [138]–[141]. cf. *Raban v Romania* (25437/08) (ECHR) [2011] 1 F.L.R. 1130; [2011] Fam. Law 121.

[284] *In re E (Children) (Abduction: Custody Appeal)* [2011] UKSC 27; [2012] 1 AC 144 at [1]; and *In the Matter of S (A Child)* [2012] UKSC 10; [2012] 2 A.C. 257 at [37]–[38].

[285] *In re E (Children) (Abduction: Custody Appeal)* [2011] UKSC 27; [2012] 1 AC 144 at [22].

[286] *Sneersone v Italy* (1437/09) [2011] 2 F.L.R. 1322; (2013) 57 E.H.R.R. 39; [2011] Fam. Law 1188.

[287] *Sneersone v Italy* (1437/09) [2011] 2 F.L.R. 1322; (2013) 57 E.H.R.R. 39; [2011] Fam. Law 1188 at H9(b) and [85]–[86].

[288] e.g. *In re E (Children) (Abduction: Custody Appeal)* [2011] UKSC 27; [2012] 1 A.C. 144 at [52].

[289] *X v Latvia* (27853/09) [2014] 1 F.L.R. 1135; (2014) 59 E.H.R.R. 3; [2014] Fam. Law 269.

violation of art.8 of the ECHR.[290] The change of wording from "in-depth" to "effective" (examination) recognises that the *Neulinger* test was inappropriately stringent and time-consuming, and appears to have averted a collision between ECHR and Hague Convention jurisprudence. Case law will reveal the extent to which a successful alignment has been achieved.

Concluding remarks

14–75   The profile of the typical abductor, as envisaged in 1980, has changed. Case law demonstrates that, at the point of separation of an "international couple", the tendency of the principal carer, frequently the mother, who has been living in a legal system other than that of her origin, is to secure her return to her legal system of origin with her child(ren), in the hope, if not expectation, of re-settling in that place, irrespective of the interests of the other parent. Other cases can arise in which the circumstances fall outside the contemplation of the Convention drafters, as, for example, where all members of a family depart, in a final manner, from the legal system of habitual residence, and thereafter the choice of residence for the children lies between the forum and a third state.[291]

The Hague principle of swift summary return after wrongful removal or retention[292] is under challenge as a result of ECtHR jurisprudence and over-creative and over-refined judicial interpretation of the Convention at the highest level in the UK, in a manner which threatens to destabilise it. This is frequently observable through manipulation of the meaning of habitual residence, combined with a more expansive attitude to the weight to be given, in this context, to children's views. The cascade effect of the notable change in approach to interpretation of the Hague scheme is visible[293]; Scottish judges and judges lower in the English hierarchy must follow the line from time to time cast by the Supreme Court.

Doubt has been thrown on "principles" relatively recently adhered to as firm, such as the inability of a parent unilaterally to change the habitual residence of a child in law.[294] The scheme is being undermined by overworking, to the point where, though apparently operating within the framework of the Hague rules, in practice decisions are being handed down based largely on the individual forum's opinion of the merits of the case, in a manner not dissimilar to common law practice in the UK. A striking example is *Re LC (Children) (International Abduction: Child's Objections to Return)*.[295] Older authorities on which reliance

---

[290] *X v Latvia* (27853/09) [2014] 1 F.L.R. 1135; (2014) 59 E.H.R.R. 3; [2014] Fam. Law 269 at H10(d) and [118]–[120].

[291] *O v O* [2013] EWHC 2970 (Fam).

[292] e.g. *P v P* [2013] GWD 12-253; and *P v M,* 2014 S.C. 518.

[293] *R, Petitioner* [2014] CSIH 95; 2014 S.L.T. 1080 (and, on appeal, at [2015] UKSC 35; [2015] 2 W.L.R. 1583); and *Re M (Children) (Child's Objections: Joinder of Children as Parties to Appeal)* [2015] EWCA Civ 26.

[294] e.g. *A v A (Children) (Habitual Residence)* [2013] UKSC 60; [2014] A.C. 1, per Lord Hughes at [73].

[295] *Re LC (Children) (International Abduction: Child's Objections to Return)* [2014] UKSC 1; [2014] A.C. 1038.

hitherto has been placed have been dismissed as judicial "excrescence".[296] There has always been difficulty in the analysis of Hague abduction cases insofar as one point segues into another, and most cases demonstrate a number of elements, each of potential legal significance and all having the potential to bear upon the other factors. This difficulty is intensifying as a consequence of recent decisions by the Supreme Court, e.g. the state of a child's mind affecting his habitual residence.[297]

The Court of Appeal held in *Re S (A Child) (Habitual Residence and Child's Objections: Brazil)*,[298] that in exercising its discretion under the Convention, a court must have regard to the wider considerations of the child's rights and welfare. "The Hague policy must be put into the balance, but there is no limitation on the other factors that could be considered and the weighting of individual features was not prescribed."[299] While this does not mean that the discretionary stage in a Hague Convention case must involve a full-blown welfare enquiry (for the Hague process is a summary one, designed to be concluded very quickly), the schizophrenic approach of the courts is increasingly evident:

> "So far, the concentration has been on that aspect of the Convention policy which is concerned with the benefits to children of a speedy return. But the Convention has to be viewed as a whole. It is an instrument which is designed to protect children and to put their interests first and it recognizes that there will be cases where a prompt return will not serve the child's interests. It is the purpose of the exceptions to cater for this. It would potentially defeat the object if, once an exception was established, the discretion stage which followed were to be confined as has been suggested, preventing the court from acting on whatever welfare considerations appear to be important in the individual child's case."[300]

At the same time, it must be conceded that the worst of the threat from the ECtHR appears to have been contained.

Abduction cases governed by common law rules

The facts of a case, including geography[301] and the timing of events,[302] may render it one for common law regulation.

14–76

---

[296] cf. *In re S (A Child) (Abduction: Rights of Custody)* [2012] UKSC 10, per Lord Wilson at [31]; *DL v EL (Hague Abduction Convention: Effect of Reversal of Return Order on Appeal)* [2013] UKSC 75; [2014] A.C. 1017 at [21]; and *Re LC (Children) (International Abduction: Child's Objections to Return)* [2014] UKSC 1; [2014] A.C. 1038.

[297] *Re LC (Children) (International Abduction: Child's Objections to Return)* [2014] UKSC 1; [2014] A.C. 1038.

[298] *Re S (A Child) (Habitual Residence and Child's Objections: Brazil)* [2015] EWCA Civ 2; [2015] Fam. Law 254.

[299] *Re S (A Child) (Habitual Residence and Child's Objections: Brazil)* [2015] EWCA Civ 2; [2015] Fam. Law 254, per Black L.J. at [54].

[300] *Re S (A Child) (Habitual Residence and Child's Objections: Brazil)* [2015] EWCA Civ 2; [2015] Fam. Law 254 at [57].

[301] Abductions from and to certain parts of the world, e.g. Islamic states, are always likely to be common law cases.

[302] In judging whether any international instrument is applicable, the initial act complained of must take place after the coming into force of the relevant instrument between the countries in question (*Kilgour*, 1987 S.L.T. 568; *Re H (Minors) (Abduction: Custody Rights)* [1991] 3 All E.R. 230 HL).

At common law in Scotland questions of custody[303] were regarded as pertaining to status. Accordingly, the court of the father's domicile was regarded as the court of pre-eminently suitable jurisdiction,[304] and custody orders made by the court of the father's domicile were accorded the greatest respect.[305] As time passed, this was tempered by an appreciation that the Scots court, in granting a custody order or withholding recognition of a foreign custody order, should regard as paramount the best interests of the child, and should be sensitive also to the need to return the child to the "natural" forum, if foreign, to have the substantive custody issue determined there.[306] This remains the approach of the Scots court in its treatment of incoming common law cases of alleged child abduction.

Incoming common law cases, that is, involving children brought from a non-Convention country, or involving a Convention countries in circumstances where the Convention(s) does not apply,are dealt with in Scotland on a fair-minded basis of return of the child to a court of closer connection, if it is obvious that such a court exists.[307] On the other hand, if not convinced of the existence of a more appropriate forum, or if unsure about the conditions which await the child on return, the Scots court will retain the child and decide the custody issue.[308] Many years have elapsed since the era when the decree of the court of the father's domicile was entitled to unquestioned acceptance.[309]

As regards outgoing common law cases, Scots law, obviously, is unlikely to be able to influence the handling of such cases, and advice to parents is of a practical nature, seeking to stop the "abductor" from removing the child beyond the jurisdiction of the Scots courts.[310] Removal of a child to a non-Convention country of a very different culture from the UK will render unlikely a foreign court order directing return of the child to Scotland.

---

[303] The terminology has changed. For English law, see the Children Act 1989. For Scotland, the Children (Scotland) Act 1995 replaced "custody" and "access" with "residence" and "contact"; the current language speaks of "parental responsibilities" and "parental rights".

[304] Hence the Scots court would consider itself of pre-eminent jurisdiction if the father was of Scots domicile: *Ponder v Ponder*, 1932 S.C. 233; *McLean v McLean*, 1947 S.C. 79; *Re B's Settlement* [1940] Ch. 54; *Brown v Brown*, 1948 S.L.T. 129; *Babington v Babington*, 1955 S.C. 115; *Kitson v Kitson*, 1945 S.C. 434; *McShane v McShane*, 1962 S.L.T. 221; and *Shanks v Shanks*, 1965 S.L.T. 330. E.B. Crawford, "International Child Abduction" (1990) 35 J.L.S.S. 277.

[305] *Westergaard v Westergaard*, 1914 S.C. 977; *Radoyevitch v Radoyevitch*, 1930 S.C. 619.

[306] *McKee v McKee* [1951] A.C. 352; *Battaglia v Battaglia*, 1967 S.L.T. 49; *Sargeant v Sargeant*, 1973 S.L.T. (Notes) 27; *Kelly v Marks*, 1974 S.L.T. 118; *Lyndon v Lyndon*, 1978 S.L.T. (Notes) 7; *Campbell v Campbell*, 1977 S.L.T. 125; and *Thomson, Petitioner*, 1980 S.L.T. (Notes) 29.

[307] *Lyndon*, 1978 S.L.T. (Notes) 7; *Campbell v Campbell*, 1977 S.C. 103; *Thomson, Petitioner*, 1980 S.L.T. (Notes) 29.

[308] *Sinclair v Sinclair*, 1988 S.L.T. 87 (before Germany became a Hague Convention country); and *Basinski v Basinski*, 1993 G.W.D. 8-533.

[309] *McKee* [1951] A.C. 352 at 365; and also Family Law Act 1986 s.26.

[310] Family Law Act 1986 ss.17, 33–37; and *Robertson, Petitioner*, 1911 S.C. 1319. The first source of advice if the destination is a non-Convention country is the Foreign and Commonwealth Office, and then "Reunite", a UK charity specialising in handling international child abduction cases.

Non-application of Hague Convention principles to non-Convention cases

An interesting question is whether Scots and English courts should apply to **14–77** "non-Convention" incoming cases a Convention-type approach. A Scots common law case of significance is *Calleja v Calleja*,[311] where the court opined that "physical or moral injury" (the terminology of the older common law cases) might not be the best expression in modern times, preferring the "psychological harm" wording used in the Hague Convention art.13, though not applying it directly.[312]

There were some early indications that an English court in its discretion might wish to take account of as much of the Hague Convention as it felt appropriate in a particular case.[313] However, there was cautious retrenchment by the Court of Appeal in *Re A (A Minor) (Abduction: Non-Convention Country)*,[314] where the non-Convention country was the United Arab Emirates. Similarly, in *Re P*[315] the Court of Appeal held that it was not bound to apply the spirit of the Convention to a non-Convention case. In *Re J (A Child) (Custody Rights: Jurisdiction)*[316] Baroness Hale of Richmond stated firmly that:

> "There is no warrant, either in statute or authority, for the principles of the Hague Convention to be extended to countries which are not parties to it . . . This is so even in a case where a friendly foreign state has made orders about the child's future."[317]

The House of Lords held that:

> "[I]n all non-Convention cases, the courts have consistently held that they must act in accordance with the welfare of the individual child. If they do decide to return the child, that is because it is in his best interests to do so, not because the welfare principle has been superseded by some other consideration . . . the specialist rules and concepts of the Hague Convention are not to be applied by analogy in a non-Convention case".[318]

Under any system of rules, Convention or common law, the weight given to the views of the child must increase as the child grows older. An added dimension may present in that in some legal systems girls may be of marriageable age earlier

---

[311] *Calleja v Calleja,* 1997 S.L.T. 579; and *Perendes v Sim*, 1998 S.L.T. 1382.

[312] *Calleja v Calleja,* 1997 S.L.T. 579 at 603.

[313] *Re F (A Minor) (Abduction; Jurisdiction)* [1990] 3 All E.R. 97; *D v D (Child Abduction: Non-Convention Country)* [1994] 1 F.L.R. 137 CA; *Re S (Minors) (Abduction)* [1994] 1 F.L.R. 297; *Re A (Minors) (Abduction: Habitual Residence)* [1996] 1 All E.R. 24; and *Re Z (Abduction: Non-Convention Country)* [1999] 1 F.L.R. 1270.

[314] *Re A (A Minor) (Abduction: Non-Convention Country)* [1998] 1 F.L.R. 231. See also *Re S (Minors) (Abduction)* [1994] 1 F.L.R. 297 CA; *Re A (Minors) (Abduction: Habitual Residence)* [1996] 1 All E.R. 24; *Osborne v Matthan (No.3)*, 1998 S.L.T. 1264; *Re JA (A Minor) (Abduction: Non-Convention Country)* [1998] 2 F.C.R. 159; and *Re J (A Child) (Return to Foreign Jurisdiction: Convention Rights)* [2005] 3 All E.R. 291 HL.

[315] *Re P (A Minor: Abduction), The Times*, 19 July 1996.

[316] *Re J (A Child) (Custody Rights: Jurisdiction)* [2006] 1 A.C. 80.

[317] *Re J (A Child) (Custody Rights: Jurisdiction)* [2006] 1 A.C. 80 at [22].

[318] *Re J (A Child) (Custody Rights: Jurisdiction)* [2006] 1 A.C. 80 at [25]. cf. *Re R (A Child) (Prohibited Steps Order)* [2013] EWCA Civ 1115; [2014] 1 F.L.R. 643; and *Re JXN (A Child) (otherwise SXX v KRN)* [2014] EWFC 17.

than 16 years, and parents may be in agreement that they wish to remove the child from the UK to, for example, India, in order to have the child married there.[319] In an instance of this type,[320] Singer J. in the Family Division of the English High Court held that the courts in England, while not insensitive to the traditions and concepts of family authority held by minority communities, must nevertheless uphold the integrity of the individual child or young person, whose views must prevail in the "...highly personal context of an arranged or forced marriage. Accordingly, the courts would not permit what was, at best, the exploitation of an individual, and might, in the worst case, amount to outright trafficking for financial consideration."

UK–Pakistan Consensus on Child Abduction

14–78   A protocol was reached in 2003, reflecting agreement between senior members of the UK judiciary and the Pakistan judiciary, in the matter of protection of children from the harmful effects of wrongful removal or retention, and having the aim of promoting judicial co-operation between the legal systems concerned.[321] The Protocol recognises that in normal circumstances the welfare of the child is best determined by the courts of the country of the child's habitual/ordinary residence.

The criminal law aspect of international child abduction

14–79   The Child Abduction Act 1984 amends the criminal law of England[322] and Scotland[323] relating to the abduction of children (i.e. the taking or sending of a child under the age of 16 out of the UK without the appropriate consent, where there is in force a parental responsibility order, or a UK order prohibiting the removal of the child from the UK).

These provisions were conceived as English measures, but it was feared that their effectiveness would be weakened if a parent or other person could take a child abroad from a Scottish airport or port without fear of criminal sanction. Hence, s.6, of application to Scotland only, was inserted at a late stage into the 1984 Act. Scots law on this subject comprises, in addition to s.6 (which defines the offence, the penalties being specified in s.8), the common law crimes of *plagium* (child stealing) and abduction.[324] The matter was considered by the Scottish Law Commission,[325] which recommended abolition of *plagium*, reform of abduction, and the creation of a statutory offence of taking or detaining a child

---

[319] These cases may overlap with issues of forced marriage. Paras 11–30 and 12–52, above.

[320] *Re KR (A Child) (Abduction: Forcible Removal by Parents)* [1999] 4 All E.R. 954.

[321] [2003] Fam. Law 199. See also comments at [2004] Fam. Law 359; [2004] Fam. Law 609; and [2006] 1 F.L.R. 5, where it is reported that the Protocol, at least "in spirit", had been used as at that date in 52 cases. Further *Re Z (A Child)* [2006] EWCA Civ 1219 at [31]; *A v N*, 2007 GWD 01-2; *Re I (A Child) (Contact Application: Jurisdiction)* [2009] UKSC 10; [2010] 1 All E.R. 445, per Lady Hale at 458, 459.

[322] Pt 1 of the Act.

[323] Pt 2 of the Act.

[324] Both criminal and civil aspects may arise from one set of circumstances: *Deans v Deans*, 1988 S.C.L.R. 192 Sh Ct.

[325] Scottish Law Commission, *Child Abduction* (HMSO, 1985), Scot. Law Com. Memo. No.67; Scottish Law Commission, *Report on Child Abduction* (HMSO, 1987), Scot. Law Com. No.102, Cm.64.

under 16 from the control of any person having lawful control of that child, but there has been no implementing legislation.

INTERNATIONAL PARENTAL RELOCATION[326]

Difficult tensions, personal and legal, emerge in cases where the parent of a child wishes to relocate, taking the child with him/her, against the wishes of the other parent. The subject concerns the lawful, as opposed to wrongful, removal of children to a new jurisdiction. The intended removal may be temporary or short-medium term in nature, or permanent, prompted, e.g. by the desire of the custodial parent to cohabit with a new spouse; and/or the pursuit of enhanced economic security and financial prospects; and/or the repatriation of one parent to his/her country of origin. Short-term intentions readily metamorphose into longer-term realities; the notion of staying in a new place for a fixed, short period may mutate if conditions are set fair in the view of the relocating parent. In *Payne v Payne*,[327] the paradigm English case on the subject, the Court of Appeal observed that the applicant for permission to remove the child is invariably the child's mother and the primary carer; the motivation for the move arises typically out of the mother's re-marriage[328] (following "her" new spouse to "his" country), or from her repatriation, that is, the urge to return "home", usually following marital or relationship breakdown with the child's father[329]; and the father's opposition commonly is based on the resultant reduction, actual or threatened, in his contact with the child, and his influence over the child.[330]

14–80

The relocating parent enjoys a right of mobility, expressed in art.2 of Protocol 4 to the ECHR. How does, or should, one parent's right to mobility weigh against the right of the non-relocating parent to respect for his private and family life, enshrined in art.8 of the ECHR?[331] In a comment which is indicative of the stance of the English courts, Thorpe L.J. remarked in *Payne* that, "Once a family unit disintegrates the separating members' separate rights can only be to a fragmented family life … the absent parent has the right to participation to the extent and in what manner the complex circumstances of the individual case dictate".[332]

---

[326] See, for detail, J.M. Carruthers, "International Family Relocation: Recent UK Experience", 2012 (3) Juridical Review 187.
[327] *Payne v Payne* [2001] EWCA Civ 166; [2001] Fam. 473.
[328] e.g. *Re B (Children) (Removal from Jurisdiction)* [2001] 1 FCR 108; and *Re S (Children) (Removal from Jurisdiction)* [2003] EWCA Civ 1149; [2003] 2 F.L.R. 1043.
[329] As in *Payne v Payne* [2001] EWCA Civ 166; [2001] Fam. 473; *Re S (Children: Application for Removal from Jurisdiction)* [2004] EWCA Civ 1724; [2005] 1 F.C.R. 471. *Contra Re G (Removal from Jurisdiction)* [2005] EWCA Civ 170; [2005] 2 F.L.R. 166; and *Re J (Children)*[2006] EWCA Civ 1897; [2007] 2 F.C.R. 149.
[330] *Payne v Payne* [2001] EWCA Civ 166; [2001] Fam. 473 at 483–484. See N.J. Taylor and M. Freeman, "International Research Evidence on Relocation: Past, Present, Future" (2010) 44(3) F.L.Q. 317; and C.S. Bruch and J. Bowermaster, "The Relocation of Children and Custodial Parents: Public Policy, Past and Present" (1996) 30(2) F.L.Q. 245.
[331] *Re A (Permission to Remove Child from Jurisdiction: Human Rights)* [2000] 2 F.L.R. 225.
[332] *Payne v Payne* [2001] EWCA Civ 166; [2001] Fam. 473 at 486.

In *Payne* the Court of Appeal carried out a review of UK relocation jurisprudence over a 30 year period.[333] The case itself fell into the repatriation category, concerning a mother's desire to return to New Zealand, her country of origin, following the failure of her marriage to the child's father. The Court concluded that, over 30 years, relocation cases consistently had been decided on the basis of two propositions: (a) although each member of the fractured family has rights to assert, the welfare of the child is the paramount consideration[334]; and (b) refusing the primary carer's reasonable proposals for the relocation of her family life is likely to impact detrimentally on the welfare of dependent children,[335] especially in cases where the applicant has forged a new family unit by marriage or other relationship. Therefore, the position in England was that the primary carer's application to relocate ought to be granted unless the court concludes that it is incompatible with the welfare of the children. A fundamentally important factor in the court's decision-making process is the reasonableness or otherwise of the relocation proposal. The court cannot presume that the proposal is reasonable. To assess the question of reasonableness, Thorpe L.J. suggested a discipline which was to become a decision-making formula,[336] viz.: the questions an English judge should ask himself are:

(a) is the applicant's proposal genuine and realistic, i.e. can it be said that it is not motivated by selfish desire to reduce or terminate contact between the other parent and the child, and is it founded upon well conceived and well researched proposals?;[337]

(b) is the respondent parent's opposition inspired by genuine concern for the future of the child's welfare or is it driven by an ulterior motive?;

(c) what would be the impact upon the applicant parent of a refusal of a genuine and realistic proposal?[338]; and

(d) what does an overriding review of the child's welfare as the paramount consideration indicate is best for the child?

---

[333] Including *Poel v Poel* [1970] 1 W.L.R. 1469; *Nash v Nash* [1973] 2 All E.R. 704; *Re A v A (Child: Removal from Jursidiction)* [1979] 1 F.L.R. 380; *Moodey v Field* unreported 13 February 1981; *Chamberlain v de la Mare* [1982] 4 F.L.R. 434; *Lonslow v Hennig* [1986] 2 F.L.R. 378; *Belton v Belton* [1987] 2 F.L.R. 343; *Tyler v Tyler* [1989] 2 F.L.R. 158; *MH v GP (Child: Emigration)* [1995] 2 F.L.R. 106; *Re H (Application to Remove from Jurisdiction)* [1998] 1 F.L.R. 848; *Re C (Leave to Remove from Jurisdiction)* [2000] 2 F.L.R. 457; and *Re L (A Child) (Contract: Domestic Violence)* [2001] Fam. 260.

[334] e.g. *Re H (Children: Residence Order: Relocation)* [2001] EWCA Civ 1338; [2001] 2 F.L.R. 1277.

[335] e.g. *Re B (Children) (Removal from Jurisdiction)* [2001] 1 F.C.R. 108, *Re S (Children) (Removal from Jurisdiction)* [2003] EWCA Civ 1149; [2003] 2 F.L.R. 1043; *Re B (Children) (Leave to Remove: Impact of Refusal)* [2004] EWCA Civ 956; [2005] 2 F.L.R. 239; *Re A (A Child) (Temporary Removal from Jurisdiction)* [2004] EWCA Civ 1587; [2005] 1 F.L.R. 639; and *Re G (Removal from Jurisdiction)* [2005] EWCA Civ 170; [2005] 2 F.L.R. 166.

[336] *K v K (Relocation: Shared Care Arrangement)*(also known as *MK v CK)* [2011] EWCA Civ 793, per Black L.J. at [122].

[337] *H v F* [2005] EWHC 2705; [2006] 1 F.L.R. 776. *Contra Re A (Leave to Remove: Cultural and Religious Considerations)* [2006] EWHC 421; [2006] 2 F.L.R. 572.

[338] *Re C (Children) (Permission to Relocate)* [2014] EWCA Civ 705; [2014] Fam. Law 1255.

In *Re D*,[339] a rare successful appeal against the proposed relocation of a child to Australia, the Court of Appeal observed that, as a result of *Payne*, little attention tended to be paid to the damage caused to the child by the loss of the relationship with the non-relocating parent, and too much to the departing parent's predilections.[340] Forcefully, in *Re AR (A Child) (Relocation) (also known as F v M)*,[341] Mostyn J. said that *Payne* supplies a tendency, "… and that tendency is the almost invariable success of the application, save in those cases where it is demonstrably irrational, absurd or malevolent. This ideology has not been uncritically accepted. Indeed there is a strong view that the heavy emphasis on the emotional reaction of the thwarted primary carer represents an illegitimate gloss on the purity of the paramountcy principle."

Payne and its predecessors, and the cases in which it has been consistently applied in English law, are strongly reliant on the primary carer status of the applicant. However, the Court of Appeal approved the *Payne* guidelines in *Re F (A Child) (Permission to Relocate)*,[342] and indicated that they could be utilised in relocation cases other than those where the applicant was the primary carer, provided the judge considered it helpful and appropriate to do so.

Although the volume of case law is notably smaller, it can be said that Scots law has not followed the approach adopted in *Payne*. The perspective of the Scottish courts is to view the matter exclusively through the "presumption-free"[343] prism of the welfare of the child.[344] In 2011, in *M v M*,[345] the Inner House held that the ratio of *Payne* formed no part of the law of Scotland.[346] The welfare of the children is the paramount consideration, and no special significance is accorded to the wishes of the primary carer.[347] Scottish courts, in practice as well as in theory, eschew the use of any rule or guideline which tends to favour the wishes or interests of either parent.[348] The approach of courts in Scotland is neither pro-relocation, nor anti-relocation: the welfare and best interests of the child are paramount, and fall to be judged "without any preconceived leaning in favour of the rights and interests of others."[349] In terms of burden of proof, however, Scots law, on the face of things, could be thought to be anti-relocation,

---

[339] *Re D* [2010] EWCA Civ 593.

[340] See also, however, *Re D* [2010] EWCA Civ 50, per Wall L.J.; and *Re W (Children)* [2011] EWCA Civ 345, per Wall L.J. at [128]; and *K v K (Relocation: Shared Care Arrangement) (also known as MK v CK)* [2011] EWCA Civ 793; [2011] 3 F.C.R. 111.

[341] *Re AR (A Child) (Relocation) (also known as F v M)* [2010] EWHC 1346 (Fam); [2010] 2 F.L.R. 157, per Mostyn J. at [7]–[8].

[342] *Re F (A Child) (Permission to Relocate)* [2012] EWCA Civ 1364; [2013] 1 F.L.R. 645.

[343] *Donaldson v Donaldson* [2014] CSIH 88; [2014] Fam. L.R. 126.

[344] *M v M* [2011] CSIH 65; [2011] Fam. L.R. 124, per Lord Emslie at [6]. cf. *G v G* [2014] CSOH 88; 2014 G.W.D. 17-323; and *H v H*, 2015 G.W.D. 19-318.

[345] *M v M* [2011] CSIH 65; [2011] Fam. L.R. 124. Also *S v S* [2012] GWD 11-209; [2012] Fam. L.R. 32.

[346] *M v M* [2011] CSIH 65; [2011] Fam. L.R. 124 at [15]. cf. *DY v LY* 2012 GWD 5-89, per Sheriff Thornton at [6] and [9].

[347] *M v M* [2011] CSIH 65; [2011] Fam. LR 124 at [39]. cf. *D v K*, 2011 GWD 20-469, per Sheriff Holligan, at [36]; and *M v G*, 2010 GWD 17-339 at [14]. *Sed quaere* approach of Sheriff McFarlane in *M v M*, 2010 GWD 39-790, who addressed herself expressly to the factors highlighted in *Payne*.

[348] cf. *Osborne v Matthan (No.2)*, 1998 S.C. 682, per Lord Caplan, at 704; and *S v S*, 2012 GWD 11-209; [2012] Fam. L.R. 32, per Lady Paton at [31].

[349] *M v M* [2011] CSIH 65; [2011] Fam. LR 124 at [9]. cf. *DY v LY*, 2012 GWD 5-89, per Sheriff Thornton at [9].

since the applicant spouse is required to discharge the onus that, from the child's perspective, it would be better that an order be made than that no order be made at all.[350]

Efforts have been made to advance the possibility of an international solution to tackle this social and legal problem, but there is as yet only a soft law instrument,[351] of the type which, invariably, has limited success.[352]

ADOPTION

14–81   Adoption is the form of procedure by which a person, the adoptee, becomes a member of the family of another person, the adopter. It has been said that adoption is a culture-specific legal entity. In this, it is perhaps unlike anything else so far studied under the heading of personal status, for while it is true that there are different types of marriage (monogamous, polygamous, etc.), and there are different methods of divorce (judicial, extrajudicial, etc.), the status of being married, or of being divorced, arguably has an agreed core of incidents. However, when considering recognition of foreign adoption orders, one of the difficulties which arises is that some legal systems favour "full" adoption, in which an individual who has the status of adopted person thereby extinguishes all links of parental influence, rights of aliment, support, property and succession, with his biological family; whereas other systems favour "simple" adoption, in which the break from the biological family is less absolute. Further, there is a difference between adoption by strangers, and adoption by blood relatives. In the latter case, contact with the biological family obviously will continue. Valid adoptions frequently bring in train benefits of citizenship, meaning that the topic often is closely linked with immigration issues.[353] The area of inter-country adoption, however, requires to be closely regulated and monitored due to the clear possibilities which exist for criminal behaviour and the exploitation of vulnerable persons.[354]

Within the domestic laws of Scotland and England, the state has a much stronger role in adoption than was the case in earlier days, and the subject of adoption straddles public and private law. The topic has an enhanced public profile in the conflict of laws, in view of the increased opportunity to "rescue" children from overseas, which may give rise to controversial cases often lacking statutory or Convention regulation.

Prior to the introduction of the Adoption and Children (Scotland) Act 2007 ("the 2007 Act"), adoption in Scots law was regulated primarily by the Adoption (Scotland) Act 1978,[355] incidentally by Pt III of the Children (Scotland) Act 1995

---

[350] Children (Scotland) Act 1995 s.11(7).

[351] e.g. *Washington Declaration on International Family Relocation*.

[352] cf. *Re H (A Child)* [2010] EWCA Civ 915; [2010] 2 F.L.R. 1875.

[353] *Re H (A Minor) (Adoption: Non-Patrial)* [1983] 4 F.L.R. 85. Contrast *Re B (A Minor) (Adoption Order: Nationality)* [1999] 1 F.L.R. 907.

[354] *Re F (A Minor) (Abduction: Custody Rights)* [1991] Fam. 25; and *Northumberland CC v Z* [2009] EWHC 498 (Fam).

[355] Based on the Adoption Act 1976 for England and Wales. For adoption law in England, see now the Adoption and Children Act 2002 (Ch.6 ss.83–91A re adoptions with a foreign element); the Adoptions with a Foreign Element Regulations 2005 (SI 2005/392); and the Adoptions with a Foreign

and also, as regards inter-country and overseas adoption, by the Adoption (Inter-country Aspects) Act 1999, an Act which made provision for giving effect in the UK to the 1993 Hague Convention on Protection of Children and Co-operation in Respect of Inter-country Adoption. The 2007 Act, which was introduced to modernise and improve adoption law in Scotland, repeals and very largely replaces the 1978 Act,[356] repeals Pt III of the 1995 Act, and repeals also very many of the provisions in the 1999 Act which applied in Scotland. Accordingly, in relation to inter-country adoptions, the relevant law now is to be found in Pt 1 Ch.6[357] of the 2007 Act, supplemented by the Adoptions with a Foreign Element (Scotland) Regulations 2009.[358]

An important distinction must be drawn between "Convention" adoptions and "non-Convention" (or overseas) adoptions. With regard to the former, the process involves a country which, like the UK, is a signatory to the 1993 Hague Convention. Non-Convention or overseas adoptions,[359] by contrast, concern a country which is on the UK's list of designated countries, set out in the Adoption (Designation of Overseas Adoptions) Order 1973.[360] In the main, the identity of the non-UK legal system involved in the inter-country adoption, be it the state of origin of the child in question, or the receiving state, will determine the classification of the adoption as Convention or non-Convention, and in turn the body of law which will regulate the adoption process.

Recognition of adoption orders

Intra-UK

There is reciprocal recognition of adoption orders intra-UK.[361]   **14–82**

Convention adoptions

The Adoption (Inter-country Aspects) Act 1999 brought into force in the UK the   **14–83**
1993 Hague Convention. The aim of the Convention is to improve certainty, orderliness and fairness in inter-country adoption, and to attempt to stop the trafficking of children. To this end, as with the 1980 Hague Convention on

---

Element (Amendment) Regulations 2009 (SI 2009/2563), all examined in *Cheshire, North and Fawcett: Private International Law*, 14th edn (2008), pp.1155–1177.

[356] With the exception of Pt IV ("Status of adopted children"), which remains in force in order to ensure that the status of such children is unaffected by the repeal of the 1978 Act.

[357] As amended by the Adoptions with a Foreign Element (Special Restrictions on Adoptions from Abroad) (Scotland) Regulations 2008 (SSI 2008/303).

[358] Adoptions with a Foreign Element (Scotland) Regulations 2009 (SSI 2009/182), as amended by the Adoptions with a Foreign Element (Scotland) Amendment Regulations 2010 (SSI 2010/173); and Registration of Foreign Adoptions (Scotland) Regulations 2003 (SSI 2003/67).

[359] Fn.377 re s.67(1) definition.

[360] Adoption (Designation of Overseas Adoptions) Order 1973 (SI 1973/19); and Adoption (Designation of Overseas Adoptions) (Variation) Order 1993 (SI 1993/690); and Adoption (Designation of Overseas Adoptions) (Variation) (Scotland) Order 1995 (SI 1995/1614). Designated countries include all western European countries, most members of the Commonwealth and UK dependent territories, South Africa, and USA. See, for England and Wales, Adoption and Children Act 2002 s.87.

[361] Adoption and Children (Scotland) Act 2007 s.77; and Adoption and Children Act 2002 s.105.

international child abduction, the Central Authorities of Contracting States play an important facilitating and safeguarding role.[362]

Part 3 of the Adoptions with a Foreign Element (Scotland) Regulations 2009[363] concerns Convention adoptions. Part 3 Ch.1[364] regulates the procedure which must be followed in Scotland when the UK is the receiving state, that is, for incoming adoptions, where a child is brought from outwith the British Islands to the UK for adoption, in accordance with the Convention, by a person or couple who is/are habitually resident in Britain. Part 3 Ch.2 of the 2009 Regulations regulates the procedure which must be followed in Scotland in the rarer case of an outgoing, i.e. where the UK is the state of origin, and a child who is habitually resident[365] in Britain is to be adopted, in accordance with the Convention, by a person or a couple who is/are habitually resident outwith Britain.[366]

Convention framework

14–84 The 1993 Convention shall apply where a child habitually resident in one Contracting State ("the state of origin") has been, is being, or is to be, moved to another Contracting State ("the receiving state"), either after his adoption, in the state of origin, by spouses or a person habitually resident in the receiving state, or for the purposes of such an adoption in the receiving state, or in the state of origin.[367] By art.2(2), the Convention covers only adoptions which create a permanent parent-child relationship. Certain agreements, for example of Central Authorities in the state of origin and the receiving state, must be obtained; the Convention ceases to apply if these agreements have not been given before the child attains the age of 18 years.[368]

Requirements for inter-country adoptions

14–85 In terms of art.4, an adoption within the scope of the Convention shall take place only if the competent authorities of the state of origin have established that the child is adoptable, and have determined, after giving due consideration to placement of the child within the state of origin, that an inter-country adoption is in the child's best interests. Presumably the criteria of "adoptability" (in all its aspects) and what is in the child's best interests must be tested according to the domestic law of the state of origin.

Further, the competent authorities of the state of origin must ensure that the persons, institution, and authorities whose consent is necessary for adoption have been counselled and informed of the effects of their consent, in particular on the matter whether the adoption will result in the termination of the legal relationship between the child and his family of origin; that such persons, etc. have given their consent freely in the required form, not induced by payment, and their consent has not since been withdrawn; and that the consent of the mother, where required,

---

[362] 1993 Hague Convention Ch.3 arts 6–13.
[363] Adoptions with a Foreign Element (Scotland) Regulations 2009 (SSI 2009/182), as amended.
[364] Adoptions with a Foreign Element (Scotland) Regulations 2009 regs 10–37.
[365] cf. in England, *Greenwich LBC v S* [2007] EWHC 820 (Fam).
[366] Adoptions with a Foreign Element (Scotland) Regulations 2009 regs 38–52.
[367] 1993 Convention art.2(1).
[368] 1993 Convention art.3.

has been given only after the birth of the child. Further, the authorities must ensure that the child has been counselled and informed of the effects of the adoption; that consideration has been given to the child's wishes and opinions; and that his consent, where required, has been given freely in the required legal form, uninduced by payment. These latter requirements are to be given effect having regard to the age and degree of maturity of the child.

In terms of art.5, a Convention adoption shall take place only if the competent authorities of the receiving state have determined that the prospective adoptive parents are eligible and suited to adopt; have been counselled, as may be necessary; and have determined that the child is or will be authorised to enter and reside permanently in that state. Presumably "eligibility", in all its aspects, must be tested according to the domestic law of the receiving state.

Jurisdiction—applications to adopt

There is no chapter in the 1993 Convention specifically devoted to jurisdiction. It **14–86** would appear that the only criterion to enable parties to utilise the inter-country adoption process provided is that the parties be habitually resident in a Contracting State, and that the child be habitually resident in another Contracting State. But perhaps this approach to jurisdiction provision is appropriate in the circumstances which the Convention seeks to address.

By art.14, persons habitually resident in a Contracting State who wish to adopt a child habitually resident in another Contracting State[369] shall apply to the Central Authority in the state of their habitual residence.

If that Central Authority is satisfied that the applicants are eligible, and suited to adopt, it shall prepare a background report, to be transmitted to the Central Authority of the state of origin. If that Central Authority is satisfied that the child is adoptable, it shall prepare a background report (e.g. on the child's medical history and cultural background), ensuring that consents have been obtained in accordance with art.4; and shall determine whether the envisaged placement is in the best interests of the child. This report shall be transmitted to the Central Authority of the receiving state, with proof that the necessary consents have been obtained, taking care not to reveal the identity of the natural parents, if in the state of origin these identities may not be disclosed.

In terms of art.17, any decision in the state of origin that a child should be entrusted to prospective adoptive parents, may be made only if the Central Authority of that state has ensured that the prospective adoptive parents agree; that the Central Authority of the receiving state has approved such a decision, where such approval is necessary by the law of that state or by the Central Authority [*sic*] of the state of origin; that the Central Authorities of both states have agreed that the adoption will proceed; and that, in accordance with art.5, the prospective adoptive parents are eligible and suited to adopt, and that the child is or will be authorised to enter and reside permanently in the receiving state. The Central Authorities of both states shall take all necessary steps to obtain permission for the child to leave the state of origin, and to enter and reside permanently in the receiving state.

---

[369] This is the (only) qualifying scenario.

Where the adoption is to take place after the transfer of the child to the receiving state, and it appears to the Central Authority of that state that the continued placement of the child with the prospective adoptive parents is not in the child's best interests, such Central Authority shall take the necessary measures to protect the child (which may include arranging temporary care, or a new placement, or, as a last resort, arranging the return of the child to the state of origin, if his interests so require). Having regard to the age and degree of maturity of the child, he shall be consulted, and where appropriate, his consent to these measures obtained.[370]

Recognition and effects of adoption

14–87   The main challenge for the draftsmen of the Convention was the crafting of recognition provisions which are apt to cover recognition of a status which varies from country to country, some adoption laws effecting full adoption, and others only simple adoption. An adoption certified by the competent authority of the state of the adoption (being the state of origin, or the receiving state, as the case may be), as having been made in accordance with the Convention, shall be recognised as having operation of law in the other Contracting States.[371] The recognition of an adoption may be refused in a Contracting State only if the adoption is manifestly contrary to its public policy, taking into account the best interests of the child.[372]

What does recognition of an adoption connote? In terms of art.26(1), the recognition of an adoption includes recognition of (a) the legal parent-child relationship between the child and his/her adoptive parents; (b) parental responsibility of the adoptive parents for the child; and (c) the termination of a pre-existing legal relationship between the child and his/her biological parents, if the adoption has this effect in the Contracting State where it was made. By art.26(2), where an adoption has the effect of terminating a pre-existing legal parent-child relationship, the child shall enjoy in the receiving state, and in any other Contracting State where the adoption is recognised, rights equivalent to those resulting from adoptions having this effect in each such state.[373] Conversely, by art.27(1), where an adoption granted in the state of origin is less than full, it may, in the receiving state which recognises the adoption under the Convention, be converted into a full adoption (a) if the law of the receiving state so permits; and (b) if the consents referred to in art.4 have been, or are, given for the purpose of such adoption. If so, recognition of the conversion will be guaranteed by art.23 in the same way as recognition of any other qualifying adoption.

---

[370] 1993 Convention art.21.
[371] 1993 Convention art.23.
[372] 1993 Convention art.24.
[373] Hence, if an adoption is carried out under a law which operates "full adoptions", then that full status shall be enjoyed in the receiving state and essentially in all other Contracting States. However, art.26(3) provides that the child shall have the benefit of any more favourable provision which is in force in a recognising Contracting State.

General provisions

Chapter VI contains general provisions, of an administrative or a policy[374] nature. By art.28, the Convention does not affect any law of the state of origin which requires that the adoption of a child habitually resident within that state take place in that state, or which prohibits the child's placement in, or transfer to, the receiving state prior to adoption.

14–88

The 1993 Convention is an important contribution in an area of law which is difficult to regulate. Its provisions appear to contain many safeguards for the child, and for those whose consent to inter-country adoption is necessary. Its value will be judged according to the degree of international support which it commands.[375] The dual responsibility of the state of origin and the receiving state is a noteworthy characteristic. The Convention contains ex facie fewer conflict rules than might be expected; indeed they must be searched out, and/or inferred. The most notable absence is of any express mention of choice of law amid much facilitative and precautionary provision. There are many problems of a factual and evidential nature in this branch of the conflict of laws, e.g. location of the biological parents of a child, and obtaining sufficient evidence of their consent to removal of the child, and in any given case such problems are likely to be as, or more, acute than the legal problems.

Non-Convention adoptions[376]

As explained above, non-Convention or overseas adoptions,[377] are adoptions to or from a country which is on the UK's list of designated countries, set out in the Adoption (Designation of Overseas Adoptions) Order 1973.[378] Many countries designated for this purpose also are party to the 1993 Hague Convention, but an adoption from such a Contracting State still may be treated as an overseas adoption if, for some factual reason, the adoption does not satisfy the particular requirements of the Convention. An overseas adoption will have equivalent effect in Scotland to a Scottish adoption.

14–89

The requirements for non-Convention cases are set out in Pt 1 Ch.6 of the Adoption and Children (Scotland) Act 2007. The 2007 Act places restrictions on

---

[374] e.g. art.32: no-one shall derive improper financial or other gain from an activity related to an inter-country adoption.

[375] As of 1 July 2015 there are 95 Contracting States to the 1993 Convention. Recognition of adoptions from certain specified countries can be suspended because of concerns about child trafficking. In *R (on the application of Thomson) v Minister of State for Children* [2006] 1 F.L.R. 175 claimant British citizens unsuccessfully applied for judicial review of a decision by the Secretary of State to impose a temporary suspension on inter-country adoptions from Cambodia, and forbidding them to proceed. See, for England and Wales, Children and Adoption Act 2006 Pt 2 ss.9–14.

[376] "Overseas adoptions" per s.67(1) of the 2007 Act.

[377] Section 67(1) of the 2007 Act defines an overseas adoption as one effected under the law of any country or territory outwith the British Islands (that is, the UK, Channel Islands and Isle of Man), and which is not a Convention adoption.

[378] Adoption (Designation of Overseas Adoptions) Order 1973 (SI 1973/19); and Adoption (Designation of Overseas Adoptions) (Variation) Order 1993 (SI 1993/690); and Adoption (Designation of Overseas Adoptions) (Variation) (Scotland) Order 1995 (SI 1995/1614). Designated countries include all western European countries, most members of the Commonwealth and UK dependent territories, South Africa, and USA. See, for England and Wales, Adoption and Children Act 2002 s.87.

incoming adoptions of children to the UK, as well as on outgoing adoptions of children from the UK. Additionally, Pt 2[379] of the Adoptions with a Foreign Element (Scotland) Regulations 2009[380] makes provision for non-Convention adoptions.

Part 2 Ch.1[381] lays down rules for cases where a child is brought into the UK in circumstances where s.58 of the 2007 Act applies.[382] Regulations 3 and 4 prescribe the requirements which must be met and the conditions which must be satisfied by prospective adopters before a child may be brought into the UK. Regulation 5 imposes functions on the local authority which apply when the child has been brought into the UK and the prospective adopters have given notice of their intention to apply for an adoption order. Part 2 Ch.2 applies to the more unusual case of where a child is to be taken out of the UK for overseas adoption. Regulations 7 and 8 lay down the requirements which must be met before an order may be made under s.59[383] of the 2007 Act.[384]

Section 60 of the 2007 Act makes it an offence for any person to take or send a protected child[385] out of Great Britain to any place outwith the British Islands with a view to the adoption of that child. By virtue of s.62 of the 2007 Act,[386] if Scottish Ministers have reason to believe that, because of adoption practices taking place in an overseas country, it would be contrary to public policy to further the bringing of children into the UK from such countries, special restrictions may be ordered to prevent such movement.[387]

Adoption orders at common law

14–90   Where a foreign adoption does not qualify as a Convention case under the 2009 Regulations, or as an overseas adoption under the 2007 Act, a question of recognition will arise at common law. In such a case, where the matter falls to be decided without legislative guidance, there is support for application of old principles of recognition on the basis of domicile,[388] or "recognition by"[389] the

---

[379] With the exception of reg.9.

[380] Foreign Element (Scotland) Regulations 2009 (SSI 2009/182), as amended.

[381] Foreign Element (Scotland) Regulations 2009 (SSI 2009/182) regs 3–6.

[382] That is, where a British resident brings or causes another to bring a child into the UK for the purposes of adoption or where they bring or cause another to bring a child adopted by a British resident under an external adoption effected within a period of 12 months from that adoption. Section 58(3) makes clear that the provision has no application if a child is intended to be adopted under a Convention adoption order.

[383] That is, a preliminary order vesting parental responsibilities and rights in the prospective adopters where a child is to be adopted abroad.

[384] cf. in England and Wales, *Re G (A Child) (Adoption: Placement outside Jurisdiction) (aka C v X Local Authority)* [2008] EWCA Civ 105; and *A LBC v Department for Children, Schools and Families* [2009] EWCA Civ 41; [2010] Fam. 9.

[385] Defined in s.60(9) as a child who is habitually resident in the UK or a Commonwealth citizen.

[386] Also the Adoptions with a Foreign Element (Special Restrictions on Adoptions from Abroad) (Scotland) Regulations 2008 (SSI 2008/303); and, for England and Wales, the Adoptions with a Foreign Element (Special Restrictions on Adoptions from Abroad) Regulations 2008 (SI 2008/1807).

[387] cf. for England and Wales, suspensions on inter-country adoption per Children and Adoption Act 2006 Pt 2 ss.9–14.

[388] *Re Wilson (Deceased)* [1954] Ch. 733; *Re Wilby* [1956] P. 174; *Re Marshall* [1957] Ch. 507; *Re Valentine's Settlement* [1965] Ch. 831; *Re N (Recognition of Foreign Adoption Order)* [2010] 1 F.L.R. 1102; [2010] Fam. Law 12; and *T v OCC* [2010] EWHC 964 (Fam); [2011] 1 F.L.R. 1487; [2011] Fam. Law 337. In *Re R (A Child) (Recognition of Indian Adoption)* [2012] EWHC 2956 (Fam);

law of domicile of the adoptive parents, or one of them. Recognition of an adoption order at common law does not necessarily require giving effect to all the incidents of that adoption.[390] Moreover, a foreign adoption may be denied recognition if recognition would be contrary to public policy, or to the best interests of the child.[391]

CROSS-BORDER SURROGACY

Domestic legal systems vary markedly in their attitudes to surrogacy, that is, the practice whereby a woman, on a commercial or altruistic basis, and whether or not using her own eggs, becomes pregnant with the intention of giving the child to someone else upon birth. At present, there is no UK or EU private international law measure which regulates cross-border surrogacy agreements, or the legal effects thereof. The question has been asked whether there is a need for the articulation of rules and the establishment of standards legally binding on EU Member States[392] in connection with cross-border surrogacy,[393] and work is under way at the Hague Conference to address the question whether or not there is a need for an international legal response to seek to regulate the phenomenon on a global level.[394]

14–91

One of the basic difficulties in seeking to regulate this area is that there is no uniform cross-border surrogacy arrangement. In general, the main participants

---

[2013] 1 F.L.R. 148, Hedley J. at [14] followed *Re Valentine's Settlement*, as interpreted in light of the abolition of spousal unity of domicile. See further, in England, *Re G (Children) (Recognition of Brazilian adoption)* [2014] EWHC 2605 (Fam); and, in Scotland, *Brown, Petrs*, 2015 G.W.D. 20-341.

[389] On analogy of *Armitage v Att Gen* [1906] P. 135 (divorce); and *Abate v Abate* [1961] P. 29 (nullity), though this principle has ceased to apply in "proceedings" divorce and nullity recognition: Family Law Act 1986 s.46(1).

[390] Ch.10, above.

[391] e.g. *Re MN (Non-recognised Adoptions: Unlawful Discrimination: India)* [2008] EWCA Civ 38; and *A County Council v M* [2013] EWHC 1501 (Fam); [2014] 1 F.L.R. 881; [2013] Fam. Law 933. *Contra D v D* [2008] EWHC 403 (Fam).

[392] See, for detailed analysis, European Parliament, Directorate General for Internal Policies Policy Department C: Citizens' Rights And Constitutional Affairs Legal Affairs: "A Comparative Study on the Regime of Surrogacy in the EU Member States" [PE 474.403] (2013), Ch 4 – Legal Analysis: Private International Law (pp.159–191) (J.M. Carruthers).

[393] If a regional, EU regime were to be proposed, there would have to be determined the extent to which only minimal factual connection with an EU Member State would bring the case *within* the remit of the putative EU regime, e.g. if neither the surrogate mother nor the intended parent(s) were habitually resident in an EU Member State, but some element of the reproductive procedure should take place within the EU, or the agency has a presence in an EU Member State, or the egg donor is habitually resident in the EU. Conversely, it would require to be determined to what extent one or more connection(s) with a Third State would remove the case beyond the reach of a putative EU regime.

[394] Hague Conference on Private International Law: *Project on the private international law issues surrounding the status of children, including issues arising from international surrogacy arrangements*: http://www.hcch.net/index_en.php?act=text.display&tid=178 [accessed 20 June 2015]. See, e.g. Hague Conference Permanent Bureau, *The Desirability and Feasibility of Further Work on The Parentage / Surrogacy Project* (Prel. Doc. No 3 B) (April 2014); Hague Conference Permanent Bureau, *A Study of Legal Parentage and the Issues arising from International Surrogacy Arrangements* (Prel. Doc. No 3 C) (March 2014). See also K. Trimmings and P. Beaumont (eds), *International Surrogacy Arrangements: Legal Regulation at the International Level* (Oxford: Hart Publishing) (2013).

are the surrogate mother; the surrogacy services provider ("the agency"); the intended parent(s); the egg donor, in cases of gestational surrogacy/collaborative use of bodily materials; the putative child; and other consenting parties, such as the surrogate mother's spouse/partner.

Legal complications emerge where the factual matrix of the surrogacy arrangement involves more than one legal system. A number of legal systems potentially will be interested in the form and content of the arrangement, including the state of origin (i.e. the personal law, say, habitual residence) of the surrogate mother; the receiving state (i.e. the personal law, say, habitual residence) of the intended parent(s); the principal place of business of the surrogacy services provider (if any), and any branch office thereof; the locus of reproductive procedure/services; the place of birth of child (which is likely to coincide with state of origin of the surrogate mother); and the personal law of the child (say, its habitual residence, arguably coinciding with the state of origin, depending on the facts). Potentially, on the facts, there are many more links to different legal systems than normally are present in an international family dispute, by reason of the number of persons, and contracts, likely to be present.

Viewing the subject through a conflict of laws lens, it is a notable lack that there are, at present, no harmonised rules allocating jurisdiction in the cross-border surrogacy context, even though disputes potentially requiring court determination may arise pertaining to any one or more of the following issues:

— the process of negotiation of contractual terms between the surrogate mother and the putative intended parent(s), with or without an intermediate surrogacy services provider ("contractual issues")[395];

— the process of enforcement of agreements entered into by the surrogate mother and intended parent(s), and resolution of disputes pertaining to, e.g. alleged non-performance or defective performance of the contractual terms, including (non-) payment of expenses/compensation to the surrogate mother; and, on the other side, the production and delivery of a child ("enforcement issues");

— the process of assessment of participants' eligibility/suitability to act as surrogate mother or putative intended parent(s), respectively, and of securing due consents ("regulatory issues");

— the conferral of legal parenthood in respect of a child born or to be born, and the attribution of parental rights and responsibilities ("parental civil status issues"); and/or

— the determination of a child's status, incidents of his status, and rights, including his permitted departure from the state of origin, entry to the receiving state, and citizenship ("child civil status issues").

With regard to applicable law, the question of what law governs the various legal issues which arise in connection with cross-border surrogacy is one of pivotal importance. At present, since there is no harmonised private international law regulation of surrogacy per se, an individual forum will apply to the facts and

---

[395] There may be an anterior or parallel contract between/among the surrogate mother, the intended parent(s), the surrogacy services provider, and an egg donor, from which contractual issues may derive.

circumstances of a particular case its own national choice of law rules, on a case by case basis. In the UK, however, as in many countries, there are no national choice of law rules to deal in a systematic way with cross-border surrogacy.

Insofar as a surrogacy arrangement is contractual in nature, it is important, at the outset, to note the non-applicability of Rome I; by art.1.2(a) and (b), contractual obligations involving the status or legal capacity of natural persons, and contractual obligations arising out of family relationships are excluded from the scope of the instrument.[396] Hence, any EU court currently must apply its own international private law rules pertaining to contractual obligations in order to assess the validity and enforceability of a cross-border surrogacy contract. Contractual issues might arise pertaining to the capacity to contract of the intended parents and of the surrogate mother; the question of the formal, essential and material[397] validity of the arrangement, and matters of interpretation thereof. Moreover, performance issues may arise, such as satisfactory discharge of contract, and remedies for non-performance by surrogate mother, including frustration by way, e.g. of miscarriage or abortion, or responsibility for "over-performance" by way of multiple birth. Equivalent questions may emerge vis-à-vis non-performance by the intended parents, including total or partial non-payment, or repudiation of contract. An important issue is likely to be that of payment of compensation/remuneration to the surrogate mother, as well as her costs and expenses. Familiar contractual questions such as the application of mandatory protective provisions, e.g. of the forum are likely to be relevant, as is the public policy of that court.

In speculating as to the formulation of choice of law rules for this subject area, it is impossible to ignore the essential contractual component of cross-border surrogacy arrangements, which is stronger than, e.g. in inter-country adoption. On the other hand, there is a close parallel with inter-country adoption, and of the patent need for child welfare safeguards, which tend to the conclusion that matters cannot be left entirely to party autonomy/contractual regulation. There is an important difference between the contractual consequences of a cross-border surrogacy arrangement, and issues of personal status *contra mundum*.

Civil status issues liable to arise include the matter of legal parentage (i.e. the parent/child relationship based on bio-genetic affinity), and the legal effects thereof; and legal parenthood (being the attribution of parental status, i.e. the attribution of legal status to someone as the parent of a child), and the legal effects thereof. Related issues include authorisation of a child's departure from his state of origin and entry to the receiving state; and the conferral of citizenship/nationality of a child born from surrogacy. The choice of law governance of these issues currently is unregulated, though probably, in a UK court, would be distributed between the law of the state of origin and the law of the receiving state, perhaps according to which coincides with the *lex fori*.

It should be appreciated that against a background of widely varying attitudes to surrogacy, ranging between the extremes of absolute prohibition and an anti-commercialisation agenda, on the one hand, and the direct encouragement of

14–92

---

[396] cf. non-applicability of Rome II (art.1.2(a)), meaning that a claim in unjust enrichment would not be regulated thereby.

[397] e.g. ensuring a party giving consent understands the effect and consequences of that decision; and ensuring that consent was given freely, and not induced.

commercial arrangements and of "reproductive tourism", on the other, striking international accord on this subject is likely to be difficult to achieve. If, as a matter of policy, however, it should be deemed appropriate to seek to negotiate a common EU or global approach to the range of possible issues arising, rules of jurisdiction allocation may be less appropriate than would be a framework of regulation and co-operation through central authorities, such as is found in the 1993 Hague Adoption Convention.[398] Although the Adoption Convention does not lay down *expressis verbis* rules of jurisdiction or applicable law, nonetheless it may yield assistance as a template for rules of cross-border surrogacy. The model of that Convention, which does not require national adoption laws to be uniform, could be a workable basis for formulating an international instrument on cross-border surrogacy, principally by establishing minimum standards and safeguards, and by facilitating international co-operation, co-ordination and supervision through the creation and use of central authorities.

Section 54 parental orders

14–93   Such cross-border cases as presently come before UK courts tend to present as applications, under s.54 of the Human Fertilisation & Embryology Act 2008,[399] for a "parental order", namely, one which provides "for a child to be treated in law as the child of the applicants". Section 54 contains many requirements, e.g. as to jurisdiction[400]; substance, namely, that the surrogate mother has freely and unconditionally agreed to the making of the order[401]; that no money or other benefit has been given or received[402]; and that the applicants must apply for the order within six months of the child's birth.[403] An examination of UK case law reveals the facilitative character of the judgments, recognising the reality of the situation; the domestic UK prohibition and associated policy objection against payment for surrogacy services cannot be upheld in a cross-border situation in which the child has a putative home in the UK with the commissioning parents, and no home or status in the legal system of the surrogate mother.[404] Typically the English forum will find that payments made by commissioning parents were not so disproportionate to expenses reasonably incurred by the surrogate mother that the granting of the parental order in favour of the former is an affront to public policy,[405] and in many cases there is retrospective judicial authorisation of

---

[398] Para.14–84 et seq., above.

[399] Human Fertilisation & Embryology Act 1990 ex-s.30.

[400] Human Fertilisation & Embryology Act 2008 s.54(4): at the time of the application and the making of the order—(a) the child's home must be with the applicants; and (b) either or both of the applicants must be domiciled in the United Kingdom or in the Channel Islands or the Isle of Man. See e.g. *Re A (Parental Order: Domicile) (orwise A) v SA* [2013] EWHC 426 (Fam); and *Re Q (A Child) (Parental Order: Domicile)* [2014] EWHC 1307 (Fam); [2014] Fam. Law 1256.

[401] Human Fertilisation & Embryology Act 2008 s.54(6).

[402] Human Fertilisation & Embryology Act 2008 s.54(8).

[403] Human Fertilisation & Embryology Act 2008 s.54(3). Though see *Re X (A Child) (Surrogacy: Time Limit)* [2014] EWHC 3135.

[404] *Re IJ (A Child) (Foreign Surrogacy Agreement: Parental Order)* [2011] EWHC 921 (Fam).

[405] e.g. *Re L (A Child) (Parental Order: Foreign Surrogacy)* [2010] EWHC 3146 (Fam); [2011] Fam. 106; *J v G (Parental Orders)* [2013] EWHC 1432 (Fam); [2014] 1 F.L.R. 297; and *Re G (Parental Orders)* [2014] EWHC 1561 (Fam); [2014] Fam. Law 1114.

payment.[406] Equally, where the necessary consents have not and cannot be obtained, often for the reason that the surrogate mother cannot be found, the court will dispense with that requirement.[407] Case law shows that it will normally be in a child's best interests for the court to grant the s.54 application,[408] and applications for parental orders regularly are granted, *faute de mieux*.

SUMMARY 14

1. Status.   **14–94**
    The status of legitimacy and of legitimation have the potential to be relevant in Scots conflict cases. By s.41 of the Family Law (Scotland) Act 2006, any question arising as to the effect on a person's status of his/her parents being, or having been, married to each other, or not being, or not having been, married to each other, shall be determined by the law of that person's domicile at the time at which the question arises.
2. Parental rights and responsibilities.
    Article 61 of Brussels II *bis* ranks that Regulation above the relevant provisions of the 1996 Hague Convention where the child in question is habitually resident in an EU Member State.
    Brussels II *bis* shall apply: (a) where the child concerned has his or her habitual residence on the territory of a Member State; and (b) as concerns the recognition and enforcement of a judgment given in a court of a Member State on the territory of another Member State, even if the child concerned has his or her habitual residence on the territory of a third State which is a contracting Party to the said Convention.
    If the child in question is not habitually resident in an EU Member State, but is habitually resident in a (non-EU) state which is a Contracting State to the 1996 Hague Convention, the Convention will apply.
    Where neither Brussels II *bis*, nor the 1996 Hague Convention, applies, the residual rules of Scots law contained in the Family Law Act 1986 are available.
    Allocation of jurisdiction and conflicting jurisdictions: see Brussels II *bis*, arts 8–15; 1996 Hague Convention arts 5–14; failing which, Family Law Act 1986 ss.8–18.
    Choice of law: the 1996 Hague Convention lays down rules concerning applicable law (arts 15–22). The general rule under art.15(1) is that the forum, in exercising jurisdiction under Ch.II (arts 5–14) of the Convention, shall apply its own law. By way of exception to art.15(1), art.15(2) provides that, insofar as the protection of the person or the property of the child requires, the court may apply or take into consideration the law of another state with which the situation has a substantial connection, even if the law designated is the law of a non-Contracting State.

---

[406] e.g. *Re X (Children) (Parental Order: Retrospective Authorisation of Payments)* [2011] EWHC 3147; [2012] 1 F.L.R. 1347.

[407] Human Fertilisation & Embryology Act 2008 s.54(7); e.g. *Re D (Minors) (Surrogacy)* [2012] EWHC 2631 (Fam); [2013] Fam. Law 38; [2013] 1 W.L.R. 3135.

[408] *Re C (A Child) (Parental Order)* [2013] EWHC 2413 (Fam); [2014] 1 F.L.R. 654. cf. *C v S*, 1996 S.L.T. 1387.

The reference to Ch.II in art.15 of the Convention is to be read as including a reference to Ch.II of Brussels II *bis* (arts 8–20), meaning that the applicable law provisions of the 1996 Convention will apply also where a UK forum is exercising jurisdiction under Brussels II *bis*.

The residual rules of Scots law are to be found in s.14 of the Children (Scotland) Act 1995.

Recognition and enforcement of parental responsibility orders: see Brussels II *bis* arts 21–36; 1996 Hague Convention arts 23–28; failing which, Family Law Act 1986 ss.27–29.

3.   Guardianship and administration of property.

Under Brussels II *bis*, the definition of parental responsibility, and of the holder thereof, is apt to cover a person who in Scots law would be regarded as a guardian. Likewise, under art.3(c) of the 1996 Hague Convention, the measures referred to in art.1 as protecting the person or property of a child, may deal with guardianship, curatorship and analogous institutions. Accordingly, in relation to guardianship, as for other aspects of parental responsibility, the pre-existing jurisdictional rules of Scots law contained in the Family Law Act 1986 ss.9–12, now operate only as residual national rules.

With regard to orders concerning the administration of a child's property, the Children (Scotland) Act 1995 ss.9, 10, and 14 apply, subject to the rules contained in Brussels II *bis* and the 1996 Hague Convention. For residual cases, s.14(3) directs the forum to apply the law of the child's habitual residence, subject to a discretionary power, in terms of the 1995 Act, to regard the welfare of the child as the paramount consideration.

4.   International child abduction.

The primary legislation in the UK is the Child Abduction and Custody Act 1985, which brought into effect the 1980 Hague Convention on the civil aspects of international child abduction. In a qualifying (intra-EU) case, the 1980 Convention is complemented by Brussels II *bis* arts 10 and 11.

In incoming common law cases falling outside the scope of the above instruments, the Scottish court will act in what it perceives in its discretion to be the best interests of the child. There is no warrant, in statute or authority, for the principles of the Hague Convention to be extended to abductions involving countries which are not party to the Convention.

5.   Inter-country adoption

The relevant legislation for Scotland is the Adoption and Children (Scotland) Act 2007 Pt I Ch.6, supplemented by the Adoptions with a Foreign Element (Scotland) Regulations 2009.

The categories of foreign adoptions are:

(a)   Convention adoptions, regulated by the 1993 Hague Convention and Pt 3 of the Adoptions with a Foreign Element (Scotland) Regulations 2009 (SSI 2009/182);

(b)   non-Convention or overseas adoptions, regulated by Pt 1 Ch.6 of the Adoption and Children (Scotland) Act 2007; and Pt 2 of the Adoptions with a Foreign Element (Scotland) Regulations 2009; and referring to adoptions to or from a country designated in the Adoption (Designation of Overseas Adoptions) Order 1973; and

(c)   common law adoptions.

6.   Cross-border surrogacy

There is no international or regional instrument governing this practice. In the UK, consideration of the validity and effect of a cross-border surrogacy arrangement typically presents as an application on behalf of commissioning parents for a parental order under s.54 of the Human Fertilisation and Embryology Act 2008.

CHAPTER 15

The law of contractual obligations

GENERAL MATTERS AND GOVERNING LAW

Classification

The question whether a cross-border case is to be treated as pertaining to contract, or to some other legal category, is determined by the *lex fori*.[1] For conflict of laws purposes it is not essential, in order to characterise a problem as contractual, that there be present all the domestic requirements of the *lex fori* for the constitution of a contract; it is sufficient that, in the view of the forum, the broad elements of a contractual obligation exist.[2]

15–01

Legislative background to choice of law

Choice of law rules in contract are contained in Regulation 593/2008 on the law applicable to contractual obligations (Rome I)[3] (henceforth "Rome I Regulation"). This Regulation replaces the Rome Convention on the law applicable to contractual obligations (henceforth "Rome I Convention"), and applies, in situations involving a conflict of laws,[4] to contractual obligations in civil and commercial matters.

15–02

It is clear from art.24.2 of the Rome I Regulation that insofar as the Regulation replaces the provisions of the Rome I Convention, any reference (in any instrument) to that Convention shall be understood as a reference to the Regulation. It is to be assumed that, apart from autonomous definitions newly inserted in the Regulation,[5] and where the provisions of the Regulation do not differ substantially in their meaning and purpose from those in the Convention,

---

[1] *De Nicols v Curlier (No.1)* [1900] A.C. 21; *Earl of Stair v Head* (1846) 6 D. 904; and *Krupp Uhde GmbH v Weir Westgarth Ltd* unreported 31 May 2002, CSOH, per Lord Eassie.

[2] *Re Bonacina* [1912] 2 Ch. 394. cf. Private International Law (Miscellaneous Provisions) Act 1995 s.9(2).

[3] See F. Ferrari and S. Lieble (eds), *Rome I Regulation: The Law Applicable to Contractual Obligations in Europe* (Munich: Sellier, 2009); and R. Plender and M. Wilderspin, *The European Private International Law of Obligations*, 4th edn (London: Sweet & Maxwell, 2014).

[4] Contrast the wording used by the Rome I Convention, the rules of which applied to contractual obligations "in any situation involving a choice of law between the laws of different countries" (art.1.1).

[5] e.g. Regulation arts 9(1) and 19.

the principle of continuity of interpretation ("vertical continuity")[6] should apply, leading to the conclusion that the body of jurisprudence interpretative of the Rome I Convention may be referred to and relied on in interpretation of the Regulation. It is desirable that the related principle of "horizontal continuity" should apply in the interpretation of cognate instruments. This means that the substantive scope and content of the Rome I Regulation should be construed consistently with the Rome II Regulation, and with the relevant jurisdiction provisions in the Brussels I and Brussels I Recast Regulations.[7]

In this chapter, all references to legislation, unless otherwise specified, are to the Regulation, not the Convention. The body of case law interpretative of the Regulation, though growing, is still small, and so, unless otherwise stated, cases cited in this chapter have been decided according to the Rome I Convention or the common law. Rarely, a case on its facts may require application both of the Convention and the Regulation, as where, for example, there is a series of contracts between the transacting parties, some of which pre-date and some of which post-date application of the Rome I Regulation.[8]

The Rome I Convention was brought into force in the UK, with effect from 1 April 1991, by means of the Contracts (Applicable Law) Act 1990, in respect of contracts entered into after that date.[9] On 14 January 2003 the EC Commission published a Green Paper entitled "Conversion of the Rome Convention of 1980 on the Law Applicable to Contractual Obligations into a Community Instrument and its Modernisation" ("Green Paper").[10] The Commission sought views on whether the Convention should be converted into a Regulation, and upon whether, in any event, the substantive provisions ought to be amended in light of experience. The Commission pointed out that at Community level the Rome Convention was the only international private law instrument then still in the form of an international treaty, and suggested that in this important commercial area, the rules of jurisdiction, on the one hand, and of choice of law, on the other, should not be governed by different types of instrument. Proceeding by way of Regulation, rather than, say, by Directive, was said to be appropriate where an entire subject area (the private international law of contractual obligations) was to be harmonised, not simply a particular aspect of that area, and, being directly applicable, meant that harmonisation measures would enter into force in all Member States contemporaneously. The separate argument that a Regulation would achieve the desirable aim of clothing the Court of Justice of the EU ("CJEU") with jurisdiction to hear appeals on matters concerning the interpretation of Rome I (with the aim of having legal concepts common to Brussels and Rome interpreted in like manner), was less persuasive since the entry into force of the Brussels Protocol, q.v.[11]

---

[6] i.e. from foundation instrument to current instrument, e.g. 1968 Brussels Convention, Brussels I Regulation, and Brussels I Recast; cf. para.7–13, above. See E.B. Crawford and J.M. Carruthers, "Connection and Coherence between and among European Instruments in the Private International Law of Obligations" (2014) 63 I.C.L.Q. 1.

[7] Rome I Regulation recital (7).

[8] e.g. *OJSC TNK-BP Holding v Lazurenko* [2012] EWHC 2781 (Ch).

[9] Rome I Convention art.17.

[10] COM(2002) 654 final.

[11] Green Paper para.3.2.11.

In December 2005 the Commission presented a Proposal for a Regulation of the European Parliament and the Council on the law applicable to contractual obligations (Rome I).[12] Publication of the proposal was greeted in the UK with scepticism, since it could be seen that the draft instrument went further than an updating exercise and proposed certain fundamental changes and new provisions likely, in the UK view, to introduce uncertainty in complex international contracts. The initial reaction of the UK government was against opting-in.[13] Nonetheless, the Government continued to participate in negotiations with a view to securing improvements in the text from the UK's point of view. Eventually, an accommodation or compromise having been reached, and following consultation of interested parties,[14] a request[15] was made by the UK to permit acceptance of, and participation in, the Regulation. The Commission gave a positive response,[16] with the result that the Rome I Regulation entered into force in the UK on 22 December 2008.[17] The Regulation is applied by Member State courts, including those of the UK, to qualifying cases concerning contracts concluded on and after[18] 17 December 2009.[19]

Although there are similarities between the provisions of the Rome I Regulation and its Convention predecessor, and the pre-existing common law rules of Scotland and England, it would be wrong to regard the Regulation or the Convention as a codification of common law rules.[20] Where the Rome I Regulation does not apply (art.1: scope), or where it is silent on an issue,[21] the common law continues to apply, as it does to all contracts entered into before 1 April 1991.[22] As a result, Scots and English choice of law rules in contract are found principally in the Regulation, but subsidiarily in the common law, which should be regarded as the backdrop.

The coming into force of the Rome I Regulation does not prejudice the application of other international conventions to which a Member State is a party and which lay down conflict of laws rules relating to contractual obligations (e.g. conventions on carriage).[23] But, as between Member States, the Regulation shall take precedence over conventions concluded exclusively between two or more of them insofar as such conventions concern matters governed by the Regulation.[24]

---

[12] COM(2005) 650 final.
[13] Rome I Regulation recital (45).
[14] Ministry of Justice, *Rome I—Should the UK opt in?* (The Stationery Office, 2008), Consultation Paper CP05/08.
[15] Notified under Doc. C(2008) 8554 [2008] O.J. L177.
[16] Commission Opinion, COM(2008) 730 final.
[17] Decision 2009/26/EC on the request of the United Kingdom to accept Regulation (EC) No.593/2008 on the law applicable to contractual obligations [2009] O.J. L10/22.
[18] Corrigendum to the Rome I Regulation 13497/1/09, REV 1, JUR369 [2008] O.J. L177, correcting art.28 of the Rome I Regulation.
[19] The Law Applicable to Contractual Obligations (Scotland) Regulations 2009 (SSI 2009/410); The Law Applicable to Contractual Obligations (England and Wales and Northern Ireland) Regulations 2009 (SI 2009/3064); and The Financial Services and Markets Act 2000 (Law Applicable to Contracts of Insurance) Regulations 2009 (SI 2009/3075). Also E.B. Crawford, "Applicable Law of Contract: Some Changes Ahead", 2010 S.L.T. (News) 17.
[20] *Cheshire, North and Fawcett: Private International Law*, 14th edn (2008), pp.676, 677.
[21] Certain rules of the Regulation are not comprehensive, e.g., art 13 (capacity).
[22] e.g. *Zebrarise Ltd v De Nieffe* [2005] 1 Lloyd's Rep. 154.
[23] Rome I Regulation art.25.1.
[24] Rome I Regulation art.25.2.

Interpretation of the Convention and Regulation

15–03   With regard to interpretation of the Rome I Convention, reference to the Giuliano and Lagarde report on the Rome Convention[25] (henceforth "Giuliano and Lagarde") was permitted in order to ascertain the meaning and effect of any provision.[26] Questions of interpretation were required to be determined in accordance with the principles laid down by the European Court of Justice, and any relevant decision of that court. From 1990 a body of Scottish and English decisions interpretative of the Convention accumulated. Only from 1 March 2005 were (appellate) courts in the United Kingdom permitted to refer cases raising issues concerning the interpretation of the Rome I Convention to the ECJ for decision,[27] but it might have been expected, in light of the Brussels Protocol, that a body of ECJ/CJEU decisions would develop thereafter, possibly demonstrating methods of purposive interpretation different from those to which the UK is accustomed. However, before this process could become established, the Rome I Regulation came into effect. The CJEU has jurisdiction to give preliminary rulings on interpretation of the Rome I Regulation submitted by national courts.[28] Any court or tribunal of a Member State may submit a request for a preliminary ruling to the CJEU on the interpretation of a rule of European Union law if it considers it necessary to do so in order to resolve the dispute brought before it.[29] Courts or tribunals against whose decisions there is no judicial remedy under national law must bring such a request before the CJEU, unless the Court has already ruled on the point, or unless the correct interpretation of the rule of law in question is obvious.[30]

The Regulation contains no provision equivalent to art.18 of the Convention, which stated that "In the interpretation and application of the preceding uniform rules, regard shall be had to their international character and to the desirability of achieving uniformity in their interpretation and application." This deliberate omission recognises that uniform interpretation by EU Member States now is expected.

---

[25] Giuliano and Lagarde, "Report on the Convention on the Law Applicable to Contractual Obligations" [1980] O.J. C282/1.

[26] Contracts (Applicable Law) Act 1990 s.3(1), (2), (3)(a).

[27] The Contracts (Applicable Law) Act 1990 (Commencement No.2) Order 2004 (SI 2004/3448). The Brussels Protocol 1998, permitting such references, could not come into force earlier as it had not been ratified by all the EC Member States. The first reported case decided by the ECJ on interpretation of the Convention is *Intercontainer Interfrigo (ICF) SC v Balkenende Oosthuizen BV* (C-133/08) [2010] I.L.Pr. 3.

[28] Treaty on European Union ("TEU") art.19(3)(b) and art.267 of the Treaty on the Functioning of the European Union ('TFEU'); and "Recommendations of CJEU to national courts and tribunals in relation to the initiation of preliminary ruling proceedings" [2012] O.J. C338/1.

[29] "Recommendations of CJEU to national courts and tribunals in relation to the initiation of preliminary ruling proceedings" [2012] O.J. C338/1 rec.11.

[30] "Recommendations of CJEU to national courts and tribunals in relation to the initiation of preliminary ruling proceedings" [2012] O.J. C338/1 rec.12.

Governing law of a contract: general principles

Although a contract may contain elements connecting it with a number of different legal systems, if it is closely analysed, it will be found that its main elements can be localised, and that it has, or is deemed to have, a closer connection with one law than with any other. This law, the governing law, was known at common law as the "proper law of the contract". Its successor under the Rome I Convention, and now under the Rome I Regulation, is termed "the applicable law". It is the legal centre of gravity of the contract, and in it there is to be found the origin and determinant of the rights and obligations of the contracting parties.

15–04

Nature of the governing law

The governing law must be determined according to the facts as they exist at the date of making the contract, not taking into account actings after conclusion of the contract.[31] A contract must have a governing law from the outset: the governing law is held to attach at the time the contract is concluded, even though it may not be explicit and may require subsequently to be identified by the court. It has been said that the governing law cannot float[32]: a contract cannot be "anarchic" since, should a problem arise immediately upon conclusion thereof, there must be a law to determine the existence and extent of a remedy.

15–05

(a)   More than one governing law

There are unusual cases in which different parts of a contract may have closer connections with different systems of law. There is no reason why the provisions of a contract should not be severable,[33] and the result, exceptionally, is that parties may choose to have different laws govern different parts of a contract. This position is confirmed by the Rome I Regulation art.3.1.

15–06

---

[31] *Compagnie Tunisienne de Navigation SA v Compagnie d'Armement Maritime SA* [1970] 3 All E.R. 71; *James Miller & Partners Ltd v Whitworth Street Estates (Manchester) Ltd* [1970] 1 All E.R. 796.
[32] *Armar Shipping Co v Caisse Algerienne d'Assurance et de Reassurance (The Armar)* [1981] 1 All E.R. 498; *EI du Pont de Nemours & Co v Agnew (No.1)* [1987] 2 Lloyd's Rep. 585 CA; *Libyan Arab Foreign Bank v Bankers' Trust Co* [1987] 2 F.T.L.R. 509; and *Mauritius Commercial Bank Ltd v Hestia Holdings Ltd, Sujana Universal Industries Ltd* [2013] EWHC 1328 (Comm). See R. Fentiman, *International Commercial Litigation*, 2nd edn (2015, OUP), para 5.33.
[33] G.C. Cheshire, *International Contracts* (Glasgow: Jackson, Son & Co, 1948), p.42; Wolff, *Private International Law*, 2nd edn (1950), p.422; *Greer v Poole* (1880) L.R. 5 Q.B.D. 272; *Adelaide Electric Supply Co Ltd v Prudential Assurance Co Ltd* [1934] A.C. 122 at 151; *R. v International Trustee for the Protection of Bondholders AG* [1937] A.C. 500; *Mount Albert BC v Australasian Temperance & General Mutual Life Assuarnce Society Ltd* [1938] A.C. 224; *Forsikringsaktieselskapet Vesta v Butcher* [1986] 2 All E.R. 488 at 504, 505; affirmed [1988] 1 Lloyd's Rep. 19 at 29–33, 34, 35 CA; and [1989] 2 W.L.R. 290 HL; and *Libyan Arab Foreign Bank v Bankers' Trust Co* [1989] Q.B. 728.

(b)   Change of governing law

15–07   By agreement, the parties may change the governing law after conclusion of the contract. This is confirmed by the Regulation art.3.2,[34] subject to the proviso that such variation shall not prejudice the contract's formal validity, or adversely affect the rights of third parties.

(c)   Change in substance of governing law

15–08   The governing law of a contract is not static and does not remain fixed or frozen according to the provisions of that law at the date of formation of the contract.[35] The applicable law, as it stands from time to time, governs. Changes in substantive law may bring private law advantages and disadvantages, respectively, to the parties.[36]

Choice of law rules in contract under the Rome I Regulation

Material scope of Rome I Regulation

15–09   Article 1 of the Rome I Regulation provides that:

"1.   This Regulation shall apply, in situations involving a conflict of laws, to contractual obligations in civil and commercial matters.

It shall not apply, in particular, to revenue, customs or administrative matters.

2.   The following shall be excluded from the scope of this Regulation:

(a)   questions involving the status or legal capacity of natural persons, without prejudice to Article 13;

(b)   obligations arising out of family relationships and relationships deemed by the law applicable to such relationships to have comparable effects, including maintenance obligations;

(c)   obligations arising out of matrimonial property regimes, property regimes of relationships deemed by the law applicable to such relationships to have comparable effects to marriage, and wills and succession;

(d)   obligations arising under bills of exchange, cheques and promissory notes and other negotiable instruments to the extent that the obligations under such other negotiable instruments arise out of their negotiable character[37];

(e)   arbitration agreements[38] and agreements on the choice of court;

---

[34] Rome I Regulation cases: *Mauritius Commercial Bank Ltd v Hestia Holdings Ltd, Sujana Universal Industries Ltd* [2013] EWHC 1328 (Comm), per Popplewell J., at para.30; *In the Matters of Apcoa Parking Holdings GmbH, Apcoa Parking Deutschland GmbH (Companies Incorporated In Germany) v In the Matter of Apcoa Parking Austria GmbH (A Company Incorporated In Austria)* [2014] EWHC 3849 (Ch) at [230]. Under the Convention: *ISS Machinery Services Ltd v Aeolian Shipping SA (The Aeolian)* [2001] 2 Lloyd's Rep. 641.

[35] Para.4–08, above.

[36] *Re Chesterman's Trusts* [1923] 2 Ch. 466; *Kahler v Midland Bank Ltd* [1950] A.C. 24; and *Ralli Bros v Compania Naviera Sota y Aznar* [1920] 2 K.B. 287.

[37] i.e. not simply because payment under a contract was made by cheque. Characterisation as a negotiable instrument is governed by the *lex fori*. Giuliano and Lagarde, p.11.

[38] Para.15–14, below.

(f)   questions governed by the law of companies[39] and other bodies, corporate or unincorporated, such as the creation, by registration or otherwise, legal capacity, internal organisation or winding-up of companies and other bodies, corporate or unincorporated, and the personal liability of officers and members as such for the obligations of the company or body;

(g)   the question whether an agent is able to bind a principal, or an organ to bind a company or other body corporate or unincorporated, in relation to a third party[40];

(h)   the constitution of trusts and the relationship between settlors, trustees and beneficiaries[41];

(i)   obligations arising out of dealings prior to the conclusion of a contract[42];

(j)   insurance contracts arising out of operations carried out by organisations other than undertakings referred to in Article 2 of Directive 2002/83/EC of the European Parliament and of the Council of 5 November 2002 concerning life assurance the object of which is to provide benefits for employed or self-employed persons belonging to an undertaking or group of undertakings, or to a trade or group of trades, in the event of death or survival or of discontinuance or curtailment of activity, or of sickness related to work or accidents at work.[43]

3.   This Regulation shall not apply to evidence and procedure, without prejudice to Article 18.[44]

4.   In this Regulation, the term 'Member State' shall mean Member States to which this Regulation applies. However, in Article 3(4) and Article 7 the term shall mean all the Member States."

Principle of universality

The courts of Member States must apply the rules in the Rome I Regulation to any qualifying case, meaning that any law specified[45] by the instrument shall be applied by a Member State court whether or not it is the law of a Member State.[46] Hence the Rome I Regulation has the characteristic, like its predecessor the Convention,[47] of "universality" or "universal application".   **15–10**

---

[39] i.e. concerning internal operation of the business entity. Contracts made with such bodies, and not otherwise excluded by art.1, are subject to the Rome I Regulation. See e.g. *Integral Petroleum SA v SCU-Finanz AG* [2015] EWCA Civ 144.

[40] But contracts made between agent and principal are governed by the Rome I Regulation. See paras 15–29—15–30, below; and Giuliano and Lagarde, p.13.

[41] See Recognition of Trusts Act 1987.

[42] Recital (10) explains that such obligations are covered by art.12 of the Rome II Regulation. Such matters (e.g. standard of conduct at the pre-contractual stage, and good faith in negotiating—an area termed *culpa in contrahendo*, from German law) generally are regarded in civilian legal systems as pertaining to tort or restitution.

[43] Contrast Rome I Convention art.1.3, and see Rome I Regulation art.7, para.15–26, below. The rules of the Rome I Convention did not apply to contracts of insurance which cover risks situated in the territories of EEC Member States (though this exclusion did not apply to contracts of re-insurance).

[44] As to burden of proof, see para.15–50, below, and generally Ch.8.

[45] This means the rules of law in force in that country other than its rules of private international law, unless provided otherwise in the Regulation: art.20. See para.15–52, below.

[46] Rome I Regulation art.2.

[47] And its sibling, Rome II: art.3.

The Rome I Regulation applies also in the case of conflicts of laws between the different jurisdictions of the UK.[48]

Freedom of choice of applicable law by the parties[49]

15–11 The Regulation endorses[50] the principle of freedom of choice of applicable law by parties.[51] The current, legislative formulation of the rule is as follows:

> "Article 3
> Freedom of choice
> 1. A contract shall be governed by the law chosen by the parties. The choice shall be made expressly or clearly demonstrated by the terms of the contract or the circumstances of the case. By their choice the parties can select the law applicable to the whole or to part only of the contract.
> 2. The parties may at any time agree to subject the contract to a law other than that which previously governed it, whether as a result of an earlier choice made under this Article or of other provisions of this Regulation. Any change in the law to be applied that is made after the conclusion of the contract shall not prejudice its formal validity under Article 11 or adversely affect the rights of third parties.
> 3. Where all other elements relevant to the situation at the time of the choice are located in a country other than the country whose law has been chosen, the choice of the parties shall not prejudice the application of provisions of the law of that other country which cannot be derogated from by agreement.
> 4. Where all other elements relevant to the situation at the time of the choice are located in one or more Member States, the parties' choice of applicable law other than that of a Member State shall not prejudice the application of provisions of Community law, where appropriate as implemented in the Member State of the forum, which cannot be derogated from by agreement.
> 5. The existence and validity of the consent of the parties as to the choice of the applicable law shall be determined in accordance with the provisions of Articles 10, 11 and 13."

---

[48] Rome I Regulation art.22. cf. 1990 Act s.2(3); and Rome II art.25.

[49] For in-depth treatment of party autonomy in contract, see P.E. Nygh, *Autonomy in International Contracts* (Oxford: Clarendon Press, 1999).

[50] The principle of party autonomy was upheld at common law in the UK; the contracting parties' expressed intention determined the proper law of a contract. For treatment of the common law position, see the 2nd edition of this book (2006), paras.15-11–15-12. The guide was taken to be provided by Lord Wright in *Vita Food Products Inc v Unus Shipping Co Ltd (In Liquidation)* [1939] A.C. 277 at 290, namely that the law selected must have been (a) chosen in good faith; (b) the choice must have been legal; and (c) the choice must not have been contrary to public policy. The requirements were readily accepted at a superficial level, but soon were queried: at what point does (legitimate?) self-interest extinguish or grievously impair good faith?; "legal" by which law? See further *Ocean Steamship Co v Queensland State Wheat Board* [1941] 1 K.B. 402; *Stirling's Trustees v Legal & General Assuarnce Society Ltd*, 1957 S.L.T. 73; *English v Donnelly*, 1958 S.C. 494; *Golden Acres v Queensland Estates* (1969) St. R. Qd. 738 (Australia); and *Queensland Estates v Collas* [1971] St. R. Qd. 75.

[51] Rome I Regulation recital (11). See, e.g. under the Regulation, *Aquavita International SA v Ashapura Minecham Ltd* [2014] EWHC 2806 (Comm); and *Toyota Tsusho Sugar Trading Ltd v Prolat S.R.L.* [2014] EWHC 3649 (Comm). Under the Convention: *Duarte v Black & Decker Corp* [2007] EWHC 2720 (QB).

Article 3 permits contracting parties to agree the applicable law. The choice may be made expressly, or it may be "clearly demonstrated"[52] by the terms of the contract or the circumstances of the case.[53] It was clearly understood that under the Rome I Convention the court might not infer a choice of law which the parties might have made, where it was apparent that they had no clear intention of making a choice. This position, which must be taken to continue into the Regulation, is to be contrasted with the common law position in the UK where courts considered themselves free to "find" the intention of parties albeit never expressed and even in the absence of evidence that parties had given any thought to the matter of choice of law.[54]

If the court should find that, despite the averments of the contending parties, there was no consensus as to choice of law, art.3 is not satisfied, and the court must seek to identify the applicable law per art.4, q.v.[55] If, however, on the face of a deed, the parties have consented to a choice of law, the fact of consent may be difficult to challenge.[56] The issue whether a party later may say that his consent to a contract, including a choice of law and jurisdiction clause, was not real or genuine, or existent, at the time of purported conclusion of the contract, was raised in *Horn Linie GmbH & Co v Panamericana Formas E Impresos SA (The Hornbay),*[57] in which Morison J. held the parties to their bargain, stating that: " ... looking at the matter dispassionately, the Defendants have entered into a contract, by which they are bound, with a choice of law and jurisdiction clause in it and there is no reason why they should be heard to say that their consent was not real or genuine or was not given."[58] Further, his Lordship thought it reasonable to judge the consent of the defendants by the putative applicable law of the contract.[59]

There is no reason why parties' choice of law per art.3.1 of the Regulation should not fall on a "neutral" law; commercial and/or personal considerations

---

[52] There was a slight change of wording from that adopted in the Rome I Convention, where the words were: "The choice must be express or demonstrated with reasonable certainty". Notable cases interpretative of the art.3 of the Rome I Convention include *Egon Oldendorff v Libera Corp (No.2)* [1996] 1 Lloyd's Rep. 380; *Morin v Bonham & Brooks Ltd* [2004] 1 Lloyd's Rep. 702 (express choice of law contained in general conditions of sale in an auction catalogue deemed to have been accepted by all bidders); *FR Lurssen Werft GmbH & Co KG v Halle* [2009] EWHC 2607 (Comm); *Faraday Reinsurance Co Ltd v Howden North America Inc* [2011] EWHC 2837 (Comm); *Cox v Ergo Versicherung AG (formerly Victoria)* [2014] UKSC 22; and *Lawlor v Sandvik Mining and Construction Mobile Crushers and Screens Ltd* [2013] EWCA Civ 365.

[53] For cases under the Rome I Convention where the choice can be inferred through, for example, an earlier course of dealing or standard conditions of the trade, see Giuliano and Lagarde, p.17.

[54] *The Assunzione* [1954] P. 150; *Amin Rasheed Shipping Corp v Kuwait Insurance Co (The Al Wahab)* [1983] 2 All E.R. 884; and *Wasa International Insurance Co Ltd v Lexington Insurance Co* [2009] UKHL 40.

[55] *Iran Continental Shelf Oil Co v IRI International Corp* [2002] EWCA Civ 1024.

[56] cf. in the context of choice of court, *Deutsche Bank AG v Asia Pacific Broadband Wireless Communications Inc* [2009] I.L.Pr. 36.

[57] *Horn Linie GmbH & Co v Panamericana Formas E Impresos SA (The Hornbay)* [2006] EWHC 373 (Comm).

[58] *Horn Linie GmbH & Co v Panamericana Formas E Impresos SA (The Hornbay)* [2006] EWHC 373 (Comm) at [20].

[59] *Horn Linie GmbH & Co v Panamericana Formas E Impresos SA (The Hornbay)* [2006] EWHC 373 (Comm) at [19].

might lead parties to choose such a law.[60] Particular provisions of a foreign law can be expressly incorporated as terms of a contract; this is not the same as making the whole of that foreign law the applicable law.[61]

It would not be acceptable for parties to choose, under authorisation of the Rome I Regulation, the common law of England or Scotland pertaining to contract as it stood prior to the coming into force of the Regulation, i.e. parties cannot use Rome I to contract out of Rome I.

The parties' choice of applicable law is subject to overriding provisions discussed below, namely, arts 3.3 (an anti-avoidance provision repeating what was contained in the corresponding article of the Rome I Convention) and 3.4 (a provision seeking to ensure the application of "mandatory Community law"), as well as to "overriding mandatory rules" (art.9) and the public policy of the forum (art.21).

Choice of non-State law

15–12   Under the Rome I Convention, as at common law, parties might choose, by means of art.3, only the law of a country (i.e. a body of State law), capable of ascertainment, and capable of answering any problem which might arise concerning the contract. The Rome I Convention did not contemplate or permit choice of a non-State system of law, such as the *lex mercatoria*, nor the choice of a body of religious law.[62]

The Court of Appeal decision in *Halpern v Halpern* provides a useful elaboration of the limits of the use which could be made of non-State law within the bounds of the Rome I Convention. While the court was clear that the English applicable law of the agreement alone must govern matters of substance, Jewish law as a distinct body of law could be relied on "as part of the contractual framework",[63] with the effect of permitting it to govern questions of interpretation. Waller L.J. alluded to the problems of enforcing remedies granted in terms of religious rules: "remedies, if they were to be effective, would have to flow from a system of law in the sense of the law of a country."[64]

The contractual arrangement in *Halpern* is to be contrasted with that made in *Shamil Bank of Bahrain EC v Beximco Pharmaceuticals Ltd*,[65] in which the Court of Appeal had difficulty in finding the true intention of the parties, and in particular in construing the clause, "subject to the principles of the glorious Sharia'a, this agreement shall be governed by and construed in accordance with the laws of England". Not only was it held to be impossible for there to be two

---

[60] At common law in the UK, opinion varied as to whether or not there required to be some factual connection between the identity of the chosen law and the facts of the contract. See *Cheshire and North's Private International Law*, 11th edn (1987), pp.471, 472, where the view was expressed that, at common law, an unconnected choice would be ineffective.

[61] *Dicey, Morris and Collins on the Conflict of Laws*, 15th edn (2012), para.32–056. See *Amin Rasheed Shipping Corp v Kuwait Insurance Co (The Al Wahab)* [1984] A.C. 50, per Lord Wilberforce at 69, 70; and *Forsikringsaktieselskapet Vesta v Butcher* [1988] 1 Lloyd's Rep. 19; affirmed on other grounds [1989] A.C. 852.

[62] See *Shamil Bank of Bahrain EC v Beximco Pharmaceuticals Ltd* [2004] 1 W.L.R. 1784, per Potter L.J. at [48].

[63] *Halpern v Halpern* [2008] Q.B. 195, per Waller L.J. at [33].

[64] *Halpern v Halpern* [2008] Q.B. 195, per Waller L.J. at [39].

[65] *Shamil Bank of Bahrain EC v Beximco Pharmaceuticals Ltd* [2004] 1 W.L.R. 1784.

governing laws (English law and Sharia law being incapable of operating jointly), but also there was the problem that the reference to "principles of the glorious Sharia'a" is a phrase of very uncertain meaning when there can be different schools of thought as to what Sharia law lays down.[66] References to Sharia law were held merely to reflect the Islamic religious principles according to which the Shamil Bank did business; the form of words used did not incorporate Sharia law as the governing law of the contract. The attempt to have Sharia law apply was inept, procedurally as well as substantively.

It was expected that the Rome I Regulation would expand party choice in the matter of what could be chosen, but that which materialised was less generous than anticipated.[67] The Regulation does not sanction party choice of a non-State body of rules per art.3.1. As has always been the case, however, this can be done obliquely by parties choosing to submit their dispute to arbitration, and to have the substantive issue so regulated.[68] All that survives expressly in the Regulation is the guidance contained in recitals (13) and (14). Recital (13) permits parties to incorporate by reference into their contract a non-State body of law or an international convention (e.g. UNIDROIT Principles of International Commercial Contracts), or the rules of a Convention, such as the 1980 United Nations Convention on Contracts for the International Sale of Goods (the Vienna Convention). Moreover, parties, by choice of the law of a State which is a contracting party, e.g. to the Vienna Convention, thereby will import into their contract the terms of that Convention.[69] In any event non-State bodies of law may be found to have gaps in coverage, meaning that such rules require to be supplemented by the relevant provisions of what is deemed by the court to be the governing law of the contract. Recital (14) provides that, "Should the Community adopt, in an appropriate legal instrument, rules of substantive contract law, including standard terms and conditions, such instrument may provide that the parties may choose to apply those rules",[70] and in so doing it opens the door to a less restrictive approach.

Link between choice of law and choice of court

A proposed presumption in a draft version of art.3 of the Regulation, that if parties have agreed to confer jurisdiction on a court or tribunal of a Member State to hear and determine disputes that had arisen or might arise out of the contract, **15–13**

---

[66] *Shamil Bank of Bahrain EC v Beximco Pharmaceuticals Ltd* [2004] 1 W.L.R. 1784 at [33].

[67] For background detail, see *Cheshire, North and Fawcett: Private International Law*, 14th edn (2008), p.699.

[68] *Halpern v Halpern* [2008] Q.B. 195, per Waller L.J. at [38], " . . .if parties wish some form of rules or law not of a country to apply to their contract, then it is open to them to so agree, provided that there is an arbitration clause. The court will give effect to the parties' agreement in that way." See also *Musawi v RE International (UK) Ltd* [2008] 1 Lloyd's Rep. 326, which demonstrates that while the arbitrator was required by agreement of the parties to apply to the subject matter of the dispute and its resolution the principles of Shia Sharia law, a distinction has to be drawn between that agreement and the identification of the governing laws of the underlying contracts.

[69] e.g. *Mimusa v Yves Saint-Laurent Parfums* [2008] E.C.C. 30 (Cour de Cassation).

[70] e.g. European Commission Proposal for a Regulation of the European Parliament and of the Council on a Common European Sales Law (COM/2011/0635 final – 2011/0284 (COD)) (11 October 2011).

they should be presumed also to have chosen the law of that Member State, was abandoned during the negotiation process. However, a hint to this effect remains through the medium of recital (12):

> "An agreement between the parties to confer on one or more courts or tribunals of a Member State exclusive jurisdiction to determine disputes under the contract should be one of the factors to be taken into account in determining whether a choice of law has been clearly demonstrated".

Relegation of the proposed "rule" to the recitals is wise. If it had been implemented in the body of the Regulation, it would have operated, as a matter of practice, to undermine the contract-specific rules set out in art.4 of the Regulation.[71] On the basis of recital (12), choice of court *may* supply choice of law. Choice of law cannot supply choice of court.[72] "Agreements on the choice of court" are excluded from the scope of the Rome I Regulation by art.1.2.e, which means that finding the governing law of such an agreement is an exercise which must be performed according to common law rules.

Link between choice of law and arbitration clause

15–14   Until 1968, an arbitration clause was held to be a very important factor in ascertaining the proper law of the contract: if differences were to be settled by arbitration in a particular place, or by an arbiter to be appointed in such a place, it was presumed that the parties intended that their contractual rights and duties should be governed by the law of that place.[73] Morris, in 1968,[74] stated that, "there is an almost irrebuttable presumption that the law of that country is the proper law of the contract as a whole". Decisions of the House of Lords of 1970[75] show, however, that although an arbitration clause was still a very strong factor, it was not conclusive and might give way to other indications.[76]

---

[71] Though it is conceded that a contract which contains a choice of court clause is likely also to contain an applicable law clause, bringing the case under art.3 of the Regulation.

[72] *Pace, Shekar v Satyam Computer Services Ltd* [2005] I.C.R. 737 (employment tribunal, per Judge PT Wallington at [52]). At common law see *NV Kwik Hoo Tong Handel Maatschappij v James Findlay & Co Ltd* [1927] A.C. 604; and *Dunbee Ltd v Gilmour & Co (Australia) Pty Ltd* [1968] 2 Lloyd's Rep. 394.

[73] *Hamlyn & Co v Talisker Distillery* (1894) 21 R. (H.L.) 21; *Girvin Roper and Co v Monteith* (1895) 23 R. 129; *Spurrier v La Cloche* [1902] A.C. 446; *Austrian Lloyd Steamship Co v Gresham Life Assurance Society Ltd* [1903] 1 K.B. 249; *Robertson v Brandes Schonwald and Co* (1906) 8 F. 815; *Johannesburg Municipal Council v D Stewart & Co (1902) Ltd*, 1909 S.C. (H.L.) 53; *Kirchner & Co v Gruban* [1909] 1 Ch. 413; *Pena Copper Mines v Rio Tinto Co Ltd* (1911) 103 L.T. 846; *Norske Atlas Insurance Co Ltd v London General Insurance Co Ltd* (1972) 43 T.L.R. 541; *Perry v Equitable Life Assurance Society* (1929) 45 T.L.R. 468; *Kennedy v London Express* [1931] I.R. 532; *National Bank of Greece and Athens SA v Metliss* [1958] A.C. 509; *Tzortzis v Monark Line A/B* [1968] 1 W.L.R. 406.

[74] Morris, *Cases on Private International Law*, 4th edn (1968), p.280.

[75] *Compagnie Tunisienne de Navigation SA v Compagnie d'Armement Maritime SA* [1970] 3 All E.R. 71; and *James Miller & Partners Ltd v Whitworth Street Estates (Manchester) Ltd* [1970] 1 All E.R. 796.

[76] See also *Astro Vencedor Compania Naviera SA v Mabanaft GmbH (The Damianos)* [1971] 2 Q.B. 588; *Tracomin SA v Sudan Oil Seeds Co Ltd (No.2)* [1983] 2 All E.R. 129; *Astro Venturoso Compania Naviera v Hellenic Shipyards SA (The Mariannina)* [1983] 1 Lloyd's Rep. 12; *Furness Withy*

The position has changed under the Convention and the Regulation because "arbitration agreements" are excluded from the scope of each instrument.[77] In a cross-border commercial situation involving arbitration, four contracts potentially are discernible,[78] viz.: first, the main contract (of sale of goods/provision of services etc) between the parties ("the matrix contract"), the applicable law of which is likely to be determinable by the Rome I Regulation; secondly, the agreement of the contracting parties to have any dispute arising from the matrix contract referred to arbitration ("the agreement to go to arbitration"). This agreement to go to arbitration might be freestanding, but usually is found in the matrix contract, in the form of an arbitration clause. This agreement, qualifying as an "arbitration agreement" within the meaning of art.1.2.e is excluded from the scope of the Rome I Regulation, and consequently its governing law must be determined according to common law rules. In essence, this is done by a three-stage process, viz. express choice of law, failing which inferred choice, and failing both, identification of the law of closest connection. Thirdly, if dispute should arise and the parties to the matrix contract proceed to arbitration, their engaging the services of the arbiter constitutes a separate contract, which likewise must fall outside the scope of the Rome I Regulation. Finally, the arbitral procedure itself has a governing law (the "curial law"), which is likely to be that of the law of the place where the arbitration is conducted (the "seat of the arbitration"[79]), and typically will be different from the law governing the matrix contract (which law, however, it must ascertain and apply to the substance of the contractual dispute). It is important to bear in mind this sequence of contractual relationships while recognising that "the parties would not be expected to have chosen pointlessly to resort to numerous different systems to govern their affairs, and so an express choice of a law to govern them in one respect is a strong indication that they might have understood or intended that it should apply to others."[80] Hence, indirectly, although arbitration agreements are excluded from the Regulation's scope, a choice of applicable law per art.3 to govern the matrix contract, may influence the court's identification of the law governing the arbitration agreement.

(Australia) Ltd v Metal Distributors (UK) (The Amazonia) [1990] 1 Lloyd's Rep. 236. See now, as to Scots curial law, Arbitration (Scotland) Act 2010 Sch.1; certain of these rules have been designated mandatory rules of the *lex curiae* (s.8).

[77] Rome I Regulation art.1.2.e; and Rome I Convention art.1.2.d.

[78] cf. *Arsanovia Ltd, Burley Holdings Ltd, Unitech Ltd v Cruz City 1 Mauritius Holdings* [2012] EWHC 3702 (Comm), per Andrew Smith J. at [9]; *Sul América Cia Nacional De Seguros SA v Enesa Engenharia SA* [2012] 1 Lloyd's Rep. 671, per Moore-Bick L.J. at [26]–[27]; and *Habas Sinai Ve Tibbi Gazlar Istihsal Endustrisi AS v VSC Steel Company Ltd* [2013] EWHC 4071 (Comm), Hamblen J. at [101]–[102].

[79] *James Miller & Partners Ltd v Whitworth Street Estates (Manchester) Ltd* [1970] 1 All E.R. 796: since the parties by their subsequent conduct had acquiesced in Scottish arbitration proceedings, Scots law governed the curial procedure.

[80] *Arsanovia Ltd, Burley Holdings Ltd, Unitech Ltd v Cruz City 1 Mauritius Holdings* [2012] EWHC 3702 (Comm), per Andrew Smith J. at [10]; citing Lord Mustill in *Channel Tunnel Group Ltd v Balfour Beatty Construction Ltd* [1993] AC 334 at 357F.

Determination of applicable law in the absence of choice of law

15–15   The provisions on determination of the applicable law in the absence of choice were re-drawn in the Rome I Regulation. Article 4.1 of the Regulation is "contract-specific", with particular rules for particular categories of contract.[81] Such a formulation has the effect of ousting from its central role under the Rome Convention the connecting factor of "habitual residence of the party who is to effect the performance which is characteristic of the contract".[82] Under the Regulation the "characteristic performer" retains but a minor part.

> "Article 4
>   Applicable law in the absence of choice
>   1.   To the extent that the law applicable to the contract has not been chosen in accordance with Article 3 and without prejudice to Articles 5 to 8,[83] the law governing the contract shall be determined as follows:
>   (a)   a contract for the sale of goods shall be governed by the law of the country where the seller[84] has his habitual residence[85];
>   (b)   a contract for the provision of services[86] shall be governed by the law of the country where the service provider has his habitual residence;
>   (c)   a contract relating to a right *in rem* in immovable property or to a tenancy of immovable property shall be governed by the law of the country where the property is situated[87];
>   (d)   notwithstanding point (c), a tenancy of immovable property concluded for temporary private use for a period of no more than six consecutive months shall be governed by the law of the country where the landlord has his habitual residence, provided that the tenant is a natural person and has his habitual residence in the same country;
>   (e)   a franchise contract shall be governed by the law of the country where the franchisee has his habitual residence;
>   (f)   a distribution contract shall be governed by the law of the country where the distributor has his habitual residence;

---

[81] See Z. Tang, "Law Applicable in the Absence of Choice—The New Article 4 of the Rome I Regulation", 2008 M.L.R. 785.

[82] Rome Convention art.4.2.

[83] Special rules pertaining to contracts of carriage; consumer contracts; insurance contracts; and individual employment contracts, explained at paras 15–23—15–30, below.

[84] Recital (17) states that the concept of "sale of goods" should be interpreted in the same way as when applying art.5 of the Brussels I Regulation (cf. Brussels I Recast art.7) insofar as sale of goods are covered by that Regulation. But the effect of insertion into the Brussels I Regulation of a community definition of "place of performance" (indicating, in sale of goods contracts, the place of delivery) appears to have the result of clothing with jurisdiction the court of the buyer's legal system. Thus when art.4.1(a) is applied, the effect is that the buyer's court is enjoined to apply the seller's law.

[85] Article 19 of the Regulation provides, of new, a definition of habitual residence of companies and other bodies, corporate or unincorporated, and of a natural person acting in the course of his business activitiy, and of branches or agencies: para.15–51, below. See, under Rome Convention, *Sierra Leone Telecommunications Co Ltd v Barclays Bank Plc* [1998] 2 All E.R. 820; and *Iran Continental Shelf Oil Co v IRI International Corp* [2002] EWCA Civ 1024. Contrast *Ennstone Building Products Ltd v Stanger Ltd* [2002] 1 W.L.R. 3059.

[86] Recital (17) states that the concept of "provision of services" should be interpreted in the same way as when applying art.5 of the Brussels I Regulation (cf. Brussels I Recast art.7) insofar as provision of services are covered by that Regulation. The same outcome of mismatch between court and applicable law can be seen as arises in relation to sale of goods: cf. fn.84, above.

[87] cf. exclusive jurisdiction provisions contained in Brussels I Regulation art.22.1 (cf. Brussels I Recast art.24).

     (g)   a contract for the sale of goods by auction shall be governed by the law of the country where the auction takes place, if such a place can be determined;

     (h)   a contract concluded within a multilateral system which brings together or facilitates the bringing together of multiple third-party buying and selling interests in financial instruments, as defined by Article 4(1), point (17) of Directive 2004/39/EC, in accordance with non-discretionary rules and governed by a single law, shall be governed by that law.

2.   Where the contract is not covered by paragraph 1 or where the elements of the contract would be covered by more than one of points (a) to (h) of paragraph 1, the contract shall be governed by the law of the country where the party required to effect the characteristic performance[88] of the contract has his habitual residence.

3.   Where it is clear from all the circumstances of the case that the contract is manifestly more closely connected with a country other than that indicated in paragraphs 1 or 2, the law of that other country shall apply.

4.   Where the law applicable cannot be determined pursuant to paragraphs 1 or 2, the contract shall be governed by the law of the country with which it is most closely connected."

Where the drafting device adopts a list of contract-specific rules, it is clearly essential to include a provision governing contracts which fall outside the list, or which straddle different categories within the list. This is contained in art.4.2. Article 4.3 is the displacement rule. It is not unusual in modern European choice of law instruments[89] to include a displacement provision for use at the discretion of the forum in cases where the law identified by the general rule cannot be regarded, in the view of the forum, as the law of closest connection.[90]

The precursor to art.4.3 and 4.4 of the Regulation is the Rome I Convention art.4.5. Essentially the thrust of these provisions is the same. The effect of the Convention art.4.5 was that the forum could use its unfettered discretion to identify the applicable law if the characteristic performance could not be determined, or if it appeared from the circumstances as a whole that the contract was more closely connected with another country. Changes in format in art.4.3 and 4.4 of the Regulation do not appear to be substantial, and two exit routes remain.

Article 4.4 of the Regulation permits the forum discretion to take an overview in order to identify the applicable law. Where the forum is a UK forum, it seems plausible that a range of factors could be advanced as indicators of closeness of connection, such as to justify a finding as to applicable law. It is not inconceivable that aid might be had from the wealth of common law cases which illustrated the English and Scots approaches to finding the proper law in the absence of choice.[91]

---

[88] Discussed below, para.15–18.

[89] cf. Rome II art.4.3.

[90] Rome I Regulation recital (16). cf. equivalent provision in Rome I Convention art.4.5, in respect of which see Crawford and Carruthers, *International Private Law in Scotland*, 2nd edn (2006), paras 15–14 to 15–16 and paras 15–12—15–15, below.

[91] See the 3rd edition of this book (2010), paras 15–19 to 15–23.

Continuing relevance of Rome I Convention

15–16 Insofar as cases concerning contracts concluded before 17 December 2009 continue to be litigated under the Rome I Convention, examination of such provisions of the Convention as differ from the Regulation, with accompanying case law, continues to be relevant.

Rome I Convention article 4: applicable law in the absence of choice

15–17 Article 4 provided as follows:

"1.   To the extent that the law applicable to the contract has not been chosen in accordance with Article 3, the contract shall be governed by the law of the country with which it is most closely connected. Nevertheless, a severable part of the contract which has a closer connection with another country may by way of exception be governed by the law of that other country.

2.   Subject to the provisions of paragraph 5 of this Article, it shall be presumed that the contract is most closely connected with the country where the party who is to effect the performance which is characteristic of the contract has, at the time of conclusion of the contract, his habitual residence, or, in the case of a body corporate or unincorporate, its central administration.[92] However, if the contract is entered into in the course of that party's trade or profession, that country shall be the country in which the principal place of business is situated or, where under the terms of the contract the performance is to be effected through a place of business other than the principal place of business, the country in which that other place of business is situated.

3.   Notwithstanding the provisions of paragraph 2 of this Article, to the extent that the subject matter of the contract is a right in immovable property or a right to use immovable property it shall be presumed that the contract is most closely connected with the country where the immovable property is situated. ...[93]

5.   Paragraph 2 shall not apply if the characteristic performance cannot be determined, and[94] the presumptions in paragraphs 2, 3 and 4 shall be disregarded if it appears from the circumstances as a whole that the contract is more closely connected with another country."

Rome I Convention article 4.2

15–18 The Rome I Convention introduced a significant change in its choice of the connecting factor of "habitual residence of the characteristic performer". The choice was idiosyncratic. The concept of "characteristic performance", deriving from Swiss conflict rules, was new to the UK in 1990.[95] Giuliano and Lagarde explain it thus:

---

[92] *Sierra Leone Telecommunications Co Ltd v Barclays Bank Plc* [1998] 2 All E.R. 821.

[93] Re art.4.4, see Contracts of Carriage at para.15–24, below.

[94] The disjunctive "and" should be read as "or".

[95] While it is true that at common law in the UK application qua "proper law" of the *lex loci solutionis* usually was preferred to the *lex loci contractus* where the two laws differed, and that while, in identifying the place of performance, "performance" by means of manufacture or creative work was rated more meaningful than "performance" by way of payment made by the other party, the Convention effected a significant change.

"In addition it is possible to relate the concept of characteristic performance to an even more general idea, namely the idea that his performance refers to the function which the legal relationship involved fulfils in the economic and social life of any country. The concept of characteristic performance essentially links the contract to the social and economic environment of which it will form a part."[96]

Difficulty occasionally was encountered under the Convention in ascertaining what was the "characteristic performance",[97] or in identifying the party who was to effect it.[98] Under the Rome I Convention manufacture or supply of goods was more characteristic than payment[99]; provision of a service more characteristic than payment for the service[100]; and performance by a banker of his side of a contract with a customer more characteristic than the customer's counterpart obligation.[101] The tendency was to favour the party effecting the "positive" performance rather than the reciprocal pecuniary obligation. This is likely to be true still of characteristic performance for the purposes of Rome I Regulation art.4.2.

The relative strengths of Rome I Convention article 4.2 and 4.5[102]

A court applying art.4 of the Convention was permitted to disregard art.4.2 if characteristic performance could not be determined; and if it appeared from the circumstances as a whole that the contract was more closely connected with another country. This latter clause of art.4.5 permitted UK courts, in their view at least, in a qualifying case, to draw upon the pre-existing body of common law case law concerning determination of the proper law of a contract.

    The relationship between art.4.2 and 4.5, i.e. their relative strengths, was a matter of controversy. The height of the controversy has passed given that the Rome I Convention is on an exit trajectory and "uniform interpretation" is aided now by the permitted reference to the CJEU. The extent to which discretion remains to the forum under the Rome I Regulation art.4, is considered above.

    According to art.4.5, the presumptions in art.4.2, 4.3 and 4.4 were to be disregarded if it appeared from the circumstances as a whole that the contract was

15–19

---

[96] Giuliano and Lagarde, p.20.

[97] *Print Concept GmbH v GEW (EC) Ltd* [2001] EWCA Civ 352; *Kenburn Waste Management Ltd v Bergmann*[2002] EWCA Civ 98; *Hogg Insurance Brokers Ltd v Guardian Insurance Co Inc* [1997] I Lloyd's Rep. 412; and *Apple Corps Ltd v Apple Computer Inc* [2004] EWHC 768.

[98] *Iran Continental Shelf Oil Co v IRI International Corp* [2002] EWCA Civ 1024; *Ennstone Building Products Ltd v Stanger Ltd* [2002] 1 W.L.R. 3059.

[99] *Sapporo Breweries Ltd v Lupofresh Ltd* [2013] EWCA Civ 948; [2014] 1 All E.R. (Comm) 484.

[100] *Naraji v Shelbourne* [2011] EWHC 3298 (QB) at [167].

[101] *Bank of Baroda v Vysya Bank Ltd* [1994] 2 Lloyd's Rep. 87. See also *Ark Therapeutics Plc v True North Capital Ltd* [2006] 1 All E.R. (Comm) 138 (a "unilateral contract"); and (re indemnity agreement) *Ophthalmic Innovations International (UK) Ltd v Ophthalmic Innovations International Inc* [2005] I.L.Pr. 10.

[102] J. Hill, "Choice of Law in Contract under the Rome Convention" (2004) 53 I.C.L.Q. 325; and S. Atrill, "Choice of Law in Contract: the Missing Pieces of the Article 4 Jigsaw" (2004) 53 I.C.L.Q. 549.

more closely connected with another country. The wording of art.4.5, and choice of the verb "disregard",[103] suggested that a variety of interpretative approaches might justifiably be taken.

The EU Commission favoured the approach taken in the decision of the Dutch Hoge Raad in *Société Nouvelle des Papeteries de l'Aa SA v BV Machinenfabriek BOA*,[104] which found the Dutch law of the place of business of the sellers to be the applicable law in circumstances where all other factual contacts were with French law. The decision represented a strong preference for the certainty which application of art.4.2 delivered, over the possible benefits of appropriateness inherent in displacement of art.4.2 by means of art.4.5 and the discretion which the latter provision conferred. In the instant case the decision permitted the forum to apply its own Dutch law. The effect of the decision was that art.4.2 was to be displaced only if the factor of the habitual residence of the characteristic performer had "no real value" as a connecting factor.

The earliest English case interpretative of art.4.2 of the Rome I Convention is *Bank of Baroda v Vysya Bank Ltd*,[105] concerning a letter of credit. The contract between the issuing and the confirming banks was English law, per art.4.2. Although the applicable law of the principal contract (for which the inter-bank contract was facilitative) would have been governed by Indian law per art.4.2, Mance J. (as he then was) held that, for clarity and simplicity, it was desirable that all aspects of this contractual nexus be governed by the same applicable law (English law). Article 4.5 was the means by which to secure this result. The line of English authority[106] evinced a preference for use of art.4.5 to confer wider discretion upon the forum in its identification of the applicable law, a discretion which, in a number of instances, resulted in the selection of English law as the applicable law. The forum may hold it appropriate to apply to an ancillary contract related to the main contract (as, for example, a guarantee) the same governing law as regulates the main contract.[107]

---

[103] See generally *Definitely Maybe (Touring) Ltd v Marek Lieberberg Konzertagentur GmbH (No.2)* [2001] 4 All E.R. 283, per Morison J. at 287, 288; *Credit Lyonnais v New Hampshire Insurance Co Ltd* [1997] 2 Lloyd's Rep. 1, per Hobhouse L.J. at 5; *Samcrete Egypt Engineers & Contractors SAE v Land Rover Exports Ltd* [2001] EWCA Civ 2019; and *Iran Continental Shelf Oil Co v IRI International Corp* [2002] EWCA Civ 1024.

[104] *Société Nouvelle des Papeteries de l'Aa SA v BV Machinenfabriek BOA* (1992) No.750, RvdW (1992) No.207.

[105] *Bank of Baroda v Vysya Bank Ltd* [1994] 2 Lloyd's Rep. 87. See also *Marconi Communications International Ltd v PT Pan Indonesian Bank TBK* [2005] 2 All E.R. (Comm) 325.

[106] e.g. *Bank of Baroda v Vysya Bank Ltd* [1994] 2 Lloyd's Rep. 87; *Definitely Maybe (Touring) Ltd v Marek Lieberberg Konzertagentur GmbH (No.2)* [2001] 4 All E.R. 283, per Morison J. at 287, 288; *Credit Lyonnais v New Hampshire Insurance Co Ltd* [1997] 2 Lloyd's Rep. 1, per Hobhouse L.J. obiter at 5; *Kenburn Waste Management Ltd v Bergmann* [2002] EWCA Civ 98; *Samcrete Egypt Engineers & Contractors SAE v Land Rover Exports Ltd* [2002] C.L.C. 533; *Marconi Communications International Ltd v PT Pan Indonesian Bank TBK* [2005] 2 All E.R. (Comm) 325; *British Arab Commercial Bank plc v Bank of Communications* [2011] 1 Ll's Rep. 664; and *Deutsche Bank (Suisse) SA v Kahn* [2013] EWHC 482 (Comm). But see *Ophthalmic Innovations International (UK) Ltd v Ophthalmic Innovations International Inc* [2005] I.L.Pr. 10; and *Martrade Shipping & Transport GmbH v United Enterprises Corp* [2015] 1 W.L.R. 1.

[107] *Star Reefers Pool Inc v JFC Group Ltd* [2011] EWHC 339 (Comm); [2011] 2 Lloyd's Rep. 215; and *Golden Ocean Group Ltd v Salgaocar Mining Industries Pvt Ltd* [2012] EWCA Civ 265. The same reasoning may apply where the governing law of the main contract has been expressly chosen by the parties: *Aquavita International SA v Ashapura Minecham Ltd* [2014] EWHC 2806 (Comm).

The leading Scots case on the point is *Caledonia Subsea Ltd v Micoperi Srl*,[108] which showed a clear preference for adhering to the art.4.2 presumption.[109] The circumstances revealed a factual and legal nexus with Egyptian law, but the business of the characteristic performer was situated in Scotland. Lord President Cullen's opinion gave firm dominance to the art.4.2 presumption:

> "I consider that the presumption under para 2 should not be 'disregarded' unless the outcome of the comparative exercise referred to in para 5 . . .demonstrates a clear preponderance of factors in favour of another country."[110]

The outcome in *Caledonia Subsea* of holding to art.4.2 was application of the forum's own (Scots) law. In order for the forum to "walk home", it was not necessary always to have resort to art.4.5.

The European Court of Justice in *Intercontainer Interfrigo (ICF) SC v Balkenende Oosthuizen BV and MIC Operations BV*,[111] gave voice to a moderate view that, "article 4(5) of the Convention must be construed as meaning that, where it is clear from the circumstances as a whole that the contract is more closely connected with a country other than that determined on the basis of one of the criteria set out in article 4(2) to (4) of the Convention, it is for the court to disregard those criteria and apply the law of the country with which the contract is most closely connected."[112]

The interpretative history of art.4 has been narrated at length on the rationale that in the re-cast art.4 contained in the Rome I Regulation, effectively the same discretion remains for use by the forum. The enlarged appearance of art.4 of the Regulation perhaps distracts attention from the fact that where the law applicable cannot be determined pursuant to the many rules contained in art.4.1 and 4.2, or where it is clear from all the circumstances of the case that the contract is manifestly more closely connected with a country other than that indicated in art.4.1 or 4.2, it shall be the function of the forum to take a view on the identity of the law of the country of manifestly closer connection (art.4.3) or most close connection (art.4.4). It is unlikely that a UK forum will, or can, ignore the hinterland to art.4 of the Regulation, but it is to be expected that the influence of the CJEU in interpreting the Regulation will reduce the scope for individual Member State forum variation in the manner of exercise of its judicial discretion.

---

[108] *Caledonia Subsea Ltd v Micoperi Srl*, 2002 S.L.T. 1022. Also *William Grant & Sons International Ltd v Marie Brizard Espana SA*, 1998 S.C. 536. Contrast *Ferguson Shipbuilders Ltd v Voith Hydro GmbH & Co KG*, 2000 S.L.T 229, obiter per Lord Penrose.

[109] cf. *Krupp Uhde GmbH v Weir Westgarth Ltd* unreported 31 May 2002, CSOH, per Lord Eassie.

[110] *Caledonia Subsea Ltd v Micoperi Srl*, 2002 S.L.T. 1022 at 1029G.

[111] *Intercontainer Interfrigo (ICF) SC v Balkenende Oosthuizen BV and MIC Operations BV* Case C-133/08 [2008] O.J. C158/10. See also *Haeger & Schmidt GmbH v Mutuelles du Mans assurances IARD (MMA IARD)* (C-305/13) [2015] 2 W.L.R. 175.

[112] *Intercontainer Interfrigo (ICF) SC v Balkenende Oosthuizen BV and MIC Operations BV* Case C-133/08 [2008] O.J. C158/10, para.64.

Continuing relevance of common law choice of law rules in contract

15–20 In cases which fall outside the subject-matter scope of the Regulation and the Convention,[113] and outside the scope of any European harmonisation instrument, common law principles and approaches remain applicable in the UK courts. Under the Convention, it was clear that the common law rules of Scotland and England retained residual influence insofar as the Convention was not exhaustive in its provision, and a UK forum might legitimately resort to common law authorities where the Convention did not supply a rule, or supplied an incomplete rule. In that certain matters continue to fall outside the scope of the Regulation, and certain rules continue to be incomplete,[114] the same reasoning must obtain, namely, that the common law may be permitted to supply the lack.

In the different scenario demonstrated by art.4.3 and 4.4. of the Regulation, in which the EU forum is entitled to depart, at its discretion, from the rules contained in the instrument, the question arises whether the forum is entitled to summon to its aid common law authorities peculiar to its own jurisdiction. While this was thought to be permissible under art.4.5 of the Convention, constrained only by the terms of art.18,[115] the correctness of this approach is doubted with regard to the Regulation. The very fact that the Regulation contains no provision equivalent to art.18 of the Convention admits that uniform interpretation is expected, and impliedly conveys that reference to national common law authorities is generally inappropriate.

Restrictions on choice of law

Mandatory rules and the Rome I Convention

15–21 The approach which the Rome I Convention adopted to the subject of party autonomy was to allow choice of law in principle, but to circumscribe that choice by means of the compulsory application of rules of certain other laws. Reference was made in the Convention to two types of mandatory provision, internal and overriding. While the French text made clear in its use of the terms "*dispositions imperatives*" (art.3.3) and "*lois de police*" (art.7) that there was a difference between the two types of mandatory provision, this difference was not apparent in the English language text.

The phrase "mandatory rules" in relation to art.3.3 (which applied only in instances of party choice of applicable law) embraced, "rules which cannot be derogated from by contract", i.e. as a matter of the forum's domestic law. Article 3.3 secured application of the mandatory rules of the law of the country to which, "all the other elements [apart from the parties' choice of law] relevant to the situation at the time of the choice are connected".[116]

---

[113] e.g. marriage contracts (art.1.2(c) of the Regulation).

[114] e.g. Rome I Regulation art.13 (contractual capacity).

[115] "In the interpretation and application of the preceding uniform rules, regard shall be had to their international character and to the desirability of achieving uniformity in their interpretation and application."

[116] *Caterpillar Financial Services Corp v SNC Passion* [2004] 2 Lloyd's Rep. 99.

Article 7 (applicable regardless of whether or not parties exercised choice of law), in contrast, referred to rules which, "must be applied whatever the law applicable to the contract", i.e. as a matter of the forum's choice of law rules. The latter usage used to be termed in UK law, "overriding legislation of the forum" (referring to legislation which applied no matter what the content of the foreign proper law[117]), and was a type of directory provision, which superimposed itself upon, or countermanded, normal choice of law rules.

Article 7.2 provided for application of the rules of the law of the *forum* in a situation where they were mandatory irrespective of the law otherwise applicable to the contract. A court of a Rome Convention Contracting State was required to take its own view on the question whether or not a rule of its domestic law was an overriding mandatory provision for the purpose of art.7.2. Article 7.1, which permitted "effect to be given"[118] to the overriding mandatory rules of the law of *another country* with which the situation had a close connection, did not apply in the UK, reservation having been entered in respect of this provision. A number of Contracting State delegations regarded art.7.1 with misgiving, as novel and uncertain.[119]

A point of dubiety under the Convention was the relationship in the area of consumer protection between arts 5 (mandatory rules of the law of the country in which the consumer is habitually resident) and 7. It was not clear whether or not art.7 was available to protect the consumer in a case where, in the circumstances, he failed to qualify for art.5 protection.[120]

Rome I Regulation

It was recognised at the negotiation and drafting stage of the Regulation that it would clearly be desirable in the English language text to make some distinction in verbal form between the meaning of "mandatory provisions" as they had been used in art.3.3 of the Convention, and art.7, respectively.[121] Article 3.3 of the Convention is replaced by art.3.3 and 3.4 of the Regulation.

15–22

> "Article 3
> Freedom of choice . . .
> 3.   Where all other elements relevant to the situation at the time of the choice are located in a country other than the country whose law has been chosen, the choice of the parties shall not prejudice the application of provisions of the law of that other country which cannot be derogated from by agreement.[122]
> 4.   Where all other elements relevant to the situation at the time of the choice are located in one or more Member States, the parties' choice of applicable law other than that of a Member State shall not prejudice the application of provisions of Community law, where appropriate as implemented in the Member State of the forum, which cannot be derogated from by agreement."

---

[117] UK legislation may exhibit overriding and/or self-denying provisions, e.g. Unfair Contract Terms Act 1977 s.27; Late Payment of Commercial Debts (Interest) Act 1998 s.12; and Timeshare, Holiday Products, Resale and Exchange Contracts Regulations 2010/2960 reg. 5. See also *Trident Turboprop (Dublin) Ltd v First Flight Couriers Ltd* [2009] EWCA Civ 290.

[118] See decision of Cour de Cassation in *Viol Frères v Philippe Fauveder & Co* (2010) (X 08-21.511).

[119] The UK and six other states exercised the right to enter a reservation. Giuliano and Lagarde, p.27.

[120] See also para.15–25 below.

[121] Rome I Regulation recital (37).

[122] See also Rome I Regulation recital (15). cf. Rome II Regulation art.14 and recital (32).

Characterisation of a rule of law for the purposes of art.3.3 and 3.4, as one which cannot be derogated from by agreement, is a task for the forum. Article 3.3 of the Regulation serves essentially the same purpose as did art.3.3 of the Convention.[123] Mandatory provision for the purpose of art.3 of the Regulation (which is relevant only in circumstances where a choice of law has been made by the parties) must be read as referring to provisions of the law of a country which cannot be derogated from by agreement.

Article 3.4 is an innovation, seeking to ensure, in cases where the choice of applicable law is that of a non-Member State, the application of provisions of Community law which cannot be derogated from by agreement. This elevates the status of Community law, ensuring that all Member State courts are mindful of it—but possibly the application of such provisions would have been safeguarded in any case by art.9.2 q.v. (and under the Convention, by art.7.2). Where the parties' choice of law falls upon the law of a Member State, art.3.4 has no application.

Article 7 of the Convention is replaced by art.9 of the Regulation.

> "Article 9
> Overriding mandatory provisions
> 1.   Overriding mandatory provisions are provisions the respect for which is regarded as crucial by a country for safeguarding its public interests, such as its political, social or economic organisation, to such an extent that they are applicable to any situation falling within their scope, irrespective of the law otherwise applicable to the contract under this Regulation.
> 2.   Nothing in this Regulation shall restrict the application of the overriding mandatory provisions of the law of the forum.
> 3.   Effect may be given to the overriding mandatory provisions of the law of the country where the obligations arising out of the contract have to be or have been performed, in so far as those overriding mandatory provisions render the performance of the contract unlawful. In considering whether to give effect to those provisions, regard shall be had to their nature and purpose and to the consequences of their application or non-application."

In relation to art.9, there are three principal points to note: first, art.9 applies regardless of whether or not the parties have exercised freedom of choice of law; secondly, a definition has been supplied in art.9.1 of "overriding mandatory provisions"; and thirdly, that which was optional under the Rome I Convention[124] has become compulsory under the Regulation—a mandatory provision in respect of mandatory provisions (which, paradoxically, contains within its own terms discretion for the forum).

There has been an important change of wording between art.7.1 of the Convention and art.9.3 of the Regulation, such as partially to allay the anxiety on the part of the UK and some other Member States that the provision was unreasonably vague.[125] While the introductory words of art.9.3 remain precatory (effect *may* be given), the identity of the country the law of which may be applied

---

[123] Rome I Regulation recital (15).

[124] Since Contracting States were permitted to enter a reservation under art.7.1.

[125] These concerns were sufficiently serious to influence the decision by the UK as to opting-in or not to the Regulation. It is, therefore, highly significant that as a result of negotiation (during which it became clear that the UK's preference for deletion of what became art.9.3 would not secure sufficient support among Member States), a compromise rule was reached that is narrower in scope than the

is, ex facie at least, clear. This is an improvement on the approach of the Convention, in terms of art.7.1 of which effect might be given to the mandatory rules, "of the law of another [i.e. any] country with which the situation has a close connection".

Characterisation, per art. 9.3, of a provision of the law of the country where the obligations arising out of the contract have to be or have been performed as an "overriding mandatory provision" is a task for the forum, which must heed the Community meaning supplied in art.9.1. However, it can be anticipated that identification, by any given forum on any given facts, of "the law of the country where the obligations arising out of the contract have to be or have been performed" will give rise to a line of interpretative case law, including references to CJEU.

Though art.11.5 (formal validity of contracts concerning immoveable property) is essentially the same as art.9.6 of the Convention, the draftsmen have taken care to specify that mandatory provisions of the *lex situs* must be observed.

In this commercial sphere, the exercise by the forum of its public policy is rarely seen. Nonetheless, public policy could apply to trump even mandatory provisions. In the event of a battle of policies under art.9 of the Regulation, the forum's policy, by virtue of art.21, could prevail. Strictly this would be true also in relation to art.3.3, though such a contest seems most unlikely.

SPECIAL CONTRACTS

Under the Rome I Regulation, bespoke and elaborate provision is made for four categories of special contract, viz.: contracts of carriage (art.5); consumer contracts (art.6); insurance contracts (art.7); and individual employment contracts (art.8). The rationale for the last three is explained in recital (23), to the effect that parties perceived to be at a disadvantage should be protected by choice of law rules that are more favourable to their interests than are the general rules.

15–23

Contracts of carriage

The Rome I Regulation in art.5 makes detailed provision regarding the applicable law of contracts for the carriage of goods and of passengers. The Rome I Convention made provision, under the aegis of art.4.4,[126] only for the carriage of goods.[127] The terms of the Rome I Regulation are subordinate to the terms of

15–24

Commission's original proposal (which resembled more closely art.7.1 of the Convention). See Ministry of Justice, *Rome I—Should the UK opt in?* 2008, Consultation Paper CP05/08, paras 77, 78.

[126] *Intercontainer Interfrigo (ICF) SC v Balkenende Oosthuizen BV and MIC Operations BV* Case C-133/08 [2008] O.J. C158/10; and *Haeger & Schmidt GmbH v Mutuelles du Mans assurances IARD (MMA IARD)* (C-305/13) [2015] 2 W.L.R. 175.

[127] Contracts for the carriage of persons fell within art.4.2 of the Rome Convention, and potentially, art 5.5, as "a contract which, for an inclusive price, provides for a combination of travel and accommodation". Charters by demise, where the contract was for the hire of the ship rather than for the carriage of goods, were not covered by the special presumption in art.4.4, but rather by art.4.2, the characteristic performance being delivery of the ship by the ship owner.

other conventions to which a Member State is, or may become a party, and which lay down conflict of laws rules relating to contractual obligations (art.25).[128]

The contracting parties may exercise freedom of choice of law to govern their contract, but, in the case of contracts for the carriage of passengers, that choice is limited, within the terms of art.5.2. The parties may choose only the law of the country where: (a) the passenger has his habitual residence; or (b) the carrier has his habitual residence; or (c) the carrier has his place of central administration; or (d) the place of departure is situated; or (e) the place of destination is situated.

In the absence of choice of law, the applicable law of the contract for the carriage of *goods* (art.5.1) shall be the law of the carrier's habitual residence,[129] provided that the place of receipt, or of delivery, or of consignor's habitual residence, is also situated in that country; which failing, the applicable law shall be the law of agreed place of delivery.

In the absence of choice of law, the applicable law of the contract for the carriage of *passengers* (art.5.2) shall be the law of the passenger's habitual residence, provided that either the place of departure or the place of destination is situated in that country; which failing, the law of the carrier's habitual residence shall apply.

By virtue of art.5.3, where no choice of law has been made by the parties, and it is clear from all the circumstances of the case that the contract is manifestly more closely connected with a country other than that indicated in art.5.1 or 5.2, the law of that other country shall apply.

Consumer contracts

15–25   At common law, there was no such species of person as a "consumer" for the purpose of international private law.[130] However, prior to the Contracts (Applicable Law) Act 1990, British domestic legislation sought to recognise and compensate cases of uneven bargaining power, principally in the cases of consumers and employees. An early example of conflict of laws awareness in a domestic statute is the Unfair Contract Terms Act 1977,[131] which contains in s.27(1) a self-denying provision, and in s.27(2) an overriding provision.

Certain "qualifying" consumer contracts were singled out for special treatment in the Rome I Convention art.5. In short, the benefit resided, first, in securing for the consumer the mandatory rules of the law of his habitual residence, notwithstanding choice by the parties of another law to govern their contract; and secondly, if the parties had made no express choice of law, the swift ascription to the contract as its applicable law of the law of the consumer's habitual residence.

---

[128] Hence, for example carriage of goods by sea continues to be regulated by the Hague-Visby Rules in terms of the Carriage of Goods by Sea Act 1971. A list of countries in which the Hague-Visby Rules are in force is set out in the Carriage of Goods by Sea (Parties to Convention) Order 1985 (SI 1985/443), as amended by Carriage of Goods by Sea (Parties to Convention) (Amendment) Order 2000 (SI 2000/1103). See, e.g. *Jindal Iron & Steel Co Ltd v Islamic Solidarity Shipping Co Jordan Inc* [2005] 1 Lloyd's Rep 57.

[129] As to which, see art.19.

[130] Though see *English v Donnelly*, 1958 S.C. 494 (Scots hire-purchase legislation held to apply irrespective of the proper law of the contract). cf. Generally *Stirling's Trustees v Legal & General Assurance Society Ltd*, 1957 S.L.T. 73.

[131] As amended by Contracts (Applicable Law) Act 1990 s.5, Sch.4 para.4. Other examples were Employment Protection (Consolidation) Act 1978 and Wages Act 1986, both now repealed.

These benefits arose only if the circumstances of the transaction satisfied the criteria set out in art.5.2. Care was taken, for example, by oblique wording to cover such circumstances as "cross-border excursion selling".

Article 6 of the Rome I Regulation provides as follows:

"1.   Without prejudice to Articles 5 and 7,[132] a contract concluded by a natural person for a purpose which can be regarded as being outside his trade or profession (the consumer)[133] with another person acting in the exercise of his trade or profession (the professional) shall be governed by the law of the country where the consumer has his habitual residence, provided that the professional:
    (a)   pursues his commercial or professional activities in the country where the consumer has his habitual residence, or
    (b)   by any means, directs such activities to that country or to several countries including that country,
and the contract falls within the scope of such activities.

2.   Notwithstanding paragraph 1, the parties may choose the law applicable to a contract which fulfils the requirements of paragraph 1, in accordance with Article 3. Such a choice may not, however, have the result of depriving the consumer of the protection afforded to him by provisions that cannot be derogated from by agreement by virtue of the law which, in the absence of choice, would have been applicable on the basis of paragraph 1.

3.   If the requirements in points (a) or (b) of paragraph 1 are not fulfilled, the law applicable to a contract between a consumer and a professional shall be determined pursuant to Articles 3 and 4.

4.   Paragraphs 1 and 2 shall not apply to:
    (a)   a contract for the supply of services where the services are to be supplied to the consumer exclusively in a country other than that in which he has his habitual residence;
    (b)   a contract of carriage other than a contract relating to package travel within the meaning of Council Directive 90/314/EEC of 13 June 1990 on package travel, package holidays and package tours;
    (c)   a contract relating to a right *in rem* in immovable property or a tenancy of immovable property other than a contract relating to the right to use immovable properties on a timeshare basis within the meaning of Directive 94/47/EC;
    (d)   rights and obligations which constitute a financial instrument and rights and obligations constituting the terms and conditions governing the issuance or offer to the public and public take-over bids of transferable securities, and the subscription and redemption of units in collective investment undertakings in so far as these activities do not constitute provision of a financial service;
    (e)   a contract concluded within the type of system falling within the scope of Article 4(1)(h)."

The Rome I Regulation is less prescriptive in relation to qualifying contracts. However, since it was felt that the rules of applicable law as contained in the Rome I Convention had not kept pace with the provisions contained in the

---

[132] Contracts of carriage; and insurance contracts.

[133] Assuming consistency of approach with the definition of consumer in the Brussels I and Recast Regulations (cf. recital (24) of the Rome I Regulation), see case law at paras 7–32—7–34, above.

Brussels I Regulation to protect consumers in jurisdictional terms,[134] the Rome I Regulation now contains, in art.6.1, the phrase "by any means, directs" such (commercial or professional) activities to the country of the consumer's habitual residence, a form of words which matches the wording used in art.15.1(c) of the Brussels I Regulation and art.17.1(c) of the Brussels I Recast. The insertion of this phrase at the time of drafting the Brussels I Regulation was regarded as a success for consumers. It is thought that it should cover internet purchases.[135]

One source of conjecture under the Rome I Convention was the matter of ranking in a case where the mandatory rules of the consumer's habitual residence were less favourable than those of the applicable law by way of the parties' choice of law per art.3. The argument that the supplier would have been prevented from setting up the less favourable rules of the habitual residence appears to be supported by the tone of recital (23) of the Rome I Regulation. As alluded to above,[136] the relationship between arts 5 (mandatory rules of the law of the country in which the consumer is habitually resident) and 7 of the Convention was not clear. Under the Regulation, it must be asked whether or not the relationship between arts 6 and 9 ("overriding mandatory provisions") is any clearer. In particular, is art.9 available to protect the consumer in a case where, in the circumstances, s/he fails to qualify for art.6 protection? It is clear from the text of art.6 that its provisions are without prejudice to arts 5 (contracts of carriage) and 7 (insurance contracts). Recital (32) explains that owing to the particular nature of these contracts, specific provisions are required to ensure an adequate level of protection of passengers and policy holders. Article 6 does not apply in the context of those particular contracts, even if the law putatively applicable under art.6 were more generous, in the circumstances, than the law applicable per arts 5 or 7. But by the same token, since there is no explicit ranking of arts 6 and 9 (nor arts 5 and 7, and 9), it may be taken that art.9 can operate in the context of a consumer (or carriage or insurance) contract, to the effect of securing for the weaker party the most advantageous outcome.

A particular rule is contained in art.11.4 (formal validity), to the effect that the form of a consumer contract shall be governed by the law of the country where the consumer has his habitual residence, overriding all other connecting factors set out in art.11. While art.11.4 is clearly intended to provide a simple rule for the benefit of consumers, the usual doubt arises viz.: what should happen if, by the law of the consumer's habitual residence, the "contract" is invalid as to form, but by the law of the country where the consumer happened to be present at the time of conclusion of the "contract" (art.11.2), the contract is formally valid? The tenor of the weaker party protections is to take an approach which favours the weaker party; it is not clear whether a court would be justified in taking an *in favorem* (upholding the contract) or *contra proferentem* (denying the contract) approach, as best suits the consumer.

---

[134] In respect of the vertical continuity of which, see *Ilsinger v Dreschers* (C-180/06) [2009] O.J. C153/3); E.B. Crawford, "The right of a consumer to seek payment of a prize apparently won" 2009 (4) European Journal of Consumer Law 861.

[135] See, however, recital (24).

[136] Para.15–21, above.

While much effort in the process of EC private international law harmonisation has been, and continues to be, made[137] to secure for cross-border consumers a body of rules, both of jurisdiction and of choice of law, which operates to their advantage, and to cut the costs of settling such disputes,[138] a salutary reminder has been given[139] that such persons often may seek a remedy for their grievance by extrajudicial means such as through negotiation or alternative dispute resolution, and that, in any event, the monetary amount involved may not be sufficiently large to warrant litigation.

Insurance contracts

The rules of the Rome I Convention did not apply to contracts of insurance covering risks situated in the territories of EC Member States.[140] This was explicable as there were several sectoral Directives governing the conflict of laws aspects of insurance. Contracts of reinsurance, however, were governed by the Convention.[141] Insured parties receive protective treatment in jurisdictional terms under the Brussels I Regulation.[142] As well as its being desirable to have a comprehensive and coherent system in place as between rules of jurisdiction and those of choice of law, criticism was expressed regarding the lack of transparency of choice of law provision in the insurance area.[143] Consequently, after consultation, specific provision for insurance contracts was made in art.7 of the Rome I Regulation.[144]

15–26

Article 7 applies to qualifying[145] insurance contracts whether or not the risk covered is situated in a Member State, and to all other insurance contracts covering risks situated inside the territory of Member States. The Regulation does not apply to reinsurance contracts, which are excluded from the scope of the instrument[146] (in contrast with the situation obtaining under the Convention).

---

[137] Rome I Regulation art.27.1(b) provides that by June 17, 2013, the Commission shall submit a report including an evaluation of the application of art.6, in particular as regards the coherence of Community law in the field of consumer protection. No report has yet been forthcoming.

[138] Rome I Regulation recital (24).

[139] J Hill, *Cross-Border Consumer Contracts* (Oxford: Oxford University Press, 2008).

[140] Rome I Convention art.1.3. To determine whether a risk is situated in these territories, the Convention provided that the forum should apply its internal law (art.1.3). Under the Regulation, see art.7.6.

[141] Rome I Convention art.1.4.

[142] Brussels I Regulation arts 8–14; and Brussels I Recast arts 10–16. These instruments also, in arts 14 and 16, respectively, differentiate between the generality of risks and particular risks (including "large risks" as defined in Directive 73/239/EC, as amended), described therein.

[143] 2003 Green Paper on Conversion of the Rome Convention of 1980 on the Law Applicable to Contractual Obligations into a Community Instrument and its Modernisation (COM(2002) 654 final), para.3.2.2.

[144] Article 27.1(a) provides that by 17 June 2013, the Commission shall submit a report including a study on the law applicable to insurance contracts and an assessment of the impact of any amendments proposed. The timetable has slipped: only in August 2014 did the European Commission issue its Open call for tender (JUST/2014/JCOO/PR/CIVI/0050 – Study on the law applicable to insurance contracts).

[145] Contracts covering "large risks" as defined: art.7.2. In the absence of party choice of law, the applicable law for contracts covering large risks normally shall be the law of habitual residence of the insurer.

[146] Rome I Regulation art.7.1.

In the case of insurance contracts other than those covered by art.7.2 (i.e. contracts other than those which cover "large risk"), only limited party autonomy to choose the applicable law is permitted, within the terms of art.7.3,[147] the rationale being to protect the policyholder. In the absence of choice of applicable law by the parties, the contract shall be governed by the law of the Member State in which the risk is situated at the time of conclusion of the contract.[148]

Individual employment contracts[149]

15–27   Article 8 of the Rome I Regulation is worded as follows:

> "1.   An individual employment contract shall be governed by the law chosen by the parties in accordance with Article 3. Such a choice of law may not, however, have the result of depriving the employee of the protection afforded to him by provisions that cannot be derogated from by agreement under the law that, in the absence of choice, would have been applicable pursuant to paragraphs 2, 3 and 4 of this Article.
>
> 2.   To the extent that the law applicable to the individual employment contract has not been chosen by the parties, the contract shall be governed by the law of the country in which or, failing that, from which the employee habitually carries out his work[150] in performance of the contract. The country where the work is habitually carried out shall not be deemed to have changed if he is temporarily employed in another country.
>
> 3.   Where the law applicable cannot be determined pursuant to paragraph 2, the contract shall be governed by the law of the country where the place of business through which the employee was engaged is situated.[151]
>
> 4.   Where it appears from the circumstances as a whole that the contract is more closely connected with a country other than that indicated in paragraphs 2 or 3, the law of that other country shall apply.[152]"

The provision is specific and leans towards application of the law of the place where the employee habitually carries out his work,[153] not only in securing to him

---

[147] Following the model of the rule in art.5.2 (contracts of carriage of passengers). See also The Financial Services and Markets Act 2000 (Law Applicable to Contracts of Insurance) Regulations 2009 (SI 2009/3075) regs 4, 5.

[148] Additional rules for situations where a Member State imposes an obligation to take out insurance are contained in art.7.4; and provision for risks situated in more than one Member State is made in art.7.5.

[149] For detail: L. Merrett, *Employment Contracts in Private International Law* (Oxford: Oxford University Press, 2011).

[150] In respect of which (under art.6.2 of the Rome Convention), see *Koelzsch v Luxembourg* (C-29/10) [2012] Q.B. 210.

[151] On the operation of the equivalent rule under art.6.2.b of the Rome I Convention, see *Voogsgeerd v Navimer SA* (C-384/10) [2012] I.L.Pr. 16.

[152] On the operation of the equivalent displacement rule under art.6.2 of the Rome I Convention, see *Schlecker (t/a Firma Anton Schlecker) v Boedeker* (C-64/12) [2014] Q.B. 320: in the absence of choice of law by the parties, the national court could disregard the law applicable in the country where the work was habitually carried out if it appeared from the circumstances as a whole that the contract was more closely connected with another country.

[153] See further explanation in recital (36). In *Koelzsch v Luxembourg* (C-29/10) [2012] Q.B. 210, the CJEU held that where an employee carries out his activities in more than one contracting state, the country in which he "habitually carries out his work" in performance of the contract is that in which or from which, in the light of all the factors which characterise that activity, the employee performed the greater part of his obligations towards his employer.

the benefit of the mandatory provisions of that law,[154] but also in identifying that law as the applicable law in the absence of choice.[155]

As with consumer contracts, the weaker party (the employee) should have the best outcome from his perspective. Within the operation of art.8, if the rules of the "chosen" law confer less benefit on him in the instant case than do the rules of the laws specified in art.8.2, 8.3 and 8.4, which cannot be derogated from by agreement, then the latter should prevail.[156] As regards the relationship between arts 8 and 9, it must be asked whether art.9 can operate in the context of an employment contract, to the effect of securing for the employee the most advantageous outcome. The answer must be that the employee can insist upon the application of the overriding mandatory provisions of the law of the forum, per art.9.2, if they are more generous.[157] Due to the likely coincidence between the place of habitual employment (art.8.2) and the country where the obligations arising out of the contract have to be performed (art.9.3), art.9.3 is not likely to be of assistance.

International sale of goods[158]

Various international instruments make special provision for contracts for the **15–28** international sale of goods. The Rome I Regulation does not follow this approach except for the particular provision in art.4.1(a).

There have been various attempts by the Hague Conference on Private International Law to regulate contracts for the sale of goods, including: 1955 Convention on the Law Applicable to International Sales of Goods; 1958 Convention on the Law governing Transfer of Title in International Sales of Goods; and 1958 Convention on the Jurisdiction of the Selected Forum in the case of International Sales of Goods.[159] Other international efforts in this area include the 1980 United Nations Convention on Contracts for the International Sale of Goods (also known as the Vienna Convention). These conventions aim to harmonise the substantive domestic laws of Contracting States in one particular area of law, and in so doing to provide an alternative to the traditional conflict of laws method of resolving disputes.[160] None, however, has been adopted by the UK.

By the Uniform Law on International Sales Act 1967, the UK implemented two Conventions, namely, the Uniform Law on the International Sale of Goods, and the Uniform Law on the Formation of Contracts for the International Sale of Goods.[161] Since art.25.1 of the Rome I Regulation saves the application of international conventions to which a Member State is, or becomes, a party, this

---

[154] *Duarte v Black & Decker Corp* [2007] EWHC 2720 (QB).

[155] *Shekar v Satyam Computer Services Ltd* [2005] I.C.R. 737.

[156] Rome I Regulation recital (35).

[157] Which effectively was the outcome in 1973 in *Brodin v A/R Seljan*, 1973 S.C. 213.

[158] For detail: J.J. Fawcett, J.M. Harris and M. Bridge, *International Sale of Goods in the Conflict of Laws* (Oxford: Oxford University Press, 2005).

[159] The 1955 Convention entered into force in nine states, but not in the UK. The two 1958 Conventions did not enter into force.

[160] See also European Commission Proposal for a Regulation of the European Parliament and of the Council on a Common European Sales Law (COM/2011/0635 final – 2011/0284 (COD)) (11 October 2011).

[161] Both concluded at The Hague on 1 July 1964.

means that, in theory, the two Uniform Law Conventions take precedence over the solution dictated by the general provisions of the Rome I Regulation.[162] But in practice hitherto, parties very rarely agreed to adopt, for application to their contract, the body of substantive rules contained in the Uniform Laws (assuming such a choice was/is competent[163]). Additionally, certain factual conditions must be fulfilled before the *corpus* of Uniform Law rules shall operate,[164] and these uniform rules, in any event, are subordinate to the mandatory provisions of the law which otherwise would be applicable. Hence, the option is not wholly attractive. Not only is the UK party only to a minority of these instruments, but those conventions which it has implemented are not in their substantive rules comprehensive.

Agency

15–29   Article 1.2(g) excludes from the scope of the Rome I Regulation the question whether an agent is able to bind a principal, or an organ to bind a company or body corporate or unincorporated, to a third party.[165] Other contractual aspects of agency, including disputes between principal and agent, will be subject to the Regulation, and identification of the applicable law for such matters is regulated by arts 3 or 4, as the case may be.[166] Since, perhaps surprisingly, agency is not one of the types of contract having a bespoke rule under art.4.1,[167] identification of the applicable law of the principal/agent contract, in the absence of choice of law by the parties, must be governed by art.4.2 of the Regulation, from which one might infer that, in the majority of cases, the applicable law will be that of the habitual residence of the agent.

Commercial agents

15–30   The activities of commercial agents in Great Britain are regulated by the Commercial Agents Directive 1986,[168] brought into effect in Great Britain by the Commercial Agents (Council Directive) Regulations 1993.[169]

---

[162] Subject, however, to art.25.2: as between Member States, the Regulation shall take precedence over conventions concluded exclusively between two or more of them in so far as such conventions concern matters governed by the Regulation.

[163] See discussion at para.15–12, above.

[164] See Uniform Law on International Sales Act 1967 Sch.1 art.1.

[165] cf. Rome I Convention art.1.2(f); and Giuliano and Lagarde, p.13. See also *Cheshire, North and Fawcett: Private International Law*, 14th edn (2008), pp.685, 686.

[166] Consider *Presentaciones Musicales SA v Secunda* [1994] Ch. 271; and *Lawlor v Sandvik Mining and Construction Mobile Crushers and Screens Ltd*[2013] EWCA Civ 365.

[167] An earlier proposal by the Commission to include a special rule for contracts concluded by an agent (covering (i) the applicable law governing the contractual relations between principal and agent; (ii) the relationship between the principal and third parties, whether the agent acted within or outside his powers; and (iii) the relationship between agent and third party) did not survive negotiations. See Ministry of Justice, *Rome I—Should the UK opt in?*, 2008, Consultation Paper CP05/08, para.74.

[168] Directive 86/653 on the co-ordination of the laws of the Member States relating to self-employed commercial agents [1986] O.J. L382/17.

[169] Commercial Agents (Council Directive) Regulations 1993 (SI 1993/3053), amended by Commercial Agents (Council Directive) (Amendment) Regulations 1993 (SI 1993/3173) and Commercial Agents (Council Directive) (Amendment) Regulations 1998 (SI 1998/2868). For examination of agency and the conflict of laws, see P. Watt and F.M.B. Reynolds (eds), *Bowstead &*

The 1986 Directive was introduced due to differences in the national laws of EC Member States concerning commercial representation, and the resultant inhibition upon conclusion and operation of commercial representation contracts where principal and commercial agents were established in different Member States. Since conflict of laws rules in the matter of commercial representation do not remove inconsistencies in national law, some degree of harmonisation of substantive law was required. The Directive gives priority to the legal relationship between commercial agent and principal.

The 1993 Regulations, as amended, have the general effect of protecting the agent, whereas domestic Scots law might be said to have shown particular awareness of the potential liabilities of the principal, and therefore, to be more protective of the latter party. A commercial agent is defined in reg.2(1) as:

> "…a self-employed intermediary who has continuing authority to negotiate the sale or purchase of goods on behalf of another person (the 'principal'), or to negotiate and conclude the sale or purchase of goods on behalf of and in the name of that principal."[170]

By Schedule to the Regulations, it is made clear that the type of agent to which they apply is one who devotes, "substantially the whole of his time to representative activities".[171] It is a complex matter to decide as regards any individual whether the Regulations apply.[172]

It has been seen that the relationship between principal and agent is subject to the Rome I Regulation (and the Convention before it). In a British forum, it is likely that the 1993 Regulations (application whereof is determined by the location of the activities of the agent, and not by personal law factors pertaining to the principal or agent) will have the status of mandatory provision of the forum for the purposes of the Rome I Regulation. In terms of reg.1, courts are directed to apply the law which the parties have agreed (under Rome I Regulation art.3) will govern their agency contract, to the extent that the choice is the law of a Member State. But it may be assumed, given the nature of the Directive, that there will be equivalent derivative/secondary legislation in each Member State, and that such legislation will share the characteristic of being mandatory in nature. Therefore, in any case where the activities of the agent are being performed in an EU state, it seems likely, regardless of the applicable law under the Rome I Regulation (be it the law of an EU Member State, or otherwise), that the contract will be subject to the mandatory rules of the (EU) forum (Rome I Regulation art.9.2), and possibly of the law of another state under arts 3.3 or 9.3, or provisions of Community law per art.3.4. This important point, that parties whose activities take place in a Member State cannot evade the protective provisions concerning commercial representations by choosing as the applicable

---

Reynolds on Agency, 20th edn (2014) (Sweet & Maxwell), Ch.12 (and on commercial agency and the conflict of laws, paras 11–006 to 11–011); and L.J. Macgregor, *The Law of Agency in Scotland* (Edinburgh: W. Green, 2013), Ch.9.

[170] Though see express exclusions from this category in reg.2.

[171] 1993 Regulations Sch.1 para.3(c).

[172] *McAdam v Boxpak Ltd*, 2006 S.L.T. 217. Also J.M. Carruthers, "Commercial Agency and the Conflict of Laws – What Place for Party Autonomy?" in D. Busch, L.J. Macgregor and P. Watt, *Agency Law in Commercial Practice* (OUP, 2015), forthcoming.

law under the Rome I Regulation the law of a non-EU State, was confirmed by the ECJ in *Ingmar GB Ltd v Eaton Leonard Technologies Inc*.[173]

In cases where the agent's activities are to be performed outside the EU, presumably the effectiveness of a choice of law clause in the principal-agent contract (even where those parties have Scottish connection), for application of the law of a non-EU Member State, will depend upon the choice of law rules of the *lex fori*. If ensuing litigation should take place in Scotland in respect of such a scenario, it would seem difficult as a matter of interpretation for the Scots court to hold that the Commercial Agents Regulations, which govern the activities of commercial agents in Great Britain, are mandatory under art.9.2.

INCIDENTS OF A CONTRACT

15–31   In cases covered by the Rome I Regulation, as under the Convention, the applicable law will govern most issues, but another law may govern a particular incident as an alternative to the generally applicable law, or in substitution for it. This approach reflects the position at common law.

Consent and material validity

15–32   Article 10 of the Rome I Regulation echoes the Convention (art.8), which itself affirmed and supplemented the common law:

> "1.   The existence and validity of a contract, or of any term of a contract, shall be determined by the law which would govern it under this Regulation if the contract or term were valid.
> 2.   Nevertheless, a party, in order to establish that he did not consent, may rely upon the law of the country in which he has his habitual residence if it appears from the circumstances that it would not be reasonable[174] to determine the effect of his conduct in accordance with the law specified in paragraph 1."

According to Guiliano and Lagarde, art.8 of the Convention was intended to cover all aspects of formation of the contract "other than general validity".[175] "General validity" must be taken to mean that which at common law in the UK was referred to as "essential validity" (validity of the contract as to its whole purpose, and/or as to particular terms thereof[176]), as opposed to "material validity" (establishing the fact of agreement).

---

[173] *Ingmar GB Ltd v Eaton Leonard Technologies Inc* [2001] All E.R. (Comm) 329 (in respect of which see H.L.E. Verhagen, "The Tension between Party Autonomy and European Union Law: Some Observations on *Ingmar GB Ltd v Eaton Leonard Technologies Inc*" (2002) 51 I.C.L.Q. 135). See also *United Antwerp Maritime Agencies (Unamar) NV v. Navigation Maritime Bulgare* Case C-184/12, CJEU 17 October 2013. cf. from jurisdiction, *Accentuate Ltd v Asigra Inc* [2009] EWHC 2655 (QB); [2009] 2 Lloyd's Rep. 599; [2010] 2 All E.R. (Comm) 738; and *Fern Computer Consultancy Ltd v Intergraph Cadworx & Analysis Solutions Inc* [2014] EWHC 2908 (Ch).

[174] *Toyota Tsusho Sugar Trading Ltd v Prolat SRL* [2014] EWHC 3649 (Comm).

[175] Giuliano and Lagarde, p.29.

[176] In respect of which, see art.12, below.

At common law, the question whether a contract had been formed was governed by the law which would have been the proper law of the contract if it were held that a contract had been validly concluded (the putative proper law),[177] exemplified in *Albeko Schuhmaschinen AG v Kamborian Shoe Machine Co Ltd*.[178] This workable approach can be seen to have been adopted by the Convention and the Regulation (the putative applicable law), subject to addition by way of art.10.2.

The rule on material validity covers the questions whether or not there has been sufficient consent to contract (i.e. sufficient by the putative applicable law), and agreement necessary to constitute a binding bargain. Hence, questions of substance as to what constitutes acceptance, as well as "technical" questions, such as the effect of posting an acceptance (i.e. whether or not receipt by the offeror is necessary for the constitution of the contract), are referred to the putative applicable law.

The reason for the inclusion of the discretionary power in art.10.2 is to guard against the consequences of operation of a rule of some legal systems that silence on the part of the offeree connotes acceptance.[179]

Formal validity

The matter is governed by art.11 of the Regulation, in which the list of potentially relevant connecting factors has been expanded from that available under the Convention, which, in turn, was more expansive than the common law.[180] The approach remains generous. Difficulties occasionally may arise, however, as to the meaning of formal validity.[181] The rules traditionally have taken, and the Regulation continues to take, an *in favorem* approach, finding, where possible, a contract to be formally valid.

15–33

> "1.   A contract concluded between persons who, or whose agents, are in the same country at the time of its conclusion is formally valid if it satisfies the formal requirements of the law which governs it in substance under this Regulation or of the law of the country where it is concluded.
>
> 2.   A contract concluded between persons who, or whose agents, are in different countries at the time of its conclusion is formally valid if it satisfies the formal requirements of the law which governs it in substance under this

---

[177] *Mackender v Feldia AG* [1967] 2 Q.B. 590; and *Euro-Diam Ltd v Bathurst* [1987] 2 All E.R. 113; affirmed [1990] 1 Q.B. 1. See E.B. Crawford, "The Uses of Putativity and Negativity in the Conflict of Laws" (2005) 54 I.C.L.Q. 829, 830–832.

[178] *Albeko Schuhmaschinen AG v Kamborian Shoe Machine Co Ltd* (1961) 111 L.J. 519. See also *Compania Naviera Micro SA v Shipley International Inc (The Parouth)* [1982] 2 Lloyd's Rep. 351 CA.

[179] Giuliano and Lagarde, p.28.

[180] At common law a contract was formally valid if it complied with the provisions of either the proper law or the *lex loci contractus: Guepratte v Young* (1851) 4 De G. & Sm. 217; *Van Grutten v Digby* (1862) 31 Beav. 561; *Purvis's Trustees v Purvis's Executors* (1861) 23 D. 812 (per Lord Justice-Clerk Inglis at 831 re testamentary writings); *Valery v Scott* (1876) 3 R. 965.

[181] See, e.g. *Integral Petroleum SA v Scu-Finanz AG* [2015] EWCA Civ 144, per Floyd L.J. at [39] on the question of the correct characterisation of the issue between the parties: "The issue is one of the authority of a single prokurist [registered officer] to bind the company. That is a matter for the company's constitution, as broadly interpreted, and is not governed by the Rome I Regulation, but instead by the common law principles...".

Regulation, or of the law of either of the countries where either of the parties or their agent is present at the time of conclusion, or of the law of the country where either of the parties had his habitual residence at that time.[182]

3. A unilateral act intended to have legal effect relating to an existing or contemplated contract is formally valid if it satisfies the formal requirements of the law which governs or would govern the contract in substance under this Regulation, or of the law of the country where the act was done, or of the law of the country where the person by whom it was done had his habitual residence at that time.

4. Paragraphs 1, 2 and 3 of this Article shall not apply to contracts that fall within the scope of Article 6.[183] The form of such contracts shall be governed by the law of the country where the consumer has his habitual residence.

5. Notwithstanding paragraphs 1 to 4, a contract the subject matter of which is a right *in rem* in immovable property or a tenancy of immovable property shall be subject to the requirements of form of the law of the country where the property is situated if by that law:

(a) those requirements are imposed irrespective of the country where the contract is concluded and irrespective of the law governing the contract; and

(b) those requirements cannot be derogated from by agreement."[184]

Scope of the law applicable

15–34 Whereas art.10 of the Regulation concerns material validity (establishing the fact of agreement), art.12 concerns matters of general or essential validity (validity of the contract as to its whole purpose, and/or as to particular terms thereof). Article 12, headed "Scope of the law applicable", provides as follows:

"1. The law applicable to a contract by virtue of this Regulation shall govern in particular[185]:

(a) interpretation;

(b) performance;

(c) within the limits of the powers conferred on the court by its procedural law, the consequences of a total or partial breach of obligations, including the assessment[186] of damages[187] in so far as it is governed by rules of law[188];

(d) the various ways of extinguishing obligations, and prescription and limitation of actions[189];

(e) the consequences of nullity of the contract."

Since art.12 does not provide an exhaustive list of topics falling within the scope of the law applicable, authorities residing in the common law or Rome

---

[182] There has been an enlargement of potentially applicable laws through the addition of the habitual residence of either party at the time of contracting.

[183] Of the "weaker" parties for whom special treatment is set out in arts 6–8, the consumer alone receives special treament in relation to formal validity.

[184] With regard to contracts concerning immoveable property, art.11.5 does not differ in substance from its precursor, art.9.6 of the Convention.

[185] The list is not comprehensive.

[186] cf. Rome II art.15.1(c). See discussion at Ch.8, above.

[187] cf. at common law *J D'Almeida Araujo LDA v Sir Frederick Becker & Co Ltd* [1953] 2 Q.B. 329.

[188] See paras 8–35 and 16–38.

[189] See discussion at paras 8–07—8–10, above.

Convention[190] background still may be of assistance. At common law, the essential validity of a contract was governed by its proper law, or putative proper law.[191] Essential validity was deemed to include all questions pertaining to substance, and to the rights and obligations of the contracting parties generally, including matters such as the need for consideration; liability for non-performance; interest[192]; acquiescence in allegedly inadequate performance; rejection of goods as disconform to contract[193]; retention of payment[194]; liability for damages; third party rights under the contract (*jus quaesitum tertio*); the effect of a moratorium; the effect of war; the effects of exemption and indemnity clauses, etc. The proper law therefore determined all questions as to the rights of parties and defences, subject to the qualification that contractual rights might not have been enforceable if illegal by the law of the forum, or contrary to its public policy.

(a) Interpretation

Article 12.1(a) of the Regulation, in referring the matter of interpretation entirely to the applicable law, is rather more restrictive than the common law according to which the construction or interpretation of a contract was determined by the law chosen by the parties to govern that aspect. At common law, in the absence of a clause providing for interpretation, the law indicated by the contract applied; in the majority of cases, this was the proper law, but that law did not necessarily apply and probably would not apply if the contract were written in a language different from that of the proper law.[195]

15–35

(b) Performance

Adequacy of performance of obligations due under the contract will be governed by the applicable law. This will include the effect of partial performance and non-performance, as well as defective or delayed performance. Cognate topics

15–36

---

[190] e.g. *OJSC TNK-BP Holding, OJSC TNK-BP Management v Lazurenko* [2012] EWHC 2781 (Ch); and *Sapporo Breweries Ltd v Lupofresh Ltd* [2013] EWCA Civ 948; [2014] 1 All E.R. (Comm) 484.
[191] e.g. *Jacobs Marcus & Co v Credit Lyonnais* (1884) 12 Q.B.D. 589; *The Leon XIII* (1883) L.R. 8 P.D. 121; *Hansen v Dixon* (1906) 23 T.L.R. 56; *Kremezi v Ridgway* [1949] 1 All E.R. 662; *Equitable Trust Co of New York v Henderson* (1930) 47 T.L.R. 90; *Société des Hotels Reunis v Hawker* (1913) 29 T.L.R. 578; *Re Bonacina* [1912] 2 Ch. 394; *Re Claim by Helbert Wagg & Co Ltd* [1956] Ch. 323; *McCormick v Rittmeyer* (1869) 7 M. 854; *Gow v Caledonian Scrap Co* (1893) 7 Sh.Ct Rep. 65; *Keiner v Keiner* [1952] 1 All E.R. 643; *Hamlyn and Co v Talisker Distillery* (1894) 21 R. (H.L.) 21; *St Pierre v South American Stores* [1936] 1 K.B. 382; *The Al Wahab* [1983] 2 All E.R. 884; *The Rosso* [1982] 3 All E.R. 841; *Gill & Duffus Landauer Ltd v London Export Corp* [1982] 2 Lloyd's Rep. 627; *The Mariannina* [1983] 1 Lloyd's Rep. 12; *Armour v Thyssen Edelstahlwerke AG*, 1986 S.L.T. 94 OH; 1990 S.L.T. 891 HL; *Zahnrad Fabrik Passau GmbH v Terex Ltd*, 1986 S.L.T. 84.
[192] *Parken v Royal Exchange Assurance Co* (1846) 8 D. 365.
[193] *Benaim & Co v Debono* [1924] A.C. 514; *Sellar and Sons v Gladstone and Co* (1868) 5 S.L.R. 417; *Gow v Caledonian Scrap Co* (1893) 7 Sh.Ct Rep. 65.
[194] cf. *Bank of East Asia Ltd v Scottish Enterprise*, 1997 S.L.T. 1213.
[195] *Bonython v Australia* [1951] A.C. 201; [1952] A.C. 493; *The Assunzione* [1954] P. 150; *Re Claim by Helbert Wagg & Co Ltd* [1956] Ch. 323; *Corocraft Ltd v Pan American Airways Inc* [1969] 1 Q.B. 616; *Total Societa Italiana per Azioni v Liberian Transocean Navigation Corp (The Alexandria I)* [1972] 1 Lloyd's Rep. 399; *Woodhouse AC Israel Cocoa SA v Nigerian Produce Marketing Co Ltd* [1972] A.C. 741; *WJ Alan & Co Ltd v El Nasr Export & Import Co* [1972] 2 Q.B. 189.

such as impossibility of performance, and excuses for non- or partial performance, are likely to arise, and equally are substantive matters to be referred to the *lex causae*.

The law applicable to the contract governs performance, but art.12.2 provides that in relation to the manner of performance and the steps to be taken in the event of defective performance, regard shall be had to the law of the country in which performance takes place. This acts as a discretionary restriction on the operation of the law applicable to the contract, and is expressed merely in precatory terms. With regard to the precursor provision of the Convention, art.10.2, the Giuliano and Lagarde Report noted the absence of any definition of the phrase "manner of performance", and suggests that matters such as the rules governing public holidays and the manner in which goods are to be examined would fall within this rule.

Money obligations

15–37　With regard to the counterpart obligation of payment, it was found to be important at various points in the common law development of the subject, in decades in which a currency crisis had arisen, to draw a distinction between the discharge of the substance of an obligation, on the one hand, and, on the other, the performance of the obligation by payment of the debt in the currency which, by agreement of the parties, was to be used.[196] Insofar as these matters still might be of importance, the "money of account of a contract" (being the amount of money due by the debtor, and representing the currency in which his obligation must first be calculated) will be governed by the applicable law, by virtue of art.12.1(b). In contrast, the "money of payment of a contract" (being the kind of money or currency which the debtor must proffer in order to discharge his obligation, that is, the currency in which the money due is to be paid) traditionally was regarded as procedural, and governed by the law of the place of performance. Conceivably, the latter aspect now may be considered to fall within art.12.1(d), and so subject too to the law applicable to the contract, rendering the distinction irrelevant.

Likewise, contractual obligations may be affected, and even invalidated, by exchange control legislation, if the legislation forms part of the governing law of the contract,[197] or is regarded as an overriding mandatory provision of the forum[198] or of the place of performance.[199]

Revalorisation laws (laws revaluing a particular currency) apply only to contracts and debts the applicable law of which is the law of the country concerned.[200]

---

[196] *Adelaide Electric Supply Co Ltd v Prudential Assurance Co Ltd* [1934] A.C. 122; *Mayor of Auckland v Alliance Assurance Co Ltd* [1937] A.C. 587; *Mount Albert BC* [1938] A.C. 224; *Bonython v Australia* [1951] A.C. 201; *National Mutual Life Association of Australasia v Att Gen of New Zealand* [1956] A.C. 369.

[197] Subject to the public policy of the forum (art.21). cf. At common law *Re Claim by Helbert Wagg & Co Ltd* [1956] Ch. 323.

[198] Rome I Regulation art.9.2. See at common law, *Boissevain v Weil* [1950] A.C. 327.

[199] Rome I Regulation art.9.3.

[200] cf. at common law, *Anderson v Equitable Life Assurance Co* (1926) 41 T.L.R. 123; *Re Schnapper* [1936] 1 All E.R. 322; *Kornatzki v Oppenheimer* [1937] 4 All E.R. 133.

Effect of illegality of a contract

The Rome I Regulation, in common with the Convention, does not make express **15–38** provision regarding the matter of illegality, but a rule can be inferred by reference to art.12, namely, that a contract which in its terms breaches its own applicable law will not be enforced by any Member State court. There must be considered as potentially relevant, in addition, rules which cannot be derogated from by agreement (under art.3.3 or 3.4), and account has to be taken of the public policy of the forum (art.21).[201] Application of any of these provisions may lead to unenforceability of a contract in the UK.[202]

Under the Rome I Convention, while a provision illegal by the mandatory rules of the forum was caught by art.7.2, art.7.1 was not available to UK courts to assist in cases where, initially or subsequently, there was illegality by some law of close connection (other than the applicable law).[203] Now, under the Rome I Regulation, reference must be made to art.9.3, which provides expressly for cases of performance illegal by the law of the country where the obligation arising out of that contract has to be or has been performed. As has been noted,[204] art.9.3 is phrased as a guide, not a direction. Its potential application can be tested conveniently against the facts which arose in an English forum in *Ralli Bros v Compania Naviera Sota y Aznar*.[205] The case concerned the carriage of jute on a Spanish ship from Calcutta to Barcelona, at a rate of freight which, en route, became illegal by the Spanish law of the nationality of the ship (taken to be the law of the place of performance), and thus provides an example of supervening, as opposed to initial, illegality of contractual terms by the law of the place of performance. The proper law of the contract of carriage was English. Since the English forum refused to enforce the contractual rate of freight, the inference was drawn that, if the proper law of a contract is English, illegality by the *lex loci solutionis* would render the contract unenforceable in England. There was debate about whether this rule was one of English domestic or English conflict law, but it seemed reasonable, and in accordance with principle, further to infer from the decision that the effect of illegality by the *lex loci solutionis* was a matter which an English court would refer to the applicable law.[206] The common law position is that a contract would not have been enforceable in England or Scotland if it was illegal according to the proper law of the contract[207]; or it offended against

---

[201] cf. at common law, *Foster v Driscoll* [1929] 1 K.B. 470; *Regazzoni v KC Sethia (1944) Ltd* [1958] A.C. 301; and *Lemenda Trading Co Ltd v African Middle East Petroleum Co Ltd* [1988] Q.B. 448.

[202] *Soleimany v Soleimany* [1999] Q.B. 785. See *Cheshire, North and Fawcett: Private International Law*, 14th edn (2008), pp.658–660.

[203] cf. notable Dutch decision, *Cie européenne des pétrôles SA v Sensor Nederlands BV Hague 1982* (1983) 23 Int. Legal Mat. 66 (see *Dicey, Morris and Collins on the Conflict of Laws*, 15th edn (2012), para.32–085).

[204] Para.15–22, above.

[205] *Ralli Bros v Compania Naviera Sota y Aznar* [1920] 2 K.B. 287; cf. *Regazzoni v KC Sethia (1944) Ltd* [1958] A.C. 301.

[206] cf. Reynolds, "Illegitimacy by *Lex Loci Solutionis*" (1992) 108 L.Q.R. 553.

[207] *Heriz v Riera* (1840) 11 Sum. 318; *Rousillon v Rousillon* (1880) L.R. 14 Ch. D. 351; *Re Missouri Steamship Co* (1889) L.R. 42 Ch. D. 321; *Kaufman v Gerson* [1904] 1 K.B. 591; *Ralli Bros v Compania Naviera Sota y Aznar* [1920] 2 K.B. 287; *Foster v Driscoll* [1929] 1 K.B. 470; *De Beeche v South American Stores(Gath & Chaves) Ltd* [1935] A.C. 148; *R. v International Trustee for the Protection of Bondholders AG* [1937] A.C. 500; *O'Toole v Whiterock Quarry Co Ltd*, 1937 S.L.T. 521; *Kahler v Midland Bank Ltd* [1950] A.C. 24; contrast *Kleinwort Sons & Co v Ungarische*

the public policy of the *lex fori*.[208] Applying the Rome I Regulation to the facts of *Ralli Bros*, it seems that the English forum simply would exercise its discretion whether or not to give effect to the supervening Spanish law, assuming that the English forum considered the provision in question to be an overriding mandatory provision of the law of the place of performance. There are, therefore, two steps of discretion.

(c)   The consequences of breach

15–39   The consequences of a total or partial breach of obligations, including the assessment of damages insofar as it is governed by rules of law,[209] is referred by the Regulation to the law applicable to the contract. Questions of fact will always be matters of procedure for the forum,[210] but the wording of this provision of the Regulation denotes a shift in damages awards[211] between the provinces of the *lex causae* and the *lex fori*, respectively, to the effect of enlarging that of the *lex causae*.

(d)   The various ways of extinguishing obligations

Discharge of obligations

15–40   Obligations under a contract may be affected, or even discharged, by subsequent events. A general discharge of obligations, or some other act purporting to discharge obligations, is effective if it is effective under the applicable law of the contract. Thus, the governing law determines the effect of supervening impossibility, war, moratorium, and confiscatory and other legislation.[212] Similarly the effects of novation, delegation,[213] and acceptilation must be determined by the governing law of the principal obligation (rather than that of the derivative agreement). Excuses for non-performance or defences attributable to statutory provision which are part of the applicable law of the contract under the Rome I Regulation will operate. Excuses and defences which are not part of the applicable law will be effective only where those provisions qualify as overriding mandatory provision under art.9.[214]

Baumwolle Industrie AG [1939] 2 K.B. 678; *Addison v Brown* [1954] 1 W.L.R. 779; *Arab Bank Ltd v Barclays Bank (Dominion, Colonial and Overseas)* [1954] A.C. 495; *Prodexport State Co for Foreign Trade v ED&F Man Ltd* [1973] Q.B. 389.

[208]   cf. *Lemenda Trading Co Ltd v African Middle East Petroleum Co Ltd* [1988] Q.B. 448; and see Clarkson and Hill, *Conflict of Laws*, 4th edn (2011), p.55.

[209]   See para.8–35, above.

[210]   Giuliano and Lagarde, p.33.

[211]   The shift is visible in non-contractual obligations as well as contractual obligations: cf. Rome II art.15(c): para.16–38.

[212]   See, at common law, *Watson v Renton* (1792) M. 4582; *Ellis v McHenry* (1871) L.R. 6 C.P. 228; *Jacobs Marcus and Co v Credit Lyonnais* (1884) 12 Q.B.D. 589; *Gibbs and Sons v Société Industrielle et Commerciale des Metaux* (1890) L.R. 25 Q.B.D. 399; *Re Anglo-Austrian Bank (Vogel's Application)* [1920] 1 Ch. 69; and *Adams v National Bank of Greece and Athens SA* [1961] A.C. 255.

[213]   *Re United Railways of Havana and Regla Warehouses Ltd* [1961] A.C. 1007.

[214]   Or less likely, as rules that cannot be derogated from by agreement, in terms of art.3.3 and 3.4. At common law, the general rule was that statutory provisions, whether Scottish, UK or foreign, affected a contract only if they were part of the proper law. *Kleinwort Sons & Co v Ungarische Baumwolle*

The same principle applies with regard to the universal discharge of all obligations following upon insolvency proceedings conducted under the same law as the law governing the principal obligation. Likewise, a discharge under a trust deed will be a complete discharge, if granted under the same law as the law applicable to the principal obligation. If, however, the governing law differs from the law of the insolvency proceedings or the trust deed, a discharge would have no extraterritorial effect[215] except that under the British bankruptcy statutes a discharge in a Scots sequestration will be effective as a discharge in England in respect of a claim arising from any contractual obligation, regardless of its governing law.[216]

Where the discharge arises in the context of collective insolvency proceedings in relation to a debtor whose main interests are centred in an EU Member State, account must be taken of Regulation 1346/2000 on Insolvency Proceedings.[217] Article 4.2 of that Regulation, and art.7 of the Recast Insolvency Regulation, respectively states that the law of the state of the opening of proceedings (the *lex concursus*)[218] (regarding main or secondary proceedings, respectively)[219] shall determine the effects of insolvency proceedings upon current contracts to which the debtor is party (para.(e)), and on creditors' rights after closure of such proceedings (para.(k)). As regards contracts relating to immoveable property, however, the effect of insolvency proceedings on a contract conferring the right to acquire or use such property, is governed solely by the law of the Member State within the territory of which the property is situated (art.8 of the Insolvency Regulation; art.11 of the Recast Insolvency Regulation).[220]

With regard to the relationship between Regulation 1346/2000 and the Rome I Regulation, reference may be made to art.23 of Rome I, which provides that, "...this Regulation shall not prejudice the application of provisions of Community law which, in relation to particular matters, lay down conflict-of-law rules relating to contractual obligations". It is to be presumed, therefore, that art.12.1(d) is without prejudice to the particular rules contained in Regulation 1346/2000 and, in turn, the Recast Regulation by virtue of art.91 thereof.

Industrie AG [1939] 2 K.B. 678; *Vita Food Products Inc v Unus Shipping Co Ltd (In Liquidation)* [1939] A.C. 277; *Arab Bank Ltd v Barclays Bank* [1954] A.C. 495; *English v Donnelly*, 1959 S.L.T. 2; *National Bank of Greece and Athens SA v Metliss* [1958] A.C. 509; *Adams v National Bank of Greece and Athens SA* [1961] A.C. 255; *Rossano v Manufacturers Life Insurance Co* [1963] 2 Q.B. 352.

[215] See *Gibbs and Sons v Société Industrielle et Commerciale des Metaux* (1890) L.R. 25 Q.B.D. 399.

[216] Bankruptcy (Scotland) Act 1985 ss.54, 55(1). For English law, see *Dicey, Morris and Collins on the Conflict of Laws*, 15th edn (2012), rr.213, 215, and comment at paras 31–054 to 31–057, 31–068 to 31–071.

[217] The Regulation applies only to collective insolvency proceedings where the centre of the debtor's main interests is located in the EU; recitals (13), (14). See also Regulation (EU) 2015/848 of the European Parliament and of the Council of 20 May 2015 on Insolvency Proceedings (Recast) Recital (23) and (25). Ch.17, below.

[218] Regulation 1346/2000 recital (23).

[219] Regulation 1346/2000 art.3 and Regulation (EU) 2015/848, art.3. See Ch.17, below.

[220] cf. Regulation 1346/2000 recital (25).

Set-off[221]

15–41   The Rome I Regulation contains, in art.17, a new rule on set-off, which is a method of extinguishing, wholly or partly, an indebtedness. Impliedly under the Rome Convention, the subject of set-off fell within art.10.1(d) (the various ways of extinguishing obligations). Article 17 of the Regulation, however, sets out a special rule, to the effect that where the right to set-off is not agreed by the parties, set-off shall be governed by the law applicable to the claim against which the right to set-off is asserted. This new rule aims to resolve the more complex situation where a conflict arises because more than one obligation is involved, each obligation is governed by a different law, and the substantive laws contain different rules concerning set-off. But if the right to set-off is agreed between or among the parties, the applicable law of that agreement per art.3 (or potentially arts 5–8), in combination with art.12.1(d), must govern, in the same way as before.

Multiple liability

15–42   Multiple liability now is dealt with in a freestanding article of the Regulation, art.16, but the substantive import is unchanged from art.13.2 of the Convention. The article provides that:

> "If a creditor has a claim against several debtors who are liable for the same claim, and one of the debtors has already satisfied the claim in whole or in part, the law governing the debtor's obligation towards the creditor also governs the debtor's right to claim recourse from the other debtors. The other debtors may rely on the defences they had against the creditor to the extent allowed by the law governing their obligations towards the creditor."

Prescription and limitation of actions

15–43   In terms of art.12.1(d), prescription and limitation of actions shall be governed by the law applicable to the contract. This is in accord with pre-existing Scots and English law.[222]

(e)   The consequences of nullity of the contract

15–44   By art.12.1(e) of the Rome I Regulation, the law applicable to a contract will govern the consequences of nullity of the contract, which will include the repayment of sums due under a void or nullified contract. By UK reservation the equivalent provision of the Rome I Convention, art.10.1(e), did not apply in a UK court since the consequences of nullity were regarded by Scots and English law

---

[221] See M. Hellner in Ferrari and Leible (eds), *Rome I Regulation: The Law Applicable to Contractual Obligations in Europe* (2009), p.251.

[222] Prescription and Limitation (Scotland) Act 1973, as amended by the Prescription and Limitation (Scotland) Act 1984. See also reg.3 of The Law Applicable to Contractual Obligations (Scotland) Regulations 2009 (SSI 2009/410). For England, see Foreign Limitation Periods Act 1984; and reg.3 of The Law Applicable to Contractual Obligations (England and Wales and Northern Ireland) Regulations 2009 (SI 2009/3064). See Ch.8, above.

as pertaining to rules of restitution. In many cases the applicable law identified by these two routes would be the same. While in principle there is no reason, therefore, for UK lawyers to feel unease about the inclusion of the consequences of nullity of contract within art.12, it is important to realise the extent of regulation of this area given that in Ch.III of the Rome II Regulation there are provisions regulating the subjects of unjust enrichment, *negotiorum gestio* and *culpa in contrahendo*. The relationship between the Rome I and Rome II Regulations in this area may be productive of difficulties of demarcation.[223]

Capacity to contract

Article 13 of the Rome I Regulation contains a provision, introduced in art.11 of the Convention, which is remarkably specific in its terms.[224]   **15–45**

> "Article 13
> Incapacity
> In a contract concluded between persons who are in the same country, a natural person who would have capacity under the law of that country may invoke his incapacity resulting from the law of another country, only if the other party to the contract was aware of that incapacity at the time of the conclusion of the contract or was not aware thereof as a result of negligence."

This topic in practice is not simple, and there are conflicting policy considerations.[225] Where the case does not fall within the complex prerequisites of art.13, the common law continues to apply. Early Scots and English cases at common law indicated that contractual capacity was governed by the *lex loci contractus*,[226] but preference later was shown for the putative proper law.[227] Cheshire, when he delivered the David Murray Lecture[228] at the University of Glasgow in 1948 suggested, first, that a contract is not void for incapacity if the parties are fully capable by the putative proper law (that is, the law objectively ascertained, for parties could not at common law confer on themselves capacity by simple choice of a law unconnected) and, secondly, that a party who is incapable by the putative proper law should not succeed in pleading incapacity if he is of full capacity by the law of his domicile.

In *Haugesund Kommune v Depfa ACS Bank*,[229] the English Court of Appeal endorsed the approach of the judge at first instance in referring the question of the capacity of a corporation to enter into a legal transaction to both its constitution and the applicable law of the putative contract.

---

[223] Further, para.15–62 et seq.

[224] See commentary per *Cheshire, North and Fawcett: Private International Law*, 14th edn (2008), pp.750–753.

[225] See D. McClean and V. Ruiz Abou-Nigm, *Morris – The Conflict of Laws*, 8th edn (2012), paras 11–065 to 11–068.

[226] *Male v Roberts* (1800) 3 Esp. 163; *McFeetridge v Stewarts & Lloyds Ltd*, 1913 S.C. 773.

[227] *Bodley Head Ltd v Alec Flegon (t/a Flegon Press)* [1972] 1 W.L.R. 680. See also, in Canada, *Bondholders Securities Corp v Manville* (1933) 4 D.L.R. 699; *Charron v Montreal Trust* (1958) 15 D.L.R. (2d.) 240.

[228] Printed as Geoffrey C. Cheshire, *International Contracts* (Glasgow: Jackson, Son & Co, 1948).

[229] *Haugesund Kommune v Depfa ACS Bank* [2012] Q.B. 549.

Voluntary assignment

15–46 Articles 14–17 of the Regulation have in common the feature that the contractual circumstances which they address involve, or are capable of involving, a third or further party in addition to the original contracting parties.

Articles 14–16 of the Regulation have re-cast and amplified provisions which were to be found in arts 12 and 13 of the Convention.[230]

Article 14

15–47 A triangular situation arises where the creditor in an original claim against a debtor assigns his right to pursue that claim to a third party assignee. The contract between the original parties (debtor and creditor) has a governing law, ascertained by reference to arts 3 or 4 of the Regulation, provided that the contract falls within its scope. The assignation too, from creditor to assignee, has its own law, so determined. The third side of the triangle is the relationship between assignee and debtor.

Article 14, the successor to the criticised art.12 of the Convention, in seeking to regulate this tripartite scenario, provides as follows:

> "1.   The relationship between assignor and assignee under a voluntary assignment[231] or contractual subrogation of a claim against another person (the debtor) shall be governed by the law that applies to the contract between the assignor and assignee under this Regulation.
>
> 2.   The law governing the assigned or subrogated claim shall determine its assignability, the relationship between the assignee and the debtor, the conditions under which the assignment or subrogation can be invoked against the debtor and whether the debtor's obligations have been discharged.
>
> 3.   The concept of assignment in this Article includes outright transfers of claims, transfers of claims by way of security and pledges or other security rights over claims."

The non-exhaustive explanation of the concept of assignment, in art.14.3, is new, but the meaning and effect of the remainder of art.14 largely repeats art.12 of the Convention, viz.: the relationship between assignor and assignee shall be governed by the applicable law of the contract between them[232]; and the law governing the assigned or subrogated claim shall determine not only its assignability, but also the relationship between the assignee and the debtor, and the conditions under which the assignment or subrogation can be invoked against the debtor, and whether the debtor's obligations have been discharged.[233]

The problem is that art.14, like its predecessor, makes no provision for tangential or external complexities, namely, the relationship between or among two or more competing assignees. Opportunity was not taken in the Regulation, through lack of time, to select the law which shall govern the effectiveness of an assignment or subrogation of a claim vis-à-vis third parties; nor to address the

---

[230] See R.L.E. Verhagen and S. van Dongen, "Cross-Border Assignments under Rome I" (2010) 6 J.P.I.L. 1.

[231] Or, in Scots terminology, "assignation".

[232] Rome I Regulation art.14.1 (ex-art.12.1 of the Convention).

[233] Rome I Regulation art.14.2 (ex-art.12.2 of the Convention).

problem of finding a rule to govern the priority of an assigned or subrogated claim over competing claims made by other parties. These points currently must be dealt with by each Member State according to its own conflict rules.[234] A report has been produced in response to art.27.2 of the Regulation, but a proposal for a revised rule is awaited.[235] Given the commercial importance of assignment, in that assignation of bundles of incorporeal rights is a commonly utilised means of raising finance, consideration needs to be given to finding a European solution, whether it be a single rule, or a general rule with exceptions for specialised cases.

Subrogation

Article 14: contractual subrogation

The title of the new art.14 makes clear that its remit concerns voluntary **15–48** assignment and contractual subrogation, i.e. subrogation by means of a contract (*not* subrogation of a claim in contract). The treatment of contractual subrogation (of a contractual or possibly of a non-contractual[236] claim), therefore, has been aligned with the treatment of voluntary assignments, discussed above.

Article 15: legal subrogation

Article 15 of the Regulation, which replicates in effect art.13 of the Convention, **15–49** concerns legal subrogation, i.e. subrogation by operation of law,[237] as for example the subrogation of a motor insurance company to the victim's claim against the wrongdoer, where the insurer itself has compensated the victim, and is as follows:

> "Where a person (the creditor) has a contractual claim against another (the debtor) and a third person has a duty to satisfy the creditor, or has in fact satisfied the creditor in discharge of that duty, the law which governs the third person's duty to satisfy the creditor shall determine whether and to what extent the third person is entitled to exercise against the debtor the rights which the creditor had against the debtor under the law governing their relationship."

---

[234] Ch.17, below.

[235] British Institute of International and Comparative Law "Final Report (2012): Study on the question of effectiveness of an assignment or subrogation of a claim against third parties and the priority of the assigned or subrogated claim over a right of another person", which is intended to serve as a basis for the report that the Commission must present according to art.27(2) and for a potential future proposal to amend art. 14 to provide a new European conflict of laws solution for the third-party aspects of assignment. With regard to earlier discussion within the UK, see Ministry of Justice Discussion Paper, *Rome I: European Commission Review ECR of Article 14: Assignment* (The Stationery Office, 2009), which is restricted to voluntary assignations.

[236] The transferability of which is governed by the Rome II Regulation art.15(e).

[237] The article in terms begins: "Where a person...has a contractual claim against another...". Subrogation where a person has a non-contractual claim upon another is governed by Rome II Regulation art.19.

Burden of proof

15–50 Rules of evidence and procedure fall within the province of the forum, for reasons of long held tradition and convenience.[238] The Rome I Regulation upholds this by excluding such matters from its scope (art.1.3), but the exclusion is subject to art.18, in the following terms:

> "1. The law governing a contractual obligation under this Regulation shall apply to the extent that, in matters of contractual obligations, it contains rules which raise presumptions of law or determine the burden of proof.
>
> 2. A contract or an act intended to have legal effect may be proved by any mode of proof recognised by the law of the forum or by any of the laws referred to in Article 11 under which that contract or act is formally valid, provided that such mode of proof can be administered by the forum."

Habitual residence

15–51 As indicated in Ch.6, above,[239] an innovation is contained in the Rome I Regulation, in that art.19.1 defines, for the purposes of the Regulation, the habitual residence of companies and other bodies, corporate or unincorporated, as the place of central administration.[240] Further, it defines the habitual residence of a natural person acting in the course of his business activity as his principal place of business. With regard to *tempus inspiciendum*, the relevant point in time shall be the time of conclusion of the contract.[241]

Where a contract is concluded in the course of the operations of a branch, agency or any other establishment, or if, under the contract, performance is the responsibility of such a branch, agency or establishment, the place where the branch, agency or any other establishment is located shall be treated as the place of habitual residence.

Exclusion of *renvoi* (article 20)

15–52 The application of the law of any country specified by the Rome I Regulation means the application of the rules of law in force in that country other than its rules of private international law, unless provided otherwise[242] in the Regulation.

Public policy of the forum (article 21)

15–53 The application of a rule of the law of any country specified by the Rome I Regulation may be refused only if such application is manifestly incompatible with the public policy ("*ordre public*") of the forum.

---

[238] Ch.8, above.

[239] Para.6–50, above.

[240] See Rome I Regulation recital (39).

[241] Rome I Regulation art.19.3.

[242] The solitary example is to be found in art.7.3 final paragraph, concerning parties' freedom to choose the law governing an insurance contract which is not concerned with large risk. In such a case, party choice is restricted to certain specified laws, but if those laws themselves should grant greater freedom of choice, parties may take advantage thereof.

ELECTRONIC COMMERCE

Electronic advances have removed the firm basis of understanding, and **15–54** consequent assumptions, that the world is divided into legal systems based on territorial areas, and have thrown into confusion certain established methods of approaching and solving conflict problems. This does not mean that "traditional" rules may not be adapted to service the electronic age. The conflict of laws was able to accommodate "remote" methods of contracting such as telegrams and telexes by identifying what it deemed to be the *lex loci contractus* and the proper law.[243] UK government policy, recognising the growth of electronic commerce, is to encourage and facilitate such transactions and to attempt to safeguard UK interests. One of the main concerns is to secure the principle of "medium neutrality", i.e. to ensure that there is no difference in legal effectiveness between traditional and electronic methods of transacting. It is interesting that the EU Commission, in its 2009 Report on cross-border e-commerce in the EU,[244] noted that while the use of e-commerce is increasing on a national level, it was, at that date, "still relatively uncommon for consumers to use the internet to purchase goods or services in another Member State."[245] The Commission attributed this to cross-border barriers to online trade. In recent years, a number of legislative responses have been made to meet technological developments.

Electronic signature: Electronic Communications Act 2000

The Electronic Communications Act 2000 (which implemented certain provi- **15–55** sions of the EU Electronic Signatures Directive,[246] intended to facilitate the use of electronic signatures and to provide for their legal recognition throughout the EU) is part of the legislative framework to facilitate and encourage confidence in electronic transactions. The 2000 Act is in three Parts. Part I makes arrangements for registering providers of cryptography support services, providing, e.g. electronic signature services and confidentiality services[247]; Pt II provides for the legal recognition of electronic signatures, regulating the process under which such signatures may be "generated, communicated or verified"; and Pt III deals with miscellaneous and supplemental issues.[248]

---

[243] *Entores Ltd v Miles Far East Corp* [1955] 2 Q.B. 327; *Brinkibon Ltd v Stahag Stahl* [1982] 1 All E.R. 293.

[244] Commission Report on cross-border e-commerce in the EU SEC(2009) 283 final.

[245] Commission Report on cross-border e-commerce in the EU SEC(2009) 283 final, executive summary. This seems scarcely credible, even at 2009.

[246] Directive 1999/93/EC on a Community framework for electronic signatures [2000] O.J. L13/12, superseded by Regulation (EU) No.910/2014 of the European Parliament and of the Council of 23 July 2014 on electronic identification and trust services for electronic transactions in the internal market and repealing Directive 1999/93/EC.

[247] The use of cryptography can secure confidentiality, and provide a means for delivering a signature electronically. By s.7 of the 2000 Act, electronic signatures can be admitted as evidence in court. Sections 1–6, however, were repealed (never in force) on 25 May 2005, by operation of s.16(4) of the Act. The statutory scheme contained in Pt I was to be commenced only if the industry-led self-regulation failed.

[248] 2000 Act Pt III ss.11, 12 were repealed: Communications Act 2003 Sch.19 para.1.

Electronic Commerce Directive

15–56 The EU Electronic Commerce Directive,[249] adopted on 4 May 2000, encourages the development of electronic commerce in the internal market. There is "no overlap in the detailed provisions" of the Electronic Commerce Directive and the 2000 Act.[250] Two main areas addressed in the Directive are the ensuring of the legal validity of electronic contracts and limitation of the liability of intermediary service providers.

Recital (58) makes clear that while the Electronic Commerce Directive does not apply to services supplied by providers established in non-EU states, nevertheless, in view of the global dimension of electronic commerce, it is appropriate to ensure that European rules are consistent with international rules. Development of the EU internal market requires co-ordination at EU level of regulatory measures so as not adversely to affect the competitiveness of European industry.

Article 1.4 of the Electronic Commerce Directive declares that it does not establish additional rules on private international law, nor does it deal with the jurisdiction of courts.[251] However, art.9 (treatment of contracts) begins with the requirement that Member States shall ensure that their legal systems allow contracts to be concluded by electronic means, and that their legal requirements do not create obstacles for the use of electronic contracts, nor deprive them of legal effectiveness by reason of their having been made by electronic means. Article 9.2 permits Member States to make certain exceptions[252] to this *desideratum* in respect of all or certain contracts falling into one of the following categories:

"(a)   contracts that create or transfer rights in real estate, except for rental rights;
(b)   contracts requiring by law the involvement of courts, public authorities or professions exercising public authority;
(c)   contracts of suretyship granted and on [*sic*] collateral securities furnished by persons acting for purposes outside their trade, business or profession;
(d)   contracts governed by family law or by the law of succession."

The Electronic Commerce (EC Directive) Regulations 2002

15–57 Certain provisions of the Electronic Commerce Directive were implemented in the UK by the Electronic Commerce (EC Directive) Regulations 2002.[253] The 2002 Regulations seek to promote the internal market in Europe, by securing the free movement of "information society services", meaning, essentially, all

---

[249] Directive 2000/31/EC on certain legal aspects of information society services, in particular electronic commerce, in the Internal Market [2000] O.J. L178/1 (henceforth "EU Electronic Commerce Directive").
[250] Explanatory note to the 2000 Act p.6.
[251] cf. Electronic Commerce Directive recitals (23), (55).
[252] Member States which make such exceptions are required to submit to the Commission every five years a report explaining why they consider it necessary to maintain excluded category/ies of contract.
[253] Electronic Commerce (EC Directive) Regulations 2002 (SI 2002/2013), as extended by the Electronic Commerce (EC Directive) (Extension) Regulations 2003 (SI 2003/115), Electronic Commerce (EC Directive) (Extension) (No. 2) Regulations 2003 (SI 2003/2500); and Electronic Commerce (EC Directive) (Extension) Regulations 2004 (SI 2004/1178).

commercial online services.[254] The 2002 Regulations apply to those who advertise or sell goods or services online to businesses or consumers. Generally the Regulations require online service providers to comply with certain information requirements, which can be divided into three categories: (i) information requirements, which require providers to give full information about themselves to "end users"[255]; (ii) commercial communications requirements; and (iii) electronic contracting requirements, which require the online services provider to provide end users with a description of the different technical steps to be taken to conclude a contract online.

For present purposes, the principal feature of interest is the limited guidance as to choice of law applicable to online services. The 2002 Regulations direct that UK-established service providers must comply with UK laws, even if they are providing those services in another EU Member State, and they prevent the UK from restricting the provision in the UK of online services from another EU Member State. The regulatory structure is authorised by reg.4 of the 2002 Regulations, but it does not apply to those fields set out in the Schedule to the Electronic Commerce Directive (the Schedule permitting the contracting parties, in such excluded fields, freedom to choose the applicable law and not affecting the law applicable to a consumer contract, so that the consumer may not be deprived of the mandatory rules otherwise applicable to his situation by the law of the Member State in which he has his residence).[256] Otherwise parties are free to choose the law applicable to individual contracts. The 2002 Regulations do not deal with the matter of jurisdiction.[257]

Consumer Protection (Distance Selling) Regulations 2000[258]

The 2000 Regulations regulate "distance contracts", which are defined generally as any contract concerning goods or services concluded between a supplier and a consumer under an organised distance sales or service provision scheme run by the supplier, who, for the purpose of the contract, makes exclusive use of one or more means of distance communication, up to and including the moment at which the contract is concluded.[259] The Regulations are without conflict of laws content, except to the extent that reg.25(1) prohibits contracting out of the consumer protection provisions of the regulations, and reg.25(5) stipulates that the regulations shall apply if the contract has a close connection with the territory of a Member State, notwithstanding any contract term which applies or purports to apply the law of a non-Member State.[260] The effect of these provisions is to secure for the consumer in his electronic dealings the same protections as have been constructed in relation to traditional forms of consumer contract.

15–58

---

[254] Electronic Commerce Directive recital (18).
[255] These information requirements are in addition to existing requirements, such as contained in the Consumer Protection (Distance Selling) Regulations 2000 (SI 2000/2334).
[256] Electronic Commerce Directive recital (55).
[257] Which must be determined according to normal commercial rules: Ch.7.
[258] Consumer Protection (Distance Selling) Regulations 2000 (SI 2000/2334), implementing Directive 97/7/EC on the protection of consumers in respect of distance contracts [1997] O.J. L144/19 ("Distance Selling Directive"), as amended by Consumer Protection (Distance Selling)(Amendment) Regulations 2005 (SI 2005/689).
[259] 2000 Regulations reg.3(1).
[260] cf. Distance Selling Directive reg.12(2).

Application of the Rome I Regulation to electronic commerce transactions

15–59   None of these complex modern instruments addresses systematically the conflict of laws implications of electronic contracting, and so the conclusion must be that electronic contracts, their constitution and effects are subject to the Rome I Regulation. The absence of bespoke choice of law rules regarding electronic contracts is noticeable, particularly when one considers the exponential growth of electronic contracting, and the fact that a far higher number of such contracts have international implications than has been the case with traditional contracts. This is especially true, in theory at least, of consumer contracts.[261] The challenge is to interpret the Rome I Regulation in a manner compatible with modern electronic conditions of commerce.

The questions to be answered are the same as arise with regard to "traditional" contracts. With regard to electronic contracting, conflict disputes are likely to concern: (i) pre-contractual issues[262]; (ii) evidencing that consensus has been reached between identified parties; (iii) ascertaining the identity of the governing law and assessing the substantive validity of the contract, including any choice of court and/or choice of law clauses; (iv) performance-related issues, including the main obligation and counter-obligation (supply and payment); and (v) post-contractual issues of dispute resolution, including application of relevant rules of jurisdiction (because despite the extent and rapidity of technological change, carrying with it the impression that territorial frontiers no longer are significant, the contractual dealings, however ethereal, must be brought down to earth for the purpose of securing a remedy in some territorial law unit).

The first matter to be ascertained is whether the contracting parties have made a choice of law, express or clearly demonstrated.[263] If such a choice is evident, the body of law applicable by parties' choice to the contract will be augmented, in the usual way, by the mandatory rules of another system of law, in terms of the Rome I Regulation arts 3.3, 3.4 and 9. It may be that in the act of ordering online one party accepts the other's express choice of law. Whether the parties have reached consensus is governed, in the usual way, by the putativity principle in the Rome I Regulation art.10.

In terms of art.4.1(a) and (b) of the Rome I Regulation, in the absence of choice of law by the parties, the law governing a contract for the sale of goods, or for the provision of services, shall be the habitual residence of the seller or service provider, respectively. This is as true of an online transaction as of a conventional transaction. Articles 4.3 and 4.4 afford to the court discretion to identify the applicable law on a wider basis and could reasonably justify consideration of factors such as the location of internet service providers. If, as in many cases of online transacting, the purchaser/user is a "consumer", he will have the benefit of the Rome I Regulation art.6. Article 6.1(b) provides that a contract concluded by a natural person acting outside his trade or profession (the consumer), with another person acting in the exercise of his trade or profession

---

[261] J. Hill, *Cross-Border Consumer Contracts* (2008); and Z.S. Tang, *Electronic Consumer Contracts in the Conflict of Laws* (Oxford: Hart, 2009).

[262] Rome II Regulation art.12. Ch.16, below.

[263] Rome I Regulation art.3.1.

(the professional), shall be governed by the law of the consumer's habitual residence, provided that the professional pursues his activities in the country of the consumer's habitual residence, or, by any means, directs[264] such activities to that country or to several countries including that country. Provided that the contract falls within the scope of the professional's commercial or professional activities, the contract will confer upon the consumer the benefit of a "consumer contract" with its attendant advantages[265] from his point of view.

As to formal validity, the Rome I Regulation art.11.1 provides that for contracts "concluded between persons who, or whose agents, are in the same country at the time of its conclusion" it is sufficient that the contract comply with the formal requirements of the applicable law, or of the law where it is concluded. This provision demonstrates the extent to which territorial situation remains important in traditional contracts, and at the same time reveals its inappropriateness with regard to electronic contracting.[266] The qualifications contained in art.11.1 are unlikely to be satisfied in electronic contracts, and therefore one is led to the enlarged rule of alternative reference in art.11.2, to the effect that with regard to persons who, or whose agents, "are in different countries at the time of its conclusion", it is sufficient to comply with the formal validity rules of the applicable law, or "of the law of either of the countries where either of the parties or their agent is present at the time of conclusion, or the law of the country where either of the parties had his habitual residence at that time."[267]

With regard to contractual capacity, it has been seen that art.13 supplies a specific rule, applicable in cases of "face-to-face" contracting, which rule obviously is not helpful in the case of remote transactions. The answer, for electronic commerce, should be to apply the putative applicable law to the question of capacity.

WHERE CONTRACT MEETS OTHER AREAS OF LAW

Where contractual obligations meet non-contractual obligations

The Rome I and Rome II Regulations are intended to be interlocking instruments, furnishing for Member State courts a set of rules of applicable law governing issues arising out of contractual and non-contractual obligations. They are mutually consistent, and in places are interdependent.[268] For example, the applicable law rules in contract may have a part to play in identifying the law

15–60

---

[264] "[B]y any means, directs" employs the same wording as art.15.1(c) of the Brussels I Regulation and art.17.1(c) of the Brussels I Recast, bringing the choice of law provision into line with the jurisdiction provision. cf. recital (24).

[265] Rome I Regulation recital (25).

[266] Electronic Commerce Directive recital (55).

[267] The rule though generous, is not as explicitly inclusive as the medium-neutrality rule contained in art.23.2 of the Brussels I Regulation and art.25.2 of the Brussels I Recast: any communication by electronic means which provides a durable record of the agreement shall be equivalent to "writing". See para.7–42, above (prorogation).

[268] E.B. Crawford and J.M. Carruthers, "Connection and Coherence between and among European Instruments in the Private International Law of Obligations" (2014) 63 I.C.L.Q. 1.

applicable to a non-contractual obligation; in other words, the applicable law under the Rome I Regulation may influence identification of the applicable law under the Rome II Regulation.

Interface between contract and Rome II Chapter II (delict)[269]

15–61   Symbiosis between the two instruments is observable, e.g. in Rome II art.4.3 (applicable law in tort and delict), in the provision conferring discretion on the forum, in effect, to override both the principal *lex loci damni* rule in art.4.1 and the rule of commonality in art.4.2, in order to secure as the governing law in delict that law which, in the view of the forum, is manifestly more closely connected with the delict. In exercising that discretion, the forum is given a hint that such a manifestly closer connection might be based upon a pre-existing relationship between the parties, *such as a contract* that is closely connected with the delict in question.[270]

Article 4.3 of the Rome II Regulation is loosely drawn, both by use of the word "might" and by the reference, at second remove, to a contract. In the employer-employee situation, or carrier-passenger situation, the provision might be relevant, e.g. re a claim falling within the category of economic delicts, such as inducement of breach of contract; or an accident which occurred in a work place where the injured party/employee would not have been but for the contract of employment. One might think that the facts found in *Johnson v Coventry Churchill International Ltd*[271] would satisfy application of art.4.3 in that the relationship between the parties was the contractual one of employer/employee, and the allegedly tortious incident happened on a building site in Germany. The claimant, an English employee working as a joiner, was injured when the plank on which he was crossing a trench collapsed, in circumstances in which under English law, but not under German law, the employer would be liable for failure to provide a safe system of work. The contract of employment in that instance was expressly governed by English law.

If, in the view of the forum, the employment and carriage situations fall within art.4.3 of Rome II, reference will be made, not to the applicable law identified per the general rules contained in the Rome I Regulation,[272] but to the particular rules contained in arts 5–8 thereof. This exercise would involve an incursion into the detail of the rules of the Rome I Regulation in order to arrive at a conclusion under Rome II. That said, perhaps it is implausible to suggest that the court would look beyond Rome II art.4.1 or 4.2 in this specialised situation of employee (or passenger), for it is unlikely that there will be a manifestly more closely connected country than that identified by the principal rules.

The defender may adduce a defence in contract to a claim laid in delict, and the task then for the court is to prioritise the forum's own choice of law rules in these areas, and to assess their interaction. This occurs in cases where parties engaged in litigation arising out of an allegedly delictual situation are linked by a

---

[269]   With regard to Ch.II of Rome II, see para.16–02 et seq., below.

[270]   The particularity of expression is important: the delict in question, seemingly, must derive from, or have a close association with the contract.

[271]   *Johnson v Coventry Churchill International Ltd* [1992] 3 All E.R. 14.

[272]   Rome I Regulation arts 3 and 4.

pre-existing contractual relationship, commonly that of employer and employee, or carrier and passenger. If one considers in this connection the celebrated problem which arose at common law of a party adducing a contractual defence to a delictual/tortious claim, such as occurred in *Brodin v A/R Seljan*[273] or *Sayers v International Drilling Co NV*,[274] is it right to assume that the forum, in the new world of harmonised rules, still would look first to the applicable law of the delict in order to ascertain whether by that law a contractual defence can be offered,[275] and thereafter ascertain, by the law governing the contract as determined under the Rome I Regulation, whether the contract and the relevant term thereof are valid, apt and sufficient to provide a defence? This approach still seems commendable, at least where the applicable law in delict is determined per art.4.1 or 4.2; but, if art.4.3 of Rome II were used in order to establish, by reference to the pre-existing contract between the parties, the applicable law in delict, confusing circularity surely would result.

A further link between Rome I and Rome II can be identified, underpinning the party autonomy rule for non-contractual obligations in art.14 of Rome II. By that provision, parties may agree to submit non-contractual obligations to the law of their choice by an agreement entered into after the event giving rise to the damage occurred, or where all the parties are pursuing a commercial activity, by an agreement freely negotiated before that event. Such a contract embodying the art.14 choice of law will be governed as to its validity by the Rome I Regulation.

Where a consumer is injured by the defective product which was the subject of his consumer contract, the Rome I/Rome II borderland must be closely examined. A different outcome might be produced by application of Rome I art.6 (consumer contracts), rather than Rome II art.5 (product liability). Both provisions point initially to the law of the habitual residence of the consumer. But, especially under Rome II, there are other possibilities, which not implausibly the court might follow, such as the law of the country of acquisition of the product,[276] or the law of the country in which the damage occurred,[277] and account also would require to be taken of a general sweeper discretion available to the forum under art.5 of Rome II.[278] Moreover, party choice of law appears to be unfettered in relation to product liability under Rome II,[279] whereas it is restricted vis-à-vis consumers under the Rome I Regulation art.6.2. It is impossible to say which instrument, in any given situation, would prove more beneficial to the consumer, but the Rome I Regulation appears to provide greater certainty as to governing law than does the Rome II Regulation. This is not to say that a claimant necessarily will have freedom to choose between applicable law instruments because he may be constrained by the special jurisdiction rules of the Brussels regime.[280]

---

[273] *Brodin v A/R Seljan*, 1973 S.C. 213.

[274] *Sayers v International Drilling Co NV* [1971] 1 W.L.R. 1176.

[275] Reference to art.15(b) of the Rome II Regulation suggests such an approach.

[276] Rome II art.5.1(b).

[277] Rome II art.5.1(c).

[278] Rome II art.5.2. Rome I Regulation art.6 affords the forum no such discretion.

[279] Contrast Rome II arts 6.4 (unfair competition) and 8.3 (infringement of intellectual property rights).

[280] Para.7–19 et seq., above.

Interface between contract and Rome II Chapter III (unjust enrichment, negotiorum gestio, and culpa in contrahendo)[281]

(a) Relational unjust enrichment

15–62 In many cases arising under the head of unjust enrichment, there is found to have existed an element or semblance of a contract. The first limb of the legislative solution in art.10 of the Rome II Regulation is concerned to treat this situation. By art.10.1, non-contractual obligations arising out of unjust enrichment, including payment of amounts wrongly received, *where they concern a pre-existing relationship between the parties such as one arising out of a contract or a tort* (i.e. "relational unjust enrichment") shall be governed by the law which governs that relationship, that is to say, by the applicable law identified according to the Rome I (contract) or Rome II (tort/delict) Regulation, as the case may be. Seemingly, under art.10.1 of Rome II, the applicable law in contract will govern the obligation arising out of unjust enrichment *only* if that unjust enrichment derives from, or is closely associated with, that contract.[282]

(b) Nullity of contract

15–63 In light of the Rome I Regulation, there is pan-European agreement that the subject of nullity of contract be governed by the putative applicable law of the allegedly null contract. It is possible, therefore, that the co-existence of this rule with the choice of law rules under the Rome II Regulation Ch. III, may prompt problems of characterisation and distribution of application of choice of law rules between the Rome I and Rome II Regulations.

In the jurisdictional aspect also, the area of void and nullified contracts is productive of doubt.[283] Difficulties of demarcation present in borderline cases.[284] Turf wars between art.12 of Rome I[285] and art.10.1 of Rome II[286] can be envisaged.

(c) Culpa in contrahendo

15–64 Like the consequences of nullity of contract, this subject too weaves about on either side of the line between contractual and non-contractual obligations. Article 1.2(i) of the Rome I Regulation expressly excludes from the scope of Rome I obligations arising out of dealings prior to the conclusion of a contract. Article 12.1 of the Rome II Regulation applies to what it classes as a

---

[281] With regard to Ch.III of Rome II, see para.16–56 et seq., below.

[282] cf. art.11.1 (*negotiorum gestio*). See also Rome II arts 4.3, 5.2.

[283] Para.7–21, above.

[284] S. Pitel, "Rome II and Choice of Law for Unjust Enrichment" in Binchy and Ahern (eds), *The Rome II Regulation: The Law Applicable to Non-contractual Obligations* (Leiden: Brill, 2009), p.236.

[285] Rome I Regulation art.12.1: "The law applicable to a contract by virtue of this Regulation shall govern in particular:...(b) performance;...(e) the consequences of nullity of the contract."

[286] Rome I Regulation art.10.1: "If a non-contractual obligation arising out of unjust enrichment, including payment of amounts wrongly received, concerns a relationship existing between the parties, such as one arising out of a contract or a tort/delict, that is closely connected with that unjust enrichment, it shall be governed by the law that governs that relationship."

non-contractual obligation (albeit one arising out of dealings prior to the conclusion—or not—of a contract) the applicable law of the contract, or the putative applicable law. This choice of law rule applies whether or not a contract was actually concluded. If, however, the law applicable cannot be determined under art.12.1 of Rome II, then the rule which must be applied under art.12.2 is in the same terms as the general rule for delict contained in art.4.

Where contract meets property

The terms of a contract, valid by the governing law thereof, nevertheless may contravene, in detail or in policy, the law of some other interested legal system, most frequently in practice that of the *situs* of moveable property[287] which is the subject of the contract. Thus, while title to property may have passed according to the applicable law of the contract, it may not have passed according to the governing law of property, namely, the *lex situs* of the goods at the time when ownership is purported to have passed. The *situs* of the property at the time of conclusion of the contract may differ from its *situs* when dispute arises and litigation ensues. Both time and space, therefore, may be significant. Circumstances may present in which a forum must segregate and rank issues, e.g. of contractual obligation, of proprietary right, and of trust.[288]

    15–65

An interconnection is seen also between contractual assignation of incorporeal rights, and the choice of law property principles governing the transfer of incorporeal rights. It has been noted above that art.14 of the Rome I Regulation lacks a provision to guide the court as to choice of law to determine the effectiveness of a voluntary assignation of a claim against another person (the debtor) against third parties, and the priority of the assigned claim over the right of another person. In such cases, it is impossible to divorce the proprietary aspects of the assignation from the contractual aspects. In *Raiffeisen Zentralbank Österreich AG v Five Star General Trading LLC (The Mount I)*,[289] Mance L.J.[290] found it impossible to conclude that the draftsmen of the Rome I Convention art.12.2 had intended to make any such distinction. Consequently, both with regard to the Rome Convention, and now in relation to the Regulation, albeit that each instrument purports to deal only with contractual obligations, it is accepted that art.12 of the Convention, and art.14 of the Regulation, are intended also to encompass the property implications of voluntary assignments.

SUMMARY 15

1.   General

    15–66

---

[287] i.e. the law of the situation of the property at the point of contracting, or more likely, the law of the subsequent situation of the property at litigation; e.g. *Hammer and Sohne v HWT Realisations Ltd*, 1985 S.L.T. (Sh. Ct.) 21.

[288] *Joint Administrators of Rangers Football Club Plc, Noters* 2012 S.L.T. 599. See Ch.17, below.

[289] *Raiffeisen Zentralbank Österreich AG v Five Star General Trading LLC (The Mount I)* [2001] 1 Lloyd's Rep. 597.

[290] *Raiffeisen Zentralbank Österreich AG v Five Star General Trading LLC (The Mount I)* [2001] 1 Lloyd's Rep. 597 at [45].

Classification of a matter as contractual or otherwise is determined by the *lex fori*.

The Rome I Regulation shall apply, in any EU Member State court, in situations involving a conflict of laws, to regulate contractual obligations, in civil and commercial matters, when the contract was entered into on or after December 17, 2009, and the contract does not fall within an exception to the scope of the Regulation per art.1. Cases which, by type, fall outside the ambit of the Rome I Regulation, because the instrument is incomplete or inapplicable in terms of scope, will be governed by common law rules.

Cases which, by time, fall outside the ambit of the Rome I Regulation (i.e. those entered into before December 17, 2009), will be governed by the Rome I Convention, as embodied in the Contracts (Applicable Law) Act 1990, failing which, by the common law.

2.   Applicable Law

Identification of the applicable law is effected through application of art.3 of the Rome I Regulation where a choice of law has been made expressly, or is clearly demonstrated by the terms of the contract or the circumstances of the case; or of art.4 of that Regulation in the absence of party choice of law.

Article 4 provides contract-specific rules to identify the applicable law, subject to a discretion afforded to the forum to select instead the law with which, in its view, the contract is manifestly more closely connected.

Restrictions on freedom of party choice are imposed through the mandatory application of rules of Community law or a national law, which cannot be derogated from by contract, in terms of art.3.3 and 3.4.

All contracts, whether or not there has been a choice of law by parties, are subject to art.9 (overriding mandatory provisions).

Article 19 contains a definition, for the purpose of the Regulation, of the habitual residence of companies and other bodies, corporate or unincorporated, and of natural persons acting in the course of business.

The operation of *renvoi* is excluded by art.20, unless provided otherwise in the Regulation.

By art.21, the application of a provision of an otherwise applicable law may be refused effect if its application is manifestly incompatible with the public policy of the forum.

3.   Special Contracts

The Regulation contains stand-alone applicable law rules to govern:

—   contracts of carriage of goods, and of persons: art.5;
—   consumer contracts: art.6;
—   contracts of insurance: art.7; and
—   individual employment contracts: art.8.

As was the case in the Convention, the question whether an agent can bind a principal, or an organ bind a company, to a third party, is excluded from the scope of the Regulation. The contract between the principal and the agent, however, is governed by the Regulation.

4.   Incidents of a Contract

Consent and material validity (whether or not there is deemed to be agreement such as to constitute a contract) is governed by the putative applicable law in accordance with art.10.1, subject to a forum discretion contained in art.10.2.

Formal validity is governed by art.11.

Scope of the law applicable is treated by means of non-exhaustive list in art.12. A change for the UK is that art.12.1(e) subjects to the applicable law the consequences of nullity of contract, a matter which had been excluded under the Rome Convention by means of UK reservation.

The rule concerning contractual incapacity is contained in art.13. It is specific in its terms, and when on the facts of the case the article has no application, common law rules will apply.

Voluntary assignment and contractual subrogation are treated in art.14, and legal subrogation in art.15.

5.   Electronic commerce

The Rome I Regulation applies in tandem with special sectoral legislative provision.

6.   Hybrid cases

In certain circumstances, the forum's choice of law rules in areas of private law other than contract (principally of property and of delict), may impinge upon a situation involving a contractual obligation. The forum must prioritise and reconcile its own choice of law rules in these different areas. In particular, any EU Member State forum must apply the Rome II Regulation in respect of non-contractual obligations, including unjust enrichment, and must be aware of the interdependence of the Rome I and Rome II Regulations.

CHAPTER 16

The law of non-contractual obligations

DELICT

Choice of law background

The history of this area of Scots and English international private law **16–01** demonstrates the use of a variety of approaches to choice of law in delict. Various theories have underpinned the choice of law applied by UK courts in cases involving delicts with foreign elements. The subject is one which, in the past at least, was more productive of academic writing than of case law.

If a court were to apply only its own law, substantive as well as procedural (a *lex fori* approach), not only would this be objectionable in encouraging forum shopping, but also, in obliterating the input of the law of the place of occurrence of the alleged wrongdoing, could result in a successful claim in respect of an act which was not actionable by the law of the place where it was committed, an outcome which seems inherently unfair and contrary to legitimate party expectations.

Conversely, were a court to apply only the law of the place where the allegedly delictual act or omission was committed (a *lex loci delicti* approach), objections could be raised on the bases that the place of occurrence of the delict might be entirely fortuitous and/or difficult to determine,[1] and that application of that law might result in the forum having to grant a decree for damages for an act which was not wrongful by its own law, something which is likely to jar on the conscience of the judge. An approach akin to, but one step removed from, the *lex loci delicti* theory, originating in the judgment of Holmes J. in the American case, *Slater v Mexican National Railroad Co*,[2] is that delictual actings give rise to an *obligatio* attaching to the person and enforceable wherever the alleged wrongdoer may be found.

In reality, there was developed in the Scots and English courts, a rule of "double actionability",[3] requiring actionability both by the *lex loci delicti* and by the *lex fori*. The rule, though apparently even-handed, was prone, through cumulative application of two laws, to work adversely for the claimant, and to favour the defendant.[4]

---

[1] Para.16–18, below.
[2] *Slater v Mexican National Railroad Co,* 194 U.S. 120 (1904).
[3] For content and (residual) application of the rule, see paras 16–56—16–59, below.
[4] cf. infamously *McElroy v McAllister*, 1949 S.C. 110.

Innovative thinking, prompted by the problematic Scots decision of *McElroy v McAllister*,[5] generated a "proper law" approach to identification of the governing law in delict. The progenitor of the theory was Morris, writing in the late 1940s.[6] According to this theory the rights of parties should be governed by the proper law of the delict, that is, the law with which, objectively, it has the closest connection. Parties' rights and liabilities, it was argued, should be judged according to the social environment in which the delict was committed. This mode of thinking conferred upon courts a notable degree of discretion within a jurisdiction-selecting framework, and foreshadowed more revolutionary juridical developments in the USA concerning choice of law in tort. The preferred approach in the USA long had been strict adherence to the sole application of the *lex loci delicti*. However, when this connecting factor plainly was unsuitable in the view of the forum, recourse sometimes was had to the device of manipulative characterisation to secure a different result.[7] From the early 1960s, there emerged in the USA a broader, rule-selecting approach, unorthodox in method, though arguably similar in effect to the proper law theory of English law.[8]

In the 1980s in the UK, the Law Commission and the Scottish Law Commission in their thorough reviews of English and Scots choice of law rules in tort and delict, and in their suggestions for possible reform of the double actionability rule, concluded that the American "revolution", though interesting, and having the merit of giving due warning against over-rigidity of choice of law connecting factor, was more suited to the inter-state, than the international, situation, and decided against recommending the adoption of such approaches in the UK.[9] Nonetheless change was required, for the rule of double actionability was idiosyncratic and unsatisfactory.

The modern era began with the enactment by the UK Parliament of the Private International Law (Miscellaneous Provisions) Act 1995 (hereinafter "1995 Act"). This, in turn, has been largely overtaken through the EU harmonisation process by Regulation 864/2007 of the European Parliament and of the Council of 11 July 2007 on the Law Applicable to Non-Contractual Obligations ("Rome II").[10]

---

[5] *McElroy v McAllister,* 1949 S.C. 110.

[6] J. Morris, "The Proper Law of a Tort" (1949) 12 M.L.R. 248, expanded in (1951) 64 Harv. L. Rev. 881; C.J.G. Morse, *Torts in Private International Law* (1978); and P.M. North, "Torts in the Dismal Swamp: Choice of Law Revisited" in *Essays in Private International Law* (1993).

[7] Para.4–05, above.

[8] Famously in *Babcock v Jackson*, 12 N.Y. 2d. 473, 191 N.E. 2d. 279 (1963). Also *Macey v Rozbicki*, 18 N.Y.2d. 289, 221 N.E. 2d. 380 (1966); *Griffith v United Airlines Inc*, 203 A. 2d. 796 (1964); *Tooker v Lopez*, 12 N.Y. 2d. 569, 249 N.E. 2d. 394 (1969); *Reich v Purcell*, 67 Cal. 2d. 551, 423 P. 2d. 727 (1967); *Kell v Henderson*, 26 A.D. 2d. 595, 270 N.Y.S. 2d. 552 (1966); *Bernhard v Harrah's Club*, 128 Cal. Rptr. 215, 546 P.2d. 709 (1976). Ch.3, above regarding policy evaluation methods.

[9] Law Commission and Scottish Law Commission, *Private International Law: Choice of Law in Tort and Delict* (HMSO, 1984), Law Com. Working Paper No.87; Scot. Law Com. Memo. No.62, paras 4.35–4.54.

[10] Rome II Regulation [2007] O.J. L199/40. See, for background, European Commission Proposal for a Regulation of the European Parliament and the Council on the Law Applicable to Non-Contractual Obligations ("Rome II") COM(2003) 427 final (2003/0168(COD)); and accompanying Explanatory Memorandum ("Explanatory Memorandum"). See also House of Lords European Union Committee, *The Rome II Regulation, 8th Report of Session 2003–04* (The Stationery Office, 2004), HL Paper No.66 (Session 2003/04) ("Scott Report"). In relation to the negotiation and drafting process, see J.M. Carruthers and E.B. Crawford, "Variations on a Theme of Rome II. Reflections on Proposed Choice of Law Rules for Non-Contractual Obligations" (2005) 9 Edin. L.R. 65 (Pt I), and 238 (Pt II). For

Despite the attainment of a harmonised set of choice of law rules through the introduction of a European Regulation, it cannot be said that the 1995 Act, nor even the common law, is extinct, for account yet must be taken, in UK courts, by reason of subject matter and/or of date, of these pre-existing rules.[11] The area presents, therefore, an acute example of the layering problem characteristic of modern conflict of laws rules.[12]

The Rome II Regulation[13]

Rome II constitutes the major scheme of applicable law rules to be applied by EU Member State courts in cases concerning the law governing all qualifying non-contractual obligations arising out of a tort or delict, and restitutionary claims under the heads of unjust enrichment, *negotiorum gestio* and *culpa in contrahendo*.

16–02

Temporal scope

Particular care is necessary in the drafting of legislative provisions as to the temporal scope of application of rules.[14] By art.31, Rome II applies to events giving rise to damage which occur after[15] its entry into force.[16] The date of entry

16–03

---

information as to the protracted negotiations, see Dickinson, *The Rome II Regulation* (2008), para.1.44. As to possible future reform of the Regulation, see, in response to the review clause contained in art.30, EU Commission Questionnaire to the Member States on the application of Regulation (EC) No.864/2007 on the Law Applicable to Non-Contractual Obligations (Rome II) (August 2012); responses to the Questionnaire and any proposed change to the instrument are awaited.

[11] The Law Applicable to Non-contractual Obligations (England and Wales and Northern Ireland) Regulations 2008 (SI 2008/2986), inserting s.15A into the 1995 Act; and The Law Applicable to Non-contractual Obligations (Scotland) Regulations 2008 (SSI 2008/404), inserting s.15B into the 1995 Act, operate to restrict the application of the statutory choice of law rules contained in Pt III of the 1995 Act, and give precedence to the operation of Rome II.

[12] Account may have to be taken also of sectoral provision, such as package travel, etc. regulations (as in *Japp v Virgin Holidays Ltd* [2013] EWCA Civ 1371), and motor insurance legislation, (e.g. *Jacobs v Motor Insurers Bureau* [2010] EWCA Civ 1208).

[13] A. Dickinson, *The Rome II Regulation* (Oxford: OUP, 2008 & Supplement 2010); P. Huber (ed.) *Rome II Regulation: Pocket Commentary* (Munich: Sellier European Law Pub, 2011); and J. Ahern and W. Binchy (eds), *The Rome II Regulation on the Law Applicable to Non-Contractual Obligations* (Oxford: Hart, 2011).

[14] e.g. *Bacon v Nacional Suiza Cia Seguros Y Reseguros SA* [2010] EWHC 2017 (QB); a decision handed down prior to the ECJ ruling in *Homawoo v GMF Assurance SA* [2012] I.L.Pr. 2, and superseded thereby; and *Alliance Bank JSC v Aquanta Corp* [2012] EWCA Civ 1588.

[15] Contrast the position under the Rome I Regulation: Corrigendum to the Rome I Regulation 13497/1/09, REV 1, JUR369 [2008] O.J. L177, correcting art.28 of the Rome I Regulation, providing that that Regulation will be applied by Member State courts, including those of the UK, to qualifying cases concerning contracts concluded as from (i.e. on and after) December 17, 2009. There is no express mention in Rome II of the law to govern events which occur *on* January 11, 2009, but it is assumed that Rome II was intended to apply in such cases. Further, A. Dickinson, *The Rome II Regulation: the law applicable to non-contractual obligations* (Oxford: Oxford University Press, 2008), paras 3.315–3.324.

[16] The date of entry into force, 20 August 2007, is tied to the date of publication of the instrument in the Official Journal, namely, 31 July 2007 ([2007] O.J. L199/40).

into force of the Regulation must be distinguished from the date of its application. By art.32, the Regulation shall apply from 11 January 2009.[17]

Doubt was entertained in the UK about the proper interpretation of arts 31 and 32 of Rome II. In *Homawoo v GMF Assurance SA*,[18] the English High Court made a reference to the ECJ on interpretation of art.32, asking the ECJ to determine, as a preliminary issue, if Rome II applied to a claim for personal injury sustained in a road traffic accident in France on 29 August 2007. The ECJ responded that arts 31 and 32 must be interpreted as requiring a national court to apply the Regulation only to events giving rise to damage occurring after 11 January 2009.[19] The date on which the proceedings seeking compensation for damage are brought, or the date on which the applicable law is determined by the court seised, has no bearing on determining the scope *ratione temporis* of the Regulation.[20] A subtle question of interpretation remained, however, in the phrase "events giving rise to damage occurring after January 11, 2009": does the date refer to the date of the "event" or the date of the ensuing "damage"? The better view, in line with art.31, is that the date qualifies the "event", not the "damage", meaning that the relevant date is the date of the occurrence of the event, and not any later date on which harm may become manifest. In short, Rome II applies only to events occurring after 11 January 2009. The first task, therefore, for a court is to identify the event giving rise to the damage, and to determine the date of that event. The difficulty of this task can be compounded by the nature of the delict, such as when the delict is constituted by a series of actings.[21]

With regard to events which occur before 11 January 2009, the governing rules are contained in the 1995 Act, provided that the act or omission giving rise to the claim occurred on or after 1 May 1996.[22] In relation to acts or omissions which precede 1 May 1996, the common law rules shall apply.[23]

Temporal issues of this kind are notoriously difficult, but the problem will wear itself out through the process of time itself.

Subject-matter scope

16–04   Article 1 of Rome II lays down the subject matter scope of the Regulation. In terms of art.1.1, Rome II shall apply in situations involving a conflict of laws, to non-contractual obligations in civil and commercial matters, including non-contractual obligations that are likely to arise.[24] It is clear from recital (11) that the concept of a non-contractual obligation varies from one Member State to

---

[17]   Except for art.29 (List of conventions), which applied from 11 July 2007.

[18]   *Homawoo v GMF Assurance SA* [2010] EWHC 1941 (QB).

[19]   *Homawoo v GMF Assurance SA* [2012] I.L.Pr. 2.

[20]   *Homawoo v GMF Assurance SA* [2012] I.L.Pr. 2 at [36] and [37].

[21]   e.g. in cases of product liability, as for example, the insertion of an allegedly defective hip implant: *Allen v Depuy International Ltd* [2014] EWHC 753 (QB). cf. in jurisdiction *Kainz v Pantherwerke AG* (Case C-45/13) [2015] Q.B. 34.

[22]   1995 Act s.14(1); and the Private International Law (Miscellaneous Provisions) Act 1995 (Commencement) Order 1996 (SI 1996/995) reg.2.

[23]   e.g. *Re T&N Ltd* [2005] EWHC 2990 (Ch).

[24]   Rome II art.2.2.

another, and that, for the purposes of the Regulation, "non-contractual obligation" should be understood as an autonomous concept.[25] The Regulation shall not apply to evidence and procedure.[26]

By virtue of art.1.1, the Regulation shall not apply to revenue, customs or administrative matters or the liability of the state for acts and omissions in the exercise of state authority.[27] Article 1.2 adds to the list of matters excluded from the Regulation's scope. These comprise, in outline, non-contractual obligations arising out of:

(a)   family and comparable relationships[28];
(b)   matrimonial property and comparable regimes, and wills and succession;
(c)   bills of exchange, cheques, promissory notes and other negotiable instruments to the extent that the obligations under such other negotiable instruments arise out of their negotiable character;
(d)   the law of companies and other bodies corporate or unincorporated, including the personal liability of officers and members and the personal liability of auditors to a company or its members;
(e)   the relations between the settlors, trustees and beneficiaries of a trust created voluntarily;
(f)   nuclear damage;
(g)   violations of privacy and rights relating to personality, including defamation.

Excluded matters fall to be regulated in a UK court by the pre-existing law, which, in almost all cases, means the 1995 Act Pt III. In the case of the art.1.2(g) exclusion (violations of privacy and rights relating to personality, including defamation), however, reference must be made to the 1995 Act s.13, which preserves the application of the common law for the determination of "issues arising in any defamation claim". Section 13(2) of the 1995 Act defines "defamation claim" as meaning: (a) any claim under the law of any part of the UK for libel or slander or for slander of title, slander of goods or other malicious falsehood and any claim under the law of Scotland for verbal injury; and (b) any claim under the law of any other country corresponding to or otherwise in the nature of a claim mentioned in para.(a) above. The effect of this provision is that the determination of defamation claims having a conflict aspect must be treated by a Scots or English court in accordance with the pre-existing common law rule (double actionability, q.v.), as interpreted and applied in Scots and English law, respectively. The definition contained in s.13(2) of the 1995 Act is not coterminous with the exclusion in art.1.2(g) of Rome II, with the effect that

---

[25] A. Scott, "The Scope of Non-Contractual Obligations" in Ahern and Binchy (eds), *The Rome II Regulation on the Law Applicable to Non-Contractual Obligations* (2009). Also *Jacobs v Motor Insurers Bureau* [2010] EWCA Civ 1208; and *Maher v Groupama Grand Est* [2009] EWCA Civ 1191; [2010] 1 W.L.R. 1564 (liability of driver's insurer to the victim characterised by the forum as tortious).
[26] e.g. *Wall v Mutuelle de Poitiers Assurances* [2014] EWCA Civ 138; [2014] 1 W.L.R. 4263, a dispute concerning the manner in which expert evidence was to be adduced to the court. The English court characterised the matter in issue (namely the number of experts, and manner of their giving evidence) as procedural, and therefore outside the scope of Rome II. Further paras 8–35 and 16–38.
[27] Rome II recital (9).
[28] Rome II recital (10).

violations of privacy and personality rights, though excluded from the scope of Rome II, do not appear to be regulated by the common law via s.13, and so must be governed by the 1995 Act. However, in order to be regulated by Pt III of the 1995 Act, such claims must be characterised by the forum, for the purposes of private international law, as issues relating to tort or delict.[29] By art.1.3, the Regulation shall not apply to evidence and procedure.

Principle of universal application

16–05   The choice of law rules contained in Rome II have universal application, that is, any law specified by the Regulation must be applied in qualifying cases in any EU forum regardless of whether or not the contending law is that of an EU Member State.[30]

States with more than one legal system

16–06   In the case of a Member State comprising several territorial units, each having its own rules of law in respect of non-contractual obligations, each such unit shall be considered as a country for the purpose of identifying the applicable law under the Regulation.[31]

Exclusion of renvoi

16–07   Article 24 of Rome II provides that the application of the law of any country specified by the Regulation means the application of the rules of law in force in that country other than its rules of private international law.[32]

Applicable law

General rule

16–08   "Article 4...
1.   Unless otherwise provided for in this Regulation, the law applicable to a non-contractual obligation arising out of a tort/delict shall be the law of the country in which the damage occurs irrespective of the country in which the event giving rise to the damage occurred and irrespective of the country or countries in which the indirect consequences of that event occur.
2.   However, where the person claimed to be liable and the person sustaining damage both have their habitual residence in the same country at the time when the damage occurs, the law of that country shall apply.
3.   Where it is clear from all the circumstances of the case that the tort/delict is manifestly more closely connected with a country other than that indicated in paragraphs 1 or 2, the law of that other country shall apply. A manifestly closer connection with another country might be based in particular on a pre-existing relationship between the parties, such as a contract, that is closely connected with the tort/delict in question."

---

[29]   1995 Act s.9(2). Further, para.16–48, below.
[30]   Rome II art.3.
[31]   Rome II art.25.1. See, in respect of intra-UK situations, para.16–45, below.
[32]   For detail, Ch.5, above.

Chapter II of Rome II provides for application in all qualifying cases of the law of "a country", i.e. a territorial unit with a common body of law. For the purposes of maritime delicts,[33] the territorial waters of the litoral state are to be treated as equivalent to the territory of a country.[34]

One difference in principle between the civilian and UK approaches to choice of law in tort and delict is the preference of the former for fixed, certain rules, contrasted with the UK preference for flexibility. At common law and in application of the 1995 Act, English courts showed confidence in utilising discretion in applying the choice of law rules in tort, in order to find what they considered to be the most appropriate law. It is trite to say that in crafting a rule for choice of law in delict the draftsmen must set that rule at some point on the line between certainty and flexibility.[35] In Rome II the most appropriate connecting factor to achieve the objectives of securing legal certainty and the need to effect individual justice has been determined to be the law of the place of damage, subject to certain "escape clauses", and subject to the exercise of party choice, so far as permitted.

Article 4.1—lex loci damni rule

Article 4.1 contains a rule of general application, applicable where no choice of law has been made by the parties under art.14 (q.v.), and designating as applicable to the obligation[36] in question the law of the country in which the damage occurs or is likely to occur.[37] This is termed in recital (16) the *lex loci damni*. The law of the country in which the damage occurs applies irrespective of the country or countries in which the indirect consequences of the event giving rise to the damage occurred. In terms of art.2.1, "damage" covers, "any consequence arising out of the tort or delict". This should be construed as "any direct consequence", for otherwise the aim of art.4.1 would be subverted.

16–09

It is said that application of the *lex loci damni* strikes a fair balance between the interests of the person claimed to be liable and the person sustaining the damage, and also that it reflects the modern approach to civil liability and the development of systems of strict liability.[38]

In cases of personal injury or damage to property, art.4.1 should lead to application of the law of the country where the victim was when the injury was sustained, or where the property was situated when it was damaged.[39]

---

[33] Para.16–53, below.

[34] *Cheshire, North and Fawcett: Private International Law*, 14th edn (2008), p.859.

[35] cf. Rome II recital (14).

[36] Rome II art.4, in contrast with s.12 of the 1995 Act, identifies the law applicable to the "obligation" arising out of the tort or delict, and not the law applicable to a particular "issue", meaning, in effect, that the Regulation excludes the possibility of dépeçage.

[37] Rome II art.2.3(b). e.g. *Wall v Mutuelle de Poitiers Assurances* [2014] EWCA Civ 138; [2014] 1 W.L.R. 4263; and *Stylianou v Toyoshima* [2013] EWHC 2188 (QB).

[38] Rome II recital (16).

[39] Rome II recital (17).

Dealing with double/multiple locality delicts[40]

16–10   The solution preferred in Rome II art.4.1 is to apply the law of the country in which the damage occurs. No regard is paid per the general rule to the location of the event which gave rise to the damage (the place of acting), or to the place of occurrence of indirect consequences of the event.[41]

The Regulation assumes that it is possible in all cases to identify the place of damage, but there will be instances in which the localisation of the place of damage is difficult or impossible, such as where goods in transit across a number of countries arrive damaged at their destination. While it would be possible to argue in favour of application of the law of the place of discovery of harm as the notional place of damage; or, relying on a "mosaic" principle, in favour of application of the law of each of the different countries through which the goods have passed,[42] use of art.4.3 (q.v.) might commend itself more readily to the forum, enabling it to apply to the "whole" a law of closer connection.[43]

There will be cases in which direct damage to the same victim occurs in more than one country. In such cases, art.4.1 must be applied by the forum on a distributive basis, requiring application in turn of each *lex causae* (*"mosaikbetrachtung"* principle).[44]

Equally, difficulties can arise at common law and under the 1995 Act where allegedly delictual conduct is spread over intervals of time and place. Is the delict to be regarded as having been committed at (i) the place where it began, or was instigated (the place of acting); (ii) the place where it ended and its effects were felt (the place of result); or (iii) either/both places, as an option of pleading.[45] In many English cases[46] the point at issue in the consideration of *locus delicti* was

---

[40] Carruthers and Crawford, "Variations on a Theme of Rome II. Part 2" (2005) 9 Edin. L.R. 238, 242.

[41] In a European context, given that a claimant, as a result of the ECJ decision in *Handelswekerij GJ Bier BV v Mines de Potasse d'Alsace SA* (21/76) [1976] E.C.R. 1735, has the option to sue in the place of acting or the place of result, the outcome in choice of law terms will be that whichever EU forum is seised must apply, at least under the general rule, the law of the place of direct result. For discussion of horizontal continuity between or among EU legislative instruments, see E.B. Crawford and J.M. Carruthers, "Connection and Coherence between and among European Instruments in the Private International Law of Obligations" (2014) 63 I.C.L.Q. 7–11.

[42] *Cheshire, North and Fawcett: Private International Law*, 14th edn (2008), p.797.

[43] cf. *Congentra AG v Sixteen Thirteen Marine SA (The Nicholas M)* [2008] EWHC 1615 (Comm) (decided under 1995 Act); and, in jurisdiction, *Reunion Europeene SA v Spliethoffs Bevrachtingskantoor BV* (C-51/97) [1998] E.C.R. I-6511.

[44] Dickinson, *The Rome II Regulation* (2008), para.4.69; and A. Mills, "The Application of Multiple Laws under the Rome II Regulation" in Ahern and Binchy (eds), *The Rome II Regulation on the Law Applicable to Non-Contractual Obligations* (2009).

[45] cf. *Dow Jones & Co Inc v Gutnick* [2002] HCA 56, per Kirby J. at [140]: to adopt the law of the place of the wrong as the applicable law in international tort claims, "is not the end of the inquiry, it is merely the beginning. It leads immediately to the additional question of identifying the place of the wrong . . . much controversy can exist in relation to the proper identification of where the place of the wrong is."

[46] *R. v Peters* (1886) 16 Q.B.D. 636; *George Monro Ltd v American Cyanamid & Chemical Corp* [1944] 1 K.B. 432; *Bata v Bata* [1948] W.N. 366; *Jenner v Sun Oil Co* (1952) 2 D.L.R. 526 (defamatory broadcast in USA heard in Canada); *Cordova Land Co Ltd v Victor Bros Inc* [1966] 1 W.L.R. 793; *R. v Robert Millar (Contractors) Ltd* [1969] 3 All E.R. 247; *Distillers Co (Biochemicals) Ltd v Thompson* [1971] A.C. 458.

one of jurisdiction,[47] and when that point was settled, no further discussion of *locus* was made for the purposes of choice of law. Not infrequently at common law such problems of ascertaining the *locus delicti* were resolved by means of the forum paying close attention to the nature of the delict or tort in question,[48] and/or to the manner in which the complaint was framed. More generally, the court sometimes resorted to a consideration of where the substance of the alleged tort took place.[49] Much depended on localisation of the actings which constituted the tort or delict; or on the precise description in the pleadings of the wrongdoing alleged, e.g. the putting on the market of a product/medication without due warning, rather than the negligent manufacture thereof.[50] In *Ennstone Building Products Ltd v Stanger Ltd*[51] (in which it was necessary to identify the *locus delicti*, in circumstances where allegedly negligent advice was given in England and acted upon in Scotland), Keane L.J. accepted the argument that where the tort consisted in essence in the giving of negligent advice, it was committed where the advice was communicated, in this case, England.

A great deal of the difficulty engendered in common law cases was removed by the introduction in the 1995 Act of detailed rules, in s.11(2) (a) and (b), which specify where the country in which the events constituting the tort or delict occurred is to be taken to be.[52]

The indirect consequences of the event giving rise to the damage

In most cases of personal injury (physical or psychiatric) or damage to property, **16–11** the country in which the injury was sustained or the property damaged will be easily ascertained. Difficulties may emerge in cases where a victim's condition deteriorates, potentially resulting in a claim for aggravated damage. In jurisdiction terms, for the purposes of special jurisdiction in tort, the decision in *Henderson v Jaouen*[53] concerning deterioration of the victim's condition was to deny that a fresh cause of action arose at the place of deterioration. Where a primary victim who suffered physical harm in state A, suffers derivative economic loss in state B, the latter should be deemed to be an indirect consequence and therefore incapable of engaging the applicable law rule under art.4.1.

---

[47] e.g. *Diamond v Bank of London and Montreal* [1979] Q.B. 333; *Ark Therapeutics Plc v True North Capital Ltd* [2006] 1 All E.R. (Comm) 138. See para.7–23, above in relation to Brussels I Regulation art.5.3 and Brussels I Recast art.7.2.

[48] e.g. *Soutar v Peters*, 1912 1 S.L.T. 111.

[49] *Metall und Rohstoff AG v Donaldson Lufkin & Jenrette Inc* [1990] 1 Q.B. 391; *Morin v Bonham & Brooks Ltd* [2004] 1 Lloyd's Rep. 702. cf. *Protea Leasing Ltd v Royal Air Cambodge Co Ltd* [2002] EWHC 2731; and *Ashton Investments Ltd v OJSC Russian Aluminium (Rusal)* [2006] EWHC 2545 (Comm). See J.M. Carruthers and R.B. Crawford, "Variations on a Theme of Rome II. Part 2" (2005) 9 Edin. L.R. 238, 240.

[50] *Castree v ER Squibb & Sons Ltd* [1980] 1 W.L.R. 1248; *Distillers Co (Biochemicals) Ltd v Thompson* [1971] A.C. 458.

[51] *Ennstone Building Products Ltd v Stanger Ltd* [2002] EWCA Civ 916 (common law case); cf. *Diamond v Bank of London and Montreal* [1979] Q.B. 333.

[52] e.g. *Anton Durbeck GmbH v Den Norske Bank ASA* [2002] EWHC 1173; [2003] Q.B. 1160; and *Morin v Bonham & Brooks Ltd* [2004] 1 Lloyd's Rep. 702.

[53] *Henderson v Jaouen* [2002] 1 W.L.R. 2971.

Rarely, though occasionally, there may be difficulty in distinguishing between primary or direct physical harm and the indirect consequences thereof. In *Edmunds v Simmonds*, a case which arose for decision under the 1995 Act, Garland J. referred to the complainant's damages, particularly the major heads, costs of care and loss of future earnings as "consequences of the events constituting the tort."[54] Strictly, however, these heads are not so much indirect consequences of the wrongful event, as elements of the actual damage, or at the very least, "direct consequences" of the wrongful event.

A more complicated situation will be where the primary loss is financial or economic.[55] What is the place of damage in such cases? The search must be for the centre of the victim's loss, the place where the loss was sustained and the financial resources depleted.[56] More difficult perhaps is to draw the line between direct financial damage (the law of the country in which that occurs being the *lex causae* per art.4.1), and the indirect consequences of such damage (irrelevant for the purposes of art.4.1).[57] The crux of the matter may be the difficulty of distinguishing between primary financial loss suffered in state A and secondary financial loss suffered in state B by the same victim.

By contrast, where A, in Scotland, suffers psychiatric or financial loss as a result of physical injury caused to B, in France, the country in which the damage to A occurs is Scotland, not France. This is a situation of direct harm to a secondary victim, a scenario for which art.4.1 makes no special provision. It cannot be said that the separate cause of action accruing to A is an indirect consequence of the event giving rise to the damage to B. Rather, A's situation should be viewed as a separate harm, in respect of which the applicable law will be determined, in the first instance, by art.4.1, on the basis of location. The extent of the alleged wrongdoer's liability to a secondary victim in a cross-border case is likely to form the basis of a freestanding claim under Rome II.

The direction in art.4.1 to disregard the indirect consequences of the event giving rise to the damage is, of course, a direction limited to the process of ascertainment of applicable law under that paragraph. The indirect consequences of the event, and the country in which the event occurred each may be relevant for the purposes of art.4.3 (q.v.). Further, the question whether or not redress can be had from the alleged wrongdoer for indirect consequences of the event will be referred under art.15 (a)–(c) (*q.v.*) to the applicable law as ascertained.

---

[54] *Edmunds v Simmonds* [2001] 1 W.L.R. 1003 at 1009C; cf. *Harding v Wealands* [2006] UKHL 32.

[55] Dickinson, *The Rome II Regulation* (2008), paras 4.36–4.37, 4.66–4.68; and *Cheshire, North and Fawcett: Private International Law*, 14th edn (2008), p.798.

[56] *Hillside (New Media) Ltd v Baasland* [2010] EWHC 3336 (Comm). cf. *Fortress Value Recovery Fund I LLC v Blue Skye Special Opportunities Fund LP* [2013] EWHC 14 (Comm); [2013] 1 All E.R. (Comm) 973, per Flaux J at [56] – [75].

[57] cf. *Dumez France SA v Heissische Landesbank* [1990] E.C.R. I-49; *Réunion Européenne SA v Spliethoff's Bevractingskantoor BV* (C-51/97) [2000] Q.B. 690; *Protea Leasing Ltd v Royal Air Cambodge Co Ltd* [2002] EWHC 2731 (Comm); and *Marinari v Lloyds Bank Plc* [1996] Q.B. 217, discussed in Carruthers and Crawford, "Variations on a Theme of Rome II. Part 2" (2005) 9 Edin. L.R. 238, 247.

Article 4.2—rule of commonality

Article 4.2 inserts an exception[58] to the general rule in art.4.1, leading to **16–12** application of the law of the common habitual residence of the defendant (the person claimed to be liable)[59] and the victim (the person sustaining the damage). Article 4.1 thereby is rendered subject to a commonality clause, to the effect that the obligation shall be governed instead by the law of the common habitual residence of the alleged wrongdoer and the victim at the time when the damage occurs, if such commonality is present.

The rule of commonality in so many words is a novelty to UK lawyers, but instances can be cited of decisions by English courts under the 1995 Act in which the existence of a shared personal law was a relevant factor in the decision whether or not to displace the prima facie applicable law.[60]

The concept of habitual residence is partly defined in the Regulation:

> "Article 23
> Habitual residence
> 1. For the purposes of this Regulation, the habitual residence of companies and other bodies, corporate or unincorporated, shall be the place of central administration.
>   Where the event giving rise to the damage occurs, or the damage arises, in the course of operation of a branch, agency or any other establishment, the place where the branch, agency or any other establishment is located shall be treated as the place of habitual residence.
> 2. For the purposes of this Regulation, the habitual residence of a natural person acting in the course of his or her business activity shall be his or her principal place of business."

The habitual residence of a natural person acting otherwise than in the course of business activity will be construed by the forum in accordance with existing ECJ jurisprudence and its own national law.[61]

Article 4.2 is inflexible in the sense that it must oust the application of art.4.1 if common habitual residence is present, and that legal system is different from the *lex loci damni*. But art.4.2 is subservient to art.4.3.

Article 4.3—rule of displacement and forum discretion[62]

Recital (18) states that: **16–13**

> "Article 4(3) should be understood as an 'escape clause' from Article 4(1) and (2), where it is clear from all the circumstances of the case that the tort/delict is manifestly more closely connected with another country."

---

[58] Rome II recital (18).
[59] *Winrow v Hemphill* [2014] EWHC 3164 (QB), in which the "person claimed to be liable" is the tortfeasor, not the compensation body named as defendant.
[60] *Edmunds v Simmonds* [2001] 1 W.L.R. 1003; *Harding v Wealands* [2006] UKHL 32. At common law, see *Chaplin v Boys* [1971] A.C. 356 ("this was a very British occurrence"). *Sed contra McElroy v McAllister*, 1949 S.C. 110, where the parties had a common habitual residence.
[61] Cf. paras 6–43 et seq. and 15–51, above.
[62] R. Fentiman, "The Significance of Close Connection" in Ahern and Binchy (eds), *The Rome II Regulation on the Law Applicable to Non-Contractual Obligations* (2009).

A similar approach can be seen in the 1995 Act, which in s.12,[63] confers upon the forum discretion to displace the otherwise applicable law in favour of a law which appears to it in all the circumstances to be substantially more appropriate. Since, as has been noted, art.4.3, in contrast with s.12 of the 1995 Act, identifies the law applicable to the obligation arising out of the tort or delict, and not the law applicable to a particular issue,[64] it is not possible for a Member State court applying art.4 to displace the law otherwise applicable in relation to only one or some of the issues presented.[65]

The implicit warning to the forum against over-use of its art.4.3 discretion, by the explicit setting of the displacement threshold at "manifestly more closely connected"—a high bar—will not necessarily deter a forum from freely exercising the discretion to which, in the UK at least, courts have become accustomed.[66]

Some guidance, of an unusually specific nature, is given in the last sentence of art.4.3, which suggests that a manifestly closer connection with another country might be based in particular on a pre-existing relationship between the parties, such as a contract that is closely connected with the tort/delict in question.[67] A pre-existing contractual relationship is relevant only insofar as it is closely connected with the delict in question. Article 4.3, in singling out the existence of a pre-existing relationship between the parties, raises that factor to prominence. It is questionable to what extent the factor has particular significance in the evaluation process which art.4.3 necessitates. Other factors which, one may conjecture, may be taken into account in the comparison exercise include factors relating to the parties (e.g. common domicile and/or common nationality), the events constituting the delict (including the place of acting), and, as stated above, even the consequences, direct and indirect, of the delict in question; once art.4.3 is triggered, art.4.1 cannot inhibit the discretion of the forum. It has been suggested, however, that since art.4.2 provides a rule based on common habitual residence, thereby taking out one important factor in the art.4.3 exercise, art.4.3 is less significant than it appears.[68]

Notably, art.4.3, unlike arts 4.1 and 4.2, contains no temporal limitation on the factors to be taken into account.[69] That being the case, when the court is undertaking the "balancing exercise" necessitated by art.4.3, "the link of the

---

[63] Para.16–47, below.

[64] The displacement rule contained in s.12 of the 1995 Act provides that, in certain cases, the issues arising in a case, or any of those issues, may be governed by a law other than the prima facie applicable law.

[65] Carruthers and Crawford, "Variations on a Theme of Rome II. Part 2" (2005) 9 Edin. L.R. 238, 249.

[66] e.g. *O v A* [2014] EWCA Civ 1277, in which the Court of Appeal was open to an argument for displacement in favour of English law. *Sed contra Stylianou v Toyoshima* [2013] EWHC 2188 (QB), in which displacement per art.4.3 in favour of English law was denied.

[67] This raises interesting questions about the interdependence and mutual assistance of cognate harmonisation instruments. E.B. Crawford and J.M. Carruthers, "Connection and Coherence between and among European Instruments in the Private International Law of Obligations" (2014) 63 I.C.L.Q. 7 at 11–12. Symbiosis between the Rome I Regulation and Rome II Regulation is observable, e.g. in art.4.3.

[68] R. Fentiman, "The Significance of Close Connection" in Ahern and Binchy (eds), *The Rome II Regulation on the Law Applicable to Non-Contractual Obligations* (2009), p.91.

[69] *Winrow v Hemphill* [2014] EWHC 3164 (QB), per Slade J. at [51].

consequences of the tort [i.e. after the event causing the damage] to a particular country will be considered as a relevant factor".[70]

The delict-specific rules

Application of the general rule is modified for cases where the general rule is not thought to strike a reasonable balance between the interests at stake.[71] Accordingly, a series of delict-specific rules are contained in arts 5–9. Delict-specific rules are more familiar to civilian lawyers than to UK lawyers. The approach taken in Rome II, which never featured in Scots and English choice of law rules in delict/tort (apart from the defamation exception contained in s.13 of the 1995 Act), presaged the contract-specific approach adopted in art.4 of the Rome I Regulation.[72]

    16–14

A specific-category approach has its drawbacks in that there will always be potential for argument where the categorisation is debateable in a particular case, or where the factual and legal circumstances cross more than one category,[73] or where the categories themselves seem inadequate for the complexity of the situation. Moreover, the presence of an abundance of categories could be said to weaken the so-called general rule.

Product liability

"Article 5[74]...

    16–15

1.   Without prejudice to Article 4(2), the law applicable to a non-contractual obligation arising out of damage caused by a product shall be:
   (a)   the law of the country in which the person sustaining the damage had his or her habitual residence when the damage occurred, if the product was marketed in that country; or, failing that,
   (b)   the law of the country in which the product was acquired, if the product was marketed in that country; or, failing that,
   (c)   the law of the country in which the damage occurred, if the product was marketed in that country.

   However, the law applicable shall be the law of the country in which the person claimed to be liable is habitually resident if he or she could not reasonably foresee the marketing of the product, or a product of the same type, in the country the law of which is applicable under (a), (b) or (c).

2.   Where it is clear from all the circumstances of the case that the tort/delict is manifestly more closely connected with a country other than that indicated in paragraph 1, the law of that other country shall apply. A manifestly closer connection with another country might be based in particular on a pre-existing relationship between the parties, such as a contract, that is closely connected with the tort/delict in question."

Recital (20) states that:

---

[70] *Winrow v Hemphill* [2014] EWHC 3164 (QB), per Slade J. at [50].
[71] Rome II recital (19).
[72] Para.15–15, above.
[73] Note the solution to this problem adopted by art.4.2, and 4.3, 4.4 of the Rome I Regulation. No such solution is provided in Rome II.
[74] P. Stone, "Product Liability under the Rome II Regulation" in Ahern and Binchy (eds), *The Rome II Regulation on the Law Applicable to Non-Contractual Obligations* (2009), p.175.

"The conflict-of-law rule in matters of product liability should meet the objectives of fairly spreading the risks inherent in a modern high-technology society, protecting consumers' health, stimulating innovation, securing undistorted competition and facilitating trade. Creation of a cascade system of connecting factors, together with a foreseeability clause, is a balanced solution in regard to these objectives . . .".

Article 5, which is elaborate in its drafting, is subject *expressis verbis* to the rule of commonality in art.4.2. Article 5.2 is equivalent to the displacement rule contained in art.4.3.

The sequence of rules in art.5.1 is self-explanatory, subject perhaps only to noting (a) the use of "failing that", a drafting formula which closes debate as soon as a rule, on the facts, is satisfied; and (b) the meaning and significance of the term "marketing",[75] which includes the sale of products, as well as other commercial dealings such as hire, and promotional gift.[76]

Interesting questions arise where a consumer is injured by a defective product which was the subject of his consumer contract. The aggrieved party may require to be advised as to his best course of action, given that a remedy, ex facie, may be available in contract and in delict. Leaving aside possible difficulties with regard to the basis of jurisdiction on which he may seise a court,[77] it will be necessary to consider on his behalf whether the outcome afforded to him under the favourable consumer contract provisions contained in the Rome I Regulation[78] will produce a better result for him in his particular circumstances than that achieved through utilising the bespoke product liability rule in art.5 of Rome II.

Unfair competition and acts restricting free competition[79]

16–16

"Article 6 . . .
1. The law applicable to a non-contractual obligation arising out of an act of unfair competition shall be the law of the country where competitive relations or the collective interests of consumers are, or are likely to be, affected.
2. Where an act of unfair competition affects exclusively the interests of a specific competitor, Article 4 shall apply.
3. (a) The law applicable to a non-contractual obligation arising out of a restriction of competition shall be the law of the country where the market is, or is likely to be, affected.
  (b) When the market is, or is likely to be, affected in more than one country, the person seeking compensation for damage who sues in the

---

[75] In detail: Dickinson, *The Rome II Regulation* (2008), para.5.18; and Stone, "Product Liability under the Rome II Regulation" in Ahern and Binchy (eds), *The Rome II Regulation on the Law Applicable to Non-Contractual Obligations* (2009), pp.188 et seq.

[76] That online purchases, it is thought, must be included is consonant with art.15.1(c) of the Brussels I Regulation/art.17.1(c) of the Brussels I Recast, and art.6.1(b) of the Rome I Regulation.

[77] A factor possibly inhibiting choice as a result of the nature and internal ranking of the special jurisdiction rules contained in art.5.1 (contract) and 5.3 (delict) of the Brussels I Regulation/art.7.1 and 7.2 of the Brussels I Recast. Para.7–27, above. The problem arises because special jurisdictions, being derogations from the general rule, must be construed strictly.

[78] Article 6, discussed at para.15–25, above; and E.B. Crawford and J.M. Carruthers, "Connection and Coherence between and among European Instruments in the Private International Law of Obligations" (2014) 63 I.C.L.Q. 7 at 25–26.

[79] J. Fitchen, "Choice of Law in International Claims Based on Restrictions of Competition: Article 6(3) of the Rome II Regulation" (2009) 5 J. Priv. Int. Law 337.

court of the domicile of the defendant, may instead choose to base his or her claim on the law of the court seised, provided that the market in that Member State is amongst those directly and substantially affected by the restriction of competition out of which the non-contractual obligation on which the claim is based arises; where the claimant sues, in accordance with the applicable rules on jurisdiction, more than one defendant in that court, he or she can only choose to base his or her claim on the law of that court if the restriction of competition on which the claim against each of these defendants relies directly and substantially affects also the market in the Member State of that court.

4.   The law applicable under this Article may not be derogated from by an agreement pursuant to Article 14."

It is claimed in recital (21) that the special rule in art.6 is not an exception to the general rule in art.4.1, but rather a clarification of it. The aim of the provision is very widely stated, viz. to protect competitors, consumers and the general public and ensure that the market economy functions properly. It is said that the adoption qua applicable law of the law of the country where competitive relations or the collective interests of consumers are, or are likely to be, affected generally satisfies these objectives.[80] At the outset, it is possible that there will be problems of characterisation in relation to this article, especially in the UK, where there is no known category of delict, *sub nom.* "acts of unfair competition". There may be scope for applying art.6 to the economic delicts, such as inducement/procurement of breach of contract, conspiracy, or causing loss by unlawful means.

Environmental damage[81]

"Article 7...   **16–17**
     The law applicable to a non-contractual obligation arising out of environmental damage or damage sustained by persons or property as a result of such damage shall be the law determined pursuant to Article 4(1),[82] unless the person seeking compensation for damage chooses to base his or her claim on the law of the country in which the event giving rise to the damage occurred."

This type of damage does not attract special treatment in the domestic Scots law of delict. Recital (24) explains that "environmental damage" should be understood as meaning:

"...adverse change in a natural resource, such as water, land or air, impairment of a function performed by that resource for the benefit of another natural resource or the public, or impairment of the variability among living organisms."[83]

The inclusion of a specific rule to deal with delicts under this head proved controversial during Rome II negotiations. Although at one point the removal of

---

[80] Rome II recitals (22) and (23). e.g. *Innovia Films Ltd v Frito-Lay North America, Inc* [2012] EWHC 790 (Pat), per Arnold J. at [109].

[81] M. Bogdan, "The Treatment of Environmental Damage in the Regulation Rome II" in Ahern and Binchy (eds), *The Rome II Regulation on the Law Applicable to Non-Contractual Obligations* (2009), p.219.

[82] But not pursuant to art.4.2 and 4.3, which do not apply in the case of environmental damage.

[83] Article 1.2(f) provides that non-contractual obligations arising out of nuclear damage are excluded from the scope of the Regulation.

this special choice of law rule was proposed, ultimately the option was preferred[84] of providing that the law applicable to a non-contractual obligation arising or likely to arise out of a violation of the environment, including damage caused to persons or property, shall be the law determined by application of the general rule in art.4.1, unless the person[85] seeking compensation elects to base his claim on the law of the country in which the event giving rise[86] to the damage occurred (i.e. the place where the harm was triggered, rather than the place where its environmental effects were felt). This introduces a unilateral party autonomy rule, in contrast to the bilateral rule contained in art.14 (q.v.).

The characterisation of a non-contractual obligation as one arising out of environmental damage is a significant one for the claimant, since it favours the victim in a manner consistent with the interpretation famously given by the ECJ in the jurisdiction case of *Bier BV v Mines de Potasse d'Alsace SA*,[87] viz. elective power of the victim. The question of when the claimant can make the choice of law is to be determined in accordance with the law of the Member State forum.[88] Following this line of thought, the victim has a choice in the matters both of jurisdiction and choice of law, provided that the incident qualifies as one falling under art.7, a decision which is for the forum selected, taking account of recital (24).

Although the wording of art.7 suggests that its remit is confined to identification of applicable law for *compensation claims* for damage, it is thought[89] that it is not intended to be so limited, and there is no reason why the applicable law rules contained therein should not also extend to applications for interdict/injunctions to prevent such damage.

Infringement of intellectual property rights

16–18

"Article 8...

1.   The law applicable to a non-contractual obligation arising from an infringement of an intellectual property right shall be the law of the country for which protection is claimed.

2.   In the case of a non-contractual obligation arising from an infringement of a unitary Community intellectual property right, the law applicable shall, for any question that is not governed by the relevant Community instrument, be the law of the country in which the act of infringement was committed.

---

[84] The reason for including the rule is explained in recital (25).

[85] A question arises to what extent legal, as well as natural, persons are competent to bring or defend a claim under the Regulation. The Regulation applies to "civil and commercial matters" (art.1.1). The Brussels regime as a whole does not extend to public authorities exercising their public powers (*Lufttransportunternehmen GmbH & Co KG v Organisation Europeenne pour la Securite de la Navigation Aerienne (Eurocontrol)* (29/76) [1977] 1 C.M.L.R. 88), but if a state or local authority were to be seen to be acting in a private capacity, as for example, as the owner of land, it would appear that Rome II will apply.

[86] Contrast formulation (favouring application of the law of the place of harm) used in the general rule in art.4.1. This is justified on the basis of policy, to ensure that the law of the place of acting, if it imposes the more exacting standard, shall apply, at the option of the claimant.

[87] *Bier BV v Mines de Potasse d'Alsace SA* (Case 21–76) [1978] 1 Q.B. 708 ECJ: para.7–23, above.

[88] Rome II recital (25).

[89] Bogdan, "The Treatment of Environmental Damage in the Regulation Rome II" in Ahern and Binchy (eds), *The Rome II Regulation on the Law Applicable to Non-Contractual Obligations* (2009), p.221.

3.　　The law applicable under this Article may not be derogated from by an agreement pursuant to Article 14."

Article 8.1 enshrines the principle of the *lex loci protectionis*,[90] and this, combined with the prohibition in art.8.3 upon derogation therefrom by the parties through choice of applicable law per art.14, demonstrates the strength of application of the territoriality approach.[91] The term "intellectual property rights" is to be interpreted as including copyright, related rights, the sui generis right for the protection of databases, and industrial property rights. Characterisation by the forum of the issue as one of infringement of an intellectual property right such as covered by art.8 means that the matter must be regarded as non-contractual and regulated in an EU Member State court by the terms of art.8.[92] Though the word "damage" is not mentioned in this article, in referring to "protection" and "infringement", it appears nonetheless to cover both bases of claim, namely, preventative and compensatory measures.

Industrial action

> "Article 9...
> 　　Without prejudice to Article 4(2), the law applicable to a non-contractual obligation in respect of the liability of a person in the capacity of a worker or an employer or the organisations representing their professional interests for damages caused by an industrial action, pending or carried out, shall be the law of the country where the action is to be, or has been, taken."

16–19

No definition of "industrial action" is included in the Regulation, and the reference[93] to each Member State's internal rules is not helpful, at least in the case of the UK, where, in Scots and English law, there is no special category of delicts pertaining to industrial action. Additionally, it is not clear whether the law applicable under art.9 determines its own applicability; one cannot be as confident that characterisation falls within the province of the forum, as one can be in relation to the other delict-specific rules.

　　Article 9 is subject to the rule of commonality in art.4.2, but (unlike, for example, art.5.2) contains within its short terms no equivalent to the displacement rule contained in art.4.3. Therefore, it would seem that there is no possibility of displacement in favour of a law of manifestly closer connection.

---

[90] e.g. *Actavis UK Ltd v Eli Lilly & Co* [2014] EWHC 1511 (Pat); [2014] 4 All E.R. 331, and [2015] EWCA Civ 555.

[91] Rome II recital (26).

[92] Cheshire, North and Fawcett, *Private International Law*, 14th edn (Oxford: OUP, 2008), p.815.

[93] Recital (27) states that: "The exact concept of industrial action, such as strike action or lock-out, varies from one Member State to another and is governed by each Member State's internal rules. Therefore, this Regulation assumes as a general principle that the law of the country where the industrial action was taken should apply, with the aim of protecting the rights and obligations of workers and employers." Further, according to recital (28): "The special rule on industrial action in Article 9 is without prejudice to the conditions relating to the exercise of such action in accordance with national law and without prejudice to the legal status of trade unions or of the representative organisations of workers as provided for in the law of the Member States."

Road traffic accidents[94]

16–20 The final version of Rome II does not contain a special rule for road traffic accidents. This being so, the general rules in art.4 (and in arts 17 and 18) will apply, leading to concerns that victims of road traffic accidents in Member States other than the Member State of their habitual residence ("visiting victims") may have applied to their claims a law which, in their circumstances, may be inappropriate, with regard to the size of the award of compensation and the limitation period within which the claim must be brought.[95] Recital (33) of Rome II contains a guide to the effect that:

> "According to the current national rules on compensation awarded to victims of road traffic accidents, when quantifying damages for personal injury in cases in which the accident takes place in a State other than that of the habitual residence of the victim, the court seised should take into account all the relevant actual circumstances of the specific victim, including in particular the actual losses and costs of after-care and medical attention."[96]

As has been said elsewhere in this book, the status of the recitals is not clear, particularly in respect of a sentiment which is not supported in a specific article.

In light of these concerns, a consultative document was issued in 2009 by the European Commission,[97] seeking views on a variety of options to address this perceived problem.[98] The most striking option was to apply the law of the country of the visiting victim's residence, which would entail the consequence that in certain accidents, e.g. on a coach tour, where the passengers are each of different habitual residences, there could be multiple *leges causae*, and the defendant, if liable, could be liable to different victims to varying extents, depending on an individual victim's circumstances, legal and factual. Another possibility would be to require pan-European agreement between insurance companies, in order to produce a system whereby visiting victims could settle their claims with their own third party liability motor insurer, and on the fiction that the accident took place in the victim's country of residence, in order to receive compensation in accordance with that law. The UK Government favours the status quo.[99]

An additional complexity in this subject area is the relationship between Rome II and the 1971 Hague Convention on the Law Applicable to Traffic Accidents, to

---

[94] See J. von Hein, "Article 4 and Traffic Accidents" in Ahern and Binchy (eds), *The Rome II Regulation on the Law Applicable to Non-Contractual Obligations* (2009).

[95] But this is true of many victims of various types of delict which occur outside their country of residence.

[96] M. Chapman, "The Rome II Regulation and 'European Law Enforcement Area': harmony and discord in the assessment of damages" [2010] J. Priv. Int. Law 10.

[97] European Commission Consultation Paper on the Compensation of Victims of Cross-Border Road Traffic Accidents in the European Union MARKT/H2/RM markt.h2(2009)61541. Further, European Commission Public Consultation on Limitation Periods for Compensation Claims of Victims of Cross-Border Road Traffic Accidents in the European Union (2012) http://ec.europa.eu/justice/newsroom/civil/opinion/121031_en.htm [accessed 21 June 2015].

[98] Views were also sought on nine proposed options to address the fact that limitation periods vary among Member States.

[99] UK Government Response to a Consultative Document issued by the European Commission dated March 26, 2009 (June 2009).

which many EU Member States (though not the UK) are parties. Article 30 of Rome II required the Commission to produce, not later than 20 August 2011, a study on the effects of art.28 (relationship with existing international conventions) with respect to the 1971 Hague Convention. In 2009, a report was published,[100] recommending, in the first place, that solutions should be proportionate to the objectives pursued; and that at the EU level solutions should be proportionate to the significance of the issues for the internal market. Specifically, the difference in compensation levels and limitation periods lead to a great amount of uncertainty, and risks of under- and over-compensation. However, it is not clear that the distortions created by these differences have a significant impact on the internal market, "visiting victims" being few in number. Therefore, given the relatively small number of people concerned, an appropriate solution would not involve overhauling the whole legal framework as it pertains to victim compensation. It is unclear whether the impetus to date among some Member States for the creation of a special choice of law rule for traffic accidents will maintain its momentum.

DIRECT ACTION AGAINST THE INSURER OF THE PERSON LIABLE[101]

Although Rome II does not contain a specific rule for road traffic accidents, of interest and relevance in this connection is art.18, which provides that: **16–21**

> "The person having suffered damage may bring his or her claim directly against the insurer of the person liable to provide compensation if the law applicable to the non-contractual obligation or the law applicable to the insurance contract so provides."

This victim-friendly rule may be said to amount in effect to a delict-specific rule for motor accidents. It offers the victim a choice of defendant (and thereby possibly also of forum). Clearly it will often be advantageous to proceed immediately to sue the insurer. This can be done, by virtue of art.18, if a direct claim against the insurer of the wrongdoer is permitted either by the law governing the delict or by the law applicable to the insurance contract. In jurisdiction terms the victim already is assisted by interpretation of the Brussels I Regulation, case law[102] having clarified that the Regulation confers on him, in his action against the wrongdoer's insurers, the benefits provided in s.3 of the Regulation, in particular art.9.1(b).[103] Few topics demonstrate so cogently the interrelationship of applicable law rules in non-contractual and contractual obligations; and between applicable law and jurisdiction rules.

---

[100] Hoche (Demolin, Brulard, Barthelemy), *Compensation of Victims of Cross-Border Road Traffic Accidents in the EU: Comparison of National Practices, Analysis of Problems, and Evaluation of Options for Improving the Position of Cross-Border Victims*, Contract ETD/2007/IM/H2/116.

[101] cf. *Maher v Groupama Grand Est* [2009] EWCA Civ 1191; [2010] 1 W.L.R. 1564; and, under the 1995 Act, *Knight v Axa Assurances* [2009] EWHC 1900 (QB); and *Jones v Assurances Generales de France (AGF) SA* [2010] I.L.Pr. 4.

[102] *FBTO Shadeverzekeringen NV v Odenbreit* (C-463/06) [2007] ECR I-11321; [2008] I.L.Pr. 12.

[103] Para.7–31, above.

Violations of privacy and rights relating to personality

16–22 Despite lengthy and arduous negotiations, it was not possible to agree a harmonised choice of law rule to deal with these subjects.[104] Article 30.2 of Rome II stipulated that, not later than 31 December 2008, the Commission should submit to the European Parliament, the Council and the European Economic and Social Committee a study on the situation in the field of the law applicable to non-contractual obligations arising out of violations of privacy and rights relating to personality, taking into account rules relating to freedom of the press and freedom of expression in the media, and conflict of laws issues related to Directive 95/46/EC on the protection of individuals with regard to the processing of personal data and on the free movement of such data. The timescale slipped, and in February 2009 there was published the final report, entitled, *Comparative study on the Situation in the 27 Member States as regards the law applicable to non-contractual obligations arising out of violations of privacy and rights relating to personality*.[105] The matter remains controversial, and consensus is elusive.

On 10 May 2012, the European Parliament passed a resolution with recommendations to the Commission on the amendment of Rome II, including a suggested choice of law rule.[106] The Parliament requested that the Commission submit a proposal designed to insert in Rome II a provision to deal with the law applicable to non-contractual obligations arising out of violations of privacy and rights relating to personality, including defamation. The Commission did not formally respond,[107] but included the topic within its 2012 Questionnaire on Rome II. There the matter rests. In the absence of a harmonised rule, national choice of law rules continue to apply.[108]

Collective redress

16–23 The existing choice of law rules in Rome II make no overt reference to mass claims or actions for collective redress. Application of the harmonised rules in Rome II might lead to the application of several different laws to the substance of claims arising out of one grievance.[109] To date, the European Commission has not been persuaded that it would be appropriate to introduce into Rome II a tort-specific rule for collective claims, requiring the forum to apply a single *lex causae*. On 11 June 2013, the European Commission issued a non-binding Recommendation on common principles for injunctive and compensatory

---

[104] For background: Dickinson, *The Rome II Regulation* (2008), paras 3.217–3.228.

[105] *Comparative study on the Situation in the 27 Member States as regards the law applicable to non-contractual obligations arising out of violations of privacy and rights relating to personality* (University of the Basque Country, 2009), JLS/2007/C4/028; see also Annex 1 Survey Questionnaires.

[106] P7_TA(2012)0200.

[107] European Parliament, Committee on Legal Affairs, "Stocktaking of parliamentary committee activities during the 7th legislature Committee", p.8.

[108] For Scotland and England, see paras16–48—16–52, below.

[109] "Towards a European Horizontal Framework for Collective Redress" COM(2013) 401 final (Strasbourg, 11 June 2013), para.3.7.

collective redress mechanisms in the Member States concerning violations of rights granted under Union Law.[110] These are discussed in Ch.7.[111]

Freedom of choice

Whether, and to what extent, party autonomy should be permitted in the area of non-contractual obligations has been the subject of much discussion. Recital (31) of the Rome II Regulation encapsulates the rationale for art.14, as follows:

16–24

> "To respect the principle of party autonomy and to enhance legal certainty, the parties should be allowed to make a choice as to the law applicable to a non-contractual obligation.... Protection should be given to weaker parties by imposing certain conditions on the choice."

Article 14 is in the following terms:

> "Article 14[112]...
> 1.   The parties may agree to submit non-contractual obligations to the law of their choice:
>   (a)   by an agreement entered into after the event giving rise to the damage occurred;
>   or
>   (b)   where all the parties are pursuing a commercial activity, also by an agreement freely negotiated before the event giving rise to the damage occurred.
>   The choice shall be expressed or demonstrated with reasonable certainty by the circumstances of the case and shall not prejudice the rights of third parties.
> 2.   Where all the elements relevant to the situation at the time when the event giving rise to the damage occurs are located in a country other than the country whose law has been chosen, the choice of the parties shall not prejudice the application of provisions of the law of that other country which cannot be derogated from by agreement.
> 3.   Where all the elements relevant to the situation at the time when the event giving rise to the damage occurs are located in one or more of the Member States, the parties' choice of the law applicable other than that of a Member State shall not prejudice the application of provisions of Community law, where appropriate as implemented in the Member State of the forum, which cannot be derogated from by agreement."

---

[110] Recommendation on common principles for injunctive and compensatory collective redress mechanisms in the Member States concerning violations of rights granted under Union Law 2013/396/EU ([2013] O.J. L201/60). See also European Commission, Communication from the Commission to the European Parliament, the Council, the European Economic and Social Committee and the Committee of the Regions, "Towards a European Horizontal Framework for Collective Redress" (COM(2013) 401 final) (Strasbourg, 11 June 2013).

[111] Paras 7–65—7–68, above.

[112] T. Kadner Graziano, "Freedom to Choose the Applicable Law in Tort—Articles 14 and 4(3) of the Rome II Regulation" in Ahern and Binchy (eds), *The Rome II Regulation on the Law Applicable to Non-Contractual Obligations* (2009), p.219.

Party choice in relation to choice of law in commercial law, and to some extent elsewhere,[113] increasingly is permitted, even encouraged—though generally it is reined in by the concept and imposition of "mandatory rules"; and in the case of choice of jurisdiction, by provisions designed to protect weaker parties from making choices which are perceived to be against their best interests.[114]

In 1984[115] the Law Commissions, when scrutinising the subject of choice of law in tort and delict, recommended that, "It should be possible (before or after a tort or delict has occurred) to agree by means of contract what law should govern the parties' mutual liability in tort or delict. Such agreement should be effective whether or not it results in the application of the law of the forum."[116] Oddly, the issue of party autonomy was not addressed in the ensuing report,[117] nor does it feature in Pt III of the 1995 Act.[118] Sir Peter North remarked in 1993 that it would be "prudent and practical" to legislate for party autonomy in tort and delict since it was, "…highly improbable that courts would feel free to develop at common law a concept of party autonomy in tort alongside a regime of statutory choice of law rules."[119] The decision in *Morin v Bonham & Brooks Ltd*[120] suggests that not only would courts have felt reluctant to develop such a concept under the 1995 Act, but also would have been powerless so to do.

When may the parties exercise choice under Rome II?

16–25 In most cases, delictual events are not contemplated or anticipated. Article 14 sanctions freedom of choice ex post: art.14.1 provides that the parties may agree to submit non-contractual obligations to the law of their choice by an agreement entered into after the event giving rise to the damage occurred. However, choice ex post facto is not necessarily *informed* choice; permission to choose the applicable law *after* the event is no guarantee that advantage will not be taken of a weaker party. The theory behind the limitation of parties to choice ex post facto seems to be that they will be protected thereby from inadvertently waiving their

---

[113] J.M. Carruthers, "Party Autonomy in the Legal Regulation of Adult Relationships: What Place for Party Choice in Private International Law?" (2012) 61 I.C.L.Q. 881; J.M. Carruthers, "Party Autonomy and Children: A View from the UK" *Nederlands Internationaal Privaatrect*, Special Issue 2012: Party Autonomy and International Family Law 562; E.B. Crawford and J.M. Carruthers, "Speculation on the Operation of Succession Regulation 650/2012: Tales of the Unexpected" (2014) 22(6) European Review of Private Law 847 at 866 et seq.

[114] cf. protective wording of arts 13 (insured persons), 17 (consumers) and 21 (employees) in Brussels I Regulation/ arts 15, 19 and 23 of Brussels I Recast.

[115] Law Commission and Scottish Law Commission, *Private International Law: Choice of Law in Tort and Delict*, 1984, Law Com. Working Paper No.87; Scot. Law Com. Memo. No.62 (followed by *Private International Law: Choice of Law in Tort and Delict* (HMSO, 1990), Law Com. No.193; Scot. Law Com. No.129).

[116] Law Commission and Scottish Law Commission, *Private International Law: Choice of Law in Tort and Delict*, 1984, Law Com. Working Paper No.87; Scot. Law Com. Memo. No.62, p.265, para.7.3.1(a).

[117] Law Commission and Scottish Law Commission, *Private International Law: Choice of Law in Tort and Delict*, 1990, Law Com. No.193; Scot. Law Com. No.129.

[118] Sir Peter North described this as the "sin of omission" ("Torts in the Dismal Swamp: Choice of Law Revisited" in *Essays in Private International Law* (1993), p.85). The issue, he writes, "disappeared without trace" ("Choice in Choice of Law" in *Essays* (1993), p.190).

[119] North, *Essays* (1993), p.190.

[120] *Morin v Bonham & Brooks Ltd* [2003] 2 All E.R. (Comm) 36; [2003] I.L.Pr. 25.

rights, or yielding to the will of the other party in advance of the dispute (by virtue perhaps of a standard form contract). Thus, in the Brussels I and Brussels I Recast Regulations, parties deemed to be weak (where there is obvious inequality in bargaining power) are restricted in their exercise of free will to the making of choices of court after the event and within certain safeguards.[121]

Only where all the parties are pursuing a commercial activity may choice be exercised by an agreement freely negotiated before the event giving rise to the damage occurred. It is clear that the provisions of art.14.1(b), concerning choice *ex ante*, can apply only to the minority of cases in which parties were known to each other commercially before the occurrence of the event giving rise to the damage.

In the absence of choice of law to govern any non-contractual liability which may arise, where the parties are linked by contract, the governing law of that commercial relationship may be identified by the court as the applicable law to govern the non-contractual obligation, in terms of art.4.3, even if the parties had made no anterior choice of law within that contract to govern any delictual liability which might eventuate. For the applicable law of the contract to be utilised in the context of art.4.3, the delict would require to be closely connected with the contract.[122]

Greater freedom of choice (albeit freedom restricted by overriding mandatory provisions and public policy, q.v.) is a welcome development in this area; and of particular benefit in cases lying on the cusp where there exist parallel claims in contract and in tort, and where application of a common applicable law to the contractual and non-contractual aspects of a claim would be desirable.[123]

Although art.14.1 appears to apply to all non-contractual obligations, choice of law is prohibited for certain delicts, by virtue of the terms of the specific choice of law rules set out in arts 6 (unfair competition and acts restricting free competition)[124] and 8 (infringement of intellectual property rights).[125]   **16–26**

What may the parties choose?

Leaving aside the question of *when* parties can exercise choice, we must ask *what*   **16–27**
is it that parties may choose? This subject last came to the forefront of discussion in contract, in relation to the conversion of the Rome I Convention into a Regulation.[126] Parties may choose "the law of their choice",[127] choice being

---

[121] Para.7–61, above.

[122] cf. *Sapporo Breweries Ltd (a company incorporated under the laws of Japan) v Lupofresh Ltd* [2012] EWHC 2013 (QB), per Bean J. at [41]–[46]; and on appeal at [2013] EWCA Civ 948; [2014] 1 All E.R. (Comm) 484: in respect of Lupofresh's counterclaim in tort, the judge at first instance held that it was substantially more appropriate for the law of Japan to be applied to the tort since Japanese law was the applicable law of the contracts.

[123] As, e.g. employer/employee disputes: *Brodin v A/R Seljan*, 1973 S.C. 213; *Coupland v Arabian Gulf Oil Co* [1983] 3 All E.R. 226; and *Sayers v International Drilling Co NV* [1971] 1 W.L.R. 1176. cf. The "proper law of the issue", as Lord Denning, alone among his peers, sought to get to the heart of the matter in the mixed contract/tort case of *Sayers v International Drilling Co NV*. Para.16–46, below, and from a contractual perspective, paras 15–60—15–61, above.

[124] Rome II art.6.4. But see Dickinson, *The Rome II Regulation* (2008), para.6.75.

[125] Rome II art.8.3. Explanatory Memorandum, p.22.

[126] Para.15–12, above.

limited to the domestic, internal rules of the chosen law,[128] with no possibility of recourse to *renvoi*. Exclusion of *renvoi* is a necessary handmaid to effective choice of law where the law selected by parties is that of a Member State; were it otherwise, circularity would ensue.[129] There can be no getting away from regulation by the Regulation as, for example, by choosing national rules of applicable law in delict operating before Rome II.

The contract by which the parties exercise their choice under article 14

16–28   The contractual vehicle by which the parties exercise their choice will be subject to the Rome I Convention/Regulation, as appropriate. Where the agreement on choice of law is one permitted by art.14 of the Rome II Regulation, it must be referred to the Rome I Convention/Regulation, for assessment as to formal validity, interpretation, material validity (at least so far as demonstrating consensus), and performance obligations. To the issue of contractual capacity in art.13 of the Rome I Regulation, must be added the antecedent proviso supplied by Rome II art.14, that only "parties pursuing a commercial activity" are eligible to make such an agreement before the event giving rise to the damage occurs.[130]

With regard to essential validity of the terms of the choice of law agreement, the position is less clear: for example, A and B, commercial parties, agree in advance of any potential delictual incident, that liability will be governed by the law of Evasia, by which, let it be assumed, there is no principle of vicarious liability of an employer for an employee. The contract by which A and B make this "Rome II art.14 agreement", contains a clause to the effect that the law governing the contract as a whole shall be Scots law (per Rome I Regulation art.3). Insofar as vicarious liability is a principle of Scots law which cannot be derogated from by agreement,[131] the question arises whether the essential validity of the delictual choice of law agreement must be judged by the applicable law of the contract (Scots law) or by the applicable law, contractually agreed by the parties, to govern the non-contractual obligation (Evasian law). Rome II appears to anticipate this problem through its mandatory rules provision in art.14.2,[132] but this will not cover all cases. In a situation in relation to which more than two laws have an interest in being applied, it is arguable that the policing mechanisms operative under the Rome I Regulation, namely, arts 8 (employment contracts), 9 (overriding mandatory provisions), and 21 (public policy of the forum) will apply so as to temper the choice of law agreement made under art.14 of Rome II.

---

[127] Although the rules in Ch. II of Rome II are restricted to application of "the law of a country", the wording of art.14 is not so restricted: see suggestion in Kadner Graziano, "Freedom to Choose the Applicable Law in Tort" in Binchy & Ahern (eds), *The Rome II Regulation: The Law Applicable to Non-contractual Obligations* (Leiden: Brill, 2009), p.119, that a resource such as the Principles of European Tort Law, drawn up by the European Group on Tort Law, could be viewed in the same light as the Common Frame of Reference in choice of law in contract.

[128] Rome II art.24.

[129] E.B. Crawford, "The Use of Putativity and Negativity in the Conflict of Laws" (2005) 54 I.C.L.Q. 829.

[130] Subject to the prohibitions upon freedom of choice contained in Rome II arts 6, 8.

[131] Law Reform (Personal Injuries) Act 1948, abolishing the doctrine of common employment. cf. *Brodin v A/R Seljan*, 1973 S.C. 213.

[132] So too per art.14.3 (mandatory provision of Community law).

Viewed from this perspective, the extent of party autonomy in the non-contractual sphere, where it now appears for the first time, is restricted by the rules governing party autonomy in contractual obligations. This conclusion suggests that the non-contractual obligation is subjugated to the larger contractual choice of law provision. By this mode of reasoning, any attempt by parties to evade a principle such as the vicarious liability of an employer for the wrongful actings of employees in the scope of employment would be difficult to achieve.[133]

Restrictions on choice of law

Parties' choice of law in terms of art.14 will be subject,[134] per art.14.2, to the provisions of the law of another country which cannot be derogated from by agreement where all the elements relevant to the situation at the time when the event giving rise to the damage occurs are located.[135] This provision is intended to deal with a situation which is "purely internal" to one Member State, and which falls within the scope of the Regulation only because the parties have agreed on a choice of foreign law.[136] It deals with a country's rules of *internal* policy, that is, rules which are mandatory in the domestic sense, but not necessarily in the international context:

16–29

> "...*internal* public policy rules are not necessarily mandatory in an international context. Such rules must be distinguished from the rules of international public policy of the forum [art.26] and overriding mandatory rules [art.16]."[137]

By reason of art.14.3, where all the elements relevant to the situation at the time when the event giving rise to the damage occurs are located in one or more of the EU Member States, the parties' choice of applicable law other than that of a Member State, shall not prejudice the application of provisions of Community law, where appropriate as implemented in the Member State of the forum, which cannot be derogated from by agreement. This is a novel provision, replicated in art.3.4 of the Rome I Regulation.[138] In order for the provision in art.14.3 of Rome II (as in art.3.4 of the Rome I Regulation) to apply, the choice of law of the parties must be that of a non-EU Member State. Therefore the provision can be seen as having the aim of ensuring the application of "Community law". Where the parties' choice falls upon the law of a Member State, art.16, preserving overriding mandatory provisions of the (EU) forum, may operate to preserve the application of such provisions of Community law as bind Member State forums.

---

[133] Even on the different hypothesis that Evasian law was both the governing law of the contract and the chosen applicable law in delict, any rule of that law exonerating the employer for allegedly delictual actings of his employees might be refused effect in a Scots forum through operation by the forum of the public policy discretion endowed by art.26 (q.v.).

[134] cf. Rome II recital (32).

[135] cf. Rome I Regulation art.3.3. Para.15–22, above.

[136] Explanatory Memorandum, p.22.

[137] Explanatory Memorandum, p.22.

[138] Para.15–22, above.

Overriding mandatory provisions

16–30   "Article 16...
        Nothing in this Regulation shall restrict the application of the provisions of the law of the forum in a situation where they are mandatory irrespective of the law otherwise applicable to the non-contractual obligation."

The applicable law (whether found by application of art.4, or by the delict-specific rules, or through party choice exercised in terms of art.14) is subject to the overriding mandatory provisions of the *lex fori*.[139] Characterisation of the provision in question as mandatory for the purpose of art.16 must be done by the forum according to its own law. Rome II, in contrast with art.9.1 of the Rome I Regulation, does not contain any definition of mandatory provisions which would guide or restrict the forum.

Rules of safety and conduct

16–31   "Article 17...
        In assessing the conduct of the person claimed to be liable, account shall be taken, as a matter of fact and in so far as is appropriate, of the rules of safety and conduct which were in force at the place and time of the event giving rise to the liability.
        Recital (34) provides useful elaboration, thus:

> 'In order to strike a reasonable balance between the parties, account must be taken, in so far as appropriate, of the rules of safety and conduct in operation in the country in which the harmful act was committed, even where the non-contractual obligation is governed by the law of another country. The term 'rules of safety and conduct' should be interpreted as referring to all regulations having any relation to safety and conduct, including, for example, road safety rules in the case of an accident'."

In an instrument which, by its general rule, identifies the *lex loci damni* as the applicable law, art.17 requires account to be taken of certain provisions of the *lex loci delicti* ("place...of the event giving rise to the liability"). The wording of art.17 gives rise to ambiguities of interpretation and of application. With regard to interpretation, it is not easy to understand the extent of the forum's discretion to disregard a particular rule ("in so far as appropriate") when account "shall"/ "must" be taken thereof.[140] "Rules of safety and conduct", although capable of very broad interpretation, possibly will be taken to refer principally (but not exclusively[141]) to road safety rules, as recital (34) suggests.

Public policy of the forum

16–32   "Article 26[142]...

---

[139] cf. Rome I Regulation art.9.1, 9.2. Rome II has no equivalent to art.9.3.

[140] Dickinson, *The Rome II Regulation* (2008), suggests at para.15.33 that Member State courts have a wide margin of appreciation in deciding whether, and if so for what purpose and to what extent, to take account of any such rule. See para.15–36, above re art.12.2 of the Rome I Regulation.

[141] Rome II art.17, for example, may have particular significance in relation to claims for environmental damage under art.7.

[142] Also recital (32).

The application of a provision of the law of any country specified by this Regulation may be refused only if such application is manifestly incompatible with the public policy (*ordre public*) of the forum."

According to the Commission Explanatory Memorandum, the public policy provision can be distinguished from the provision on overriding mandatory rules[143] in that with regard to the latter, "the courts apply the law of the forum automatically, without first looking at the content of the foreign law."[144] Public policy, on the other hand, may be invoked only *after* the content of the foreign law and the result of its application has been considered by the forum. Article 16 represents, in effect, a positive exercise of the forum's policy: policy operating as a sword, i.e. the strength of the forum's policy is such that it precludes the operation of a contradictory rule of any potentially applicable foreign law. Article 26, in contrast, represents a negative exercise of the forum's public policy: policy operating as a shield, i.e the strength of the forum's policy prevents application of the prima facie relevant foreign law. It is normally the case that the effect of exercise of the forum's public policy in a matter of governing law in any context is preventative of the *application* of the *lex causae* for some reason that is deeply important to the forum, but conceivably, in a minority of instances, a *prohibition* (such as an inter-spousal immunity from suit) found in the content of the *lex causae*'s rules is itself so offensive to the forum that the forum's refusal to give effect to that prohibition has the result of producing a positive effect.

By its nature, the tool of public policy is a tool of the forum, for use sparingly. At the negotiation stage of Rome II, the Commission Proposal[145] contained a provision which would have given strong guidance to a forum not to give effect to a provision of the *lex causae* deemed in advance to be contrary to "Community public policy". The Proposal's ambit was limited to one particular point in the law of damages. In the result, such a provision does not appear in Rome II, but traces of it can be found in recital (32).[146]

Scope of the law applicable[147]

"Article 15...   **16–33**
The law applicable to non-contractual obligations under this Regulation shall govern in particular:
(a)   the basis and extent of liability, including the determination of persons who may be held liable for acts performed by them;
(b)   the grounds for exemption from liability, any limitation of liability and any division of liability;
(c)   the existence, the nature and the assessment of damage or the remedy claimed;
(d)   within the limits of powers conferred on the court by its procedural law, the measures which a court may take to prevent or terminate injury or damage or to ensure the provision of compensation;

---

[143] Rome II art16.
[144] Explanatory Memorandum, p.28.
[145] Rome II art.24, Commission Proposal COM(2003) 427 final (2003/0168(COD)).
[146] See "Damages", para.16–39, below.
[147] J.M. Carruthers, "Has the Forum Lost its Grip?" in Ahern and Binchy (eds), *The Rome II Regulation on the Law Applicable to Non-Contractual Obligations* (2009), p.25.

(e)   the question whether a right to claim damages or a remedy may be transferred, including by inheritance;

(f)   persons entitled to compensation for damage sustained personally;

(g)   liability for the acts of another person;

(h)   the manner in which an obligation may be extinguished and rules of prescription and limitation, including rules relating to the commencement, interruption and suspension of a period of prescription or limitation."

Once the applicable law is identified, its scope of application is fixed by art.15, which confirms the authority of the *lex causae*, but does not foreclose its authority in matters not listed. The list of issues which are subject to regulation by the *lex causae* is therefore not exhaustive, but the article is useful since different Member States traditionally have adopted different classifications, the same issue in one forum being treated as substantive and therefore subject to application of the *lex causae*, and in another forum as procedural, for the *lex fori*. From a UK perspective, it is significant that listed in art.15 are matters that a UK court otherwise might have characterised as procedural and thus referred to the *lex fori*, both as a matter of principle and by virtue of the exclusions of evidence and procedure per art.1.3 from the scope of the regulation. The manner of drafting of art.15 gives the *lex causae* an expansive scope of application, conferring upon it a very wide function. The Commission's justification for this expansive approach is certainty.[148]

Paragraph (a)

16–34   By para.(a), "the basis and extent of liability, including the determination of persons who may be held liable for acts performed by them" shall be governed by the applicable law in delict. This provision is intended to refer to *intrinsic* factors of liability,[149] including issues such as, "...nature of liability (strict or fault-based); the definition of fault, including the question whether an omission can constitute a fault; the causal link between the event giving rise to the damage and the damage; the persons potentially liable; etc."[150] "Extent of liability", on the other hand, is intended to refer to, "...the limitations laid down by law on liability, including the maximum extent of that liability and the contribution to be made by each of the persons liable for the damage which is to be compensated for".[151] Article 15(a) is to be construed as covering not only what was referred to, traditionally in Scots law, as *remoteness of injury* (the existence of liability), but also *remoteness of damage* (the extent of liability).

The phrase, "including the determination of persons who may be held liable for acts performed by them" is ambiguous. The matter of determination of persons liable in (a) arguably covers the same thing (vicarious liability) as art.15(g) (liability for the acts of another person). The duplication is not problematic insofar as the applicable law is the same under both paragraphs, but the drafting could have been more careful. Paragraph (a) probably is intended to refer to issues such as whether an *incapax* person, by reason of non-age, or

---

[148] Explanatory Memorandum, p.23.
[149] Explanatory Memorandum, p.23.
[150] Explanatory Memorandum, p.23.
[151] Explanatory Memorandum, p.23.

mental in-capacity, etc., may be held liable for his potentially tortious acts and omissions. In order to avoid potential conflicts of characterisation, it might have been sensible expressly to include in para.(a) the matter of tortious capacity. Curiously, although the question of capacity to incur liability in tort/delict is not expressly listed in art.15, it is narrated in recital (12) as being a matter which is governed by the *lex causae*. Why this is relegated to the recitals is not apparent. The drafters' intention, at least, is that it should not be possible under Rome II to seek to characterise tortious capacity as a matter for the choice of law rules on status and capacity, and thus governed by the putative wrongdoer's personal law, be that his domicile, habitual residence or nationality.

Paragraph (b)

The grounds for exemption from liability, any limitation of liability and any division of liability are governed by the applicable law in delict. These, it is said, are *extrinsic* factors of liability,[152] or "conditions for exoneration from liability".[153] The grounds for release from liability could include *force majeure*; necessity; third-party fault; and fault by the victim,[154] by way of contributory negligence or voluntary assumption of risk.

16–35

Contributory negligence on the part of the victim possibly deserved an express mention in para.(b), for it, normally, is the most important reason for a division of liability. A useful case on the subject of defences is *Dawson v Broughton*.[155] A car driven by Broughton in France was involved in a collision with another vehicle driven by a French driver. Of the passengers in Broughton's car, two were injured and one was killed. Broughton's primary liability was not disputed, but a defence of contributory negligence was entered on the ground that the individual who died had not been wearing a seat belt. Under s.11 of the 1995 Act, the applicable law was French. In terms of French law, under the *Loi Badinter*, failure to wear a seat belt does not result in any reduction in damages. A question arose as to whether that provision of French law was substantive or procedural, a matter of significance because, by effect of s.14(3)(b) of the 1995 Act (q.v.), matters of evidence and procedure were to be determined by English law. The court held that contributory negligence was relevant to the scope of a defendant's liability and the identification of actionable damage, and therefore, that the matter was substantive, and not to be regarded as merely part of the quantification of damages. On this line of reasoning, the French provision applied (subject only to displacement under s.12 of the 1995 Act, q.v.). If contributory negligence falls within "exemption from liability, any limitation of liability and any division of liability", Rome II requires that the rules of the *lex causae* on this matter will govern, rendering the substance/procedure debate irrelevant.

---

[152] Explanatory Memorandum, p.23.

[153] *Cheshire, North and Fawcett: Private International Law*, 14th edn (2008), p.842.

[154] Explanatory Memorandum, p.23.

[155] *Dawson v Broughton* (2007) 151 S.J.L.B. 1167; and "Case Comment", 2007 J. Priv. Int. Law C186. See also *Middleton (A Child) v Allianz Iard SA* [2012] EWHC 2287 (QB).

Paragraph (c)

16–36 The most contentious aspect of art.15 is para.(c). The damages debate has long been the subject of particular interest in the UK.[156]

PRE-ROME II

16–37 The pre-existing UK choice of law rule relating to damages was said to be partly substantive and partly procedural: the applicable law in delict determined what heads of damages were available, whereas the monetary assessment or quantification of damages, and the mode of calculation (e.g. by judge or jury) were governed by the law of the forum, since these were deemed to be aspects of procedure. No Scottish or English case at common law or under the 1995 Act applied the principles of a *foreign* applicable law to the task of quantification. There are two main elements in the assessment of damages[157]:

(a) Determination of liability, traditionally deemed to be a matter of substance determined in accordance with the delictual *lex causae*. The applicable law would govern all matters such as remoteness of damage and the heads under which damages may be claimed.

(b) Quantification of the amount of damages, traditionally considered to be a matter of procedure determined by the *lex fori* alone.[158]

The result of s.14(2) and (3)(b) of the 1995 Act seemingly produced no change in this area, but the matter of distinguishing between issues of substance and of procedure revealed itself in practice to be complex.[159]

Opportunity for the House of Lords to revisit the "damages rule", and to review its merits arose in *Harding v Wealands*,[160] a case decided according to the 1995 Act. The claimant, Giles Harding, an English national, domiciled in England, was rendered tetraplegic as a result of a motor accident in New South Wales in February 2003. The car in which he was a front-seat passenger was being driven at the time of the accident by his partner, Tania Wealands, an Australian national who had lived in Australia until June 2001, at which time she moved to England to live with the claimant. Ms Wealands conceded liability (no

---

[156] Notably in *Harding v Wealands* [2007] 2 A.C. 1. See J.M. Carruthers, "Substance and Procedure in the Conflict of Laws: A Continuing Debate in relation to Damages" (2004) 53 I.C.L.Q. 691; G. Panagopoulos, "Substance and Procedure in Private International Law" (2005) 1(1) J. Priv. Int. Law 69; J.M. Carruthers, "Damages in the Conflict of Laws—the Substance and Procedure Spectrum: *Harding v Wealands*" (2005) 1(2) J. Priv. Int. Law 323; C. Dougherty and L. Wyles, "*Harding v Wealands*" (2007) 56 I.C.L.Q. 443; R. Weintraub, "Choice of Law for Quantification of Damages: A Judgment of the House of Lords makes a Bad Rule Worse" (2007) 43 Texas Int. Law J. 311; and R. Garnett, *Substance and Procedure in Private International Law* (OUP, 2012), Ch.11.

[157] *Kohnke v Karger* [1951] 2 All E.R. 179; *J D'Almeida Araujo LDA v Sir Frederick Becker & Co Ltd* [1953] 2 Q.B. 329 (contract); *Chaplin v Boys* [1971] A.C. 356; *Mitchell v McCulloch*, 1976 S.L.T. 2.

[158] *Maher v Groupama Grand Est* [2009] EWCA Civ 1191; [2010] 1 W.L.R. 1564; *Knight v Axa Assurances* [2009] EWHC 1900 (QB); and *Mapfre Mutilidad Compania De Seguros Y Reaseguros SA v Keefe* [2015] EWCA Civ 598.

[159] e.g. *Edmunds v Simmonds* [2001] 1 W.L.R. 1003; *Roerig v Valiant Trawlers Ltd* [2002] 1 Lloyd's Rep. 681; and *Iraqi Civilians v Ministry of Defence* [2014] EWHC 3686 (QB).

[160] *Harding v Wealands* [2007] 2 A.C. 1.

other vehicle was involved in the incident), but a preliminary issue arose before Elias J. concerning the law applicable to the assessment of damages.[161]

There were two potentially applicable laws: the law of New South Wales ("NSW"), being the law of the country where the tort occurred; and English law, being the law of the forum and also, the claimant argued, the "substantially more appropriate" law to apply. New South Wales law, unlike English law, imposed various limitations on the nature and amount of damages recoverable by the claimant in terms of the Motor Accidents Compensation Act 1999 ("MACA"). It was in the claimant's interests that English law apply to the assessment of damages.

At first instance, Elias J. found in favour of the claimant on two grounds. First, it was accepted that English law should apply to all aspects of the assessment of damages in terms of s.12 of the 1995 Act (on the basis of coincidence of *lex causae* and *lex fori*). But in any event, his Lordship concluded that, even if NSW law applied under s.11, nevertheless English law, as master of procedure in its own house, should govern the quantification of damages qua *lex fori*. Ms Wealands appealed. Two issues arose on appeal: first, whether Elias J. was correct to disapply the general rule in s.11 of the 1995 Act (which, it was concluded, ultimately, he was not); and, secondly, whether the NSW damages provisions were to be classified as substantive or procedural, the significance being that if they were held to be rules of substance, they would apply (given the s.11 application of NSW law) even in an English forum.

The majority[162] of the Court of Appeal found in favour of Ms Wealands. This was not an appropriate case for s.12 displacement. Moreover, English law should not govern assessment of the claimant's damages. In the Court of Appeal Arden L.J. endeavoured to propel English law in a new direction, stating that the applicable law in tort (in this case, NSW law) should govern, as far as possible, the assessment of damages, including quantification of damages. The *lex fori* should apply only as a back-up or secondary provision, where it is not possible, or just, to apply the proper law. Mr Harding appealed.

The House of Lords allowed Mr Harding's appeal, restoring the judgment of Elias J., and affirming the "damages principle". Their Lordships, retreating from Arden L.J.'s statement of the law, cleaved to the traditional British view, that questions of quantification of damages are procedural, to be determined by the law of the forum. This is at odds, however, with the harmonised European solution.

ROME II

Article 15(c) of Rome II refers "the existence, the nature and the assessment of damage or the remedy claimed" to the applicable law in tort. Thus, the forum's approach to quantification of damages in tort will be adopted only if the *lex fori* happens also to be the law governing substantive liability, i.e. if the *lex fori* applies qua *lex causae*. This wrought a significant change of position for United

16–38

---

[161] *Harding v Wealands* [2004] EWHC 1957 (QB). All references henceforth to Elias J. are to this citation.
[162] Arden L.J. and Sir Wm Aldous; Waller L.J., dissenting. See *Harding v Wealands* [2005] 1 W.L.R. 1539 CA, per Arden L.J. at [52].

Kingdom courts. There is no scope under art.15 to displace application of the pre-determined *lex causae*; the only way in which displacement is possible is to revisit the subject of identification of the *lex causae*, or to reassess the applicability of arts.16 or 26.[163]

It is well known that the distinction between substance and procedure in damages is not always as clear-cut as might be expected.[164] However, the choice of law distinction between liability and quantification has been rendered meaningless for the purposes of awards of damages under Rome II now that all such matters are to be referred, in any event, to the same law, the *lex causae*. There may yet be matters in the area of the award of damages which remain the province of the forum, on the rationale that the point is procedural ("evidence and procedure" being excluded from the scope of Rome II per art 1.3), as, for example, in *Wall v Mutuelle de Poitiers Assurances*.[165]

Moreover, the delivery to the applicable law by art.15(c) of the matter of the assessment of damage can fail in circumstances such as encountered in *Jacobs v Motor Insurers Bureau*.[166] A road traffic accident occurred in Spain, in which the claimant, a UK resident, was injured by a car driven, uninsured, by a German national. The claimant utilised reg.13 of the UK Motor Vehicles (Compulsory Insurance) (Information Centre and Compensation Body) Regulations 2003[167] in order to claim compensation from the Motor Insurers' Bureau. Since the facts fell precisely within the terms of the 2003 Regulations, the MIB was directed thereby to compensate the injured party as if "the accident had occurred in Great Britain". The decision at first instance, that compensation had to be assessed in accordance with Spanish law as the applicable law per art.4.1 of Rome II, was reversed by the English Court of Appeal on the ground that reg.13 of the 2003 Regulations was not a choice of law provision. Regulation 13 merely defined the existence and extent of the MIB's obligation to compensate. While it was implicit that the claimant was required to show that the uninsured driver was liable to him in tort (a question determinable by reference to the applicable law per Rome II), the MIB's obligation to compensate victims of accidents occurring abroad involving uninsured drivers was subject to the 2003 Regulations' rule that the accident must

---

[163] Paras 16–30 and 16–32, above.

[164] Para.8–35, above.

[165] *Wall v Mutuelle de Poitiers Assurances* [2014] EWCA Civ 138; [2014] 1 W.L.R. 4263. The manner in which expert evidence was to be offered was classified by the court as procedural. The defendant's contrary submission, that art.15 should receive a broad construction so as to include within the scope of the (French) applicable law practices regularly used by the French court in assessing damages under French law, did not find favour with the English Court of Appeal.

[166] *Jacobs v Motor Insurers' Bureau* [2010] EWCA Civ 1208; [2011] 1 W.L.R. 2609. cf. *Bloy v Motor Insurers' Bureau* [2013] EWCA Civ 1543), in which English law was applied to the quantification of compensation: a cap on damages by the Lithuanian applicable law per Rome II art.4.1, was dislodged by operation of reg.13 of the 2003 Regulations, permitting the outcome that the accident was deemed to have occurred in England. But see doubts expressed per Gilbart, J in *Moreno v Motor Insurers' Bureau* [2015] EWHC 1002 (QB), para. [11] and [73]–[82]. Also *Actavis UK Ltd v Eli Lilly & Co* [2015] EWHC Civ 555, per Floyd, LJ obiter at [136]–[149].

[167] UK Motor Vehicles (Compulsory Insurance) (Information Centre and Compensation Body) Regulations 2003 (SI 2003/37), implementing in the UK Directive No.2000/26/EC of the European Parliament and the Council of 16 May 2000 on the approximation of laws of the member States relating to insurance against civil liability in respect of the use of motor vehicles and amending Council Directives 73/239/EEC and 88/357/EEC (Fourth Motor Insurance Directive) ([2000] O.J. L181/65).

be treated as having occurred in Great Britain. Hence the assessment of damages was performed by English law qua notional or deemed locus.

The two-pronged approach to damages was not without defect: in quantifying novel claims, for example, how was the forum to quantify a head of loss which was available under the *lex causae*, but which the *lex fori* did not know or recognise? This problem did not generally arise at common law because of the requirement of double actionability,[168] but that is not true of operation of the 1995 Act. Whatever the merit of art.15(c), it short-circuits this particular problem.

If it is the aim of the Rome II Regulation to achieve uniformity and foreseeability of outcome (in applicable law terms at least) there is a strong case for arguing that quantification should depend on the applicable law, rather than on the law of the particular forum in which the claim happens to be brought. There is certainly something to be said for applying the foreign law, and having regard to the foreign remedy so long as its application would be consistent with the procedural possibilities available in the forum. Trouble may be encountered, however, where its application would be inconsistent with the procedural possibilities of the forum, e.g. where the *lex causae* prefers payment of interim or provisional damages, or damages in instalments,[169] or where the decision on quantum is one for a jury, but the *lex fori* has no such procedural device or mechanism. Article 15(c), unlike art.15(d),[170] does not, apparently, offer an escape route from this problem. The view has been expressed that, "...common sense requires that Article 15(c) should be interpreted as being implicitly procedurally limited in the same way as Article 10(1)(c)[171] of the Rome Convention is explicitly so limited".[172] It is to be hoped that this common sense interpretation will be adopted.

A further significant difference in wording exists between art.10(1)(c) of the Rome I Convention/art.12.1(c) of the Rome I Regulation and its sibling, art.15(c) of Rome II, viz.: Rome I provides that the contractual *lex causae* shall determine the assessment of damages, "in so far as it is governed by *rules of law*", a proviso which does not feature in Rome II.[173] The wording of Rome I is intended to draw a distinction between circumstances when the assessment of damages raises questions of fact and those when it raises questions of law. If the issue raises a question of law,[174] then the contractual *lex causae* per Rome I will apply. If, however, the question in relation to assessment is one only of fact (e.g. if a jury is to calculate the amount of damages) this is a matter purely for the *lex fori*, and the applicable law under Rome I will not apply.

Rome II does not, ex facie, vouchsafe such a role for the *lex fori*. Article 15(c) apparently is less restrictive than Rome I in this respect, and a literal approach to

---

[168] Para.16–49, below.

[169] Although these matters, potentially, could be characterised as relating to "forms of compensation" and subject, therefore, to art.15(d), which is subject to the proviso that the forum is obliged to act only within the limits of powers conferred by its own procedural law.

[170] Discussed, para.16–40, below.

[171] Which is prefaced by the words, "within the limits of the powers conferred on the court by its procedural law". cf. Rome I Regulation art.12.1(c).

[172] *Cheshire, North and Fawcett: Private International Law*, 14th edn (2008), p.846.

[173] Notably, it did feature in the corresponding provision (art.11(e)) of the original Commission Proposal for a Regulation. For detail: *Cheshire, North and Fawcett: Private International Law*, 14th edn (2008), p.845, fn.591.

[174] e.g. Giuliano and Lagarde, p.33.

interpretation indicates that the applicable law in tort will apply, regardless of whether the issue of assessment arising is one of fact or of law. Strictly, therefore, and anomalously, the role of the *lex fori* is more significantly reduced in assessment of damage in *non-contractual* obligations, than in relation to *contractual* obligations. It remains to be seen whether courts applying this paragraph will adopt a strict, literal construction of the provision, or whether they will take the view that omission of the proviso from Rome II was inadvertent. As a matter of practice, the latter approach would be the more sensible.

Non-compensatory, exemplary or punitive damages

16–39   During the negotiations of Rome II, there was an attempt by the European Parliament to include rules directing Member State courts on the manner of treatment of awards of non-compensatory, exemplary or punitive damages of an excessive nature.[175] Within the UK there was strong concern at the prospect of development of the concept of "Community public policy".[176] Ultimately, the clause as drafted in the Commission Proposal[177] did not survive, but a residue remains in the form of recitals (32)[178] and (33).[179]

Paragraph (d)

16–40   This paragraph is intended to refer to, "...forms of compensation, such as the question whether the damage can be repaired by payment of damages, and ways of preventing or halting the damage, such as an interlocutory injunction, though without actually obliging the court to order measures that are unknown in its own procedural law."[180] This caveat ensures that the forum cannot be required to order measures that have no place in its procedural law.

Paragraph (e)

16–41   This provision, providing that the applicable law will govern, "the question whether a right to claim damages or a remedy may be transferred, including by inheritance" is self-explanatory. The rule should operate effectively, so long as it is accepted that the matter is one which properly belongs to the law of delict and not to that of succession or procedure. The Commission Memorandum states that, "...in succession cases, the designated law[181] governs the question whether an

---

[175] Carruthers and Crawford, "Variations on a Theme of Rome II. Part 1" (2005) 9 Edin. L.R. 65, 95–97.

[176] Scott Report, Evidence, House of Lords Committee, 8th Report, e.g. Briggs, para.16.

[177] Commission Proposal ex-arts 23 and 24.

[178] Recital (32) provides that: "Considerations of public interest justify giving the courts of the Member States the possibility, in exceptional circumstances, of applying exceptions based on public policy and overriding mandatory provisions. In particular, the application of a provision of the law designated by this Regulation which would have the effect of causing non-compensatory exemplary or punitive damages of an excessive nature to be awarded may, depending on the circumstances of the case and the legal order of the Member State of the court seised, be regarded as being contrary to the public policy (*ordre public*) of the forum."

[179] Para.16–39, above.

[180] Explanatory Memorandum, p.24.

[181] i.e. the applicable law under the Rome II Regulation.

action can be brought by a victim's heir to obtain compensation for damage sustained by the victim.[182] In assignment cases, the designated law[183] governs the question whether a claim is assignable, and also the relationship between assignor and debtor."[184]

Paragraph (f)

The applicable law will govern, "persons entitled to compensation for damage sustained personally". On first sight the meaning of this clause is not clear. The wording is opaque and arguably the matter could be treated under art.15(c). The Commission Memorandum, however, explains that the concept particularly refers to the question whether a secondary victim, that is, a person other than the "direct victim", can obtain compensation for damage sustained on a "knock-on" basis, following damage sustained by the primary victim.[185] "Such damage might be non-material, as in the pain and suffering caused by a bereavement, or financial, as in the loss sustained by the children or spouse of a deceased person."[186] The heading appears to cover both the question of availability of an award of damages in principle, and the entitlement to claim such award.

At common law, the subject of title and interest to sue is normally a matter of procedure to be determined by the *lex fori*, but examples of more manipulative classification in the USA demonstrate that this largely procedural subject, which is of the first importance in every sense, may merge into a matter of substance. For example, claims within the family may be regarded as pertaining to the law of domestic relations and may be referred to the law of the domicile. While title to sue in a technical sense is procedural, interest to sue is a substantive matter; sometimes this distinction is not clearly drawn, and the expression "title to sue" may encompass both aspects.[187]

16–42

Paragraph (g)

Paragraph (g) provides that vicarious liability shall be determined by the applicable law, and not the *lex fori*. It would cover the liability of parents for their children, and of principals for their agents, and is to the same effect as the pre-Rome II position in the United Kingdom. Article 15(g) would appear to extend to natural and to legal persons (e.g. within a corporate group, as regards the liability of a parent company for the acts or omissions of its subsidiaries).

16–43

Paragraph (h)

Lastly, paragraph (h) provides that, "the manner in which an obligation may be extinguished and rules of prescription and limitation, including rules relating to the commencement, interruption and suspension of a period of prescription or

16–44

---

[182] The *lex successionis* will determine who benefits from survival of the cause of action.
[183] i.e. the applicable law under the Rome II Regulation, being "the proper law of the right".
[184] Explanatory Memorandum, p.24.
[185] Explanatory Memorandum, p.24. Also para.16–11, above.
[186] Explanatory Memorandum, p.24.
[187] e.g. *FMC Corp v Russell*, 1999 S.L.T. 99. See E.B. Crawford, "The Adjective and the Noun: Title and Right to Sue in International Private Law", 2000 J.R. 347; and para.8–06, above.

limitation" shall be referred to the applicable law under the Regulation. In line with the existing UK legislation, the law designated as applicable by Rome II will govern the loss of a right following failure to exercise it, whether by the *lex causae* such provisions are deemed substantive or procedural.[188]

Article 15 does not eliminate the difficult interface between the applicable law and the law of the forum, that is, between substance and procedure; indeed, it makes no reference as such to substance and procedure. However, by expanding the territory over which the *lex causae* explicitly extends, Rome II reduces the size of the debateable land between substance and procedure.

The range of matters set out in art.15 as falling under the governance of the *lex causae* tilts the balance in favour of the *lex causae* in a manner which is explicit. There is no overt means in art.15 by which the forum is able to inhibit the application of the *lex causae*.

Intra-UK cases

16–45   Typically, European conflict of laws harmonisation instruments confer upon states with more than one legal system the opportunity not to apply the harmonised rules to conflicts solely between the laws of such units. This provision is contained in art.25.2 of Rome II. The UK typically declined to take up the opportunity not to apply Rome II to intra-UK conflicts.[189]

Under the 1995 Act, a difficulty of interpretation arose in relation to the combined effect of ss.9(6),[190] 10 and 14(2).[191] Where allegedly delictual actings took place entirely within one territorial unit of the UK, and were litigated upon in that same unit, it was unclear whether the statutory rules were to be regarded as applicable. This matter now is of much decreased importance, and reference should be made to the previous edition of this work.[192]

Where delict meets contract[193]

16–46   Although delictual actings usually are not premeditated, it may happen that there is a pre-existing relationship between the alleged wrongdoer and the victim. As noted above, the existence of the contractual nexus may influence the identification of the applicable law in delict,[194] and indeed may lead to the conclusion that the law applicable to the contractual and non-contractual

---

[188]   cf. Rome I Regulation art.12.1(d).

[189]   1995 Act s.15A; and The Law Applicable to Non-Contractual Obligations (England and Wales and Northern Ireland) Regulations 2008 (SI 2008/2986) reg.6; and 1995 Act s.15B; and The Law Applicable to Non-Contractual Obligations (Scotland) Regulations 2008 (SSI 2008/404) reg.4, respectively, extend the scope of Rome II to conflicts solely between the laws of England and Wales, Scotland, Northern Ireland and Gibraltar.

[190]   "This Part applies in relation to events occurring in the forum as it applies in relation to events occurring in any other country".

[191]   "Nothing in this Part affects any rules of law (including rules of private international law) except those abolished by section 10".

[192]   Crawford and Carruthers, *International Private Law in Scotland*, 2nd edn (2006), paras 16–10, 16–23; and E.L.R 70 et seq.; also para.16–50, below.

[193]   E.B. Crawford and J.M. Carruthers, "Connection and Coherence between and among European Instruments in the Private International Law of Obligations" (2014) 63 I.C.L.Q. 7 at 11–12, and 23.

[194]   Rome II arts 4.3 and 18.

obligation, respectively, is the same. The choice of law process under Rome II may necessitate identification of the applicable law in contract.

Where, however, this is not the case, and the parties stand to each other, for example, as employer/employee, or carrier/passenger, the defender in an action founded in delict may wish to try to use a term of the contract agreed between the parties to oust or mitigate his potential delictual liability,[195] as where a Scots employee entered into an employment contract under which he agreed to waive certain provisions of Scots law regarding the law of damages for personal injuries, and agreed instead to accept the provisions of some other (presumably less favourable) law, or an exclusion or limitation of liability on the part of the employer. If such a person is injured through an act of negligence for which his employer prima facie is responsible,[196] is his right of action to be regarded as a right based on delict governed by the conflict rules stated, or as a contractual right governed (i.e. limited) by the provisions of the contract? In *Sayers v International Drilling Co NV*,[197] the judges took different views, but it is suggested that if the approach of Lord Denning M.R. in that case, and of Lord Kissen in *Brodin v A/R Seljan*,[198] is followed, the Scots courts will treat the matter, first, as one involving delict and apply the conflict rules of delict prior to those of contract.[199]

Hence, applying the choice of law rule in delict (under Rome II, the 1995 Act, or at common law, as the case may be), the court would decide whether contractual exclusion or limitation of delictual liability on the part of the alleged wrongdoer would be permitted by the delictual *lex/leges causae*. Only if such a defence is allowed according to the delictual *lex/leges causae* would the court proceed to consider whether the contract and/or contractual term in question is valid by its own applicable law, as determined by the Rome I Regulation, and relevant in the circumstances.[200]

---

[195] cf. *Matthews v Kuwait Bechtel Corp* [1959] 2 All E.R. 345; and *Coupland v Arabian Gulf Oil Co* [1983] 3 All E.R. 226.

[196] In terms of art.15(g) of Rome II, the question of vicarious liability would fall to be governed by the applicable law determined per arts 4–14.

[197] *Sayers v International Drilling Co NV* [1971] 1 W.L.R. 1176. See also *Comex Houlder Diving Ltd v Colne Fishing Co Ltd*, 1987 S.L.T. 443 (right of contribution under Law Reform (Miscellaneous Provisions) (Scotland) Act 1940 s.3(2)).

[198] *Brodin v A/R Seljan*, 1973 S.L.T. 198. In this case no doubt an element of policy was present. Lord Kissen was not inclined to the view that the thrust of the provisions of the UK Law Reform (Personal Injuries) Act 1948 could be displaced by the Norwegian contract of employment of a sailor injured in Scotland by a fellow employee, who sued his employer in Scotland.

[199] *Coupland v Arabian Gulf Oil Co* [1983] 3 All E.R. 226; *Henderson v Merrett Syndicates Ltd (No.1)* [1994] 3 All E.R. 506 (domestic law). See C.G.J. Morse, *Torts in Private International Law* (1978), pp.187 et seq.; and North, "Contract as a Tort Defence in the Conflict of Laws", reprinted in *Essays* (1993), p.89: "The availability of the contractual defence is a matter of tort law but the validity of the contract in which it is to be found is a matter of contract law" (p.108).

[200] Paras 15–60 and 15–61, above.

Private International Law (Miscellaneous Provisions) Act 1995[201]

16–47   As stated, while Rome II represents the major scheme of applicable law rules to be applied by Member State courts in qualifying cases arising under the head of non-contractual obligations,[202] account still must be taken, in UK courts, of the 1995 Act, by reason of subject matter and/or date. With regard to events giving rise to damage which occur before 11 January 2009, the governing rules are those contained in the 1995 Act, provided that the act or omission giving rise to the claim occurred on or after 1 May 1996.[203] Furthermore, violations of privacy and personality rights are excluded from the scope of Rome II by art.1.2(g), and so fall to be regulated by Pt III of the 1995 Act, provided the claim is characterised by the forum, for the purposes of private international law, as one relating to tort or delict.[204]

The 1995 Act sprang from the work and consultation undertaken by the Law Commissions in the 1980s,[205] which in turn was prompted by long-running academic discussion and speculation.[206]

Section 11 provides the general rule, in the following terms:

"(1)   The general rule is that the applicable law[207] is the law of the country in which the events constituting the tort or delict in question occur.[208]

(2)   Where elements of those events occur in different countries, the applicable law under the general rule is to be taken as being—

(a)   for a cause of action in respect of personal injury caused to an individual or death resulting from personal injury, the law of the country where the individual was when he sustained the injury[209];

---

[201] C.G.J. Morse, "Torts in Private International Law: A New Statutory Framework" (1996) I.C.L.Q. 888; and P.J. Rogerson, "Choice of Law in Tort: A Missed Opportunity?" (1995) I.C.L.Q. 650.

[202] The Law Applicable to Non-Contractual Obligations (England and Wales and Northern Ireland) Regulations 2008 (SI 2008/2986), inserting s.15A into the 1995 Act; and The Law Applicable to Non-Contractual Obligations (Scotland) Regulations 2008 (SSI 2008/404), inserting s.15B into the 1995 Act, operate to restrict the application of the statutory choice of law rules contained in Pt III of the 1995 Act and give precedence to the operation of Rome II.

[203] 1995 Act s.14(1); and the Private International Law (Miscellanous Provisions) Act 1995 (Commencement) Order 1996 (SI 1996/995) reg.2.

[204] 1995 Act s.9(2).

[205] Law Commission and Scots Law Commission, *Private International Law: Choice of Law in Tort and Delict*, 1984, Law Com. Working Paper No.87; Scot. Law Com. Memo. No.62; *Private International Law: Choice of Law in Tort and Delict*, 1990, Law Com. No.193; Scot. Law Com. No.129.

[206] For detail: Crawford and Carruthers, *International Private Law in Scotland*, 2nd edn (2006), para.16–16.

[207] The applicable law shall exclude any choice of law rules forming part of the applicable law: s.9(5). cf. at common law *McElroy v McAllister*, 1949 S.C. 110, per Lord Russell at 126; and under Rome II art.24.

[208] e.g. *Equitas Ltd v Wave City Shipping Co Ltd* [2005] 2 All E.R. (Comm) 301; *Langlands v SG Hambros Trust Co (Jersey) Ltd* [2007] EWHC 627 (Ch); *R. (on the application of Al-Jedda) v Secretary of State for Defence* [2008] 1 A.C. 332; *OJSC Oil Co Yugraneft v Abramovich* [2008] EWHC 2613 (Comm); *The Nicholas M* [2008] EWHC 1615 (Comm); *Parker v TUI UK Ltd* [2009] EWCA Civ 1261; *Jones v Assurances Generales de France (AGF) SA* [2010] I.L.Pr. 4; and *Donkers v Storm Aviation Ltd* [2014] EWHC 241 (QB).

[209] e.g. *Edmunds v Simmonds* [2001] 1 W.L.R. 1003; *Hulse v Chambers* [2002] 1 All E.R. (Comm) 812; *Hornsby v James Fisher Rumic Ltd* [2008] EWHC 1944 (QB); *Jones v Assurances Generales de France (AGF) SA* [2010] I.L.Pr. 4; *Saldanha v Fulton Navigation Inc* [2011] EWHC 1118 (Admlty);

(b) for a cause of action in respect of damage to property, the law of the country where the property was when it was damaged[210]; and

(c) in any other case, the law of the country in which the most significant element or elements of those events occurred."[211]

The general rule is subject to the rule of displacement supplied by s.12, viz.:

"(1) If it appears, in all the circumstances, from a comparison of—
(a) the significance of the factors which connect a tort or delict with the country whose law would be the applicable law under the general rule; and
(b) the significance of any factors connecting the tort or delict with another country,
that it is substantially more appropriate for the applicable law for determining the issues arising in the case, or any of those issues, to be the law of the other country, the general rule is displaced and the applicable law for determining those issues or that issue (as the case may be) is the law of that other country.

(2) The factors that may be taken into account as connecting a tort or delict with a country for the purposes of this section include, in particular, factors relating to the parties, to any of the events which constitute the tort or delict in question or to any of the circumstances or consequences of those events."

The decision to displace is a matter for the discretion of the forum; upon the frequency and boldness of the forum's exercise of that discretion depends the strength of the general rule. The words "substantially more appropriate" sound a warning against overuse. The decision to displace is based on the preponderance and distribution of factors. The list of factors in s.12(2) is not exhaustive. Morse argued that, if the surrounding circumstances include "factors relating to the parties", it might be possible to segregate pairs of parties, so that a different applicable law might apply between different pairs of litigants, even where all claims arose out of the same incident. There might be displacement in respect of a particular issue, as well as in respect of the whole claim, unlike the position under Rome II art.4.3. Displacement might be in favour of the *lex fori* or a third (or conceivably more) law(s).

Several English decisions have been reported since the entry into force of the 1995 Act, and interpretative guidance continues to be handed down despite the

---

Naraji v Shelbourne [2011] EWHC 3298 (QB); *Rahmatullah v Ministry of Defence* [2014] EWHC 3846 (QB); *Middleton (A Child) v Allianz Iard SA* [2012] EWHC 2287 (QB); *Wylie v Omniasig SA* 2013 S.L.T. 46; *Cox v Ergo Versicherung AG (formerly Victoria)* [2014] UKSC 22 and *Mapfre Mutilidad Compania De Seguros Y Reaseguros SA v Keefe* [2015] EWCA Civ 598.

[210] e.g. *Glencore International AG v Metro Trading International Inc (No.2)* [2001] 1 Lloyd's Rep. 284; *West Tankers Inc v RAS Riunione Adriatica di Sicurta SpA (The Front Comor)* [2005] EWHC 454 (Comm).

[211] e.g. *Protea Leasing Ltd v Royal Air Cambodge Co Ltd* [2002] EWHC 2731; *Anton Durbeck GmbH v Den Norske Bank ASA* [2002] EWHC 1173 (Comm); [2006] 1 Lloyd's Rep. 93; *Morin v Bonham & Brooks Ltd* [2004] 1 Lloyd's Rep. 702; *Trafigura Beheer BV v Kookmin Bank Co* [2006] EWHC 1450 (Comm); *Dornoch Ltd v Mauritius Union Assurance Co Ltd* [2006] EWCA Civ 389 CA (Civ Div); *Ark Therapeutics Plc v True North Capital Ltd* [2006] 1 All E.R. (Comm) 138; *Middle Eastern Oil v National Bank of Abu Dhabi* [2008] EWHC 2895 (Comm); *Hillside (New Media) Ltd v Baasland* [2010] EWHC 3336 (Comm); *Berezovsky v Abramovich* [2012] EWHC 2463 (Comm); *Excalibur Ventures LLC v Texas Keystone Inc* [2013] EWHC 2767 (Comm); *Fiona Trust & Holding Corp v Skarga* [2013] EWCA Civ 275; and *Constantin Medien AG v Ecclestone* [2014] EWHC 387 (Ch), per Newey J at [309]–[320].

fact that Rome II is in force.[212] Early guidance was to be had from *Roerig v Valiant Trawlers Ltd,*[213] the decision of Waller L.J. serving as a useful guide to the steps which a court ought to take in deciding whether or not to displace the general rule. His Lordship stated that: "The first exercise [is] to identify the issue in relation to which it might be suggested that the general rule should not be applicable."[214] Thereafter, the next task is to identify the factors which connect the tort with the countries whose laws are competing for application. An important task for the forum is to assess the significance of the contacts, requiring the court to make a value judgment. The general rule in s.11 is not to be dislodged easily. "Substantially" is to be strictly construed, courts being careful not to displace the general rule too readily, particularly where they are displacing in favour of the *lex fori.*[215]

Supreme Court direction was handed down in 2013, in *VTB Capital Plc v Nutritek International Corp,*[216] a case concerned principally with jurisdiction, but also with the relationship between jurisdiction and choice of law. Against a complex and evenly balanced factual background, differences in manner of approach to s.11(2)(c) and s.12 are observable at each level of the judicial hierarchy. Guidance in the approach to application of s.11(2)(c) was provided in the Court of Appeal by Lloyd L.J.,[217] and endorsed by the Supreme Court.[218] The necessarily open-textured nature of s.11(2)(c), which requires the forum to evaluate the location of the most significant elements of the events constituting the delict (i.e. localising the delict in cases which often demonstrate factual complexity), leads the court into taking a broader perspective, which, in turn, renders less likely displacement per s.12, either at that court's own hand or by an appellate court.[219]

---

[212] e.g. *Hornsby v James Fisher Rumic Ltd* [2008] EWHC 1944 (QB); and *Fiona Trust & Holding Corp v Skarga* [2013] EWCA Civ 275 (reported at first instance as *Fiona Trust & Holding Corp v Privalov* [2010] EWHC 3199 (Comm) (Andrew Smith J.)); *Kingspan Environmental Ltd v Borealis A/S* [2012] EWHC 1147 (Comm); and *Donkers v Storm Aviation Ltd* [2014] EWHC 241 (QB). *Sapporo Breweries Ltd v Lupofresh Ltd* [2012] EWHC 2013 (QB), per Bean J. at [46].

[213] *Roerig v Valiant Trawlers Ltd* [2002] 1 Lloyd's Rep. 681; and, more recently, *Fiona Trust & Holding Corp v Skarga* [2013] EWCA Civ 275.

[214] *Roerig v Valiant Trawlers Ltd* [2002] 1 Lloyd's Rep. 681 at [12](ii).

[215] *Dornoch Ltd v Mauritius Union Assurance Co Ltd* [2006] EWCA Civ 389; *Hornsby v James Fisher Rumic Ltd* [2008] EWHC 1944 (QB); and *Wylie v Omniasig SA,* 2013 S.L.T. 46.

[216] *VTB Capital Plc v Nutritek International Corp* [2013] UKSC 5; [2013] 2 A.C. 337, per Lord Clarke of Stone-cum-Ebony, at [161] et seq. 317 Although Lord Clarke was one of two dissenting judges in the case, the majority judgments did not take issue with his approach to interpretation of ss.11 and 12, and his Lordship's words subsequently were adopted by the Court of Appeal in *Fiona Trust & Holding Corp v Skarga* [2013] EWCA Civ 275. See also *Constantin Medien AG v Ecclestone* [2014] EWHC 387 (Ch), per Newey J. at [317].

[217] *VTB Capital Plc v Nutritek International Corp* [2012] EWCA Civ 808, [148] – [149].

[218] *VTB Capital Plc v Nutritek International Corp* [2013] UKSC 5, per Lord Clarke of Stone-cum-Ebony at [199].

[219] *Constantin Medien AG v Ecclestone* [2014] EWHC 387 (Ch), per Newey J. at [327].

The *lex causae* identified under the 1995 Act governs all questions of liability, available defences of a substantive nature,[220] and heads of damages.[221] Quantification of damages under the Act, as at common law, is a matter for the forum.

The 1995 Act has generated, in its short and fading life, a sizeable body of case law and concomitant expertise, at least in English courts. The approach to identification of applicable law in non-contractual matters in terms of Rome II is not fundamentally dissimilar to that employed in the Act, but national authorities interpretative of the 1995 Act cannot be considered relevant in the interpretation of Rome II.

Defamation and related claims

As explained,[222] non-contractual obligations arising out of violations of privacy **16-48** and rights relating to personality, including defamation, are excluded from the scope of Rome II by virtue of art.1.2(g), and therefore in litigation arising under this head, Member State courts must continue to apply their own national choice of law rules. The difficulty of striking a balance between respect for private life and preservation of reputation, on the one hand, and the upholding of freedom of expression on the other, and the fact that legal systems vary in where they strike that balance, means that the task of designing an acceptable choice of law rule defeated the draftsmen of Rome II, just as it defeated the draftsmen of the 1995 Act. At the time of UK parliamentary debate in the 1990s, particular disquiet[223] was felt by the British Press that, as a result of loss of forum control, which was a defining feature of the changes introduced by the 1995 Act, its freedom might be compromised if, following publication of material in a UK newspaper, it were possible for proceedings for conduct not delictually actionable by the *lex fori* to be brought in the UK[224] by a party aggrieved by the incidental dissemination of the material elsewhere. The success of the press lobby resulted, at a late stage, in s.13 (defamation claims) of the 1995 Act, viz.:

> "(1) Nothing in this Part applies to affect the determination of issues arising in any defamation claim.
>
> (2) For the purposes of this section 'defamation claim' means—
>
> (a) any claim under the law of any part of the United Kingdom for libel or slander or for slander of title, slander of goods or other malicious falsehood and any claim under the law of Scotland for verbal injury; and
>
> (b) any claim under the law of any other country corresponding to or otherwise in the nature of a claim mentioned in paragraph (a) above."

---

[220] Defences under the *lex fori* of a procedural nature are available, but avail cannot be taken in a UK forum of procedural defences of the *lex loci delicti*: *Scott v Lord Seymour* (1862) 158 E.R. 865.

[221] Claims under the 1995 Act arising after 11 January 2009, are unaffected by the (different) approach taken in Rome II art.15(c).

[222] Paras 16–04 and 16–48, above.

[223] But see Morse (1996) I.C.L.Q. 888, n.53, at 892.

[224] As to the jurisdictional rules in this area, Ch.7, above.

Consequently, liability for allegedly delictual actings under the head of defamation claims continues to be judged by the double actionability rule.[225] Few (if any) cases have been litigated upon the point whether s.13, in principle, applies to a given claim, but the extent of the category of "defamation claims" is not free from doubt. The definition in s.13(2) of the 1995 Act is not coterminous with the exclusion in art.1.2(g) of Rome II. Issues such as alleged violations of alleged rights of privacy, or alleged breach of alleged personality rights, though excluded from the scope of Rome II, are not expressly covered by s.13 (and therefore do not appear to be regulated by the common law). The conclusion must be that, provided that such issues arising in such a claim are characterised by the forum, per s.9(2) of the 1995 Act, as relating to tort or delict, they must be governed in a UK court by ss.11 and 12 of that Act.[226]

The common law rule: double actionability

16–49   The choice of law rules which were applied at common law in the UK, and continue to be applied with regard to "defamation claims", vary according to the place where the delict was committed.

Delicts committed within Scotland

16–50   As regards delicts committed within Scotland but having foreign elements (e.g. through connection of parties), Scots law applies, irrespective of whether there is a right of action in delict under the personal law of the alleged wrongdoer and/or victim.[227] The English courts apply an equivalent rule.[228] One might say of such cases simply that the *lex fori* applied, or alternatively that, since there was a coincidence of the *lex fori* and *lex loci delicti*, this was an example of operation of the double actionability rule (q.v.).

Where the opposing parties share the same personal law, it might be thought that the occurrence of allegedly delictual conduct in a different country (which also happens to be the *lex fori*) should result at least in the possibility of displacement of the *lex fori* by a law of closer connection to the parties, for it could be said that the parties were walking in a bubble of their own law, or, more elegantly, that they were, "politically and psychologically insulated from their geographical environment."[229] Nevertheless, in *Szalatnay-Stacho v Fink*[230] the English court applied English law to the substantive issue (libel), stating that the principle of comity of nations did not compel or entitle the court to apply foreign (in this case, Czech) law to acts done in England, even though both parties to the

---

[225] *Skrine & Co v Euromoney Publications Plc* [2002] E.M.L.R. 15; *Vassiliev v Amazon.Com Inc* [2003] EWHC 2302 (Comm); *Metropolitan International Schools Ltd (t/a SkillsTrain and t/a Train2Game) v Designtechnica Corp (t/a Digital Trends)* [2009] EWHC 1765 (QB); *Valmoria v Hynes* [2012] EWHC 193 (QB); and *Ontulmus v Collett* [2013] EWHC 980 (QB). cf. Early example of *Maclarty v Steele* (1881) 8 R. 435.

[226] Unless, ingeniously, presented as a claim in restitution: see *Douglas v Hello! Ltd (No.6)* [2005] EWCA Civ 595; [2005] 4 All E.R. 128 (para.16–56, below).

[227] *Convery v Lanarkshire Tramways Co* (1905) 8 F. 117.

[228] *Szalatnay-Stacho v Fink* [1947] 1 K.B. 1; and *Al-Fayed v Al-Tajir* [1987] 3 W.L.R. 102.

[229] D. McLean and K. Beevers, *Morris: The Conflict of Laws,* 6th edn (London: Sweet & Maxwell, 2005), para.14–012.

[230] *Szalatnay-Stacho v Fink* [1947] 1 K.B. 1.

litigation were Czech nationals. It is arguable that after *Chaplin v Boys*,[231] an English court would be entitled to use the flexible exception to achieve the aim, if it thought fit, of substituting the law of the parties' common personal law as the *lex causae*.

Delicts committed furth of Scotland (other than on the high seas)

SCOTS LAW[232]

There was no suggestion or possibility at common law of giving effect to any **16–51** choice of law expressed by the parties to an action. The applicable law was determined independently of the parties' intentions or wishes.

The Scots courts referred, in the first place, to the *lex loci delicti* as the origin of the pursuer's right, if any. If, by that law, the conduct was actionable, the court referred to Scots law as the *lex fori* to ensure that it was actionable also by that law.[233] The rule of Scots common law was that an act committed outside Scotland would be actionable as a delict in the Scots courts if:

(a) it was actionable as a delict, in general and in the particular circumstances, by the *lex loci delicti* at the date of the action; and

(b) it was actionable as a delict by the *lex fori* at the date of the action; and

(c) both systems of law conferred a right of action on the same person in the same capacity for substantially the same remedy.

In defamation claims, there may be particular difficulties in ascertaining the *locus delicti*. In *Evans & Sons v Stein & Co*,[234] allegedly defamatory letters, while in transit from Scotland to their destination in England were, "as safe as if they were still locked up in the defender's desk". The *locus delicti* was the place of receipt, by the (English) law of which no right of action arose. Clear favour was shown to the place of harm, being the place where the aggrieved person saw or heard the allegedly defamatory material or broadcast. By the same token, as regards online defamation, it was held in *Dow Jones & Co Inc v Gutnick*,[235] a decision of the High Court of Australia, that the tort of defamation is committed where the

---

[231] *Chaplin v Boys* [1971] A.C. 356.

[232] Leading Scottish cases at common law include: *Goodman v LNWR* (1877) 14 S.L.R. 449; *Rosses v Bhagvat Sinhjee* (1891) 19 R. 31; *Evans and Sons v John G Stein and Co* (1904) 7 F. 65; *Thomson v Kindell*, 1910 2 S.L.T. 442; *Soutar v Peters*, 1912 1 S.L.T. 111; *Naftalin v London Midland & Scottish Railway Co*, 1933 S.C. 259; *McElroy v McAllister*, 1949 S.C. 110; *Mackinnon v Iberia Shipping Co*, 1955 S.C. 20; *Rodden v Whatlings Ltd*, 1961 S.C. 132; *Mitchell v McCulloch*, 1976 S.L.T. 2; *James Burrough Distillers Plc v Speymalt Whisky Distributors Ltd*, 1989 S.L.T. 561; and *William Grant & Sons Ltd v Glen Catrine Bonded Warehouse Ltd*, 1995 S.L.T. 936.

[233] J.M. Thomson, "Delictual Liability in Scottish International Private Law" (1976) 25 I.C.L.Q. 873.

[234] *Evans and Sons v John G Stein and Co* (1904) 7 F. 65. See earlier *Longworth v Hope* (1865) 3 M. 1049. Also *Parnell v Walter* (1889) 16 R. 917; *Thomson v Kindell*, 1910 2 S.L.T. 442. cf. *Diamond v Bank of London and Montreal* [1979] 1 All E.R. 561 (fraudulent misrepresentation by telex held to have been committed where received).

[235] *Dow Jones & Co Inc v Gutnick* [2002] HCA 56; and *Jameel v Dow Jones & Co Inc* [2005] EWCA Civ 75.

material complained of is downloaded.[236] In this area, there are many more cases dealing with jurisdiction than with choice of law.[237] If jurisdiction is established in Scotland (or England), the balance of opinion favours application *qua lex loci delicti* of the law of the place where the online material was accessed, on the basis that the publisher of the material must be taken to have known the extent of its possible dissemination given the current state of electronic communication development. If online material has been accessed in multiple countries, there would be multiple *leges loci delicti*. This rule of double actionability continues to regulate available defences and the heads under which damages might be awarded.[238]

ENGLISH LAW[239]

16–52   The English courts adopt a slightly different, more forum-dominant approach than did the Scots courts, but they arrive at a similar result. In the first place, they require actionability by the *lex fori*.[240] If that condition is satisfied, reference is made to the *lex loci delicti*. The conflict rule which was applied for many years was based on the opinion of Willes J. (later Lord Penzance) in *Phillips v Eyre*,[241] in which, after saying that, in order to found a suit in England, a tort must be actionable by the *lex fori*, he said that it must also be "not justifiable" according to the *lex loci delicti*. As a result, the choice of law rule of English law prior to *Chaplin v Boys*,[242] was that an allegedly tortious act committed in a foreign country would be actionable as such in England only if it was both:

(a)   *actionable* as a tort according to English law; and

(b)   *not justifiable* according to the law of the country where it was committed.

---

[236] Further: Law Commission, *Aspects of Defamation Procedure* (The Stationery Office, 2002), Scoping Study, and Law Commission, *Defamation and the Internet: A Preliminary Investigation* (The Stationery Office, 2002), Scoping Study No.2, Pt IV ("Jurisdiction and Applicable Law"). It was held in *Al-Amoudi v Brisard* [2006] 3 All E.R. 294 that in the case of an internet libel, it is for the claimant to prove that the material in question has been accessed and downloaded (*Loutchansky v Times Newspapers Ltd (No.2)* [2001] E.M.L.R. 36, applied).

[237] e.g. *King v Lewis* [2004] I.L.Pr. 31; and *Metropolitan International Schools Ltd v Designtechnica Corp* [2009] EWHC 1765 (QB) (liability of ISPs and search engines).

[238] For detail: Crawford and Carruthers, *International Private Law in Scotland*, 2nd edn (2006), para.16–13.

[239] Leading English cases at common law include: *Dobree v Napier* (1839) 2 Bing. N.C. 781; *The Halley* (1868) L.R. 2 P.C. 193; *Phillips v Eyre* (1870) L.R. 6 Q.B. 1; *The Mary Moxham* (1876) 1 P.D. 107; *Machado v Fontes* [1897] 2 Q.B. 231; *Carr v Fracis Times and Co* [1902] A.C. 176; *Canadian Pacific Railway Co v Parent* [1917] A.C. 195; *Walpole v Canadian Northern Railway Co* [1923] A.C. 113; *Mcmillan v Canadian Northern Railway Co* [1923] A.C. 120; *M Isaacs & Sons Ltd v Cook* [1925] 2 K.B. 391; *Owners of the Seirstad v Hindustan Shipping Co Ltd (The Waziristan and The Seirstad)* [1953] 1 W.L.R. 1446; *Chaplin v Boys* [1971] A.C. 356; [1969] 2 All E.R. 1085; *John Walker & Sons Ltd v Henry Ost & Co Ltd* [1970] 1 W.L.R. 917; *Church of Scientology of California v Commissioner of Police for the Metropolis (No.1)* (1976) 120 S.J. 690; *MacShannon v Rockware Glass Ltd* [1978] 1 All E.R. 625; *Def Lepp Music v Stuart-Brown* [1986] R.P.C. 273; *Black v Yates* [1991] 4 All E.R. 722; *Tyburn Productions Ltd v Conan Doyle* [1991] Ch. 75; *Johnson v Coventry Churchill International Ltd* [1992] 3 All E.R. 14; *Red Sea Insurance Co Ltd v Bouygues SA* [1994] 3 All E.R. 749 PC; *Bank of Credit & Commerce International SA v Ali* [2006] EWHC 2135 (Ch).

[240] A tenacious requirement traceable to *The Halley* (1868) L.R. 2 P.C. 193.

[241] *Phillips v Eyre* (1870) L.R. 6 Q.B. 1.

[242] *Chaplin v Boys* [1971] A.C. 356.

This is an unusual choice of law rule, concerned rather with the laying down of jurisdictional requirements in a broad sense, and placing the main emphasis on the *lex fori*, as gatekeeper *and* as judge of substance, if the case was allowed to proceed through the gate, in a manner not generally found in other English and Scots conflict rules. In requiring actionability by two laws, the claimant was placed at a disadvantage.

A difficulty was introduced by *Machado v Fontes*,[243] a libel case in which the words "not justifiable" were held to include an act which was wrongful in general (i.e. criminal) terms, but which did not confer a civil right of action by the *lex loci delicti*. This case, which had no influence in Scotland, was rejected in the leading and notorious case of *McElroy v McAllister*,[244] and was overruled in *Chaplin v Boys*.[245] Nonetheless, it is probably true to say that the Scots courts tended to accord greater weight to the *lex loci delicti* than did the English courts.

From the date of *Boys*, the English courts, unlike the Scots, displayed willingness to use discretion in applying a *flexible exception* to the double rule, either to the whole claim, or to one or more issues.[246] While Scotland adhered to the double rule strictly, it was accepted in England[247] that the effect of the flexible exception was not only that the *lex loci delicti* might be displaced in favour of the *lex fori*, but also that the reverse process of displacement in favour of the *lex loci delicti* might take place, or even displacement in favour of a third law. The English courts, in the years immediately preceding the 1995 Act, became rather bolder in the exercise of this discretionary exception,[248] but willingness to make the rule more flexible was not evident in Scottish judicial practice.[249] It follows that Scottish courts operating the double rule, perforce now only in defamation claims, can be expected to apply it strictly, while the English courts will have at their disposal an element of discretion.

Maritime delicts[250]

Incidents in foreign territorial waters

The rules of Rome II are postulated upon the occurrence of allegedly delictual events in a "country". Events occurring in the territorial waters of a country are deemed to be equivalent to events occurring in that country. Therefore, any allegedly delictual actings resulting in damage in the territorial waters of a country fall to be regulated by the choice of law rules in Ch.II, as the circumstances dictate.

16–53

---

[243] *Machado v Fontes* [1897] 2 Q.B. 231.
[244] *McElroy v McAllister,* 1949 S.C. 110.
[245] *Chaplin v Boys* [1971] A.C. 356; affirming *Boys v Chaplin* [1968] 2 Q.B. 1.
[246] *Red Sea Insurance Co Ltd v Bouygues SA* [1994] 3 W.L.R. 926.
[247] *Johnson v Coventry Churchill International Ltd* [1992] 3 All E.R. 14.
[248] *Johnson v Coventry Churchill International Ltd* [1992] 3 All E.R. 14; *Red Sea Insurance Co Ltd v Bouygues SA* [1994] 3 All E.R. 749 PC.
[249] e.g. *James Burrough Distillers Plc v Speymalt Whisky Distributors Ltd*, 1989 S.L.T. 561.
[250] J. Basedow, "Rome II at Sea—General Aspects of Maritime Torts" (2010) 74 RabelsZ 118; K. Siehr, "The Rome II Regulation and Specific Maritime Torts: Product Liability, Environmental Damage, Industrial Action" (2010) 74 RabelsZ 139.

In the past, the double actionability rule,[251] and the 1995 Act, in turn, applied to incidents in foreign territorial waters. The *locus delicti* was the law of the country in whose territorial waters the incident occurred. Where, however, there was no significant link with the litoral state, use could be made of the rule of displacement in s.12 of the 1995 Act, in favour of the law of the flag (i.e. the law of the port of registry) or some other substantially more appropriate law.[252]

Incidents internal to a ship on the high seas

16–54 Since Ch.II of Rome II requires application of the law "of a country", it has no application to allegedly delictual incidents occurring on the high seas.[253] Accordingly, incidents internal to a ship on the high seas continue to be regulated by the 1995 Act. For the purposes of s.11 of the 1995 Act, such incidents are to be regarded as having occurred within the country whose flag the ship was flying. The applicable law per s.11 is subject to displacement in the usual way by s.12.

Incidents external to a ship on the high seas (including collisions)

16–55 There is no justification for application of Rome II to any collision incident on the high seas. However, the 1995 Act, to which resort might have been had, never was applied to such incidents, because in such cases the courts applied a general maritime law, so-called.[254] It may be doubted, however, whether such a body of law truly existed. It is perhaps rather more likely in these cases that the forum applied its own law, whether or not by its own name.[255] A UK forum may require to apply provisions in the Merchant Shipping Act 1995 to a question, for example, of the liability of the shipowner(s), within the ambit of operation laid down by that Act.

This subject area is difficult and unclear, as is the (rare) subject of wrongful actings taking place aboard an aircraft during flight, and (rarer still!) the occurrence of collisions between aircraft. The rules applying to maritime delicts presumably would apply, mutatis mutandis. As to incidents (such as assault, defamation, or personal injury, as, for example, by the provision of contaminated food) on board an aircraft in foreign (as opposed to uncontrolled, international)

---

[251] *Mackinnon v Iberia Shipping Co Ltd*, 1955 S.C. 20, an accident internal to a ship lying in the territorial waters of San Domingo. San Domingo, as the littoral state, was the *locus delicti*. The Scots forum applied the double rule in circumstances where arguably a proper law of delict, or rule of commonality, approach would have been more suitable.

[252] *Hornsby v James Fisher Rumic Ltd* [2008] EWHC 1944 (QB); contrast *Saldanha v Fulton Navigation Inc* [2011] EWHC 1118 (Admlty).

[253] *Cheshire, North and Fawcett: Private International Law*, 14th edn (2008), p.859.

[254] *Boettcher v Carron C* (1861) 23 D. 322; *Aberdeen Artic Co v Sutter* (1862) 4 Macq. 355; (1862) 24 D. (H.L.) 4; *The Amalia* (1863) 1 Moore P.C. (N.S.) 471; *Submarine Telegraph Co v Dickson* (1864) 15 C.B. (N.S.) 759; *The Leon* (1881) L.R. 6 P.D. 148; *Chartered Mercantile Bank of India, London and China v Netherlands India Steam Navigation Co Ltd* (1883) L.R. 10 Q.B.D. 521; *Currie v McKnight* (1897) 24 R. (H.L.) 1; *Kendrick v Burnett (Owners of the SS Marsden)* (1897) 25 R. 82; *Owners of the SS Reresby v Owners of the SS Cobetas*, 1923 S.L.T. 719; *The Tubantia (No.2)* [1924] P. 78; *Sheaf Steamship Co Ltd v Compania Transmediterranea*, 1930 S.C. 660; *Chung Chi Cheung v R.* [1929] A.C. 16; *The King Alfred* [1914] P. 84.

[255] *Cox v Owners of the The Esso Malaysia (The Esso Malaysia)* [1974] 2 All E.R. 705 (applying *Davidsson v Hill* [1900–1903] All E.R. 997).

airspace, the comparison with maritime delicts is not entirely helpful since application of the law of the country in whose airspace the plane happens to be at the point of the allegedly delictual conduct would produce difficult problems of proof. In all cases involving wrongful actings aboard aircraft,[256] it would be preferable to apply the law of the place of registration of the aircraft.[257]

NON-CONTRACTUAL OBLIGATIONS ARISING OUT OF RESTITUTIONARY CLAIMS

From the latter part of the 20th century this area of law in its domestic aspect was the subject of much academic exploration and discussion in England and Scotland. Initially the writing was concerned with domestic law, but increasingly there was interest in its conflict dimensions.[258] Conflictually, the relative paucity of decisions[259] on jurisdiction[260] and choice of law[261] afforded opportunity for speculation as to applicable law[262] and reason for caution. Generally it was thought that this area provided an opportunity for creation of, "a principled and reasoned approach to the question of the proper choice of law rule for restitutionary issues."[263] Until the advent of Rome II, the subject as treated in UK courts was a common law hybrid, governed neither by the Rome I Convention, nor by the Private International Law (Miscellaneous Provisions) Act 1995. Rome II, in providing for these topics, accelerated the process of producing clear rules—which rules, however, rarely are called in issue.

16–56

---

[256] Assuming liability does not exist under Ch.III of the 1929 Warsaw Convention on International Carriage by Air.

[257] *Dicey, Morris and Collins on the Conflict of Laws*, 15th edn (2012), para.35–034.

[258] J. Blaikie, "Unjust Enrichment in the Conflict of Laws", 1984 J.R. 112; and R.D. Leslie, "Unjustified Enrichment in the Conflict Laws" (1998) 2 Edin. L.R. 233.

[259] Though see *Batthyany v Walford* (1887) L.R. 36 Ch. D. 269; *Cantiere San Rocco SA (Shipbuilding Co) v Clyde Shipbuilding & Engineering Co Ltd* [1924] A.C. 226; *Fibrosa Spolka Akcyjna v Fairbairn Lawson Combe Barbour Ltd* [1943] A.C. 32; *Re Jogia (A Bankrupt)* [1988] 1 W.L.R. 484; *El Ajou v Dollar Land Holdings Plc (No.1)* [1993] 3 All E.R. 717; [1994] 2 All E.R. 685; *Baring Bros & Co Ltd v Cunninghame DC*, 1997 C.L.C. 108.

[260] *Kleinwort Benson Ltd v Glasgow City Council (No.2)* [1997] 4 All E.R. 641; and *Strathaird Farms Ltd v GA Chattaway & Co*, 1993 S.L.T. (Sh. Ct.) 36. Paras 7–21 and 7–22, above.

[261] *Baring Bros & Co Ltd v Cunninghame DC*, 1997 C.L.C. 108; *Macmillan Inc v Bishopsgate Investment Trust Plc (No.3)* [1996] 1 W.L.R. 387 CA; *Arab Monetary Fund v Hashim (No.9)* [1996] 1 Lloyd's Rep. 589 CA; and cf. *Douglas v Hello! Ltd (No.6)* [2005] EWCA Civ 595; [2005] 4 All E.R. 128 (the issue of breach of confidence being treated as restitutionary).

[262] Even to the extent of arguments in favour of *renvoi: Barros Mattos Junior v MacDaniels Ltd* [2005] I.L.Pr. 45, per Collins J. at [121]; and *Blue Sky One Ltd v Mahan Air* [2010] EWHC 631 (Comm).

[263] G. Panagopoulos, *Restitution in Private International Law* (Oxford: Hart, 2000), p.111.

The Rome II Regulation

16–57   Rome II deals in Ch.III (arts 10–13) with the law applicable to non-contractual obligations arising out of a restitutionary claim[264] under the heads of unjust enrichment, *negotiorum gestio* and *culpa in contrahendo*.[265]

Unjust enrichment

16–58   "Article 10...
1.   If a non-contractual obligation arising out of unjust enrichment, including payment of amounts wrongly received, concerns a relationship existing between the parties, such as one arising out of a contract or a tort/delict, that is closely connected with that unjust enrichment, it shall be governed by the law that governs that relationship.
2.   Where the law applicable cannot be determined on the basis of paragraph 1 and the parties have their habitual residence in the same country when the event giving rise to unjust enrichment occurs, the law of that country shall apply.
3.   Where the law applicable cannot be determined on the basis of paragraphs 1 or 2, it shall be the law of the country in which the unjust enrichment took place.
4.   Where it is clear from all the circumstances of the case that the non-contractual obligation arising out of unjust enrichment is manifestly more closely connected with a country other than that indicated in paragraphs 1, 2 and 3, the law of that other country shall apply."

The rules which now are contained in art.10 are, at least ex facie, fairly straightforward and, like the other rules in Ch.III, are framed in what now are familiar drafting terms.

A substantial proportion of problems arising under the head of unjust enrichment has a foundation in a pre-existing relationship, usually contractual, between the parties. This fact was reflected in the terms in which, at common law, the embryonic choice of law rule in Scots and English law was emerging. Such cases are instances of "relational" unjust enrichment. While to differentiate between relational and non-relational unjust enrichment was broadly agreed at common law, a degree of criticism of this approach could be found, both generally and on the particular ground[266] that insofar as parties can choose the applicable law of their contract, it would follow that they can choose, indirectly (possibly inadvertently) and perhaps with inappropriate effect, the law to govern related restitutionary obligations.

---

[264] The inference of recital (29) is that "damage" (art.2.1) is a prerequisite for the application of the rules under Ch.III: "Provision should be made for special rules where damage is caused by an act other than a tort/delict, such as unjust enrichment, *negotiorum gestio* and *culpa in contrahendo*."

[265] For drafting background: Proposal for a Regulation on the Law Applicable to Non-Contractual Obligations COM(2003) 427 final (2003/0168(COD)), accompanying Explanatory Memorandum; House of Lords European Union Committee, *The Rome II Regulation*, 2004, HL Paper No.66 (Session 2003/04) ("Scott Report"). See also Carruthers and Crawford, "Variations on a Theme of Rome II. Part 2" (2005) 9 Edin. L.R. 238; and S. Pitel, "Rome II and Choice of Law for Unjust Enrichment" in Ahern and Binchy (eds), *The Rome II Regulation on the Law Applicable to Non-Contractual Obligations* (2009).

[266] e.g. *Cheshire and North's Private International Law*, 13th edn (1999), pp.679, 686, 691, 692.

NON-CONTRACTUAL OBLIGATIONS ARISING OUT OF RESTITUTIONARY CLAIMS

It is not surprising that the first limb of the legislative solution in art.10 of Rome II is concerned to treat cases of relational unjust enrichment. By art.10.1 non-contractual obligations arising out of unjust enrichment, including payment of amounts wrongly received, *where they concern a pre-existing relationship between the parties such as one arising out of a contract or a tort*, shall be governed by the law which governs that relationship, that is to say, by the applicable law identified according to the Rome I Regulation (contract) or Rome II Regulation (tort/delict),[267] as the case may be. The gateway to the operation of art.10.1 is that the alleged non-contractual obligation can be said to "concern" such a pre-existing relationship, but the applicable law in contract (or delict) will be held to govern the obligation arising out of unjust enrichment *only* if that unjust enrichment derives from, or is closely associated with, that very contract (or, seldom, delict).[268]

It is notable that there is to be no express application of the *lex situs* in cases where the unjust enrichment is connected with a transaction concerning immoveable property. This is the only significant difference between the rules in Rome II and the pre-existing UK approach. Presumably, at least in the operation of art.10.1, the applicable law would be very likely to be the *lex situs*.

Under art.10.2, where the law applicable cannot be determined on the basis of identification of the law governing the relationship between the parties, i.e. "non-relational" enrichment cases, and the parties have a common habitual residence when the event giving rise to the enrichment occurs, the law of that country shall apply.

Further, in terms of art.10.3, where the law applicable cannot be determined on the basis of the rules contained in art.10.1 or 10.2, the law of the country in which the unjust enrichment took place shall be the applicable law. In the common law consideration of this subject, opinion in the UK was divided as to the quality of the connecting factor of place of occurrence of the enrichment.[269] Enrichment may occur in several places, and those places may be artificial or casual. Yet, on occasion, the territorial place of enrichment may be regarded by the court as (also) the country with which the alleged obligation has its closest and most real connection, as in *OJSC Oil Co Yugraneft v Abramovich*.[270]

A tangential comment is provided by a consideration of the case of *Douglas v Hello! Ltd (No.6)*,[271] in which the Court of Appeal treated the claimant's claim relating to invasion of privacy not as a tort, but rather as a restitutionary claim for

---

[267] Dickinson, *The Rome II Regulation* (2008), paras 10.25, 10.26 on the subject of a pre-existing relationship arising out of tort/delict.

[268] Rome II art.10.1 would not apply, therefore, to a situation where, in a road traffic accident outside the scope of employment, an employer wrongfully caused injury to an employee.

[269] Blaikie, "Unjust Enrichment and the Conflict of Laws", 1984 J.R. 112; Bird J. "Choice of Law", in Francis Rose (ed.), *Restitution and the Conflict of Laws* (Oxford: Mansfield Press, 1995); Leslie, "Unjustified Enrichment and the Conflict of Laws" (1998) 2 Edin. L.R. 233; *Cheshire and North's Private International Law*, 13th edn (1999), Ch.20; Panagopoulos, *Restitution in Private International Law* (2000). See also decision of Lawrence Collins J. in *Barros Mattos Junior v MacDaniels Ltd* [2005] I.L.Pr. 45, where approval was not given to a mechanical application of the law of the place of enrichment. In *Dicey, Morris and Collins on the Conflict of Laws*, 14th edn (2006) (preceding Rome II), r.230 retains support for the proper law, in residual cases, being the law of the country in which the enrichment occurs.

[270] *OJSC Oil Co Yugraneft v Abramovich* [2008] EWHC 2613 (Comm).

[271] *Douglas v Hello! Ltd (No.6)* [2005] EWCA Civ 595; [2005] 4 All E.R. 128.

unjust enrichment. Utilising therefore the connecting factor of "place where the enrichment occurred", the court, by inference, proceeded to hold in effect that England was the place of enrichment, based upon publication in England of the offending material.[272]

Finally, art.10.4 gives the forum discretion to identify as the applicable law the law of a country other than that indicated under the three preceding paragraphs of art.10, which it considers in the light of all the circumstances of the case to be manifestly more closely connected to the non-contractual obligation in question. The resulting article, while a familiar amalgam of European drafting devices in applicable law rules, is in keeping with the choice of law approach observable in the UK before the advent of Rome II in the few cases in which the question arose.

Parties may agree to subject non-contractual obligations arising out of a restitutionary claim under the head of unjust enrichment to the law of their choice under art.14 of the Regulation.[273] It is possible to envisage a situation in which the parties, under art.14, might choose a law to govern their non-contractual relations, which law might differ from the law which governs their contract, by express choice under art.3 of the Rome I Regulation, or by operation of art.4 thereof.

Consequences of nullity of contract (Rome I) and problems of unjust enrichment (Rome II)

16–59   Although the rules in art.10 of Rome II are clear in themselves, careful thought must be given to their interrelationship with those of the Rome I Regulation[274]; and to the contribution to the subject made by cases interpretative of the Brussels I Regulation.

By art.12.1(e) of the Rome I Regulation,[275] the law applicable to a contract will govern the consequences of nullity of the contract, which will include the repayment of sums[276] due under a void or nullified contract. By UK reservation, the equivalent provision of the Rome I Convention art.10.1(e), did not apply in a UK court since the consequences of nullity were regarded by Scots and English law as pertaining to rules of restitution. In many cases the applicable law identified by these two routes would be the same. Now, however, since there is pan-European agreement that the subject of nullity of contract be dealt with by the putative applicable law of the necessarily putative contract, it is time to address the possibility that the co-existence of this rule with the choice of law rules under the Rome II Regulation Ch.III, may prompt problems of characterisation and distribution of application of choice of law rules between the Rome I and Rome II Regulations.

The area of void and nullified contracts is productive of doubt in the jurisdictional aspect too. A claim arising in restitution from a *void* contract does

---

[272] *Douglas v Hello! Ltd (No.6)* [2005] EWCA Civ 595; [2005] 4 All E.R. 128 at [96]–[102].
[273] Para.16–24, above.
[274] Para.15–62, above.
[275] Rome I art.12.1: "The law applicable to a contract by virtue of this Regulation shall govern in particular:...(b) performance;...(e) the consequences of nullity of the contract."
[276] Giuliano and Lagarde, p.33 reveals that the equivalent provision under the Rome I Convention art.10.1(e), was inserted to make it clear that the applicable law under the Convention governed this issue.

not fall, for the purpose of Scots and English jurisdiction rules under Sch.4, under
art.5.1 special jurisdiction in contract.[277] On the other hand, matters relating to a
contract can include matters relating to a *disputed* contract.[278] Arguably
(especially from a European perspective), the consequences of nullity of a
contract *should* be characterised as contractual for the purposes of jurisdiction,
chiming with the Rome I Regulation for choice of law. It is hoped that the matter
will be considered by the ECJ in such a way as to place a restitutionary claim of
this sort under the head of special justiciary in contract. It seems not unreasonable
that in all Member State courts the remedy for such claims be regulated by the
content of what must be the putative applicable law of the void contract, and that
the court properly seised to implement this remedy be, as it were, the "putative
court" under art.5.1 of Brussels I Regulation/art.7.1 of Brussels Recast
Regulation. To say that claims resulting from *void* contracts fall outside the ambit
of art.5.1/art.7.1, but those which arise out of *voidable or unenforceable* contracts
fall within its ambit, is not a helpful dividing line.[279]

Negotiorum gestio

"Article 11 ...   **16–60**
1.   If a non-contractual obligation arising out of an act performed without due
      authority in connection with the affairs of another person concerns a
      relationship existing between the parties, such as one arising out of a contract
      or a tort/delict, that is closely connected with that non-contractual obligation,
      it shall be governed by the law that governs that relationship.
2.   Where the law applicable cannot be determined on the basis of paragraph 1,
      and the parties have their habitual residence in the same country when the
      event giving rise to the damage occurs, the law of that country shall apply.
3.   Where the law applicable cannot be determined on the basis of paragraphs 1
      or 2, it shall be the law of the country in which the act was performed.
4.   Where it is clear from all the circumstances of the case that the
      non-contractual obligation arising out of an act performed without due
      authority in connection with the affairs of another person is manifestly more
      closely connected with a country other than that indicated in paragraphs 1, 2
      and 3, the law of that other country shall apply."

The formulation of choice of law rules by which to deal with cases of *negotiorum
gestio* presents a challenge, to be relished more as an academic exercise than with
any expectation that resort in practice will have to be made to the carefully
crafted rules. Within the UK such cases are exceedingly rare, and so rarely do
they have a conflict dimension that one might say the subject was arcane.
Moreover, controversy will arise only if the content of the potentially applicable
laws varies (although variation, admittedly, is likely, and some legal systems will

---

[277] *Kleinwort Benson Ltd v Glasgow City Council (No.2)* [1999] 1 A.C. 153, discussed at para.7–21,
above (though *Kleinwort* is not an ECJ decision, and the ECJ might take a different view). Vertical
continuity indicates that the same will be true of art.7.1 of Brussels I Recast Regulation.
[278] *Boss Group Ltd v Boss France SA* [1996] 4 All E.R. 970; *Halki Shipping Corp v Sopex Oils Ltd
(The Halki)* [1997] 3 All E.R. 833; *Belgian International Insurance Group SA v McNicol*, 1999
G.W.D. 22–1065.
[279] J. Hill and A. Chong, *International Commercial Disputes in English Courts*, 4th edn (Oxford:
Hart, 2010), para.5.6.16, paraphrasing the views of Lord Nicholls (dissenting) in *Kleinwort*.

have no knowledge of the concept).In relational cases of *negotiorum gestio*[280] under art.11.1, the law governing the relationship, be it contractual, delictual or other, shall apply. In non-relational cases, by art.11.2, the law of the common habitual residence at the time when the event giving rise to the damage occurs, shall apply, failing which,[281] by art.11.3, the applicable law shall be the law of the country in which the act (i.e. that performed without due authority in connection with the affairs of another person) took place. There is discretion in art.11.4 permitting recourse in both relational and non-relational cases to the law of a country of manifestly more close connection.

As with claims in unjust enrichment, parties may agree to subject non-contractual obligations arising out of a restitutionary claim under the head of *negotiorum gestio* to the law of their choice under art.14 of the Regulation.

In terms of art.15 (scope of the law applicable), the applicable law shall govern, inter alia, the basis and extent of liability, including determination of persons who may be held liable for acts performed by them; grounds for exemption from liability, any limitation, and any division of liability; and liability for the acts of another person. Points where there might be a variation among the domestic laws of potentially applicable *leges causae* include:

(a) the circumstances which justify an individual person becoming an agent or *gestor*;

(b) the *gestor's* right to payment, or only to reimbursement, and the effect thereon of the *gestor's* efforts having proved fruitless or detrimental;

(c) the right of action by an individual reasonably employed by the *gestor* to sue the beneficiary (i.e. principal) by direct action;

(d) the standard of care to be exercised by the *gestor*, and liability of the *gestor* to the principal if that standard is not exhibited; and

(e) whether the *gestor*, having intervened, must attempt to bring matters to a conclusion, and the legal consequences of quitting the task prematurely.

Culpa in contrahendo

16–61

"Article 12 . . .

1. The law applicable to a non-contractual obligation arising out of dealings prior to the conclusion of a contract, regardless of whether the contract was actually concluded or not, shall be the law that applies to the contract or that would have been applicable to it had it been entered into.

2. Where the law applicable cannot be determined on the basis of paragraph 1, it shall be:

(a) the law of the country in which the damage occurs, irrespective of the country in which the event giving rise to the damage occurred and irrespective of the country or countries in which the indirect consequences of that event occurred; or

(b) where the parties have their habitual residence in the same country at the time when the event giving rise to the damage occurs, the law of that country; or

---

[280] One must speculate that examples of this would be, e.g. actings by a parent/guardian on behalf of a child concerning his property; or where an agent acts, on an ongoing basis, by virtue perhaps of a power of attorney.

[281] i.e. where the applicable law cannot be determined under either art.11.1 or 11.2.

> (c)   where it is clear from all the circumstances of the case that the non-contractual obligation arising out of dealings prior to the conclusion of a contract is manifestly more closely connected with a country other than that indicated in points (a) and (b), the law of that other country."

The concept of *culpa in contrahendo*, originating in German customary law, signifies those rules of national legal systems concerning the standard of conduct required of parties in pre-contractual negotiations. Whether a contract comes into existence or not, it can be seen that allegations of inadequate disclosure, misrepresentation, and failure to display good faith and decent dealing, have potential to import liability and have a hybrid character within the law of obligations. In Scots law such circumstances often are treated purely as contractual, the issue being whether *consensus in idem* has been reached in the circumstances.[282] In many European systems, such questions are regarded as delictual or restitutionary. Recital (30) of Rome II states that *culpa in contrahendo* for the purposes of the Regulation is an autonomous concept:

> "...and should not necessarily be interpreted within the meaning of national law. It should include the violation of the duty of disclosure and the breakdown of contractual negotiations. Article 12 covers only non-contractual obligations presenting a direct link with the dealings prior to the conclusion of a contract. This means that if, while a contract is being negotiated, a person suffers personal injury, Article 4 or other relevant provisions of this Regulation should apply."

The symbiosis and order maintained between the Rome I and Rome II Regulations is evidenced by the express exclusion from the scope of Rome I, per art.1.2(i), of obligations arising out of dealings prior to the conclusion of a contract, and the express inclusion in Rome II of an applicable law provision specifically to address such obligations.

For the type of situation which can be characterised as pertaining to *culpa in contrahendo*, as illustrated above, the special rule provided in art.12.1 diverts attention from the non-contractual character of the obligation by nominating as applicable the putative applicable law of the (putative)[283] contract. The rule formulated leads to the same result as would have eventuated had such cases of *culpa in contrahendo* been characterised as cases of relational unjust enrichment. Moreover, though the topic falls under Rome II (non-contractual obligations), the (restitutionary) choice of law rule, as it applies to *culpa in contrahendo*, is indistinguishable from the "putative applicable law" solution to problems of material validity of contract contained in the Rome I Regulation art.10.

If the law applicable cannot be determined under art.12.1 of Rome II (which surely must be a very rare case),[284] then the rule which must be applied under art.12.2 is in the same terms as the general rule for delict contained in art.4.

---

[282] e.g. *WS Karoulias SA v Drambuie Liqueur Co Ltd,* 2005 S.L.T. 813.

[283] The provision is available whether a contract has resulted or not.

[284] Consider *Cheshire, North and Fawcett: Private International Law,* 14th edn (2008), pp.835, 836, where the case postulated is that during negotiations each party had tried to impose without success its preferred choice of law clause on the other, but the parties never reached consensus on the point. Or if contractual negotiations had broken off at a very early stage, it may be impossible to ascertain the applicable law; in such circumstances, art.12.2 must be intended to govern liability for any loss,

Finally, parties may agree, though this seems highly unlikely,[285] to subject non-contractual obligations arising out of a restitutionary claim under the head of *culpa in contrahendo* to the law of their choice under art.14 of the Regulation.

SUMMARY 16

16–62 1. Choice of law in delict: sources.

The rules are contained in three sources:
  (a) Regulation 864/2007 on the law applicable to non-contractual obligations ("Rome II");
  (b) Private International Law (Miscellaneous Provisions) Act 1995 Pt III;
  (c) The common law rule of double actionability.

In order to ascertain which set of rules applies in an individual case, careful attention must be paid to the date of occurrence of the event giving rise to the damage, and to the subject matter of the claim.

2. Choice of law in delict: rules.

Rome II comprises:

Article 4: a *lex loci damni* rule, with one mandatory exception (rule of commonality) and one discretionary exception (rule of displacement);
Articles 5–9: a series of delict-specific rules;
Article 14: a party autonomy rule;
Article 15: scope of the law applicable.

The 1995 Act comprises:

Section 11: a *lex loci delicti* rule;
Section 12: a discretionary rule of displacement.

The double actionability rule (applicable now only to "defamation claims" as defined in s.13(2) of the 1995 Act) is to the effect that alleged wrongdoing is actionable as a delict in a Scots court if:
  (a) it was actionable as a delict by the *lex loci delicti* at the date of the action; and
  (b) it was actionable as a delict by the *lex fori* at the date of the action; and
  (c) both systems of law confer a right of action on the same person in the same capacity for substantially the same remedy.

3. Choice of law rules in non-contractual obligations arising out of restitutionary claims.

Rules are provided by Rome II Ch.III, for the particular subjects of:

Article 10: unjust enrichment;
Article 11: negotiorum gestio;
Article 12: culpa in contrahendo;
Article 14: party autonomy.

---

though if negotiations were at a very early stage one would imagine that reparable loss such as to give rise to litigation engaging art.12.2 would be infrequently encountered.
[285] Choice of law ex ante is not competent unless all parties are pursuing a commercial activity: art.14.1(b).

CHAPTER 17

The law of property (including insolvency)

Different rules govern the transfer of property according to whether the transfer **17–01** in question is particular in nature, that is, affecting one or more specific assets, by means of gift, sale, mortgage, etc.; or universal in nature, that is, affecting an individual's entire estate, such as upon the events of marriage, insolvency or death. This chapter will examine, first, the rules governing particular transfers, and secondly, the rules which apply to general transfers in the event of insolvency. General transfers upon marriage are treated in Ch.13, and those occurring on the event of succession are the subject of Ch.18.

PARTICULAR TRANSFERS OF PROPERTY

Terminology and classification

That this is one of the very few areas of Scots and English international private **17–02** law which rests mainly on the common law, largely untouched by statute and convention, is both refreshing and alarming.[1]

Note should be taken of the following differences in terminology:

(a)   domestic Scots law—heritage and moveables;
(b)   domestic English law—real and personal property;
(c)   conflict of laws—immoveables and moveables.[2]

In a Scots or English forum the terms and classification "immoveable" and "moveable" are utilised,[3] so as to accommodate differences in property categorisations adopted by different legal systems.[4] Examples can be cited of cases where the classification of property arrived at as a result of application of a

---

[1] The contributions of writers are influential. See J.M. Carruthers, *Transfer of Property in the Conflict of Laws* (2005); P.A. Lalive, *The Transfer of Chattels in the Conflict of Laws* (London: OUP, 1955); and G. Zaphiriou, *The Transfer of Chattels in Private International Law* (London: University of London, The Athlone Press, 1956).

[2] *Macdonald*, 1932 S.C. (H.L.) 79, per Lord Tomlin at 84; cf. *Re Hoyles* [1911] 1 Ch. 179, per Farwell L.J. at 185, and *Re Cutcliffe's Will Trusts* [1940] Ch. 565.

[3] The preferred Scottish spelling is "immoveable"/ "moveable"; "immovable"/ "movable" is favoured in England.

[4] *Dicey, Morris and Collins on the Conflict of Laws* (15th edn), 2012, para.22–004. The distinction is made in the conflict of laws on the basis of the factual difference between moveable and immoveable

legal system's conflict rules differs from that which would be accorded by its domestic law, for example, English leaseholds[5]; foreign land[6] and mortgages over land[7]; stocks and shares[8]; Scots bonds and dispositions in security[9]; and land held upon trust for sale.[10]

Property is always classified for the purposes of a conflict case as moveable or immoveable in accordance with the *lex situs* (q.v.).[11]

A different problem of classification may arise in relation to categorisation of a cause of action, for example, as between property and contract, or property and unjustified enrichment,[12] or property and trust.[13] A claim for restitution of property is a claim to which, if there are foreign elements, it may be appropriate for the choice of law rules of property to be applied in preference to those of contract.[14] The characterisation proposed in the pleadings of parties may not be that which ultimately is adopted by the court in its resolution of the dispute.[15] The initial characterisation by the forum of a cause of action (e.g. as being one of intestate succession to moveable property) will indicate to that court the identity of its relevant choice of law rule, and the applicable law to apply (i.e. last domicile of the deceased). But to follow through the application of the *lex causae*, re-characterisation of the property by use of the domestic law of the *lex causae* occasionally may be necessary.[16] Thus, characterisation of the nature of

---

property, and not on technical nicety or historical grounds, such as, e.g. Scots law of "fixtures" where, in domestic law, a right over what is physically moveable is regarded as being a right over an immoveable.

[5] *Freke v Carbery* (1873) L.R. 16 Eq. 461; *Re Gentili* (1875) I.R. 9 Eq. 541; *Duncan v Lawson* (1889) L.R. 41 Ch. D. 394; *Pepin v Bruyere* [1902] 1 Ch. 24; *De Fogassieras v Duport* (1881) 11 L.R. Ir. 123.

[6] *Re Berchtold* [1923] 1 Ch. 192; *Macdonald*, 1932 S.C. (H.L.) 79.

[7] *Marquess of Breadalbane's Trustees* (1843) 15 S.L. 389; *Downie v Downie's Trustees* (1866) 4 M. 1067; and *Monteith v Monteith's Trustees* (1882) 9 R. 982.

[8] *Moss's Trustees v Moss*, 1916 2 S.L.T. 31 (but see A.E. Anton, *Private International Law*, 1st edn (1967), pp.387, 388); *Re Hoyles* [1911] 1 Ch. 179; *Macmillan Inc v Bishopsgate Investment Trust Plc (No.3)* [1996] 1 All E.R. 585 CA.

[9] The chameleon nature of these security rights has caused difficulties, e.g. *Train v Train's Executor* (1899) 2 F. 146; cf. *Moss's Trustees v Moss*, 1916 2 S.L.T. 31. See A.E. Anton, *Private International Law*, 1st edn (1967), pp.387, 388; and explanation by Leslie, *Stair Memorial Encyclopaedia*, Vol.17, p.318. Such bonds were immoveable by the conflict rule of Scots law, although moveable in the succession of the creditor in the domestic law of Scotland in terms of the Titles to Land Consolidation (Scotland) Act 1868 s.117, as amended. The standard security, which replaced them per the Conveyancing and Feudal Reform (Scotland) Act 1970, is a heritable security which forms a heritable debt in the estate of the debtor, and is not subject to legal rights in the estate of the creditor.

[10] The interest of a beneficiary in such land in Scotland or England is immoveable until the power of sale is exercised. *Murray v Champernowne* [1901] 2 I.R. 232; *Re Lyne's Settlement Trusts* [1919] 1 Ch. 80; *Re Berchtold* [1923] 1 Ch. 192; *Re Cartwright* [1939] Ch. 90; *Re Cutcliffe's Will Trusts* [1940] Ch. 565; *Re Middleton's Settlement* [1947] Ch. 583; *Re Stoughton* [1941] I.R. 166.

[11] *Ross v Ross's Trustees*, 4 July 1809 FC; *Hall's Trustees v Hall* (1854) 16 D. 1057; *Macdonald*, 1932 S.C. (H.L.) 79. Though see *Iran v Berend* [2007] EWHC 132 (QB) where the parties, by agreement, directed that the court should treat the asset in question (fragment of limestone relief) as moveable; and further *Martin v Secretary of State for Work and Pensions* [2009] EWCA Civ 1289.

[12] R. Leslie, *Stair Memorial Encyclopaedia*, Vol.17, p.312.

[13] *Joint Administrators of Rangers Football Club Plc, Noters* 2012 S.L.T. 599.

[14] Bearing in mind also that art.10 of the Rome II Regulation contains choice of law rules concerning non-contractual obligations arising out of unjust enrichment, including payment of amounts wrongly received. Ch.16, above.

[15] *Macmillan Inc v Bishopsgate Investment Trust Plc (No.3)* [1996] 1 All E.R. 585.

[16] As explained by Leslie, *Stair Memorial Encyclopaedia*, Vol.17, p.318.

property as moveable or immoveable, whether or not straightforward at the outset, conceivably may require to be revisited at a later stage.

Meaning of lex situs

In view of the importance which traditional conflict rules place upon the *lex situs* as a connecting factor in the resolution of title disputes, it is necessary to be clear about the meaning of this factor.

17–03

Identification of "situs"

The definition of *situs* in relation to immoveable property normally gives rise to no difficulty, the *situs* being the place where the property is situated. No further definition or qualification is required, subject only in the rare case of the re-drawing of territorial boundaries.

17–04

With regard to moveable property, localising property in a spatial sense is not generally difficult but, crucially, in disputes concerning moveable property, there is an important temporal dimension in the ascertainment of the *lex situs*. The spatial definition (the "situation" of the asset) is of no use without a temporal qualification (the "situation" at what point in time?). Although it is the nature of the *situs* of a moveable asset to change, *at any given time* the situation of a corporeal moveable normally is fixed. The *lex situs* (or *lex loci rei sitae*) of a corporeal moveable, for the purposes of conflict of laws assessment of title thereto, is the law of the place where the property is situated at the time of the transaction in question,[17] i.e. when ownership or other proprietary right is alleged to have passed.

Particular care is required in the ascertainment of the *situs* of certain types of corporeal property, including cultural property,[18] aircraft[19] and ships. It is arguable that, though physically moveable, aircraft and ships have a quasi-permanent *situs* at their place of registration. However, in *Air Foyle Ltd v Center Capital Ltd*,[20] Gross J. firmly supported the ascription as the *situs* of an aircraft of its physical situation for the time being, at least unless the aircraft is over the high seas or over a territory which is not under the sovereignty of any state.[21] The

---

[17] *Macmillan Inc v Bishopsgate Investment Trust Plc (No.3)* [1996] 1 W.L.R. 387, per Staughton L.J. at 400.

[18] Within the EU particular rules have been laid down, such as Directive 2014/60/EU of the European Parliament and of the Council of 15 May 2014 on the return of cultural objects unlawfully removed from the territory of a Member State and amending Regulation (EU) No.1024/2012 (Recast). Essentially, however, from a conflict of laws viewpoint, the normal rules on title to moveable property apply (cf. Directive 2014/60/EU art.13, which declares that ownership of a qualifying cultural object, after its return to a requesting Member State, shall be governed by the law of that State). See J.M. Carruthers, *Transfer of Property in the Conflict of Laws* (2005), Ch.5, especially paras 5.31–5.34; *Cheshire, North and Fawcett: Private International Law*, 14th edn (2008), pp.1223, 1224; C. Roodt, *Private International Law, Art and Cultural Heritage* (2015); and *Iran v Barakat Galleries Ltd* [2009] Q.B. 22. See also paras 3-05—3-06.

[19] UNIDROIT Convention on International Interests in Mobile Equipment and Aircraft Equipment Protocol (2001), in relation to which see Decision 2009/370/EC on the accession of the European Community to the Convention [2009] O.J. L121/3.

[20] *Air Foyle Ltd v Center Capital Ltd* [2004] I.L.Pr. 15.

[21] *Air Foyle Ltd v Center Capital Ltd* [2004] I.L.Pr. 15 at [40].

same preference was shown by Beatson J. in *Blue Sky One Ltd v Mahan Air*.[22] Similarly, with regard to ships,[23] strong judicial preference for the physical *situs* of the vessel (over the notional or artifical *situs* thereof at the place of registration) was shown by Tomlinson J. in *Dornoch Ltd v Westminster International BV*.[24]

In the case of goods in transit, the physical location of which is casual or fortuitous, and transient,[25] a more flexible approach requires to be taken to the ascertainment of the *situs*.[26] Property will be classified as being in transit if it has left the country of despatch without having arrived at its intended destination.

A more difficult concept is the *situs* of incorporeal moveables. Since by nature an intangible right has no physical location, the practice has been to impute to such property an artificial legal *situs* according to the choice of law rule of the forum.[27] Rules have emerged in terms of which certain classes of intangible rights have been accorded a fictional *situs*, for example a money debt is deemed to be situated at the place where the debtor resides, being the place, it is presumed, where the debt may be enforced[28]; registered shares generally are deemed to be situated in the country in which they can be effectively dealt with as between the shareholder and the company[29]; and rights of action in contract, delict or unjustified enrichment are deemed to be situated in the country in which they can be effectively pursued.

Interpretation of "lex" situs

17–05   Whilst it would be possible to argue, as with immoveables,[30] so with moveables, that a reference to the law of the *situs* includes a reference to its rules of international private law (a possibility that was kept alive by Slade J. in

---

[22] *Blue Sky One Ltd v Mahan Air* [2010] EWHC 631 (Comm) at [156].

[23] As to which the early cases dealt with the distinction between personal and proprietary rights in ships by applying the law of the flag to contractual rights, and the *lex situs* in cases involving third parties and raising proprietary questions: *Schultz v Robinson and Niven* (1861) 24 D. 120; *Simpson v Fogo* (1863) 1 H. & M. 195; *Liverpool Marine Credit Co v Hunter* (1867) L.R. 4 Eq. 62; *Hooper v Gumm* (1867) L.R. 2 Ch. App. 282; *Castrique v Imrie* (1870) L.R. 4 H.L. 414.

[24] *Dornoch Ltd v Westminster International BV (The WD Fairway)* [2009] EWHC 889 (Admlty) at [96], [97], [103].

[25] *Standard Chartered Bank Ltd v Inland Revenue Commissioners* [1978] 1 W.L.R. 1160; and *Hardwick Game Farm v Suffolk Agricultural Poultry Producers Association* [1966] 1 W.L.R. 287.

[26] Carruthers, *Transfer of Property in the Conflict of Laws* (2005), Ch.5, paras 1.27–1.30.

[27] *Smelting Company of Australia Ltd v Inland Revenue Commissioners* [1897] 1 Q.B. 175.

[28] *English, Scottish and Australian Bank Ltd v Inland Revenue Commissioners* [1932] A.C. 238; *Re Banque des Marchands de Moscou (Koupetschesky) (No.3)* [1954] 1 W.L.R. 1108; *F&K Jabbour v Custodian of Israeli Absentee Property* [1954] 1 W.L.R. 139; and *Wight v Eckhardt Marine GmbH* [2003] UKPC 37.

[29] *Brassard v Smith* [1925] A.C. 371; *R. v Williams* [1942] A.C. 541. If there should be more than one share register the *situs* will be the country in which the transaction, according to the ordinary course of business, would be registered. See *Macmillan Inc v Bishopsgate Investment Trust Plc (No.3)* [1996] 1 W.L.R. 387. Difficulties arise where the place of the issuer's incorporation differs from the place where the share register is maintained, and from the place where the shareholding can be dealt with effectively as between the investor and the issuer. Further, para.17–35, below.

[30] *Re Duke of Wellington* [1947] Ch. 506; affirmed [1948] Ch. 118. Para.5–21, above.

Winkworth v Christie, Manson & Woods Ltd[31]), subsequent decisions tend to suggest that the argument in favour of *renvoi* is unlikely to succeed before an English court.[32]

Immoveable property

Capacity and powers

Capacity and power generally to transact in relation to land are governed by the *lex situs*.[33]

17–06

Contracts

A distinction should be drawn between an agreement to transfer an interest in land or other immoveable property, or otherwise to transact in relation to such property (i.e. a matter concerning only personal rights), and the actual transfer/conveyance of a right in rem in immoveable property (i.e a matter concerning real rights).[34]

17–07

As regards the essential validity of contracts concerning immoveable property, the rights of the parties are governed by the governing law of the contract which usually,[35] but not necessarily,[36] will be the *lex situs*. This is reinforced by art.4.1(c) of the Rome I Regulation.[37]

The formal validity of contracts the subject-matter of which is a right in immoveable property or a right to use immoveable property is subject to the mandatory requirements of form of the *lex situs* by virtue of art.11.5 of the Rome I Regulation.[38]

Proprietary rights

The existence and nature of real rights in land or other immoveables are governed by the *lex situs*.[39] The *lex situs*, besides being capable of clear identification, is generally thought to have an unassailable claim to be applied, as of right and common sense. Any question pertaining to the creation, including alienability,

17–08

---

[31] *Winkworth v Christie, Manson & Woods Ltd* [1980] Ch. 496 at 514.

[32] *Macmillan Inc v Bishopsgate Investment Trust Plc (No.3)* [1996] 1 W.L.R. 387 at 405; *Iran v Berend* [2007] EWHC 132 (QB); *The WD Fairway* [2009] EWHC 889 (Admlty); and *Blue Sky One Ltd v Mahan Air* [2010] EWHC 631 (Comm), all discussed at para.5–13, above.

[33] *Bank of Africa Ltd v Cohen* [1909] 2 Ch. 129 (but this case has been criticised: see Carruthers, *Transfer of Property in the Conflict of Laws* (2005), para.4.04); *Harris's Trustees,* 1919 S.C. 432; *Ogilvy v Ogilvy's Trustees*, 1927 S.L.T. 83; *Waring, Petitioner,* 1933 S.L.T. 190; *Black v Black's Trustees*, 1950 S.L.T. (Notes) 32; *Bondholders Securities Corp v Manville* (1933) 4 D.L.R. 699; *Charron v Montreal Trust* (1958) 15 D.L.R. (2d.) 240. See also Rome I Regulation art.13.

[34] *Hamilton v Wakefield*, 1993 S.L.T. (Sh. Ct.) 30.

[35] *Cood* (1863) 33 Beav. 314; *Re Smith* [1916] 2 Ch. 206; see also *Mackintosh v May* (1895) 22 R. 345.

[36] *British South Africa Co v De Beers Consolidated Mines Ltd* [1912] A.C. 52.

[37] See, however, art.4.1(d) introducing a special choice of law rule for short-term tenancies, echoing the jurisdiction rule contained in art.22.1 of the Brussels I Regulation.

[38] Ex-art.9.6 of the Rome I Convention.

[39] *Dicey, Morris and Collins on the Conflict of Laws*, 15th edn (2012), r.132.

acquisition (including by means of prescription),[40] use, disposal, gift, or transfer of an interest in immoveable property, and its effect on the proprietary rights of any person claiming, by any law, to be interested therein, is governed by the *lex situs*.[41]

All deeds of title must comply with the *lex situs* both as regards form[42] (including formalities of execution) and essentials.[43]

Real rights in security

17–09   The grant of a security interest over immoveable property must comply with the *lex situs* both as regards form and essentials.[44]

If, however, a security over land in Scotland is taken by a foreign creditor by way of equitable mortgage or some other form of security not known to Scots domestic law, it cannot prevail against a valid security in Scots form, though it may confer a preference on the holder thereof over unsecured creditors in a Scots bankruptcy or liquidation. If there are no securities valid by the *lex situs*, or if after such securities have been satisfied, there are no prior claims valid by that law, there will then be a competition between purely personal rights,[45] which will be determined by the law common to the litigants' claims, if there is one, and failing that, by the *lex situs*.[46]

Moveable property

Preliminary

17–10   For the purpose of the resolution of conflict disputes, it is important to note certain distinctions concerning:

(a)   *The nature of the property in question*: different rules apply to the treatment of corporeal moveables (choses in possession/chattels, e.g. a motor vehicle or a painting) from incorporeal moveables (choses in action, e.g. a money debt, or the interest under a life insurance policy).

(b)   *The nature of the purported transfer*: different rules govern voluntary assignations (e.g. by means of gift,[47] sale, or other consensual exchange) from those which govern involuntary assignations (by virtue of diligence or bankruptcy).

---

[40] *Beckford v Wade* (1805) 17 Ves. Un. 87 (positive prescription); *Re Peat* (1869) L.R. 7 Eq. 302; *Pitt v Lord Dacre* (1876) 3 Ch. D. 295 (negative).

[41] Erskine's *Institute*, III, 2, 40 on formal validity of conveyances of immoveable property. See also *Hewitt's Trs v Lawson* (1891) 18 R. 793.

[42] *Adams v Clutterbuck* (1883) L.R. 10 Q.B.D. 403. This is reinforced by Rome I Regulation art.11.5.

[43] *Norton v Florence Land and Public Works Co* (1887) L.R. 7 Ch. D. 332.

[44] *Ballachulish Slate Quarries Co Ltd v Bruce or Menzies* (1908) 16 S.L.T. 48. For a rare illustration of the prevailing of another law over the *lex situs*: *Carse v Coppen*, 1951 S.C. 233.

[45] *Re Courtney Ex p. Pollard* (1840) Mont. & Ch. 239; *Coote v Jecks* (1872) L.R. 13 Eq. 597; *Ex p. Holthausen* (1874) L.R. 9 Ch. App. 722; *Re Anchor Line (Henderson Bros) Ltd* [1937] Ch. 483.

[46] In respect of insolvency, see para.17–41 et seq., below.

[47] *Cochrane v Moore* (1890) L.R. 25 Q.B.D. 57; *Re Korvine's Trust* [1921] 1 Ch. 343. Whether or not a gift will be recognised as effective to transfer a real right in property and all questions of proprietary

(c)   *The basis of the dispute as contractual or proprietary*: contractual rights
involve the rights of the parties to a transfer of moveables *only as between
themselves*, and are purely personal in nature. Proprietary rights may, and
usually do, involve questions with third parties relating to rights in the
object which is the subject of the transfer and are real rather than personal,
i.e. rights enforceable *against all the world* (*contra mundum*). Certain types
of transfer have an existence which is independent of contract (e.g.
donations), whereas other transfers are rooted in contract (e.g. conditional
sale agreements). Whilst personal rights are governed by the law governing
the contract, proprietary questions are referred to the applicable law in
property.[48] This chapter is concerned mainly with the existence and ranking
of proprietary (real) rights, rather than with contractual (personal) rights.

The Scottish Law Commission's 2011 Discussion Paper on Moveable Transactions[49] is concerned with three strands of property law investigation, viz.: (i)
outright transfer (assignation) of incorporeal moveable property; (ii) security over
incorporeal moveable property; and (iii) security over corporeal moveable
property. The project does not encompass the outright transfer of corporeal
moveable property. More significantly, the project is confined to the domestic
Scots law of moveable transactions. The Discussion Paper notes[50] that, while it
would be possible to address the international private law aspects of secured
transactions within the project, the project required to be kept within
"manageable bounds". The constant refrain throughout the Paper is that the
international private law aspect (though frequently germane to moveable
transactions) is to be "left on one side", showing sustained disinclination on the
part of the Commissioners to engage in this area of property law in its
international private law dimension.[51]

Corporeal moveables

The laws which might contend to be applied in order to determine conflict   **17–11**
questions relating to the validity of the creation, acquisition, use and/or transfer
of real rights in corporeal moveables are:

(a)   *lex domicilii* (of transferor and/or transferee)[52]; or

---

rights must be matters for the *lex situs* at the time of alleged donation. Personal rights as between
donor and donee may be governed by the proper law of the gift, which need not necessarily be the *lex
situs*: *Stiftung v Lewis* [2004] EWHC 2589.
[48] *Joint Administrators of Rangers Football Club Plc, Noters* 2012 S.L.T. 599, per Lord Hodge at
[19]; *Glencore International AG v Metro Trading International Inc (No.2)* [2001] 1 All E.R. (Comm)
103; and *Pattni v Ali* [2007] 2 A.C. 85, per Lord Mance at [25].
[49] Discussion Paper No.151, June 2011.
[50] Discussion Paper No.151, June 2011, para.1.16.
[51] Discussion Paper No.151, June 2011. Cf. the conflict-of-laws-blind proposed rule on "Acquisition
of corporeal moveable property by prescription" contained in Ch.1, Prescription and Title to
Moveable Property (Scotland) Bill in Scottish Government "Consultation on a draft Bill to clarify the
law on when possessing an object can become full ownership" (July 2015).
[52] *Sill v Worswick* (1791) 1 H.B. 1 665 at 690; and *Re Ewin* (1830) 1 Cr. & J. 151 at 156. Historically,
the maxim *mobilia sequuntur personam* (questions of moveable property are governed by the
personal law) operated in questions relating to corporeal moveables, but now the principle applies

(b)   *lex loci actus* (the law of the place where the transaction/transfer took place)[53]; or

(c)   *lex actus* (proper law of the transfer, being the law of deemed closest connection); or

(d)   *lex situs* or *lex loci rei sitae* (the law of the situation of the asset at the time of the transfer alleged to have given rise to proprietary rights therein).

The development of the law to date shows the increasing application of the *lex situs*; the *lex situs* generally[54] has final say over title to corporeal moveables and determines all questions involving proprietary rights in respect thereof.[55] Counsel for the claimant in *Winkworth v Christie, Manson & Woods Ltd*[56] failed to persuade the court of the possible existence of a "proper law of property" based on the law of closest connection, preference being shown for the more easily ascertained factor of *lex situs*.[57]

The validity of a transfer

17–12   The purported transfer of a corporeal moveable assets must be considered as regards:

(a)   Alienability of property

The *lex situs* decides whether or not property is alienable, and determines also the legal nature of any document or other thing connected with property, such as title deeds or keys.[58] In *Duc de Frias v Pichon*[59] the saleability of sacred vessels stolen from a monastery in Spain was referred to the law of France, their situation at the time of the purported sale: by French law, but not by Spanish law, they were capable of being sold.

The assignability of incorporeal moveable property is a more complex matter, discussed at para.17–26, below.

(b)   Legal and proprietary capacity of transferor and transferee

The legal capacity of the transferor (i.e. age, insanity, etc.) could be governed either by the putative applicable law of the transfer, being the *lex situs*, or by the transferor's personal law.

---

only as a rule of succession on death, to the effect that succession, testate or intestate, to moveable estate is regulated by the law of the deceased's last domicile.

[53] Suggested by Kay L.J. in *Alcock v Smith* [1892] 1 Ch. 238 at 267.

[54] Para.17–15 regarding exceptions to the *lex situs* rule.

[55] *Re Anziani* [1930] 1 Ch. 407; *Bank voor Handel en Scheepvaart NV v Slatford (No.2)* [1953] 1 Q.B. 248; *F&K Jabbour v Custodian of Israeli Absentee Property* [1954] 1 W.L.R. 139; *Iran v Berend* [2007] EWHC 132 (QB).

[56] *Winkworth v Christie, Manson & Woods Ltd* [1980] 1 All E.R. 1121.

[57] See Carruthers' suggested "lex proprietatis" in *Transfer of Property in the Conflict of Laws* (2005), Chs 5, 8, 9. cf. *Glencore International AG v Metro Trading International Inc (No.2)* [2001] 1 All E.R. (Comm) 103.

[58] *Duc de Frias v Pichon* (1886) 13 *Journal du Droit International* 593; *Lushington v Sewell* (1827) 1 Sim. 435; *Stewart v Garnett* (1830) 3 Sim. 398; *Dominion Bridge Co v British American Nickel Co Ltd* (1925) 2 D.L.R. 138.

[59] *Duc de Frias v Pichon* (1886) 13 *Journal du Droit International* 593.

The proprietary capacity of the transferor (i.e. entitlement to deal with the property) is governed by the *lex situs*.[60]

(c) Formal validity of transfer

If the transfer is by means of contract, reference should be made to art.11 of the Rome I Regulation[61]; if otherwise than by means of contract, e.g. by gift, the governing law would be, by analogy, the *lex loci actus* or the *lex actus*, that is, the proper law of the transfer, being the law of deemed closest connection.

Rules for determining proprietary rights

As a general rule, proprietary rights in corporeal moveable property are governed by the *lex situs*. In a question between an "original" owner and a subsequent transferee, the latter will be preferred if he has acquired a title valid by the *lex situs* at the time of the purported transfer in his favour, or if he has acquired from an intermediate owner who has obtained such a title, that is, one which extinguishes the rights and title of the original owner.[62] Thus, if a valid transfer has taken place in the country in which an object was situated at that time, any proprietary right which it confers on the transferee will be recognised in Scotland, whether the transfer took place by way of public or private sale, donation, pledge, order of court,[63] Act of Parliament or equivalent, or otherwise. Essentially, the law of the latest transfer (whether it favours the latest transferee or a party earlier in the chain)[64] will govern.

17–13

Fraud/sale by non-owner

The case of transfer "tainted" by fraud is singled out only for emphasis, and not because the choice of law rule applied differs from any other purported transfer case. If a transferee has been guilty of fraud or if he has acquired from a non-owner (e.g. a thief), that transferee will not obtain good title to the property in question unless in either case the transfer in his favour is valid according to the *lex situs* of the property at the time of that transfer.[65] The general principle is that a transferee takes the property subject to all restrictions on the right of the

17–14

---

[60] As to the capacity of the transferee, some assistance can be derived from *Republica de Guatemala v Nunez* [1927] 1 K.B. 669 CA. Compare generally, legal capacity of a beneficiary to succeed, para.18–12, below.

[61] Para.15–33, above.

[62] *Todd v Armour* (1882) 9 R. 901; *Inglis v Usherwood* (1801) 1 East 515; *Cammell v Sewell* (1860) 5 H. & M. 728; *Castrique v Imrie* (1870) L.R. 4 H.L. 414; *Re Korvine's Trust* [1921] 1 Ch. 343; *Re Craven's Estate (No.1)* [1937] Ch. 423; *Princess Paley Olga v Weisz* [1929] 1 K.B. 718; *Winkworth v Christie, Manson & Woods Ltd* [1980] 1 All E.R. 1121.

[63] *Castrique v Imrie* (1870) L.R. 4 H.L. 414.

[64] *Goetschius v Brightman*, 245 N.Y. 186 (1927); *Century Credit Corp v Richard* (1962) 34 D.L.R. (2d.) 291 (discussed in *Cheshire, North and Fawcett: Private International Law*, 14th edn (2008), p.1216).

[65] *Winkworth v Christie, Manson & Woods Ltd* [1980] 1 All E.R. 1121; and *Kurtha v Marks* [2008] EWHC 336 (QB).

transferor, unless the *lex situs* at the time of the purported transfer has had an overriding effect which extinguishes any prior right.[66]

Exceptions to the situs rule

17–15 Certain exceptions to the *situs* rule were conceded by the defendant in the leading case of *Winkworth*,[67] namely:

> "The first 'if goods are in transit and their *situs* is casual or not known, a transfer which is valid and effective by its proper law will (semble) be valid and effective in England'[68]…The second exception…arises where a purchaser claiming title has not acted bona fide.[69] The third exception is the case where the English court declines to recognise the particular law of the relevant *situs* because it considers it contrary to English public policy. The fourth exception arises where a statute in force in the country which is the forum in which the case is heard obliges the court to apply the law of its own country…Fifthly…special rules might apply to determine the relevant law governing the effect of general assignments of movables on bankruptcy or succession."[70]

Competing claims to the same property

17–16 In this area of conflict of laws, the most difficult problem will be that concerning the ranking of competing claims to the same property. It is necessary to consider first the validity of each particular claim, and the transfer upon which it is based. If all such claims are governed by the *same* law, a Scots or English forum will apply that "common" law to determine which claim succeeds.[71] However, in

---

[66] *Freeman v The East India Co* (1822) 5 B. & Ald. 617; *Mehta v Sutton* (1913) 108 L.T. 514; *Goetschius v Brightman*, 245 N.Y. 186 (1927); *Universal Credit Co v Marks* (1932) 163 A. 810; *Century Credit Corp v Richard* (1962) 34 D.L.R. (2d.) 291; *Winkworth v Christie, Manson & Woods Ltd* [1980] 1 All E.R. 1121.

[67] *Winkworth v Christie, Manson & Woods Ltd* [1980] Ch. 496 at 501.

[68] The proper law of the transfer, being the law having closest connection to the transfer, seems an appropriate contender regarding transfers of goods in transit. In ascertaining that law, account will be taken of the country of despatch, and the country of intended destination. See Carruthers, *Transfer of Property in the Conflict of Laws* (2005), paras 3.32–3.35.

[69] An explanatory gloss is needed, viz. any requirement of good faith on the part of the transferee in order that title shall pass should depend entirely on the content of the law which is the *lex situs* at the time of the transfer on which a party relies (see Carruthers, *Transfer of Property in the Conflict of Laws* (2005), para.8.38). A more general point is that there is a division among legal systems between those favouring the instant transaction (*en fait des meubles, la possession vaut titre*), and those which find it impossible to disregard a *vitium reale* in the subject-matter purported to be transferred (i.e. that stolen property has an ineradicable taint: *nemo dat quod non habet*). Clearly the well-informed art thief should seek to dispose of his spoils in the former.

[70] See also *Glencore International AG v Metro Trading International Inc (No.2)* [2001] 1 All E.R. (Comm) 103.

[71] *North Western Bank Ltd v John Poynter Son and MacDonalds* (1894) 22 R. (H.L.) 1: [1895] A.C. 56. In the time-honoured (but later, by the speaker, amended) words of Lord Watson, at 75: "[w]hen a moveable fund, situated in Scotland admittedly belongs to one or other of two domiciled Englishmen, the question to which of them it belongs is prima facie one of English law." The gloss is that the reference to two domiciled Englishmen must be taken to mean "two men claiming under the same [English] law". *City Bank v Barrow* (1880) L.R. 5 App. Cas. 664; *Inglis v Robertson*; sub nom. *Irvine v Inglis*; *Irvine & Robertson v Baxter & Inglis* [1898] A.C. 616; *Connal and Co v Loder* (1868) 6 M. 1095; *Dinwoodie's Executor v Carruthers' Executor* (1895) 23 R. 234.

competitions between voluntary and involuntary transfers, or between transfers having *different* governing laws, competing proprietary claims are resolved by application of the *lex situs* at the time of the competition.

Governmental seizure of property

The territoriality principle applies, but this in turn may have private law repercussions outside the territory. The topic is treated at paras 3–05 and 3–06, above.

17–17

Where contract meets property[72]

The terms of a contract, valid by the governing law of the contract, may contravene the law of some other interested legal system. In a purely contractual sphere, this is regulated by the "overriding mandatory provisions" rules of the Rome I Regulation, and by that instrument's preservation of the forum's public policy. However choice of law rules of property typically may impinge in any given case, and there have been cases in Scotland[73] concerning the effect of advanced or elaborate forms of retention/reservation of title ("Romalpa") clauses,[74] which, while acceptable by the governing law of the contract of which they form part, are found to contravene the principles of the Scottish *lex situs* at the point of conclusion of the contract or at the date of subsequent litigation. Where there is a collision between a legal system's rules, conflict and/or domestic, of contract and property, in a Scots forum the property rules prevail, at least if the dispute is one of proprietary right.

17–18

Much interest in this area was shown in Scotland in the 1980s and 1990s.[75] Although it seemed that the Scots courts were being true to Scots law, both domestic (that generally there can be no security without possession), and conflict (that the validity of security rights are judged by the *lex situs*), there was a problem of their being out of step in international commercial terms. A solution, by means of change in forms of security in domestic law, was considered,

---

[72] Para.15–65, above. Background writing: see K. Reid and G. Gretton, "Retention of Title in Romalpa Clauses", 1983 S.L.T. (News) 77; "Retention of Title: Lord Watson's Legacy", 1983 S.L.T. (News) 105; Stewart, "Romalpa Clauses: Choosing the Law", 1985 S.L.T. (News) 149; P. Sellar, "Romalpa and Receivables—Choosing the Law", 1985 S.L.T. (News) 313; H. Patrick "Romalpa: the International Dimension", 1986 S.L.T. (News) 265 and 277; Clark, "All-Sums Retention of Title", 1991 S.L.T. (News) 155; C.G.J. Morse, "Retention of Title in English Private International Law" [1993] J.B.L. 168; and Gerard McCormack, *Reservation of Title*, 2nd edn (London: Sweet & Maxwell, 1995).

[73] *Hammer and Sohne v HWT Realisations Ltd*, 1985 S.L.T. (Sh.Ct.) 21; *Zahnrad Fabrik Passau GmbH v Terex Ltd*, 1986 S.L.T. 84; *Armour v Thyssen Edelstahlwerke AG*, 1986 S.L.T. 452 OH; 1990 S.L.T. 891 HL; *Emerald Stainless Steel Ltd v South Side Distribution Ltd*, 1983 S.L.T. 162; *Deutz Engines Ltd v Terex Ltd*, 1984 S.L.T. 273; *E Pfeiffer Weinkellerei-Weinenkauf GmbH v Arbuthnot Factors Ltd* [1988] 1 W.L.R. 150.

[74] So-called because of the name of the case in which such a clause was first noted: *Aluminium Industrie Vaassen BV v Romalpa Aluminium Ltd* [1976] 1 W.L.R. 676 (conflict issues not discussed).

[75] Department of Trade and Industry, *Security Over Moveable Property in Scotland: A Consultation Paper* (HMSO, 1994); also commentary by Murray, "Security over Moveable Property", 1995 S.L.T. (News) 31.

originally by the Halliday Committee for Scotland in 1986,[76] and the Diamond Committee[77] for England (though the growth of Romalpa clauses did not occasion an equivalent flurry of conflict cases on the point in that jurisdiction), and most recently by the Scottish Law Commission in its Discussion Paper on Moveable Transactions.[78] Another solution might have been to redefine the *lex situs* in these cases as, say, the place of despatch in terms of the contract,[79] or to place the problem in a wider context of distribution in bankruptcy (for such was often the situation which brought the case to court). However, in *Armour v Thyssen Edelstahlwerke AG*[80] the House of Lords ruled that, in the courts below, the nature of the retention of title clause in the contract in question had been misconstrued; that it could not be offensive to Scots law as a security right without possession, because on a true construction only possession and not property was transferred before payment. There the matter rests.

Incorporeal moveables

17–19   This is an area concerning the transfer of such rights as debts, shares and securities, funds in bank accounts, insurance policies, decrees, claims for damages and other causes of action, intellectual property rights, and interests in trust estates.[81] Assignation of bulk claims as a means of raising finance is a specialised sub-topic.[82]

Situs

17–20   As explained above, such rights have their *situs* at the place where the right is enforceable.[83]

---

[76] Scottish Law Commission Working Party on Security Over Moveable Property, chaired by Professor J.M. Halliday, *Report by Working Party on Security Over Moveable Property* (HMSO, 1986).

[77] Professor A.L. Diamond, *A Review of Security Interests in Property* (HMSO, 1989).

[78] Discussion Paper No.151, June 2011, Ch.3. Paragraph 3.43 states that no changes will be made per the instant project to international private law rules, which will remain in their current form and role of determining when domestic Scots law would apply.

[79] Stewart, "Romalpa Clauses: Choosing the Law", 1985 S.L.T. (News) 149.

[80] *Armour v Thyssen Edelstahlwerke AG*, 1990 S.L.T. 891.

[81] *Clare & Co v Dresdner Bank* [1915] 2 K.B. 576; *N Joachimson (A Firm) v Swiss Bank Corp* [1921] 3 K.B. 110; *Swiss Bank Corp v Boechmische Industrial Bank* [1923] 1 K.B. 673; *New York Life Insurance Co v Public Trustee* [1924] 2 Ch. 101; *Richardson v Richardson* [1927] P. 228; *Sutherland v Administrator of German Property* (1934) 50 T.L.R. 107; *Arab Bank Ltd v Barclays Bank* [1954] A.C. 495; *Re Claim by Helbert Wagg & Co Ltd* [1956] Ch. 323; *Re Banque des Marchands de Moscou (No.3)* [1954] 1 W.L.R. 1108 at 1115; *Reuter v Mulhens (No.2)* [1954] Ch. 50; *Westminster Bank Execcutor & Trustee Co (Channel Islands) Ltd v National Bank of Greece SA* [1971] 2 W.L.R. 105; *Compania Colombiana de Seguros v Pacific Steam Navigation Co (The Colombiana)* [1965] 1 Q.B. 101; *Trendtex Trading Corp v Credit Suisse* [1982] A.C. 679; *Macmillan Inc v Bishopsgate Investment Trust Plc (No.3)* [1996] 1 All E.R. 585; and *Raiffeisen Zentralbank Osterreich AG v Five Star General Trading LLC (The Mount I)* [2000] 2 Lloyd's Rep. 684; [2001] 1 Lloyd's Rep. 597.

[82] As to which: para.17–35, below.

[83] Paragraph 17–04, above; e.g. *F&K Jabbour v Custodian of Israeli Absentee Property* [1954] 1 W.L.R. 139; *Power Curber International Ltd v National Bank of Kuwait SAK* [1981] 3 All E.R. 607; *Kwok Chi Leung Karl v Commissioner of Estate Duty* [1988] 1 W.L.R. 1035 PC; and *Wight v Eckhardt Marine GmbH* [2003] UKPC 37.

Choice of law

The possible laws which contend to govern assignations[84] of incorporeal rights, **17–21**
and questions arising therefrom, are as follows:

(a)   *lex domicilii* of the creditor or the debtor; or
(b)   *lex loci actus* (the law of the place where the transaction takes place: the law of the paper transfer); or
(c)   *lex actus* (the law governing the assignation, being the law of deemed closest connection); or
(d)   proper law of the right purportedly assigned, that is, the *lex situs* of the right (normally the residence of the debtor).

One difficulty in the early cases is that the reason for application by the forum of a particular *lex causae* is not always clear,[85] especially where the *lex domicilii*, the *lex loci actus* and the *lex situs* happened to coincide. Thus, in the early leading case of *Republica de Guatemala v Nunez*,[86] which concerned both the formal validity of an assignation, and the legal capacity of the assignee to take (the flaw alleged being infancy), both issues were referred to the law of Guatemala which, on a revisionist view, has been said to be the (putative) proper law of the assignation.[87]

Triangular relationship

Typically, cases involving the assignation of incorporeal moveable rights concern **17–22**
a triangular scenario, where a creditor in an original claim against a debtor assigns his right to pursue that claim to a third party assignee. The relationship between the original parties (debtor and creditor) has a governing law, ascertained, if contractual, in accordance with the Rome I Regulation (so long as the contract falls within the scope of Rome I); if non-contractual, the relationship between debtor and creditor is governed by the proper law of the right purportedly assigned, being the law where the right may be enforced. Likewise, the assignation (from creditor to assignee) has its own governing law. The third side of the triangle is the relationship between assignee and debtor. It is important in any conflict case arising in this area to ascertain *which* parties the dispute in question concerns.

Effect of article 14 of the Rome I Regulation

Although the principal concern of this chapter is the proprietary, not the **17–23**
contractual, aspects of transfers, in relation to the assignation of incorporeal

---

[84] Termed in English law "assignment".
[85] Contrast close discussion in more modern authorities such as *Trendtex Trading Corp v Credit Suisse* [1982] A.C. 679; *Macmillan Inc v Bishopsgate Investment Trust Plc (No.3)* [1996] 1 W.L.R. 387; and *Raiffeisen Zentralbank Osterreich AG v Five Star General Trading LLC (The Mount I)* [2000] 2 Lloyd's Rep. 684; [2001] 1 Lloyd's Rep. 597.
[86] *Republica de Guatemala v Nunez* [1927] 1 K.B. 669.
[87] cf. *Lee v Abdy* (1886) L.R. 17 Q.B.D. 309 where it was clear that the putative proper law of the assignation was the law of Cape Colony, South Africa.

moveables of a contractual nature (e.g. a contractual debt),[88] it is difficult, and probably artificial, to sever the proprietary aspect from the contractual aspect, since the property right is a right arising under contract. Contractual assignations[89] of incorporeal moveable rights (whether contractual or non-contractual in nature) are governed by art.14 of the Rome I Regulation.[90]

Article 14: Voluntary assignment and contractual subrogation[91]

17–24

1. The relationship[92] between assignor and assignee under a voluntary assignment or contractual subrogation of a claim against another person ("the debtor") shall be governed by the law that applies to the contract between the assignor and assignee under the Rome I Regulation.
2. The law governing the assigned or subrogated claim shall determine its assignability, the relationship between the assignee and the debtor, the conditions under which the assignment or subrogation can be invoked against the debtor and whether the debtor's obligations have been discharged.
3. The concept of assignment in this article includes outright transfers of claims, transfers of claims by way of security as well as pledges or other security rights over claims.[93]

Article 14 applies to claims assigned by means of contract *irrespective* of the nature of the claim itself, which may be contractual or non-contractual.[94] The validity of a contractual assignation falling outside the scope of the Rome I Regulation is governed by the common law rules of assignation, i.e. the common law choice of law rules pertaining to contract. Likewise, non-contractual assignations, even of a contractual right such as a money debt, are not governed

---

[88] Rights which are capable of being assigned can be contractual, or non-contractual, e.g. the benefit arising under a right of copyright, or a right to sue (*Trendtex Trading Corp v Credit Suisse* [1982] A.C. 679).

[89] An assignation of property can be contractual, but might also be effected in a non-contractual manner, e.g. by gift or bequest.

[90] ex-Rome I Convention art.12.

[91] See, on art.14 and art.15 (legal subrogation), paras 15–46 and 15–49, above. The remit of art.14 extends to voluntary assignments and contractual subrogations (and does not encompass involuntary assignment), it being thought that these transfers are similar in nature. "Contractual subrogation" refers to subrogation by means of a contract; it does not mean that the nature of the claim subrogated necessarily is contractual.

[92] Rome I Regulation recital (38) provides that: "In the context of voluntary assignment, the term 'relationship' should make it clear that Article 14.1 also applies to the property aspects of an assignment, as between assignor and assignee, in legal orders where such aspects are treated separately from the aspects under the law of obligations. However, the term 'relationship' should not be understood as relating to any relationship that may exist between assignor and assignee. In particular, it should not cover preliminary questions as regards a voluntary assignment or a contractual subrogation. The term should be strictly limited to the aspects which are directly relevant to the voluntary assignment or contractual subrogation in question". Although the remit of the Rome I Regulation is contractual obligations in situations involving a conflict of laws, the wording of recital (38) is evidence that the competence of the instrument or amendments thereto to deal with the property aspects of voluntary assignment is assumed.

[93] Article 14.3 provides of new a non-exhaustive definition of the concept of assignment.

[94] For the law governing the transferability of a non-contractual claim, see Rome II Regulation art.15(e) (para.16–41, above).

by the Rome I Regulation, but fall to be governed by the common law rules, e.g. of donation or bequest, as appropriate. It is important, therefore, to distinguish between contractual and non-contractual assignations of incorporeal moveable rights.[95]

Article 14, which very largely replicates the wording of art.12 of the Rome I Convention, defines the ambit of operation, or authority, of the law applicable; it does not seek to identify what shall be the law applicable.

Article 14.1 issues: relationship between the assignor and the assignee

In the case of contractual assignations, the relationship between the assignor and assignee falls, as a contractual matter, within art.14.1 of the Rome I Regulation. This means that the applicable law of the assignation governs that relationship. The applicable law will be determined according to the rules in the Rome I Regulation, principally contained in arts 3 and 4. In the case of non-contractual assignations, matters of essential validity are governed at common law by the proper law of the assignation,[96] but an assignation will be essentially valid also if it complies with the proper law of the right transferred.[97]

17–25

Article 14.2 issues

(a) Assignability

As regards contractual assignations, art.14.2 of the Rome I Regulation applies to the effect that assignability is governed by the law governing the assigned or subrogated claim.[98]

17–26

As regards non-contractual assignations (e.g. by means of gift), assignability is governed by the proper law of the right[99] (i.e. the same result as art.14.2). The common law rule is clearly seen in the case of *Pender*,[100] in which the assignability of an insurance policy, taken out with reference to the English Married Women's Property Act 1882, was categorised by the Scots court as an assignation of a Scottish right, as to which assignability and the separate issue of capacity to assign were referred to Scots law qua, respectively, the law of closest connection and the domicile of the transferor. By Scots law the married woman granter was under a personal incapacity to assign the benefits of such a policy. Hence, her purported assignation to a bank was ineffective.

These facts illustrate that within the one broad heading of assignability, the issue of capacity to assign may take precedence: "...the rule as to assignability is subordinate to the rule governing capacity to assign; personal (in)capacity to

---

[95] Carruthers, *Transfer of Property in the Conflict of Laws* (2005), Ch.6, para.6.12.

[96] *Scottish Provident Institution v Cohen* (1888) 16 R. 112; *Libertas-Kommerz GmbH v Johnson*, 1977 S.C. 191.

[97] *Re Anziani* [1930] 1 Ch. 407.

[98] Logically, it would have been expected that the subject of assignability would have been treated first in order, but the drafting of art.14 follows the sequence adopted by art.12 of the Rome I Convention, producing the odd result that the general rule comes second.

[99] *Grant's Trustees v Ritchie's Executor* (1886) 13 R. 646; *Pender v Commercial Bank of Scotland Ltd*, 1940 S.L.T. 306; *Campbell Connelly & Co Ltd v Noble* [1963] 1 W.L.R. 252; *Libertas-Kommerz GmbH v Johnson*, 1977 S.C. 191.

[100] *Pender v Commercial Bank of Scotland Ltd*, 1940 S.L.T. 306.

assign must be regarded as an essential component of assignability."[101] In *Pender*, the *two leges causae* (law of closest connection and the domicile of the transferor) coincided in Scotland, but clearly this might not always be the case.

(b) Relationship between the assignee and the debtor

17–27 As between assignee and debtor (i.e. under the right transferred):

> "[I]t is easy to understand why the intrinsic validity of the assignment should be governed by the proper law of the assignation; but, when issues of validity (other perhaps than mere formal validity) arise between the assignee and the other party to the original contract, the argument in support of the application of the proper law of the assignation, in preference to the proper law both of the original contract and of the debt claimed, is in my opinion, inconsistent with both logic and equity."[102]

Assuming that the right in question is assignable, and that there is capacity on the part of the assignor to assign, and of the assignee to accept, art.14.2 of the Rome I Regulation states, in relation to contractual assignations, that the law governing the right to which the assignment relates (i.e. the proper law of the right) governs the relationship between the assignee and the debtor, as well as the conditions under which the assignment can be invoked against the debtor and any question whether the debtor's obligations have been discharged.

(c) Miscellaneous

17–28 Capacity to make or to accept an assignation: In the past, the *lex loci actus* or the law of the domicile of the purported transferor (or transferee) was applied, but it is submitted that capacity to make or to accept an assignation of incorporeal moveable property should be governed by the proper law of the assignation or by the proper law of the right purportedly assigned,[103] according to whichever of these laws confers capacity earlier.[104] In the case of contractual assignations, the putative applicable law of the contract, subject to art.13 of the Rome I Regulation,[105] will apply.

17–29 Formal validity: At common law, there were three possibly applicable laws, to the effect that an assignation, contractual or non-contractual, would be formally valid if it complied with any one of the *lex loci actus*, the proper law of the assignation, or the proper law of the right assigned.[106] In cases of contractual assignations regulated by the Rome I Regulation art.11 governs formal validity.[107]

---

[101] Carruthers, *Transfer of Property in the Conflict of Laws* (2005), para.6.08.

[102] *Bankhaus H Aufhauser v Scotboard Ltd*, 1973 S.L.T. (Notes) 87, per Lord Hunter at 89.

[103] *Lee v Abdy* (1886) L.R. 17 Q.B.D. 309; *Republica de Guatemala v Nunez* [1927] 1 K.B. 669.

[104] Since arguably "the conditions under which the assignment can be invoked against the debtor" encompasses the questions of incapacity of assignor and/or assignee, by virtue of art.14.2 these matters should be referred to the law governing the assigned or subrogated claim (i.e. "the proper law of the right").

[105] Ch.15, above.

[106] *Republica de Guatemala v Nunez* [1927] 1 K.B. 669; *Stirling's Trustees v Legal & General Assurance Society*, 1957 S.L.T. 73.

[107] At common law: *Scottish Provident Institution v Cohen* (1888) 16 R. 112; and *Bankhaus H Aufhauser v Scotboard Ltd*, 1973 S.L.T. (Notes) 87.

The effectiveness of an assignment of a claim against third parties, and priorities

That which was unregulated by the Rome Convention, and was left unregulated by the Rome I Regulation, is the effectiveness of a voluntary assignment vis-à-vis third parties. No guidance is given in the Regulation as to how a Member State forum should prioritise competing claims,[108] governed by different laws, to the same right.

17–30

The current approach

Currently, these points must be dealt with by each Member State according to its own conflict rules. Questions involving competing proprietary rights must be considered as regards: (i) the debtor's liability under the right in question; (ii) the validity of each assignation, as to form and essentials; and (iii) the ranking of competing claims inter se.

17–31

In Scots law, the *lex situs* regulates the proprietary rights of the parties, and governs in particular (i) the debtor's liability to pay; and (ii) competitions between assignations valid by their own proper laws; and between voluntary and involuntary assignations and diligences. There are, however, certain qualifications to this rule: in a competition between two or more assignations having the same proper law and derived from the same debtor, or between a voluntary and an involuntary assignation both governed by the same proper law, the parties' rights are governed and regulated by that law.[109] This rule applies only to the determination of the rights of creditors inter se when they hold assignations with the same proper law.[110] The competing rights inter se of creditors holding "rights" under assignations which have different proper laws are regulated by the *lex situs*.[111] Any question of priority between the holders of voluntary and involuntary transfers,[112] such as arising as a result of diligence, also are governed by the *lex situs*.

In practice, questions are solved as follows:

(1)   The debtor's liability will be determined by the *lex situs* of the right which is the subject of the assignation(s).

(2)   Assuming the right in question is enforceable against the debtor, the following process is applied:

---

[108] Most likely to be by creditors of the assignor, who somehow managed to raise money or gain some kind of consideration by assigning or depositing the same right twice.

[109] cf. *North Western Bank v John Poynter Son and MacDonalds* (1894) 22 R. (H.L.) 1, per Lord Watson at 12.

[110] *Scottish Provident Institution v Robinson* (1892) 29 S.L.R. 733; *Dinwoodie's Executor v Carruthers' Executor* (1895) 23 R. 234; *Forbes v Official Receiver in Bankruptcy*, 1924 S.L.T. 522; *Republica de Guatemala v Nunez* [1927] 1 K.B. 669.

[111] *Le Feuvre v Sullivan* (1855) 10 Moo. P.C. 389; *Kelly v Selwyn* [1905] 2 Ch. 117.

[112] *Strachan v McDougle* (1835) 13 S. 954; *Donaldson v Ord* (1855) 17 D. 1053; *Re Maudslay Sons & Field* [1900] 1 Ch. 602; *Re Queensland Mercantile & Agency Co Ex p. Australian Investment Co* [1892] 1 Ch. 219; *F&K Jabbour v Custodian of Israeli Absentee Property* [1954] 1 W.L.R. 139.

(a)   the validity of each assignation, contractual or non-contractual, is determined by its governing law[113];

(b)   if there is more than one valid assignation, and each competing assignation has the same proper law, that law will regulate the rights of assignees inter se;

(c)   if there is more than one valid assignation, and the competing assignations have different proper laws, or if there is a competition between voluntary and involuntary transfers, such as diligence, priority will be regulated by the *lex situs* of the right.

Prospective European reform

17–32   Article 27(2) of the Rome I Regulation required the European Commission to submit to the European Parliament, the Council and the European Economic and Social Committee a report on the question of the effectiveness of an assignment or subrogation of a claim against third parties and the priority of the assigned or subrogated claim over a right of another person, together with a proposal to amend the Rome I Regulation (art.14).[114]

In 2009, the UK Ministry of Justice published a discussion paper entitled, "Rome I: European Commission Review of Article 14: Assignment".[115] Consultation was restricted to the question of voluntary assignations; the anticipated review of art.14 did not embrace the ranking of involuntary assignations inter se (in respect of which reference may require to be made to Regulation 1346/2000 or its successor), or the ranking between/among involuntary and voluntary assignations. The reaction of the UK Government to the 2009 European Commission review was that the general rule to govern the effectiveness of an assignation against third parties and the priority of assigned claims over the same right should be the law governing the claim assigned ("the proper law of the right" in "old'" parlance). It is thought that this factor, being constant and not liable to change, would promote certainty. However, in this complex area,[116] it was thought that there is a case for the creation of specific exceptions to the general rule. Special provision has been considered for the bulk assignment of debts (debt factoring).[117] In respect of special cases of this type, it was proposed that the question of the effectiveness of the assignment against third parties and priority of the assigned claims over a right of another person should be governed by the law of the country where the assignor has his habitual residence. Despite the usual concerns with regard to the connecting factor of habitual residence, namely, its uncertainty of meaning, and, in this context, the doubts which will arise if the habitual residence of the assignor changes during

---

[113] e.g. *Scottish Provident Institution v Cohen* (1888) 16 R. 112.

[114] For background: Conversion of the Rome Convention of 1980 on the Law Applicable to Contractual Obligations into a Community Instrument and its Modernisation COM(2002) 654 final, paras 3.2.13, 3.2.14.

[115] "Rome I: European Commission Review of Article 14: Assignment" The Stationery Office, 2009.

[116] Epitomised by *Raiffeisen Zentralbank Osterreich AG v Five Star General Trading LLC (The Mount I)* [2000] 2 Lloyd's Rep. 684; [2001] 1 Lloyd's Rep. 597.

[117] And also for assignments by a natural person acting outside the course of his business or profession. Other areas considered in the Ministry of Justice Discussion Paper for special treatment were assignments of judgment debts; intellectual property rights; shares in companies; transferable securities; letters of credit; insurance policies; and claims in tort or delict.

the crucial period, it was thought to be apt to deal with the bulk assignment case, in respect of which it would be awkward for the assignee (the financier) to ascertain the applicable law of each and every debt. A problem would arise, however, should there be a competition between or among claims, one or some of which fall to be regulated by the general rule, and others by the special rule; for such cases there would require to be a pre-eminent, tie-breaking rule.

Subsequent to the 2009 discussion paper, and as a precursor to its compliance with the substance, if not the timescale, of art.27(2), the European Commission commissioned from the British Institute of International and Comparative Law a study, which was published in 2012.[118] The BIICL Report, which should serve as a basis for the European Commission's expected report on, and proposal to amend, art.14, concludes that there is a need for a new rule in art.14. It accepts that in this area of law and practice, it will be difficult to achieve consensus as to the "best" rule. The Report notes the importance of seeking to create a new rule which will support trade. While recognising that one rule will not suit all interested parties and industries, it recommends that there should be only "moderate" use of sector-specific rules.[119] It is concerned also with clarifying the relationship between a revised version of art.14 of the Rome I Regulation and EU Regulation 1346/2000 on Insolvency Proceedings (and its successor). Rejecting less well supported options, the Report formulates three possible drafting proposals, reflecting the conflict of laws solutions favoured by a significant number of stakeholders and/or experts.[120] Proposal (A) is based on an application of the law governing the contract between assignor and assignee; proposal (B) applies the law governing the claim assigned, under exception of a special sub-rule for "future claims" and assignments by way of factoring; and Proposal (C) advocates application of the law of the assignor's habitual residence, again subject to a possible exception for a limited group of financial contracts. The Commission's reaction and proposal are awaited.

Bills of exchange

Conflict rules in relation to bills of exchange (and promissory notes) were laid down early, by statute, in terms of the Bills of Exchange Act 1882.[121] There are excluded from the Rome I Regulation by art.1(2)d: **17–33**

> "obligations arising under bills of exchange, cheques and promissory notes and other negotiable instruments to the extent that the obligations under such other negotiable instruments arise out of their negotiable character."[122]

---

[118] Final Report: Study on the question of effectiveness of an assignment or subrogation of a claim against third parties and the priority of the assigned or subrogated claim over a right of another person (15 May 2012) ("BIICL Report"). For background: P.R. Wood, *Conflict of Laws and International Finance* (Sweet & Maxwell, London, 2007); J. Perkins, "A Question of Priorities: Choice of Law and Proprietary Aspects of the Assignment of Debts" (2008) L.F.M.R. 238; and M. Bridge, "The Proprietary Aspects of Assignment and Choice of Law" (2009) L.Q.R. 1.

[119] Final Report, p.412.

[120] The BIICL Report empirical study was based on responses to a questionnaire which "... reached thousands of stakeholders, but [of whom] only 36 have responded." (Final Report, p.373).

[121] The meaning of bills of exchange is defined in ss.3, 4.

[122] Rome I Regulation art.1.2(d).

The wording of the exclusion is identical to that in art.1.2(c) of the Rome I Convention, and so by the principle of continuity of interpretation, it can be taken that, as under the Convention, so too under the Regulation, the qualifying phrase "to the extent that...negotiable character" applies only to "other negotiable instruments". Bills of exchange, cheques and promissory notes[123] are excluded from the Rome I Regulation without reservation.[124] A commercial letter of credit is not a negotiable instrument and is not subject to exclusion as above.[125]

Conflict rules concerning bills of exchange are contained in the 1882 Act s.72,[126] which provides that where a bill drawn in one country is negotiated, accepted, or payable in another, the rights, duties, and liabilities of the parties thereto shall be determined in accordance with that section.[127] The general effect of s.72 as regards foreign bills[128] is to make the validity of each of the interdependent contracts depend upon its own law and not on the law of the bill. This "several laws" approach attracts widespread international agreement.[129] Section 72 provides as follows:

(1)   The formal validity of a bill and of each indorsement is governed by the law(s) of the place(s) of issue,[130] but it will be sufficient for enforcement of payment in this country that the law of the UK is complied with. By s.72(1), lack of a stamp in accordance with the law of the place of issue does not make a bill invalid in the UK.

(2)   Essential validity is governed by the law of the place where the bill and indorsements are made. The word used in s.72(2) of the Act is "interpretation" of the drawing, indorsement, acceptance or acceptance

---

[123] *Zebrarise Ltd v De Nieffe* [2005] 1 Lloyd's Rep. 154.

[124] Giuliano and Lagarde, p.11.

[125] Conflict cases on letters of credit include *Offshore International SA v Banco Central SA* [1976] 3 All E.R. 749 (Elizabeth B. Crawford, "Oil on Troubled Waters: proper law of letter of credit" (1977) 22 J.L.S. 434); *Power Curber International Ltd v National Bank of Kuwait SAK* [1981] 3 All E.R. 607; *United City Merchants (Investments) Ltd v Royal Bank of Canada (The American Accord)* [1983] 1 A.C. 168 HL; *Bank of Baroda v Vysya Bank* [1994] 2 Lloyd's Rep. 87; and *Marconi Communications International Ltd v PT Pan Indonesia Bank Ltd* [2005] 2 All E.R. (Comm) 325.

[126] Cases following the Act: *Re Marseilles Extension Railway and Land Co* (1885) L.R. 30 Ch. D. 598; *Re Commercial Bank of South Australia* (1887) L.R. 36 Ch. D. 522; *Bank of Montreal v Exhibit and Trading Co Ltd* (1906) 22 T.L.R. 722; *Guaranty Trust Co of New York v Hannay & Co* [1918] 1 K.B. 43; [1918] 2 K.B. 623; *Alcock v Smith* [1892] 1 Ch. 238; *Embiricos v Anglo Austrian Bank* [1904] 2 K.B. 870; [1905] 1 K.B. 677; *F Koechlin et Cie v Kestenbaum Bros* [1927] 1 K.B. 889; *Moulis v Owen* [1907] 1 K.B. 746; *Re Francke & Rasch* [1918] 1 Ch. 470; *Koch v Dicks* [1933] 1 K.B. 307; *Bank Polski v KJ Mulder & Co* [1941] 2 K.B. 266; [1942] 1 K.B. 497; *Cornelius v Banque Franco-Serbe* [1942] 1 K.B. 29; [1942] 1 K.B. 29; *Syndic in Bankruptcy of Khoury v Khayat* [1943] A.C. 507.

[127] But only where there is a conflict: *Karafarin Bank v Mansoury-Dara* [2009] EWHC 3265 (Comm); [2010] 1 Lloyd's Rep. 236.

[128] "Defined" in s.4(1) thus: "An inland bill is a bill which is or on the face of it purports to be (a) both drawn and payable within the British Islands, or (b) drawn within the British Islands upon some person resident therein. Any other bill is a foreign bill."

[129] *Dicey, Morris and Collins on the Conflict of Laws*, 15th edn (2012), para.33–328.

[130] 1882 Act s.72(1). A contract is made (s.21) when the instrument is delivered in order to give effect to the contract: delivery means transfer of possession, actual or constructive.

supra protest of a bill,[131] but it is thought that this term relates not merely to construction but to all questions of essential validity.[132]

(3)   Procedure as to protest on dishonour, etc. is governed by the law of the place where the act is done.[133]

(4)   The due date is determined by the law of the place where the bill is payable.[134]

The 1882 Act does not provide conflict rules to govern all conflict questions which might arise in relation to a bill, and leaves aside, in particular, capacity, and the proprietary, as opposed to the contractual, aspects.[135] In their residual contractual aspect, and by dint of art.1.2(d) of the Rome I Regulation, they will be governed by common law choice of law rules in contract, and not by the Regulation.[136]

Negotiable instruments

The choice of law rules on this subject are based on those relating both to the law of contract and of property. A negotiable instrument is an order involving a contract to pay money to a person to be named or to his order, to be signified by indorsement of the document. No intimation to the debtor is required. A document recognised as being a negotiable instrument has certain privileges which do not apply to documents not recognised as such; a holder acquiring a document not having this characteristic does not necessarily acquire a good title even if he acquires it in good faith and for value.

17–34

The general view is that the question whether or not a particular document is to be regarded as a negotiable instrument is to be determined by the law of the place where its negotiation takes place, which almost invariably will be the *lex fori,* that is, the law of the place in which the instrument is situated at the time of the delivery.[137] For a document to be regarded as a negotiable instrument, the true test is that it must be recognised as such by the *lex fori* but possibly it should also have that quality according to the law under which it was created.[138]

---

[131] Provided that where an inland bill is indorsed in a foreign country the indorsement as regards the payer shall be interpreted according to the law of the United Kingdom (s.72(2)).

[132] *Alcock v Smith* [1892] 1 Ch. 238; *Embiricos v Anglo Austrian Bank* [1904] 2 K.B. 870; *F Koechlin et Cie v Kestenbaum Bros* [1927] 1 K.B. 889.

[133] 1882 Act s.72(3).

[134] 1882 Act s.72(5).

[135] *Dicey, Morris and Collins on the Conflict of Laws*, 15th edn (2012), para.33–332.

[136] The Act has put the *lex loci contractus* in a dominant position in matters of form and interpretation and Dicey, Morris and Collins recommend that "gaps" in the Act be filled by ascribing to this law regulation of capacity and everything pertaining to the formation of the contract (*Dicey, Morris and Collins on the Conflict of Laws*, 15th edn (2012), para.33–332).

[137] *Dicey, Morris and Collins on the Conflict of Laws*, 15th edn (2012), para.33–383.

[138] *Goodwin v Robarts* (1876) L.R. 1 App. Cas. 476; *Picker v London and County Banking Co Ltd* (1887) L.R. 18 Q.B.D. 515; *London Joint Stock Bank v Simmons* [1892] A.C. 201.

Shares and other securities[139]

17–35   Questions of choice of law may arise in relation to (a) the effect of transfers as regards the issuing company; (b) the effect of transfers as between the parties themselves (i.e. issuer and investor); and (c) the situation of shares for the purposes of inheritance tax, stamp duties, income tax and other similar matters.

Choice of law rules in relation to shares and other securities traditionally were based upon the assumption of a direct relationship between the issuer and the investor, evidenced, in the case of registered securities, by registration of the investor's name in the books of the issuer, and in the case of bearer securities, by physical possession by the investor of a certificate. The following rules apply to directly-held securities[140]: normally the *situs* of shares of a company is the place where the company is registered and the share register is kept.[141] In order to divest the transferor and give the transferee a good title which will be effective as a real right against third parties, it is essential to comply with the *lex situs*.[142] The personal rights of the transferor and transferee merely as between themselves (that is, contractual rights) are regulated by the proper law of the transfer which is usually the law of the place where the transfer occurs, and may be different from the *lex situs* of the shares.

Technological developments, and market demands have led to the development of a more efficient holding pattern, namely, one which permits holding via an intermediary, and which allows for the transfer of interests by means of electronic book-entry to securities accounts. The traditional, materialised system in many instances has been replaced by a dematerialised (electronic), intermediated holding system. The choice of law rule traditionally applied to govern the proprietary aspects of a transfer of shares or other securities (namely, the law of the *situs* of those shares or other right) is not easily applied to the transfer of "intermediated securities". To meet the demands of the global financial market for certainty and predictability of securities transactions, there was produced the 2006 Hague Convention on the Law Applicable to Certain Rights in respect of Securities Held with an Intermediary. The purpose of the Convention is to harmonise rules of choice of law concerning rights in respect of intermediated securities. It applies in all cases where securities are held with an intermediary (i.e. where securities are credited to a securities account), but it has no application to directly held securities, which continue to be governed by pre-existing, national choice of law rules.

---

[139] Carruthers, *Transfer of Property in the Conflict of Laws* (2005), Ch.7.

[140] *Williams v Colonial Bank* (1888) L.R. 38 Ch.D. 388 (right to hold share certificates distinguished from substantive rights in shares); *Colonial Bank v Cady* (1890) L.R. 15 App. Cas. 267; *Brassard v Smith* [1925] A.C. 371; *Baelz v Public Trustee* [1926] Ch. 863; *London and South American Investment Trust Ltd v British Tobacco Co (Australia) Ltd* [1927] 1 Ch. 107; *Erie Beach Co Ltd v Att Gen of Ontario* [1930] A.C. 161; *R. v Williams* [1942] A.C. 541; *Re Middleton's Settlement* [1947] Ch. 583; *Re Fry (Deceased)* [1946] Ch. 312; *Macmillan Inc v Bishopsgate Investment Trust Plc (No.3)* [1996] 1 W.L.R. 387; and *International Credit and Investment Co (Overseas) Ltd v Adham* [1994] 1 B.C.L.C. 66. But consider Stevens, "The Law Applicable to Priority in Shares" (1996) 112 L.Q.R. 198.

[141] *Macmillan Inc v Bishopsgate Investment Trust Plc (No.3)* [1996] 1 W.L.R. 387. See further, *Dicey, Morris and Collins on the Conflict of Laws*, 15th edn (2012), para.22–044.

[142] *Akers v Samba Financial Group* [2014] EWHC 540 (Ch).

Article 2 (Scope of the Convention and of the applicable law) provides in para.(1) that the Convention operates to determine the law applicable to the following issues in respect of securities held with an intermediary, namely:

(a)   the legal nature and effects against the intermediary and third parties of the rights resulting from a credit of securities to a securities account;

(b)   the legal nature and effects against the intermediary and third parties of a disposition of securities held with an intermediary;

(c)   the requirements, if any, for perfection of a disposition of securities held with an intermediary;

(d)   whether a person's interest in securities held with an intermediary extinguishes or has priority over another person's interest;

(e)   the duties, if any, of an intermediary to a person other than the account holder who asserts in competition with the account holder or another person an interest in securities held with that intermediary;

(f)   the requirements, if any, for the realisation of an interest in securities held with an intermediary;

(g)   whether a disposition of securities held with an intermediary extends to entitlements to dividends, income, or other distributions, or to redemption, sale or other proceeds.

The primary rule of choice of law is contained in art.4 of the Convention, and gives effect to an express agreement on governing law between an account holder and its immediate intermediary, subject however to the requirement that the law chosen will apply only if the relevant intermediary has, at the time of the agreement, a qualifying office in the state the law of which has been chosen. If the applicable law is not determined under art.4, art.5 contains a series of "fall-back" rules. Article 6 deliberately severs any link with traditional *situs* thinking, insofar as it is expressly stated that in determining the applicable law under the Convention no account should be taken, inter alia, of the place where the issuer is incorporated, the place where securities certificates are located, or the place where a securities register is located or maintained.

The 2006 Hague Convention has not entered into force, and has been signed only by Mauritius, Switzerland and the USA.

Intellectual property rights

Though this heading encompasses a number of different types of right, including copyright, patents, and trade marks,[143] each appears to be treated in broadly the same way, in that the *situs* is taken to be the country in which they may be effectively transferred, i.e. the legal system of their creation.[144] Intellectual property rights have a definite connection with a particular place,[145] and if

                                              17–36

---

[143] Infringement thereof being subject to the applicable law rules contained in art.8 of the Rome II Regulation (para.16–18, above).

[144] See, for specialist treatment, J.J. Fawcett and P. Torremans, *Intellectual Property and Private International Law*, 2nd edn (Oxford: Oxford University Press, 2011).

[145] *Campbell Connolly & Co v Noble* [1963] 1 W.L.R. 252. On jurisdiction of the English courts with regard to alleged breach of a foreign statutory intellectual property right, see *Pearce v Ove Arup*

created in the UK are effective only there unless they receive extra-territorial effect in foreign countries under the conflict rules there applicable.

The goodwill of a business is deemed to be situated in the legal system of the situation of the asset to which the goodwill attaches.[146]

UNIVERSAL TRANSFERS OF PROPERTY: INSOLVENCY[147]

Common law theories

17–37   In the development of this subject, favour has been shown to one or other of two main theories, which will be outlined before attention is turned to recent legislative development.

Unity of bankruptcy

17–38   According to the theory of unity, a bankruptcy should be one and indivisible, and when a person is sequestrated or grants a trust deed for creditors, the process should attach and convey to the trustee in bankruptcy all property, wherever situated, belonging to the bankrupt, with the result that only one set of bankruptcy proceedings is permissible. A separate bankruptcy in each country should not be permissible.

At common law, the Scots courts favoured the unity theory[148] and therefore would not grant a sequestration if the bankrupt already had been sequestrated in another country, unless perhaps for some reason the foreign bankruptcy was no longer effective.

Separate bankruptcies

17–39   According to this theory, the opposite of the unity theory, the bankrupt's assets should be distributed separately in each jurisdiction for the benefit of creditors in that jurisdiction. Hence it should be permissible to have multiple bankruptcies. This is the "territoriality" approach, favoured at common law in England.[149] The English courts declined to allow the existence of concurrent proceedings, or the factor of priority of date, to be decisive in the question whether or not there should be a stay of English bankruptcy proceedings.[150]

Partnership Ltd [1997] 3 All E.R. 31; *Tyburn Productions Ltd v Conan Doyle* [1990] 3 W.L.R. 167; and *Coin Controls Ltd v Suzo International (UK) Ltd* [1997] 3 All E.R. 45.

[146] *Inland Revenue Commissioners v Muller & Co's Margarines Ltd* [1901] A.C. 217, per Lord Macnaghten at 224. Contrast dissenting judgment of Lord Halsbury L.C. at 240; and *Reuter v Mulhens (No.2)* [1954] Ch. 50 at 95, 96.

[147] For a full treatment, see I.F. Fletcher, *Insolvency in Private International Law: National and International Approaches*, 2nd edn (Oxford: Oxford University Press, 2005), Supplement (2007).

[148] *Goetze v Aders and Co* (1874) 2 R. 100; *Bank of Scotland v Youde* (1908) 15 S.L.T. 847; and *Home's Trustee v Home's Trustees*, 1926 S.L.T. 214.

[149] *Re Artola Hermanos Ex. p Chale* (1890) L.R. 24 Q.B.D. 640; *Felixstowe Dock & Railway Co v United States Lines Inc* [1988] 2 All E.R. 77; and *Re Thulin* [1995] 1 W.L.R. 165.

[150] *Cheshire and North's Private International Law*, 12th edn (1992), p.907; and Smart, "Forum Non Conveniens in Bankruptcy Proceedings" [1989] J.B.L. 126.

Universality of bankruptcy

Under this principle, bankruptcy proceedings should receive extraterritorial **17–40** effect, and therefore, unless proceedings clearly conferred a territorially limited title on the trustee, they should be regarded as passing to the trustee all estate, moveable and immoveable, in the country where the bankruptcy was granted and all moveable estate (but not immoveable estate) abroad. At common law, both the Scots and English systems accepted the principle of universality, which is the logical result of the unity theory.[151] "Unity" and "universality" therefore mean, as has been well put, "one set of proceedings (unity) effective in every jurisdiction (universality)".[152]

Overview of regulatory schemes

There are four schemes of rules operative in Scottish courts to regulate **17–41** insolvency proceedings having a cross-border dimension, viz.:

(a)   The EU Insolvency Regulation: Council Regulation (EC) No.1346/2000 of 29 May 2000 on Insolvency Proceedings, to be repealed by Regulation (EU) 2015/848 of the European Parliament and of the Council of 20 May 2015 on insolvency proceedings (recast) ("Insolvency Regulation Recast");
(b)   Insolvency Act 1986 s.426;
(c)   Cross-Border Insolvency Regulations 2006,[153] giving force of law in Great Britain to the UNCITRAL Model Law on cross-border insolvency, as modified for application in Great Britain;[154] and
(d)   pre-existing Scottish conflict of laws rules.

The scope of each scheme of rules, and the manner in which the schemes interact, will be addressed below.

The EU Insolvency Regulation[155]

Non-application of rules of jurisdiction in Regulations 1215/2012 and 44/2001

Bankruptcy of individuals, and similar proceedings in relation to insolvent **17–42** companies, are excluded from the scope of the Brussels I Recast Regulation and its predecessor Regulation 44/2001.[156] However, a company winding up can

---

[151] In England, despite adherence to the separate bankruptcies theory, the status and claims of a foreign trustee would be accepted provided that there were no English proceedings.
[152] Donna McKenzie-Skene, "The EC Convention on Insolvency Proceedings" (1996) 4(3) E.R.P.L. 181.
[153] Cross-Border Insolvency Regulations 2006 (SI 2006/1030).
[154] Cross-Border Insolvency Regulations 2006 (SI 2006/1030), regs 1 and 2, and Sch.1.
[155] G. Moss, I. Fletcher and S. Isaacs, *The EC Regulation on Insolvency Proceedings: A Commentary and Annotated Guide*, 2nd edn (Oxford: Oxford University Press, 2009).
[156] Regulation 44/2001 art.1.2(b). *SCT Industri AB (In Liquidation) v Alpenblume AB* (C-111/08) [2009] I.L.Pr. 43; *Byers v Yacht Bull Corp* [2010] EWHC 133 (Ch); *German Graphics Graphische Maschinen GmbH v van der Schee* (C-292/08) [2010] I.L.Pr. 1; and *Polymer Vision R&D Ltd v Van*

occur when a company is solvent, as well as when insolvent, and in the former case, Brussels I Recast Regulation/ Regulation 44/2001, as appropriate, will apply, directing the matter by way of the exclusive jurisdiction provision[157] to the court which is defined for constitutional purposes as the "seat" of the company.[158]

Company winding-up is excluded from the intra-UK allocation effected by the Civil Jurisdiction and Judgments Acts 1982 and 1991 Sch.4,[159] and must be governed by the rules contained in the Insolvency Act 1986. Scottish rules of jurisdiction in respect of personal bankruptcy are contained in the Bankruptcy (Scotland) Act 1985 (q.v.).

Regulation 1346/2000

17–43   The Council of Europe produced in 1990 a Convention on Certain International Aspects of Bankruptcy (the Istanbul Convention). The Convention[160] was not signed by the UK, in view of anticipated EU intervention in this area,[161] and in time was overtaken by Council Regulation (EC) No.1346/2000 on Insolvency Proceedings, which came into force on 31 May 2002,[162] directly applicable in all EU Member States except Denmark,[163] with effect from that date.[164]

The aim of the Insolvency Regulation is to establish a framework, applicable to the insolvency of natural and legal persons, for the administration of insolvencies within the EU. After 31 May 2002, whenever the "centre of the debtor's main interests" (q.v.) is located within an EU Member State (excluding Denmark, but including the UK), proceedings must be regulated by the Regulation; this is a mandatory scheme. Where the debtor's centre of main interests is outside the EU, the Insolvency Regulation has no application.[165] Notably, in determining whether the Regulation applies, there is no general and absolute condition that there have to be cross-border elements; a fortiori, it is not

---

Dooren [2012] I.L.Pr. 14. Contrast *F-Tex SIA v Lietuvos-Anglijos UAB Jadecloud-Vilma* (C-213/10) ECJ (First Chamber) [2012] I.L.Pr. 24. See cases under the Brussels Convention such as *Gourdain v Nadler* [1979] E.C.R. 733 at [4]; and *Thoars' Judicial Factor v Ramlort Ltd*, 1998 G.W.D. 29-1504, in respect of which see note by E.B. Crawford, 1999 J.R. 203. By recital (7) of the Insolvency Regulation Recast, that instrument and Brussels I Recast Regulation are to be interpreted to avoid regulatory loopholes between the two instruments.

[157] Brussels I Recast art.24.2; and Brussels I Regulation art.22.2.

[158] Civil Jurisdiction and Judgments Acts 1982 and 1991 s.43; and Regulation 44/2001 art.60/Brussels I Recast art.63.

[159] Now Civil Jurisdiction and Judgments Order 2001 (SI 2001/3929).

[160] The Virgós-Schmit Report on the European Convention on Insolvency Proceedings was never formally adopted, but may be regarded as an authoritative commentary on the Convention and Regulation 1346/2000 which derives from it (*Re Olympic Airlines SA* [2013] EWCA Civ. 643, per Sir Bernard Rix at [19]).

[161] D. McKenzie-Skene, "The EC Convention on Insolvency Proceedings" (1996) 4(3) E.R.P.L. 181, 182, 183.

[162] Regulation 1346/2000 art.47.

[163] Regulation 1346/2000 recital (33).

[164] In *Re Staubitz-Schreiber* (C-104) [2006] I.L.Pr. 30, the ECJ held that the Insolvency Regulation was applicable if no judgment opening insolvency proceedings had been delivered before the Regulation's entry into force on 31 May 2002, albeit that the request to open proceedings was lodged prior to that date. On the other hand, in *SCT Industri AB (In Liquidation) v Alpenblume AB* (C-111/08) [2009] I.L.Pr. 43, the Insolvency Regulation was held not to apply since the insolvency proceedings had been opened before its entry into force.

[165] *HSBC Plc, Petitioner*, 2010 S.L.T. 281.

the case that for the Regulation to apply the circumstances must involve connecting factors with two or more Member States.[166]

In the manner of many EU instruments of recent years in the conflict of laws, the scheme of the Regulation is to provide harmonised rules of jurisdiction, which in turn justify rules of mutual recognition and enforcement of judgments. The Regulation contains also provisions as to applicable law, and cross-border co-operation where there is more than one set of bankruptcy proceedings. The Regulation is a compromise between the unity and territoriality approaches, to the effect that insolvency proceedings may be opened in more than one Member State, but only one set of proceedings can have extraterritorial effect. Any other proceedings will have only intra-territorial effect.

The Regulation applies to "collective insolvency proceedings which entail the partial or total divestment of a debtor and the appointment of a liquidator".[167] For the purposes of the UK, this comprises winding up by or subject to the supervision of the court; creditors' voluntary winding up with confirmation by the court; administration; voluntary arrangements under insolvency legislation; and bankruptcy or sequestration.[168] Notably, the Regulation does not apply to receivership since that essentially is an action at the instance of one creditor, and is not a collective procedure. Moreover, the Regulation shall not apply to insolvency proceedings concerning insurance undertakings, credit institutions, investment undertakings[169] which provide services involving the holding of funds or securities for third parties, or to collective investment undertakings.[170]

Jurisdiction rules under Regulation 1346/2000

Main proceedings (article 3)

The Regulation applies to any debtor having the centre of his main interests in a Member State.[171] The connecting factor of "centre of a debtor's main interests" (henceforth "COMI") is the crux of the matter; the COMI must first be identified, and found to be within the EU (except Denmark) before the Regulation applies.[172] As explained above, application of art.3.1 does not, as a general rule, depend on the existence of a cross-border link involving two or more Member States[173]; the somewhat paradoxical rationale is that to hold up proceedings until such time as the locations of various ancillary aspects are determined would

17–44

---

[166] *Schmid v Hertel* [2014] I.L.Pr. 11.
[167] Insolvency Regulation art.1(1).
[168] Regulation 1346/2000 Annex A.
[169] *Re Phoenix Kapitaldienst GmbH* [2008] B.P.I.R. 1082; and *Re HIH Casualty & General Insurance Ltd* [2008] UKHL 21.
[170] Insolvency Regulation art.1(2).
[171] *Skjevesland v Geveran Trading Co Ltd (No.4)* [2003] B.P.I.R. 924; *Re BRAC Rent-A-Car International Inc* [2003] EWHC 128; [2003] 1 W.L.R. 1421; *Re Salvage Association* [2003] EWHC 1028; *Re Daisytek-ISA Ltd* [2004] B.P.I.R. 30; *Re Eurofood IFSC Ltd* (C-341/04) [2006] Ch. 508; *France v Klempka* [2006] B.C.C. 841 Cour de Cassation (France); *Hans Brochier Holdings Ltd v Exner* [2006] EWHC 2594 (Ch); and *Re BenQ Mobile Holding BV (Amsterdam)* [2008] B.C.C. 489.
[172] Insolvency Regulation Preamble, recital (14). cf. *Official Receiver v Mitterfellner* [2009] B.P.I.R. 1075.
[173] *Schmid v Hertel* [2014] I.L.Pr. 11, paras [29]–[30].

frustrate the Regulation's objectives of efficiency and effectiveness of insolvency proceedings having cross-border effects.

The COMI, the key concept of the Regulation, must be interpreted in a uniform way by reference to EU law.[174] Article 3.1 provides that the courts of the Member State within the territory of which the COMI is situated shall have jurisdiction to open[175] insolvency proceedings (the "main proceedings"). Such jurisdiction confers competence to hear and determine actions which derive directly from the main proceedings and are closely connected to them.[176] This means that the Regulation may affect a company incorporated outside the EU as long as the COMI is situated within the EU.[177]

Determination of the COMI will necessitate a detailed factual inquiry.[178] While there is no conclusive definition of this important connecting factor, identification is assisted by the provision in art.3.1 of a presumption that, with regard to companies and legal persons, the place of the registered office shall be presumed to be the COMI, in the absence of proof to the contrary.[179] That presumption can be rebutted only by factors that are both objective and ascertainable by third parties, i.e. potential creditors.[180] Where a debtor company is a subsidiary company whose registered office and that of its parent company are situated in different Member States, the presumption that the COMI of the subsidiary is situated in the Member State in which its registered office is situated can be rebutted only if factors, objective and ascertainable by third parties, enable it to be established that the actuality is different from that which location at that registered office is deemed to reflect.[181] If a party seeks to establish that a company or legal person has its COMI at a place other than its registered office, then the court will examine the "totality of evidence",[182] including the location of the company's bank account, the place of preparation of financial statements, and the place of employment of the majority of employees.[183]

---

[174] *Interedil Srl (in liquidation) v Fallimento Interedil Srl* (Case C/396/09) [2011] W.L.R. (D) 334.

[175] *Re Eurofood IFSC Ltd* [2006] Ch. 508.

[176] *Seagon v Deko Marty Belgium NV* (C-339/07) [2009] I.L.Pr. 25, in which the German court was thereby enabled to set aside a transaction on the grounds of insolvency of the debtor against a defendant having its statutory seat in Belgium; and *Re Jurisdiction to Set Aside a Transaction on Grounds of Insolvency* [2010] I.L.Pr. 6.

[177] Insolvency Regulation recital (14).

[178] e.g. *Re Ci4Net.com.Inc* [2004] EWHC 1941 (Ch).

[179] *Re Stanford International Bank Ltd (in receivership)* [2011] Ch. 33; and *Interedil Srl (in liquidation) v Fallimento Interedil Srl* (Case C/396/09) [2011] W.L.R. (D) 334.

[180] *Re Eurofood IFSC Ltd* [2006] Ch. 508; and *Re Stanford International Bank Ltd (in receivership)* [2011] Ch. 33.

[181] *Re Eurofood IFSC Ltd* [2006] Ch. 508. Contrast *MPOTEC GmbH* [2006] B.C.C. 681 *Tribunal de Grande Instance* (Nanterre); and *Re Energotech Sarl* [2007] B.C.C. 123 *Tribunal de Grande Instance* (France) (relevant factors included the location of board meetings and of creditors, and locus of dealings with clients). As to a global group of companies, see *Bank of America NA v Minister for Productive Industries* [2008] I.L.Pr. 25 *Consiglio di Stato* (Italy); *Re Nortel Networks SA* [2009] EWHC 1482 (Ch); and *Re Lennox Holdings Plc* [2009] B.C.C. 155.

[182] *Hans Brochier Holdings Ltd v Exner* [2006] EWHC 2594 (Ch); and *Sparkasse Hilden Ratingen Velbert v Benk* [2012] EWHC 2432 (Ch).

[183] e.g. *Re Daisytek-ISA Ltd* [2004] B.P.I.R. 30, which concerned a petition for administration orders to be made in an English court in respect of the English holding company of a pan-European group of companies, many of the members of which had registered offices in France and Germany. The English court had to perform a balancing exercise, assessing the size and importance of interests administered in England and elsewhere, respectively. The court held that there was sufficient evidence to rebut the

There is no presumption in relation to individuals, but recital (13) indicates that the COMI should correspond to the place where the debtor conducts the administration of his interests on a regular basis, being therefore ascertainable by third parties.[184]

Although a debtor reasonably may be held to have interests in one, or more than one, Member State(s), the Regulation does not apply unless one of these business bases can be said to be the "centre" of his interests. The criterion assumes in law that a debtor has only one centre of main business interests,[185] but this might not always be the case in fact. In principle, the COMI of an individual, who is neither a professional nor someone carrying on business in his own right, is his place of habitual residence.[186]

There is no temporal element in the COMI criterion as set out in art.3.1, a fact which may generate problems given that in business one would expect to find that the COMI of an individual or company might change over time. This issue was met with in *Shierson v Vlieland-Boddy*,[187] in which the English court recognised the fact that the debtor's COMI had moved from England to Spain. The Court of Appeal held that the debtor's COMI was to be determined at the time when the court was required to decide whether to open insolvency proceedings and in the light of the facts as they were at the relevant time, which included historical facts. Moreover, the court held that it was important to have regard not only to what the debtor was doing, but also to what he was perceived to be doing by an objective observer, and to have regard to the need for an element of permanence. In this regard, the place where the debtor lives and has his home is likely to be relevant to a determination of where s/he conducts the administration of his interests. The court in *Shierson* took the view that there is no principle of immutability, and that a debtor should be free to choose where he carries on activities falling within the concept of administration of his interests. Since such a decision might be made for a self-serving purpose, for example, to alter the insolvency rules which would apply to him in respect of existing debts, the court would need to scrutinise the facts which are said to give rise to a change in the COMI, and be satisfied that a change in the place where the activities which fell within the concept of "administration of his interests" were carried on was based on substance and not an illusion. In 2014 the CJEU in *Schmid v Hertel*[188] confirmed that in order to determine which court had jurisdiction to open insolvency proceedings, the COMI had to be determined at the time when the request to open insolvency proceedings was lodged.

---

presumption that the place of the registered office was the COMI, with the result that the English forum was competent. A large majority of potential creditors by value was aware that many important functions of the group companies were carried out in England.

[184] cf. *X v Fortis Bank (Nederland) NV* [2004] I.L.Pr. 37 Hoge Raad (NL).

[185] G. Maher and B. Rodger, "Jurisdiction in Insolvency Proceedings" (2003) 48 J.L.S.S. 26, 30.

[186] *Stojevic v Komercni Banka AS* [2006] EWHC 3447 (Ch); and *O'Donnell v Bank of Ireland* [2012] EWHC 3749 (Ch).

[187] *Shierson v Vlieland-Boddy* [2005] 1 W.L.R. 3966. Followed in *Cross Construction Sussex Ltd v Tseliki* [2006] EWHC 1056 (Ch); *Official Receiver v Eichler* [2007] B.P.I.R. 1636; and *Official Receiver v Mitterfellner* [2009] B.P.I.R. 1075.

[188] *Schmid v Hertel* [2014] I.L.Pr.11. Further, the Court held that jurisdiction conferred on the courts of COMI included international jurisdiction to hear and determine actions which derived directly from those proceedings and were closely connected with them, irrespective of whether the persons against whom the actions were brought were resident in another Member State or in a third country.

In *Re Opening of Insolvency Proceedings*,[189] the Bundesgerichtshof decided to refer to the ECJ the question whether the court of the Member State which receives a request for the opening of insolvency proceedings retains jurisdiction to open insolvency proceedings if the debtor moves his/her COMI to the territory of another Member State after filing the request, but before the proceedings are opened, or whether the court of that other Member State acquires jurisdiction. The ECJ responded, in *Staubitz-Schreiber*,[190] to the effect that art.3.1 must be interpreted as meaning that the court of the Member State within which the COMI is situated at the time when the request is lodged to open insolvency proceedings retains jurisdiction to open those proceedings if the debtor moves the COMI to another Member State after the request has been lodged, but before the proceedings are opened.

Averments as to jurisdiction must acknowledge the primacy of the Regulation, and in a qualifying petition at the outset must aver that the COMI is in the forum petitioned.

Allocation of jurisdiction within the UK

17–45 The rules of jurisdiction set out in the Insolvency Regulation establish only international jurisdiction, i.e. they designate the Member State the courts of which may open insolvency proceedings. Territorial jurisdiction within that Member State must be established by the national law of the Member State concerned.[191] In other words, if the debtor's COMI is found to be in the UK, "UK national law" must determine the further allocation among the legal systems of the UK.

There is no set of rules equivalent to the Civil Jurisdiction and Judgments Act 1982 Sch.4 to serve to allocate jurisdiction among the courts of the constituent units of the UK. Assuming it can be established that the COMI is in the UK, the allocation thereafter will be done according to the pre-existing (i.e. non-Regulation) domestic insolvency rules (q.v.).[192]

Secondary proceedings

17–46 To protect the diversity of interests, the Regulation allows "secondary proceedings" to be opened in parallel with the main proceedings.[193] Jurisdiction in respect of secondary proceedings is conferred upon the legal system of a Member State in which the debtor has an "establishment", meaning "any place of operations where the debtor carries out a non-transitory economic activity with human means and goods".[194] The mere presence of assets in a Member State will

---

[189] *Re Opening of Insolvency Proceedings* (IX ZB 418/02) [2005] I.L.Pr. 4 Bundesgerichtshof (Germany).

[190] *Re Staubitz-Schreiber* (C-104) [2006] I.L.Pr. 30.

[191] Insolvency Regulation recital (15).

[192] G. Maher and B. Rodger, *Civil Jurisdiction in the Scottish Courts* (W. Green, 2010), para.11–13.

[193] Insolvency Regulation art.27. e.g. *Bank Handlowy w Warszawie SA v Christianapol sp z oo* (C-116/11) [2013] I.L.Pr. 21.

[194] Insolvency Regulation art.2(h). Sir Bernard Rix, in *Re Olympic Airlines SA* [2013] EWCA Civ 643 (affirmed in Supreme Court: [2015] UKSC 27) at [19], places some reliance on the Virgós-Schmit commentary (para.71) in respect of the meaning of "establishment".

not be sufficient to confer secondary jurisdiction. The issue of whether or not a debtor has an "establishment" for this purpose arises at the date on which the jurisdiction of the insolvency court is invoked.[195] There must be an element of permanence to the establishment, though the existence of a branch office is not necessary. More than one set of secondary proceedings may take place concurrently. Secondary insolvency proceedings, as well as protecting local interests, serve a useful purpose in cases of complex estates which are difficult to administer as a unit, or where there is wide variation in the laws of the jurisdictions in which the debtor has assets. The liquidator in the main proceedings may request the opening of secondary proceedings if it seems to him that the efficient administration of the estate so requires.[196]

Effect of main and secondary proceedings

The main proceedings have extraterritorial effect, encompassing all of the debtor's assets. Article 3.1, therefore, can be seen to enshrine the principle of universality.

17–47

The effect of secondary proceedings is limited to assets situated within the Member State in which they are opened (i.e. they have intra-territorial effect only).

Given the different consequences attaching to main and secondary proceedings, respectively, it is important for a court to make clear the capacity in which it is acting.

If the COMI is situated in another Member State, main proceedings cannot be opened in Scotland, even though jurisdiction appears to exist in terms of pre-existing Scottish conflict of laws rules, e.g. where the registered office of an insolvent company is in Scotland. The jurisdiction of the Member State where the debtor's main interests are centred obliterates the jurisdiction otherwise available to the Scots court under its residual national rules, but without prejudice to the jurisdiction of the Scots court in relation to secondary proceedings under the Insolvency Regulation.

Relationship between main and secondary proceedings

There must be co-operation between the liquidator in the main proceedings and the liquidator(s) in the secondary proceedings (art.31).[197] A creditor may lodge his claim both in the main proceedings and in any secondary proceedings (art.32). The main liquidator can request that the secondary proceedings be stayed (art.33). The stay will be refused only if the stay is manifestly of no interest to the creditors in the main proceedings. In the event of a stay, the main liquidator must guarantee the interests of creditors in the secondary proceedings. Any surplus assets in the state of secondary proceedings following payment of claims in that state must be remitted to the main liquidator (art.35).

17–48

---

[195] *Re Olympic Airlines SA* [2015] UKSC 27.
[196] Insolvency Regulation Preamble, recital (19).
[197] In *Bank Handlowy w Warszawie SA v Christianapol sp z oo* (C-116/11) [2013] I.L.Pr. 21, the ECJ referred to principles of "sincere co-operation" and "mandatory co-ordination" between the courts in which the main and secondary proceedings, respectively, are opened. Assistance from the courts of other Member States also may require to be sought: *Re Nortel Networks SA* [2009] I.L.Pr. 42.

Choice of law rules under Regulation 1346/2000 (articles 4 and 28)

17–49   The Regulation harmonises conflict rules, not substantive rules. Article 4 directs that the applicable law shall be the law of the state in which the proceedings (main[198] or secondary,[199] respectively) are opened. In other words, the opening, conduct and closure of the proceedings[200] will be conducted according to the law of the forum, termed the "*lex concursus*".

More importantly, under art.4.2 the *lex concursus* also determines many essential matters, including the ascertainment of assets and liabilities[201]; the lodging and verification of claims; the ranking of claims; distribution of proceedings; the debtor's and liquidator's powers; the effects of the insolvency proceedings on contracts to which the debtor is a party and on proceedings brought by individual creditors[202]; any protection afforded by legal professional privilege[203]; the conditions for, and effects of, closure of insolvency proceedings (in particular by composition); and creditors' rights after closure.

Articles 5–15

17–50   Account must be taken of arts 5–15 which prescribe, by way of exception to arts 4 and 28, the circumstances in which certain other laws shall take precedence over the *lex concursus*. For example, the effect of insolvency proceedings on a contract conferring the right to acquire or make use of immoveable property shall be governed solely by the law of the state in which that property is situated[204]; and their effect upon employment contracts shall be governed solely by the law of the state applicable to the contract of employment.[205] It is obvious that the admission of a claim, if contractual, depends upon the validity of the claim according to its own (contractual) governing law, each EU forum applying to this question the relevant provisions, if applicable, of the Rome I Regulation.

More complex is art.7, which provides that the opening of insolvency proceedings against the purchaser of an asset shall not affect the seller's rights based on a reservation of title where, at the time of opening proceedings, the asset is situated within the territory of a Member State other than the state of opening proceedings. This rule gives precedence, therefore, to the *lex situs*, where it differs from the *lex concursus*.[206] Similarly, by art.5 (third parties' rights in rem), the opening of insolvency proceedings shall not affect the rights in rem of creditors or third parties in respect of assets (of all types) belonging to the debtor which are situated at that date within the territory of another Member State.

---

[198]   Insolvency Regulation art.4. *Also MG Probud Gdynia sp z oo* (C-444/07) [2010] B.C.C. 453.
[199]   Insolvency Regulation art.28.
[200]   Insolvency Regulation recital (23).
[201]   *German Graphics Graphische Maschinen GmbH v van der Schee* (C-292/08) [2010] I.L.Pr. 1.
[202]   *Syska v Vivendi Universal SA* [2009] EWCA Civ 677.
[203]   *Re Hellas Telecommunications (Luxembourg) II S.C.A.* unreported Companies Court (Chancery Division), 24 July 2013.
[204]   Insolvency Regulation art.8 and recital (25).
[205]   Insolvency Regulation art.10 and recital (28).
[206]   Contrast the situation in *German Graphics Graphische Maschinen GmbH v van der Schee* (C-292/08) [2010] I.L.Pr. 1, in which German Graphics' assets, over which a reservation of title existed, were situated at the time of opening of insolvency proceedings in the Netherlands, the same Member State in which those proceedings had been opened.

Articles 5–15 represent substantial, albeit defensible, derogations from the basic *lex concursus* rule.

Recognition rules under Regulation 1346/2000 (articles 16–26)

The principle in art.16 is that any judgment opening[207] insolvency proceedings handed down by a court of a Member State having jurisdiction under art.3 shall be recognised in all the other Member States without those other Member States being able to review the jurisdiction of the court of the "opening State".[208] Recognition of proceedings, however, shall not preclude the opening in another Member State of secondary proceedings.[209] Article 25 lays down the principle of mutual recognition of judgments concerning the course and closure of insolvency proceedings. Grounds for non-recognition are minimal. In terms of art.26, a state may refuse to recognise the opening of insolvency proceedings, or a judgment from such proceedings, only if it is manifestly contrary to its own public policy.[210]

    One notable exception to the "revenue law exception"[211] (that revenue collection is local and cannot be enforced extra-territorially), which arises as a result of the promotion of equal treatment of creditors, is the recognition of the entitlement of tax authorities and social security authorities domiciled, habitually resident or having a registered office in a Member State other than the state of the opening of proceedings, to lodge claims in writing in any proceedings (art.39).

    In terms of art.40, when insolvency proceedings are opened in a Member State, there is a duty upon the court of that state having jurisdiction, or the liquidator appointed by it, immediately to inform known creditors having their habitual residence, domicile, or registered office in other Member States, of the opening of such proceedings. This seems hardly capable of being satisfied; not only in a complex case are assets and creditors, known and unknown, likely to be found in more than one Member State so that provisions such as art.40 seem unrealistic of attainment even within Europe, but also assets and/or creditors may exist outside Europe, so that there will be an uneasy co-existence between the EU regulated area and pre-existing national rules.

17–51

Review and reform of Regulation 1346/2000

Pursuant to art.46 of Regulation 1346/2000, in December 2012 the European Commission published its Report to the European Parliament, the Council and

17–52

---

[207] The ECJ in *Re Eurofood IFSC Ltd* [2006] Ch. 508 held that the appointment of a provisional liquidator, involving the divestment of the debtor of his powers of management over his assets, amounted to the "opening" of insolvency proceedings.

[208] *Re Eurofood IFSC Ltd* [2006] Ch. 508. Any challenge to jurisdiction must be made to the court in which it is sought to open proceedings: *France v Klempka (Administrator of ISA Daisytek SAS)* [2006] B.C.C. 841. Also *MG Probud Gdynia sp z oo* (C-444/07) [2010] B.C.C. 453. For discussion of relationship of art.16 with recognition provisions of the Brussels I Regulation, see *German Graphics Graphische Maschinen GmbH v van der Schee* (C-292/08) [2010] I.L.Pr. 1.

[209] *Re Nortel Networks SA* [2009] EWHC 1482 (Ch).

[210] *Re Eurofood IFSC Ltd* [2006] Ch. 508 at [62]–[64]; and *MG Probud Gdynia sp z oo* (C-444/07) [2010] B.C.C. 453. But see *France v Klempka (Administrator of ISA Daisytek SAS)* [2006] B.C.C. 841.

[211] Ch.3, above.

the European Economic and Social Committee on the application of Council Regulation (EC) No 1346/2000.[212] The Commission's conclusion was that "the Regulation is generally regarded as a successful instrument."[213] Various shortcomings,[214] however, were identified in relation to the operation of the Regulation in practice, namely:

— the scope of the Regulation: the Regulation does not extend to national procedures which provide for company restructuring at a pre-insolvency stage ("pre-insolvency proceedings") or to proceedings which leave existing management in place ("hybrid proceedings").

— the rules on jurisdiction: while there is wide support for granting jurisdiction to open main proceedings to the Member State where the debtor's COMI is located, the concept has proved difficult to apply in practice, giving rise, in particular, to "bankruptcy-forum shopping" by means of abusive COMI-relocation.

— the relationship between main and secondary proceedings: the opening of secondary proceedings has the effect that the liquidator in the main proceedings no longer has control over assets located in the other Member State, rendering more difficult the sale of the debtor on a going concern basis.

— the publicity of insolvency-related decisions and the lodging of claims: there is no mandatory publication or registration of the decisions in the Member States where proceedings are opened, nor in Member States where there is an establishment. Judges and creditors alike ought to be better apprised of proceedings which have commenced elsewhere.

— the absence of specific rules for the insolvency of members of a group of companies: the basic premise of the Regulation is that separate proceedings should be opened for each individual member of a corporate group. "The lack of specific provisions for group insolvency often diminishes the prospects of successful restructuring of the group as a whole and may lead to a break-up of the group in its constituting parts".[215]

The Commission proposed to modernise the rules, to shift focus from liquidation to develop a new approach to help businesses overcome financial difficulties and to rescue economically viable debtors, while simultaneously protecting creditors' rights to recover their money. There was a strong desire on the part of the Commission and Member States to improve the framework for resolving cross-border insolvency cases to ensure the smooth functioning of the internal market, and to make it more resilient in times of economic crisis.[216]

---

[212] COM(2012) 743 Final (Strasbourg, 12.12.2012).

[213] COM(2012) 743 Final (Strasbourg, 12.12.2012), para.1.2.

[214] Proposal for a Regulation of the European Parliament and of the Council amending Council Regulation (EC) No 1346/2000 on insolvency proceedings (COM/2012/0744 final 2012/0360 (COD) (Strasbourg, 12.12.2012), para.1.2.

[215] Proposal for a Regulation of the European Parliament and of the Council amending Council Regulation (EC) No 1346/2000 on insolvency proceedings (COM/2012/0744 final 2012/0360 (COD) (Strasbourg, 12.12.2012).

[216] Proposal for a Regulation of the European Parliament and of the Council amending Council Regulation (EC) No 1346/2000 on insolvency proceedings (COM/2012/0744 final 2012/0360 (COD) (Strasbourg, 12.12.2012). See also Communication from the Commission to the European Parliament,

Insolvency Regulation Recast

Regulation (EU) 2015/848 of the European Parliament and of the Council of 20 **17–53**
May 2015 on insolvency proceedings (recast) was published on 5 June 2015.[217]
By virtue of art 91 of that instrument, Regulation (EC) No.1346/2000 is repealed.
All references to the repealed Regulation shall be construed as references to the
Insolvency Regulation Recast, and are to be read in accordance with the
correlation table set out in Annex D to the recast instrument. The Insolvency
Regulation Recast entered into force on 26 June 2015, and, in terms of art 92,
shall apply, in the main, from 26 June 2017.

The UK, having opted in to the proposal to revise Regulation 1346/2000,[218]
recital (87) of the recast instrument makes clear that, in accordance with Protocol
No.21 on the position of the UK and Ireland in respect of the area of freedom,
security and justice, those countries are taking part in the adoption and
application of the Recast Regulation.

Recital (10) articulates that the scope of the Recast Regulation extends to
"proceedings which promote the rescue of economically viable but distressed
businesses and which give a second chance to entrepreneurs. It should, in
particular, extend to proceedings which provide for restructuring of a debtor at a
stage where there is only a likelihood of insolvency, and to proceedings which
leave the debtor fully or partially in control of its assets and affairs. It should also
extend to proceedings providing for a debt discharge or a debt adjustment in
relation to consumers and self- employed persons, for example by reducing the
amount to be paid by the debtor or by extending the payment period granted to
the debtor. Since such proceedings do not necessarily entail the appointment of an
insolvency practitioner, they should be covered by this Regulation if they take
place under the control or supervision of a court." Similarly, by recital (11) the
Recast Regulation applies to "procedures which grant a temporary stay on
enforcement actions brought by individual creditors where such actions could
adversely affect negotiations and hamper the prospects of a restructuring of the
debtor's business."

---

the Council and the European Economic and Social Committee: "A new European approach to
business failure and insolvency" (COM(2012) 742 final) (Strasbourg, 12.12.2012). The Communication noted that the Commission was proposing the modernisation of Regulation 1436/2000, and that
the changes suggested affect only cross-border cases. The Communication highlighted areas where
differences among domestic insolvency laws, in the Commission's view, have "the greatest potential
to hamper the establishment of an efficient insolvency legal framework in the internal market" and
sought to identify the issues, on which the new European approach to business failure and insolvency
should focus so as to develop the rescue and recovery culture across the Member States. See further
Commission Recommendation on a new approach to business failure and insolvency (C(2014) 1500
final) (Brussels, 12.3.2014)).
[217] OJ L141/19 (5.6.2015).
[218] On 15 April 2013, the Parliamentary Under-Secretary of State for Business, Innovation and Skills
(Jo Swinson) confirmed in a written ministerial statement that the UK would opt-in to the Regulation:
"... the proposed amendments to the Insolvency Regulation will benefit UK businesses affected by
insolvency in the EU. The proposals support business rescue by expanding the scope of the
Regulation to restructuring and pre-insolvency proceedings. Bankruptcy tourism will be tackled
through new rules on determining jurisdiction and increased transparency for creditors. In addition,
the proposals include new rules on publication of insolvency information via free online registers
across the EU, in line with our Digital by Default strategy ...". (15 Apr 2013: Column 1WS).

With regard to jurisdiction, art.3(1) strengthens the definition of the 'centre of main interests' by providing in the body of the instrument, rather than in the shade of the recitals[219] that, "the centre of main interests shall be the place where the debtor conducts the administration of its interests on a regular basis and which is ascertainable by third parties." The presumption regarding the COMI of a company or legal person continues to apply, but only if the registered office has not been moved to another Member State within the three-month period prior to the request for the opening of insolvency proceedings. A presumptive definition has been inserted regarding the COMI of an individual exercising an independent business or professional activity: the COMI shall be presumed to be that individual's principal place of business in the absence of proof to the contrary (as in the case of companies and legal persons, the presumption applying only if the individual's principal place of business has not been moved to another Member State within the three-month period prior to the request for the opening of insolvency proceedings). In the case of any other individual, the COMI shall be presumed to be the place of the individual's habitual residence in the absence of proof to the contrary. This last presumption shall only apply if the habitual residence has not been moved to another Member State within the six-month period prior to the request for the opening of insolvency proceedings.

A balance is to be struck between preventing fraudulent or abusive forum shopping and preserving freedom of movement on the part of the debtor, including the ability to re-structure in the place that best serves the creditors' interest. The time limits imposed in art.3 of the Recast Regulation have the objective, as narrated by recitals (29) to (31), of preventing forum shopping. Importantly, per art.4.1, a court seised of a request to open insolvency proceedings is required, of its own motion, to examine whether or not there exists a valid ground of jurisdiction pursuant to art.3. To buttress this, a judgment opening insolvency proceedings must specify the grounds on which the jurisdiction of the court is based.

Co-operation between main and secondary proceedings has been enhanced. In relation to secondary proceedings, recognising that secondary insolvency proceedings may hamper the efficient administration of the insolvency estate,[220] the Recast Regulation aims to secure a more efficient administration of proceedings by enabling a court to refuse the opening of secondary proceedings if they are not necessary to protect the interests of local creditors,[221] or to provide for a temporary stay of such proceedings.[222] Further, the requirement that secondary proceedings must be winding-up proceedings has been abolished.[223]

With regard to publicity of proceedings and the lodging of claims, the Recast Regulation, in arts 24 to 27, requires Member States to establish and maintain public "insolvency registers" in order to improve the provision of information to relevant creditors and courts, and to prevent the opening of parallel insolvency proceedings. In order to facilitate access to that information for creditors and courts domiciled or located in other Member States, this Recast Regulation requires the publication of relevant court decisions in cross-border insolvency

---

[219] cf. Recital (13), Regulation 1346/2000.
[220] Recital (41), Recast Regulation.
[221] Art.36 and recital (42), Recast Regulation.
[222] Art.38 and recital (45), Recast Regulation.
[223] cf. art.3.3, Regulation 1346/2000 and art.3.3, Recast Regulation.

cases in a publicly accessible electronic register, and provides for the interconnection of national insolvency registers.[224]

Finally, the Recast Regulation, arts 56 to 58 and Recitals (51) to (62), provides for the co-ordination of insolvency proceedings concerning different members of a corporate group by obliging the liquidators and courts involved in different sets of main proceedings to co-operate and communicate with each other.

Insolvency Act 1986 section 426

Council Regulation (EC) No.1346/2000 of 29 May 2000 on Insolvency Proceedings is pre-eminent. However, art.44(3)(b) provides that the Regulation shall not apply in the UK to the extent that is irreconcilable with the obligations arising in relation to bankruptcy and the winding-up of insolvent companies from any arrangements with the Commonwealth existing at the time the Regulation entered into force. In effect, this preserves the operation of s.426 of the Insolvency Act 1986, entitled "Co-operation between courts exercising jurisdiction in relation to insolvency".

17–54

Section 426 provides for reciprocal recognition of insolvency proceedings in the constituent parts of the UK,[225] and for an element of international co-operation. By s.426(1), an order made by any UK court in insolvency proceedings shall be enforced in any other part of the UK as if it were made by a court in the legal system addressed. However, s.426(2) provides that nothing in subs.(1) requires a court in any part of the UK to enforce, in relation to property situated in that part, any order made by a court in any other part of the UK. Further, by s.426(4) the courts having jurisdiction in relation to insolvency law in any part of the UK shall assist the courts having the corresponding jurisdiction in any other part of the UK[226] or in any "relevant country or territory".[227] By s.426(11), "relevant country or territory" means (a) any of the Channel Islands or the Isle of Man; or (b) any country or territory designated for the purposes of s.426 by the Secretary of State by order made by statutory instrument.[228]

Within the UK, there is also mutual recognition of receivers in terms of the Insolvency Act 1986 s.72.

---

[224] Recital (76).

[225] *Gerrard, Petitioner,* 2009 S.C. 593; and *KPMG LLP v Hill* unreported 20 January 2012.

[226] Such help always was available at common law: e.g. *Re Kooperman* [1928] W.N. 101; *Obers v Paton's Trustees (No.3)* (1897) 24 R. 719. See, generally, *Cheshire and North's Private International Law,* 12th edn (1992), pp.915, 916.

[227] Section 426(5) provides that for the purposes of s.426(4), a request made is authority for the requested court to apply, in relation to any matter specified in the request, the insolvency law which is applicable by either court in relation to comparable matters falling within its jurisdiction. Section 426(5) concludes, "In exercising its discretion…a court shall have regard in particular to the rules of private international law". See, e.g. *Re HIH Casualty & General Insurance Ltd* [2008] UKHL 21; *Rubin v Eurofinance SA and New Cap Reinsurance Corp Ltd (in Liquidation) v Grant* [2013] 1 A.C. 236; *McKinnon v Graham* [2013] EWHC 2870 (Ch.); and *In re Tambrook Jersey Ltd* [2014] Ch. 252.

[228] Designated countries, per Co-operation of Insolvency Courts (Designation of Relevant Countries and Territories) Order 1986 (SI 1986/2123), currently are: Anguilla, Australia, The Bahamas, Bermuda, Botswana, Canada, Cayman Islands, Falkland Islands, Gibraltar, Hong Kong, Republic Of Ireland, Montserrat, New Zealand, St. Helena, Turks and Caicos Islands, Tuvalu, Virgin Islands.

The Cross-Border Insolvency Regulations 2006[229]

17–55   In 1997 UNCITRAL adopted a Model Law on Cross-Border Insolvency, offering a legislative framework for adoption by states, and designed to assist states to equip their insolvency laws with a modern, harmonised and fair framework to address more effectively instances of cross-border insolvency.[230] By virtue of the 2006 Regulations, this Model Law was adopted, with certain modifications,[231] for Great Britain, and applies where:

(a)   assistance is sought in Great Britain by a foreign court or a foreign representative in connection with a foreign proceeding; or

(b)   assistance is sought in a foreign State in connection with a proceeding under British insolvency law; or

(c)   a foreign proceeding and a proceeding under British insolvency law in respect of the same debtor are taking place concurrently; or

(d)   creditors or other interested persons in a foreign State have an interest in requesting the commencement of, or participating in, a proceeding under British insolvency law.[232]

By inference, the provisions of the Model Law do not extend to the recognition or enforcement in one British court of insolvency proceedings in another British court, or to the recognition of an insolvency order made in another British court.[233] However, reg.7 of the 2006 Regulations provides that an order made by a court in either part of Great Britain in the exercise of jurisdiction in relation to insolvency proceedings shall be enforced in the other part of Great Britain as if it were made by a court exercising the corresponding jurisdiction in that other part.

In a sense, the Model Law overlaps in content with the rules in Regulation 1346/2000, though in scope the EC Regulation is limited to the co-ordination of insolvency proceedings within the EU, i.e. where the debtor's COMI is situated within the EU. To the extent that the Model Law conflicts with any obligation of the UK under the EC Insolvency Regulation, the requirements of that EC Regulation prevail.[234] The Model Law seeks to provide a complementary regime of regulation and co-operation where the debtor's COMI is outside the EU:

---

[229] Cross-Border Insolvency Regulations 2006 (SI 2006/1030) (entry into force 4 April 2006) ("the 2006 Regulations"). See also Act of Sederunt (Rules of the Court of Session Amendment No.2) (UNCITRAL Model Law on Cross-Border Insolvency) 2006 (SSI 2006/199); Act of Sederunt (Sheriff Court Bankruptcy Rules 1996) Amendment (UNCITRAL Model Law on Cross-Border Insolvency) 2006 (SSI 2006/197); and Act of Sederunt (Sheriff Court Company Insolvency Rules 1996) Amendment (UNCITRAL Model Law on Cross-Border Insolvency) 2006 (SSI 2006/200).

[230] Explanatory memorandum to 2006 Regulations, para.2.1.

[231] 2006 Regulations reg.2(1).

[232] 2006 Regulations Sch.1 art.1(1).

[233] *Gerrard, Petitioner,* 2009 S.L.T.659, per Lord Glennie at [6].

[234] 2006 Regulations Sch.1 art.3.On the question of the interaction among the EC Insolvency Regulation, the Model Law and pre-existing UK law, see Anton with Beaumont, *Private International Law*, 3rd edn (2011), paras.25.168 – 25.175. Further, see *Re Olympic Airlines SA* [2013] EWCA Civ. 643, per Sir Bernard Rix at [18]–[20].

"This will place Great Britain, by virtue of the operation of section 426 of the Insolvency Act 1986 in the unique position of having a suite of statutory procedures available in cross-border insolvency cases, as well as the flexibility of common law."[235]

By reg.3(1) of the 2006 Regulations, "British insolvency law" shall apply,[236] with such modification as the context requires, for the purpose of giving effect to the provisions of the 2006 Regulations, though by reg.3(2) in the case of conflict between any provision of "British insolvency law" or Pt 3 of the Insolvency Act 1986 and the 2006 Regulations, the latter shall prevail.

In terms of the Model Law, the person administering a foreign insolvency may initiate an insolvency proceeding in Great Britain in relation to a debtor who is the subject of the foreign proceedings, and may participate in those British proceedings regarding that debtor.[237] Essentially, the purpose of the Model Law is to "enable a foreign office holder to use British insolvency law to obtain the same relief against persons located in Great Britain as if the insolvency were one that was commenced and continued in [Great Britain]."[238]

The Model Law does not address jurisdiction to open insolvency proceedings. Rather, art.4 ("Competent Court") designates the Court of Session as the court in Scotland having jurisdiction to exercise the function of recognising foreign proceedings and securing suitable co-operation with foreign courts.[239] The Model Law establishes criteria for deciding whether foreign insolvency proceedings are to be recognised,[240] and if so, whether as "main" or "non-main" proceedings (depending on whether the foreign proceedings are taking place in the country where the main operations of the debtor are located[241]); and sets out the effects of recognition, and the relief available to a foreign representative.

A British court may grant discretionary relief for the benefit of any recognised foreign proceedings,[242] although it must be satisfied that the interests of local creditors are adequately protected. Recognition of foreign proceedings does not prevent local creditors from initiating or continuing insolvency proceedings in Britain concerning the same debtor.

Rules also are provided to permit foreign creditors to commence and participate in insolvency proceedings in Britain. The Model Law seeks

---

[235] Explanatory Memorandum to 2006 Regulations, para.7.4. See *Re HIH Casualty and General Insurance Ltd* [2008] UKHL 21.

[236] Guidance in practical matters as to the operation of the 2006 Regulations is to be found in *Re Rajapakse* [2007] B.P.I.R. 99.

[237] With regard to definition of debtor, see *Rubin v Eurofinance SA* [2009] EWHC 2129 (Ch) (and later on appeal at 2013] 1 A.C. 236) Strauss Q.C. held that it would be perverse, and parochial, to give the word "debtor" any other meaning than that given to it by the foreign court in the foreign proceedings. Therefore, a trust was a debtor for the purposes of the 2006 Regulations and the Model Law, even though by English law it had no legal personality as an individual or a body corporate.

[238] *Akers v Samba Financial Group* [2014] EWHC 540 (Ch), per Sir Terence Etherton at [6] (reversed [2014] EWCA Civ 1516).

[239] Article 2 defines, inter alia "foreign court", "foreign main proceeding", "foreign non-main proceeding" and "foreign proceeding".

[240] 2006 Regulations Sch.1 Ch.III; *Re Stanford International Bank Ltd (In Receivership)* [2011] Ch. 33.

[241] 2006 Regulations Sch.1 art.17(2); *Rubin v Eurofinance SA* [2011] Ch. 133 (and see, on appeal, [2012] UKSC 46).

[242] *Re Pan Ocean Co Ltd* [2014] EWHC 2124 (Ch).

co-ordination between courts in different states in relation to concurrent insolvency proceedings concerning the same debtor, and authorises courts in one state to seek assistance from courts and representatives in another.[243]

Pre-existing Scots conflict of laws rules for cross-border insolvencies

17–56   The pre-existing Scots conflict of laws rules will be invoked in two sets of circumstances:

(a)   where the centre of a debtor's main interests is situated in the UK and territorial jurisdiction in one legal system of the UK requires to be established under Council Regulation (EC) No.1346/2000[244]; or

(b)   where the centre of the debtor's main interests cannot be said to be in any EU Member State (including the UK), and "non-Regulation proceedings" are to be taken in Scotland.

In such cases, the jurisdiction of the Scots court will be founded upon the provisions of the Bankruptcy (Scotland) Act 1985 (personal insolvency), or the Insolvency Act 1986, as amended (corporate insolvency),[245] and problems of choice of law and matters of recognition will be regulated by pre-existing national rules.

Jurisdiction

17–57   The jurisdiction rules for personal bankruptcy are contained in the Bankruptcy (Scotland) Act 1985, as amended by the Bankruptcy and Diligence etc. (Scotland) Act 2007.[246] Section 9, which is subject to art.3 of the EC Insolvency Regulation,[247] establishes jurisdiction in Scotland, in the case of individuals, upon proof of an established place of business in the relevant sheriffdom, or proof of habitual residence there; and in the case of entities (such as partnerships), upon proof of an established place of business in the relevant sheriffdom, or constitution or formation under Scots law and proof that at any time it carried on business in the sheriffdom. A claim by a (foreign) creditor in a Scots sequestration will subject the claimant to the jurisdiction of the Scots court by reconvention.[248]

---

[243] 2006 Regulations Sch.1 arts 28–32. Explanatory Memorandum to 2006 Regulations, paras 7.7–7.17.

[244] Regualtion 1346/2000 recital (15).

[245] Bankruptcy (Scotland) Act 1985, Companies Act 1985, Insolvency Act 1986, Enterprise Act 2002, and Bankruptcy (Scotland) Regulations 2008 (SSI 2008/82) and Insolvency (Scotland) Rules 1986 (SI 1986/1915), each as amended. For detail: G. Maher and B.J. Rodger, *Civil Jurisdiction in the Scottish Courts* (W. Green, 2010), paras 11.14–11.36.

[246] And more recently by the Bankruptcy and Debt Advice (Scotland) Act 2014. See also Act of Sederunt (Sheriff Court Bankruptcy Rules) 2008 (SSI 2008/119); and Insolvency Act 1986 for personal insolvency law for England only.

[247] Bankruptcy (Scotland) Act 1985 s.9(6).

[248] *Wilsons (Glasgow and Trinidad) Ltd v Dresdner Bank*, 1913 2 S.L.T. 437; Anton with Beaumont, *Private International Law*, 3rd edn (2011), para.26.48, and cf. generally the salutary tale of incautious greed: *Guiard v De Clermont & Donner* [1914] 3 K.B. 145 (Morris, *Conflict of Laws*, 3rd edn (1984), p.113).

The Insolvency Act 1986 is concerned with corporate insolvency law for Scotland and England (Pts IV and V).[249] The Act contains jurisdiction provisions for the Scots courts in the matter of winding-up of companies registered in Scotland,[250] and for unregistered companies.[251] The exercise of jurisdiction by means of these provisions is subject to the operation of Regulation 1346/2000. Hence, where insolvency proceedings fall outside the scope of the Insolvency Regulation, by reason of subject-matter or time, the Bankruptcy (Scotland) Act 1985 and the Insolvency Act 1986 provisions can operate: so long as the debtor's COMI is not situated in an EU Member State,[252] the Scots court is justified in utilising the 1985 Act (personal insolvency) or 1986 Act (corporate insolvency) in order to take jurisdiction.[253]

Applicable law

Where the Scots court has jurisdiction by virtue of the pre-existing domestic insolvency rules set out above, the forum will apply, qua *lex fori*, its own domestic law, statutory or common law, to matters of administration and substance. Competing claims are decided by the *lex fori* of the bankruptcy.[254] With regard to personal insolvency, any rights acquired by the trustee in sequestration per the *lex fori* are subject, however, under national choice of law rules to the overriding provisions of a foreign *lex situs*[255]: s.31 of the Bankruptcy (Scotland) Act 1985, as amended, vests in the trustee in sequestration "the whole estate of the debtor" as at the date of sequestration, and wherever situated,[256] for the benefit of the creditors. There is no territorial limitation, but in respect of property situated abroad it is for a foreign *lex situs* to determine the effect which it gives to a Scottish sequestration vis-à-vis property situated there.[257]

The UNCITRAL Model Law, implemented in the UK *per* the Cross-Border Insolvency Regulations 2006,[258] forms part of Scots law. Where the Model Law applies in any given case,[259] the provisions of Ch.II ("Access of foreign representatives and creditors to courts in Great Britain") and Ch.IV ("Cooperation with foreign courts and foreign representatives) will prevail. Many provisions of the Model Law are facilitative and quasi-procedural, e.g. art.13, which provides that foreign creditors generally have the same rights regarding the

17–58

---

[249] J. St Clair and Lord Drummond Young, *The Law of Corporate Insolvency in Scotland*, 4th revised edn (Edinburgh: W. Green, 2011); and Greene and Fletcher, *The Law and Practice of Receivership in Scotland*, I.M. Fletcher and R. Roxburgh (eds), 3rd edn (Haywards Heath: Tottel, 2004).
[250] Insolvency Act 1986 ss.120 (jurisdiction where company is registered in Scotland) and 121.
[251] Insolvency Act 1986 ss.221 (jurisdiction where company has principal place of business in Scotland) and 225.
[252] Including the UK, but excluding Denmark.
[253] *HSBC Bank Plc, Petitioner*, 2010 S.L.T. 281.
[254] *Re Courteney Ex p. Pollard* (1840) Mont. & Ch. 239; *Re Anchor Line (Henderson Bros) Ltd* [1937] Ch. 483; *Scottish Union and National Insurance Co v James* (1886) 13 R. 928.
[255] *Re Reilly* [1942] I.R. 416.
[256] Bankruptcy (Scotland) Act 1985 s.31(1), (8).
[257] Or vice versa: *Murphy's Trustees v Aitken*; sub nom. *Morley's Trustees v Aitken*, 1983 S.L.T. 78; 1982 S.C. 73: English trustee in bankruptcy took Scottish heritage subject to any inhibition registered against the bankrupt prior in date to trustee's appointment. See now, intra-UK, 2006 Regulations reg.7.
[258] Para.17–55, above.
[259] 2006 Regulations Sch.1 art.1.

commencement of, and participation in, a proceeding under British insolvency law as creditors in Great Britain, and stipulates that the provision shall not affect the ranking of claims in a proceeding under British insolvency law, except that the claim of a foreign creditor shall not be given a lower priority than that of general unsecured claims solely because the holder of such a claim is a foreign creditor.

Where the UNCITRAL Model Law does not supply the answer, recourse must be had to residual national rules, statutory or common law. At common law, there is no difference in principle in ranking simply because a claim is foreign,[260] though ranking in general is the function of the *lex fori*.[261] If, however, such a creditor does not claim in the Scots bankruptcy, it would seem that, if he obtained the assets before the date of that bankruptcy, he may retain them, but, if he obtained them after that date and he is subject to the jurisdiction in bankruptcy of a Scots court, the Scottish trustee may recover the assets.[262]

17–59   Discharge is governed by the *lex fori*. By s.55(1) of the Bankruptcy (Scotland) Act 1985, on a debtor's discharge under s.54 of the Act, s/he shall be discharged within the UK of all debts and obligations contracted by him, or for which he was liable, at the date of sequestration.[263] Beyond this particularity, in a UK court a discharge in bankruptcy will have the effect of discharging a contractual obligation[264] only if it was granted under the same law as the proper law of the obligation.[265]

Recognition in Scotland of non-EU (or Danish) insolvency proceedings

17–60   Where a Scots court has jurisdiction under the pre-existing Scots conflict of laws rules for cross-border insolvencies,[266] the Court of Session may be required to exercise the function of recognition of foreign insolvency proceedings.[267] In that connection, the terms of Ch.III ("Recognition of a foreign proceeding and relief") and/or Ch.IV ("Cooperation with foreign courts and foreign representatives) of the Model Law, as set out above, may be relevant.

To the extent that the UNCITRAL Model Law is not comprehensive, it may be necessary for a Scots court to refer to residual national conflict of laws rules concerning recognition and enforcement of foreign insolvency proceedings. At

---

[260] *Re Kloebe* (1884) L.R. 28 Ch. D. 175.

[261] Which may disadvantage foreign creditors, e.g. if their claims have prescribed by the law of the forum, but not by their own proper law: *Re Lorillard* [1922] 2 Ch. 638.

[262] *Stewart v Auld* (1851) 13 D. 1337; *Wilsons (Glasgow and Trinidad) Ltd v Dresdner Bank*, 1913 2 S.L.T. 437; *Murphy's Trustee, Petitioner*, 1933 S.L.T. 632; *Re Courtney Ex p. Pollard* (1840) Mont. & Ch. 239; *Re Oriental Island SS Co* (1874) L.R. 9 Ch. App. 557; *Ex p. Robertson* (1875) L.R. 20 Eq. 733; *Thurburn v Steward* (1871) L.R. 3 P.C. 478; *Ex p. Melbourne* (1870) L.R. 6 Ch. App. 64; *Banco de Portugal v Waddell* (1880) L.R. 5 App. Cas. 161; *Re Anchor Line (Henderson Bros) Ltd* [1937] Ch. 483; *Rousou's Trustee v Rousou* [1955] 1 W.L.R. 545. *Cheshire and North's Private International Law*, 12th edn (1992), pp.908–911.

[263] *Dicey, Morris and Collins on the Conflict of Laws*, 15th edn (2012), para.31–100 states that this is the case, irrespective of the law applicable to the contract or debt. See also rr.213 and 215.

[264] *Gardiner v Houghton* (1862) 2 B. & S. 743; *Ellis v McHenry* (1871) L.R. 6 C.P. 228.

[265] *Bartley v Hodges* (1861) 1 B. & S. 375; *Gibbs and Sons v Société Industrielle et Commercialle des Metaux* (1890) L.R. 25 Q.B.D. 399; and Rome I Regulation art.12(1)(d).

[266] That is, where the COMI is outside the EU and the debtor company has its registered office in Scotland.

[267] 2006 Regulations Sch.1 art.4(1).

common law, a Scots court would regard a foreign court as competent if it had assumed jurisdiction on grounds similar to those assumed in Scotland, provided that the bankrupt was a party to the foreign proceedings.[268] Immoveable property in Scotland would not pass automatically at common law to the trustee under a foreign bankruptcy, but the Scottish court might assist the trustee in such a bankruptcy to deal with heritage in Scotland.[269] If so, the Scots heritage would pass subject to any charges attaching to the property under the Scots *lex situs*.[270] With regard to moveables, the Scots courts would recognise and enforce the right of a trustee under a foreign bankruptcy to all the bankrupt's moveable property without further process,[271] with the result that all such property would be attached and fall to the trustee in preference to the claims of creditors who might have attached the assets after the date of the bankruptcy.[272] The rights of Scots creditors who had taken action such as diligence in Scotland prior to the date of the foreign bankruptcy would not be adversely affected because the foreign bankruptcy, assuming it was recognised, was regarded as taking effect only from its date onwards. Scots statutory provisions about dating back applied only to Scots bankruptcies.[273] The Scots rules as to illegal preferences applied only to Scots bankruptcies and a foreign trustee did not have the right to cut down preferences, because the effect of a foreign bankruptcy in Scotland was prospective only.[274] Similarly, a Scots sequestration was regarded as taking effect abroad only from its date onwards so that it did not operate to cut down preferences already obtained there,[275] i.e. ranking or entitlement to rank is governed by the law under which the sequestration/bankruptcy order is granted.

SUMMARY 17

Particular transfers of property

1. Classification.   **17–61**
    The nature of property as moveable or immoveable is determined by the *lex situs*.
2. Meaning of the *lex situs*.
    The *lex situs* of immoveable property and corporeal moveable property is the law of the situation of the property in question at the time of the transaction allegedly giving rise to the proprietary claim.

---

[268] *Wilkie v Cathcart* (1870) 9 M. 168; *Gibson v Munro* (1894) 21 R. 840; *Obers v Paton's Trustees (No.3)* (1897) 24 R. 719; *Re Davidson* (1873) L.R. 15 Eq. 383; *Re Lawson's Trusts* [1896] 1 Ch. 175; *Re Anderson (A Bankrupt)* [1911] 1 K.B. 896; *Re Craig*, 86 L.J. Ch. 62; *Bergerem v Marsh* (1921) 91 L.J. K.B. 80.

[269] *Rattray v White* (1842) 4 D. 880; *Araya v Coghill*, 1921 S.C. 462. The English courts applied the same principle: *Re Kooperman* [1928] W.N. 101.

[270] *Murphy's Trustees v Aitken*, 1983 S.L.T. 78.

[271] *Araya v Coghill*, 1921 S.C. 462.

[272] *Goetze v Aders* (1874) 2 R. 150; *Phosphate Sewage Co v Molleson* (1876) 3 R. (HL) 77; (1876) 5 R. 1125; (1876) 6 R. (H.L.) 113; *Obers v Paton's Trustees (No.3)* (1897) 24 R. 719; *Salaman v Tod*, 1911 S.C. 1214; *Home's Trustee v Home's Trustees*, 1926 S.L.T. 214.

[273] See now 1985 Act ss.34–37.

[274] *Goetze v Aders* (1874) 2 R. 150.

[275] *Galbraith v Grimshaw* [1910] A.C. 508.

The *lex situs* of incorporeal moveables is the law of the place where the right may be enforced.

Recent case law suggests that reference to the *lex situs* is unlikely to include a reference to its rules of international private law.

3. Distinction between rights in personam and rights in rem.

Care must be taken to distinguish rights in personam from rights in rem, the latter being governed by choice of law rules in property, and the former by choice of law rules in contract.

4. Immoveable property

Contracts concerning immoveables are governed by their applicable law, usually the *lex situs* (see Rome I Regulation arts 4.1(c) and 11.5).

Proprietary rights in respect of immoveable property, and security rights in respect thereof, are governed by the *lex situs*.

5. Moveable property.

   (a) Corporeal moveables:

   Alienability is governed by the *lex situs*.

   Title validly conferred by the *lex situs* at the time of the purported transfer prevails, subject to any overriding effect accorded by a subsequent *lex situs*. The *lex situs* generally governs competing claims.

   (b) Incorporeal moveables:

   Assignability is governed by the proper law of the right purportedly assigned, that is, the *lex situs* of the right. In cases of contractual assignation regulated by the Rome I Regulation, by art.14.2 assignability shall be determined by the law governing the assigned claim.

   Capacity to make, or to accept, an assignation is governed by the governing law of the assignation, or by the proper law of the right purportedly assigned.

   The formal validity of an assignation is governed by the *lex loci actus*, the proper law of the assignation, or the proper law of the right purportedly assigned. In cases of contractual assignation regulated by the Rome I Regulation, art.11 governs.

   The essential validity of an assignation is governed by the proper law of the assignation, or the proper law of the right purportedly assigned. In cases of contractual assignation regulated by the Rome I Regulation, art.14.2 provides that the relationship between the assignee and the debtor, the conditions under which the assignation can be invoked against the debtor, and whether the debtor's obligations have been discharged, shall be determined by the law governing the assignation.

   In cases of contractual assignation regulated by the Rome I Regulation, art.14.1 provides that the relationship between the assignor and the assignee under a voluntary assignation shall be governed by the law that applies to the contract of assignation between the parties in terms of the Regulation.

   The *lex situs* of the right governs competing claims to the same right, and competitions between voluntary and involuntary transfers.

Special rules apply to bills of exchange, negotiable instruments, shares and other securities, and intellectual property rights.

Universal transfers of property: insolvency

1. Theories.   **17–62**
    Unity; separation; universality of bankruptcy.
2. Regulatory schemes.
    There are four schemes of rules operative in Scottish courts to regulate insolvency proceedings having a cross-border dimension, viz.:
    (a) The EU Insolvency Regulation: Council Regulation (EC) No.1346/2000 of 29 May 2000 on Insolvency Proceedings:
         Regulation 1346/2000 establishes a system to regulate cross-border insolvencies where the centre of a debtor's main interests is situated within an EU Member State (except Denmark). It sets up a system of main proceedings (having extraterritorial effect) and secondary proceedings (limited to assets situated in the state where the secondary proceedings are opened), and directs that the applicable law, subject to arts 5–14, shall be the law of the state in which proceedings (main or secondary) are opened (the *lex concursus*). Regulation 1346/2000 is repealed and replaced by Regulation (EU) 2015/848 of the European Parliament and of the Council of 20 May 2015 in insolvency proceedings (recast), which entered into force on 26 June 2015 and will apply, in the main, from 26 June 2017.
    (b) Insolvency Act 1986 s.426:
         Intra-UK and international co-operation among Commonwealth countries.
    (c) Cross-Border Insolvency Regulations 2006, giving force of law in Great Britain to the UNCITRAL Model Law on cross-border insolvency, as modified for application in Great Britain, and applicable where:
         (i)   assistance is sought in Great Britain by a foreign court or a foreign representative in connection with a foreign proceeding; or
         (ii) assistance is sought in a foreign State in connection with a proceeding under British insolvency law; or
         (iii) a foreign proceeding and a proceeding under British insolvency law in respect of the same debtor are taking place concurrently; or
         (iv) creditors or other interested persons in a foreign State have an interest in requesting the commencement of, or participating in, a proceeding under British insolvency law.
    (d) pre-existing Scottish conflict of laws, applicable where:
         (i)   the centre of a debtor's main interests is situated in the UK and territorial jurisdiction in one legal system of the UK requires to be established under the EU Insolvency Regulation; or

(ii)   where the centre of the debtor's main interests cannot be said to be in any EU Member State (including the UK), and "non-Regulation proceedings" are to be taken in Scotland.

The pre-existing national rules of jurisdiction are contained in the Bankruptcy (Scotland) Act 1985, as amended by the Bankruptcy and Diligence etc. (Scotland) Act 2007 (personal insolvency), and the Insolvency Act 1986, as amended (corporate insolvency).

CHAPTER 18

The law of succession

MATTERS PERTAINING TO BOTH TESTATE AND INTESTATE SUCCESSION

Confirmation to estate in Scotland

No person is entitled to take any administrative act in the estate of any deceased person who has left assets in Scotland until he has obtained confirmation in Scotland. Confirmation constitutes title to all moveable and immoveable estate in Scotland vested in a deceased, whatever his domicile. There must be property in Scotland before confirmation will be granted. The same principles apply, mutatis mutandis, in England, where probate is granted in testate cases, and letters of administration in intestate cases.[1]

The granting of confirmation[2] confers authority on the executor to intromit with assets in Scotland,[3] but not generally with assets situated elsewhere. Before the executor has authority to intromit with assets in Scotland he must complete title according to the Scots *lex loci rei sitae/lex situs*. Within the UK there used to be a system of resealing of the grant of authority made in one territorial unit in the other constituent parts, if there were assets to be dealt with there, but by the Administration of Estates Act 1971 s.3(1), resealing was dispensed with, provided that the deceased died domiciled in the legal system which issued the grant. Thus, confirmation or probate or letters of administration granted in any UK jurisdiction normally operates directly in the others.[4]

If the deceased died domiciled in a Commonwealth country, and if probate, letters of administration or similar authority has/have already been granted there, it is not necessary to apply separately for confirmation to estate in Scotland. Instead the probate or letters may be resealed in Edinburgh.[5] Before resealing can

18–01

---

[1] *Currie on Confirmation of Executors*, edited by E.M. Scobbie, 9th edn (Edinburgh: W. Green (2011), para.14–31).

[2] Or in England, probate or letters of administration, as appropriate.

[3] Or, mutatis mutandis, England.

[4] Though obtaining confirmation to Scottish estate and separate probate/letters to English estate is still competent: *Currie on Confirmation of Executors*, 9th edn (2011), para.14–39 (and generally, para.14–33).

[5] The Colonial Probate Act 1892 and the Colonial Probate (Protected States and Mandated Territories) Act 1927. If resealing is competent under these Acts, it does not matter that the executor could not have been appointed as executor in the country where resealing takes place. *Currie on Confirmation of Executors*, 9th edn (2011), para.15–02 explains that separately obtaining Scottish confirmation nonetheless may be preferable, e.g. to obtain title to individual items of estate.

take place, an inventory of the deceased's estate in Scotland must be lodged.[6] Resealing does not have retrospective effect, with the result that a resealed confirmation or probate is effective in the country where it was resealed only from the date of resealing onwards, not from the date of the original grant. Reciprocal arrangements have been made for the resealing of Scottish confirmations in Commonwealth countries.

If the deceased died domiciled outside the Commonwealth and if probate, letters of administration or similar authority has/have already been granted abroad, the Scots courts will follow the law of the deceased's domicile as regards the appointment of the executor, and confirmation will be granted in Scotland to estate in Scotland, to such person already appointed, or entitled to be appointed, under that law. Except in the case of small estates,[7] a petition will be required for the appointment in Scotland of the (foreign appointed) administrator as executor dative.

If the deceased died domiciled outside the Commonwealth, but probate, letters of administration, or similar authority has/have not been granted in the country of his domicile, and there is property to be administered in Scotland, it is necessary to prove either that the deceased's will is valid according to the law of his domicile, or that the person seeking appointment as executor dative is the person entitled by that law to the office of administrator.[8]

Some legal systems know no interposition of executor between the deceased and the heir,[9] in which case Scots law must be guided by the rules of the *lex situs* and/or the deceased's personal law. Its accommodation of the foreign law inevitably must be approximate because the connecting factor in the view of Scots law will be taken to be the law of the domicile of the deceased (even though the foreign law may favour application *qua lex causae* of the law of the deceased's nationality to all property, moveable and immoveable). Moreover, the foreign system would have that property pass directly to the heir, without the intervention of the personal representative of the deceased. Whatever the rule of the deceased's personal law, property in Scotland or England cannot pass without confirmation, probate, letters of administration, or similar authority having been obtained by the party entitled. On the other hand, Scots law will accept as executor the person identified by the deceased's personal law, whether or not such a person would be entitled to act under Scots domestic law.[10]

18–02   In summary,[11] where the deceased died domiciled in:

---

[6] *Currie on Confirmation of Executors*, 9th edn (2011), para.14–12.

[7] Confirmation to Small Estates (Scotland) Order 2011 (SSI 2011/435), which increases from £30,000 to £36,000 the limit of value of a deceased person's estate at or below which confirmation of executors may be obtained by the simplified procedures prescribed (for small intestate estates) by the Intestates Widows and Children (Scotland) Act 1875, and (for small testate estates) by the Small Testate Estates (Scotland) Act 1876, as amended by Confirmation to Small Estates (Scotland) Act 1979.

[8] So also where the deceased died domiciled in a Commonwealth country, but no authority has been granted there. Generally on procedure, and for more complex cases, see *Currie on Confirmation of Executors*, 9th edn (2011), para.2.36.

[9] *Re Haji-Ioannou (Deceased)*; sub nom. *Haji-Ioannou v Frangos* [2009] EWHC 2310 (QB).

[10] *Currie on Confirmation of Executors*, 9th edn (2011), para.2–35.

[11] *Currie on Confirmation of Executors*, 9th edn (2011), Ch.15.

MATTERS PERTAINING TO BOTH TESTATE AND INTESTATE SUCCESSION

(a)   Scotland—confirmation constitutes title to assets in Scotland, England, and Northern Ireland.[12]

(b)   England—probate or letters of administration granted in England are immediately effective in Scotland as regards title to property situated there per the Administration of Estates Act 1971 s.3(1).[13]

(c)   Northern Ireland—as for England above, mutatis mutandis, but a separate inventory must be lodged in Scotland of the deceased's Scottish estate.[14]

(d)   Channel Islands and the Isle of Man—there is no procedure for resealing, and therefore confirmation to estate in Scotland is required.

(e)   A Commonwealth country—resealing is competent under the Colonial Probate Act 1892 and the Colonial Probate (Protected States and Mandated Territories) Act 1927. A separate inventory must be lodged in Scotland of the deceased's Scottish estate, but separate Scottish confirmation is unnecessary.

(f)   A non-Commonwealth, non-EU country—[15]

  (i)   If probate or letters of administration or similar authority has/have already been granted in that country, an inventory must be lodged in Scotland of the deceased's Scottish estate, in which the executor refers to the probate, etc. as his title, and confirmation will be granted.

  (ii)   If no probate or letters of administration or similar authority has/have been granted in that country, an expert opinion on the relevant *lex/leges causae* may be required as to the validity of the will (if any), or eligibility of persons claiming appointment as executor.[16] An inventory must be lodged in Scotland of the deceased's Scottish estate, and confirmation granted.

In appropriate cases (q.v.), account must be taken of Regulation (EU) No.650/2012 of the European Parliament and of the Council on jurisdiction, applicable law, recognition and enforcement of decisions and acceptance and enforcement of authentic instruments in matters of succession and on the creation of a European Certificate of Succession (hereinafter "Rome IV").[17]

The Scots court may take evidence upon the question of the domicile of the deceased.

A foreign declarator of death is not conclusive in Scotland so that in a contested case proof of death may be necessary.[18]

---

[12]   *Re Rankine (Deceased)* [1918] P. 134.

[13]   Pre-1971: *Hutchison v Aberdeen Bank* (1837) 15 S. 1100; *Marchioness of Hastings v Executors of Marquess of Hastings* (1852) 15 D. 489.

[14]   *Burns v Campbell* [1952] 1 K.B. 15.

[15]   *In the Goods of Hill* (1870) L.R. 2 P. & D. 89; *Whiffin v Lees* (1872) 10 M. 797; *New York Breweries Co Ltd v Att Gen* [1899] A.C. 62; *In the Estate of Yahunda* [1956] P. 388.

[16]   *Re Achillopoulos* [1928] Ch. 433; *In the Estate of Leguia Ex p. Ashworth* [1934] P. 80; *In the Estate of Humphries* [1934] P. 78; *Re Kaufman (Deceased)* [1952] 2 All E.R. 261.

[17]   Para.18-40, below.

[18]   *Re Schulhof* [1948] P. 66; *Simpson's Trustees v Fox*, 1951 S.L.T. 412.

Jurisdiction in succession

18–03 The majority of successions are non-contentious.[19] Where litigation arises, the Brussels I Regulation shall not apply by reason of the exclusion of "wills and succession" from the scope of that Regulation.[20] In relation to trusts, however, art.5.6 of the Brussels I Regulation applies so as to confer jurisdiction against a settlor, trustee or beneficiary of a trust, on the courts of the Member State in which the trust is domiciled.[21] The position with regard to testamentary trusts is ambiguous. Article 5.6 of the Brussels I Regulation/Brussels I Recast, art.7.6 would appear to be concerned only with the *internal* relationships of an *inter vivos* or statutory trust, that is, among trustees inter se, or between trustees and beneficiaries. The Schlosser Report[22] explains that the expression "wills and succession...includes disputes as to the validity or interpretation of the terms of a will setting up a trust, even where the trust takes effect on a date subsequent to the death of the testator....The 1968 Convention does not, therefore, apply to any disputes concerning the creation, interpretation and administration of trusts arising under the law of succession including wills."[23] However, in his *external* relationships (e.g. in a dispute with a person who is not a beneficiary of the trust nor a fellow trustee), a trustee is not immune from suit under the Brussels I Regulation, no matter whether the trust is inter vivos or testamentary.[24]

Schedule 8,[25] constituting rules of civil jurisdiction operable in Scotland, establishes *general* jurisdiction, namely, that a person shall be sued in the courts for the place where he is domiciled[26]; and *special* jurisdiction based, inter alia, on the situation of property. There is no bespoke rule of special jurisdiction concerning wills and succession.[27] By Sch.8 para.2(h), where a defender is not domiciled in the UK, the courts for any place where (i) any moveable property belonging to him has been arrested; or (ii) any immoveable property in which he has any beneficial interest is situated, shall have jurisdiction. Furthermore, by para.2(i), in proceedings brought to assert, declare or determine proprietary or possessory rights, or rights of security, in or over moveable property, or to obtain authority to dispose of moveable property, the defender may be sued in the courts

---

[19] Notable exceptions are *Al-Bassam v Al-Bassam* [2004] EWCA Civ 857; and *Lambton (Earl of Durham) v Lady Lambton* [2013] EWHC 3566 (Ch).

[20] Brussels I Regulation art.1.2(a). See also Brussels I Recast Regulation Art.1.2(f) (see now, however, para.18–44—Rome IV jurisdiction). This exclusion does not operate (Sch.9) in relation to the residual rules of Scots law, contained in the Civil Jurisdiction and Judgments Act 1982 Sch.8.

[21] Brussels I Regulation art.60(3). Cf. Brussels I Recast Regulation arts 7(6) and 63.

[22] Schlosser Report [1979] O.J. C59/89.

[23] Schlosser Report, para 52. Further, at para.112: "If a trust has been established by a will, disputes arising from the internal relationships...are outside the scope of the 1968 Convention."

[24] Schlosser Report, para.110.

[25] Para.7–78.

[26] Civil Jurisdiction and Judgments Act 1982 Sch.8 para.1.

[27] An additional ground if jurisdiction is proposed in the Succession (Scotland) Bill (2015), cl.22 that the CJJA 1982 be amended so that, in Sch.8, r.2, a new paragraph (ga) be inserted, viz. [a person shall be sued] "in the person's capacity as an executor (where confirmation has been obtained in Scotland)—(i) in the Court of Session; or (ii) before a sheriff in the sheriffdom in which confirmation was obtained". With regard to residual rules of Scots law pertaining to trusts, see Civil Jurisdiction and Judgments Act 1982 Sch.8 para.2(g) (special jurisdiction in certain matters pertaining to trusts domiciled in Scotland); and Sch.8 paras.6(4) and (5) (prorogation of jurisdiction in certain matters pertaining to trusts).

for the place where the property is situated. In proceedings which have as their object rights in rem in immoveable property, the courts for the place where the property is situated shall have exclusive jurisdiction.[28]

Administration and distribution

In all succession cases, contentious and non-contentious, the estate must be administered in order that it be made ready for distribution. The classification between matters of administration and of distribution is determined by the *lex fori*.

18–04

The *administration* of an estate comprises all steps of procedure in completion of title and all the duties of the executor or personal representative of the deceased up to the stage of bringing the estate to the point of division. It includes obtaining confirmation or equivalent, payment of inheritance tax, collection of assets, and payment of debts.

In English law there is a presumption that, if a bequest is declared to be "free of duty" or is expressed in similar terms, such an expression covers only duties imposed by UK law unless the testator has indicated a contrary intention.[29] There is no such presumption in Scots law where the courts approach the matter purely as one of interpretation of the testator's intention.[30] If the will is silent generally about the matter of duties, taxes are paid out of the residue of the estate; and failing residue, out of the legacies, which will have to be abated.

The administration of a deceased's estate, wherever it may be, is governed by what is termed in this connection the *lex fori,* which is the law of the situation of the moveable or immoveable assets to be administered (not necessarily coinciding with the *lex domicilii* of the deceased).[31] Hence the "*lex fori*" or "*leges fori*" will derive that status from being the situation of moveable or immoveable assets. In the case of dual/multiple administrations, the procedure in a *forum rei sitae* is termed the *ancillary administration*, while that in the *forum successionis* (where the deceased was last domiciled) is termed the *principal administration*.

Thus, in the case of debts which have prescribed by the law of the deceased's domicile, but not by the *lex fori* or vice versa, it is the *lex fori* which determines whether they may be admitted and which determines priorities among competing claims on the estate.[32] The incidence and characterisation of debts as between moveables and immoveables probably is determined ultimately by the *lex situs* of the immoveables.

Distribution of an estate involves its division among the beneficiaries, and is governed by the *lex successionis*, that is, by the *lex causae* rather than the *lex fori*. When the deceased dies domiciled abroad, his assets in Scotland may be remitted

---

[28] Civil Jurisdiction and Judgments Act 1982 Sch.8 para.5(1)(a).

[29] *Re Scott* [1915] 1 Ch. 592; *Re Goetze* [1953] Ch. 96; *Re Nesbitt* [1953] 1 W.L.R. 595; and *Scarfe v Matthews* [2012] EWHC 3071 (Ch.).

[30] *Maclean's Trustees v McNair*, 1969 S.L.T. 146; *Scottish National Orchestra Society Ltd v Thomson's Executor*, 1969 S.L.T. 325.

[31] The 1973 Hague Convention concerning the International Administration of the Estates of Deceased Persons was signed, but not ratified, by the UK.

[32] *Re Lorillard* [1922] 2 Ch. 638. This case is not without its critics: if the debts were still exigible by their own applicable laws perhaps the forum overreached itself by refusing to admit the claims. Also *Re Kloebe* (1884) L.R. 28 Ch. D. 175; *Re Manifold* [1962] Ch. 1.

to the country of his domicile for distribution, but distribution at the Scots *situs* in accordance with the *lex successionis* is competent.

A decree of the court of the deceased's domicile upon a question of succession to moveables is a decree in rem entitled to recognition in Scotland, and conclusive against other claimants.[33]

Applicable law: the scission principle

18–05   The scission principle refers to the split nature of the Scottish (and English) choice of law rule in succession, which differentiates between the law governing succession to moveables (the ultimate domicile of the deceased)[34] and that governing succession to immoveables (the *lex situs*).[35]

Whether this distinction should continue to be made is a matter long debated within the UK,[36] and arguably has become more pressing in view of the adoption in Rome IV (by which the UK is not bound) of a unitary choice of law rule.[37]

The Succession (Scotland) Act 1964 removed many differences which previously had existed in domestic Scots law between succession to heritage and succession to moveables. However, remnants of the distinction remain in domestic law, and continue to permeate Scots conflict rules of succession. This can lead to difficulty, particularly where property is chameleon in character, changing its nature according to the context in which it is encountered. The result may be seen as unfair and a widow may benefit twice.[38]

---

[33] Cf. *Doglioni v Crispin* (1866) L.R. 1 H.L. 301; and *Re Trufort* (1887) L.R. 36 Ch. D. 600.

[34] *Bell v Kennedy* (1868) 6 M. (H.L.) 69; *Train v Train's Executor* (1899) 2 F. 146.

[35] *Macdonald*, 1932 S.C. (H.L.) 79; *Kerr v Mangan* 2013 S.L.T. (Sh.Ct.) 102.

[36] J. Morris, "Intestate Succession to Land in the Conflict of Laws" (1969) 85 L.Q.R. 839. *Dicey and Morris on the Conflict of Laws*, in succeeding editions, from the 10th edn (1980), r.98 up to the current 15th edn (2012), r.150, has enunciated the scission rule, but has expressed doubt about its continued appropriateness and usefulness. Similarly, by the end of the 1980s, the Scottish Law Commission came to the view that the last domicile of the deceased should regulate the devolution of the whole (intestate) estate: Scottish Law Commission, *Some Miscellaneous Topics in the Law of Succession*, 1986, Scot. Law Com. Memo. No.71, para.6.4; Scottish Law Commission, *Report on Succession*, 1990, Scot. Law Com.No.124, para.10.5; Scottish Law Commission *Discussion Paper on Succession,*2007, DP No.136, para.4.77; and *Report on Succession*, 2009, Scot. Law Com. No 215), para.5.3. Also Michael C. Meston, *The Succession (Scotland) Act 1964*, 5th edn (Edinburgh: W. Green, 2002), p.113. But see Law Commission, Intestacy and Family Provision Claims on Death: A Consultation Paper (The Stationery Office, 2009) Law Com. C.P. No.191, paras.7.38–7.39. Most recently, see Scottish Government Consultation on Technical Issues Relating to Succession (August 2014), and Analysis of the Written Responses and Scottish Government Response (June 2015), followed by introduction on 16 June 2015 by Scottish Government of the Succession (Scotland) Bill. See also Scottish Government Consultation on the Law of Succession (June 2015), in particular Ch.2 ("Intestacy") wherein the Government asks if consultees think that rights in intestacy should be "property specific", i.e. exigible regardless of nature of property, as moveable or immoveable.

[37] Para.18–46, below.

[38] *Train v Train's Executor* (1899) 2 F. 146: see criticisms in A.E. Anton, *Private International Law*, 1st edn (1967), pp.387, 388; *Re Collens (Deceased)* [1986] 1 All E.R. 611, in which the scission rule was applied. See comments in Law Commission, *Intestacy and Family Provision Claims on Death: A Consultation Paper* (The Stationery Office, 2009) Law Com. C.P. No.191, paras 7.38, 7.39, and conclusion that, since the eventuality of double benefit will arise in a limited number of cases, and may not in fact be problematic in those cases, reform of the law on this point is not warranted.

Conversion

Conversion (rules to be applied to determine the nature of property where   **18–06**
immoveables have been converted into money or vice versa) is determined
generally by the law of the testator's domicile at the date of his death, and not by
the *lex situs*.[39]

Legal rights

Most legal systems recognise rights of certain family members of the deceased to   **18–07**
claim, either against his will or in intestacy, a reserved portion of the deceased's
estate. These rights of indefeasible family provision, known in Scots domestic
law as "legal rights", constitute both rights of succession and restrictions on the
deceased's testamentary powers. The subject of protected family provision
(sometimes termed "forced heirship"), being a matter of substance, is regulated in
Scots conflict of laws by the law of the deceased's domicile at the date of his
death as regards moveables,[40] and by the *lex situs* at the date of death, as regards
immoveables.[41]

Rules of family provision per Scots law

Spouses and civil partners

Legal rights consist in Scots domestic law of the rights of a surviving spouse[42] of   **18–08**
the deceased (*jus relicti/relictae*) and of his children (*legitim*).[43] Legal rights in
Scots law, exigible now only out of moveable estate and available therefore only
where the deceased died domiciled in Scotland, can be claimed in intestate or
testate succession, though in the former case, they do not arise until prior rights of
the surviving spouse (q.v.) have been satisfied, and in the case of testacy, they
cannot be taken by a beneficiary in addition to any bequest under the will.[44] This
may not be the case in all legal systems; the matter of election is one of
substance, to be determined by the *lex successionis*. Land in Scotland is immune
to any claim for legal rights, since Scots law, the *lex situs*, no longer admits such
rights in respect of immoveables.[45]

---

[39] *Hall's Trustees v Hall* (1854) 16 D. 1057.

[40] *Bell v Kennedy* (1868) 6 M. (H.L.) 69; *Trevelyan v Trevelyan* (1873) 11 M. 516; *Train v Train's Executor* (1899) 2 F. 146; *Macdonald*, 1932 S.C. (H.L.) 79. cf. *Re Groos* [1915] 1 Ch. 572.

[41] *Lashley v Hog* (1804) 4 Pat. 581; *Bell v Kennedy* (1868) 6 M. (H.L.) 69; *Re Ogilvie* [1918] 1 Ch. 492; *Re Collens (Deceased)* [1986] 1 All E.R. 611.

[42] Or civil partner: Civil Partnership Act 2004 s.131.

[43] The Scottish Law Commission published its *Report on Succession* (The Stationery Office, 2009), Scot. Law Com. No.215, in April 2009, following *Discussion Paper on Succession* (The Stationery Office, 2007), Scot. Law Com. D.P. No.136, proposing that major changes be made to the rules on family provision (Pt 8, recommendations 1–5, 14–36). The Scottish Government Consultation on the Law of Succession (June 2015) proposes in Ch.3 ("Protection from Disinheritance") fundamentally to change the law on legal rights.

[44] The claimant is "put to his election". See "approbate and reprobate", below. cf. *Scarfe v Matthews* [2012] EWHC 3071 (Ch).

[45] Meston, *The Succession (Scotland) Act 1964*, 5th edn (2002), p.135. However, a qualifying dwelling house situated in Scotland may be subject in intestacy to "prior rights", q.v.

Cohabitants

18–09 In terms of the Family Law (Scotland) Act 2006 s.29, a surviving cohabitant may apply to the Scots court for payment from the deceased cohabitant's net intestate estate of a capital sum, and for transfer of property, heritable or moveable, from that estate, as the court may prescribe having in view the size and nature of the estate, and any benefit received or to be received by the survivor in consequence of the death.[46] The court also will take into account any other rights against, or claims on, the estate. The order shall not exceed the amount to which the survivor would have been entitled had s/he been the spouse or civil partner of the deceased. In terms of s.29(10), "net intestate estate" means so much of the intestate estate as remains after satisfaction of inheritance tax and the legal rights and the prior rights of any surviving spouse or surviving civil partner. In order for claims under s.29 to be admitted, the deceased immediately before death must have been domiciled in Scotland, and cohabiting with the survivor.[47] The decision of the Sheriff Principal in *Kerr v Mangan*,[48] upon the interpretation of s.29, is that it "innovates" on the manner in which the estate of a deceased cohabitant falls to be distributed, but ought to be read against the background of the Succession (Scotland) Act 1964, and in accordance with existing principles of international private law. Accordingly, "references to the 'net intestate estate' of the deceased...ought to be interpreted as meaning the net intestate estate that is to devolve according to Scots law including Scots private international law...".[49] Hence "net intestate estate" for the purpose of the 2006 Act does not extend to immoveable property situated outside Scotland. For completeness, however, it must be conceded that the foreign *lex situs* might make provision for a surviving cohabitant.

Collation

18–10 Collation in Scots domestic law is an equitable doctrine which requires a potential beneficiary who has received advances from the deceased during his lifetime notionally to throw these advances into the pot for division if he wishes to participate equally in the distribution of the legal rights fund upon the deceased's death. Since 10 September 1964, collation in Scots domestic law[50] has been restricted to collation *inter liberos*. In England, "hotch pot", the equivalent principle, was removed from English law by the Law Reform (Succession) Act 1995 s.1(2).

In conflict law, the subject of collation/equalisation should be regarded as a matter of substantive succession law, applicable therefore in relation to moveable

---

[46] e.g. *Simpson v Downie*, 2013 S.L.T. 178; and *Kerr v Mangan*, 2013 S.L.T. (Sh.Ct.) 102. The Scottish Government Consultation on the Law of Succession (June 2015) proposes in Ch.4 ("Cohabitants") to repeal s.29 of the 2006 Act, and to replace it with a simpler version which would enact that the new regime would apply in testate as well as intestate succession (para.4.7).

[47] Paras 11–39, 11–40 and 13–13, above. Also *Chebotareva v Khandro (King's Executrix)*, 2008 Fam. L.R. 66.

[48] *Kerr v Mangan*, 2013 S.L.T. (Sh.Ct.) 102.

[49] *Kerr v Mangan*, 2013 S.L.T. (Sh.Ct.) 102 at [23], per Sheriff Principal RA Dunlop Q.C.

[50] Gloag and Henderson, *The Law of Scotland* (ed. Eassie and MacQueen), 13th edn (Edinburgh: W. Green, 2012), para.38.13.

property only if the deceased's *lex ultimi domicilii* contains such a rule, and with regard to immoveables, only if the *lex situs* so directs.[51]

Rules of family provision per English law

In English domestic law a person who is dissatisfied by the terms of a will, and/or the effect of the rules of intestacy in the instant case, and who falls within the list of persons named in the relevant legislation, may apply to the court, within six months from the date on which representation with respect to the estate of the deceased is first taken out (i.e. probate), for the making of a discretionary order for payment or property transfer out of the estate, in terms of the Inheritance (Provision for Family and Dependants) Act 1975.[52] The list of parties entitled to claim has been extended by the Law Reform (Succession) Act 1995 s.2(3) to include a cohabitant[53] if the cohabitation has subsisted for at least two years prior to death. These rules apply only where the deceased dies domiciled in England and Wales[54]: the so-called "domicile gateway".[55] As a result of the domicile pre-condition to making a claim under the Act, a number of modern authorities on the determination of domicile have been prompted by the need for a claimant under the 1975 Act to prove to the satisfaction of the court in a contentious case that the deceased died domiciled in England and Wales.[56]

18–11

Capacity of beneficiaries

The law of the deceased's last domicile, as regards moveables, and the *lex situs*, as regards immoveables, in principle determine the legal capacity of potential beneficiaries to succeed, as well as the substantive matter of the class of persons and order of persons who shall succeed. English authorities, however, suggest that the legal capacity of a particular beneficiary to succeed to moveables may be governed by the law of the deceased's last domicile *or* by the law of the beneficiary's domicile, according to which of those laws the beneficiary acquired capacity earlier.[57] There seems no reason why a similar rule should not apply in Scotland.

18–12

---

[51] *Hay-Balfour v Scotts* (1793) 3 Pat. 300; *Robertson v Robertson* 16 February 1816 FC; *Robertson v McVean* 18 February 1817 FC; *Dundas v Dundas* (1830) 2 Dow & Cl. 349 HL; *Hewitt's Trustees v Lawson* (1891) 18 R. 793; *Brodie v Barry* (1813) 3 Ves. B. 127; *Orrell v Orrell* (1871) 6 Ch. App. 302; *Brown's Trustees v Gregson*, 1920 S.C. (H.L.) 87.

[52] As amended by the Inheritance and Trustees' Powers Act 2014.

[53] *Lindop v Agus* [2009] EWHC 1795 (Ch).

[54] Inheritance (Provision for Family and Dependants) Act 1975 s.1(1).

[55] E.B. Crawford and J.M. Carruthers, "The Law of Unintended Consequences: The Inheritance and Trustees' Powers Bill" (2014) 18 Edin. L.R. 133 for discussion of proposals at the Bill stage to "widen the gateway". In the face of opposition, the Inheritance and Trustees' Powers Act 2014 rightly did not create any additional jurisdictional criterion on which to make a family provision claim.

[56] e.g. *Gully v Dix* [2004] 1 WLR 1399; *Robinson v Bird* [2003] EWHC 30 (Ch); *Morgan v Cilento* [2004] EWHC 188 (Ch); *Agulian v Cyganik* [2006] EWCA Civ 129; *Holliday v Musa* [2010] EWCA Civ. 335; *Peters v Pinder* [2011] WTLR 1399; and *Sylvester v Sylvester* [2014] WTLR 127.

[57] *Doglioni v Crispin* (1866) L.R. 1 H.L. 301; *Re Hellman's Will* (1866) L.R. 2 Eq. 363; *Re Goodman's Trusts* (1881) L.R. 17 Ch. D. 266; *Re Hall (Deceased)* [1914] P. 1; *Re Schnapper* [1928] Ch. 420; *Re Hagerbaum* [1933] I.R. 198; in Scots law see *Seddon v Seddon* (1891) 20 R. 675; *Atherstane's Trustees* (1896) 24 R. 39; *Webb v Clelland's Trustees* (1904) 41 S.L.R. 229; and *Ogilvy v Ogilvy's Trustees*, 1927 S.L.T. 83.

Capacity to grant a discharge to trustees or executors is governed by the law of the domicile of the beneficiary (moveables) or the *lex situs* (immoveables).[58]

INTESTATE SUCCESSION

Immoveable estate

18–13 All questions of intestate succession to immoveable estate are governed by the *lex situs*.[59] The provisions of s.8 of the Succession (Scotland) Act 1964 concerning the deceased's house apply to all cases where the deceased, irrespective of his domicile, died intestate, owning a qualifying dwelling house in Scotland.[60]

Moveable estate

18–14 Intestate succession to moveable estate is governed by the law[61] of the deceased's domicile at the date of his death.[62] This law shall govern irrespective of the law of the country of the deceased's birth, death, or domicile of origin, or the situation of his moveable estate. The content of the applicable law is that of the deceased's domicile at the date of death, not subsequent thereto.[63]

Prior rights

18–15 "Prior rights" is a reference to those rights, introduced in the 1964 Act, which are capable of arising in Scots domestic law in cases of intestacy, and which comprise the right of a surviving spouse[64] to:

(a) An interest in a qualifying dwelling house[65] under s.8 (or a cash equivalent under s.8(2)). Where the value of the house exceeds a certain sum (updated

---

[58] *Ogilvy v Ogilvy's Trustees*, 1927 S.L.T. 83.

[59] *Nisbett v Nisbett's Trustees* (1835) 13 S. 517; *Train v Train's Executor* (1899) 2 F. 146; *Fenton v Livingstone* (1859) 3 Macq. 497; *Re Gentili* (1875) L.R. 9 Eq. 541.

[60] Meston, *The Succession (Scotland) Act 1964*, 5th edn (2002), p.133; and Leslie, "Prior Rights in Succession: The International Dimension", 1988 S.L.T. (News) 105.

[61] Necessarily civil law, not a body of religious law, unless the content of the law of the domicile is co-terminous with religious law: *Al-Bassam v Al-Bassam* [2004] EWCA Civ 857. cf. *Halpern v Halpern* [2008] Q.B. 195.

[62] Also *Brown* (1744) Mor. 4604; *Bruce v Bruce* (1790) 3 Pat. 163; *Lashley v Hog* (1804) 4 Pat. 581: *Nisbett v Nisbett's Trustees* (1835) 13 S. 517; *Newlands v Chalmers' Trustees* (1832) 11 S. 65; *Maxwell v McClure* (1857) 20 D. 307, affirmed 3 Macq. 852. In England: *Lynch v Provisional Government of Paraguay* (1871) L.R. 2 P. & D. 268; *Re Rea* [1902] I.R. 451; and *Re Haji-Ioannou (Deceased)*, sub nom. *Haji-Ioannou v Frangos* [2009] EWHC 2310 (QB).

[63] In *Lynch v Provisional Government of Paraguay* (1871) L.R. 2 P. & D. 268, where a foreign government sought, after the date of death, to confiscate assets of the deceased situated in England, and to alter the succession, such action was ineffective in England. However, a governmental order of that type would not be given effect in a British court for the reason also that it would fall foul of the rule that confiscations *extra territorium* have no effect. Moreover, the qualifying phrase "at death" may have been intended in *Lynch* merely to fix the date at which the domicile was to be identified.

[64] Or civil partner: Civil Partnership Act 2004 s.261(2) and Sch.28(1) para.4.

[65] Defined in s.8(4).

from time to time)[66] the survivor is entitled to receive the permitted sum in lieu of the house. This cash substitute will be regarded as immoveable qua *surrogatum*,[67] and subject therefore to regulation by the *lex situs*, i.e. the *lex situs* not the *lex domicilii* determines entitlement. No right, qua Scottish prior right, nor any *surrogatum*, arises if the (otherwise qualifying) dwelling house is situated outside Scotland.

(b)   A right to the furniture and plenishings up to a certain sum.[68] This right is classified as a right to moveables, and hence is exigible only if the deceased died domiciled in Scotland. Further, the furniture and plenishings must be those contained in the qualifying dwelling house which is the subject of s.8, which dwelling house must be situated, as explained, in Scotland.[69]

(c)   A right to a cash sum,[70] which, though apparently moveable, is to be borne rateably out of both the heritable and moveable estate of the deceased. Hence, if the deceased died domiciled in Scotland, the sum is apportioned between his moveables *wherever situated*, and his immoveables in *Scotland*. However, if domiciled outside Scotland, then the whole sum is to be taken from any immoveables in Scotland.

Caduciary rights

Difficulties may arise with regard to the succession to assets situated in Scotland in the estate of a person who died, intestate and without relatives, domiciled in a foreign country. The assets may be claimed both by the British Crown, on the basis of claimant to bona vacantia, and by the government of the country where the deceased died domiciled, qua universal successor or heir. In such a case, reference is made by the Scots forum qua *lex situs* to the law of intestate succession in the country of the deceased's domicile. The right claimed by the foreign government is analysed and classified by the *lex fori*: if it is a true right of succession, it will be recognised and its claim preferred, but if it is merely a right to bona vacantia the *lex loci rei sitae* will apply as a matter of property law and

18–16

---

[66] Presently £473,000: Prior Rights of Surviving Spouse and Civil Partner (Scotland) Order 2011 (SSI 2011/436).

[67] Meston, *The Succession (Scotland) Act 1964*, 5th edn (2002), p.134.

[68] Presently £29,000: Prior Rights of Surviving Spouse and Civil Partner (Scotland) Order 2011 (SSI 2011/436).

[69] Leslie, "Prior Rights in Succession: The International Dimension", 1988 S.L.T. (News) 105, but making reference to the contrary view expressed in Scottish Law Commission, *Some Miscellaneous Topics in the Law of Succession*, 1986, Scot. Law Com. Memo. No.71, para.6.2. If the deceased spouse died domiciled in Scotland, is the survivor entitled to the furniture and plenishings contained in an otherwise qualifying dwelling house which is excluded only by its foreign situation from forming the subject of a prior right to the house? The balance of sense of the statute suggests that the house must be in Scotland and the furniture in question must be within it, and for a successful claim to the furniture to be made by the survivor, the deceased spouse must have died domiciled in Scotland. The point was considered by the Scottish Law Commission *Discussion Paper on Succession* (DP No 136), para.4.81, but no final view was articulated. The point is not explicitly mentioned in the *Report on Succession* (Scot.Law Com. No 215) at para.5.5 on Intestacy.

[70] Presently £50,000 if the deceased left issue, and £89,000 otherwise: Prior Rights of Surviving Spouse and Civil Partner (Scotland) Order 2011 (SSI 2011/436).

the claim of the foreign (non-*situs*) government will be refused,[71] the estate falling instead to the British Crown, i.e. Exchequer.

The case of *Maldonado*[72] is renowned for the English forum's yielding to the foreign law of the domicile the power to classify the nature of its claim, and its acceptance of that classification, as expressed in the following words:

> "There might be a case where a so-called right of succession claimed by a foreign State could be shown to be in truth no more than a claim to bona vacantia…but this has not been shown to be such a case. On the contrary, it has been found (and the Crown has accepted the finding) that the State of Spain is, in the eye of Spanish law, the true heir."[73]

If the foreign rule is simply to the effect of conveying ownerless property to its fisc, the Scottish forum qua *situs* would prefer that the property fall to the UK Exchequer, and can give effect to that preference.

TESTATE SUCCESSION

Introduction

18–17   The choice of law rules of testate succession are two dimensional (or three dimensional if one includes the *renvoi* aspect), in the sense that they depend both on time and place. A will is an inchoate or ambulatory document as one cannot know a testator's final testamentary intention until the time of his death (unless he should lose mental capacity beforehand to such an extent that a later will is invalid) and, in the conflict sense, one cannot know whether the provisions of the will are essentially valid as to moveable property until the date of his death because only then can the legal system of his last domicile, the judge of essential validity, be identified.

Testamentary capacity of the testator

Legal capacity

18–18   The conflict rule of Scots law regarding legal testamentary capacity (i.e. age,[74] sanity, etc.) is that the law of the testator's domicile at the date of the will, as regards moveables, and the *lex situs*, as regards immoveables, governs.[75] By extension, challenges under the heads, e.g. of facility and circumvention, undue

---

[71] *Re Barnett* [1902] 1 Ch. 867; *Re Musurus* [1936] 2 All E.R. 1666; *Goold Stuart's Trustees v McPhail*, 1947 S.L.T. 221; *In the Estate of Maldonado* [1954] P. 223.

[72] *Maldonado* [1954] P. 223.

[73] *Maldonado* [1954] P. 223, per Jenkins L.J. at 248–250.

[74] The minimum age of testing in Scots domestic law is 12 years: Age of Legal Capacity (Scotland) Act 1991 s.2(2).

[75] *Fuld (No.3)* [1968] P. 675 (though in that case there was no change in the German domicile of the testator between the date of testing and the date of death). The Scottish Government Consultation on the Law of Succession (June 2015) proposes in Ch.5 ("Additional Matters") that capacity to make or revoke a will, whether it disposes of moveables or immoveables, be determined by the law of the testator's domicile at the time of making or revising the will (para.5.2).

influence, or force and fear, must be referred to the law of the domicile of the testator at the time of making the instrument in question,[76] or the *lex situs*, as appropriate.[77] In domestic law, in the matter of mental capacity, a testator need not be of sufficient mental capacity to test at the date of death: a will made earlier, in time of lucidity, will not be challenged on this ground.

Proprietary capacity

Proprietary testamentary capacity (i.e. entitlement to bequeath property) concerns a testator's freedom of testation. This is the correlative of the rule on legal rights or compulsory family provision, and is governed by the testator's domicile at death in relation to moveables, and by the *lex situs* in relation to immoveables.

18–19

The point is well demonstrated by *Re Groos*[78] in which a lady of Dutch domicile made a will before her marriage to another Dutch domiciliary. The terms of the will indicated that her intention was to make her future husband her heir or universal legatee, in preference to any children who might be born. Some years after their marriage, the couple came to England and her husband acquired a domicile there, as did she by virtue of the unity of spousal domicile rule then operative. The testatrix died, survived by her husband and five children. The children could not dispute the terms of their mother's will because her proprietary testamentary capacity was judged in accordance with her English domicile at death, and by that law her capacity had been expanded, since English law at that time permitted freedom of testation. It was established that by Dutch law marriage itself did not revoke a will,[79] and that the estate would have been distributed by Dutch domestic law, had it applied, in the proportion three-quarters to the children as their legitimate portion, and one-quarter to the husband.

Formal validity of wills

Common law

At common law in England, as regards immoveables, a will had to be formally valid according to the *lex situs*, and as regards moveables, English law insisted upon compliance with the law of the testator's domicile at the date of his death.[80] As time went on, however, that law was interpreted to include a law recognised by the law of the domicile at the date of death, thereby providing the genesis of *renvoi* thinking in England.[81] In *Bremer v Freeman*,[82] a will made in Paris in

18–20

---

[76] *Fuld (No.3)* [1968] P. 675. See recently in English domestic law, *Key v Key* [2010] EWHC 408 (Ch); and *Simon v Byford* [2014] EWCA Civ. 280.

[77] Unless the relevant transfer by the deceased can be characterised not as a matter of succession, but rather as an inter vivos assignation of property, as, e.g. in *Gorjat v Gorjat* [2010] EWHC 1537 (Ch).

[78] *Re Groos*; sub nom. *Groos v Groos* [1915] 1 Ch. 572 (and earlier *In the Estate of Groos* [1904] P. 269).

[79] As to conflict rules pertaining to revocation of a will by marriage: para.18–39, below.

[80] *Bremer v Freeman* (1857) 10 Moo. P.C. 306; *In the Estate of Groos* [1904] P. 269; *Re Grassi* [1905] 1 Ch. 584; *De Fogassieras v Duport* (1881) 11 L.R. Ir. 123; *Murray v Champernowne* [1901] 2 I.R. 232; *Re Moses* [1908] 2 Ch. 235; *In the Goods of Schroeder* [1949] I.R. 89.

[81] *Collier v Rivaz* (1841) 2 Curt. 855. Ch.5, above.

[82] *Bremer v Freeman* (1857) 10 Moo. P.C. 306.

English form by an Englishwoman then domiciled in England was held to be invalid because it was not also valid by the law of France, where she was domiciled at the date of her death. The decision showed that a change of domicile could have the effect of invalidating a will as to form. In consequence, the Wills Act 1861 (Lord Kingsdown's Act) was passed.

The difficulty referred to in the preceding paragraph did not arise in Scotland,[83] because the conflict rule of Scots common law was that a will was regarded as being formally valid if it had been executed in accordance with the *lex situs*, as regards immoveables; and as regards moveables, in accordance with any of the law(s) of the place of execution,[84] or of the testator's domicile at the date of execution of the will or at death.[85]

The Wills Act 1861, introduced in response to *Bremer v Freeman* (1857), was not essential therefore as regards Scots law, but it applied to both Scotland and England, and provided that a will should not be held to be revoked nor its construction altered by reason of a change of domicile of the testator. Furthermore, various options against which the formal validity of a will could be tested were provided in addition to the Scots common law rules stated above.

Wills Act 1963

18–21 The law was altered again by the Wills Act 1963, which repealed the 1861 Act, and came into operation on 1 January 1964 as regards the will of a person who died after that date. The 1963 Act represents the current law on the subject and is the result of deliberations at The Hague culminating in the 1961 Hague Convention on the Conflict of Laws relating to the Form of Testamentary Dispositions. The Act contains the following rules as to formal validity:

(a) General rule (section 1(1))

18–22 A will is to be regarded as validly executed in form if it complies with any of the following laws[86]:

(i)   the law of the place of execution[87];
(ii) the law of the testator's domicile at the date of execution or at his death;
(iii) the law of the testator's habitual residence at the date of execution or at his death;
(iv) the law of the testator's nationality at the date of execution or at his death (if he was a national of more than one country, then possibly compliance with either (any) of those laws will suffice).[88]

---

[83] *Purvis' Trustees v Purvis' Executors* (1861) 23 D. 812; *Connel's Trustees v Connel* (1872) 10 M. 627; *Bradford v Young* (1884) 11 R. 1135; *Macdonald v Cuthbertson* (1890) 18 R. 101; *Chisholm v Chisholm*, 1949 S.C. 434; *Irving v Snow*, 1956 S.C. 257.

[84] *Purvis' Trustees* (1861) 23 D. 812.

[85] cf. *Chisholm*, 1949 S.C. 434.

[86] In each case the law in question is the internal law of the country: s.6(1).

[87] Even if the testator was on a temporary visit there. *Re Wynn (Deceased)* [1983] 3 All E.R. 310.

[88] F.A. Mann, "The Formal Validity of Wills in Case of Dual Nationality" (1986) 35 I.C.L.Q. 423.

The list of applicable laws is long, yet it is still possible for a testator to fall foul of the Act. In *Re Kanani*[89] an English national and domiciliary, on holiday in Switzerland, made a will written in his own handwriting on the writing paper of his hotel. His death occurred shortly afterwards. The will was invalid as to form because it did not comply with English requirements and, although Swiss law recognised holograph wills, such wills had to be entirely holograph and the printed heading of the hotel on the writing paper was fatal to the will's validity.

(b) Additional rules (section 2)

A will is also[90] to be regarded as validly executed in form in the following circumstances:

18–23

- (i) a will executed on board a vessel[91] or aircraft (s.2(1)(a)) is properly executed if the execution conforms to the internal law of the territory with which, having regard to its registration (if any) and other relevant circumstances, the vessel or aircraft may be taken to have been most closely connected[92];
- (ii) a will so far as it disposes of immoveable property (s.2(1)(b)) is properly executed if the execution conforms to the internal law in force in the territory where the property was situated.

(c) Other relevant provisions (sections 2–6)

(i) Revocation (s.2(1)(c)). If a will purports to revoke a will valid in form under the Act, it shall itself be regarded as valid in form and thus revoking the earlier will, if it conforms to any law by reference to which the revoked will would be valid.

18–24

(ii) Powers (s.2(1)(d), (2)). If a will exercises a power of appointment, it shall be regarded as valid in form if it conforms to the law governing the essential validity of the power. Further (s.2(2)), a will which exercises a power of appointment shall not be treated as improperly executed by reason only that its execution was not in accordance with any formal requirements contained in the instrument creating the power.

18–25

(iii) Foreign law (s.3). Where a law in force outside the UK falls to be applied in relation to a will, any requirement of that law, whereby special formalities are to be observed by testators of a particular description, or witnesses are to possess certain qualifications, shall be treated as a formal requirement only.

18–26

---

[89] *Re Kanani (Deceased)* (1978) 122 S.J. 611.

[90] The rules in s.2 must be regarded as rules additionally available, over and above s.1, thereby precluding any argument that, e.g. a will purporting to dispose of immoveable property *must* comply with the formal requirements of the *lex situs*.

[91] Cases still arise concerning the privileges accorded under English domestic law, per Wills Act 1837 s.11, to wills made by soldiers in military service, and mariners or seamen, even extending to the acceptance of oral (nuncupative) wills: *Re Servoz-Gavin (Deceased)* [2011] Ch. 162.

[92] If the aircraft was on the ground, or the ship in territorial waters, at the time of the will's execution, it will be sufficient that the testator complied with the law of the place of execution.

18–27   (iv) Construction of wills (s.4). The construction of a will shall not be altered by reason of any change of domicile of the testator after the date of execution of the will.

18–28   (v) Interpretation of the Act. Section 6 defines inter alia "internal law" as the law which would apply in a case where no question of the law in force in any other territory or state arose.[93] Section 6(2) provides the solution where doubt arises in a multi-legal system state about which law to apply as the "internal law".

Registration of wills and "international wills"

18–29   The Administration of Justice Act 1982 makes provision in ss.23–25 for registration of wills, and in ss.27 and 28 for international wills.

A Convention on the Establishment of a Scheme of Registration of Wills was drawn up at Basle in 1972 under the auspices of the Council of Europe, with the aim of establishing national registration schemes and providing supplementary rules governing the international co-operation which was thought to be required between the various national authorities entrusted with registration. Sections 23–25 of the 1982 Act were put in place to allow the UK to comply with the requirements of the Convention, and thereby to ratify it, but the sections have never been implemented.

Likewise, s.27, which provides that the Annex[94] to the Convention on International Wills,[95] concluded at Washington on 26 October 1973, shall have the force of law in the UK, never entered into force. The aim of the 1973 Uniform Law was to provide a new form of will, in addition to existing forms permitted by national rules of law, for use in circumstances where a will has "some international characteristics."[96] The aim was that a will which satisfied the provisions of the Uniform Law would be regarded as formally valid in the UK or any other Contracting State to the Convention, no matter that the said will had no connection with the UK or any such other Contracting State.

It is now highly unlikely that these provisions of the 1982 Act will come into effect. The initiatives truly are a dead letter. The impetus towards some type of international register of wills was resurrected in the EU Green Paper on Wills and Succession, but wisely was not implemented in Rome IV.[97] Chapter VI of that Regulation, however, creates a European Certificate of Succession, the intended purpose of which is to make it easier for heirs and legatees to invoke their status or exercise their rights or powers throughout the EU.[98]

---

[93] i.e. there is to be no scope for *renvoi* in matters covered by the Act (in the very subject area which gave rise to *renvoi*). See, however, *Cheshire, North and Fawcett: Private International Law*, 14th edn (2008), p.1269.

[94] Set out in Sch.2 to the Administration of Justice Act 1982.

[95] UNIDROIT Convention providing a Uniform Law on the Form of an International Will.

[96] J.P. Plantard, "Explanatory Report on the Convention providing a Uniform Law on the Form of an International Will" (1974) I Uniform Law Review 91 at 92, p.2.

[97] Para.18–40, below.

[98] Rome IV arts 62 and 63. Para.18–52 re the European Certificate of Succession.

Duty of a solicitor to act timeously upon instructions to make a will

The existence, or not, of such a duty will be characterised in a Scots forum as a **18–30** matter pertaining to delict. The conflict aspect of the subject must be governed, therefore, by the applicable law determined in accordance with the Rome II Regulation.

Essential validity of wills

The essential validity of a will is governed by the *lex successionis*, which, in the **18–31** case of immoveables is the *lex situs*,[99] and in the case of moveables is the law of the testator's domicile, both as at the date of death.[100]

Essential validity is concerned with all matters pertaining to the validity and enforceability of the provisions of a will. It deals with the extent to which the provisions of a will are valid, or may be affected by any of the following matters:

(a) proof of survival[101];

(b) claims for legal rights[102];

(c) the question whether or not a beneficiary must elect between a bequest under a will and an interest outside the will: election, or approbate and reprobate[103];

(d) the validity of conditions attached to bequests, such as to marriage or religion[104];

(e) the question whether or not a bequest is contrary to public policy;

(f) the validity of bequests for religious or charitable purposes[105];

(g) the extent to which the provisions are affected by statutory provisions as to accumulation of capital and income, and perpetuities[106];

(h) the extent to which provisions may be affected by considerations of inheritance tax[107];

---

[99] *Macdonald v Macdonald,* 1932 SC (HL) 79. In England, *Nelson v Bridport* (1846) 8 Beav. 547; *Re Miller* [1914] 1 Ch. 511; *Philipson-Stow v Inland Revenue Commissioners* [1961] A.C. 727; and *Scarfe v Matthews* [2012] EWHC 3071 (Ch).

[100] *Lashley v Hog* (1804) 4 Pat. 581; *Bell v Kennedy* (1868) 6 M. HL 69; and, more recently in England, *Morris v Davies* [2011] EWHC 1773 (Ch).

[101] *Re Cohn* [1945] Ch. 5.

[102] *Re Groos* [1915] 1 Ch. 572.

[103] *Re Allen's Estate* [1945] 2 All E.R. 264; *Murray v Smith* (1828) 6 S. 690; *Alexander v Bennet's Trustees* (1829) 7 S. 817; *Hewit's Trustees v Lawson* (1891) 18 R. 793; *Brown's Trustees v Gregson,* 1920 S.C. (H.L.) 87; *Trotter v Trotter* (1829) 3 Wils. & Sh. 407; *Dundas v Dundas* (1830) 2 Dow & Cl. 349; *Douglas-Menzies v Umphelby* [1908] A.C. 224; *Re Ogilvie* [1918] 1 Ch. 492; *Re Mengel's Will Trusts* [1962] Ch. 791. As to whether a party who rejects the will can yet benefit from a beneficial tax provision contained therein, see *Scarfe v Matthews* [2012] EWHC 3071 (Ch).

[104] *Ommanney v Bingham* (1796) 3 Pat. 448.

[105] *Boe v Anderson* (1862) 24 D. 732; *Ferguson v Marjoribanks* (1853) 15 D. 637; *Hewit's Trustees v Lawson* (1891) 18 R. 793; *Re Elliot* (1891) 39 W.R. 297; *Re De Noailles* (1916) 114 L.T. 1089; *Re Egan* (1918) L.J. 633; *Re Dawson* [1915] 1 Ch. 626.

[106] *Fordyce v Bridges* (1848) 2 Ph. 497.

[107] *Philipson-Stow* [1961] A.C. 727; *Re Levick's Will Trusts* [1963] 1 WLR 311.

(i)   the operation of the conditio *si testator sine liberis decesserit*[108] or equivalent;

(j)   lapse of bequest to spouse upon the occurrence of subsequent divorce or annulment[109]; and

(k)   rules of forfeiture ("the unworthy heir").[110]

The distinction between formal validity and essential validity is clear in theory, but in exceptional cases, it may not be easy to distinguish between them. In the case of *Re Priest*,[111] for example, the English forum classified as a rule of substance, governed therefore by the law of the testator's last domicile, its own rule that bequests would be rendered void if the will in which they were made was witnessed by the spouse of a beneficiary.[112]

Construction or interpretation of wills

18–32   Just as the distinction between formal validity and essential validity is plain in theory, but occasionally in practice the one aspect may tend to merge with the other, so too the distinction between essential validity and construction may not be clear.

Construction of a will answers the question—what do the provisions of the will mean?

Essential validity answers the question—to what extent are the provisions of a will valid and enforceable?

Problems involving the following matters have been solved by the application of the rules governing interpretation:

(a)   Whether a will exercises a power of appointment (q.v.).

(b)   Application of *conditio si institutus sine liberis decesserit*.[113]
        This is exemplified by *Mitchell and Baxter v Davies*,[114] in which the application of the *conditio*, having been assigned by the Scots forum to the category of "interpretation", was referred to the Scots law governing interpretation of the will (which had been made in Scots form), rather than to the English law of the deceased's last domicile.

(c)   Accretion or intestacy as a result of the absence of a survivorship clause or a destination-over.

---

[108] i.e. the effect on a will, which makes no provision for children who may be born to the testator, of the subsequent birth of a child. Contrast characterisation of the *conditio si institutus sine liberis decesserit* (para.18–32.).

[109] cf. Family Law (Scotland) Act 2006 s.19, whereby a special destination is revoked upon the parties' divorce or annulment prior to the death of the predeceaser; and Civil Partnership Act 2004 s.124A.

[110] *Re DWS (Deceased)* [2001] 1 All E.R. 97. See further Law Commission, *The Forfeiture Rule and the Law of Succession* (The Stationery Office, 2005), Law Com. No.295.

[111] *Re Priest (Deceased)* [1944] Ch. 58.

[112] Contrast *Irving v Snow*, 1956 S.C. 257.

[113] i.e. the effect on the interpretation of a will, which makes no provision for the predecease of a beneficiary, of that beneficiary's predecease leaving issue, so as to operate in favour of that beneficiary's issue (as opposed to, e.g. accretion to existing legatees or transmission to the residuary legatee).

[114] *Mitchell and Baxter v Davies* (1875) 3 R. 208.

In the case of *Re Cunnington*,[115] the issue whether accretion to the survivors of a list of eight residuary legatees (as was the French rule) should occur, or whether the shares of the two predeceasers, neither of whom had left issue, should fall into intestacy (the English rule), was classified by the English forum, as a matter of interpretation, governed by the testator's French domicile at death.[116]

The general principle is that a will must be construed in accordance with the law by reference to which it was written, that is, the legal system contemplated by the testator,[117] which may or may not be the same as the governing law of the essentials of the will. The testator's intention, deemed or actual, is the paramount consideration.[118] In *Philipson-Stow v Inland Revenue Commissioners*,[119] Lord Denning said:

"...whilst I would agree that the construction of the will depends on the intention of the testator, I would say that in no other respect does his intention determine the law applicable to it".[120]

The following are working rules:

(1) If there is an express declaration as to the law to be applied for the purposes of interpretation, that law normally will regulate the construction of the will.

(2) In the absence of such a declaration, the law to be applied may be clearly inferred from the language of the will.[121] The use of technical terms of a particular legal system usually indicates that the will should be construed according to that law.[122]

In the special case of a will dealing with a bequest of immoveables expressed in the technical terms of the law of a country other than the *lex situs*, the meaning of the will should first be ascertained according to the law indicated by the will, and then the court should endeavour to translate it and give effect to it in terms which will be effective according to the *lex situs*.[123]

---

[115] *Re Cunnington* [1924] 1 Ch. 68.

[116] The court held that since there was no sufficient indication in the will, either express or implied, that the testator desired that his will should be construed by English law, the will was to be construed by French law.

[117] *Dellar v Zivy* [2007] I.L.Pr. 60.

[118] *Re Scott* [1915] 1 Ch. 592.

[119] *Philipson-Stow v Inland Revenue Commissioners* [1961] A.C. 727. Also *Re Levick's Will Trusts* [1963] 1 W.L.R. 311.

[120] *Philipson-Stow* [1961] A.C. 727 at 760, 761.

[121] *Re Goetze* [1953] Ch. 96; *Re Cunnington* [1924] 1 Ch. 68; *Re Price* [1900] 1 Ch. 442, per Stirling J. at 453; *Re Allen's Estate* [1945] 2 All E.R. 264.

[122] *Re McMorran* [1958] Ch. 624; *Re Manners* [1923] 1 Ch. 220; but see *Bradford v Young* (1885) L.R. 29 Ch. D. 617 in which the use of some technical terms of Scots law was held by the Court of Appeal, disapproving the court below, to be insufficient indication of the testator's intention to have the will construed by that law.

[123] *Studd v Cook* (1883) 10 R. (H.L.) 53; *Cripps' Trustees v Cripps*, 1926 S.C. 188; *Re Miller* [1914] 1 Ch. 511.

(3)   Failing an express declaration or inference from the language of the will, there is a presumption that the law of the testator's domicile at the date of the will shall apply as regards moveables[124] and probably also as regards immoveables,[125] because presumably he had that law in mind.[126] In some cases, however, the law of the domicile at the date of death has been applied.[127] In such a case, there is Scots authority[128] to the effect that the forum simply may construe the will in accordance with its own law.

(4)   The Wills Act 1963 s.4 provides that the construction of a will is not to be affected by a change of domicile by the testator after the date of execution of the will.

The width and variety of these "rules" (or guides) suggest that it is more important to be aware of the distinction between essentials and construction, to note that the *lex successionis* may not necessarily be the law which governs construction, and to be cognisant of those matters which have been assigned to the category of "interpretation", than to place great reliance on any one of the "presumptions".

Construction of bequests

18–33   To determine the validity of a claim of a beneficiary in testate succession, it will be necessary to ascertain, according to the law governing interpretation of the will, the testator's intention with regard to that beneficiary or class of beneficiaries, but there may arise thereafter the separate issue of ascertaining the status of the claimant, i.e. whether he qualifies as a member of that class of beneficiaries, e.g. of the legitimate/legitimated children of the testator.

If the succession to the estate of X, domiciled in country A, opens, in terms of his will as interpreted in accordance with the rules set out above, only to the legitimate children of Y, domiciled in country B, and a question arises as to whether or not a person is a legitimate child of Y, Scots and English choice of law rules diverge. Scots conflict law favours the application of B law to determine the status of the children of Y,[129] whereas English conflict law prefers application of A law.[130]

---

[124] *Dellar v Zivy* [2007] I.L.Pr. 60.

[125] *Mitchell and Baxter v Davies* (1875) 3 R. 208; *Smith v Smith* (1891) 18 R. 1036; *McBride's Trustees, Special Case*, 1952 S.L.T. (Notes) 59; *Re Price* [1900] 1 Ch. 442.

[126] *Re Allen's Estate* [1945] 2 All E.R. 264; *Philipson-Stow* [1961] A.C. 727, per Lord Denning at 761, 762 (so long, however, as the construction does not conflict with the rules of the *lex situs*).

[127] *Re Cunnington* [1924] 1 Ch. 68.

[128] *Griffith's Judicial Factor v Griffith's Executors* (1905) 7 F. 470.

[129] *Mitchell's Trustee v Rule* (1908) 16 S.L.T. 189; *Smith's Trustees v Macpherson's Trustees*, 1926 S.C. 983; *Goold Stuart's Trustees v McPhail*, 1947 S.L.T. 221; *Spencer's Trustees v Ruggles*, 1981 S.C. 289; *Wright's Trustees v Callender*, 1993 S.L.T. 556; *Salvesen's Trustees, Petitioners*, 1993 S.L.T. 1327. See E.B. Crawford, 1994 S.L.T. (News) 225; and R. Leslie, 1995 S.L.T. (News) 264. In *Spencer's Trustees*, 1981 S.C. 289, the question at issue was whether adopted children could succeed, but since it was established that the testator did not intend to benefit adopted children, the second stage of debating by which law the validity of a foreign adoption should be judged was not reached.

[130] *Campbell v Campbell* (1866) L.R. 1 Eq. 383; *Re Fergusson's Will* [1902] 1 Ch. 483.

Where, however, the bequest is to the "heirs", "children", "issue", "next-of-kin", etc. of the *testator*, the beneficiaries are to be identified by the *lex domicilii*[131] of the testator.

Revocation of wills

It may be necessary to consider the effect upon a will of a subsequent will; or of a subsequent marriage by the testator; or of a change of domicile by the testator after making the will.

18–34

(a) New will

The revocation of one will depends on the validity and scope of a subsequent will.[132] It is possible that a new will may be formally defective with regard to the testator's immoveable property, with the result that a prior will (if extant), valid by the *lex situs*, may continue to regulate the immoveable succession, while the new will regulates the succession to moveables.[133] In *In the Estate of Alberti,*[134] a testator made a will in England dealing, inter alia, with real estate in England. Later he made a holograph will in Switzerland which was invalid by English law although valid by Swiss law and which purported to revoke all previous wills. It was held that the English will was still effective in relation to the English real estate because only a will valid by the *lex situs* could revoke the earlier will in that regard. Different wills may apply to assets in different countries[135] where a will is regarded as having been revoked in one country, but not in another.[136]

18–35

The matter alternatively might be one of inference and interpretation, as when, without express revocation, the testator makes provision in a later will in relation to property included in an earlier one.

---

[131] There is also a temporal issue, in that the content of the applicable law may have changed between the date of testing and date of death, or between date of death and date of opening of the succession. On the same theme, in *Wright's Trustees v Callender,* 1993 S.L.T. 556 the House of Lords addressed the issue of the effect of time, and changes in the law, on the matter of *interpretation* of the truster's intentions. The effect of the decision was that the content of the applicable law as at the date of death, rather than the (much later) date of opening of the succession should prevail.

[132] *Cameron v Mackie* (1833) 7 W. & S. 16; *Cottrell v Cottrell* (1872) L.R. 2 P. & D. 397; and *Perdoni v Curati* [2012] EWCA Civ 1381.

[133] In *In the Estate of Alberti* [1955] 1 W.L.R. 1240, a testator made a will in England dealing, inter alia, with real estate in England. Later he made a holograph will in Switzerland which was invalid by English law although valid by Swiss law and which purported to revoke all previous wills. It was held that the English will was still effective in relation to the English real estate because only a will valid by the *lex situs* could revoke the earlier will in that regard.

[134] *In the Estate of Alberti* [1955] 1 W.L.R. 1240.

[135] In *Re Manifold* [1962] Ch. 1, a testatrix domiciled in Cyprus made two wills, the first valid by the laws of England and Cyprus, and the second valid only by the law of England. The court in Cyprus granted probate on the first will only, but the English court held that, as regards assets in England, the Wills Act 1861 must have an overriding effect and that probate must be granted on both wills. Thereafter, the administrators in England of the English estate were directed to distribute the assets in England according to the terms of the later will (on the basis that it had, in the English view, superseded the earlier will), and as if the assets in England were the whole estate, the legacies to abate rateably so far as necessary.

[136] *Richmond's Trustees v Winton* (1864) 3 M. 95.

(b)   A revocation clause

18–36   The effect of such a clause is considered in light of all the circumstances.[137] Again this seems a very broad guide, but it can happen on occasion that the circumstances reveal quite clearly what was the testator's intention. Thus, in *Re Wayland*[138] where the testator had separate wills to deal with his English and his Belgian estate, it was apparent that when he made a new English will, the revocation clause contained therein was intended to apply only to previous English wills; before and after making that new English will, he corresponded with his Belgian lawyer about the safekeeping of his Belgian will.

(c)   Acts involving revocation

18–37   The effectiveness of a purported act of revocation depends, as regards immoveables, upon the *lex situs*, and as regards moveables, upon the law of the testator's domicile at the date of the revocation. An excellent example is provided by *Velasco v Coney*,[139] in which the English testatrix, who had acquired Italian domicile on marriage, instructed her English solicitor to destroy her will, previously made by her in accordance with both English and Italian law. The act of destruction did not take place in her presence, presence being a requirement of English domestic law. The English court decided that such an act of revocation was sufficient to satisfy its conflict rules if the act amounted to revocation by the domicile of the testatrix at the date of the act of purported revocation—a practical decision, and one in accordance with the policy of the court, which was to, "lean towards giving effect to the intention of the testatrix."[140] By Italian law, her letter or mandate containing her instructions to revoke would have been sufficient even without the physical destruction which in fact happened.

(d)   Change of domicile

18–38   This has no effect on the formal validity or construction of a will.[141] However, change of domicile is of fundamental importance in the final outcome for, as explained, the essential validity of the will falls to be judged, vis-à-vis moveables, by the law of the testator's last domicile.[142]

(e)   Subsequent marriage

18–39   The effect of the marriage of the testator upon a previous will made by him is determined, as regards moveables, by the law of the domicile of the testator immediately after the marriage,[143] for any rule of revocation by subsequent

---

[137]   cf. Australian case of *Re Barker* [1995] 2 V.R. 439.
[138]   *Re Wayland (Deceased)* [1951] 2 All E.R. 1041. Also *Lamothe v Lamothe* [2006] EWHC 1387 (Ch).
[139]   *Velasco v Coney* [1934] P. 143.
[140]   *Velasco v Coney* [1934] P. 143 at 143.
[141]   Wills Act 1963 s.4.
[142]   *Re Groos* [1915] 1 Ch. 572.
[143]   *Re Martin* [1900] P. 211.

marriage is regarded in Scots and English conflict rules as a matter of matrimonial law rather than succession law.[144]

The effect of marriage upon any provisions in respect of immoveables must be determined by the *lex situs*.[145] By English domestic law, an ante-nuptial will is revoked by marriage of the testator, unless the will was made in contemplation of that marriage.[146] By Scots law, marriage per se does not revoke an earlier will, but if a child subsequently is born, no provision having been made for him in the will, it will be open to him to seek to have applied the presumption *conditio si testator sine liberis decesserit*. The *conditio si testator* or equivalent is regarded as a matter of substance, available, therefore, only if such a rule forms part of the *lex successionis*.

Since the domestic laws of Scotland and England differ on this matter, though their conflict rules agree, this means, in an English/Scottish context, that if a testator domiciled in England makes a will before his marriage, and is of English domicile immediately after marriage, the will is revoked and cannot revive even upon subsequent acquisition of Scots domicile. In contrast, the English courts will uphold any will made by a Scots domiciliary before marriage even though he may die domiciled in England, provided that his immediate post-nuptial domicile was Scottish.[147]

THE EU SUCCESSION REGULATION

As has been seen, the conflict of laws rules of Scots and English law in the area of succession are well-settled, and rest largely on common law.   **18–40**

Succession conflict rules were excluded from early EU private international law harmonisation agendas. Whilst harmonisation of choice of law rules concerning formal validity of wills has been accomplished,[148] initial efforts to harmonise the rules concerning essential validity proved less successful: the 1989 Hague Convention on the Law Applicable to the Estates of Deceased Persons, to which the United Kingdom did not accede, received little support and was not acceptable to the UK.[149]

A consultation process took place in 2005 to elicit opinion in EU Member States on the scope of a possible European harmonisation instrument to deal with wills and succession (choice of law and/or administration), and on the detail of proposed rules.[150] The initiative was said to be justified by the growing mobility

---

[144] *Westerman v Schwab* (1905) 8 F. 132; and *Re Groos* [1915] 1 Ch. 572.

[145] *Re Caithness* (1891) 7 T.L.R. 354.

[146] Wills Act 1837 s.18 (substituted by s.18(1) of the Administration of Justice Act 1982). The same is true of civil partnerships, per s.18B of the 1837 Act (inserted by Civil Partnership Act 2004 s.71 and Sch.4): *Court v Despallieres*; sub nom. *Re Ikin (Deceased)* [2009] EWHC 3340 (Ch).

[147] *Re Reid* (1866) L.R. 1 P. & D. 74.

[148] 1961 Hague Convention on the Conflicts of Laws Relating to the Form of Testamentary Dispositions, leading to 1963 Wills Act: para. 18–21, above.

[149] See Lord Chancellor's Department, Scottish Courts Administration, *Hague Convention on Succession: Consultation Paper* (HMSO, 1990); and Robertson, "International Succession Law. A Co-ordinated Approach" (1989) 34 J.L.S. 377.

[150] Green Paper on Succession and Wills COM(2005) 65 final; Commission Staff Working Paper, Annex to the Green Paper on Succession and Wills SEC(2005) 270; and Opinion of the European Economic and Social Committee on the Green Paper on Succession and Wills [2006] O.J. C28/1.

of European citizens in an area without internal frontiers, and the increasing frequency of personal unions between nationals of different Member States, together with the fact of acquisition by many individuals of property situated in different states.

In October 2009, the European Commission announced the publication of a proposal for a regulation on wills and succession.[151] Regulation (EU) No.650/2012 of the European Parliament and of the Council on jurisdiction, applicable law, recognition and enforcement of decisions and acceptance and enforcement of authentic instruments in matters of succession and on the creation of a European Certificate of Succession (hereinafter "Rome IV") was finalised on 4 July 2012. It shall apply to the succession of persons who die on or after 17 August 2015.[152]

The instrument is wide in technical scope, and aims to deal with all international private law aspects of the subject of succession. It is quadruple in nature, addressing itself to rules of jurisdiction (Ch.II), applicable law (Ch.III), recognition, enforceability and enforcement of decisions (Ch.IV), and introducing the European Certificate of Succession (Ch.VI).

The Regulation's essence and purpose are encapsulated in recital (37), to the effect, first, that harmonised conflict of laws rules should enable "citizens" to know in advance which law will apply to their succession; secondly, that the succession to a qualifying[153] person's estate should be governed by a predictable law of close connection; and, finally, that those harmonised rules should operate to avoid contradictory results.

Debate in the UK

18–41 Following publication of the 2009 Proposal, the UK Government directed that a public consultation exercise be undertaken[154] to address the issue of whether it would be in the UK's national interests for the Government, in accordance with art.4 of the UK's Protocol on Title IV measures,[155] to opt in to the proposed Regulation; and if so, on whether it should apply throughout the UK.[156]

The two issues of most pressing concern, identified by the House of Lords EU Committee after consideration of expert opinion,[157] were, first, the necessity for

---

[151] Proposal for a Regulation on jurisdiction, applicable law, recognition and enforcement of decisions and authentic instruments in matters of succession and the creation of a European Certificate of Succession COM(2009) 154 final (2009/0157 (COD)) ("the 2009 Proposal"); and Commission Staff Working Document accompanying the Proposal: Summary of the Impact Assessment SEC(2009) 411 final.

[152] Rome IV arts 83(1) and 84.

[153] *There's* the rub, i.e. the conflict lawyer's question—"qualifying" in whose view, and according to what criteria?

[154] UK Ministry of Justice, *European Commission proposal on succession and wills: a public consultation* (The Stationery Office, 2009), Consultation Paper CP41/09.

[155] Protocol No.21 on the position of the United Kingdom and Ireland in respect of the area of freedom, security and justice, annexed to the Treaty on European Union and to the Treaty on the Functioning of the European Union [2008] O.J. C115/295 ("Protocol 21").

[156] Article 28.2 provides the usual opt-out clause for use, if desired, by the UK and any other multi-legal system Member State.

[157] House of Lords European Union Committee, *6th Report of Session 2009–10, The EU's Regulation on Succession: Report with Evidence* (The Stationery Office, 2010), HL Paper No.75 (Session 2009/10).

further refinement of the meaning of the connecting factor of "deceased's habitual residence at time of death", and secondly, the problem of clawback.

While the House of Lords Committee found itself in agreement with the proposed change to a unitary choice of law rule to apply to the whole of the estate of a deceased,[158] and further with the 2009 Proposal to employ the connecting factor of habitual residence,[159] it concluded that a compromise needed to be struck between appropriateness and certainty, and that it was essential to define that central factor. In light of views expressed by an overwhelming number of respondents to the public consultation, the Government (with which the House of Lords EU Committee agreed) announced,[160] on 16 December 2009, that it had decided not to opt in to the proposed Regulation, concluding that the potential benefits of the Proposal were outweighed by the risks.[161]

Accordingly, recital (82) of Rome IV states that, in accordance with arts 1 and 2 of Protocol No.21, the UK and Ireland are not taking part in the adoption of Rome IV and are not bound by it or subject to its application. This is without prejudice to the possibility of the UK or Ireland, at any time after the adoption of the regulation, notifying the Council and Commission of its wish to accept the measure,[162] but there seems at present no possibility of this happening. It would be naïve, however, to assume that, by not opting in to Rome IV, the UK is "immune" from its effects. It is necessary, therefore, to examine the provisions of Rome IV, to gauge in what ways the UK, as an EU Member State which, *ex facie*, is not bound by the Regulation, nonetheless may be affected by it.

Implications of the UK's decision not to opt in: definition of "Member State"[163]

Despite early intimation of non-participation by the UK, the final version of Rome IV, though stating starkly the "opt-out" in recital (82), seems wilfully blind to the "end position", that is, that not all EU Member States adopted the Regulation, and to the repercussions of this outcome. A signal defect by way of omission in the drafting of the Regulation is the absence of an acknowledgment that, as a result of the decision by the UK and Ireland not to opt in, there exist three categories of state for the purpose of addressing cross-border successions in an EU context, namely: participating Member States, non-participating Member States (UK, Ireland and Denmark), and Third States (external to the EU), each of

18–42

---

[158] *The EU's Regulation on Succession*, 2010, HL Paper No.75 (Session 2009/10), para.58.
[159] *The EU's Regulation on Succession*, 2010, HL Paper No.75 (Session 2009/10), para.65.
[160] Hansard, HL Vol.502, Part No.17, col.141 (16 December 2009).
[161] cf. Press Release, 6 October 2005, Scottish Parliament: after consideration of expert opinion, the Justice 1 Committee of the Scottish Parliament concluded that the proposal was "fundamentally flawed and unnecessary", and strongly urged the UK Government not to opt in to any draft instrument which should emerge following the conclusion of the consultation processes. See also "Analysis of the Written Responses and Scottish Government Response" (June 2015) to the 2014 Consultation on Technical Issues Relating to Succession, para.5.8, wherein the Scottish Government stated that it would not move to implement any part of Rome IV as part of the Government's current body of work on succession.
[162] Protocol No.21 art.4.
[163] See, for detail, E.B. Crawford and J.M. Carruthers, "Speculation on the Operation of Succession Regulation 650/2012: Tales of the Unexpected" (2014) 22 European Review of Private Law 847–878.

which, by reason of the subject-matter content of the instrument, and each of whose legal systems' habitual residents, nationals or domiciliaries, potentially may be affected by Rome IV.[164]

Accurate drafting of Rome IV would have identified three categories of State, viz.: "compliant Member State",[165] "non-compliant Member State"[166] and "Third State".[167] The citizens of non-compliant Member States and property situated within such States may be affected by the provisions of Rome IV. Equally, the operation of the Regulation by compliant Member States is likely to be made more complicated, and in some cases compromised, by the refusal by the UK and Ireland to opt in. In assessing the implications of Rome IV as far as the UK is concerned, it is necessary to interpret the phrase "Member State" wherever it appears in the Regulation.

Scope of Rome IV (Chapter I)

18–43   Article 1 sets out the scope of the Regulation, excluding, inter alia, the status of natural persons (art.1.2(a)); questions regarding matrimonial property regimes (art.1.2(d)); maintenance obligations other than those arising by reason of death (art.1.2(e)); property rights, interests and assets created or transferred otherwise than by succession, e.g. by way of gifts, joint ownership with a right of survivorship, pension plans, and insurance contracts (art.1.2(g)); and the creation, administration and dissolution of trusts (art.1.2(j)[168]). Article 1 must be taken as evidence of an expectation that such excluded matters are capable of being regulated independently of a scheme of harmonised conflict rules of succession. However, issues of matrimonial property, gifts and joint ownerships frequently are intertwined with issues of succession and proprietary capacity, as exemplified classically in the House of Lords decision in *De Nicols v Curlier (No.1)*.[169] As a matter of practice, therefore, it is doubtful that the segregation of these excluded issues from succession issues will be as straightforward as the Regulation appears to envisage.

Jurisdiction (Chapter II)

18–44   As indicated above, the majority of successions are non-contentious, meaning that the creation of a set of jurisdiction rules specifically for this area is at odds with common law experience and expectations.

---

[164] Contrast the approach taken in Council Regulation (EU) No.1259/2010 implementing enhanced co-operation in the law applicable to divorce and legal separation ("Rome III"), which recognises the existence of participating and non-participating Member States. See para.12-19, above.

[165] A Member State taking part in the adoption of Rome IV and bound by it and subject to its application.

[166] A Member State not taking part in the adoption of Rome IV and not bound by it nor subject to its application; at present, UK, Ireland and Denmark.

[167] A sovereign state which is not a EU Member State.

[168] See earlier discussion of jurisdiction in relation to testamentary trusts: para.18–03.

[169] *De Nicols v Curlier (No.1)* [1900] A.C. 21. See para.13-02, above.

The scheme laid down in Rome IV is as follows: the general rule (art.4) is that the courts[170] of the Member State in which the deceased had his habitual residence at the time of death shall have jurisdiction to rule on the succession as a whole. The term "Member State", where it appears in Ch.II, must be construed to mean "compliant Member State", for it would be ultra vires the Regulation to seek to clothe with jurisdiction the courts of a non-compliant Member State.

Anticipating the party autonomy permitted in the Regulation in the matter of applicable law, art.5 provides that where the deceased has chosen the law of a Member State to govern his succession in accordance with art.22, the parties concerned (undefined) may agree[171] that a court(s) of that Member State[172] are to have exclusive[173] jurisdiction to rule on any succession matter. In such circumstances, art.6(b) directs that the court seised per art.4 shall decline jurisdiction. Furthermore, where the deceased has exercised choice of law, but "the parties concerned" have not made a choice of court agreement, the court seised per art.4 may decline jurisdiction, at the request of one of the parties, if the court considers that the courts of the (compliant) Member State whose law has been chosen are better placed to rule on the succession (art.6(a)).

Article 9 makes provision for jurisdiction based on appearance,[174] and art.10 seeks to ensure that where the habitual residence of the deceased at death is not located in a Member State, the courts of a (compliant) Member State in which assets of his estate are located may exercise subsidiary jurisdiction to rule on the succession as a whole (art.10.1), if certain conditions are fulfilled, namely, that the deceased was a national of that Member State at death, or had had his previous habitual residence there and a period of not more than five years has elapsed since the change in his habitual residence. Where these conditions are not fulfilled, the courts of the (compliant) Member State in which assets of the estate are located shall have jurisdiction to rule (only) on those assets (art.10.2). Exceptionally (art.11: *forum necessitatis*), the courts of a (compliant) Member State may rule on a succession where no other Member State court has jurisdiction pursuant to Ch.II, and if proceedings cannot reasonably be brought in a Third State, provided that the case has a sufficient connection with the Member State of the court seised.

Articles 14, 15, 17 and 18 establish a system of *lis pendens* with which we have become familiar under the Brussels regime in civil and commercial matters, and in consistorial proceedings.

---

[170] Rome IV art.3.2 defines "court" broadly, encompassing within its meaning any judicial authority or any competent authority or legal professional which exercises judicial function in matters of succession.

[171] As to form of agreement, see art.5.2.

[172] Although use of art.22 ("Choice of law") is open to nationals of a non-compliant Member State or of a Third State, and even though there is a direct drafting link between Ch.III art.22 and Ch.II art.5 ("Choice-of-court agreement"), art.5 must be interpreted as referring only to the courts of "compliant Member States".

[173] The statement of exclusivity, while binding on compliant Member States, is ultra vires as far as non-compliant Member States and Third States are concerned.

[174] The UK, as a non-compliant Member State, should be regarded as a *faux* Third State for this purpose, upon which no jurisdiction can be conferred by the rules in Ch.II, even by submission of parties.

Applicable law (Chapter III)

18–45   Article 21 (Applicable law: "General rule") provides that the law applicable to the succession as a whole shall be the law of the State in which the deceased had his habitual residence at the time of death, unless, by way of exception (art.21.2), it is clear from all the circumstances of the case that, at the time of death, the deceased was manifestly more closely connected with another State, in which case the law of that State shall apply. However, by art.22.1 ("Choice of law"), "a person" may choose[175] as the law to govern his succession as a whole the law of the state whose nationality he possesses at the time of making the choice or at the time of death. Where a person possesses multiple nationalities, he may choose the law of any of the states whose nationalities he possesses at the time of choice or death. Article 22.4 makes clear that a change of mind as to applicable law is permitted, by way of modification or revocation of the choice of law. As noted above, where a choice of law has been made, and the choice is that of a (compliant) Member State law, the "parties concerned"[176] may agree that the courts of that Member State are to have exclusive jurisdiction to rule on any succession matter (art.5).

Article 20 establishes application of the principle of universality. It is notable in this Chapter that terminology changes from reference to "Member State" to reference to "State". Moreover, the applicable law determined pursuant to the general rule in art.21 or to party choice per art.22 shall govern the succession as a whole, meaning, importantly, that a unitary principle instead of a scission principle operates and purports to govern regardless of whether the deceased's assets are located in another Member State or in a Third State.[177]

Article 35 provides the customary public policy safeguard for the forum, permitting it to refuse to apply a provision of the law of any State specified by the Regulation if such application is manifestly incompatible with the public policy of the forum.

The proposed unitary rule

18–46   Leaving for the moment the question of the quality of "last habitual residence" as a connecting factor, the replacement of the scission principle by a unitary principle is significant. This would have been a fundamental change for the UK, had the UK decided to opt in to the Regulation.[178] Yet in operating this unitary rule within the Regulation, the *lex situs* of immoveable property necessarily must have its place; art.30 ("Special rules imposing restrictions concerning or affecting the succession in respect of certain assets)", though to be construed strictly,[179] acknowledges this. On the other hand, by art.31, where a person invokes in the legal system of the *situs* a right in rem to which he is entitled under the *lex successionis*, but which is not known to the law of the Member State *situs*, the

---

[175] Rome IV recitals (38), (39) and (41).
[176] Undefined.
[177] Rome IV recital (37).
[178] In recent years, however, abandonment of the *situs* rule has been mooted, at least in the law of intestate succession. Para.18–05, above.
[179] Rome IV recital (54).

latter must seek to adapt the right to the closest equivalent right *in rem* under its own law. The Regulation refers to the *lex situs* (art.27.1(e)) the formal validity of dispositions of immoveable property.[180]

A major role for habitual residence

High among the factors causing disquiet among UK lawyers at the time of exercise of the decision to opt in, or not, was the central role to be given in the instrument to the connecting factor of habitual residence.[181] Study of the use of habitual residence across the spectrum of international private law shows it to be a weasel factor which does not always live up to its reputation as a common sense factual criterion. Habitual residence has proved to be a fruitful source of discussion and litigation. In spite of this, the Regulation does not provide a definition.[182] Recitals (24) and (25) indicate that, in the context of Rome IV, habitual residence can be established after short residence and in the face of the existence of a legal system of manifestly closer connection to the deceased. To counterbalance this, art.21.2 provides a potentially important exception to the general rule of applicable law, namely, that where it is clear[183] from all the circumstances of the case that, at the time of death, the deceased was manifestly more closely connected with a State other than the State whose law would be applicable under art.21.1 (i.e. his habitual residence at death), the law applicable to the succession shall be the law of that other State. Recital (25) explains that use of this provision might be appropriate "where, for instance, the deceased had moved to the state of his habitual residence fairly recently before his death and all the circumstances of the case indicate that he was manifestly more closely connected with another State",[184] but warns that the exception should not be resorted to as a subsidiary connecting factor whenever the determination of the habitual residence of the deceased proves complex. Article 21.2 is an exception to the general rule in art.21.1, and cannot be accessed without prior reference to art.21.1 and a preliminary finding as to the deceased's habitual residence at death. As a matter of practice, art.21.2 may prove to be a useful provision to evacuate the prima facie applicable law in favour of an essentially more appropriate law.

18–47

---

[180] Subject to the caveat contained in the disconnection clause, art.75.

[181] House of Lords European Union Committee, 6th Report of Session 2009–10, *The EU'S Regulation on Succession: Report with Evidence*, paras 54–65. On habitual residence: Ch.6, above.

[182] A definition is provided in Rome I Regulation (art.19) and the Rome II Regulation (art.23) for the purpose of each respective Regulation.

[183] Clear, presumably, to the court putatively seised under Ch.II (per art.4—the court of the putative habitual residence!).

[184] If the deceased had only recently moved to legal system A, which is less closely connected to him than legal system B, it seems wrong in principle that legal system A should be capable of being regarded as his habitual residence.

Party autonomy

18–48   Article 22 of the Regulation provides an option for a testator to choose as the law governing the succession to his estate as a whole[185] the law of the State whose nationality he possesses at the time of making the choice or at the time of death. Freedom of choice of law in the area of succession is a novelty in Scots and English conflict of laws. However, an article providing limited freedom of choice can be seen as a sensible counterbalance to a poorly conceived general rule. Against the background of the general rule in art.21.1, it is understandable that parties would wish to exercise a choice in order to align themselves legally with a point of permanence in their lives such as nationality. Party autonomy, increasingly permitted in EU private international law harmonisation instruments, normally is accompanied by mandatory rules in order to safeguard certain interests. To offset the lack of policing in Rome IV by way of mandatory rules provisions, the testator's choice is limited to the law of his nationality.

Renvoi

18–49   Typically, in EU private international law harmonisation instruments, it is provided that the application of the law of any country specified by a regulation means the application of the rules in force in that country other than its rules of private international law.[186] By contrast, in conventions produced by the Hague Conference on Private International Law, the default position is that *renvoi* reasoning may be employed unless it has been expressly excluded.[187]

The nature of the *renvoi* provision in Rome IV is to authorise the operation of *renvoi* outwards, i.e. where a (compliant) Member State court has identified as the applicable law the law of a Third State. There would be no point in admitting the *renvoi* process within the net of compliant Member States, for that would generate never-ending circularity.

Recital (57) advises that:

> "The conflict-of-laws rules laid down in this Regulation may lead to the application of the law of a third State. In such cases regard should be had to the private international law rules of that State. If those rules provide for *renvoi* either to the law of a Member State or to the law of a third State which would apply its own law to the succession, such *renvoi* should be accepted in order to ensure international consistency. *Renvoi* should, however, be excluded in situations where the deceased had made a choice of law in favour of the law of a third State."

The *renvoi* provision is one of considerable complexity, viz.:

> "Article 34 – Renvoi

---

[185] A testator is not able to use the Regulation to subvert the Regulation, by choosing, for example, the law of his nationality to govern the succession to immoveable property situated in the legal system of his nationality, and the law of his habitual residence to regulate succession to moveables wherever situated.

[186] e.g. Rome I Regulation art.20; Rome II Regulation art.24. Ch.5, above.

[187] e.g. *Re JB (Child Abduction) (Rights of Custody: Spain)* [2004] 1 F.L.R. 796.

1. The application of the law of any third State specified by this Regulation shall mean the application of the rules of law in force in that State, including its rules of private international law in so far as those rules make a renvoi:
   (a) to the law of a Member State; or
   (b) to the law of another third State which would apply its own law.
2. No renvoi shall apply with respect to the laws referred to in Article 21(2),[188] Article 22,[189] Article 27,[190] point (b) of Article 28[191] and Article 30.[192]"

A non-compliant Member State must be regarded for the purpose of art.34 as a (*faux*) Third State. Where a Third State law "in the round" makes a remission to the law of a (compliant) Member State, the *renvoi* process is permitted, and recital (57) encourages the compliant Member State to accept the reference back. Clearly it is beyond the power of the Regulation to dictate the approach which a Third State court should take to the *renvoi* process in a cross-border succession litigation.

If an English court were to engage in *renvoi* reasoning in a case where, in its view, the *lex causae* is that of a compliant Member State, that English court would be required, at second remove, to apply art.34, being part of the private international law of the compliant Member State. This constitutes one of the ways in which a UK legal system may be drawn into the operation of the Rome IV regime of rules.[193]

Scope of applicable law

Article 23 lays down that the law determined pursuant to arts 21 or 22 shall **18–50** govern the succession as a whole, including in particular (i.e. non-exhaustively) a list of topics[194] among which are the determination of beneficiaries (including the succession rights of the surviving spouse or partner), capacity to inherit, disinheritance and disqualification by conduct, and liability for the debts under the succession, together with the disposable part of the estate, the reserved shares, and other restrictions on the disposal of property on death, as well as claims which persons close to the deceased may have against the estate or the heirs (rules of compulsory family provision), plus any obligation to restore or account for gifts, advancements or legacies when determining the shares of the different beneficiaries, i.e. clawback. An example of the clawback problem is provided when a person who benefits from a forced inheritance rule is able to make a claim for that inheritance from lifetime gifts made by the deceased.[195]

The clawback provision, in particular, proved unacceptable to the UK at the time of negotiation of Rome IV and strongly influenced the Government's

---

[188] Applicable law general rule—exception.
[189] Choice of law.
[190] Formal validity of dispositions of property upon death made in writing.
[191] Validity as to form of a declaration concerning acceptance or waiver.
[192] Special rules imposing restrictions concerning or affecting the succession in respect of certain assets.
[193] Further para.18–53, below.
[194] Rome IV art.23.2(a)–(j).
[195] *The EU's Regulation on Succession*, 2010, HL Paper No.75 (Session 2009/10), para.86. While Scots law, in contrast with English law, displays a long established system of fixed family provision, it has little knowledge, now, of clawback in succession except in the limited area of *collation inter liberos*.

decision not to opt in.[196] The practical concern in the UK was that those parties, pre-eminently charities, in receipt of gifts would be uncertain whether money or property donated by an individual during his lifetime could be subject to clawback by his heirs upon the donor's death.

Clawback will operate in a Member State forum whenever the *lex successionis* contains such a rule. In terms of method, the Regulation in effect dictates the forum's ranking of its choice of law rules pertaining to lifetime transfers of moveable property, as against its rules pertaining to succession.[197] Article 23.2(i) resolves the potential conflict between the provisions of the *lex situs* of a gift as to its revocability and the corresponding provisions of the *lex successionis per* Rome IV, in favour of the latter. The inclusion of art.23.2(i) as a matter within the scope of the applicable law, and hence a matter for the harmonised rules of succession (as opposed to the unharmonised rules of title to moveable property) detracts from the ability of the forum to draw a distinction between *inter vivos* gifts and problems of succession.

Insofar as art.23.2(f) assigns to the governance of the *lex successionis* "the powers of the heirs, the executors of the wills and other administrators of the estate, in particular as regards the sale of property and the payment of creditors", problems may arise for legal systems which interpose between the deceased and the heir, one or more personal representatives, whose appointment and powers, presently in Scots international private law, are governed by the *lex fori* and not by the *lex successionis*.

Recognition, enforceability and enforcement of decisions (Chapter IV)

18–51 Chapter IV of Rome IV, in arts 39–58, contains rules of recognition and enforcement of "decisions"[198] given in a "Member State", the scheme of which, including the requirement of *exequatur* in art.43, is modelled on the equivalent rules of recognition and enforcement of judgments in civil and commercial matters contained in the Brussels I Regulation. The basic position is one of mutual recognition of decisions among Member States, subject to limited grounds of non-recognition set out in art.40. While such a corpus of rules is familiar in construct and detail, its inclusion in an area of law which is largely non-contentious is surprising.

The basic premise of mutual recognition of decisions among Member States must be construed, at first sight, as encompassing only "compliant Member States". The court of a compliant Member State addressed, if requiring to recognise and enforce a decision given in another compliant Member State, will utilise the rules in Ch.IV.

While legislative vires would suggest that, as with Ch.II, the rules in Ch.IV are intended to apply only within the net of compliant Member States, it should be considered whether, in view of the facilitative nature of Rome IV, some inroads

---

[196] House of Lords European Union Committee, 6th Report of Session 2009–10, *The EU'S Regulation on Succession: Report with Evidence*, paras 86–98.

[197] cf. generally *Stiftung v Lewis* [2004] EWHC 2589 (Ch); also *Re Korvine's Trusts* [1921] 1 Ch. 343.

[198] Defined as "any decision in a matter of succession given by a court of a Member State, whatever the decision may be called" (art.3.1(g)).

into this principle might be admitted on a teleological basis. By what rules and procedures would a "decision" given in a non-compliant Member State be recognised and enforced in a compliant Member State? Where the court of origin is in a non-compliant Member State, the question arises whether or not arts 39–58 can apply with regard to the recognition and enforcement of such a judgment in a compliant Member State. It seems possible that what was intended to be set up, on a basis of reciprocity and mutuality, was a scheme of rules operative only within and among states bound by the Regulation and subject to its application. But since Rome IV is of mandatory application in all compliant Member States, one could argue that it is the duty of a compliant Member State addressed to follow the procedures laid down *expressis verbis* in Ch.IV, whenever its assistance is sought to enforce a decision from *any* Member State.

Recital (37) contains an arrogant boast, namely, that "For reasons of legal certainty and in order to avoid the fragmentation of the succession, [the *lex successionis*] should govern the succession as a whole, that is to say, all of the property forming part of the estate, irrespective of the nature of the assets and regardless of whether the assets are located in another Member State or in a third State." This claim must be subject in relevant cases to acquiescence by a non-compliant Member State or Third State, with which the deceased had a personal law connection or in which he held assets.

Where a decision given by a compliant Member State court requires recognition and/or enforcement in a non-compliant Member State, it would not be competent for the court addressed to use the rules of Ch.IV. As to the outcome in any given case, much will depend upon the identity of the forum and upon the operation of that State's own enforcement rules. An "incoming" decision to a UK court addressed from the court of origin of a compliant Member State will require to be processed according to national common law or legislative rules as appropriate (i.e. depending on the court of origin), and subject to the exercise of public policy of the court addressed.

European Certificate of Succession (Chapter VI)

Provision for a European Certificate of Succession is made in Ch.VI, with the purpose of facilitating the administration of a succession having cross-border EU implications.[199] By art.68, the Certificate shall contain information under a number of heads, including "the law applicable to the succession and the elements on the basis of which that law has been determined."[200] The aim is that heirs, legatees, executors or administrators of an estate should be able to demonstrate easily their status and/or rights and powers in another Member State.[201]

18–52

---

[199] Also Commission Implementing Regulation (EU) No.1329/2014 of 9 December 2014 establishing the Forms referred to in Regulation (EU) No.650/2012 of the European Parliament and of the Council on jurisdiction, applicable law, recognition and enforcement of decisions and acceptance and enforcement of authentic instruments in matters of succession and on the creation of a European Certificate of Succession [2014] O.J. L359/30.

[200] Rome IV art.68(i).

[201] Rome IV recital (67).

While in administrative terms the Certificate could be useful, it is notable that use of the Certificate is not mandatory in Member States.[202] Moreover, even in cases where a Certificate is produced, there will be only a presumption of accuracy of the content thereof.[203]

A new problem of hybridity

18–53 In the context of the Europeanisation of the private international law rules of Member States, the problem of hybridity presents, notably, in the matter of ascertaining the geographical and subject-matter scope of the Brussels I Regulation and related instruments.[204] The puzzle has been to determine, under the diktat of the ECJ/CJEU, the extent to which the rules of civil jurisdiction in the Brussels regime effectively apply beyond the physical boundaries of the EU.[205] Rome IV generates a new problem of hybridity in that what presents is of a different type and level of complexity, concerning delineation of the extent of operation of that instrument within the EU vis-à-vis those EU Member States which, *ex facie*, are not bound by the Regulation.

In outline, it can be expected that, at the very least, any or all of the following circumstances will cause difficulties, viz.: the case of a UK citizen who owns assets, immoveable or moveable, in a compliant Member State; the case of an individual who is habitually resident at death in a compliant Member State and whose estate includes property situated in the UK; the case of a compliant Member State national whose estate at death includes assets in the UK; the case of a compliant Member State national whose estate includes property situated there, and who, at death, is judged (by whom?) to be habitually resident in the UK. The decision by the UK not to opt in to Rome IV does not mean that UK persons and/or assets situated in the UK will be unaffected by the Regulation; nor does it mean that estate situated in the UK and belonging to persons habitually resident in a compliant Member State will automatically be regulated by the terms of Rome IV.[206]

To this point in the EU harmonisation era, the opt-in mechanism for the UK and Ireland has been perceived as a safeguard to protect common law sensibilities and UK interests, and hitherto the effect of its operation vis-à-vis other Member States has not been the focus of attention, nor has failure on the part of the UK and/or of Ireland to opt in been perceived as having potential to undermine the successful operation of any scheme of harmonised rules.

Confusion, however, is likely to result from a split among Member States between those States which are bound by Rome IV, and those which are not. For one thing, it would appear that the constituency of electors (i.e. persons eligible to choose the applicable law to govern their succession) is not restricted to persons habitually resident in a compliant Member State. Hence, British citizens are not, it seems, excluded from availing themselves of a provision (art.22) which is

---

[202] Rome IV art.62.2.

[203] Rome IV art.69.2.

[204] Paras 1–13 to 1–17, above.

[205] Para.7–62, above.

[206] For detail, see E.B. Crawford and J.M. Carruthers, "Speculation on the Operation of Succession Regulation 650/2012: Tales of the Unexpected" (2014) 22 European Review of Private Law 847–878.

contained in a Regulation into which the UK did not opt.[207] A second illustration may be taken from the incidence of "British" persons owning immoveable property situated in a compliant Member State, e.g. where a UK national, habitually resident in Scotland and domiciled there in the Scots view, dies owning property comprising estate (heritable/immoveable and moveable) in Scotland and in France, respectively. Such a case is increasingly common as UK citizens buy second homes in the sun.

It seems inevitable that the UK involuntarily will be drawn into the operation of Rome IV.

POWERS OF APPOINTMENT AND POWERS OF APPORTIONMENT[208]

A testator (in this context, termed "the donor") may confer on his executors ("the donee") power to deal with his estate or part thereof, and to allocate the funds in question to an individual of the donee's choosing ("the appointee"). This may serve the purpose of a trust without going so far as to create a trust.[209]   **18–54**

General powers (powers of appointment) are to be distinguished from special powers (powers of apportionment). A general power of appointment is "close to full rights of ownership", though it must not be so wide as to be open to the charge of usurping the testamentary role of the testator.[210] Special powers, in contrast, refer to the case where the donee's discretion is curtailed by the donor, and his choice is limited to selecting the appointee(s) from a particular class of persons. The latter is the more usual situation, since, as noted, a wide discretion in the form of a general power might be void as a delegation to another of the power to test.

The conflict dimension

Are the capacity of the donee to take, and the validity of his exercise of a power, in form and essentials, to be governed by the law of the will conferring the power, or by the law of the domicile of the donee, or by the law of the deed by which the power is exercised? Must the law conferring the power also be the law of its exercise?[211] Lord Justice-Clerk Thomson in *Durie's Trustees v Osborne*[212] expressed the matter as follows: the question is whether the donee should be regarded as a free agent exercising the choice given to him by a testament in accordance with his own law, or as "a cog in the machinery of the donor's deed.   **18–55**

---

[207] Albeit that from a technical perspective, choice of the "law of the nationality", would need to be refined from a UK point of view.

[208] See Barr et al, *Drafting Wills in Scotland*, 2nd edn (2009).

[209] Barr et al, *Drafting Wills in Scotland*, 2nd edn (2009), para.5.59.

[210] Barr et al, *Drafting Wills in Scotland*, 2nd edn (2009), para.5.59.

[211] *Kennion v Buchan's Trustees* (1880) 7 R. 570, per Moncrieff LJC, at 573, quoting in turn Lord Brougham in *Tatnall v Hankey*, 2 Moo. P.C. 342.

[212] *Durie's Trustees v Osborne*, 1961 S.L.T. 53.

In sheer logic there is much to be said for both views", but if intention be the vital matter, "it seems better to look to a man's own law than to one arbitrarily imposed on him".[213]

The general principles to be elicited from English and Scottish authorities are as follows[214]:

General powers: the fund is regarded as being akin to the property of the donee, so that the same rules apply to a deed by the donee exercising the power, as to the donee's own will.[215]

Special powers: the fund is regarded as being still the property of the donor and the donee is seen as his agent so that the validity of a deed exercising the power is governed by the same rules as apply to the donor's will (the deed creating the power).

Capacity

18–56   The exercise of the power will be valid, as regards immoveables, if the donee has capacity per the *lex situs*, and with regard to moveables, if the donee has capacity by the law of his domicile, though it may be sufficient, certainly in the case of special powers,[216] that he has capacity by the law of the deed creating the power.

Formal validity

18–57   The provisions of the Wills Act 1963 apply equally to wills exercising powers. In addition to the general rule as to formal validity contained in s.1,[217] an additional rule provides that a will so far as it exercises a power of appointment shall be treated as properly executed if its execution conformed to the law governing the essential validity of the power.[218] With regard to immoveables, the additional rule provided by s.2(1)(b), that a will disposing of immoveable property shall be treated as properly executed if its execution conformed to the internal law of the *lex situs*, is available. Section 2(2) provides that a will so far as it exercises a power of appointment shall not be treated as improperly executed by reason only that its execution was not in accordance with any formal requirements contained in the instrument creating the power.

---

[213] *Durie's Trustees v Osborne,* 1961 S.L.T. 53 at 61.

[214] Further P.R. Beaumont and P.E. McEleavy, *Anton's Private International Law*, 3rd edn (2011), paras 24.97–24.106.

[215] *Durie's Trustees v Osborne*, 1961 S.L.T. 53; following *Anderson v Collins*, 1913 1 S.L.T. 219.

[216] *Gould v Lewal* [1918] 2 Ch. 391; *Re Langley's Settlement Trusts* [1962] Ch. 541.

[217] Para.18–21, above.

[218] Wills Act 1963 s.2(1)(d). At common law: *Kennion v Buchan's Trustees* (1880) 7 R. 570; *Anderson v Collins*, 1913 1 S.L.T. 219; *Durie's Trustees v Osborne*, 1961 S.L.T. 53; *Re Price* [1900] 1 Ch. 442; *Barretto v Young* [1900] 2 Ch. 339; *Re Wilkinson's Settlement* [1917] 1 Ch. 620.

Essential validity

General powers: the essential validity of a will (i.e. of the donee) exercising a **18–58** general power is determined by the law of that will, that is, the law of the testator's (i.e. donee's) domicile at the date of his death, as regards moveables[219]; and the *lex situs* as regards immoveables. The law of the will conferring the power is irrelevant in this case.

Special powers: the essential validity of a will exercising such a power is determined by the law governing the deed which confers the powers, that is, in respect of immoveables, the *lex situs*; and in respect of moveables, the law of the donor's domicile at the date of his death.

Construction

The following presumptions apply: **18–59**

General powers: a will exercising such power is construed according to the law which governs the construction of that will,[220] and not of the deed conferring the power. The law governing construction of the donee's will determines whether a will expressed in general terms without mentioning a power in fact operates as an exercise of the power.[221]

Special powers: the rule is that the construction of a deed exercising a special power must be governed by the law of the deed conferring the power.

Revocation

A deed by a donee purporting to revoke an earlier instrument by which the power **18–60** was exercised will be effective (i.e. as regards essentials) if it complies with either the law of the deed conferring the power, or the law of the donee's domicile at the date of revocation,[222] and as regards immoveables, with the *lex situs*.

TRUST ESTATES

Common law

Prior to the Recognition of Trusts Act 1987, the following rules applied: **18–61**

---

[219] *Pouey v Hordern* [1900] Ch. 492; *Re Pryce* [1911] 2 Ch. 286; *Re Waite's Settlement Trusts* [1958] Ch. 100; *Re Khan's Settlement* [1965] 3 W.L.R. 1291.
[220] *Durie's Trustees v Osborne*, 1961 S.L.T. 53; *Re Price* [1900] 1 Ch. 442; *Re Khan's Settlement* [1965] 3 W.L.R. 1291; *Gould v Lewal* [1918] 2 Ch. 391; *Re McMorran* [1958] Ch. 624; *Re Waite's Settlement Trusts* [1958] Ch. 100; *Re Fenston's Settlement* [1971] 1 W.L.R. 1640.
[221] Though see further P.R. Beaumont and P.E. McEleavy, *Anton's Private International Law*, 3rd edn (2011), paras 24.103–24.104.
[222] *Velasco v Coney* [1934] P. 143.

(a) Domicile

18–62   Most matters were governed by the law of what was known for convenience as the "domicile" of the trust, that is, the proper law of the trust deed or the law of the country with which the trust had the closest connection. Thus, it was the court of the domicile of the trust which had jurisdiction to determine an application to vary the trust purposes under the Trusts (Scotland) Act 1961.[223] Broadly speaking, the law of the domicile of a testamentary trust would be the law of the country in which the testator's will was lodged and a grant of confirmation or probate was first obtained. In exceptional cases the domicile of a trust might be changed.[224]

(b) Capacity to create a trust

18–63   The *lex situs* applied as regards heritage[225]; otherwise the law of the truster's domicile applied.

(c) Formal validity

18–64   It was sufficient that the deed complied with either the proper law of the trust or the law of the place of execution.[226] Where the trust was testamentary in nature, the provisions of the Wills Act 1963 applied, the definition of "will" in s.6(1) thereof including "any testamentary instrument or act".

(d) Essential validity and interpretation

18–65   Trustees' powers and variation of trust purposes were governed by the law of the domicile of the trust. So too were matters of construction.

---

[223] As to what constitutes a Scottish trust, see G. Duncan and D. Oswald Dykes, *The Principles of Civil Jurisdiction as Applied in the Law of Scotland* (Edinburgh: W. Green, 1911), p.213 quoted with approval by Lord President Clyde in *Clarke's Trustees, Petitioners*, 1966 S.L.T. 249 at 251. Article 60.3 of the Brussels I Regulation/art.63 of Brussels I Recast Regulation states that in order to determine whether a trust is domiciled in the Member State whose courts are seised of the matter, the court shall apply its rules of private international law. See further art.5(6) of Brussels I Regulation/art.7(6) of Brussels I Recast Regulation, and para.18–03, above. In respect of the UK, Civil Jurisdiction and Judgments Order 2001 (SI 2001/3929) Sch.1 para.12(3) (re Civil Jurisdiction and Judgments Act 1982 s.45) provides that a trust is domiciled in a part of the UK if and only if the system of law of that part is the system of law with which the trust has its closest and most real connection. As to definition of trust for the purposes of the Recognition of Trusts Act 1987, see Schedule to the Act, art.2.

[224] Cheshire, *Private International Law*, 8th edn (1970), pp.577, 578; Anton, *Private International Law*, 1st edn (1967), p.481; *Duke of Marlborough v Att Gen* [1945] Ch. 78; *Baroness Lloyd*, 1963 S.L.T. 231; *Re Seale's Marriage Settlement* [1961] Ch. 574; *Re Weston's Settlements* [1969] 1 Ch. 223; *Re Windeatt's Will Trusts* [1969] 1 W.L.R. 692.

[225] *Black v Black's Trustees*, 1950 S.L.T. (Notes) 32.

[226] *Thomson* (1917) 33 Sh. Ct Rep. 84; *Re Pilkington's Will Trusts* [1937] 1 Ch. 574.

(e) Sales of Scots heritage by English trustees

The powers of sale conferred upon Scots and English trustees by the Scots and **18–66** English Trusts Acts applied only to Scots and English trustees and to land in Scotland and England respectively. If an English will did not confer express power[227] of sale, power to sell land in Scotland might be obtained at the discretion of the court.[228] Retrospective sanction was not usually granted.[229] Whether this procedure, after the advent of the Recognition of Trusts Act 1987, is still required is unclear.

Recognition of Trusts Act 1987[230]

This Act gave effect in UK law to the 1986 Hague Convention on the Law **18–67** Applicable to Trusts and on their Recognition, the purpose of which is to, "ensure the international recognition of trusts and to obtain the adoption by States (even those which do not themselves have the trust concept)"[231] of a uniform choice of law rule relating to the validity, and many other aspects, of trusts. It applies to trusts regardless of their date of creation,[232] subject to individual state reservation and to the caveat that the Act shall not affect the law governing acts or omissions of trustees before the coming into force of the Act on 1 August 1987.

In terms of s.1(1), the provisions of the Convention as set out in the Schedule to the Act shall have the force of law in the UK. By s.1(2), those provisions shall, so far as applicable, have effect not only in relation to the trusts described in arts 2 and 3 of the Convention, but also in relation to any other trusts of property arising under the law of any part of the UK or by virtue of a judicial decision whether in the UK or elsewhere.

---

[227] If the power was express, no further authorisation from a Scots court was required: *Phipps v Phipps's Trustees*, 1914 1 S.L.T. 239 (though there the trustee's power to sell Scottish heritage was not express but deduced by inference from the testator's use of the words "all other my real estate whatsoever, wheresoever").

[228] In Scotland the trustees applied to the Court of Session craving power of sale under the *nobile officium* (*Allan's Trustees* (1896) 24 R. 238; (1896) 24 R. 718; *Pender's Trustees, Petitioners* (1903) 5 F. 504; 1907 S.C. 207; *Harris's Trustees, Petitioners*, 1919 S.C. 432; *Laurie's Trustees, Petitioners*, 1946 S.L.T. (Notes) 31; *Campbell-Wyndham-Long's Trustees, Petitioners*, 1952 S.L.T. 43; *Prudential Assurance Co Ltd, Petitioners*, 1952 S.L.T. 121; Anton, *Private International Law*, 1st edn (1967), pp.483, 484). In England, the trustees applied to the Court of Chancery for power to apply to the Court of Session, which power normally would be granted if it was considered expedient and in the interests of the trust estate to do so (*Forrest v Forrest* (1910) 54 S.J. 737; *Georges v Georges* (1921) 65 S.J. 311).

[229] *Dow's Trustees, Petitioners*, 1947 S.L.T. 293; *Prudential Assurance Co Ltd, Petitioners*, 1952 S.L.T. 121.

[230] P. Panico, *International Trust Laws* (Oxford: OUP, 2010); *Dicey, Morris and Collins on the Conflict of Laws*, 15th edn (2012), Ch.29; J. Harris, *The Hague Trust Convention* (Oxford: Hart, 2002); and D. Hayton, "The Hague Convention on the Law Applicable to Trusts and on their Recognition" (1987) 36 I.C.L.Q. 260.

[231] R.D. Leslie, "Trusts in Private International Law: Recognition of Trusts Act 1987" (1988) 33 J.L.S.S. 27; A.E. Anton, "The Recognition of Trusts Act 1987", 1987 S.L.T. (News) 377); and *Akers v Samba Financial Group* [2014] EWHC 540 (Ch), per Sir Terence Etherton at [75] (reversed on a *forum non conveniens* point, [2014] EWCA Civ 1516).

[232] 1987 Act Sch.1; Convention art.22.

The definition of "trust" in art.2 of the Schedule to the Act is wide, being designed to satisfy not only the requirements of a trust in the Anglo-American legal systems, but also analogous institutions in civilian systems.

These rules apply in UK courts whether or not the trust arises under the law of a contracting state, but only to "trusts created voluntarily and evidenced in writing" (art.3).

The Convention rules do not apply to preliminary issues relating to the validity of wills or of other acts by which assets are transferred to the trustee (art.4).

A trust shall be governed by the law chosen by the settlor, expressly or impliedly (art.6),[233] or, failing such choice, by the law of closest connection (art.7).[234] That law shall govern (art.8) the validity, construction, effects and administration of the trust, and in particular it shall govern matters itemised in art.8(a)–(j), including appointment and removal of trustees, trustees' rights among themselves, rights to administer and dispose of trust assets, to create security interests in the trust assets[235] or to acquire new assets, powers of investment, and liability of trustees to beneficiaries. Article 15 provides that the Convention does not prevent the application of provisions of the law designated by the conflict rules of the forum, insofar as those provisions cannot be derogated from by voluntary act, in a non-exhaustive list of matters, including, (a) the protection of minors and incapable parties; (b) the personal and proprietary effects of marriage; and (c) succession rights, testate and intestate, especially the indefeasible shares of spouses and relatives.

Article 16 preserves the application of those provisions of the law of the forum which must be applied to international situations, irrespective of rules of conflict of laws.

If the law identified as a result of the application of art.6 has no knowledge of the trust concept, the Convention, at first sight, according to art.5, appears to fall away. However, by art.6 para.2, where the law chosen by the truster does not provide for trusts, or for the category of trust involved, that choice shall not be effective. Instead, the applicable law will be identified by the forum by dint of art.7 (applicable law in the absence of choice).[236] The fact that the law of closest connection is one which does not provide for the trust envisaged does not render that law invalid as the *lex causae*, but a court will be cautious in reaching such a conclusion.[237]

Article 11 enjoins recognition of trusts falling within the scope of the Convention and the Act, and regulates the effect of such recognition. In this way, the provisions are consistent with the title of the Act, albeit that the Act, despite its name, is concerned primarily with choice of law.

---

[233] *Re Barton (Deceased)*; sub nom. *Tod v Barton* [2002] EWHC 264 (Ch).

[234] *Re Carapiet's Trusts*; sub nom. *Manoogian (Armenian Patriarch of Jerusalem) v Sonsino* [2002] EWHC 1304 (Ch); and *Akers v Samba Financial Group* [2014] EWHC 540 (Ch), per Sir Terence Etherton at paras 69–73.

[235] See saving clause in favour of the *lex situs* in art.15(d).

[236] A.E. van Overbeck, Explanatory Report on the Hague Trusts Convention, para.61.

[237] *Akers v Samba Financial Group* [2014] EWHC 540 (Ch), per Sir Terence Etherton at [75].

SUMMARY 18

Testate and intestate succession

1. Confirmation. **18–68**

   The Scots courts follow the law of the domicile of the deceased as regards title to administer moveables. If probate or letters of administration or similar authority has/have been granted to a person(s) under that law, confirmation is granted to the same person(s) as executor(s) for the purposes of estate in Scotland. A foreign executor must seek confirmation in Scotland in order to deal with Scottish estate. If there has been no grant of administration abroad, the person entitled to appointment under the law of the deceased's domicile shall be confirmed to deal with property in Scotland. Confirmation or probate granted in any of the UK jurisdictions operates directly in the other jurisdictions, and resealing will suffice in the case of Commonwealth countries.

2. Administration and distribution.

   Administration, a matter of procedure, is governed by the *lex fori*, being for this purpose the law of the situation of the moveable or immoveable assets to be administered.

   Distribution, a matter of substance, is governed by the law of the succession (*lex successionis*), being the *lex ultimi domicilii* and/or the *lex situs*.

   The *lex fori* determines classification between administration and distribution.

3. The scission principle.

   This principle, by which a different choice of law rule (the *lex situs*) applies to succession to immoveables, from that (law of deceased's last domicile) which applies to succession to moveables, operates in Scots and English choice of law rules.

4. Existence and extent of legal rights

   These are determined by the law of the domicile of the deceased at death as regards moveables, and the *lex situs* as regards immoveables.

Intestate succession

1. The laws governing intestate succession are: **18–69**
   (a) re immoveables: the *lex situs* at the date of death;
   (b) re moveables: the law of the deceased's domicile at the date of death.

2. Prior rights in moveable property available by Scots domestic law arise if the deceased died domiciled in Scotland; and the prior right to the house arises if the qualifying dwelling house is situated in Scotland.

3. Caduciary rights—the question whether the foreign government of the domicile of the deceased at death may succeed to estate in Scotland when the deceased died intestate without relatives, depends on whether or not, in the view of the UK forum, that foreign government, under the law of the deceased's last domicile, has the right to succeed as last heir as opposed to acquiring a mere right to bona vacantia.

Testate succession

18–70 The conflict rule is two-dimensional in nature, meaning that time and place are relevant.

1. Capacity.
    Legal testamentary capacity appears to be governed by the law of the domicile of the testator at the date of making the will, as regards moveable property, and by the *lex situs* at that date as regards immoveables.
    Proprietary testamentary capacity is governed by the law of the domicile of the deceased at the date of death as regards moveable property, and by the *lex situs* as regards immoveables.
2. Formal Validity.
    Under the Wills Act 1963 a will is to be regarded as validly executed in form if it complies with any one of the following laws:
    (a) place of execution;
    (b) domicile of testator at date of will or death;
    (c) habitual residence of testator at date of will or death;
    (d) nationality of testator at date of will or death;
    (e) place of registration of ship/aircraft; or
    (f) *lex situs* (immoveables only).
3. Essential Validity.
    The essential validity or legality of the substance of the provisions of a will is governed by the following laws as at the date of the death of the testator:
    (a) immoveables—the *lex situs*;
    (b) moveables—the law of the testator's domicile.
4. Construction.
    The testator's intention takes precedence and there are several working rules to identify the law to be applied as his deemed intention in the matter of construction, if his intention is not express.
5. Revocation of Wills.
    (a) new will—the extent of revocation of a previous will depends on the validity and scope of a new will;
    (b) the effect of a revocation clause is determined according to the circumstances;
    (c) the effect of a purported act of revocation depends on the law of the testator's domicile as at that date, regarding moveables; or the *lex situs* relating to immoveables;
    (d) the effect of a subsequent marriage is determined by the law of the domicile of the testator immediately *after* the marriage;
    (e) a change of domicile has no effect on the formal validity of a will, but the essential validity of testamentary provisions relating to moveables is governed by the law of the testator's last domicile.

Rome IV

The UK Government decided not to opt in to Regulation 650/2012, but the   **18–71**
instrument may prove to have effect, nonetheless, in respect of the foreign-situated property of UK nationals, and in respect of property in the UK forming part of an estate the distribution of which Rome IV purports to regulate.

The Regulation will apply to the succession of persons who die on or after 17 August 2015.

Trusts

See Recognition of Trusts Act 1987.   **18–72**

INDEX

All references are to paragraph number

INDEX

INDEX